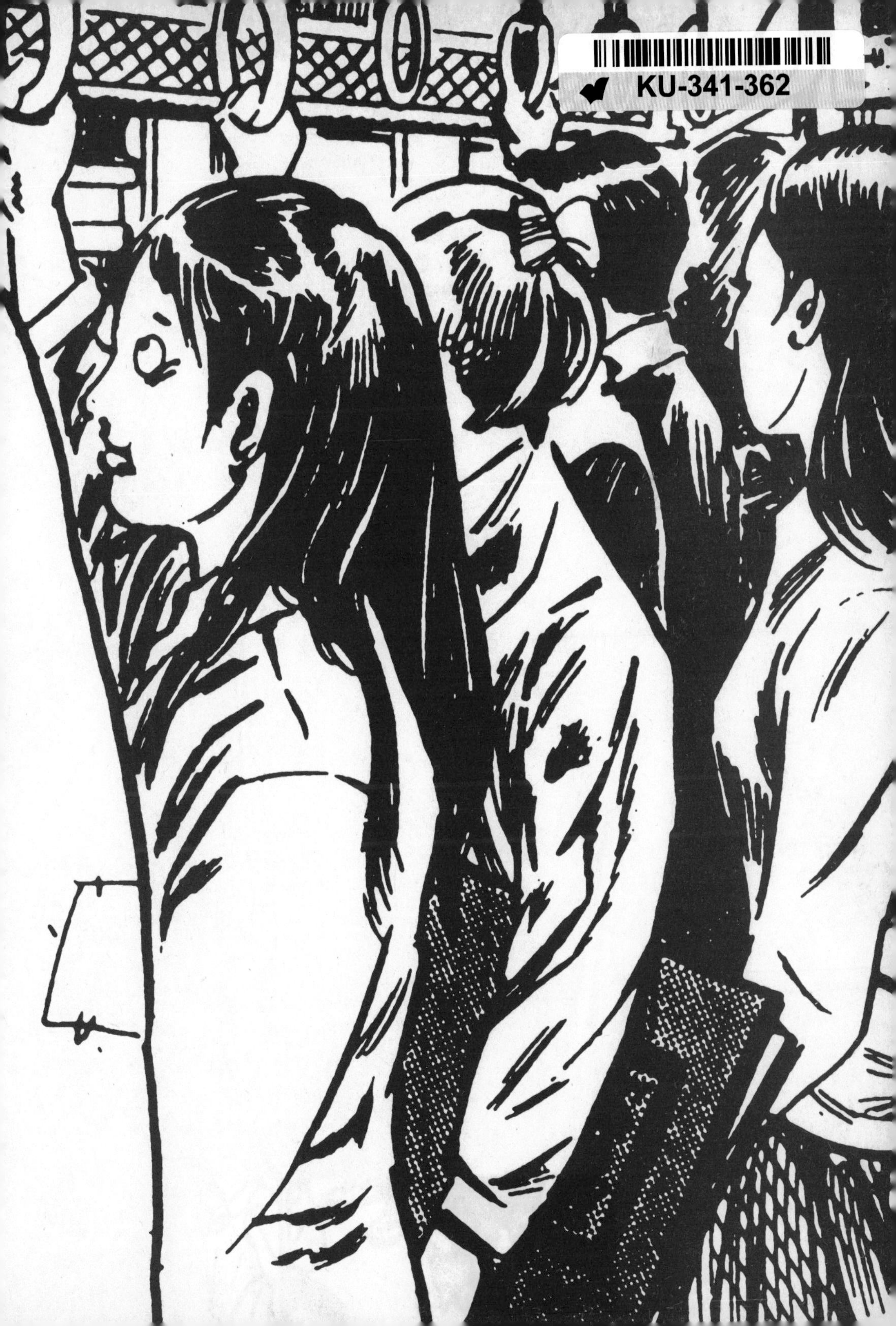

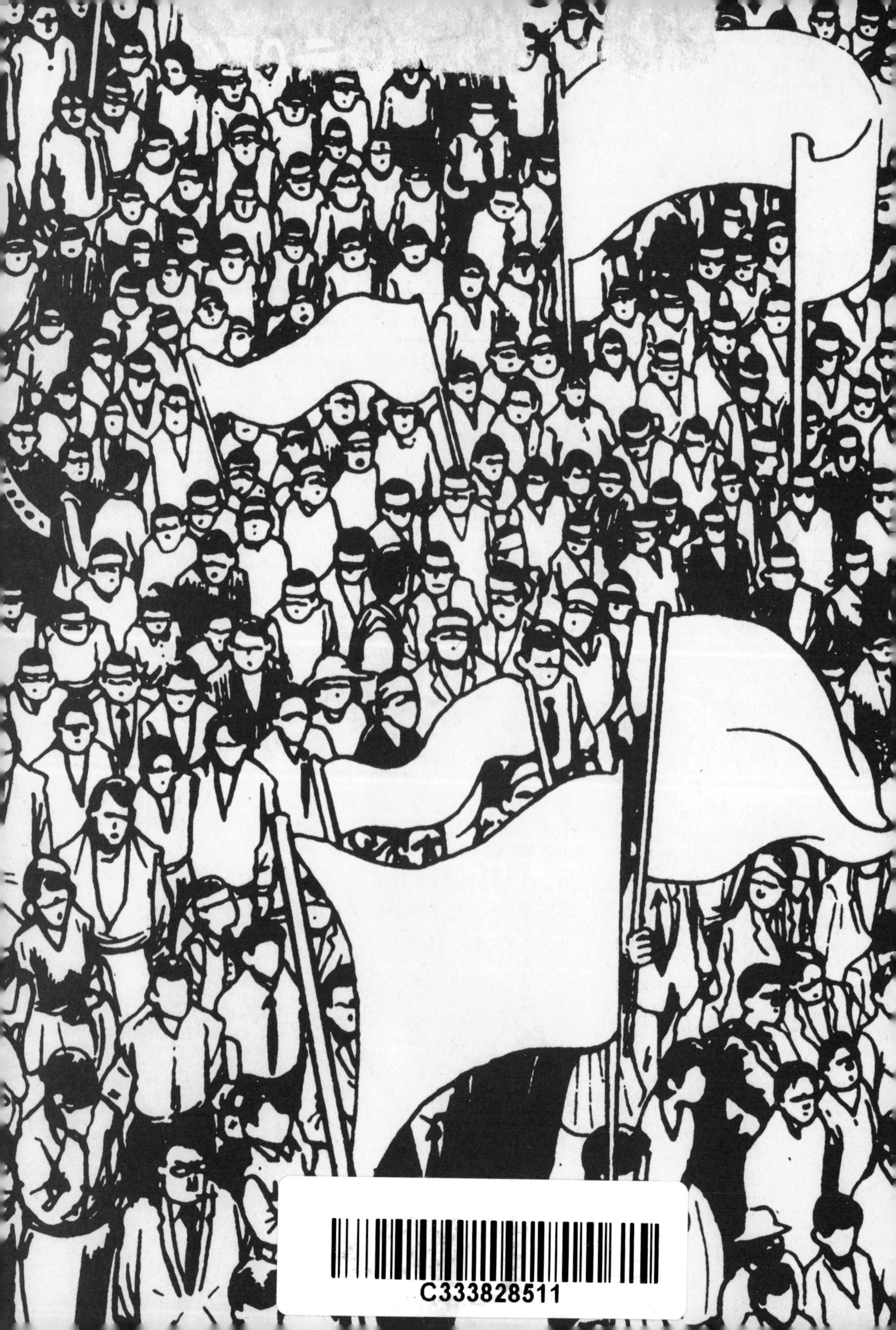

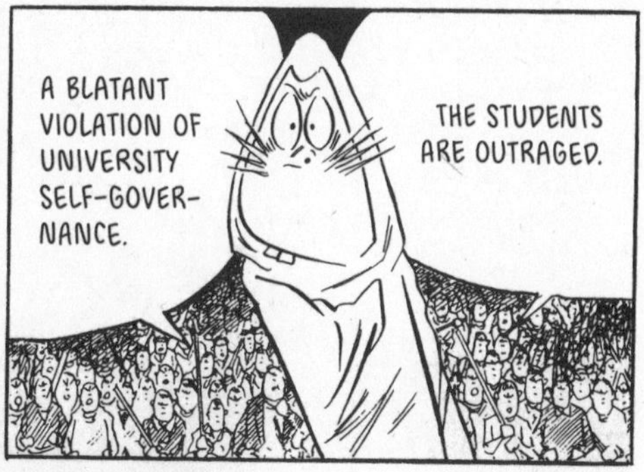
THE STUDENTS ARE OUTRAGED.
A BLATANT VIOLATION OF UNIVERSITY SELF-GOVER-NANCE.

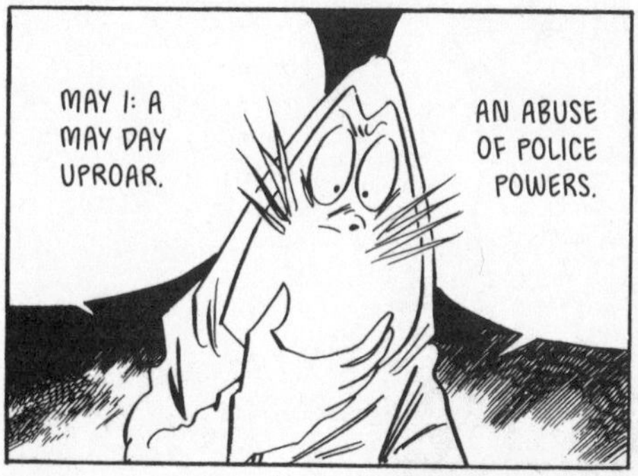
AN ABUSE OF POLICE POWERS.
MAY 1: A MAY DAY UPROAR.

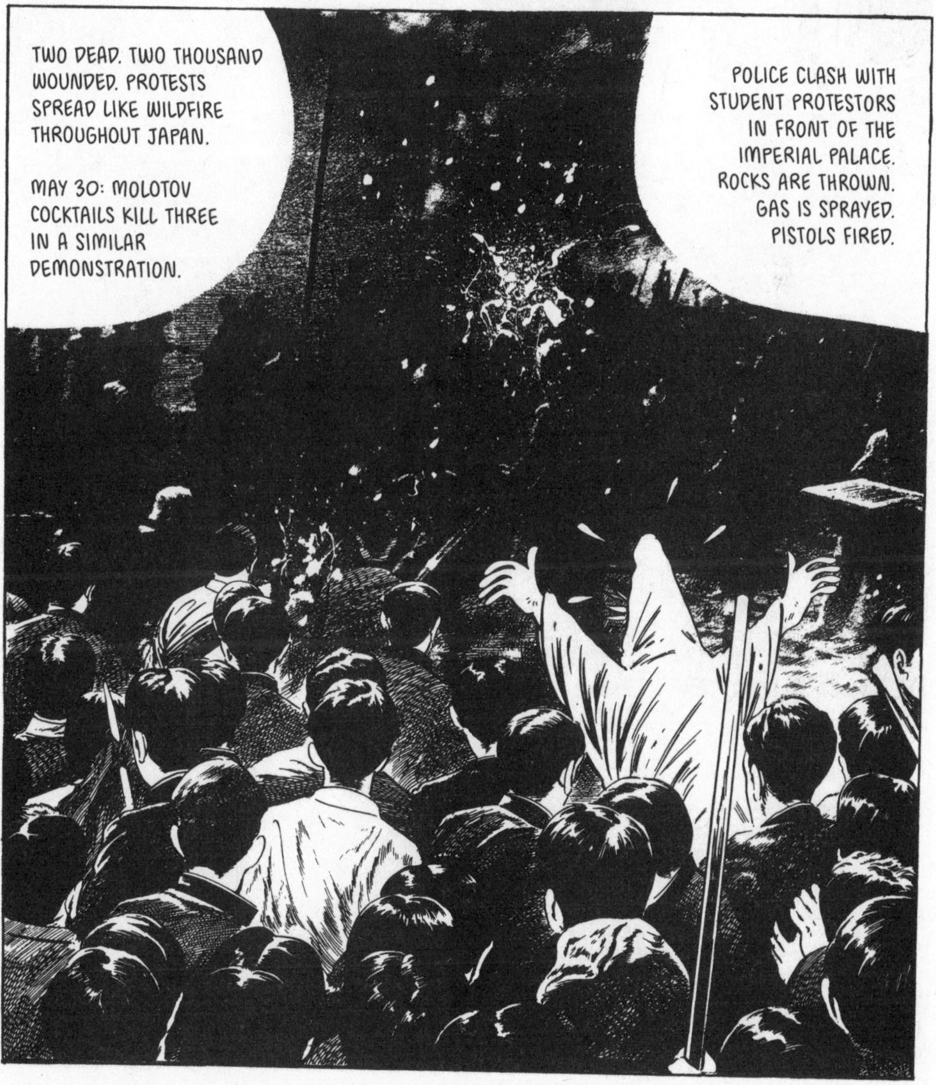
POLICE CLASH WITH STUDENT PROTESTORS IN FRONT OF THE IMPERIAL PALACE. ROCKS ARE THROWN. GAS IS SPRAYED. PISTOLS FIRED.
TWO DEAD. TWO THOUSAND WOUNDED. PROTESTS SPREAD LIKE WILDFIRE THROUGHOUT JAPAN.
MAY 30: MOLOTOV COCKTAILS KILL THREE IN A SIMILAR DEMONSTRATION.

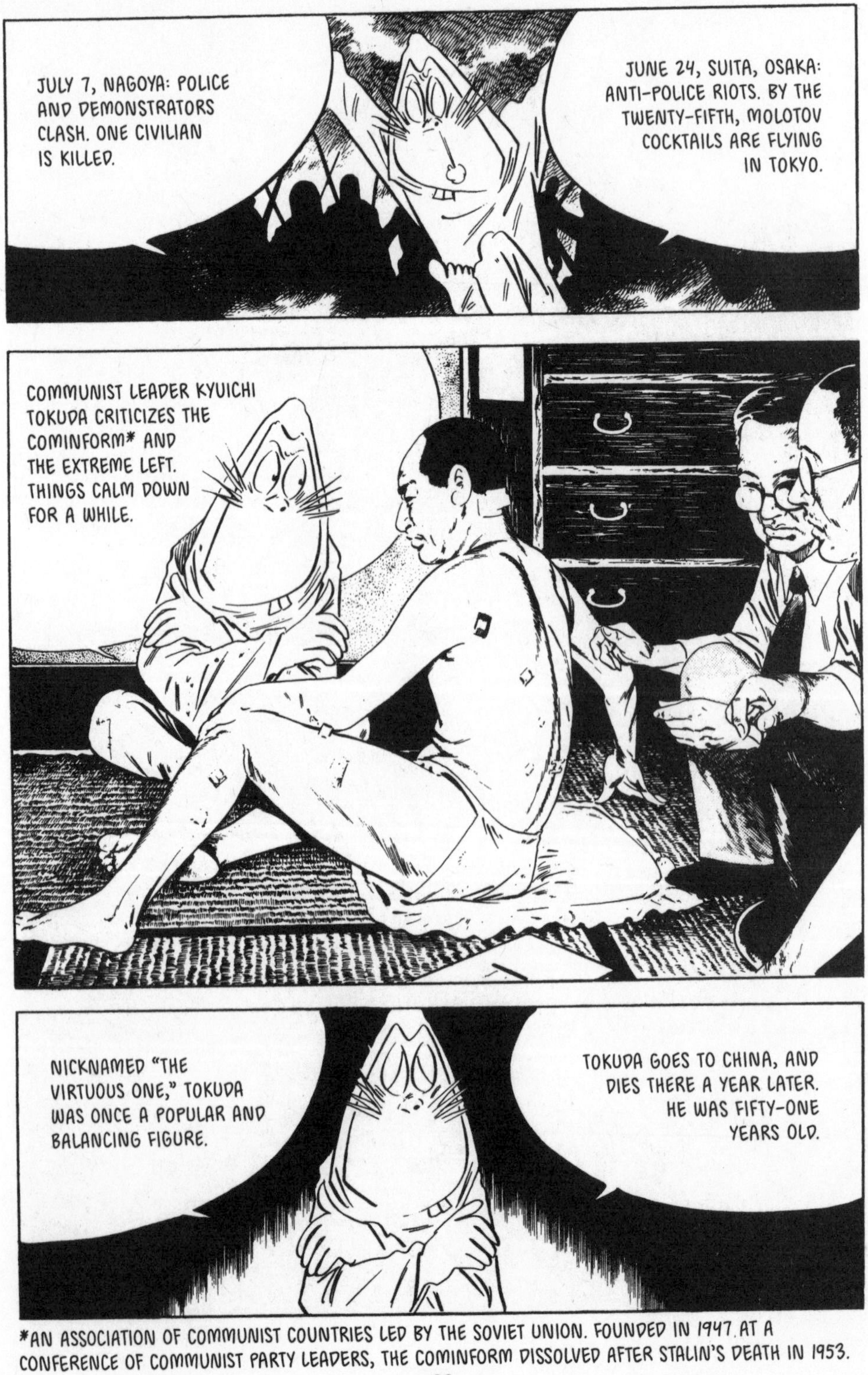
JUNE 24, SUITA, OSAKA: ANTI-POLICE RIOTS. BY THE TWENTY-FIFTH, MOLOTOV COCKTAILS ARE FLYING IN TOKYO.
JULY 7, NAGOYA: POLICE AND DEMONSTRATORS CLASH. ONE CIVILIAN IS KILLED.
COMMUNIST LEADER KYUICHI TOKUDA CRITICIZES THE COMINFORM* AND THE EXTREME LEFT. THINGS CALM DOWN FOR A WHILE.
TOKUDA GOES TO CHINA, AND DIES THERE A YEAR LATER. HE WAS FIFTY-ONE YEARS OLD.
NICKNAMED "THE VIRTUOUS ONE," TOKUDA WAS ONCE A POPULAR AND BALANCING FIGURE.

*AN ASSOCIATION OF COMMUNIST COUNTRIES LED BY THE SOVIET UNION. FOUNDED IN 1947 AT A CONFERENCE OF COMMUNIST PARTY LEADERS, THE COMINFORM DISSOLVED AFTER STALIN'S DEATH IN 1953.

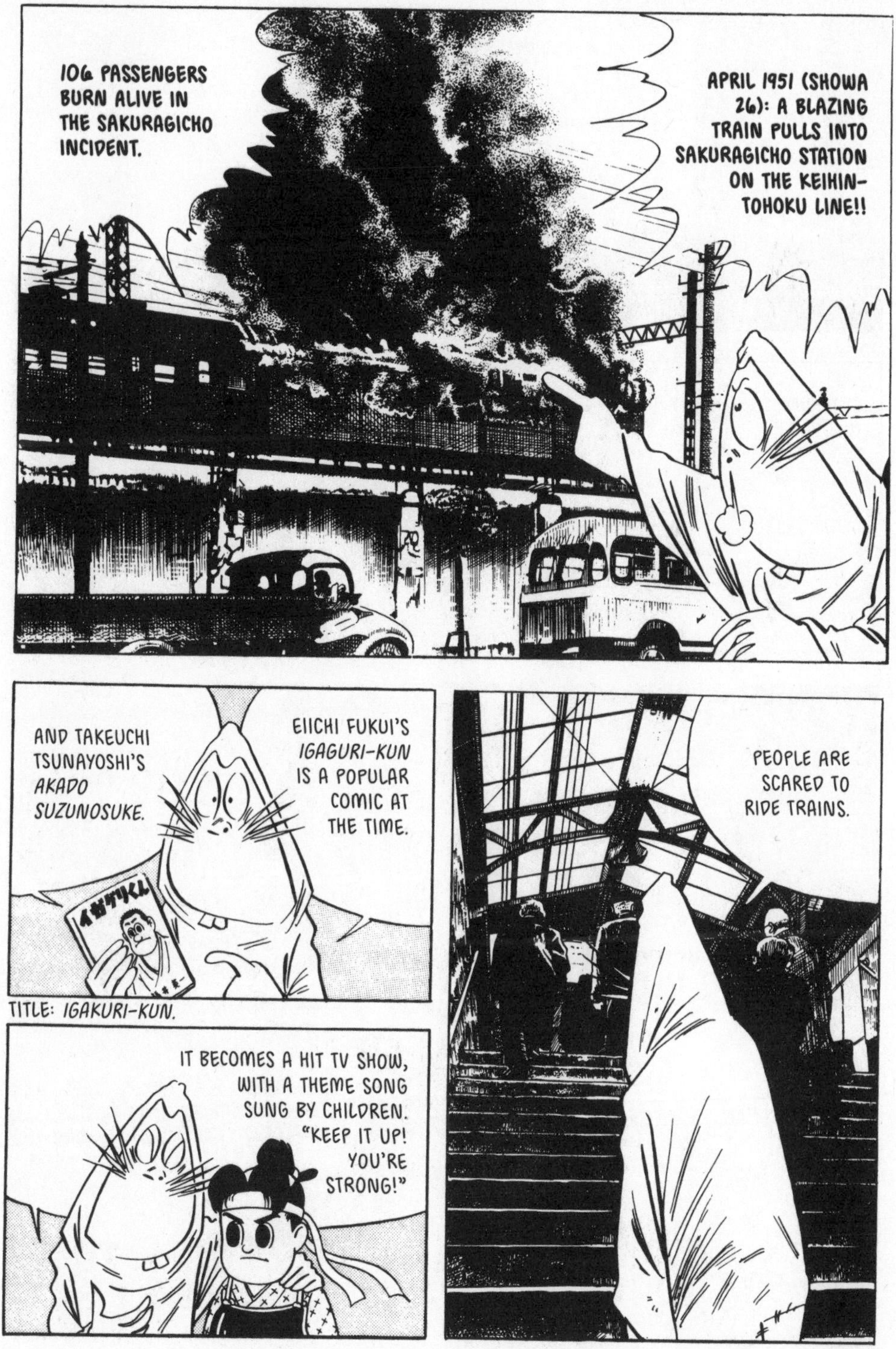
APRIL 1951 (SHOWA 26): A BLAZING TRAIN PULLS INTO SAKURAGICHO STATION ON THE KEIHIN-TOHOKU LINE!!
106 PASSENGERS BURN ALIVE IN THE SAKURAGICHO INCIDENT.
PEOPLE ARE SCARED TO RIDE TRAINS.
EIICHI FUKUI'S *IGAGURI-KUN* IS A POPULAR COMIC AT THE TIME.
AND TAKEUCHI TSUNAYOSHI'S *AKADO SUZUNOSUKE.*
TITLE: *IGAKURI-KUN.*
IT BECOMES A HIT TV SHOW, WITH A THEME SONG SUNG BY CHILDREN. "KEEP IT UP! YOU'RE STRONG!"

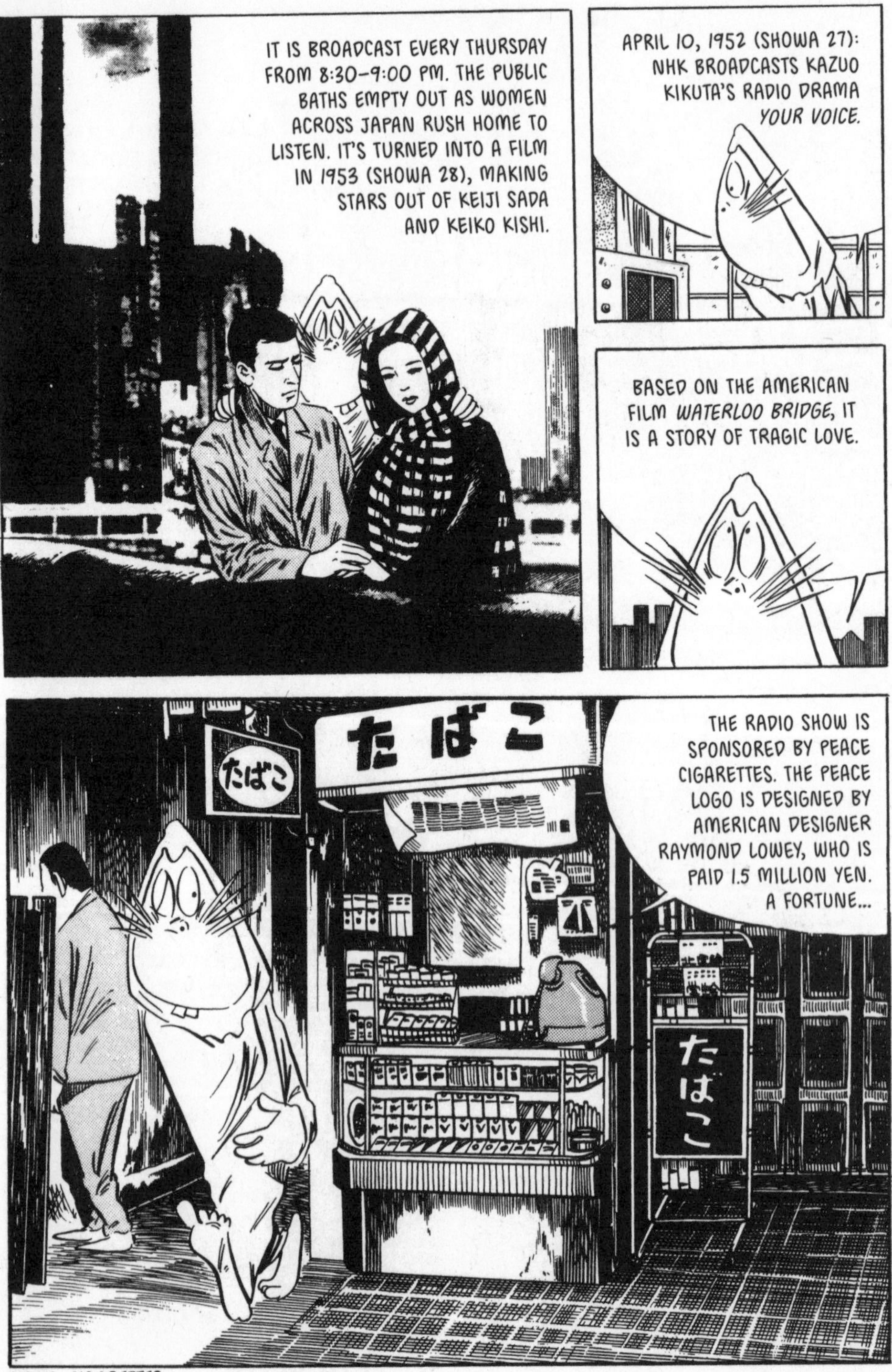
APRIL 10, 1952 (SHOWA 27): NHK BROADCASTS KAZUO KIKUTA'S RADIO DRAMA *YOUR VOICE.*
BASED ON THE AMERICAN FILM *WATERLOO BRIDGE*, IT IS A STORY OF TRAGIC LOVE.
IT IS BROADCAST EVERY THURSDAY FROM 8:30–9:00 PM. THE PUBLIC BATHS EMPTY OUT AS WOMEN ACROSS JAPAN RUSH HOME TO LISTEN. IT'S TURNED INTO A FILM IN 1953 (SHOWA 28), MAKING STARS OUT OF KEIJI SADA AND KEIKO KISHI.
THE RADIO SHOW IS SPONSORED BY PEACE CIGARETTES. THE PEACE LOGO IS DESIGNED BY AMERICAN DESIGNER RAYMOND LOWEY, WHO IS PAID 1.5 MILLION YEN. A FORTUNE...
たばこ
たばこ
たばこ
SIGNS: CIGARETTES.

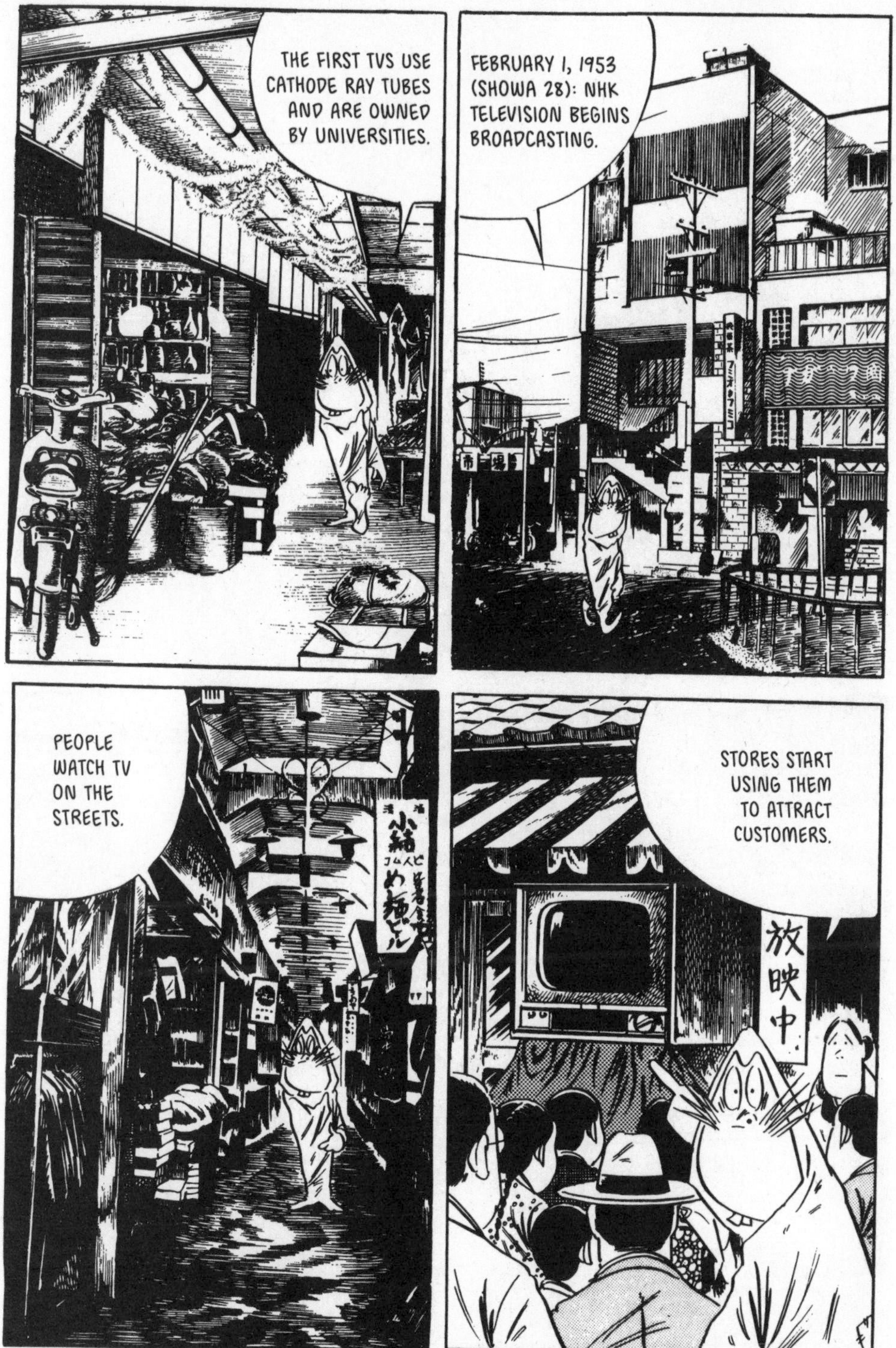
FEBRUARY 1, 1953 (SHOWA 28): NHK TELEVISION BEGINS BROADCASTING.
THE FIRST TVS USE CATHODE RAY TUBES AND ARE OWNED BY UNIVERSITIES.
STORES START USING THEM TO ATTRACT CUSTOMERS.
放映中
PEOPLE WATCH TV ON THE STREETS.
SIGN: BROADCASTING.

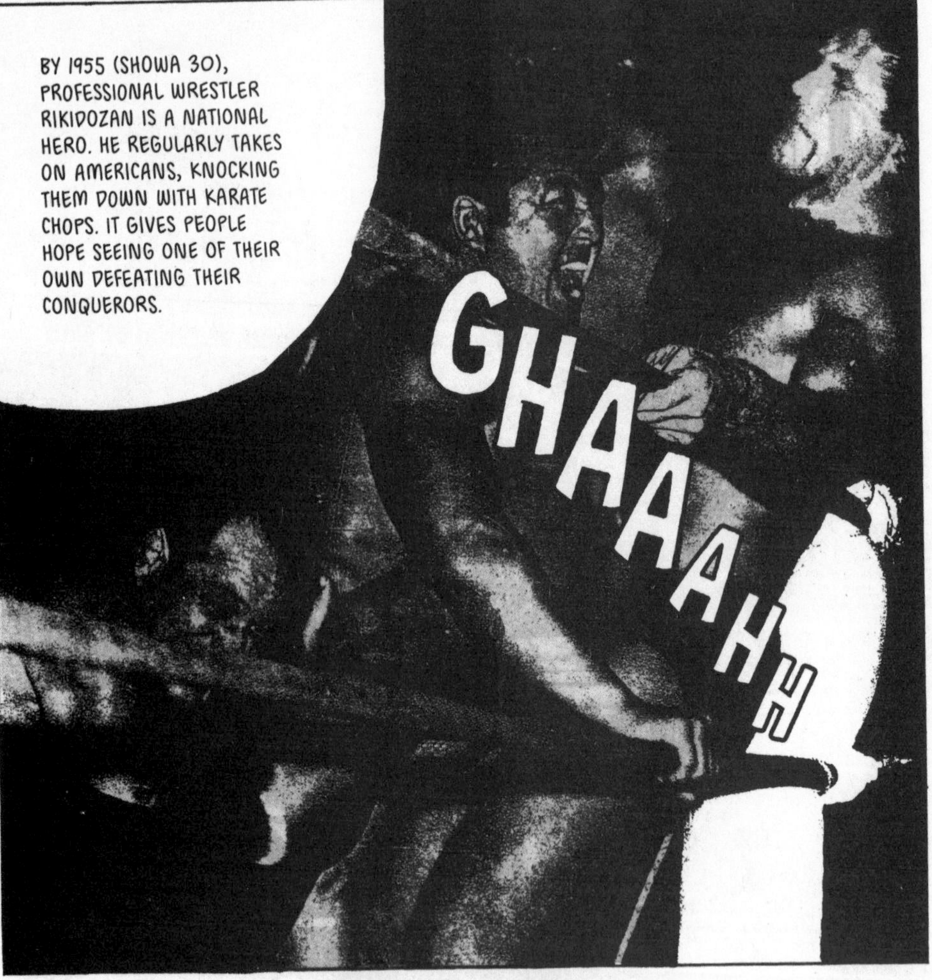
BY 1955 (SHOWA 30), PROFESSIONAL WRESTLER RIKIDOZAN IS A NATIONAL HERO. HE REGULARLY TAKES ON AMERICANS, KNOCKING THEM DOWN WITH KARATE CHOPS. IT GIVES PEOPLE HOPE SEEING ONE OF THEIR OWN DEFEATING THEIR CONQUERORS.
GHAAAAHH

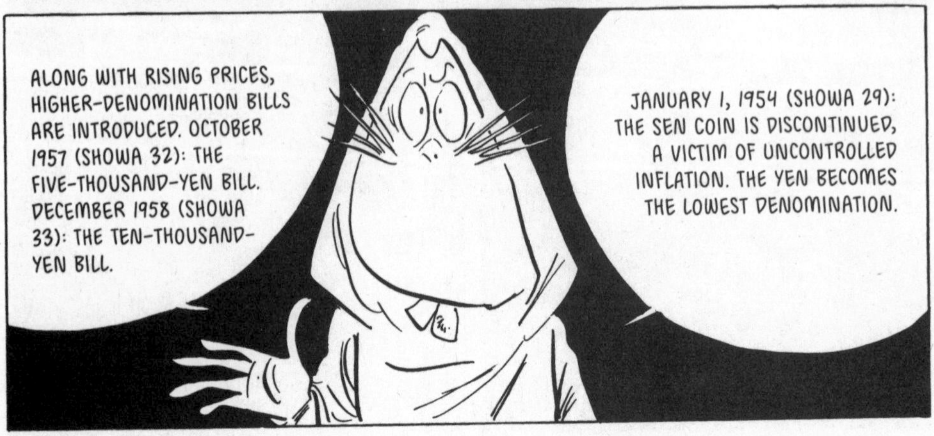
JANUARY 1, 1954 (SHOWA 29): THE SEN COIN IS DISCONTINUED, A VICTIM OF UNCONTROLLED INFLATION. THE YEN BECOMES THE LOWEST DENOMINATION.
ALONG WITH RISING PRICES, HIGHER-DENOMINATION BILLS ARE INTRODUCED. OCTOBER 1957 (SHOWA 32): THE FIVE-THOUSAND-YEN BILL. DECEMBER 1958 (SHOWA 33): THE TEN-THOUSAND-YEN BILL.

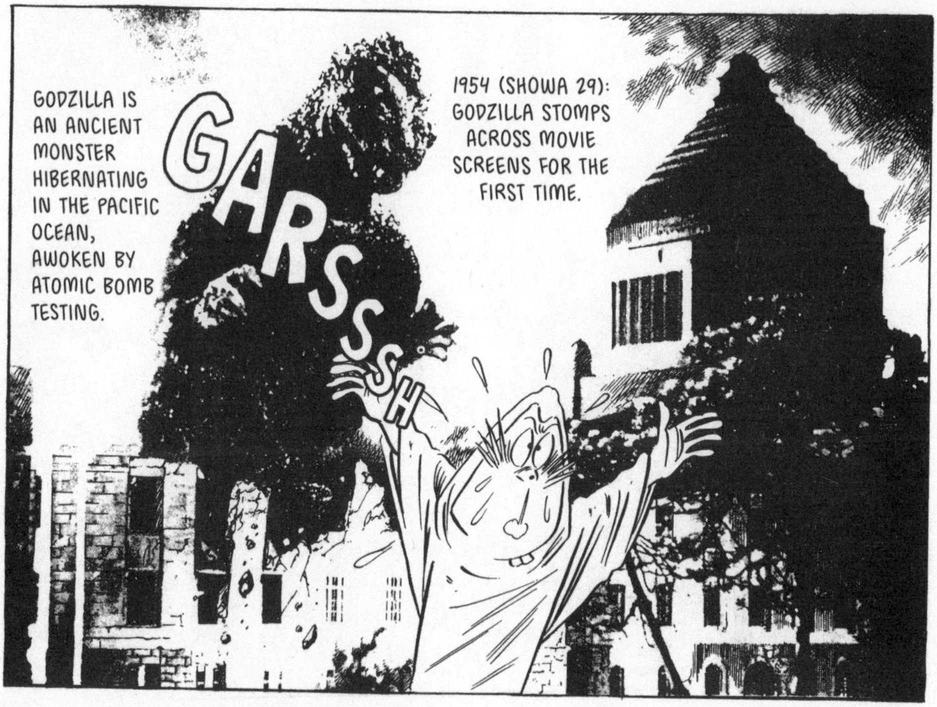
1954 (SHOWA 29): GODZILLA STOMPS ACROSS MOVIE SCREENS FOR THE FIRST TIME.
GARSSSH
GODZILLA IS AN ANCIENT MONSTER HIBERNATING IN THE PACIFIC OCEAN, AWOKEN BY ATOMIC BOMB TESTING.

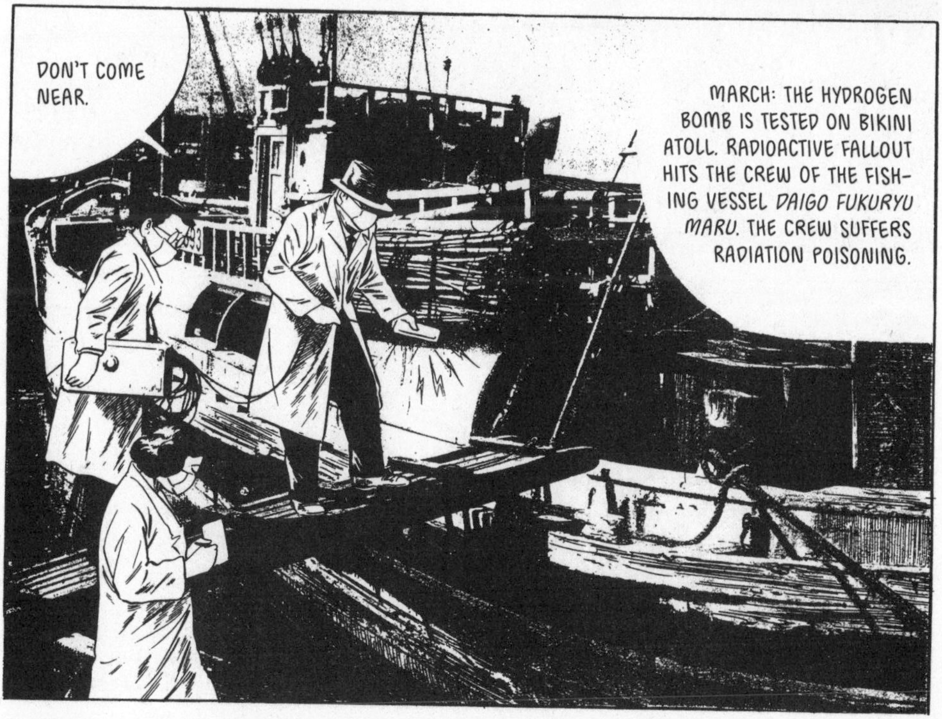
MARCH: THE HYDROGEN BOMB IS TESTED ON BIKINI ATOLL. RADIOACTIVE FALLOUT HITS THE CREW OF THE FISHING VESSEL *DAIGO FUKURYU MARU*. THE CREW SUFFERS RADIATION POISONING.
DON'T COME NEAR.

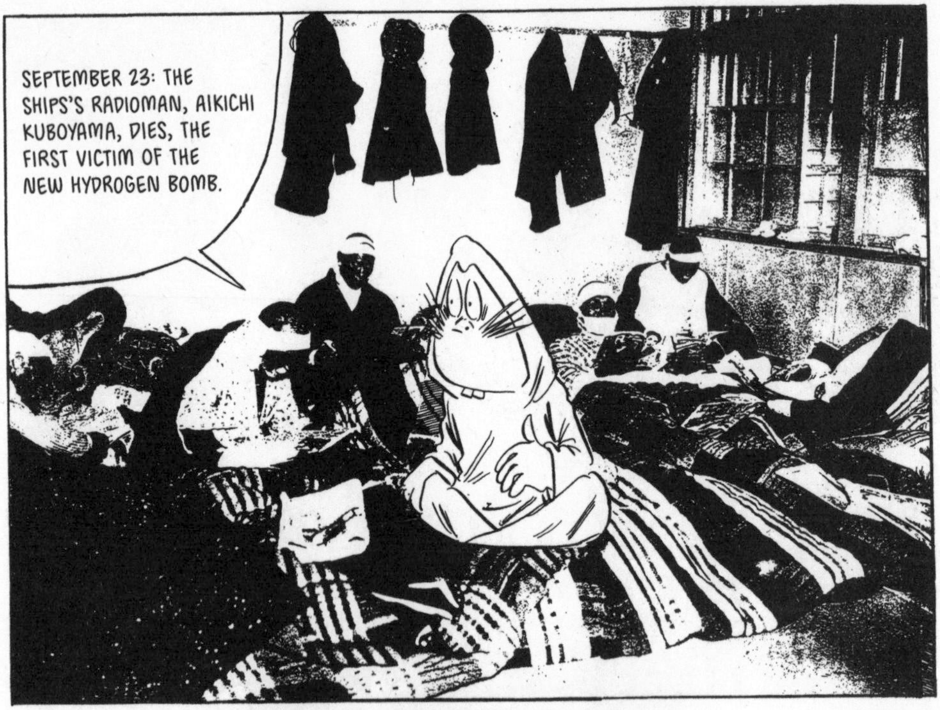
SEPTEMBER 23: THE SHIPS'S RADIOMAN, AIKICHI KUBOYAMA, DIES, THE FIRST VICTIM OF THE NEW HYDROGEN BOMB.

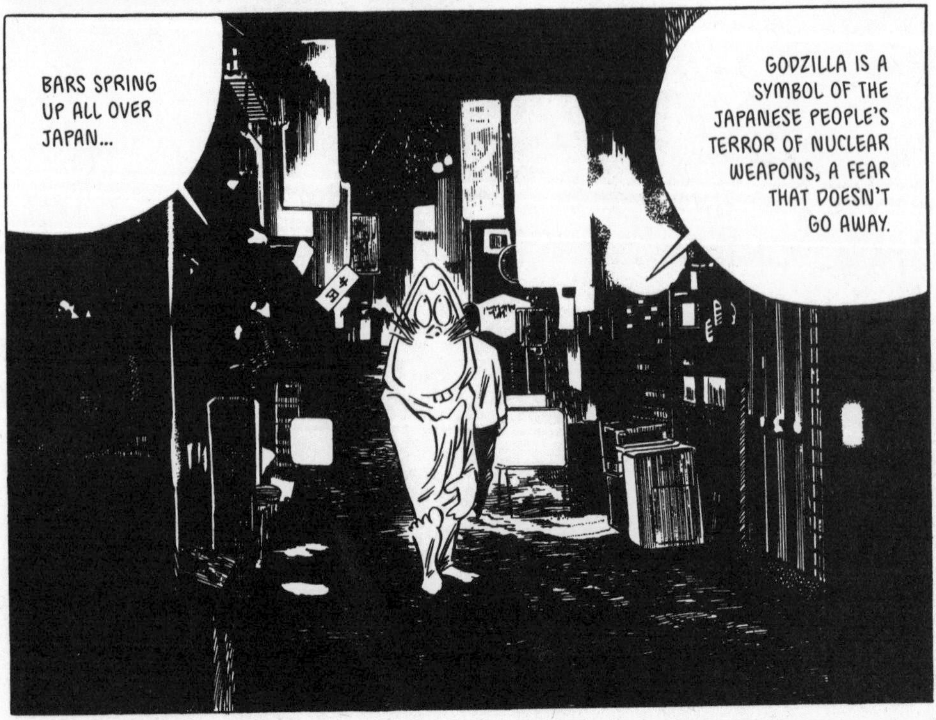
GODZILLA IS A SYMBOL OF THE JAPANESE PEOPLE'S TERROR OF NUCLEAR WEAPONS, A FEAR THAT DOESN'T GO AWAY.
BARS SPRING UP ALL OVER JAPAN...

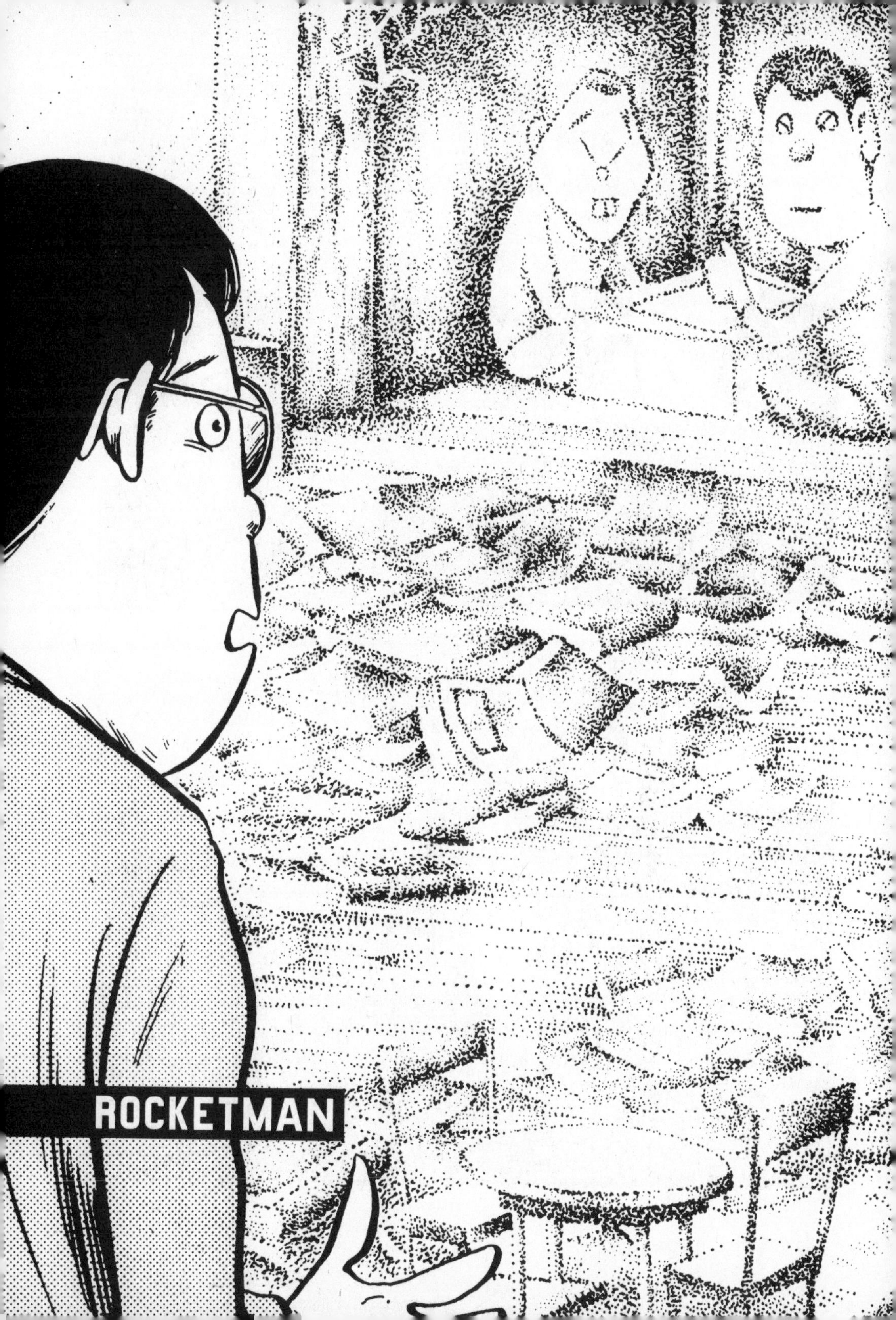
ROCKETMAN

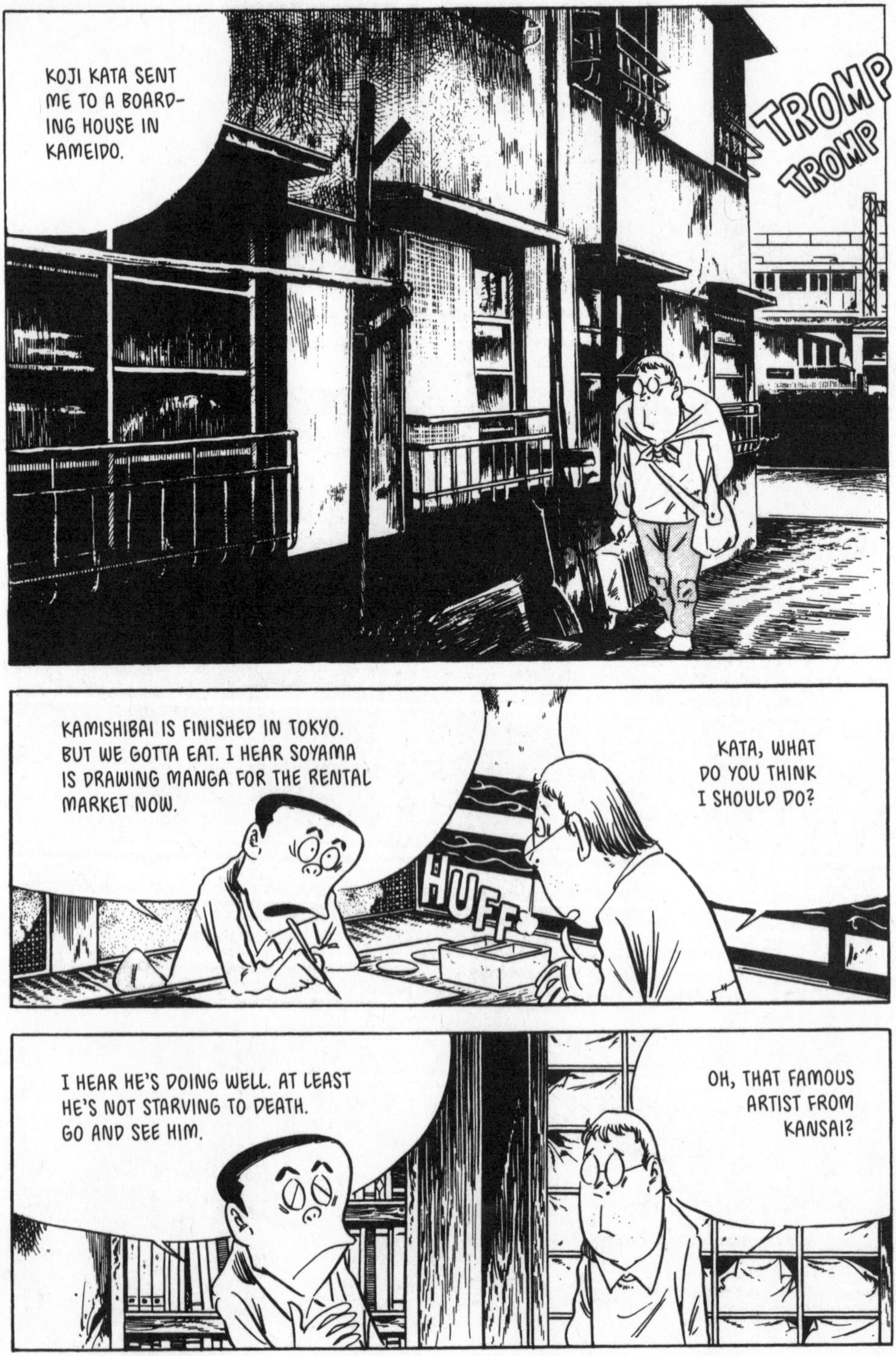
TROMP
TROMP
KOJI KATA SENT ME TO A BOARDING HOUSE IN KAMEIDO.
KATA, WHAT DO YOU THINK I SHOULD DO?
KAMISHIBAI IS FINISHED IN TOKYO. BUT WE GOTTA EAT. I HEAR SOYAMA IS DRAWING MANGA FOR THE RENTAL MARKET NOW.
HUFF
OH, THAT FAMOUS ARTIST FROM KANSAI?
I HEAR HE'S DOING WELL. AT LEAST HE'S NOT STARVING TO DEATH. GO AND SEE HIM.

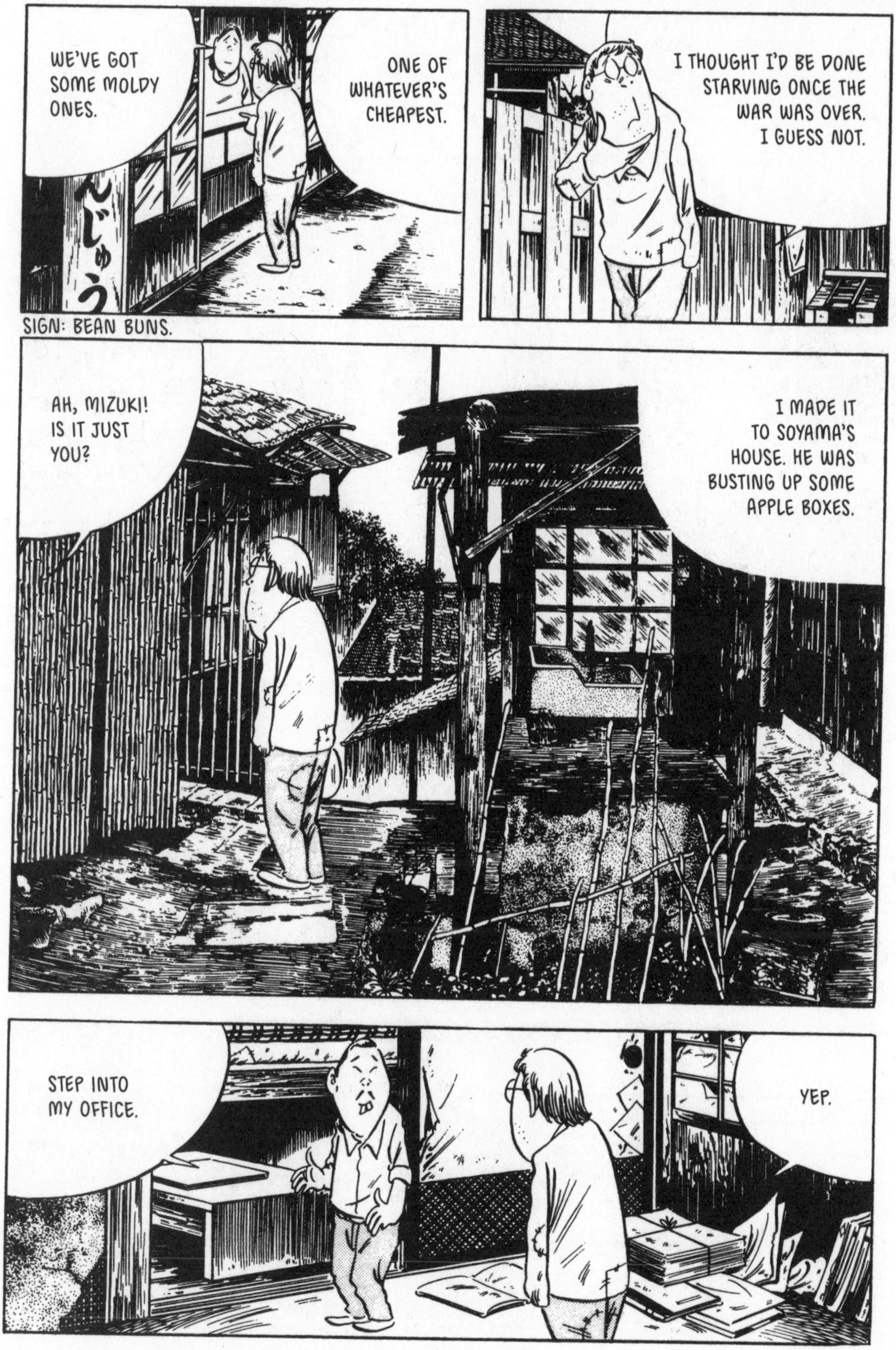
I THOUGHT I'D BE DONE STARVING ONCE THE WAR WAS OVER. I GUESS NOT.
ONE OF WHATEVER'S CHEAPEST.
WE'VE GOT SOME MOLDY ONES.
んじゅう
SIGN: BEAN BUNS.
I MADE IT TO SOYAMA'S HOUSE. HE WAS BUSTING UP SOME APPLE BOXES.
AH, MIZUKI! IS IT JUST YOU?
YEP.
STEP INTO MY OFFICE.

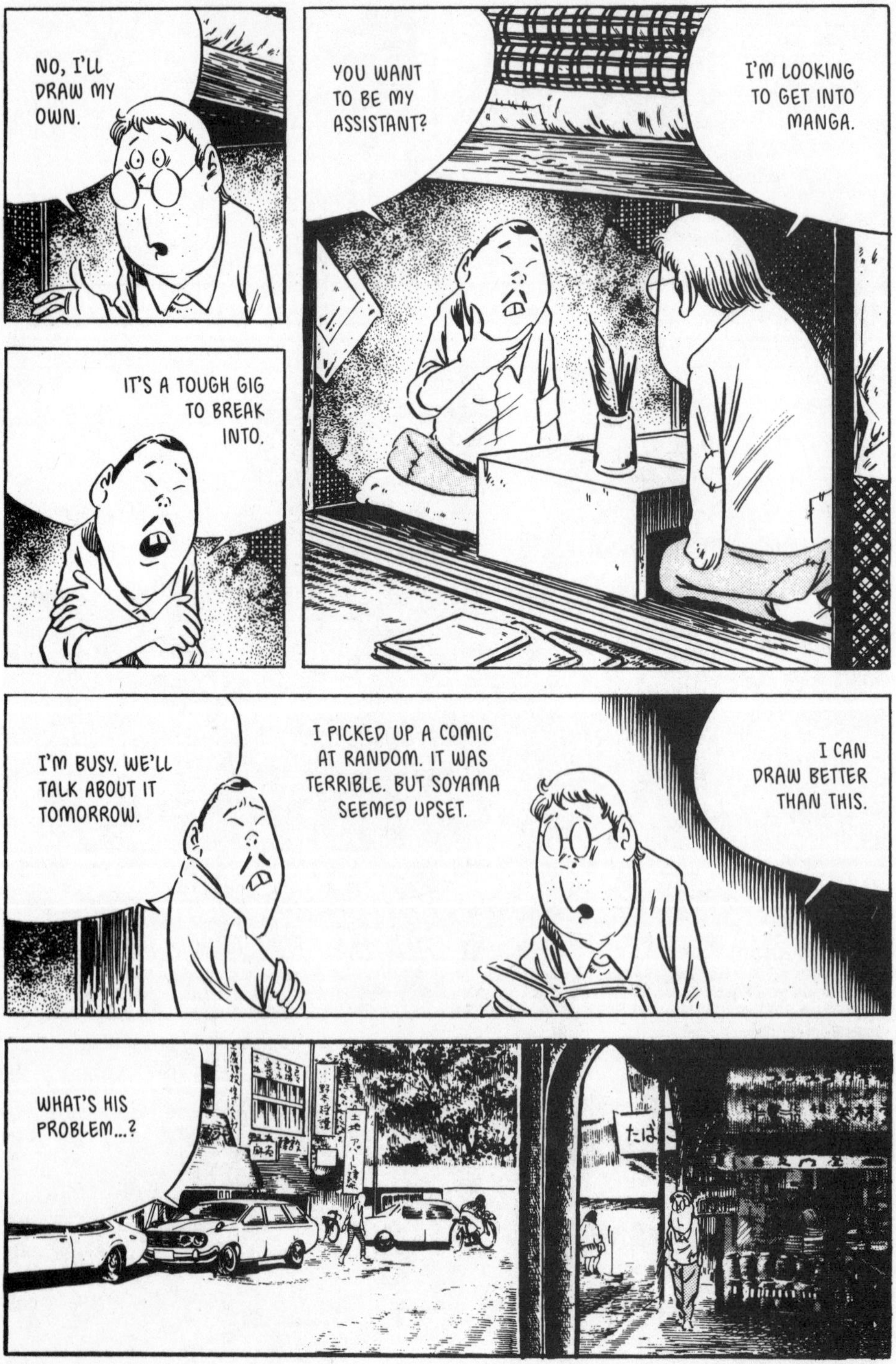
I'M LOOKING TO GET INTO MANGA.
YOU WANT TO BE MY ASSISTANT?
NO, I'LL DRAW MY OWN.
IT'S A TOUGH GIG TO BREAK INTO.
I CAN DRAW BETTER THAN THIS.
I PICKED UP A COMIC AT RANDOM. IT WAS TERRIBLE. BUT SOYAMA SEEMED UPSET.
I'M BUSY. WE'LL TALK ABOUT IT TOMORROW.
WHAT'S HIS PROBLEM...?

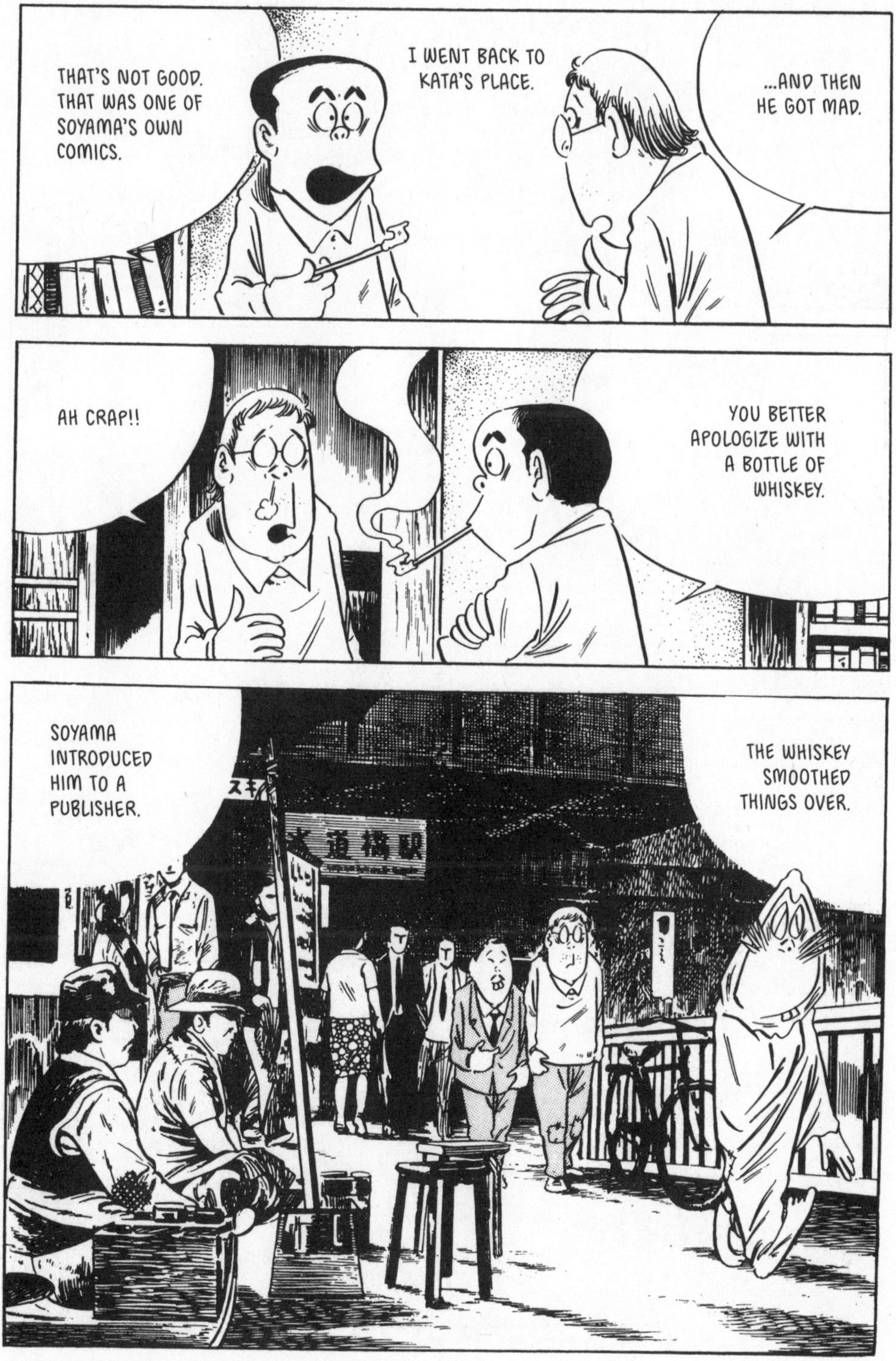
I WENT BACK TO KATA'S PLACE.
...AND THEN HE GOT MAD.
THAT'S NOT GOOD. THAT WAS ONE OF SOYAMA'S OWN COMICS.
YOU BETTER APOLOGIZE WITH A BOTTLE OF WHISKEY.
AH CRAP!!
THE WHISKEY SMOOTHED THINGS OVER.
SOYAMA INTRODUCED HIM TO A PUBLISHER.
水道橋駅

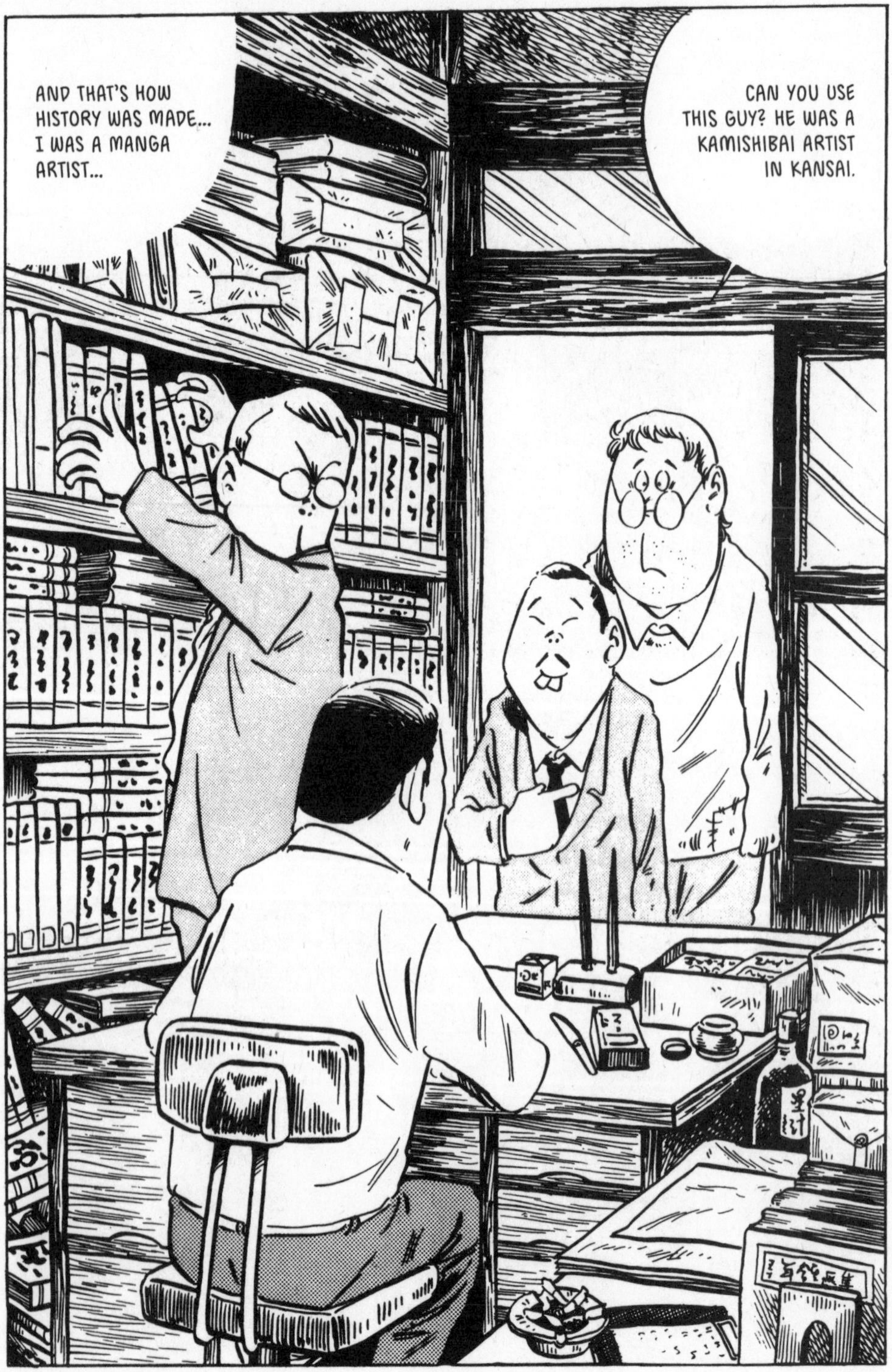
CAN YOU USE THIS GUY? HE WAS A KAMISHIBAI ARTIST IN KANSAI.
AND THAT'S HOW HISTORY WAS MADE... I WAS A MANGA ARTIST...

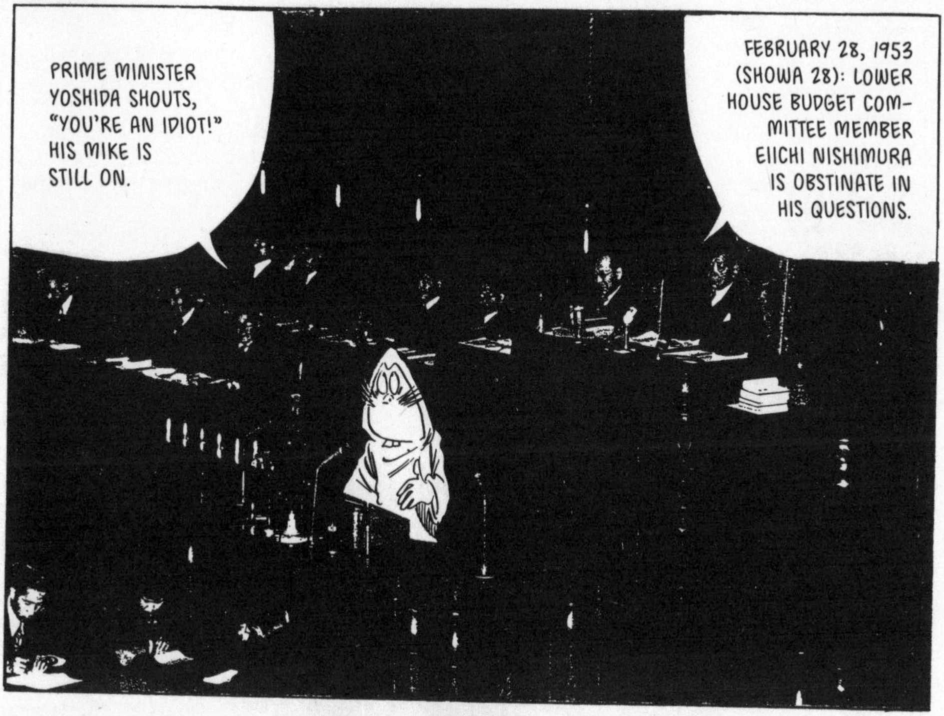
FEBRUARY 28, 1953 (SHOWA 28): LOWER HOUSE BUDGET COMMITTEE MEMBER EIICHI NISHIMURA IS OBSTINATE IN HIS QUESTIONS.
PRIME MINISTER YOSHIDA SHOUTS, "YOU'RE AN IDIOT!" HIS MIKE IS STILL ON.

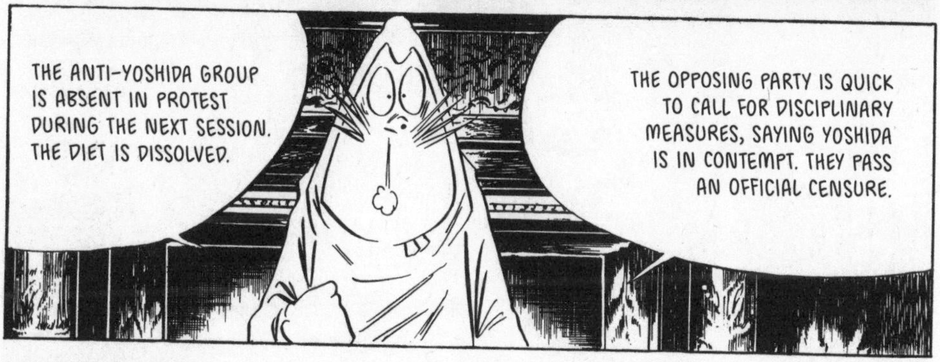
THE OPPOSING PARTY IS QUICK TO CALL FOR DISCIPLINARY MEASURES, SAYING YOSHIDA IS IN CONTEMPT. THEY PASS AN OFFICIAL CENSURE.
THE ANTI-YOSHIDA GROUP IS ABSENT IN PROTEST DURING THE NEXT SESSION. THE DIET IS DISSOLVED.

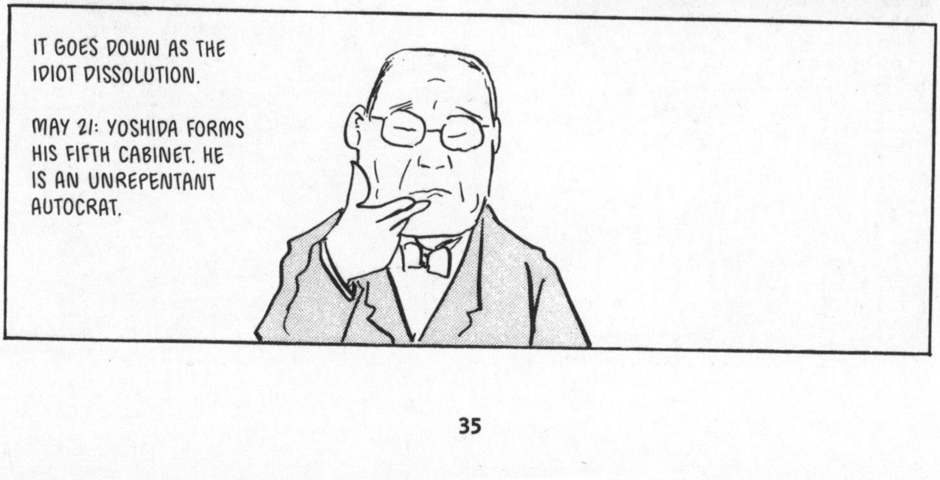
IT GOES DOWN AS THE IDIOT DISSOLUTION.
MAY 21: YOSHIDA FORMS HIS FIFTH CABINET. HE IS AN UNREPENTANT AUTOCRAT.

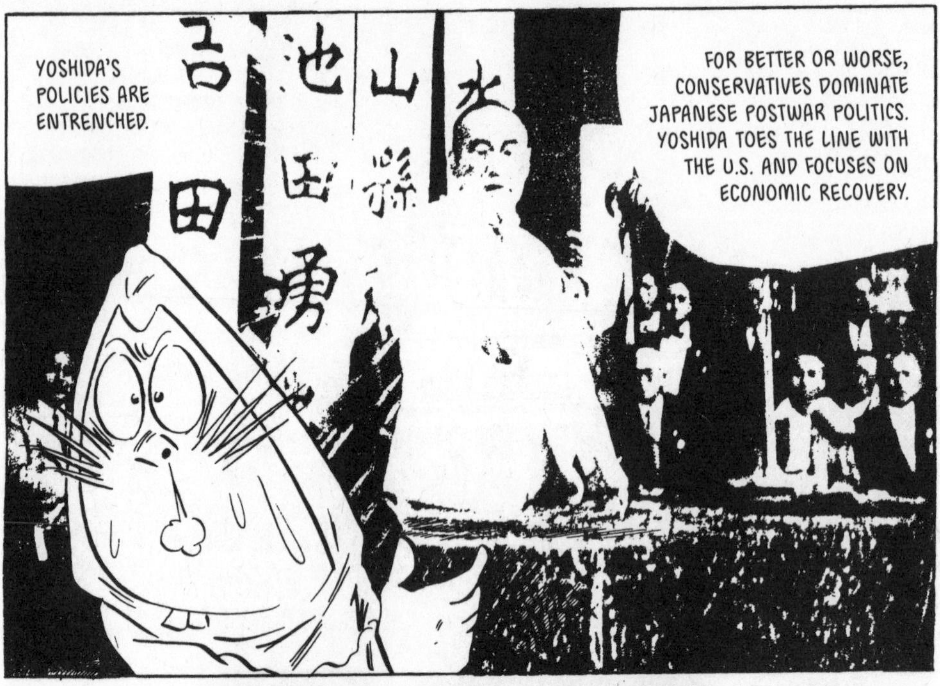
FOR BETTER OR WORSE, CONSERVATIVES DOMINATE JAPANESE POSTWAR POLITICS. YOSHIDA TOES THE LINE WITH THE U.S. AND FOCUSES ON ECONOMIC RECOVERY.
YOSHIDA'S POLICIES ARE ENTRENCHED.
吉田

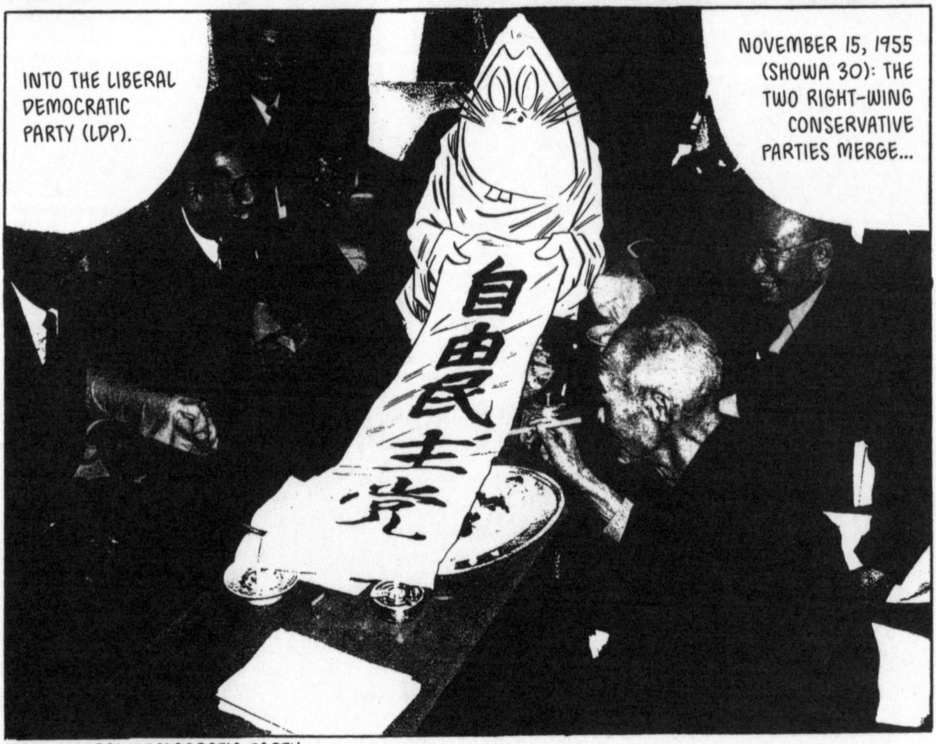
NOVEMBER 15, 1955 (SHOWA 30): THE TWO RIGHT-WING CONSERVATIVE PARTIES MERGE...
INTO THE LIBERAL DEMOCRATIC PARTY (LDP).
自由民主党

SIGN: LIBERAL DEMOCRATIC PARTY.

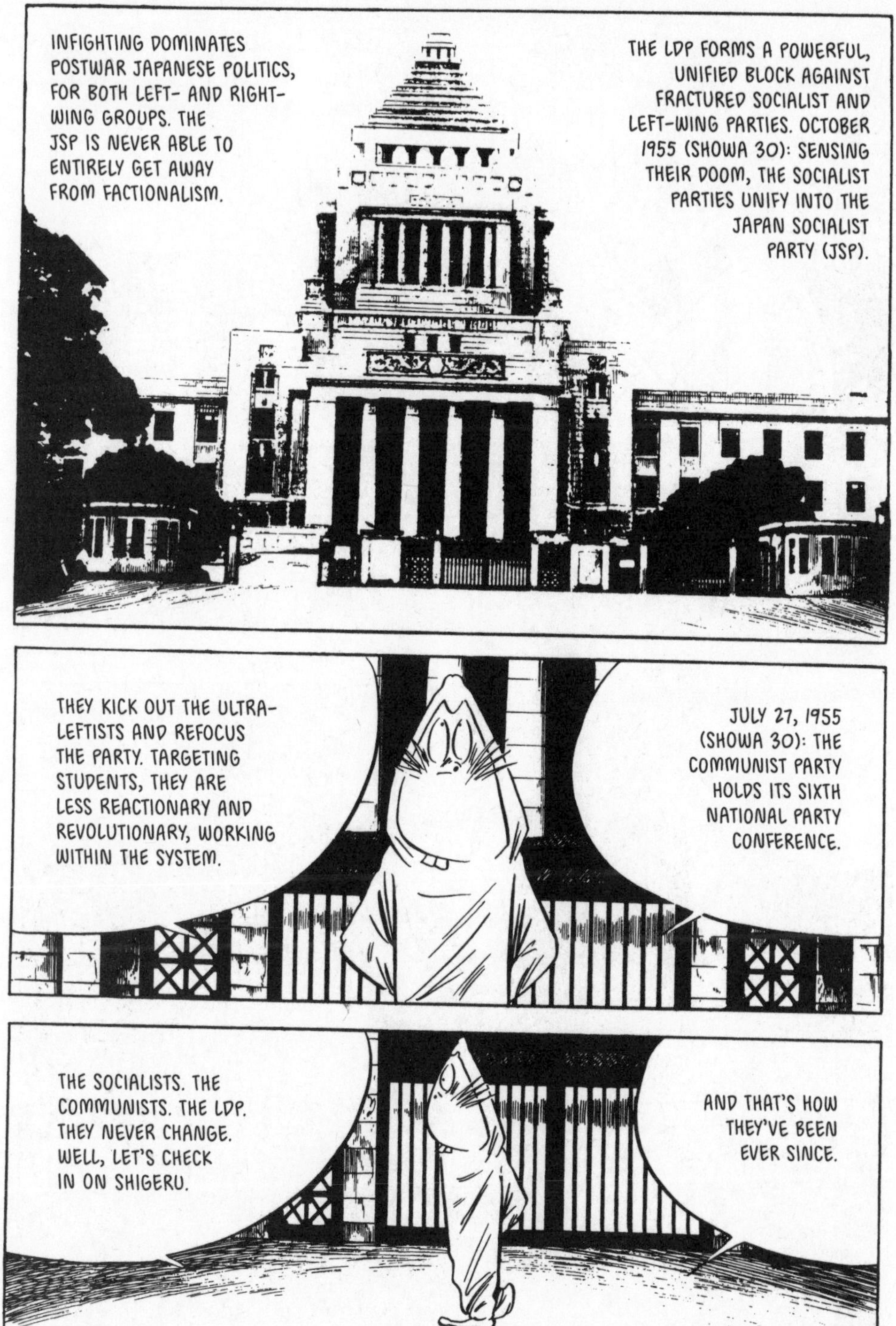
THE LDP FORMS A POWERFUL, UNIFIED BLOCK AGAINST FRACTURED SOCIALIST AND LEFT-WING PARTIES. OCTOBER 1955 (SHOWA 30): SENSING THEIR DOOM, THE SOCIALIST PARTIES UNIFY INTO THE JAPAN SOCIALIST PARTY (JSP).
INFIGHTING DOMINATES POSTWAR JAPANESE POLITICS, FOR BOTH LEFT- AND RIGHT-WING GROUPS. THE JSP IS NEVER ABLE TO ENTIRELY GET AWAY FROM FACTIONALISM.
JULY 27, 1955 (SHOWA 30): THE COMMUNIST PARTY HOLDS ITS SIXTH NATIONAL PARTY CONFERENCE.
THEY KICK OUT THE ULTRA-LEFTISTS AND REFOCUS THE PARTY. TARGETING STUDENTS, THEY ARE LESS REACTIONARY AND REVOLUTIONARY, WORKING WITHIN THE SYSTEM.
AND THAT'S HOW THEY'VE BEEN EVER SINCE.
THE SOCIALISTS. THE COMMUNISTS. THE LDP. THEY NEVER CHANGE. WELL, LET'S CHECK IN ON SHIGERU.

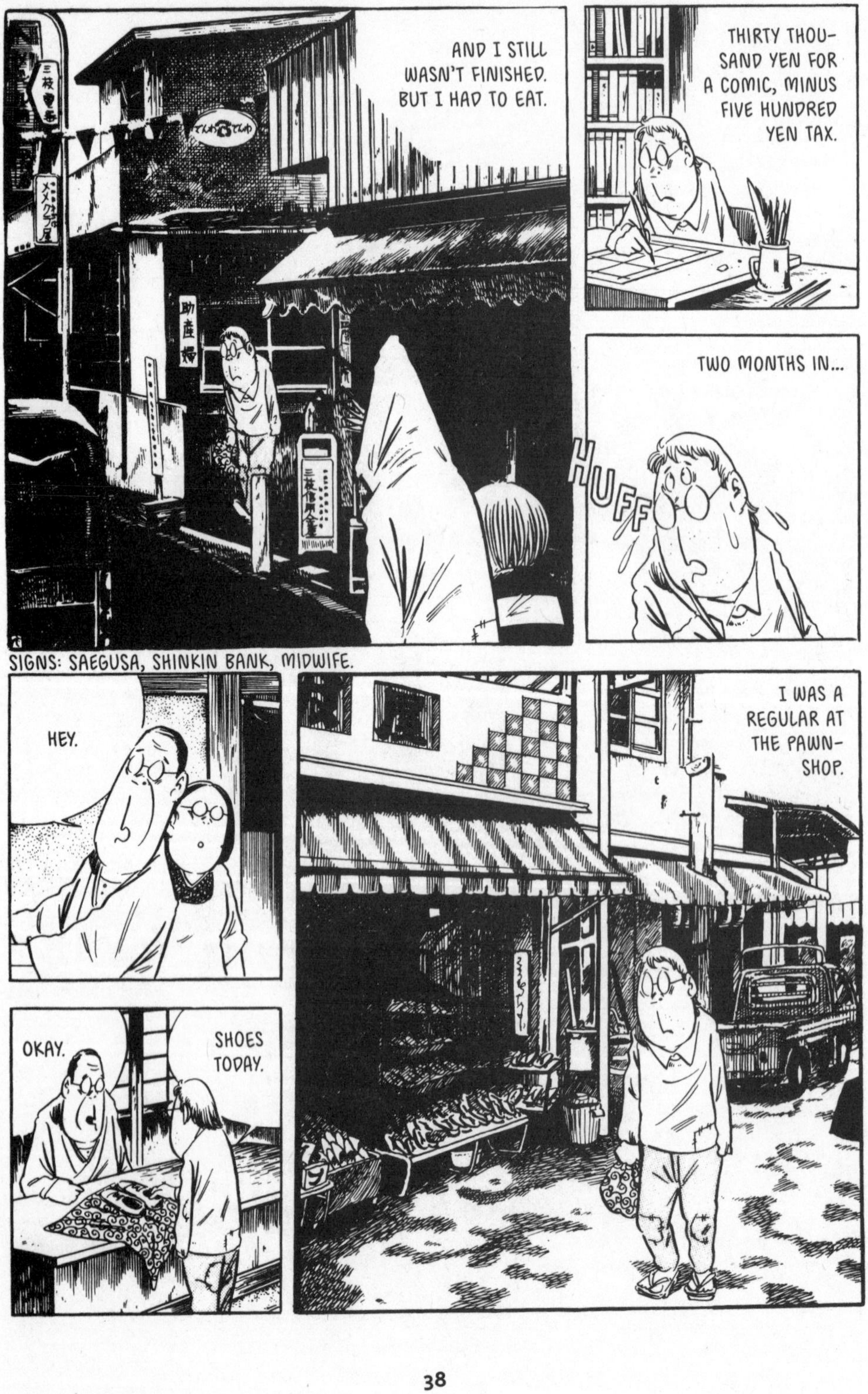
THIRTY THOUSAND YEN FOR A COMIC, MINUS FIVE HUNDRED YEN TAX.
TWO MONTHS IN...
HUFF
AND I STILL WASN'T FINISHED. BUT I HAD TO EAT.
SIGNS: SAEGUSA, SHINKIN BANK, MIDWIFE.
I WAS A REGULAR AT THE PAWNSHOP.
HEY.
SHOES TODAY.
OKAY.

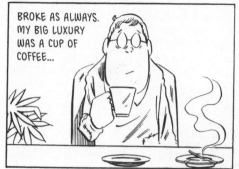

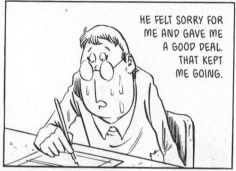

HE FELT SORRY FOR ME AND GAVE ME A GOOD DEAL. THAT KEPT ME GOING.
BROKE AS ALWAYS. MY BIG LUXURY WAS A CUP OF COFFEE...
I'D JUST FINISHED *ROCKETMAN** WHEN SUZUKI CAME FROM KOBE. HE WAS HAV-ING HARD TIMES.
I'LL BUY YOU A CUP OF COFFEE.
A COFFEE SHOP!
IT'S BEEN TWO YEARS.
AH. COFFEE...

*SHIGERU MIZUKI'S FIRST PUBLISHED COMIC. *ROCKETMAN* WAS IN EVERY WAY A SUPERMAN CLONE, EVEN WEARING AN "S" SYMBOL ON HIS CHEST.

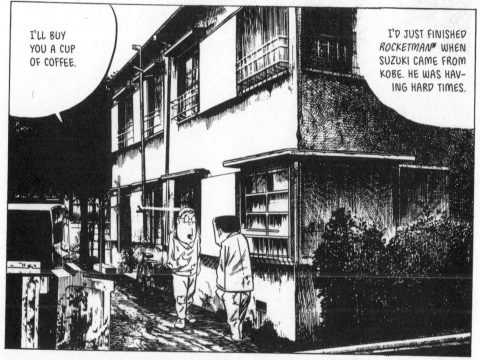

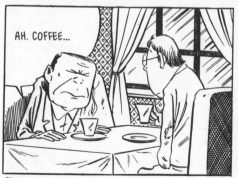

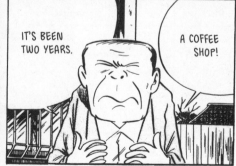

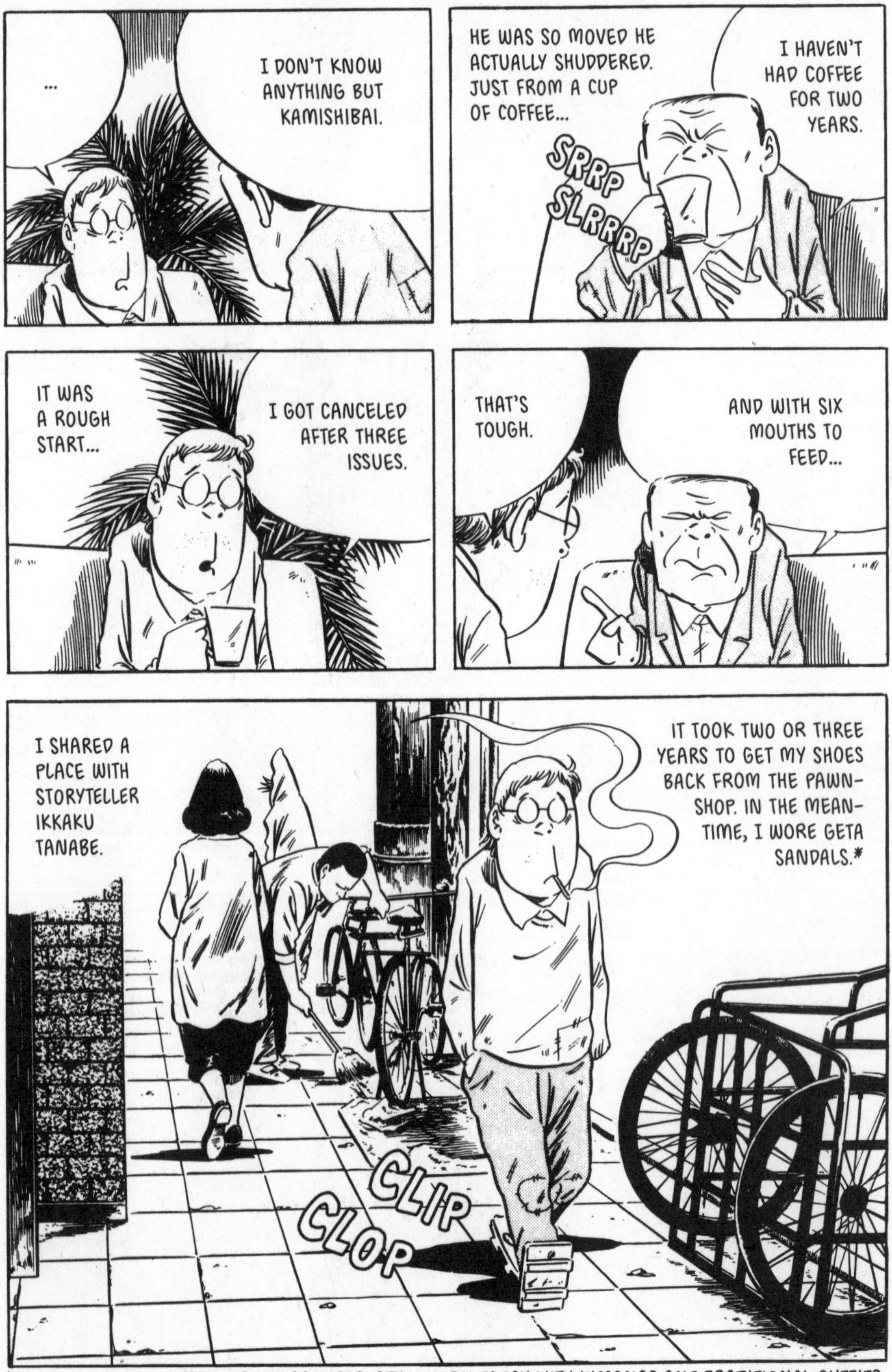

I HAVEN'T HAD COFFEE FOR TWO YEARS.
HE WAS SO MOVED HE ACTUALLY SHUDDERED. JUST FROM A CUP OF COFFEE...
SRRP
SLRRRP
I DON'T KNOW ANYTHING BUT KAMISHIBAI.
...
AND WITH SIX MOUTHS TO FEED...
THAT'S TOUGH.
I GOT CANCELED AFTER THREE ISSUES.
IT WAS A ROUGH START...
IT TOOK TWO OR THREE YEARS TO GET MY SHOES BACK FROM THE PAWN-SHOP. IN THE MEAN-TIME, I WORE GETA SANDALS.*
I SHARED A PLACE WITH STORYTELLER IKKAKU TANABE.
CLIP
CLOP

*TRADITIONAL JAPANESE WOODEN SANDALS. STILL WORN TODAY WITH KIMONOS AND TRADITIONAL OUTFITS.

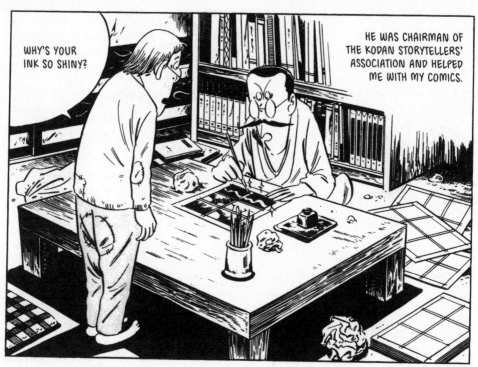

HE WAS CHAIRMAN OF THE KODAN STORYTELLERS' ASSOCIATION AND HELPED ME WITH MY COMICS.
WHY'S YOUR INK SO SHINY?
AH, I HAVE A RUNNY NOSE TODAY.
A SPECIAL SNOT AND INK MIX, HUH?
WE GOT ANY LEFTOVERS AROUND HERE?
YEAH.
GURGLE
RENT WAS SEVEN THOUSAND YEN, INCLUDING MEALS. WE WERE LATE RISERS AND ALWAYS MISSED BREAKFAST.
WE SAVED SOME RICE AND DAIKON RADISH FOR SNACKING.
NOM NOM

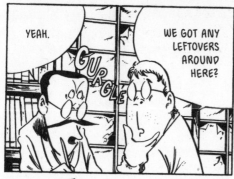

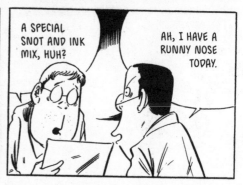

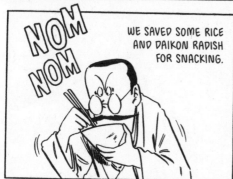

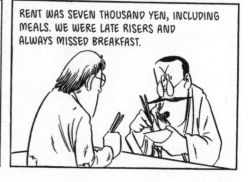

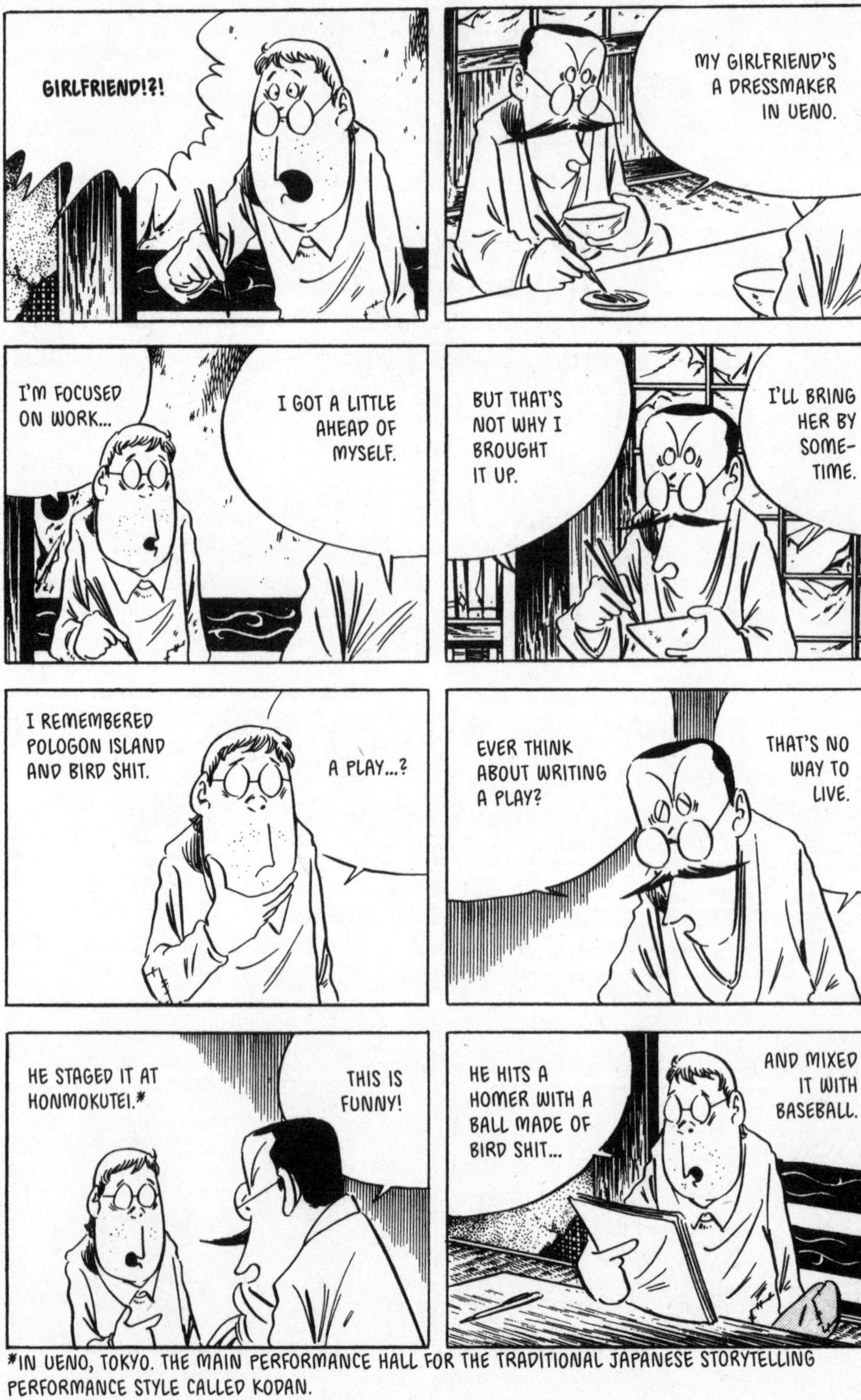
MY GIRLFRIEND'S A DRESSMAKER IN UENO.
GIRLFRIEND!?!
I'LL BRING HER BY SOME-TIME.
BUT THAT'S NOT WHY I BROUGHT IT UP.
I GOT A LITTLE AHEAD OF MYSELF.
I'M FOCUSED ON WORK...
THAT'S NO WAY TO LIVE.
EVER THINK ABOUT WRITING A PLAY?
A PLAY...?
I REMEMBERED POLOGON ISLAND AND BIRD SHIT.
AND MIXED IT WITH BASEBALL.
HE HITS A HOMER WITH A BALL MADE OF BIRD SHIT...
THIS IS FUNNY!
HE STAGED IT AT HONMOKUTEI.*

*IN UENO, TOKYO. THE MAIN PERFORMANCE HALL FOR THE TRADITIONAL JAPANESE STORYTELLING PERFORMANCE STYLE CALLED KODAN.

IT'S NOT THE POSTWAR ANYMORE

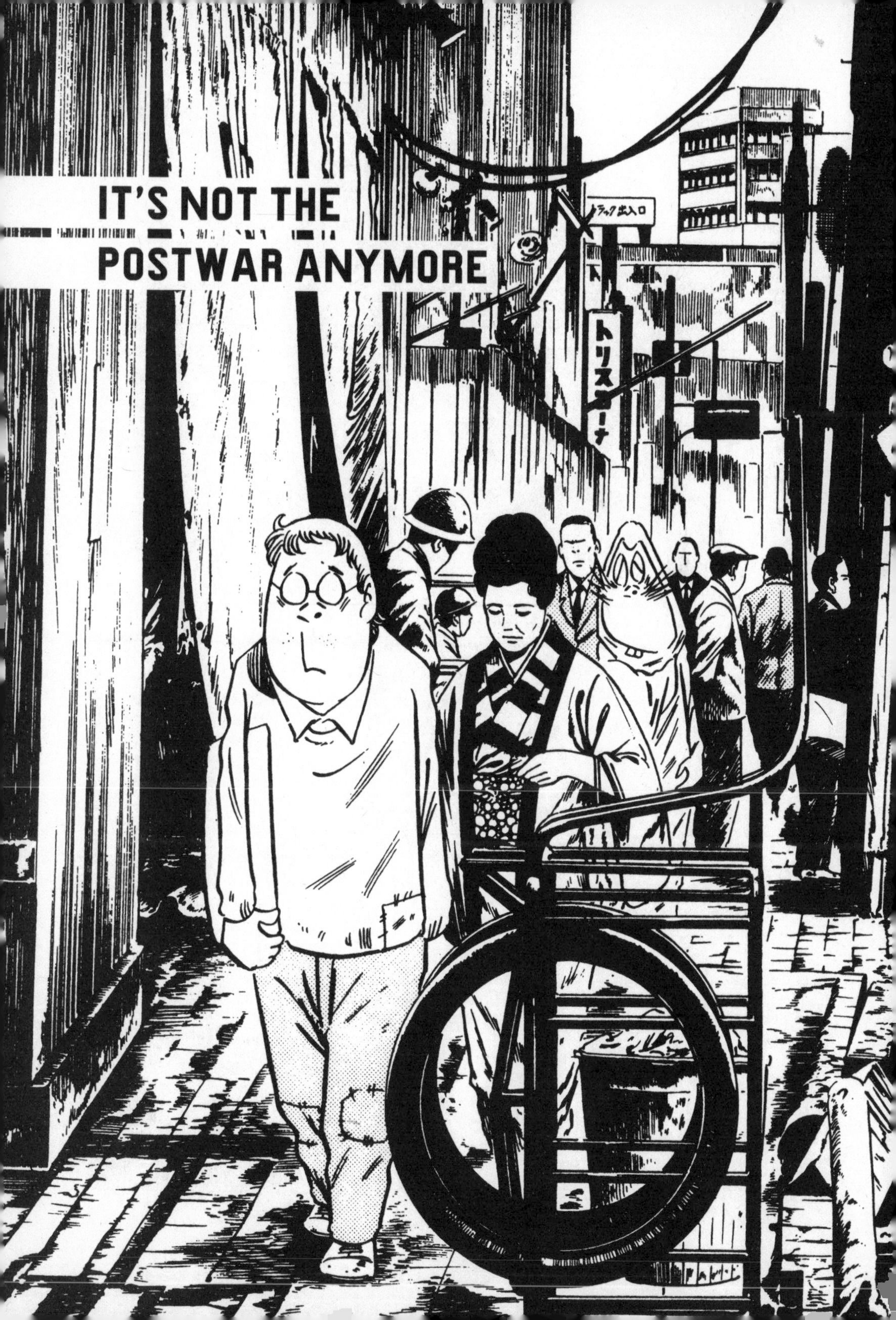

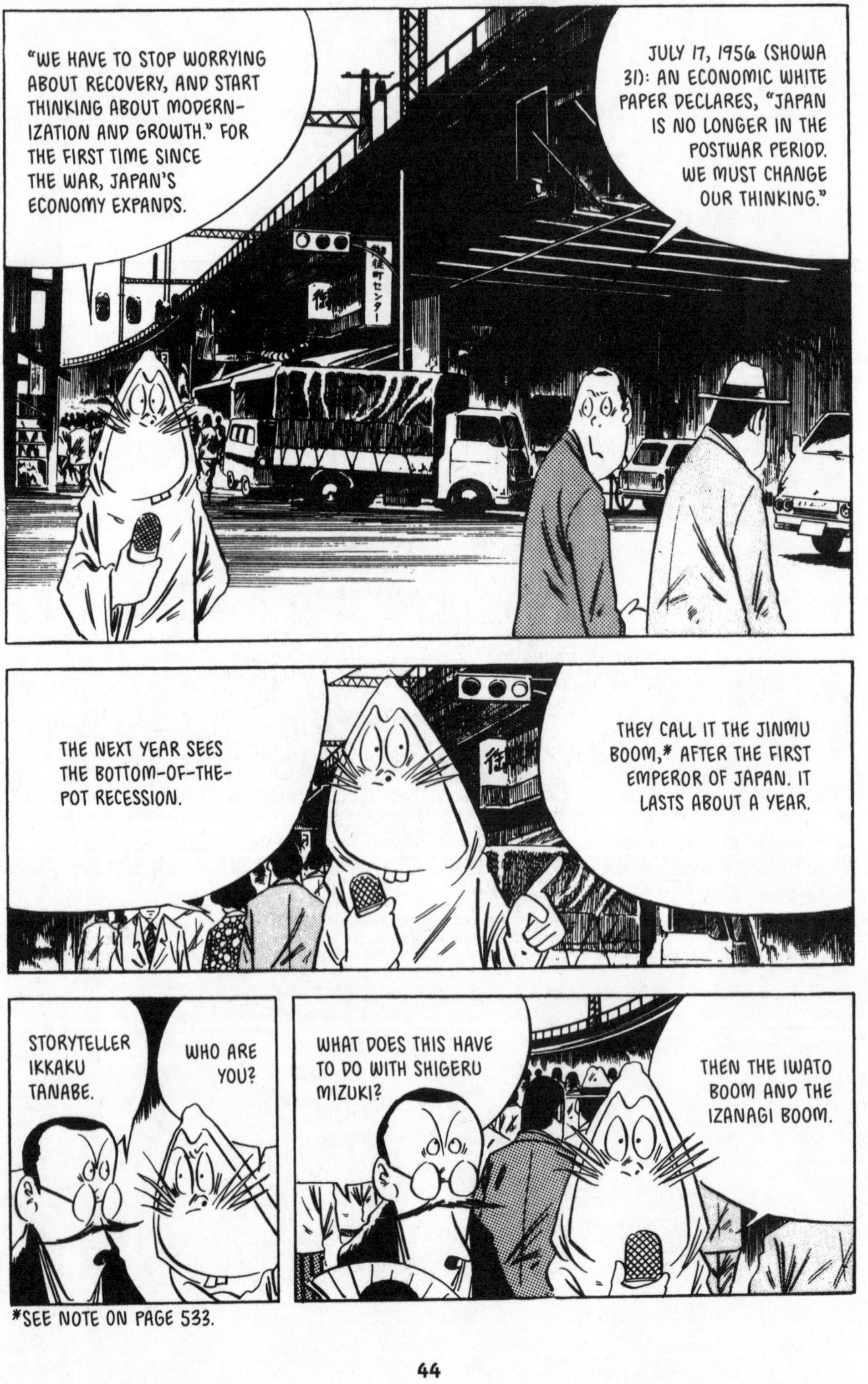
JULY 17, 1956 (SHOWA 31): AN ECONOMIC WHITE PAPER DECLARES, "JAPAN IS NO LONGER IN THE POSTWAR PERIOD. WE MUST CHANGE OUR THINKING."
"WE HAVE TO STOP WORRYING ABOUT RECOVERY, AND START THINKING ABOUT MODERN-IZATION AND GROWTH." FOR THE FIRST TIME SINCE THE WAR, JAPAN'S ECONOMY EXPANDS.
THEY CALL IT THE JINMU BOOM,* AFTER THE FIRST EMPEROR OF JAPAN. IT LASTS ABOUT A YEAR.
THE NEXT YEAR SEES THE BOTTOM-OF-THE-POT RECESSION.
THEN THE IWATO BOOM AND THE IZANAGI BOOM.
WHAT DOES THIS HAVE TO DO WITH SHIGERU MIZUKI?
WHO ARE YOU?
STORYTELLER IKKAKU TANABE.

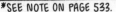

*SEE NOTE ON PAGE 533.

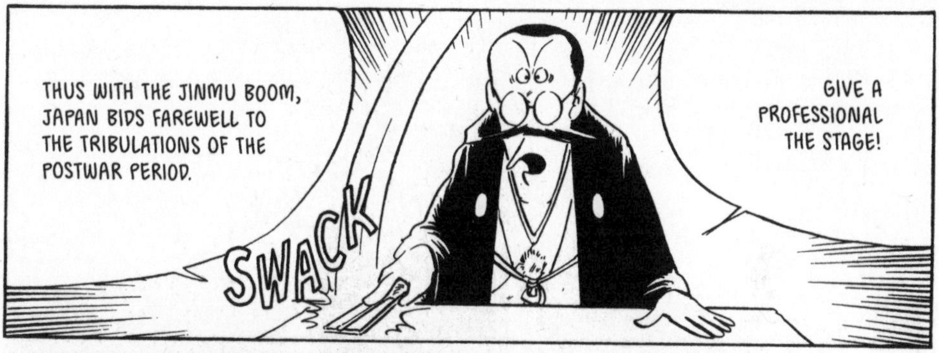
GIVE A PROFESSIONAL THE STAGE!
THUS WITH THE JINMU BOOM, JAPAN BIDS FAREWELL TO THE TRIBULATIONS OF THE POSTWAR PERIOD.
SWACK

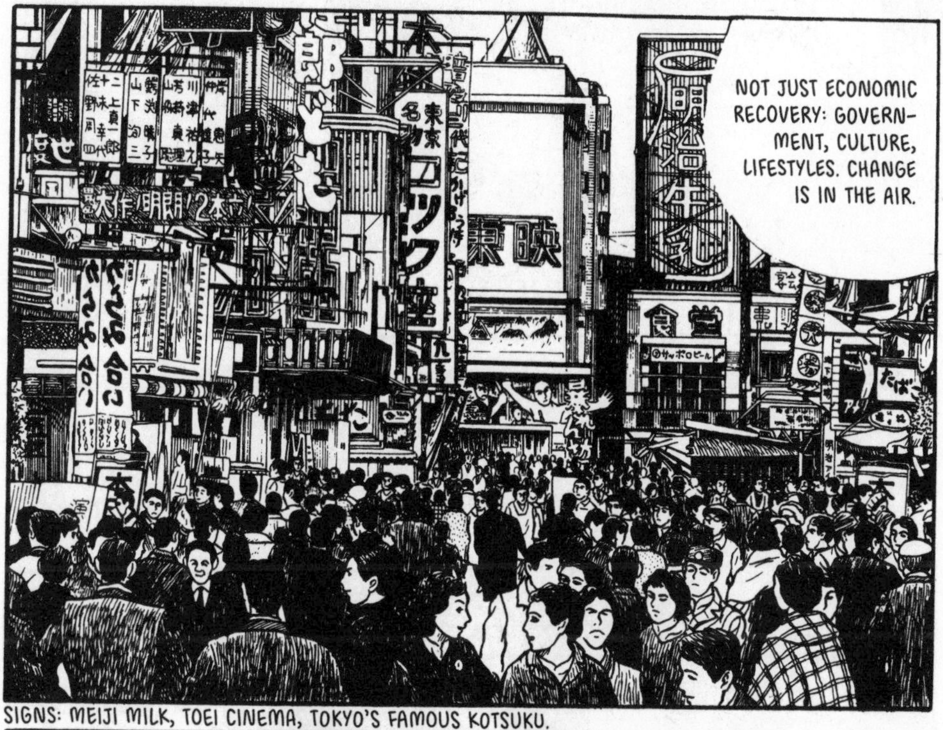
NOT JUST ECONOMIC RECOVERY: GOVERN-MENT, CULTURE, LIFESTYLES. CHANGE IS IN THE AIR.

SIGNS: MEIJI MILK, TOEI CINEMA, TOKYO'S FAMOUS KOTSUKU.

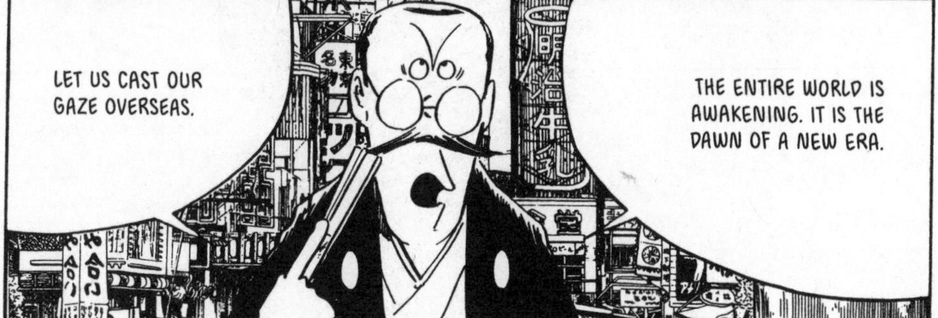
THE ENTIRE WORLD IS AWAKENING. IT IS THE DAWN OF A NEW ERA.
LET US CAST OUR GAZE OVERSEAS.

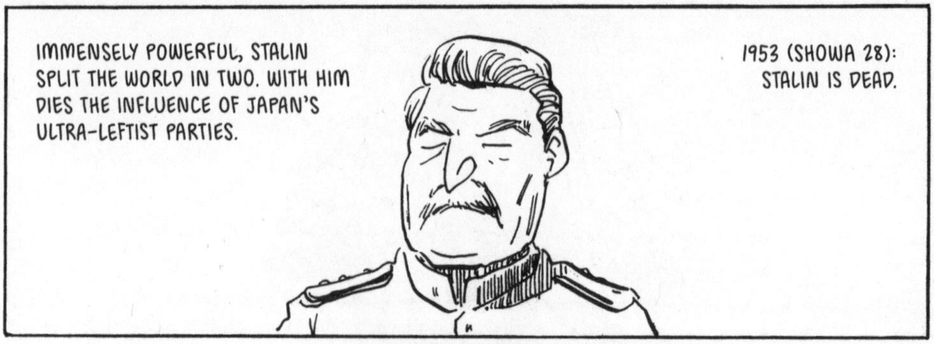
1953 (SHOWA 28): STALIN IS DEAD.
IMMENSELY POWERFUL, STALIN SPLIT THE WORLD IN TWO. WITH HIM DIES THE INFLUENCE OF JAPAN'S ULTRA-LEFTIST PARTIES.

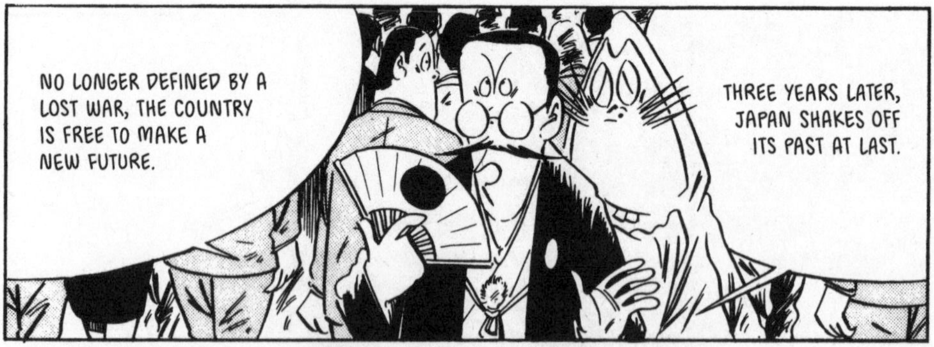
THREE YEARS LATER, JAPAN SHAKES OFF ITS PAST AT LAST.
NO LONGER DEFINED BY A LOST WAR, THE COUNTRY IS FREE TO MAKE A NEW FUTURE.

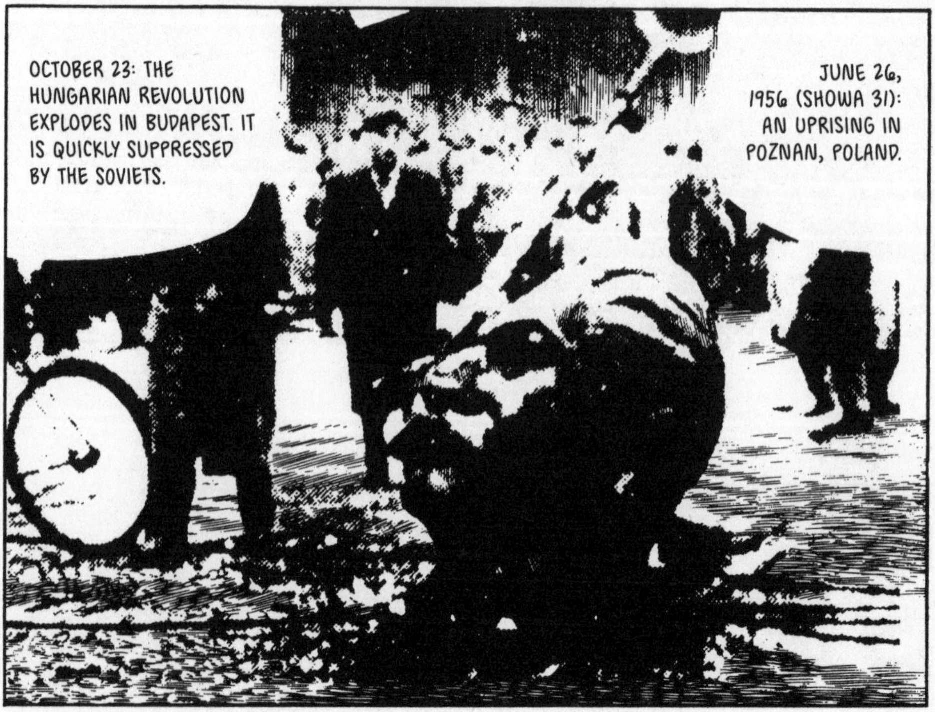
JUNE 26, 1956 (SHOWA 31): AN UPRISING IN POZNAN, POLAND.
OCTOBER 23: THE HUNGARIAN REVOLUTION EXPLODES IN BUDAPEST. IT IS QUICKLY SUPPRESSED BY THE SOVIETS.

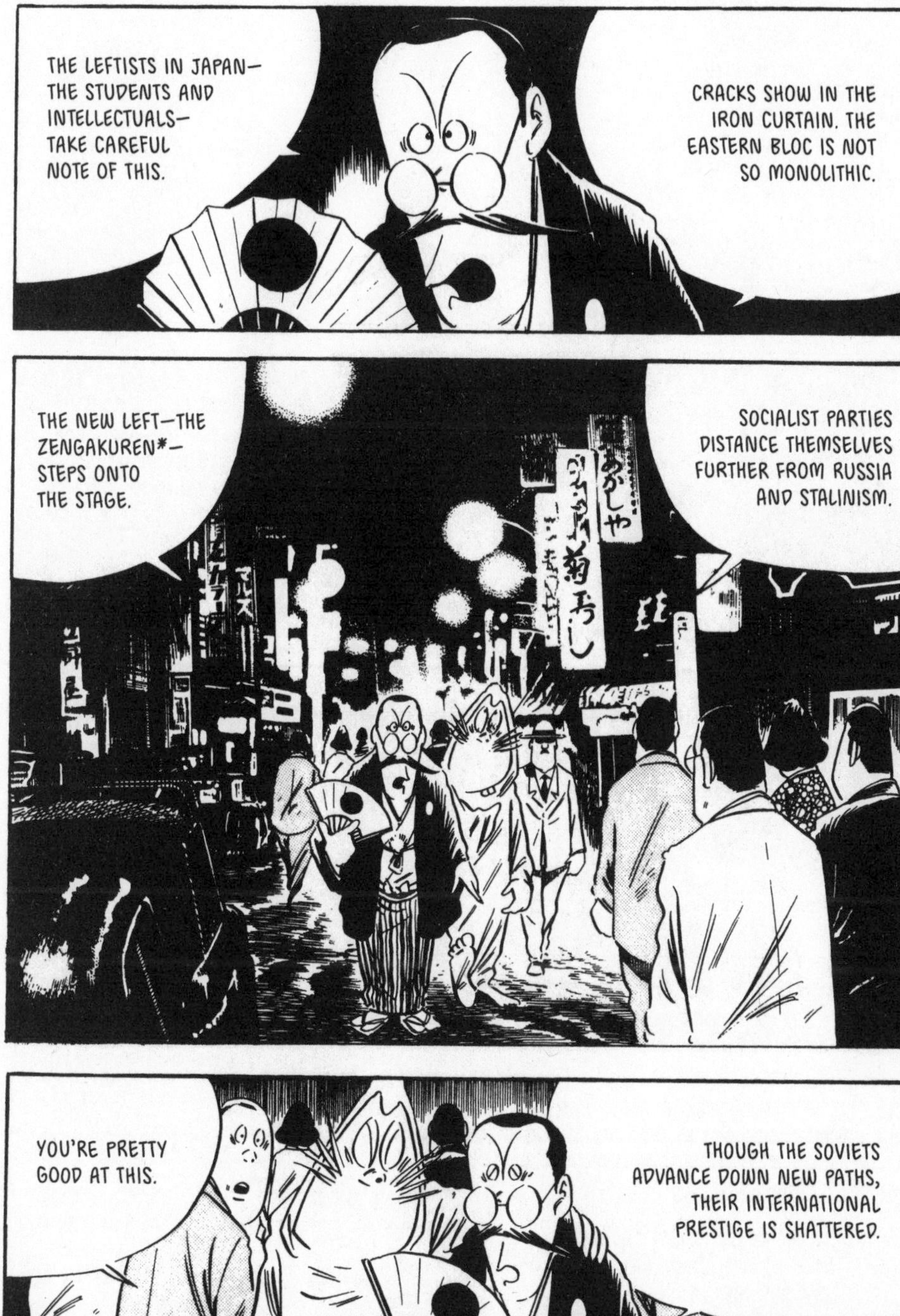
CRACKS SHOW IN THE IRON CURTAIN. THE EASTERN BLOC IS NOT SO MONOLITHIC.
THE LEFTISTS IN JAPAN—THE STUDENTS AND INTELLECTUALS—TAKE CAREFUL NOTE OF THIS.
SOCIALIST PARTIES DISTANCE THEMSELVES FURTHER FROM RUSSIA AND STALINISM.
THE NEW LEFT—THE ZENGAKUREN*—STEPS ONTO THE STAGE.
THOUGH THE SOVIETS ADVANCE DOWN NEW PATHS, THEIR INTERNATIONAL PRESTIGE IS SHATTERED.
YOU'RE PRETTY GOOD AT THIS.

*SEE NOTE ON PAGE 533.

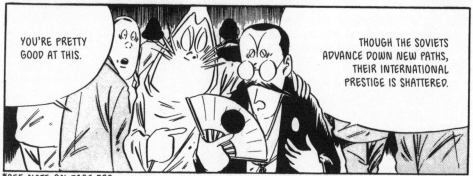

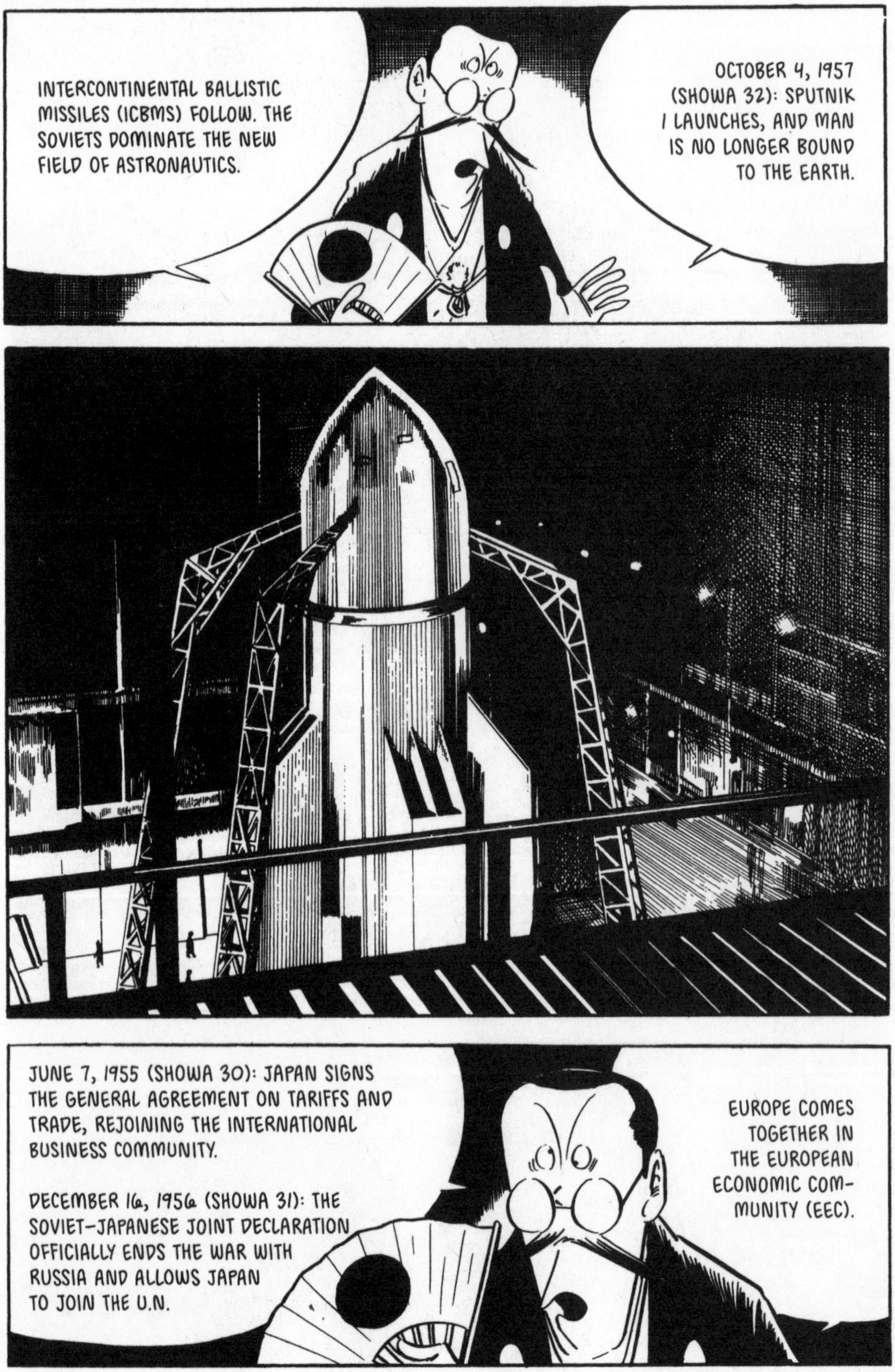
OCTOBER 4, 1957 (SHOWA 32): SPUTNIK I LAUNCHES, AND MAN IS NO LONGER BOUND TO THE EARTH.
INTERCONTINENTAL BALLISTIC MISSILES (ICBMS) FOLLOW. THE SOVIETS DOMINATE THE NEW FIELD OF ASTRONAUTICS.
EUROPE COMES TOGETHER IN THE EUROPEAN ECONOMIC COM-MUNITY (EEC).
JUNE 7, 1955 (SHOWA 30): JAPAN SIGNS THE GENERAL AGREEMENT ON TARIFFS AND TRADE, REJOINING THE INTERNATIONAL BUSINESS COMMUNITY.
DECEMBER 16, 1956 (SHOWA 31): THE SOVIET-JAPANESE JOINT DECLARATION OFFICIALLY ENDS THE WAR WITH RUSSIA AND ALLOWS JAPAN TO JOIN THE U.N.

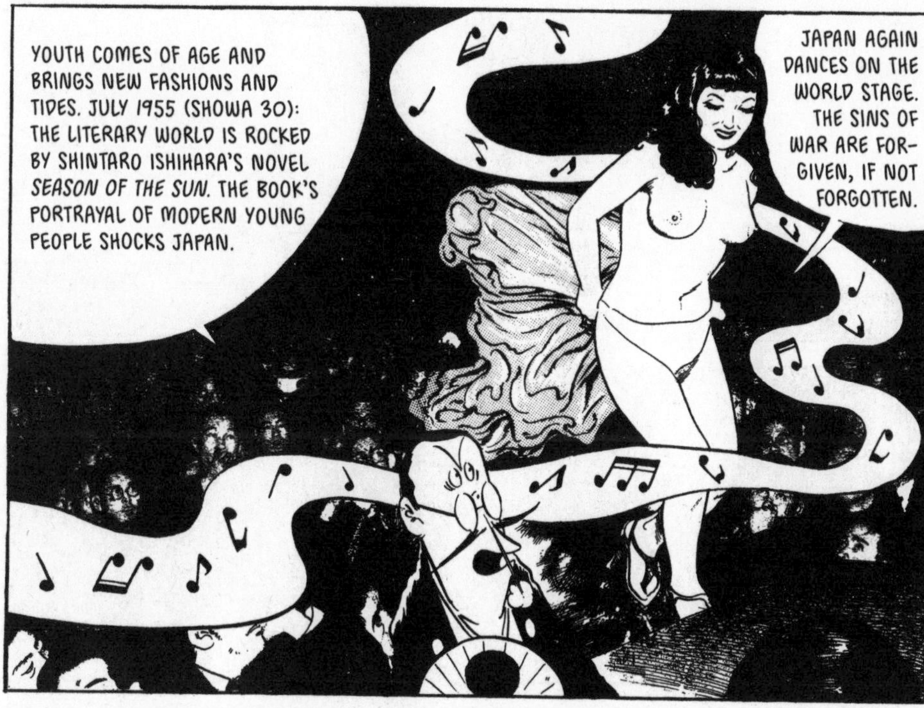
JAPAN AGAIN DANCES ON THE WORLD STAGE. THE SINS OF WAR ARE FORGIVEN, IF NOT FORGOTTEN.
YOUTH COMES OF AGE AND BRINGS NEW FASHIONS AND TIDES. JULY 1955 (SHOWA 30): THE LITERARY WORLD IS ROCKED BY SHINTARO ISHIHARA'S NOVEL *SEASON OF THE SUN*. THE BOOK'S PORTRAYAL OF MODERN YOUNG PEOPLE SHOCKS JAPAN.

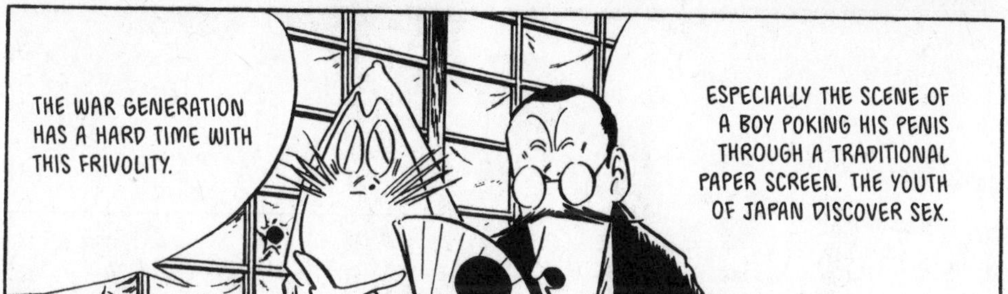
ESPECIALLY THE SCENE OF A BOY POKING HIS PENIS THROUGH A TRADITIONAL PAPER SCREEN. THE YOUTH OF JAPAN DISCOVER SEX.
THE WAR GENERATION HAS A HARD TIME WITH THIS FRIVOLITY.

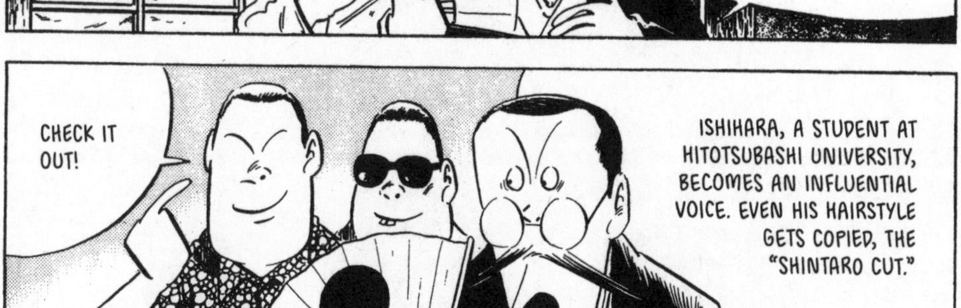
ISHIHARA, A STUDENT AT HITOTSUBASHI UNIVERSITY, BECOMES AN INFLUENTIAL VOICE. EVEN HIS HAIRSTYLE GETS COPIED, THE "SHINTARO CUT."
CHECK IT OUT!

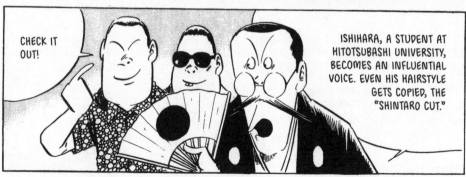

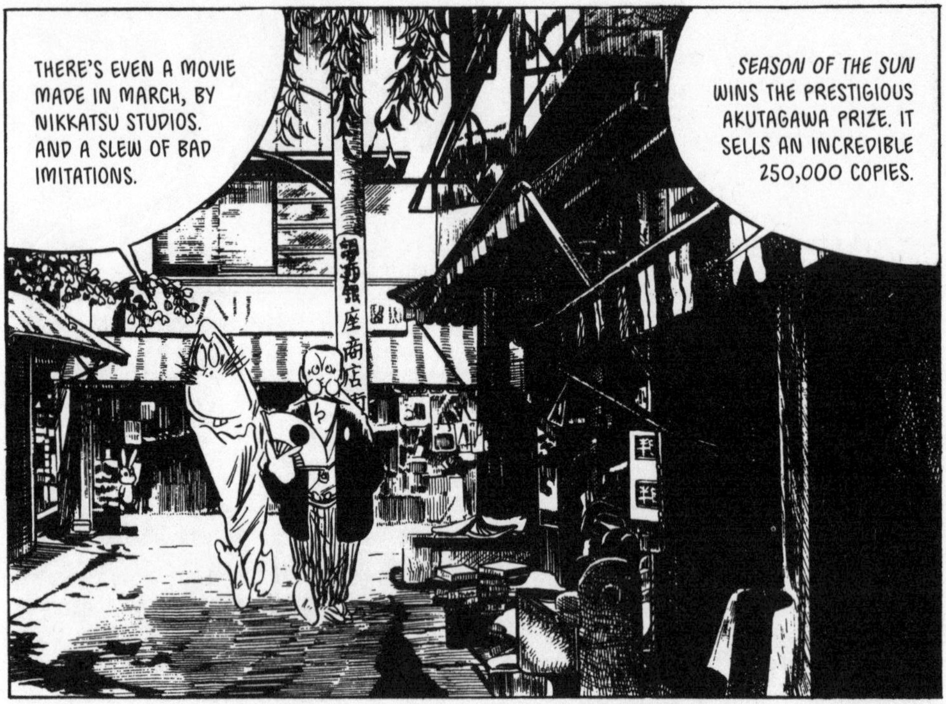
SEASON OF THE SUN WINS THE PRESTIGIOUS AKUTAGAWA PRIZE. IT SELLS AN INCREDIBLE 250,000 COPIES.
THERE'S EVEN A MOVIE MADE IN MARCH, BY NIKKATSU STUDIOS. AND A SLEW OF BAD IMITATIONS.

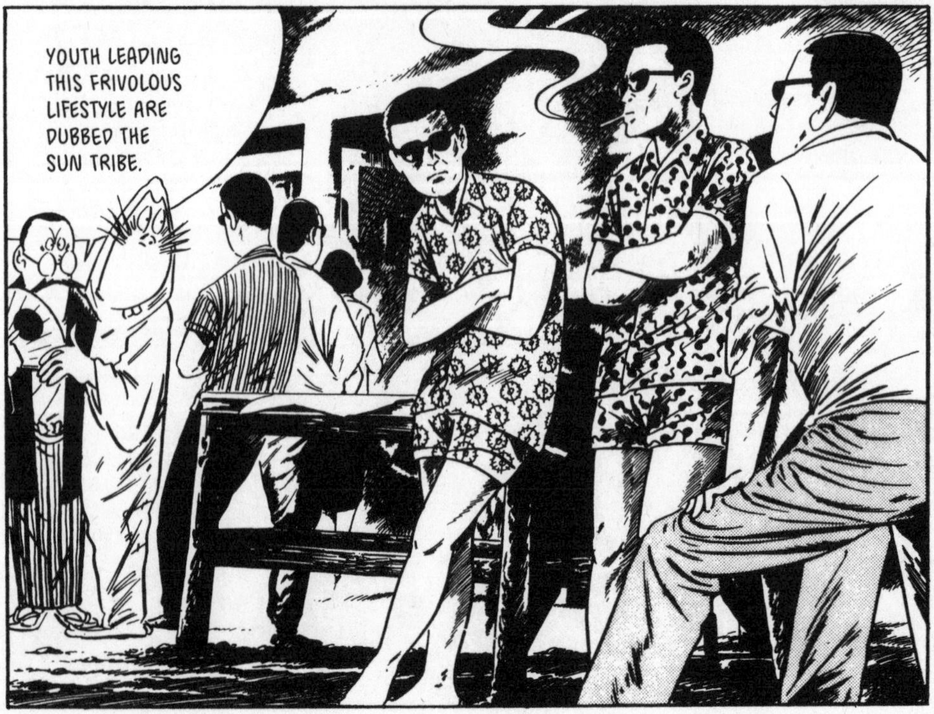
YOUTH LEADING THIS FRIVOLOUS LIFESTYLE ARE DUBBED THE SUN TRIBE.

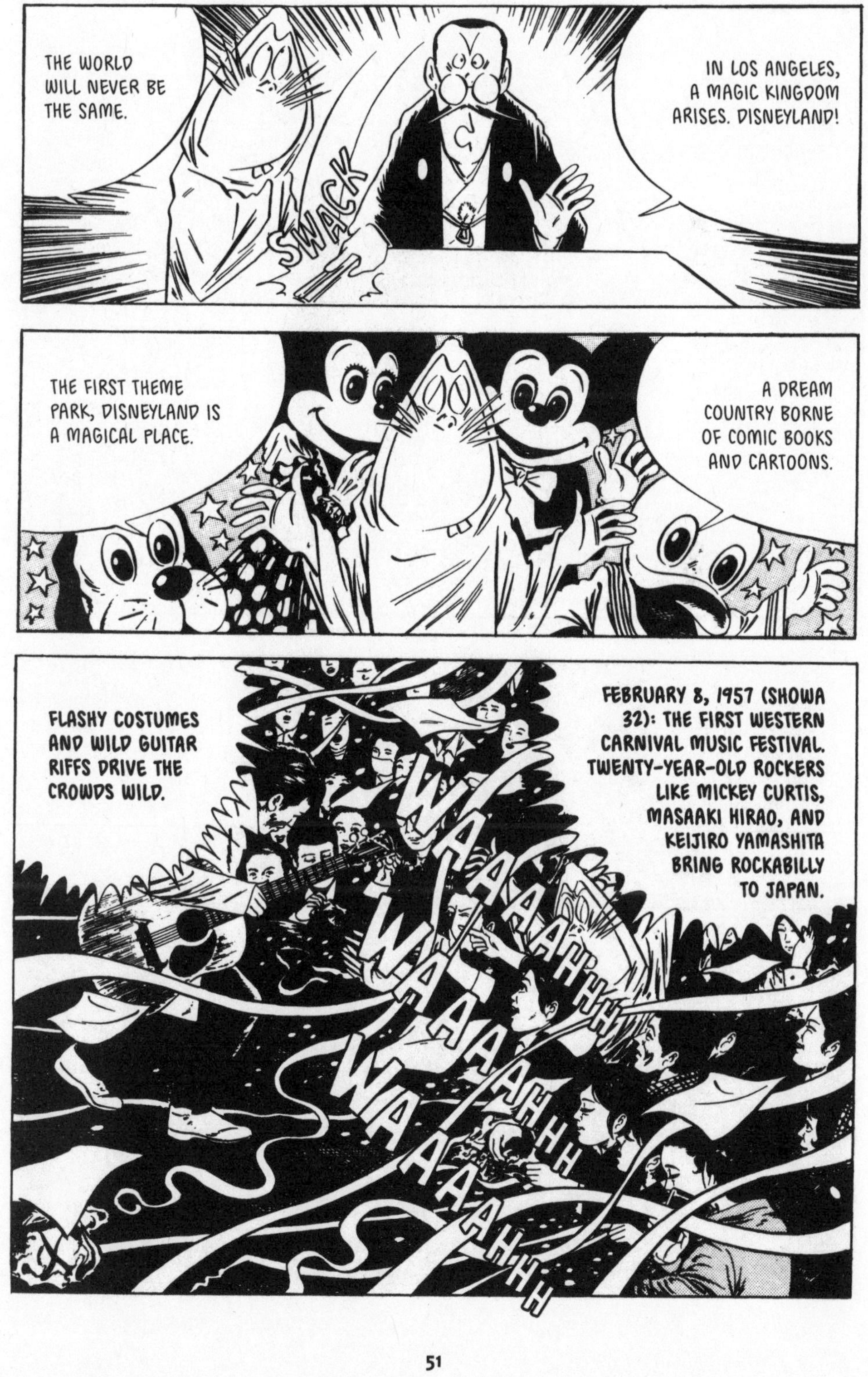
IN LOS ANGELES, A MAGIC KINGDOM ARISES. DISNEYLAND!
THE WORLD WILL NEVER BE THE SAME.
SWACK
A DREAM COUNTRY BORNE OF COMIC BOOKS AND CARTOONS.
THE FIRST THEME PARK, DISNEYLAND IS A MAGICAL PLACE.
FEBRUARY 8, 1957 (SHOWA 32): THE FIRST WESTERN CARNIVAL MUSIC FESTIVAL. TWENTY-YEAR-OLD ROCKERS LIKE MICKEY CURTIS, MASAAKI HIRAO, AND KEIJIRO YAMASHITA BRING ROCKABILLY TO JAPAN.
FLASHY COSTUMES AND WILD GUITAR RIFFS DRIVE THE CROWDS WILD.
WAAAAAHHH
WAAAAAHHHH
WAAAAAHHHH

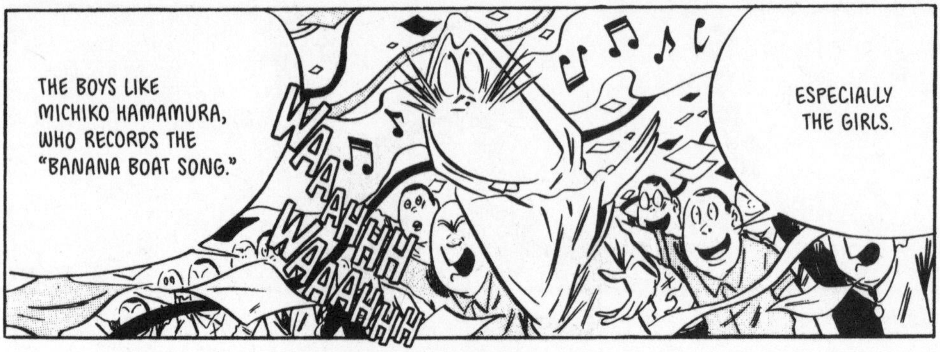
ESPECIALLY THE GIRLS.
THE BOYS LIKE MICHIKO HAMAMURA, WHO RECORDS THE "BANANA BOAT SONG."
WAAAHHHH
WAAAHHHHH

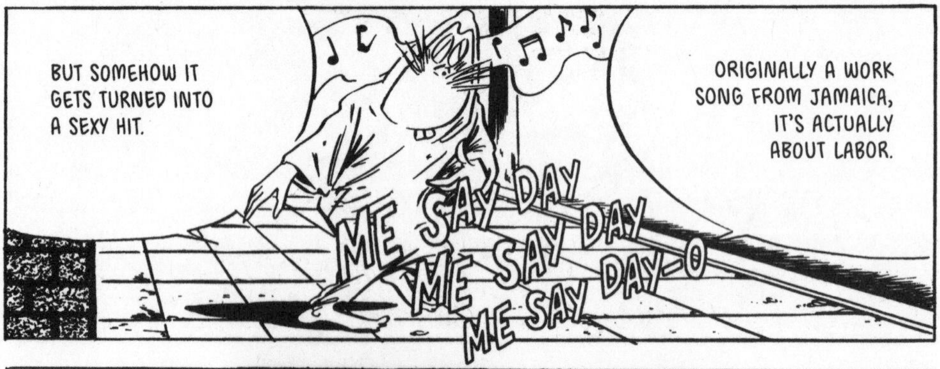
ORIGINALLY A WORK SONG FROM JAMAICA, IT'S ACTUALLY ABOUT LABOR.
BUT SOMEHOW IT GETS TURNED INTO A SEXY HIT.
ME SAY DAY
ME SAY DAY
ME SAY DAY-O

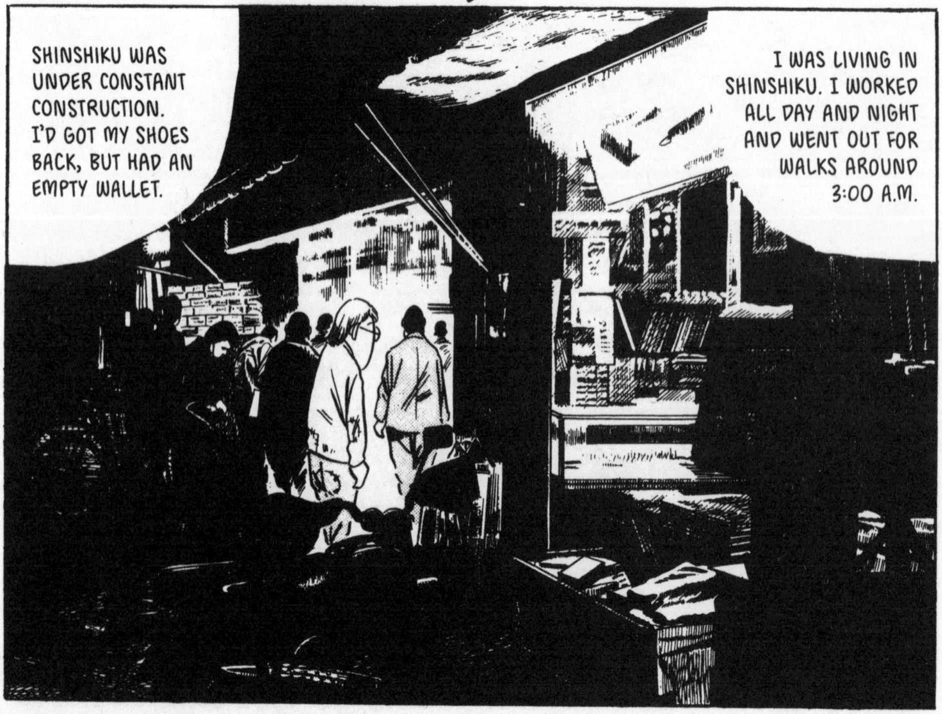
I WAS LIVING IN SHINSHIKU. I WORKED ALL DAY AND NIGHT AND WENT OUT FOR WALKS AROUND 3:00 A.M.
SHINSHIKU WAS UNDER CONSTANT CONSTRUCTION. I'D GOT MY SHOES BACK, BUT HAD AN EMPTY WALLET.

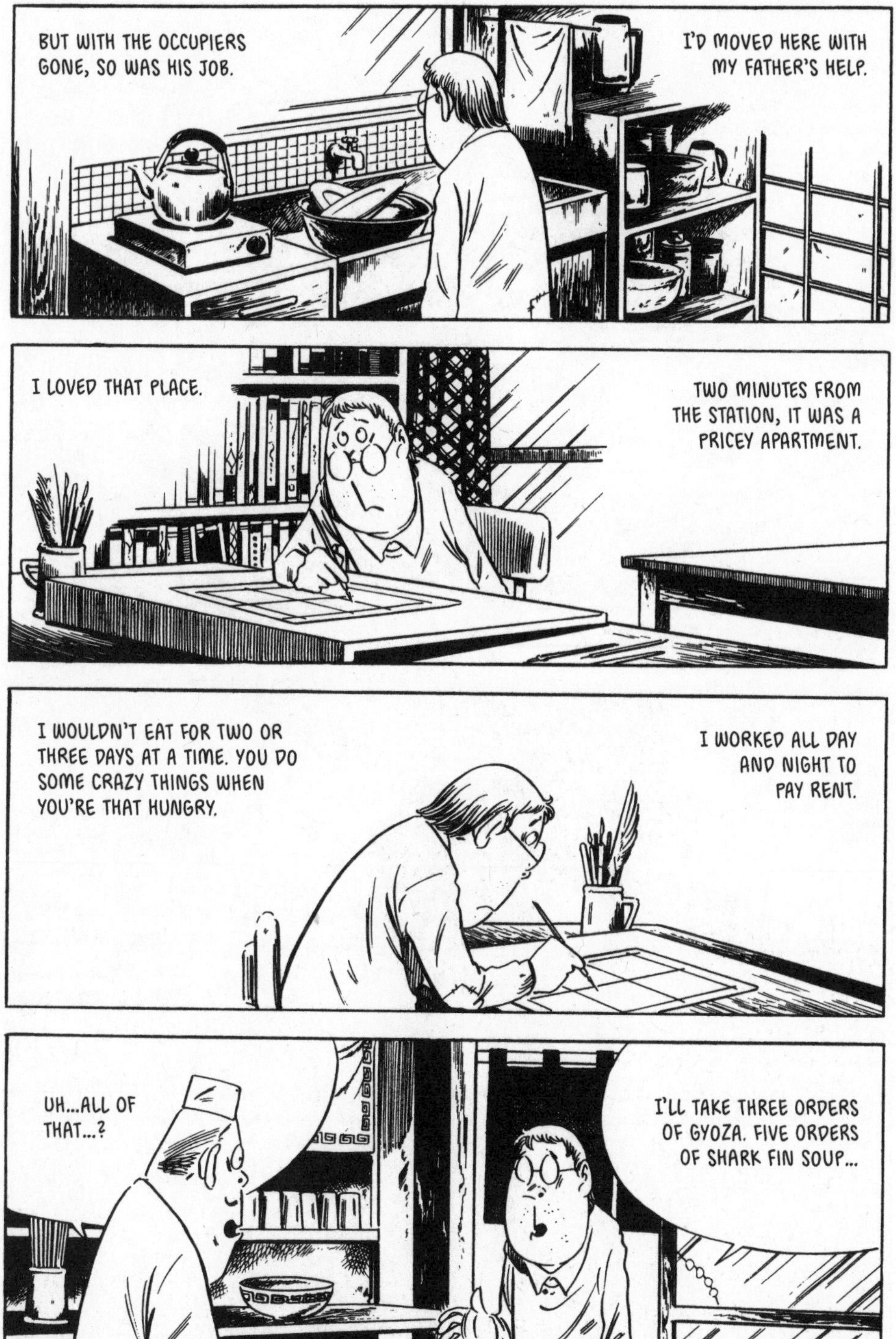
I'D MOVED HERE WITH MY FATHER'S HELP.
BUT WITH THE OCCUPIERS GONE, SO WAS HIS JOB.
TWO MINUTES FROM THE STATION, IT WAS A PRICEY APARTMENT.
I LOVED THAT PLACE.
I WORKED ALL DAY AND NIGHT TO PAY RENT.
I WOULDN'T EAT FOR TWO OR THREE DAYS AT A TIME. YOU DO SOME CRAZY THINGS WHEN YOU'RE THAT HUNGRY.
I'LL TAKE THREE ORDERS OF GYOZA. FIVE ORDERS OF SHARK FIN SOUP...
UH...ALL OF THAT...?

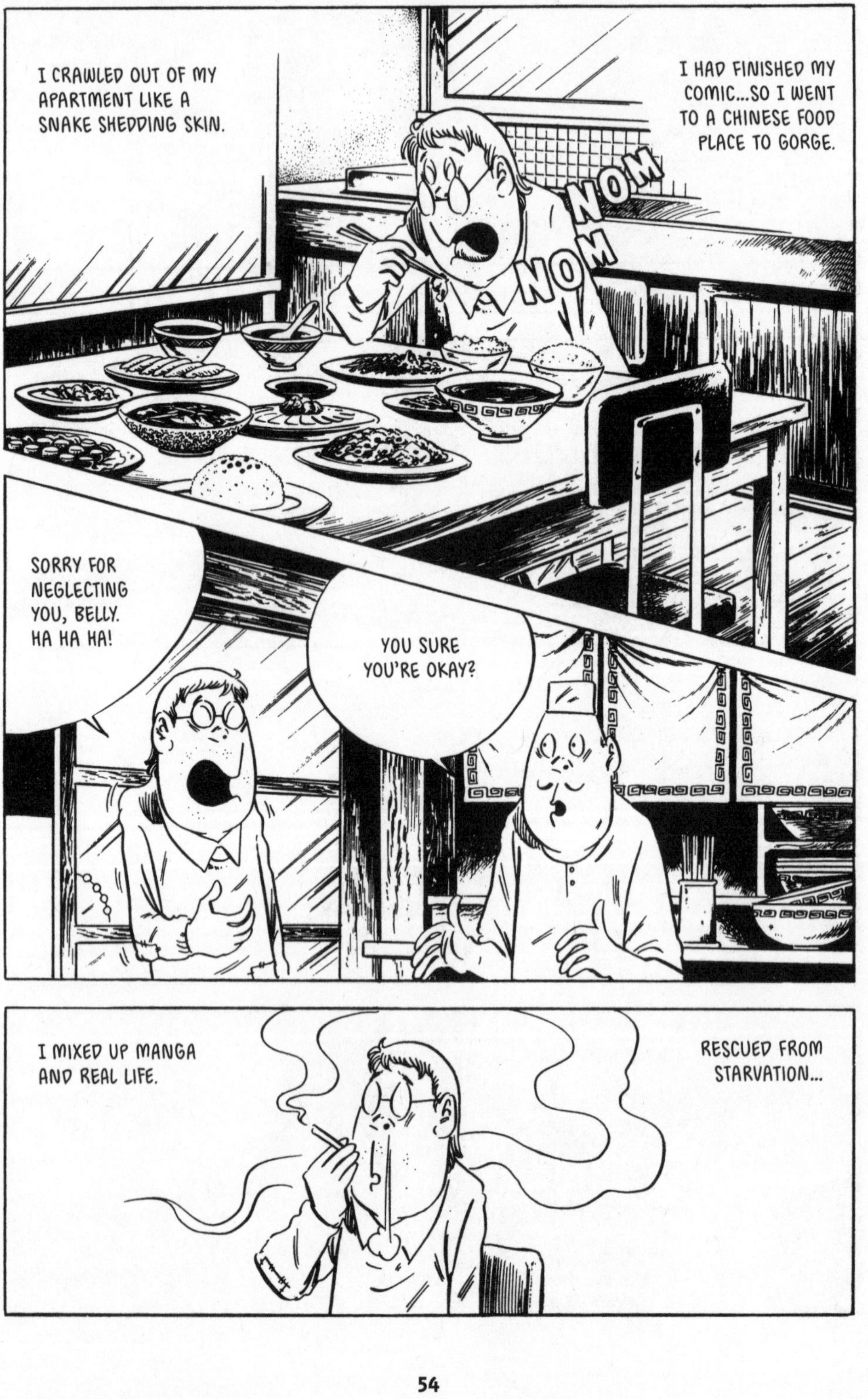
I HAD FINISHED MY COMIC...SO I WENT TO A CHINESE FOOD PLACE TO GORGE.
I CRAWLED OUT OF MY APARTMENT LIKE A SNAKE SHEDDING SKIN.
NOM
NOM
YOU SURE YOU'RE OKAY?
SORRY FOR NEGLECTING YOU, BELLY. HA HA HA!
RESCUED FROM STARVATION...
I MIXED UP MANGA AND REAL LIFE.

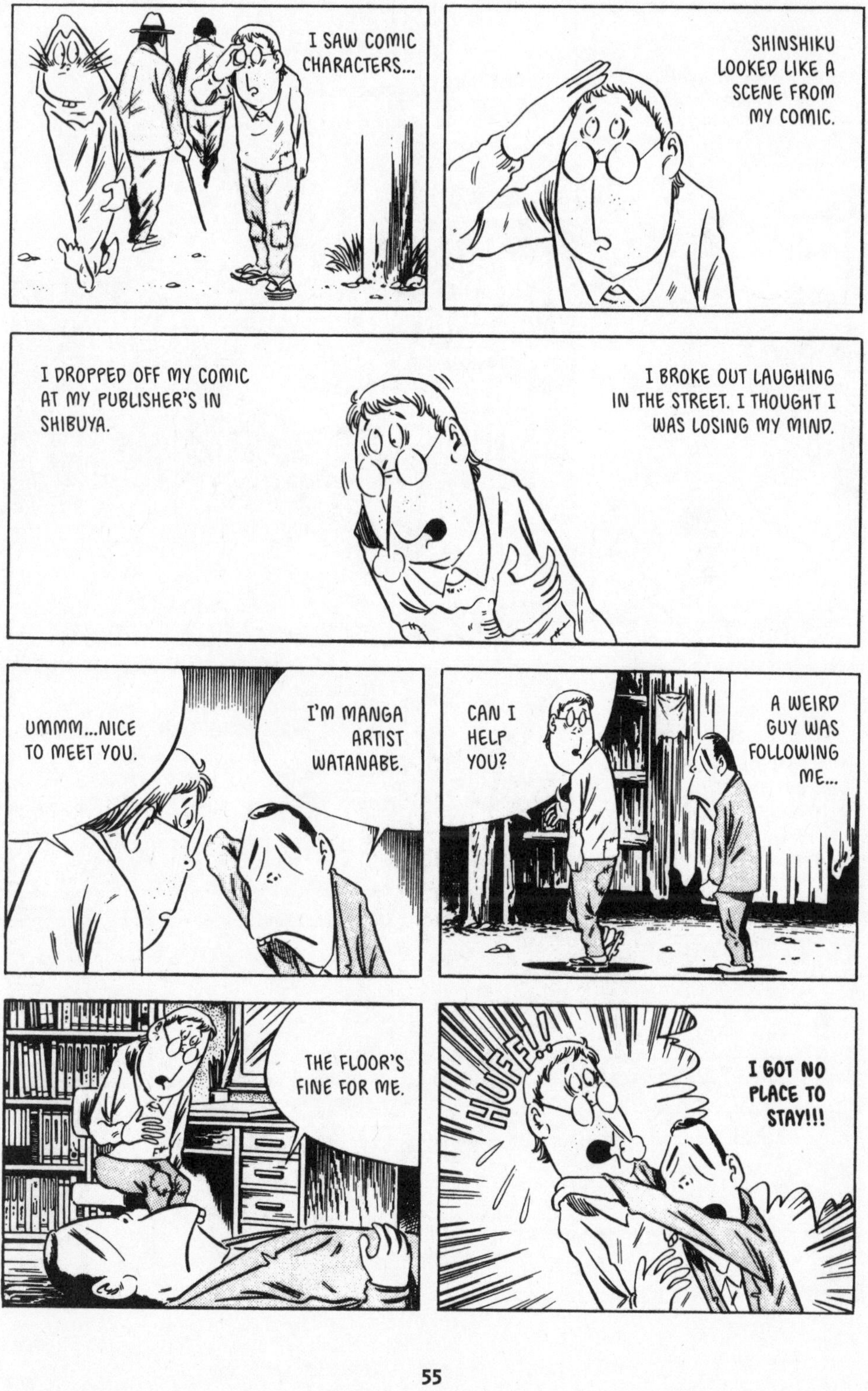
SHINSHIKU LOOKED LIKE A SCENE FROM MY COMIC.
I SAW COMIC CHARACTERS...
I BROKE OUT LAUGHING IN THE STREET. I THOUGHT I WAS LOSING MY MIND.
I DROPPED OFF MY COMIC AT MY PUBLISHER'S IN SHIBUYA.
A WEIRD GUY WAS FOLLOWING ME...
CAN I HELP YOU?
I'M MANGA ARTIST WATANABE.
UMMM...NICE TO MEET YOU.
HUFF!!
I GOT NO PLACE TO STAY!!!
THE FLOOR'S FINE FOR ME.

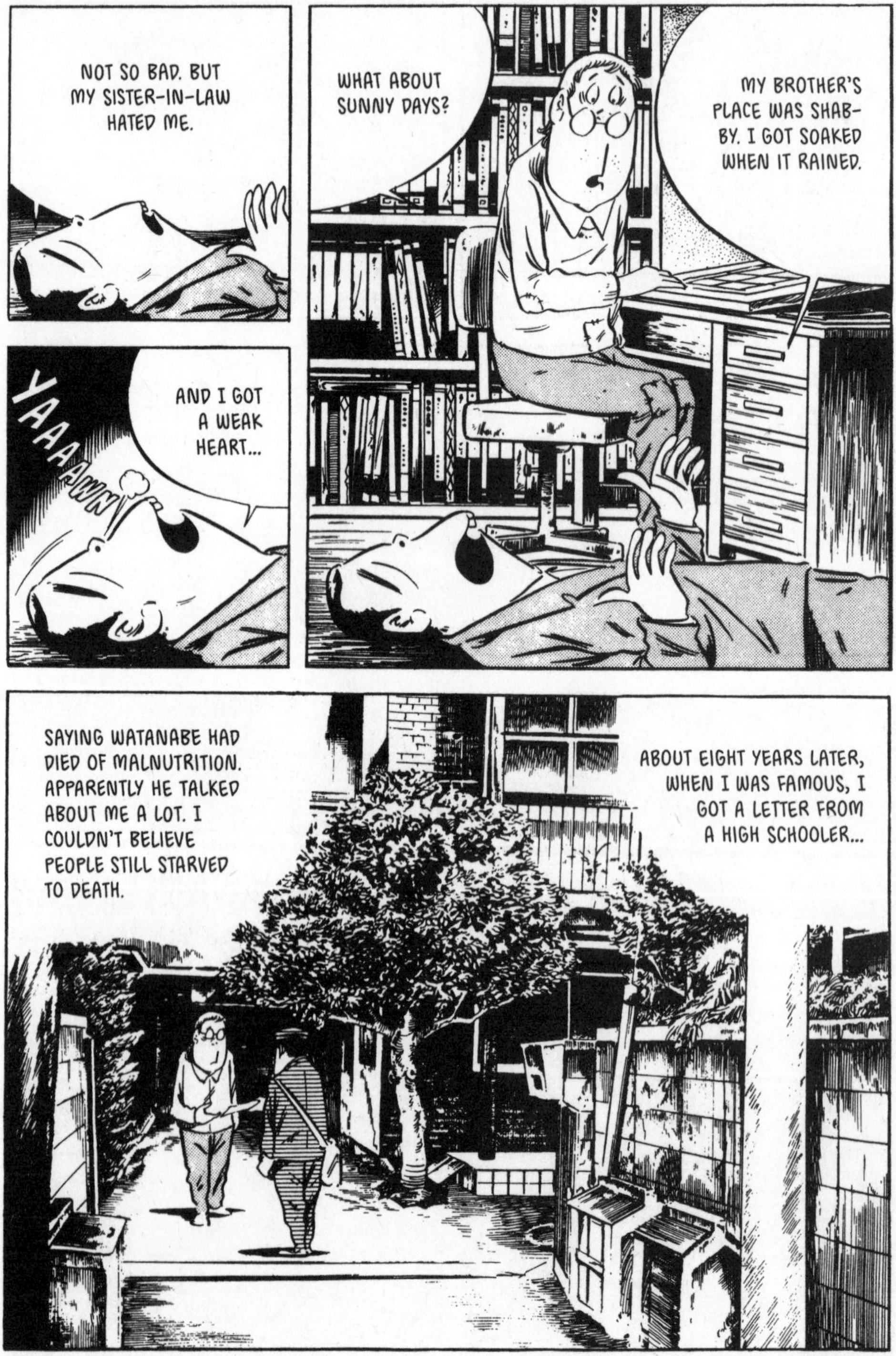
MY BROTHER'S PLACE WAS SHABBY. I GOT SOAKED WHEN IT RAINED.
WHAT ABOUT SUNNY DAYS?
NOT SO BAD. BUT MY SISTER-IN-LAW HATED ME.
AND I GOT A WEAK HEART...
YAAAAWN
ABOUT EIGHT YEARS LATER, WHEN I WAS FAMOUS, I GOT A LETTER FROM A HIGH SCHOOLER...
SAYING WATANABE HAD DIED OF MALNUTRITION. APPARENTLY HE TALKED ABOUT ME A LOT. I COULDN'T BELIEVE PEOPLE STILL STARVED TO DEATH.

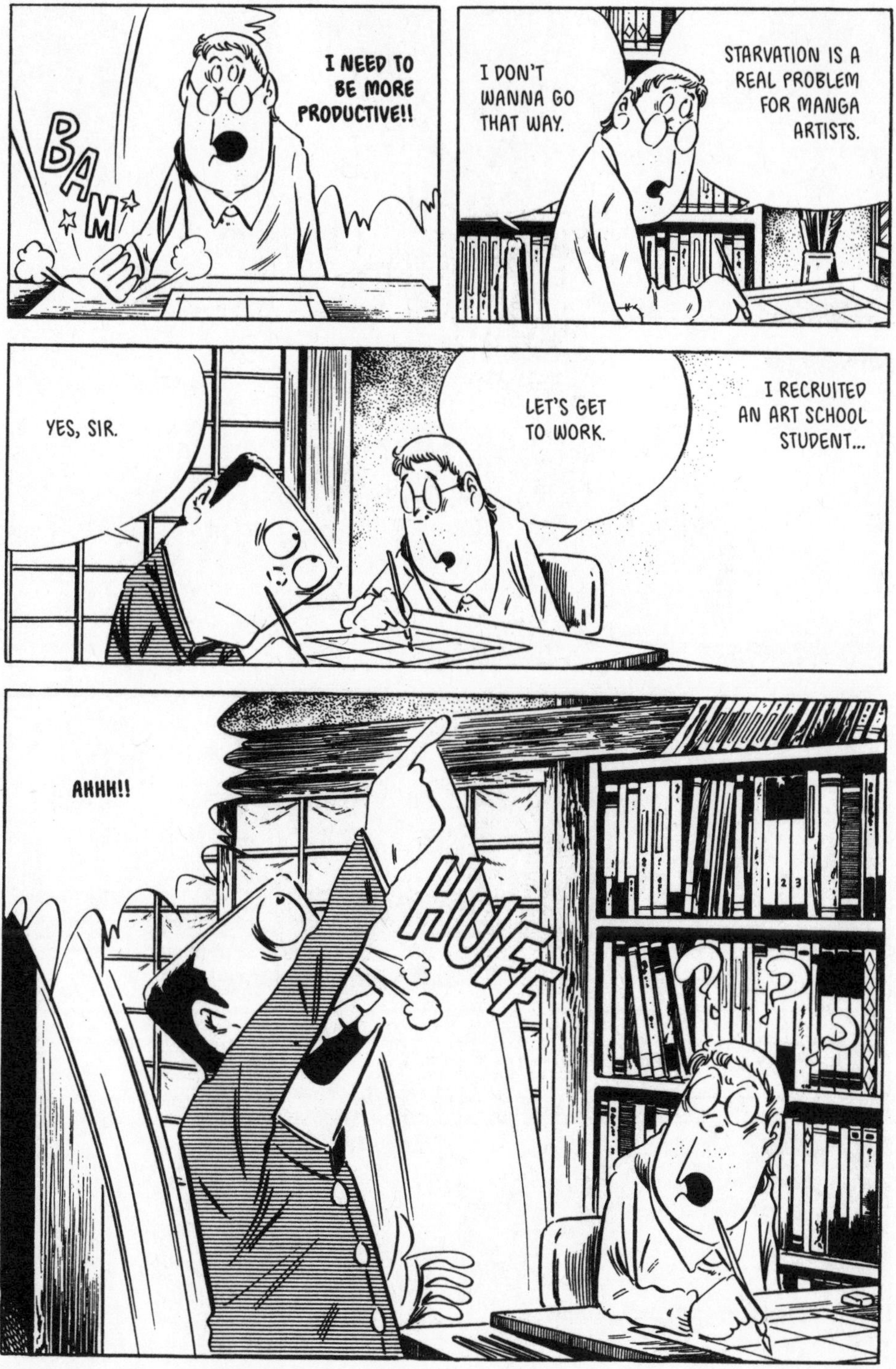
STARVATION IS A REAL PROBLEM FOR MANGA ARTISTS.
I DON'T WANNA GO THAT WAY.
I NEED TO BE MORE PRODUCTIVE!!
BAM
I RECRUITED AN ART SCHOOL STUDENT...
LET'S GET TO WORK.
YES, SIR.
AHHH!!
HUFF

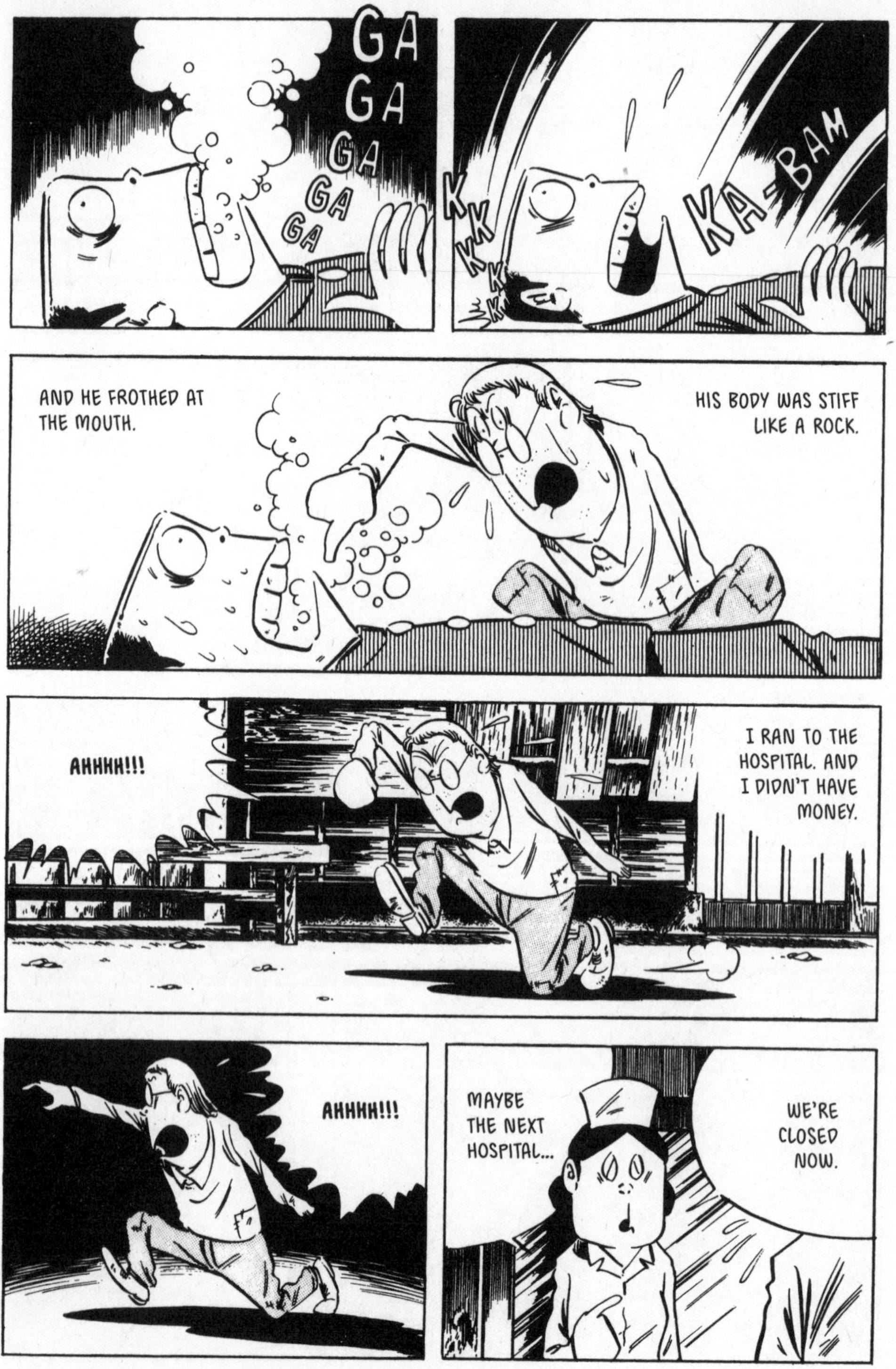
KA-BAM
KKKKKK
GA
GA
GA
GA
GA
HIS BODY WAS STIFF LIKE A ROCK.
AND HE FROTHED AT THE MOUTH.
I RAN TO THE HOSPITAL. AND I DIDN'T HAVE MONEY.
AHHHH!!!
WE'RE CLOSED NOW.
MAYBE THE NEXT HOSPITAL...
AHHHH!!!

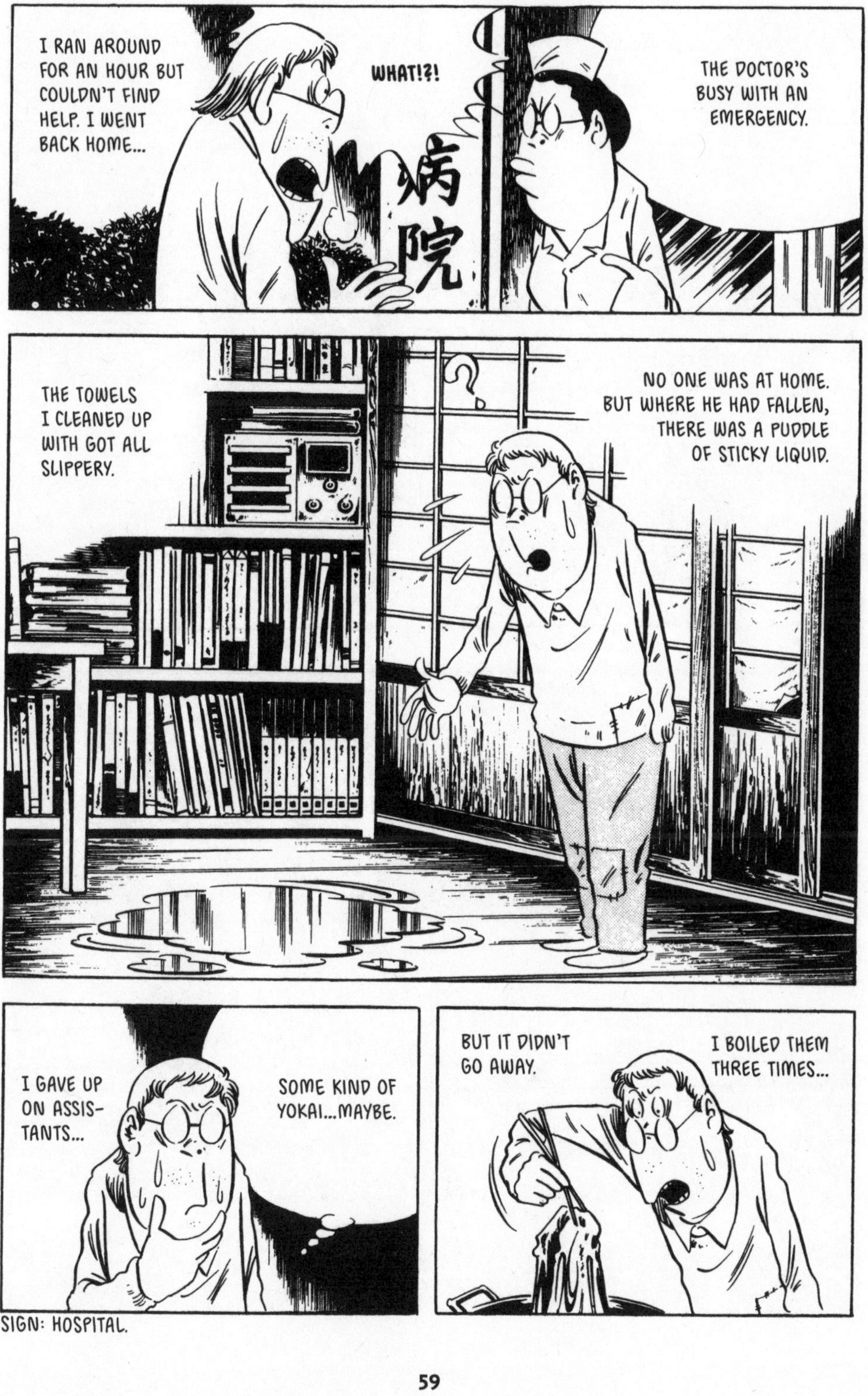
THE DOCTOR'S BUSY WITH AN EMERGENCY.
WHAT!?!
病院
I RAN AROUND FOR AN HOUR BUT COULDN'T FIND HELP. I WENT BACK HOME...
NO ONE WAS AT HOME. BUT WHERE HE HAD FALLEN, THERE WAS A PUDDLE OF STICKY LIQUID.
THE TOWELS I CLEANED UP WITH GOT ALL SLIPPERY.
I BOILED THEM THREE TIMES...
BUT IT DIDN'T GO AWAY.
SOME KIND OF YOKAI...MAYBE.
I GAVE UP ON ASSIS-TANTS...

SIGN: HOSPITAL.

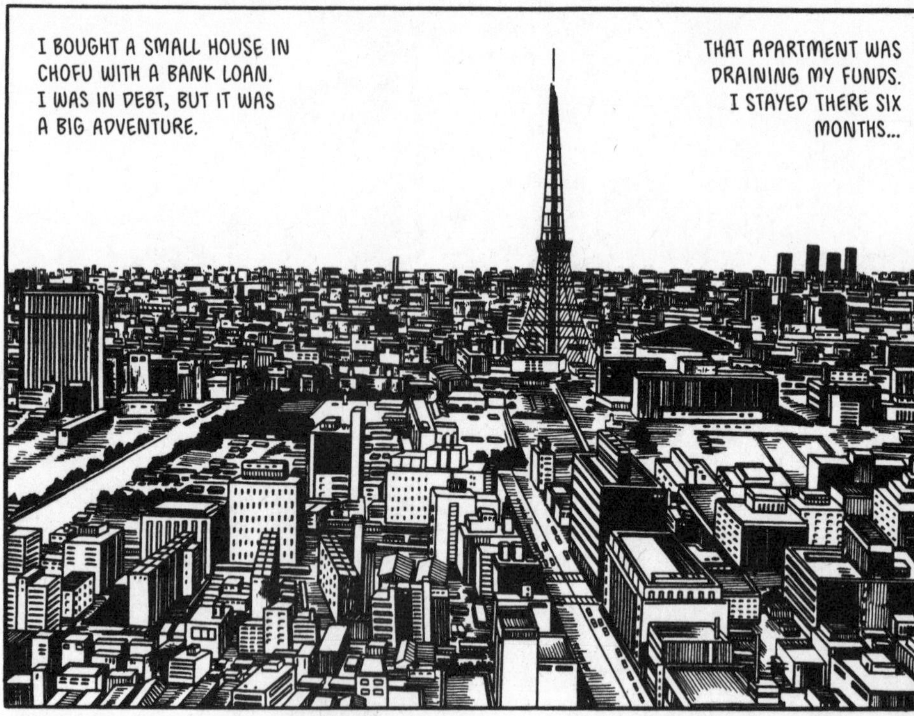
THAT APARTMENT WAS DRAINING MY FUNDS. I STAYED THERE SIX MONTHS...
I BOUGHT A SMALL HOUSE IN CHOFU WITH A BANK LOAN. I WAS IN DEBT, BUT IT WAS A BIG ADVENTURE.

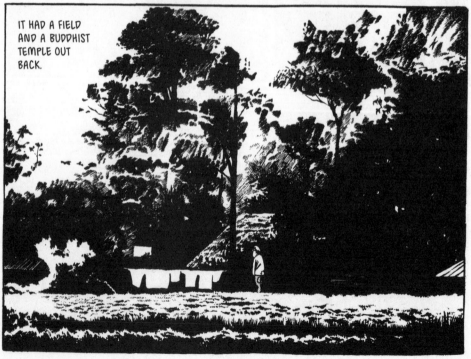

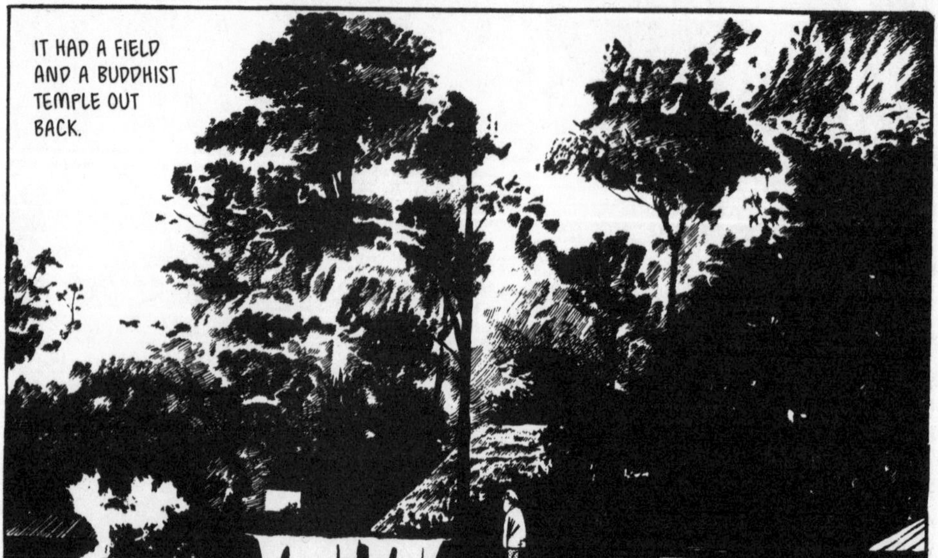
IT HAD A FIELD AND A BUDDHIST TEMPLE OUT BACK.

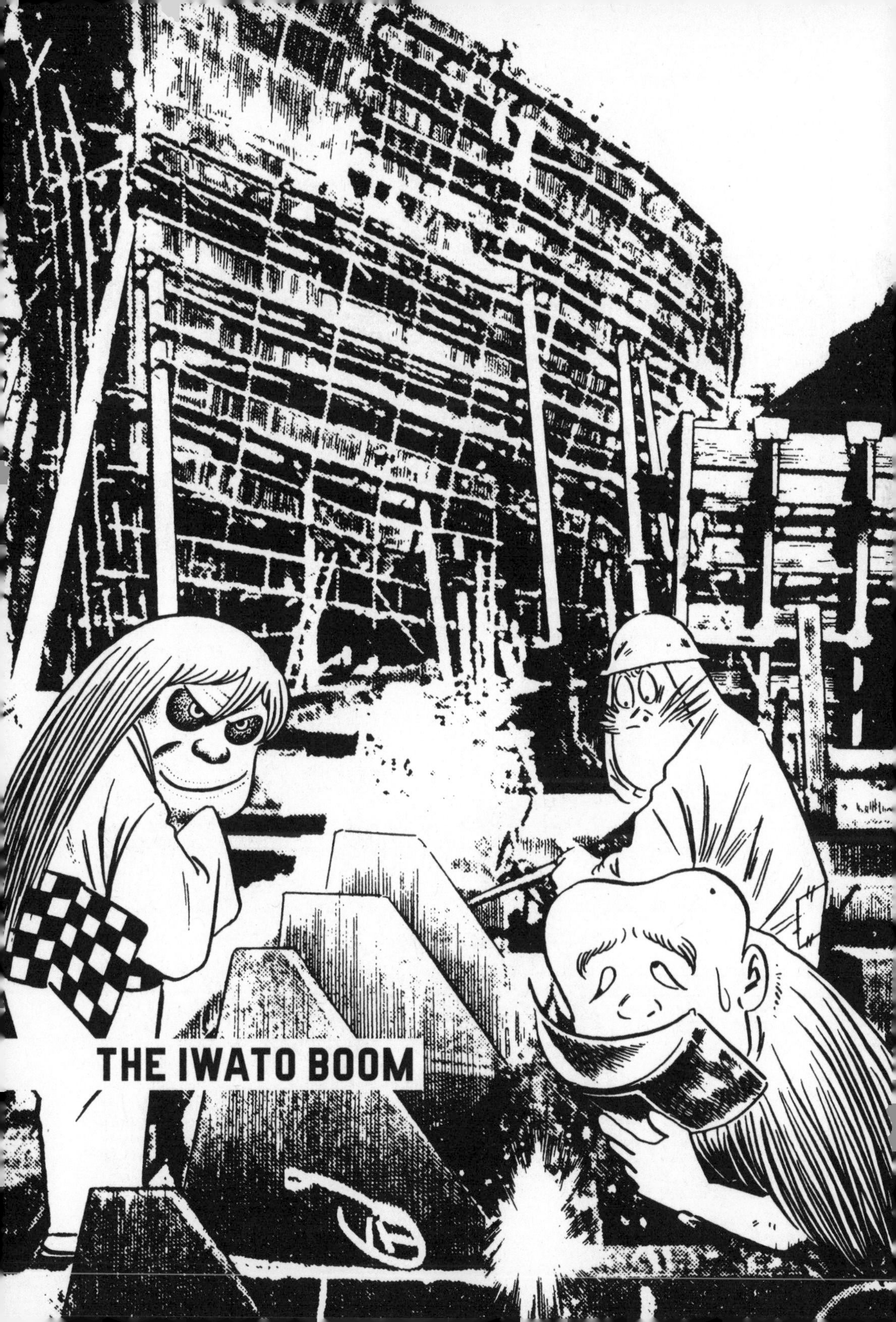
THE IWATO BOOM

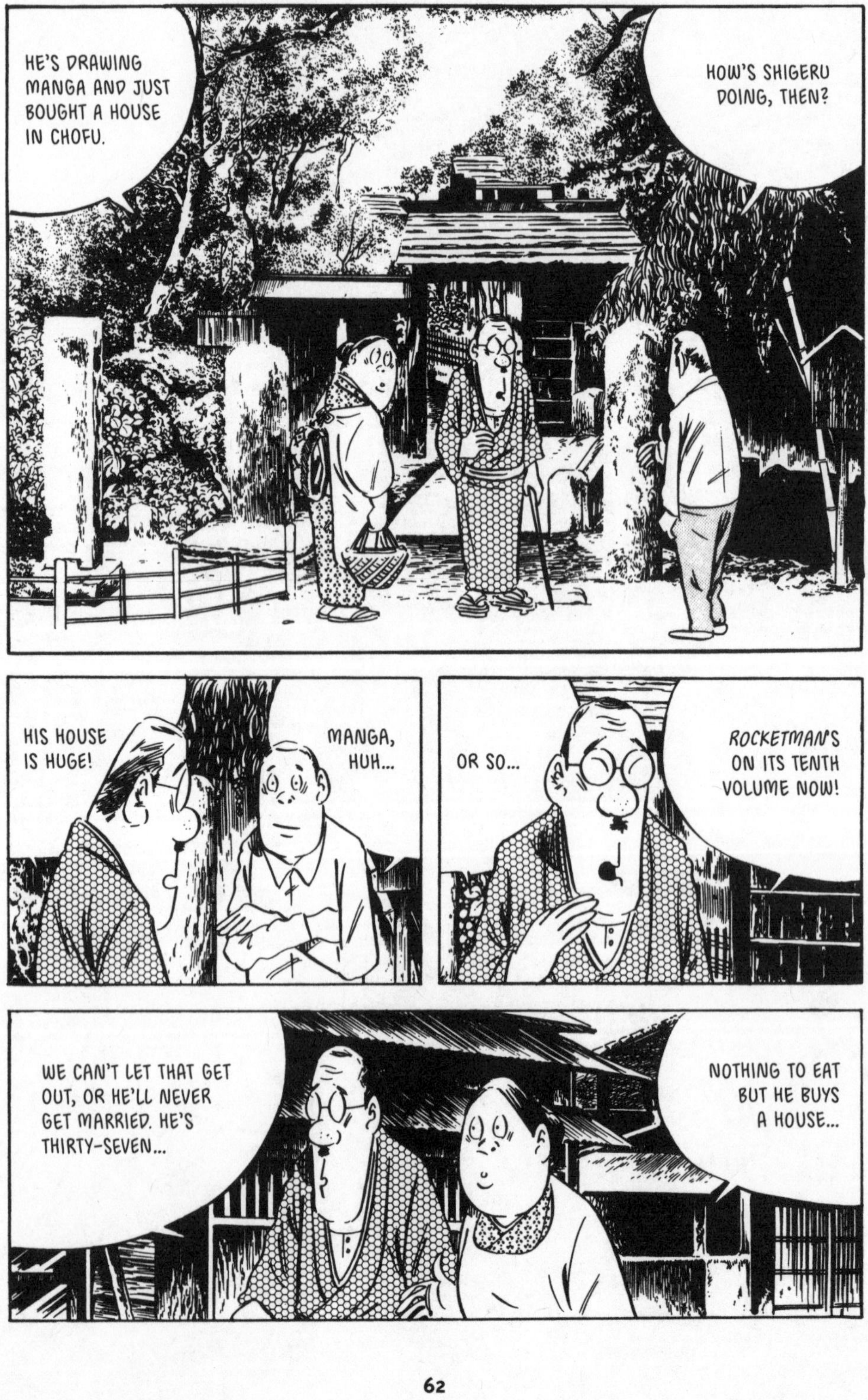
HOW'S SHIGERU DOING, THEN?
HE'S DRAWING MANGA AND JUST BOUGHT A HOUSE IN CHOFU.
ROCKETMAN'S ON ITS TENTH VOLUME NOW!
OR SO...
MANGA, HUH...
HIS HOUSE IS HUGE!
NOTHING TO EAT BUT HE BUYS A HOUSE...
WE CAN'T LET THAT GET OUT, OR HE'LL NEVER GET MARRIED. HE'S THIRTY-SEVEN...

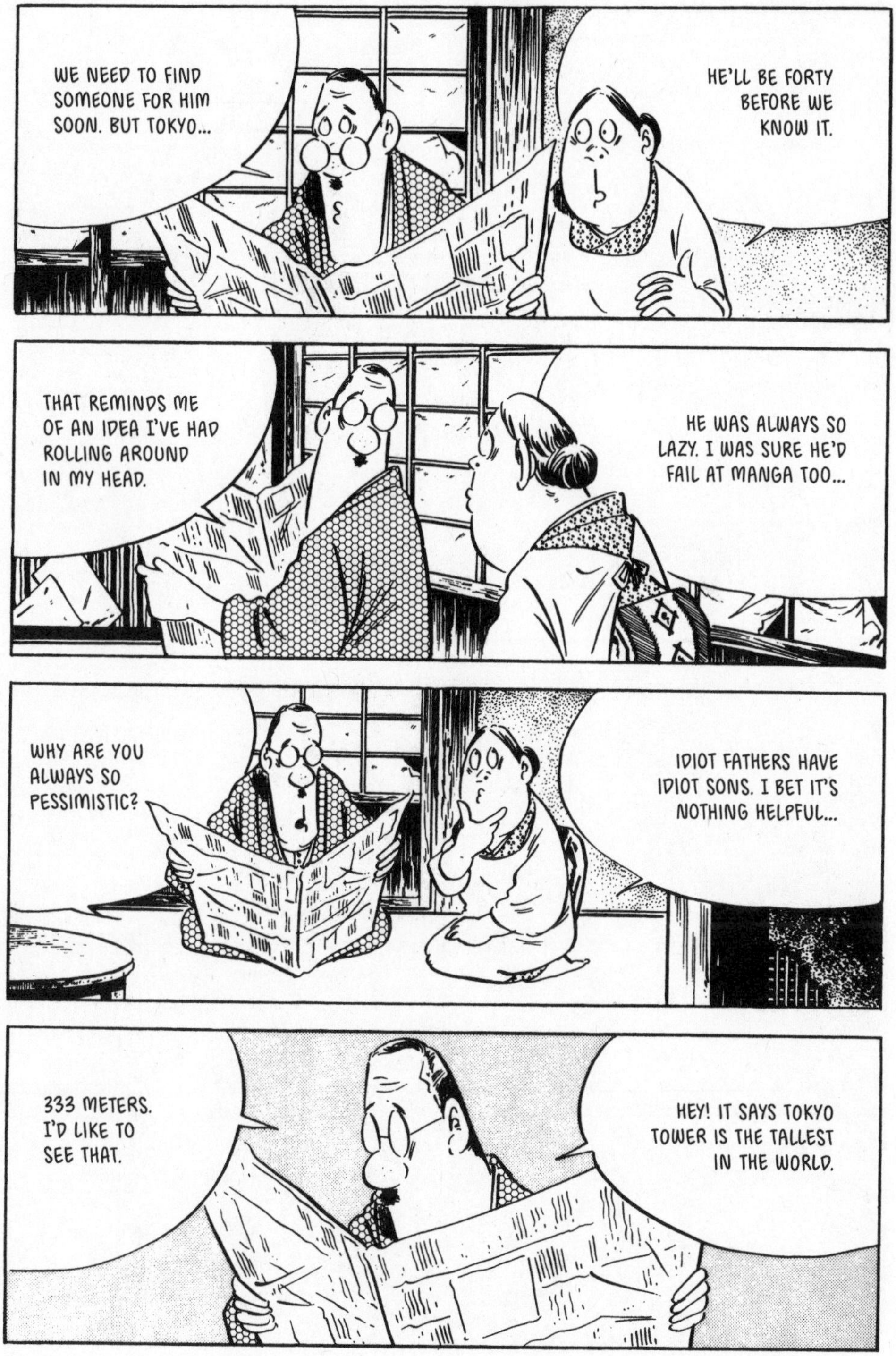
HE'LL BE FORTY BEFORE WE KNOW IT.
WE NEED TO FIND SOMEONE FOR HIM SOON. BUT TOKYO...
HE WAS ALWAYS SO LAZY. I WAS SURE HE'D FAIL AT MANGA TOO...
THAT REMINDS ME OF AN IDEA I'VE HAD ROLLING AROUND IN MY HEAD.
IDIOT FATHERS HAVE IDIOT SONS. I BET IT'S NOTHING HELPFUL...
WHY ARE YOU ALWAYS SO PESSIMISTIC?
HEY! IT SAYS TOKYO TOWER IS THE TALLEST IN THE WORLD.
333 METERS. I'D LIKE TO SEE THAT.

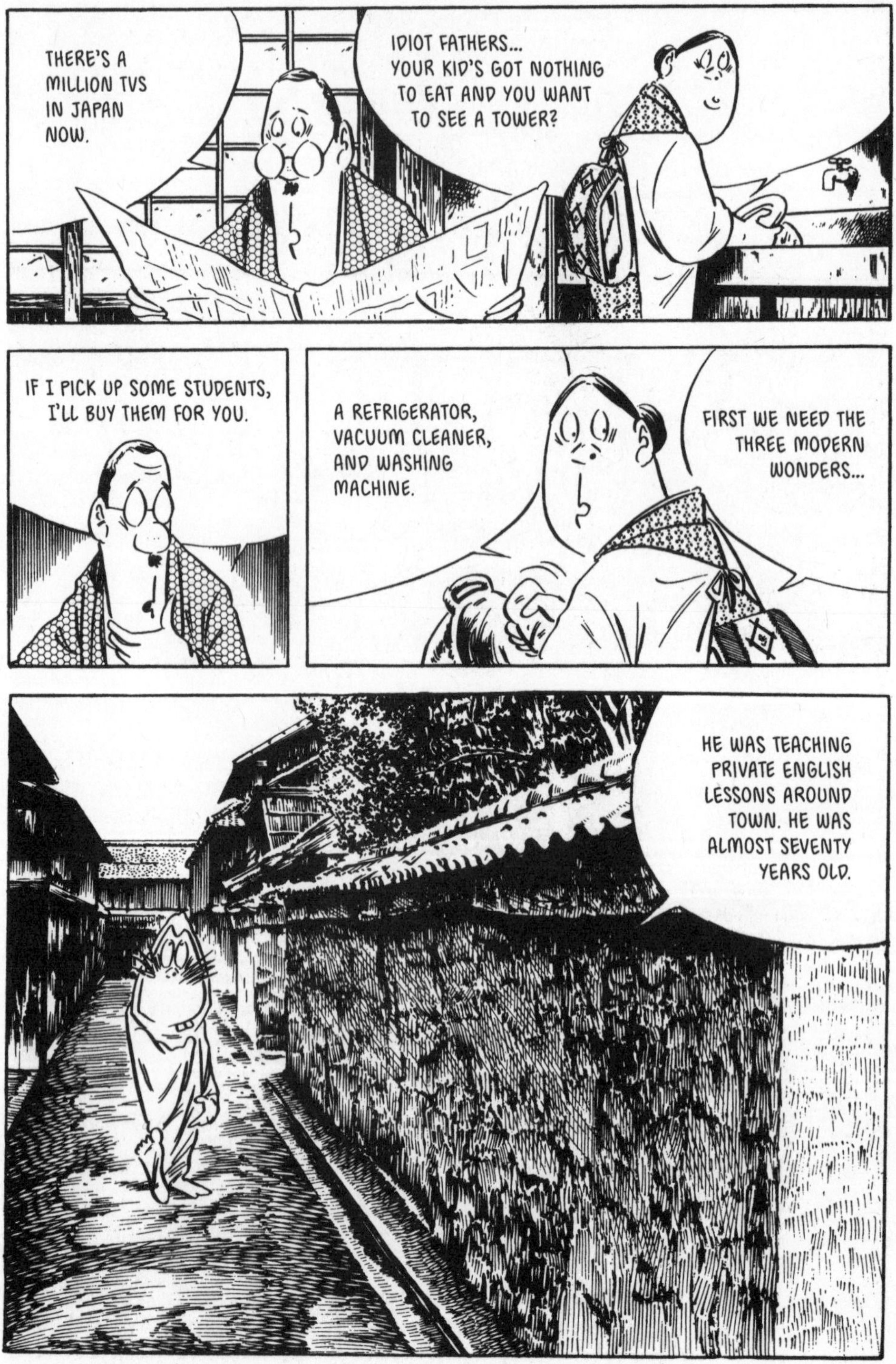
IDIOT FATHERS... YOUR KID'S GOT NOTHING TO EAT AND YOU WANT TO SEE A TOWER?
THERE'S A MILLION TVS IN JAPAN NOW.
FIRST WE NEED THE THREE MODERN WONDERS...
A REFRIGERATOR, VACUUM CLEANER, AND WASHING MACHINE.
IF I PICK UP SOME STUDENTS, I'LL BUY THEM FOR YOU.
HE WAS TEACHING PRIVATE ENGLISH LESSONS AROUND TOWN. HE WAS ALMOST SEVENTY YEARS OLD.

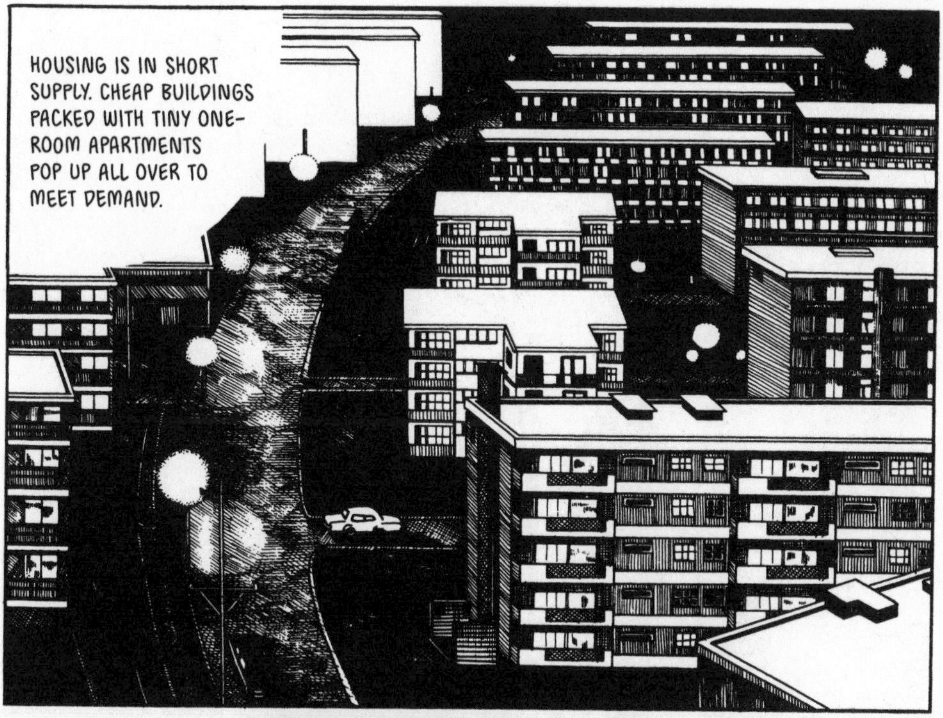
HOUSING IS IN SHORT SUPPLY. CHEAP BUILDINGS PACKED WITH TINY ONE-ROOM APARTMENTS POP UP ALL OVER TO MEET DEMAND.

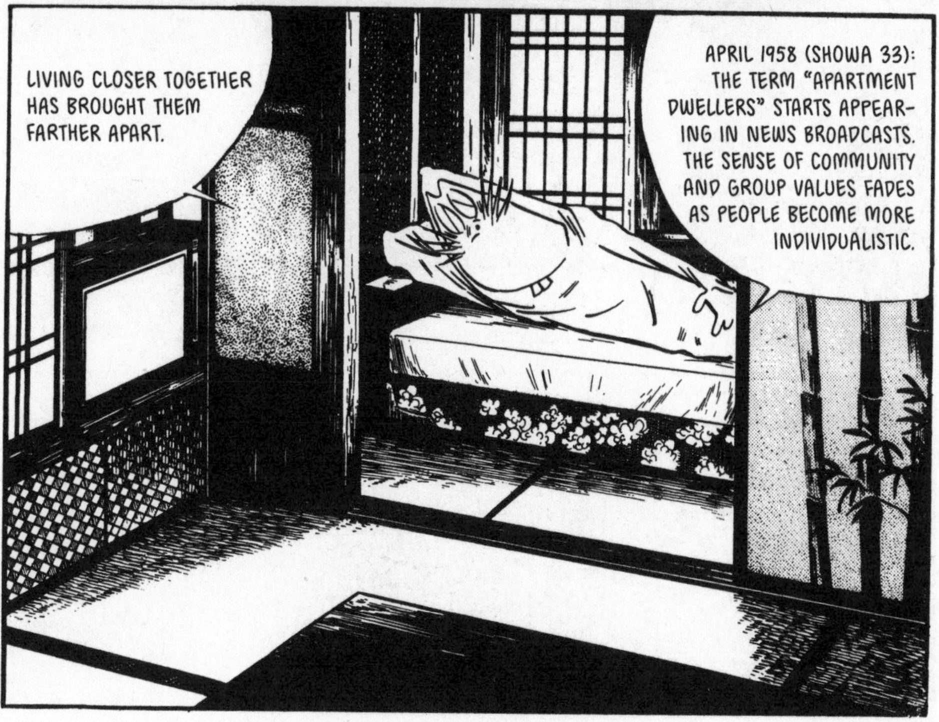
APRIL 1958 (SHOWA 33): THE TERM "APARTMENT DWELLERS" STARTS APPEARING IN NEWS BROADCASTS. THE SENSE OF COMMUNITY AND GROUP VALUES FADES AS PEOPLE BECOME MORE INDIVIDUALISTIC.
LIVING CLOSER TOGETHER HAS BROUGHT THEM FARTHER APART.

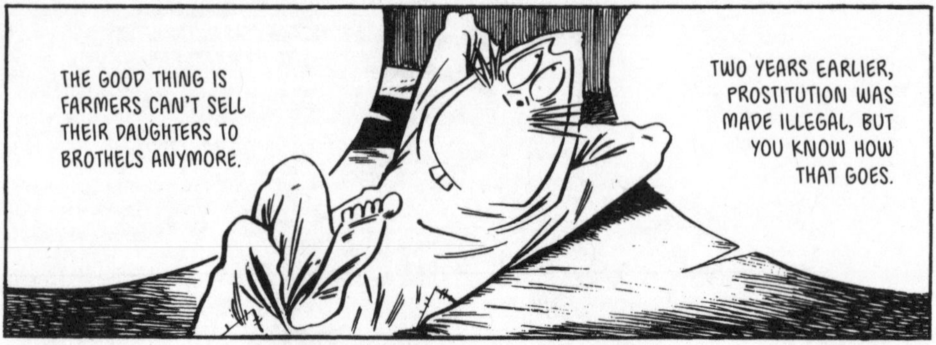
TWO YEARS EARLIER, PROSTITUTION WAS MADE ILLEGAL, BUT YOU KNOW HOW THAT GOES.
THE GOOD THING IS FARMERS CAN'T SELL THEIR DAUGHTERS TO BROTHELS ANYMORE.

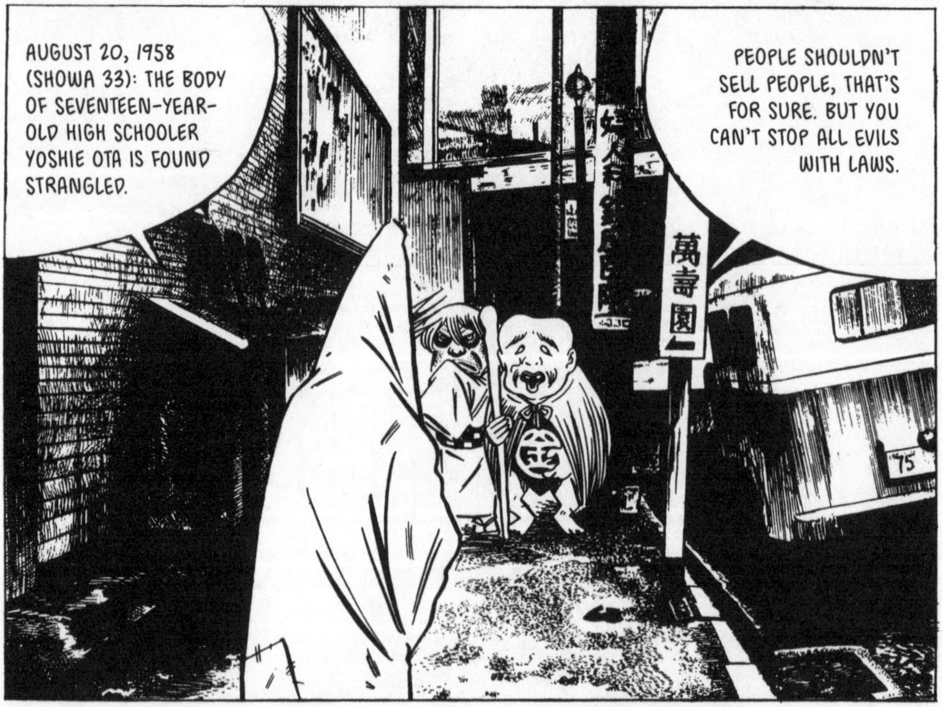
PEOPLE SHOULDN'T SELL PEOPLE, THAT'S FOR SURE. BUT YOU CAN'T STOP ALL EVILS WITH LAWS.
萬壽園
75
AUGUST 20, 1958 (SHOWA 33): THE BODY OF SEVENTEEN-YEAR-OLD HIGH SCHOOLER YOSHIE OTA IS FOUND STRANGLED.

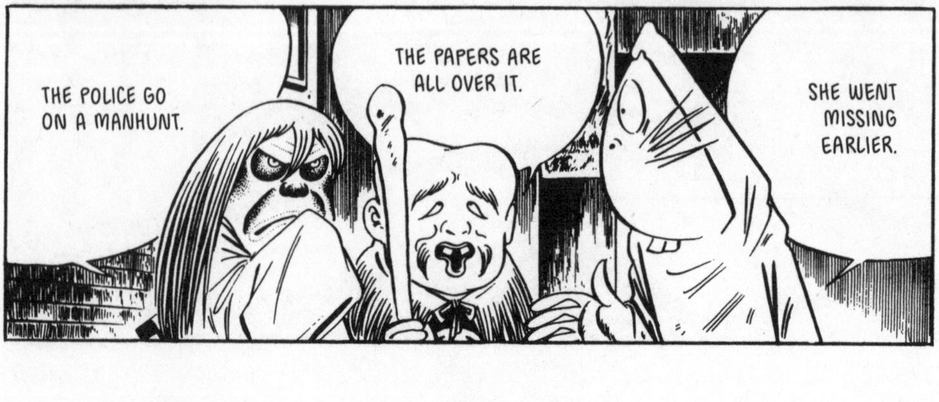
SHE WENT MISSING EARLIER.
THE PAPERS ARE ALL OVER IT.
THE POLICE GO ON A MANHUNT.

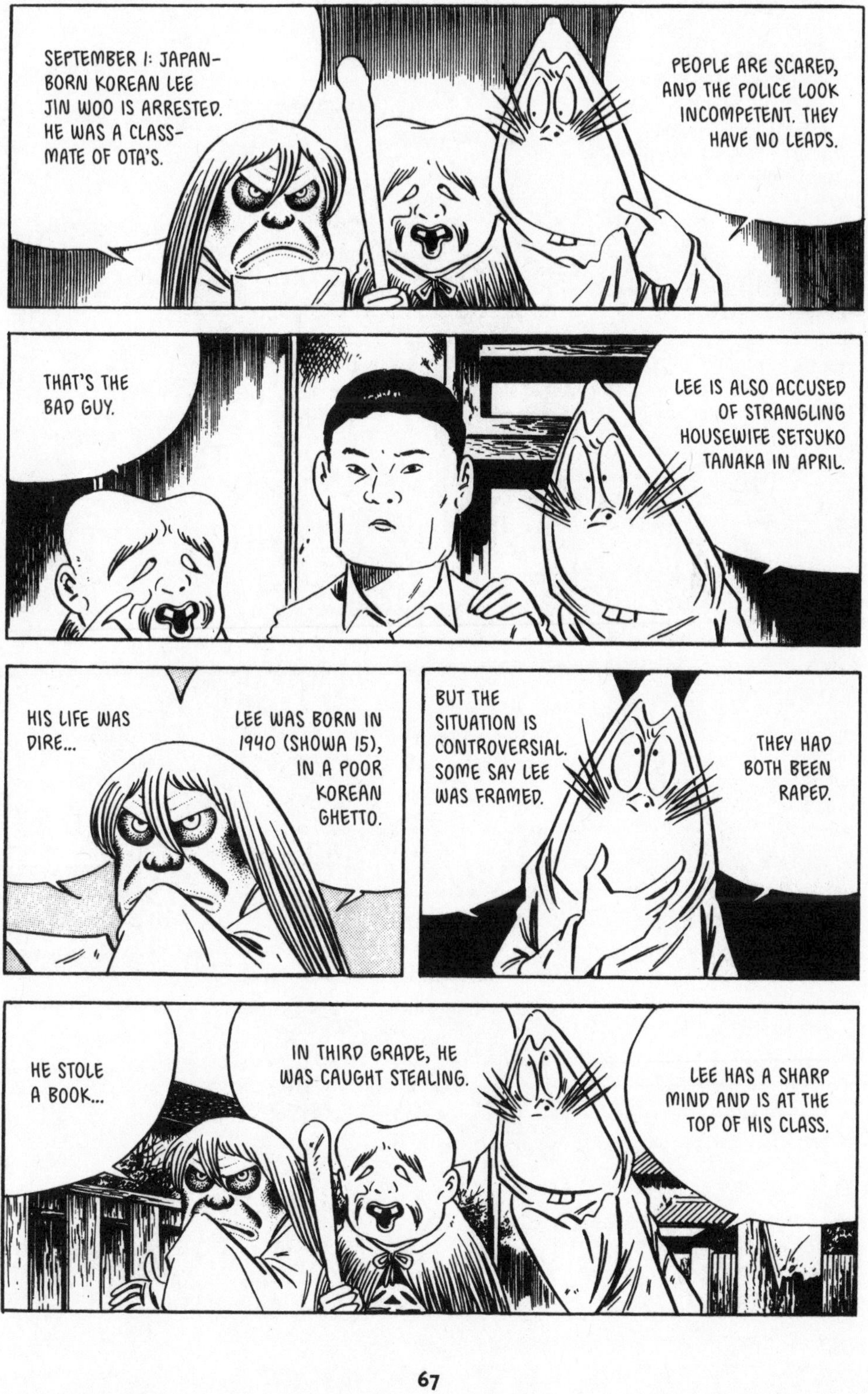
PEOPLE ARE SCARED, AND THE POLICE LOOK INCOMPETENT. THEY HAVE NO LEADS.
SEPTEMBER 1: JAPAN-BORN KOREAN LEE JIN WOO IS ARRESTED. HE WAS A CLASSMATE OF OTA'S.
LEE IS ALSO ACCUSED OF STRANGLING HOUSEWIFE SETSUKO TANAKA IN APRIL.
THAT'S THE BAD GUY.
THEY HAD BOTH BEEN RAPED.
BUT THE SITUATION IS CONTROVERSIAL. SOME SAY LEE WAS FRAMED.
LEE WAS BORN IN 1940 (SHOWA 15), IN A POOR KOREAN GHETTO.
HIS LIFE WAS DIRE...
LEE HAS A SHARP MIND AND IS AT THE TOP OF HIS CLASS.
IN THIRD GRADE, HE WAS CAUGHT STEALING.
HE STOLE A BOOK...

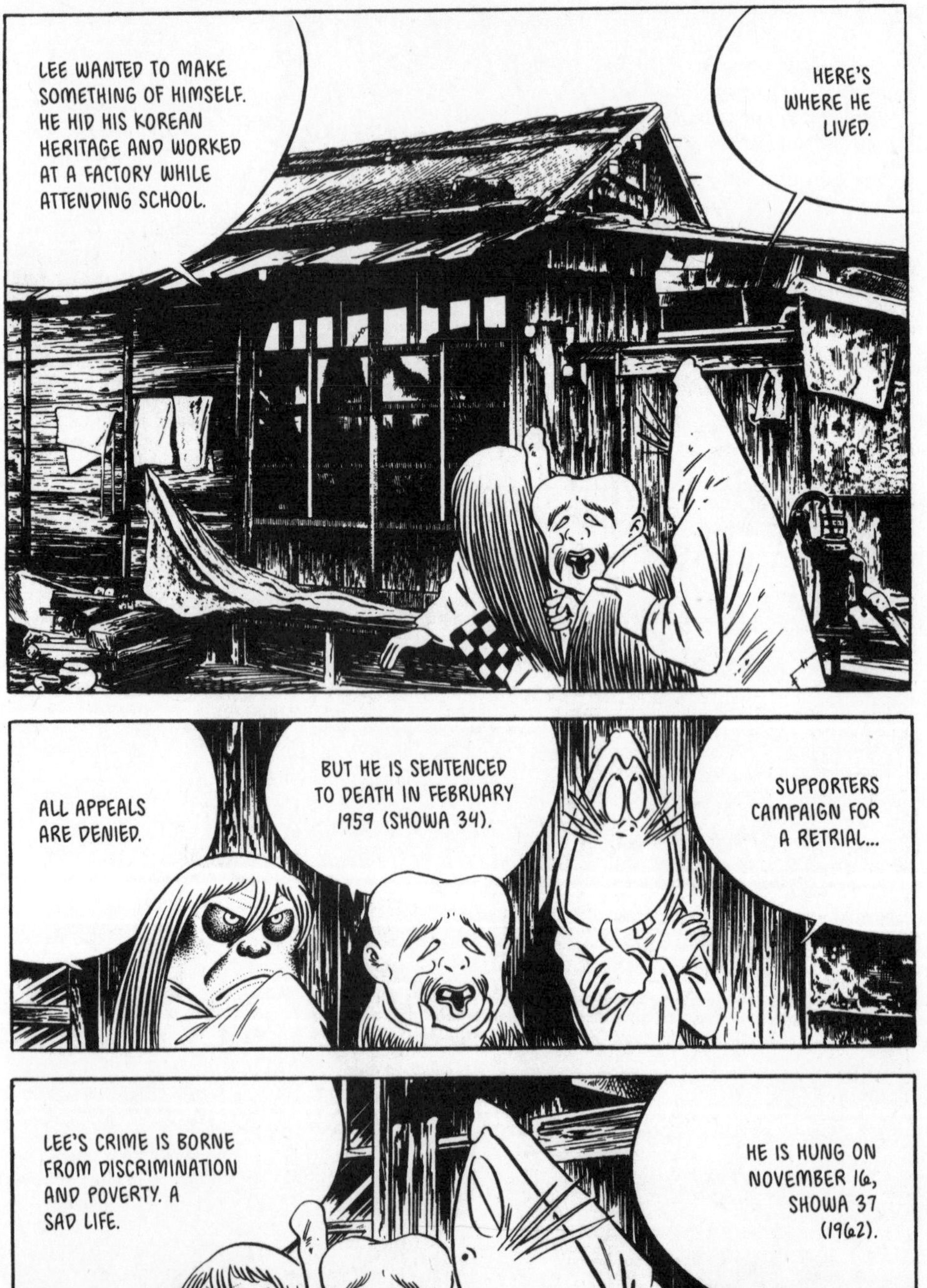
HERE'S WHERE HE LIVED.
LEE WANTED TO MAKE SOMETHING OF HIMSELF. HE HID HIS KOREAN HERITAGE AND WORKED AT A FACTORY WHILE ATTENDING SCHOOL.
SUPPORTERS CAMPAIGN FOR A RETRIAL...
BUT HE IS SENTENCED TO DEATH IN FEBRUARY 1959 (SHOWA 34).
ALL APPEALS ARE DENIED.
HE IS HUNG ON NOVEMBER 16, SHOWA 37 (1962).
LEE'S CRIME IS BORNE FROM DISCRIMINATION AND POVERTY. A SAD LIFE.

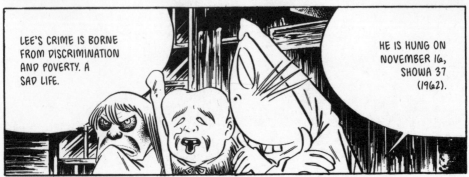

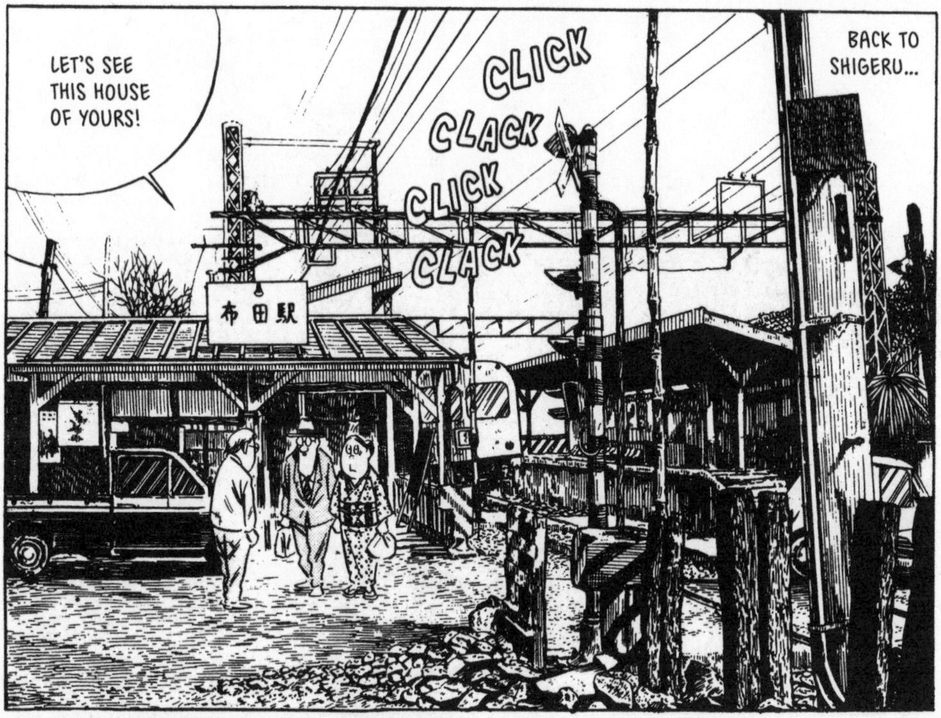
BACK TO SHIGERU...
CLICK
CLACK
CLICK
CLACK
布田駅
LET'S SEE THIS HOUSE OF YOURS!

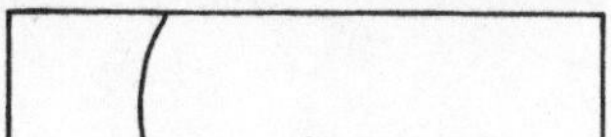
IT'S GOT ROOM FOR A WIFE!

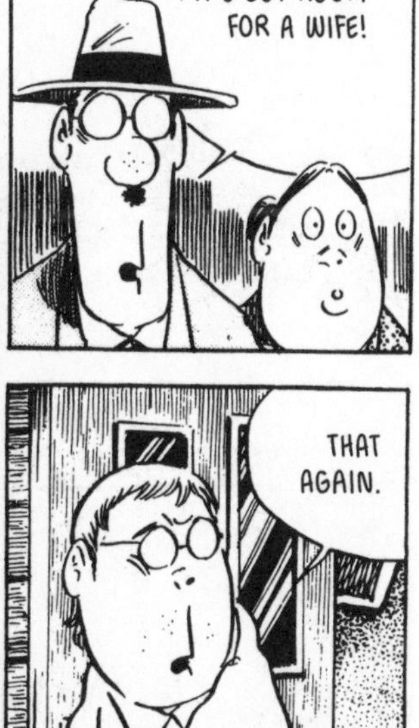
THAT AGAIN.

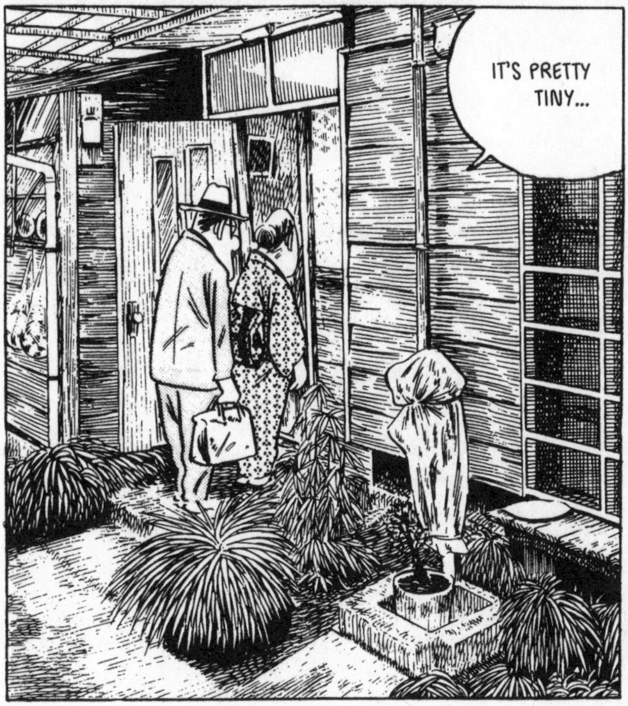
IT'S PRETTY TINY...

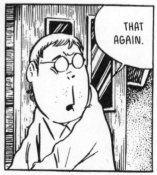

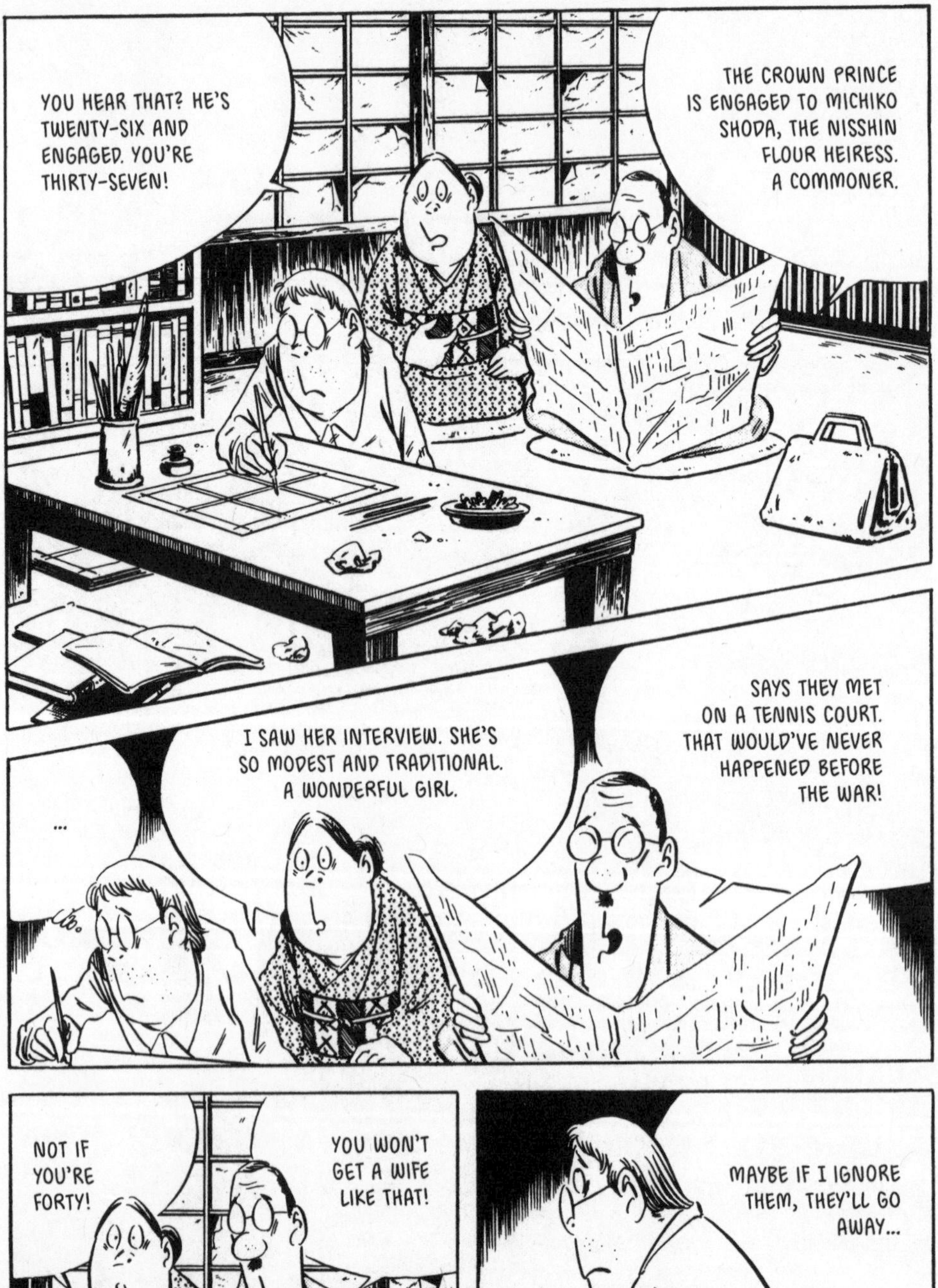
THE CROWN PRINCE IS ENGAGED TO MICHIKO SHODA, THE NISSHIN FLOUR HEIRESS. A COMMONER.
YOU HEAR THAT? HE'S TWENTY-SIX AND ENGAGED. YOU'RE THIRTY-SEVEN!
SAYS THEY MET ON A TENNIS COURT. THAT WOULD'VE NEVER HAPPENED BEFORE THE WAR!
I SAW HER INTERVIEW. SHE'S SO MODEST AND TRADITIONAL. A WONDERFUL GIRL.
...
MAYBE IF I IGNORE THEM, THEY'LL GO AWAY...
YOU WON'T GET A WIFE LIKE THAT!
NOT IF YOU'RE FORTY!

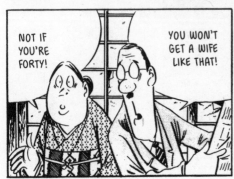

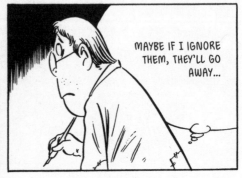

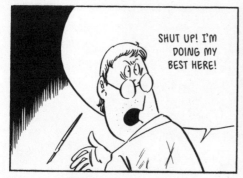

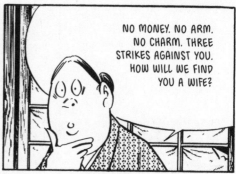

NO MONEY. NO ARM. NO CHARM. THREE STRIKES AGAINST YOU. HOW WILL WE FIND YOU A WIFE?
SHUT UP! I'M DOING MY BEST HERE!
THE MONEY'S NOT SUCH A BIG DEAL. AFTER ALL, IF ONE CAN EAT, TWO CAN EAT.
DON'T WORRY, SON. I'LL FIND YOU A GIRL.
...
APRIL 10, 1959 (SHOWA 34): MICHIKO SHODA MARRIES CROWN PRINCE AKIHITO AT THE IMPERIAL PALACE.
SOON AFTER, THE NEW ROYAL COUPLE DEPARTS IN A HORSE-DRAWN CARRIAGE FOR TOGU PALACE.

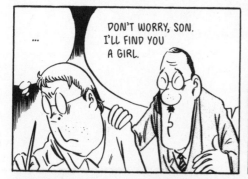

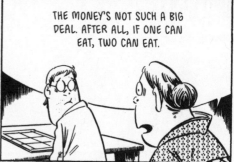

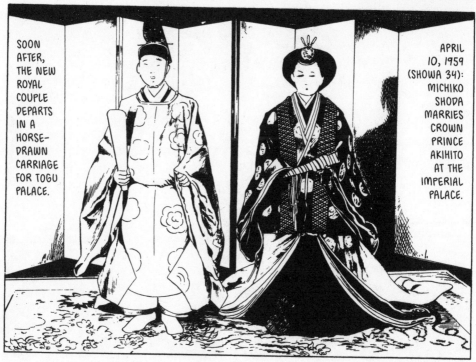

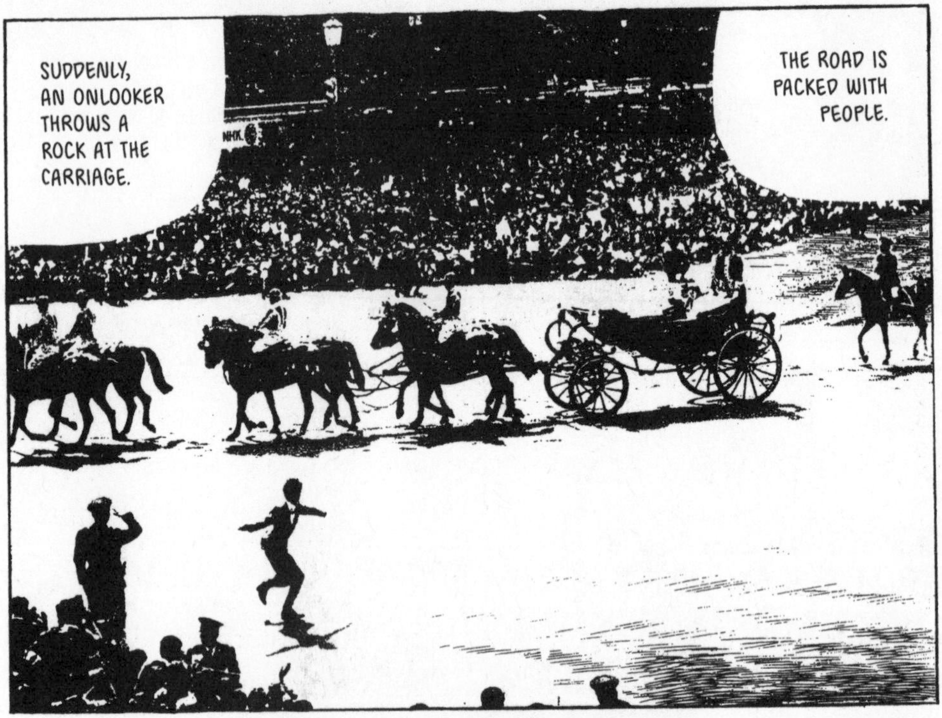
THE ROAD IS PACKED WITH PEOPLE.
SUDDENLY, AN ONLOOKER THROWS A ROCK AT THE CARRIAGE.
NHK

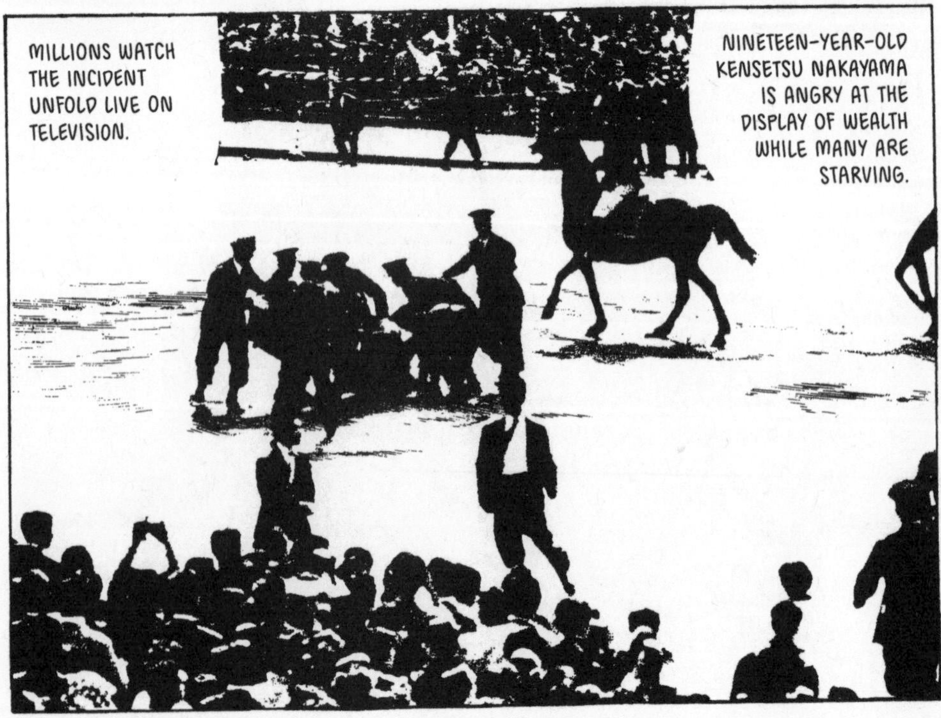
NINETEEN-YEAR-OLD KENSETSU NAKAYAMA IS ANGRY AT THE DISPLAY OF WEALTH WHILE MANY ARE STARVING.
MILLIONS WATCH THE INCIDENT UNFOLD LIVE ON TELEVISION.

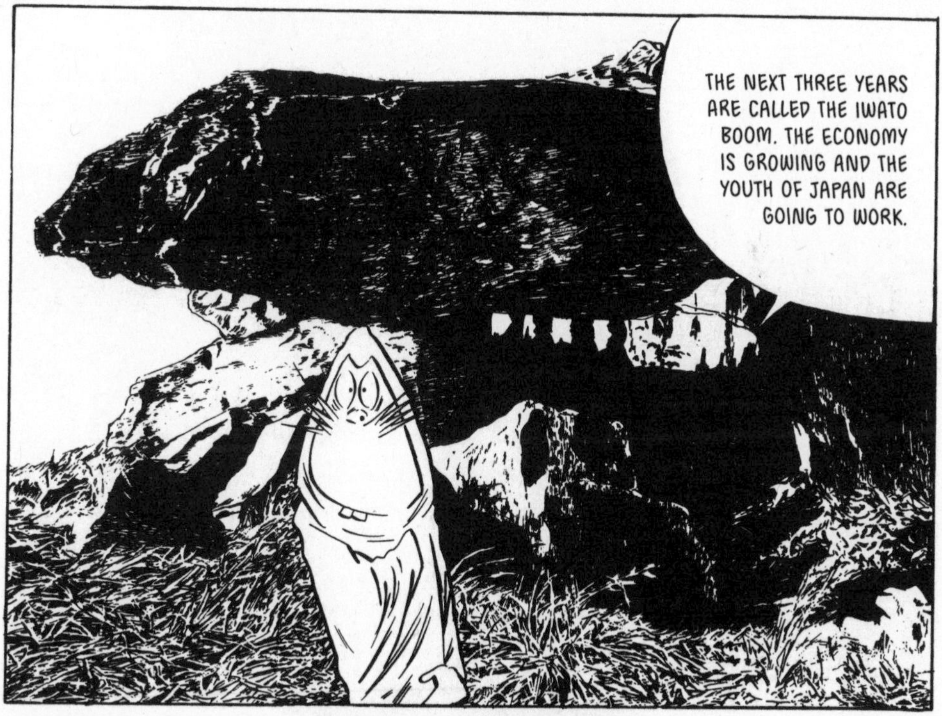
THE NEXT THREE YEARS ARE CALLED THE IWATO BOOM. THE ECONOMY IS GROWING AND THE YOUTH OF JAPAN ARE GOING TO WORK.

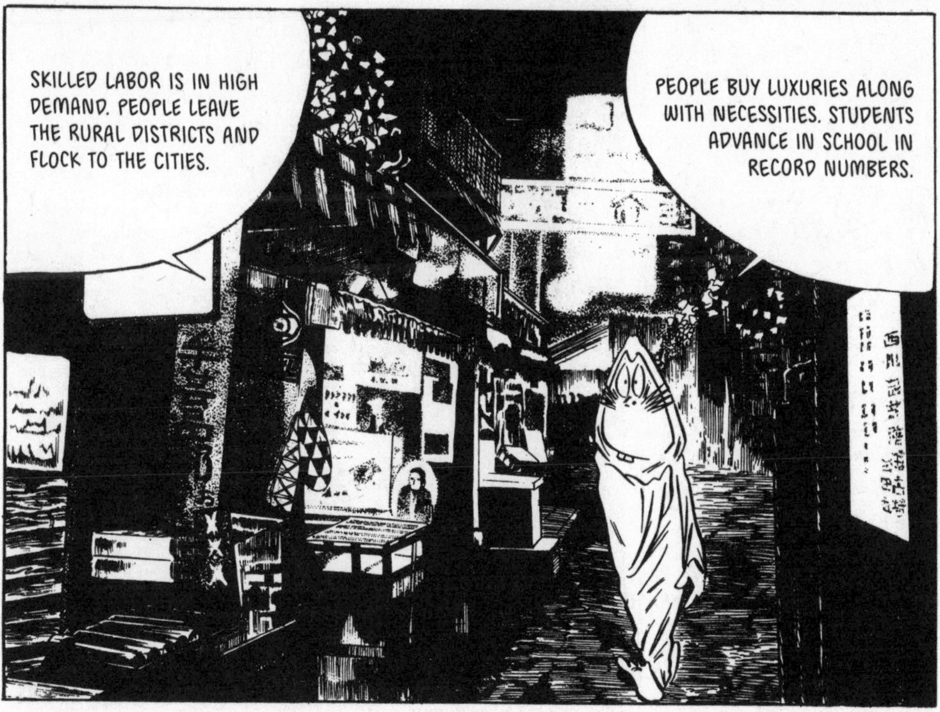
PEOPLE BUY LUXURIES ALONG WITH NECESSITIES. STUDENTS ADVANCE IN SCHOOL IN RECORD NUMBERS.
SKILLED LABOR IS IN HIGH DEMAND. PEOPLE LEAVE THE RURAL DISTRICTS AND FLOCK TO THE CITIES.

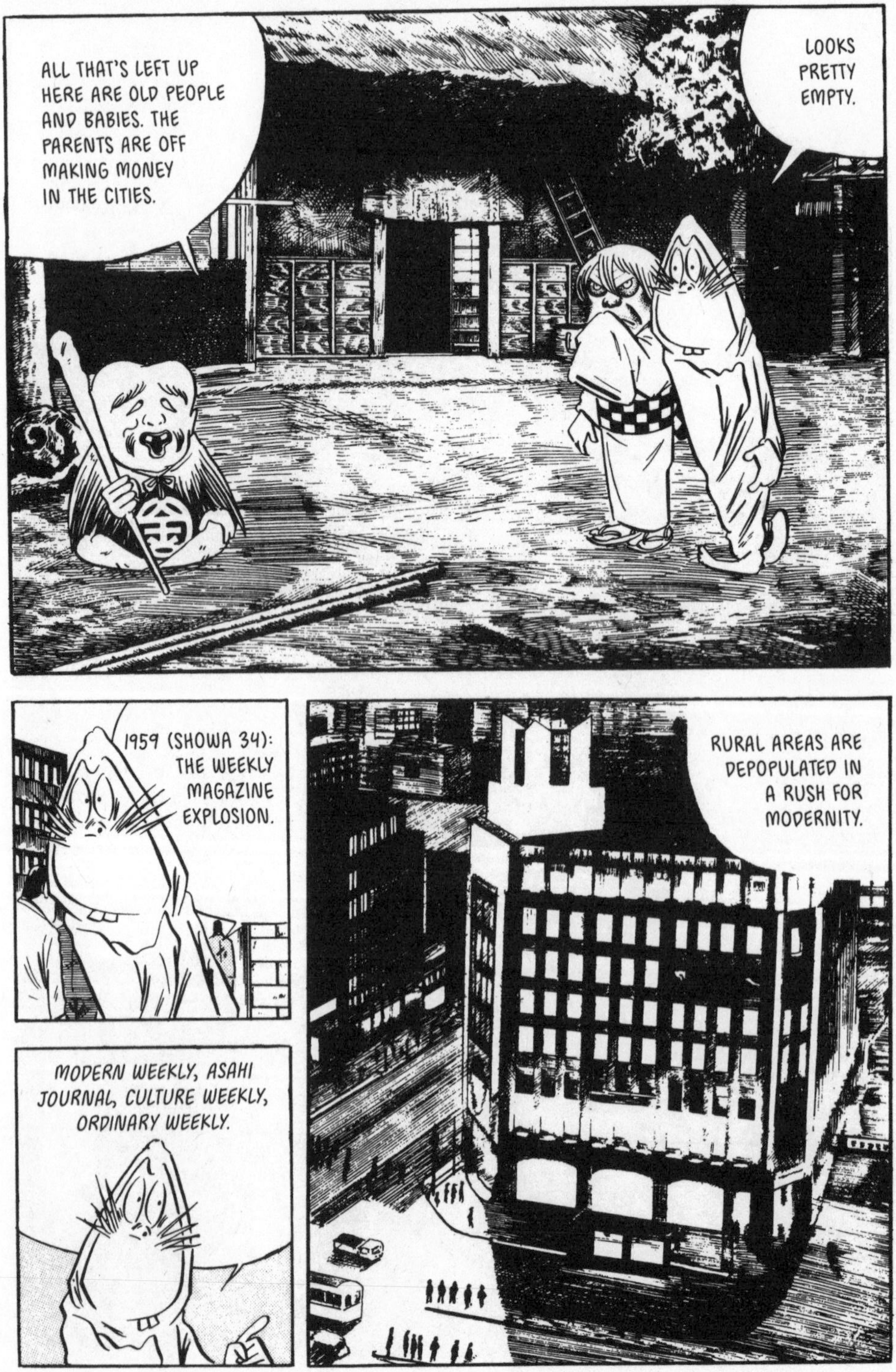
LOOKS PRETTY EMPTY.
ALL THAT'S LEFT UP HERE ARE OLD PEOPLE AND BABIES. THE PARENTS ARE OFF MAKING MONEY IN THE CITIES.
RURAL AREAS ARE DEPOPULATED IN A RUSH FOR MODERNITY.
1959 (SHOWA 34): THE WEEKLY MAGAZINE EXPLOSION.
MODERN WEEKLY, ASAHI JOURNAL, CULTURE WEEKLY, ORDINARY WEEKLY.

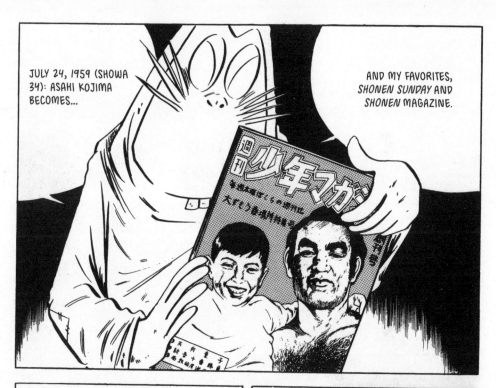

AND MY FAVORITES, SHONEN SUNDAY AND SHONEN MAGAZINE.
JULY 24, 1959 (SHOWA 34): ASAHI KOJIMA BECOMES...
THE FIRST ASIAN MISS UNIVERSE...
THAT'S A HUGE EGO BOOST TO JAPANESE WOMEN, WHO HAVE ALWAYS FELT SECOND BEST TO WESTERN WOMEN. KOJIMA BECOMES A SYMBOL OF JAPAN'S NEW ERA.
WHOOO

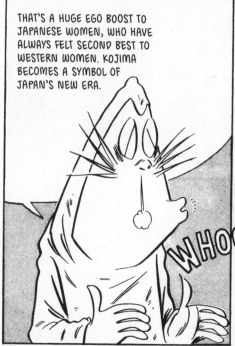

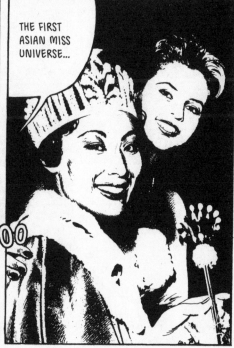

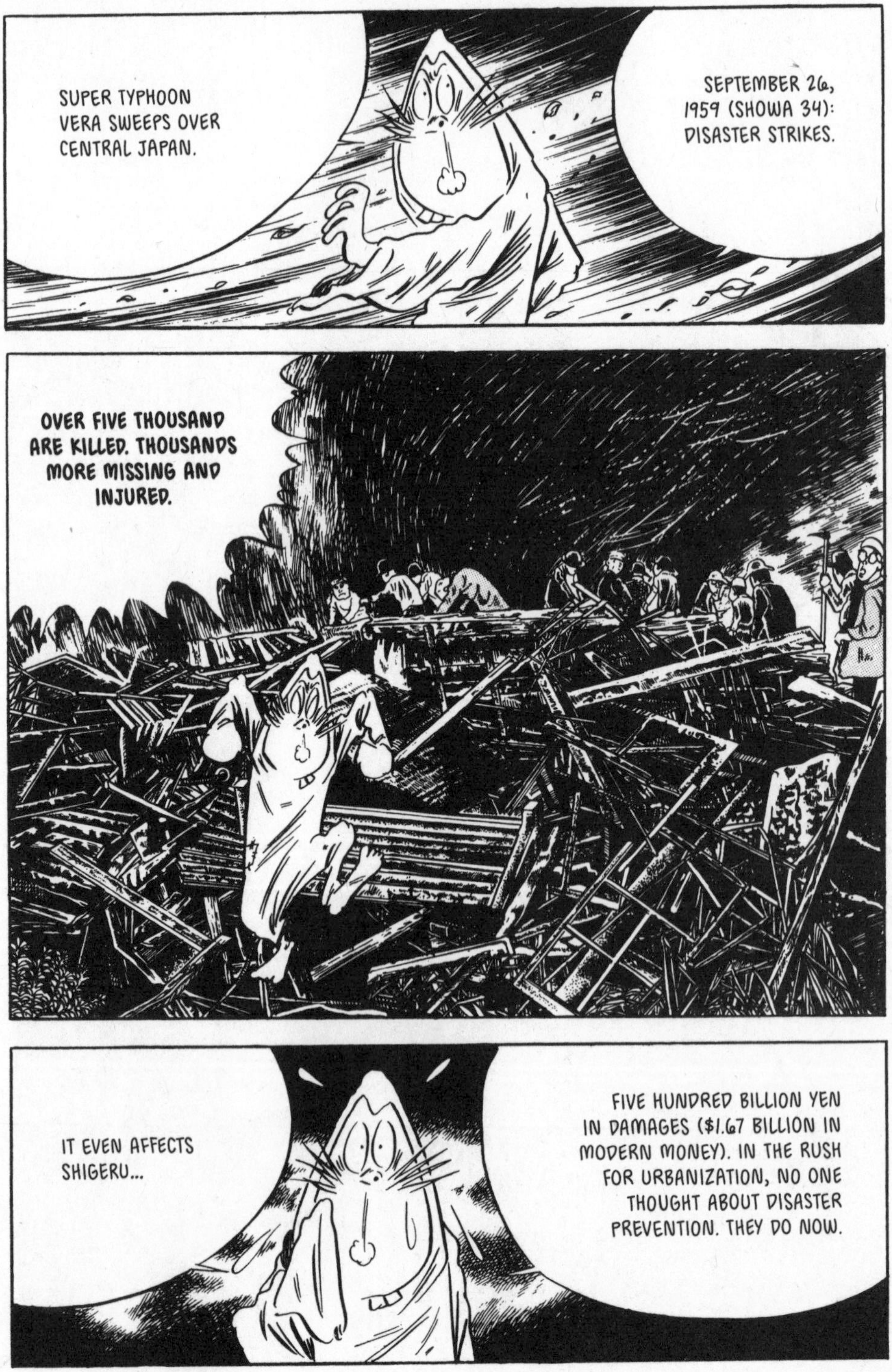
SEPTEMBER 26, 1959 (SHOWA 34): DISASTER STRIKES.
SUPER TYPHOON VERA SWEEPS OVER CENTRAL JAPAN.
OVER FIVE THOUSAND ARE KILLED. THOUSANDS MORE MISSING AND INJURED.
FIVE HUNDRED BILLION YEN IN DAMAGES ($1.67 BILLION IN MODERN MONEY). IN THE RUSH FOR URBANIZATION, NO ONE THOUGHT ABOUT DISASTER PREVENTION. THEY DO NOW.
IT EVEN AFFECTS SHIGERU...

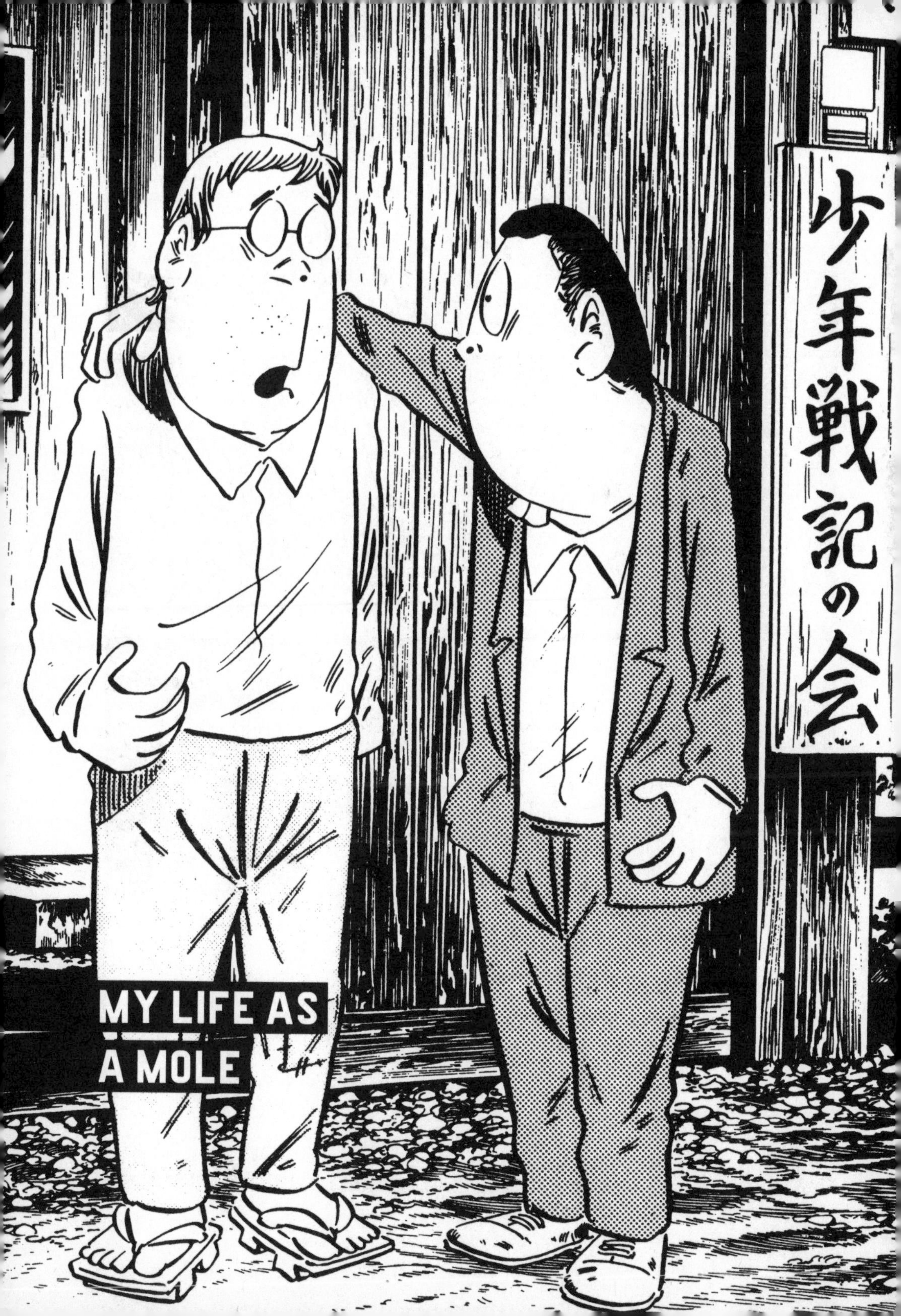
少年戦記の会
MY LIFE AS A MOLE

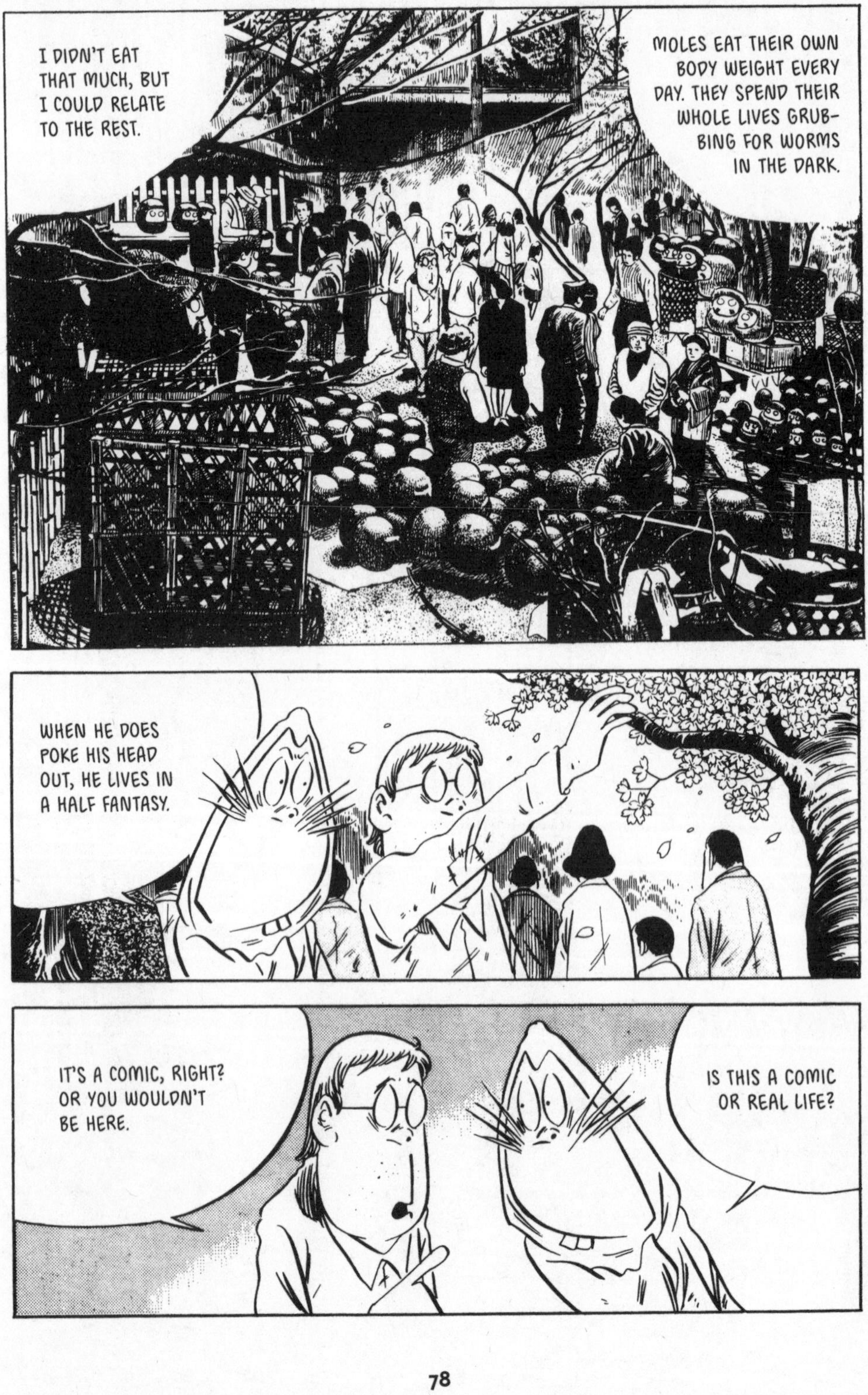
MOLES EAT THEIR OWN BODY WEIGHT EVERY DAY. THEY SPEND THEIR WHOLE LIVES GRUB-BING FOR WORMS IN THE DARK.
I DIDN'T EAT THAT MUCH, BUT I COULD RELATE TO THE REST.
WHEN HE DOES POKE HIS HEAD OUT, HE LIVES IN A HALF FANTASY.
IS THIS A COMIC OR REAL LIFE?
IT'S A COMIC, RIGHT? OR YOU WOULDN'T BE HERE.

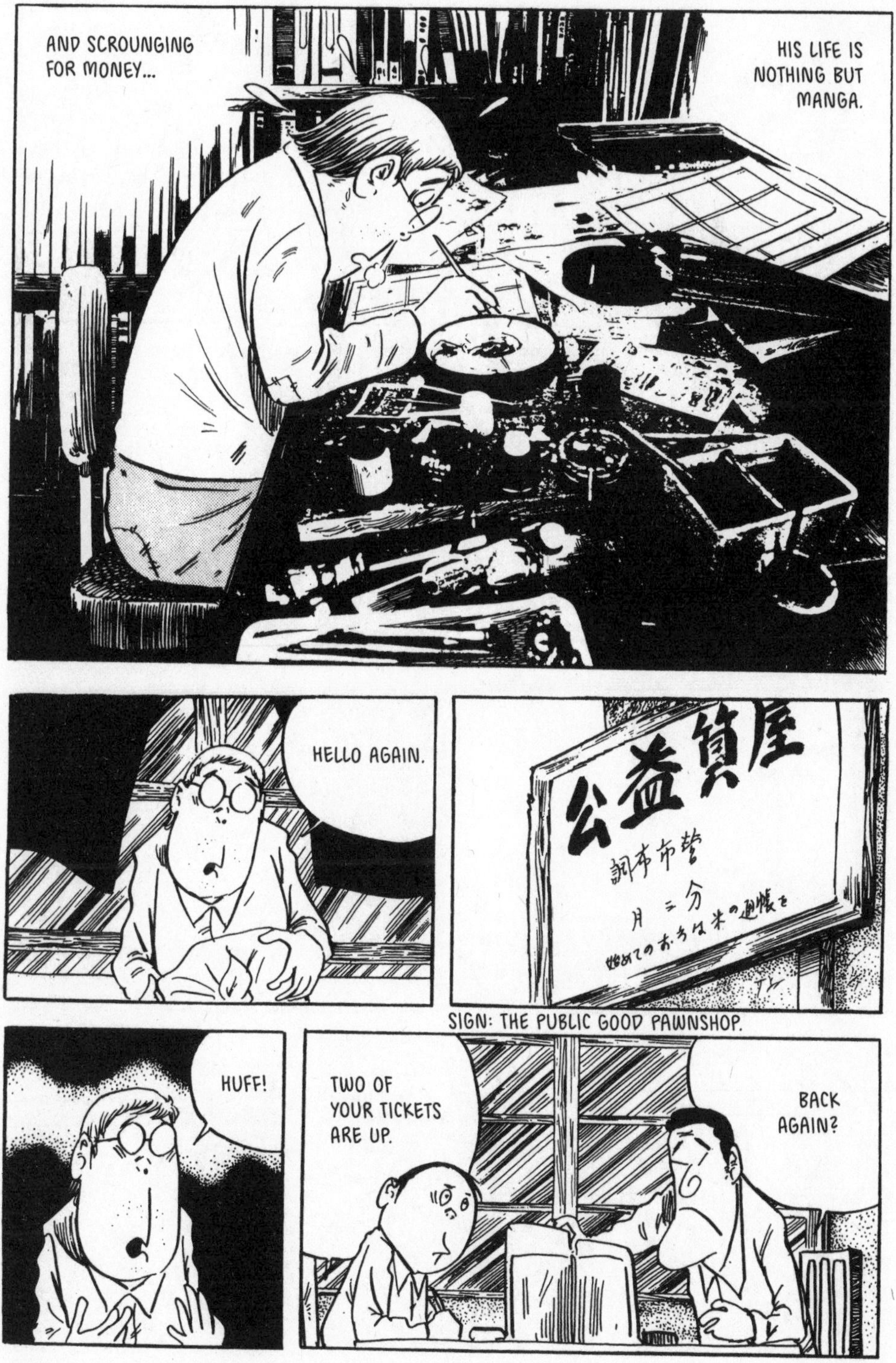
HIS LIFE IS NOTHING BUT MANGA.
AND SCROUNGING FOR MONEY...
公益質屋
SIGN: THE PUBLIC GOOD PAWNSHOP.
HELLO AGAIN.
BACK AGAIN?
TWO OF YOUR TICKETS ARE UP.
HUFF!

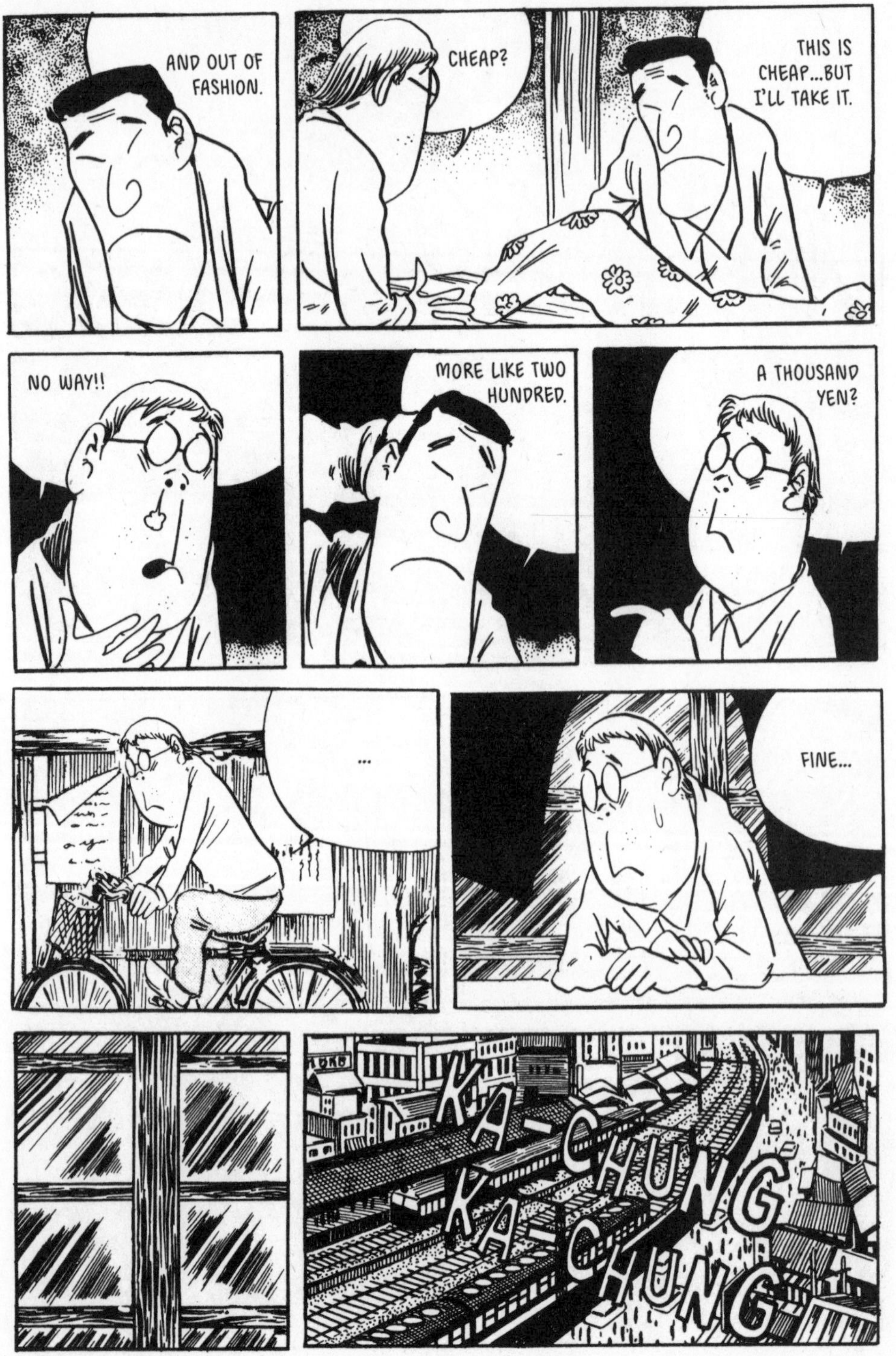
THIS IS CHEAP...BUT I'LL TAKE IT.
CHEAP?
AND OUT OF FASHION.
A THOUSAND YEN?
MORE LIKE TWO HUNDRED.
NO WAY!!
FINE...
...
KA-CHUNG
KA-CHUNG

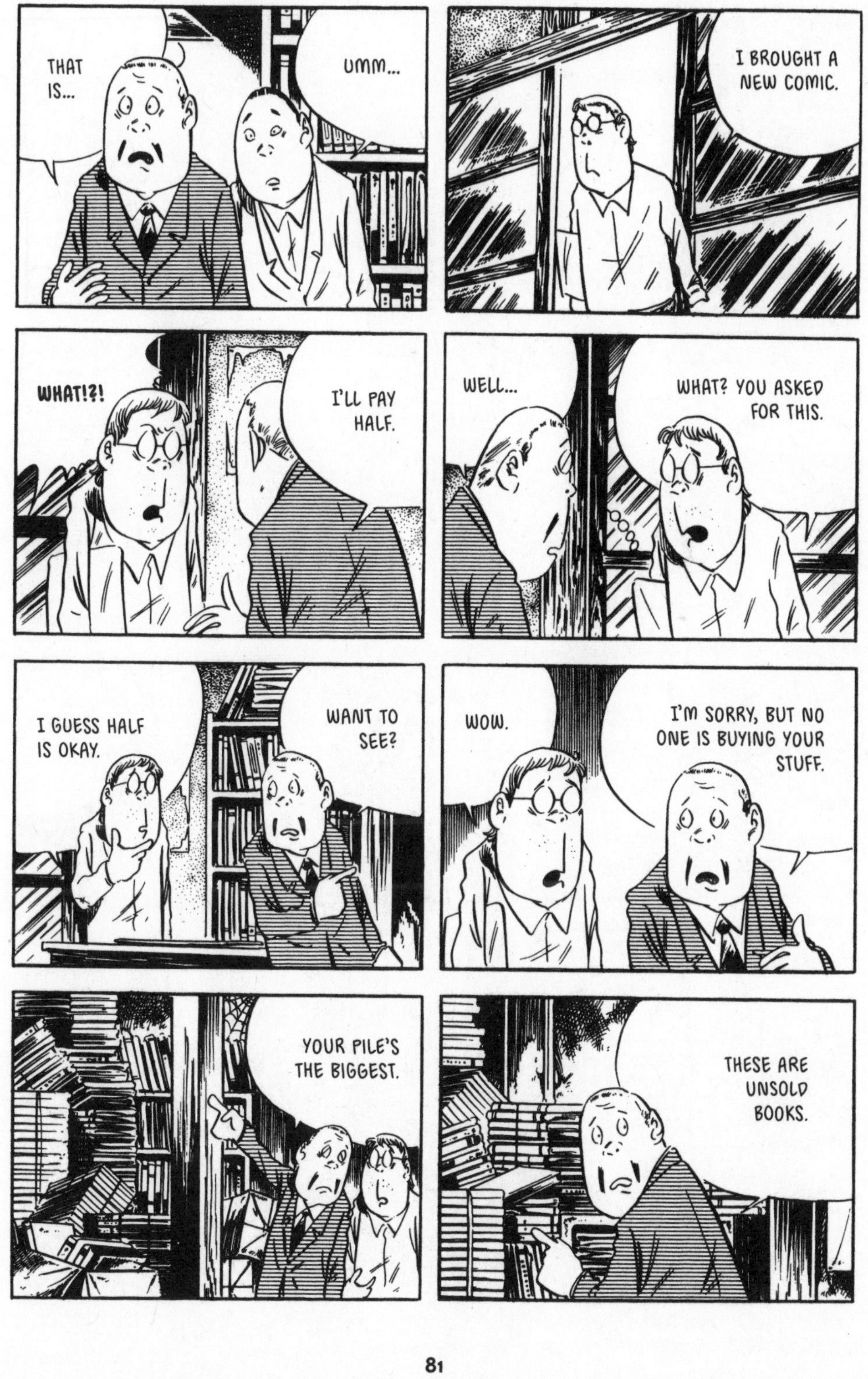
I BROUGHT A NEW COMIC.
UMM...
THAT IS...
WHAT? YOU ASKED FOR THIS.
WELL...
I'LL PAY HALF.
WHAT!?!
I'M SORRY, BUT NO ONE IS BUYING YOUR STUFF.
WOW.
WANT TO SEE?
I GUESS HALF IS OKAY.
THESE ARE UNSOLD BOOKS.
YOUR PILE'S THE BIGGEST.

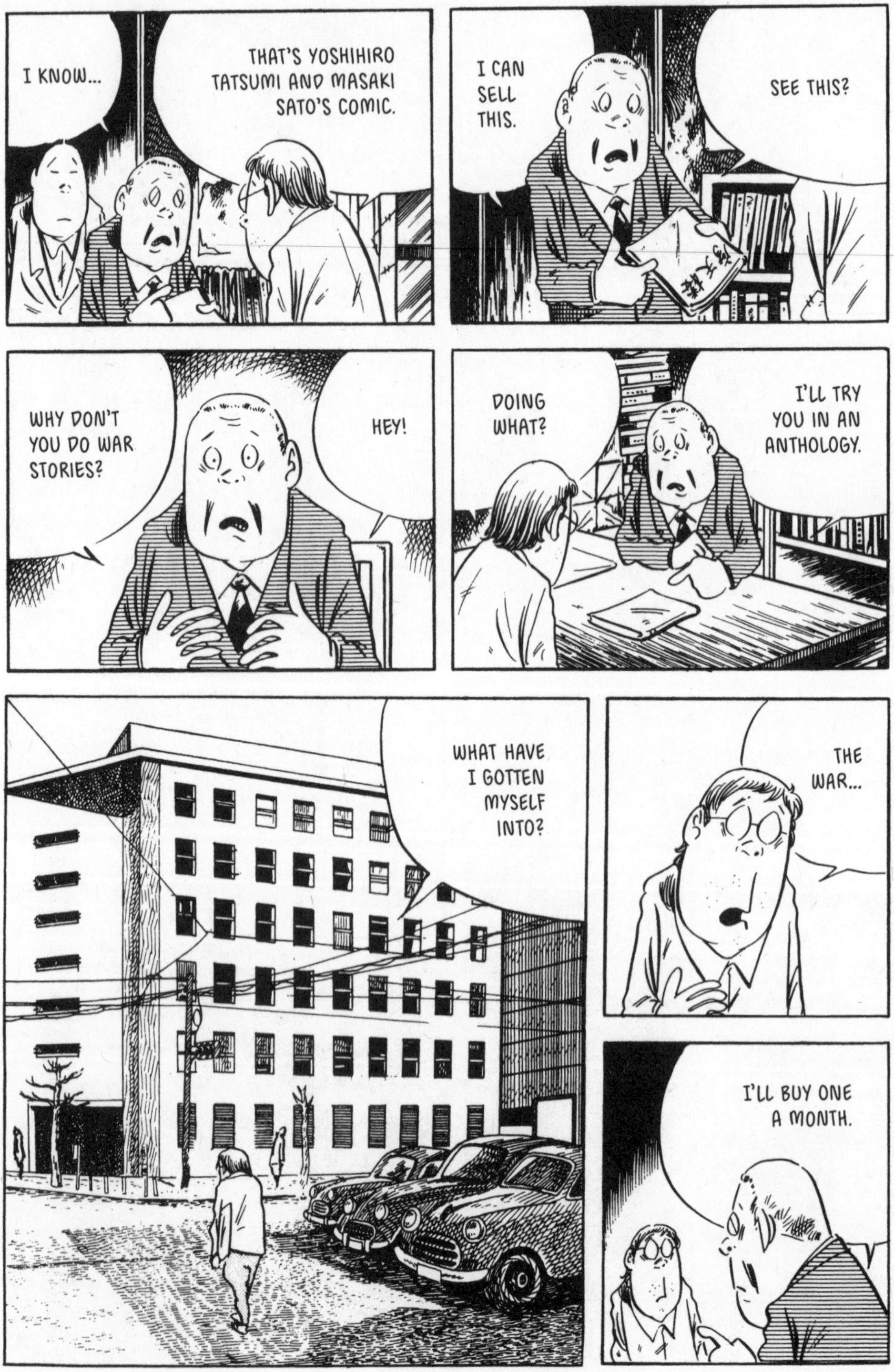
SEE THIS?
I CAN SELL THIS.
THAT'S YOSHIHIRO TATSUMI AND MASAKI SATO'S COMIC.
I KNOW...
I'LL TRY YOU IN AN ANTHOLOGY.
DOING WHAT?
HEY!
WHY DON'T YOU DO WAR STORIES?
THE WAR...
I'LL BUY ONE A MONTH.
WHAT HAVE I GOTTEN MYSELF INTO?

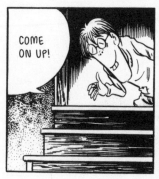

AH, MIZUKI SAN.
IS HONEJIRO SASAKI IN?
COME ON UP!
I GOT HIRED FOR *BOY'S WAR DIARIES.*
TAP TAP
THIRTY PAGES...
CHECK THIS OUT.
A HUNDRED-YEN PAGE, A TWO-HUNDRED-YEN PAGE, AND A THREE-HUNDRED-YEN PAGE.
THE CHEAP ONE'S GOT NO BACKGROUND.
BACKGROUNDS COST TWO HUNDRED YEN.
SO THEY GET WHAT THEY PAY FOR.

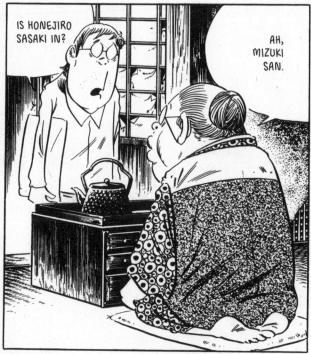

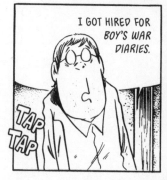

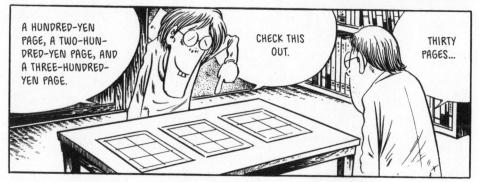

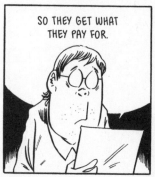

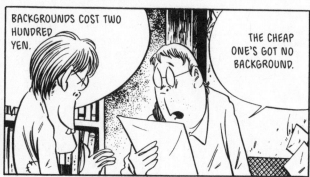

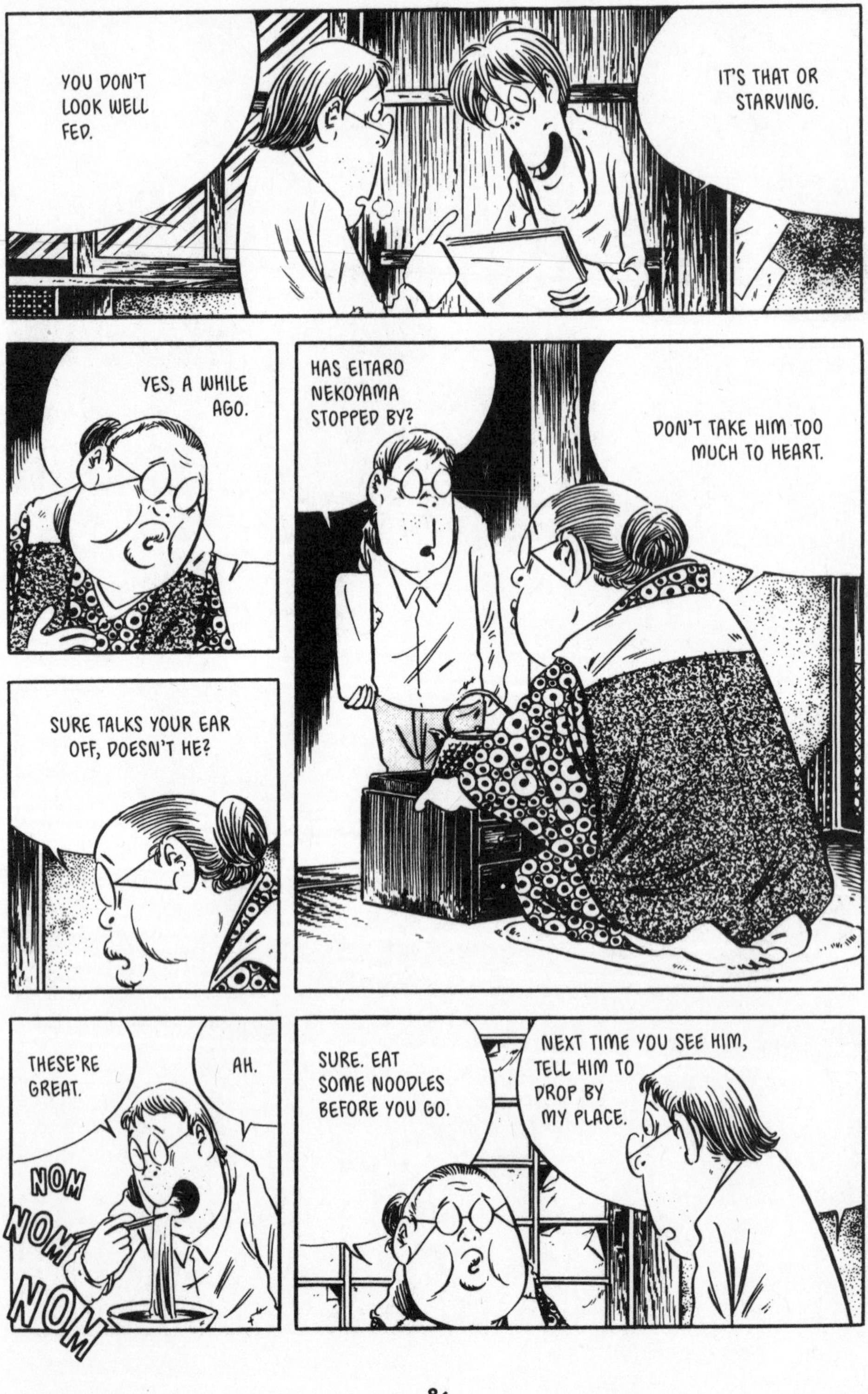
YOU DON'T LOOK WELL FED.
IT'S THAT OR STARVING.
HAS EITARO NEKOYAMA STOPPED BY?
DON'T TAKE HIM TOO MUCH TO HEART.
YES, A WHILE AGO.
SURE TALKS YOUR EAR OFF, DOESN'T HE?
NEXT TIME YOU SEE HIM, TELL HIM TO DROP BY MY PLACE.
SURE. EAT SOME NOODLES BEFORE YOU GO.
AH.
THESE'RE GREAT.
NOM
NOM
NOM

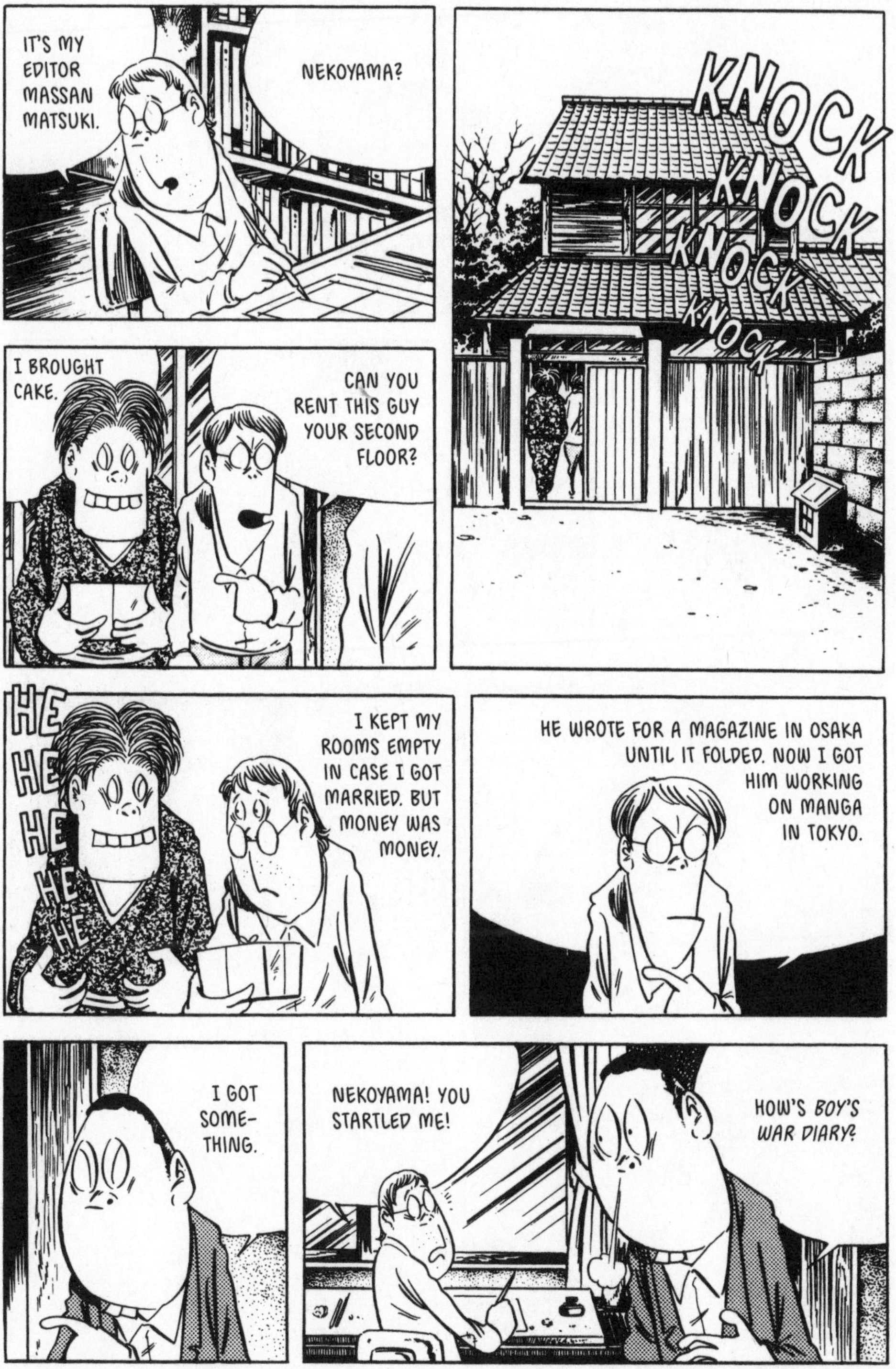
KNOCK
KNOCK
KNOCK
KNOCK
NEKOYAMA?
IT'S MY EDITOR MASSAN MATSUKI.
CAN YOU RENT THIS GUY YOUR SECOND FLOOR?
I BROUGHT CAKE.
HE WROTE FOR A MAGAZINE IN OSAKA UNTIL IT FOLDED. NOW I GOT HIM WORKING ON MANGA IN TOKYO.
I KEPT MY ROOMS EMPTY IN CASE I GOT MARRIED. BUT MONEY WAS MONEY.
HE HE HE HE HE
HOW'S *BOY'S WAR DIARY*?
NEKOYAMA! YOU STARTLED ME!
I GOT SOME-THING.

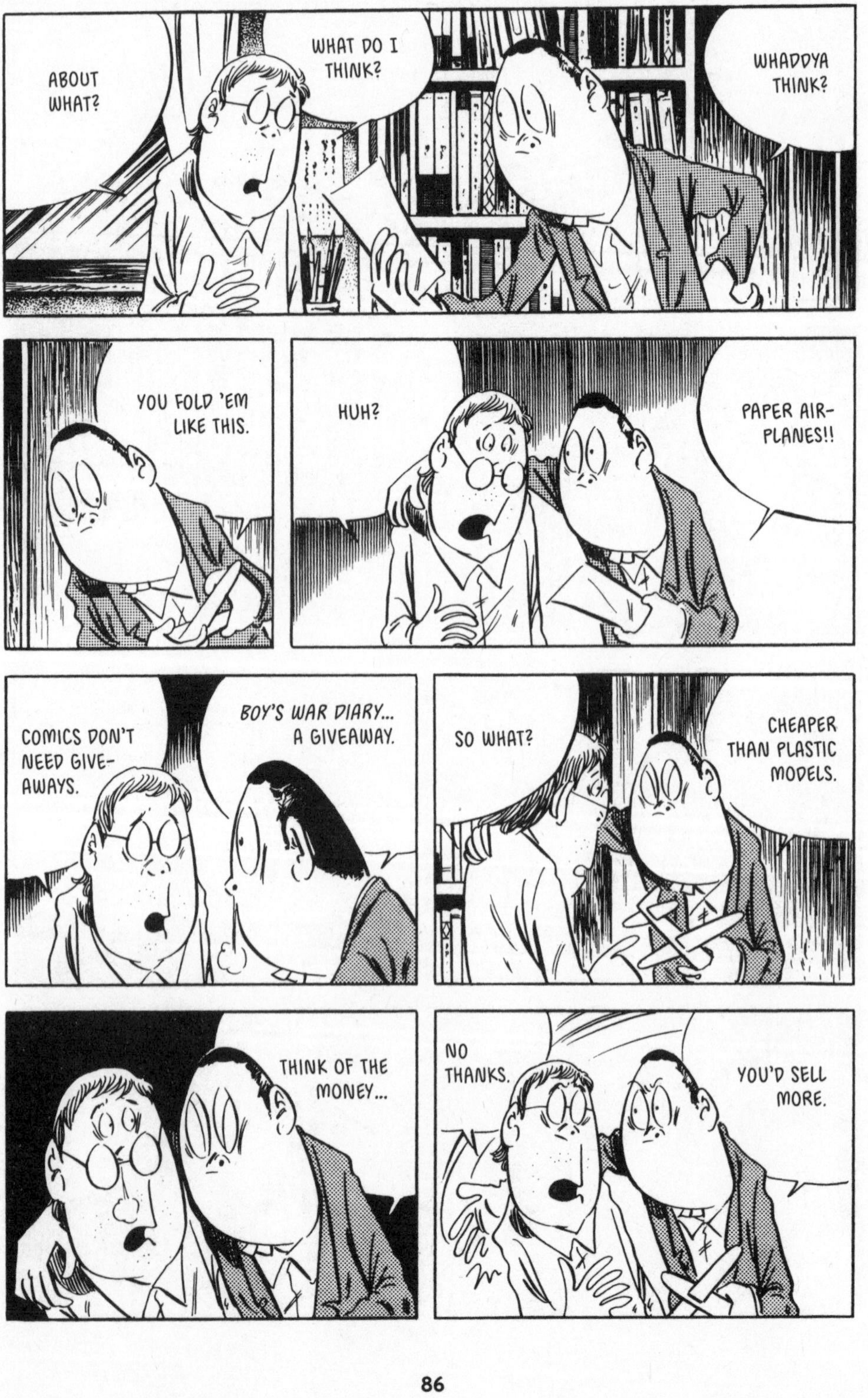
WHADDYA THINK?
WHAT DO I THINK?
ABOUT WHAT?
PAPER AIR-PLANES!!
HUH?
YOU FOLD 'EM LIKE THIS.
CHEAPER THAN PLASTIC MODELS.
SO WHAT?
BOY'S WAR DIARY... A GIVEAWAY.
COMICS DON'T NEED GIVE-AWAYS.
YOU'D SELL MORE.
NO THANKS.
THINK OF THE MONEY...

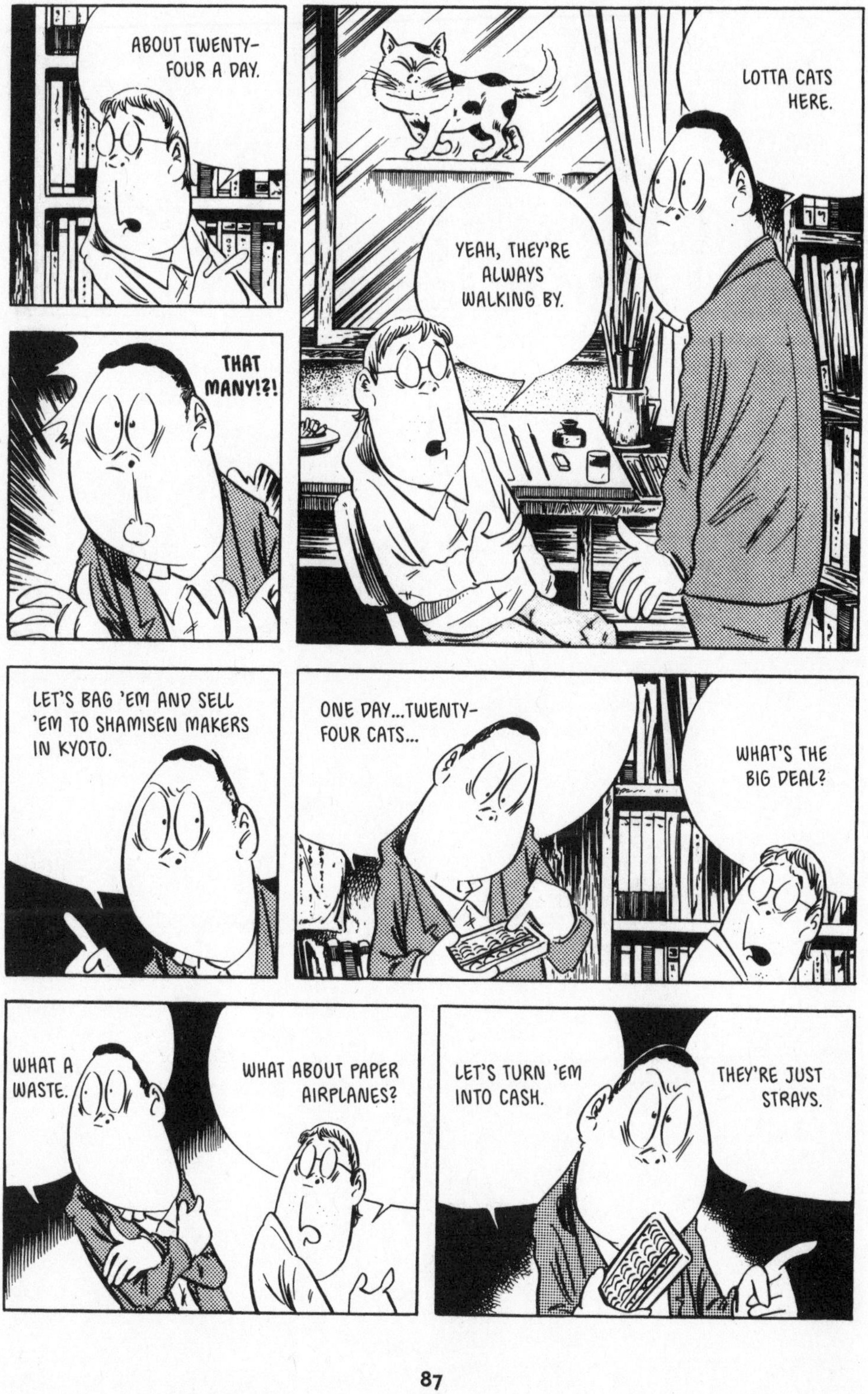
LOTTA CATS HERE.
YEAH, THEY'RE ALWAYS WALKING BY.
ABOUT TWENTY-FOUR A DAY.
THAT MANY!?!
WHAT'S THE BIG DEAL?
ONE DAY...TWENTY-FOUR CATS...
LET'S BAG 'EM AND SELL 'EM TO SHAMISEN MAKERS IN KYOTO.
THEY'RE JUST STRAYS.
LET'S TURN 'EM INTO CASH.
WHAT ABOUT PAPER AIRPLANES?
WHAT A WASTE.

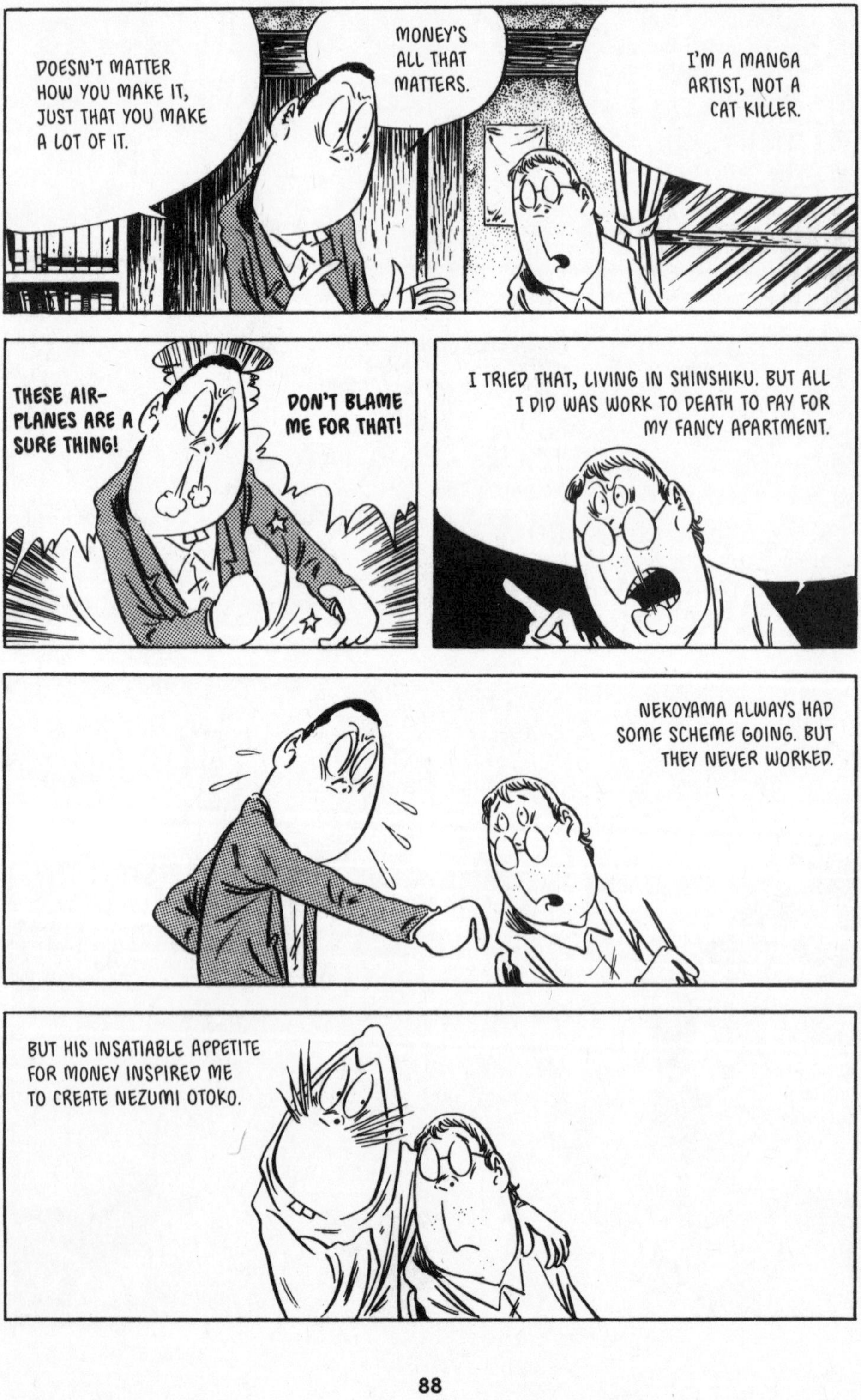
I'M A MANGA ARTIST, NOT A CAT KILLER.
MONEY'S ALL THAT MATTERS.
DOESN'T MATTER HOW YOU MAKE IT, JUST THAT YOU MAKE A LOT OF IT.
I TRIED THAT, LIVING IN SHINSHIKU. BUT ALL I DID WAS WORK TO DEATH TO PAY FOR MY FANCY APARTMENT.
DON'T BLAME ME FOR THAT!
THESE AIR-PLANES ARE A SURE THING!
NEKOYAMA ALWAYS HAD SOME SCHEME GOING. BUT THEY NEVER WORKED.
BUT HIS INSATIABLE APPETITE FOR MONEY INSPIRED ME TO CREATE NEZUMI OTOKO.

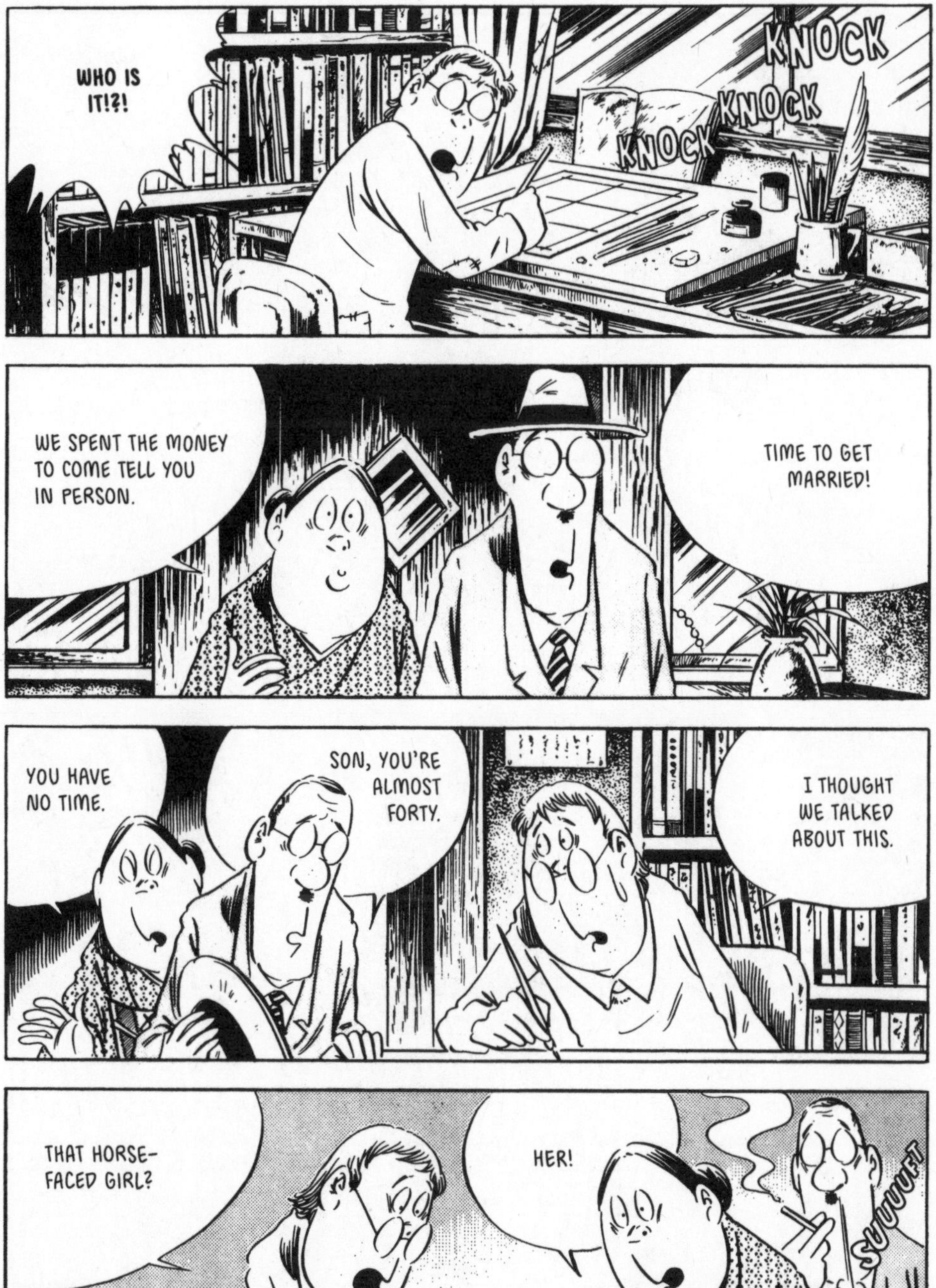
KNOCK
KNOCK
KNOCK
WHO IS IT!?!
TIME TO GET MARRIED!
WE SPENT THE MONEY TO COME TELL YOU IN PERSON.
I THOUGHT WE TALKED ABOUT THIS.
SON, YOU'RE ALMOST FORTY.
YOU HAVE NO TIME.
SUUUUFT
HER!
THAT HORSE-FACED GIRL?

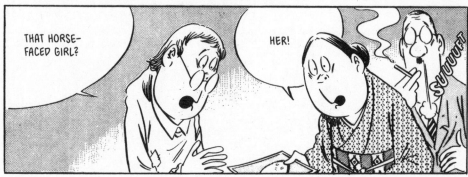

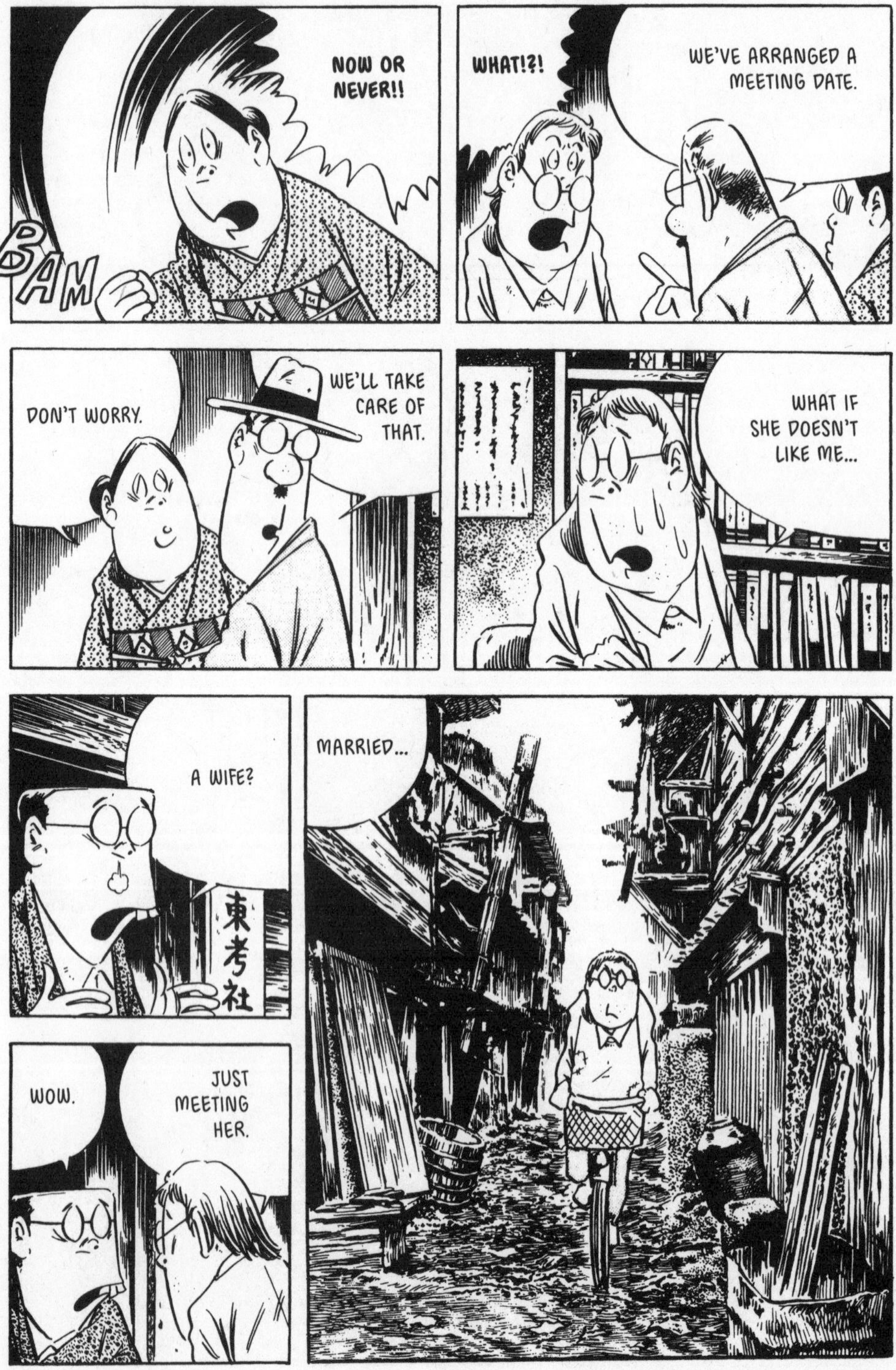
WE'VE ARRANGED A MEETING DATE.
WHAT!?!
NOW OR NEVER!!
BAM
WHAT IF SHE DOESN'T LIKE ME...
WE'LL TAKE CARE OF THAT.
DON'T WORRY.
MARRIED...
A WIFE?
東考社
JUST MEETING HER.
WOW.

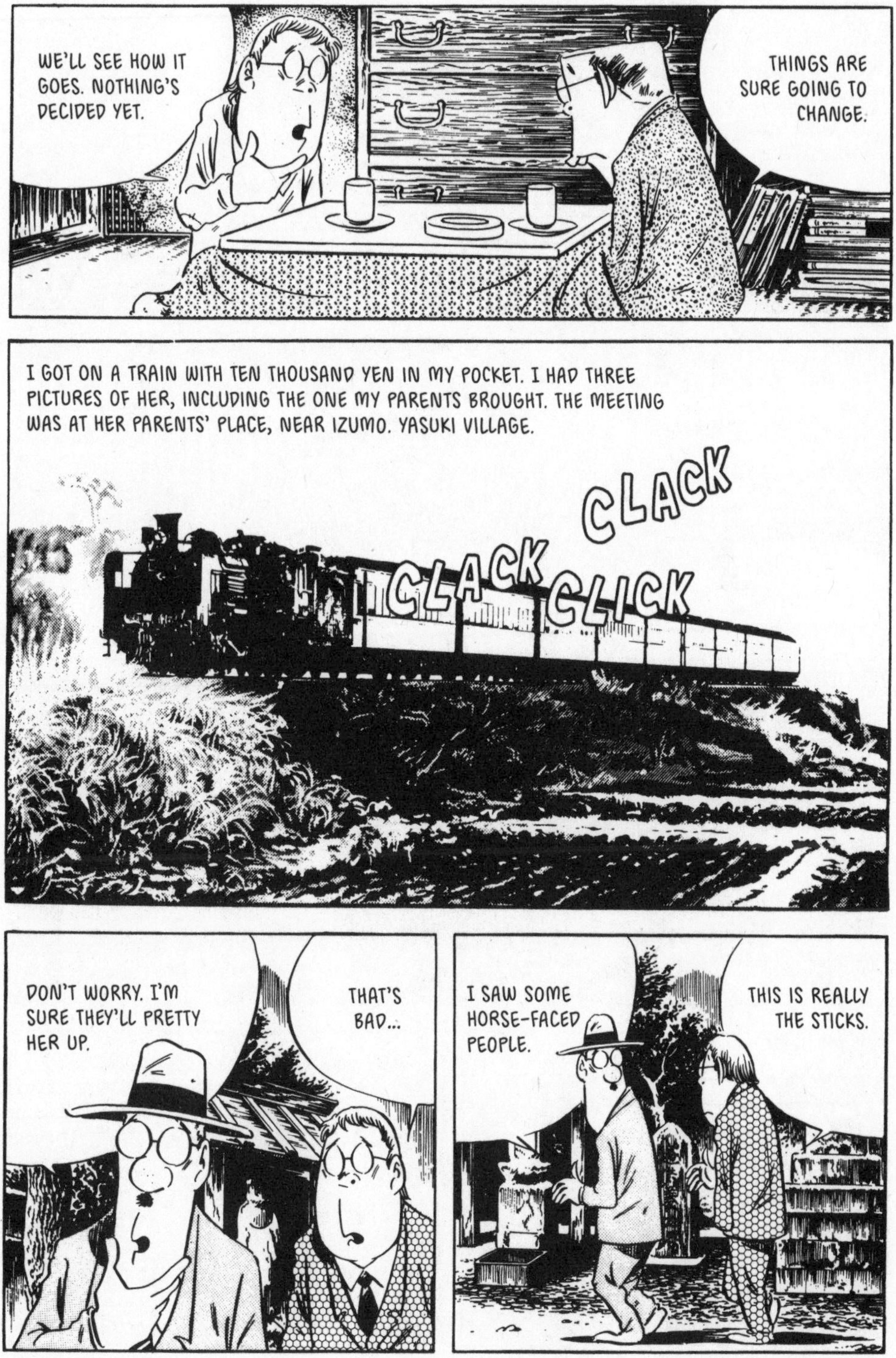
THINGS ARE SURE GOING TO CHANGE.
WE'LL SEE HOW IT GOES. NOTHING'S DECIDED YET.
I GOT ON A TRAIN WITH TEN THOUSAND YEN IN MY POCKET. I HAD THREE PICTURES OF HER, INCLUDING THE ONE MY PARENTS BROUGHT. THE MEETING WAS AT HER PARENTS' PLACE, NEAR IZUMO. YASUKI VILLAGE.
CLACK
CLACK
CLICK
THIS IS REALLY THE STICKS.
I SAW SOME HORSE-FACED PEOPLE.
THAT'S BAD...
DON'T WORRY. I'M SURE THEY'LL PRETTY HER UP.

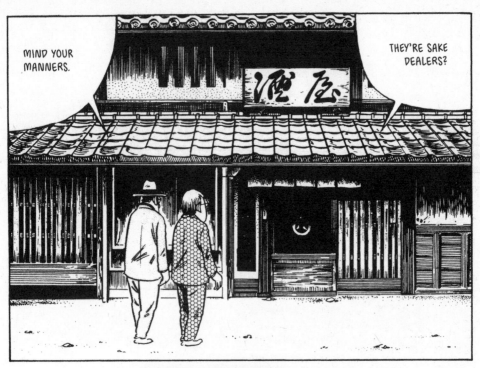

THEY'RE SAKE DEALERS?
MIND YOUR MANNERS.
THE FATHER HAD A HUGE HORSE FACE, BUT THE MOTHER WASN'T SO BAD.
HA HA HA. YOU CAN TAKE IT EASY HERE.
TOMORROW'S GOOD FOR A WEDDING...
GULP! WHAT?
I HAD TO GET BACK FOR WORK, BUT WE SET THE DATE.
HOOOOO

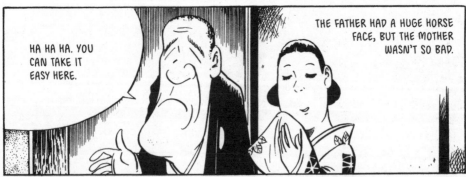

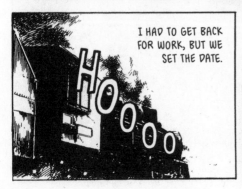

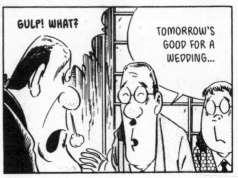

'60S SECURITY TREATY TURMOIL

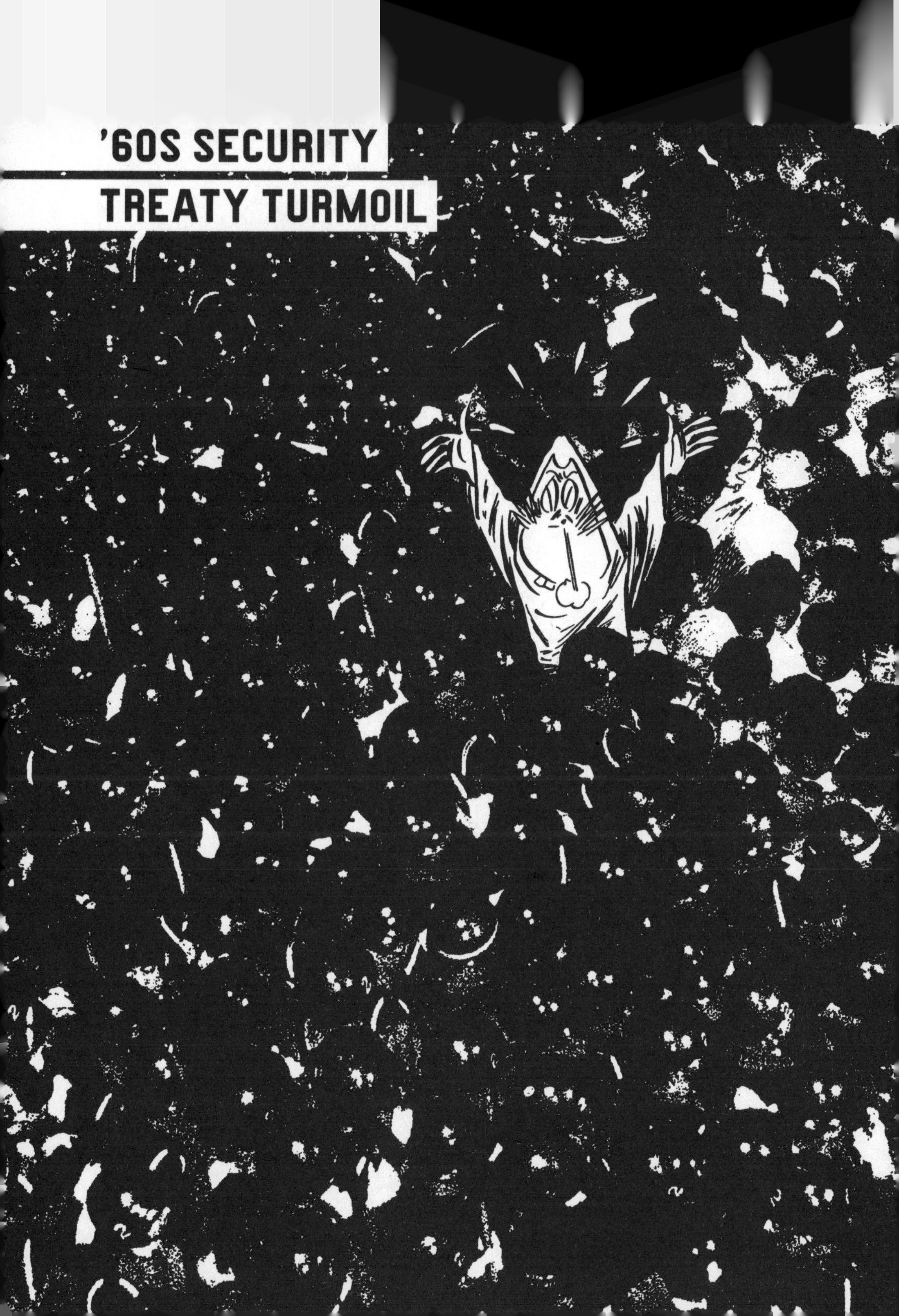

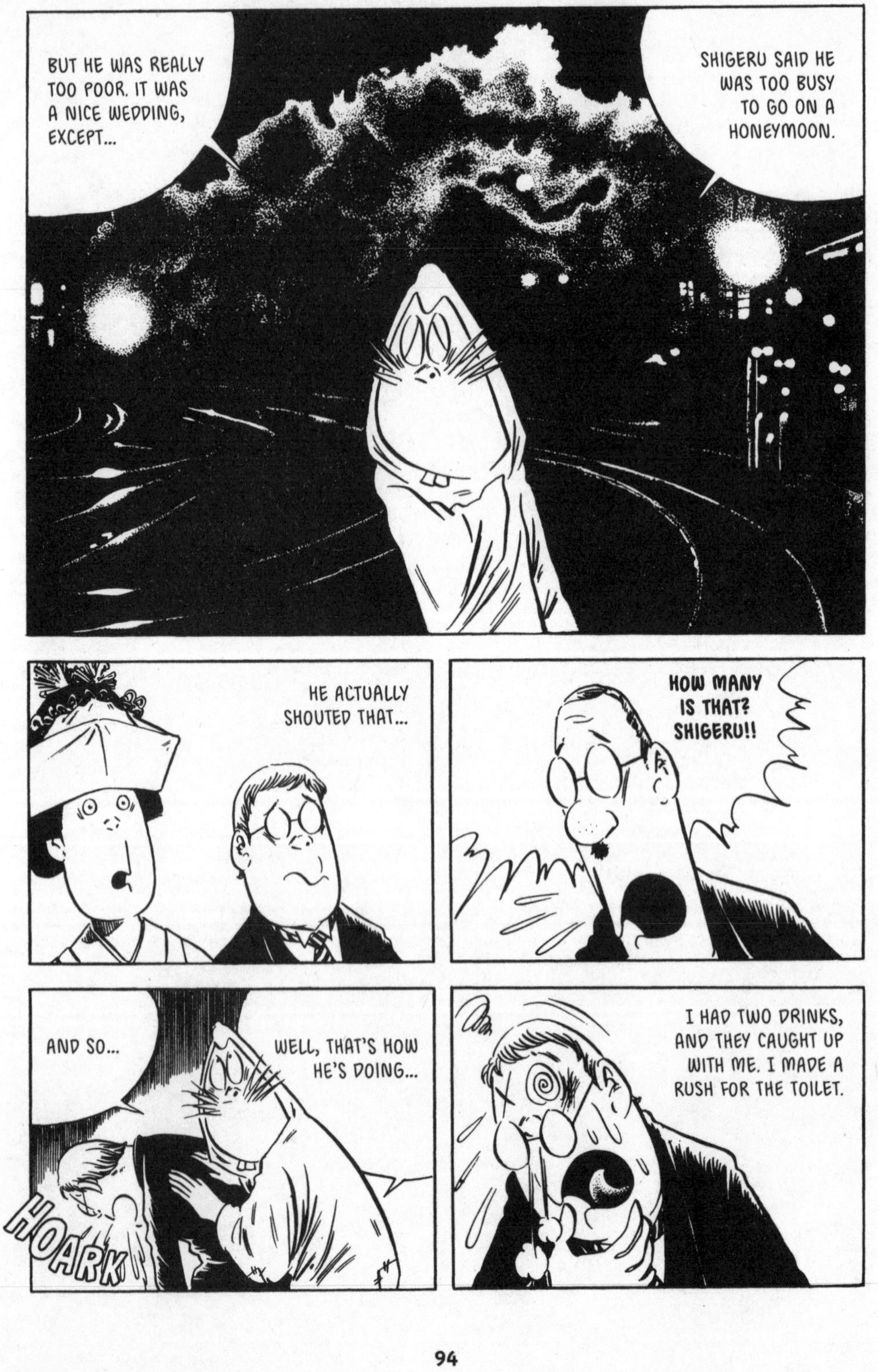
SHIGERU SAID HE WAS TOO BUSY TO GO ON A HONEYMOON.
BUT HE WAS REALLY TOO POOR. IT WAS A NICE WEDDING, EXCEPT...
HOW MANY IS THAT? SHIGERU!!
HE ACTUALLY SHOUTED THAT...
I HAD TWO DRINKS, AND THEY CAUGHT UP WITH ME. I MADE A RUSH FOR THE TOILET.
WELL, THAT'S HOW HE'S DOING...
AND SO...
HOARK

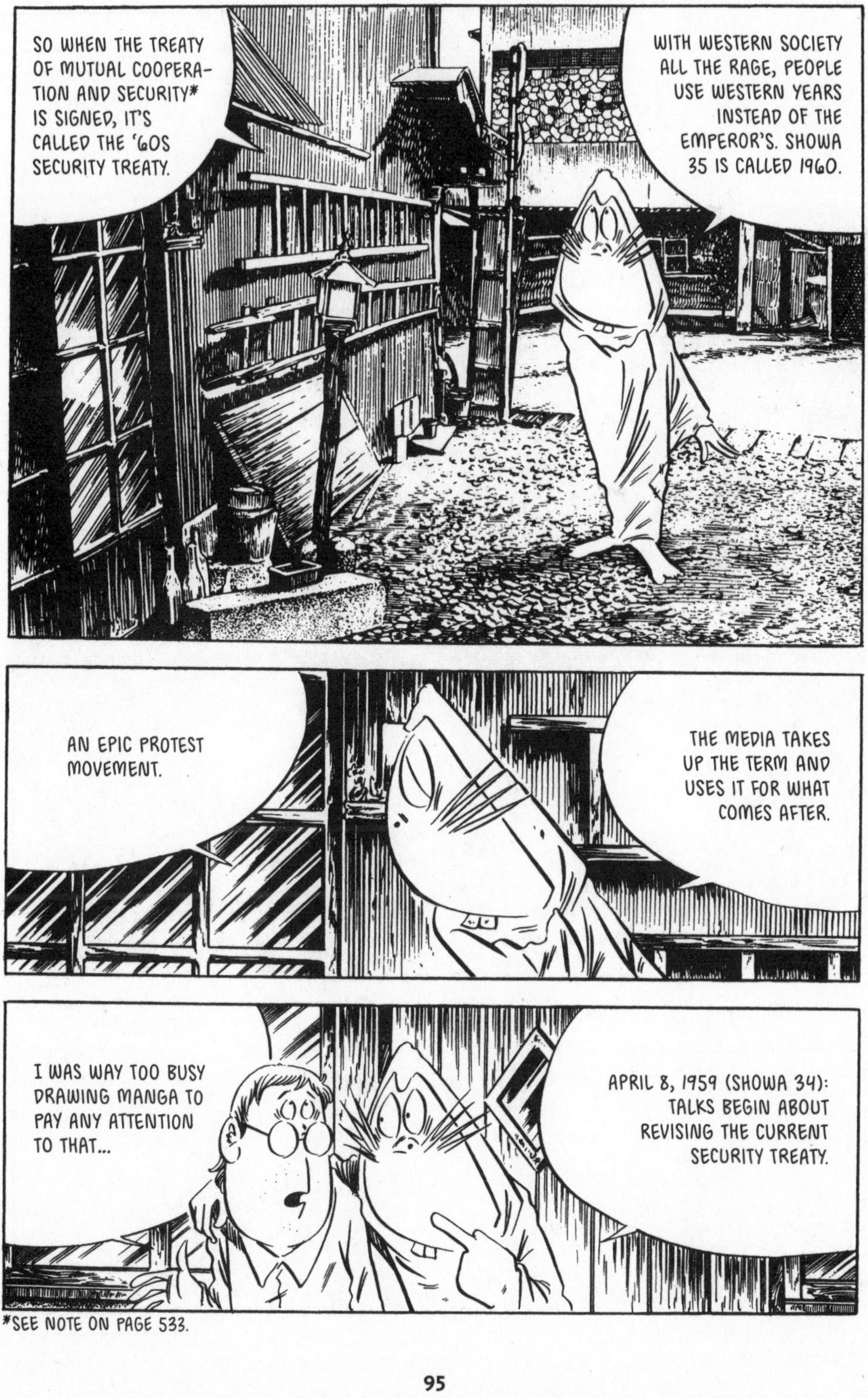
WITH WESTERN SOCIETY ALL THE RAGE, PEOPLE USE WESTERN YEARS INSTEAD OF THE EMPEROR'S. SHOWA 35 IS CALLED 1960.
SO WHEN THE TREATY OF MUTUAL COOPERATION AND SECURITY* IS SIGNED, IT'S CALLED THE '60S SECURITY TREATY.
THE MEDIA TAKES UP THE TERM AND USES IT FOR WHAT COMES AFTER.
AN EPIC PROTEST MOVEMENT.
APRIL 8, 1959 (SHOWA 34): TALKS BEGIN ABOUT REVISING THE CURRENT SECURITY TREATY.
I WAS WAY TOO BUSY DRAWING MANGA TO PAY ANY ATTENTION TO THAT...

*SEE NOTE ON PAGE 533.

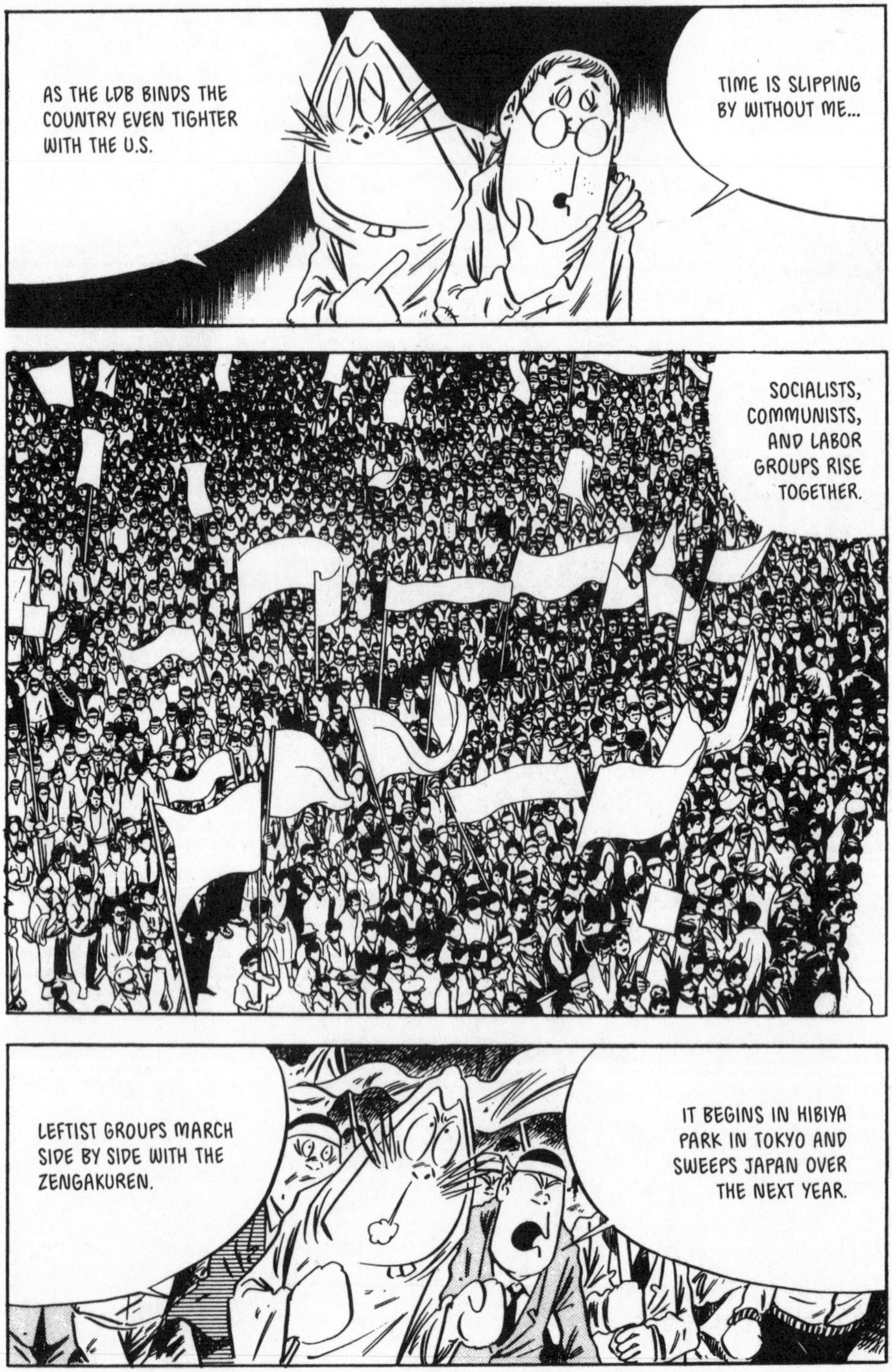
TIME IS SLIPPING BY WITHOUT ME...
AS THE LDB BINDS THE COUNTRY EVEN TIGHTER WITH THE U.S.
SOCIALISTS, COMMUNISTS, AND LABOR GROUPS RISE TOGETHER.
IT BEGINS IN HIBIYA PARK IN TOKYO AND SWEEPS JAPAN OVER THE NEXT YEAR.
LEFTIST GROUPS MARCH SIDE BY SIDE WITH THE ZENGAKUREN.

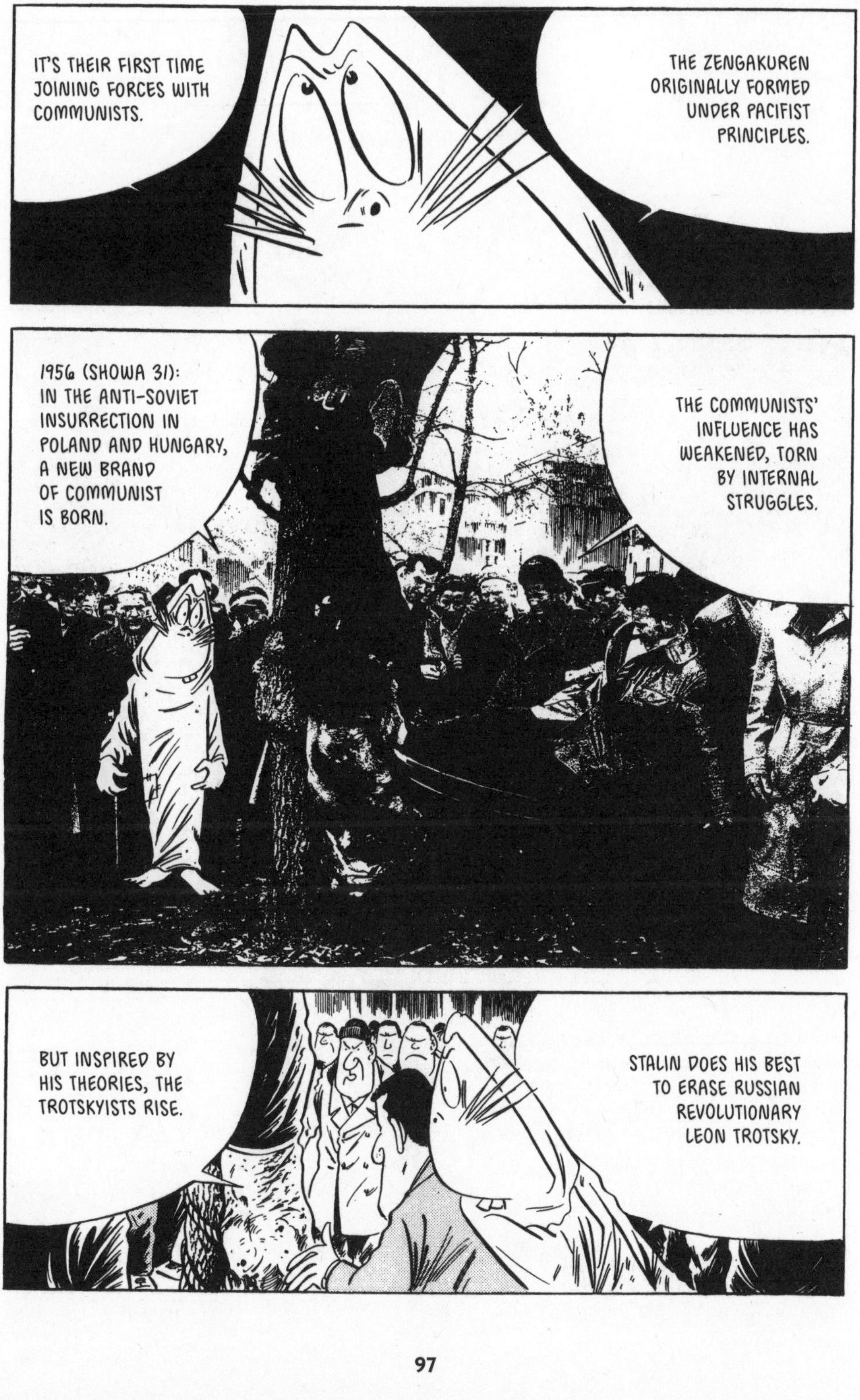
THE ZENGAKUREN ORIGINALLY FORMED UNDER PACIFIST PRINCIPLES.
IT'S THEIR FIRST TIME JOINING FORCES WITH COMMUNISTS.
THE COMMUNISTS' INFLUENCE HAS WEAKENED, TORN BY INTERNAL STRUGGLES.
1956 (SHOWA 31): IN THE ANTI-SOVIET INSURRECTION IN POLAND AND HUNGARY, A NEW BRAND OF COMMUNIST IS BORN.
STALIN DOES HIS BEST TO ERASE RUSSIAN REVOLUTIONARY LEON TROTSKY.
BUT INSPIRED BY HIS THEORIES, THE TROTSKYISTS RISE.

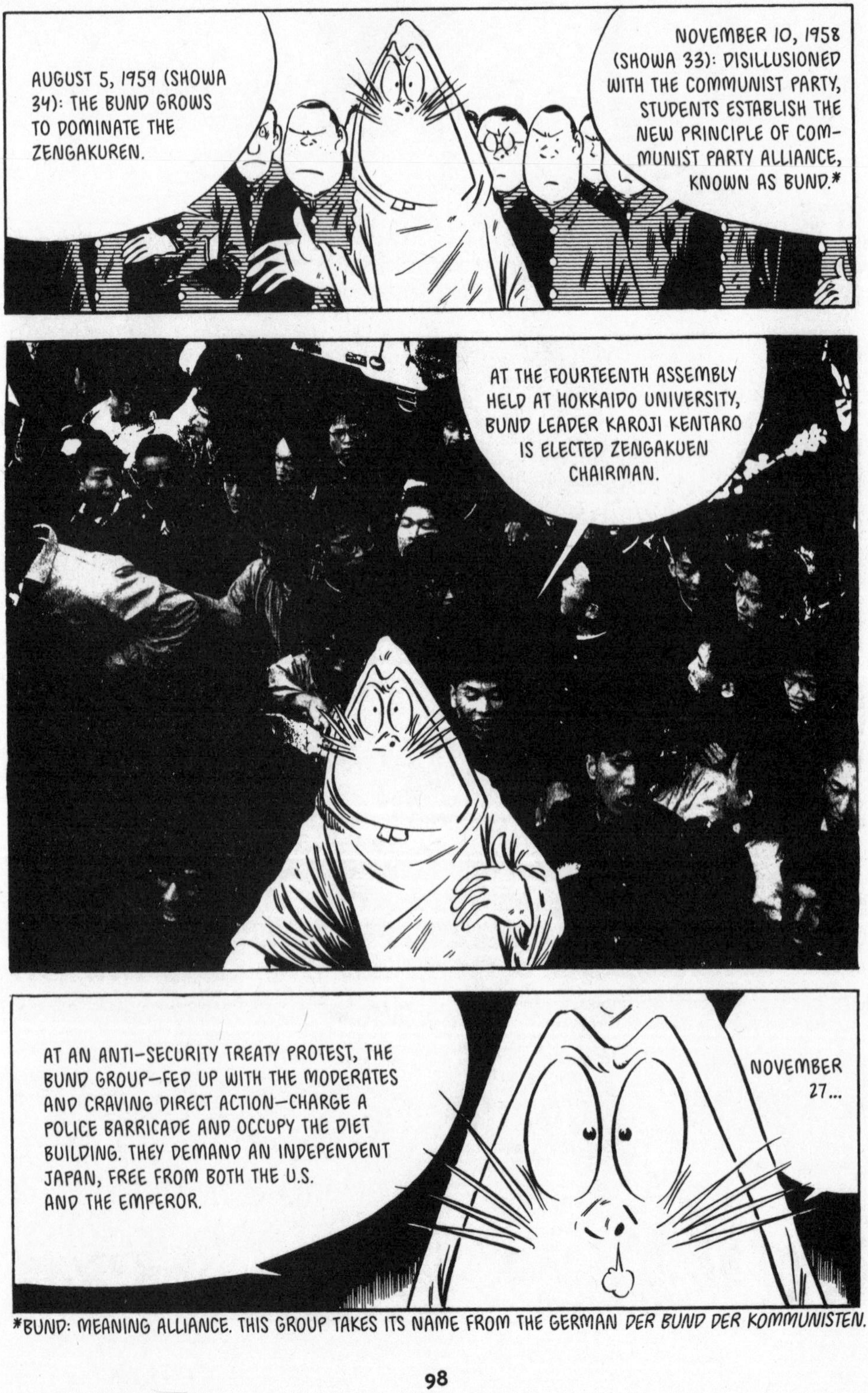
NOVEMBER 10, 1958 (SHOWA 33): DISILLUSIONED WITH THE COMMUNIST PARTY, STUDENTS ESTABLISH THE NEW PRINCIPLE OF COMMUNIST PARTY ALLIANCE, KNOWN AS BUND.*
AUGUST 5, 1959 (SHOWA 34): THE BUND GROWS TO DOMINATE THE ZENGAKUREN.
AT THE FOURTEENTH ASSEMBLY HELD AT HOKKAIDO UNIVERSITY, BUND LEADER KAROJI KENTARO IS ELECTED ZENGAKUEN CHAIRMAN.
NOVEMBER 27...
AT AN ANTI-SECURITY TREATY PROTEST, THE BUND GROUP—FED UP WITH THE MODERATES AND CRAVING DIRECT ACTION—CHARGE A POLICE BARRICADE AND OCCUPY THE DIET BUILDING. THEY DEMAND AN INDEPENDENT JAPAN, FREE FROM BOTH THE U.S. AND THE EMPEROR.

*BUND: MEANING ALLIANCE. THIS GROUP TAKES ITS NAME FROM THE GERMAN *DER BUND DER KOMMUNISTEN*.

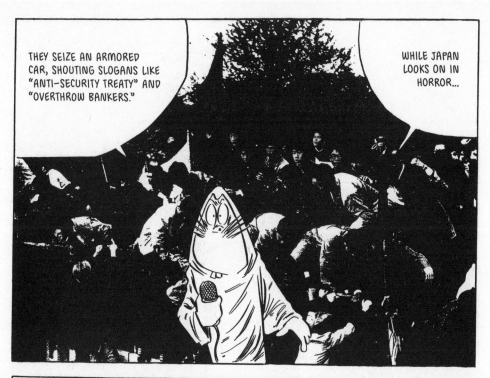

WHILE JAPAN LOOKS ON IN HORROR...
THEY SEIZE AN ARMORED CAR, SHOUTING SLOGANS LIKE "ANTI-SECURITY TREATY" AND "OVERTHROW BANKERS."
ZENGAKUREN MAKES INTERNATIONAL NEWS.
JANUARY 16, 1960 (SHOWA 35): PRIME MINISTER NOBUSUKE KISHI* LEAVES TO SIGN THE REVISED TREATY.
SEVEN HUNDRED MEMBERS OF ZENGAKUREN CLASH WITH POLICE AT THE AIRPORT LOBBY.
UWAAAAHG
UWAAAAAH
UWAAAAGH

*SEE NOTE ON PAGE 533.

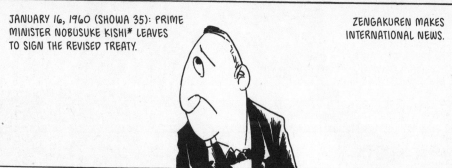

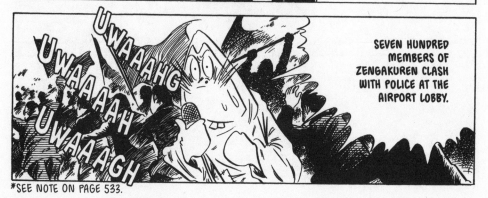

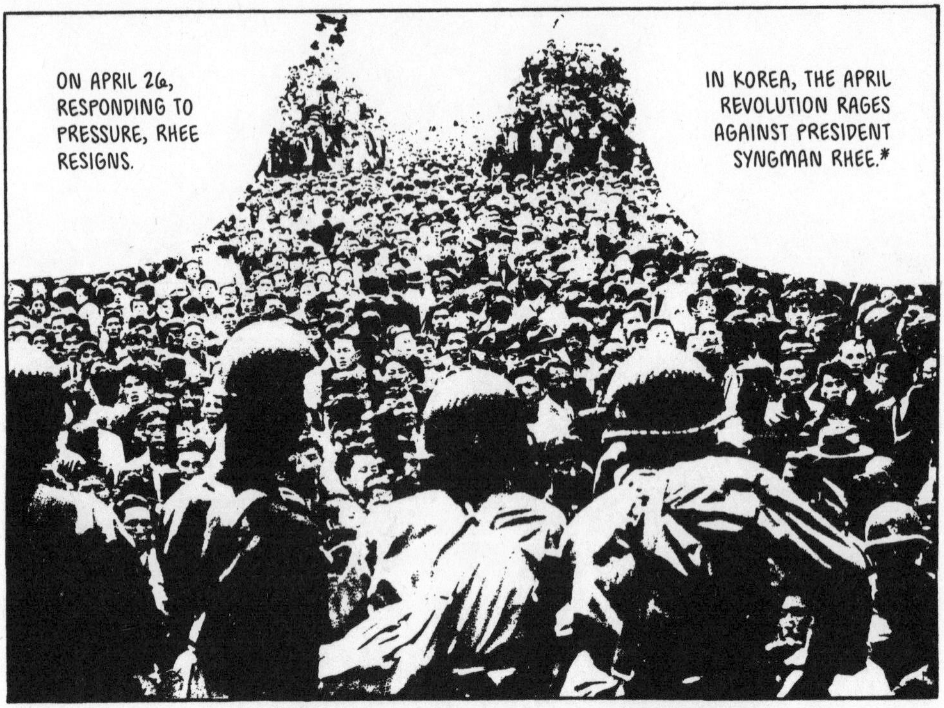
IN KOREA, THE APRIL REVOLUTION RAGES AGAINST PRESIDENT SYNGMAN RHEE.*
ON APRIL 26, RESPONDING TO PRESSURE, RHEE RESIGNS.

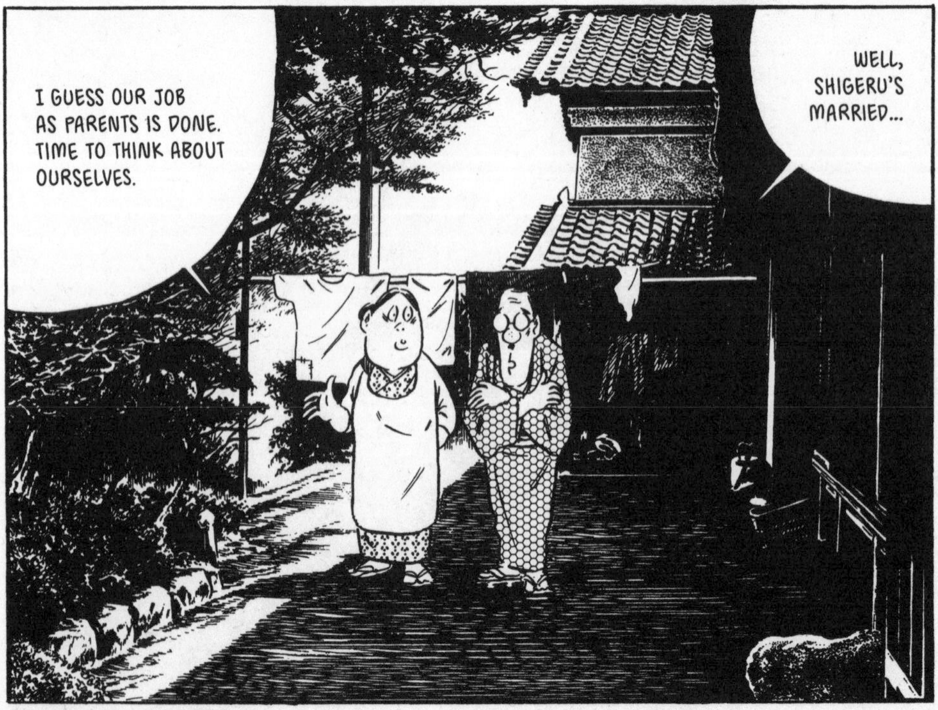
WELL, SHIGERU'S MARRIED...
I GUESS OUR JOB AS PARENTS IS DONE. TIME TO THINK ABOUT OURSELVES.

*SEE NOTE ON PAGE 533.

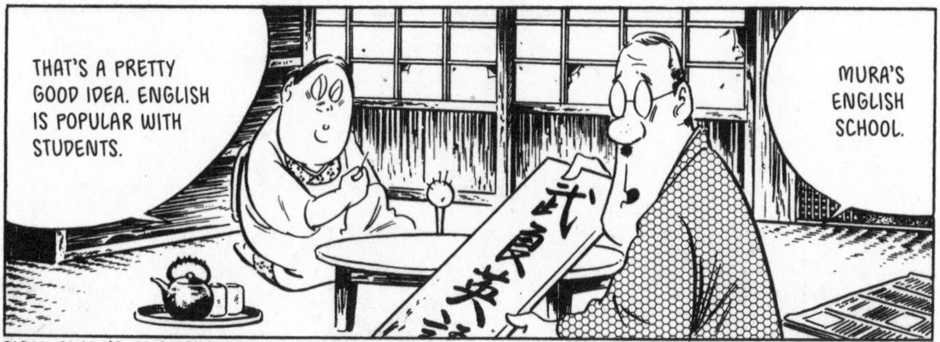
MURA'S ENGLISH SCHOOL.
THAT'S A PRETTY GOOD IDEA. ENGLISH IS POPULAR WITH STUDENTS.
SIGN: MURA'S ENGLISH SCHOOL.

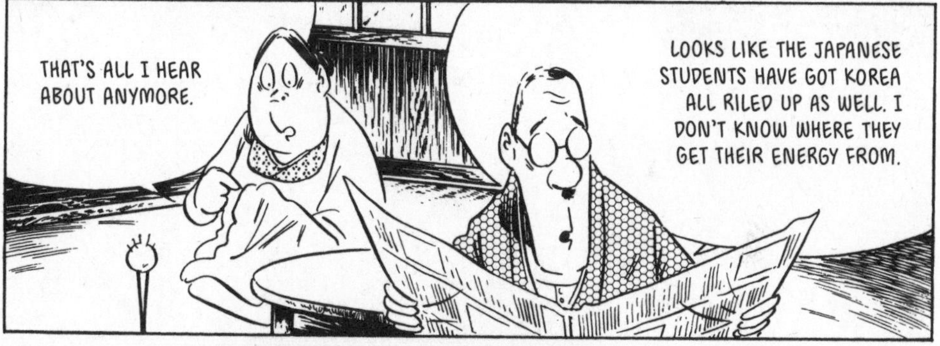
LOOKS LIKE THE JAPANESE STUDENTS HAVE GOT KOREA ALL RILED UP AS WELL. I DON'T KNOW WHERE THEY GET THEIR ENERGY FROM.
THAT'S ALL I HEAR ABOUT ANYMORE.

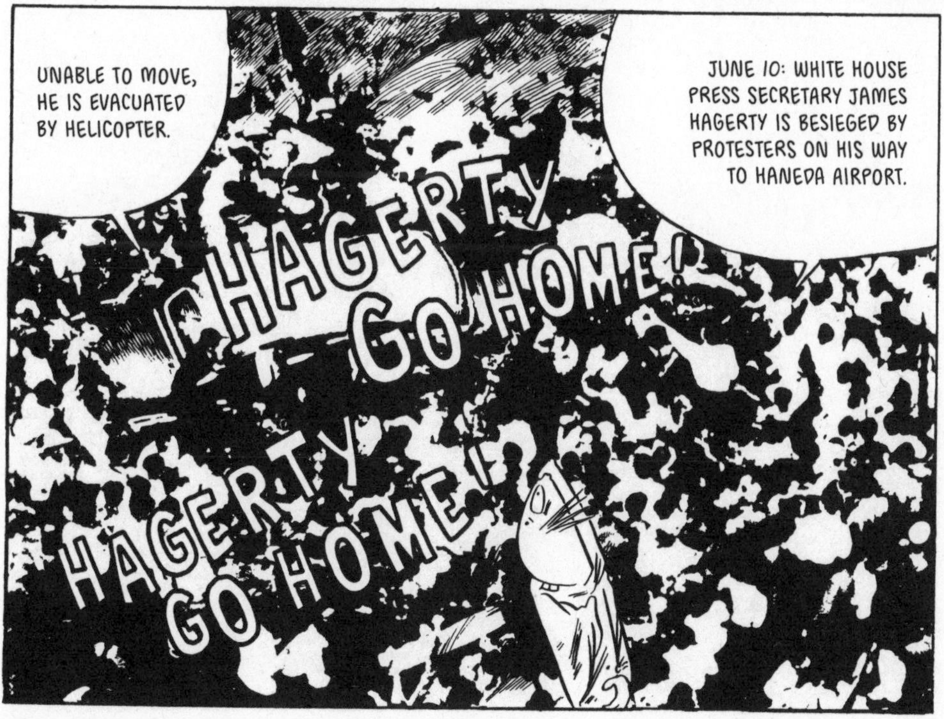
JUNE 10: WHITE HOUSE PRESS SECRETARY JAMES HAGERTY IS BESIEGED BY PROTESTERS ON HIS WAY TO HANEDA AIRPORT.
UNABLE TO MOVE, HE IS EVACUATED BY HELICOPTER.
HAGERTY GO HOME!
HAGERTY GO HOME!

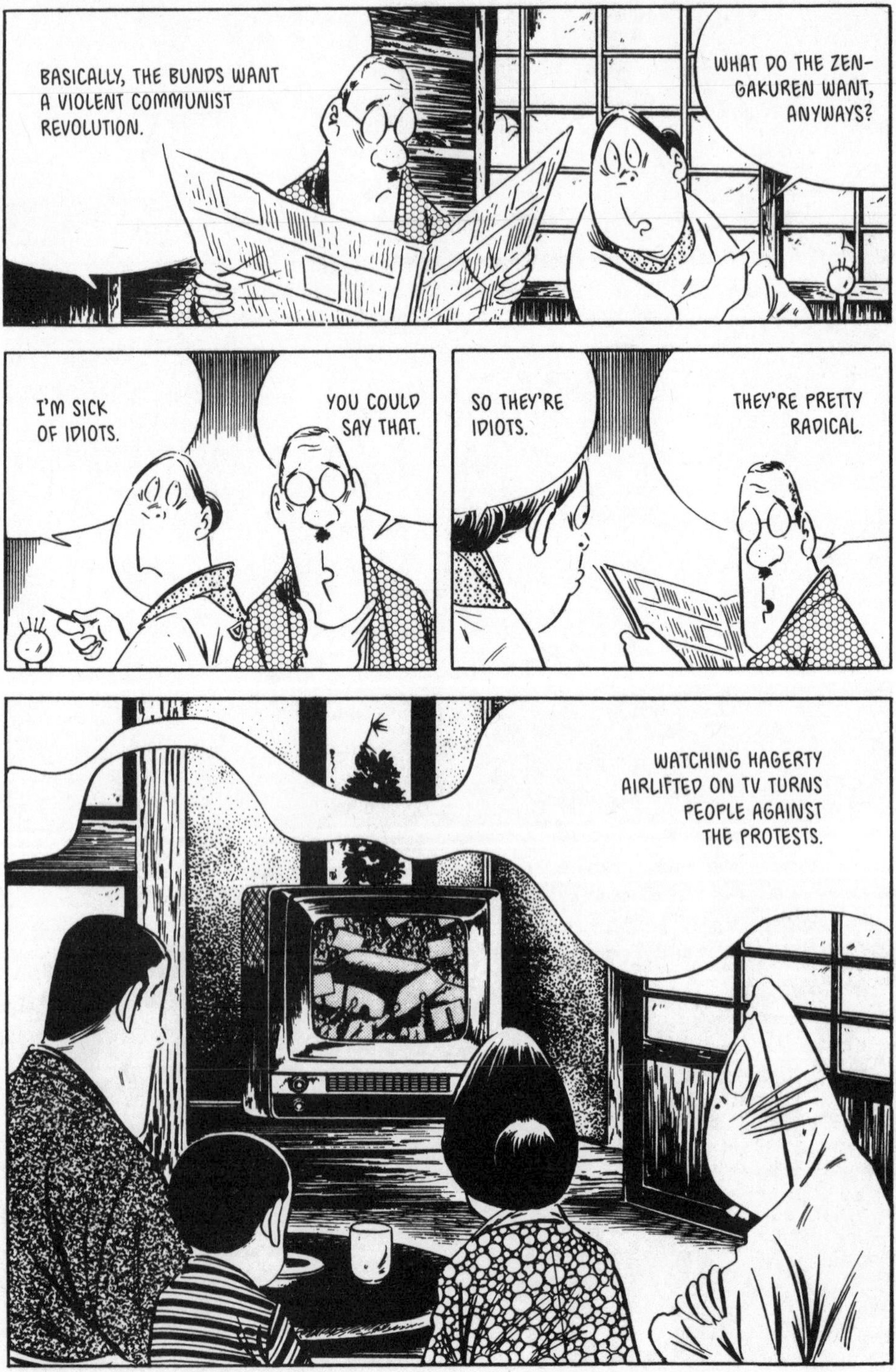
WHAT DO THE ZEN-GAKUREN WANT, ANYWAYS?
BASICALLY, THE BUNDS WANT A VIOLENT COMMUNIST REVOLUTION.
THEY'RE PRETTY RADICAL.
SO THEY'RE IDIOTS.
YOU COULD SAY THAT.
I'M SICK OF IDIOTS.
WATCHING HAGERTY AIRLIFTED ON TV TURNS PEOPLE AGAINST THE PROTESTS.

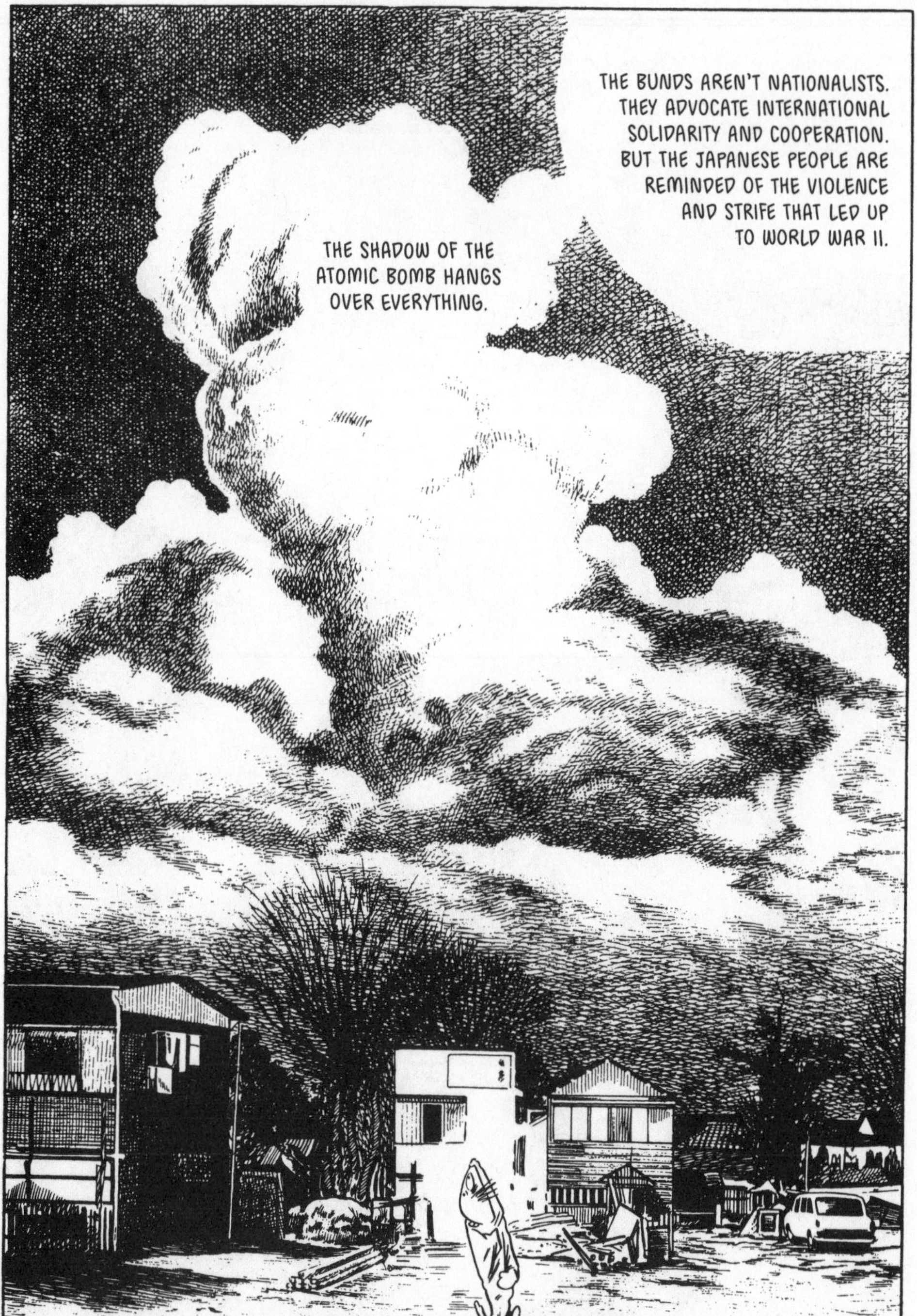
THE BUNDS AREN'T NATIONALISTS. THEY ADVOCATE INTERNATIONAL SOLIDARITY AND COOPERATION. BUT THE JAPANESE PEOPLE ARE REMINDED OF THE VIOLENCE AND STRIFE THAT LED UP TO WORLD WAR II.
THE SHADOW OF THE ATOMIC BOMB HANGS OVER EVERYTHING.

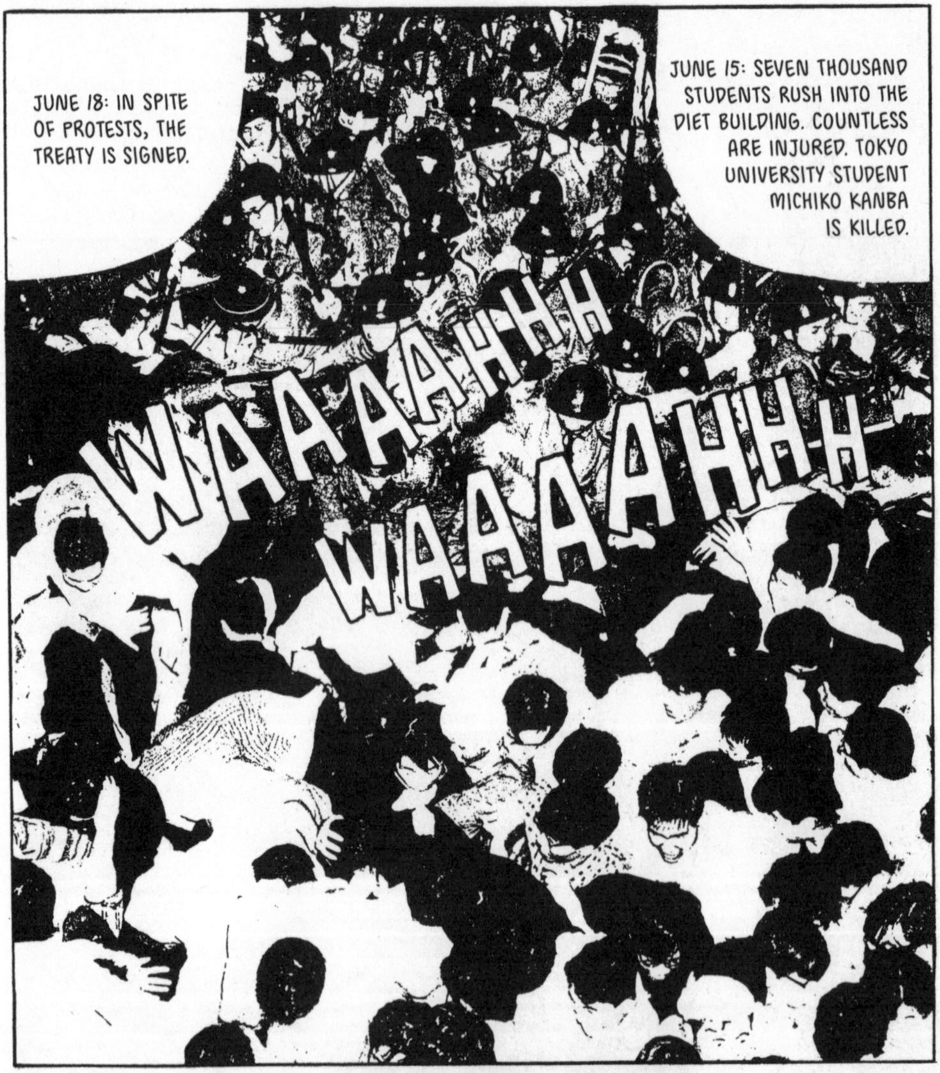
JUNE 15: SEVEN THOUSAND STUDENTS RUSH INTO THE DIET BUILDING. COUNTLESS ARE INJURED. TOKYO UNIVERSITY STUDENT MICHIKO KANBA IS KILLED.
JUNE 18: IN SPITE OF PROTESTS, THE TREATY IS SIGNED.
WAAAAHHH
WAAAAAHHH

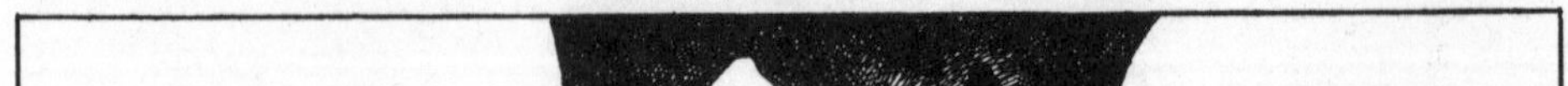
DEFEATED AND DEMORALIZED, THE FIRE GOES OUT OF MANY PROTESTERS.
BUT NOT ALL OF THEM. IN KITA-KYUSHU, WORKERS GATHER FOR THE MIIKE DISPUTE.*
昭和史

*SEE NOTE ON PAGE 534.

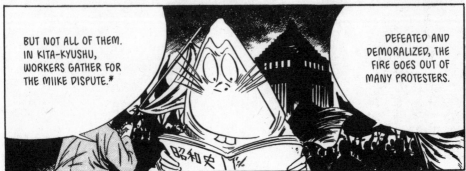

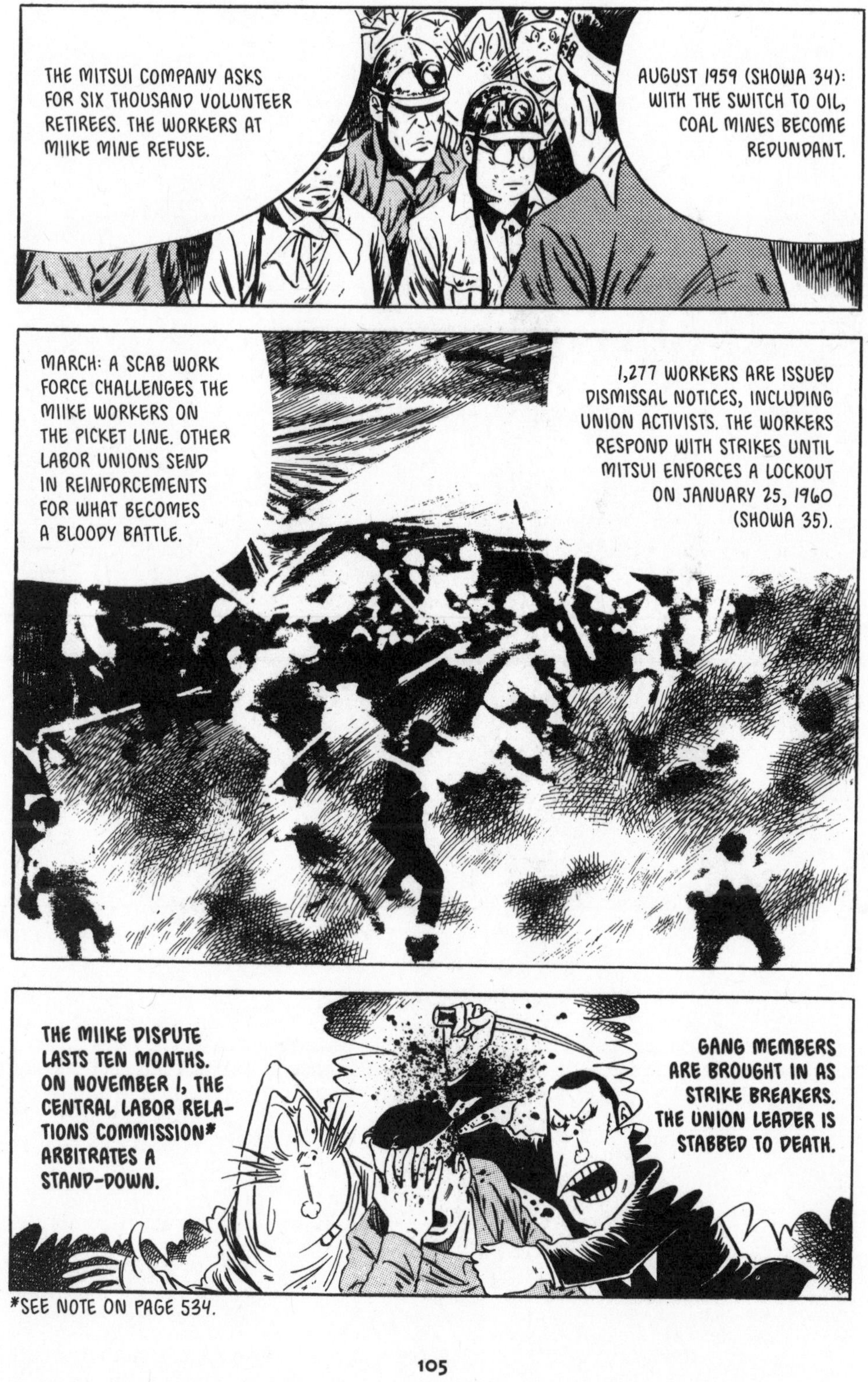
AUGUST 1959 (SHOWA 34): WITH THE SWITCH TO OIL, COAL MINES BECOME REDUNDANT.
THE MITSUI COMPANY ASKS FOR SIX THOUSAND VOLUNTEER RETIREES. THE WORKERS AT MIIKE MINE REFUSE.
1,277 WORKERS ARE ISSUED DISMISSAL NOTICES, INCLUDING UNION ACTIVISTS. THE WORKERS RESPOND WITH STRIKES UNTIL MITSUI ENFORCES A LOCKOUT ON JANUARY 25, 1960 (SHOWA 35).
MARCH: A SCAB WORK FORCE CHALLENGES THE MIIKE WORKERS ON THE PICKET LINE. OTHER LABOR UNIONS SEND IN REINFORCEMENTS FOR WHAT BECOMES A BLOODY BATTLE.
GANG MEMBERS ARE BROUGHT IN AS STRIKE BREAKERS. THE UNION LEADER IS STABBED TO DEATH.
THE MIIKE DISPUTE LASTS TEN MONTHS. ON NOVEMBER 1, THE CENTRAL LABOR RELATIONS COMMISSION* ARBITRATES A STAND-DOWN.

*SEE NOTE ON PAGE 534.

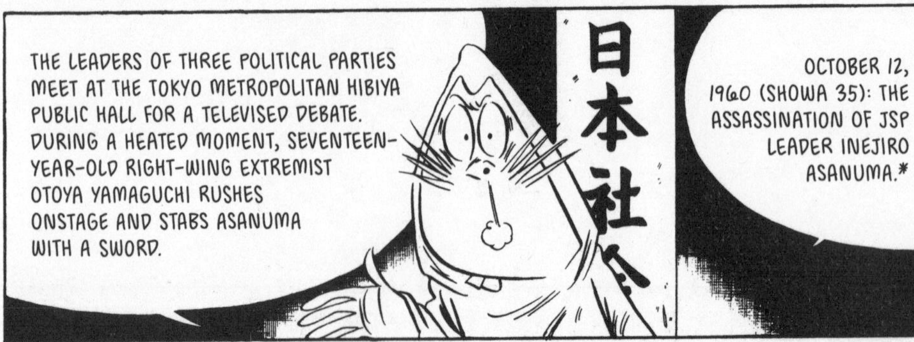
OCTOBER 12, 1960 (SHOWA 35): THE ASSASSINATION OF JSP LEADER INEJIRO ASANUMA.*
日本社
THE LEADERS OF THREE POLITICAL PARTIES MEET AT THE TOKYO METROPOLITAN HIBIYA PUBLIC HALL FOR A TELEVISED DEBATE. DURING A HEATED MOMENT, SEVENTEEN-YEAR-OLD RIGHT-WING EXTREMIST OTOYA YAMAGUCHI RUSHES ONSTAGE AND STABS ASANUMA WITH A SWORD.

SIGN: JAPAN SOCIALIST PARTY.

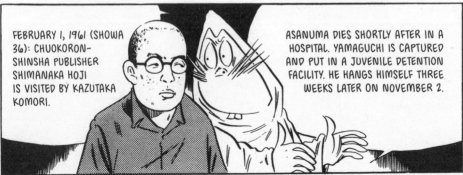

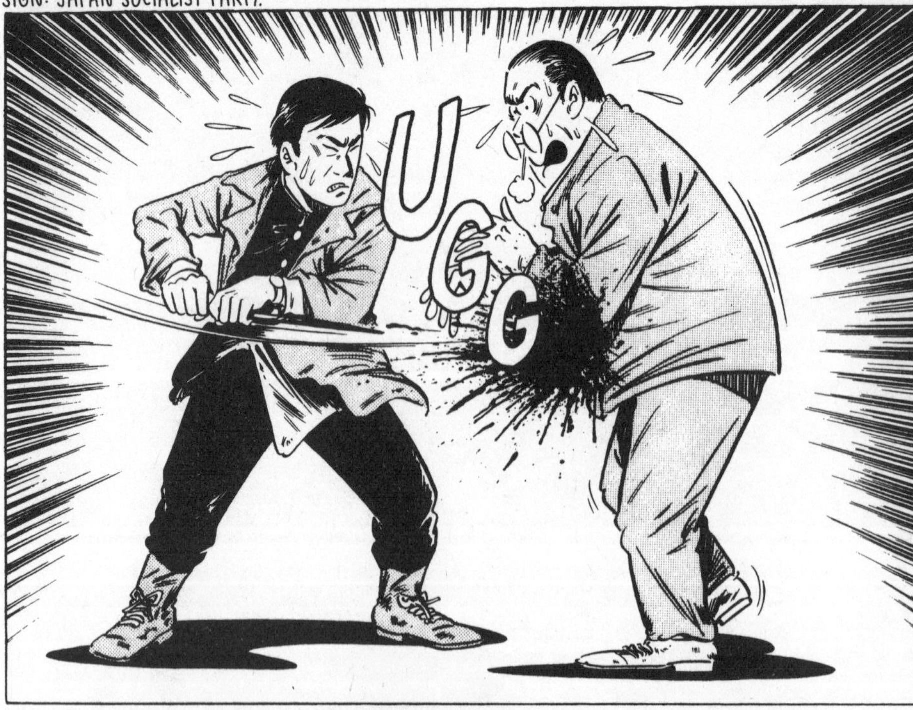
UGG

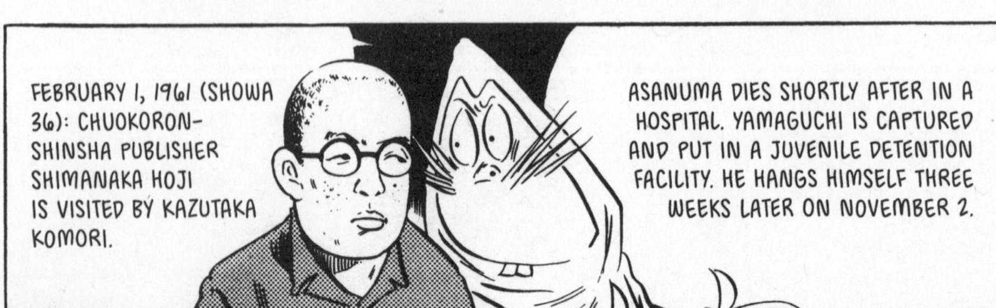
ASANUMA DIES SHORTLY AFTER IN A HOSPITAL. YAMAGUCHI IS CAPTURED AND PUT IN A JUVENILE DETENTION FACILITY. HE HANGS HIMSELF THREE WEEKS LATER ON NOVEMBER 2.
FEBRUARY 1, 1961 (SHOWA 36): CHUOKORON-SHINSHA PUBLISHER SHIMANAKA HOJI IS VISITED BY KAZUTAKA KOMORI.

*INEJIRO ASANUMA: (1898–1960) B. TOKYO CITY. POLITICIAN. ACTIVE IN THE JAPAN SOCIALIST PARTY PRE-WAR, AND CHAIRMAN OF THE PARTY POSTWAR.

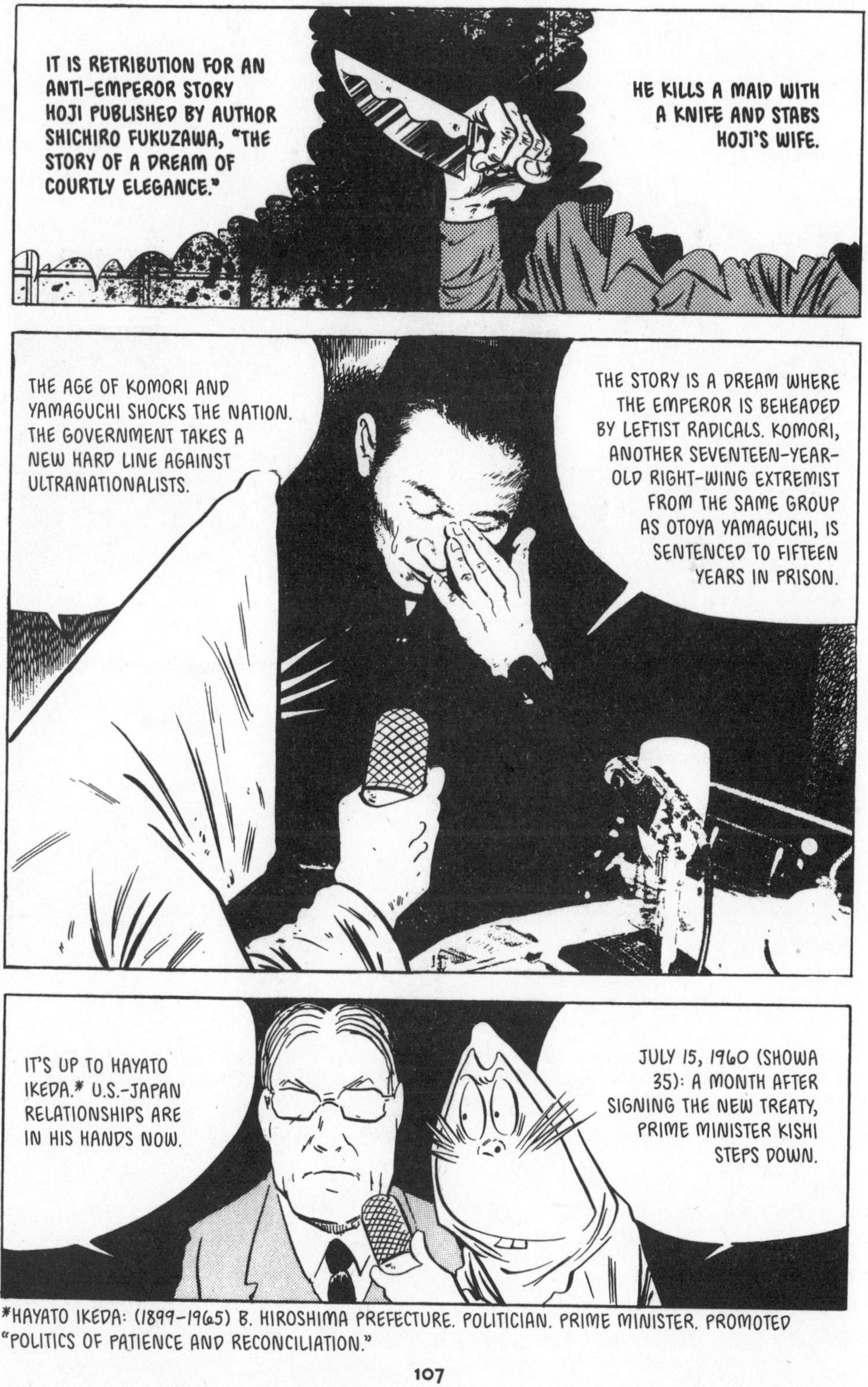
HE KILLS A MAID WITH A KNIFE AND STABS HOJI'S WIFE.
IT IS RETRIBUTION FOR AN ANTI-EMPEROR STORY HOJI PUBLISHED BY AUTHOR SHICHIRO FUKUZAWA, "THE STORY OF A DREAM OF COURTLY ELEGANCE."
THE STORY IS A DREAM WHERE THE EMPEROR IS BEHEADED BY LEFTIST RADICALS. KOMORI, ANOTHER SEVENTEEN-YEAR-OLD RIGHT-WING EXTREMIST FROM THE SAME GROUP AS OTOYA YAMAGUCHI, IS SENTENCED TO FIFTEEN YEARS IN PRISON.
THE AGE OF KOMORI AND YAMAGUCHI SHOCKS THE NATION. THE GOVERNMENT TAKES A NEW HARD LINE AGAINST ULTRANATIONALISTS.
JULY 15, 1960 (SHOWA 35): A MONTH AFTER SIGNING THE NEW TREATY, PRIME MINISTER KISHI STEPS DOWN.
IT'S UP TO HAYATO IKEDA.* U.S.-JAPAN RELATIONSHIPS ARE IN HIS HANDS NOW.

*HAYATO IKEDA: (1899–1965) B. HIROSHIMA PREFECTURE. POLITICIAN. PRIME MINISTER. PROMOTED "POLITICS OF PATIENCE AND RECONCILIATION."

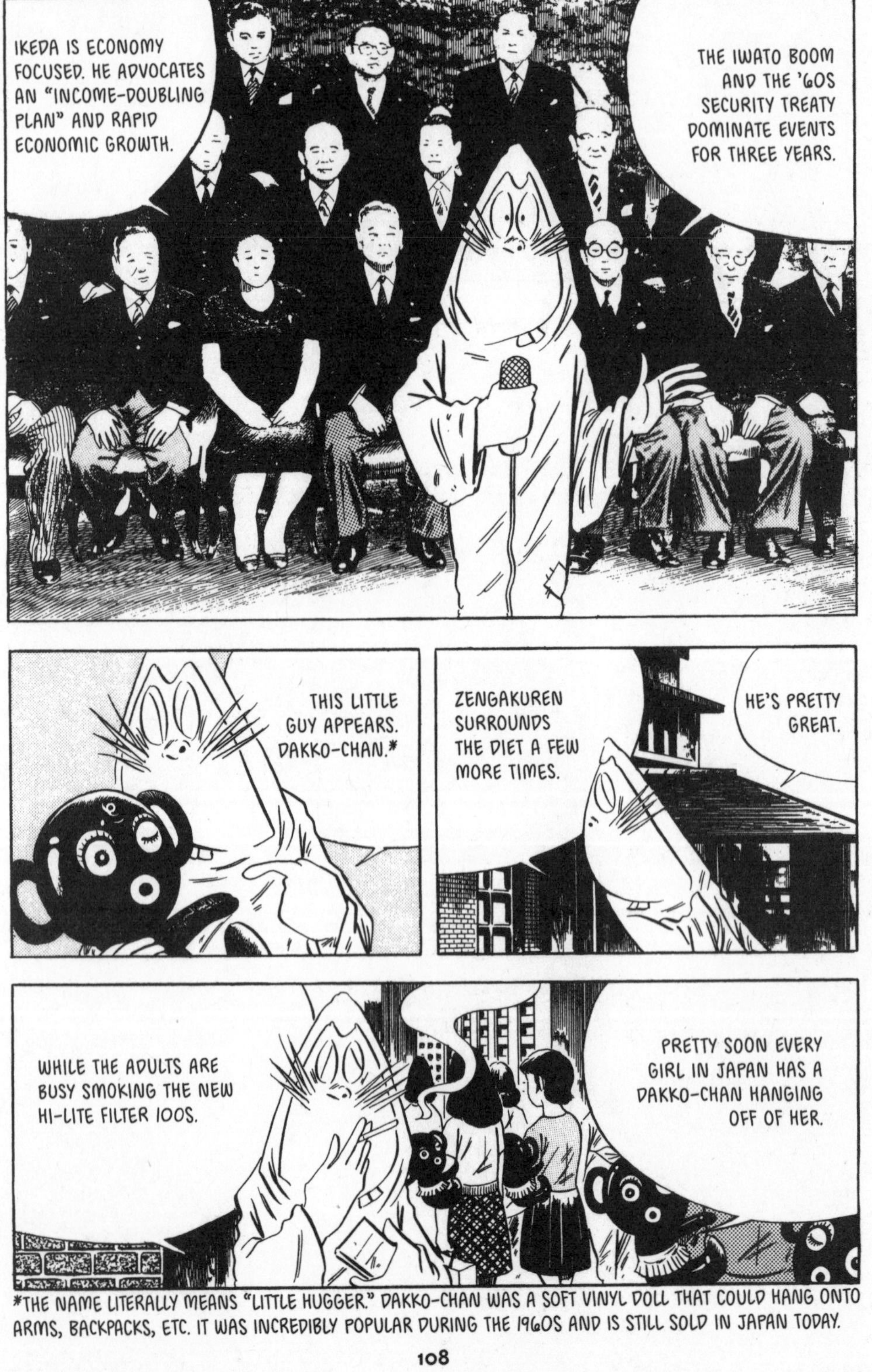
THE IWATO BOOM AND THE '60S SECURITY TREATY DOMINATE EVENTS FOR THREE YEARS.
IKEDA IS ECONOMY FOCUSED. HE ADVOCATES AN "INCOME-DOUBLING PLAN" AND RAPID ECONOMIC GROWTH.
HE'S PRETTY GREAT.
ZENGAKUREN SURROUNDS THE DIET A FEW MORE TIMES.
THIS LITTLE GUY APPEARS. DAKKO-CHAN.*
PRETTY SOON EVERY GIRL IN JAPAN HAS A DAKKO-CHAN HANGING OFF OF HER.
WHILE THE ADULTS ARE BUSY SMOKING THE NEW HI-LITE FILTER 100S.

*THE NAME LITERALLY MEANS "LITTLE HUGGER." DAKKO-CHAN WAS A SOFT VINYL DOLL THAT COULD HANG ONTO ARMS, BACKPACKS, ETC. IT WAS INCREDIBLY POPULAR DURING THE 1960S AND IS STILL SOLD IN JAPAN TODAY.

A LIFE OF EXTREME POVERTY

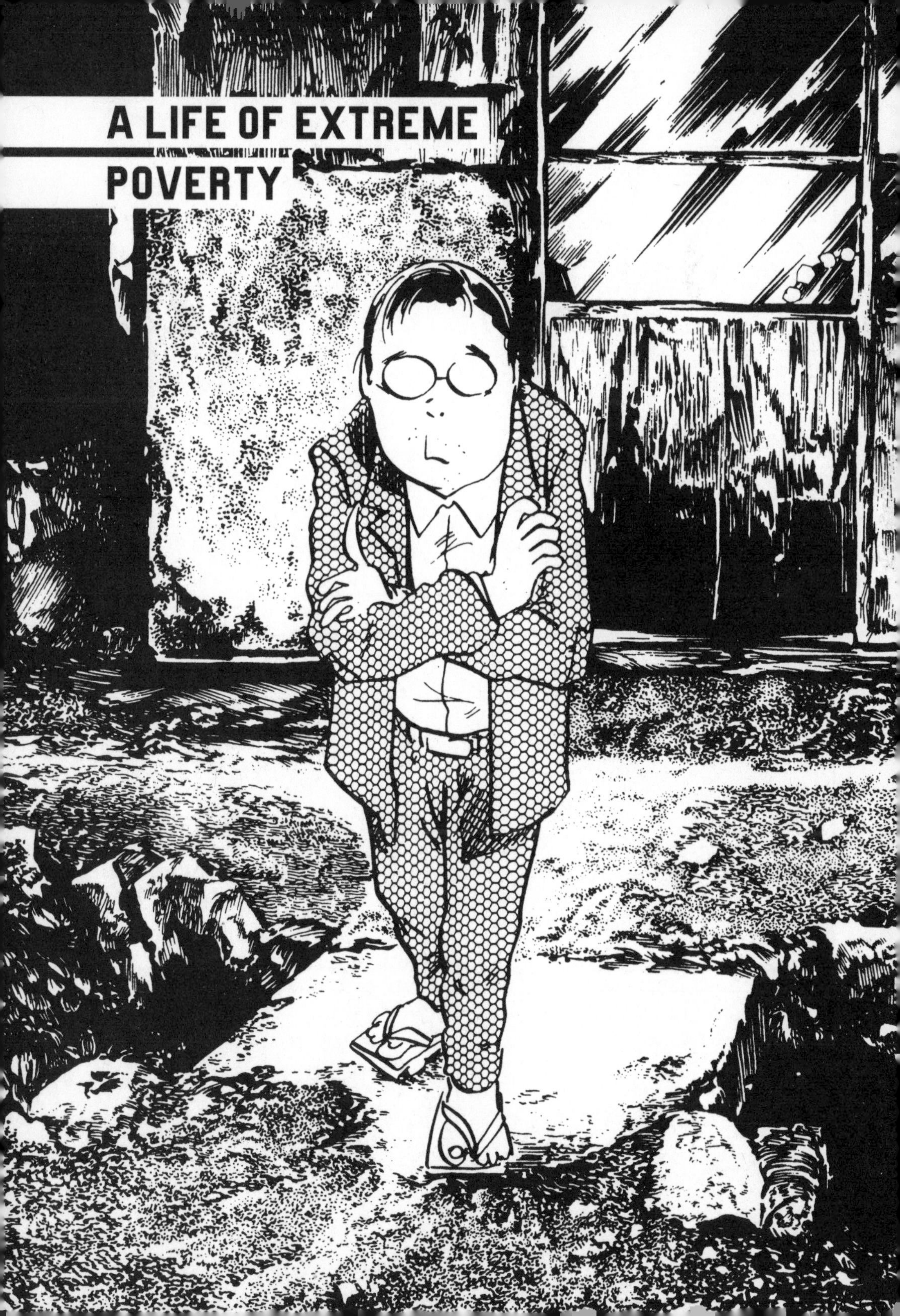

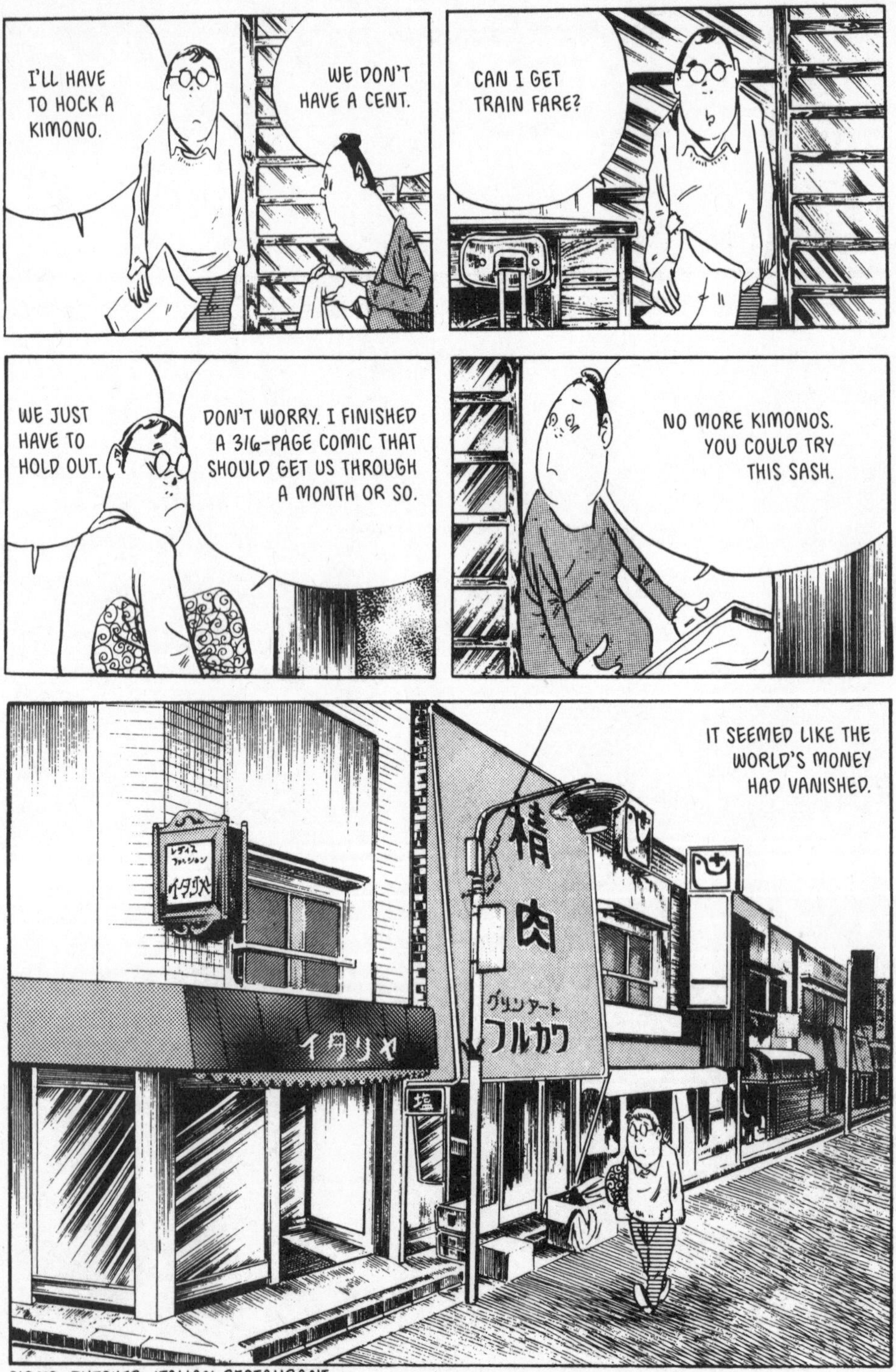
CAN I GET TRAIN FARE?
WE DON'T HAVE A CENT.
I'LL HAVE TO HOCK A KIMONO.
NO MORE KIMONOS. YOU COULD TRY THIS SASH.
DON'T WORRY. I FINISHED A 316-PAGE COMIC THAT SHOULD GET US THROUGH A MONTH OR SO.
WE JUST HAVE TO HOLD OUT.
IT SEEMED LIKE THE WORLD'S MONEY HAD VANISHED.
精肉
グリンアート
フルカワ
イタリヤ
塩

SIGNS: BUTCHER, ITALIAN RESTAURANT.

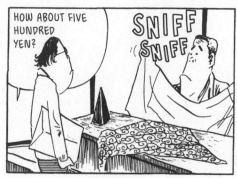

質
提質店
SIGN: PAWNSHOP.
HOW ABOUT FIVE HUNDRED YEN?
SNIFF SNIFF
IT STINKS LIKE PISS.
TWO HUNDRED'S ALL I CAN DO.
MAKE IT THREE HUNDRED?
YOUR PAWN TICKETS ARE PILING UP.
TWO HUNDRED THEN.
MONEY GOES OUT AS SOON AS IT COMES IN.

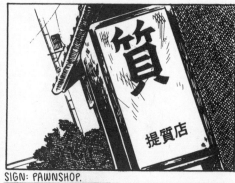

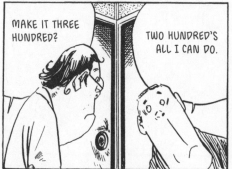

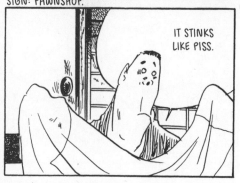

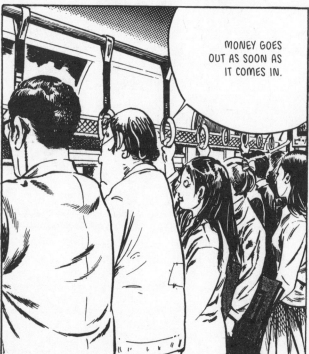

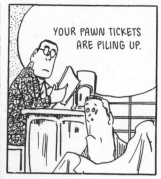

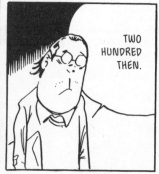

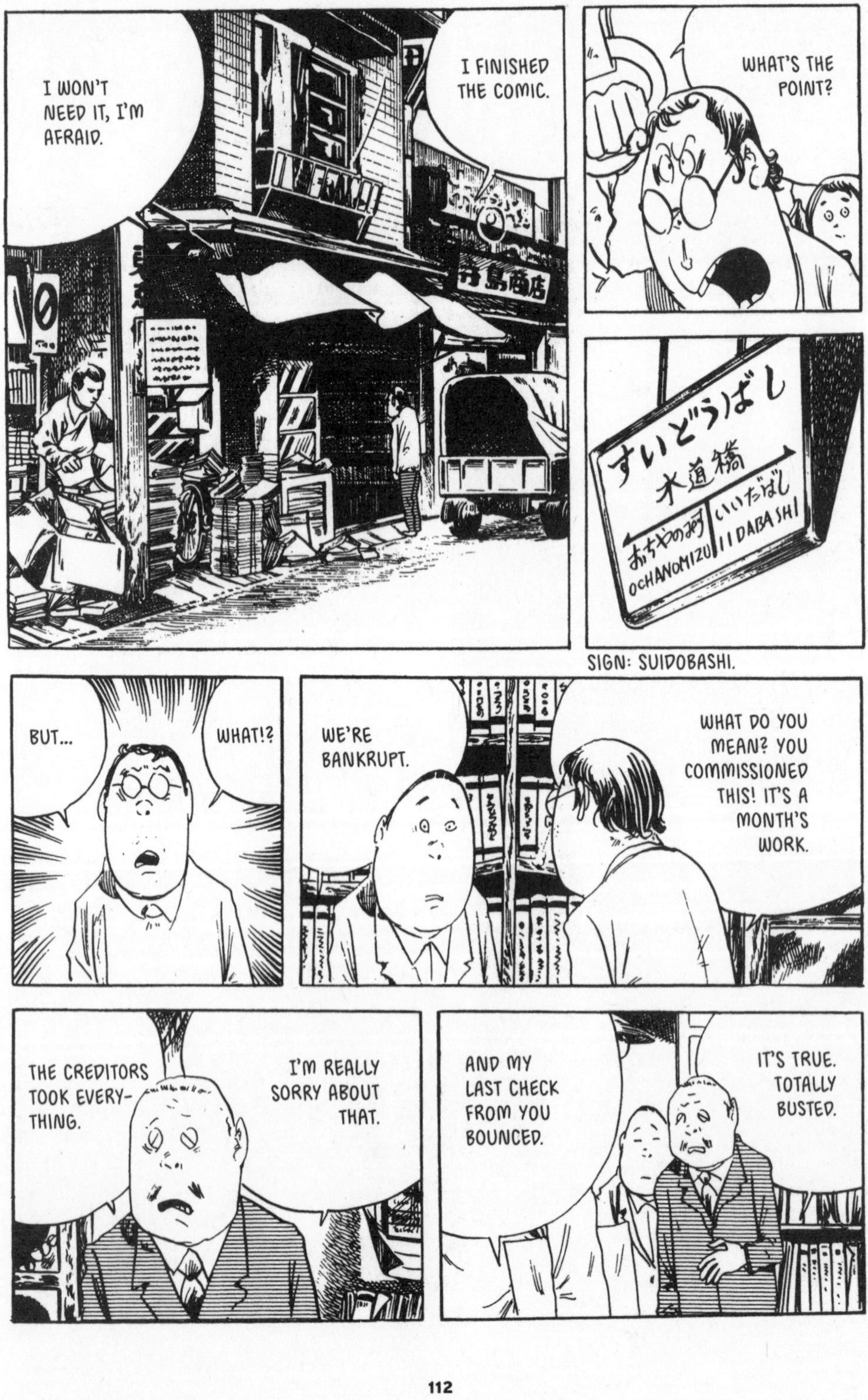
WHAT'S THE POINT?
すいどうばし
水道橋
おちゃのみず
OCHANOMIZU
いいだばし
IIDABASHI
SIGN: SUIDOBASHI.
I FINISHED THE COMIC.
I WON'T NEED IT, I'M AFRAID.
WHAT DO YOU MEAN? YOU COMMISSIONED THIS! IT'S A MONTH'S WORK.
WE'RE BANKRUPT.
WHAT!?
BUT...
IT'S TRUE. TOTALLY BUSTED.
AND MY LAST CHECK FROM YOU BOUNCED.
I'M REALLY SORRY ABOUT THAT.
THE CREDITORS TOOK EVERY-THING.

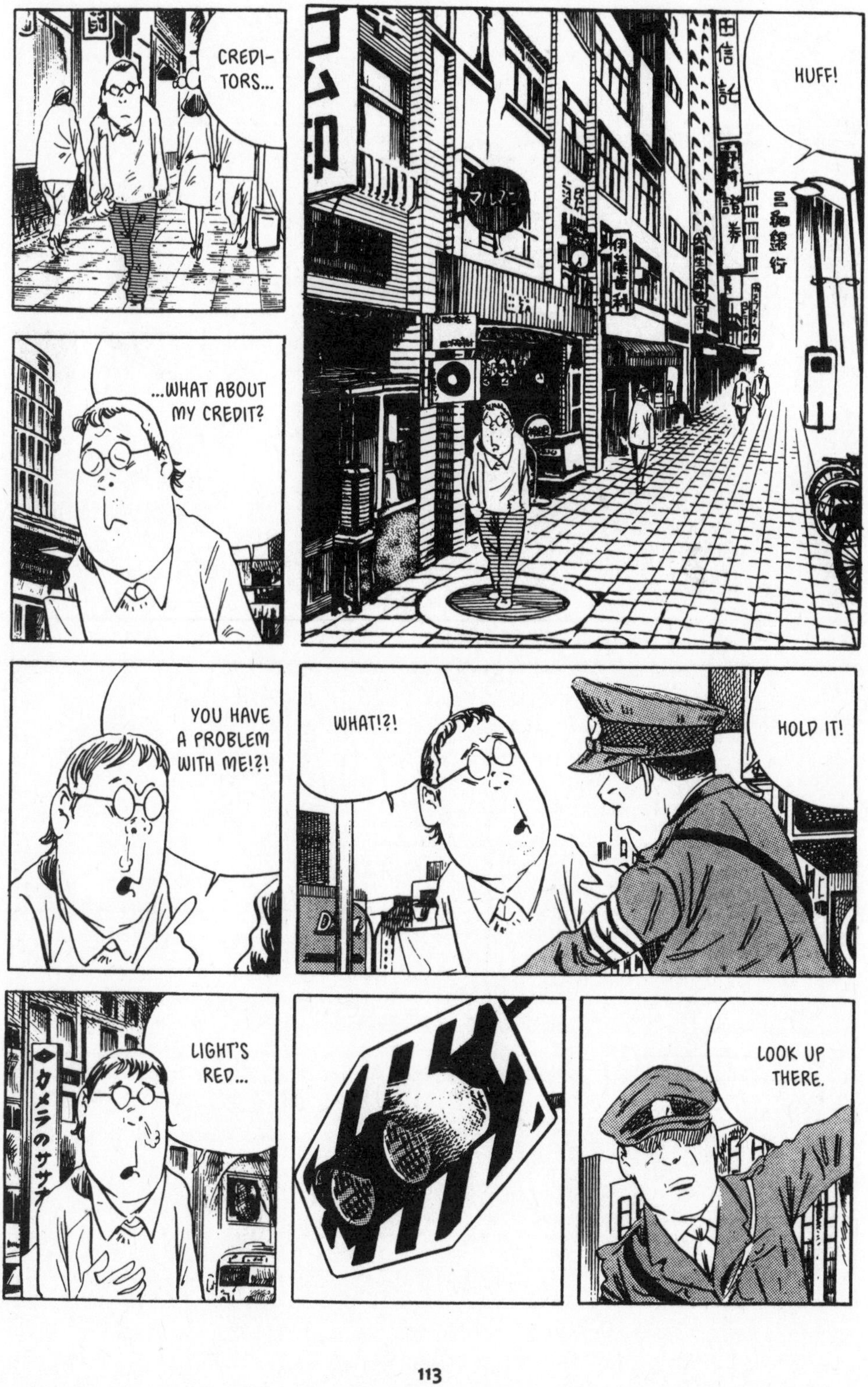
HUFF!
CREDITORS...
...WHAT ABOUT MY CREDIT?
HOLD IT!
WHAT!?!
YOU HAVE A PROBLEM WITH ME!?!
LOOK UP THERE.
LIGHT'S RED...

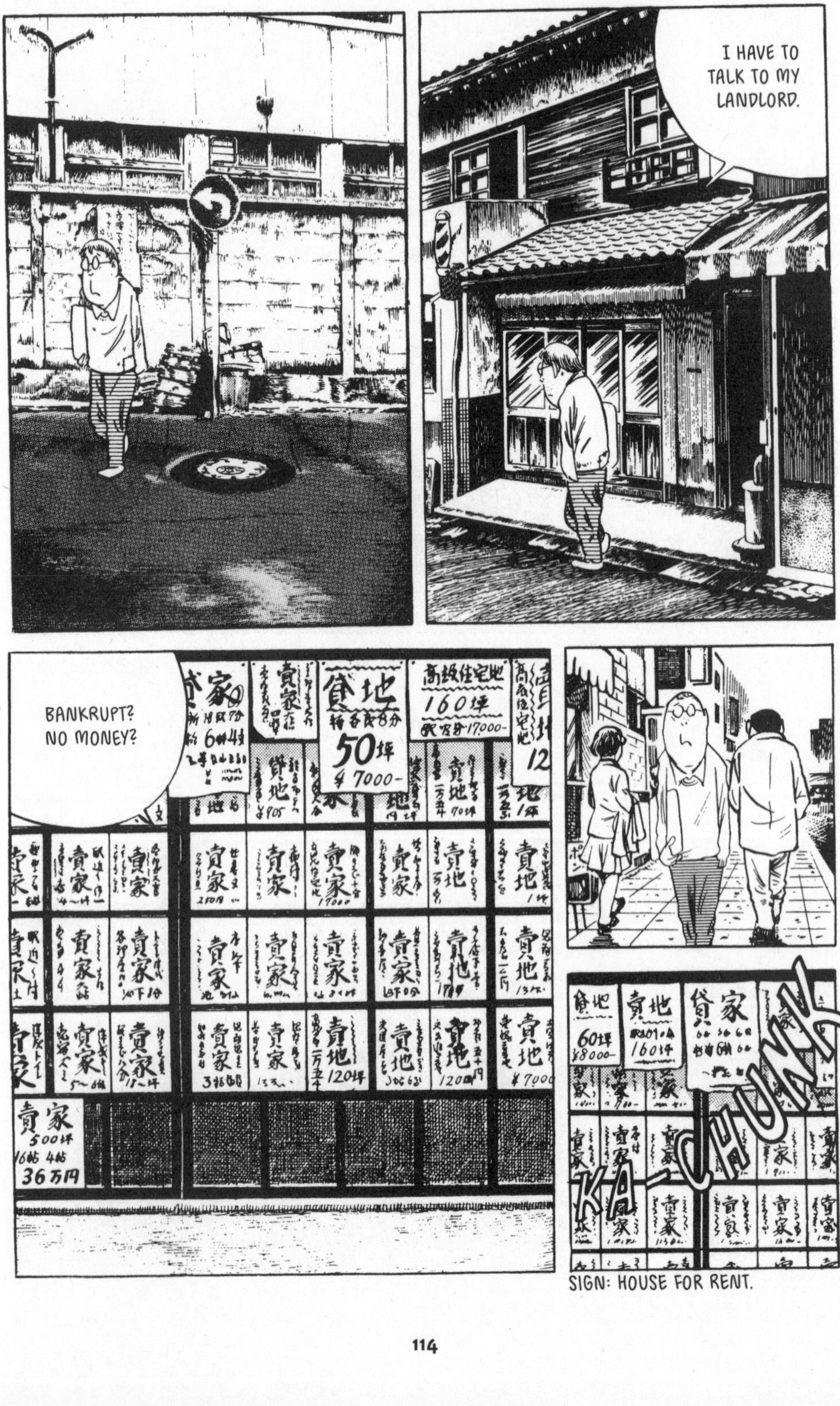
I HAVE TO TALK TO MY LANDLORD.
KA-CHUNK
SIGN: HOUSE FOR RENT.
BANKRUPT? NO MONEY?
高級住宅地
160坪
50坪
¥7000-
36万円

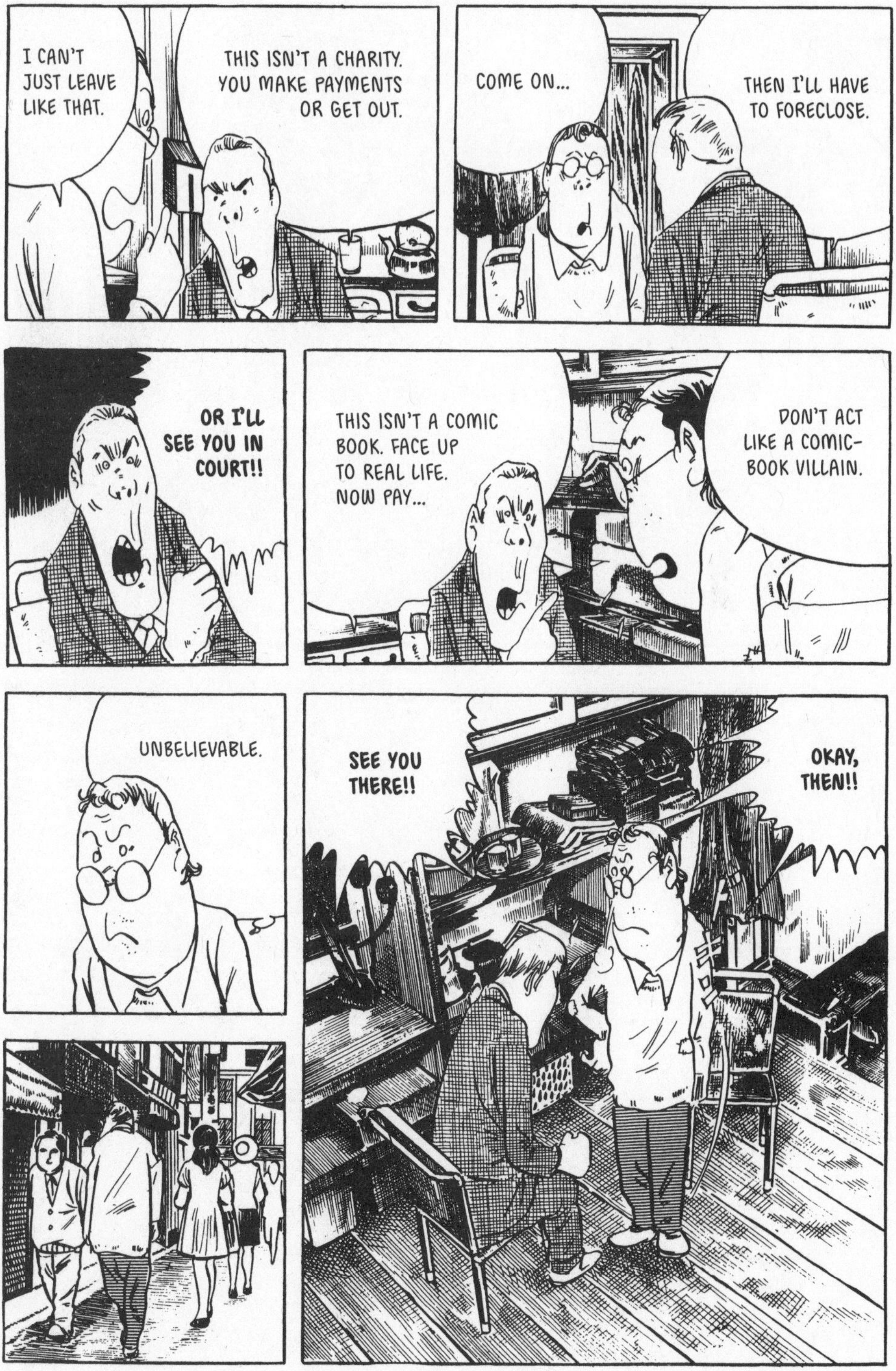
THEN I'LL HAVE TO FORECLOSE.
COME ON...
THIS ISN'T A CHARITY. YOU MAKE PAYMENTS OR GET OUT.
I CAN'T JUST LEAVE LIKE THAT.
DON'T ACT LIKE A COMIC-BOOK VILLAIN.
THIS ISN'T A COMIC BOOK. FACE UP TO REAL LIFE. NOW PAY...
OR I'LL SEE YOU IN COURT!!
OKAY, THEN!!
SEE YOU THERE!!
UNBELIEVABLE.

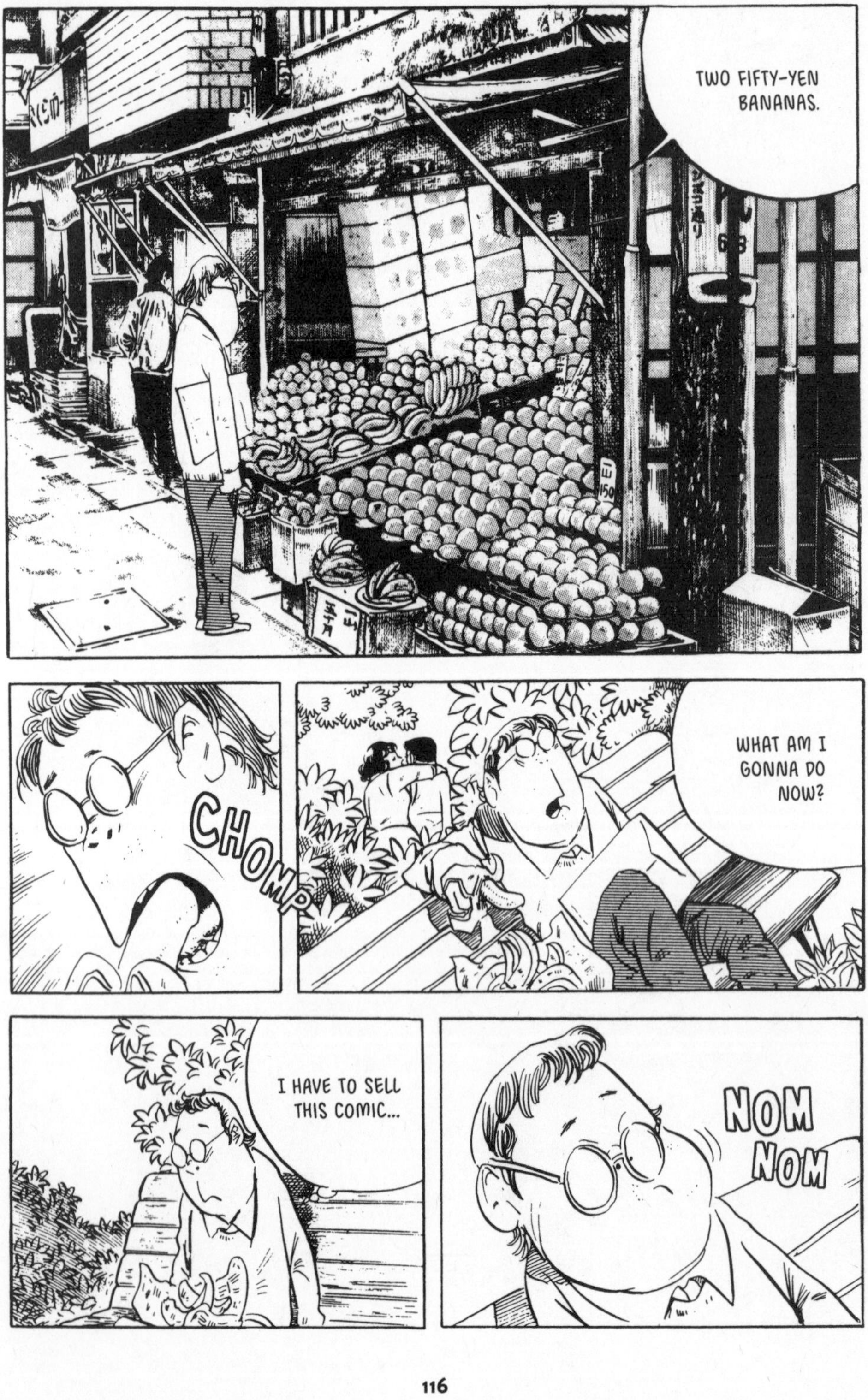
TWO FIFTY-YEN BANANAS.
WHAT AM I GONNA DO NOW?
CHOMP
NOM NOM
I HAVE TO SELL THIS COMIC...

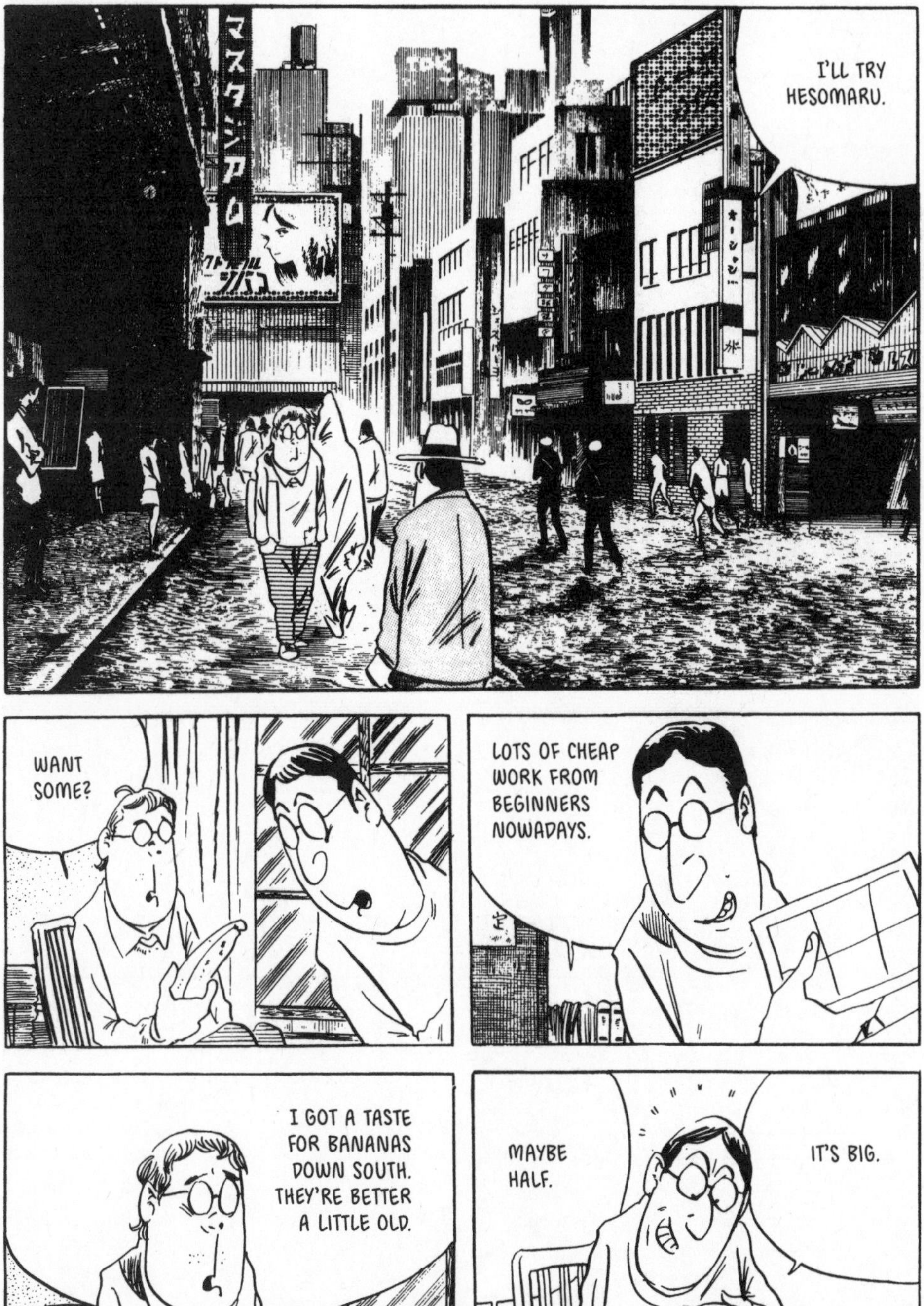
I'LL TRY HESOMARU.
LOTS OF CHEAP WORK FROM BEGINNERS NOWADAYS.
WANT SOME?
IT'S BIG.
MAYBE HALF.
I GOT A TASTE FOR BANANAS DOWN SOUTH. THEY'RE BETTER A LITTLE OLD.

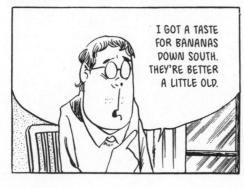

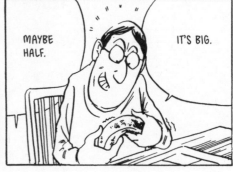

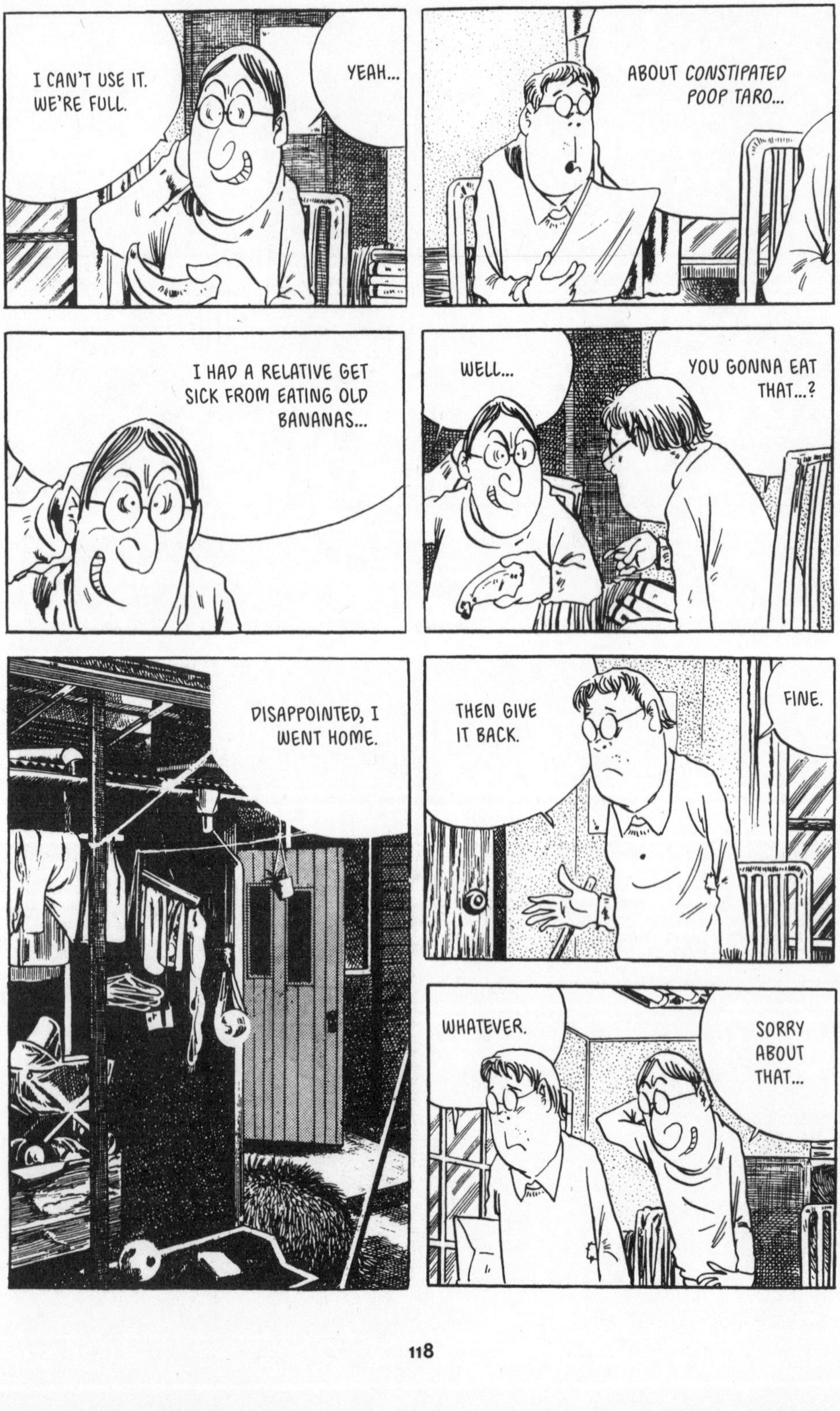
ABOUT CONSTIPATED POOP TARO...
YEAH...
I CAN'T USE IT. WE'RE FULL.
YOU GONNA EAT THAT...?
WELL...
I HAD A RELATIVE GET SICK FROM EATING OLD BANANAS...
FINE.
THEN GIVE IT BACK.
SORRY ABOUT THAT...
WHATEVER.
DISAPPOINTED, I WENT HOME.

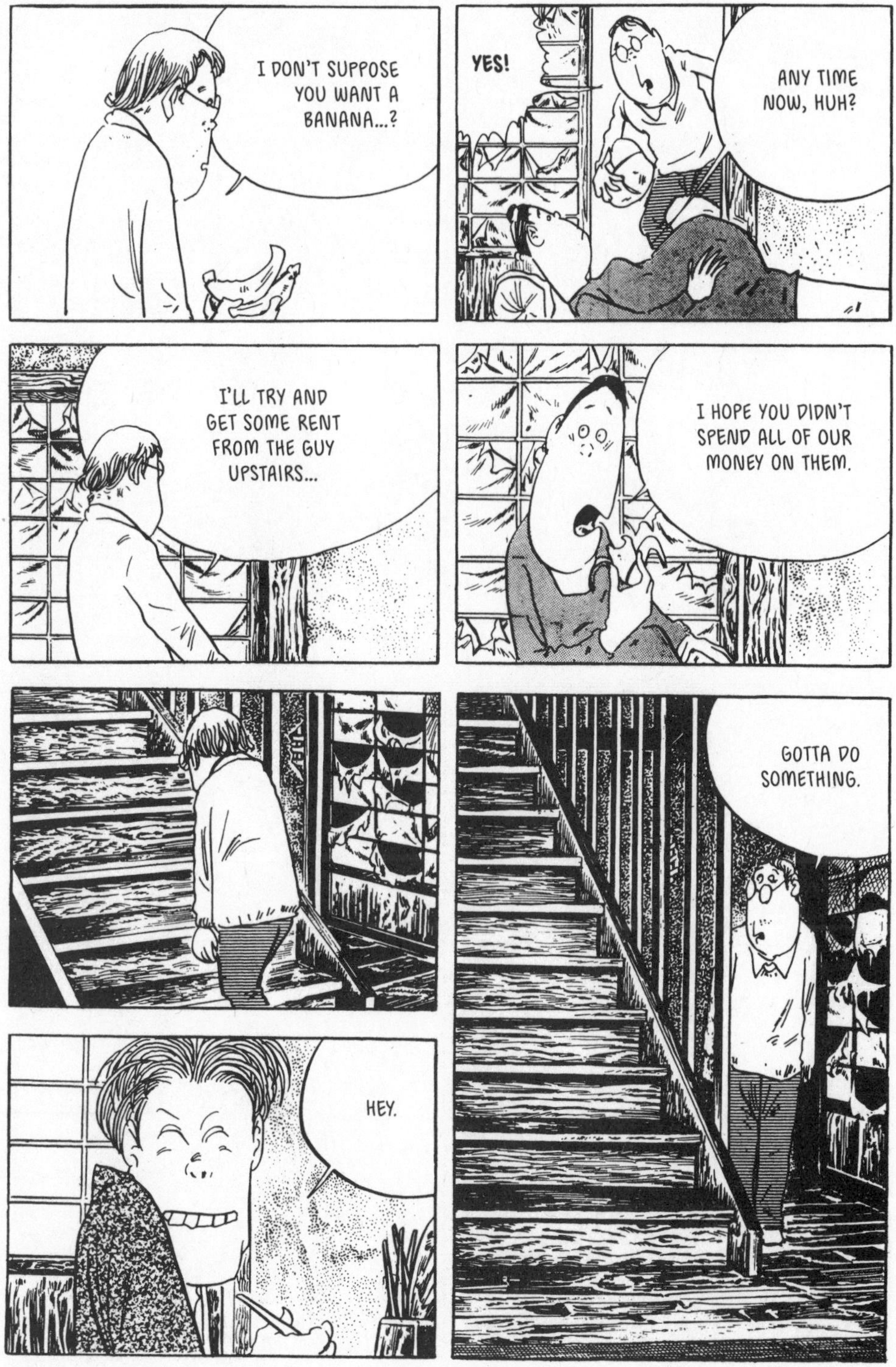
ANY TIME NOW, HUH?
YES!
I DON'T SUPPOSE YOU WANT A BANANA...?
I HOPE YOU DIDN'T SPEND ALL OF OUR MONEY ON THEM.
I'LL TRY AND GET SOME RENT FROM THE GUY UPSTAIRS...
GOTTA DO SOMETHING.
HEY.

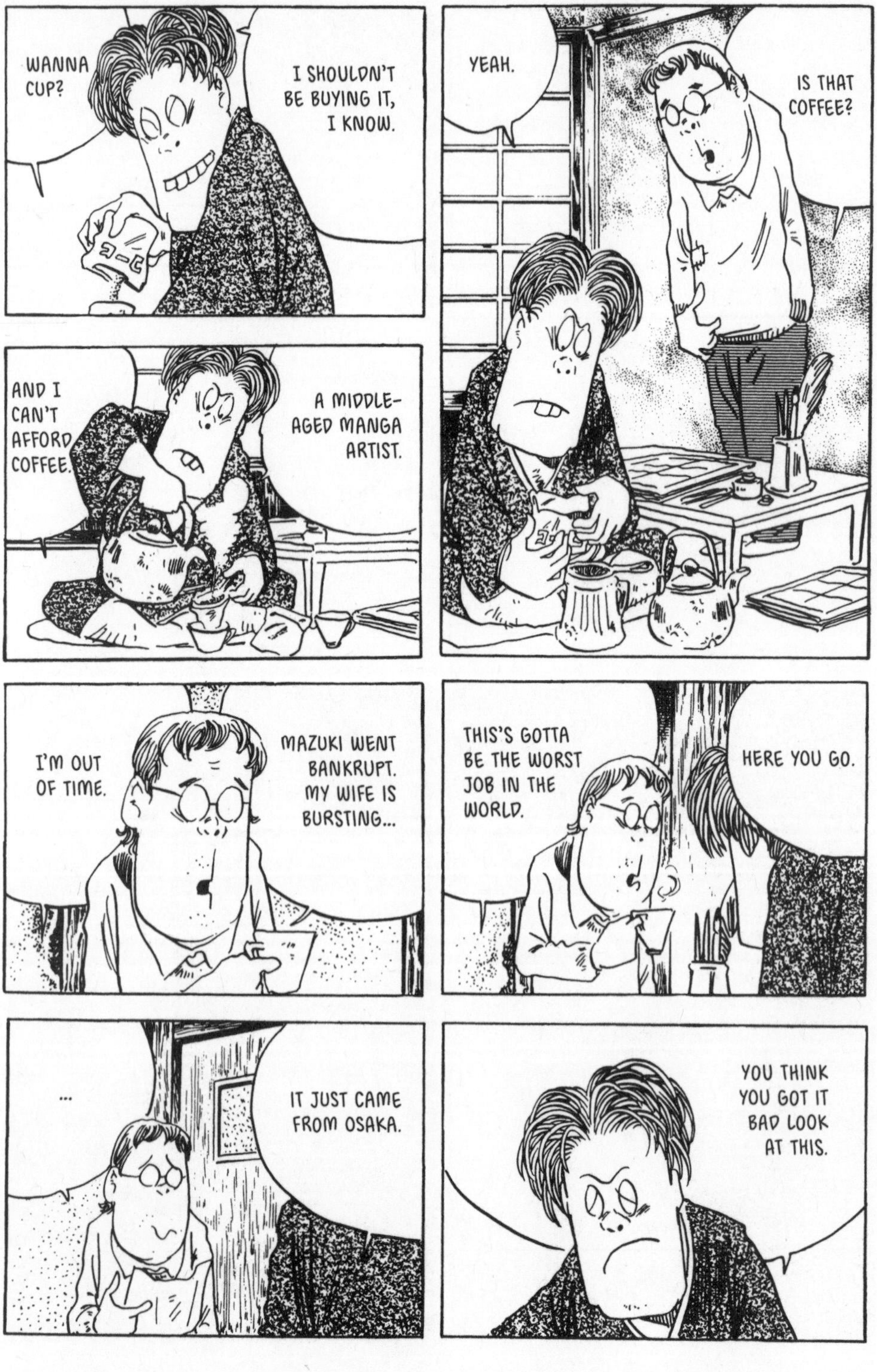
IS THAT COFFEE?
YEAH.
I SHOULDN'T BE BUYING IT, I KNOW.
WANNA CUP?
A MIDDLE-AGED MANGA ARTIST.
AND I CAN'T AFFORD COFFEE.
HERE YOU GO.
THIS'S GOTTA BE THE WORST JOB IN THE WORLD.
MAZUKI WENT BANKRUPT. MY WIFE IS BURSTING...
I'M OUT OF TIME.
YOU THINK YOU GOT IT BAD LOOK AT THIS.
IT JUST CAME FROM OSAKA.
...

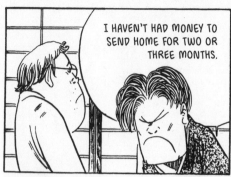

私は体の調子が悪く
病院にゆきましたところ
即日入院しなけれ
ばならないとのことで
私はとほうにく
れ病院で泣
きました。
LETTER: FELL ILL AND HOSPITALIZED. I CAN'T DO ANYTHING BUT CRY.
I HAVEN'T HAD MONEY TO SEND HOME FOR TWO OR THREE MONTHS.
A SICK WIFE AND THREE LITTLE KIDS.
WHAT CAN I DO?
WHEN I WAS WRITING FOR MAGAZINES...
I HAD ENOUGH TO BUY MY KID BROTHER A BIKE.
BUT MANGA... IT'LL BE THE DEATH OF ME.

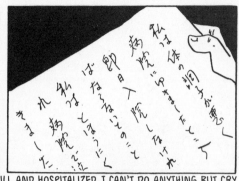

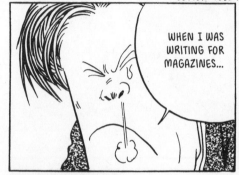

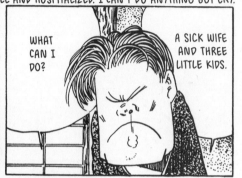

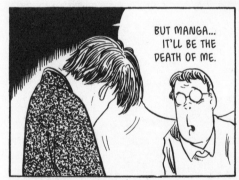

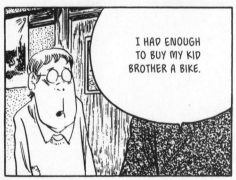

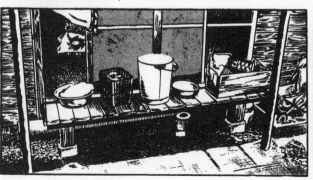

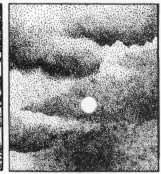

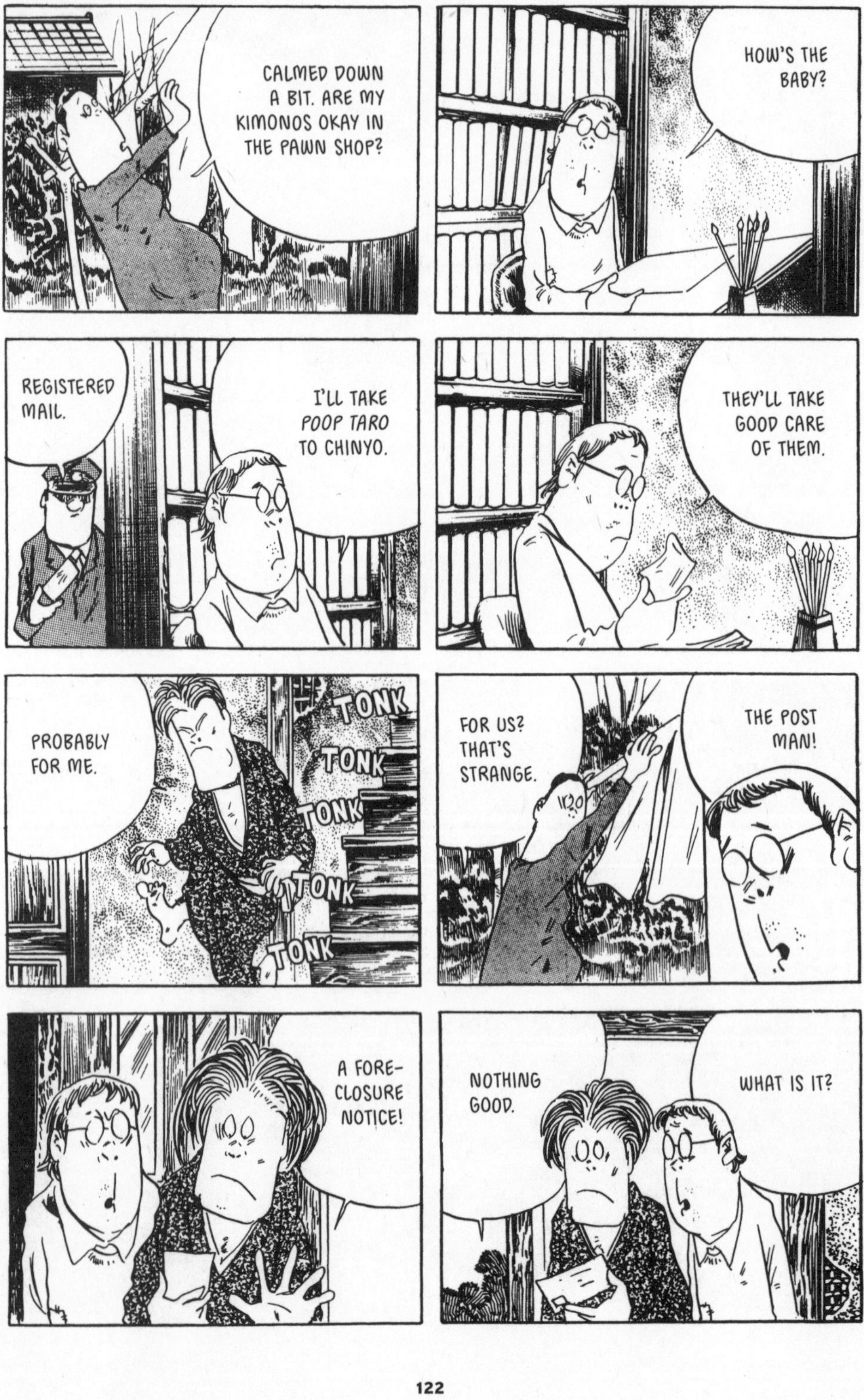
HOW'S THE BABY?
CALMED DOWN A BIT. ARE MY KIMONOS OKAY IN THE PAWN SHOP?
THEY'LL TAKE GOOD CARE OF THEM.
I'LL TAKE *POOP TARO* TO CHINYO.
REGISTERED MAIL.
THE POST MAN!
FOR US? THAT'S STRANGE.
TONK
TONK
TONK
TONK
TONK
PROBABLY FOR ME.
WHAT IS IT?
NOTHING GOOD.
A FORE-CLOSURE NOTICE!

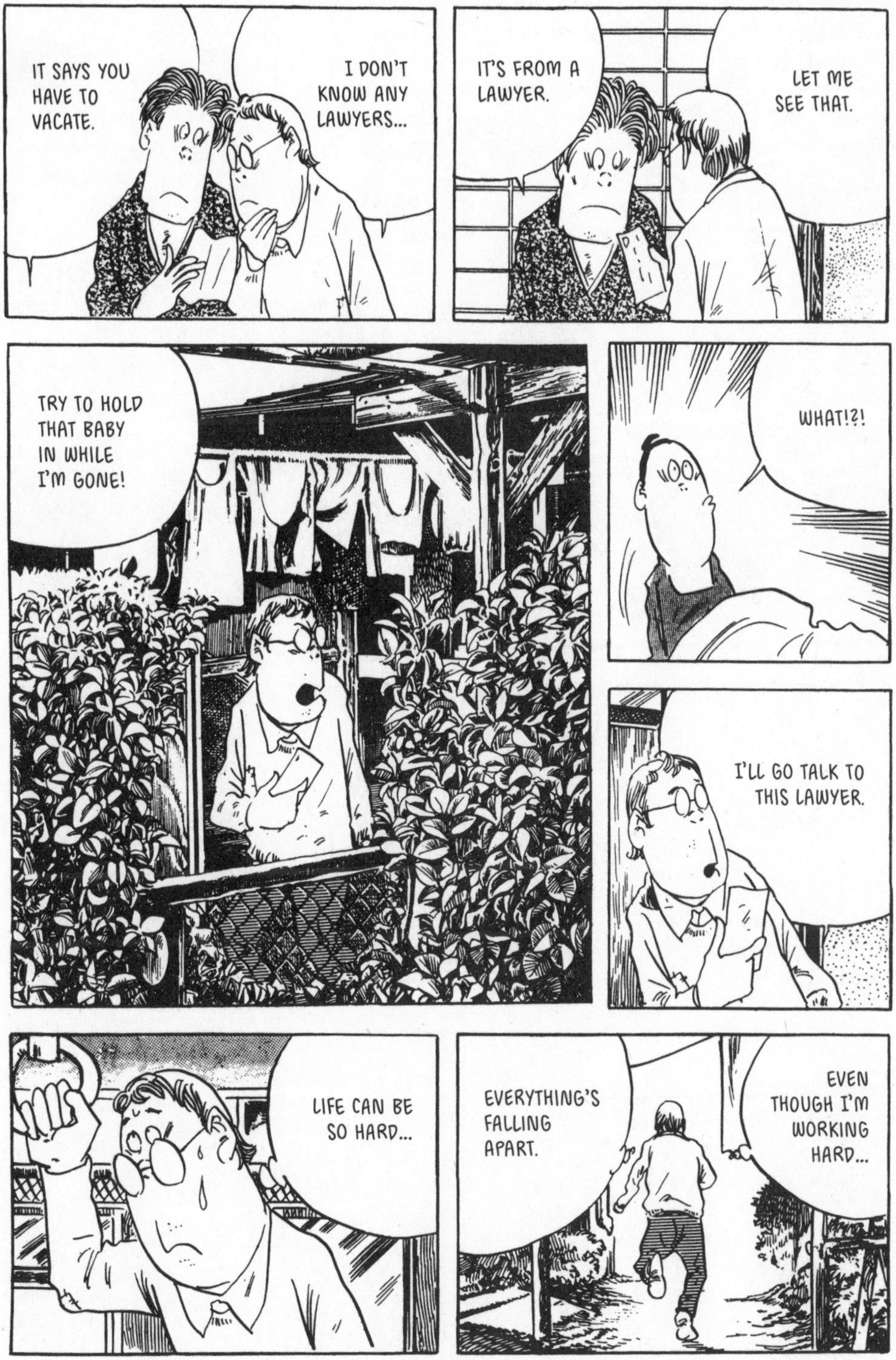
LET ME SEE THAT.
IT'S FROM A LAWYER.
I DON'T KNOW ANY LAWYERS...
IT SAYS YOU HAVE TO VACATE.
WHAT!?!
I'LL GO TALK TO THIS LAWYER.
TRY TO HOLD THAT BABY IN WHILE I'M GONE!
EVEN THOUGH I'M WORKING HARD...
EVERYTHING'S FALLING APART.
LIFE CAN BE SO HARD...

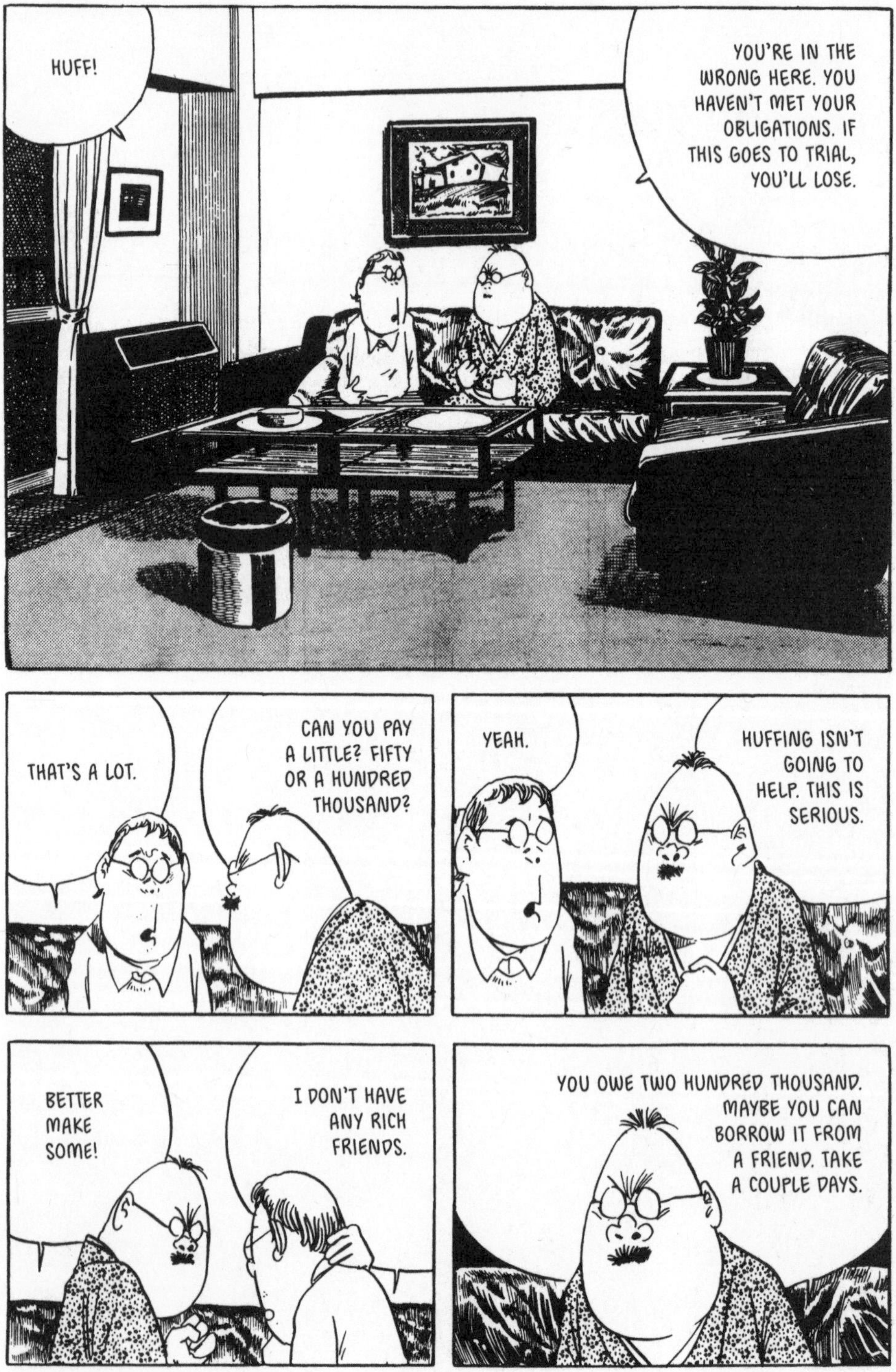
YOU'RE IN THE WRONG HERE. YOU HAVEN'T MET YOUR OBLIGATIONS. IF THIS GOES TO TRIAL, YOU'LL LOSE.
HUFF!
HUFFING ISN'T GOING TO HELP. THIS IS SERIOUS.
YEAH.
CAN YOU PAY A LITTLE? FIFTY OR A HUNDRED THOUSAND?
THAT'S A LOT.
YOU OWE TWO HUNDRED THOUSAND. MAYBE YOU CAN BORROW IT FROM A FRIEND. TAKE A COUPLE DAYS.
I DON'T HAVE ANY RICH FRIENDS.
BETTER MAKE SOME!

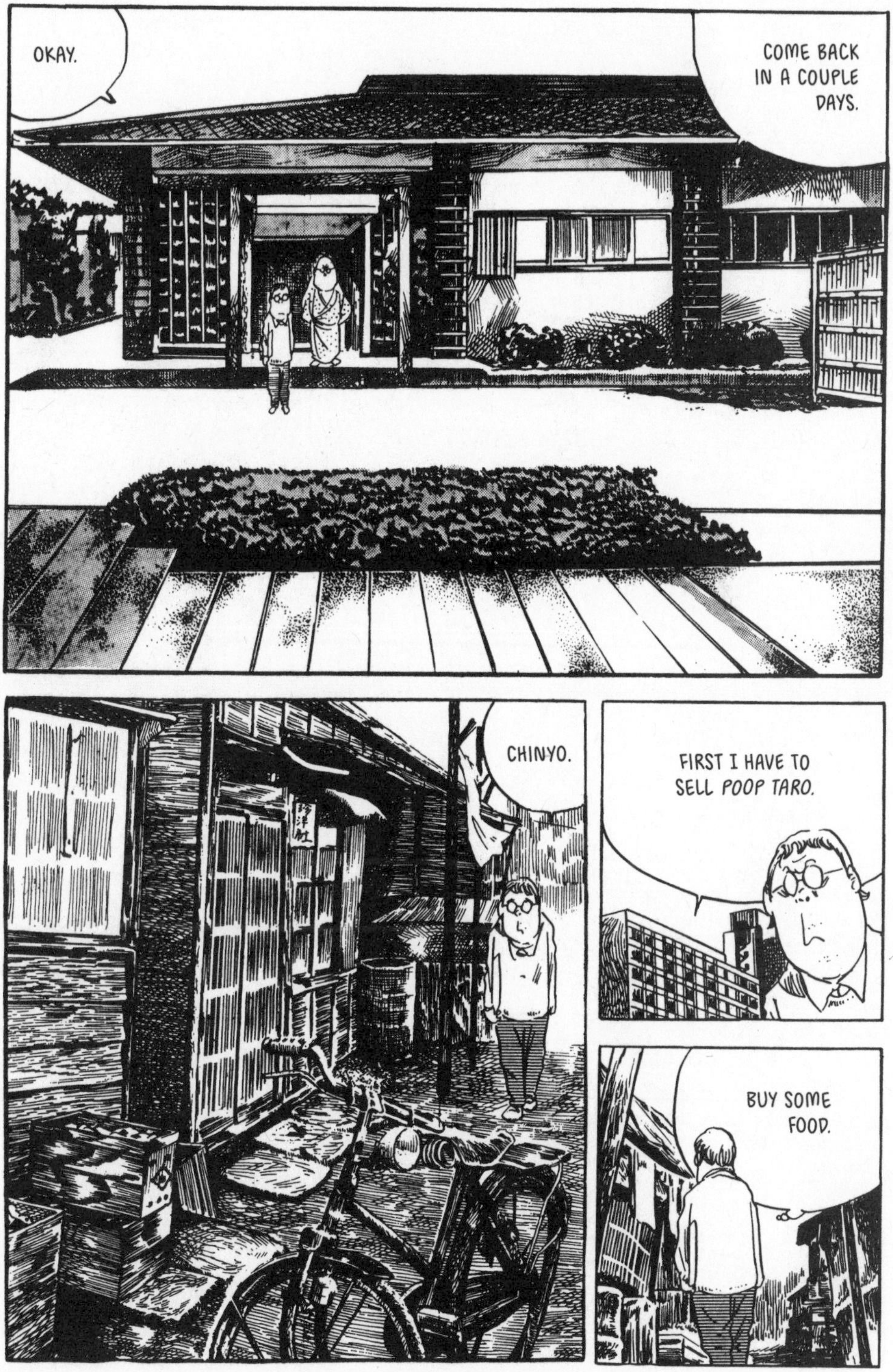
COME BACK IN A COUPLE DAYS.
OKAY.
FIRST I HAVE TO SELL *POOP TARO*.
BUY SOME FOOD.
CHINYO.

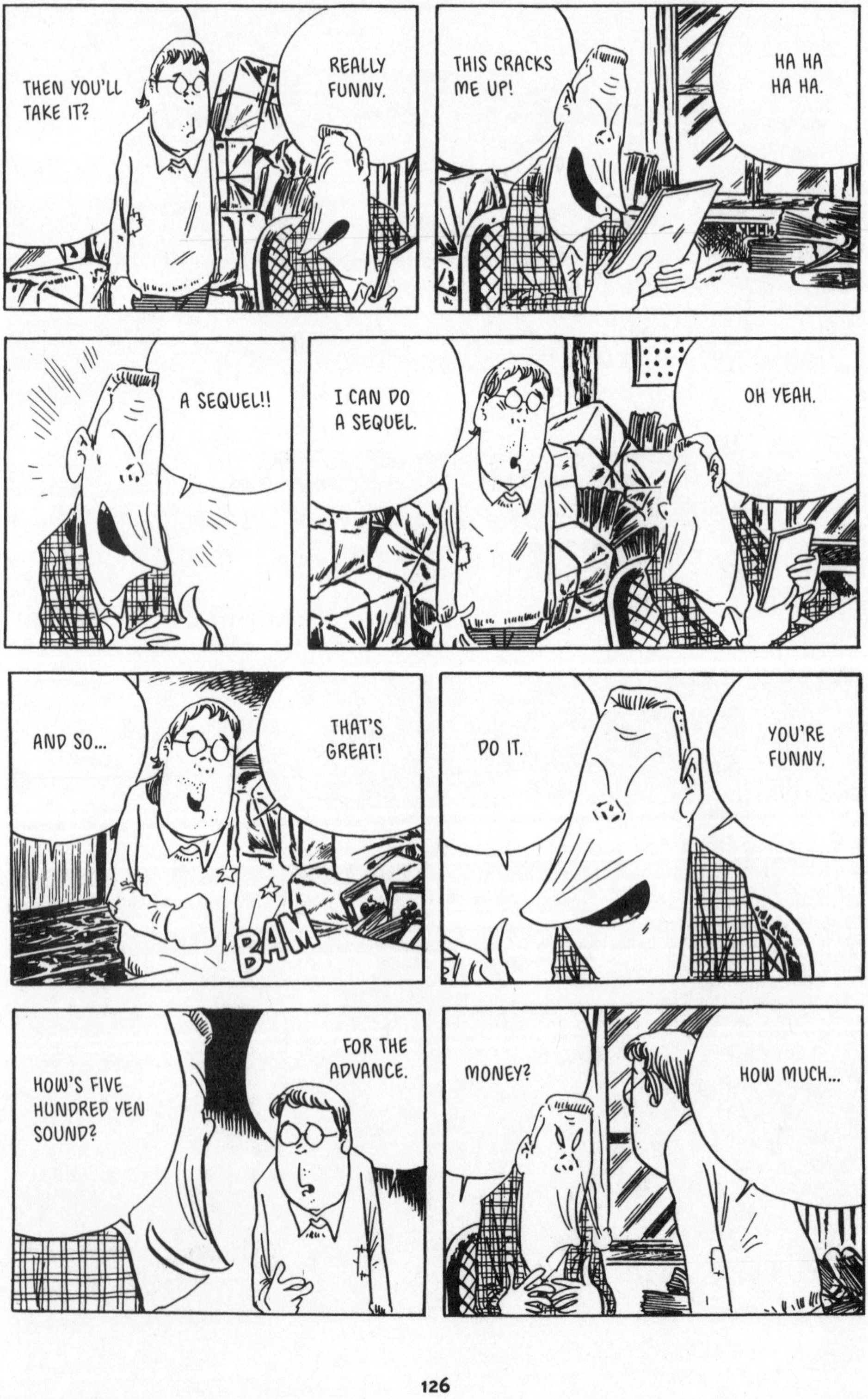
HA HA
HA HA.
THIS CRACKS ME UP!
REALLY FUNNY.
THEN YOU'LL TAKE IT?
OH YEAH.
I CAN DO A SEQUEL.
A SEQUEL!!
YOU'RE FUNNY.
DO IT.
THAT'S GREAT!
AND SO...
BAM
HOW MUCH...
MONEY?
FOR THE ADVANCE.
HOW'S FIVE HUNDRED YEN SOUND?

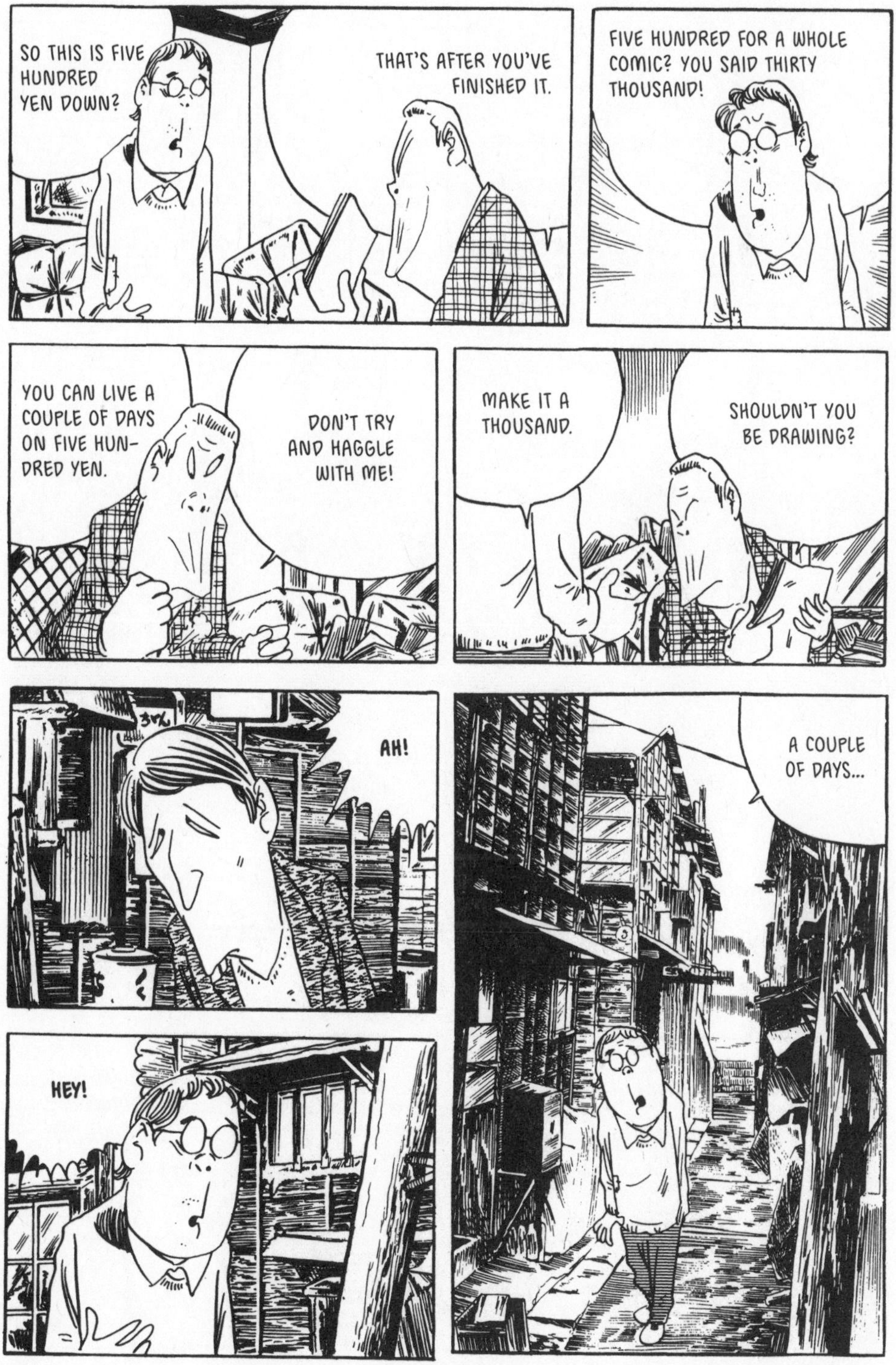
SO THIS IS FIVE HUNDRED YEN DOWN?
THAT'S AFTER YOU'VE FINISHED IT.
FIVE HUNDRED FOR A WHOLE COMIC? YOU SAID THIRTY THOUSAND!
YOU CAN LIVE A COUPLE OF DAYS ON FIVE HUN-DRED YEN.
DON'T TRY AND HAGGLE WITH ME!
MAKE IT A THOUSAND.
SHOULDN'T YOU BE DRAWING?
AH!
HEY!
A COUPLE OF DAYS...

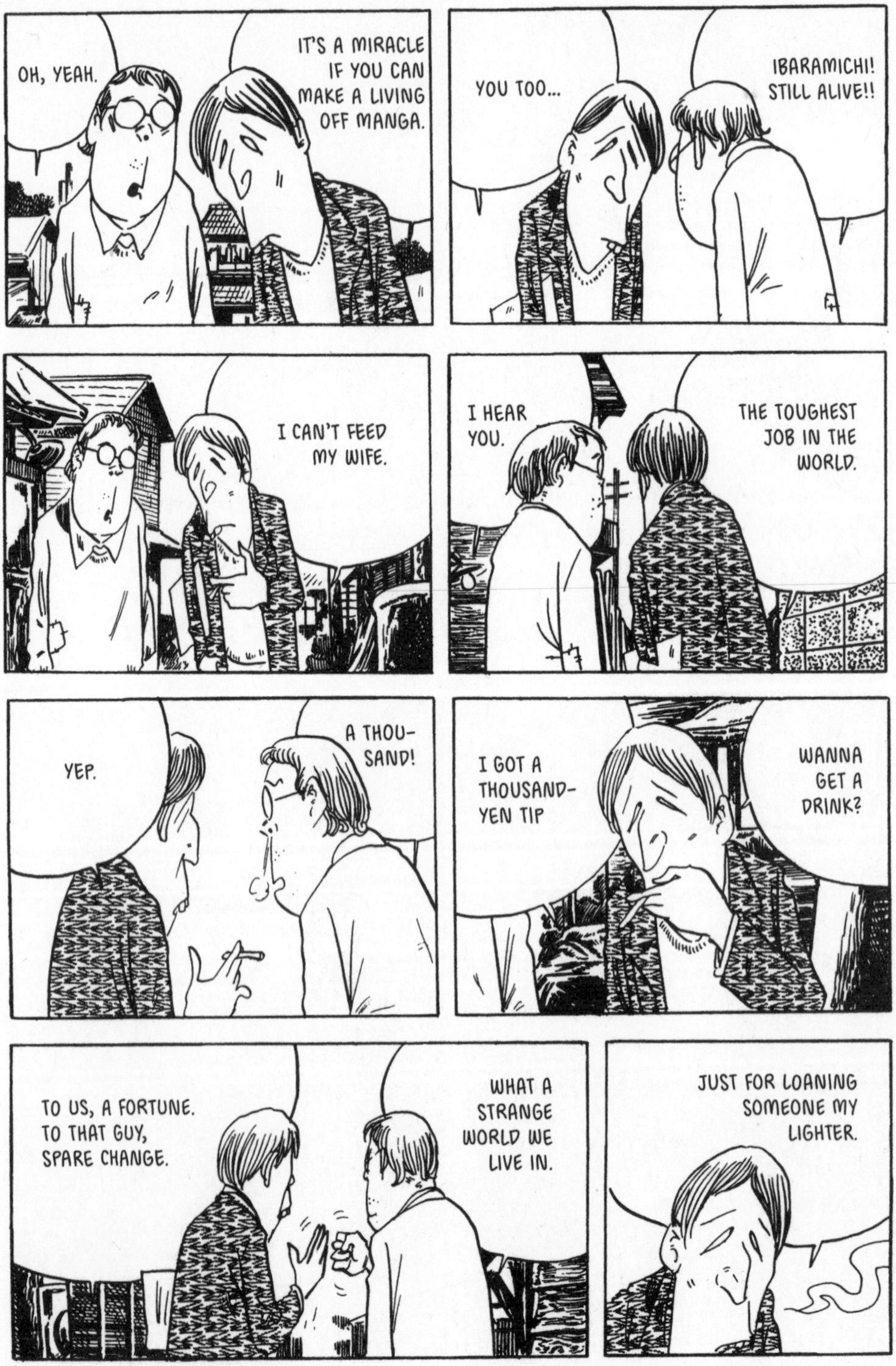
IBARAMICHI! STILL ALIVE!!
YOU TOO...
IT'S A MIRACLE IF YOU CAN MAKE A LIVING OFF MANGA.
OH, YEAH.
THE TOUGHEST JOB IN THE WORLD.
I HEAR YOU.
I CAN'T FEED MY WIFE.
WANNA GET A DRINK?
I GOT A THOUSAND-YEN TIP
A THOU-SAND!
YEP.
JUST FOR LOANING SOMEONE MY LIGHTER.
WHAT A STRANGE WORLD WE LIVE IN.
TO US, A FORTUNE. TO THAT GUY, SPARE CHANGE.

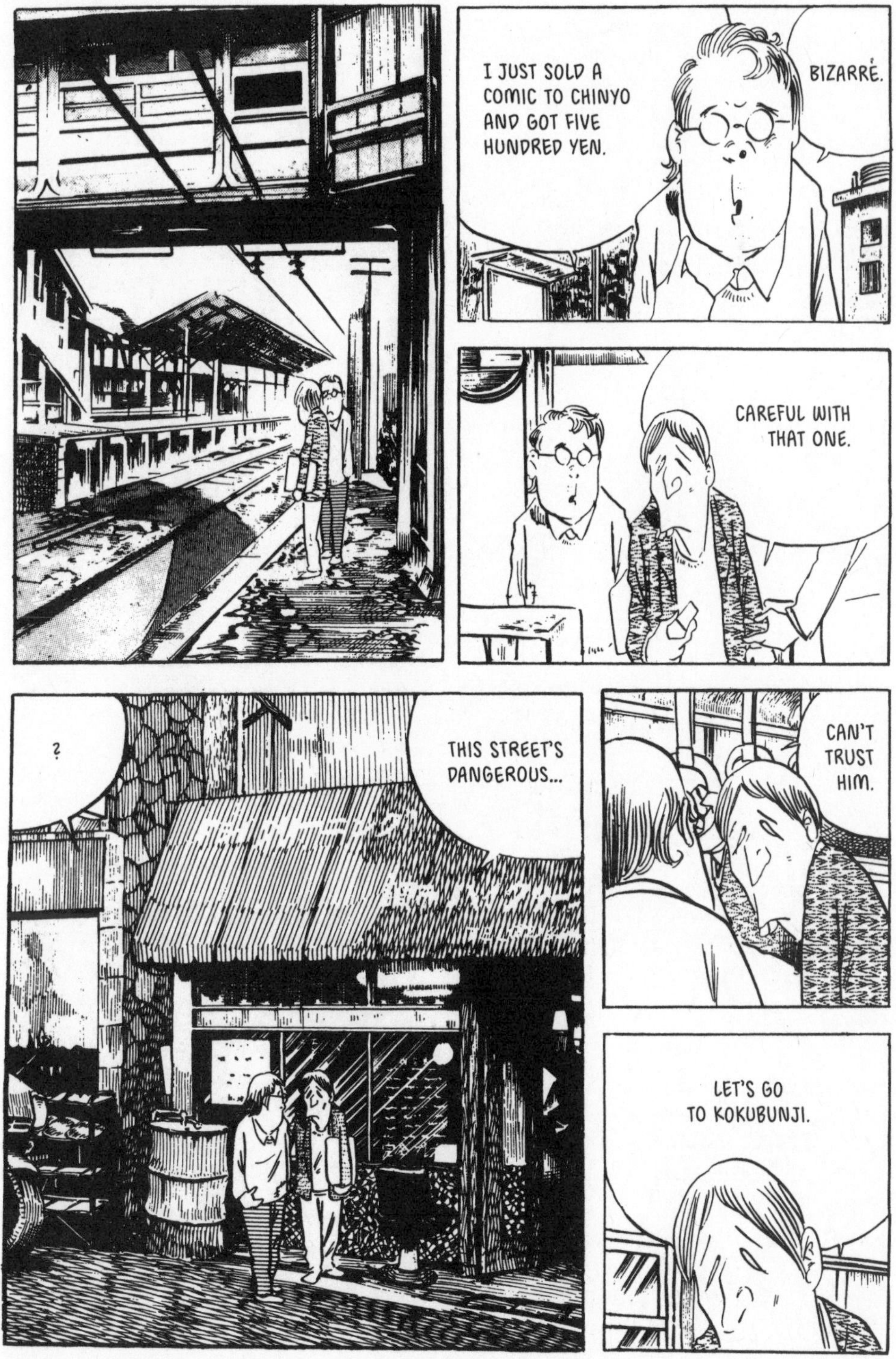
BIZARRÉ.
I JUST SOLD A COMIC TO CHINYO AND GOT FIVE HUNDRED YEN.
CAREFUL WITH THAT ONE.
CAN'T TRUST HIM.
LET'S GO TO KOKUBUNJI.
THIS STREET'S DANGEROUS...
?

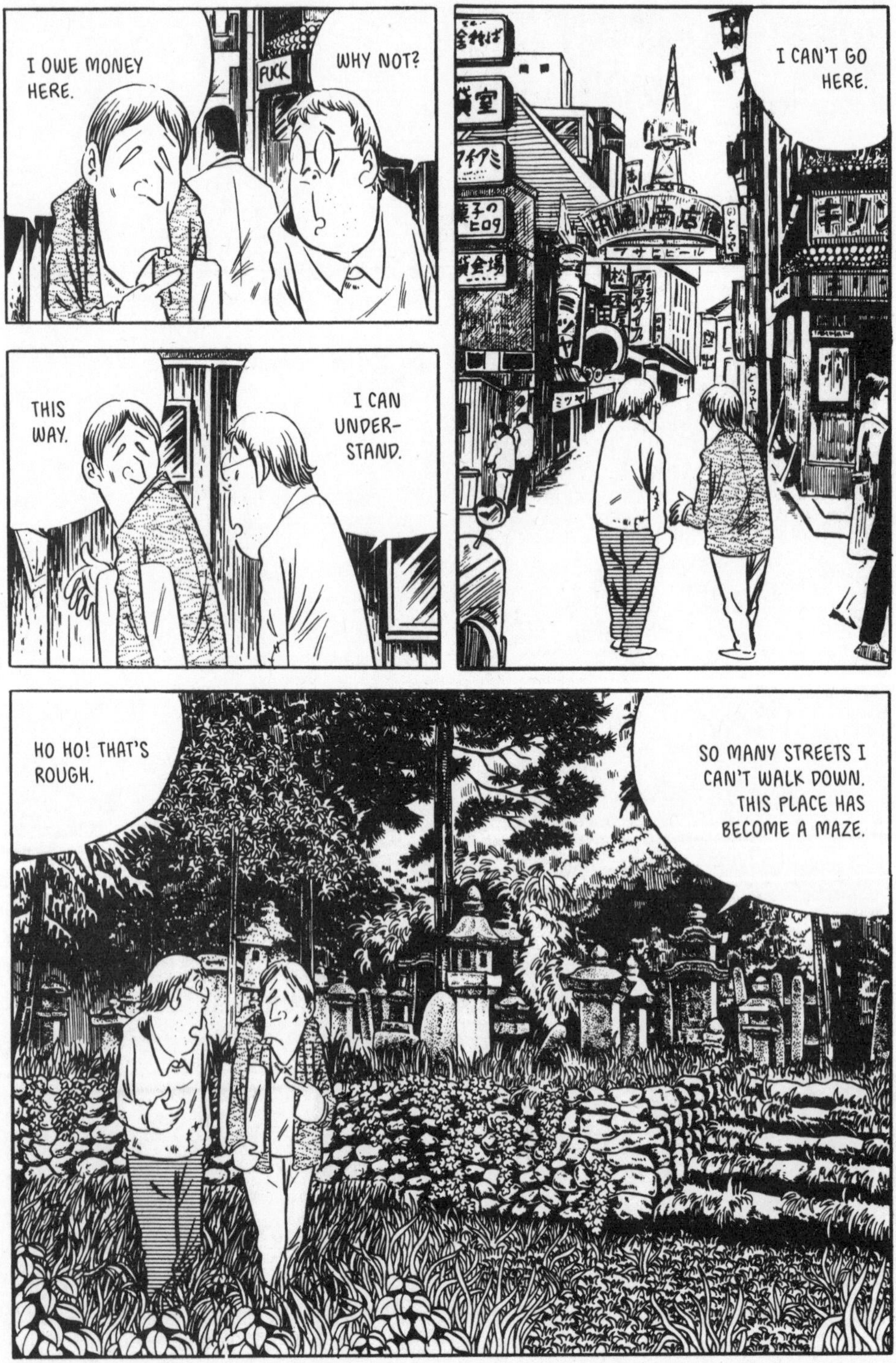
I CAN'T GO HERE.
WHY NOT?
FUCK
I OWE MONEY HERE.
I CAN UNDER-STAND.
THIS WAY.
SO MANY STREETS I CAN'T WALK DOWN. THIS PLACE HAS BECOME A MAZE.
HO HO! THAT'S ROUGH.

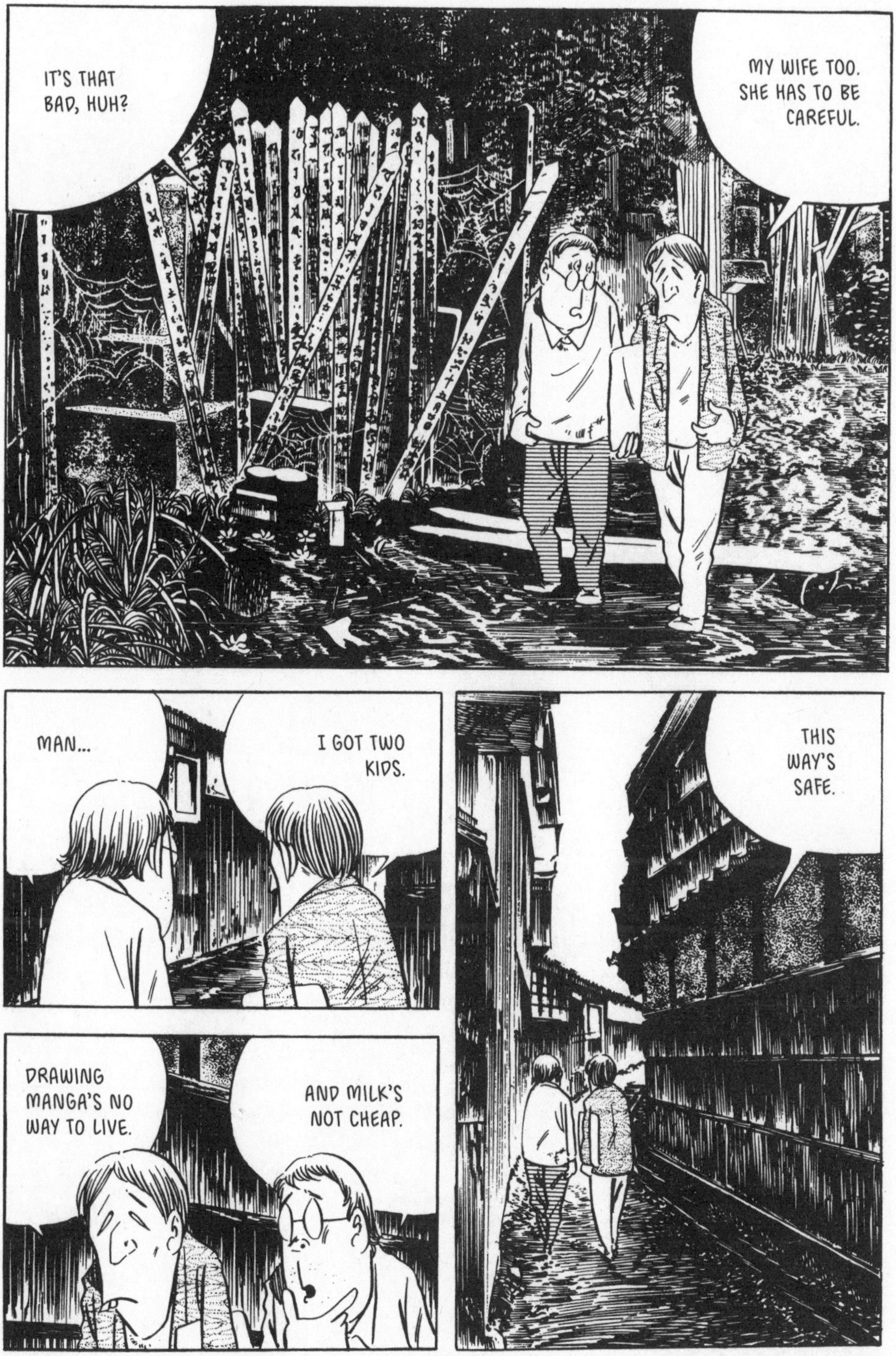
MY WIFE TOO. SHE HAS TO BE CAREFUL.
IT'S THAT BAD, HUH?
THIS WAY'S SAFE.
I GOT TWO KIDS.
MAN...
AND MILK'S NOT CHEAP.
DRAWING MANGA'S NO WAY TO LIVE.

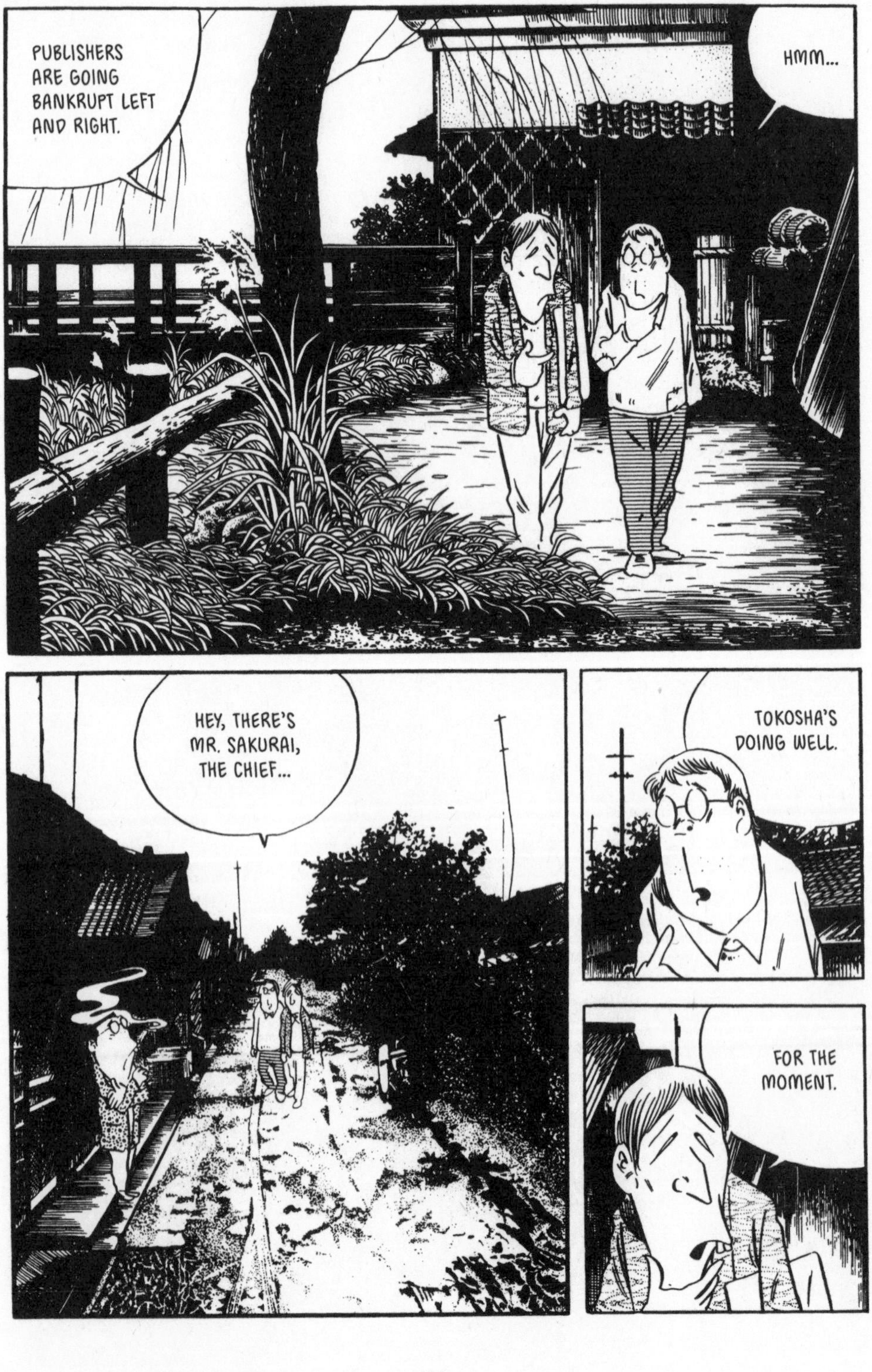
HMM...
PUBLISHERS ARE GOING BANKRUPT LEFT AND RIGHT.
TOKOSHA'S DOING WELL.
FOR THE MOMENT.
HEY, THERE'S MR. SAKURAI, THE CHIEF...

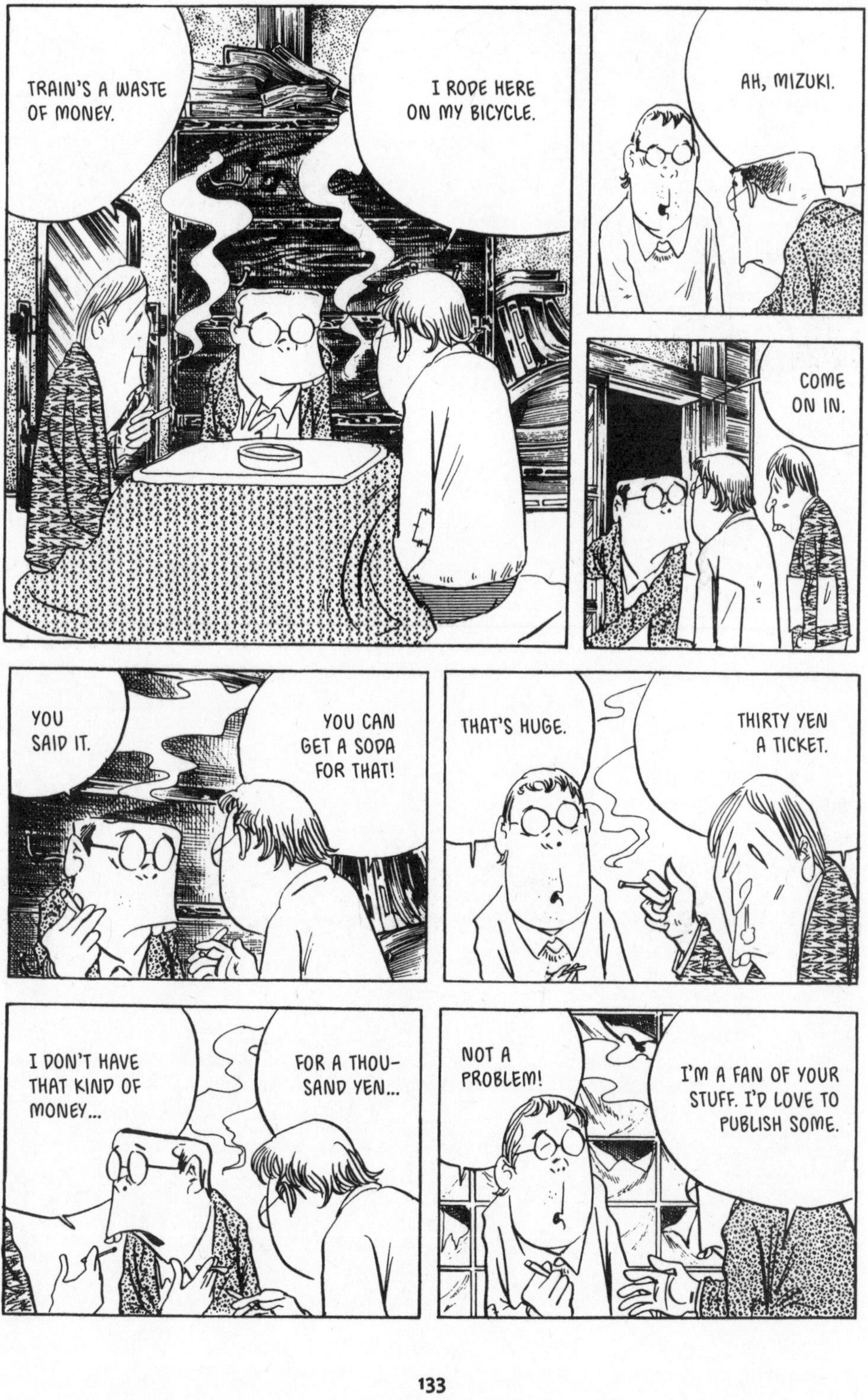
AH, MIZUKI.
COME ON IN.
I RODE HERE ON MY BICYCLE.
TRAIN'S A WASTE OF MONEY.
THIRTY YEN A TICKET.
THAT'S HUGE.
YOU CAN GET A SODA FOR THAT!
YOU SAID IT.
I'M A FAN OF YOUR STUFF. I'D LOVE TO PUBLISH SOME.
NOT A PROBLEM!
FOR A THOU-SAND YEN...
I DON'T HAVE THAT KIND OF MONEY...

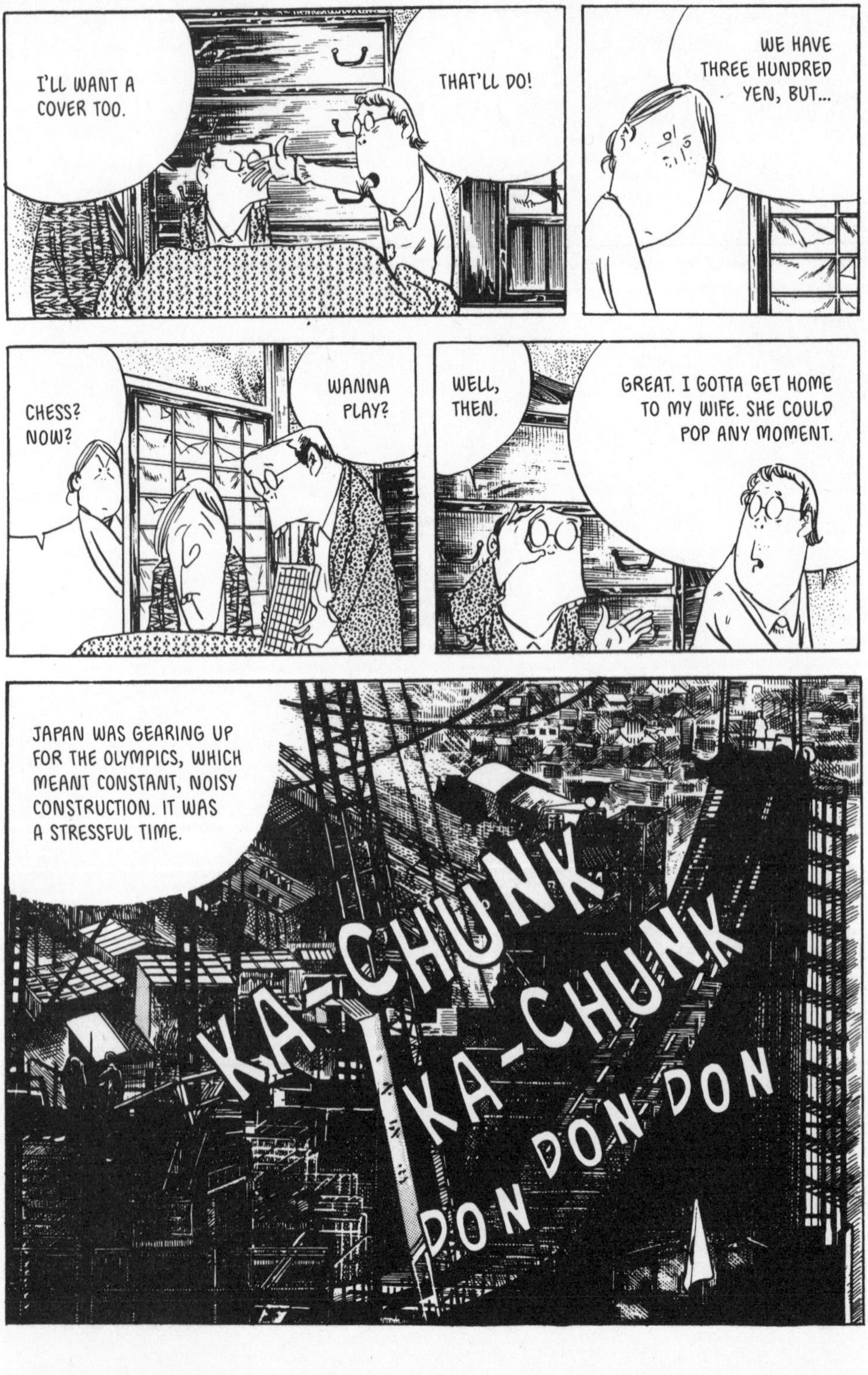
WE HAVE THREE HUNDRED YEN, BUT...
THAT'LL DO!
I'LL WANT A COVER TOO.
GREAT. I GOTTA GET HOME TO MY WIFE. SHE COULD POP ANY MOMENT.
WELL, THEN.
WANNA PLAY?
CHESS? NOW?
JAPAN WAS GEARING UP FOR THE OLYMPICS, WHICH MEANT CONSTANT, NOISY CONSTRUCTION. IT WAS A STRESSFUL TIME.
KA-CHUNK
KA-CHUNK
DON DON DON DON

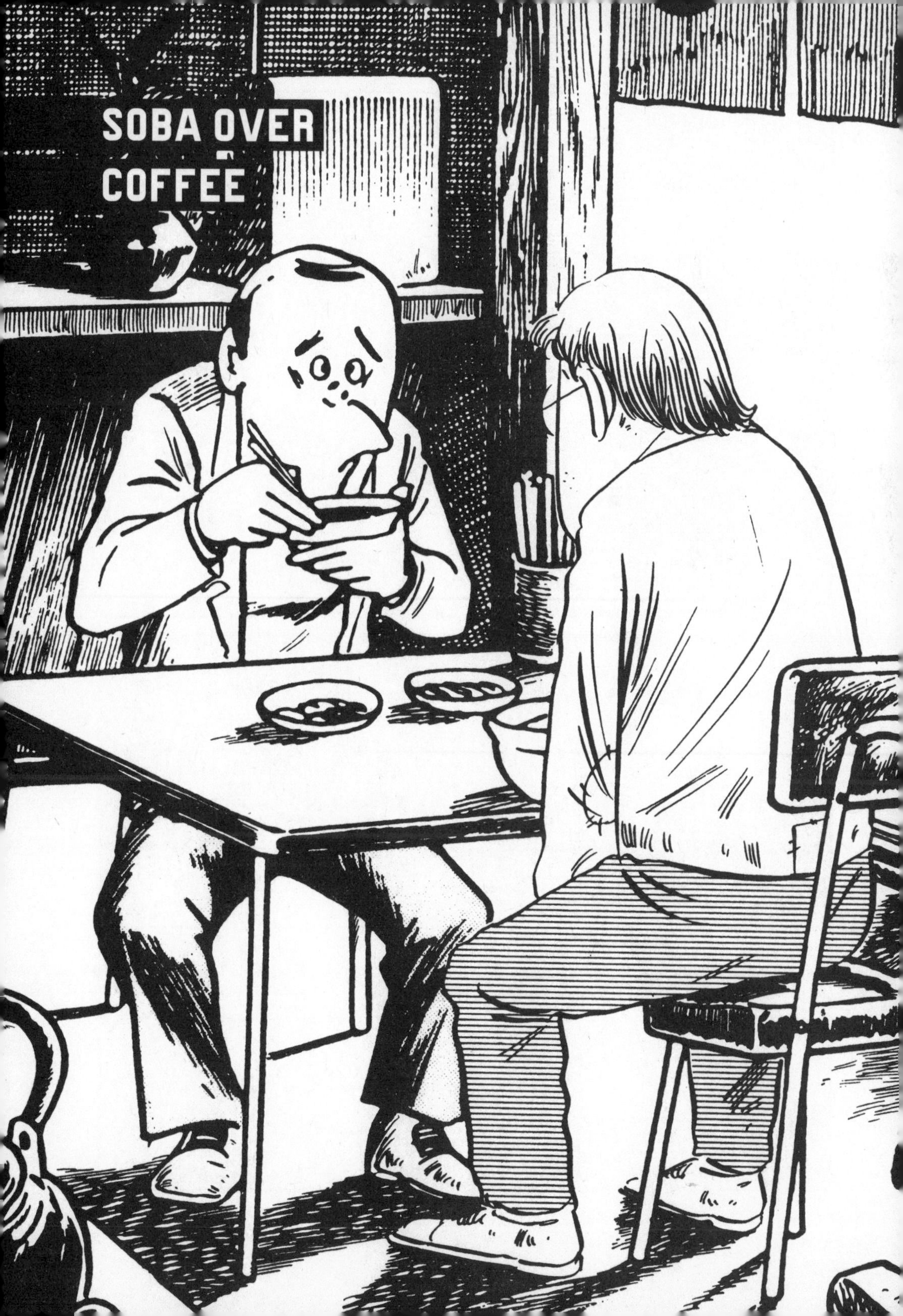
SOBA OVER
COFFEE

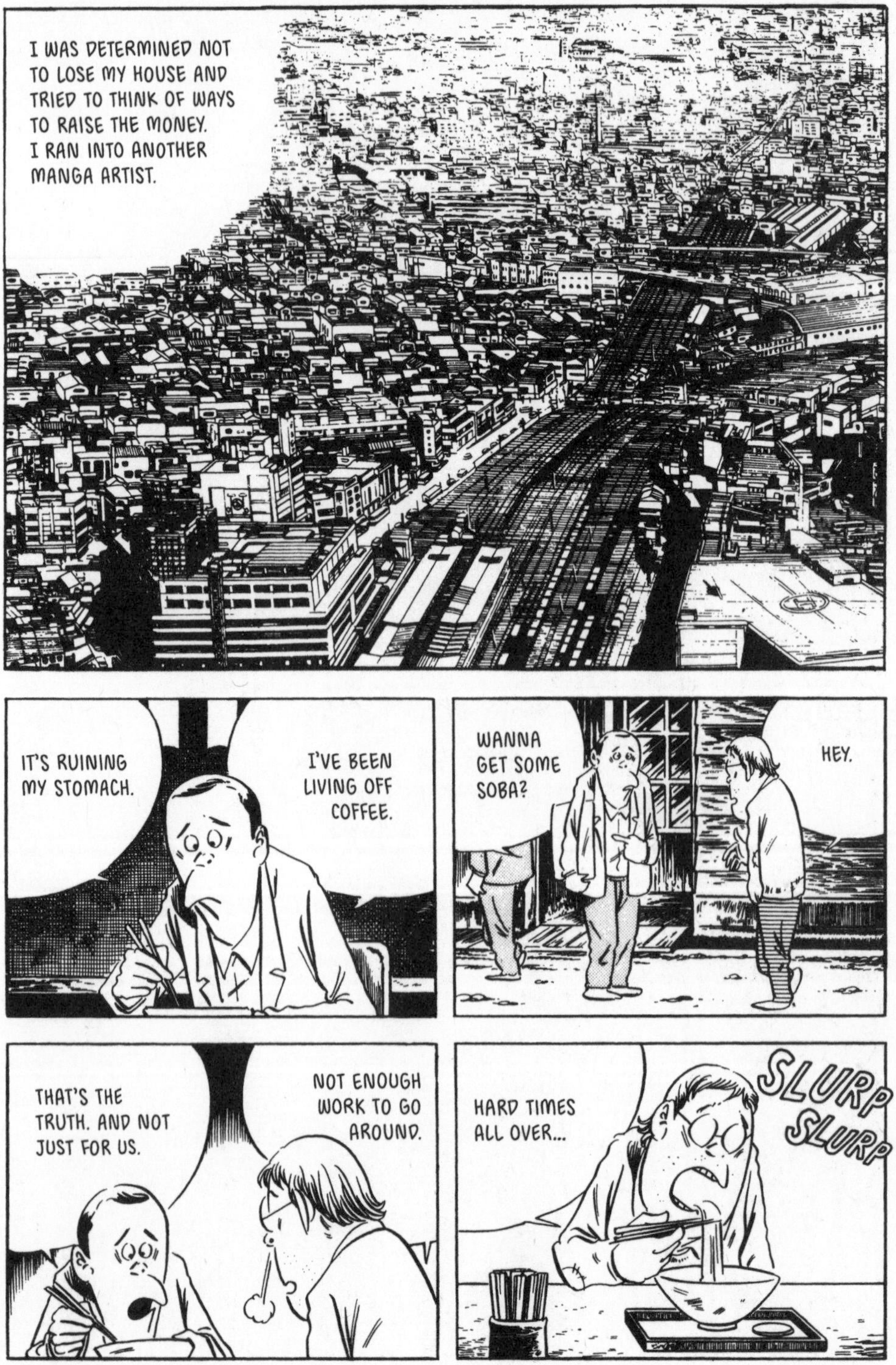
I WAS DETERMINED NOT TO LOSE MY HOUSE AND TRIED TO THINK OF WAYS TO RAISE THE MONEY. I RAN INTO ANOTHER MANGA ARTIST.
HEY.
WANNA GET SOME SOBA?
I'VE BEEN LIVING OFF COFFEE.
IT'S RUINING MY STOMACH.
SLURP SLURP
HARD TIMES ALL OVER...
NOT ENOUGH WORK TO GO AROUND.
THAT'S THE TRUTH. AND NOT JUST FOR US.

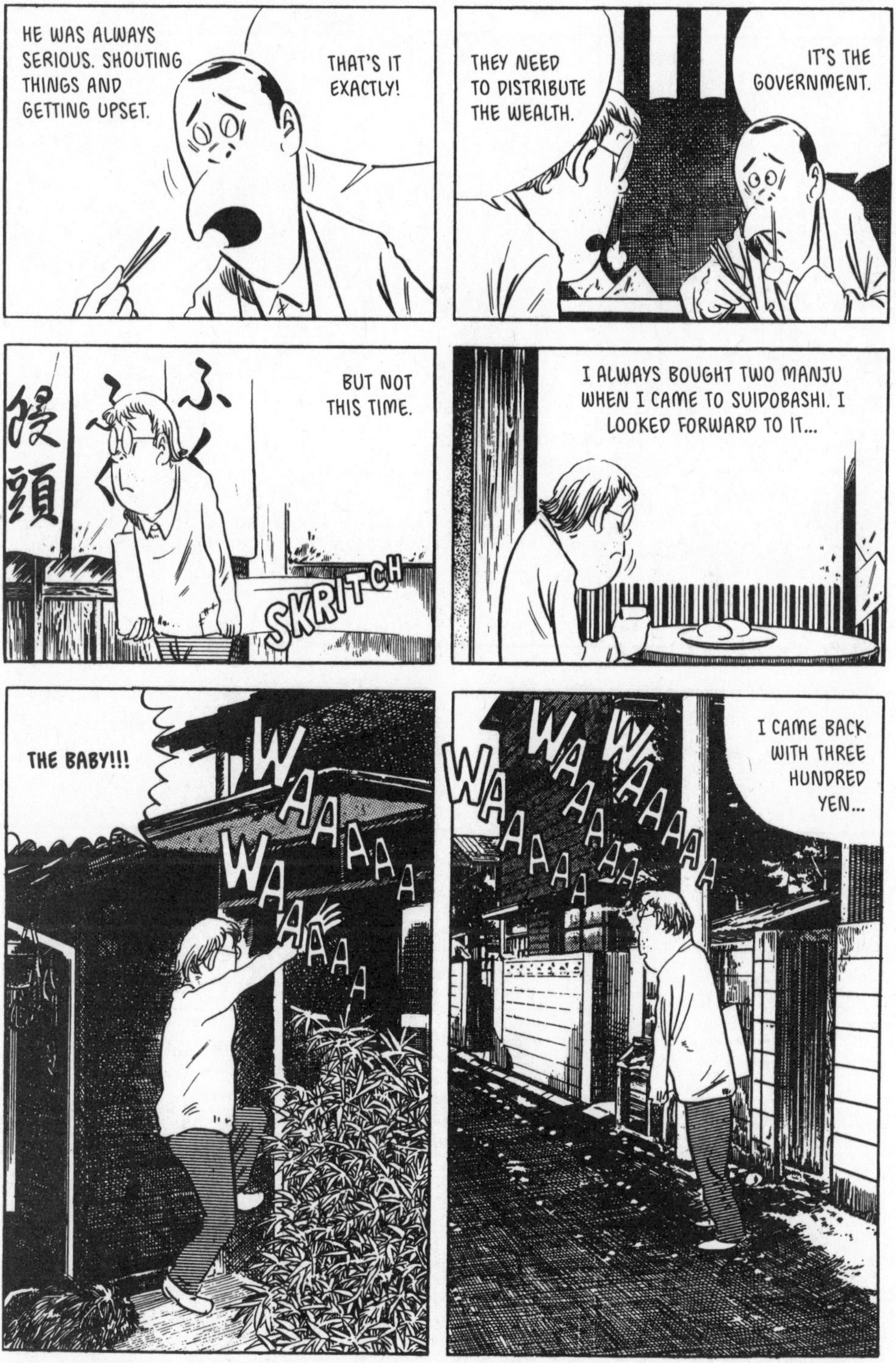
IT'S THE GOVERNMENT.
THEY NEED TO DISTRIBUTE THE WEALTH.
THAT'S IT EXACTLY!
HE WAS ALWAYS SERIOUS. SHOUTING THINGS AND GETTING UPSET.
I ALWAYS BOUGHT TWO MANJU WHEN I CAME TO SUIDOBASHI. I LOOKED FORWARD TO IT...
BUT NOT THIS TIME.
ふ
饅頭
SKRITCH
I CAME BACK WITH THREE HUNDRED YEN...
WAAAAAA
WAAAAAA
WAAAAAAA
THE BABY!!!
WAAAAA
WAAAAAA

IT'S A GIRL.
WOW...
A BABY... AND THREE HUNDRED YEN...
EXCUSE US.
WHAT?
MINISTRY OF FINANCE.
SERIOUSLY?
WHY?
WELL, HALF OF THIS LAND BELONGS TO THE MINISTRY OF FINANCE.
W...WHAT?
IF YOU LOOK AT THIS MAP, IT'S CLEAR. HERE'S THE PROPERTY LINE.
THIS IS GOVERNMENT LAND...
WHAT DOES THAT MEAN?
HALF BELONGS TO THE MINISTRY OF FINANCE.
BUT THIS IS OUR HOUSE!

YOU WANT TO CUT IT IN HALF!?!
DON'T GET SO EXCITED.
WE'VE STUDIED THE LAW. WE'RE WITHIN OUR RIGHTS.
TELL IT TO THE PEOPLE WHO BUILT THIS HOUSE. WE JUST BOUGHT IT.
BUT IT'S IN YOUR NAME.
WE WOULD CONSIDER LEASING YOU THE LAND.
WAAAAA WAAAAA!
OF ALL THE... TALK TO MY REALTOR.
I'M BUSY...
WE GOT ANYTHING TO EAT?
I THINK THERE'S SOME MOCHI.
HERE IT IS.
REGISTERED MAIL!

THAT LAWYER AGAIN.
A SUM-MONS!!
FUCK!!
THE LAWYER AND THE FINANCE MINISTER CAN FIGHT FOR IT.
ASSHOLES.
IF I HAD EVIL POWERS, I'D DESTROY THE MINISTER, THAT LITTLE-MUSTACHED LAWYER...
AND THE PAWN-SHOP OWNER! YEAH!
AND I'D SAVE ALL OF THE...
VIRTUOUS POOR.
WITH MY INCANTATION...
AND RUMBLING EARTH...

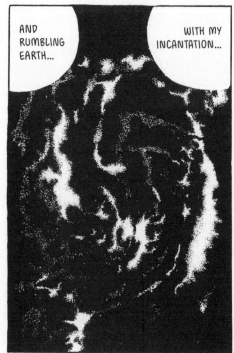

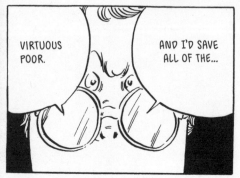

FOOOM
WHAT ARE YOU SHOUTING ABOUT?
AH.
I GUESS I WAS TOO INTO IT.
YOU NEED SOME SORT OF DEVIL POWER TO REFORM THIS WORLD.
TO FIGHT EVIL WITH EVIL.
AKUMA-KUN! THE DEVIL BOY!!
I NEED PAPER.
I'LL NEVER OWN A KIMONO AGAIN...
DON'T SAY THAT.

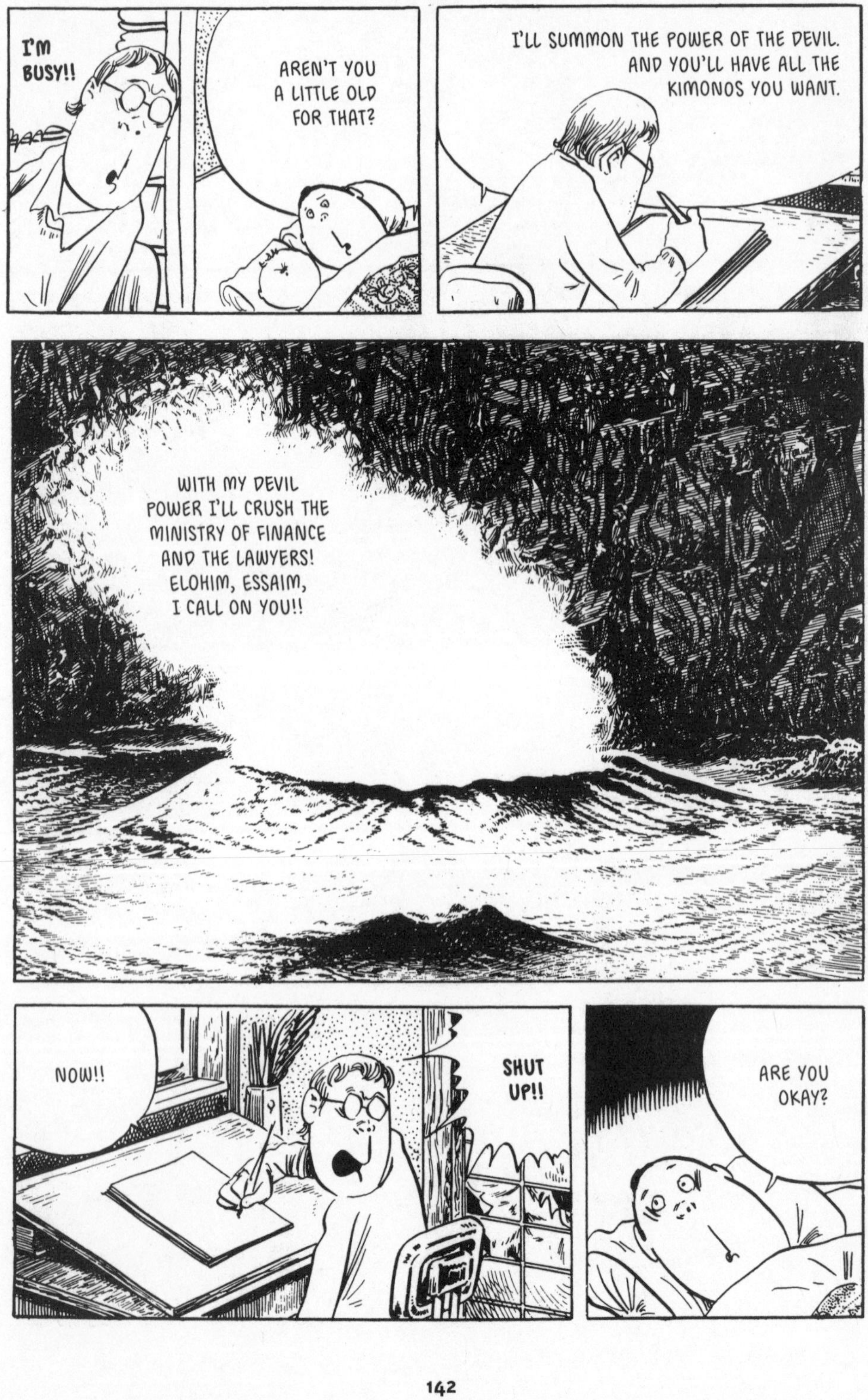
I'LL SUMMON THE POWER OF THE DEVIL. AND YOU'LL HAVE ALL THE KIMONOS YOU WANT.
AREN'T YOU A LITTLE OLD FOR THAT?
I'M BUSY!!
WITH MY DEVIL POWER I'LL CRUSH THE MINISTRY OF FINANCE AND THE LAWYERS! ELOHIM, ESSAIM, I CALL ON YOU!!
ARE YOU OKAY?
SHUT UP!!
NOW!!

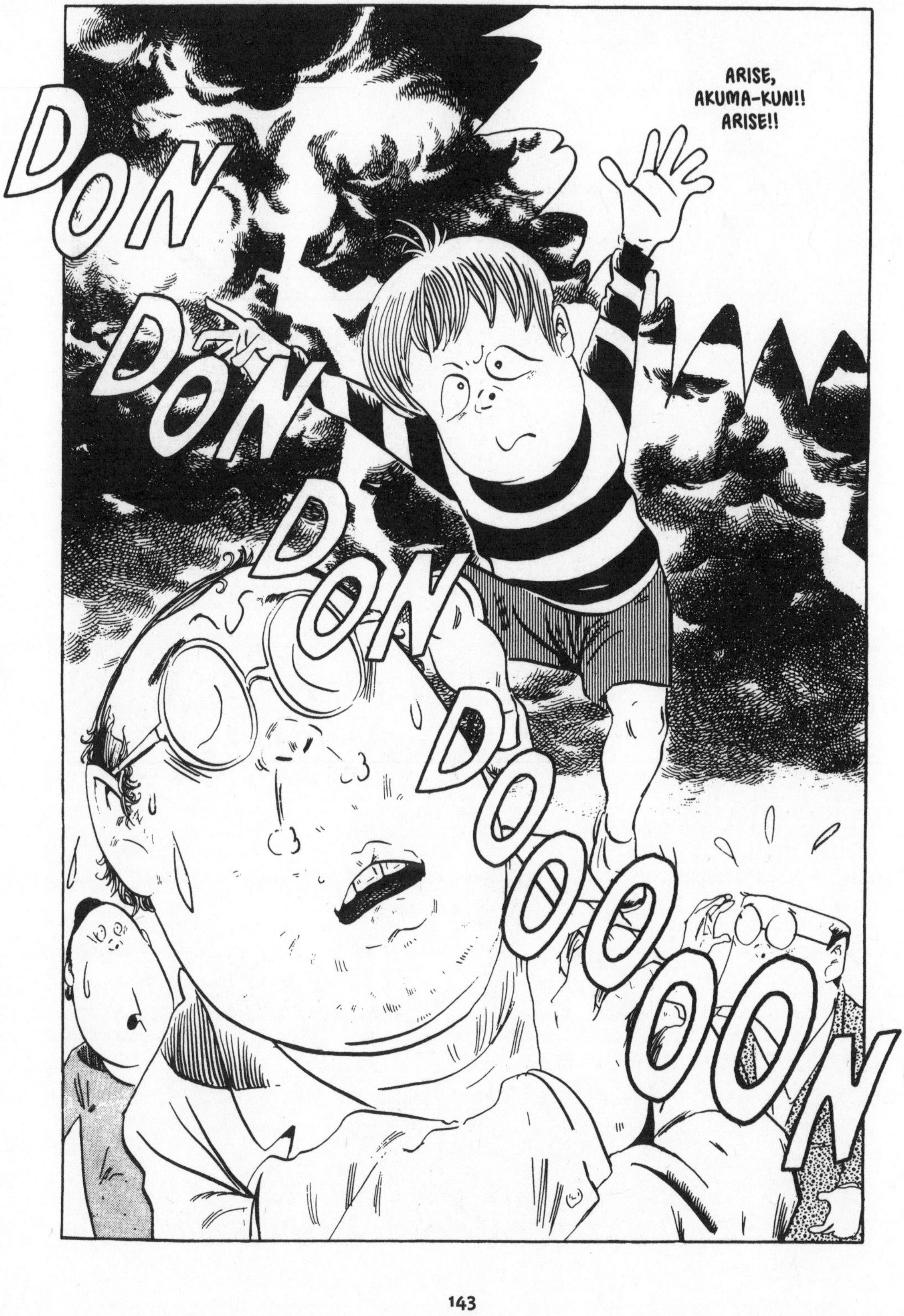
ARISE, AKUMA-KUN!! ARISE!!
DON DON DON DOOOOOOOON

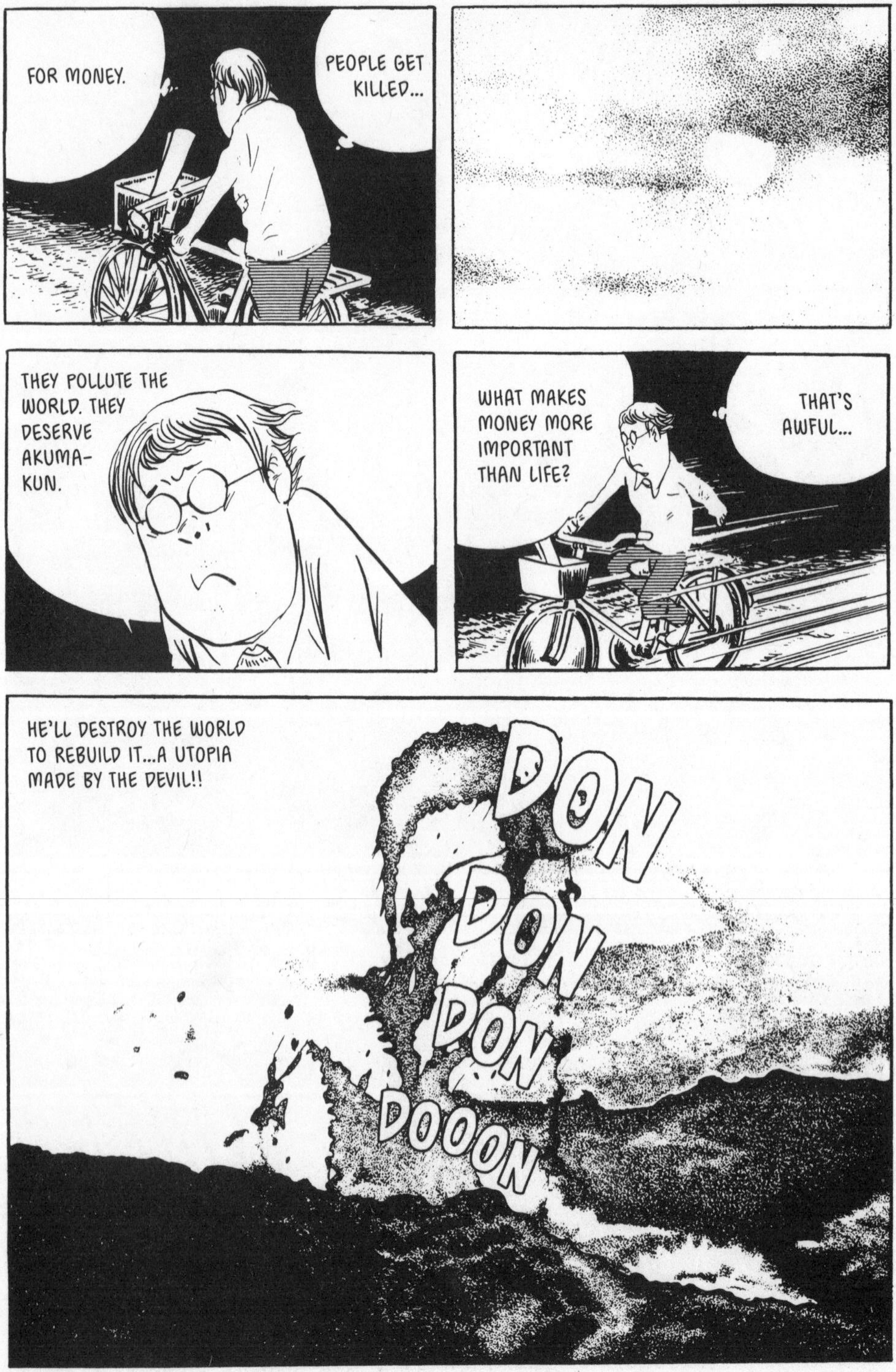
PEOPLE GET KILLED...
FOR MONEY.
THAT'S AWFUL...
WHAT MAKES MONEY MORE IMPORTANT THAN LIFE?
THEY POLLUTE THE WORLD. THEY DESERVE AKUMA-KUN.
DON DON DON DOOOON
HE'LL DESTROY THE WORLD TO REBUILD IT...A UTOPIA MADE BY THE DEVIL!!

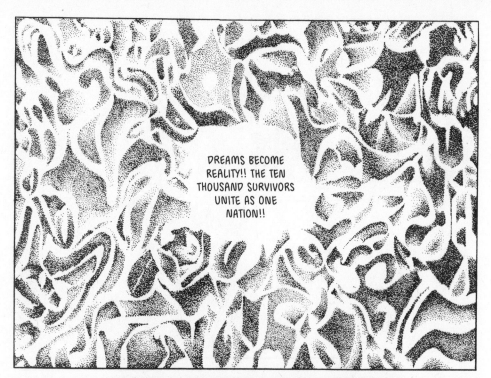

DREAMS BECOME
REALITY!! THE TEN
THOUSAND SURVIVORS
UNITE AS ONE
NATION!!

IT SERVES
YOU RIGHT.

TO THE
REST...

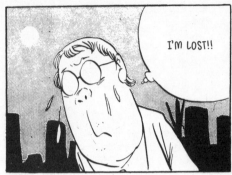

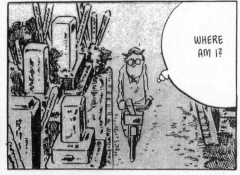

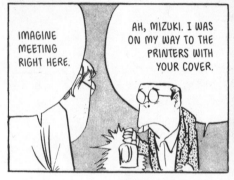

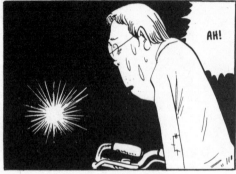

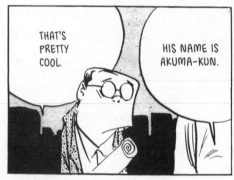

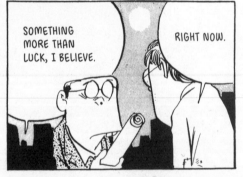

WHERE AM I?
I'M LOST!!
AH!
AH, MIZUKI. I WAS ON MY WAY TO THE PRINTERS WITH YOUR COVER.
IMAGINE MEETING RIGHT HERE.
RIGHT NOW.
SOMETHING MORE THAN LUCK, I BELIEVE.
HIS NAME IS AKUMA-KUN.
THAT'S PRETTY COOL.
I THINK IT'LL BE A HIT.
THUMP THUMP THUMP
WE'D PLANNED FOR FIVE VOLUMES OF *AKUMA-KUN* BUT ONLY PUT OUT THREE.* ABOUT THEN, THE MINISTRY OF FINANCE ADMITTED THEY'D MADE AN ERROR. BUT THE LAWYER STILL ENDED UP WITH HALF MY HOUSE.

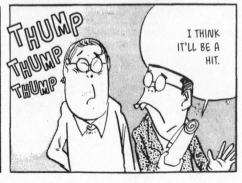

*SEE NOTE ON PAGE 534.

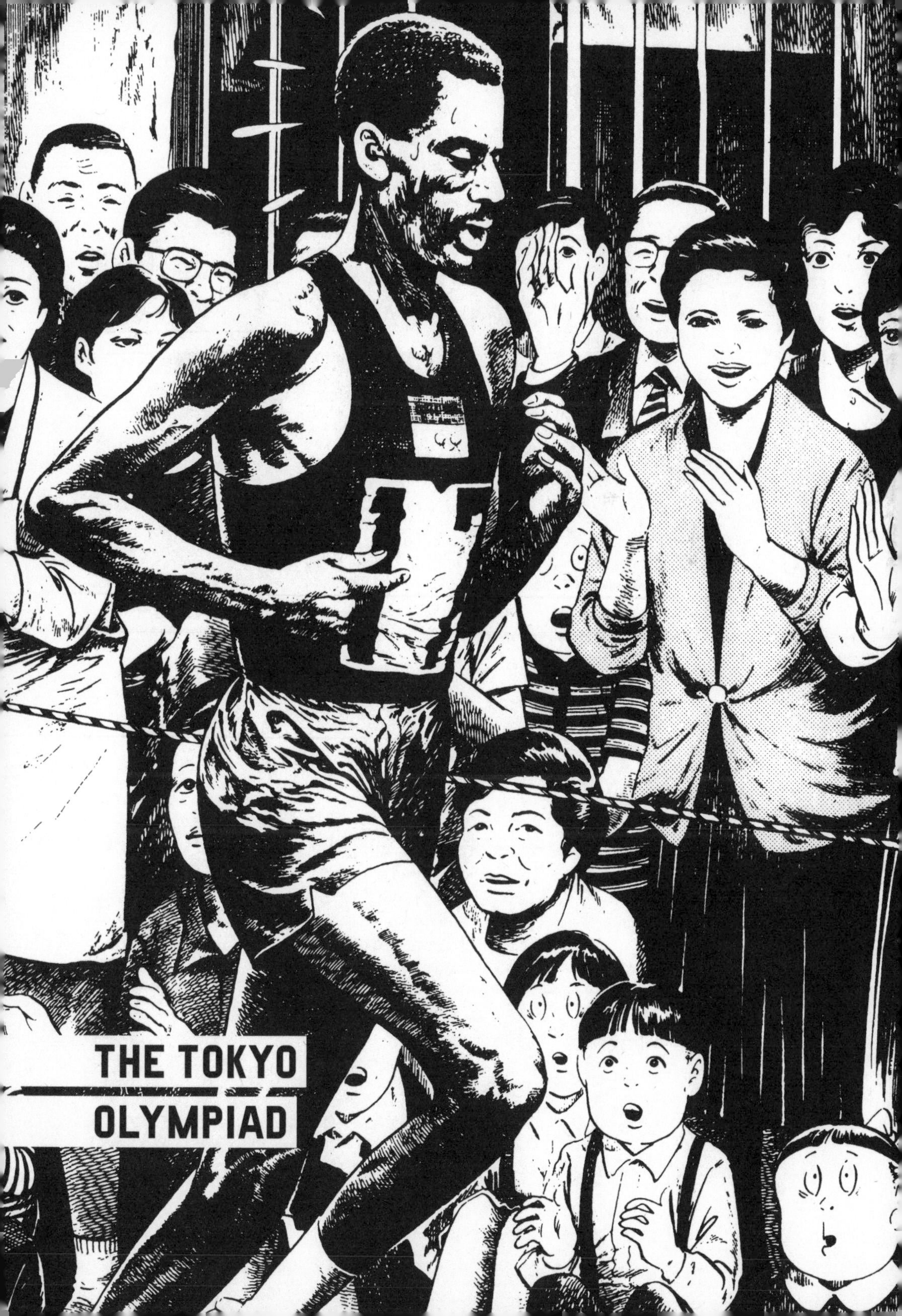
THE TOKYO
OLYMPIAD

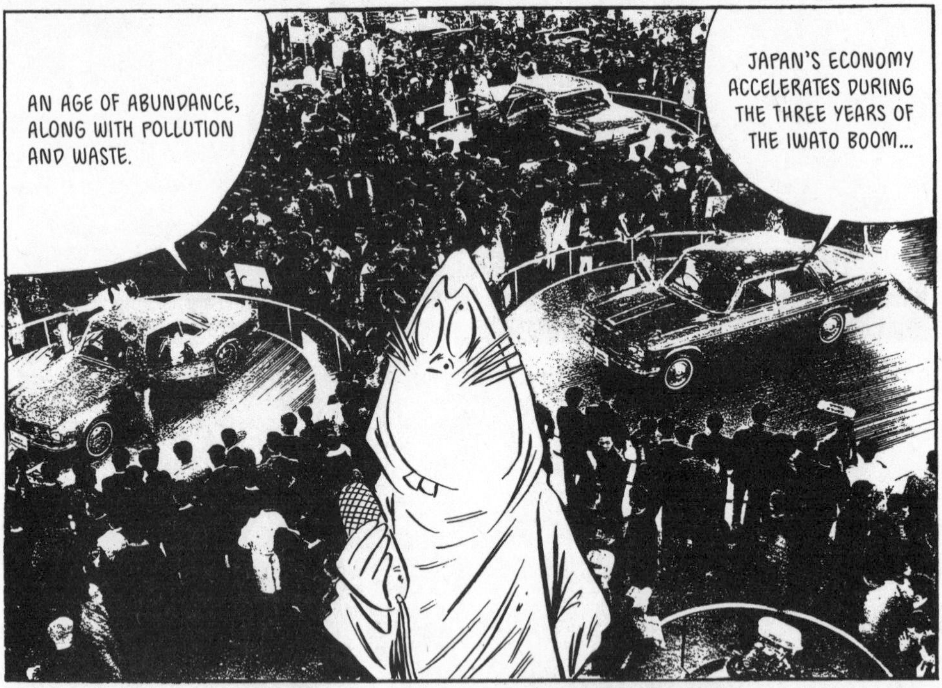
JAPAN'S ECONOMY ACCELERATES DURING THE THREE YEARS OF THE IWATO BOOM...
AN AGE OF ABUNDANCE, ALONG WITH POLLUTION AND WASTE.

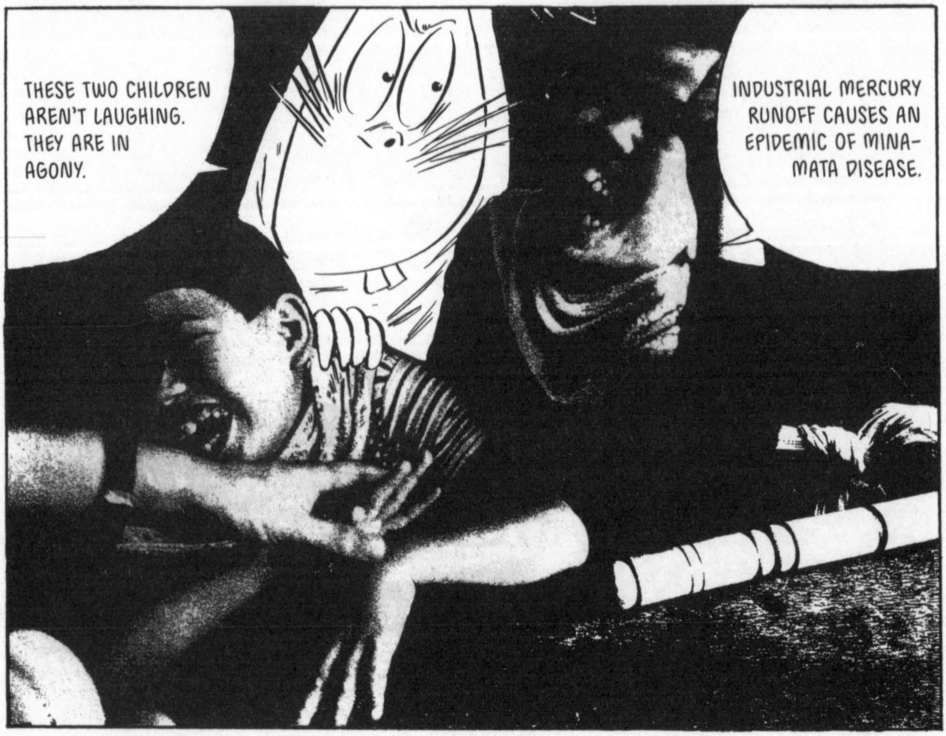
INDUSTRIAL MERCURY RUNOFF CAUSES AN EPIDEMIC OF MINA-MATA DISEASE.
THESE TWO CHILDREN AREN'T LAUGHING. THEY ARE IN AGONY.

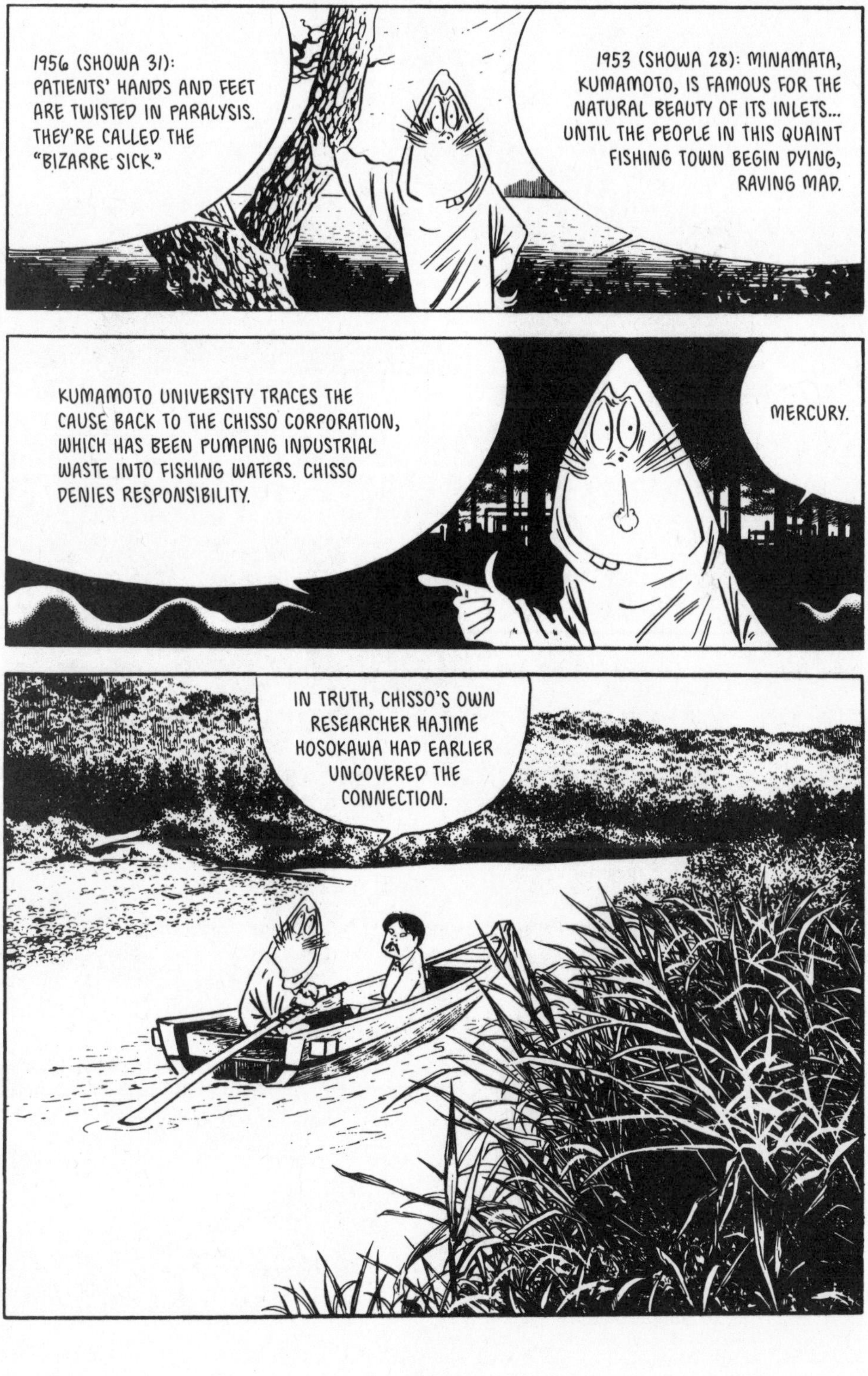
1953 (SHOWA 28): MINAMATA, KUMAMOTO, IS FAMOUS FOR THE NATURAL BEAUTY OF ITS INLETS... UNTIL THE PEOPLE IN THIS QUAINT FISHING TOWN BEGIN DYING, RAVING MAD.
1956 (SHOWA 31): PATIENTS' HANDS AND FEET ARE TWISTED IN PARALYSIS. THEY'RE CALLED THE "BIZARRE SICK."
MERCURY.
KUMAMOTO UNIVERSITY TRACES THE CAUSE BACK TO THE CHISSO CORPORATION, WHICH HAS BEEN PUMPING INDUSTRIAL WASTE INTO FISHING WATERS. CHISSO DENIES RESPONSIBILITY.
IN TRUTH, CHISSO'S OWN RESEARCHER HAJIME HOSOKAWA HAD EARLIER UNCOVERED THE CONNECTION.

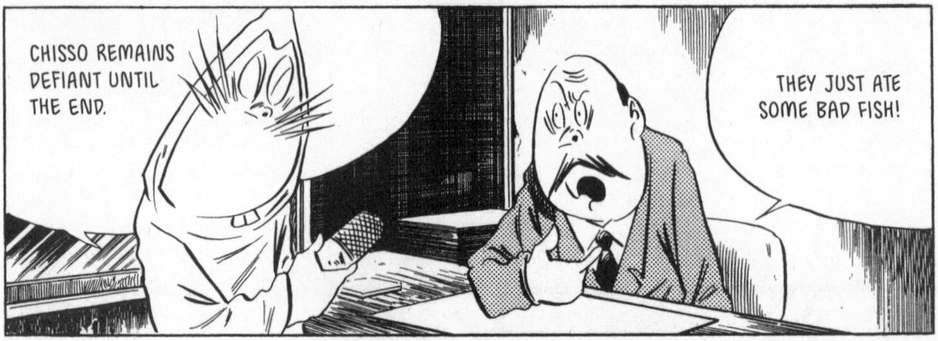
THEY JUST ATE SOME BAD FISH!
CHISSO REMAINS DEFIANT UNTIL THE END.

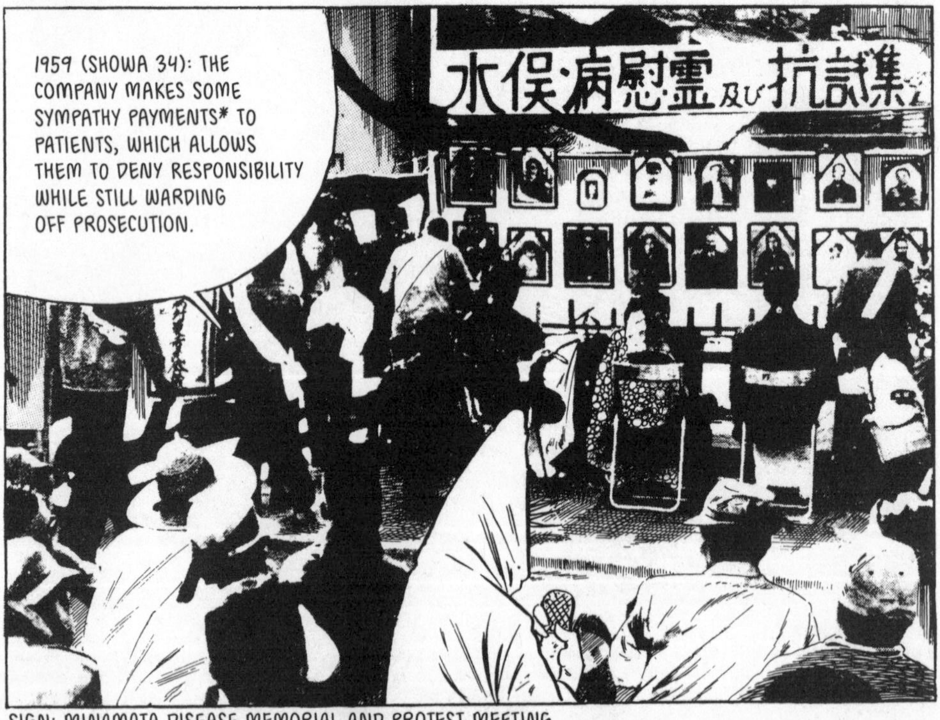
水俣·病慰霊及び抗議集
1959 (SHOWA 34): THE COMPANY MAKES SOME SYMPATHY PAYMENTS* TO PATIENTS, WHICH ALLOWS THEM TO DENY RESPONSIBILITY WHILE STILL WARDING OFF PROSECUTION.

SIGN: MINAMATA DISEASE MEMORIAL AND PROTEST MEETING.

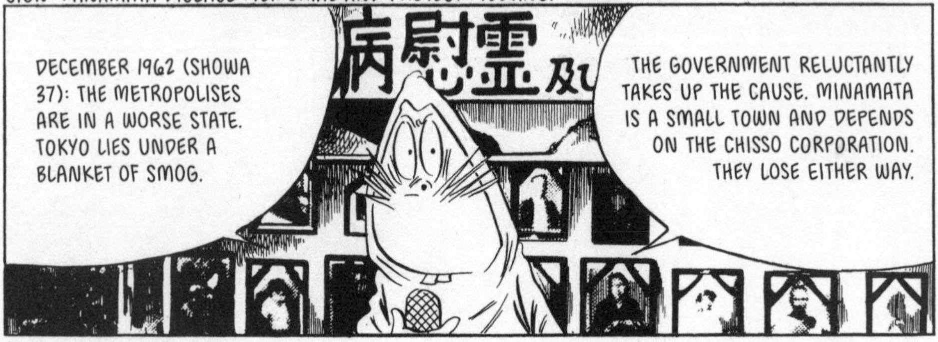
病慰霊及
THE GOVERNMENT RELUCTANTLY TAKES UP THE CAUSE. MINAMATA IS A SMALL TOWN AND DEPENDS ON THE CHISSO CORPORATION. THEY LOSE EITHER WAY.
DECEMBER 1962 (SHOWA 37): THE METROPOLISES ARE IN A WORSE STATE. TOKYO LIES UNDER A BLANKET OF SMOG.

*SEE NOTE ON PAGE 534.

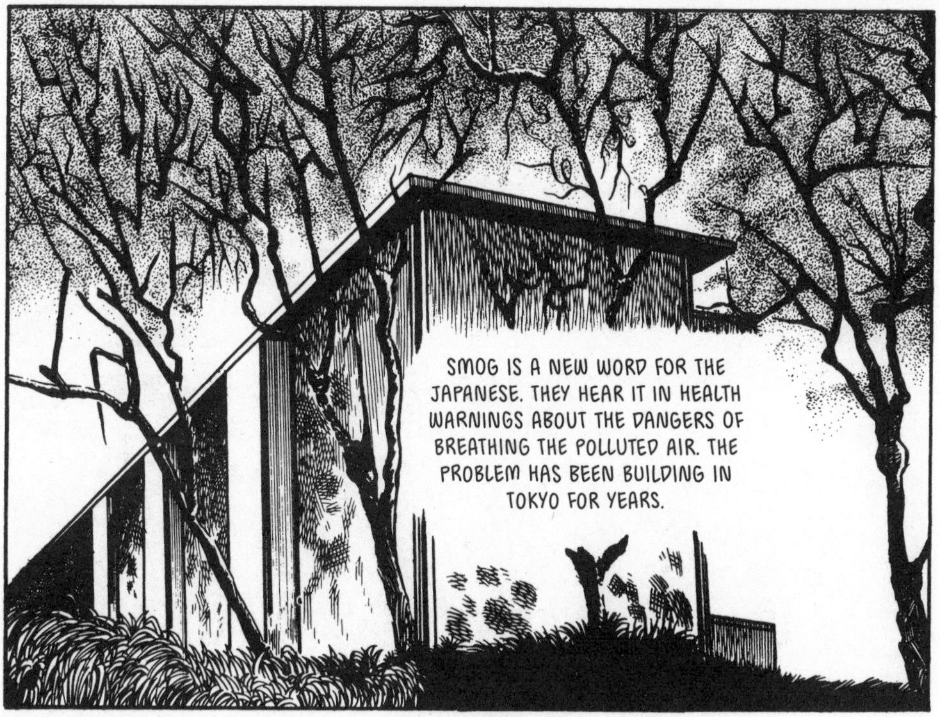
SMOG IS A NEW WORD FOR THE JAPANESE. THEY HEAR IT IN HEALTH WARNINGS ABOUT THE DANGERS OF BREATHING THE POLLUTED AIR. THE PROBLEM HAS BEEN BUILDING IN TOKYO FOR YEARS.

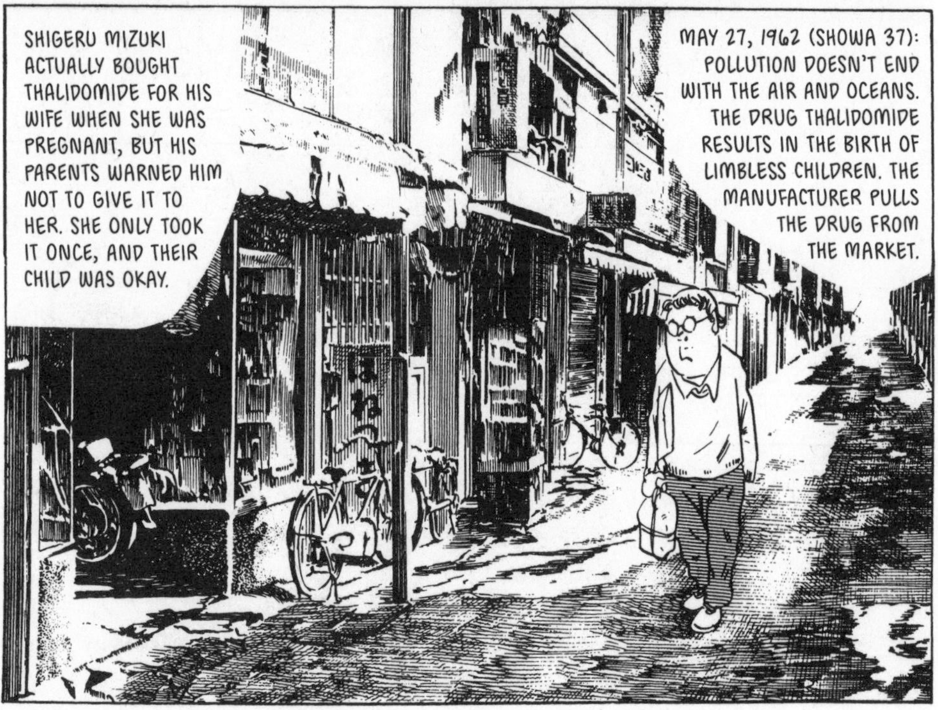
MAY 27, 1962 (SHOWA 37): POLLUTION DOESN'T END WITH THE AIR AND OCEANS. THE DRUG THALIDOMIDE RESULTS IN THE BIRTH OF LIMBLESS CHILDREN. THE MANUFACTURER PULLS THE DRUG FROM THE MARKET.
SHIGERU MIZUKI ACTUALLY BOUGHT THALIDOMIDE FOR HIS WIFE WHEN SHE WAS PREGNANT, BUT HIS PARENTS WARNED HIM NOT TO GIVE IT TO HER. SHE ONLY TOOK IT ONCE, AND THEIR CHILD WAS OKAY.

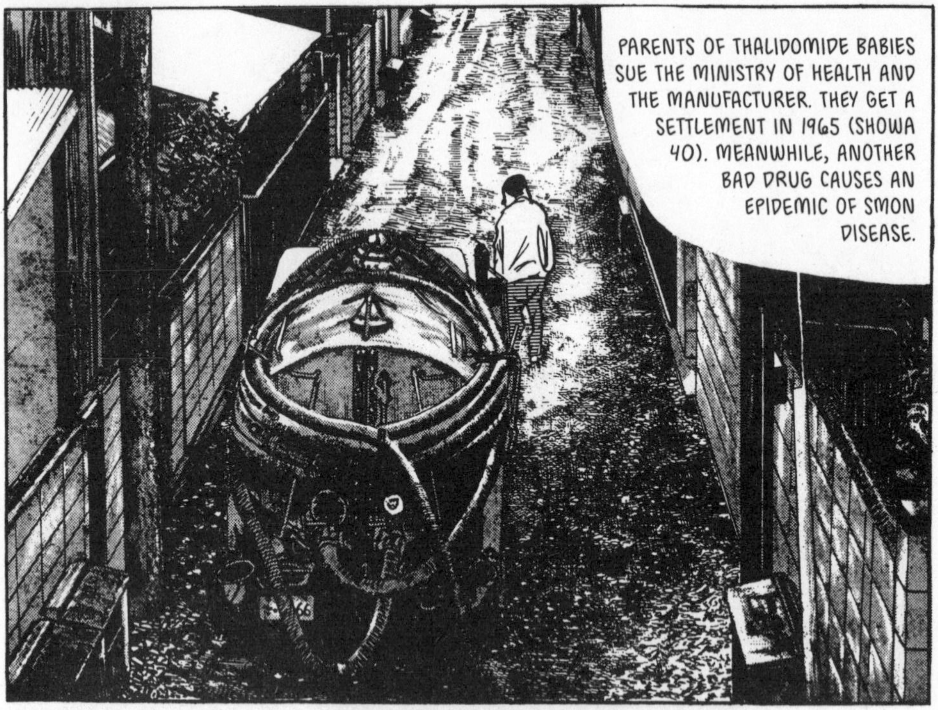
PARENTS OF THALIDOMIDE BABIES SUE THE MINISTRY OF HEALTH AND THE MANUFACTURER. THEY GET A SETTLEMENT IN 1965 (SHOWA 40). MEANWHILE, ANOTHER BAD DRUG CAUSES AN EPIDEMIC OF SMON DISEASE.

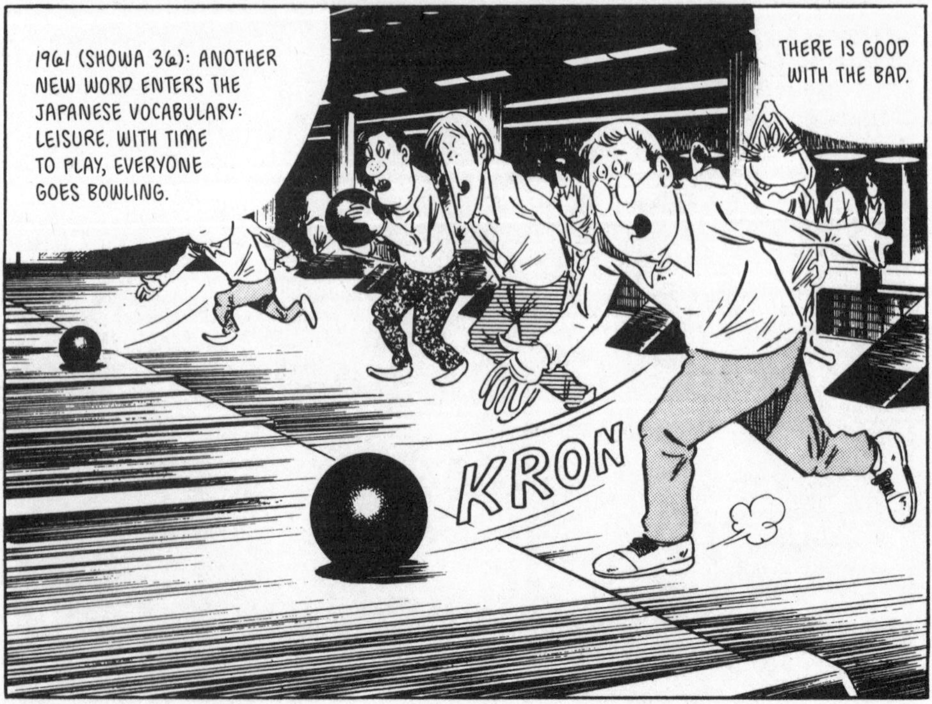
THERE IS GOOD WITH THE BAD.
1961 (SHOWA 36): ANOTHER NEW WORD ENTERS THE JAPANESE VOCABULARY: LEISURE. WITH TIME TO PLAY, EVERYONE GOES BOWLING.
KRON

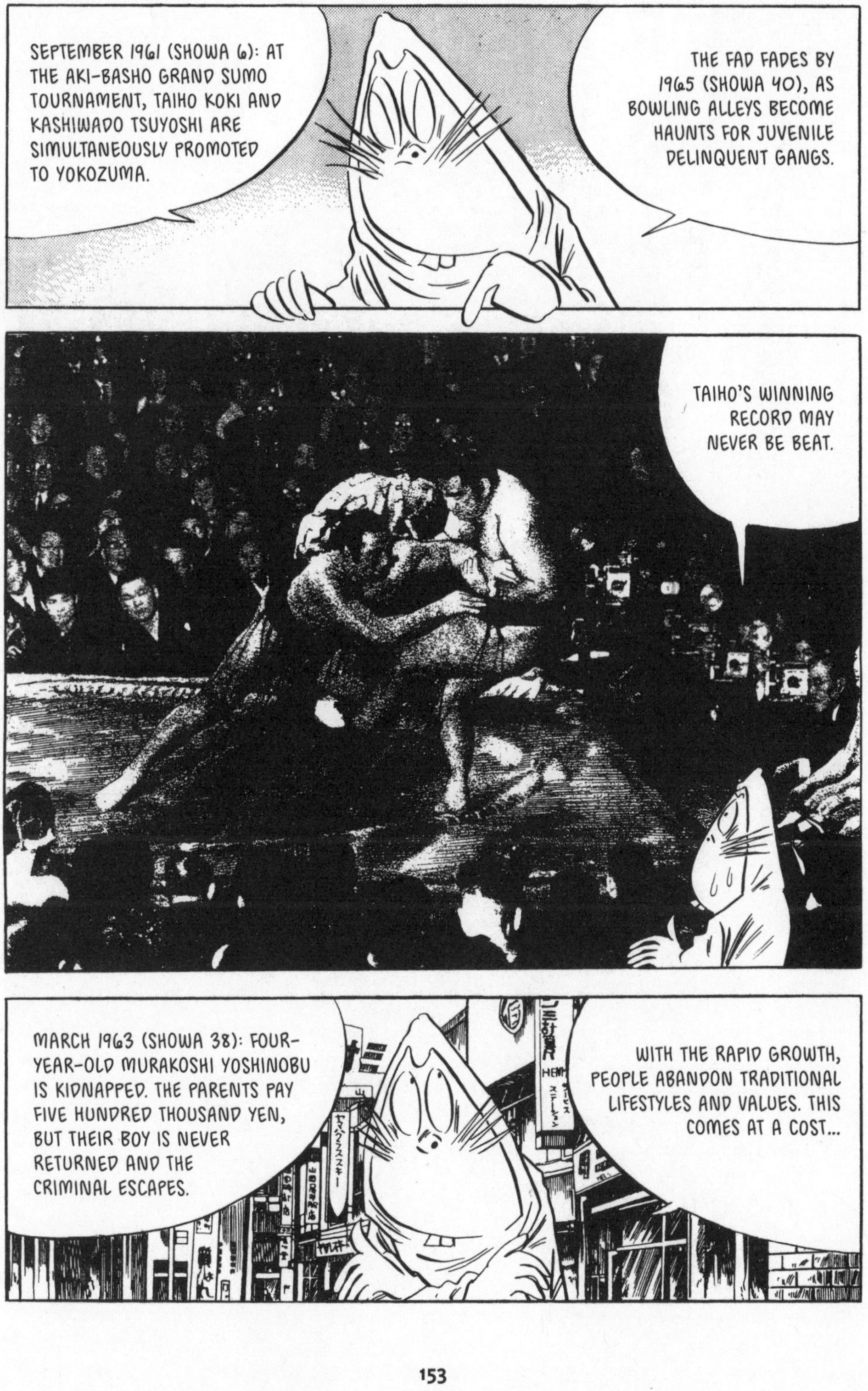
THE FAD FADES BY 1965 (SHOWA 40), AS BOWLING ALLEYS BECOME HAUNTS FOR JUVENILE DELINQUENT GANGS.
SEPTEMBER 1961 (SHOWA 6): AT THE AKI-BASHO GRAND SUMO TOURNAMENT, TAIHO KOKI AND KASHIWADO TSUYOSHI ARE SIMULTANEOUSLY PROMOTED TO YOKOZUMA.
TAIHO'S WINNING RECORD MAY NEVER BE BEAT.
WITH THE RAPID GROWTH, PEOPLE ABANDON TRADITIONAL LIFESTYLES AND VALUES. THIS COMES AT A COST...
MARCH 1963 (SHOWA 38): FOUR-YEAR-OLD MURAKOSHI YOSHINOBU IS KIDNAPPED. THE PARENTS PAY FIVE HUNDRED THOUSAND YEN, BUT THEIR BOY IS NEVER RETURNED AND THE CRIMINAL ESCAPES.

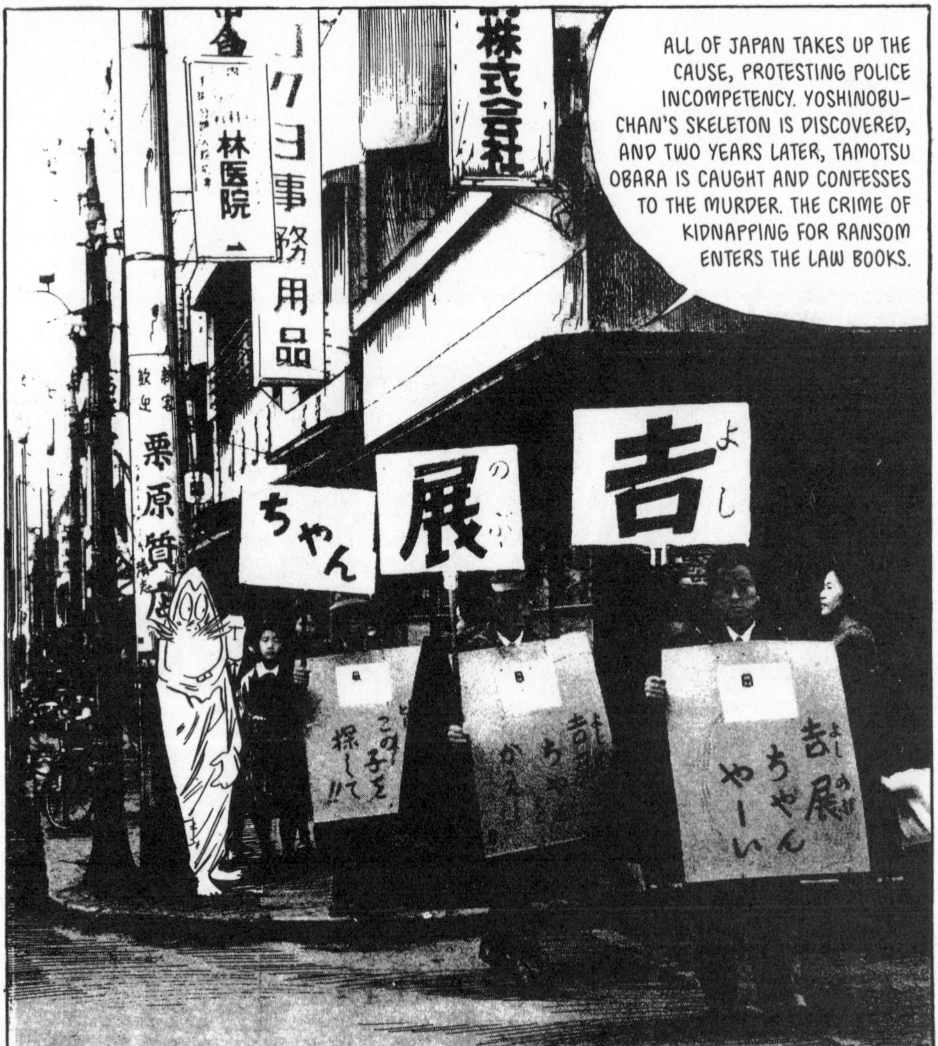
ALL OF JAPAN TAKES UP THE CAUSE, PROTESTING POLICE INCOMPETENCY. YOSHINOBU-CHAN'S SKELETON IS DISCOVERED, AND TWO YEARS LATER, TAMOTSU OBARA IS CAUGHT AND CONFESSES TO THE MURDER. THE CRIME OF KIDNAPPING FOR RANSOM ENTERS THE LAW BOOKS.
株式会社
林医院
事務用品
吉展ちゃん
吉展ちゃんやーい
この子を探して!!

SIGNS: YOSHINOBU-CHAN, HELLO YOSHINOBU, WE ARE LOOKING FOR YOU.

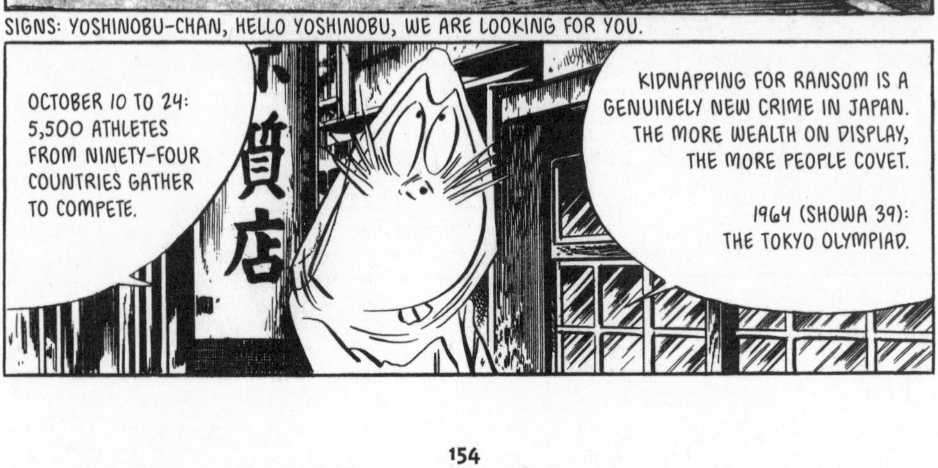
KIDNAPPING FOR RANSOM IS A GENUINELY NEW CRIME IN JAPAN. THE MORE WEALTH ON DISPLAY, THE MORE PEOPLE COVET.
1964 (SHOWA 39): THE TOKYO OLYMPIAD.
質店
OCTOBER 10 TO 24: 5,500 ATHLETES FROM NINETY-FOUR COUNTRIES GATHER TO COMPETE.

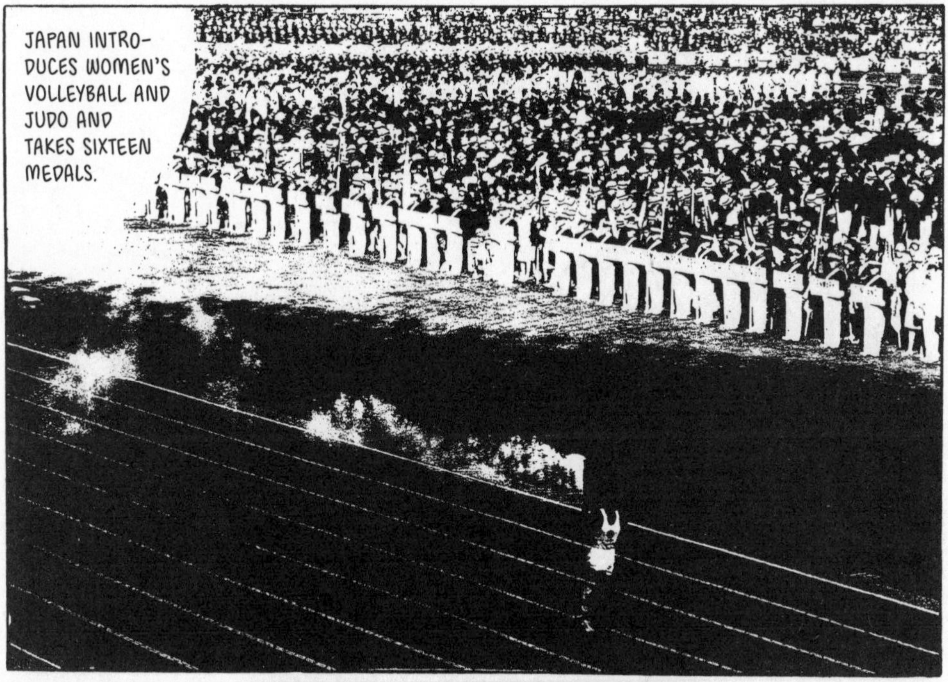
JAPAN INTRODUCES WOMEN'S VOLLEYBALL AND JUDO AND TAKES SIXTEEN MEDALS.

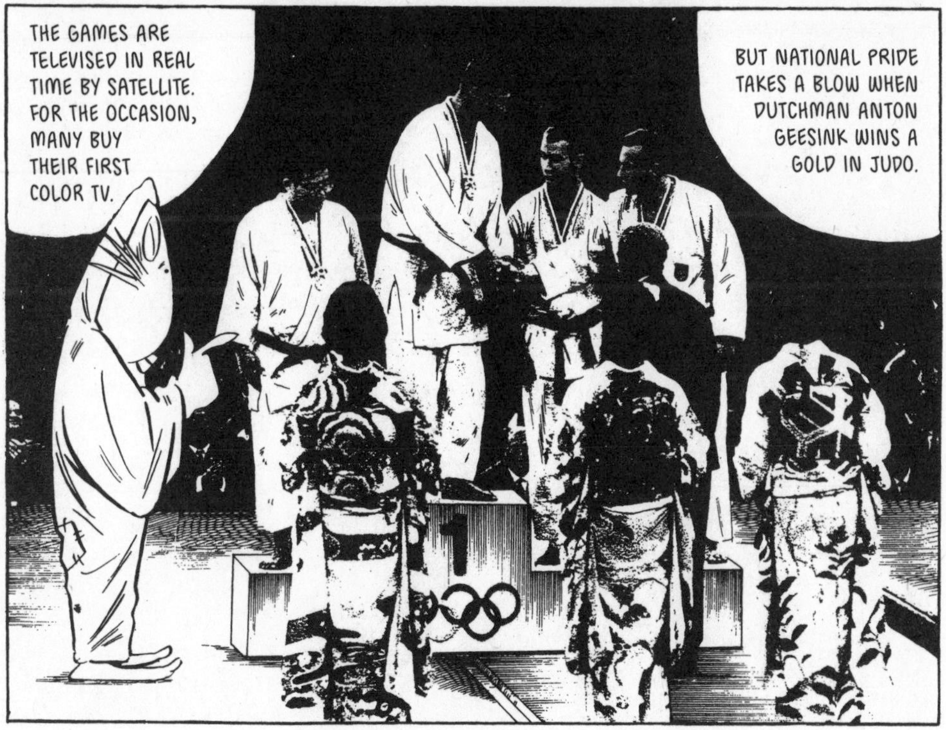
BUT NATIONAL PRIDE TAKES A BLOW WHEN DUTCHMAN ANTON GEESINK WINS A GOLD IN JUDO.
THE GAMES ARE TELEVISED IN REAL TIME BY SATELLITE. FOR THE OCCASION, MANY BUY THEIR FIRST COLOR TV.

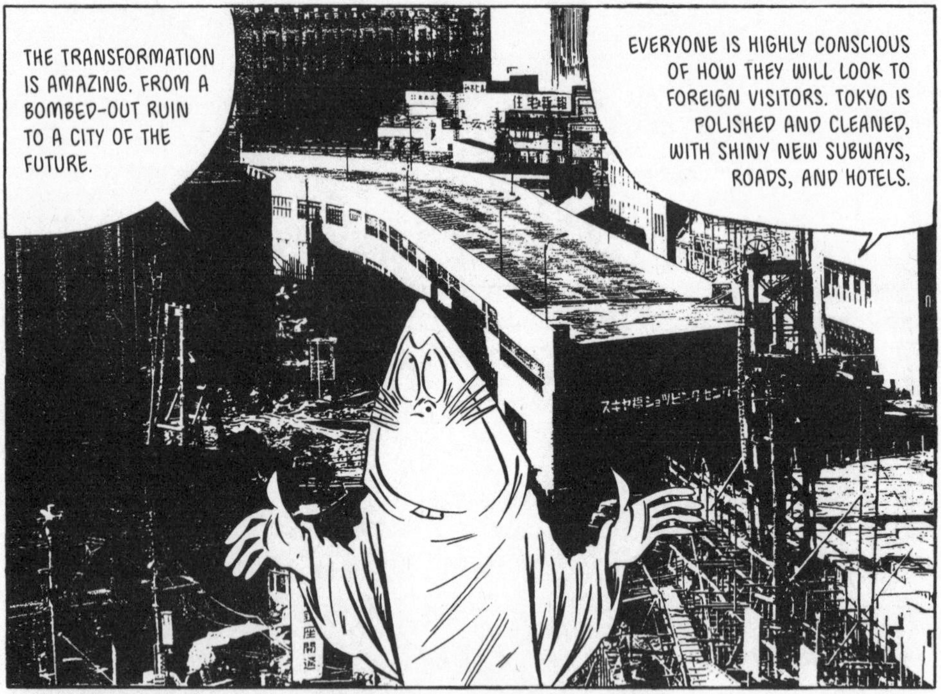
EVERYONE IS HIGHLY CONSCIOUS OF HOW THEY WILL LOOK TO FOREIGN VISITORS. TOKYO IS POLISHED AND CLEANED, WITH SHINY NEW SUBWAYS, ROADS, AND HOTELS.
THE TRANSFORMATION IS AMAZING. FROM A BOMBED-OUT RUIN TO A CITY OF THE FUTURE.

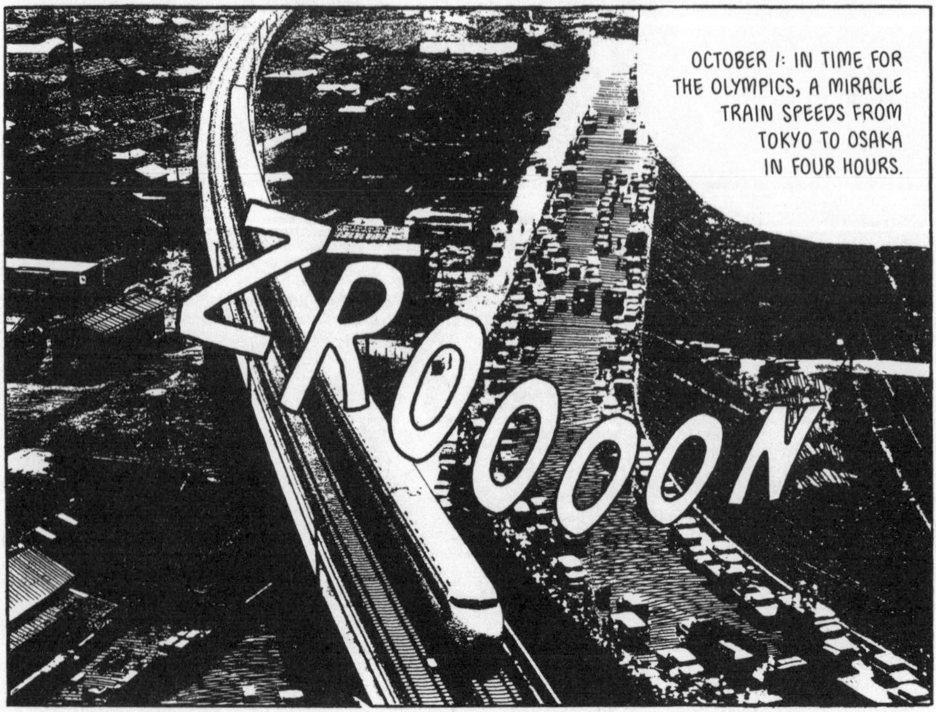
OCTOBER 1: IN TIME FOR THE OLYMPICS, A MIRACLE TRAIN SPEEDS FROM TOKYO TO OSAKA IN FOUR HOURS.
ZROOOOON

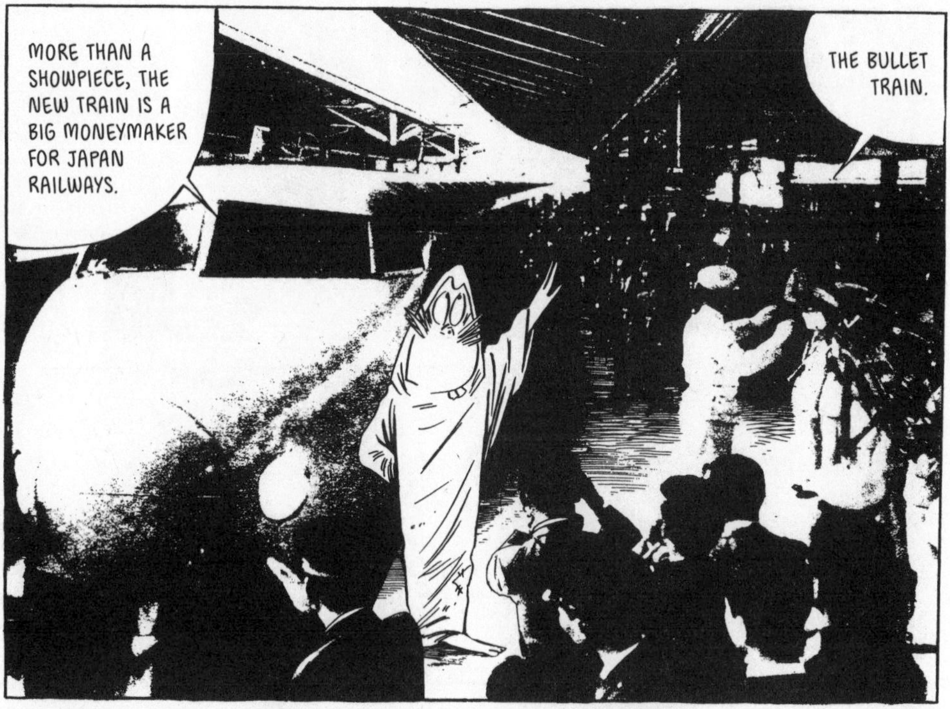
THE BULLET TRAIN.
MORE THAN A SHOWPIECE, THE NEW TRAIN IS A BIG MONEYMAKER FOR JAPAN RAILWAYS.

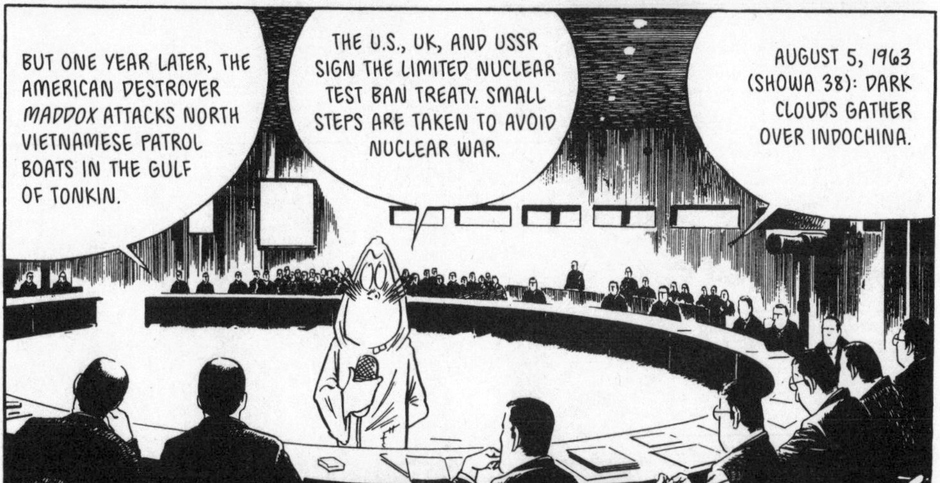
AUGUST 5, 1963 (SHOWA 38): DARK CLOUDS GATHER OVER INDOCHINA.
THE U.S., UK, AND USSR SIGN THE LIMITED NUCLEAR TEST BAN TREATY. SMALL STEPS ARE TAKEN TO AVOID NUCLEAR WAR.
BUT ONE YEAR LATER, THE AMERICAN DESTROYER *MADDOX* ATTACKS NORTH VIETNAMESE PATROL BOATS IN THE GULF OF TONKIN.

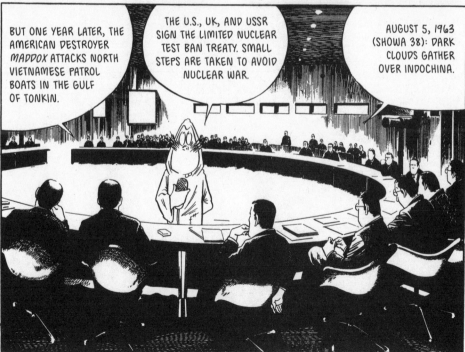

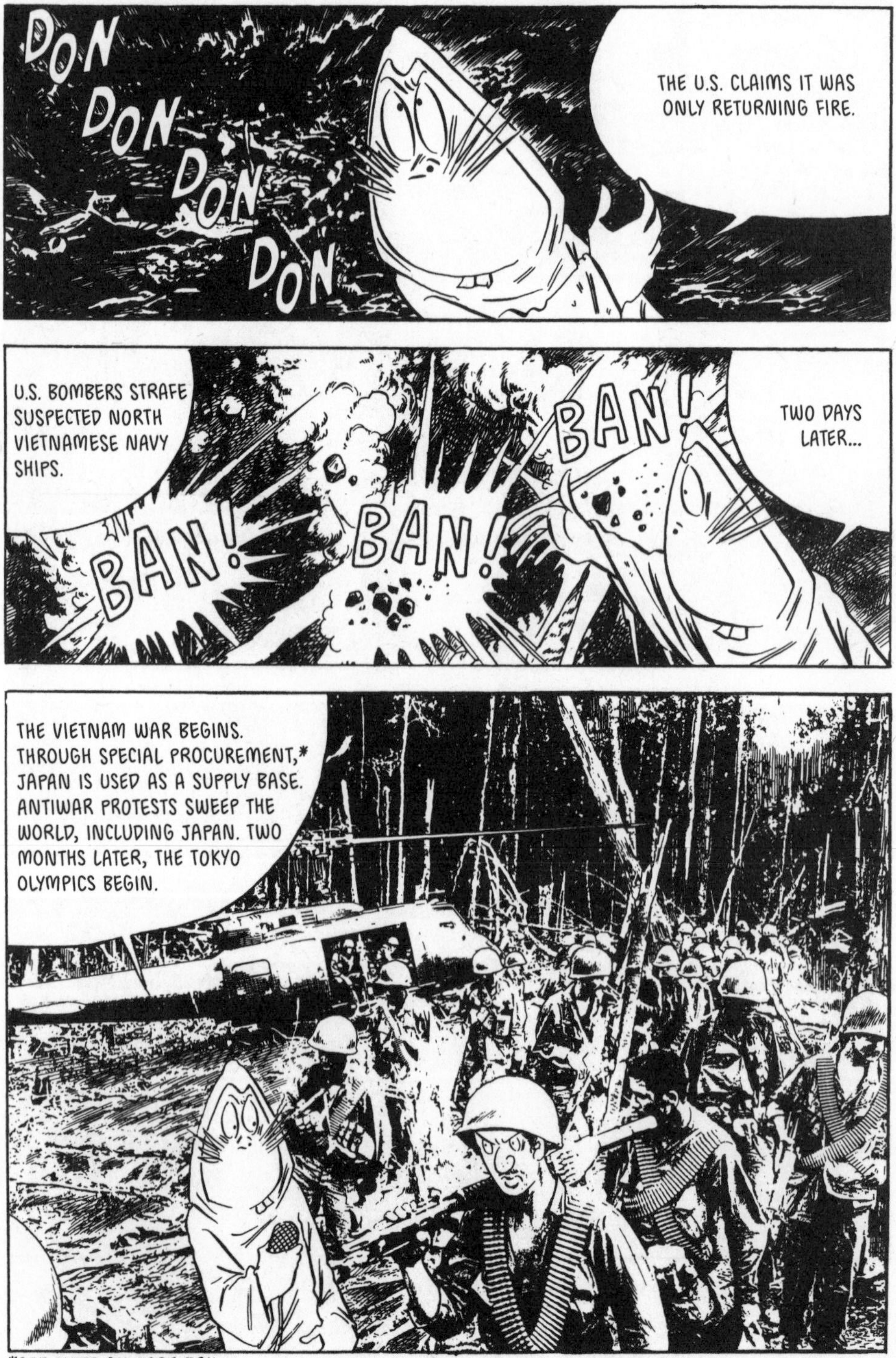
THE U.S. CLAIMS IT WAS ONLY RETURNING FIRE.
DON DON DON DON DON
TWO DAYS LATER...
BAN!
U.S. BOMBERS STRAFE SUSPECTED NORTH VIETNAMESE NAVY SHIPS.
BAN!
BAN!
THE VIETNAM WAR BEGINS. THROUGH SPECIAL PROCUREMENT,* JAPAN IS USED AS A SUPPLY BASE. ANTIWAR PROTESTS SWEEP THE WORLD, INCLUDING JAPAN. TWO MONTHS LATER, THE TOKYO OLYMPICS BEGIN.

*SEE NOTE ON PAGE 534.

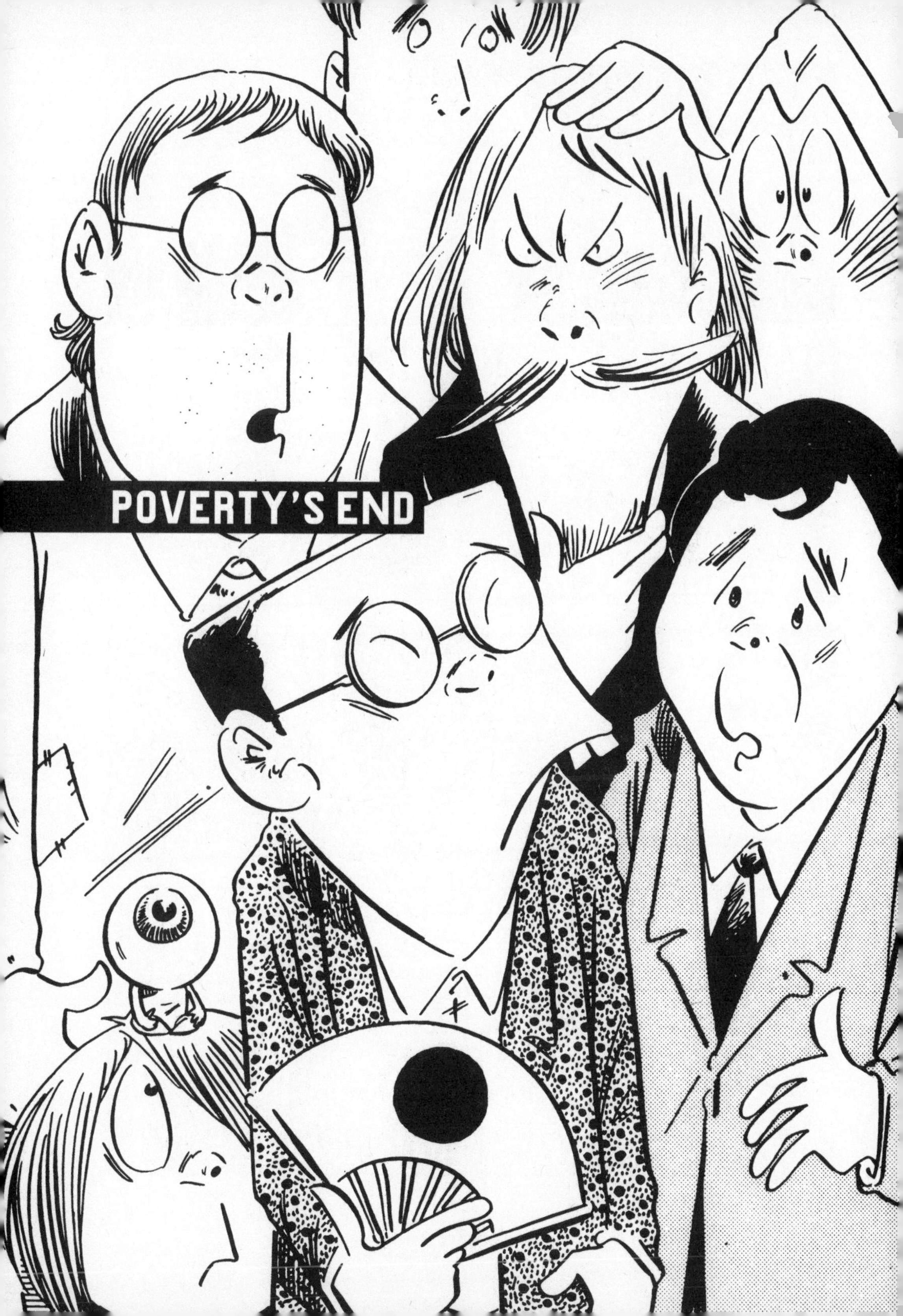
POVERTY'S END

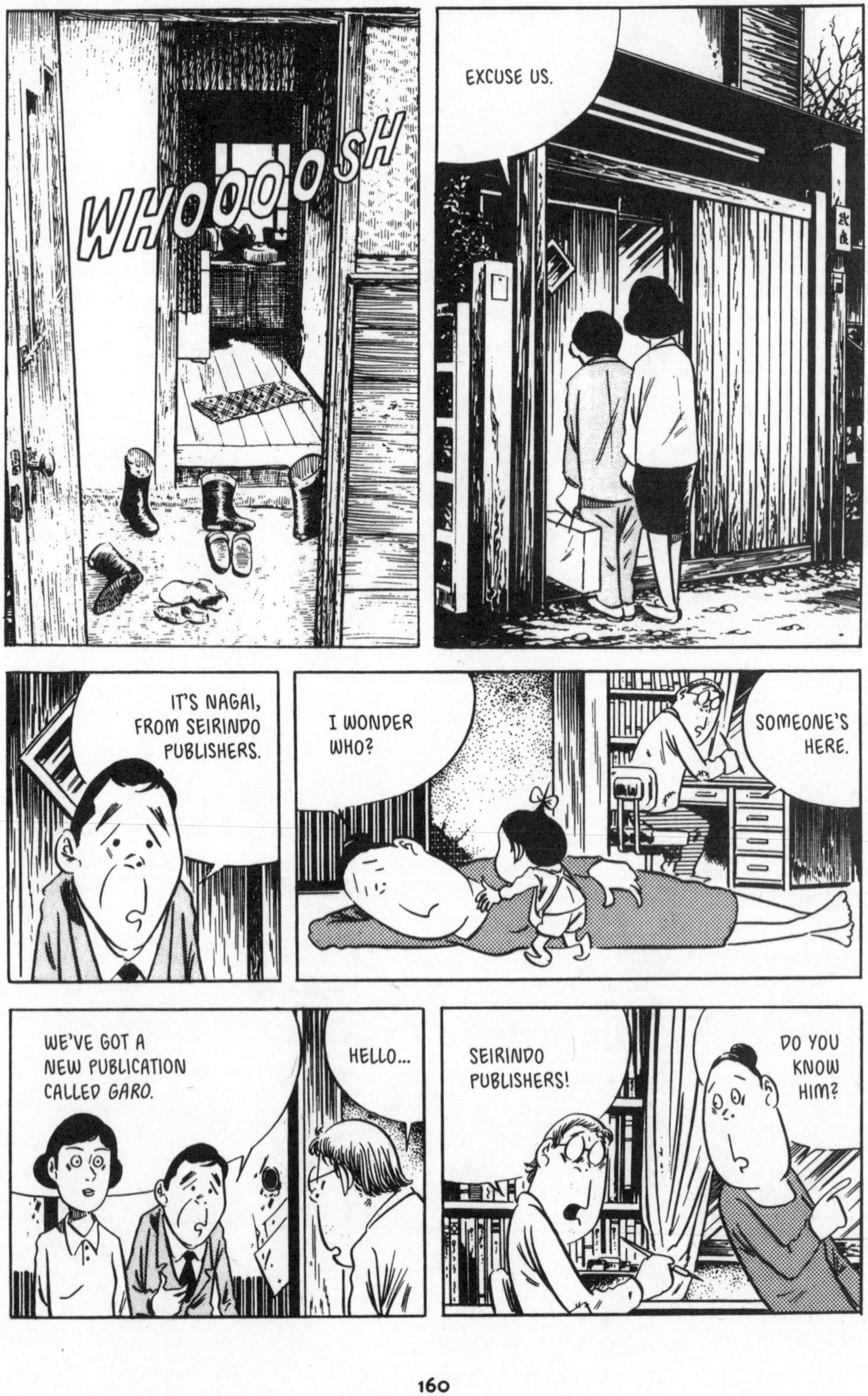
EXCUSE US.
WHOOOOOSH
SOMEONE'S HERE.
I WONDER WHO?
IT'S NAGAI, FROM SEIRINDO PUBLISHERS.
DO YOU KNOW HIM?
SEIRINDO PUBLISHERS!
HELLO...
WE'VE GOT A NEW PUBLICATION CALLED GARO.

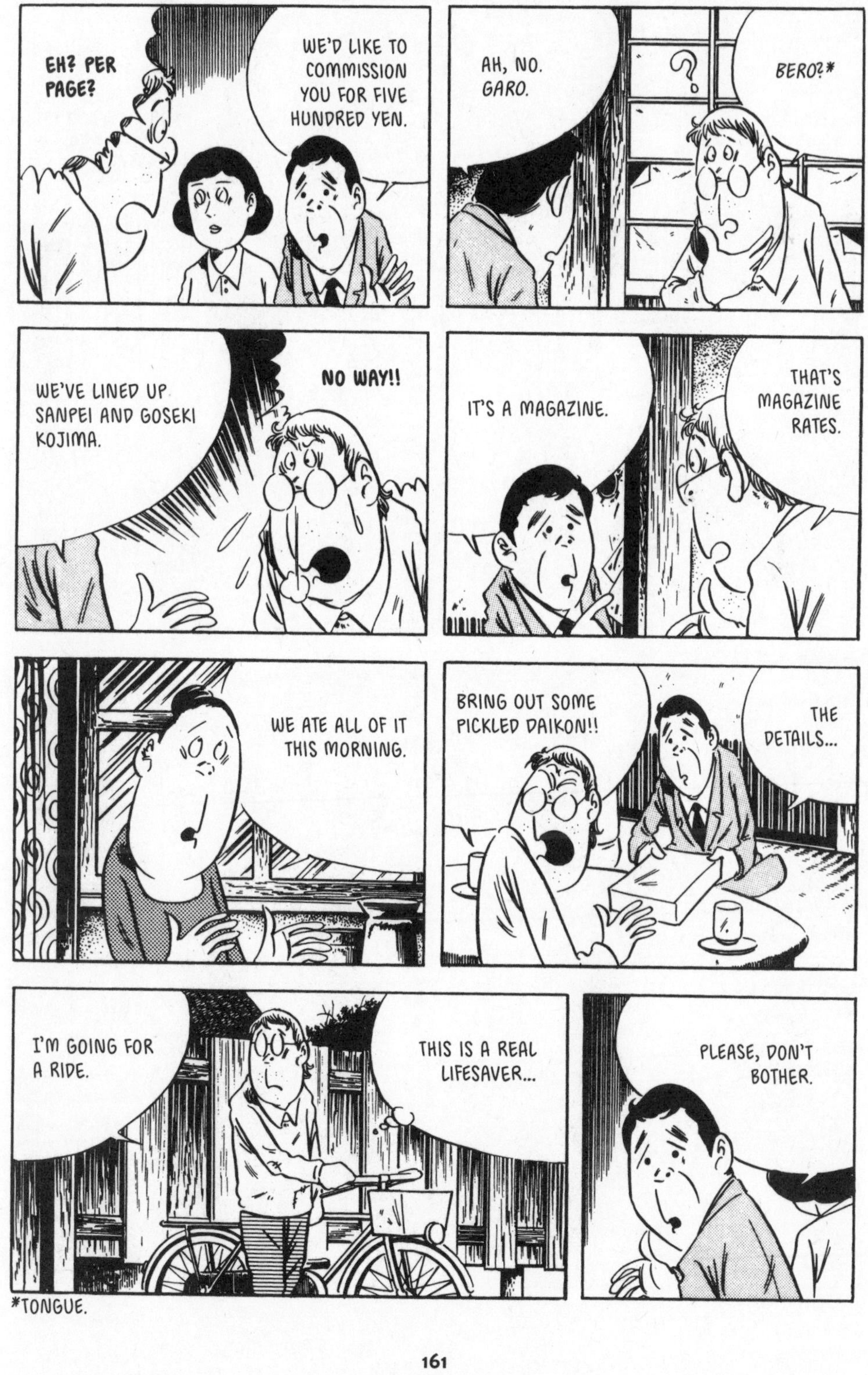
BERO?*
AH, NO. GARO.
WE'D LIKE TO COMMISSION YOU FOR FIVE HUNDRED YEN.
EH? PER PAGE?
THAT'S MAGAZINE RATES.
IT'S A MAGAZINE.
NO WAY!!
WE'VE LINED UP SANPEI AND GOSEKI KOJIMA.
THE DETAILS...
BRING OUT SOME PICKLED DAIKON!!
WE ATE ALL OF IT THIS MORNING.
PLEASE, DON'T BOTHER.
THIS IS A REAL LIFESAVER...
I'M GOING FOR A RIDE.

*TONGUE.

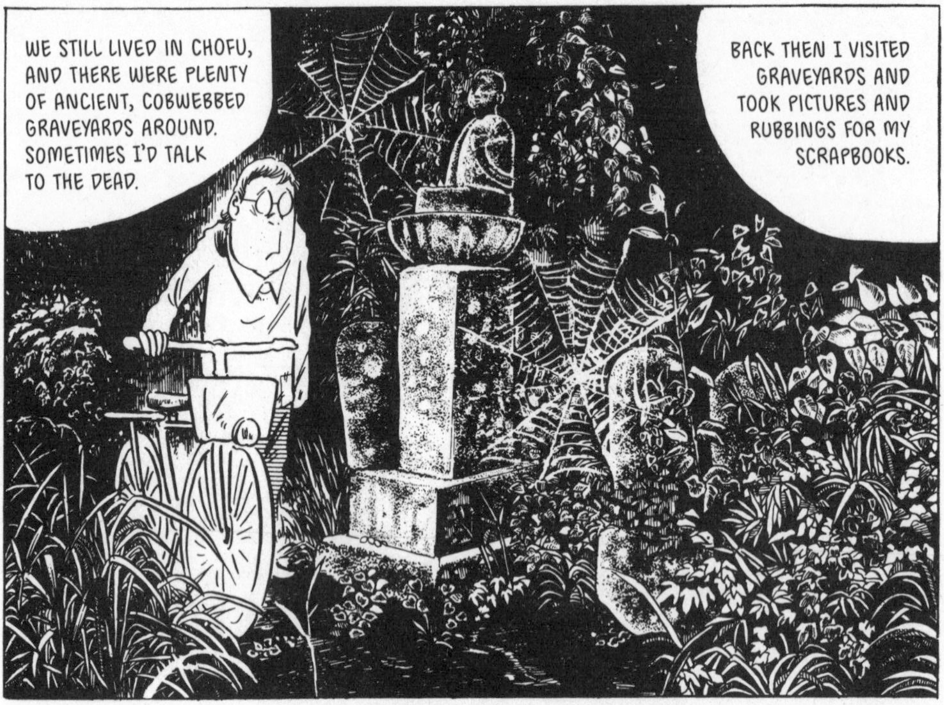
BACK THEN I VISITED GRAVEYARDS AND TOOK PICTURES AND RUBBINGS FOR MY SCRAPBOOKS.
WE STILL LIVED IN CHOFU, AND THERE WERE PLENTY OF ANCIENT, COBWEBBED GRAVEYARDS AROUND. SOMETIMES I'D TALK TO THE DEAD.

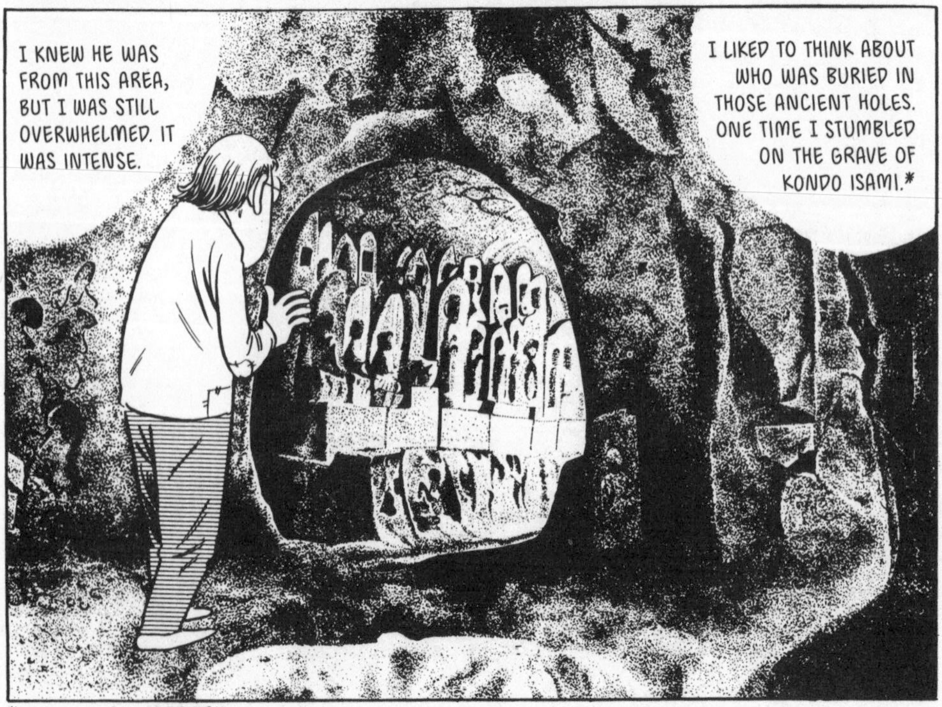
I LIKED TO THINK ABOUT WHO WAS BURIED IN THOSE ANCIENT HOLES. ONE TIME I STUMBLED ON THE GRAVE OF KONDO ISAMI.*
I KNEW HE WAS FROM THIS AREA, BUT I WAS STILL OVERWHELMED. IT WAS INTENSE.

*SEE NOTE ON PAGE 534.

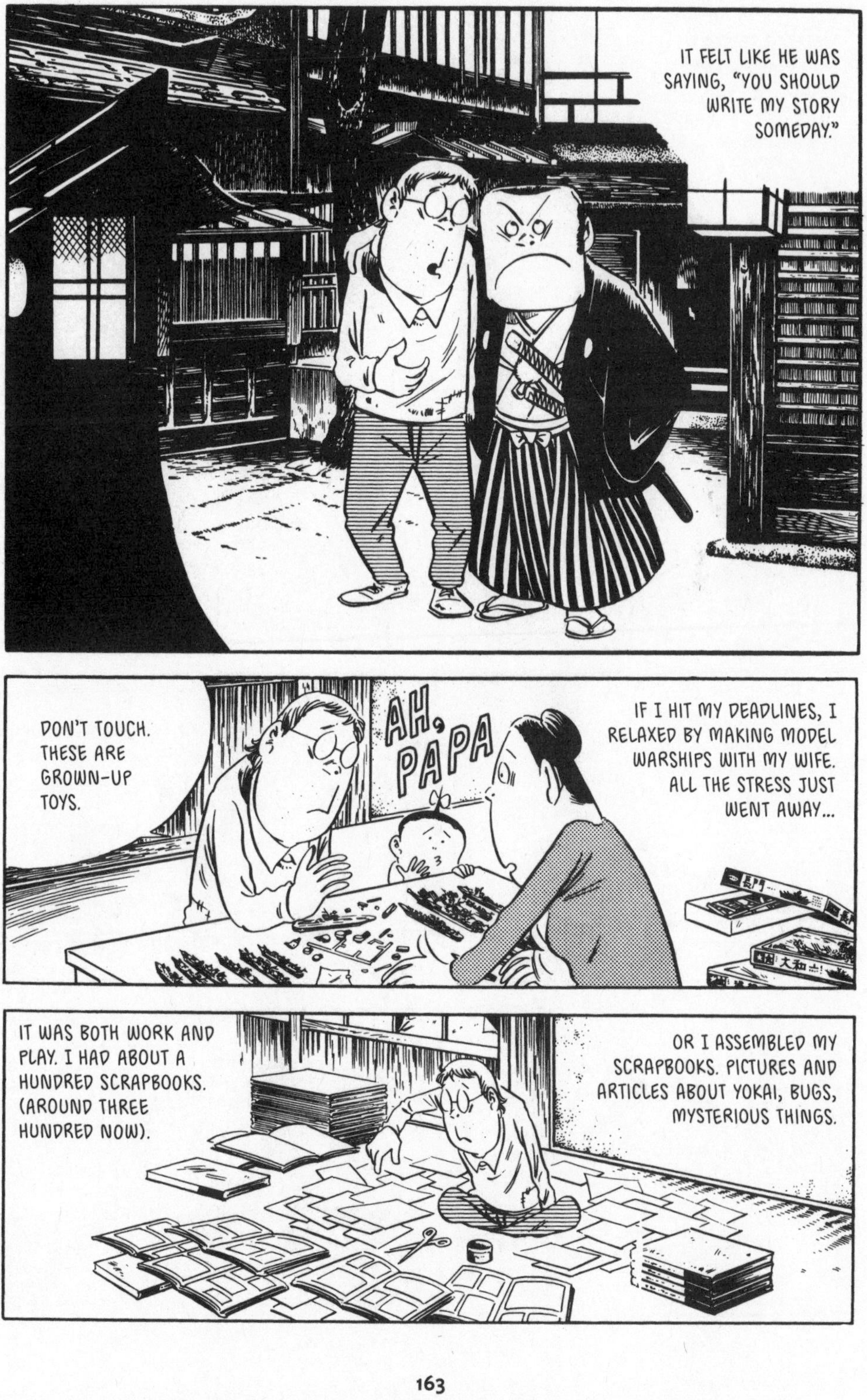
IT FELT LIKE HE WAS SAYING, "YOU SHOULD WRITE MY STORY SOMEDAY."
IF I HIT MY DEADLINES, I RELAXED BY MAKING MODEL WARSHIPS WITH MY WIFE. ALL THE STRESS JUST WENT AWAY...
AH, PAPA
DON'T TOUCH. THESE ARE GROWN-UP TOYS.
OR I ASSEMBLED MY SCRAPBOOKS. PICTURES AND ARTICLES ABOUT YOKAI, BUGS, MYSTERIOUS THINGS.
IT WAS BOTH WORK AND PLAY. I HAD ABOUT A HUNDRED SCRAPBOOKS. (AROUND THREE HUNDRED NOW).

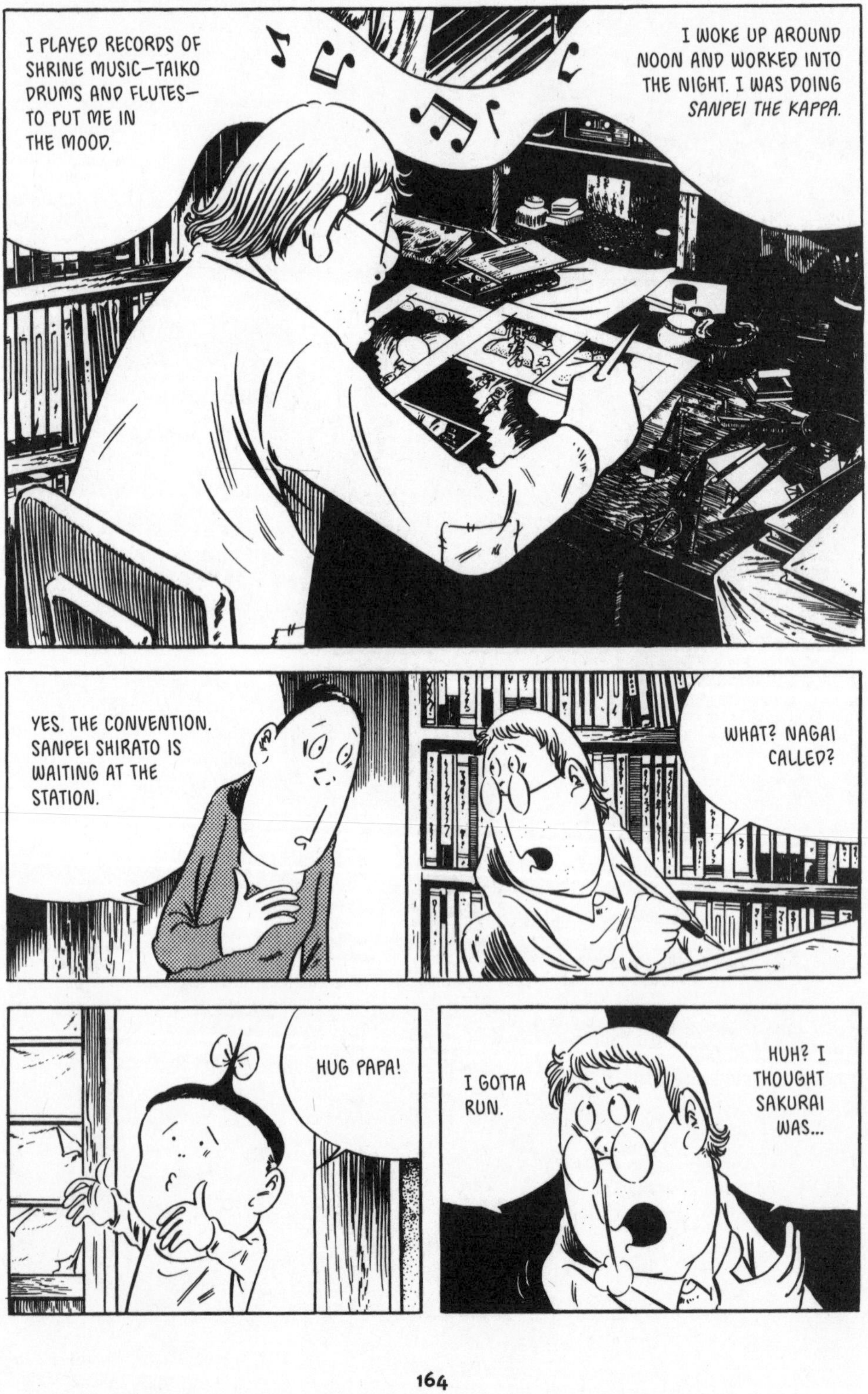
I WOKE UP AROUND NOON AND WORKED INTO THE NIGHT. I WAS DOING *SANPEI THE KAPPA.*
I PLAYED RECORDS OF SHRINE MUSIC—TAIKO DRUMS AND FLUTES—TO PUT ME IN THE MOOD.
WHAT? NAGAI CALLED?
YES. THE CONVENTION. SANPEI SHIRATO IS WAITING AT THE STATION.
HUH? I THOUGHT SAKURAI WAS...
I GOTTA RUN.
HUG PAPA!

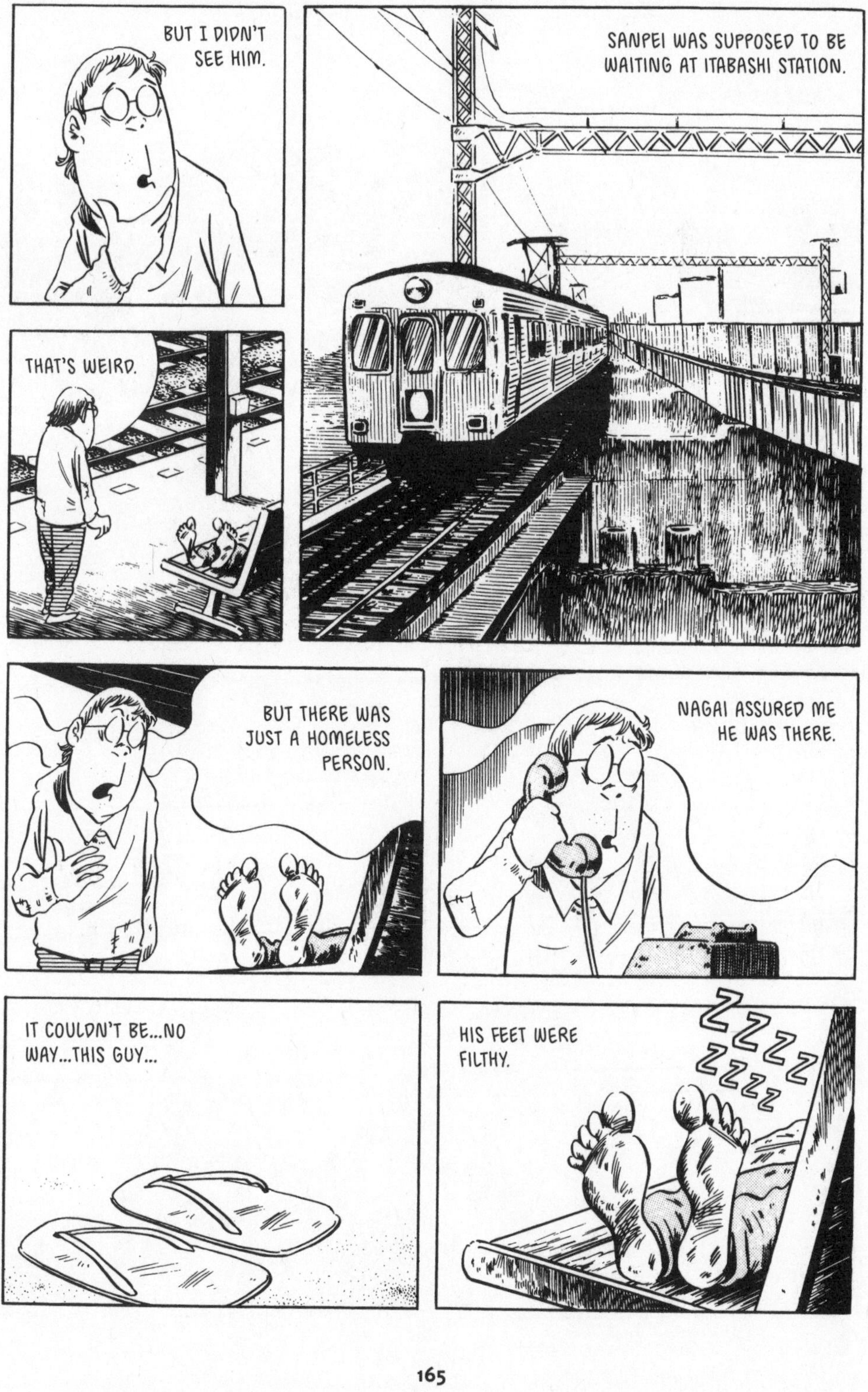
SANPEI WAS SUPPOSED TO BE WAITING AT ITABASHI STATION.
BUT I DIDN'T SEE HIM.
THAT'S WEIRD.
NAGAI ASSURED ME HE WAS THERE.
BUT THERE WAS JUST A HOMELESS PERSON.
HIS FEET WERE FILTHY.
ZZZZ ZZZZ
IT COULDN'T BE...NO WAY...THIS GUY...

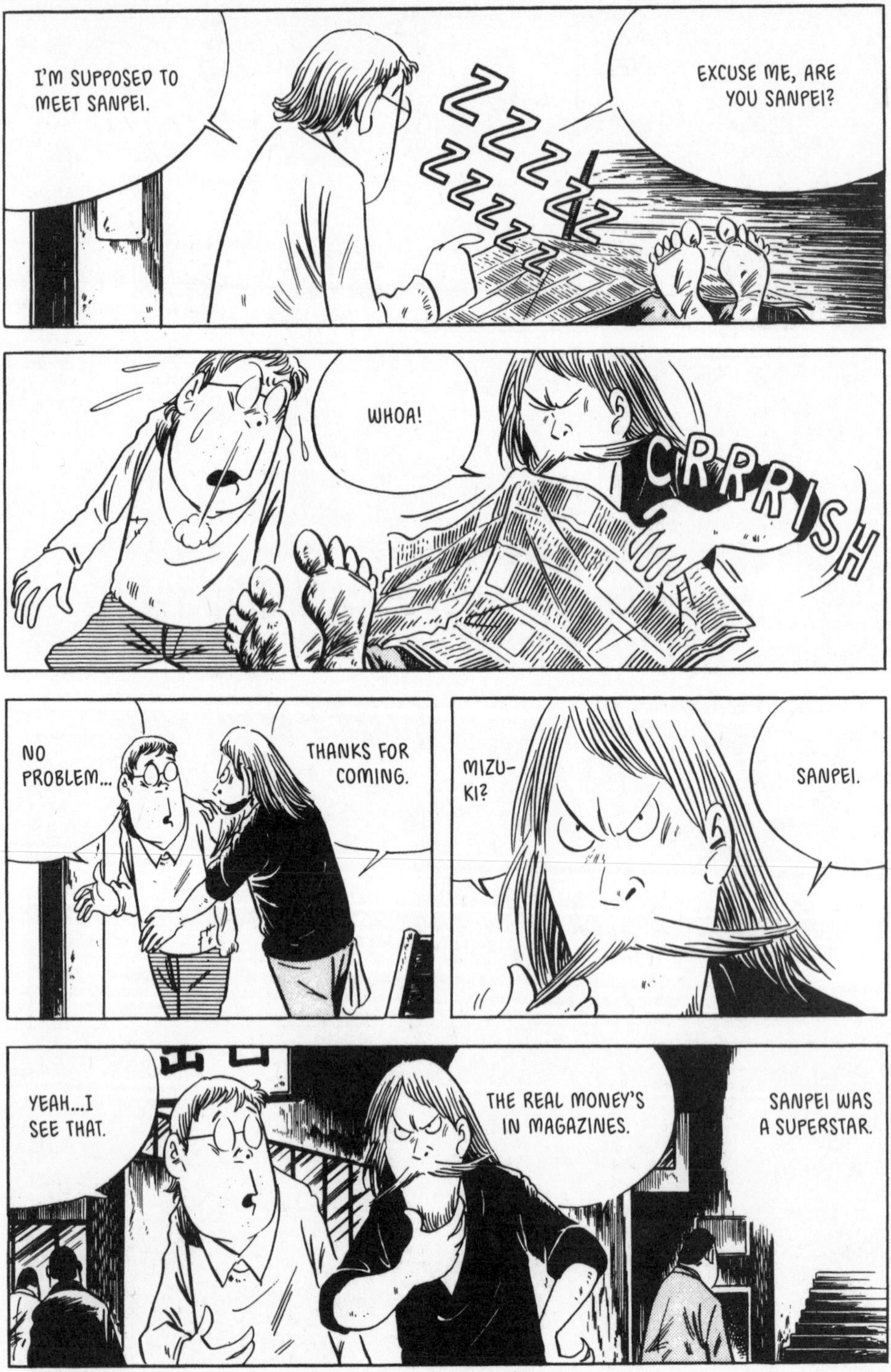
EXCUSE ME, ARE YOU SANPEI?
I'M SUPPOSED TO MEET SANPEI.
CRRRISH
WHOA!
SANPEI.
MIZU-KI?
THANKS FOR COMING.
NO PROBLEM...
SANPEI WAS A SUPERSTAR.
THE REAL MONEY'S IN MAGAZINES.
YEAH...I SEE THAT.

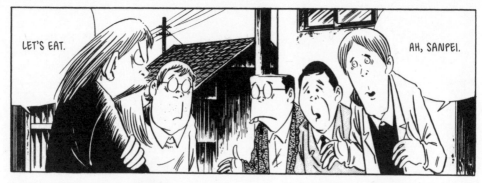

AH, SANPEI.
LET'S EAT.
I WANT...
SPAGHETTI.
I KNOW A PLACE.
I HOPE IT'S NOT EXPENSIVE...
SANPEI TREATED ALL OF US. HE WAS LOADED.
MANGA ARTISTS COULDN'T IMAGINE THAT KIND OF MONEY.
SLURP SLURP SLURP
OSAMU TEZUKA AND SHOTARO ISHINOMORI WERE THERE.
AFTER THE Q&A, WE ALL WENT HOME.

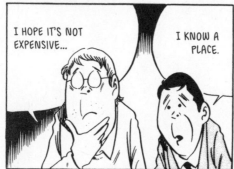

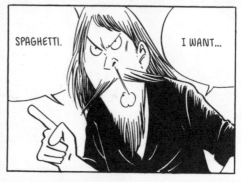

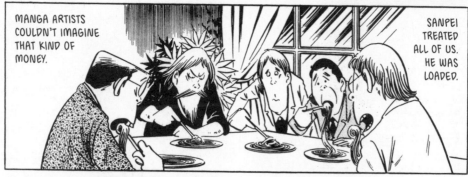

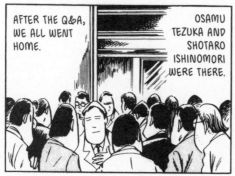

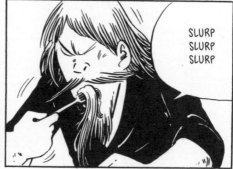

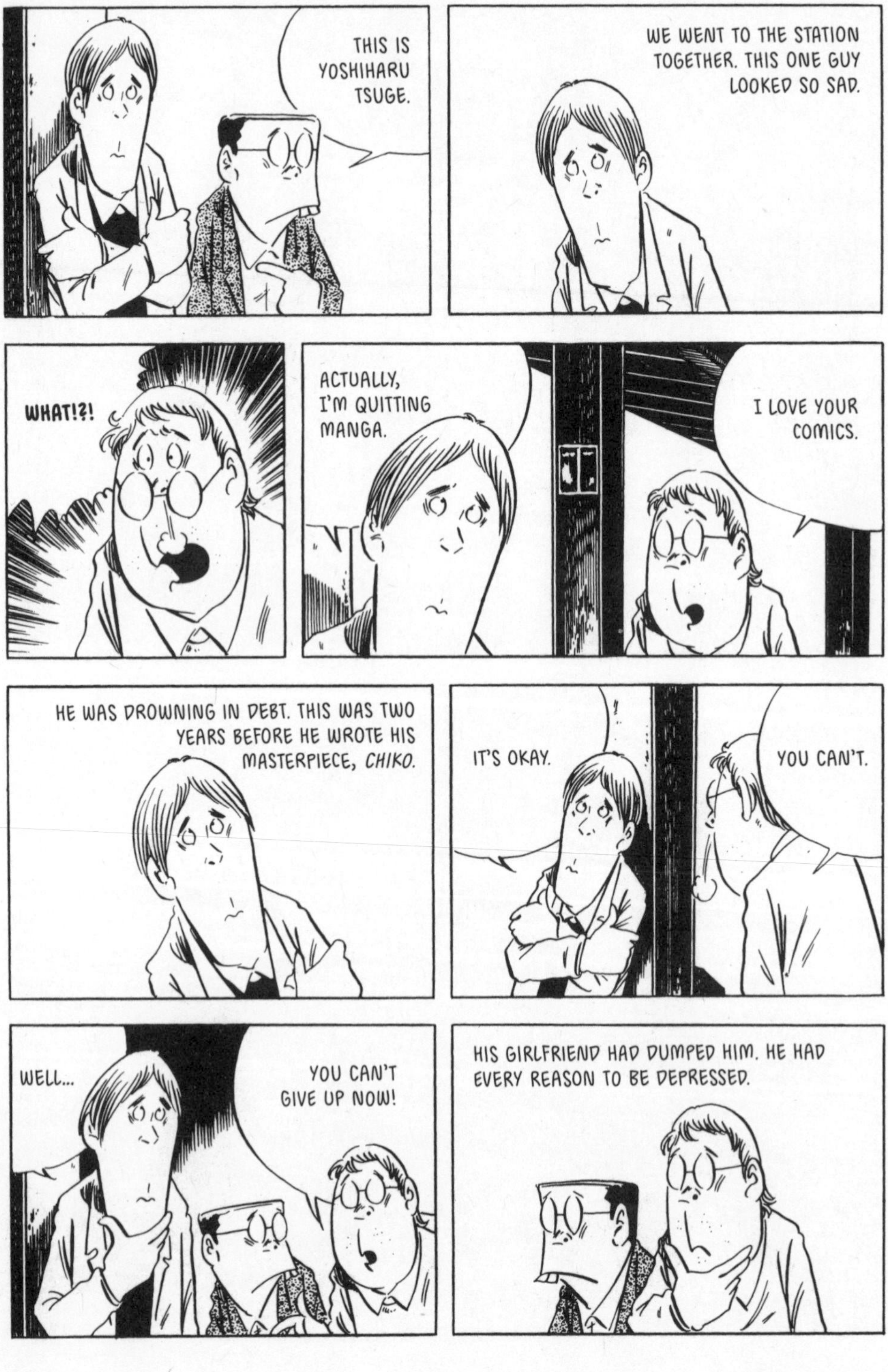
WE WENT TO THE STATION TOGETHER. THIS ONE GUY LOOKED SO SAD.
THIS IS YOSHIHARU TSUGE.
I LOVE YOUR COMICS.
ACTUALLY, I'M QUITTING MANGA.
WHAT!?!
YOU CAN'T.
!
IT'S OKAY.
HE WAS DROWNING IN DEBT. THIS WAS TWO YEARS BEFORE HE WROTE HIS MASTERPIECE, *CHIKO*.
HIS GIRLFRIEND HAD DUMPED HIM. HE HAD EVERY REASON TO BE DEPRESSED.
YOU CAN'T GIVE UP NOW!
WELL...

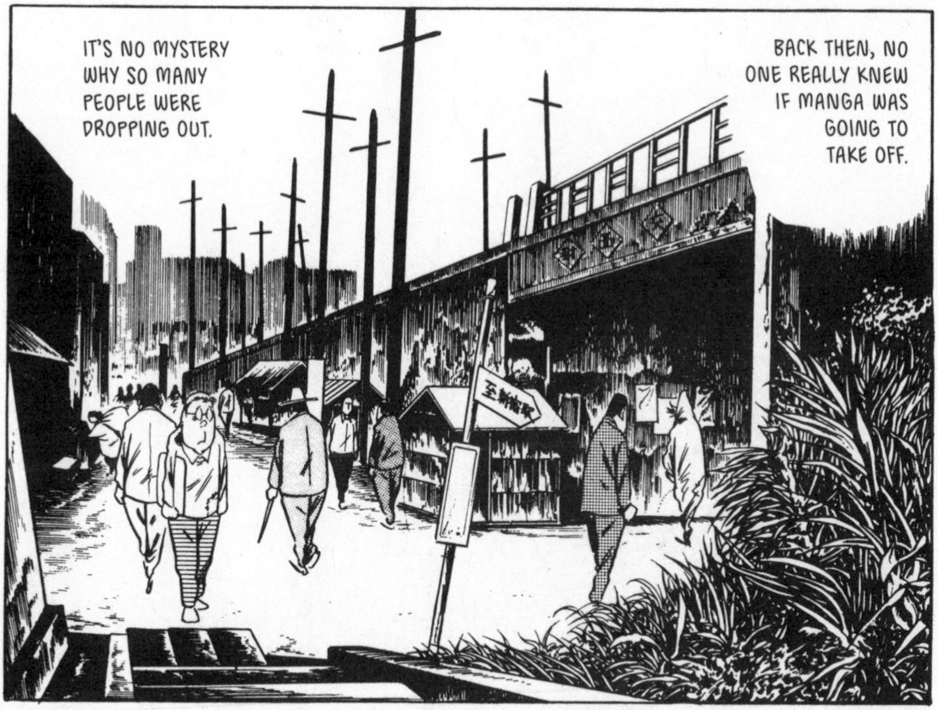
BACK THEN, NO ONE REALLY KNEW IF MANGA WAS GOING TO TAKE OFF.
IT'S NO MYSTERY WHY SO MANY PEOPLE WERE DROPPING OUT.

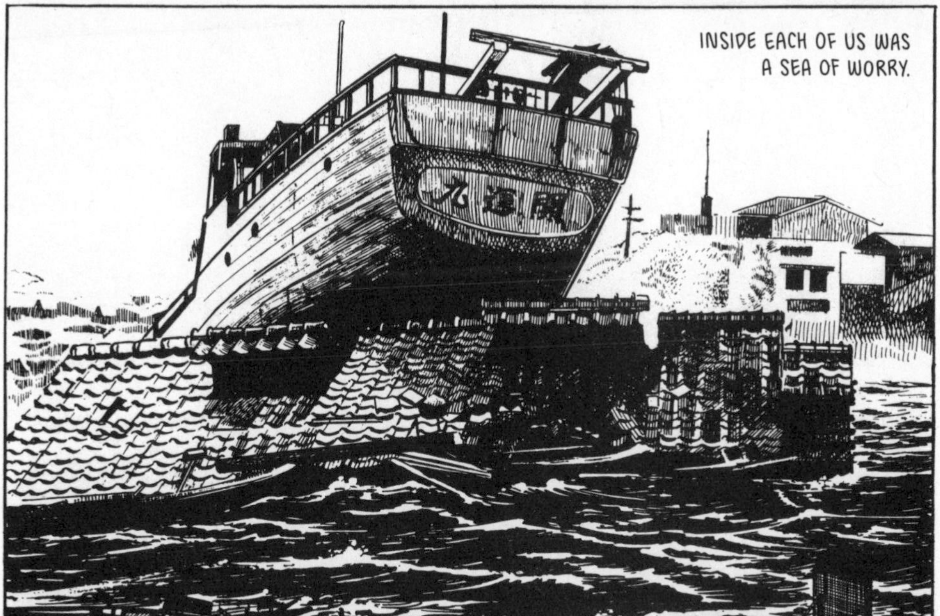
INSIDE EACH OF US WAS A SEA OF WORRY.

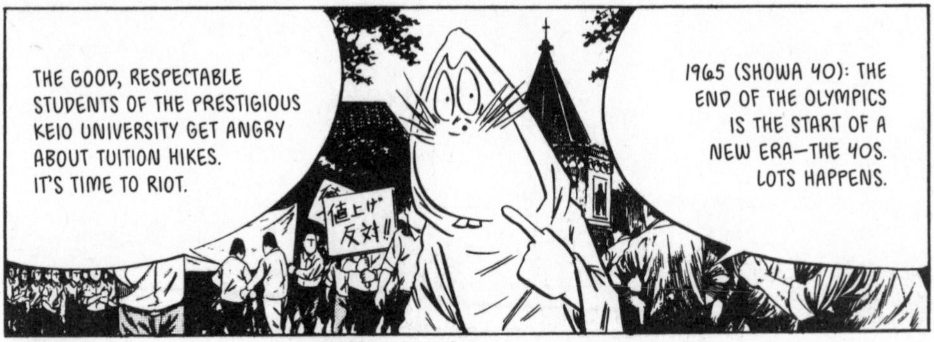
1965 (SHOWA 40): THE END OF THE OLYMPICS IS THE START OF A NEW ERA—THE 40S. LOTS HAPPENS.
値上げ反対!!
THE GOOD, RESPECTABLE STUDENTS OF THE PRESTIGIOUS KEIO UNIVERSITY GET ANGRY ABOUT TUITION HIKES. IT'S TIME TO RIOT.

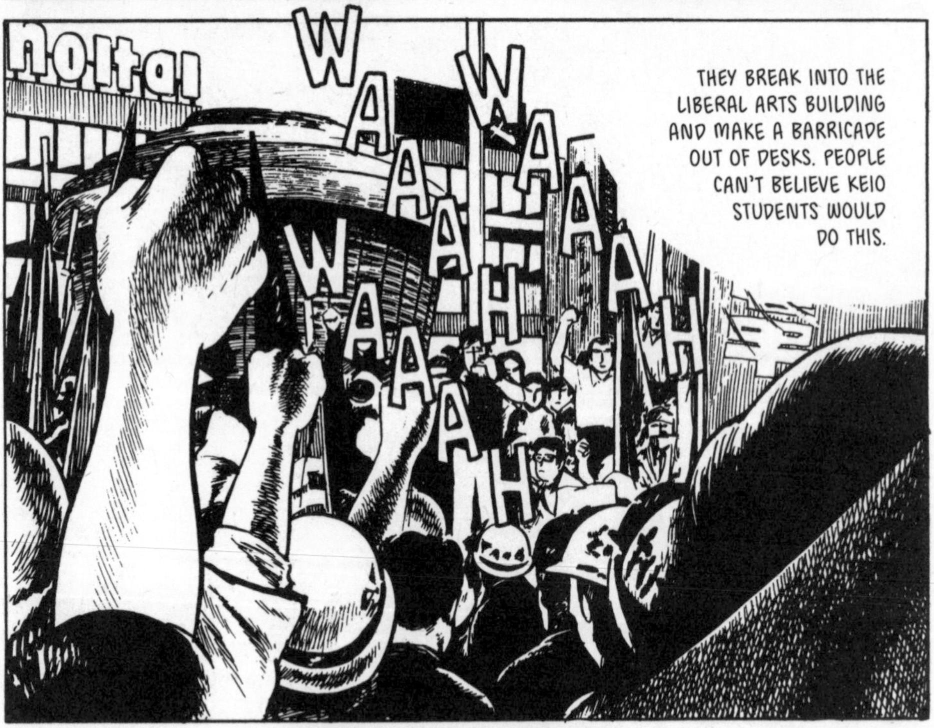
THEY BREAK INTO THE LIBERAL ARTS BUILDING AND MAKE A BARRICADE OUT OF DESKS. PEOPLE CAN'T BELIEVE KEIO STUDENTS WOULD DO THIS.
WAAAAAH
WAAAAH
WAAAAAH

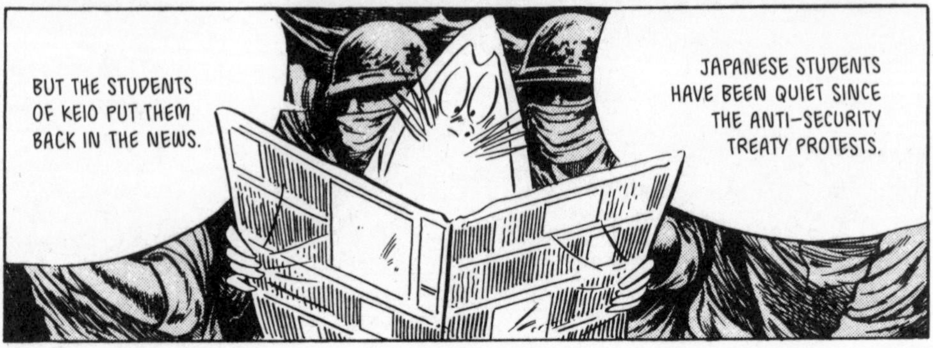
JAPANESE STUDENTS HAVE BEEN QUIET SINCE THE ANTI-SECURITY TREATY PROTESTS.
BUT THE STUDENTS OF KEIO PUT THEM BACK IN THE NEWS.

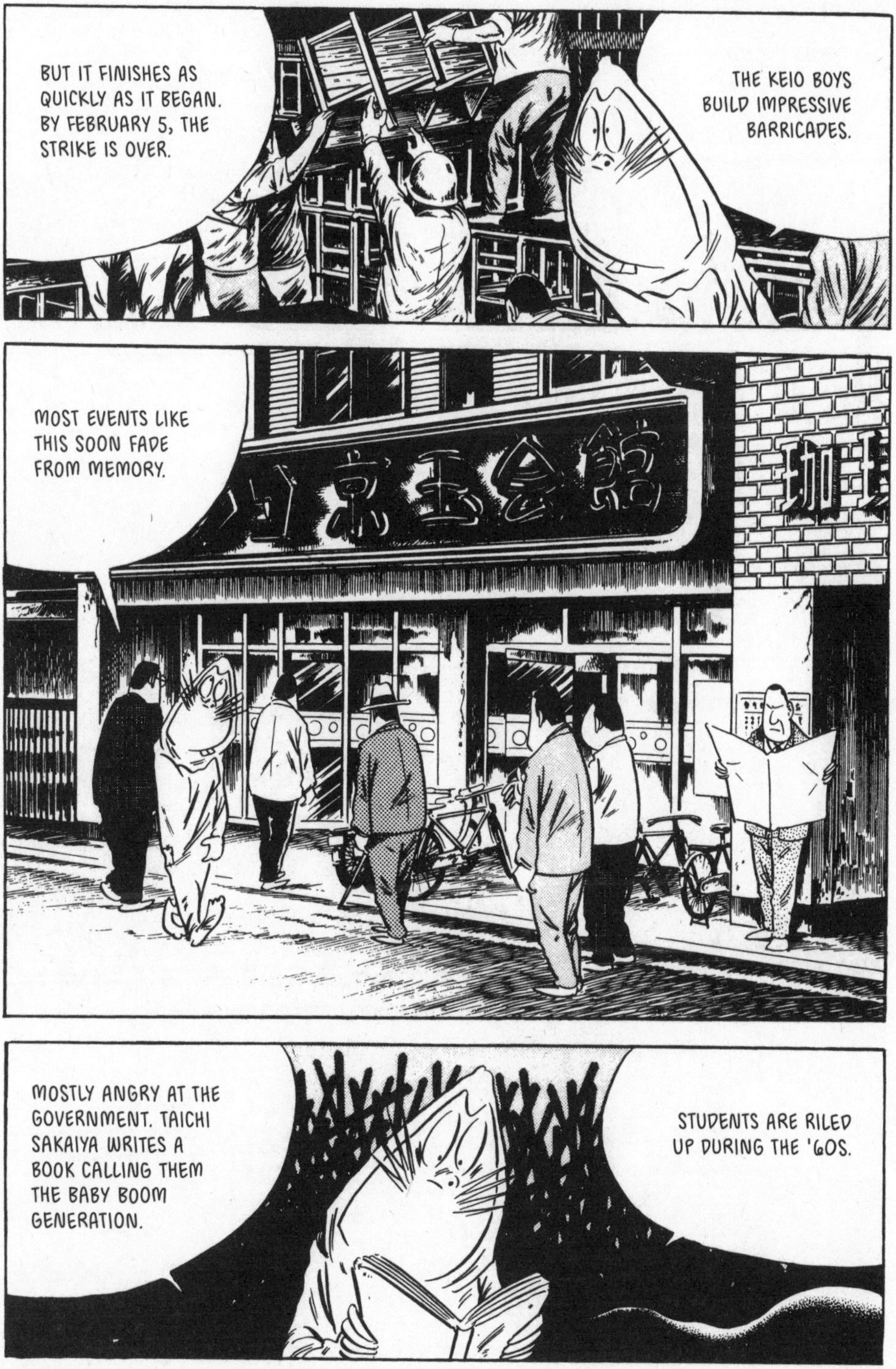
THE KEIO BOYS BUILD IMPRESSIVE BARRICADES.
BUT IT FINISHES AS QUICKLY AS IT BEGAN. BY FEBRUARY 5, THE STRIKE IS OVER.
MOST EVENTS LIKE THIS SOON FADE FROM MEMORY.
STUDENTS ARE RILED UP DURING THE '60S.
MOSTLY ANGRY AT THE GOVERNMENT. TAICHI SAKAIYA WRITES A BOOK CALLING THEM THE BABY BOOM GENERATION.

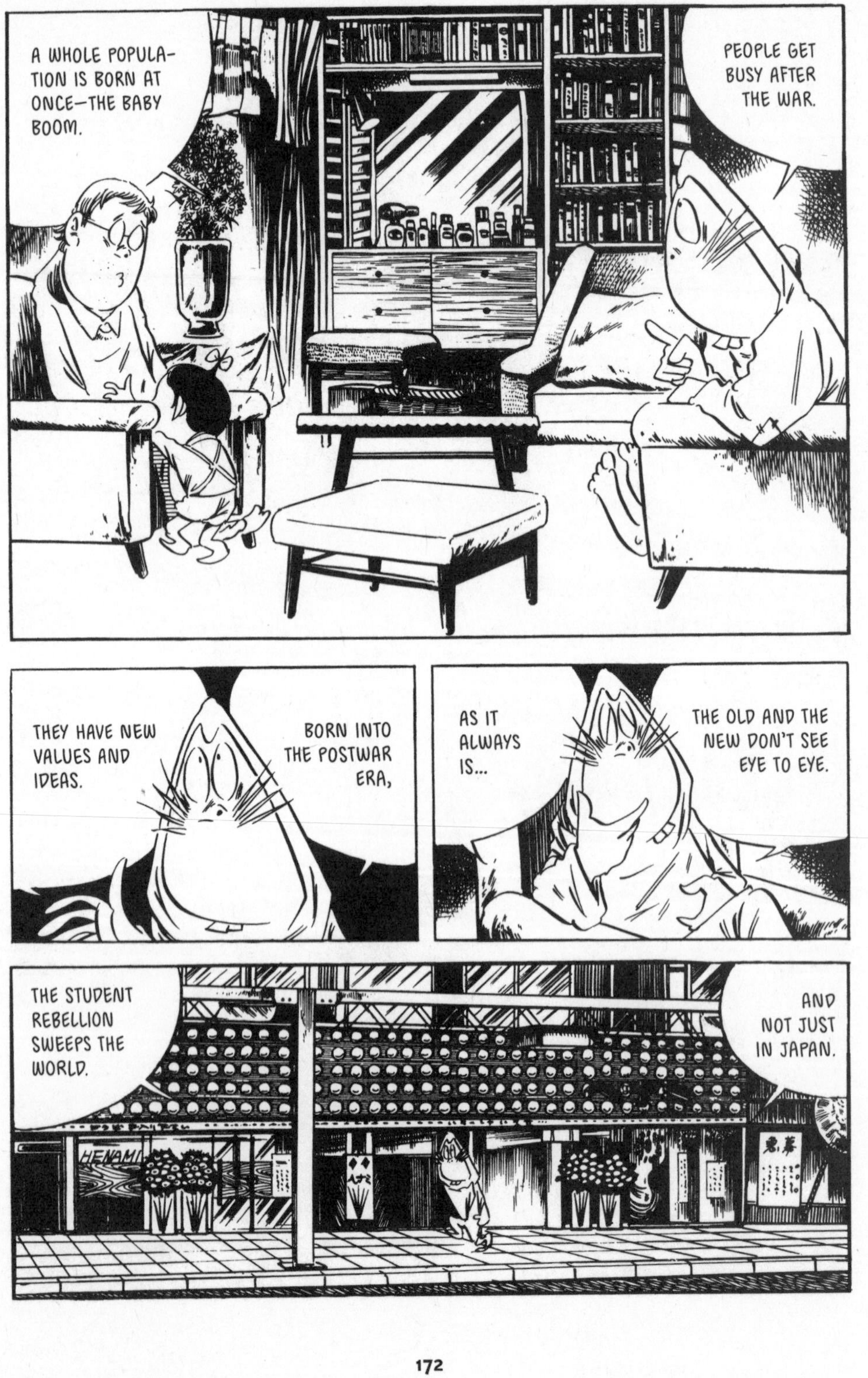
PEOPLE GET BUSY AFTER THE WAR.
A WHOLE POPULATION IS BORN AT ONCE—THE BABY BOOM.
THE OLD AND THE NEW DON'T SEE EYE TO EYE.
AS IT ALWAYS IS...
BORN INTO THE POSTWAR ERA,
THEY HAVE NEW VALUES AND IDEAS.
AND NOT JUST IN JAPAN.
THE STUDENT REBELLION SWEEPS THE WORLD.
HENAMI

THE STUDENT REBELLION

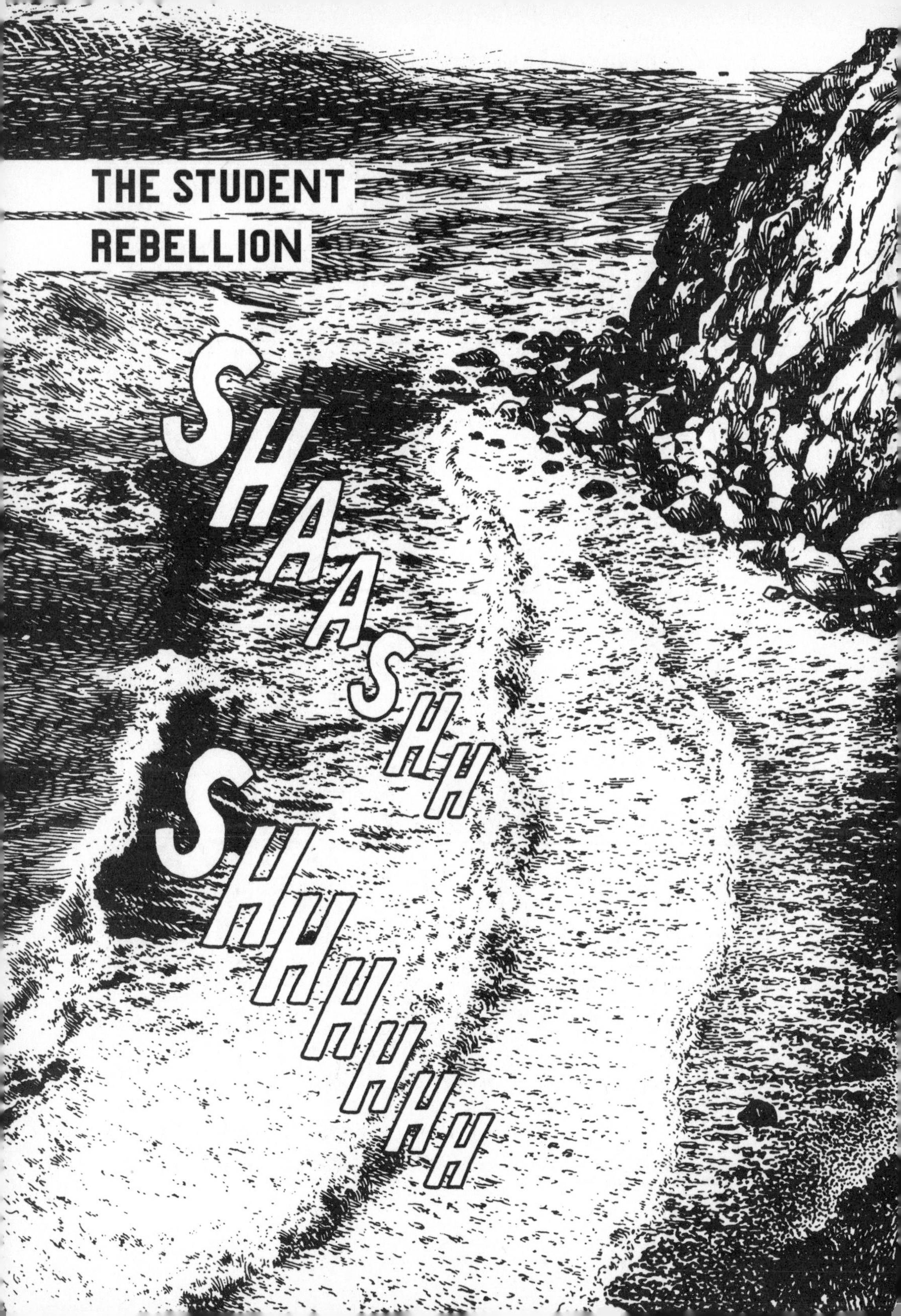
SHAASHH
SHHHHHHH

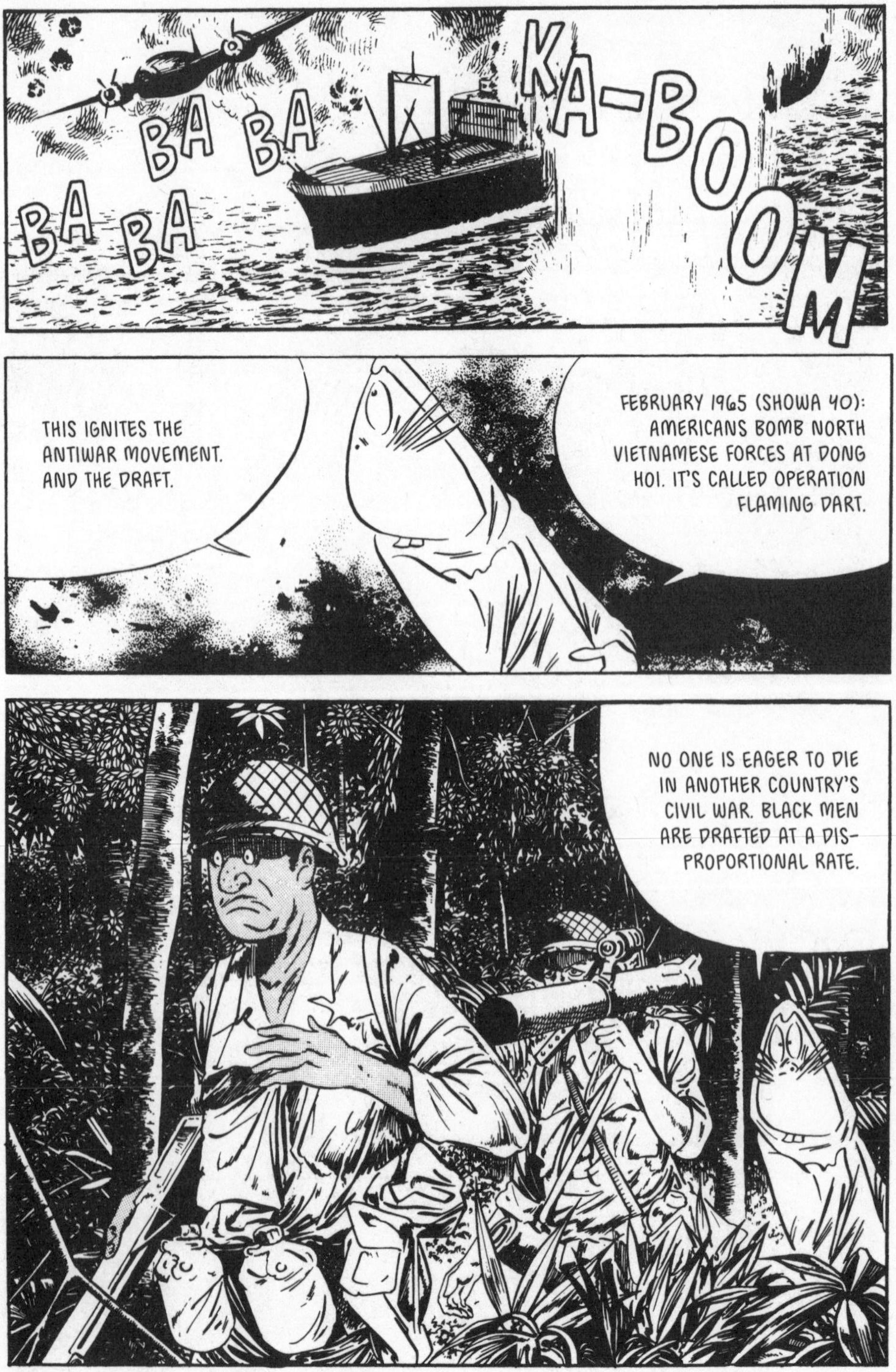
KA-BOOM
BA BA
BA BA
FEBRUARY 1965 (SHOWA 40): AMERICANS BOMB NORTH VIETNAMESE FORCES AT DONG HOI. IT'S CALLED OPERATION FLAMING DART.
THIS IGNITES THE ANTIWAR MOVEMENT. AND THE DRAFT.
NO ONE IS EAGER TO DIE IN ANOTHER COUNTRY'S CIVIL WAR. BLACK MEN ARE DRAFTED AT A DIS-PROPORTIONAL RATE.

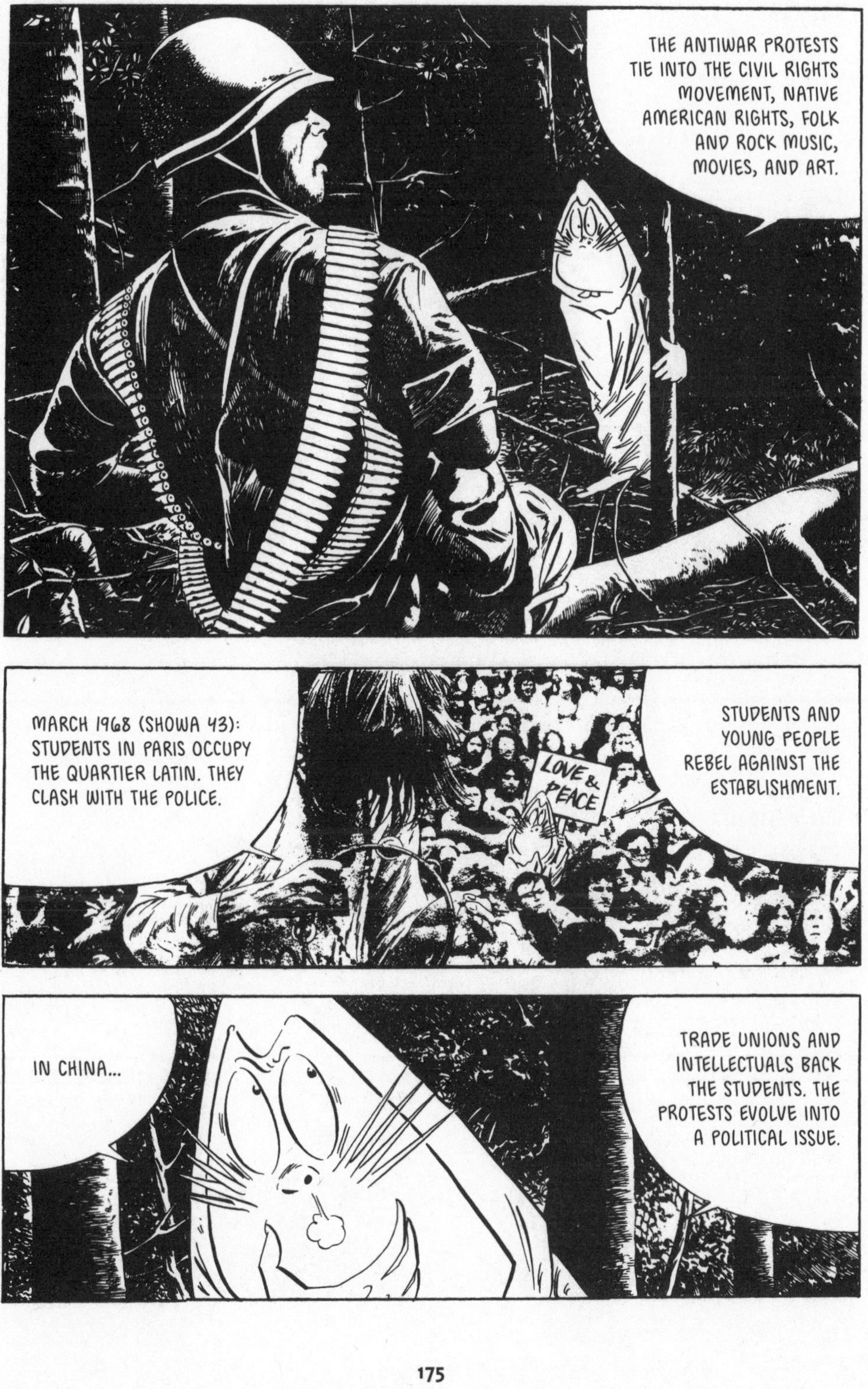
THE ANTIWAR PROTESTS TIE INTO THE CIVIL RIGHTS MOVEMENT, NATIVE AMERICAN RIGHTS, FOLK AND ROCK MUSIC, MOVIES, AND ART.
STUDENTS AND YOUNG PEOPLE REBEL AGAINST THE ESTABLISHMENT.
LOVE & PEACE
MARCH 1968 (SHOWA 43): STUDENTS IN PARIS OCCUPY THE QUARTIER LATIN. THEY CLASH WITH THE POLICE.
TRADE UNIONS AND INTELLECTUALS BACK THE STUDENTS. THE PROTESTS EVOLVE INTO A POLITICAL ISSUE.
IN CHINA...

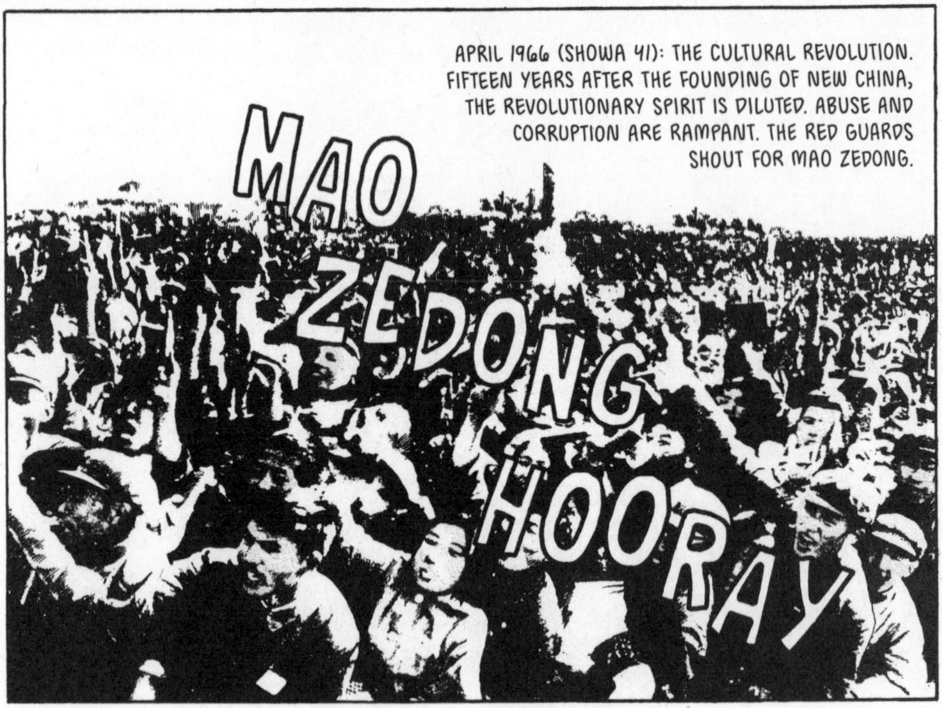
APRIL 1966 (SHOWA 41): THE CULTURAL REVOLUTION. FIFTEEN YEARS AFTER THE FOUNDING OF NEW CHINA, THE REVOLUTIONARY SPIRIT IS DILUTED. ABUSE AND CORRUPTION ARE RAMPANT. THE RED GUARDS SHOUT FOR MAO ZEDONG.
MAO ZEDONG HOORAY

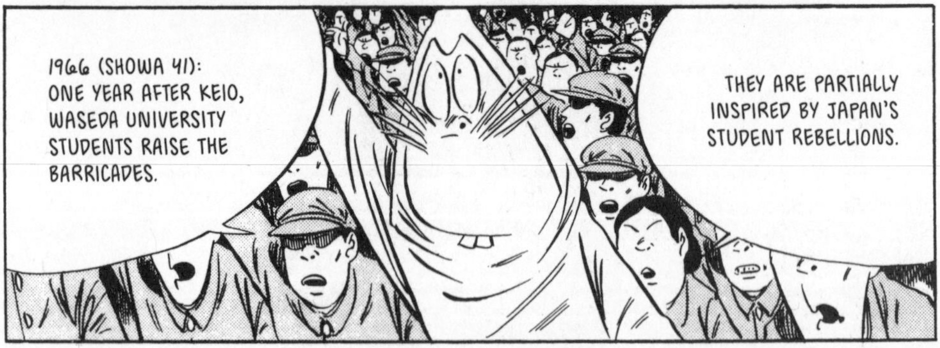
THEY ARE PARTIALLY INSPIRED BY JAPAN'S STUDENT REBELLIONS.
1966 (SHOWA 41): ONE YEAR AFTER KEIO, WASEDA UNIVERSITY STUDENTS RAISE THE BARRICADES.

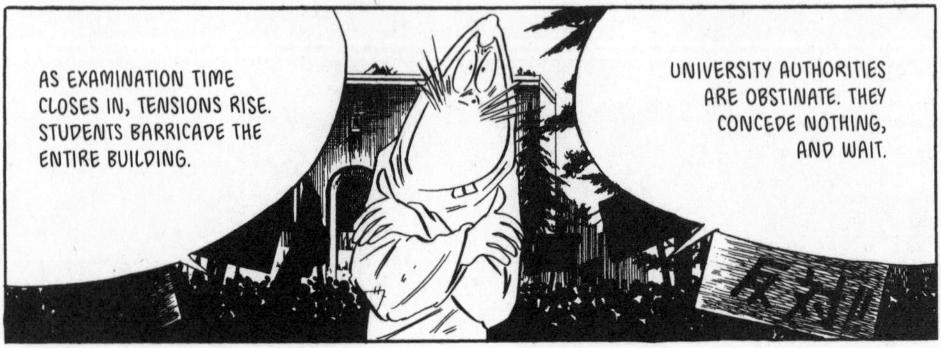
UNIVERSITY AUTHORITIES ARE OBSTINATE. THEY CONCEDE NOTHING, AND WAIT.
AS EXAMINATION TIME CLOSES IN, TENSIONS RISE. STUDENTS BARRICADE THE ENTIRE BUILDING.

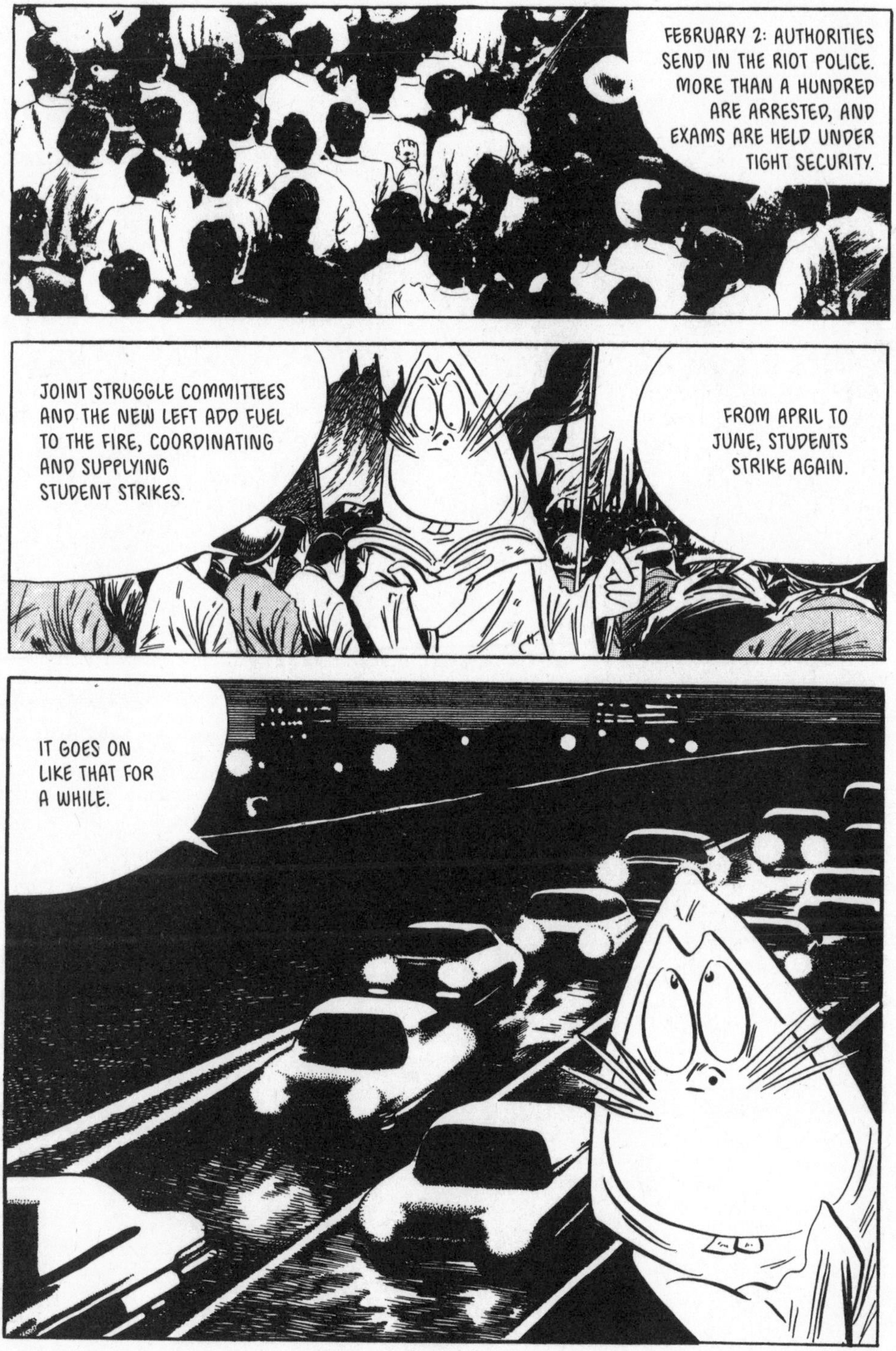
FEBRUARY 2: AUTHORITIES SEND IN THE RIOT POLICE. MORE THAN A HUNDRED ARE ARRESTED, AND EXAMS ARE HELD UNDER TIGHT SECURITY.
FROM APRIL TO JUNE, STUDENTS STRIKE AGAIN.
JOINT STRUGGLE COMMITTEES AND THE NEW LEFT ADD FUEL TO THE FIRE, COORDINATING AND SUPPLYING STUDENT STRIKES.
IT GOES ON LIKE THAT FOR A WHILE.

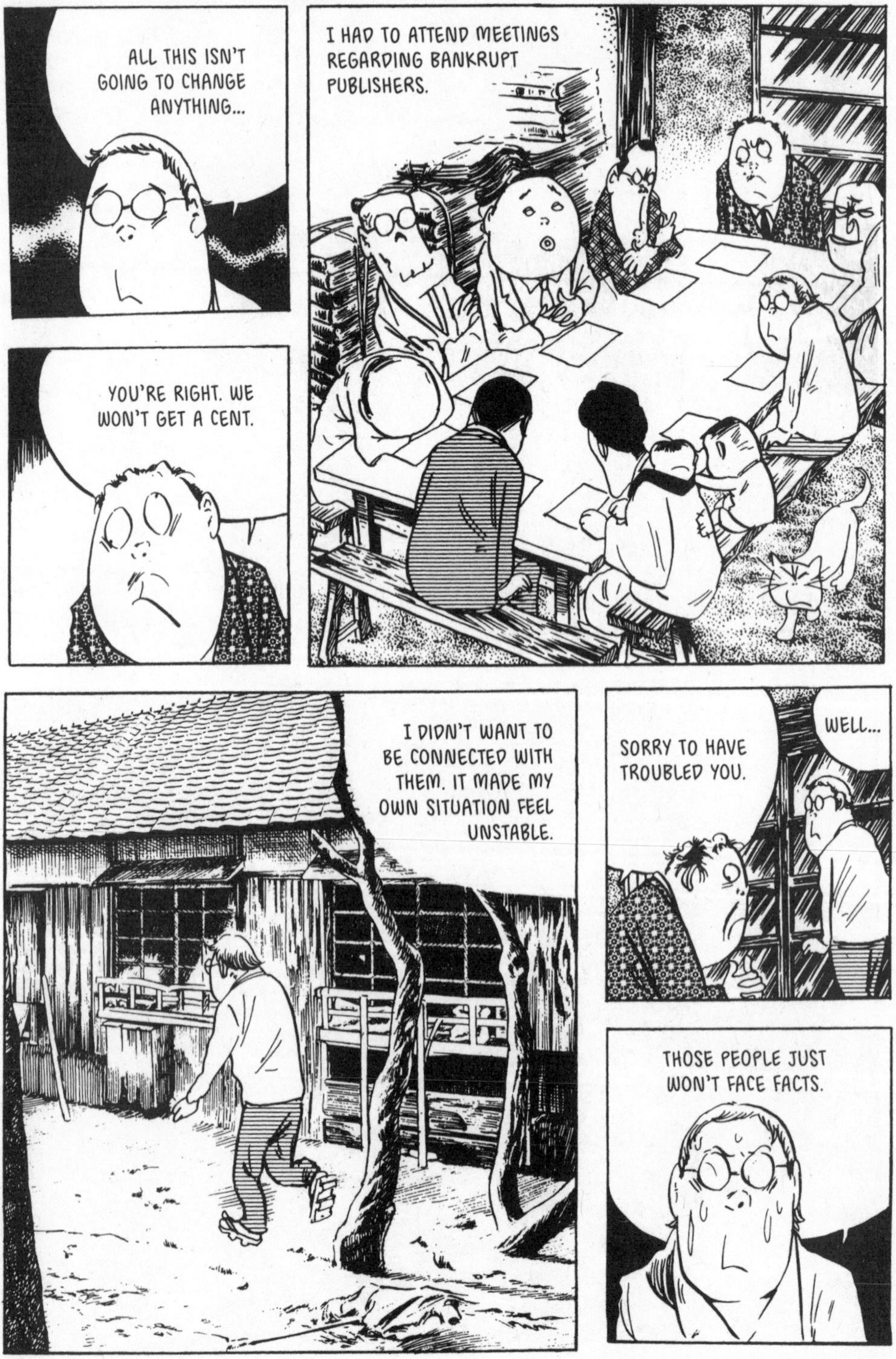
I HAD TO ATTEND MEETINGS REGARDING BANKRUPT PUBLISHERS.
ALL THIS ISN'T GOING TO CHANGE ANYTHING...
YOU'RE RIGHT. WE WON'T GET A CENT.
WELL...
SORRY TO HAVE TROUBLED YOU.
THOSE PEOPLE JUST WON'T FACE FACTS.
I DIDN'T WANT TO BE CONNECTED WITH THEM. IT MADE MY OWN SITUATION FEEL UNSTABLE.

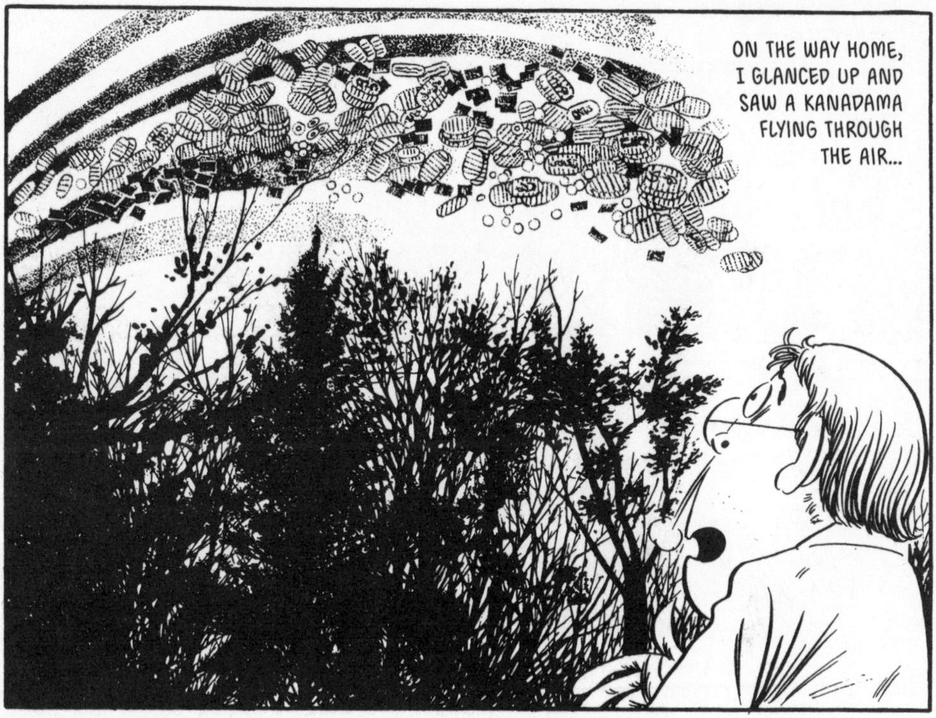
ON THE WAY HOME, I GLANCED UP AND SAW A KANADAMA FLYING THROUGH THE AIR...

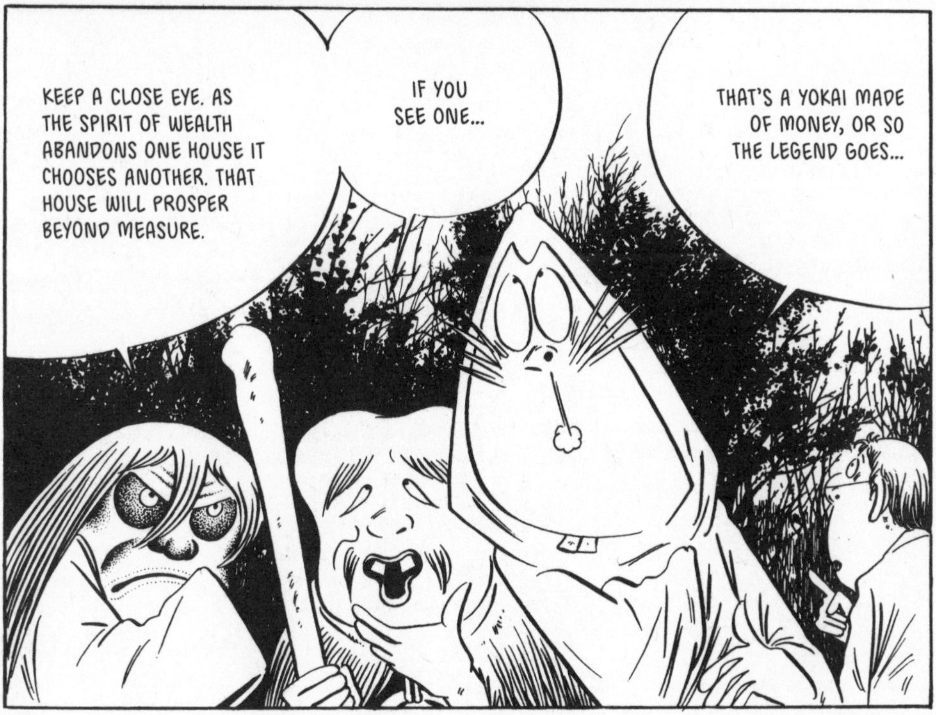
THAT'S A YOKAI MADE OF MONEY, OR SO THE LEGEND GOES...
IF YOU SEE ONE...
KEEP A CLOSE EYE. AS THE SPIRIT OF WEALTH ABANDONS ONE HOUSE IT CHOOSES ANOTHER. THAT HOUSE WILL PROSPER BEYOND MEASURE.

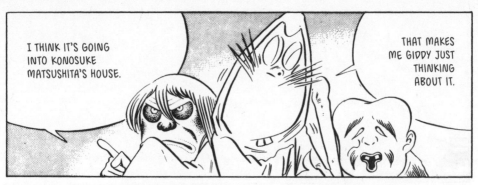

THAT MAKES ME GIDDY JUST THINKING ABOUT IT.
I THINK IT'S GOING INTO KONOSUKE MATSUSHITA'S HOUSE.
NOT MIZUKI'S...?
IDIOT!
HE'S BEEN POOR FOR SO LONG, EVEN SEEING THE KANADAMA IS A GOOD OMEN.
THAT WAS PRETTY COOL.
I WONDER IF THIS MEANS MY FORTUNES ARE CHANGING.
HUFF!
I WAS FEELING PRETTY GOOD. A STRANGER WAS WAITING FOR ME WHEN I GOT HOME...
CLACK
I'M FROM KODANSHA.

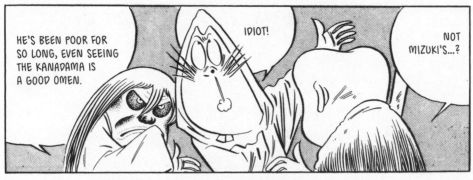

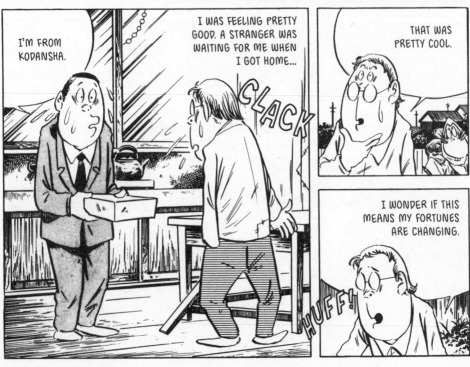

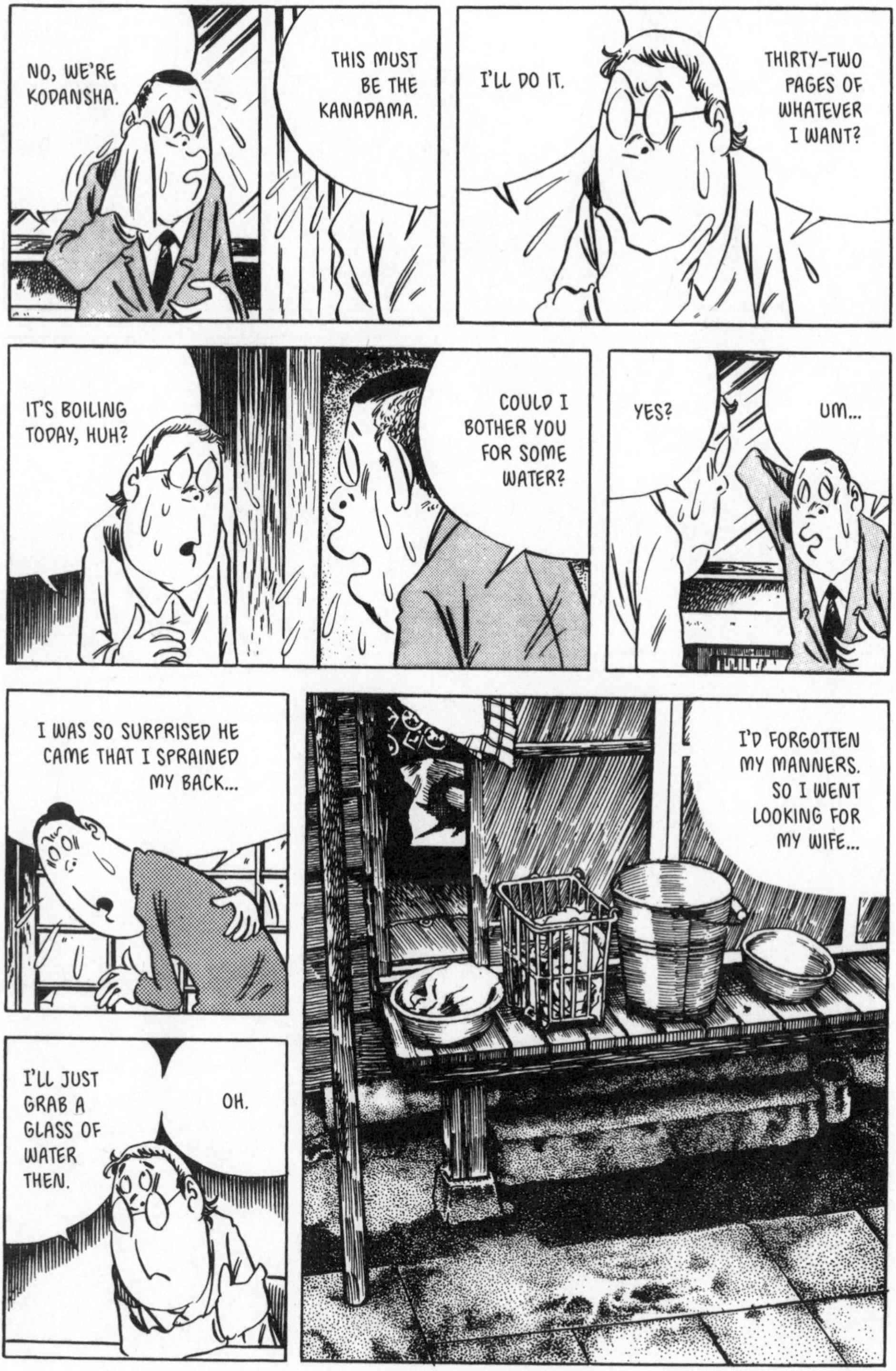
THIRTY-TWO PAGES OF WHATEVER I WANT?
I'LL DO IT.
THIS MUST BE THE KANADAMA.
NO, WE'RE KODANSHA.
UM...
YES?
COULD I BOTHER YOU FOR SOME WATER?
IT'S BOILING TODAY, HUH?
I'D FORGOTTEN MY MANNERS. SO I WENT LOOKING FOR MY WIFE...
I WAS SO SURPRISED HE CAME THAT I SPRAINED MY BACK...
OH.
I'LL JUST GRAB A GLASS OF WATER THEN.

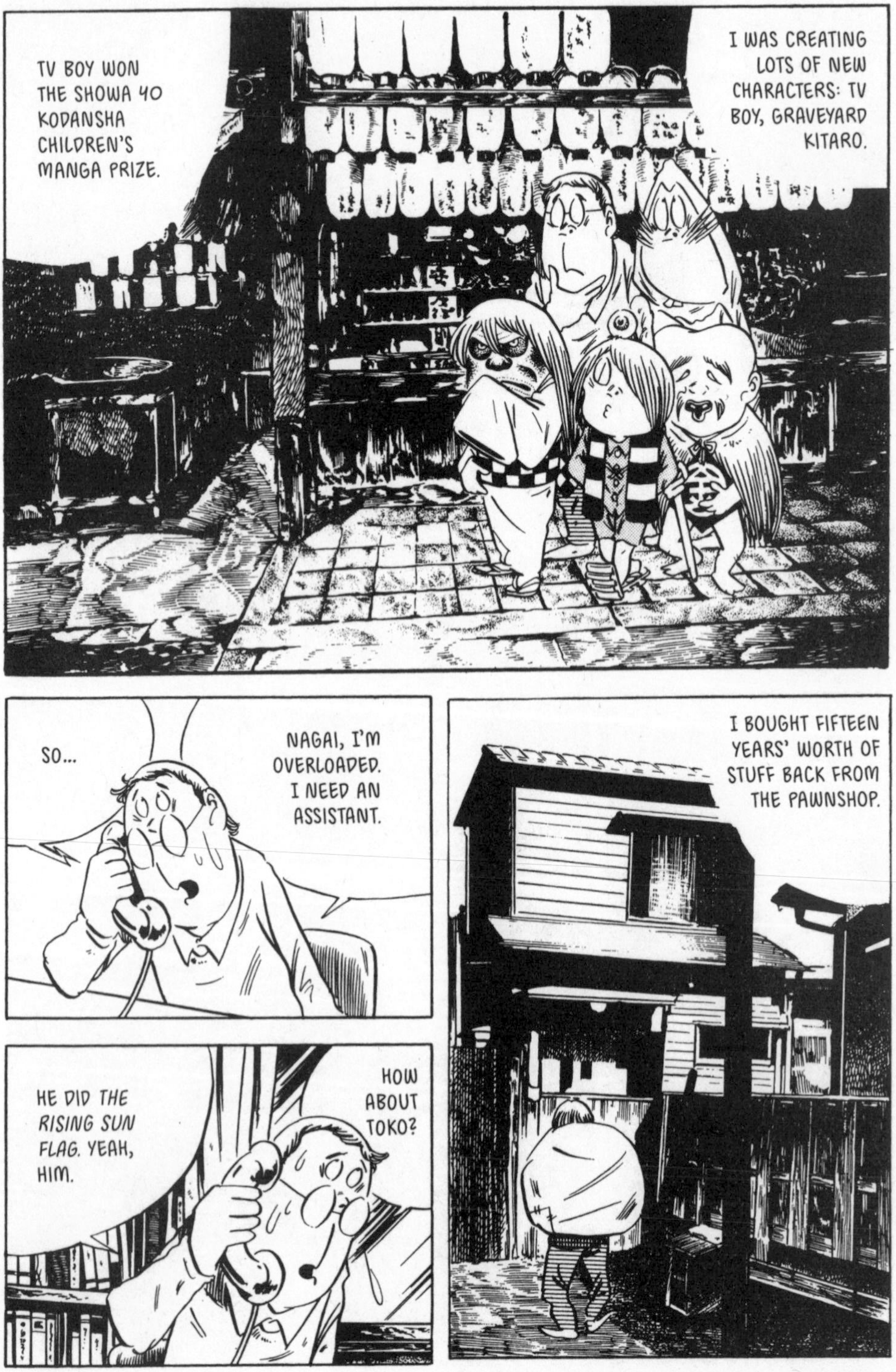
I WAS CREATING LOTS OF NEW CHARACTERS: TV BOY, GRAVEYARD KITARO.
TV BOY WON THE SHOWA 40 KODANSHA CHILDREN'S MANGA PRIZE.
I BOUGHT FIFTEEN YEARS' WORTH OF STUFF BACK FROM THE PAWNSHOP.
NAGAI, I'M OVERLOADED. I NEED AN ASSISTANT.
SO...
HOW ABOUT TOKO?
HE DID THE *RISING SUN FLAG*. YEAH, HIM.

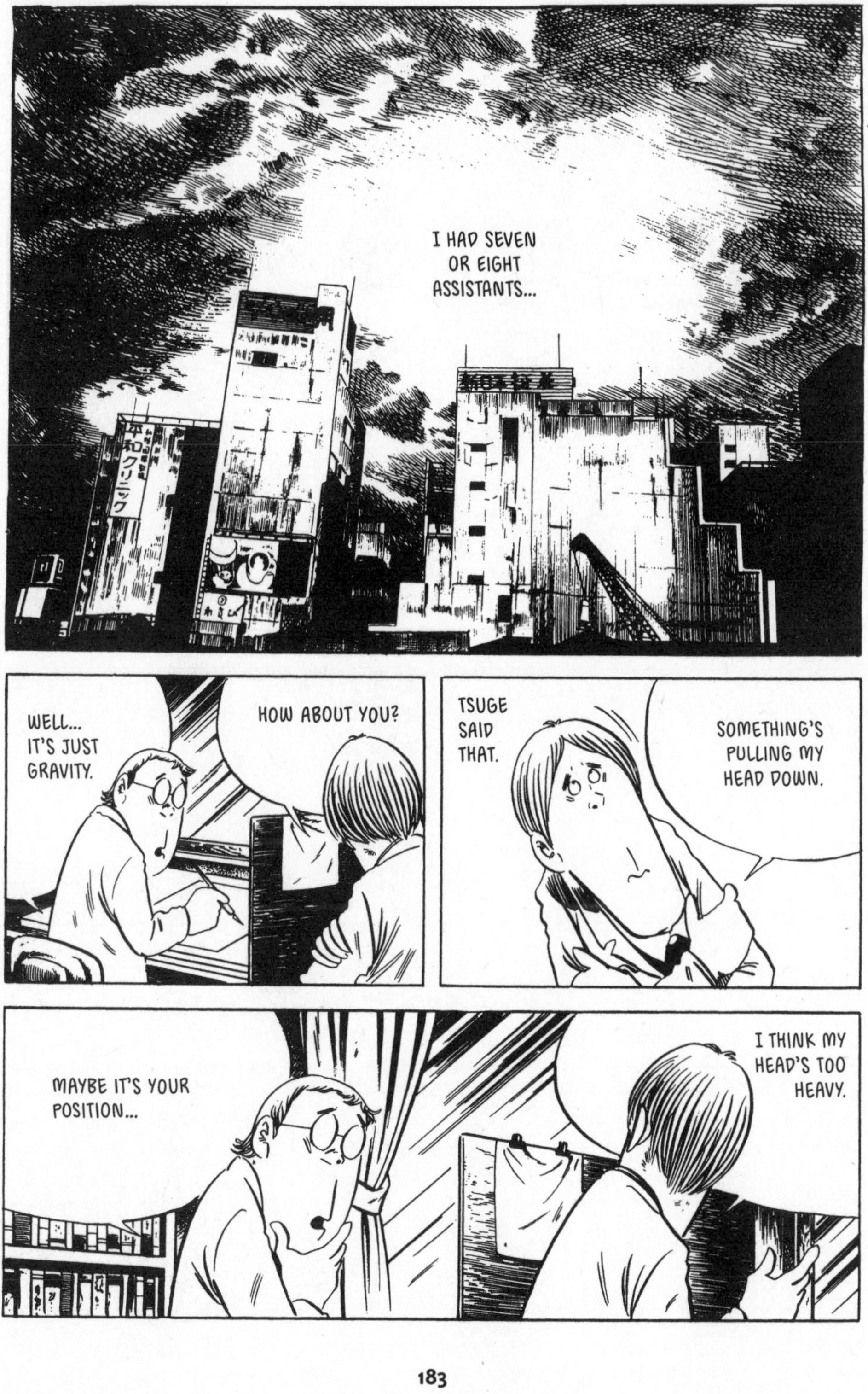
I HAD SEVEN OR EIGHT ASSISTANTS...
SOMETHING'S PULLING MY HEAD DOWN.
TSUGE SAID THAT.
HOW ABOUT YOU?
WELL... IT'S JUST GRAVITY.
I THINK MY HEAD'S TOO HEAVY.
MAYBE IT'S YOUR POSITION...

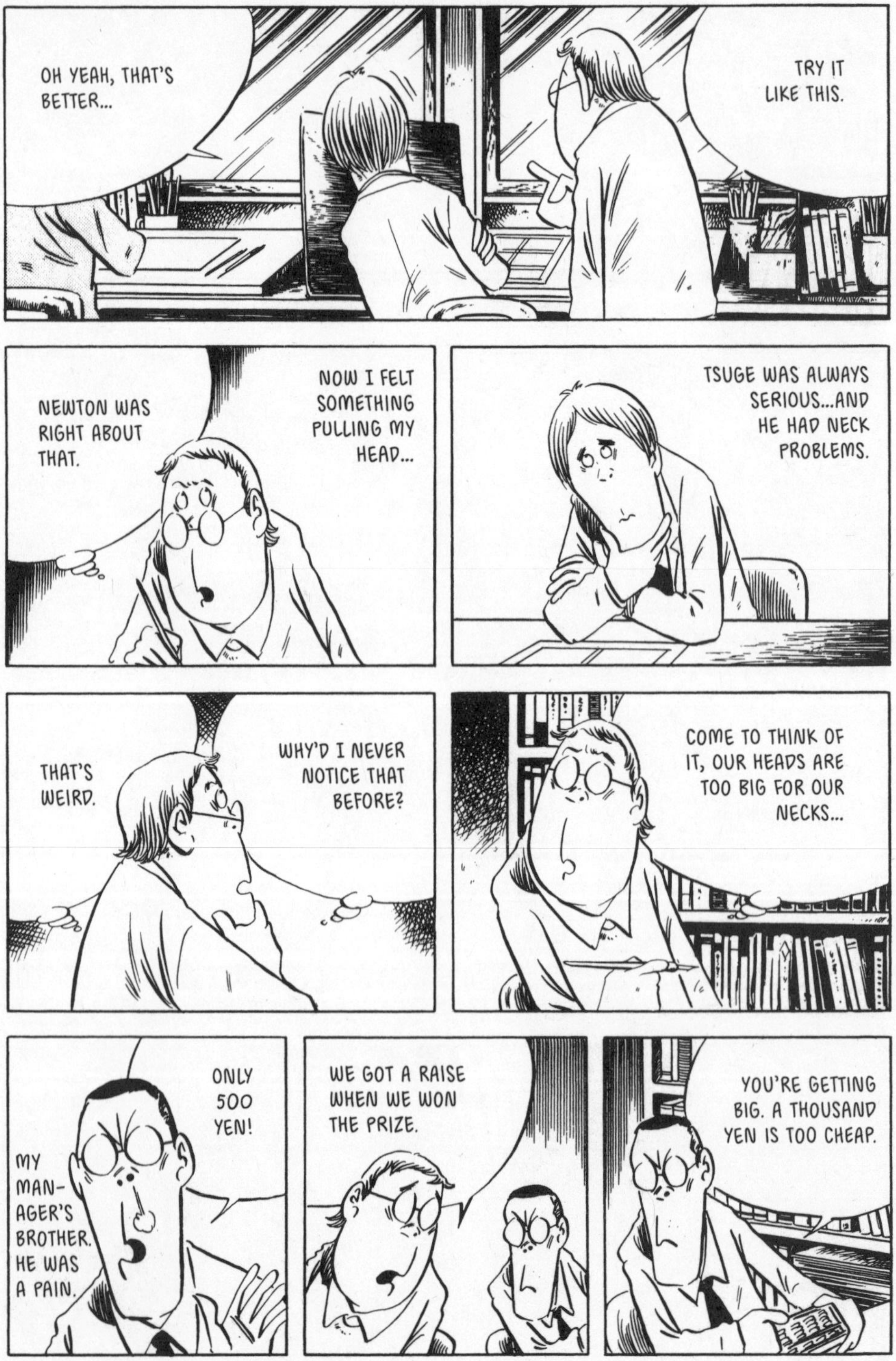
TRY IT LIKE THIS.
OH YEAH, THAT'S BETTER...
TSUGE WAS ALWAYS SERIOUS...AND HE HAD NECK PROBLEMS.
NOW I FELT SOMETHING PULLING MY HEAD...
NEWTON WAS RIGHT ABOUT THAT.
COME TO THINK OF IT, OUR HEADS ARE TOO BIG FOR OUR NECKS...
WHY'D I NEVER NOTICE THAT BEFORE?
THAT'S WEIRD.
YOU'RE GETTING BIG. A THOUSAND YEN IS TOO CHEAP.
WE GOT A RAISE WHEN WE WON THE PRIZE.
ONLY 500 YEN!
MY MANAGER'S BROTHER. HE WAS A PAIN.

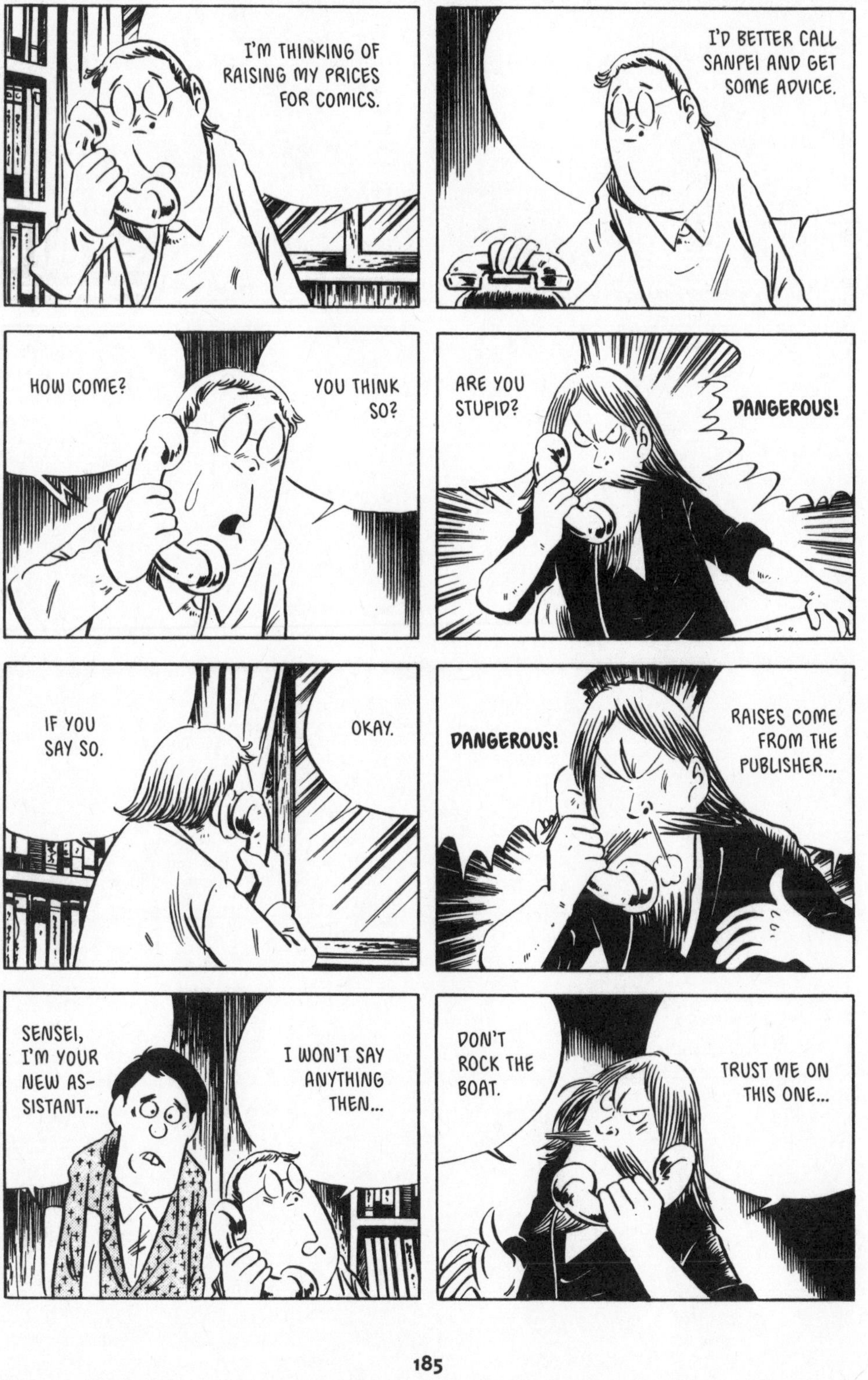
I'D BETTER CALL SANPEI AND GET SOME ADVICE.
I'M THINKING OF RAISING MY PRICES FOR COMICS.
DANGEROUS!
ARE YOU STUPID?
YOU THINK SO?
HOW COME?
RAISES COME FROM THE PUBLISHER...
DANGEROUS!
OKAY.
IF YOU SAY SO.
TRUST ME ON THIS ONE...
DON'T ROCK THE BOAT.
I WON'T SAY ANYTHING THEN...
SENSEI, I'M YOUR NEW ASSISTANT...

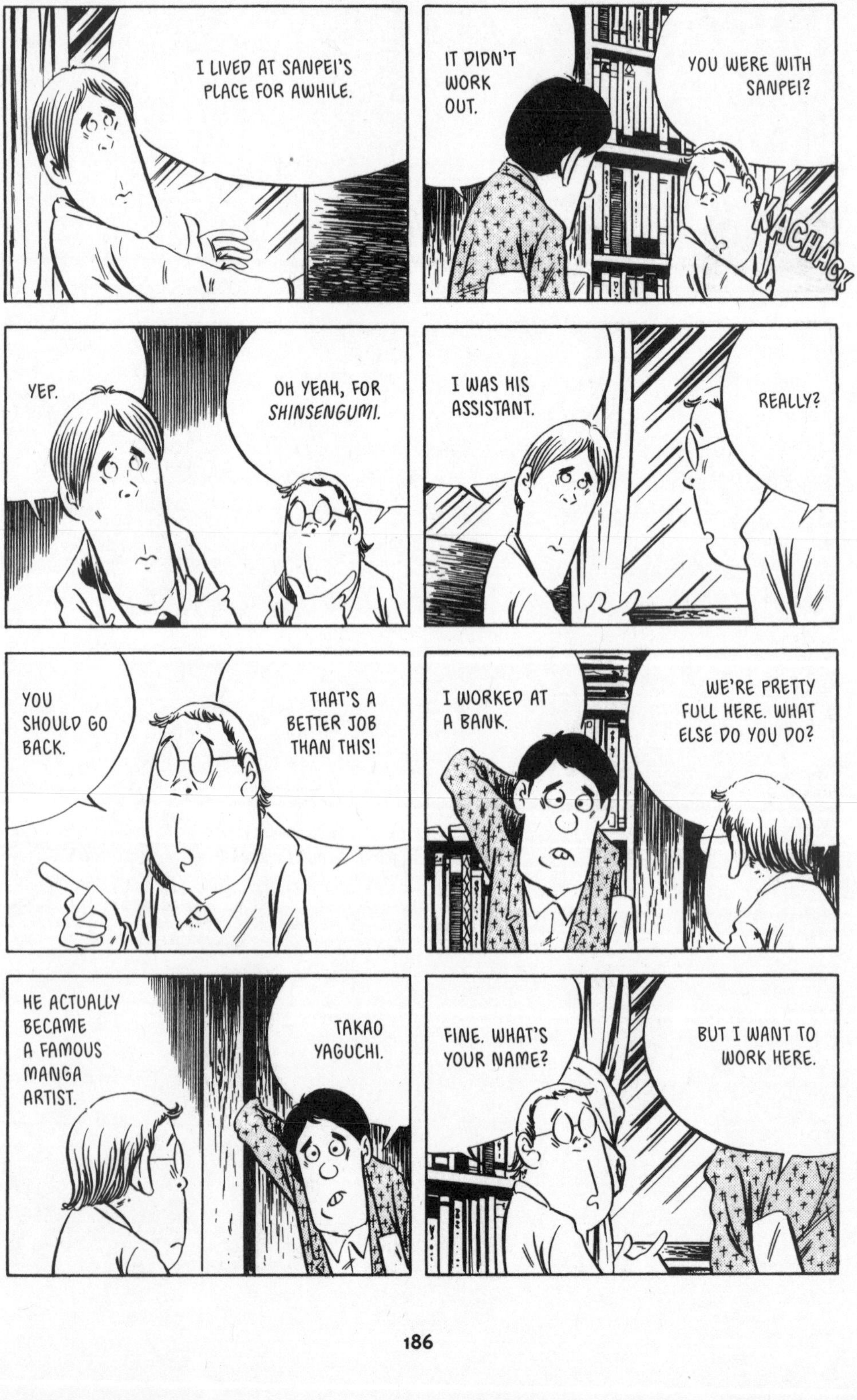
YOU WERE WITH SANPEI?
IT DIDN'T WORK OUT.
KACHACK
I LIVED AT SANPEI'S PLACE FOR AWHILE.
REALLY?
I WAS HIS ASSISTANT.
OH YEAH, FOR *SHINSENGUMI*.
YEP.
WE'RE PRETTY FULL HERE. WHAT ELSE DO YOU DO?
I WORKED AT A BANK.
THAT'S A BETTER JOB THAN THIS!
YOU SHOULD GO BACK.
BUT I WANT TO WORK HERE.
FINE. WHAT'S YOUR NAME?
TAKAO YAGUCHI.
HE ACTUALLY BECAME A FAMOUS MANGA ARTIST.

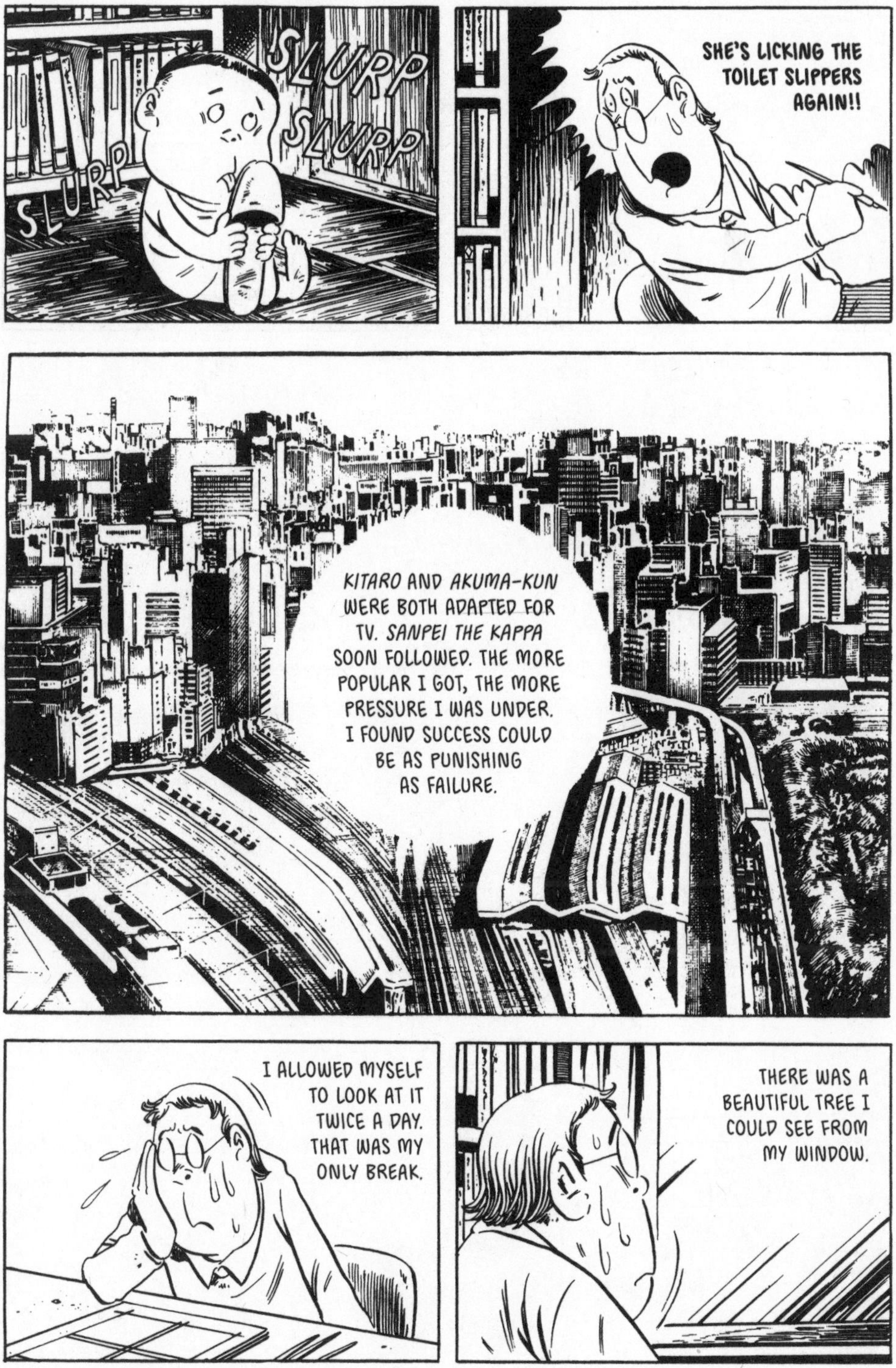
SHE'S LICKING THE TOILET SLIPPERS AGAIN!!
SLURP
SLURP
SLURP
KITARO AND *AKUMA-KUN* WERE BOTH ADAPTED FOR TV. *SANPEI THE KAPPA* SOON FOLLOWED. THE MORE POPULAR I GOT, THE MORE PRESSURE I WAS UNDER. I FOUND SUCCESS COULD BE AS PUNISHING AS FAILURE.
THERE WAS A BEAUTIFUL TREE I COULD SEE FROM MY WINDOW.
I ALLOWED MYSELF TO LOOK AT IT TWICE A DAY. THAT WAS MY ONLY BREAK.

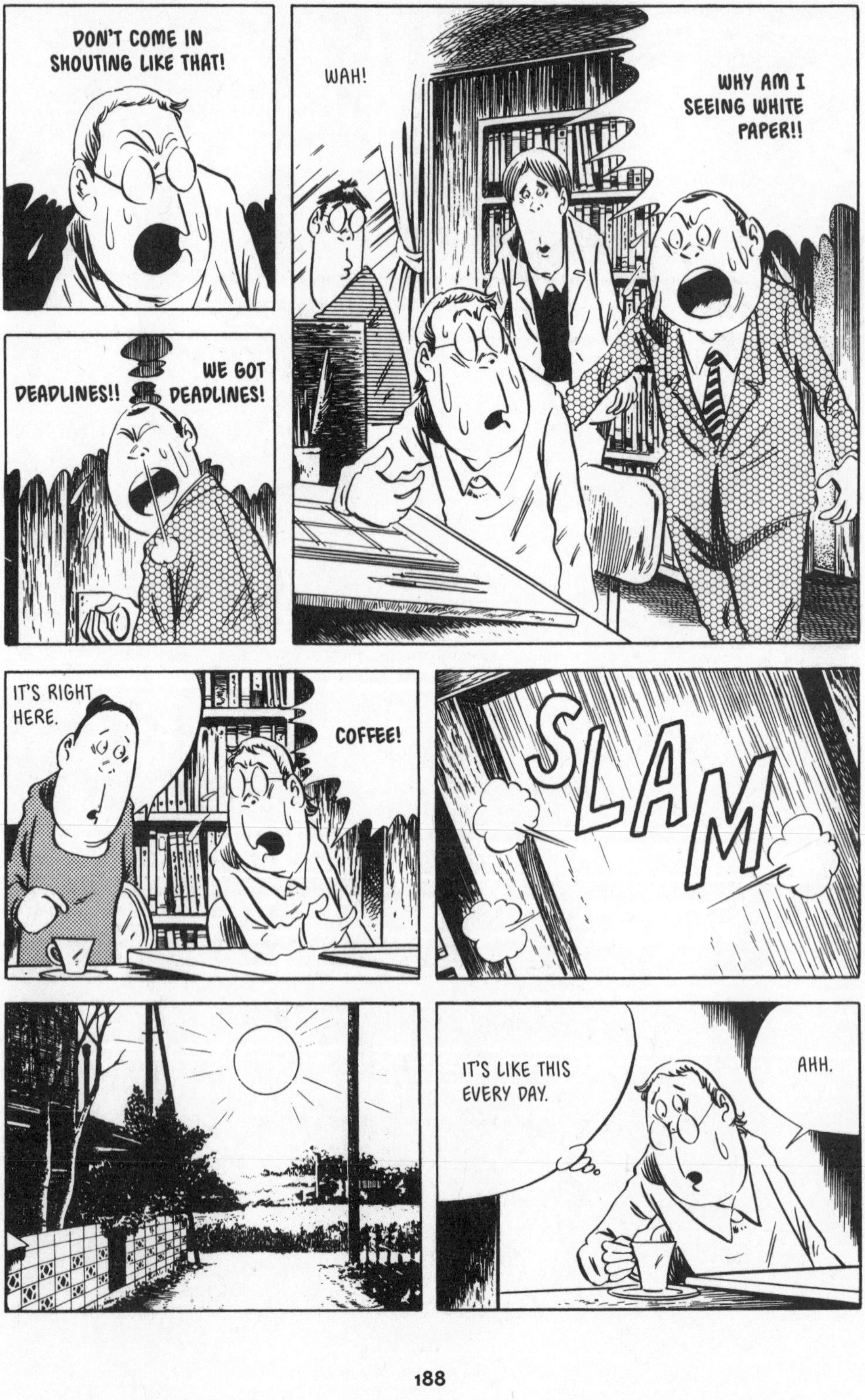
WHY AM I SEEING WHITE PAPER!!
WAH!
DON'T COME IN SHOUTING LIKE THAT!
WE GOT DEADLINES!
DEADLINES!!
SLAM
COFFEE!
IT'S RIGHT HERE.
AHH.
IT'S LIKE THIS EVERY DAY.

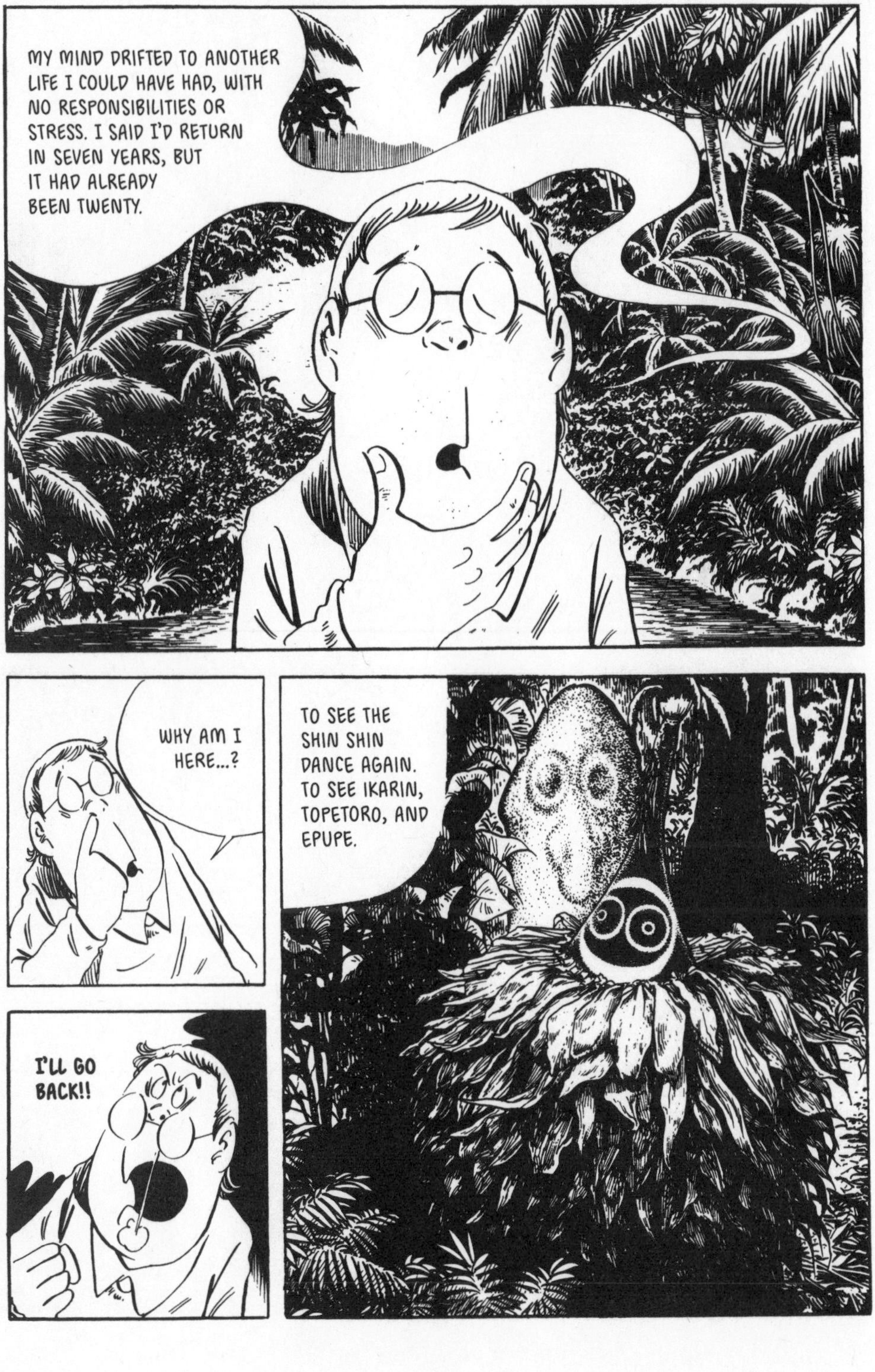
MY MIND DRIFTED TO ANOTHER LIFE I COULD HAVE HAD, WITH NO RESPONSIBILITIES OR STRESS. I SAID I'D RETURN IN SEVEN YEARS, BUT IT HAD ALREADY BEEN TWENTY.
TO SEE THE SHIN SHIN DANCE AGAIN. TO SEE IKARIN, TOPETORO, AND EPUPE.
WHY AM I HERE...?
I'LL GO BACK!!

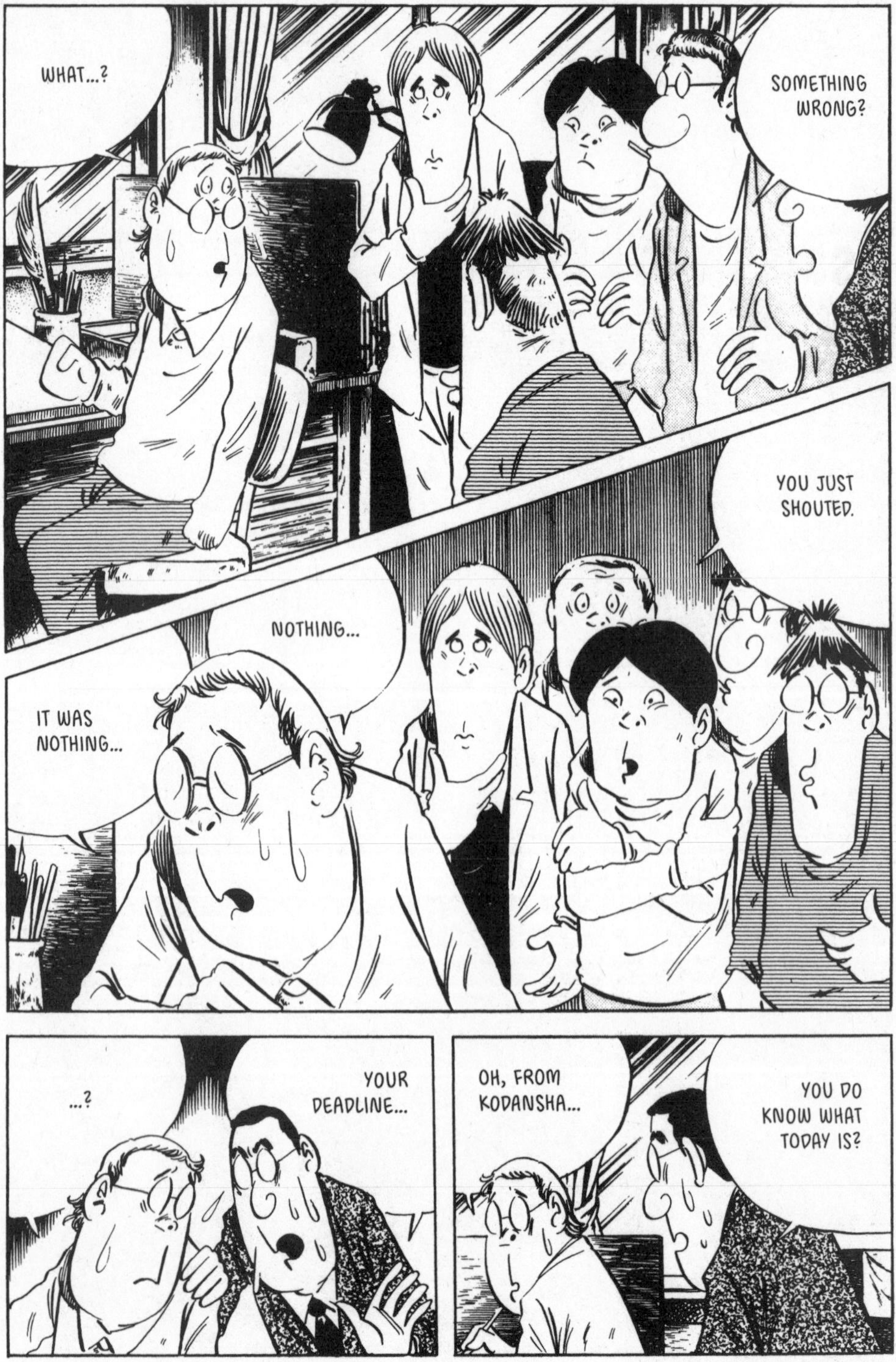
SOMETHING WRONG?
WHAT...?
YOU JUST SHOUTED.
NOTHING...
IT WAS NOTHING...
YOU DO KNOW WHAT TODAY IS?
OH, FROM KODANSHA...
YOUR DEADLINE...
...?

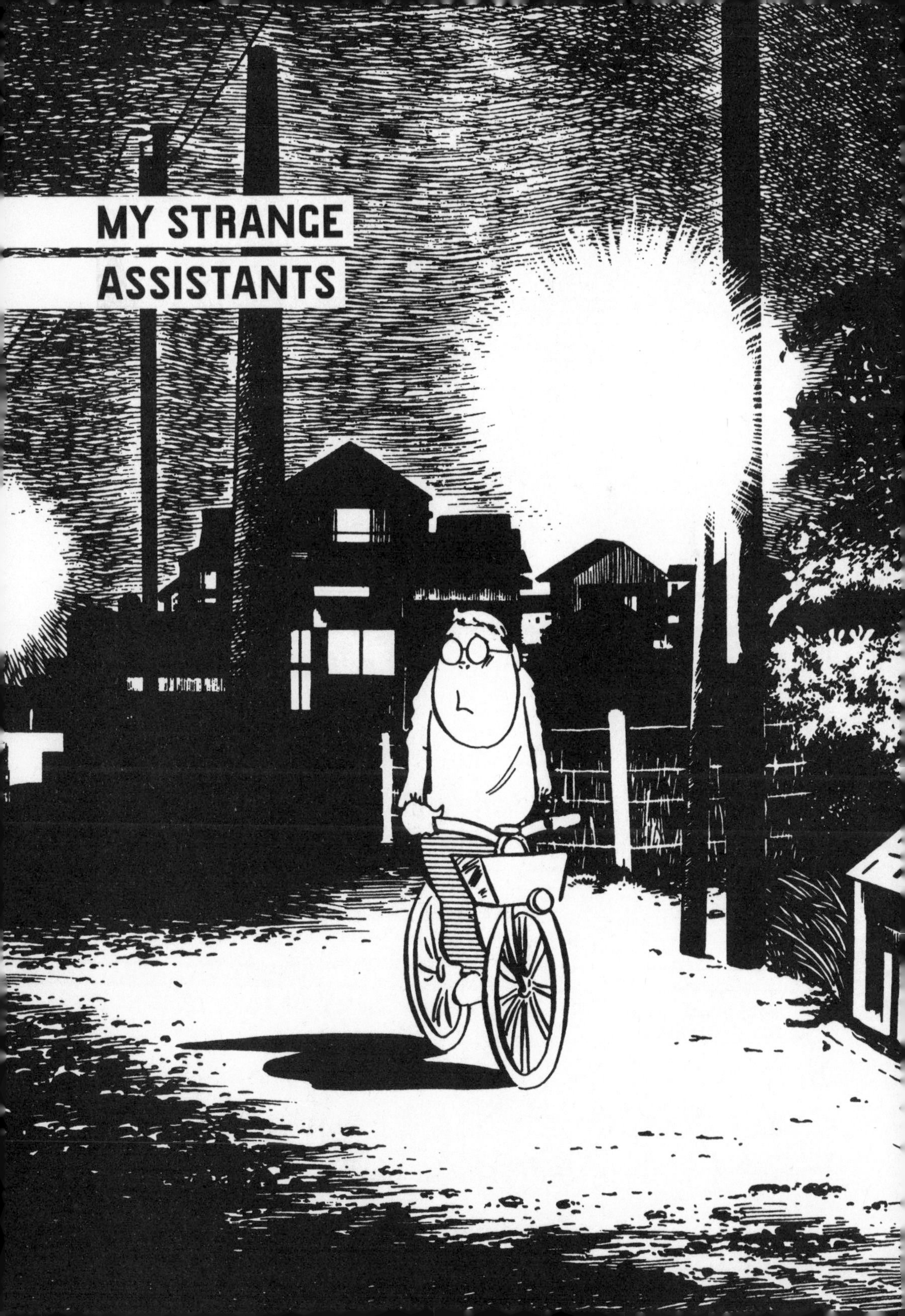
MY STRANGE
ASSISTANTS

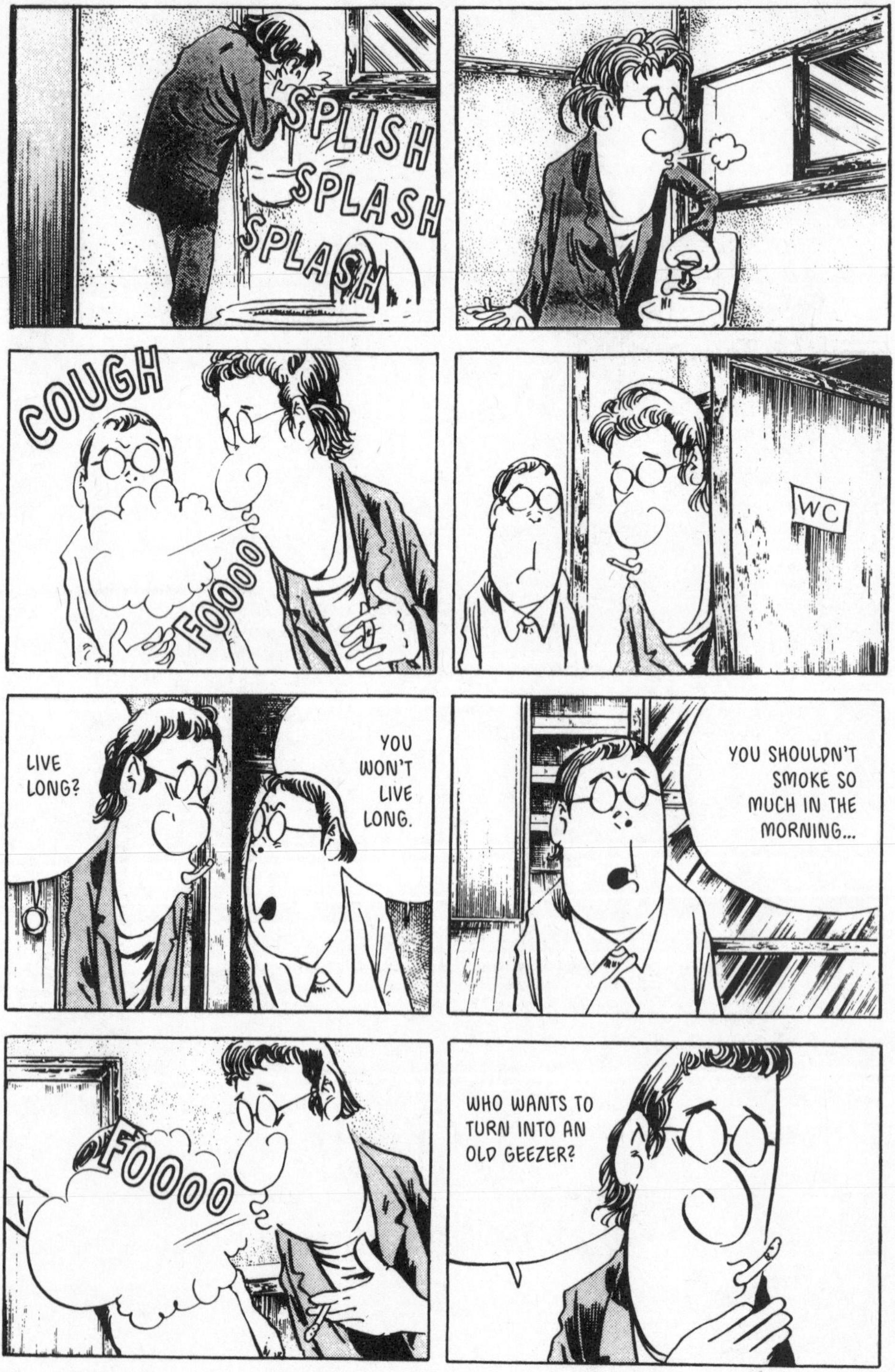
SPLISH
SPLASH
SPLASH
WC
COUGH
FOOOO
YOU SHOULDN'T SMOKE SO MUCH IN THE MORNING...
YOU WON'T LIVE LONG.
LIVE LONG?
WHO WANTS TO TURN INTO AN OLD GEEZER?
FOOOO

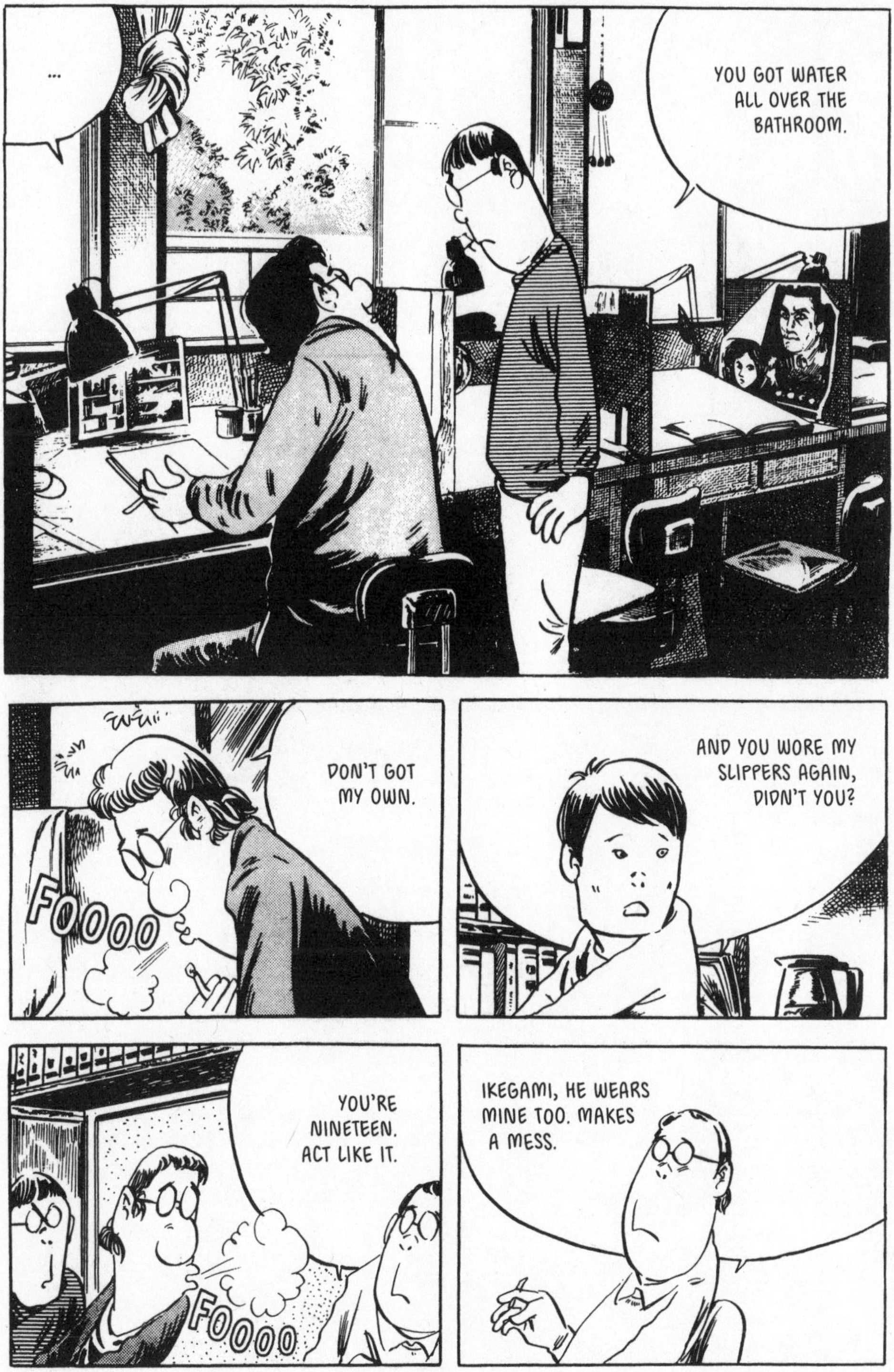
YOU GOT WATER ALL OVER THE BATHROOM.
...
AND YOU WORE MY SLIPPERS AGAIN, DIDN'T YOU?
DON'T GOT MY OWN.
FOOOO
IKEGAMI, HE WEARS MINE TOO. MAKES A MESS.
YOU'RE NINETEEN. ACT LIKE IT.
FOOOO

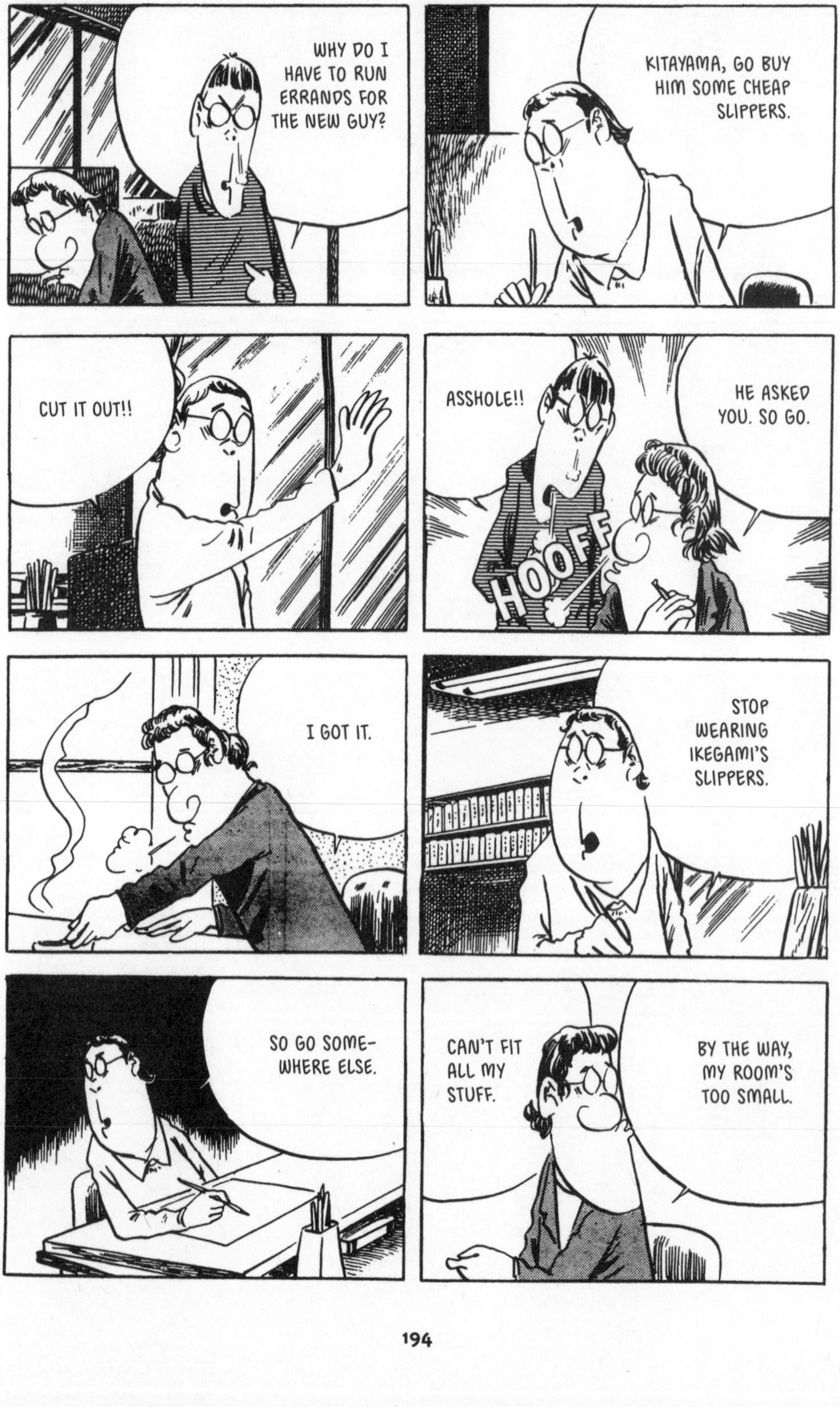
KITAYAMA, GO BUY HIM SOME CHEAP SLIPPERS.
WHY DO I HAVE TO RUN ERRANDS FOR THE NEW GUY?
HE ASKED YOU. SO GO.
ASSHOLE!!
HOOFF
CUT IT OUT!!
STOP WEARING IKEGAMI'S SLIPPERS.
I GOT IT.
BY THE WAY, MY ROOM'S TOO SMALL.
CAN'T FIT ALL MY STUFF.
SO GO SOME-WHERE ELSE.

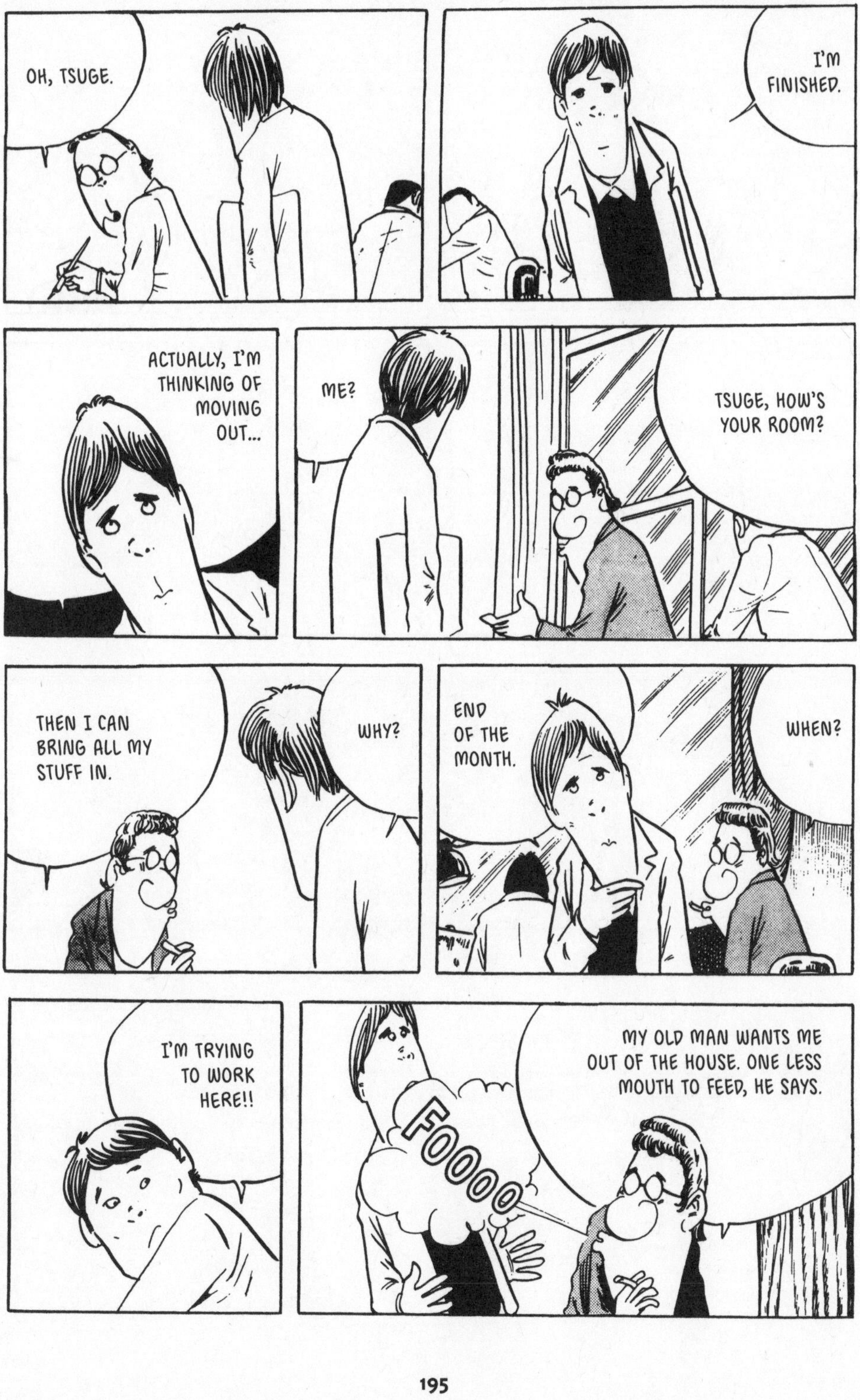
I'M FINISHED.
OH, TSUGE.
TSUGE, HOW'S YOUR ROOM?
ME?
ACTUALLY, I'M THINKING OF MOVING OUT...
WHEN?
END OF THE MONTH.
WHY?
THEN I CAN BRING ALL MY STUFF IN.
MY OLD MAN WANTS ME OUT OF THE HOUSE. ONE LESS MOUTH TO FEED, HE SAYS.
FOOOO
I'M TRYING TO WORK HERE!!

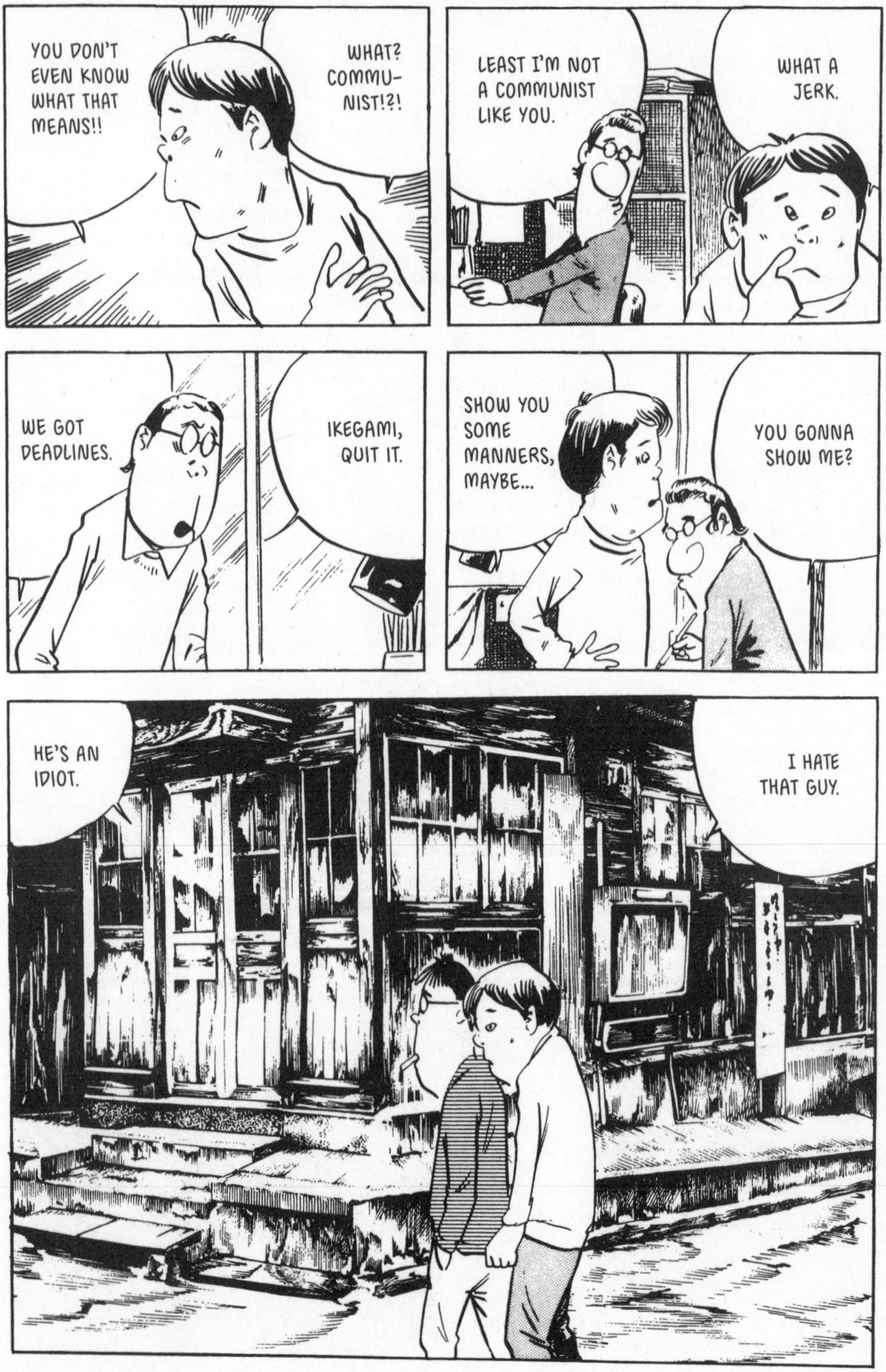
WHAT A JERK.
LEAST I'M NOT A COMMUNIST LIKE YOU.
WHAT? COMMUNIST!?!
YOU DON'T EVEN KNOW WHAT THAT MEANS!!
YOU GONNA SHOW ME?
SHOW YOU SOME MANNERS, MAYBE...
IKEGAMI, QUIT IT.
WE GOT DEADLINES.
I HATE THAT GUY.
HE'S AN IDIOT.

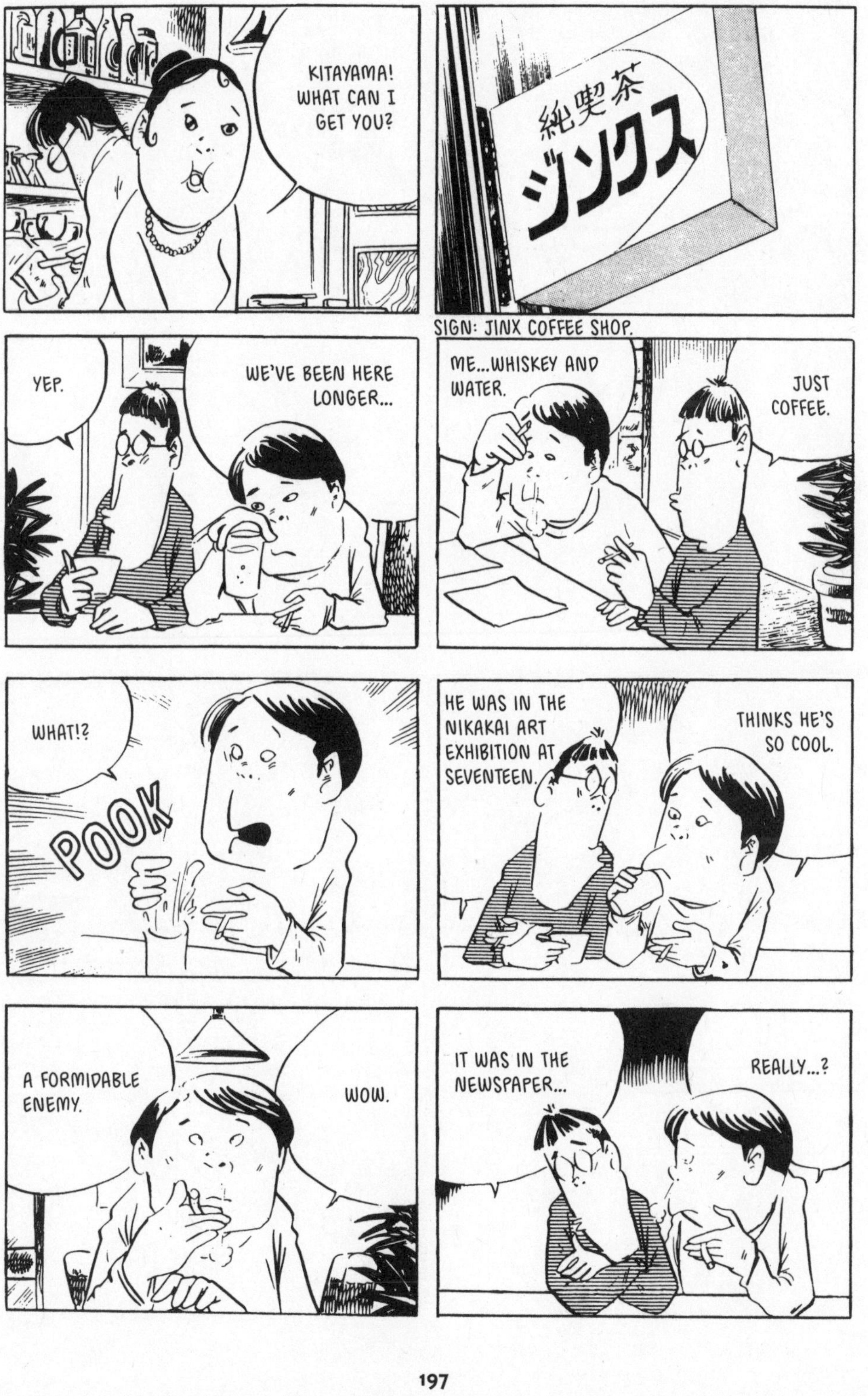
純喫茶
ジンクス
SIGN: JINX COFFEE SHOP.
KITAYAMA! WHAT CAN I GET YOU?
JUST COFFEE.
ME...WHISKEY AND WATER.
WE'VE BEEN HERE LONGER...
YEP.
THINKS HE'S SO COOL.
HE WAS IN THE NIKAKAI ART EXHIBITION AT SEVENTEEN.
WHAT!?
POOK
REALLY...?
IT WAS IN THE NEWSPAPER...
WOW.
A FORMIDABLE ENEMY.

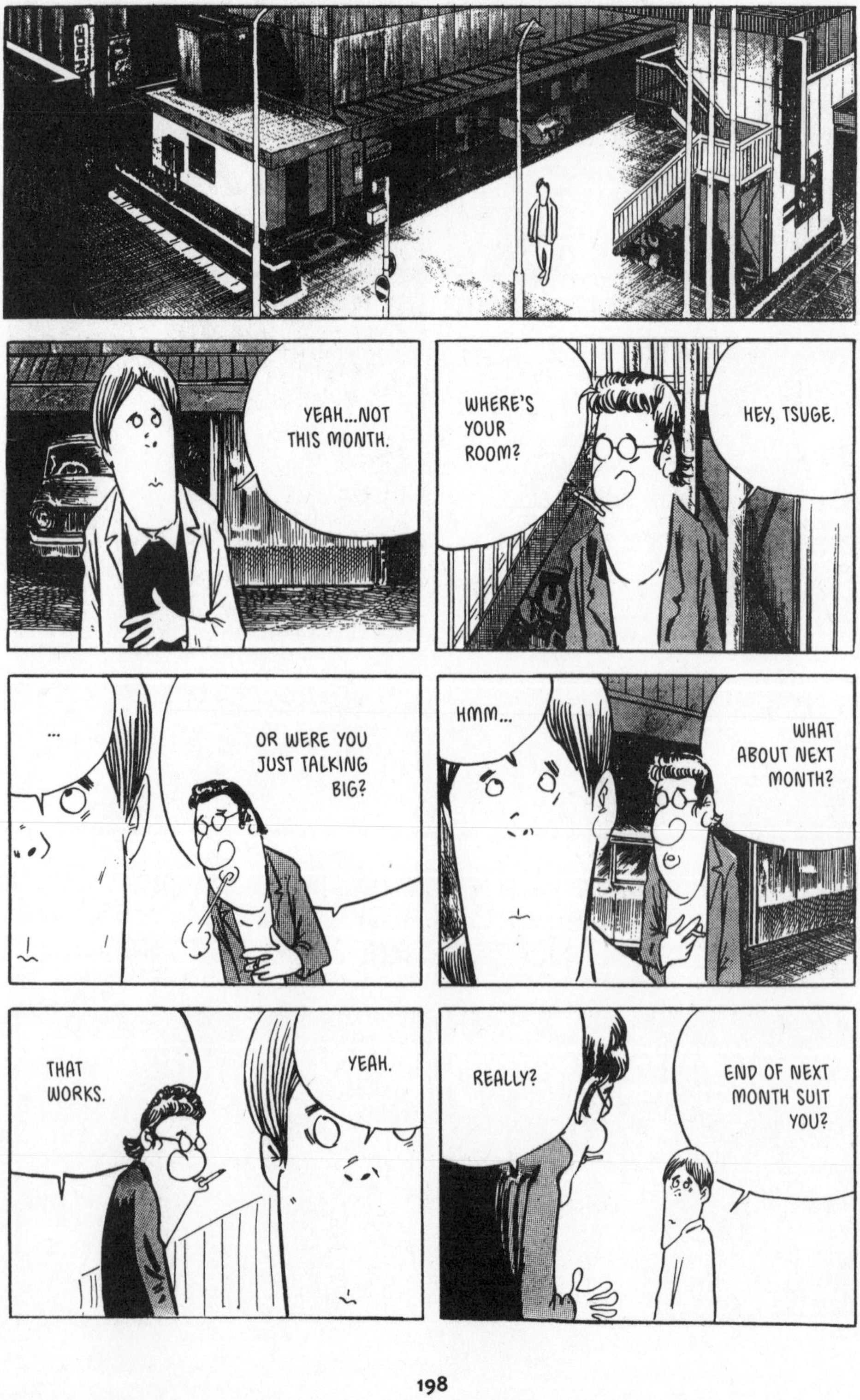
HEY, TSUGE.
WHERE'S YOUR ROOM?
YEAH...NOT THIS MONTH.
WHAT ABOUT NEXT MONTH?
HMM...
OR WERE YOU JUST TALKING BIG?
...
END OF NEXT MONTH SUIT YOU?
REALLY?
YEAH.
THAT WORKS.

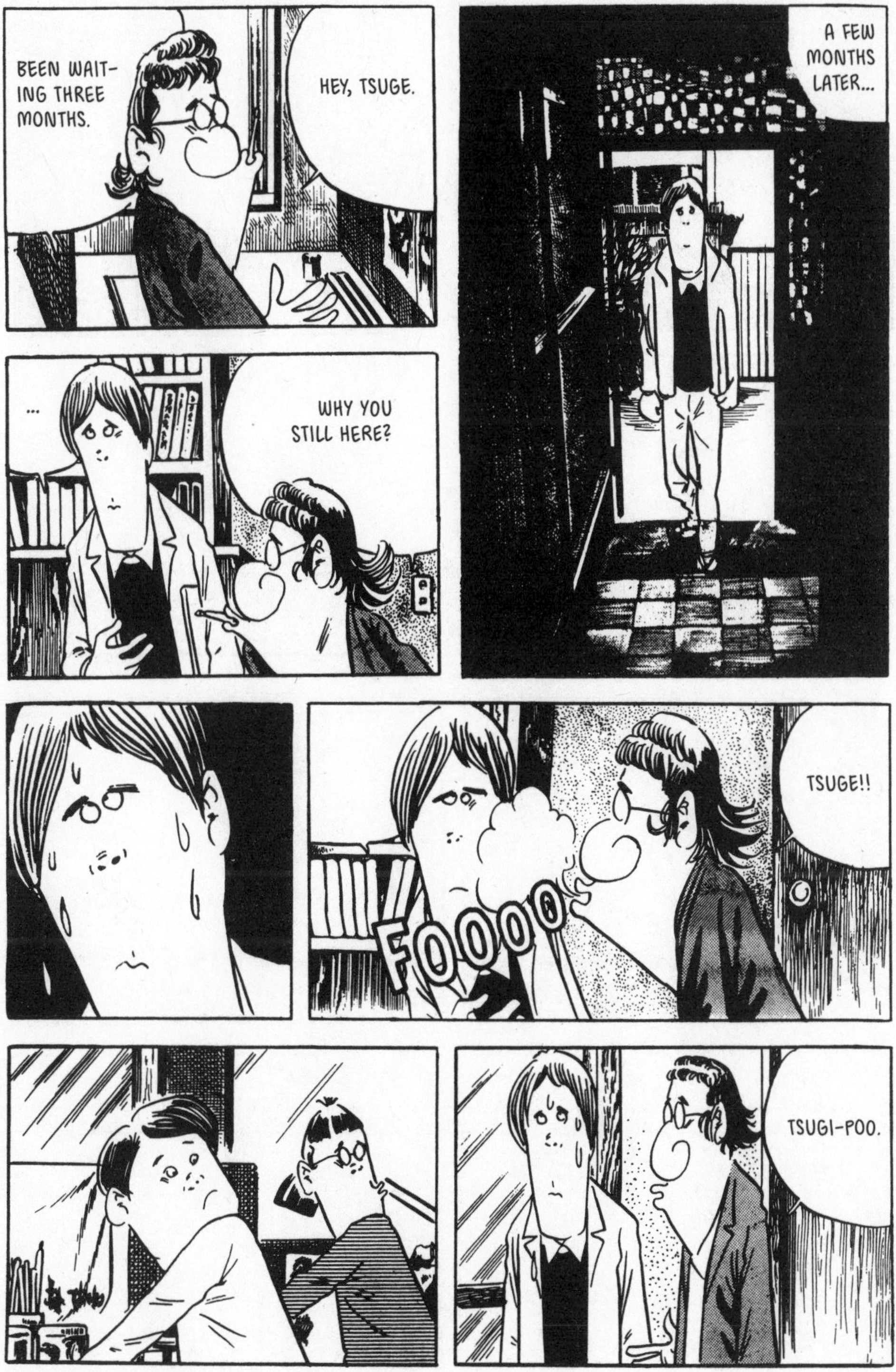
A FEW MONTHS LATER...
HEY, TSUGE.
BEEN WAIT-ING THREE MONTHS.
WHY YOU STILL HERE?
...
TSUGE!!
FOOOO
TSUGI-POO.

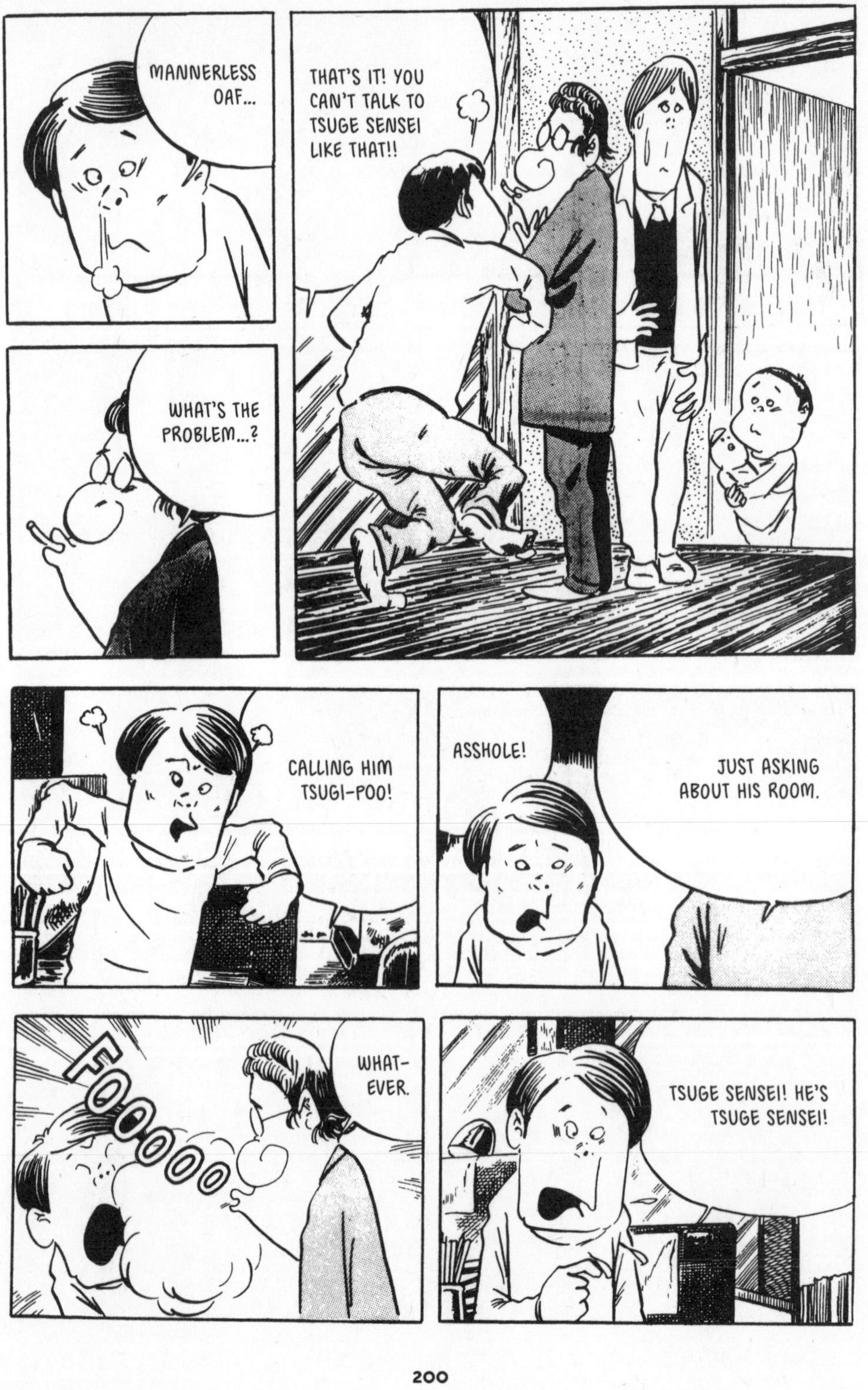
THAT'S IT! YOU CAN'T TALK TO TSUGE SENSEI LIKE THAT!!
MANNERLESS OAF...
WHAT'S THE PROBLEM...?
JUST ASKING ABOUT HIS ROOM.
ASSHOLE!
CALLING HIM TSUGI-POO!
TSUGE SENSEI! HE'S TSUGE SENSEI!
WHAT-EVER.
FOOOOO

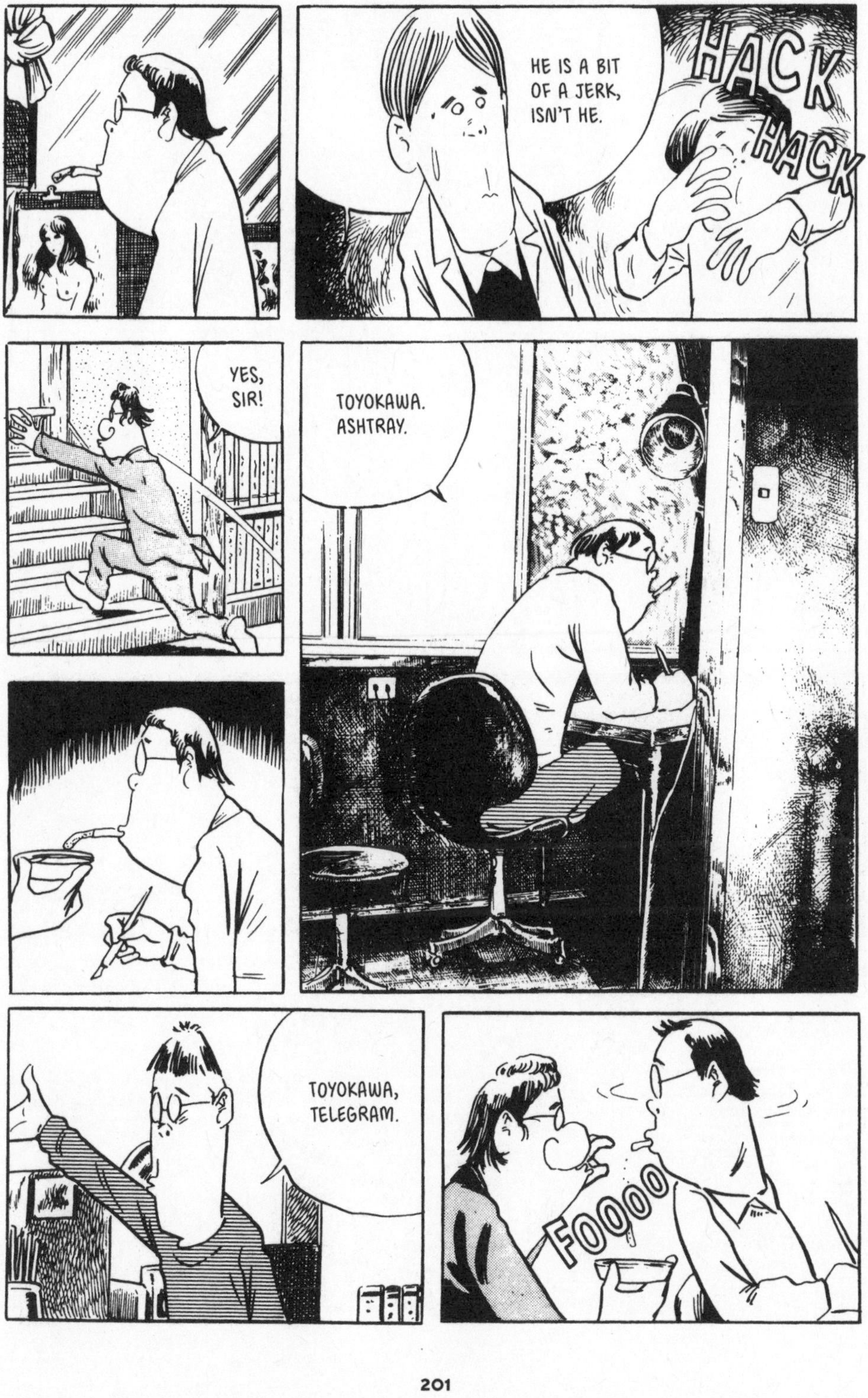
HACK
HACK
HE IS A BIT OF A JERK, ISN'T HE.
TOYOKAWA. ASHTRAY.
YES, SIR!
FOOOO
TOYOKAWA, TELEGRAM.

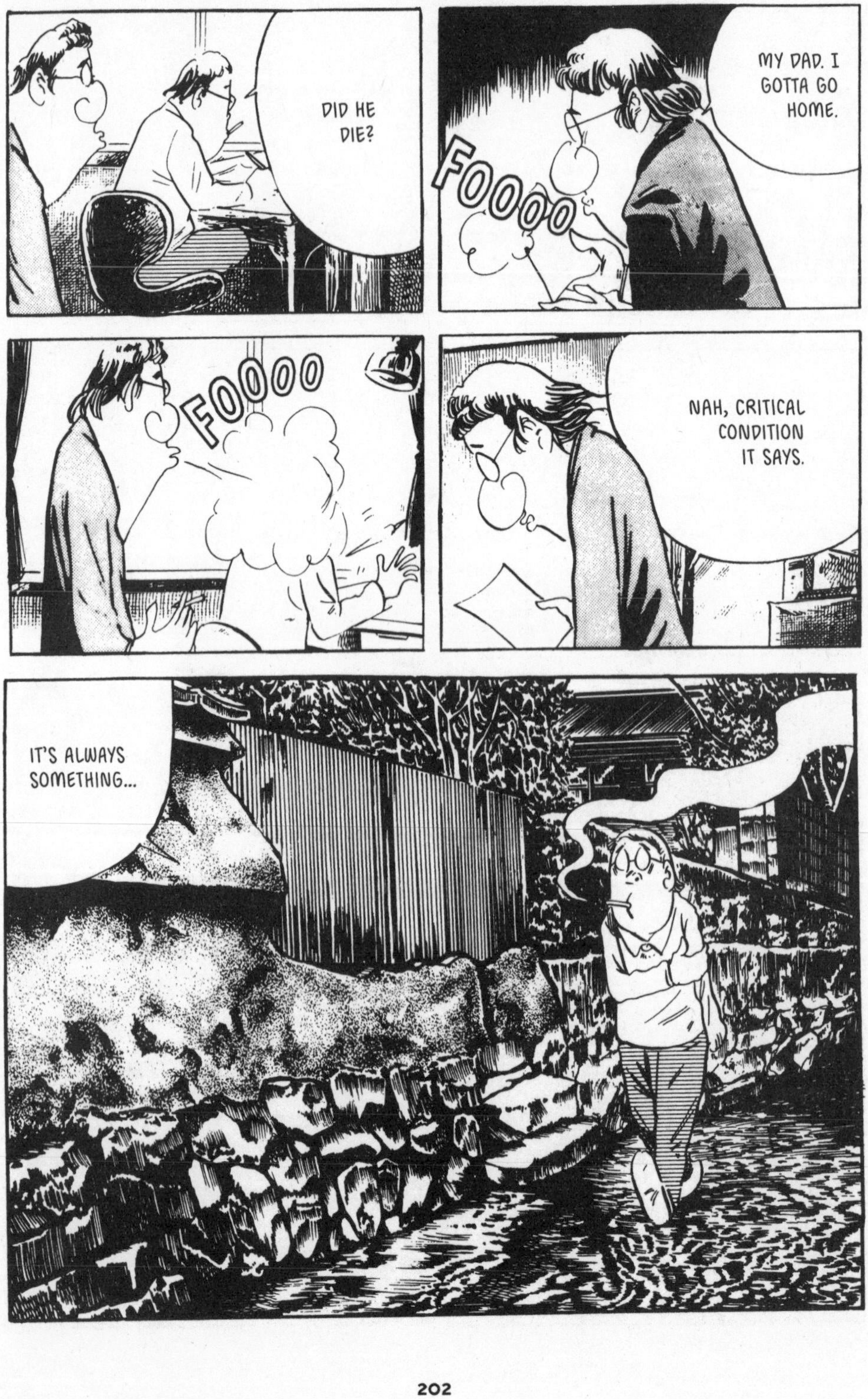
MY DAD. I GOTTA GO HOME.
FOOOO
DID HE DIE?
NAH, CRITICAL CONDITION IT SAYS.
FOOOO
IT'S ALWAYS SOMETHING...

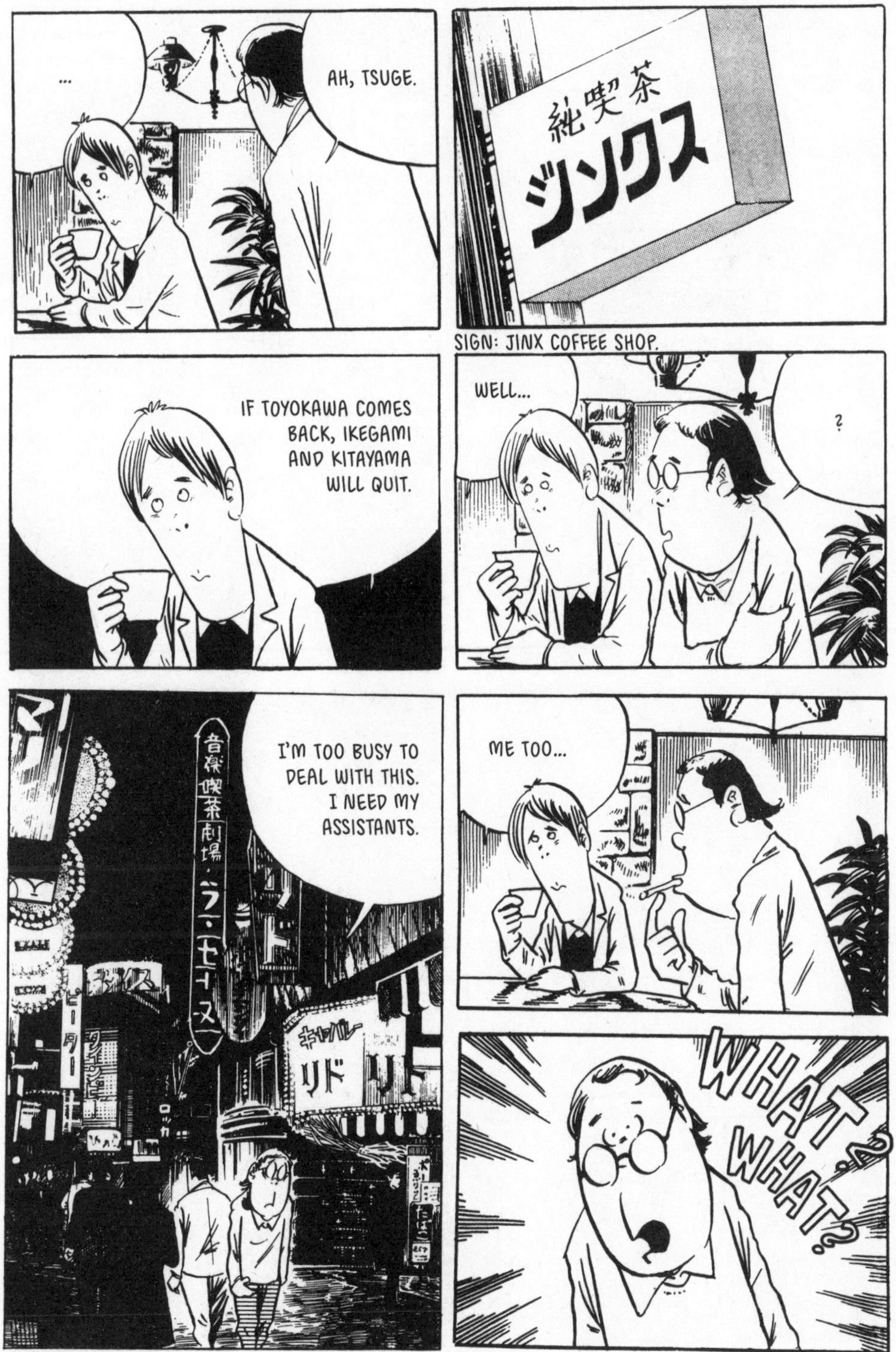

純喫茶
ジンクス
SIGN: JINX COFFEE SHOP.
AH, TSUGE.
...
?
WELL...
IF TOYOKAWA COMES BACK, IKEGAMI AND KITAYAMA WILL QUIT.
ME TOO...
WHAT? WHAT?
I'M TOO BUSY TO DEAL WITH THIS. I NEED MY ASSISTANTS.
キャバレー
リド

SIGNS: MUSIC! COFFEE SHOP!

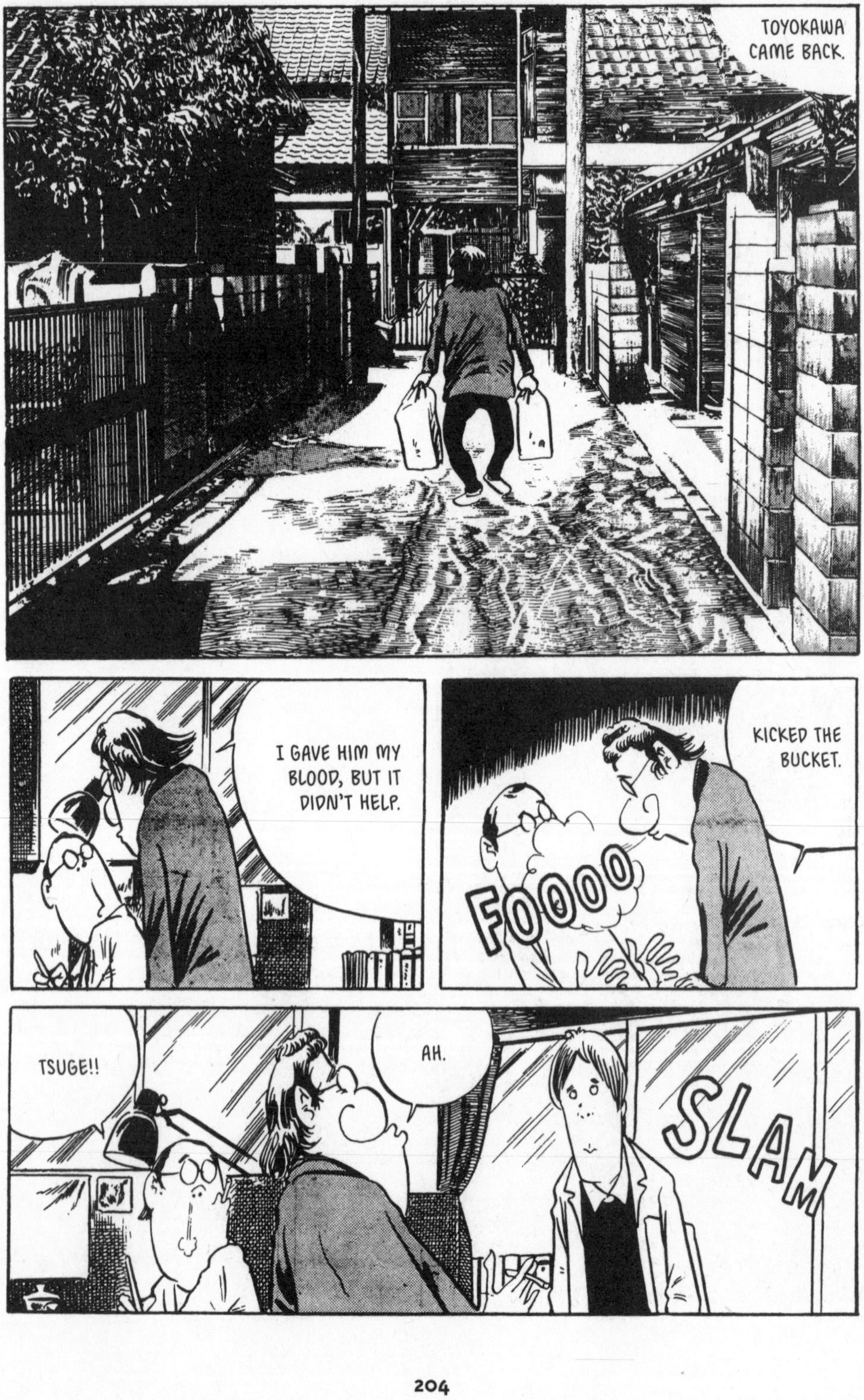
TOYOKAWA CAME BACK.
KICKED THE BUCKET.
FOOOO
I GAVE HIM MY BLOOD, BUT IT DIDN'T HELP.
SLAM
AH.
TSUGE!!

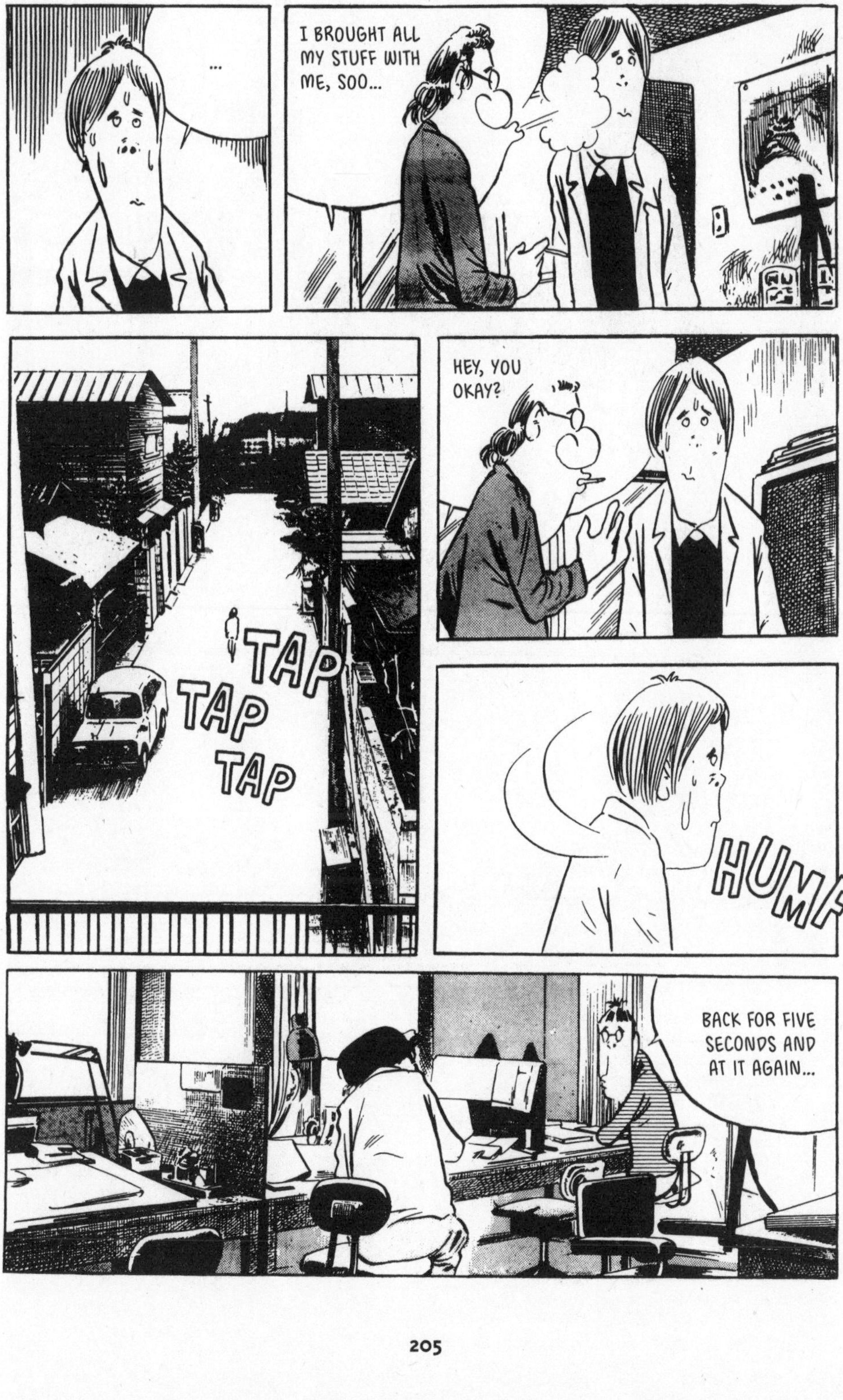
I BROUGHT ALL MY STUFF WITH ME, SOO...
...
HEY, YOU OKAY?
HUMF
TAP
TAP
TAP
BACK FOR FIVE SECONDS AND AT IT AGAIN...

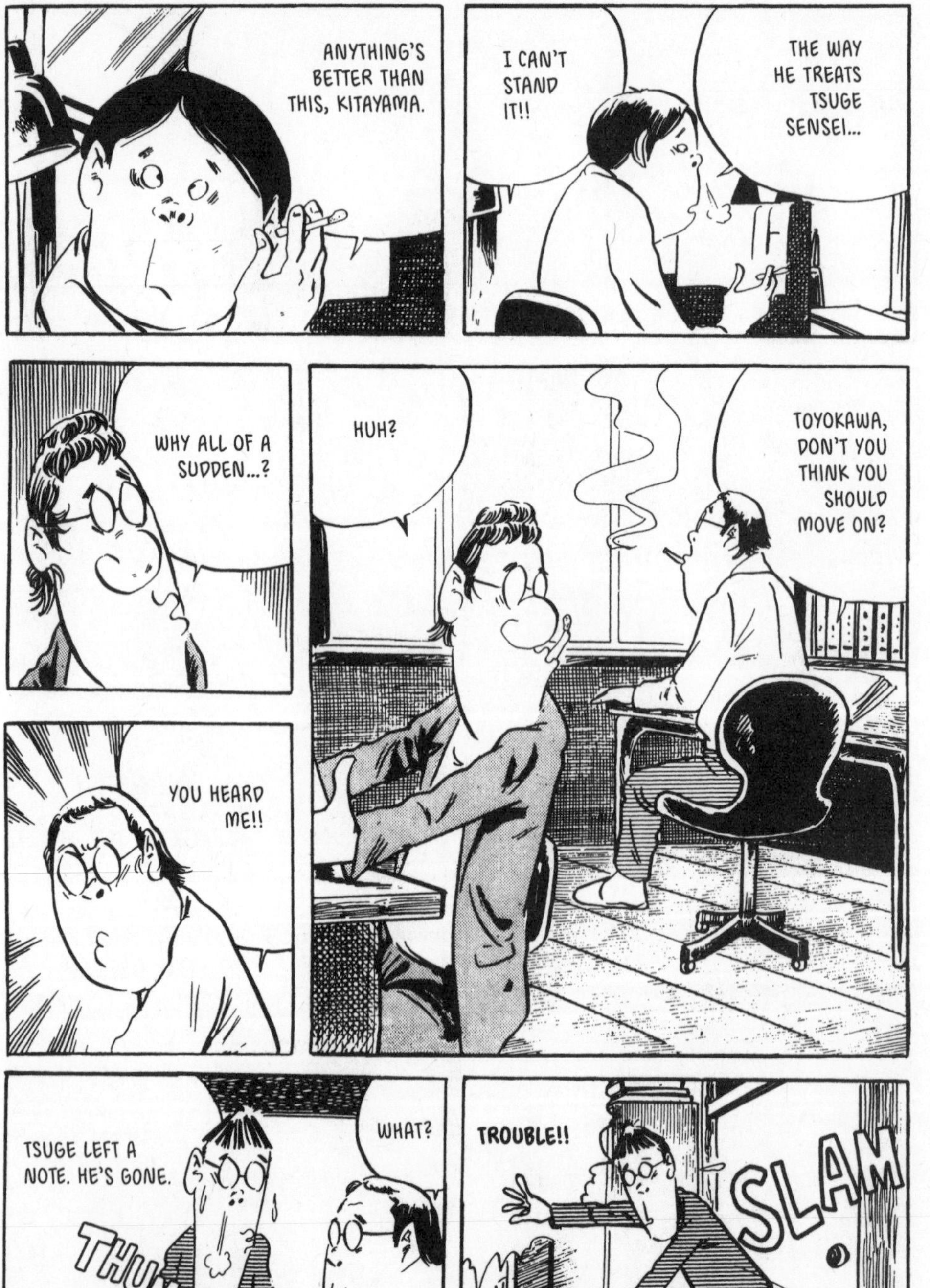
THE WAY HE TREATS TSUGE SENSEI...
I CAN'T STAND IT!!
ANYTHING'S BETTER THAN THIS, KITAYAMA.
TOYOKAWA, DON'T YOU THINK YOU SHOULD MOVE ON?
HUH?
WHY ALL OF A SUDDEN...?
YOU HEARD ME!!
SLAM
TROUBLE!!
WHAT?
TSUGE LEFT A NOTE. HE'S GONE.
THUMP THUMP

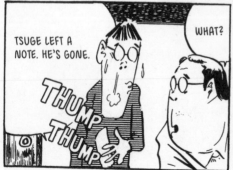

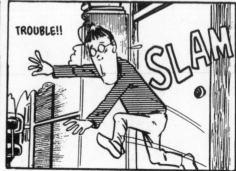

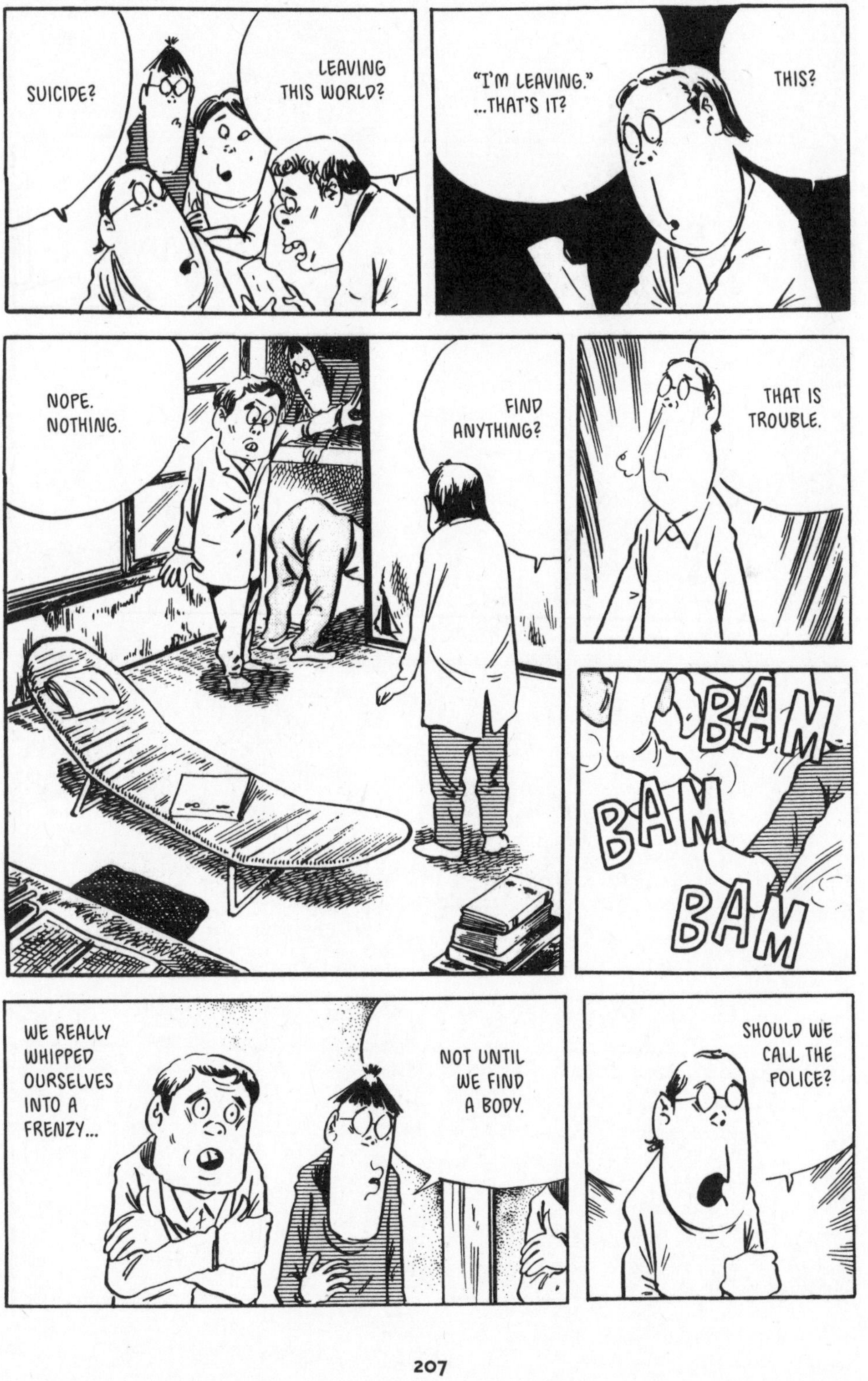
THIS?
"I'M LEAVING." ...THAT'S IT?
LEAVING THIS WORLD?
SUICIDE?
THAT IS TROUBLE.
BAM
BAM
BAM
FIND ANYTHING?
NOPE. NOTHING.
SHOULD WE CALL THE POLICE?
NOT UNTIL WE FIND A BODY.
WE REALLY WHIPPED OURSELVES INTO A FRENZY...

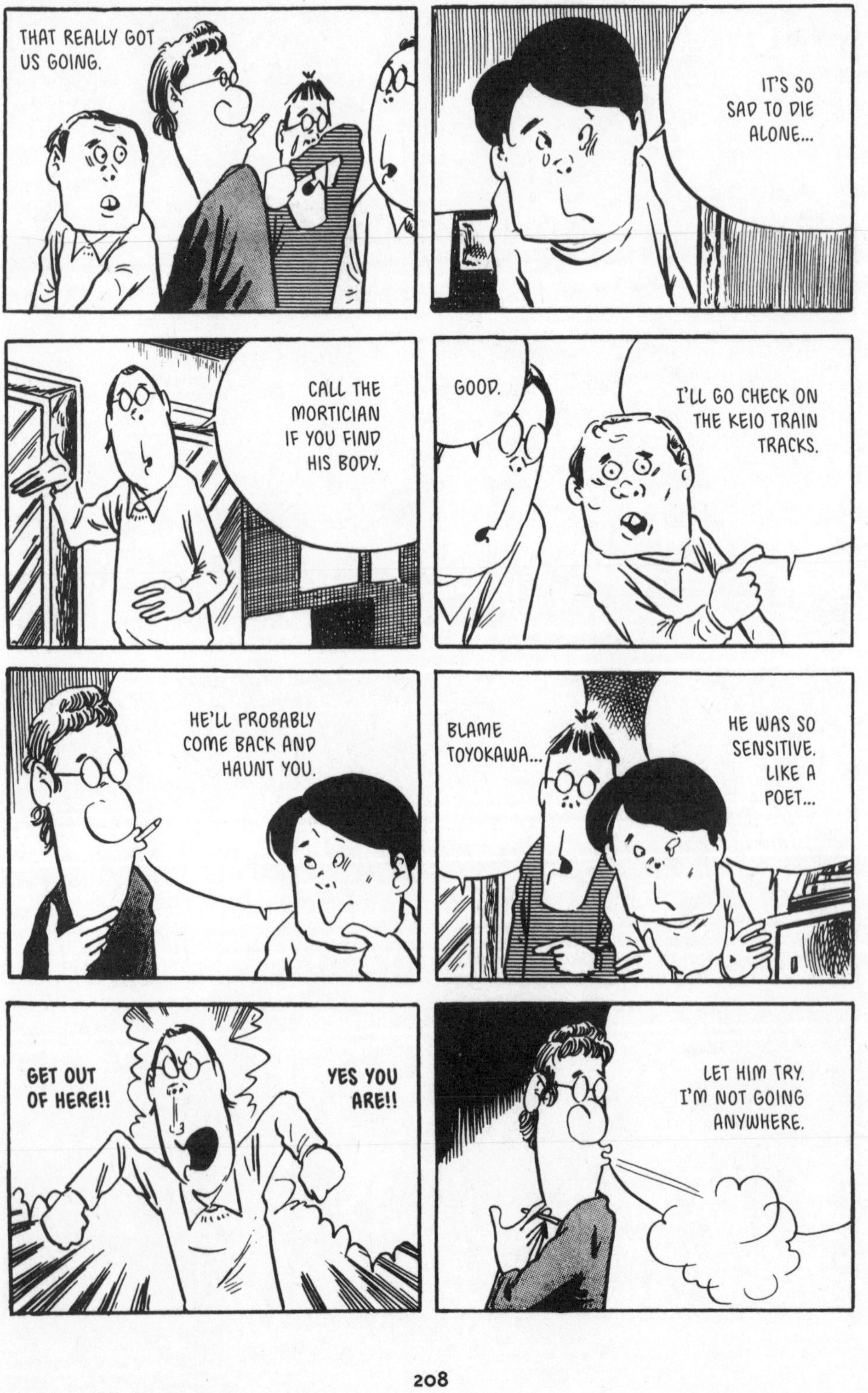
IT'S SO SAD TO DIE ALONE...
THAT REALLY GOT US GOING.
I'LL GO CHECK ON THE KEIO TRAIN TRACKS.
GOOD.
CALL THE MORTICIAN IF YOU FIND HIS BODY.
HE WAS SO SENSITIVE. LIKE A POET...
BLAME TOYOKAWA...
HE'LL PROBABLY COME BACK AND HAUNT YOU.
LET HIM TRY. I'M NOT GOING ANYWHERE.
YES YOU ARE!!
GET OUT OF HERE!!

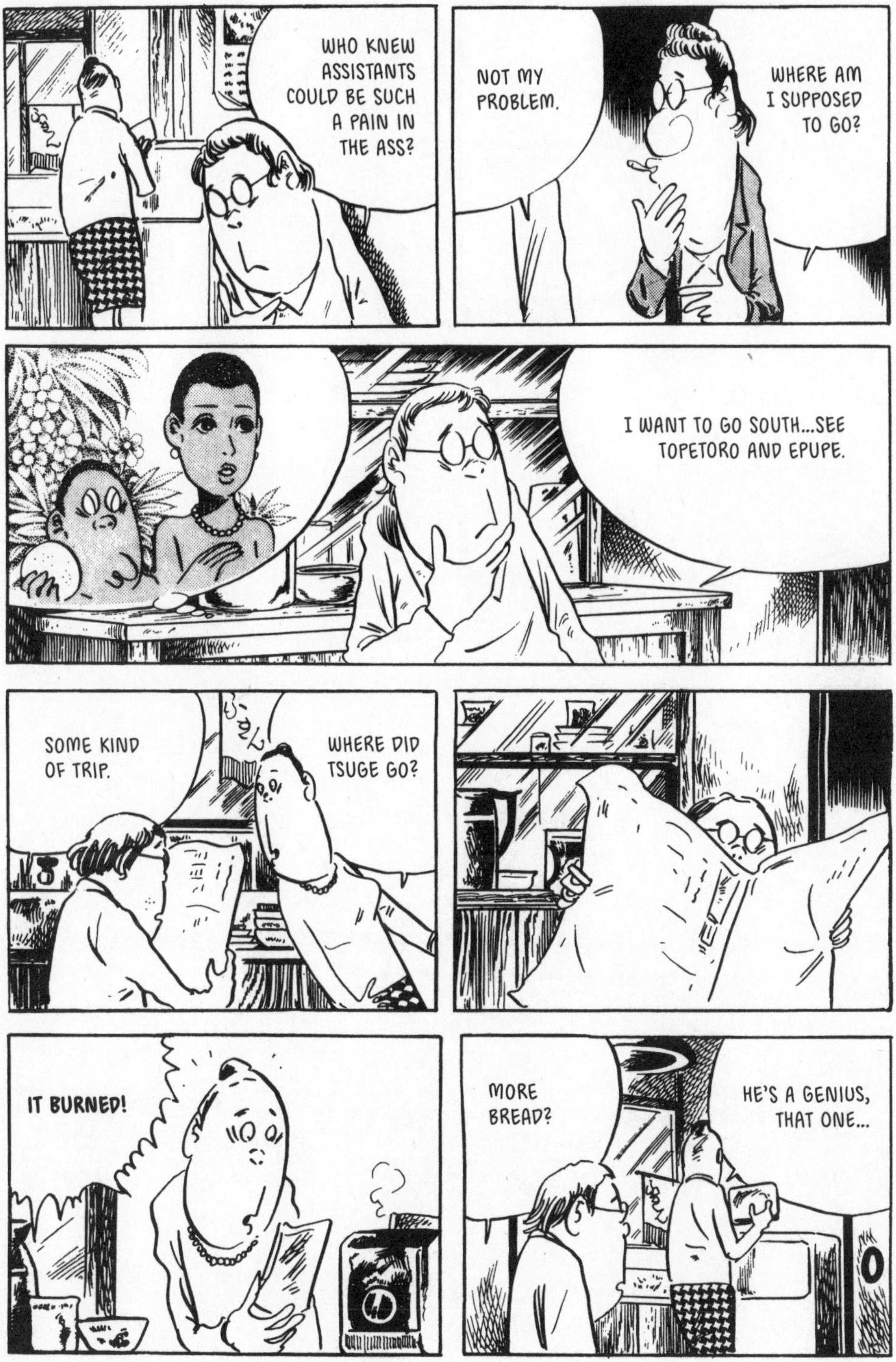
WHERE AM I SUPPOSED TO GO?
NOT MY PROBLEM.
WHO KNEW ASSISTANTS COULD BE SUCH A PAIN IN THE ASS?
I WANT TO GO SOUTH...SEE TOPETORO AND EPUPE.
WHERE DID TSUGE GO?
SOME KIND OF TRIP.
HE'S A GENIUS, THAT ONE...
MORE BREAD?
IT BURNED!

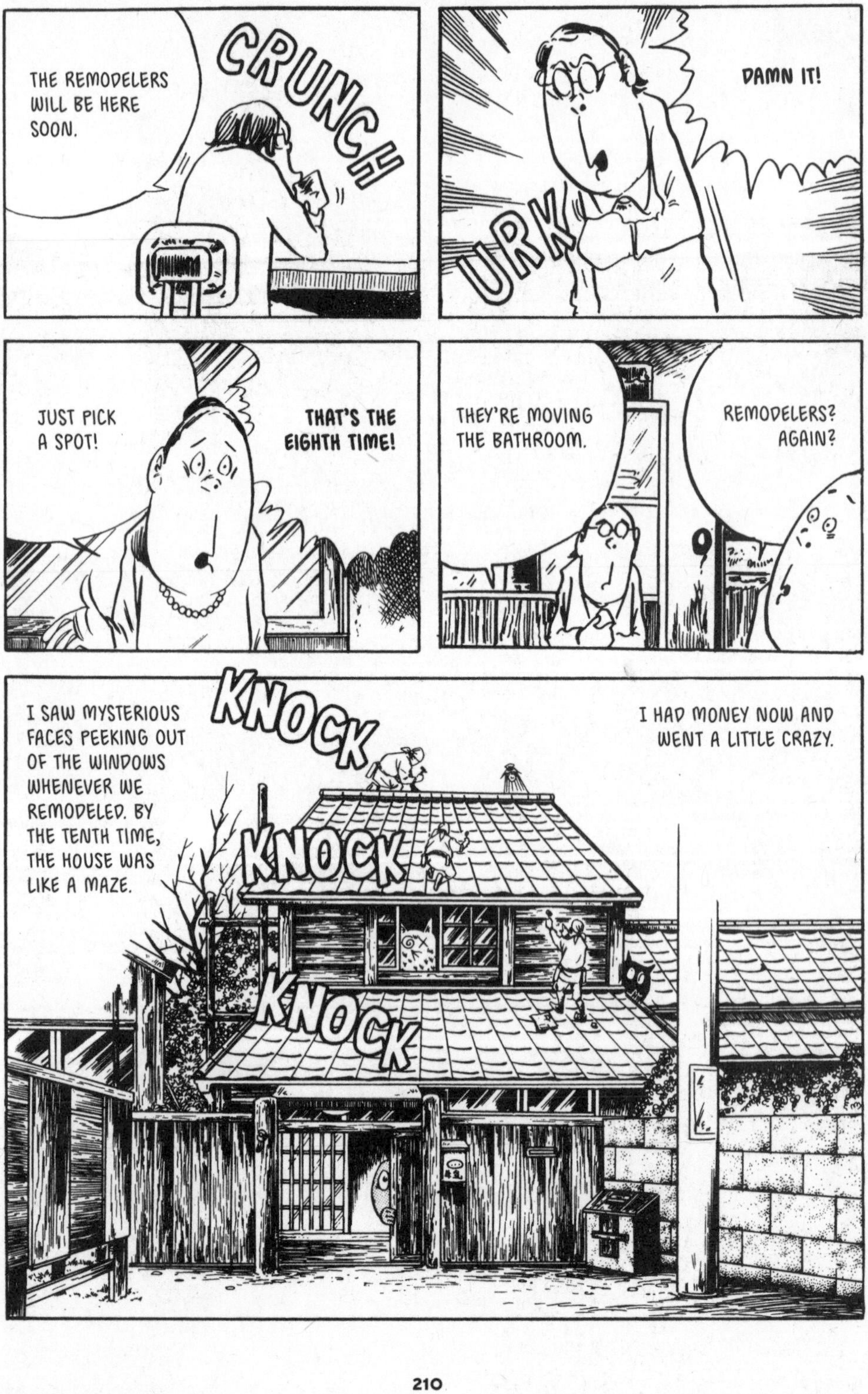
DAMN IT!
URK
CRUNCH
THE REMODELERS WILL BE HERE SOON.
REMODELERS? AGAIN?
THEY'RE MOVING THE BATHROOM.
THAT'S THE EIGHTH TIME!
JUST PICK A SPOT!
I HAD MONEY NOW AND WENT A LITTLE CRAZY.
KNOCK
KNOCK
KNOCK
I SAW MYSTERIOUS FACES PEEKING OUT OF THE WINDOWS WHENEVER WE REMODELED. BY THE TENTH TIME, THE HOUSE WAS LIKE A MAZE.

THE CONTRADICTION OF RAPID GROWTH

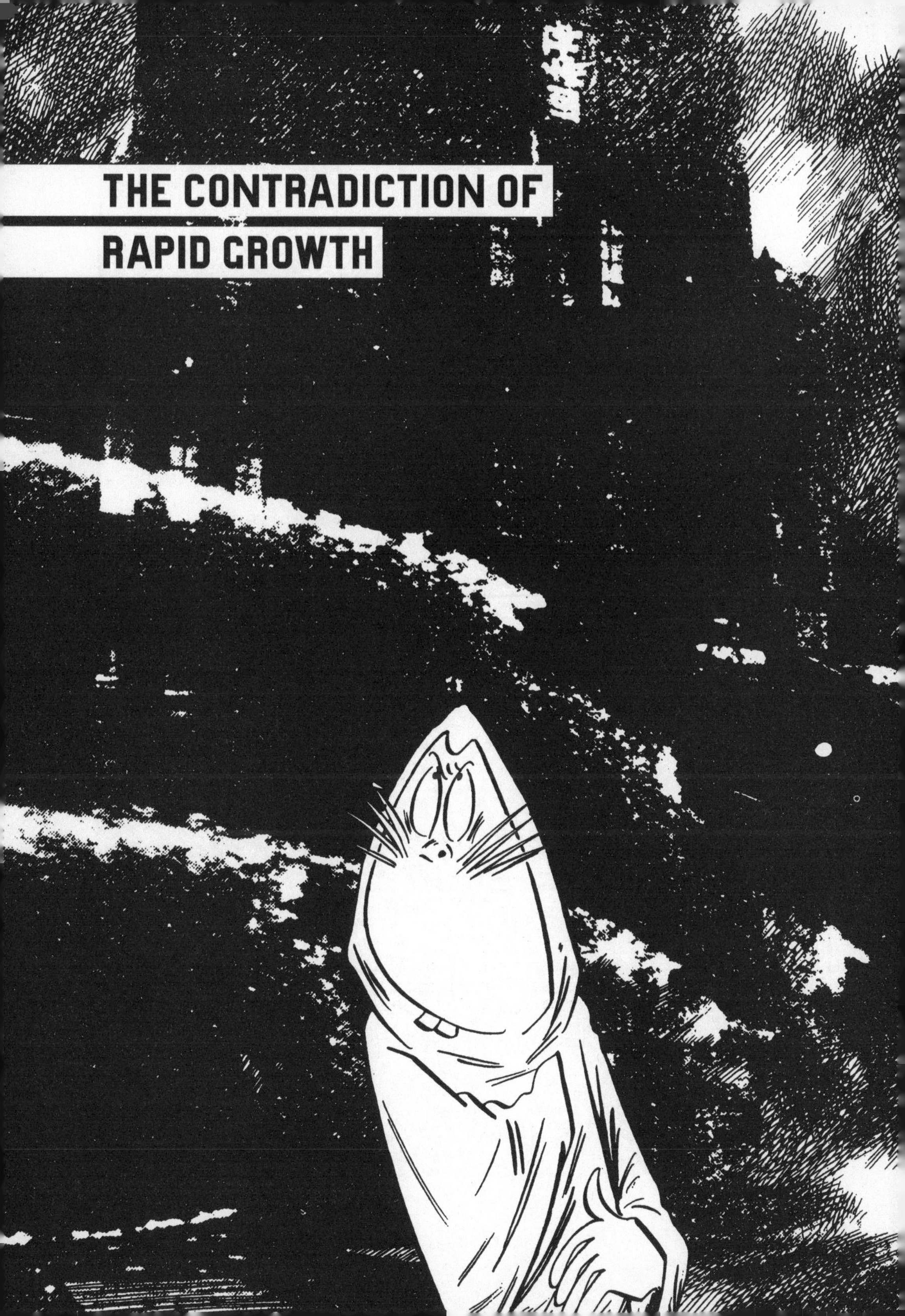

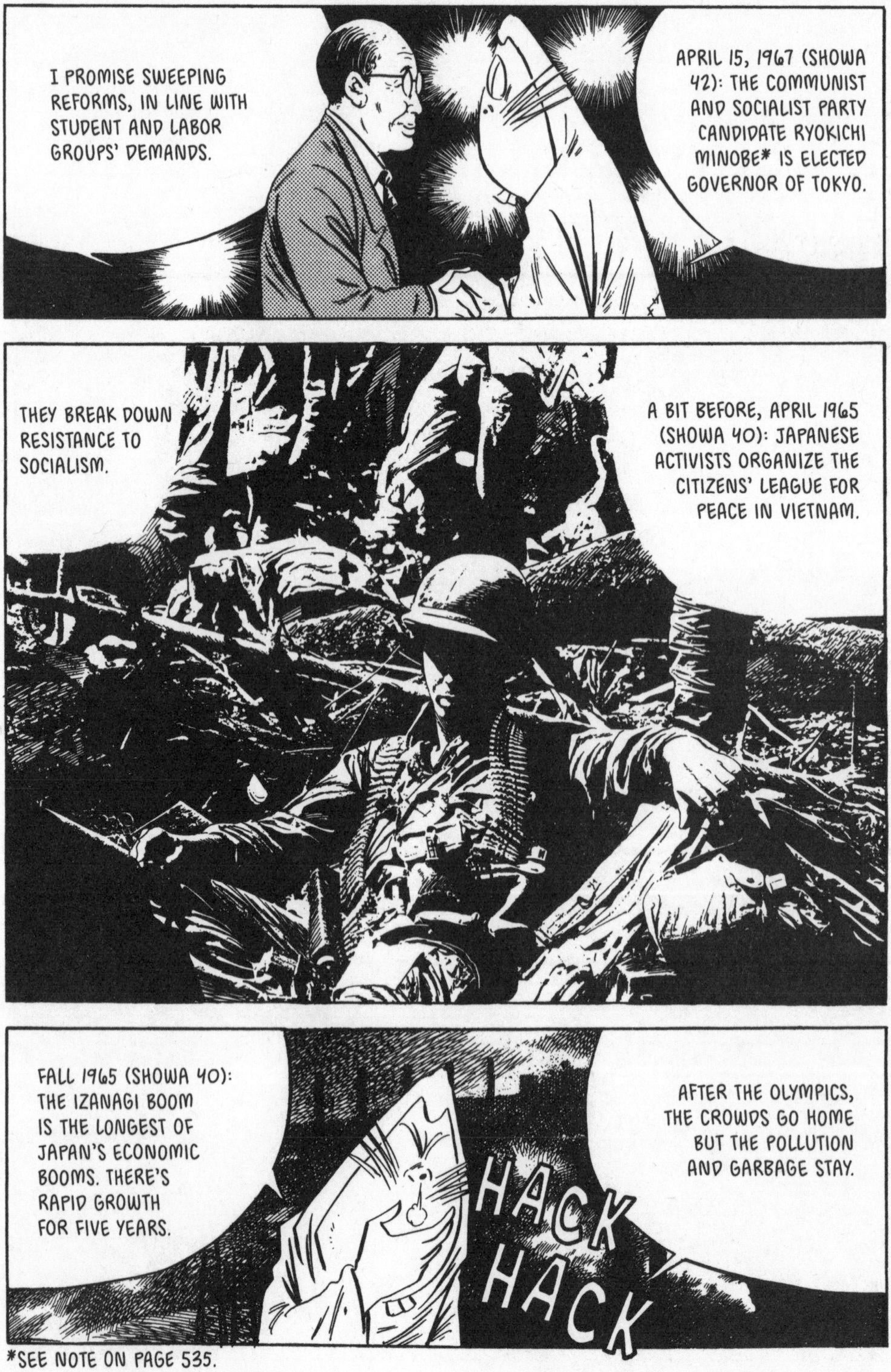
APRIL 15, 1967 (SHOWA 42): THE COMMUNIST AND SOCIALIST PARTY CANDIDATE RYOKICHI MINOBE* IS ELECTED GOVERNOR OF TOKYO.
I PROMISE SWEEPING REFORMS, IN LINE WITH STUDENT AND LABOR GROUPS' DEMANDS.
A BIT BEFORE, APRIL 1965 (SHOWA 40): JAPANESE ACTIVISTS ORGANIZE THE CITIZENS' LEAGUE FOR PEACE IN VIETNAM.
THEY BREAK DOWN RESISTANCE TO SOCIALISM.
AFTER THE OLYMPICS, THE CROWDS GO HOME BUT THE POLLUTION AND GARBAGE STAY.
HACK HACK
FALL 1965 (SHOWA 40): THE IZANAGI BOOM IS THE LONGEST OF JAPAN'S ECONOMIC BOOMS. THERE'S RAPID GROWTH FOR FIVE YEARS.

*SEE NOTE ON PAGE 535.

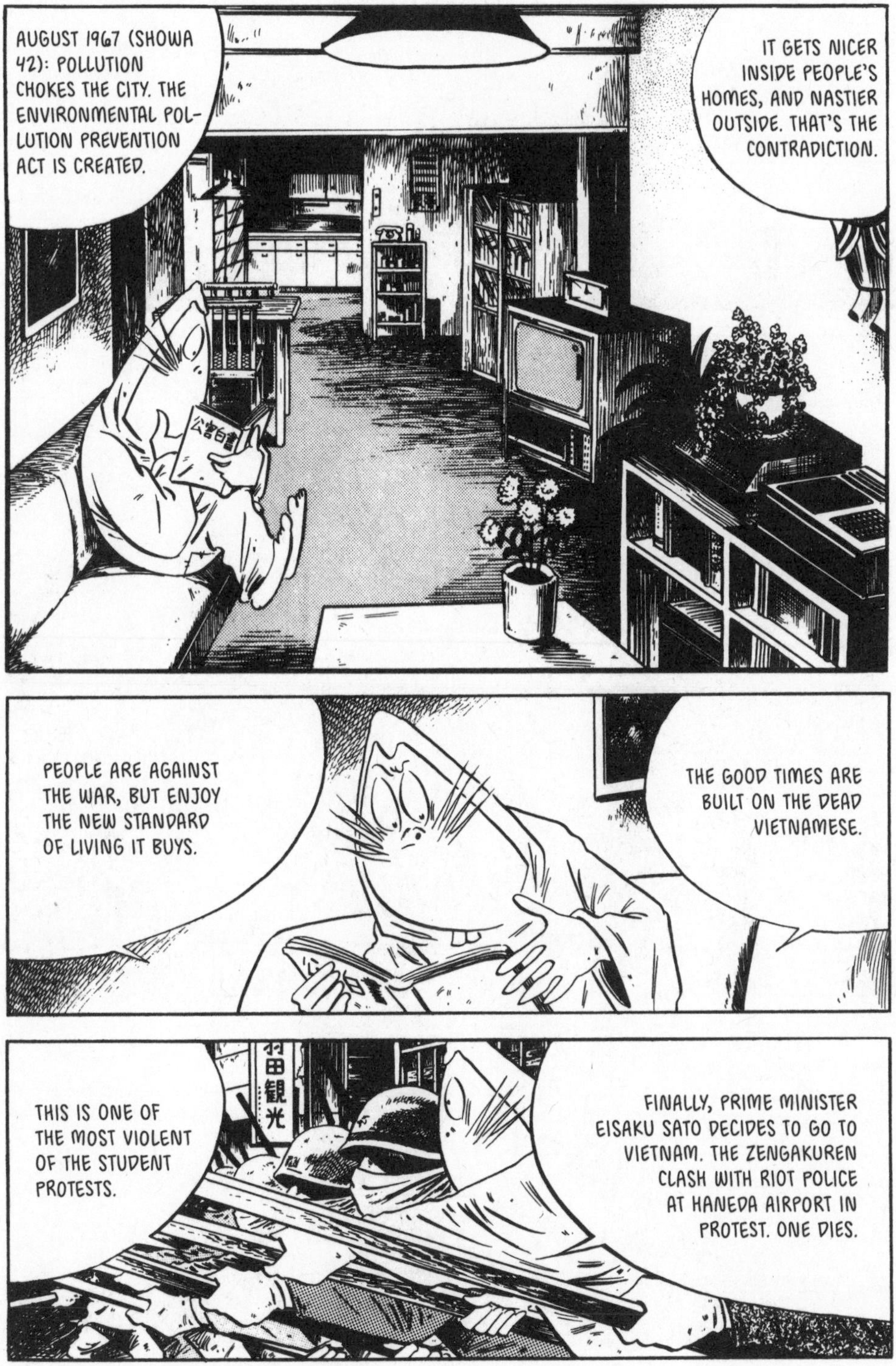
IT GETS NICER INSIDE PEOPLE'S HOMES, AND NASTIER OUTSIDE. THAT'S THE CONTRADICTION.
AUGUST 1967 (SHOWA 42): POLLUTION CHOKES THE CITY. THE ENVIRONMENTAL POL-LUTION PREVENTION ACT IS CREATED.
公害白書
THE GOOD TIMES ARE BUILT ON THE DEAD VIETNAMESE.
PEOPLE ARE AGAINST THE WAR, BUT ENJOY THE NEW STANDARD OF LIVING IT BUYS.
FINALLY, PRIME MINISTER EISAKU SATO DECIDES TO GO TO VIETNAM. THE ZENGAKUREN CLASH WITH RIOT POLICE AT HANEDA AIRPORT IN PROTEST. ONE DIES.
羽田観光
THIS IS ONE OF THE MOST VIOLENT OF THE STUDENT PROTESTS.

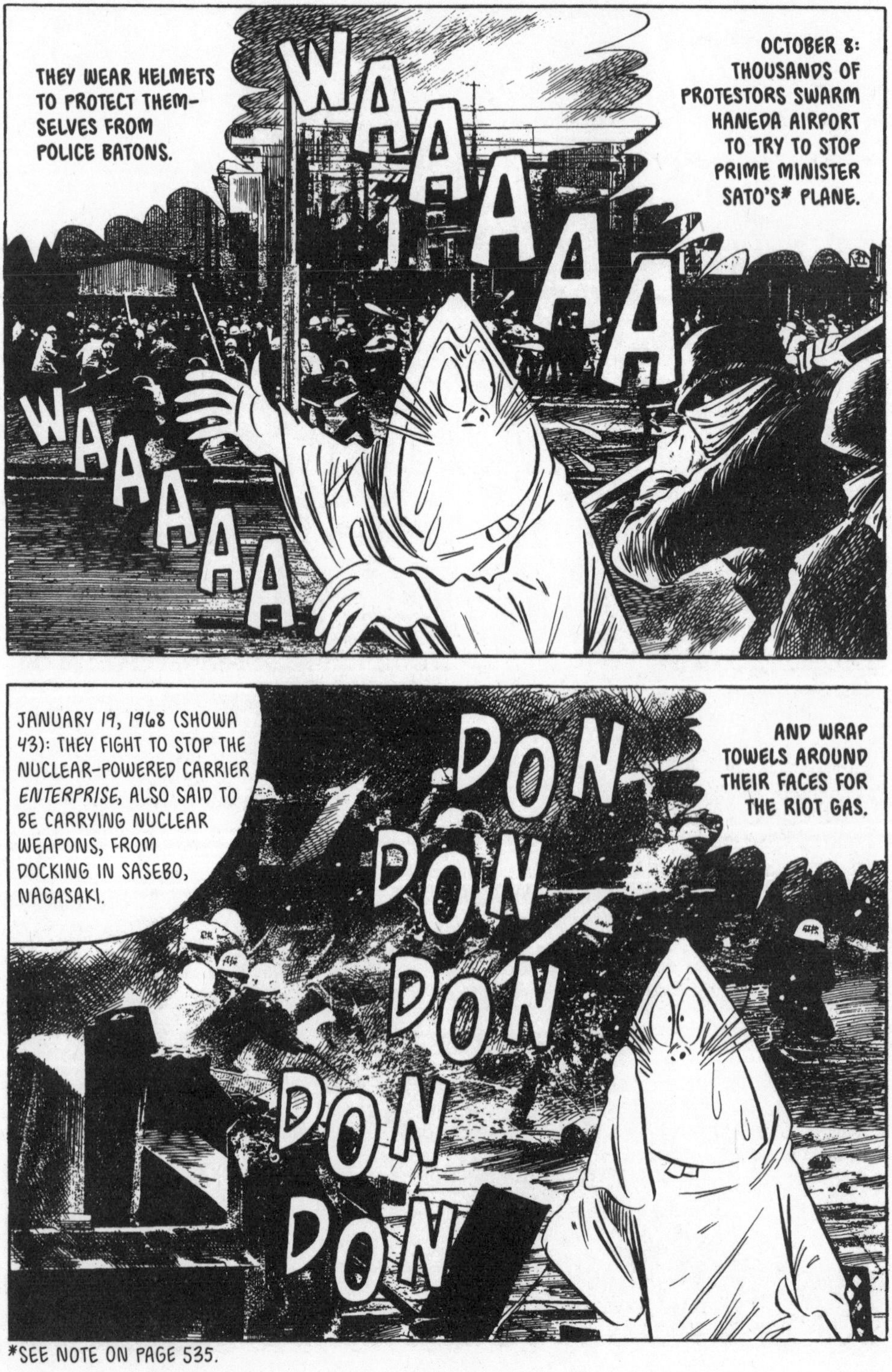
OCTOBER 8: THOUSANDS OF PROTESTORS SWARM HANEDA AIRPORT TO TRY TO STOP PRIME MINISTER SATO'S* PLANE.
WAAAAAAA
THEY WEAR HELMETS TO PROTECT THEM-SELVES FROM POLICE BATONS.
WAAAAAAA
AND WRAP TOWELS AROUND THEIR FACES FOR THE RIOT GAS.
DON DON DON DON DON
JANUARY 19, 1968 (SHOWA 43): THEY FIGHT TO STOP THE NUCLEAR-POWERED CARRIER *ENTERPRISE*, ALSO SAID TO BE CARRYING NUCLEAR WEAPONS, FROM DOCKING IN SASEBO, NAGASAKI.

*SEE NOTE ON PAGE 535.

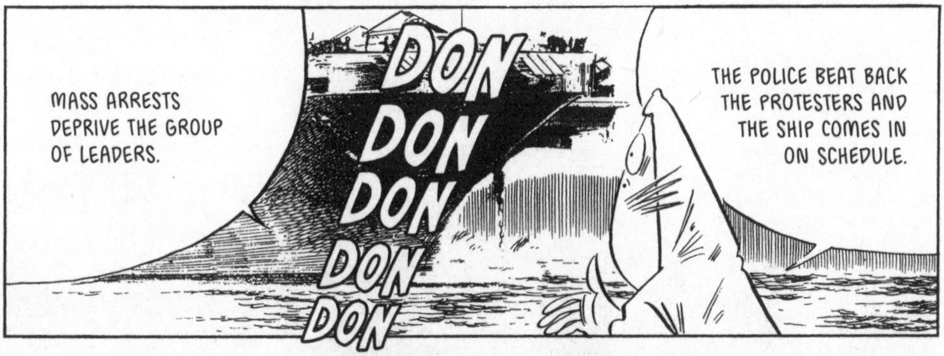
THE POLICE BEAT BACK THE PROTESTERS AND THE SHIP COMES IN ON SCHEDULE.
DON DON DON DON DON
MASS ARRESTS DEPRIVE THE GROUP OF LEADERS.

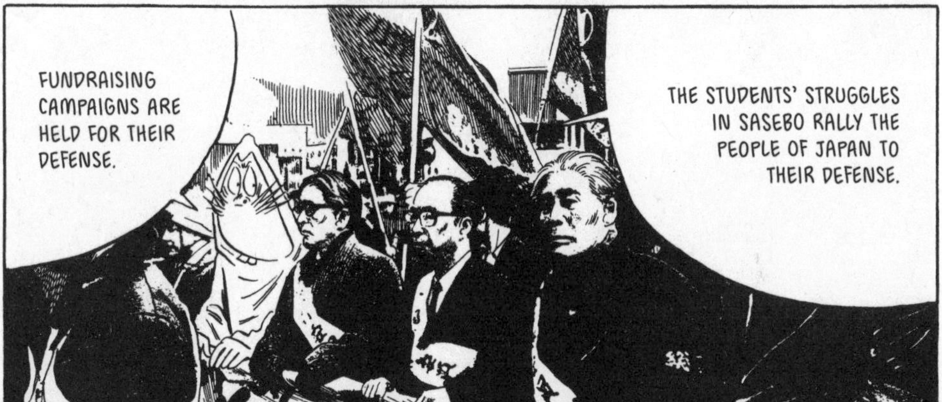
THE STUDENTS' STRUGGLES IN SASEBO RALLY THE PEOPLE OF JAPAN TO THEIR DEFENSE.
FUNDRAISING CAMPAIGNS ARE HELD FOR THEIR DEFENSE.
SIGN: NO *ENTERPRISE*! GENERAL COUNCIL OF JAPANESE TRADE UNIONS.

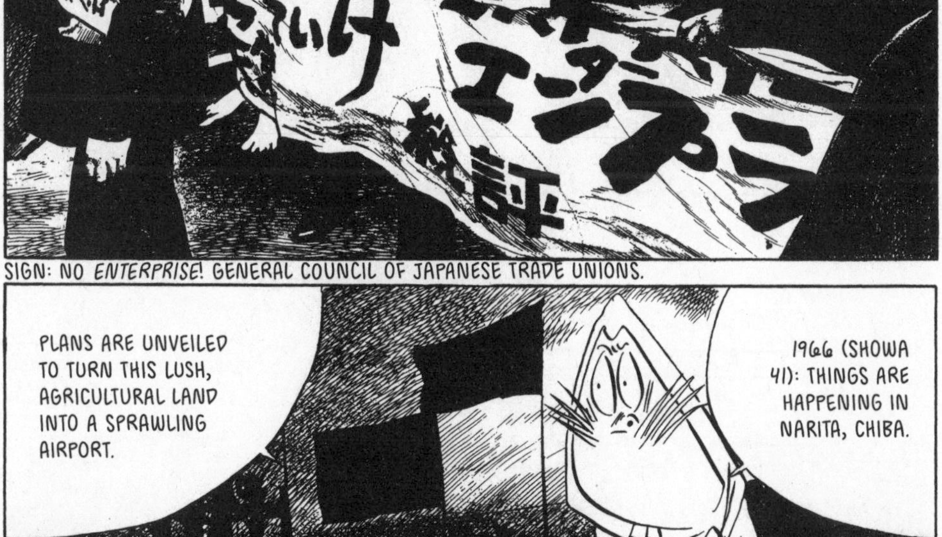
1966 (SHOWA 41): THINGS ARE HAPPENING IN NARITA, CHIBA.
PLANS ARE UNVEILED TO TURN THIS LUSH, AGRICULTURAL LAND INTO A SPRAWLING AIRPORT.

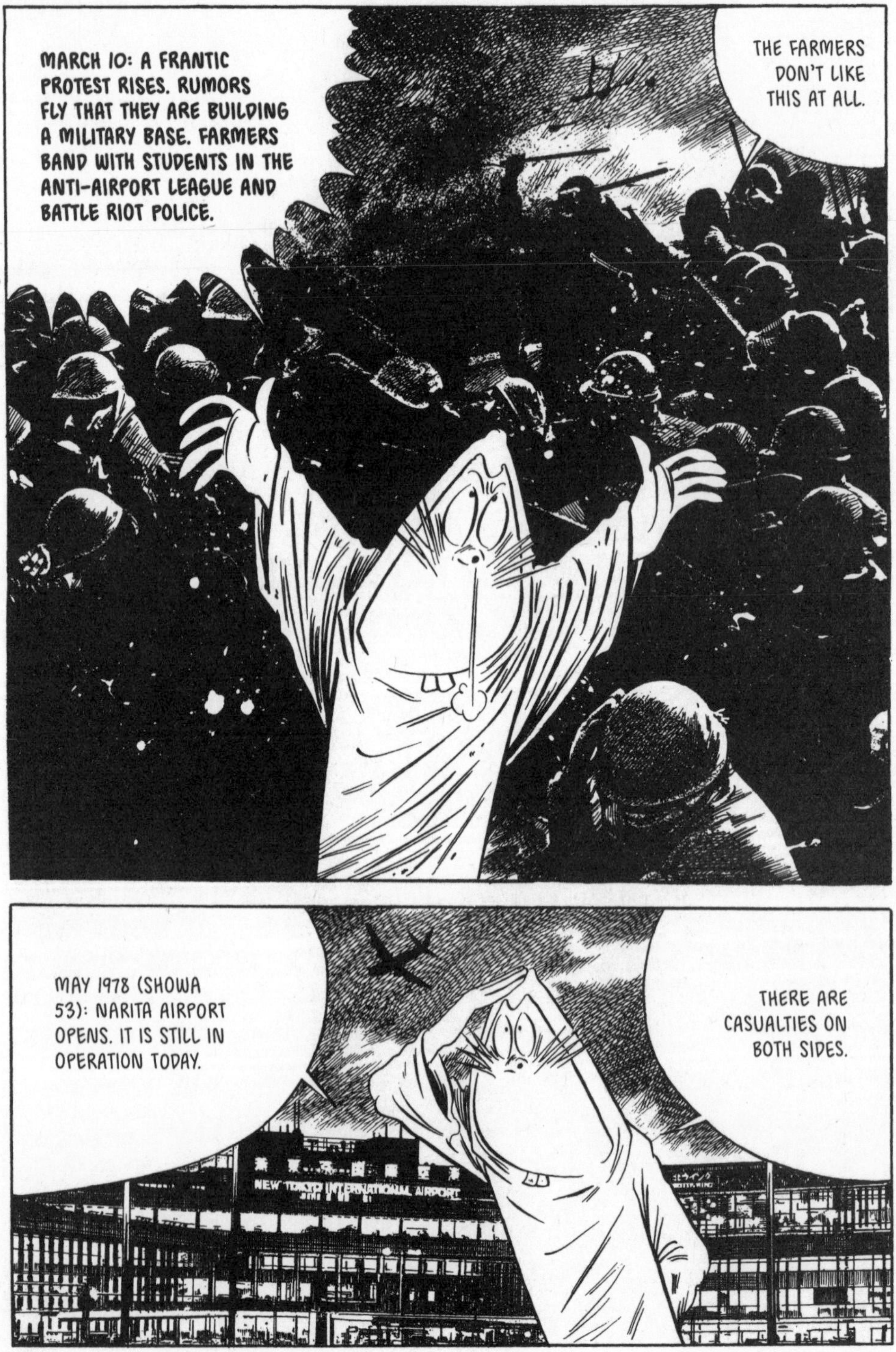
THE FARMERS DON'T LIKE THIS AT ALL.
MARCH 10: A FRANTIC PROTEST RISES. RUMORS FLY THAT THEY ARE BUILDING A MILITARY BASE. FARMERS BAND WITH STUDENTS IN THE ANTI-AIRPORT LEAGUE AND BATTLE RIOT POLICE.
THERE ARE CASUALTIES ON BOTH SIDES.
MAY 1978 (SHOWA 53): NARITA AIRPORT OPENS. IT IS STILL IN OPERATION TODAY.
NEW TOKYO INTERNATIONAL AIRPORT

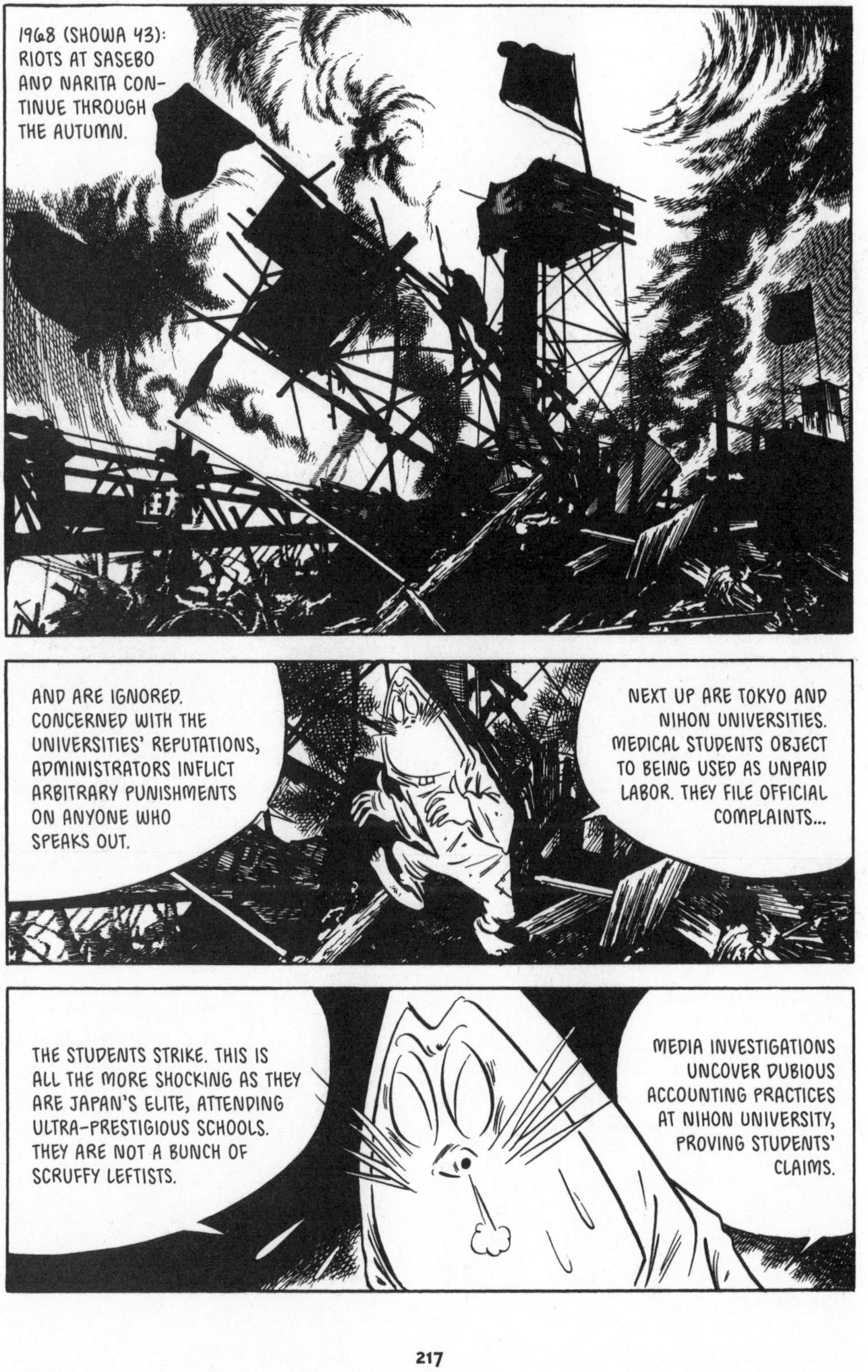
1968 (SHOWA 43): RIOTS AT SASEBO AND NARITA CONTINUE THROUGH THE AUTUMN.
NEXT UP ARE TOKYO AND NIHON UNIVERSITIES. MEDICAL STUDENTS OBJECT TO BEING USED AS UNPAID LABOR. THEY FILE OFFICIAL COMPLAINTS...
AND ARE IGNORED. CONCERNED WITH THE UNIVERSITIES' REPUTATIONS, ADMINISTRATORS INFLICT ARBITRARY PUNISHMENTS ON ANYONE WHO SPEAKS OUT.
MEDIA INVESTIGATIONS UNCOVER DUBIOUS ACCOUNTING PRACTICES AT NIHON UNIVERSITY, PROVING STUDENTS' CLAIMS.
THE STUDENTS STRIKE. THIS IS ALL THE MORE SHOCKING AS THEY ARE JAPAN'S ELITE, ATTENDING ULTRA-PRESTIGIOUS SCHOOLS. THEY ARE NOT A BUNCH OF SCRUFFY LEFTISTS.

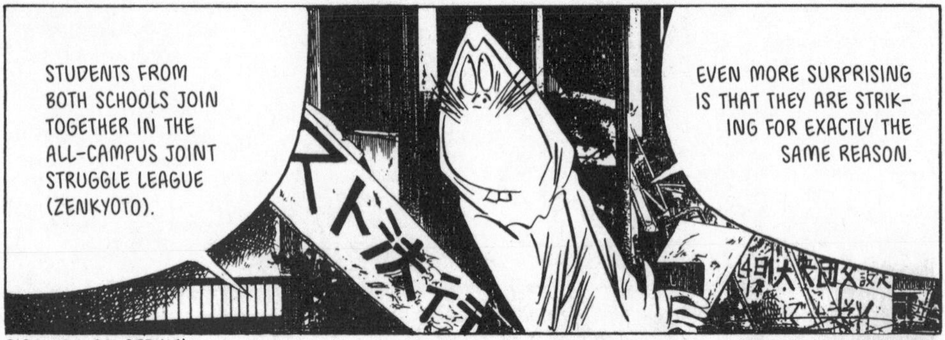
EVEN MORE SURPRISING IS THAT THEY ARE STRIKING FOR EXACTLY THE SAME REASON.
STUDENTS FROM BOTH SCHOOLS JOIN TOGETHER IN THE ALL-CAMPUS JOINT STRUGGLE LEAGUE (ZENKYOTO).

SIGN: GO ON STRIKE!

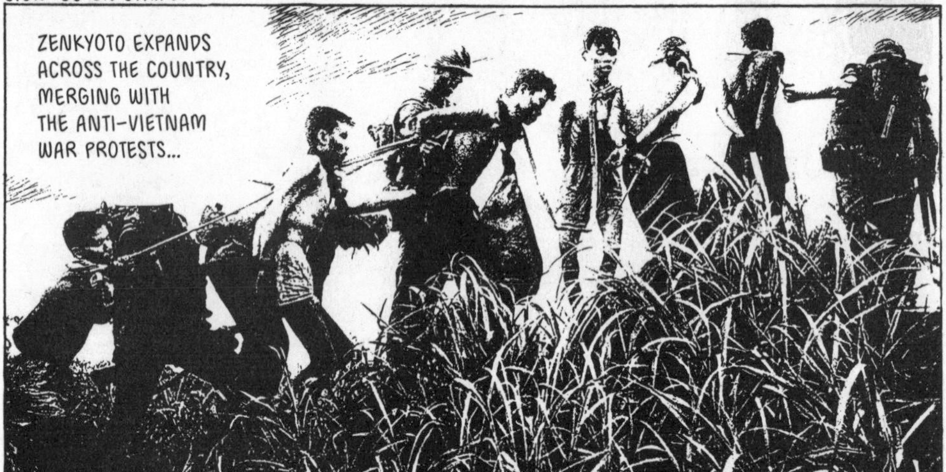
ZENKYOTO EXPANDS ACROSS THE COUNTRY, MERGING WITH THE ANTI-VIETNAM WAR PROTESTS...

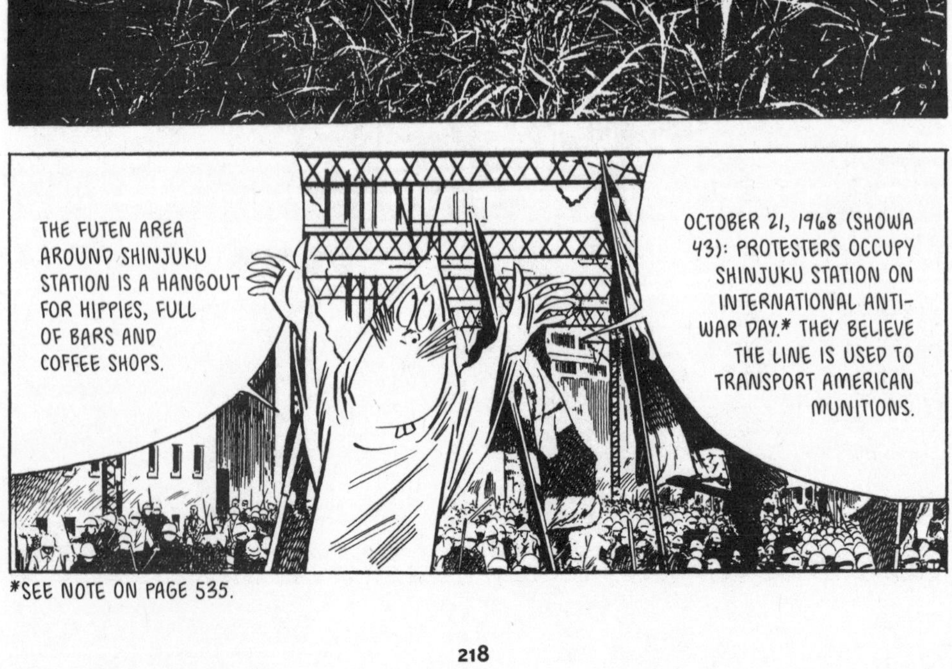
OCTOBER 21, 1968 (SHOWA 43): PROTESTERS OCCUPY SHINJUKU STATION ON INTERNATIONAL ANTI-WAR DAY.* THEY BELIEVE THE LINE IS USED TO TRANSPORT AMERICAN MUNITIONS.
THE FUTEN AREA AROUND SHINJUKU STATION IS A HANGOUT FOR HIPPIES, FULL OF BARS AND COFFEE SHOPS.

*SEE NOTE ON PAGE 535.

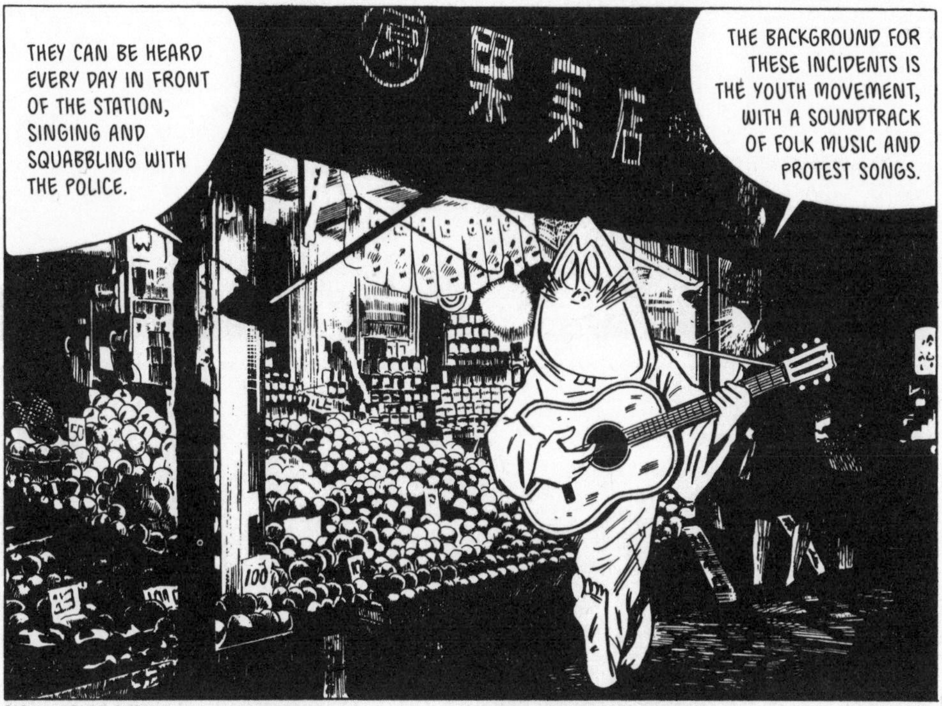
THE BACKGROUND FOR THESE INCIDENTS IS THE YOUTH MOVEMENT, WITH A SOUNDTRACK OF FOLK MUSIC AND PROTEST SONGS.
THEY CAN BE HEARD EVERY DAY IN FRONT OF THE STATION, SINGING AND SQUABBLING WITH THE POLICE.
果実店
SIGN: FRUIT STAND.

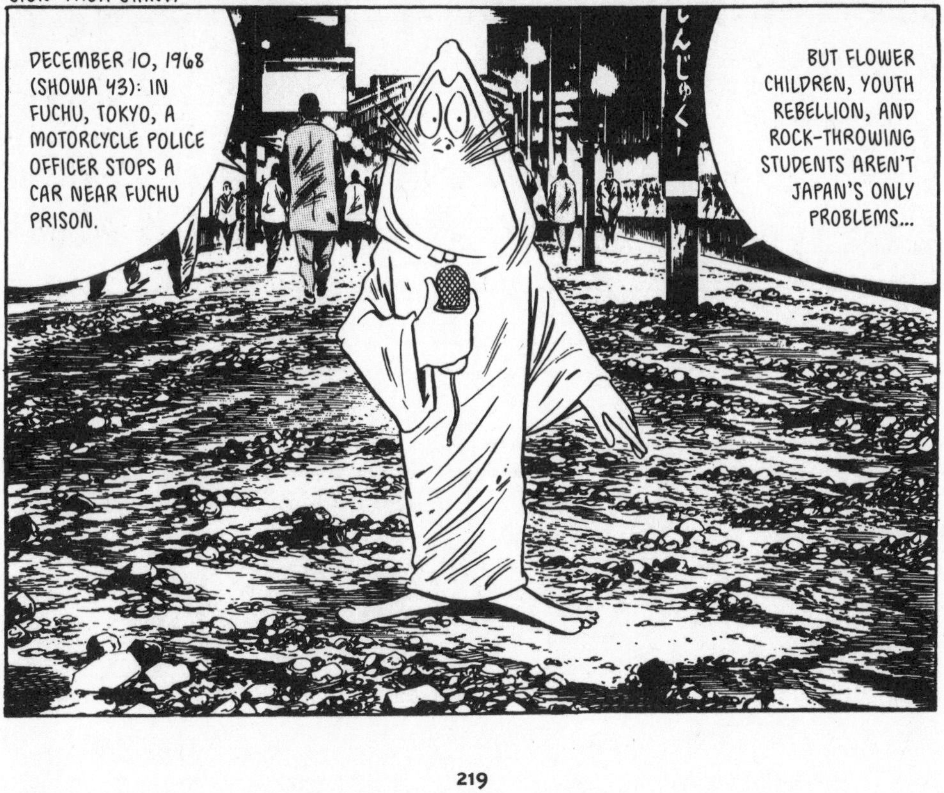
BUT FLOWER CHILDREN, YOUTH REBELLION, AND ROCK-THROWING STUDENTS AREN'T JAPAN'S ONLY PROBLEMS...
DECEMBER 10, 1968 (SHOWA 43): IN FUCHU, TOKYO, A MOTORCYCLE POLICE OFFICER STOPS A CAR NEAR FUCHU PRISON.
しんじゅく

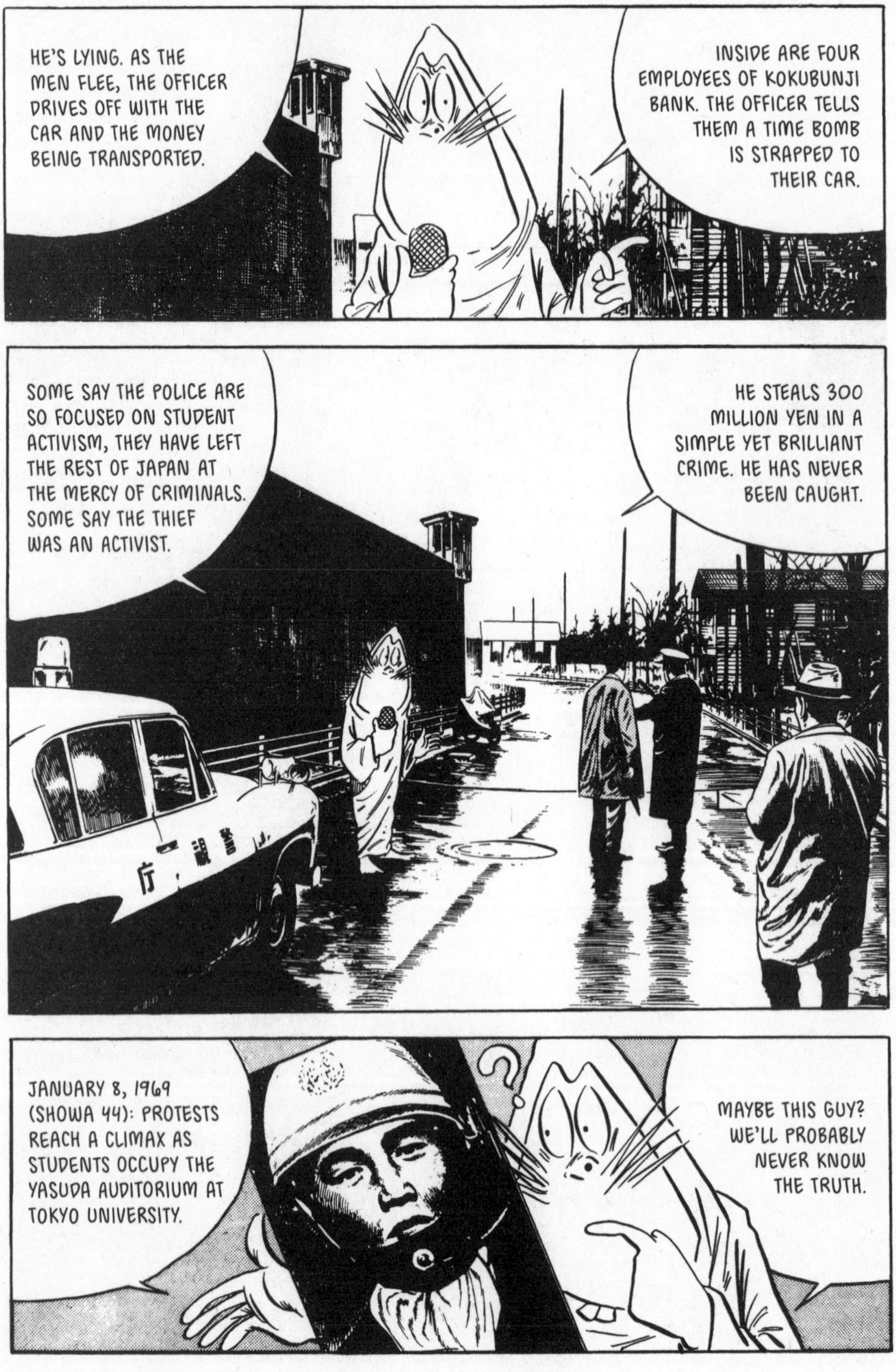
INSIDE ARE FOUR EMPLOYEES OF KOKUBUNJI BANK. THE OFFICER TELLS THEM A TIME BOMB IS STRAPPED TO THEIR CAR.
HE'S LYING. AS THE MEN FLEE, THE OFFICER DRIVES OFF WITH THE CAR AND THE MONEY BEING TRANSPORTED.
HE STEALS 300 MILLION YEN IN A SIMPLE YET BRILLIANT CRIME. HE HAS NEVER BEEN CAUGHT.
SOME SAY THE POLICE ARE SO FOCUSED ON STUDENT ACTIVISM, THEY HAVE LEFT THE REST OF JAPAN AT THE MERCY OF CRIMINALS. SOME SAY THE THIEF WAS AN ACTIVIST.
MAYBE THIS GUY? WE'LL PROBABLY NEVER KNOW THE TRUTH.
JANUARY 8, 1969 (SHOWA 44): PROTESTS REACH A CLIMAX AS STUDENTS OCCUPY THE YASUDA AUDITORIUM AT TOKYO UNIVERSITY.

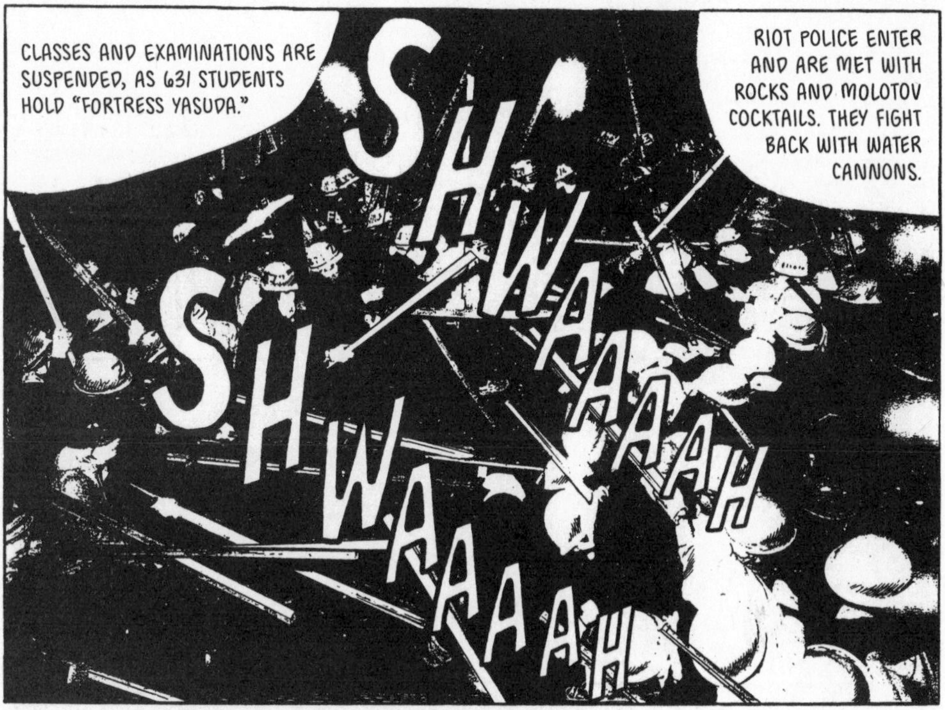
RIOT POLICE ENTER AND ARE MET WITH ROCKS AND MOLOTOV COCKTAILS. THEY FIGHT BACK WITH WATER CANNONS.
CLASSES AND EXAMINATIONS ARE SUSPENDED, AS 631 STUDENTS HOLD "FORTRESS YASUDA."
SHWAAAAH
SHWAAAAH

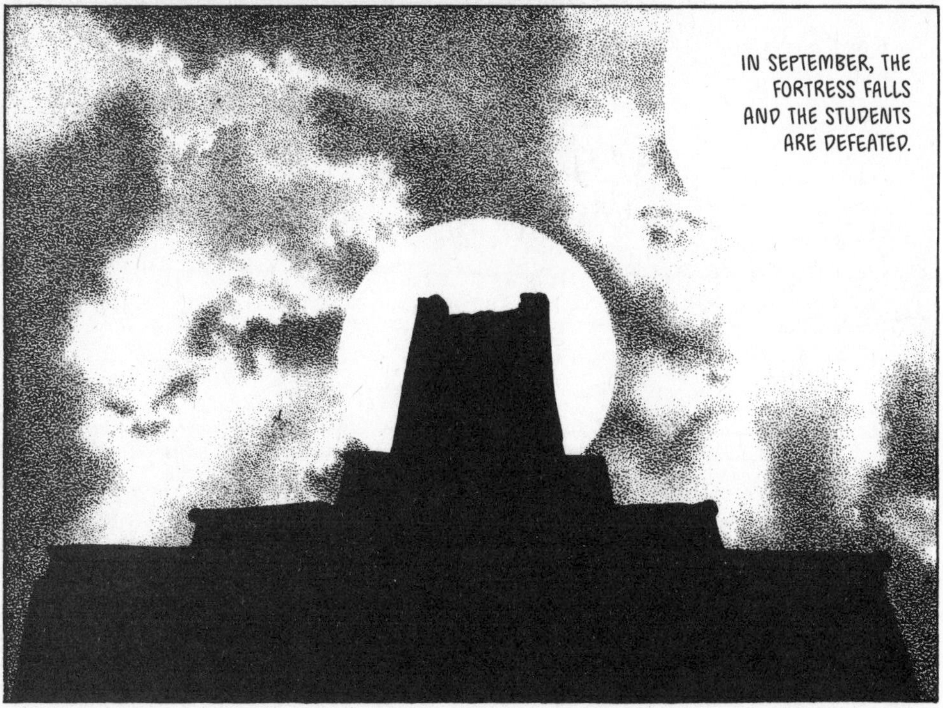
IN SEPTEMBER, THE FORTRESS FALLS AND THE STUDENTS ARE DEFEATED.

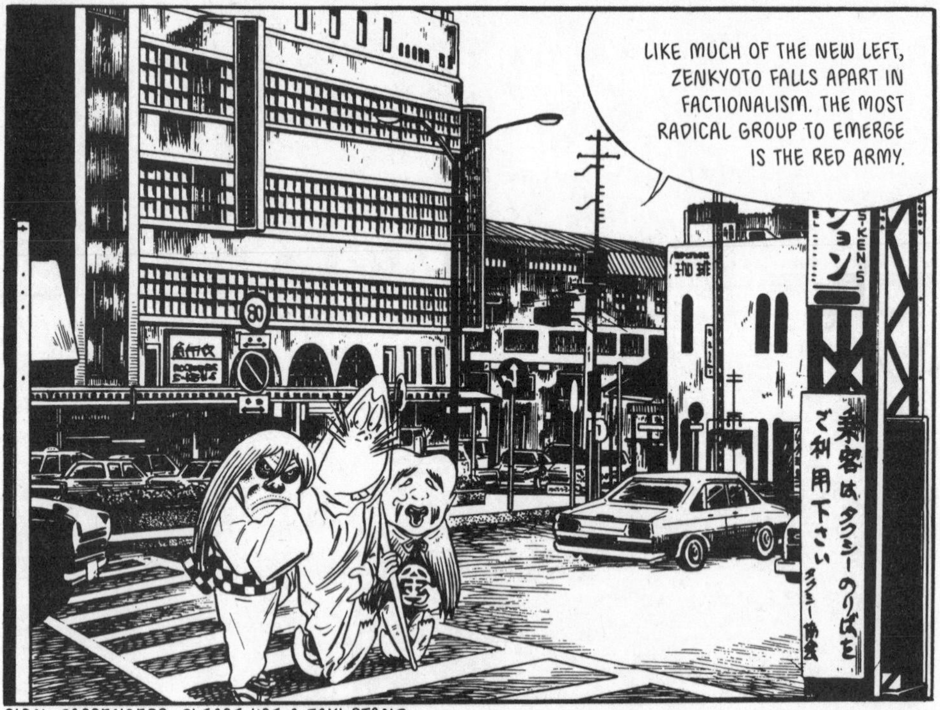
LIKE MUCH OF THE NEW LEFT, ZENKYOTO FALLS APART IN FACTIONALISM. THE MOST RADICAL GROUP TO EMERGE IS THE RED ARMY.
乗客はタクシーのりばを
ご利用下さい

SIGN: PASSENGERS, PLEASE USE A TAXI STAND.

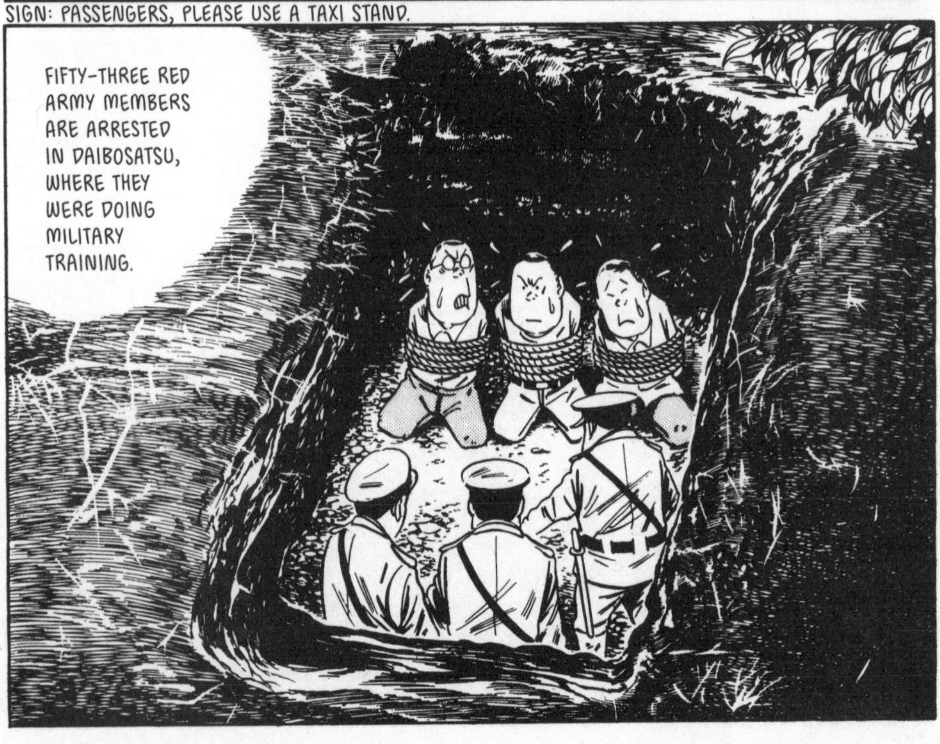
FIFTY-THREE RED ARMY MEMBERS ARE ARRESTED IN DAIBOSATSU, WHERE THEY WERE DOING MILITARY TRAINING.

THE BREAKING POINT

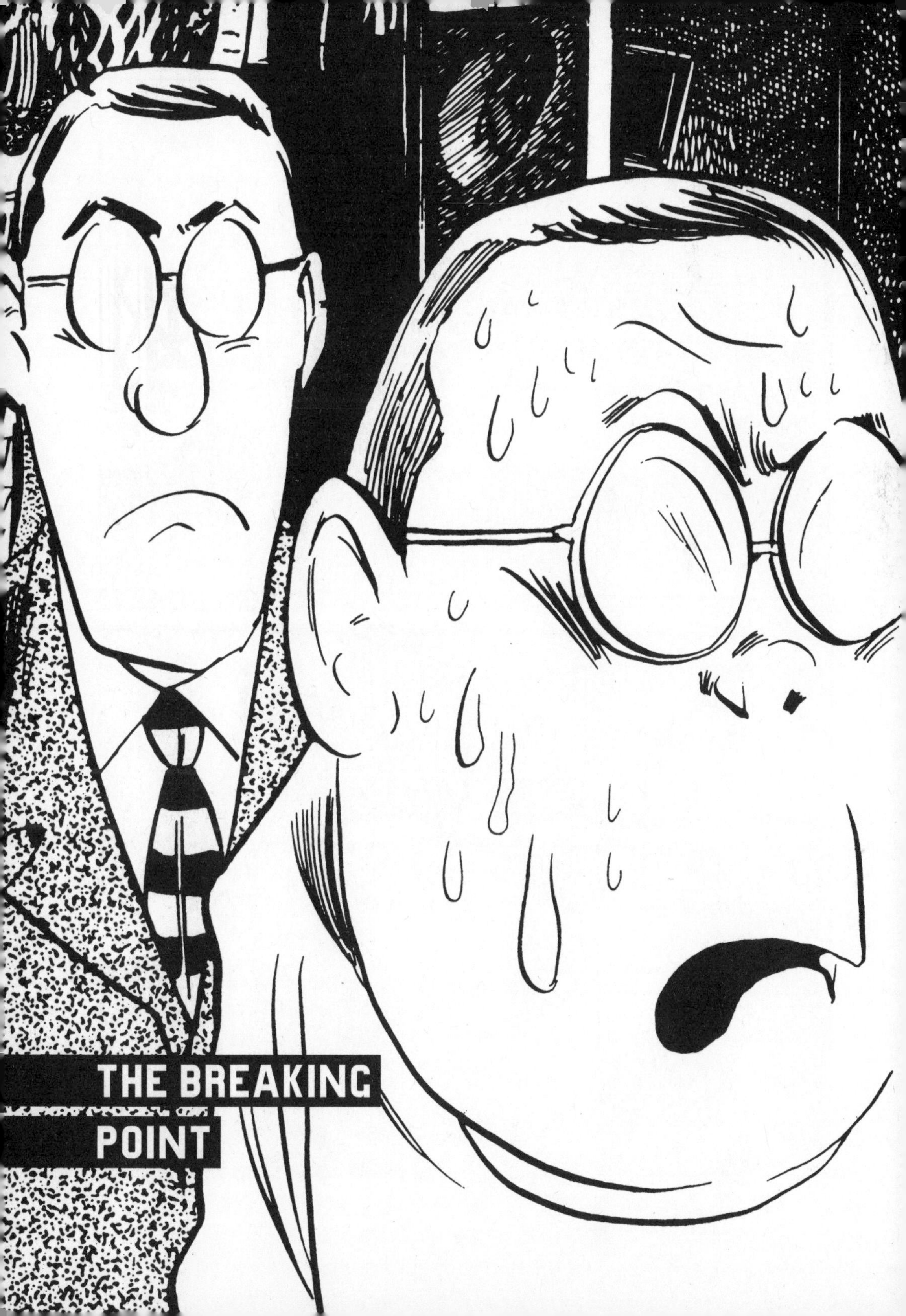

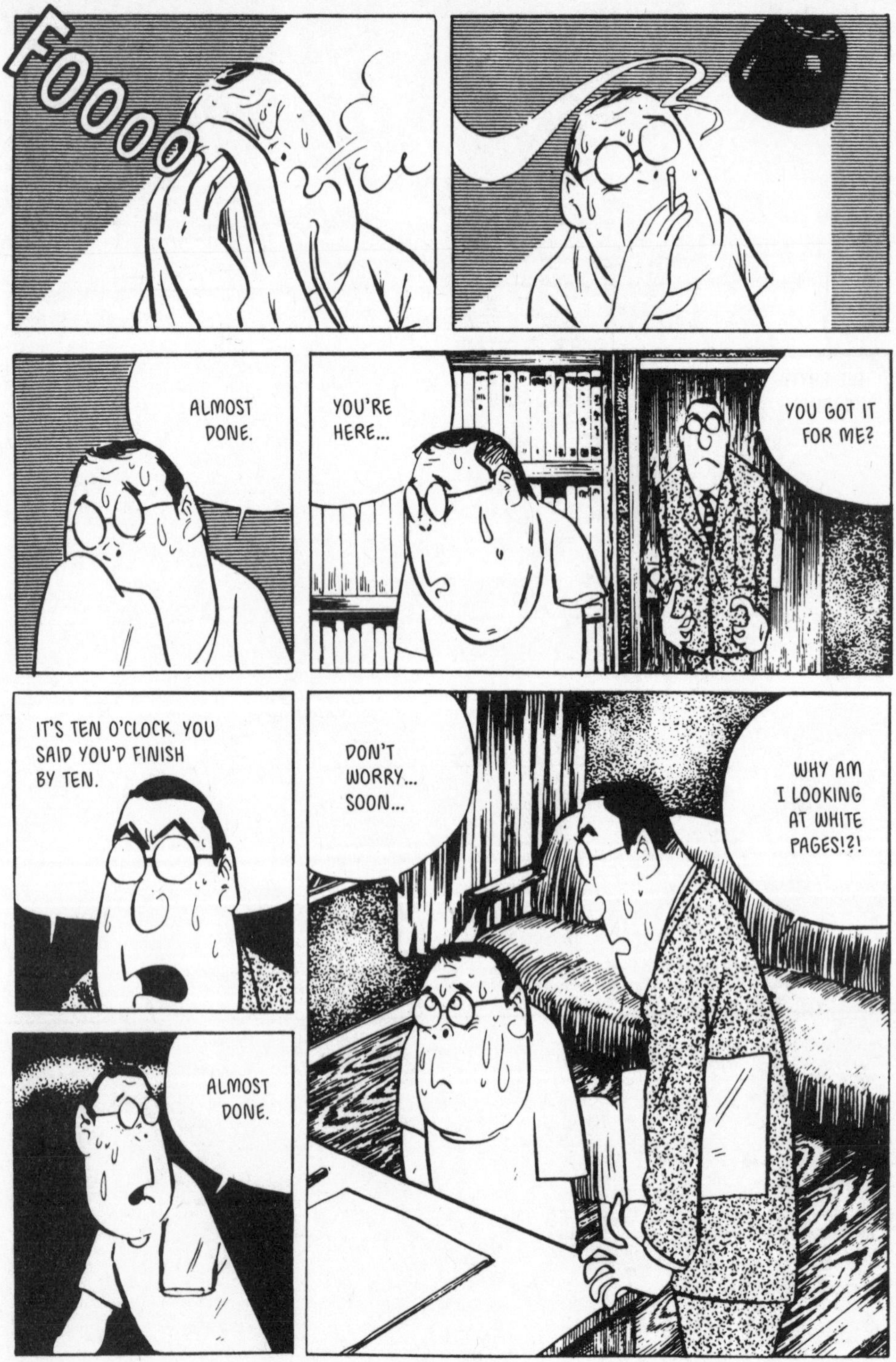
FOOOO
YOU GOT IT FOR ME?
YOU'RE HERE...
ALMOST DONE.
WHY AM I LOOKING AT WHITE PAGES!?!
DON'T WORRY... SOON...
IT'S TEN O'CLOCK. YOU SAID YOU'D FINISH BY TEN.
ALMOST DONE.

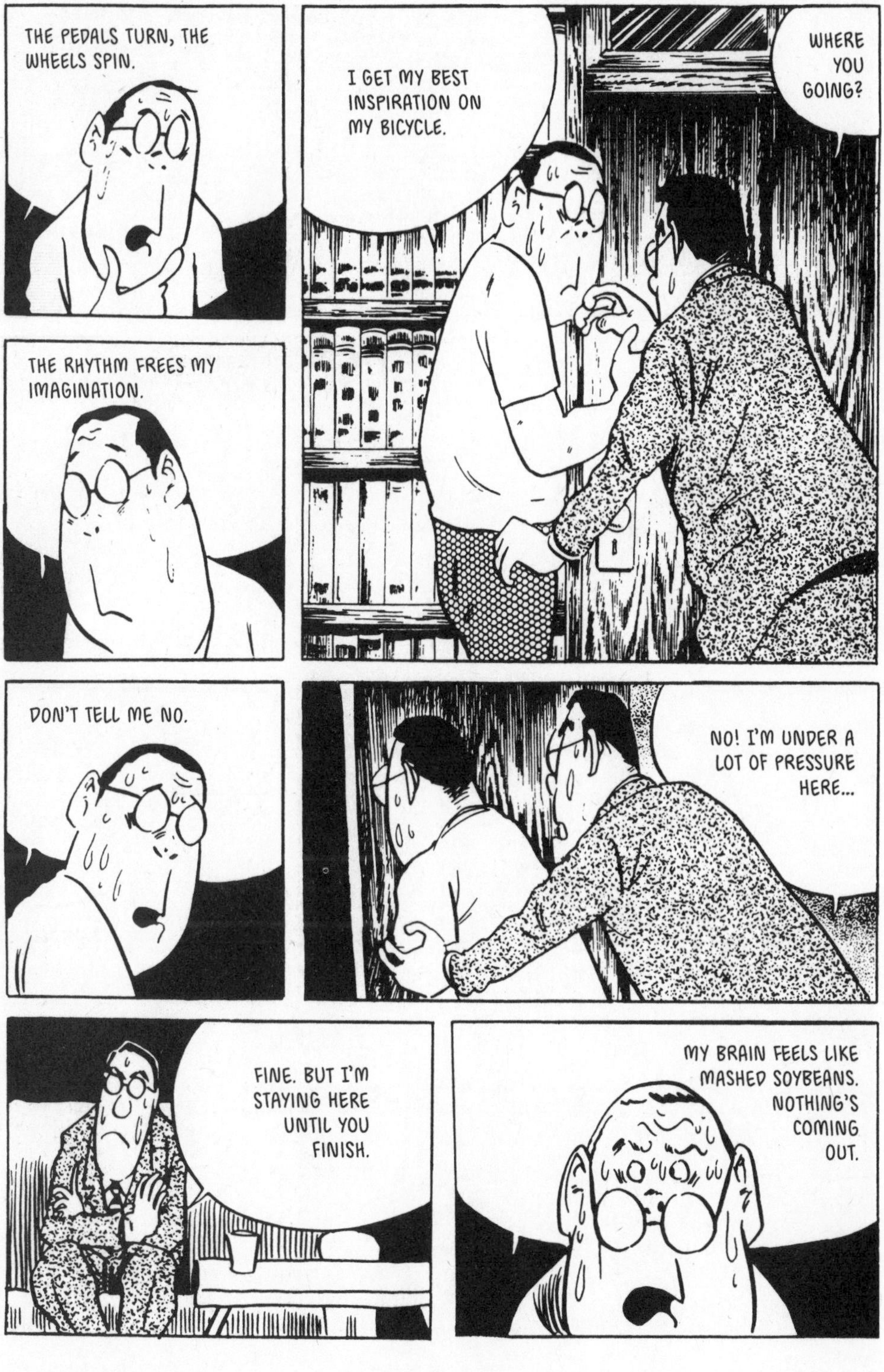
WHERE YOU GOING?
I GET MY BEST INSPIRATION ON MY BICYCLE.
THE PEDALS TURN, THE WHEELS SPIN.
THE RHYTHM FREES MY IMAGINATION.
NO! I'M UNDER A LOT OF PRESSURE HERE...
DON'T TELL ME NO.
MY BRAIN FEELS LIKE MASHED SOYBEANS. NOTHING'S COMING OUT.
FINE. BUT I'M STAYING HERE UNTIL YOU FINISH.

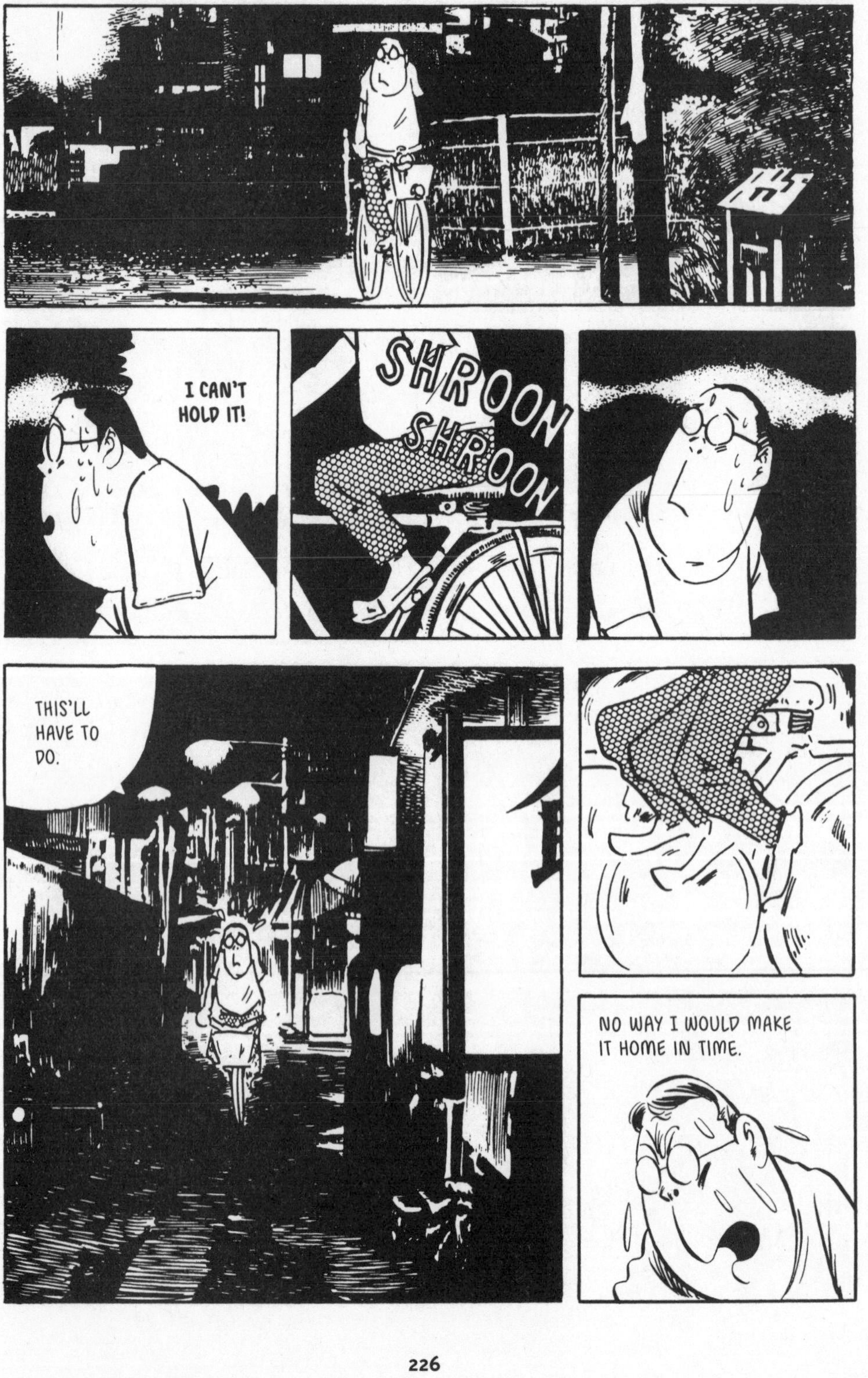
SHROON
SHROON
I CAN'T HOLD IT!
NO WAY I WOULD MAKE IT HOME IN TIME.
THIS'LL HAVE TO DO.

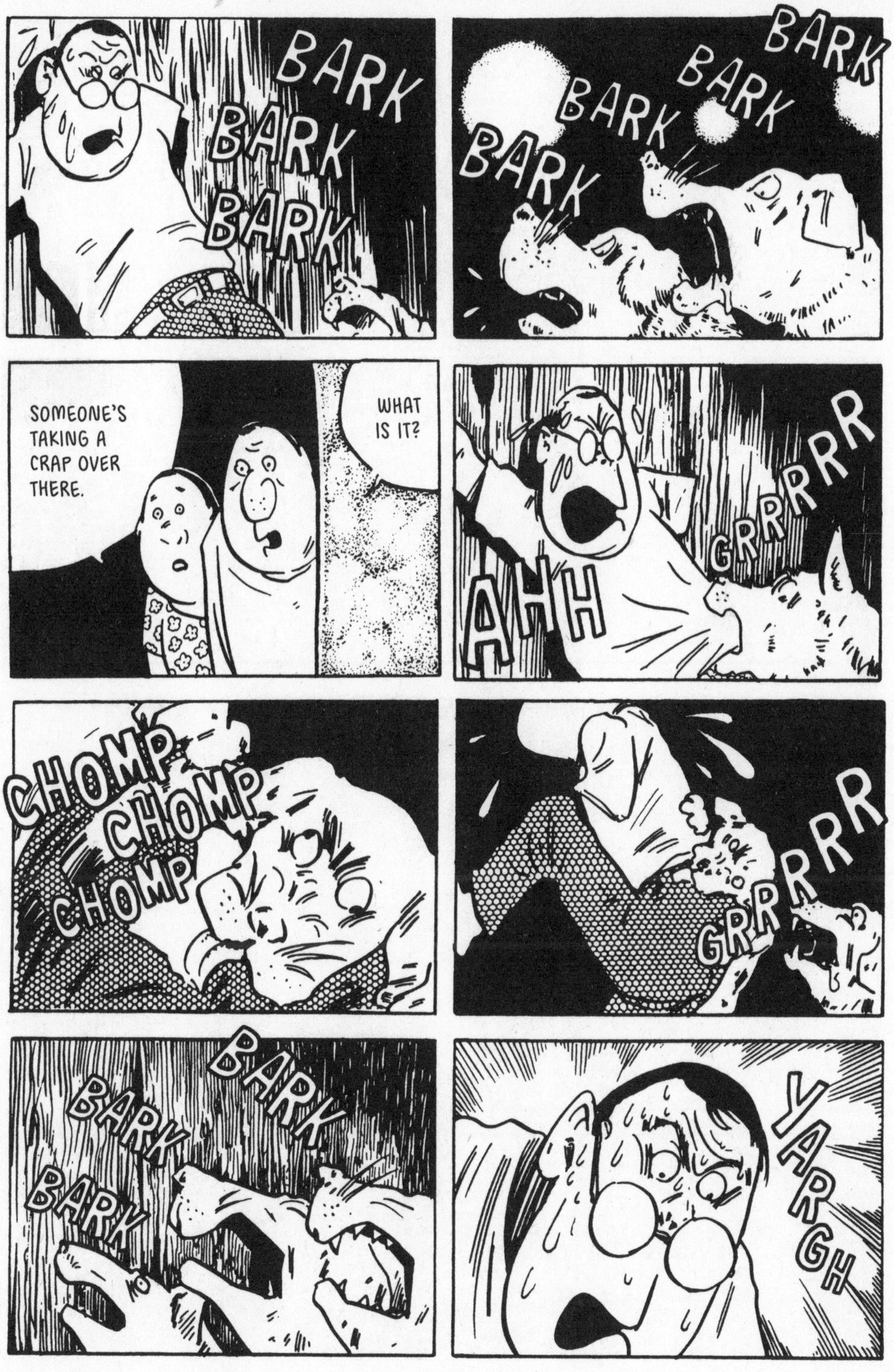
BARK
BARK
BARK
BARK
BARK
BARK
BARK
WHAT IS IT?
SOMEONE'S TAKING A CRAP OVER THERE.
GRRRRRR
AHH
GRRRRRR
CHOMP
CHOMP
CHOMP
YARGH
BARK
BARK
BARK

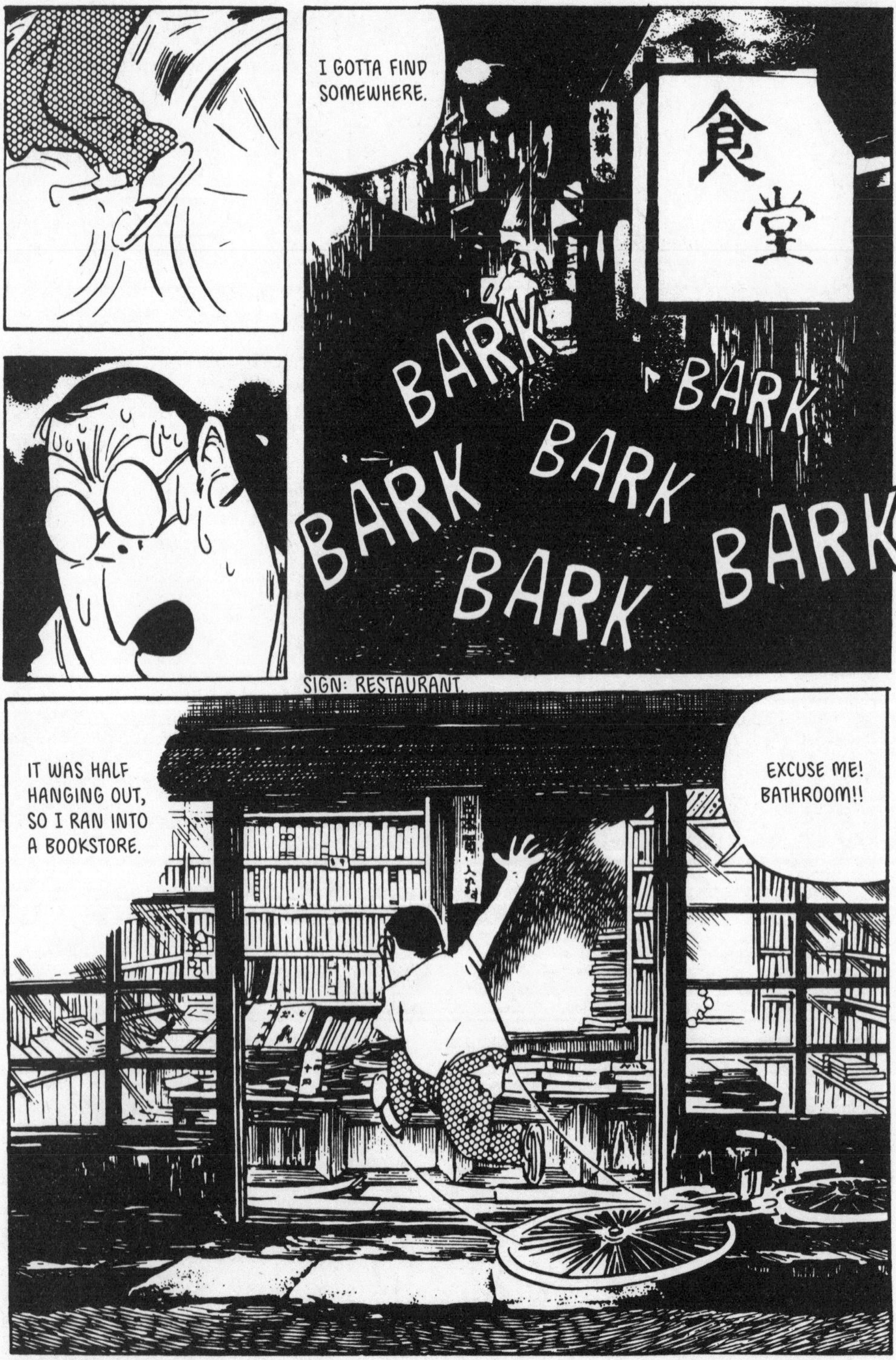
I GOTTA FIND SOMEWHERE.
食堂
BARK BARK BARK BARK BARK BARK BARK
SIGN: RESTAURANT.
EXCUSE ME! BATHROOM!!
IT WAS HALF HANGING OUT, SO I RAN INTO A BOOKSTORE.

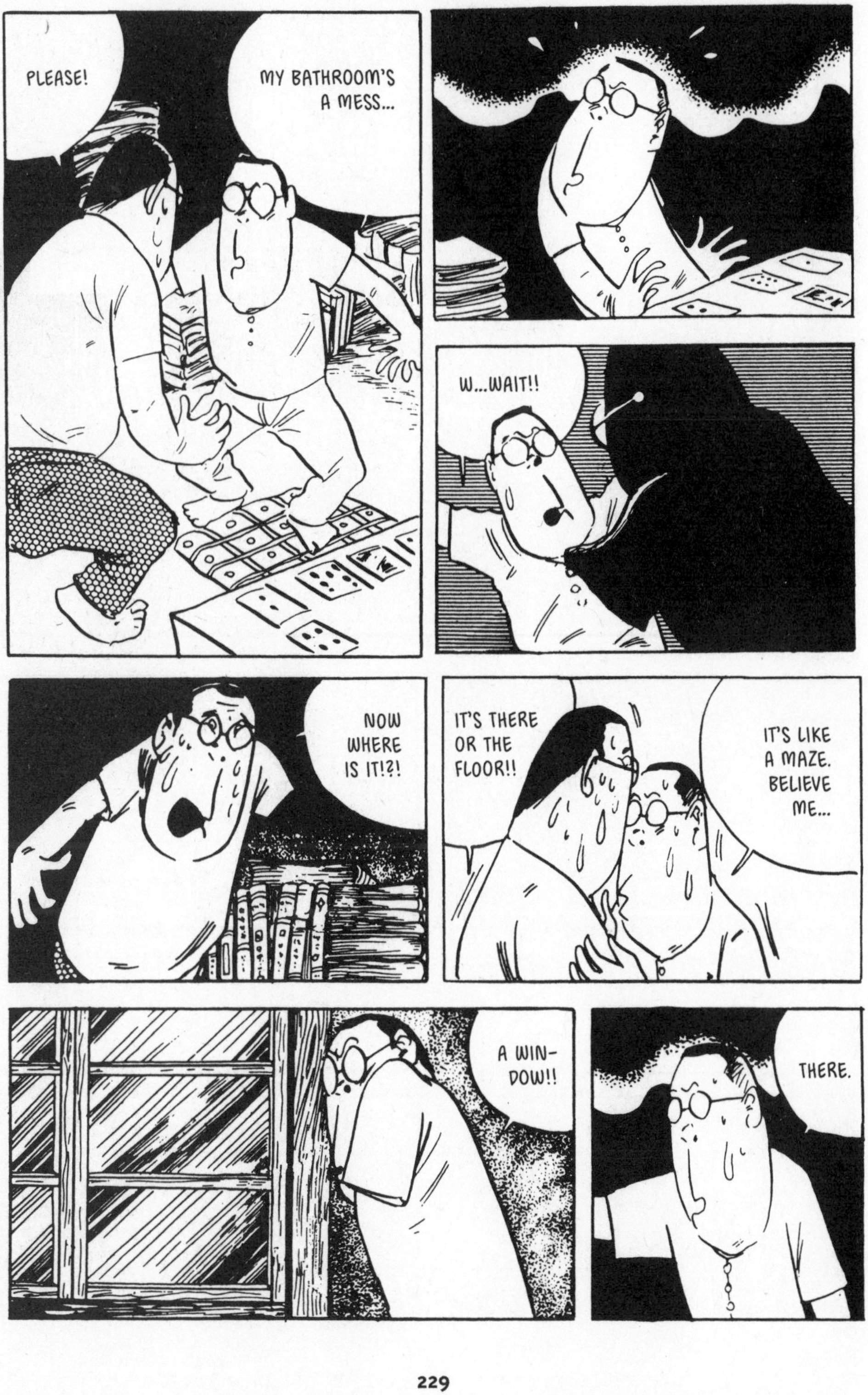
W...WAIT!!
MY BATHROOM'S A MESS...
PLEASE!
IT'S LIKE A MAZE. BELIEVE ME...
IT'S THERE OR THE FLOOR!!
NOW WHERE IS IT!?!
THERE.
A WIN-DOW!!

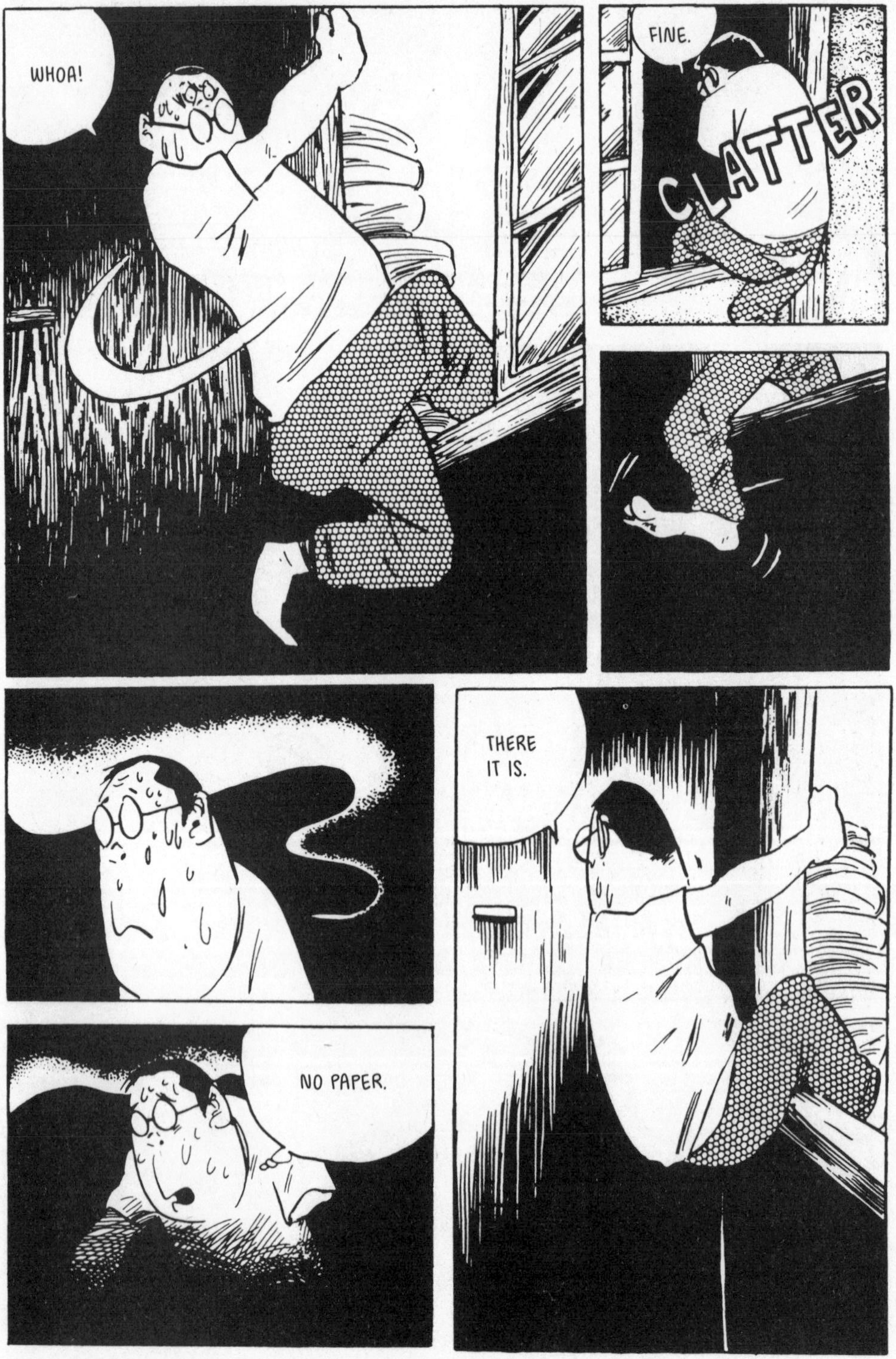
FINE.
CLATTER
WHOA!
THERE IT IS.
NO PAPER.

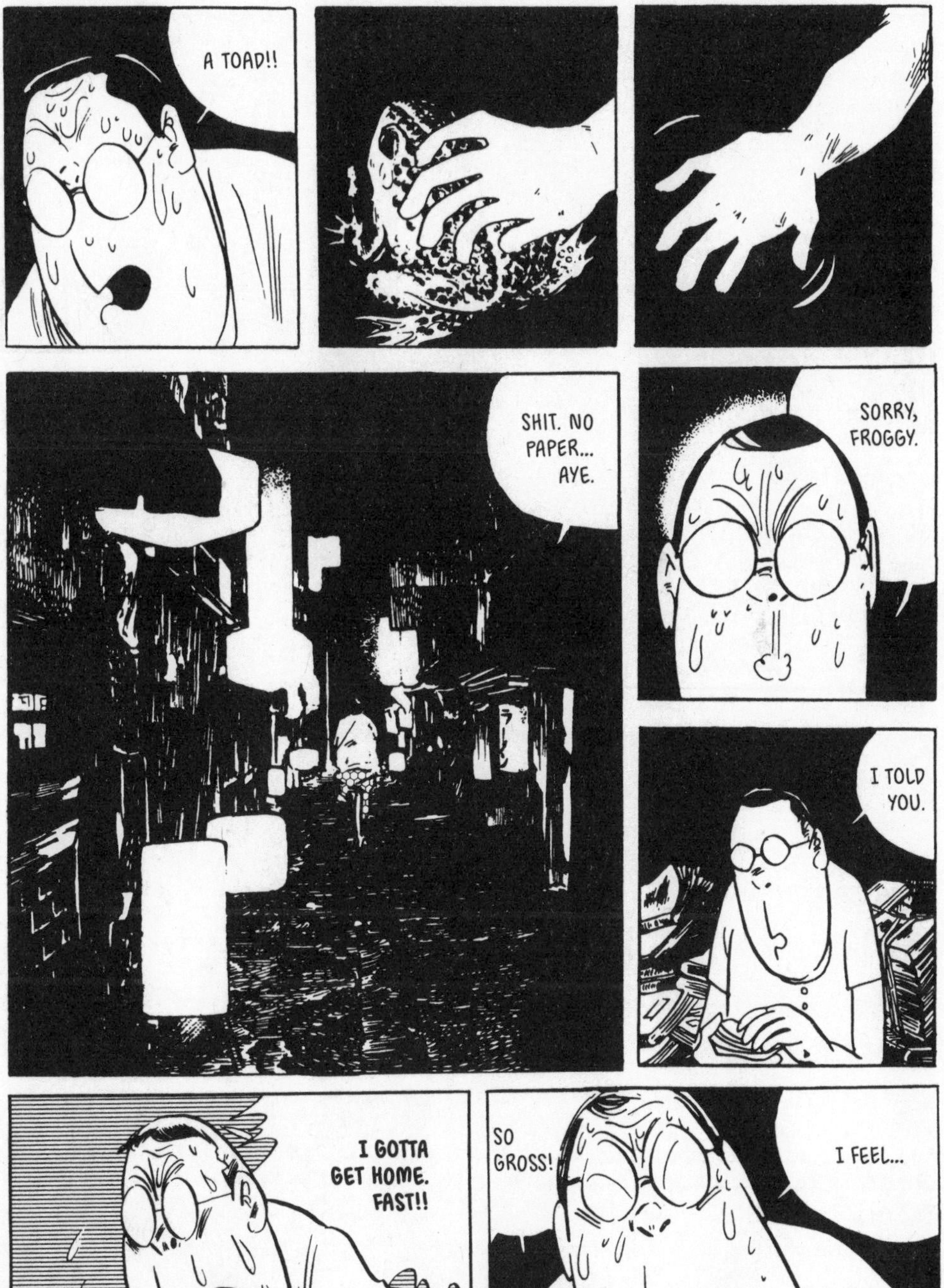
A TOAD!!
SORRY, FROGGY.
I TOLD YOU.
SHIT. NO PAPER... AYE.
I FEEL...
SO GROSS!
I GOTTA GET HOME. FAST!!

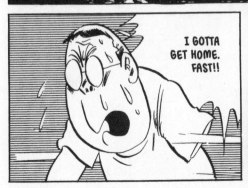

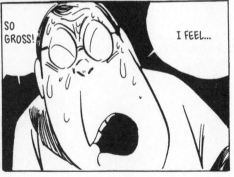

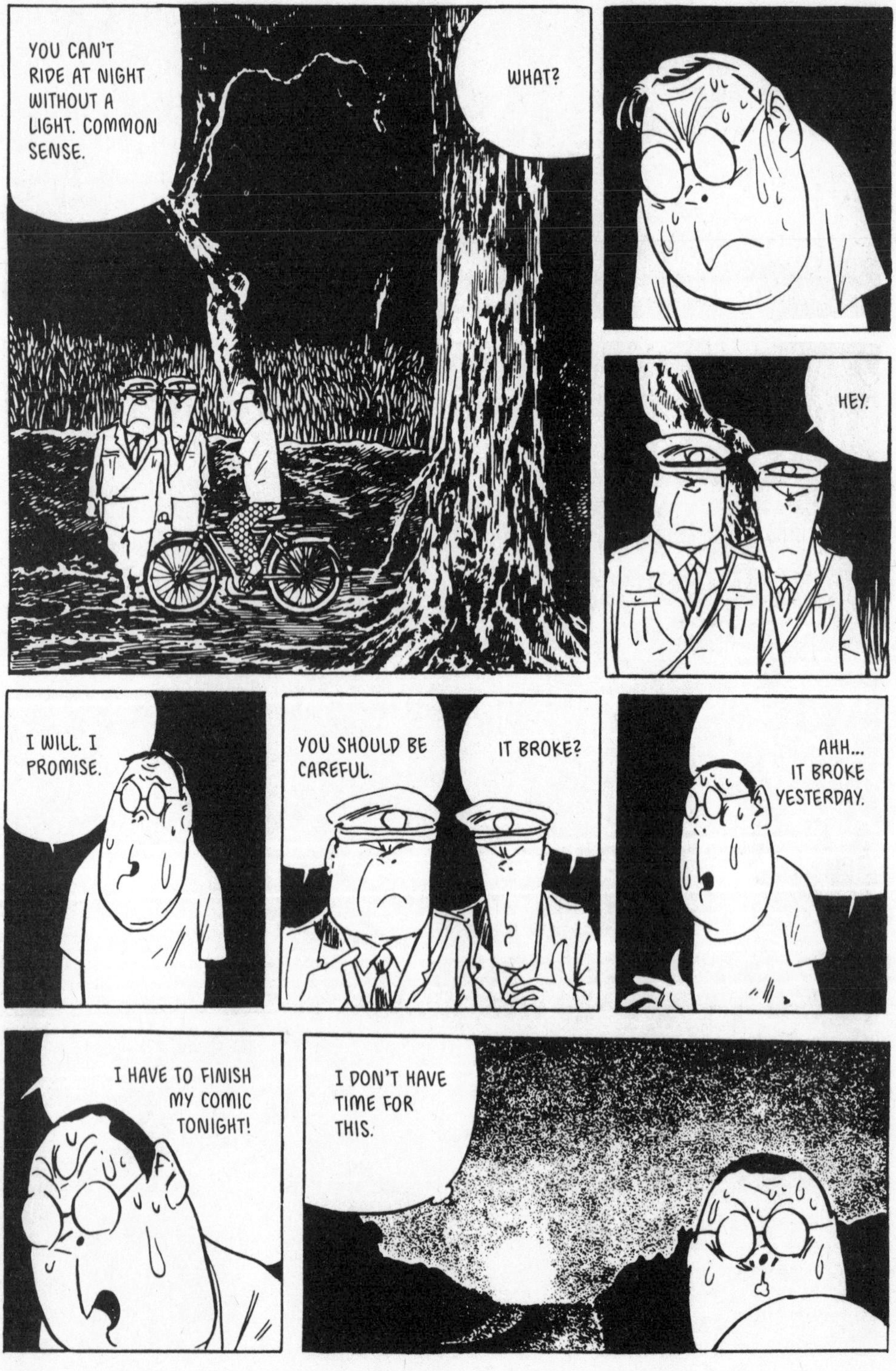
HEY.
WHAT?
YOU CAN'T RIDE AT NIGHT WITHOUT A LIGHT. COMMON SENSE.
AHH... IT BROKE YESTERDAY.
IT BROKE?
YOU SHOULD BE CAREFUL.
I WILL. I PROMISE.
I DON'T HAVE TIME FOR THIS.
I HAVE TO FINISH MY COMIC TONIGHT!

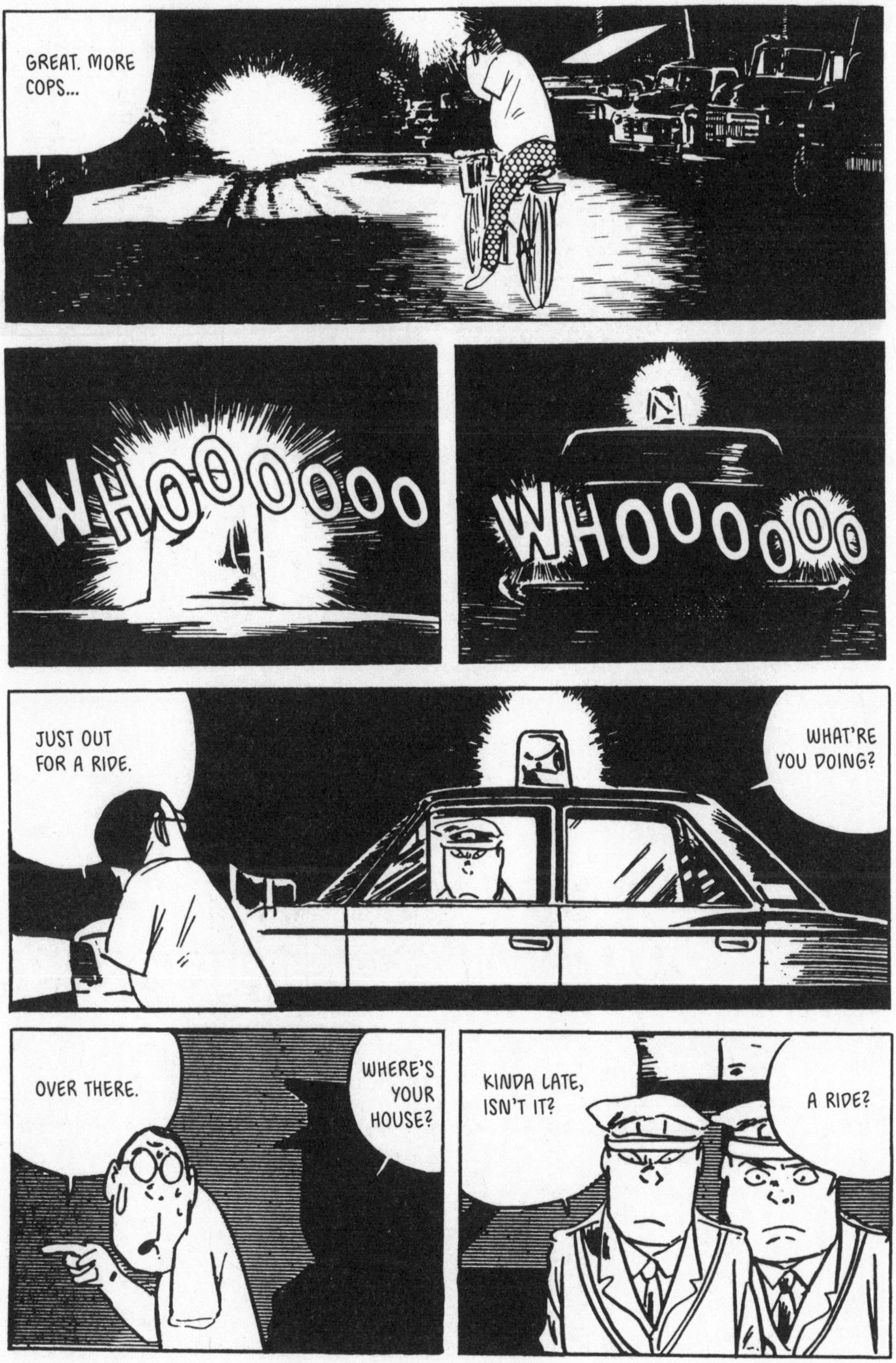
GREAT. MORE COPS...
WHOOOOOO
WHOOOOOO
WHAT'RE YOU DOING?
JUST OUT FOR A RIDE.
A RIDE?
KINDA LATE, ISN'T IT?
WHERE'S YOUR HOUSE?
OVER THERE.

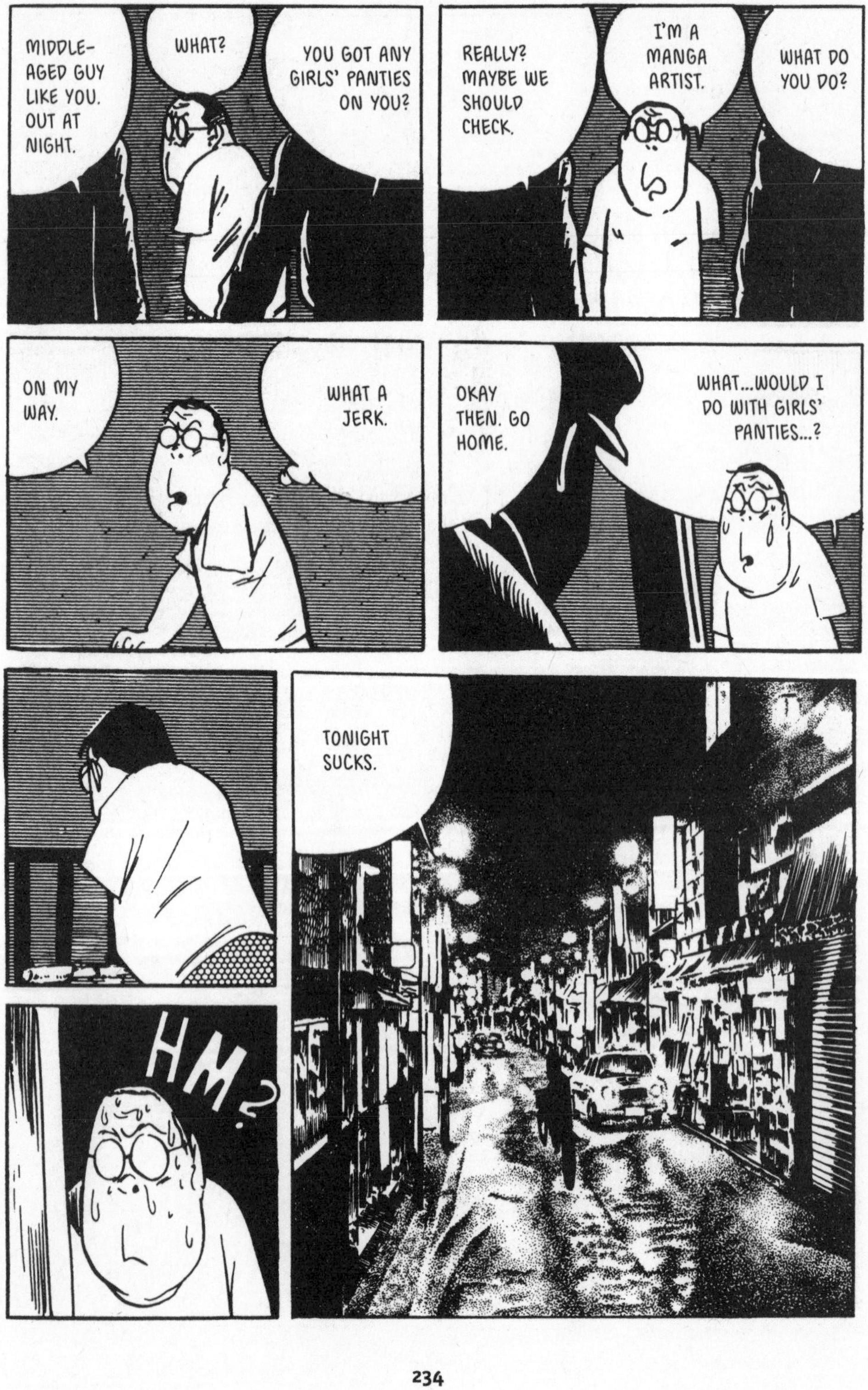
WHAT DO YOU DO?
I'M A MANGA ARTIST.
REALLY? MAYBE WE SHOULD CHECK.
YOU GOT ANY GIRLS' PANTIES ON YOU?
WHAT?
MIDDLE-AGED GUY LIKE YOU. OUT AT NIGHT.
WHAT...WOULD I DO WITH GIRLS' PANTIES...?
OKAY THEN. GO HOME.
WHAT A JERK.
ON MY WAY.
TONIGHT SUCKS.
HM?

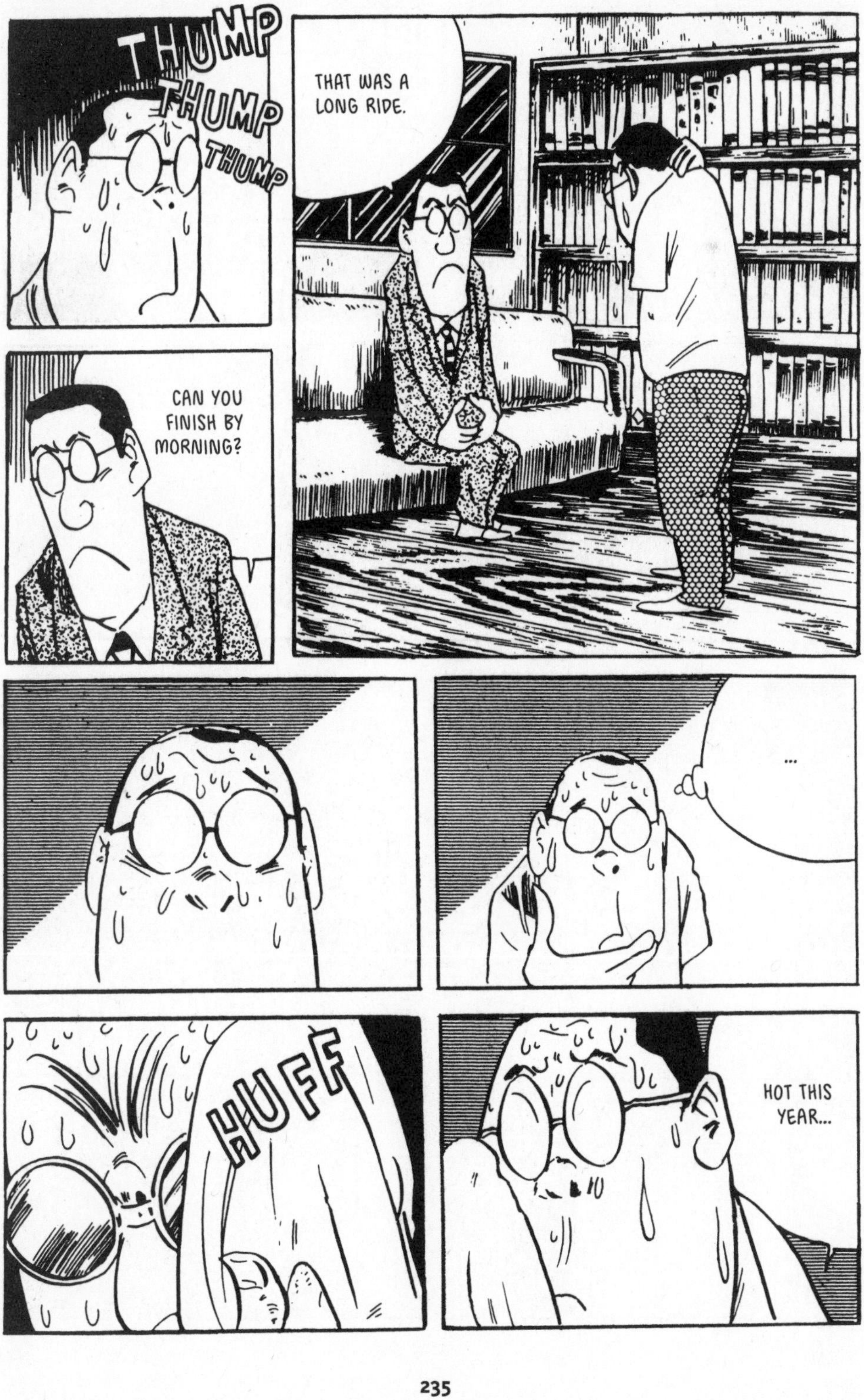
THAT WAS A LONG RIDE.
THUMP THUMP THUMP
CAN YOU FINISH BY MORNING?
...
HOT THIS YEAR...
HUFF

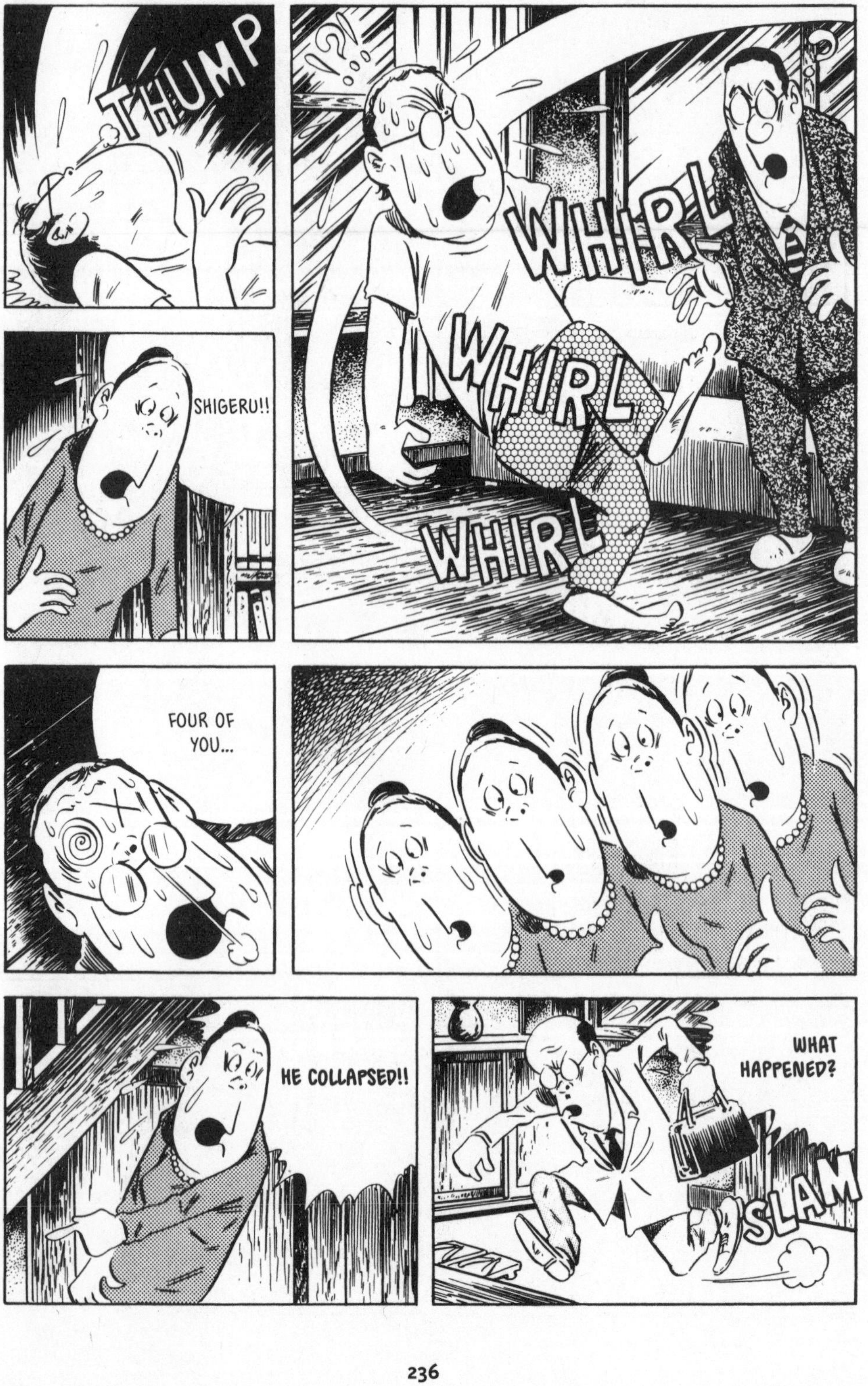
WHIRL
WHIRL
WHIRL
THUMP
SHIGERU!!
FOUR OF YOU...
WHAT HAPPENED?
SLAM
HE COLLAPSED!!

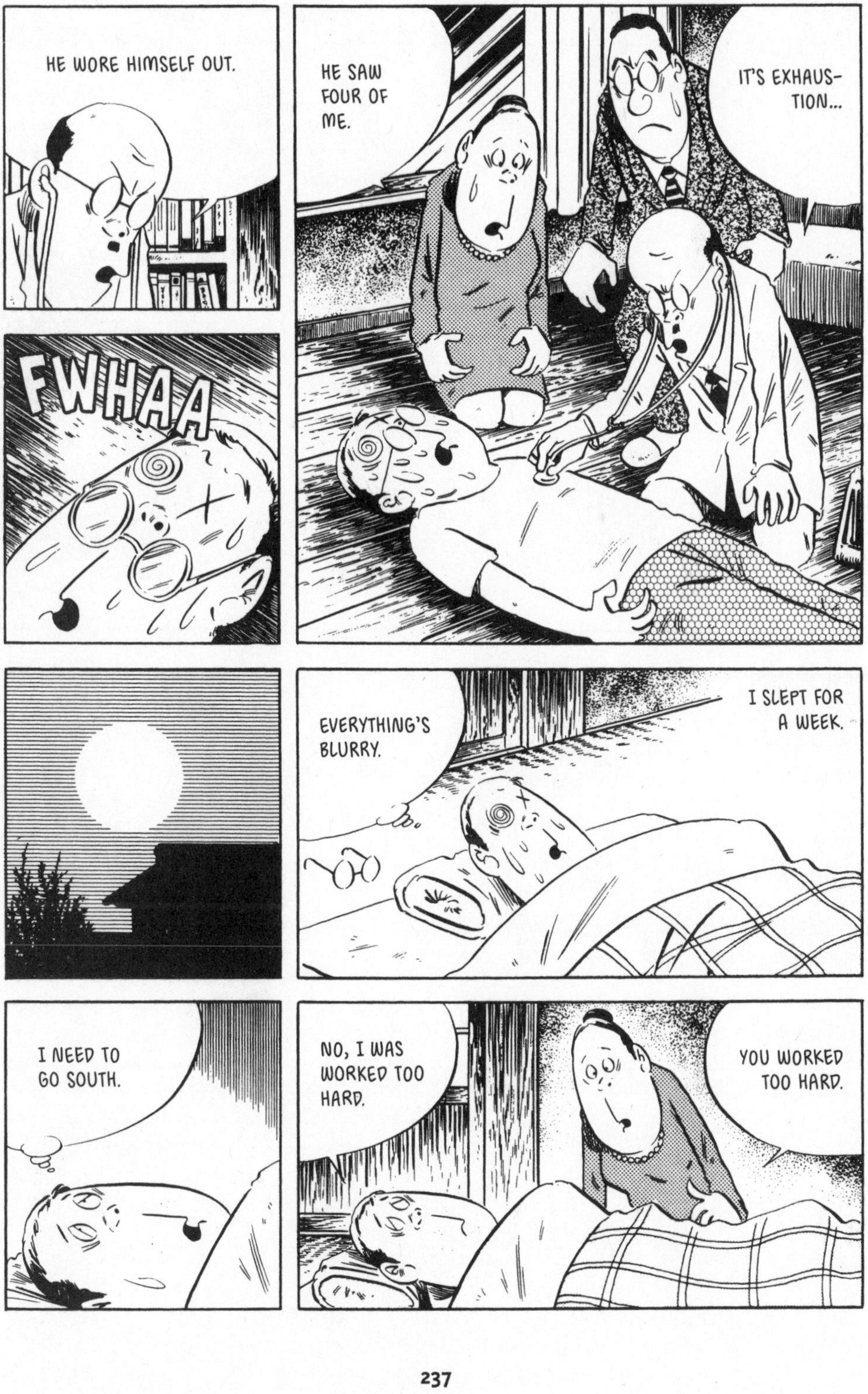
IT'S EXHAUS-TION...
HE SAW FOUR OF ME.
HE WORE HIMSELF OUT.
FWHAA
I SLEPT FOR A WEEK.
EVERYTHING'S BLURRY.
YOU WORKED TOO HARD.
NO, I WAS WORKED TOO HARD.
I NEED TO GO SOUTH.

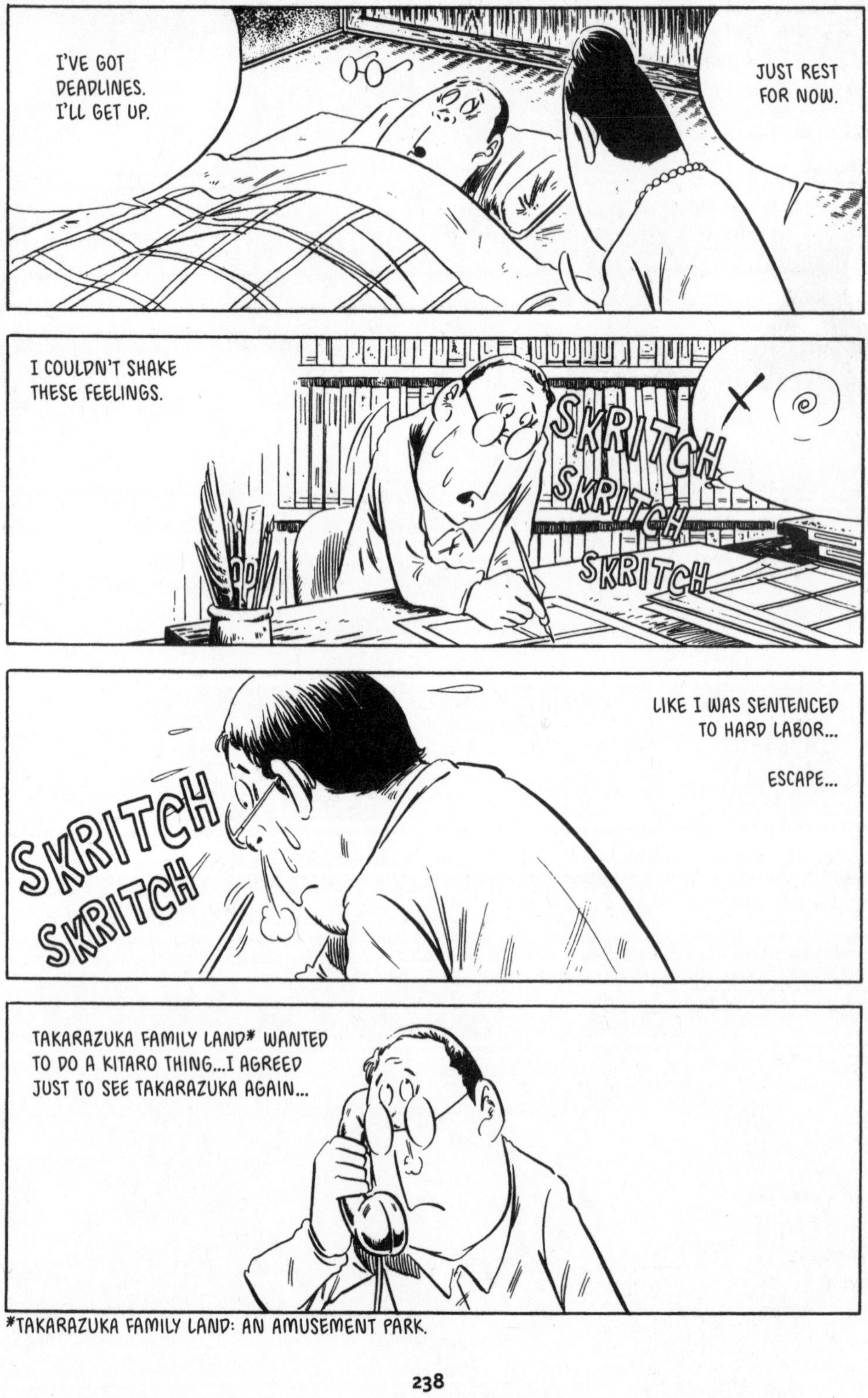
JUST REST FOR NOW.
I'VE GOT DEADLINES. I'LL GET UP.
I COULDN'T SHAKE THESE FEELINGS.
SKRITCH
SKRITCH
SKRITCH
LIKE I WAS SENTENCED TO HARD LABOR...
ESCAPE...
SKRITCH
SKRITCH
TAKARAZUKA FAMILY LAND* WANTED TO DO A KITARO THING...I AGREED JUST TO SEE TAKARAZUKA AGAIN...

*TAKARAZUKA FAMILY LAND: AN AMUSEMENT PARK.

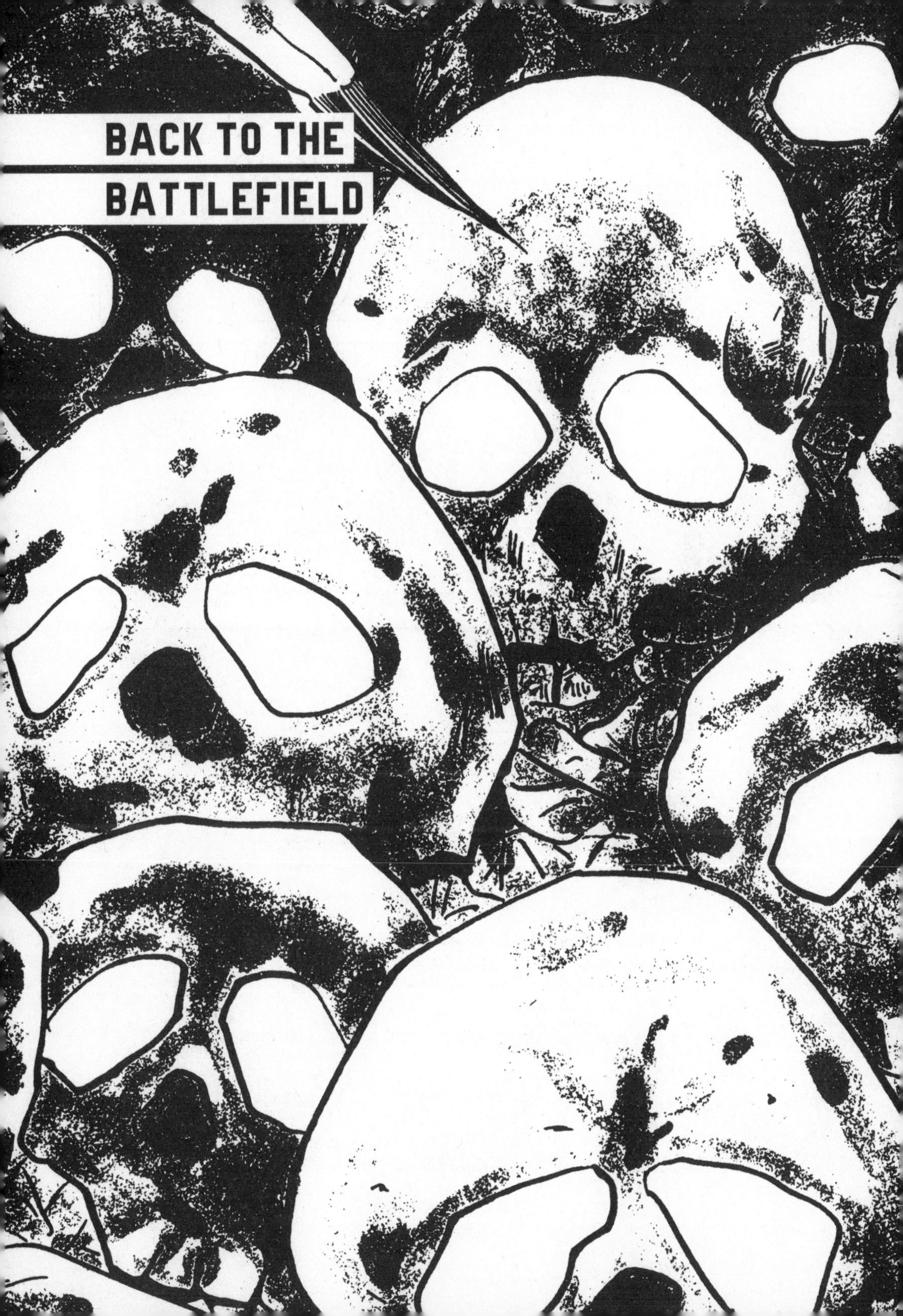
BACK TO THE
BATTLEFIELD

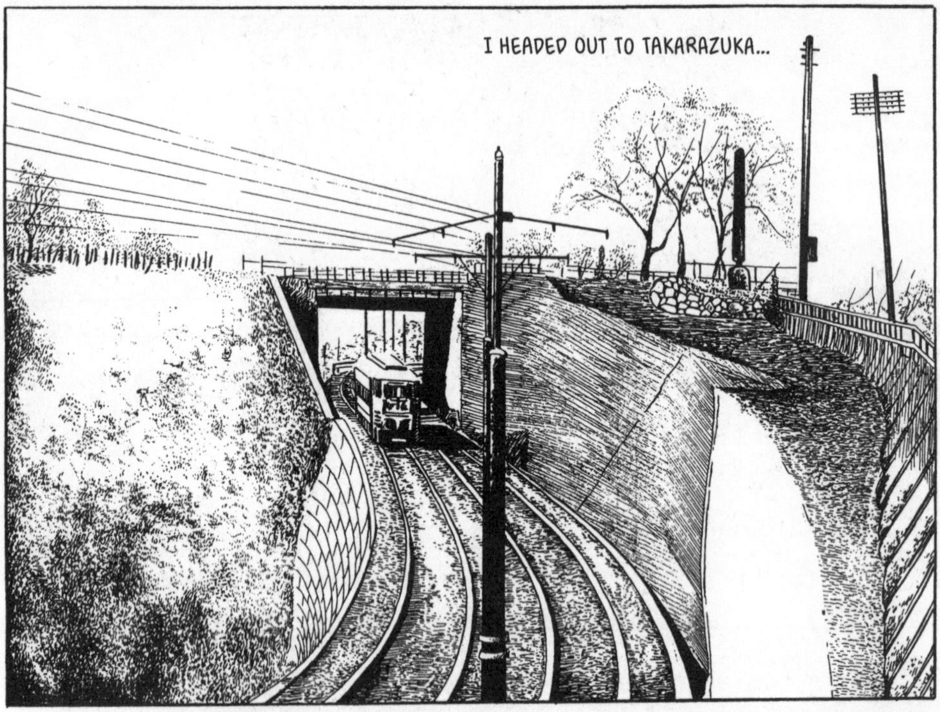
I HEADED OUT TO TAKARAZUKA...

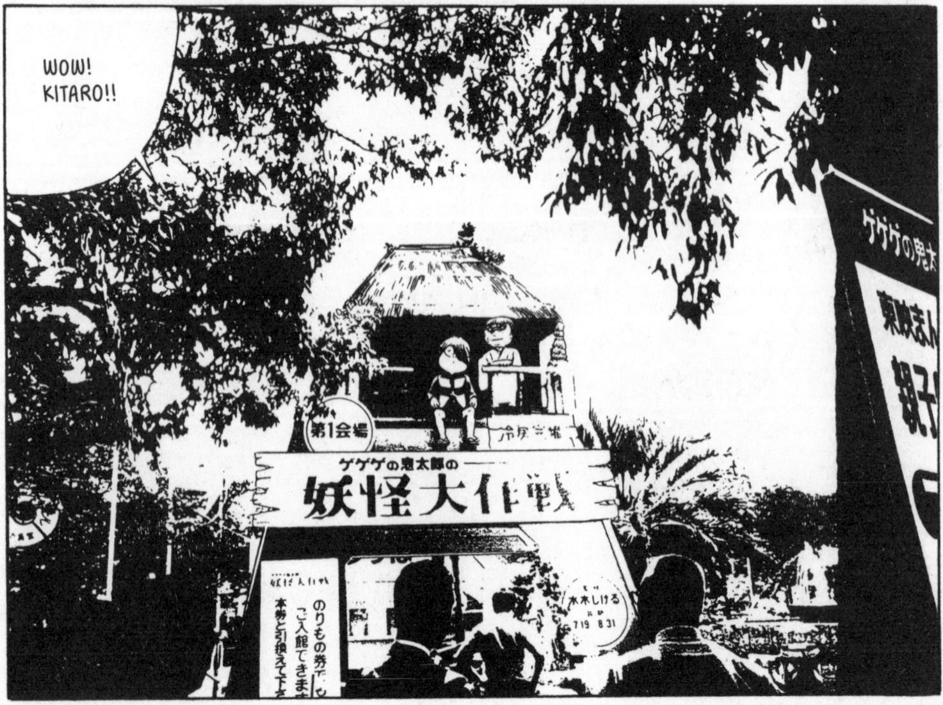
WOW! KITARO!!
第1会場
ゲゲゲの鬼太郎の
妖怪大作戦
水木しげる

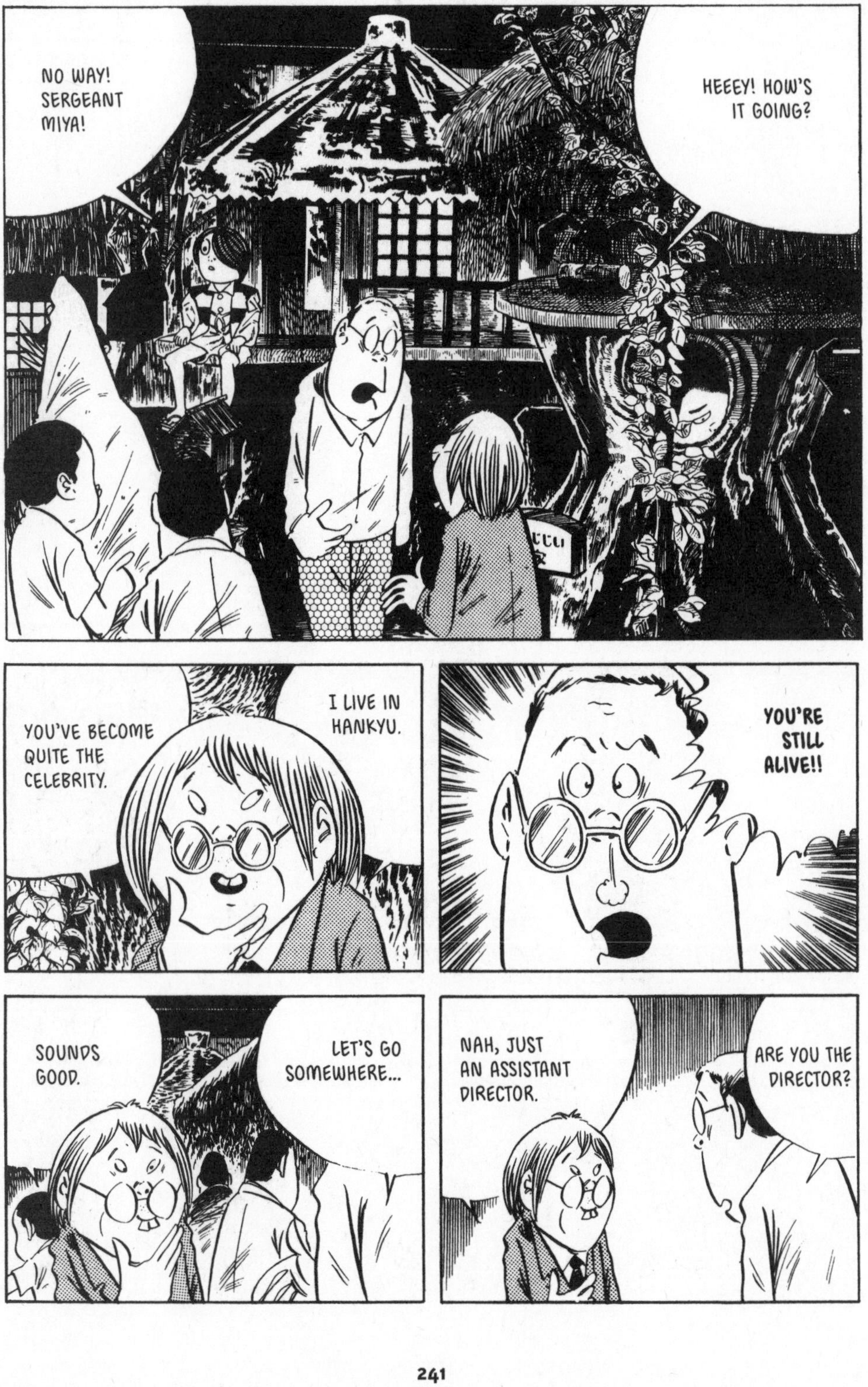
HEEEY! HOW'S IT GOING?
NO WAY! SERGEANT MIYA!
YOU'RE STILL ALIVE!!
I LIVE IN HANKYU.
YOU'VE BECOME QUITE THE CELEBRITY.
ARE YOU THE DIRECTOR?
NAH, JUST AN ASSISTANT DIRECTOR.
LET'S GO SOMEWHERE...
SOUNDS GOOD.

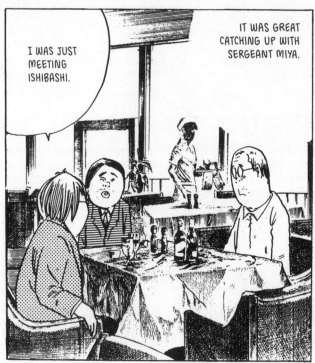

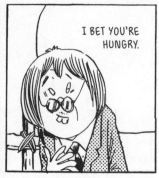

I BET YOU'RE HUNGRY.
ALWAYS.
IT WAS GREAT CATCHING UP WITH SERGEANT MIYA.
I WAS JUST MEETING ISHIBASHI.
I THOUGHT YOU DIED IN THE WAR.
I'M STILL HERE.
DISOBEYED ORDERS FOR THE SUICIDE CHARGE...
I'D LOVE TO GO BACK, AT LEAST ONCE.
WE WERE JUST TALKING ABOUT THAT.
I FIGURE IT WOULD TAKE ABOUT A MONTH.
NOT THAT LONG.

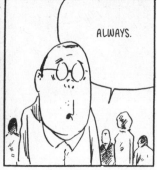

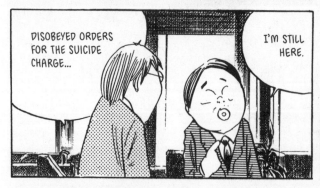

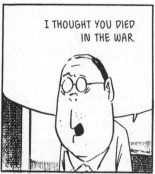

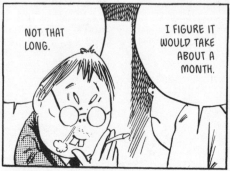

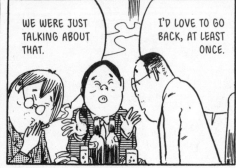

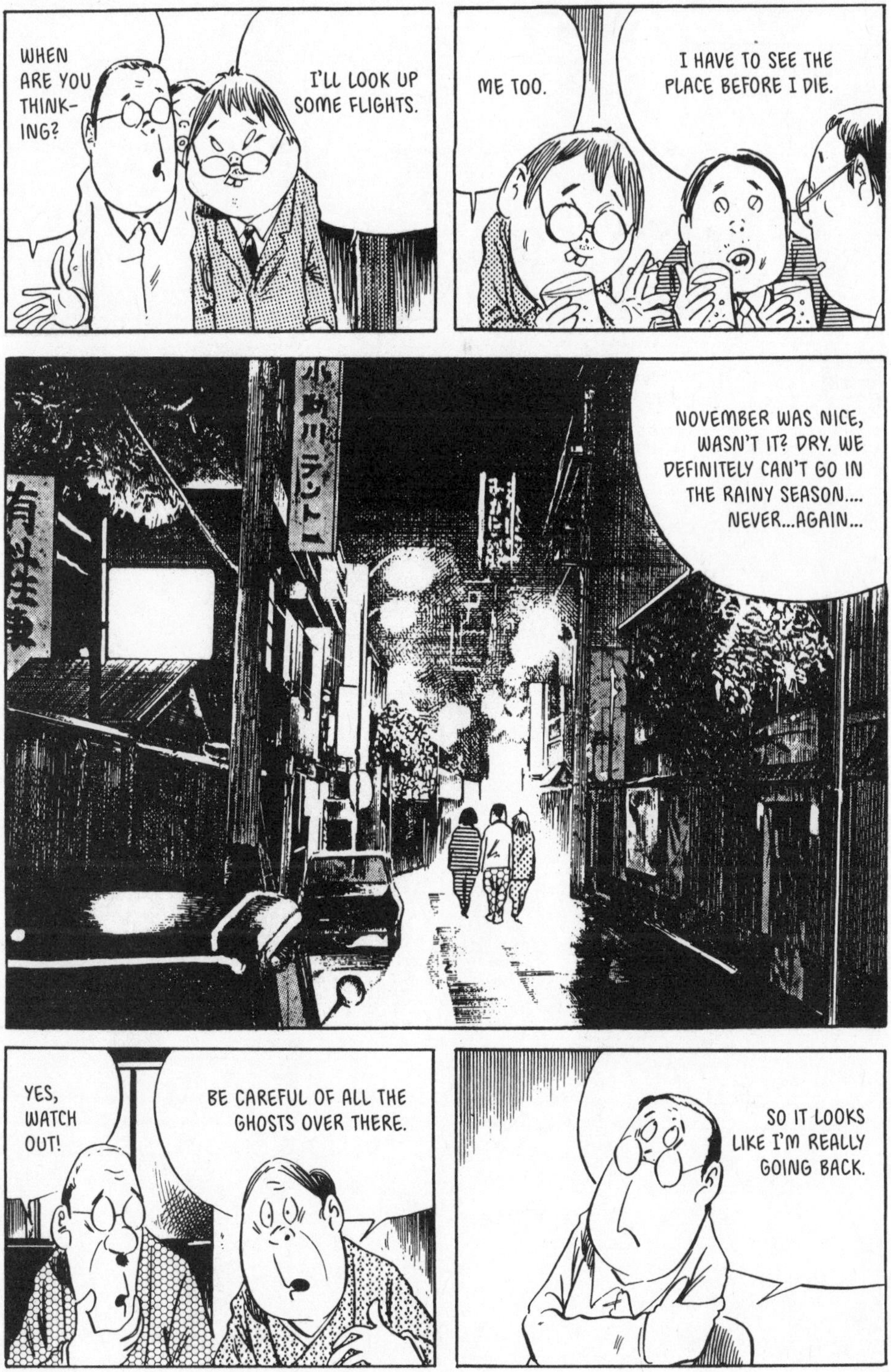
I HAVE TO SEE THE PLACE BEFORE I DIE.
ME TOO.
I'LL LOOK UP SOME FLIGHTS.
WHEN ARE YOU THINKING?
NOVEMBER WAS NICE, WASN'T IT? DRY. WE DEFINITELY CAN'T GO IN THE RAINY SEASON.... NEVER...AGAIN...
SO IT LOOKS LIKE I'M REALLY GOING BACK.
BE CAREFUL OF ALL THE GHOSTS OVER THERE.
YES, WATCH OUT!

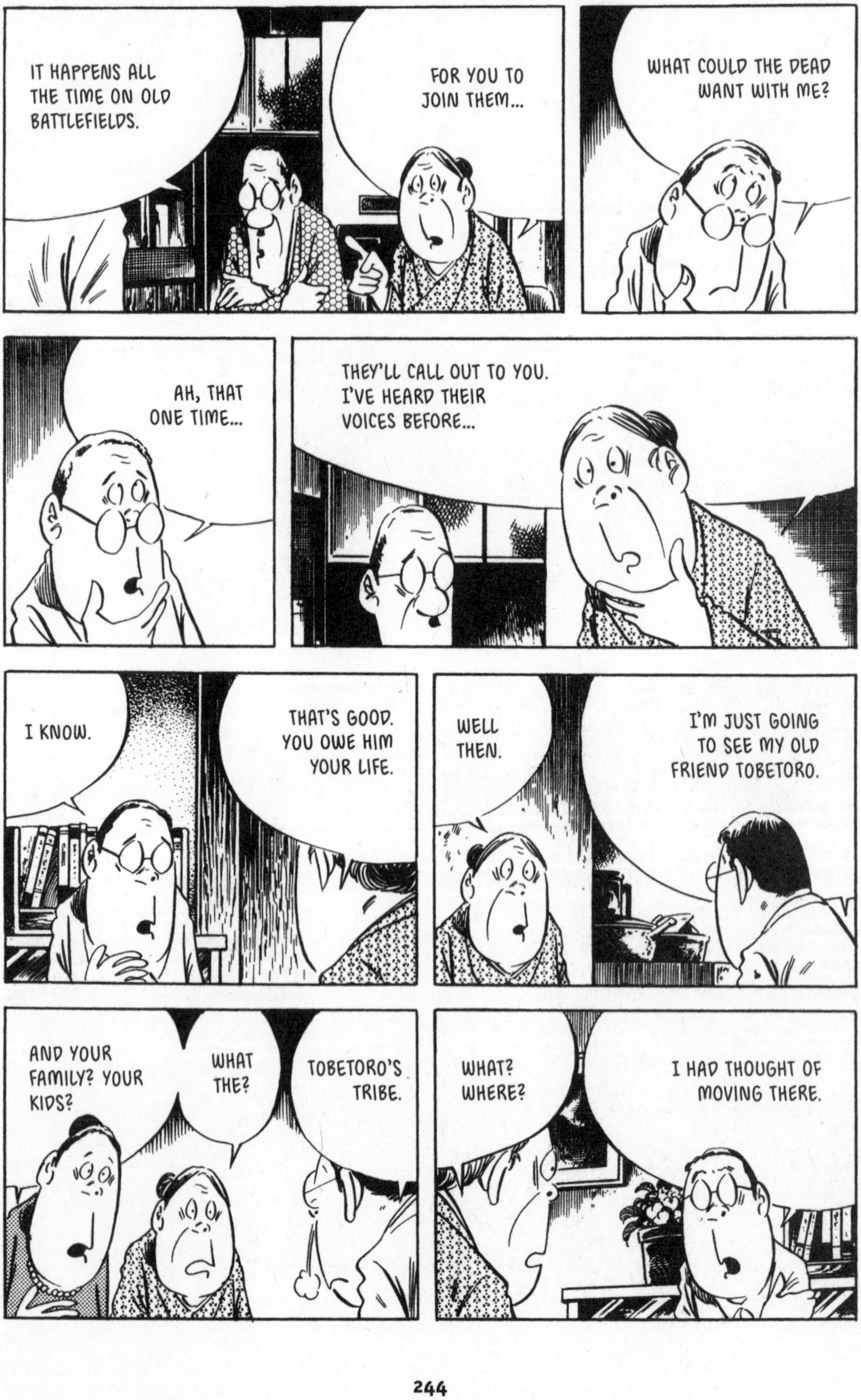
WHAT COULD THE DEAD WANT WITH ME?
FOR YOU TO JOIN THEM...
IT HAPPENS ALL THE TIME ON OLD BATTLEFIELDS.
THEY'LL CALL OUT TO YOU. I'VE HEARD THEIR VOICES BEFORE...
AH, THAT ONE TIME...
I'M JUST GOING TO SEE MY OLD FRIEND TOBETORO.
WELL THEN.
THAT'S GOOD. YOU OWE HIM YOUR LIFE.
I KNOW.
I HAD THOUGHT OF MOVING THERE.
WHAT? WHERE?
TOBETORO'S TRIBE.
WHAT THE?
AND YOUR FAMILY? YOUR KIDS?

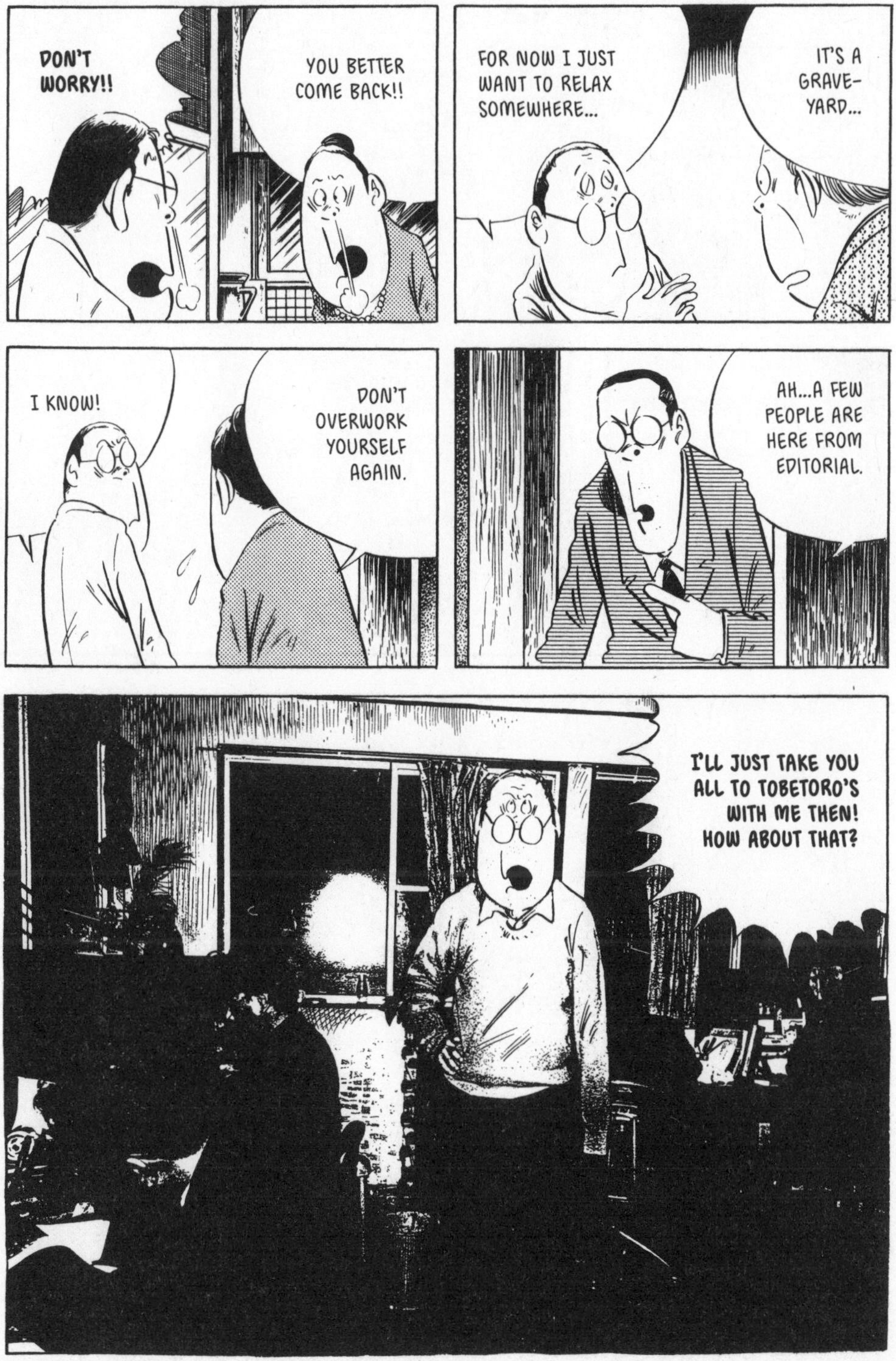
IT'S A GRAVE-YARD...
FOR NOW I JUST WANT TO RELAX SOMEWHERE...
YOU BETTER COME BACK!!
DON'T WORRY!!
AH...A FEW PEOPLE ARE HERE FROM EDITORIAL.
DON'T OVERWORK YOURSELF AGAIN.
I KNOW!
I'LL JUST TAKE YOU ALL TO TOBETORO'S WITH ME THEN! HOW ABOUT THAT?

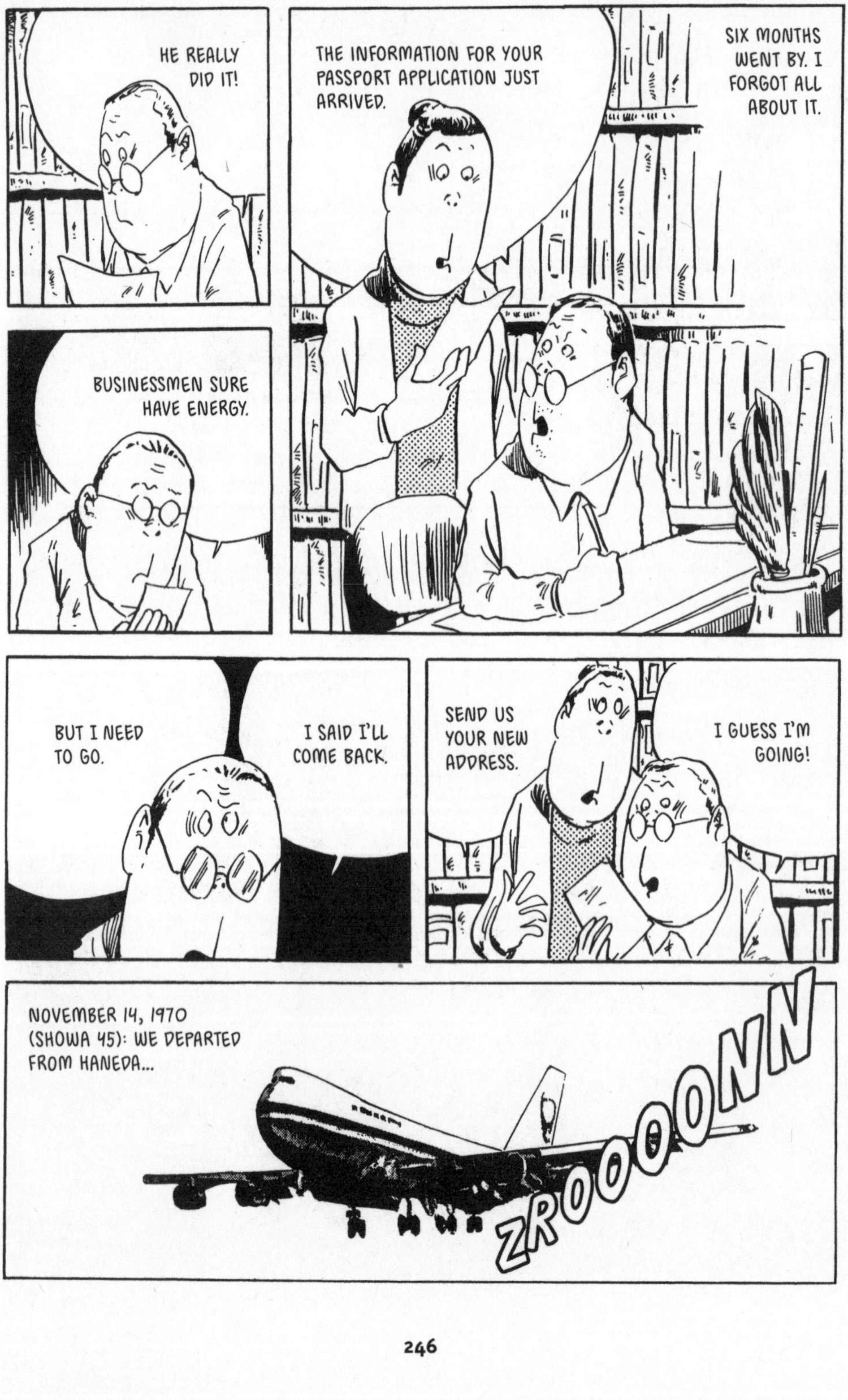
SIX MONTHS WENT BY. I FORGOT ALL ABOUT IT.
THE INFORMATION FOR YOUR PASSPORT APPLICATION JUST ARRIVED.
HE REALLY DID IT!
BUSINESSMEN SURE HAVE ENERGY.
I GUESS I'M GOING!
SEND US YOUR NEW ADDRESS.
I SAID I'LL COME BACK.
BUT I NEED TO GO.
ZROOOONN
NOVEMBER 14, 1970 (SHOWA 45): WE DEPARTED FROM HANEDA...

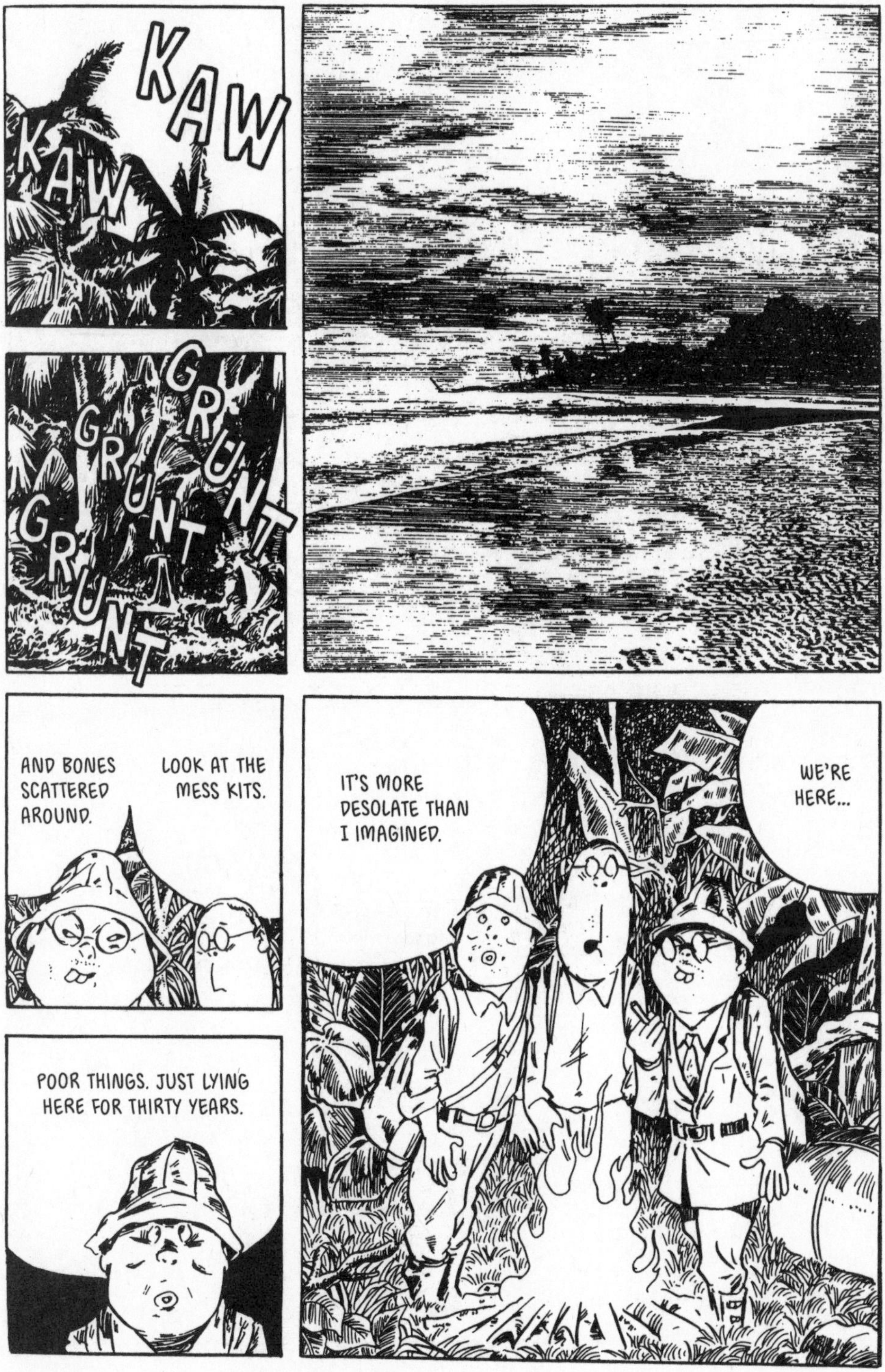
KAW
KAW
GRUNT
GRUNT
GRUNT
WE'RE HERE...
IT'S MORE DESOLATE THAN I IMAGINED.
LOOK AT THE MESS KITS.
AND BONES SCATTERED AROUND.
POOR THINGS. JUST LYING HERE FOR THIRTY YEARS.

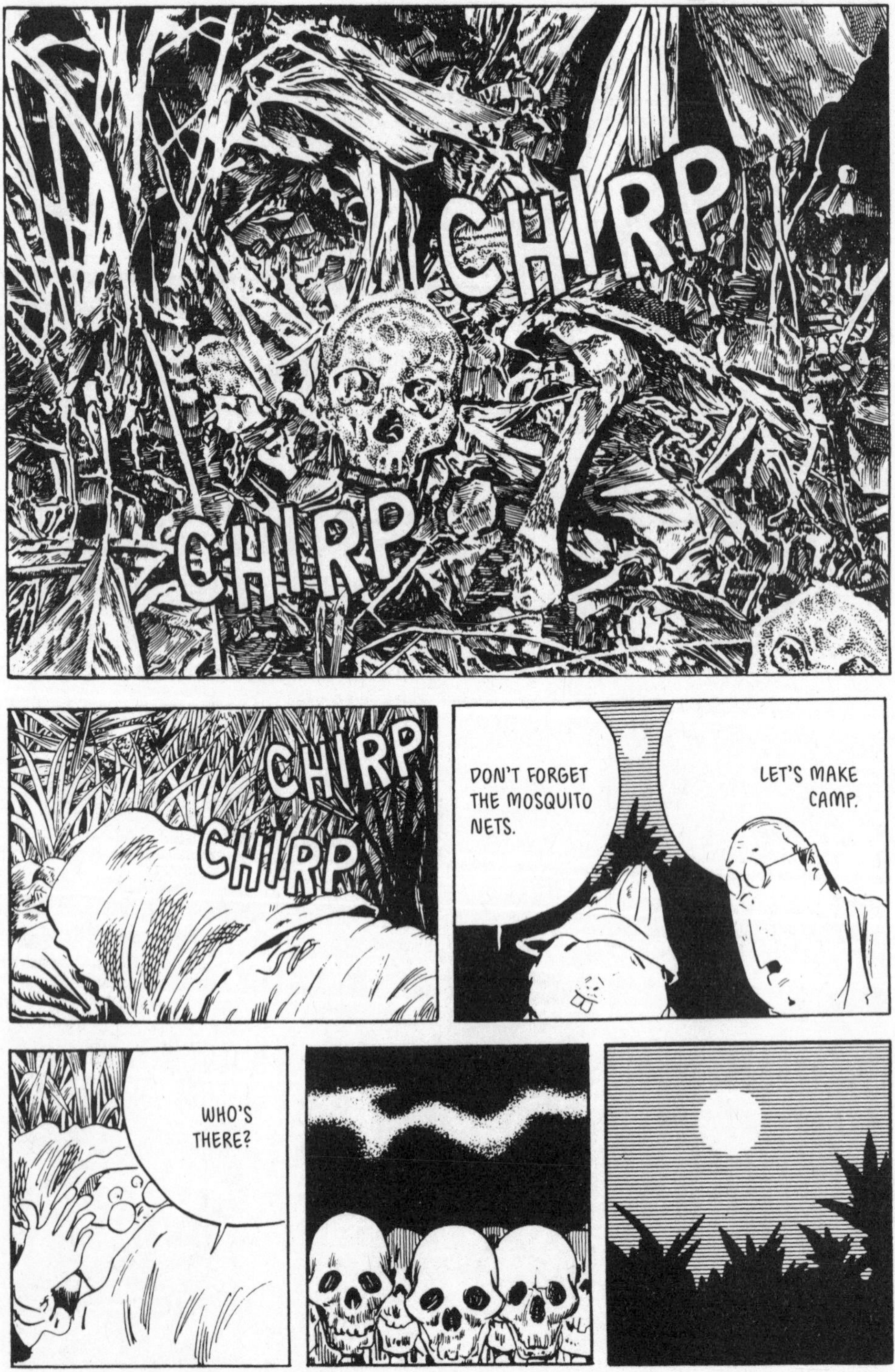
CHIRP
CHIRP
LET'S MAKE CAMP.
DON'T FORGET THE MOSQUITO NETS.
CHIRP
CHIRP
WHO'S THERE?

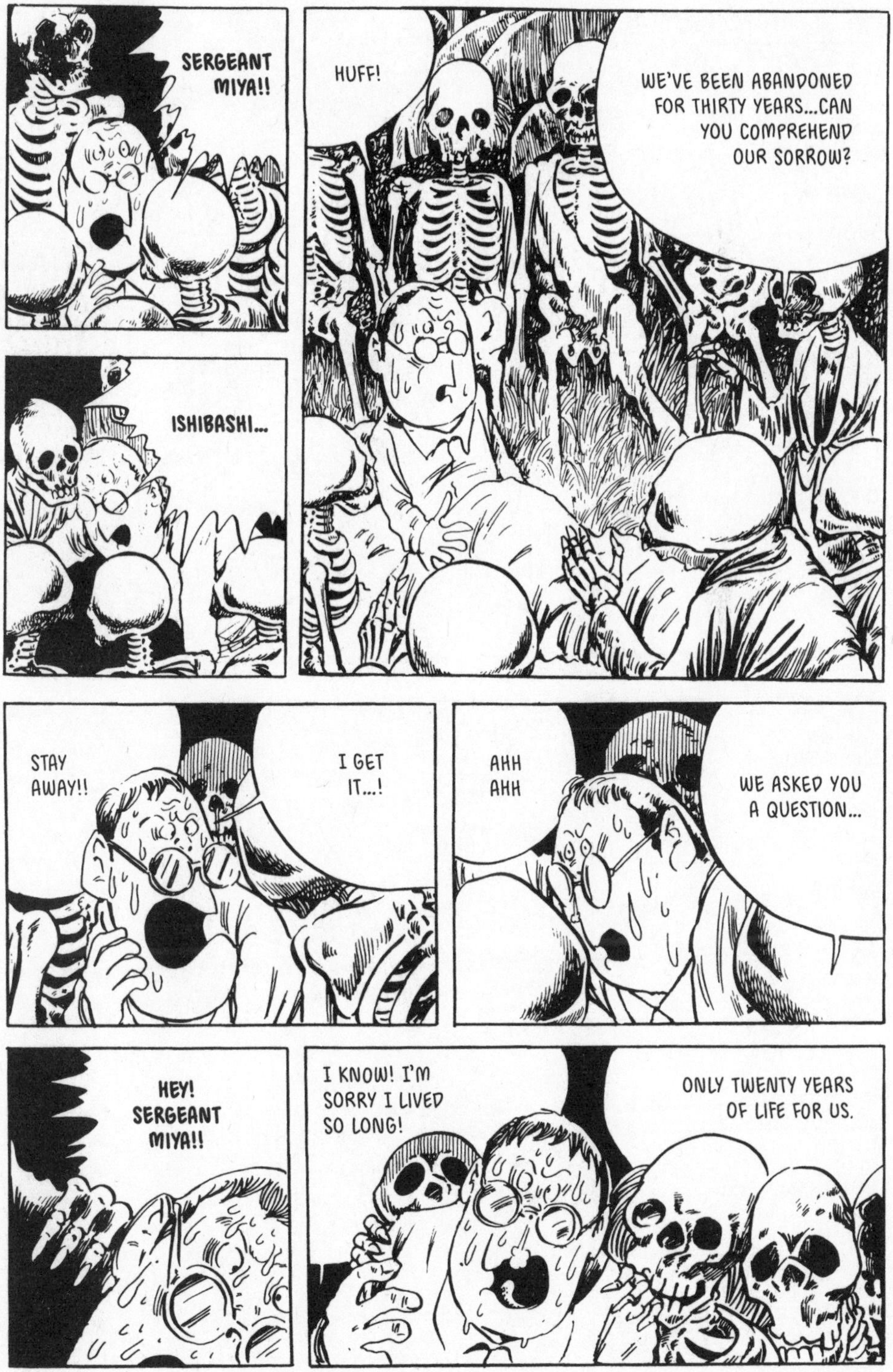
WE'VE BEEN ABANDONED FOR THIRTY YEARS...CAN YOU COMPREHEND OUR SORROW?
HUFF!
SERGEANT MIYA!!
ISHIBASHI...
WE ASKED YOU A QUESTION...
AHH AHH
I GET IT...!
STAY AWAY!!
ONLY TWENTY YEARS OF LIFE FOR US.
I KNOW! I'M SORRY I LIVED SO LONG!
HEY! SERGEANT MIYA!!

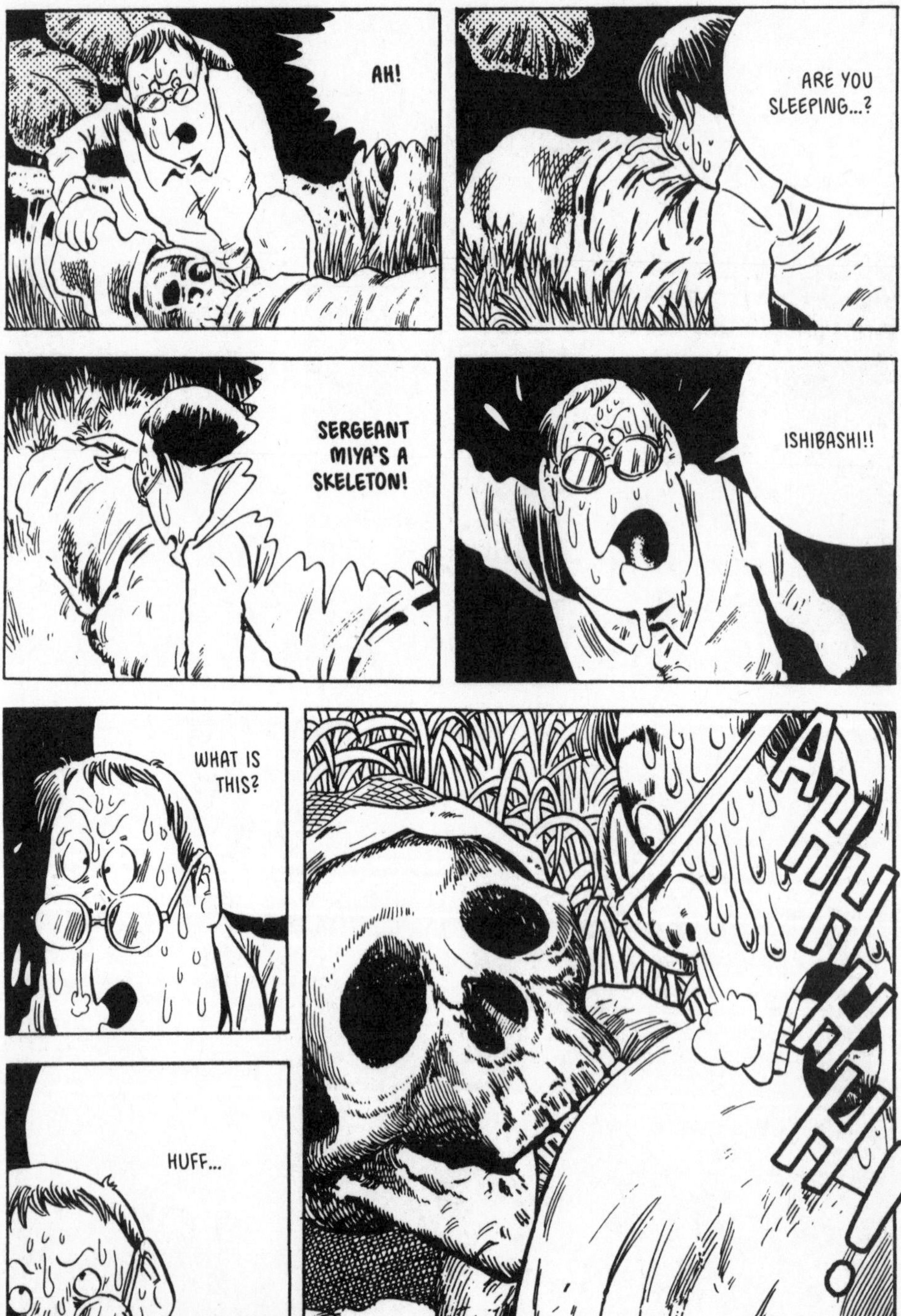
ARE YOU SLEEPING...?
AH!
ISHIBASHI!!
SERGEANT MIYA'S A SKELETON!
AHHHH!
WHAT IS THIS?
HUFF...

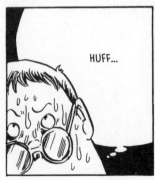

IT WAS TERRIBLE.

AHH AH AHH

A NIGHTMARE? IT'S NOON.

YEAH. US TOO. THE SAME DREAM.

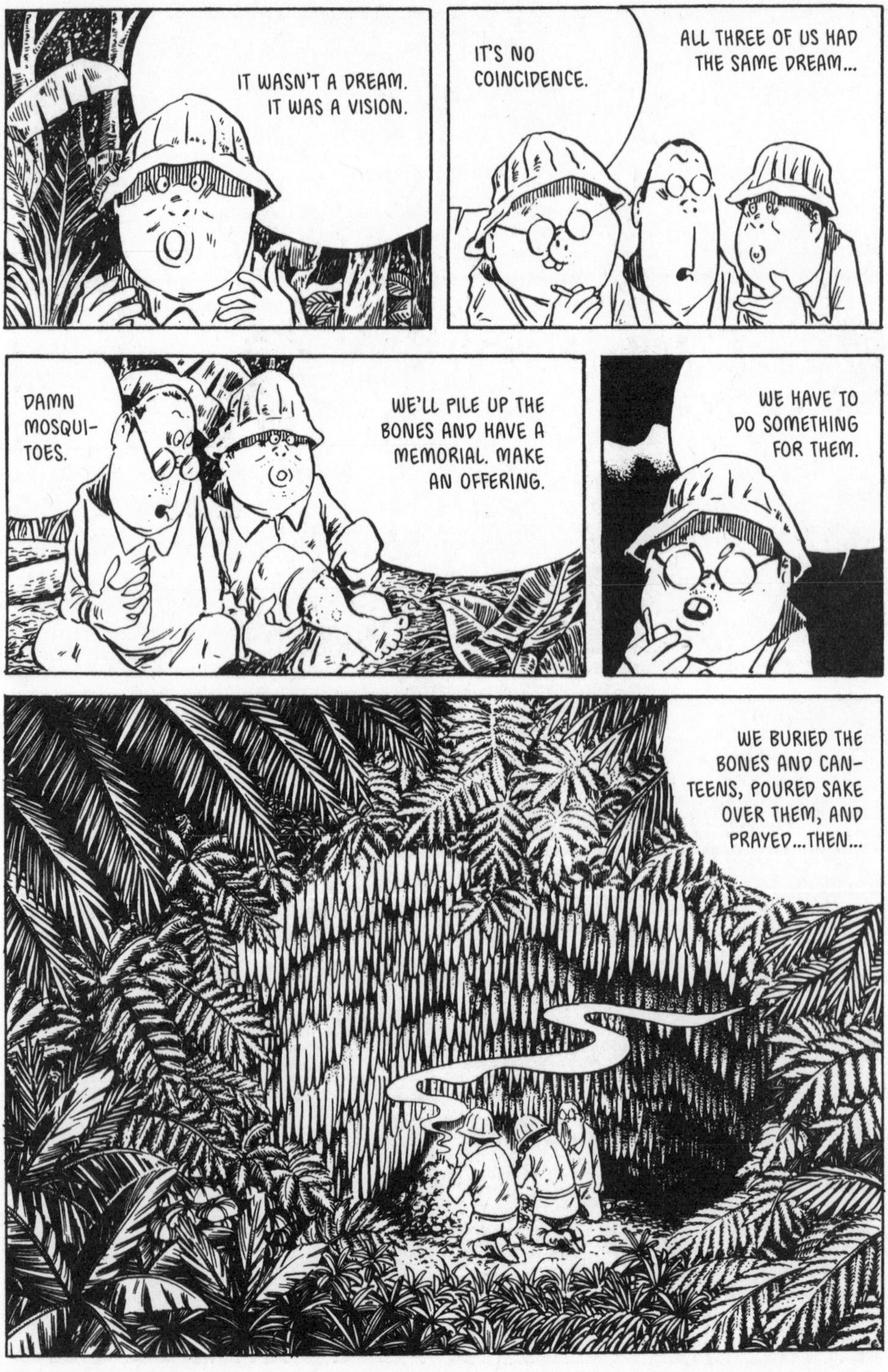
ALL THREE OF US HAD THE SAME DREAM...
IT'S NO COINCIDENCE.
IT WASN'T A DREAM. IT WAS A VISION.
WE HAVE TO DO SOMETHING FOR THEM.
WE'LL PILE UP THE BONES AND HAVE A MEMORIAL. MAKE AN OFFERING.
DAMN MOSQUI- TOES.
WE BURIED THE BONES AND CAN- TEENS, POURED SAKE OVER THEM, AND PRAYED...THEN...

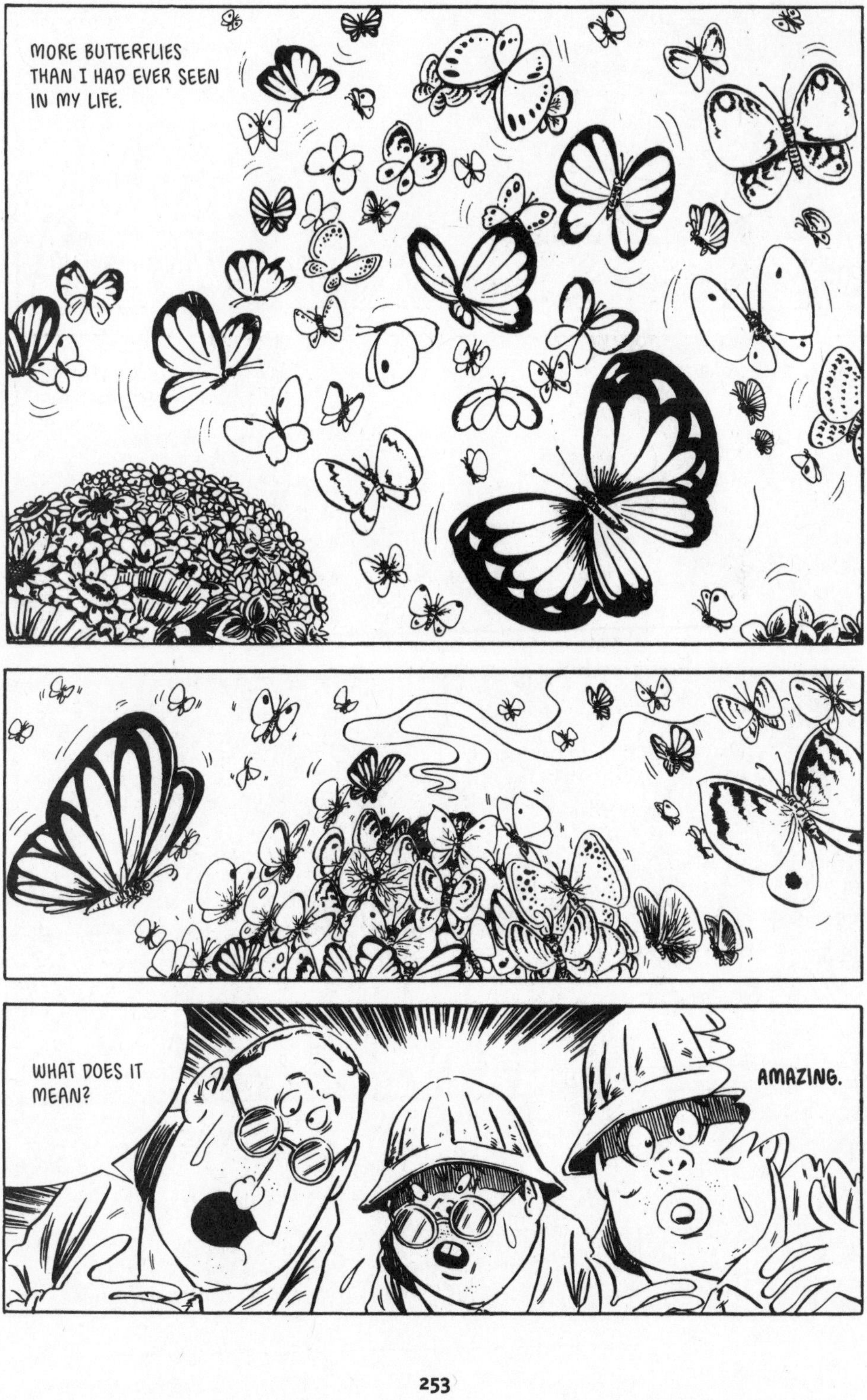
MORE BUTTERFLIES THAN I HAD EVER SEEN IN MY LIFE.
AMAZING.
WHAT DOES IT MEAN?

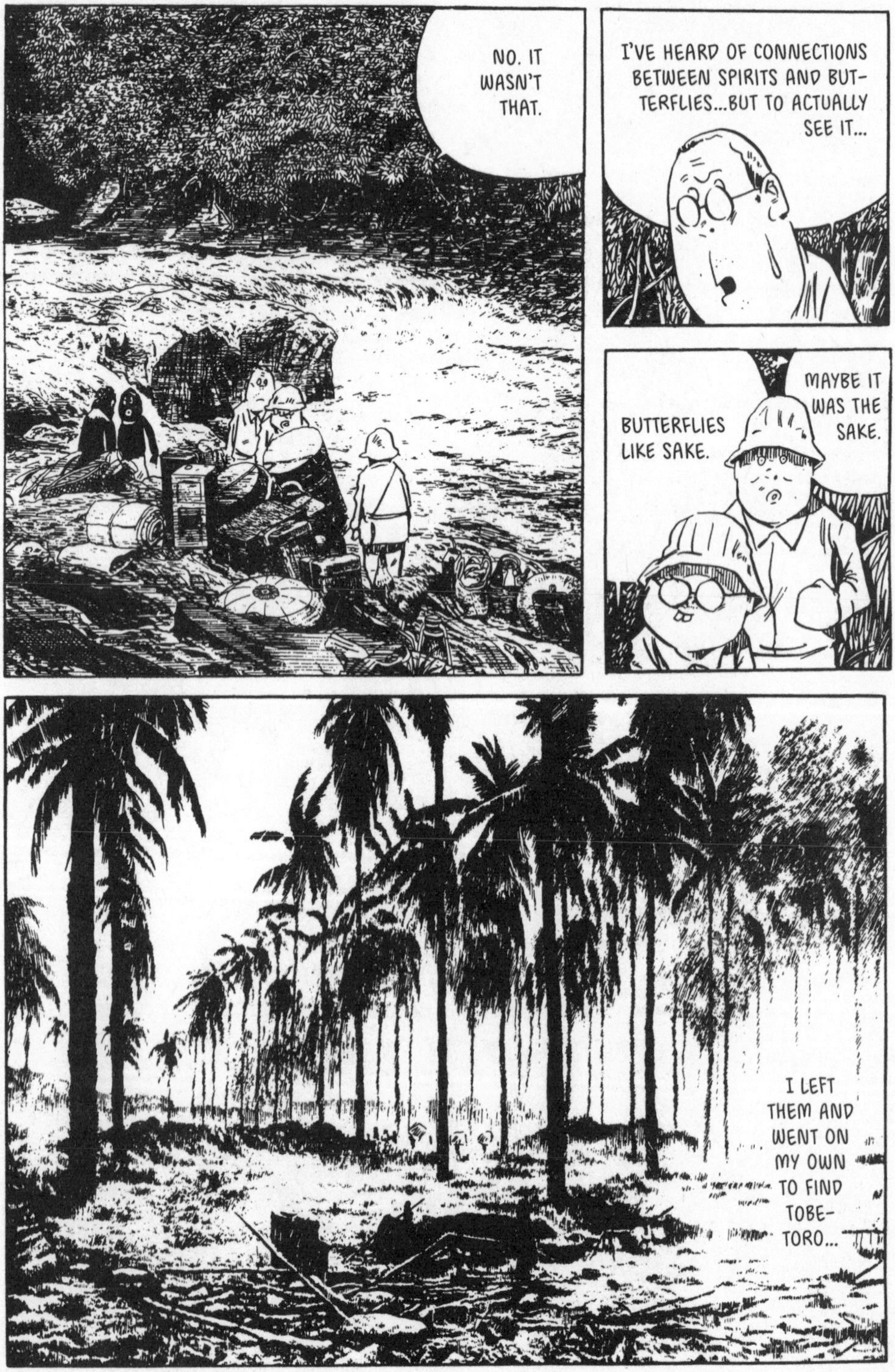
I'VE HEARD OF CONNECTIONS BETWEEN SPIRITS AND BUTTERFLIES...BUT TO ACTUALLY SEE IT...
MAYBE IT WAS THE SAKE.
BUTTERFLIES LIKE SAKE.
NO. IT WASN'T THAT.
I LEFT THEM AND WENT ON MY OWN TO FIND TOBE-TORO...

REUNION WITH TOBETORO

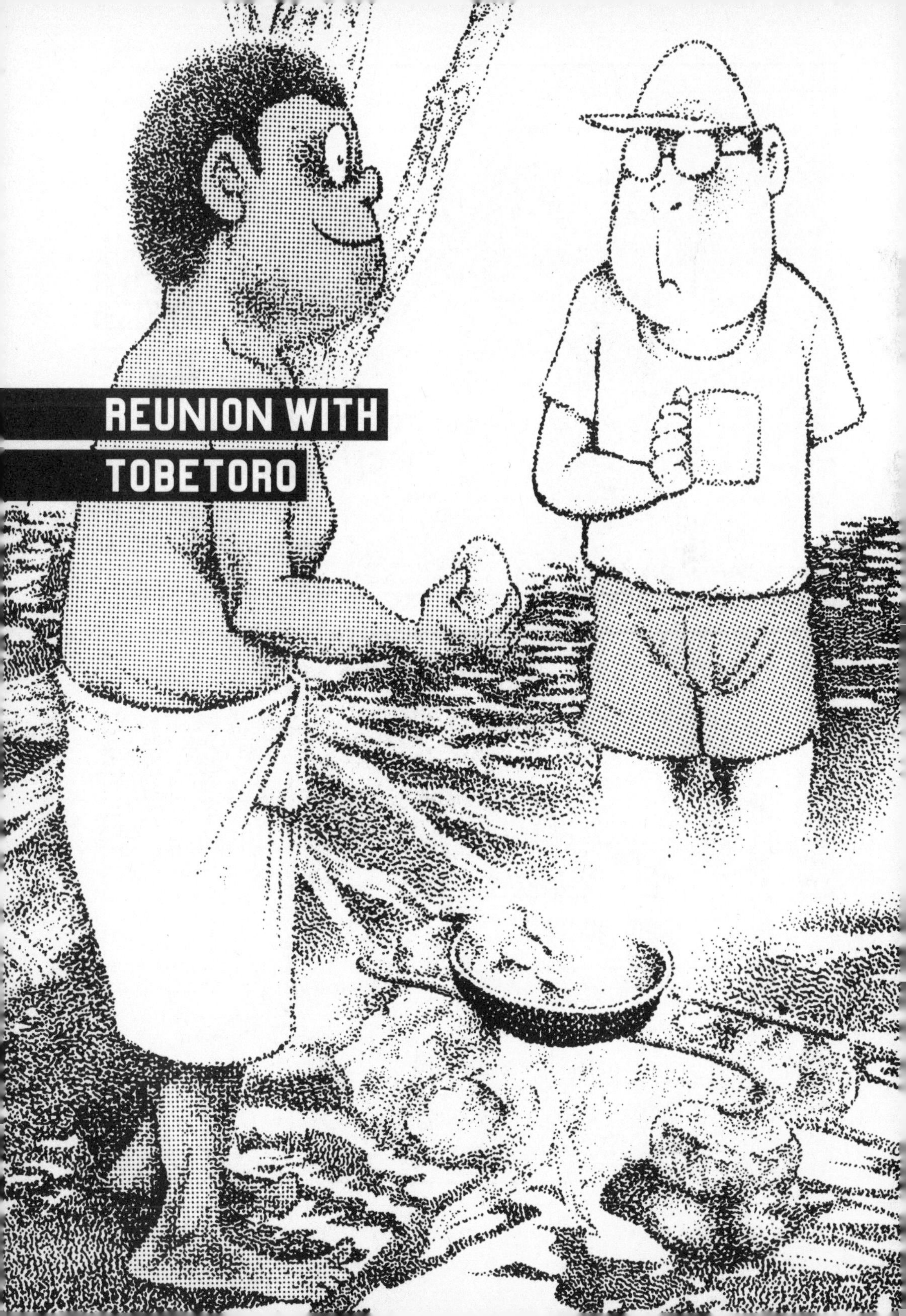

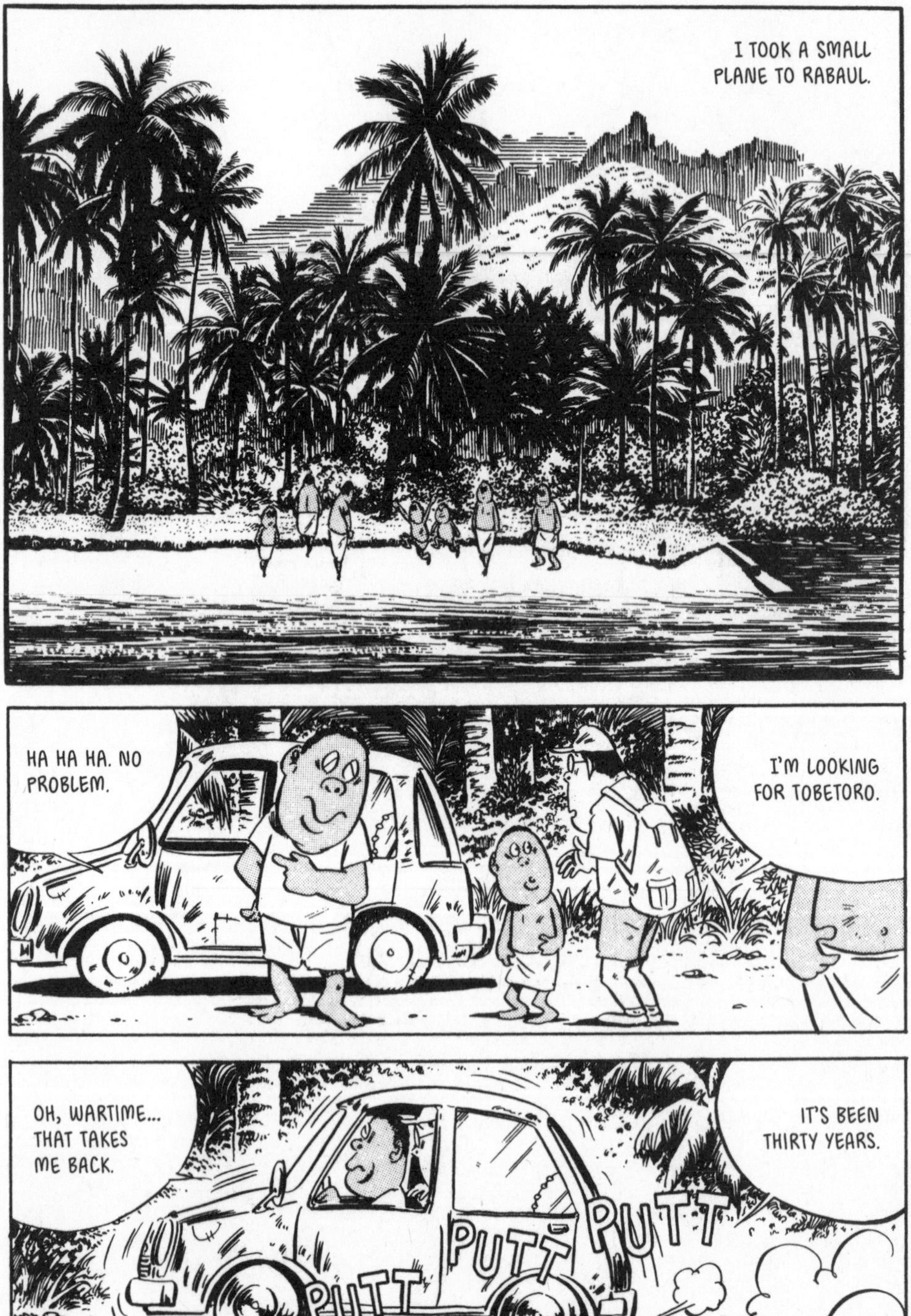
I TOOK A SMALL PLANE TO RABAUL.
I'M LOOKING FOR TOBETORO.
HA HA HA. NO PROBLEM.
IT'S BEEN THIRTY YEARS.
OH, WARTIME... THAT TAKES ME BACK.
PUTT PUTT PUTT

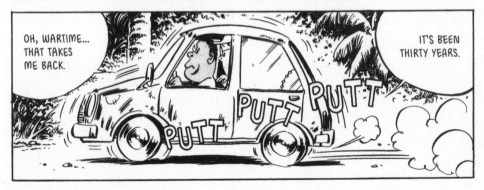

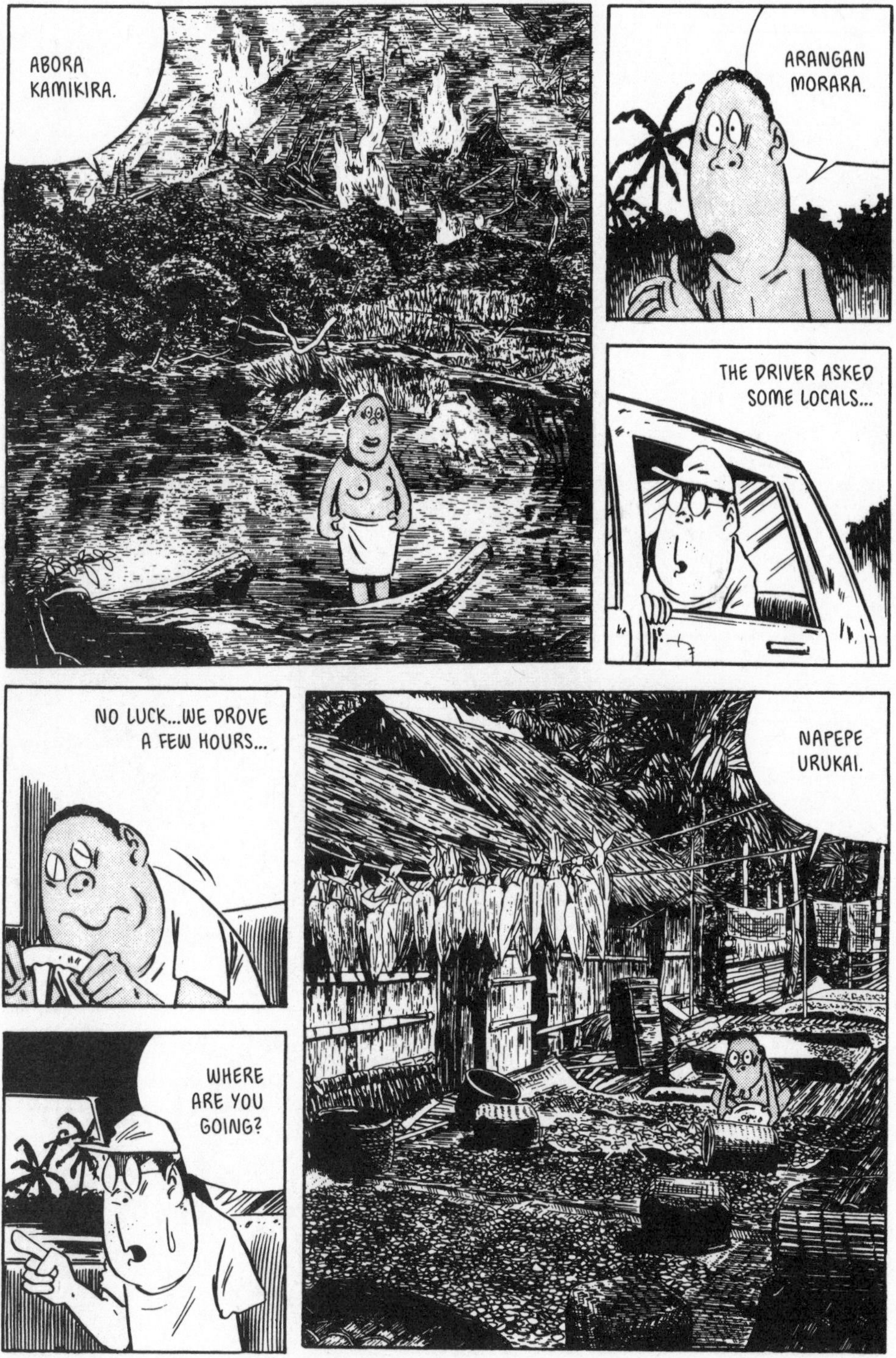
ARANGAN MORARA.
THE DRIVER ASKED SOME LOCALS...
ABORA KAMIKIRA.
NAPEPE URUKAI.
NO LUCK...WE DROVE A FEW HOURS...
WHERE ARE YOU GOING?

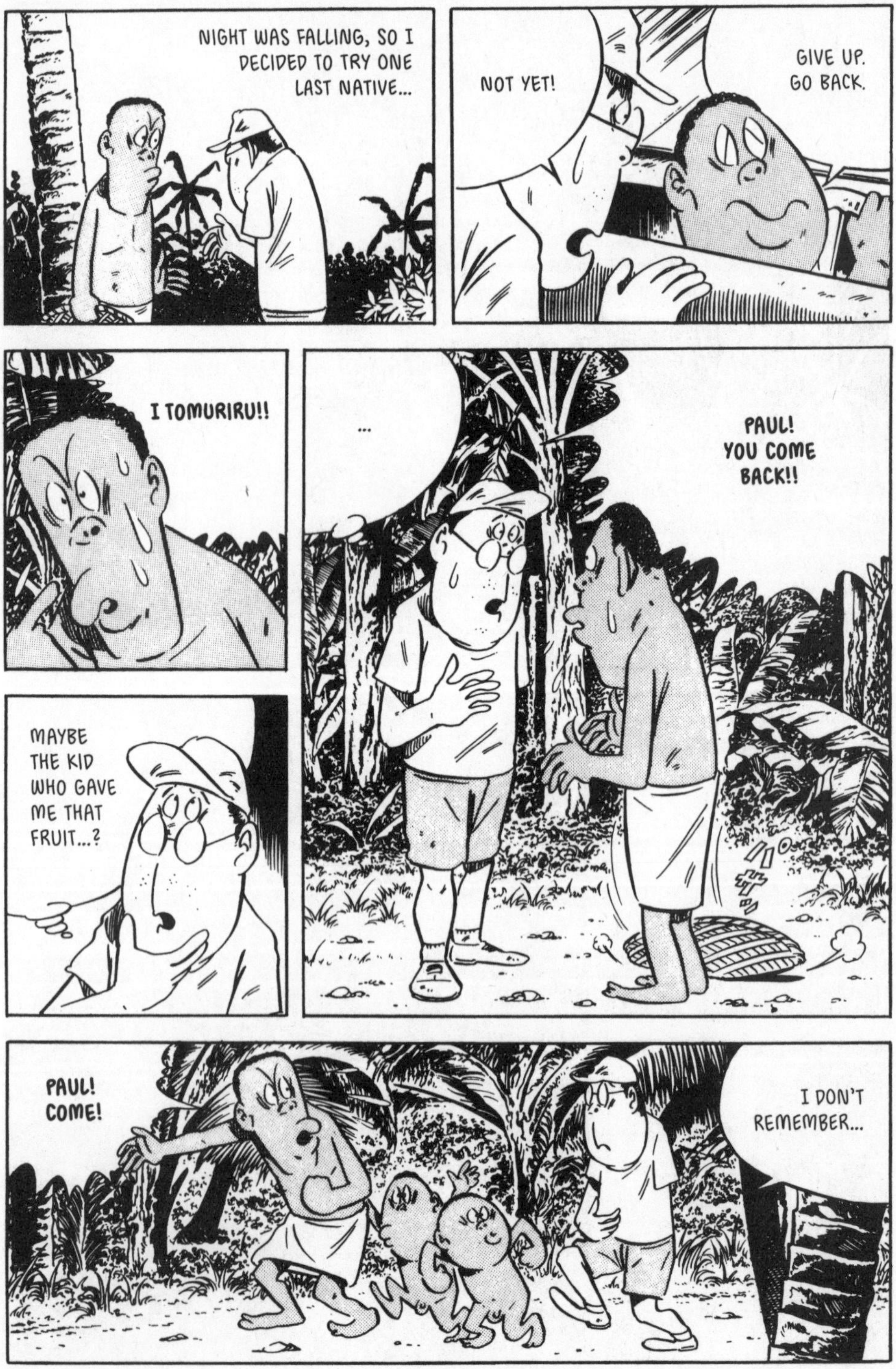
GIVE UP.
GO BACK.
NOT YET!
NIGHT WAS FALLING, SO I DECIDED TO TRY ONE LAST NATIVE...
PAUL! YOU COME BACK!!
...
I TOMURIRU!!
MAYBE THE KID WHO GAVE ME THAT FRUIT...?
I DON'T REMEMBER...
PAUL! COME!

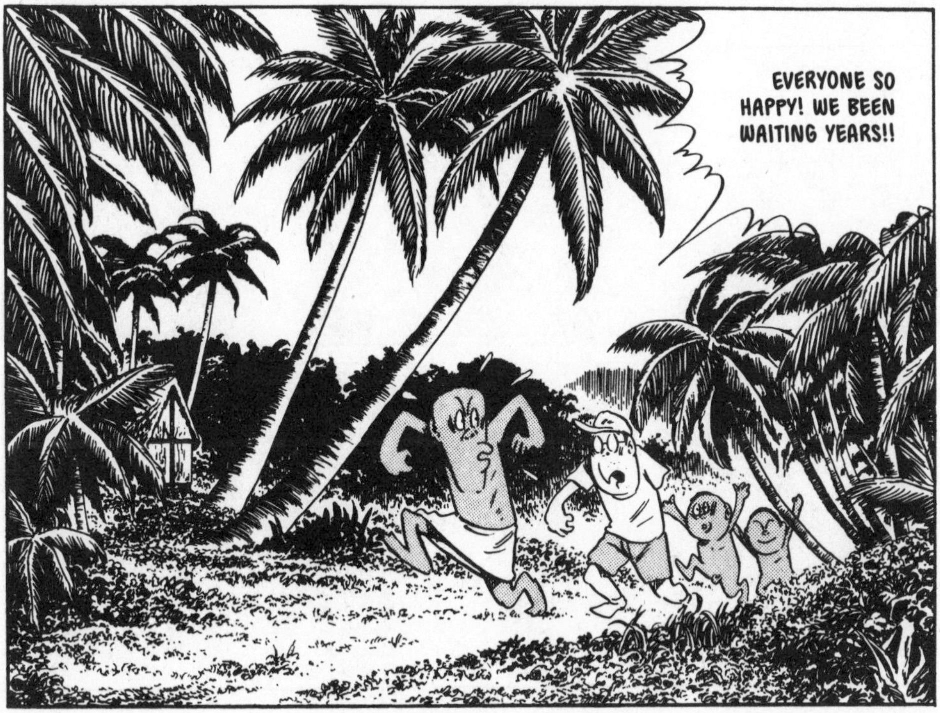
EVERYONE SO HAPPY! WE BEEN WAITING YEARS!!

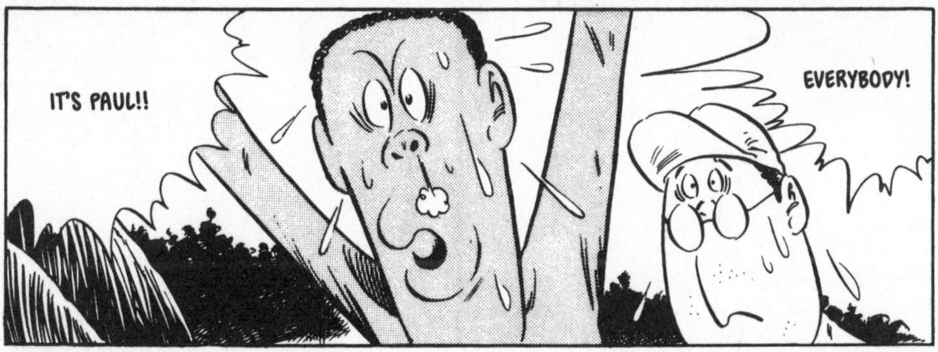
EVERYBODY!
IT'S PAUL!!

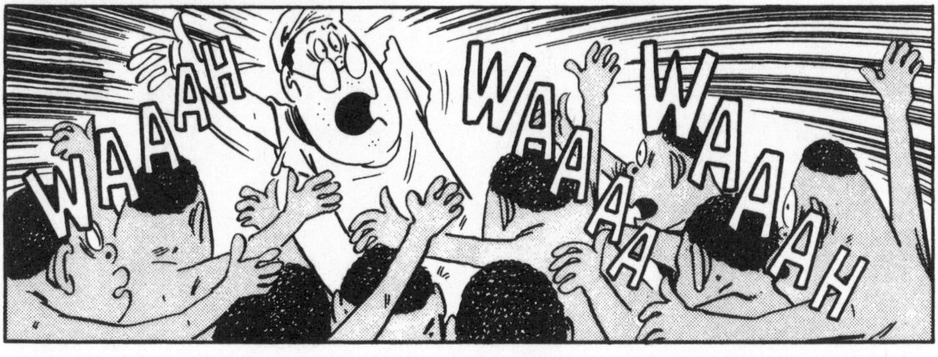
WAAAAH
WAAAAA
WAAAH

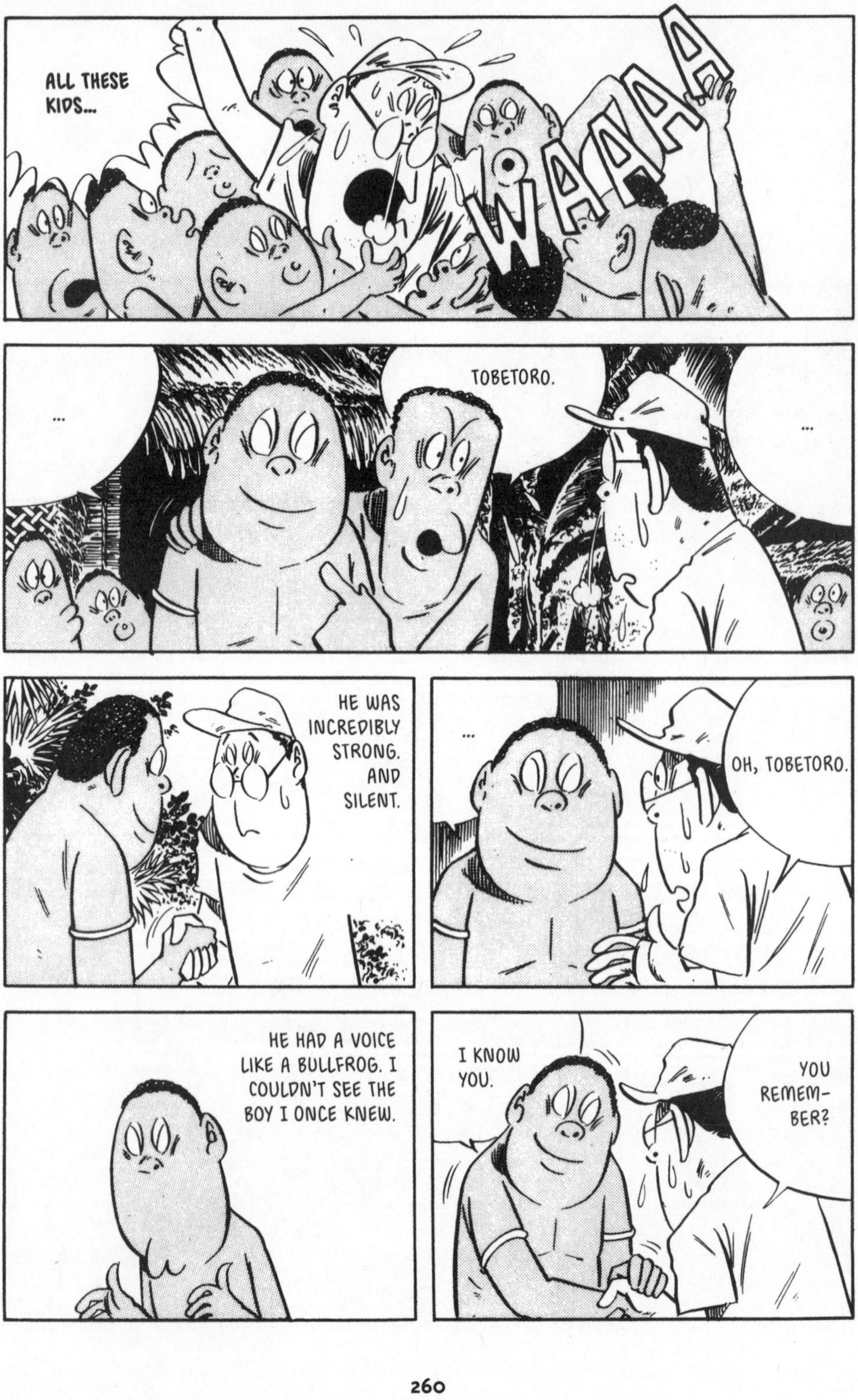
WAAAA
ALL THESE KIDS...
...
TOBETORO.
...
OH, TOBETORO.
...
HE WAS INCREDIBLY STRONG. AND SILENT.
YOU REMEMBER?
I KNOW YOU.
HE HAD A VOICE LIKE A BULLFROG. I COULDN'T SEE THE BOY I ONCE KNEW.

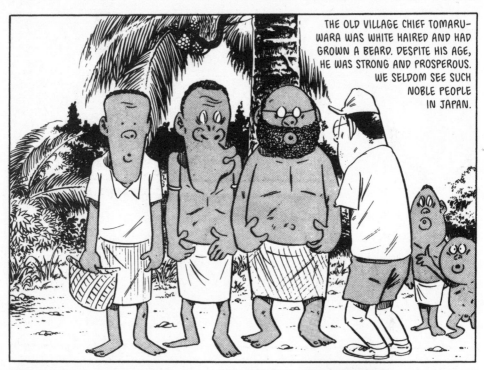

THE OLD VILLAGE CHIEF TOMARU-WARA WAS WHITE HAIRED AND HAD GROWN A BEARD. DESPITE HIS AGE, HE WAS STRONG AND PROSPEROUS. WE SELDOM SEE SUCH NOBLE PEOPLE IN JAPAN.
PAUL, WELCOME BACK.
AT LAST.
THEY SPOKE FEW WORDS, BUT ALWAYS WITH GREAT MEANING...
HOW IS IKARIEN?
SHE DIED.
ALWAYS SHE WAITING FOR YOU.

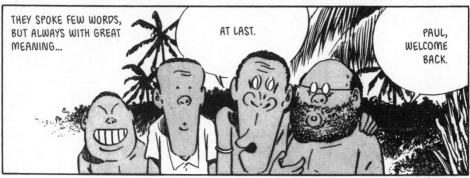

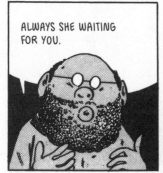

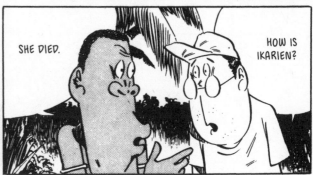

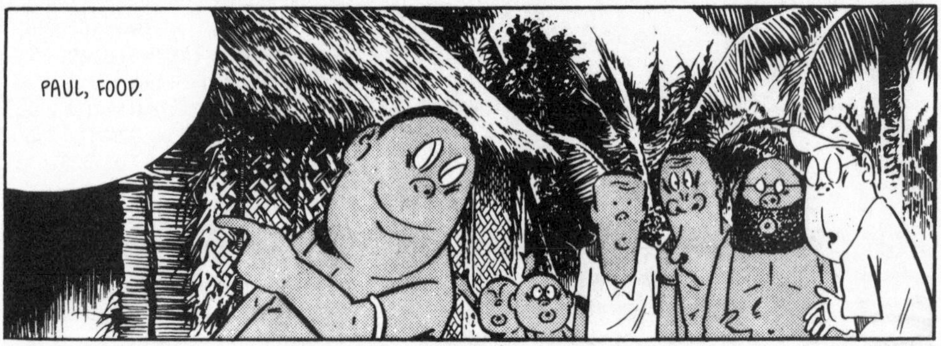
PAUL, FOOD.

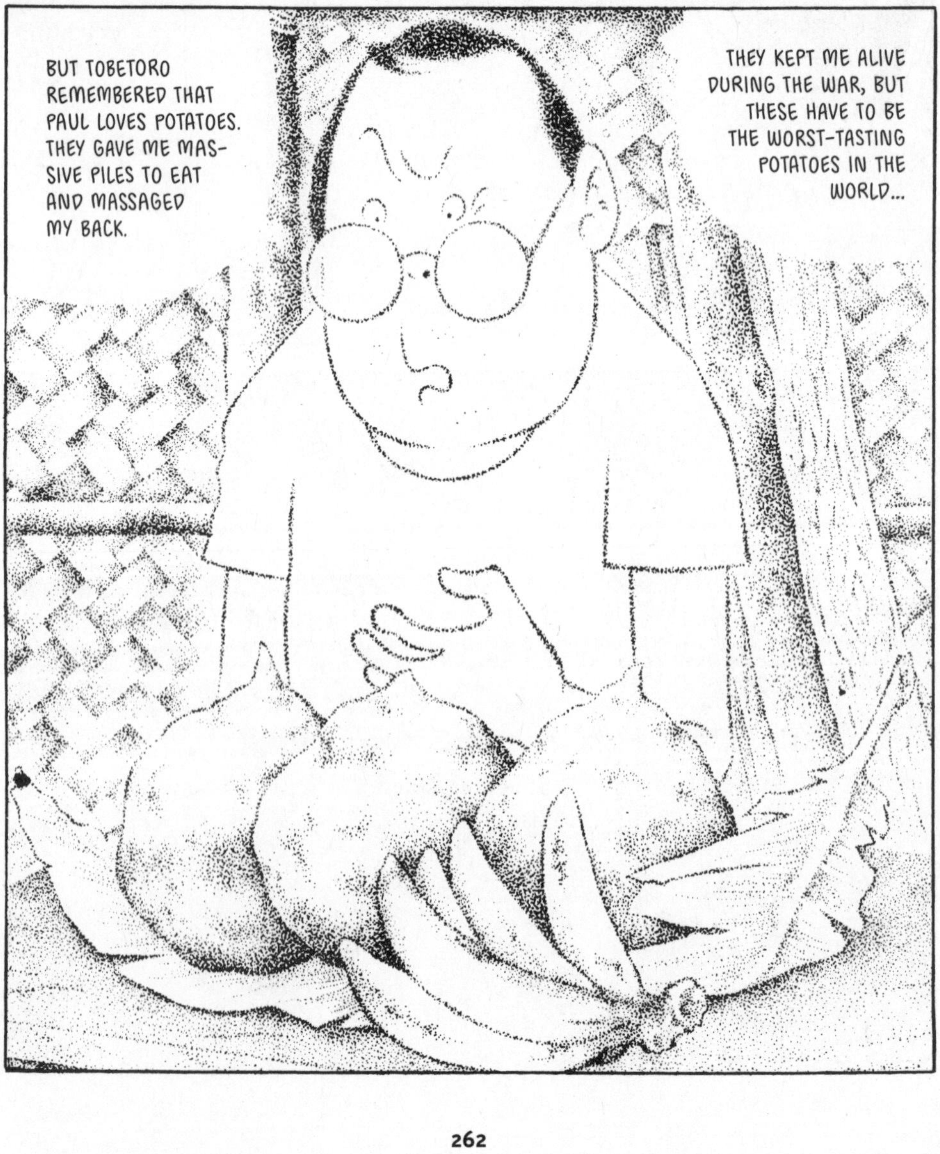
THEY KEPT ME ALIVE DURING THE WAR, BUT THESE HAVE TO BE THE WORST-TASTING POTATOES IN THE WORLD...
BUT TOBETORO REMEMBERED THAT PAUL LOVES POTATOES. THEY GAVE ME MASSIVE PILES TO EAT AND MASSAGED MY BACK.

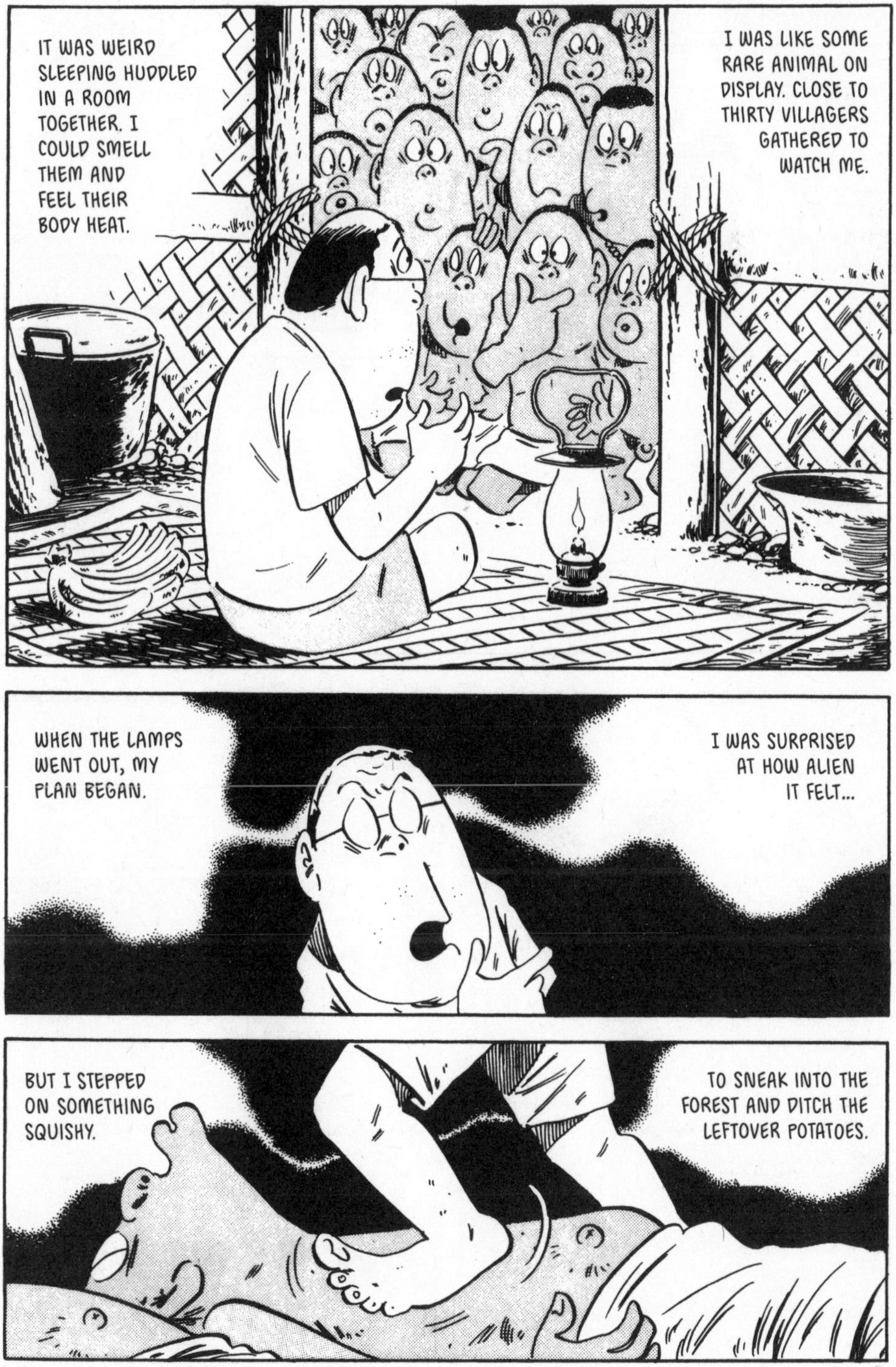
I WAS LIKE SOME RARE ANIMAL ON DISPLAY. CLOSE TO THIRTY VILLAGERS GATHERED TO WATCH ME.
IT WAS WEIRD SLEEPING HUDDLED IN A ROOM TOGETHER. I COULD SMELL THEM AND FEEL THEIR BODY HEAT.
I WAS SURPRISED AT HOW ALIEN IT FELT...
WHEN THE LAMPS WENT OUT, MY PLAN BEGAN.
TO SNEAK INTO THE FOREST AND DITCH THE LEFTOVER POTATOES.
BUT I STEPPED ON SOMETHING SQUISHY.

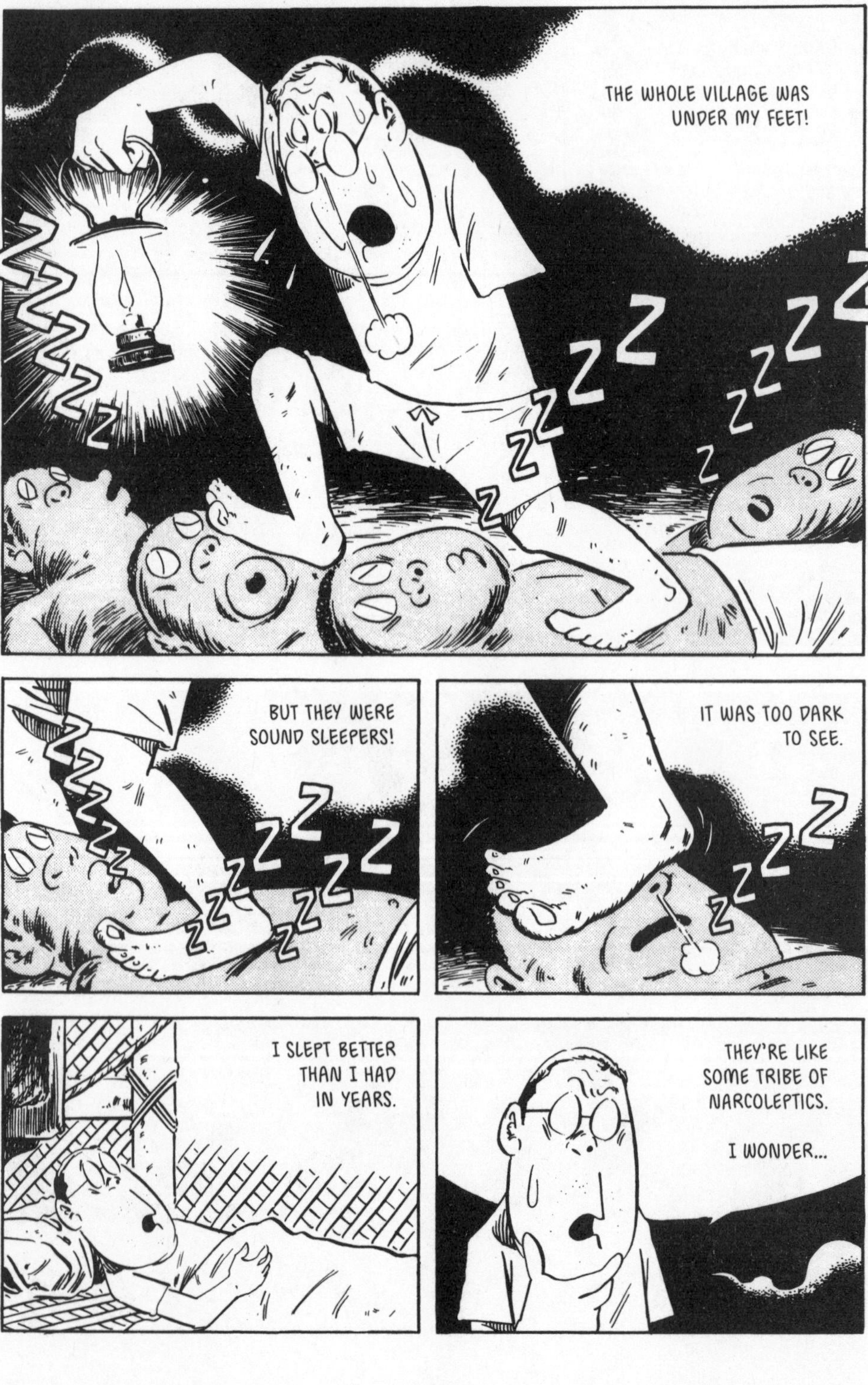
THE WHOLE VILLAGE WAS UNDER MY FEET!
IT WAS TOO DARK TO SEE.
BUT THEY WERE SOUND SLEEPERS!
THEY'RE LIKE SOME TRIBE OF NARCOLEPTICS.
I WONDER...
I SLEPT BETTER THAN I HAD IN YEARS.

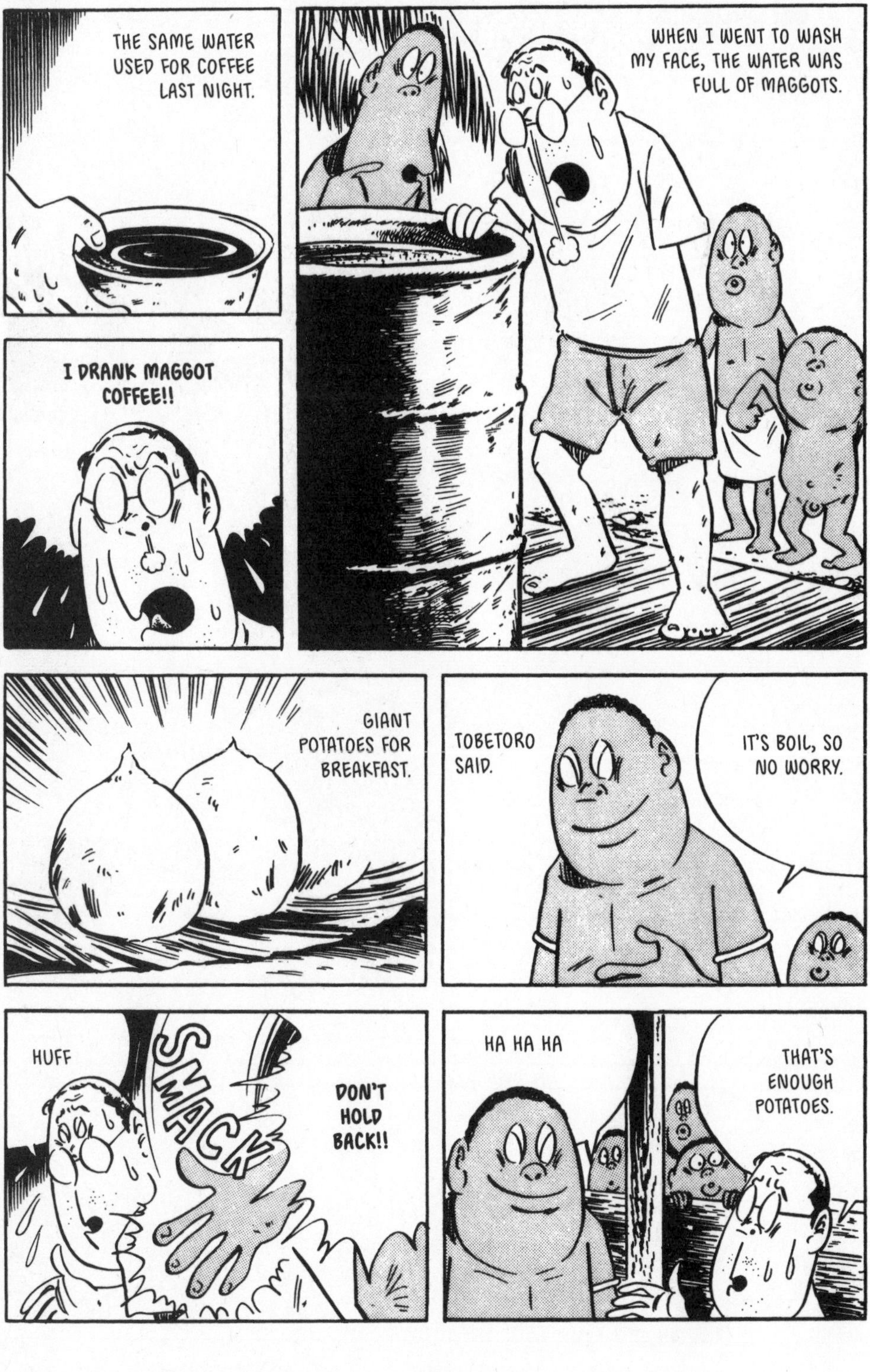
WHEN I WENT TO WASH MY FACE, THE WATER WAS FULL OF MAGGOTS.
THE SAME WATER USED FOR COFFEE LAST NIGHT.
I DRANK MAGGOT COFFEE!!
IT'S BOIL, SO NO WORRY.
TOBETORO SAID.
GIANT POTATOES FOR BREAKFAST.
THAT'S ENOUGH POTATOES.
HA HA HA
SMACK
DON'T HOLD BACK!!
HUFF

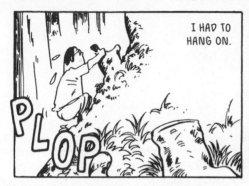

WHERE'S THE TOILET?
OVER THERE.
I HAD TO HANG ON.
PLOP
EVERYONE WATCHED.
IT CAME OUT!!
SAME AS US. SAME SHAPE.
SAME COLOR, EVEN.
WHAT SHOULD I DO WITH THAT...
DON'T WORRY. PIGS EAT ALL CLEAN.
THAT'S CONVENIENT.
THEY LOOKED AT ME WITH ADMIRATION, BUT I FELT THE SAME WAY ABOUT THEM. SUCH DIFFERENT LIVES.
AND THE BEAUTIFUL EPUPE?
AH! EPUPE!!

SORRY, BUT THE REUNION WITH EPUPE WILL HAVE TO WAIT UNTIL LATER...

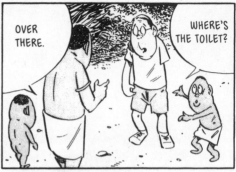

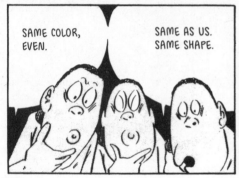

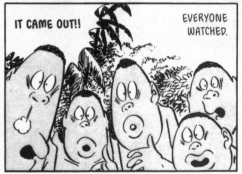

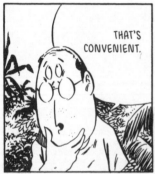

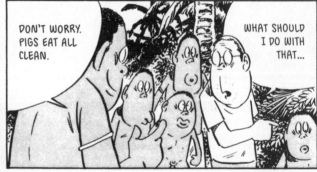

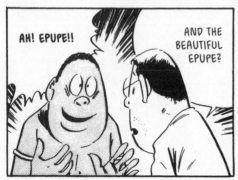

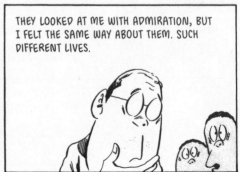

AT THE WORLD'S FAIR

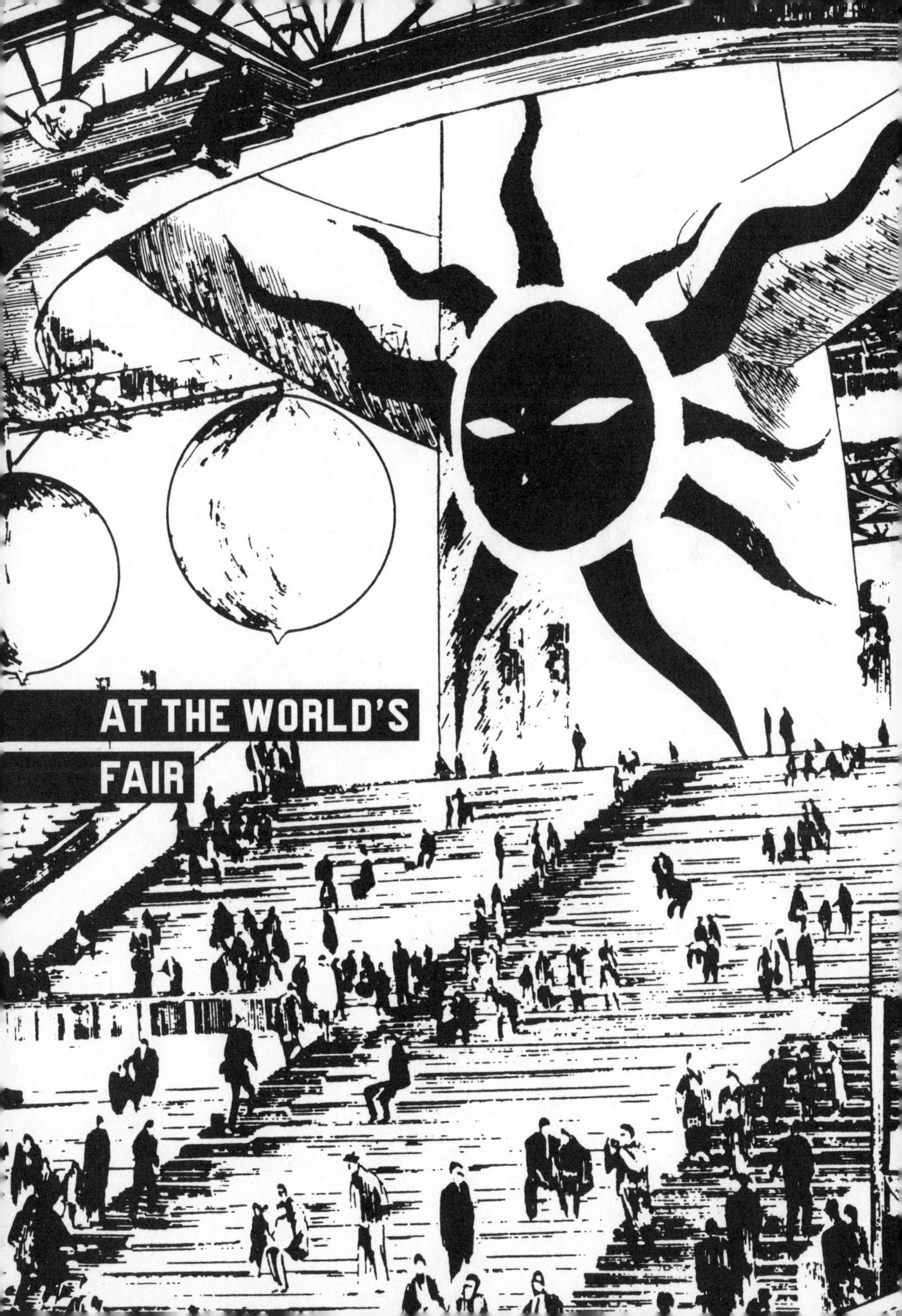

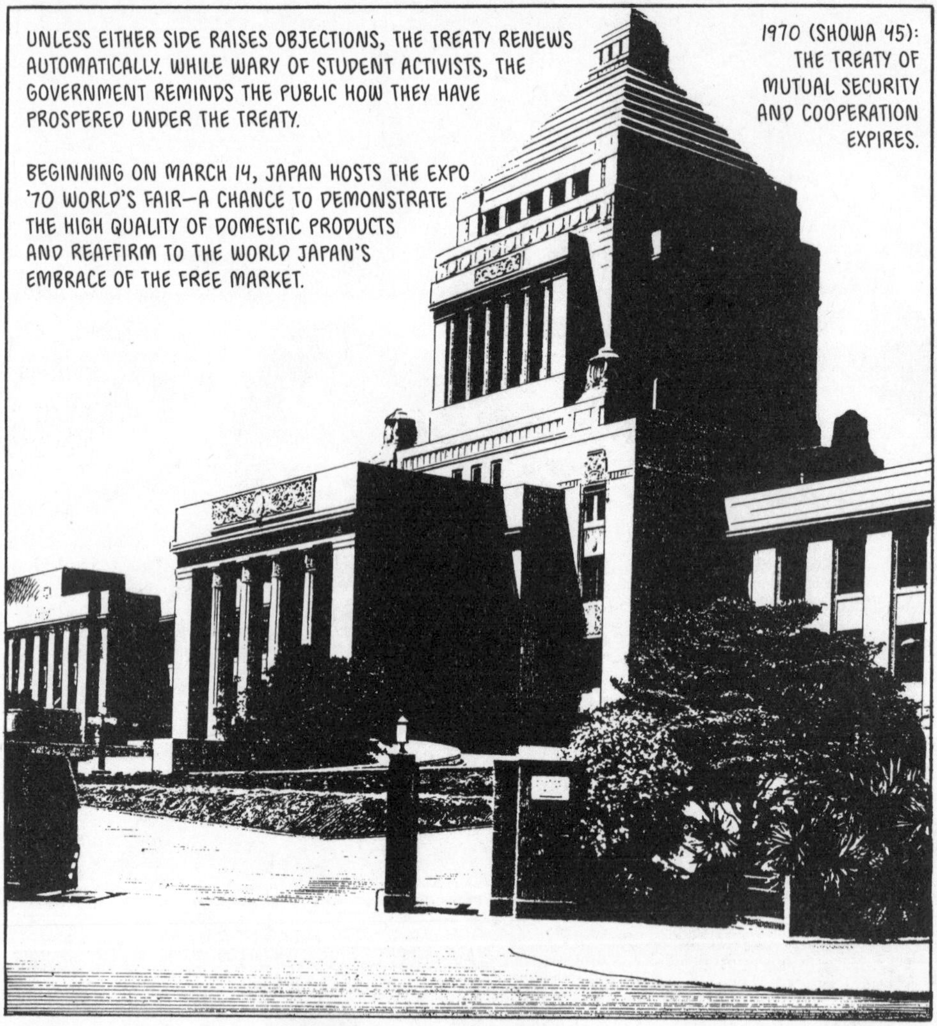
1970 (SHOWA 45): THE TREATY OF MUTUAL SECURITY AND COOPERATION EXPIRES.
UNLESS EITHER SIDE RAISES OBJECTIONS, THE TREATY RENEWS AUTOMATICALLY. WHILE WARY OF STUDENT ACTIVISTS, THE GOVERNMENT REMINDS THE PUBLIC HOW THEY HAVE PROSPERED UNDER THE TREATY.
BEGINNING ON MARCH 14, JAPAN HOSTS THE EXPO '70 WORLD'S FAIR—A CHANCE TO DEMONSTRATE THE HIGH QUALITY OF DOMESTIC PRODUCTS AND REAFFIRM TO THE WORLD JAPAN'S EMBRACE OF THE FREE MARKET.

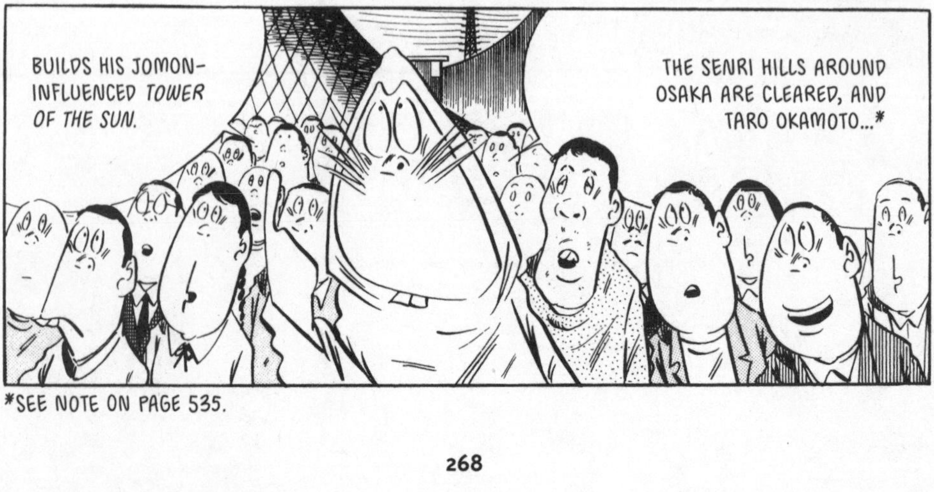
THE SENRI HILLS AROUND OSAKA ARE CLEARED, AND TARO OKAMOTO...*
BUILDS HIS JOMON-INFLUENCED *TOWER OF THE SUN.*

*SEE NOTE ON PAGE 535.

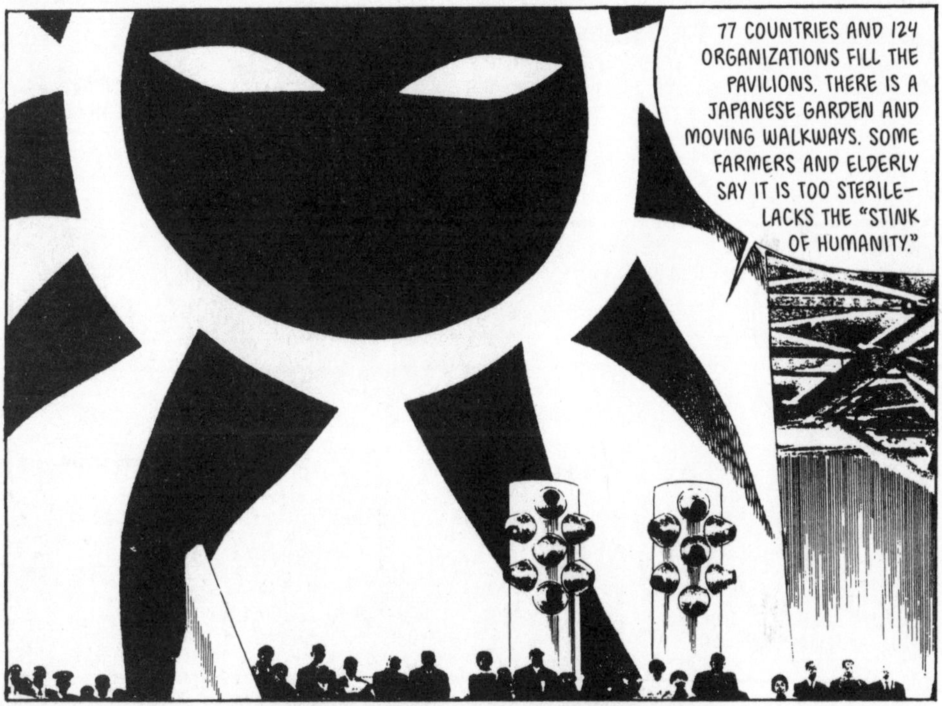
77 COUNTRIES AND 124 ORGANIZATIONS FILL THE PAVILIONS. THERE IS A JAPANESE GARDEN AND MOVING WALKWAYS. SOME FARMERS AND ELDERLY SAY IT IS TOO STERILE—LACKS THE "STINK OF HUMANITY."

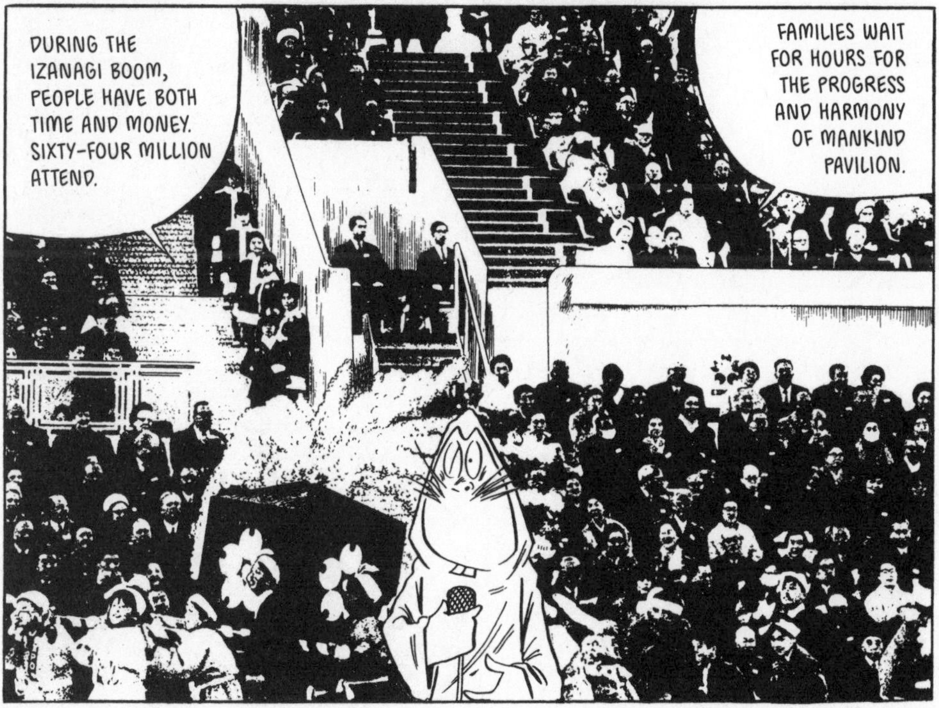
FAMILIES WAIT FOR HOURS FOR THE PROGRESS AND HARMONY OF MANKIND PAVILION.
DURING THE IZANAGI BOOM, PEOPLE HAVE BOTH TIME AND MONEY. SIXTY-FOUR MILLION ATTEND.

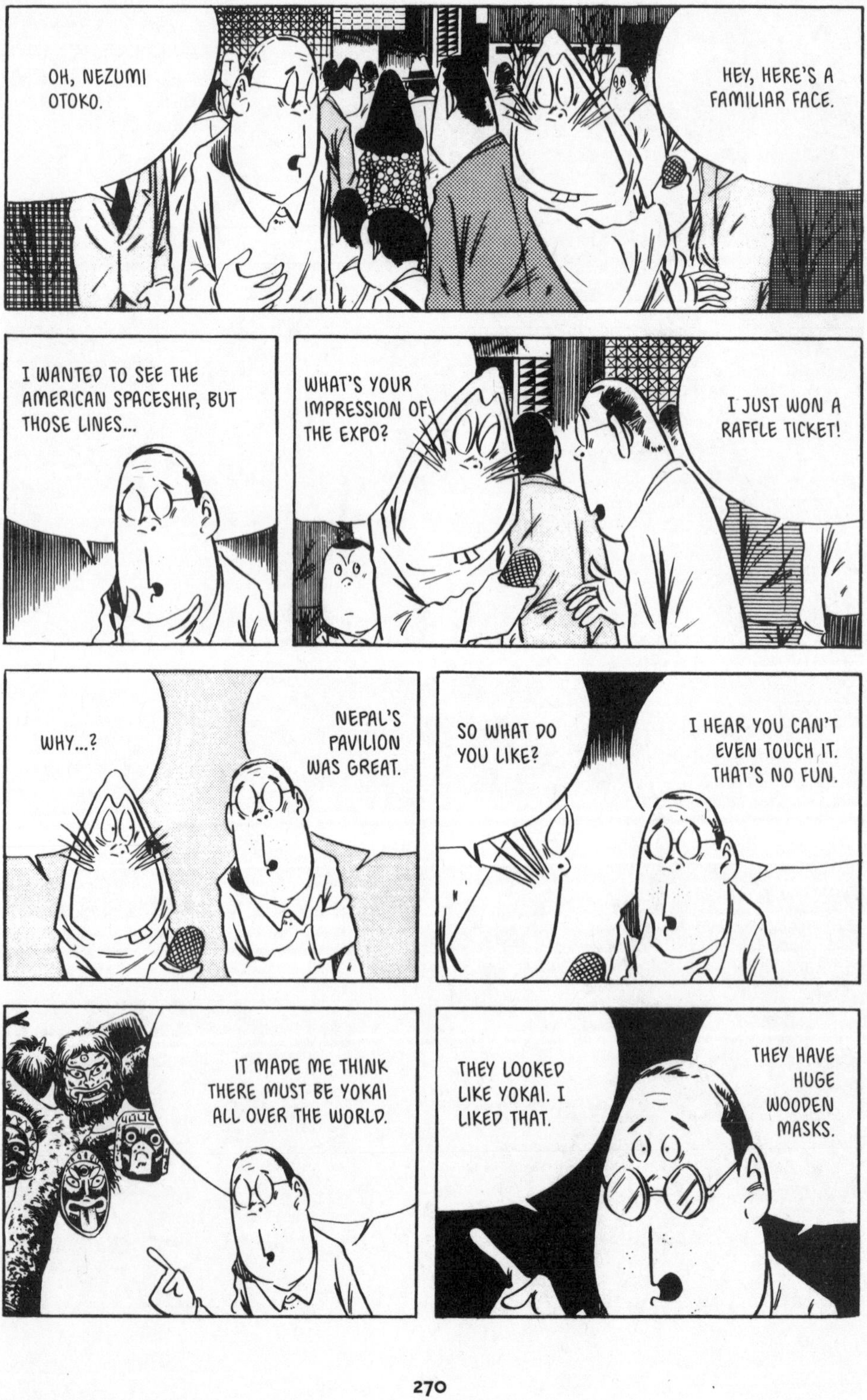
HEY, HERE'S A FAMILIAR FACE.
OH, NEZUMI OTOKO.
I JUST WON A RAFFLE TICKET!
WHAT'S YOUR IMPRESSION OF THE EXPO?
I WANTED TO SEE THE AMERICAN SPACESHIP, BUT THOSE LINES...
I HEAR YOU CAN'T EVEN TOUCH IT. THAT'S NO FUN.
SO WHAT DO YOU LIKE?
NEPAL'S PAVILION WAS GREAT.
WHY...?
THEY HAVE HUGE WOODEN MASKS.
THEY LOOKED LIKE YOKAI. I LIKED THAT.
IT MADE ME THINK THERE MUST BE YOKAI ALL OVER THE WORLD.

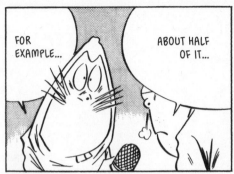

THAT'S INTERESTING.
ANYTHING YOU DIDN'T LIKE?
ABOUT HALF OF IT...
FOR EXAMPLE...
LIKE JAPAN'S CORPORATE PAVILION.
OH?
IT'S A BUNCH OF TUBES.
JUST TUBES BLOWING BUBBLES.
IT'S JUST...
A GIANT BUBBLE PIPE.
YOU WEREN'T SURPRISED?
BY A BUBBLE PIPE?
NO IMAGINATION.
JUST MAKING SOMETHING BIG DOESN'T MAKE IT INTERESTING.
WITH THE MONEY THEY SPENT...
IT SHOULD HAVE BEEN COOLER.

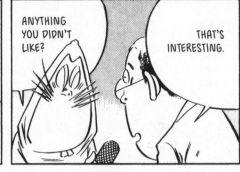

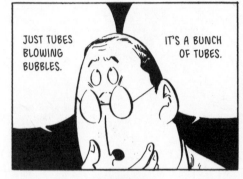

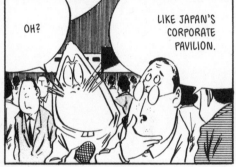

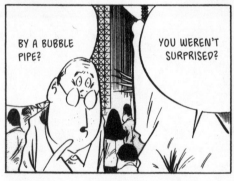

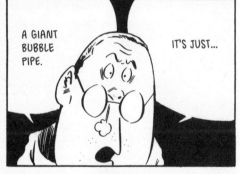

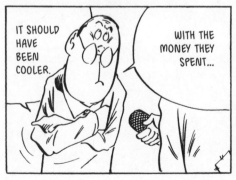

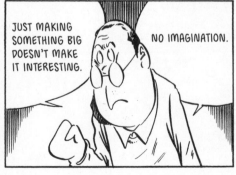

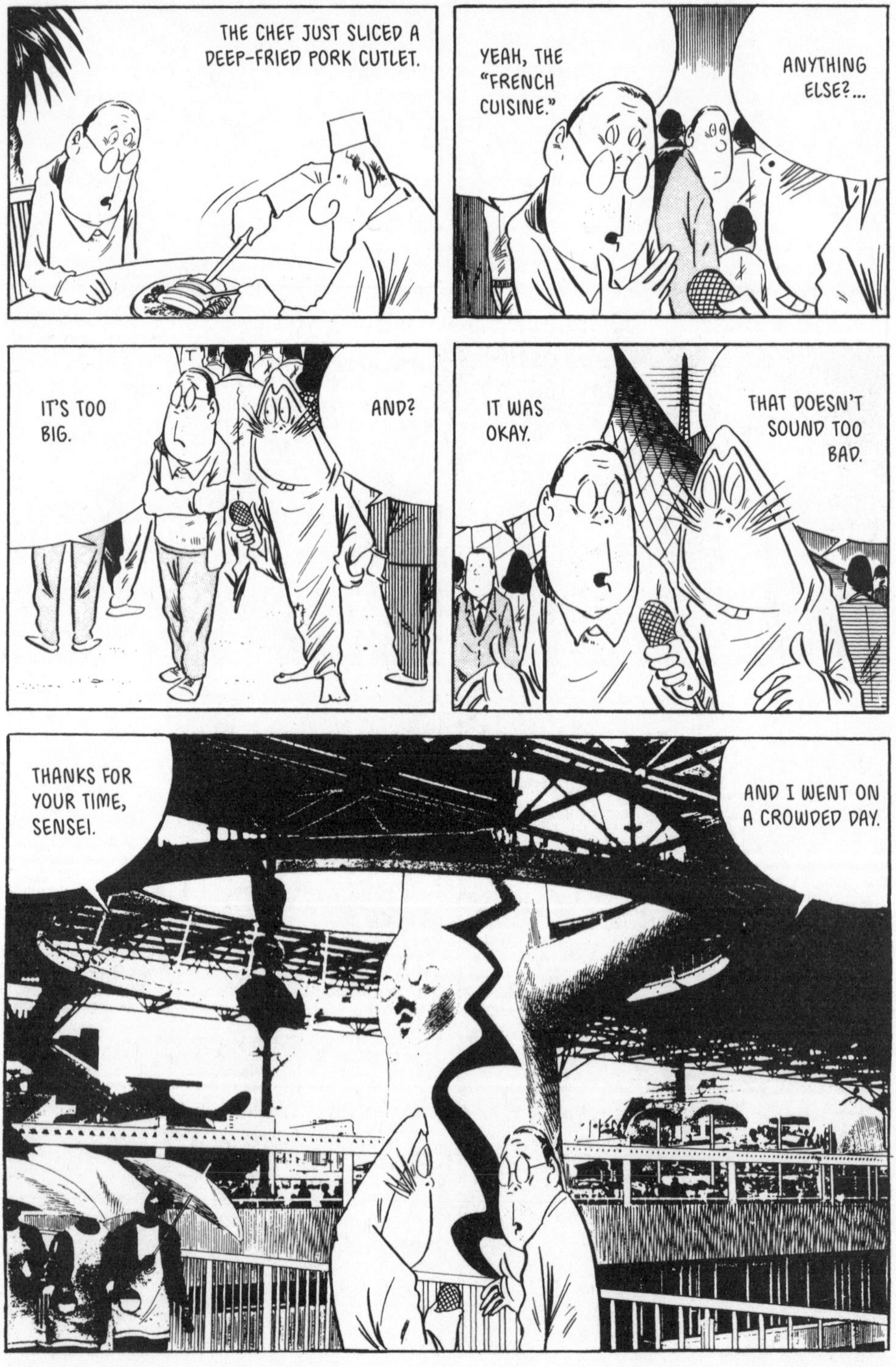
ANYTHING ELSE?...
YEAH, THE "FRENCH CUISINE."
THE CHEF JUST SLICED A DEEP-FRIED PORK CUTLET.
THAT DOESN'T SOUND TOO BAD.
IT WAS OKAY.
AND?
IT'S TOO BIG.
AND I WENT ON A CROWDED DAY.
THANKS FOR YOUR TIME, SENSEI.

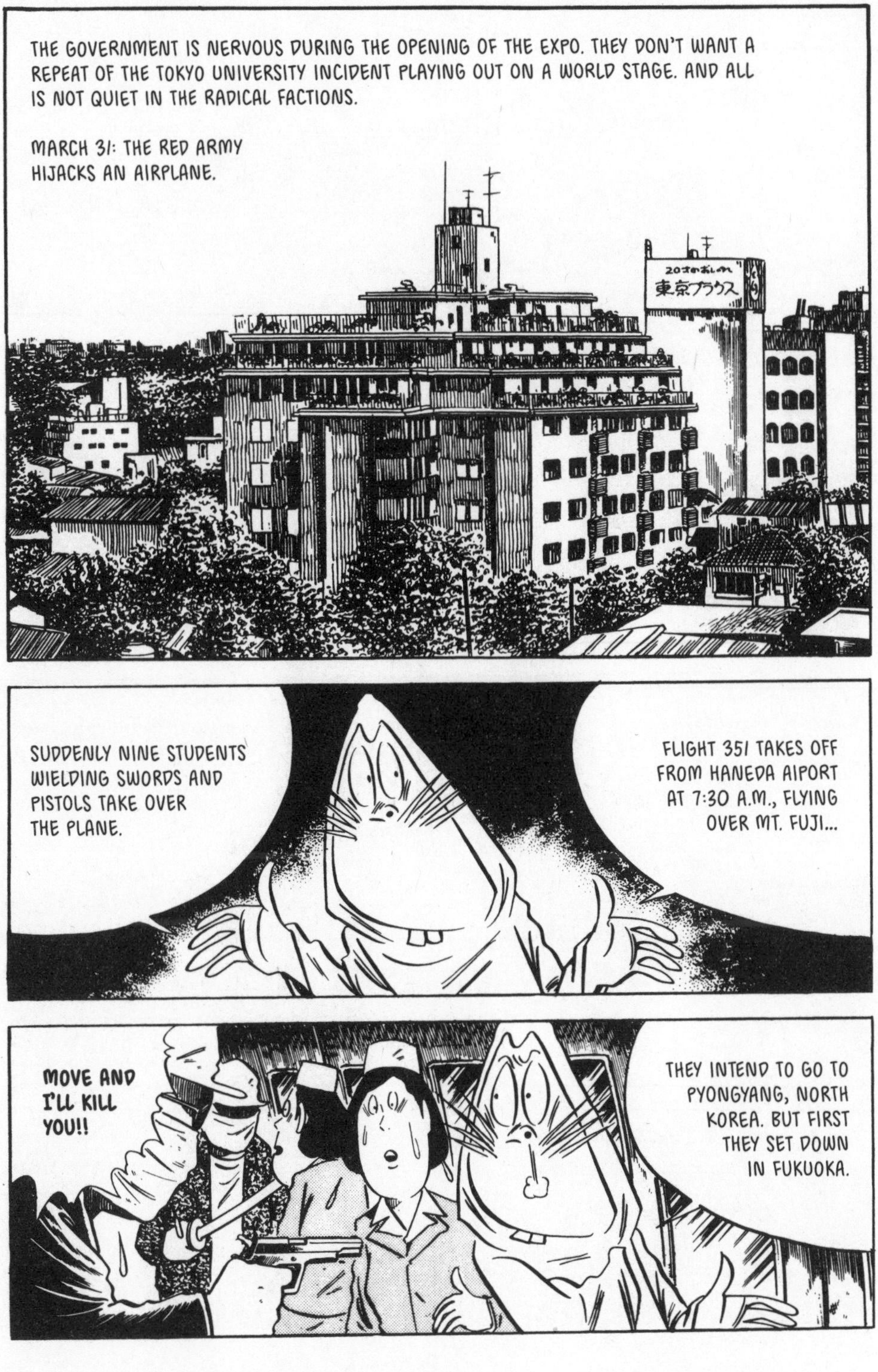
THE GOVERNMENT IS NERVOUS DURING THE OPENING OF THE EXPO. THEY DON'T WANT A REPEAT OF THE TOKYO UNIVERSITY INCIDENT PLAYING OUT ON A WORLD STAGE. AND ALL IS NOT QUIET IN THE RADICAL FACTIONS.
MARCH 31: THE RED ARMY HIJACKS AN AIRPLANE.
東京ブラウス
FLIGHT 351 TAKES OFF FROM HANEDA AIPORT AT 7:30 A.M., FLYING OVER MT. FUJI...
SUDDENLY NINE STUDENTS WIELDING SWORDS AND PISTOLS TAKE OVER THE PLANE.
THEY INTEND TO GO TO PYONGYANG, NORTH KOREA. BUT FIRST THEY SET DOWN IN FUKUOKA.
MOVE AND I'LL KILL YOU!!

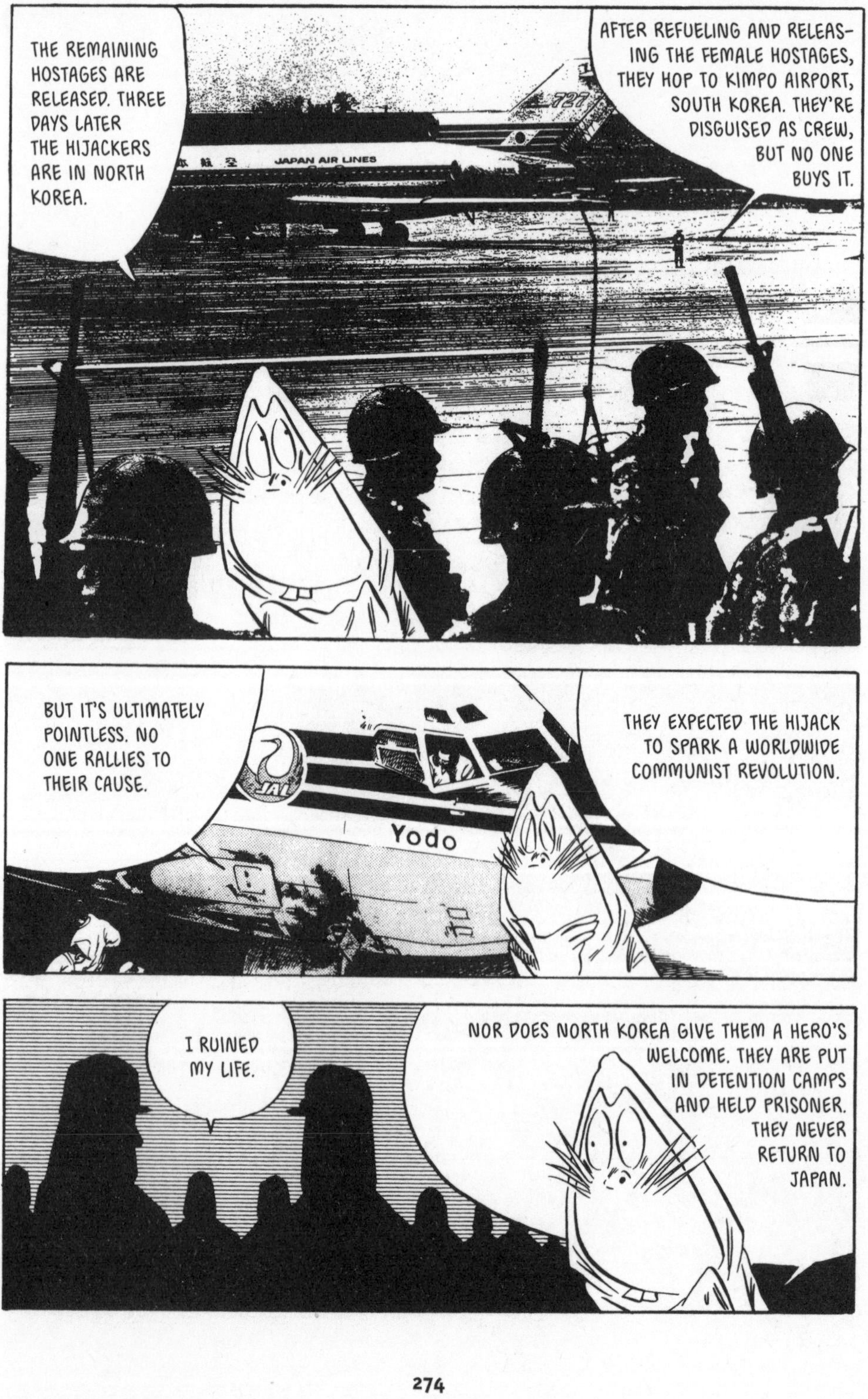
AFTER REFUELING AND RELEASING THE FEMALE HOSTAGES, THEY HOP TO KIMPO AIRPORT, SOUTH KOREA. THEY'RE DISGUISED AS CREW, BUT NO ONE BUYS IT.
THE REMAINING HOSTAGES ARE RELEASED. THREE DAYS LATER THE HIJACKERS ARE IN NORTH KOREA.
JAPAN AIR LINES
THEY EXPECTED THE HIJACK TO SPARK A WORLDWIDE COMMUNIST REVOLUTION.
BUT IT'S ULTIMATELY POINTLESS. NO ONE RALLIES TO THEIR CAUSE.
Yodo
JAL
NOR DOES NORTH KOREA GIVE THEM A HERO'S WELCOME. THEY ARE PUT IN DETENTION CAMPS AND HELD PRISONER. THEY NEVER RETURN TO JAPAN.
I RUINED MY LIFE.

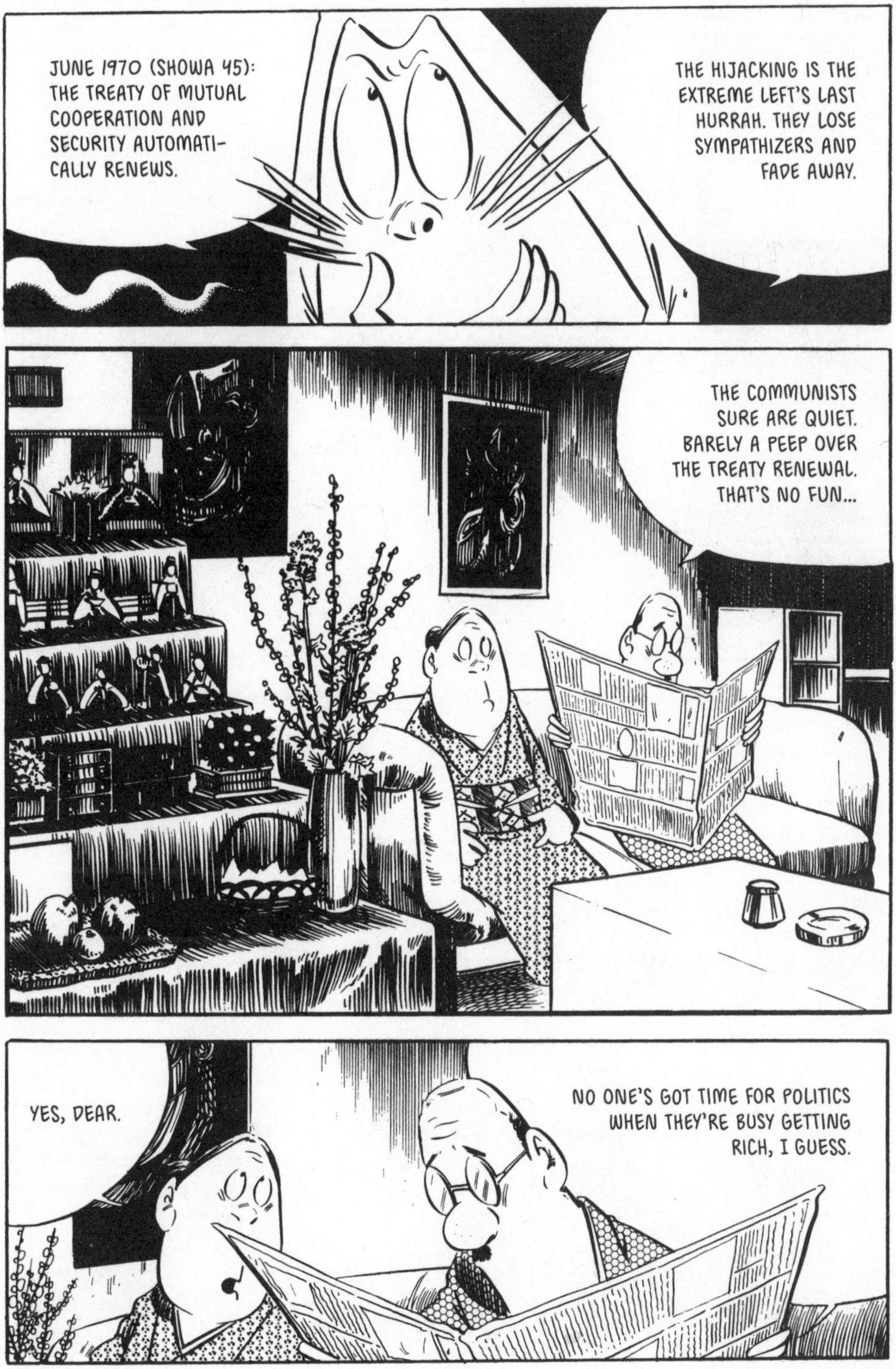
THE HIJACKING IS THE EXTREME LEFT'S LAST HURRAH. THEY LOSE SYMPATHIZERS AND FADE AWAY.
JUNE 1970 (SHOWA 45): THE TREATY OF MUTUAL COOPERATION AND SECURITY AUTOMATI-CALLY RENEWS.
THE COMMUNISTS SURE ARE QUIET. BARELY A PEEP OVER THE TREATY RENEWAL. THAT'S NO FUN...
NO ONE'S GOT TIME FOR POLITICS WHEN THEY'RE BUSY GETTING RICH, I GUESS.
YES, DEAR.

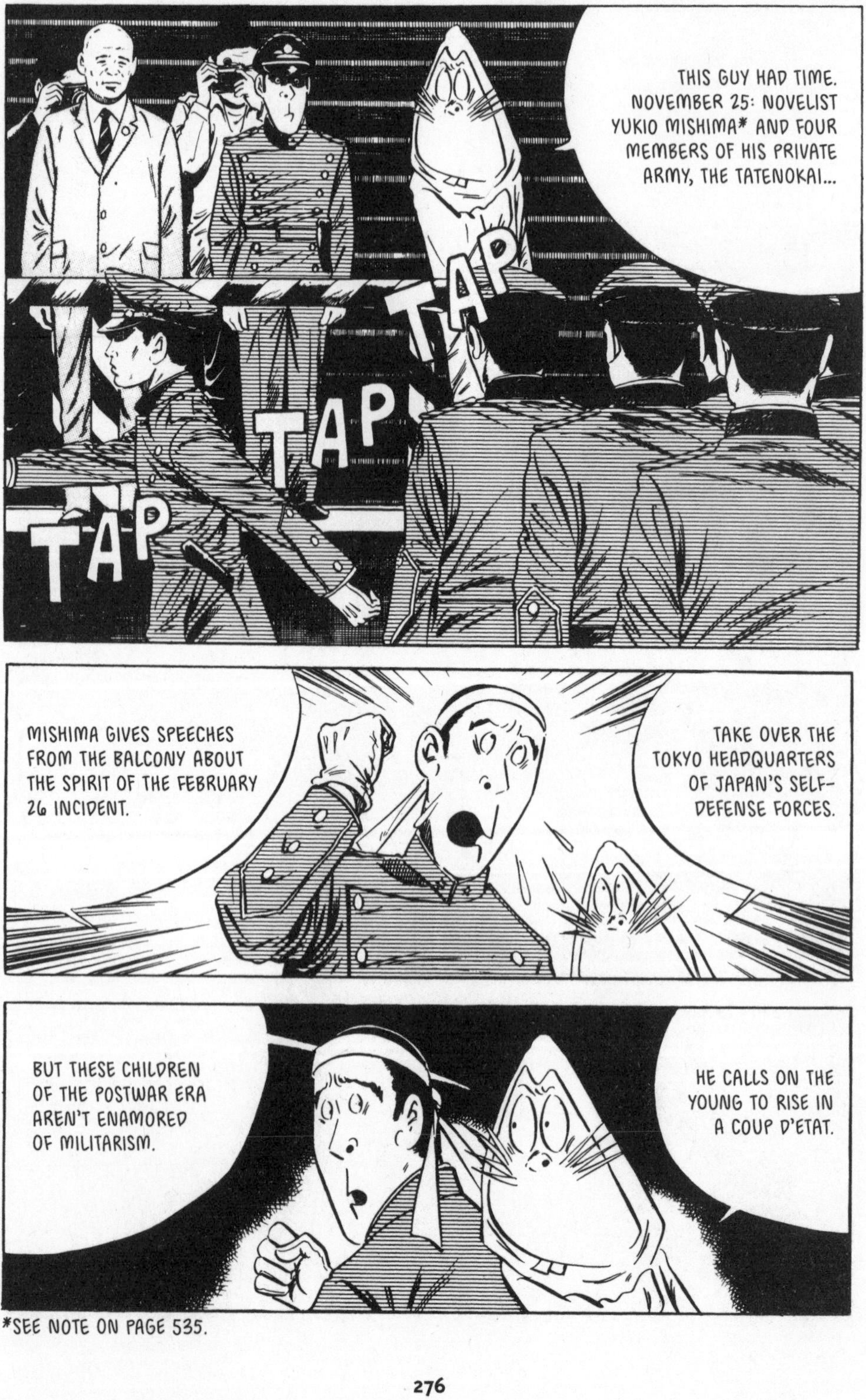
THIS GUY HAD TIME. NOVEMBER 25: NOVELIST YUKIO MISHIMA* AND FOUR MEMBERS OF HIS PRIVATE ARMY, THE TATENOKAI...
TAP
TAP
TAP
TAP
TAKE OVER THE TOKYO HEADQUARTERS OF JAPAN'S SELF-DEFENSE FORCES.
MISHIMA GIVES SPEECHES FROM THE BALCONY ABOUT THE SPIRIT OF THE FEBRUARY 26 INCIDENT.
HE CALLS ON THE YOUNG TO RISE IN A COUP D'ETAT.
BUT THESE CHILDREN OF THE POSTWAR ERA AREN'T ENAMORED OF MILITARISM.

*SEE NOTE ON PAGE 535.

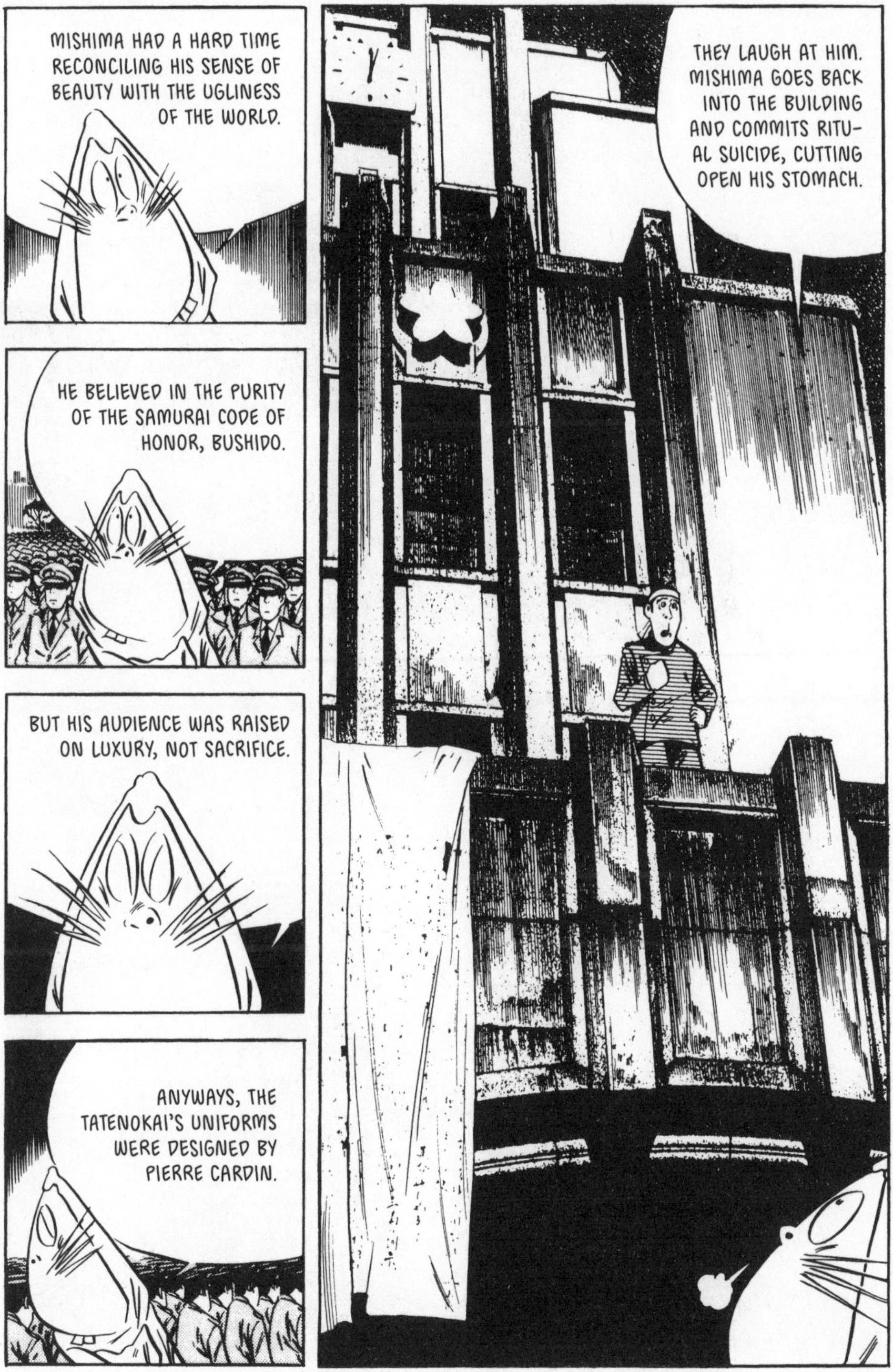
THEY LAUGH AT HIM. MISHIMA GOES BACK INTO THE BUILDING AND COMMITS RITUAL SUICIDE, CUTTING OPEN HIS STOMACH.
MISHIMA HAD A HARD TIME RECONCILING HIS SENSE OF BEAUTY WITH THE UGLINESS OF THE WORLD.
HE BELIEVED IN THE PURITY OF THE SAMURAI CODE OF HONOR, BUSHIDO.
BUT HIS AUDIENCE WAS RAISED ON LUXURY, NOT SACRIFICE.
ANYWAYS, THE TATENOKAI'S UNIFORMS WERE DESIGNED BY PIERRE CARDIN.

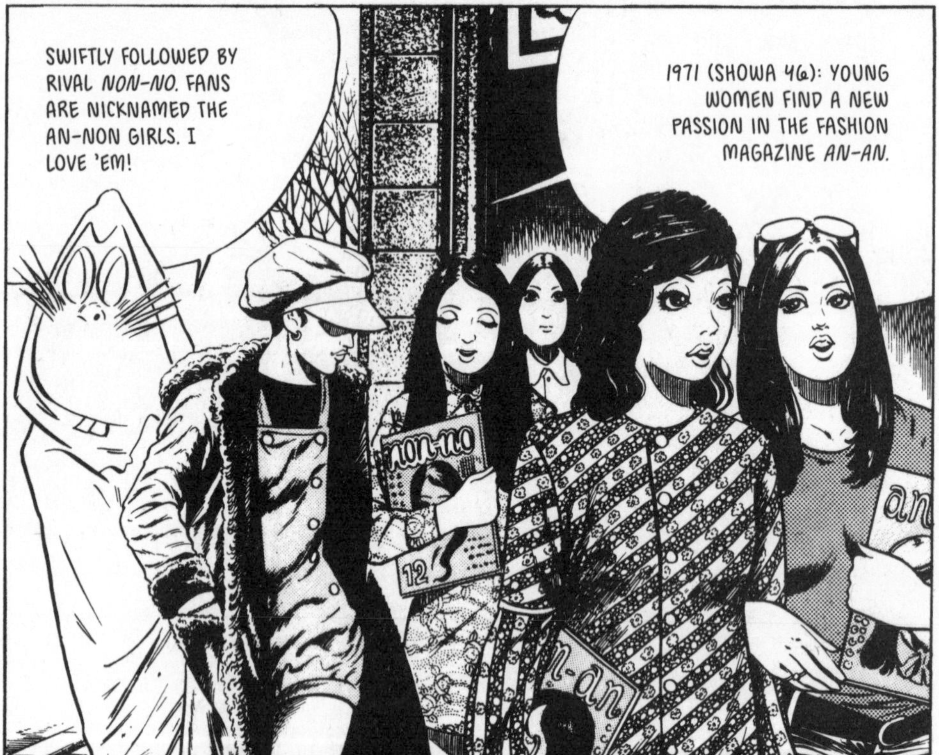
1971 (SHOWA 46): YOUNG WOMEN FIND A NEW PASSION IN THE FASHION MAGAZINE *AN-AN*.
SWIFTLY FOLLOWED BY RIVAL *NON-NO*. FANS ARE NICKNAMED THE AN-NON GIRLS. I LOVE 'EM!
non-no

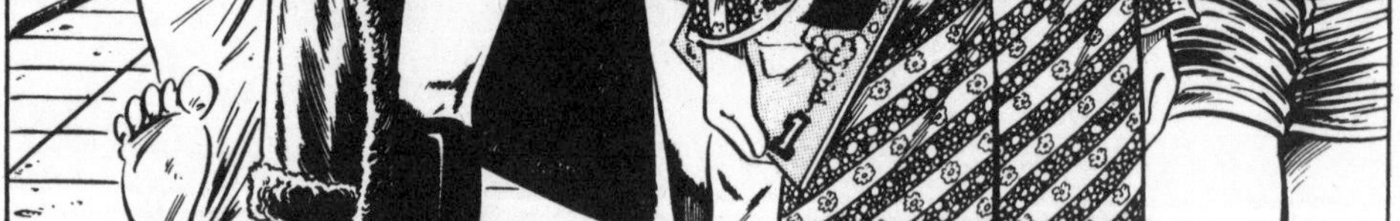
JAPAN RAILWAYS STARTS THEIR "DISCOVER JAPAN" CAMPAIGN.
MAY 1971 (SHOWA 46): KIYOSHI OKUBO APPEARS. HE'S A SMOOTH TALKER WHO ATTRACTS WOMEN WITH A SHINY WHITE CAR.

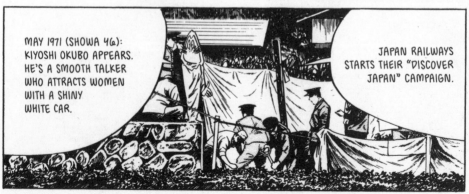

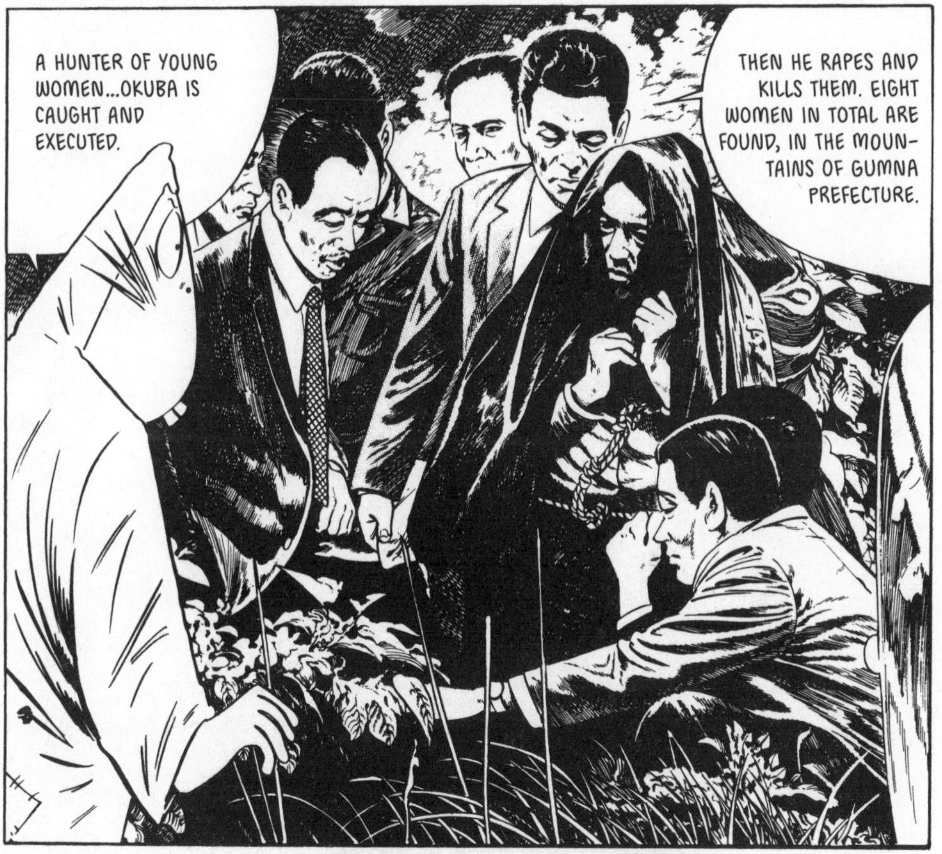
THEN HE RAPES AND KILLS THEM. EIGHT WOMEN IN TOTAL ARE FOUND, IN THE MOUNTAINS OF GUMNA PREFECTURE.
A HUNTER OF YOUNG WOMEN...OKUBA IS CAUGHT AND EXECUTED.

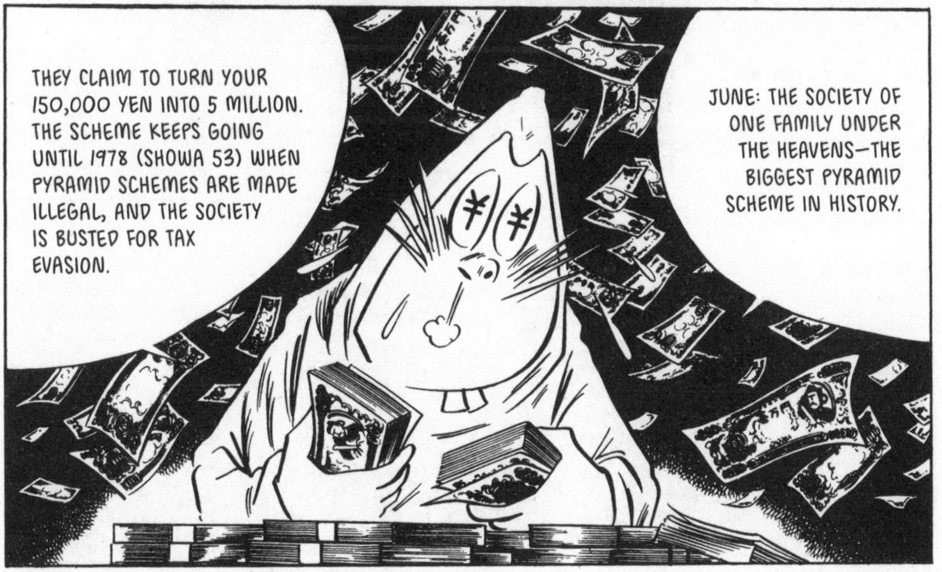
JUNE: THE SOCIETY OF ONE FAMILY UNDER THE HEAVENS—THE BIGGEST PYRAMID SCHEME IN HISTORY.
THEY CLAIM TO TURN YOUR 150,000 YEN INTO 5 MILLION. THE SCHEME KEEPS GOING UNTIL 1978 (SHOWA 53) WHEN PYRAMID SCHEMES ARE MADE ILLEGAL, AND THE SOCIETY IS BUSTED FOR TAX EVASION.

150,000 YEN = $1,500; 5M YEN = $50,000

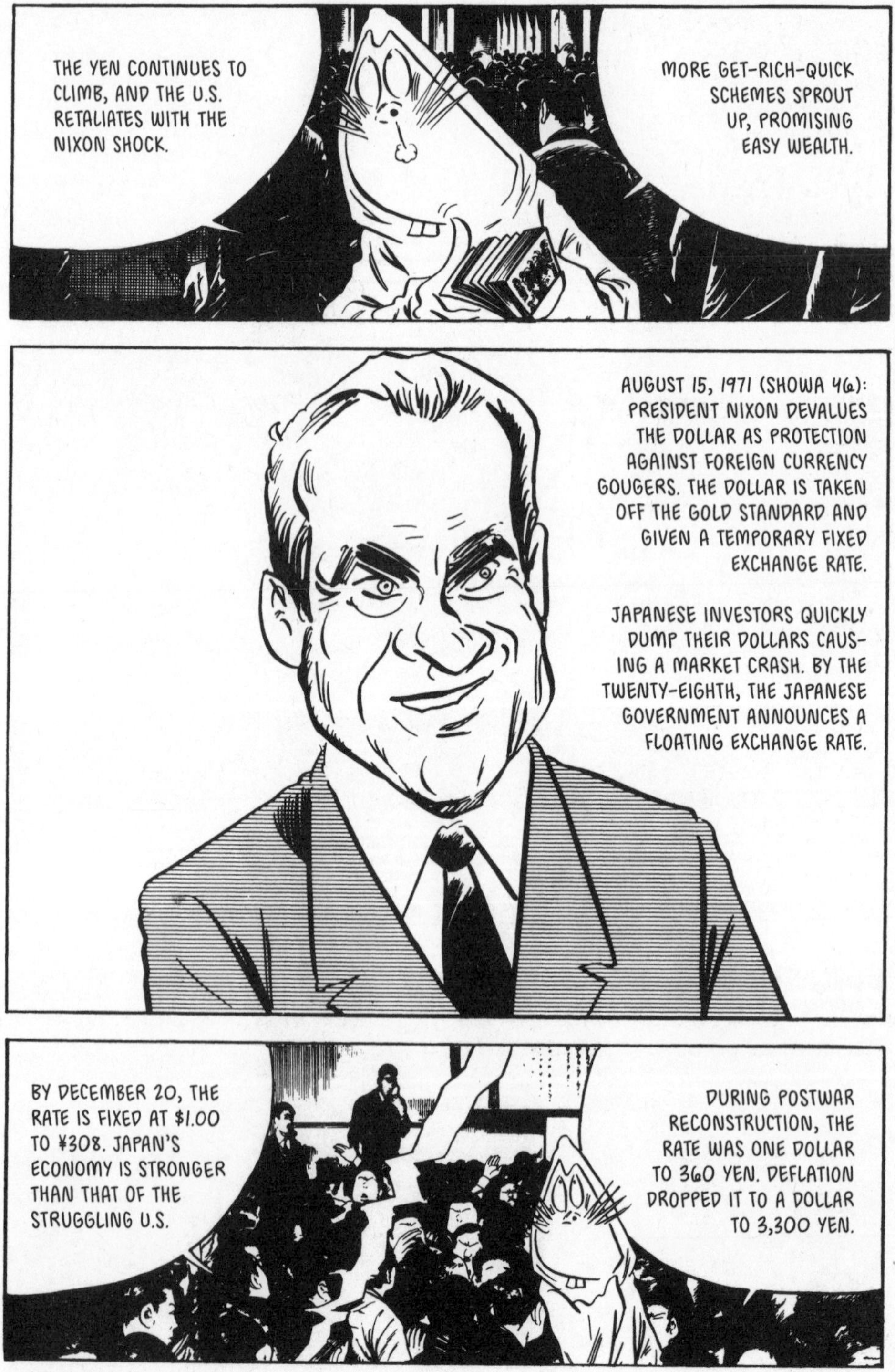
MORE GET-RICH-QUICK SCHEMES SPROUT UP, PROMISING EASY WEALTH.
THE YEN CONTINUES TO CLIMB, AND THE U.S. RETALIATES WITH THE NIXON SHOCK.
AUGUST 15, 1971 (SHOWA 46): PRESIDENT NIXON DEVALUES THE DOLLAR AS PROTECTION AGAINST FOREIGN CURRENCY GOUGERS. THE DOLLAR IS TAKEN OFF THE GOLD STANDARD AND GIVEN A TEMPORARY FIXED EXCHANGE RATE.
JAPANESE INVESTORS QUICKLY DUMP THEIR DOLLARS CAUSING A MARKET CRASH. BY THE TWENTY-EIGHTH, THE JAPANESE GOVERNMENT ANNOUNCES A FLOATING EXCHANGE RATE.
DURING POSTWAR RECONSTRUCTION, THE RATE WAS ONE DOLLAR TO 360 YEN. DEFLATION DROPPED IT TO A DOLLAR TO 3,300 YEN.
BY DECEMBER 20, THE RATE IS FIXED AT $1.00 TO ¥308. JAPAN'S ECONOMY IS STRONGER THAN THAT OF THE STRUGGLING U.S.

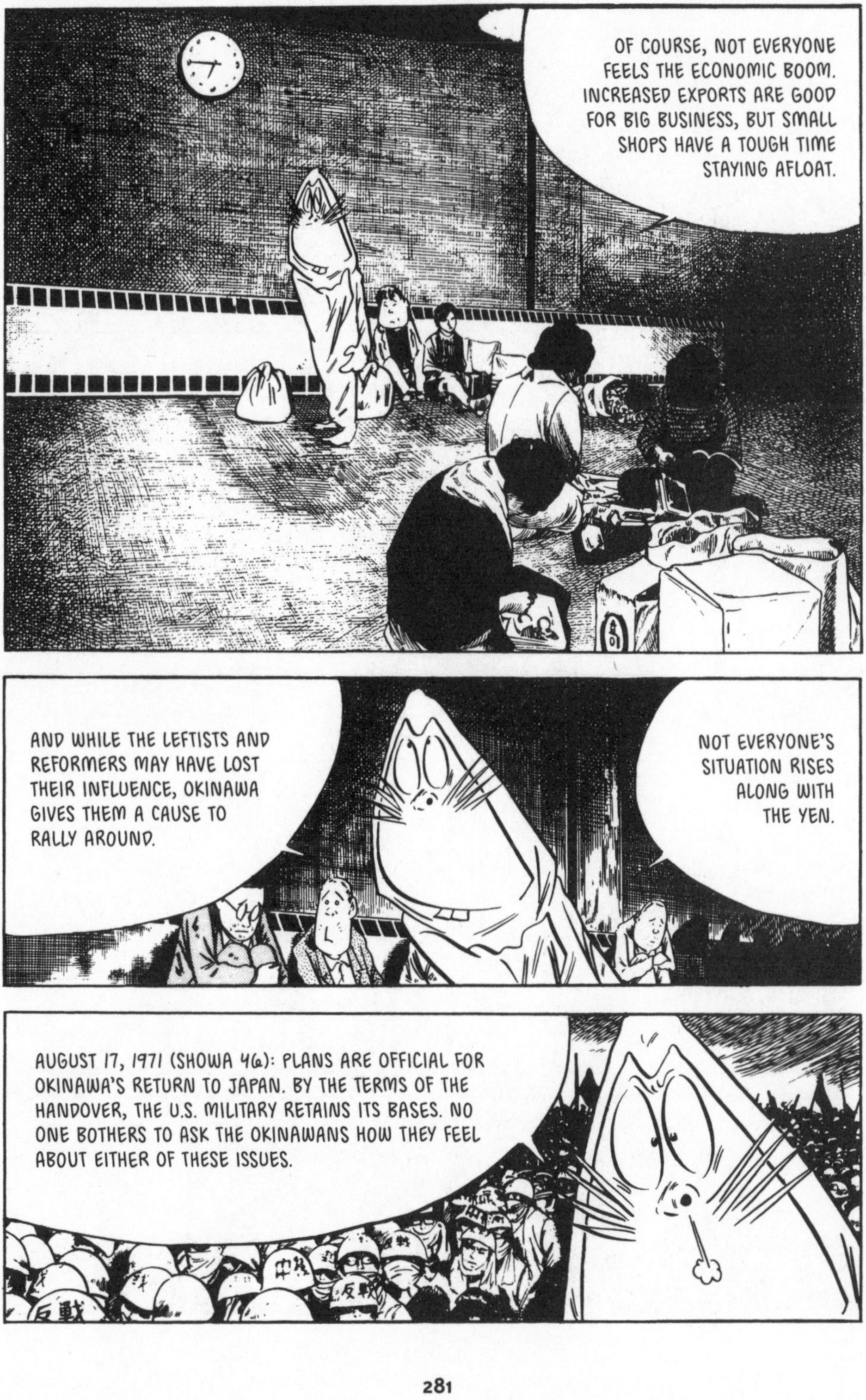
OF COURSE, NOT EVERYONE FEELS THE ECONOMIC BOOM. INCREASED EXPORTS ARE GOOD FOR BIG BUSINESS, BUT SMALL SHOPS HAVE A TOUGH TIME STAYING AFLOAT.
NOT EVERYONE'S SITUATION RISES ALONG WITH THE YEN.
AND WHILE THE LEFTISTS AND REFORMERS MAY HAVE LOST THEIR INFLUENCE, OKINAWA GIVES THEM A CAUSE TO RALLY AROUND.
AUGUST 17, 1971 (SHOWA 46): PLANS ARE OFFICIAL FOR OKINAWA'S RETURN TO JAPAN. BY THE TERMS OF THE HANDOVER, THE U.S. MILITARY RETAINS ITS BASES. NO ONE BOTHERS TO ASK THE OKINAWANS HOW THEY FEEL ABOUT EITHER OF THESE ISSUES.

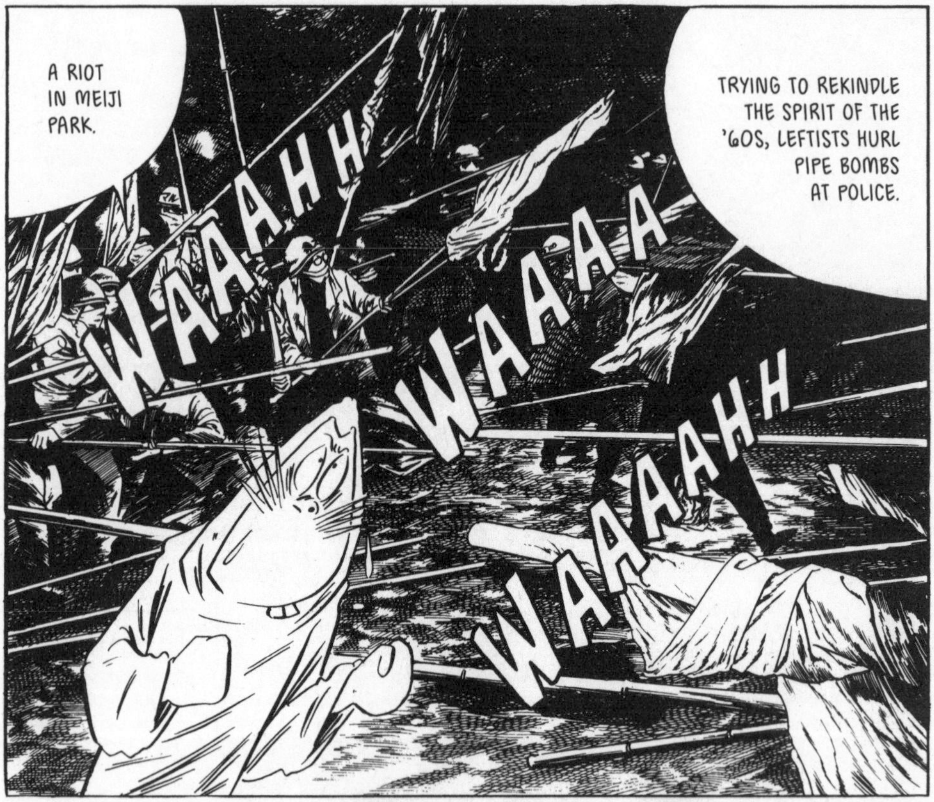
TRYING TO REKINDLE THE SPIRIT OF THE '60S, LEFTISTS HURL PIPE BOMBS AT POLICE.
A RIOT IN MEIJI PARK.
WAAAHH
WAAAAA
WAAAAAHH
WAAAAA

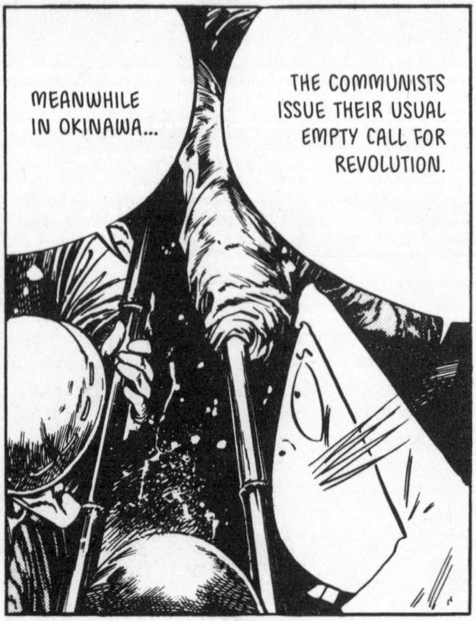
THE COMMUNISTS ISSUE THEIR USUAL EMPTY CALL FOR REVOLUTION.
MEANWHILE IN OKINAWA...

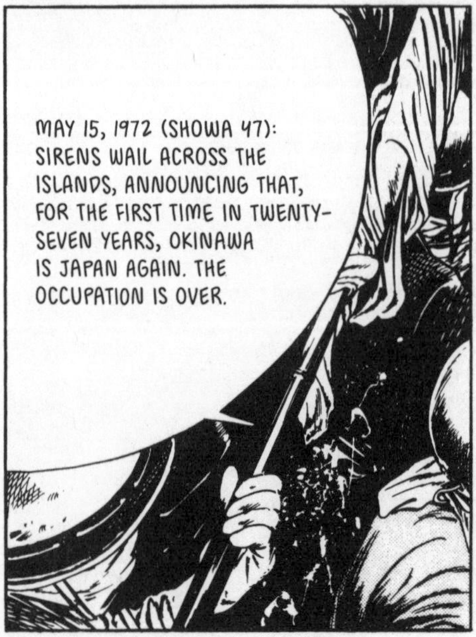
MAY 15, 1972 (SHOWA 47): SIRENS WAIL ACROSS THE ISLANDS, ANNOUNCING THAT, FOR THE FIRST TIME IN TWENTY-SEVEN YEARS, OKINAWA IS JAPAN AGAIN. THE OCCUPATION IS OVER.

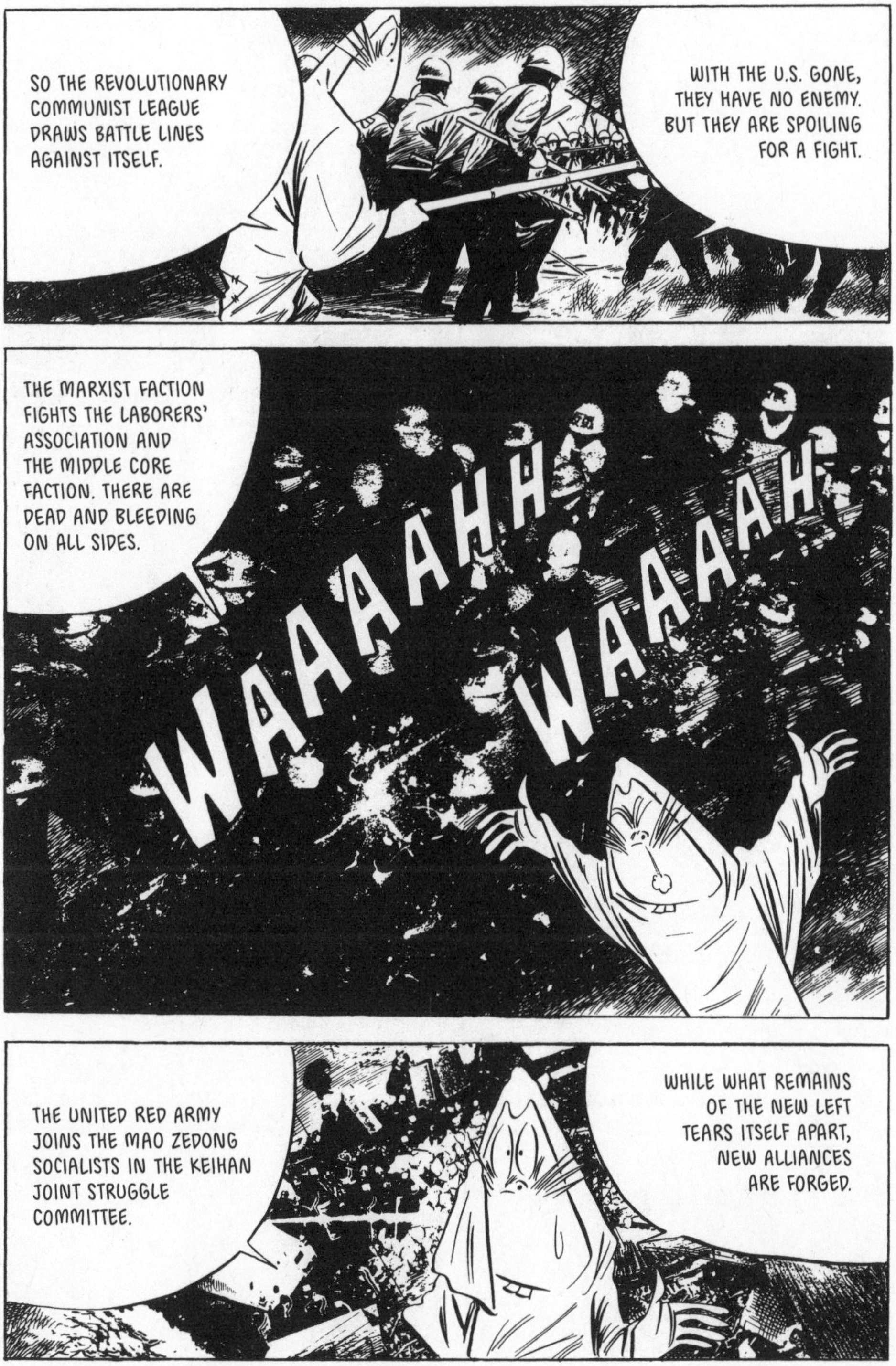
WITH THE U.S. GONE, THEY HAVE NO ENEMY. BUT THEY ARE SPOILING FOR A FIGHT.
SO THE REVOLUTIONARY COMMUNIST LEAGUE DRAWS BATTLE LINES AGAINST ITSELF.
THE MARXIST FACTION FIGHTS THE LABORERS' ASSOCIATION AND THE MIDDLE CORE FACTION. THERE ARE DEAD AND BLEEDING ON ALL SIDES.
WAAAAAH
WAAAAAHH
WHILE WHAT REMAINS OF THE NEW LEFT TEARS ITSELF APART, NEW ALLIANCES ARE FORGED.
THE UNITED RED ARMY JOINS THE MAO ZEDONG SOCIALISTS IN THE KEIHAN JOINT STRUGGLE COMMITTEE.

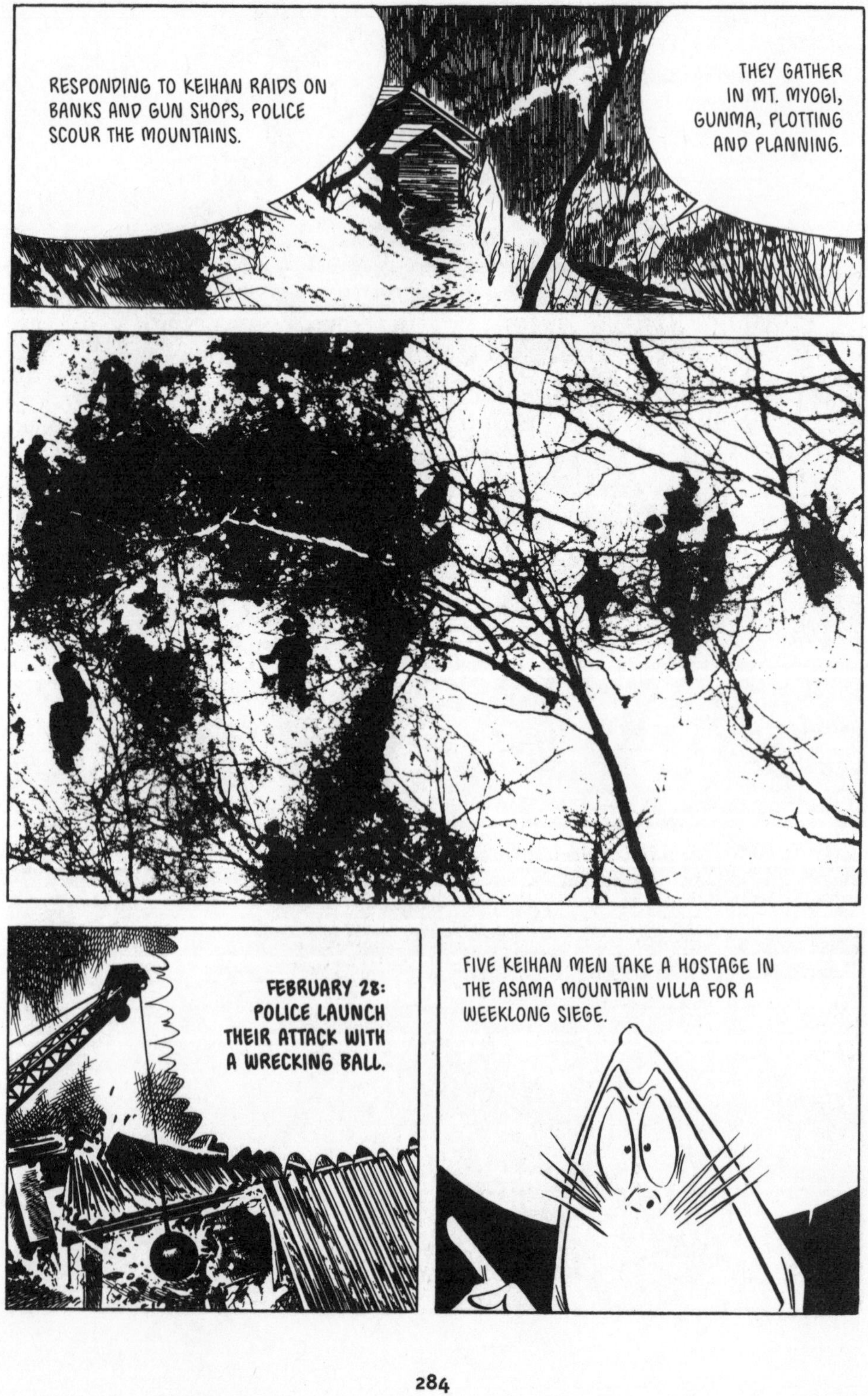
THEY GATHER IN MT. MYOGI, GUNMA, PLOTTING AND PLANNING.
RESPONDING TO KEIHAN RAIDS ON BANKS AND GUN SHOPS, POLICE SCOUR THE MOUNTAINS.
FIVE KEIHAN MEN TAKE A HOSTAGE IN THE ASAMA MOUNTAIN VILLA FOR A WEEKLONG SIEGE.
FEBRUARY 28: POLICE LAUNCH THEIR ATTACK WITH A WRECKING BALL.

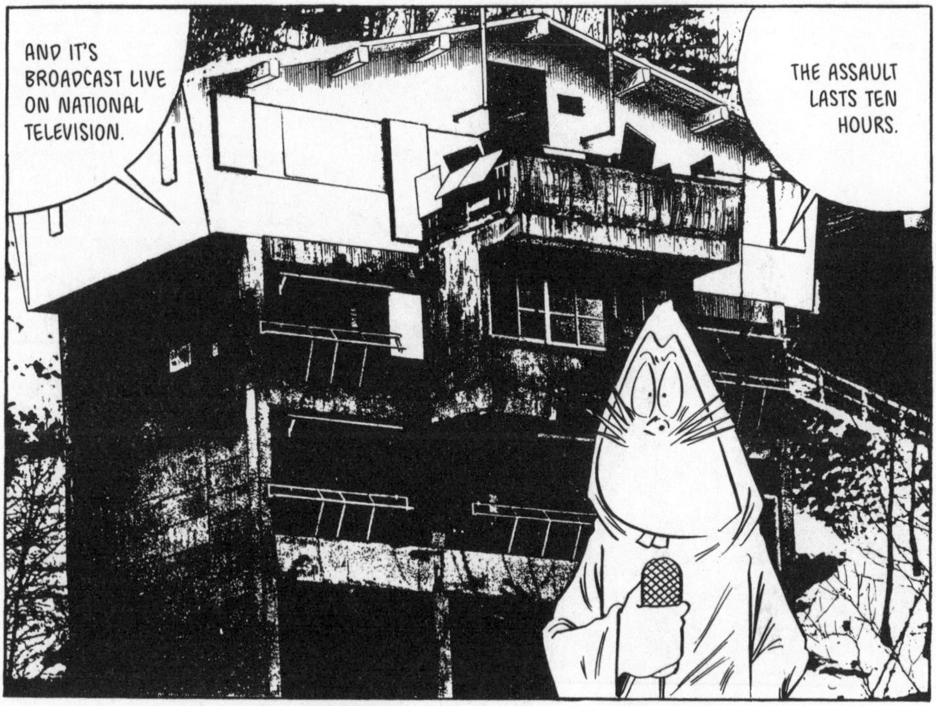
THE ASSAULT LASTS TEN HOURS.
AND IT'S BROADCAST LIVE ON NATIONAL TELEVISION.

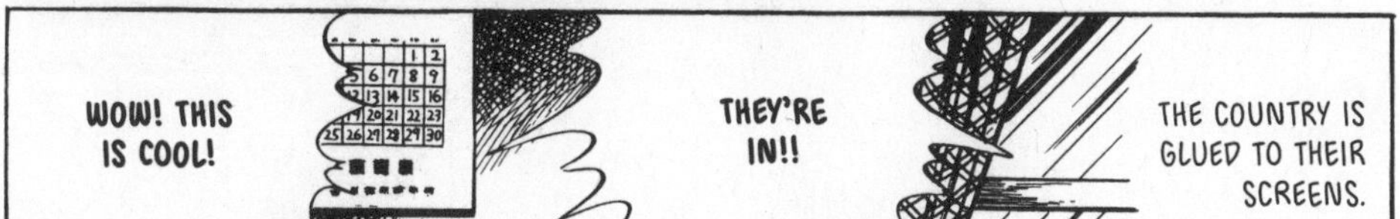
THE COUNTRY IS GLUED TO THEIR SCREENS.
THEY'RE IN!!
WOW! THIS IS COOL!

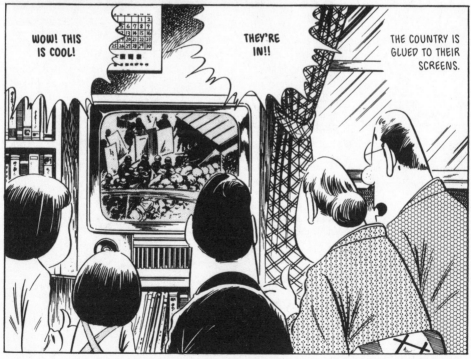

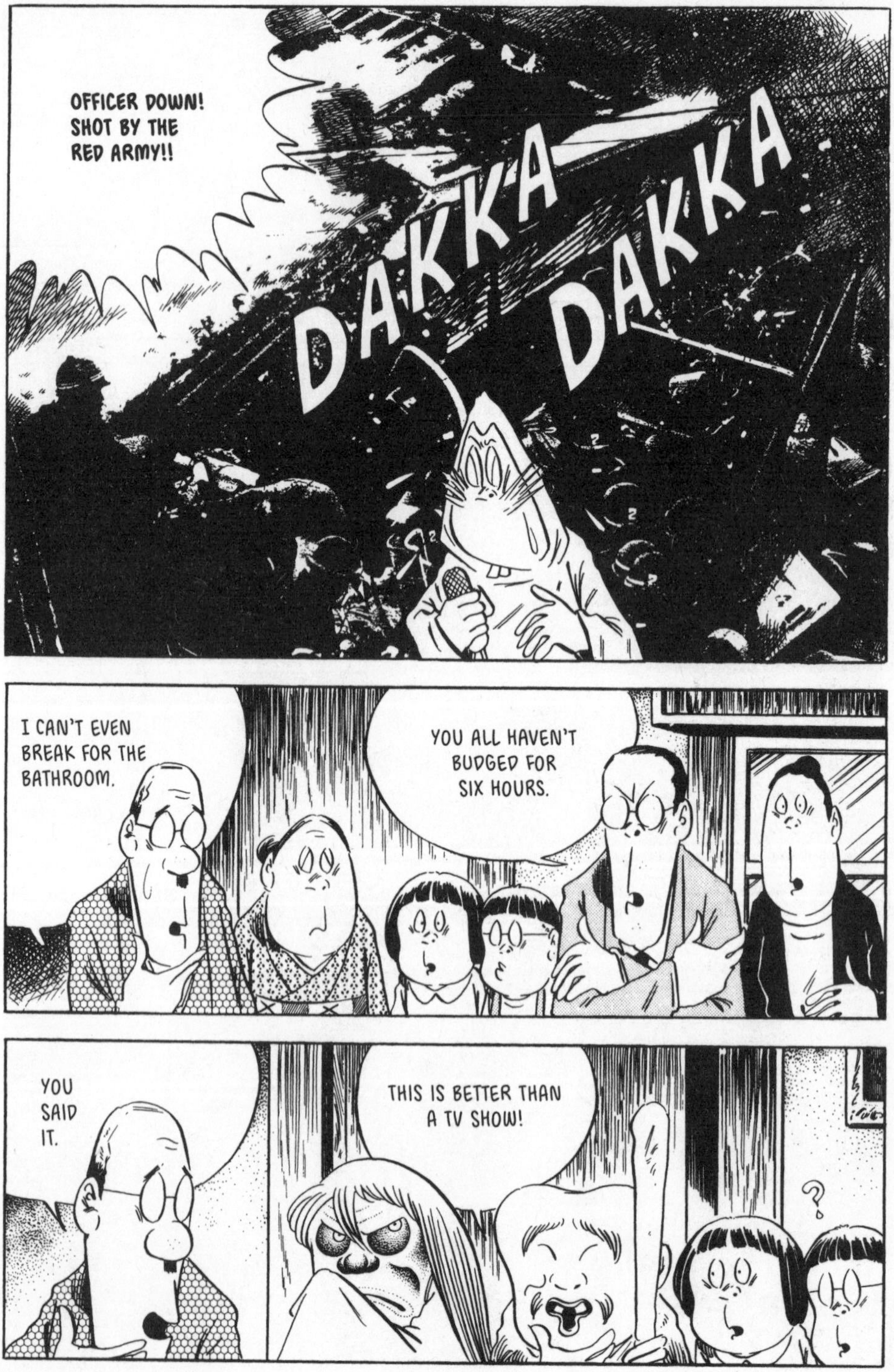
OFFICER DOWN! SHOT BY THE RED ARMY!!
DAKKA DAKKA
YOU ALL HAVEN'T BUDGED FOR SIX HOURS.
I CAN'T EVEN BREAK FOR THE BATHROOM.
THIS IS BETTER THAN A TV SHOW!
?
YOU SAID IT.

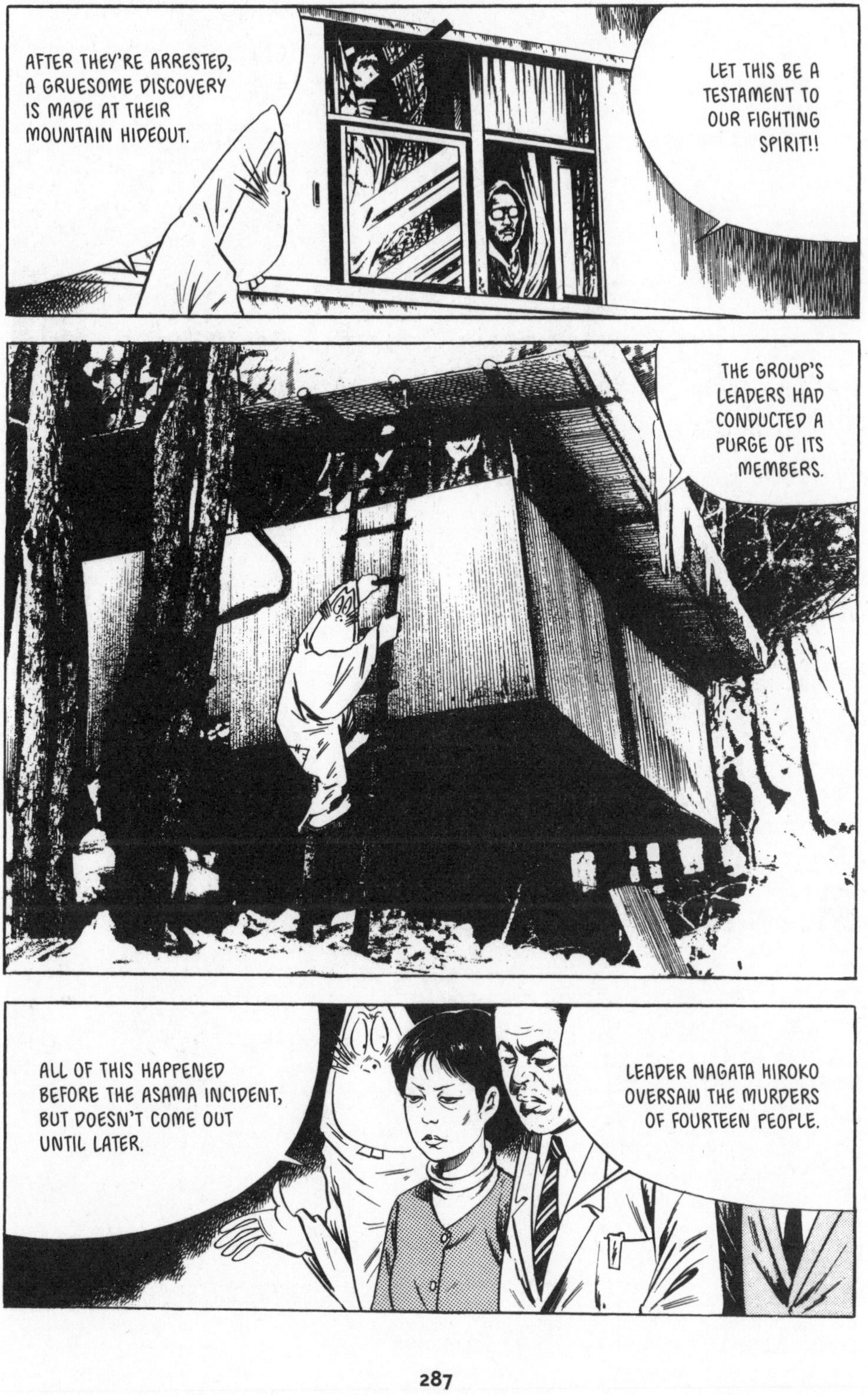
LET THIS BE A TESTAMENT TO OUR FIGHTING SPIRIT!!
AFTER THEY'RE ARRESTED, A GRUESOME DISCOVERY IS MADE AT THEIR MOUNTAIN HIDEOUT.
THE GROUP'S LEADERS HAD CONDUCTED A PURGE OF ITS MEMBERS.
LEADER NAGATA HIROKO OVERSAW THE MURDERS OF FOURTEEN PEOPLE.
ALL OF THIS HAPPENED BEFORE THE ASAMA INCIDENT, BUT DOESN'T COME OUT UNTIL LATER.

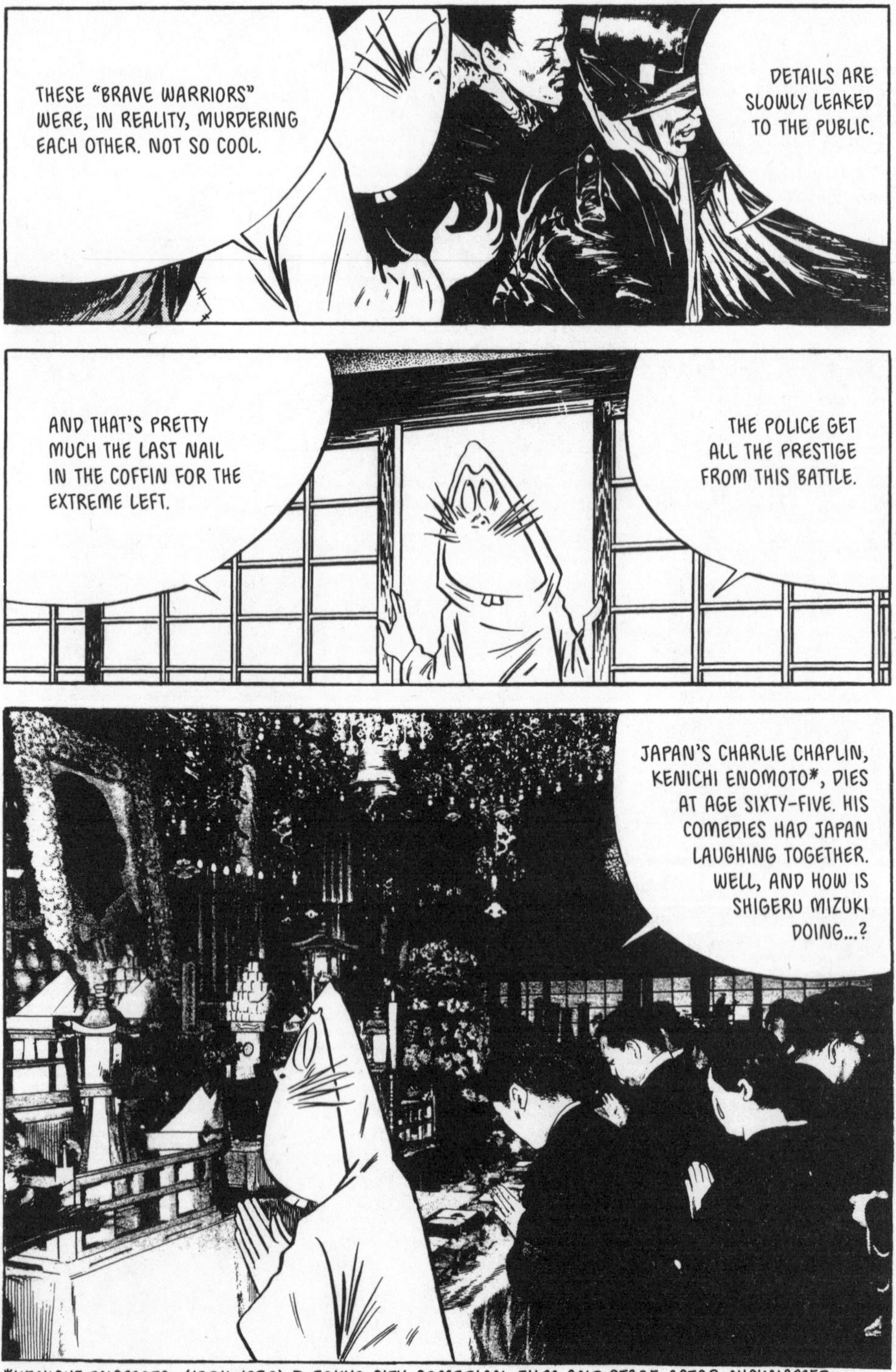
DETAILS ARE SLOWLY LEAKED TO THE PUBLIC.
THESE "BRAVE WARRIORS" WERE, IN REALITY, MURDERING EACH OTHER. NOT SO COOL.
THE POLICE GET ALL THE PRESTIGE FROM THIS BATTLE.
AND THAT'S PRETTY MUCH THE LAST NAIL IN THE COFFIN FOR THE EXTREME LEFT.
JAPAN'S CHARLIE CHAPLIN, KENICHI ENOMOTO*, DIES AT AGE SIXTY-FIVE. HIS COMEDIES HAD JAPAN LAUGHING TOGETHER. WELL, AND HOW IS SHIGERU MIZUKI DOING...?

*KENICHI ENOMOTO: (1904–1970) B. TOKYO CITY. COMEDIAN. FILM AND STAGE ACTOR. NICKNAMED ENOKEN, ENOMOTO WAS POPULAR FROM HIS DEBUT UNTIL HIS DEATH.

THE BEAUTIFUL EPUPE

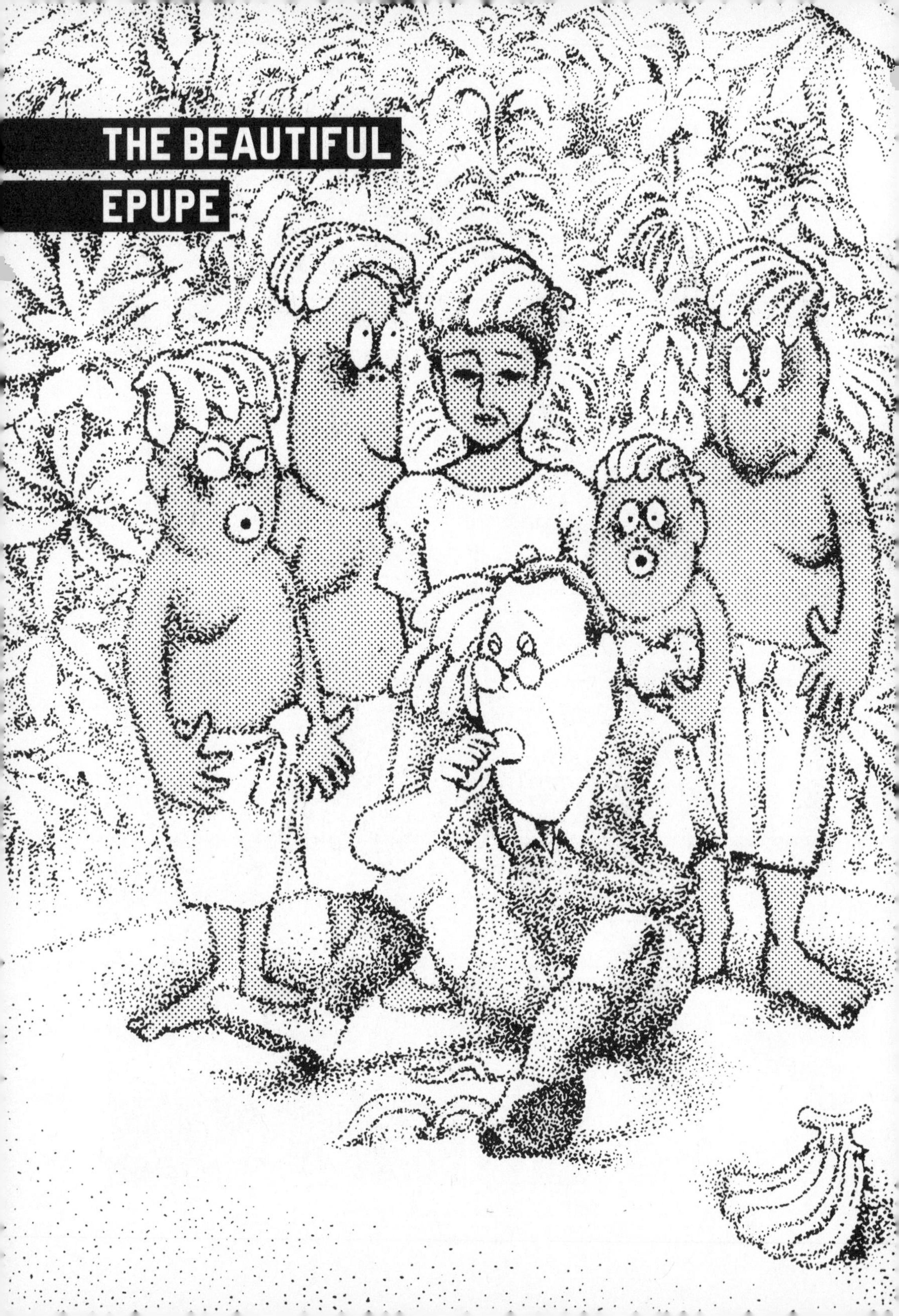

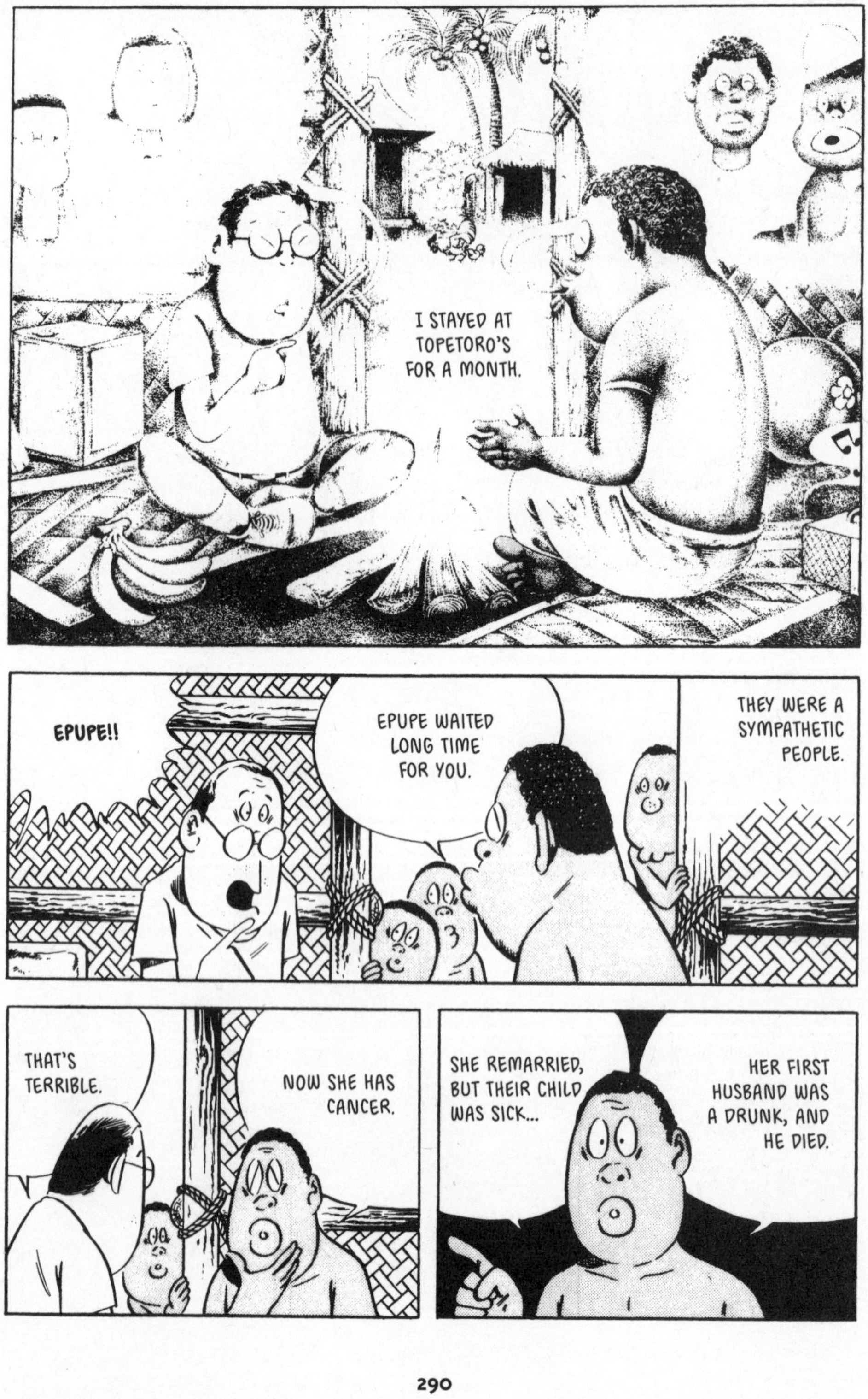
I STAYED AT TOPETORO'S FOR A MONTH.
THEY WERE A SYMPATHETIC PEOPLE.
EPUPE WAITED LONG TIME FOR YOU.
EPUPE!!
HER FIRST HUSBAND WAS A DRUNK, AND HE DIED.
SHE REMARRIED, BUT THEIR CHILD WAS SICK...
NOW SHE HAS CANCER.
THAT'S TERRIBLE.

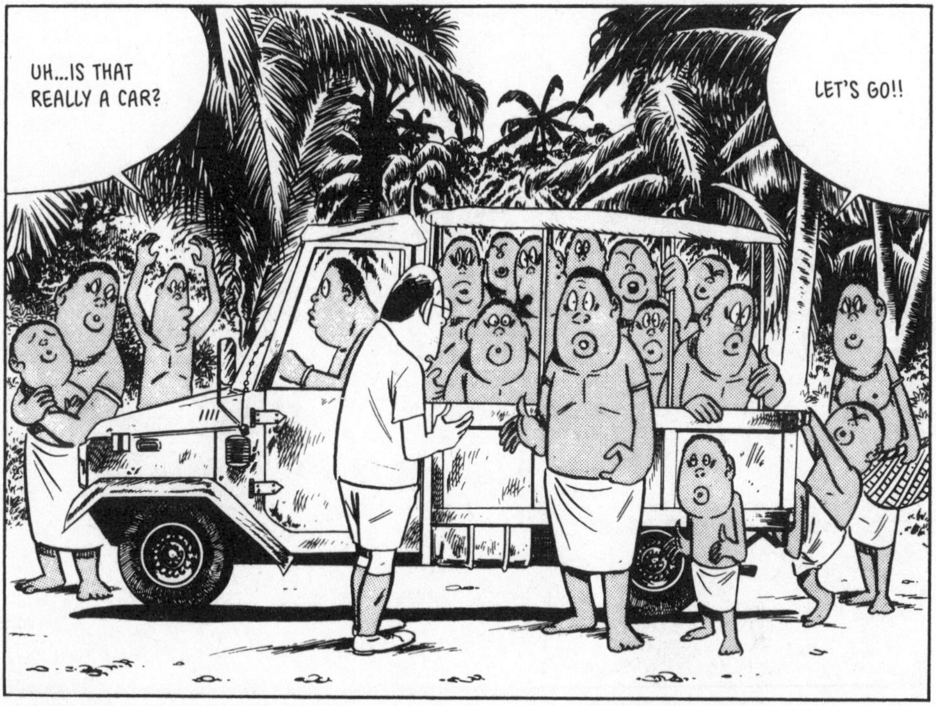
LET'S GO!!
UH...IS THAT REALLY A CAR?

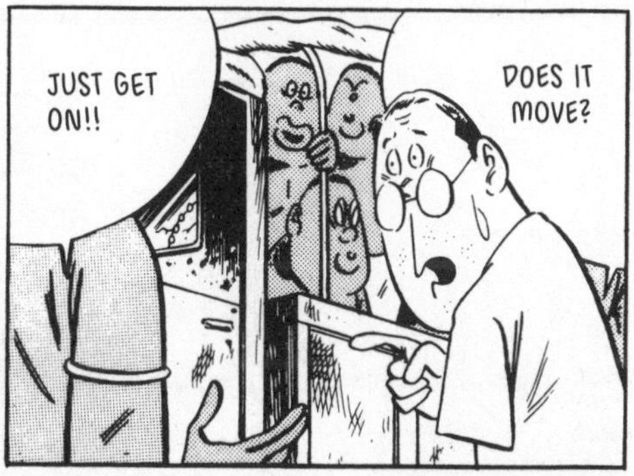
DOES IT MOVE?
JUST GET ON!!

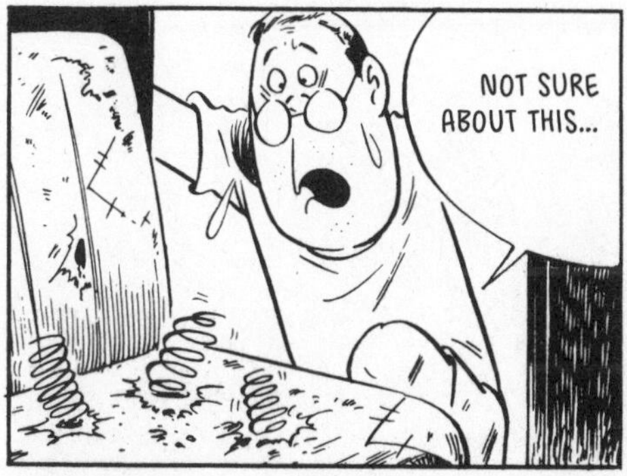
NOT SURE ABOUT THIS...

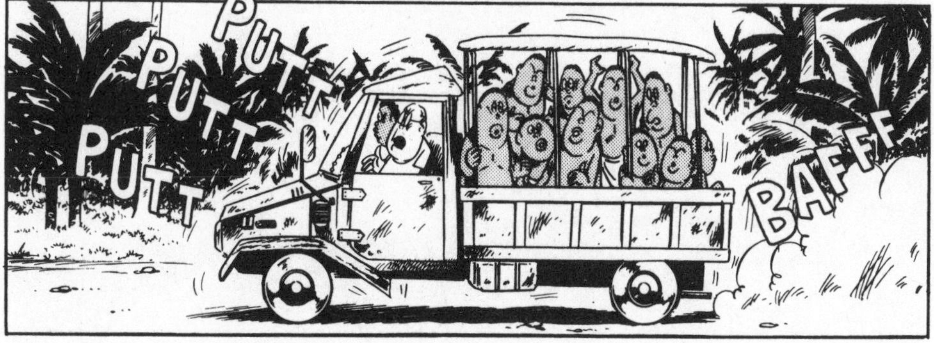
BAFFF
PUTT
PUTT
PUTT

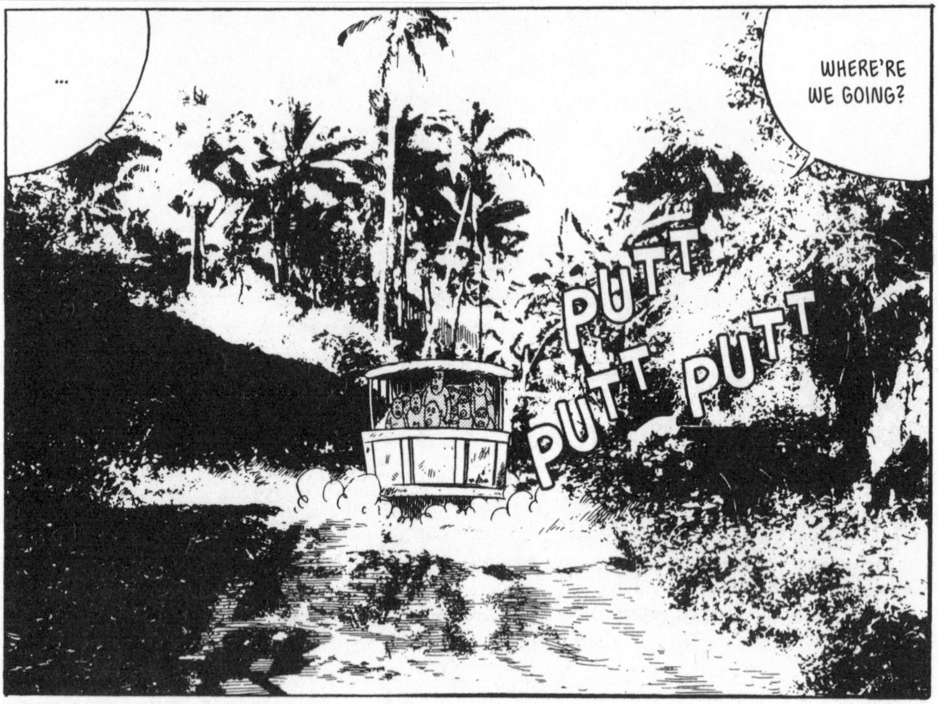
WHERE'RE WE GOING?
...
PUTT PUTT PUTT PUTT

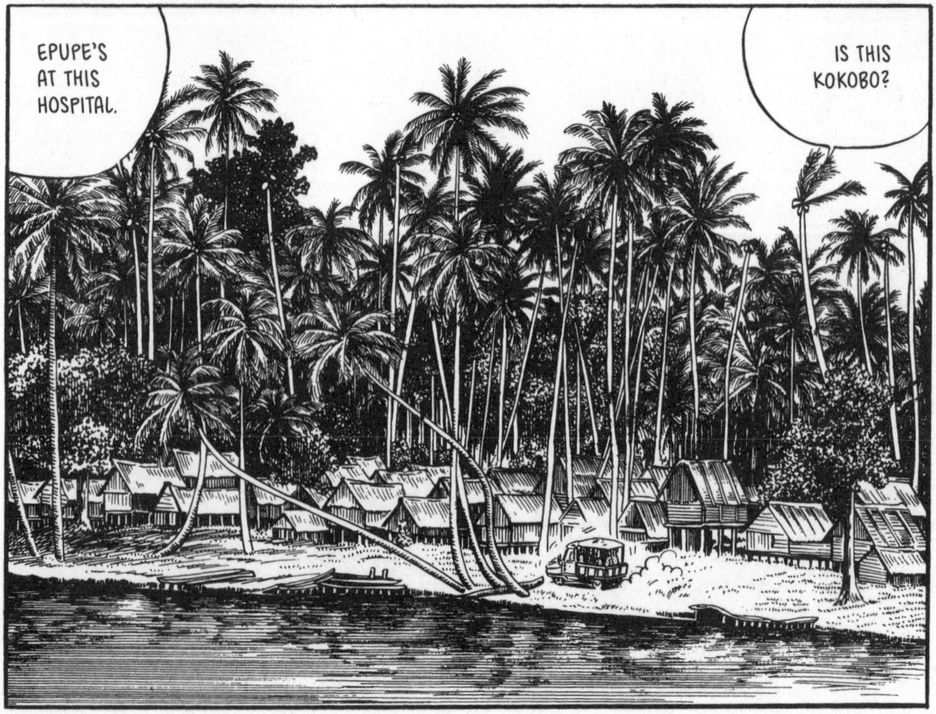
IS THIS KOKOBO?
EPUPE'S AT THIS HOSPITAL.

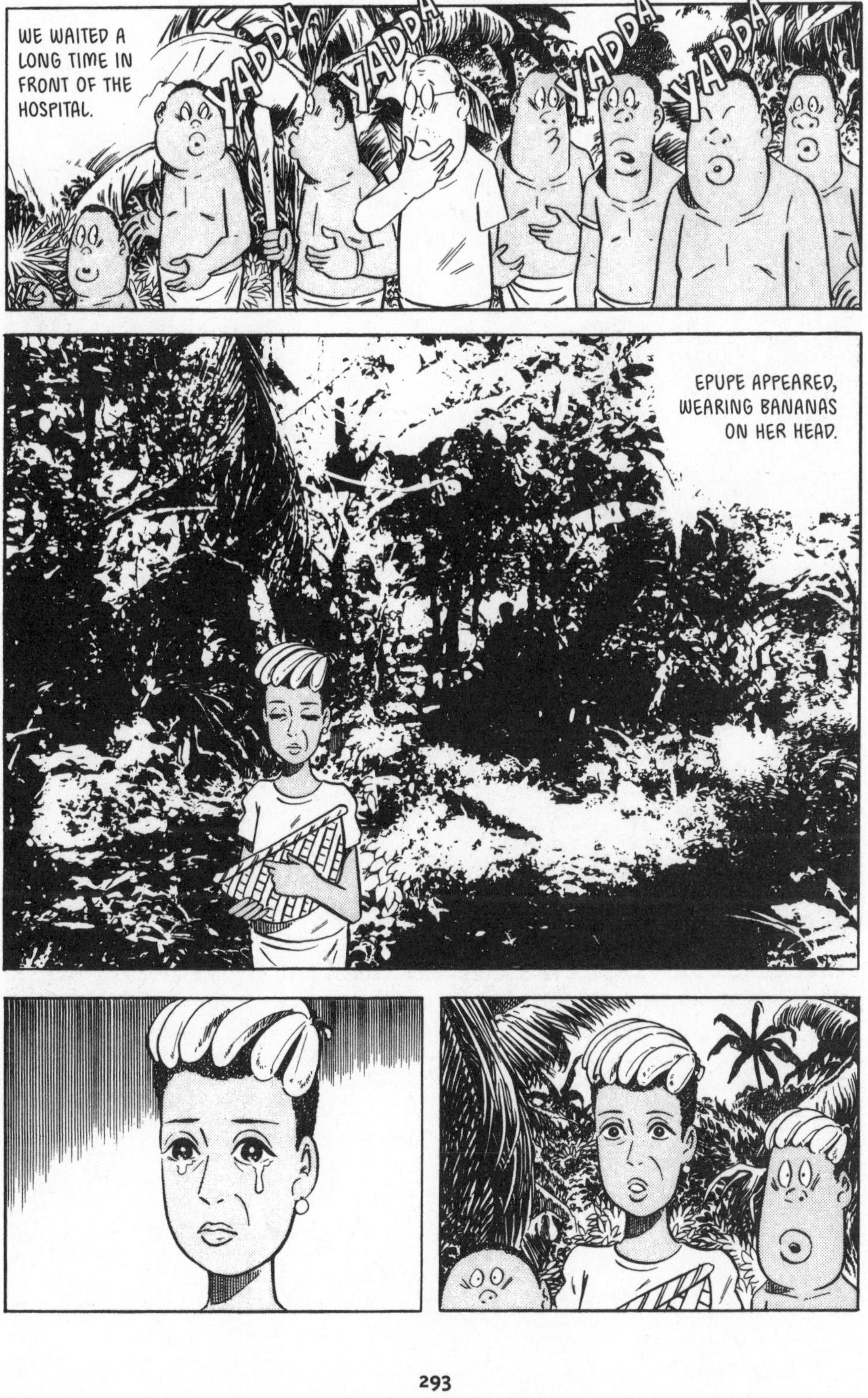
YADDA
YADDA
YADDA
YADDA
WE WAITED A LONG TIME IN FRONT OF THE HOSPITAL.
EPUPE APPEARED, WEARING BANANAS ON HER HEAD.

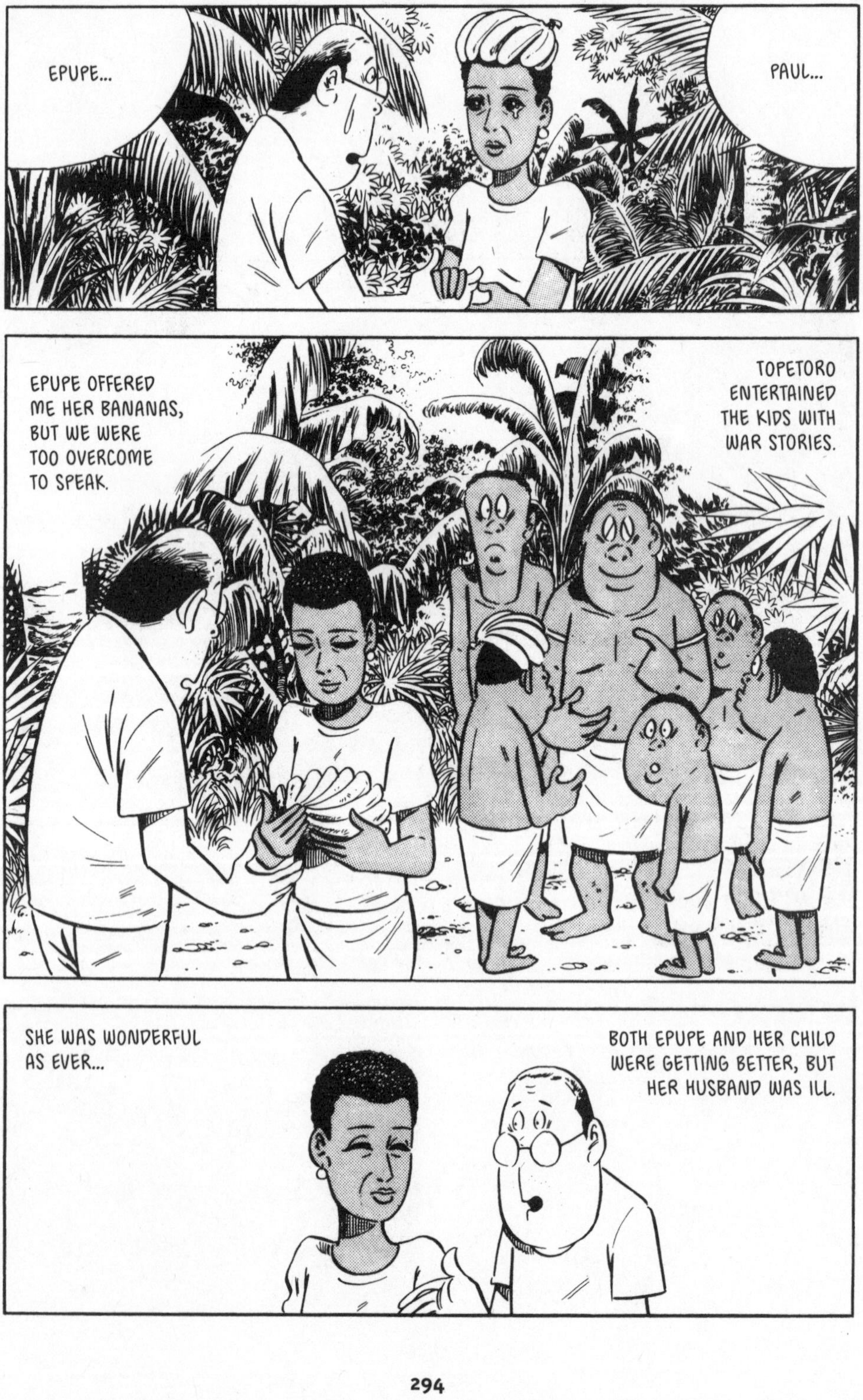
PAUL...
EPUPE...
TOPETORO ENTERTAINED THE KIDS WITH WAR STORIES.
EPUPE OFFERED ME HER BANANAS, BUT WE WERE TOO OVERCOME TO SPEAK.
BOTH EPUPE AND HER CHILD WERE GETTING BETTER, BUT HER HUSBAND WAS ILL.
SHE WAS WONDERFUL AS EVER...

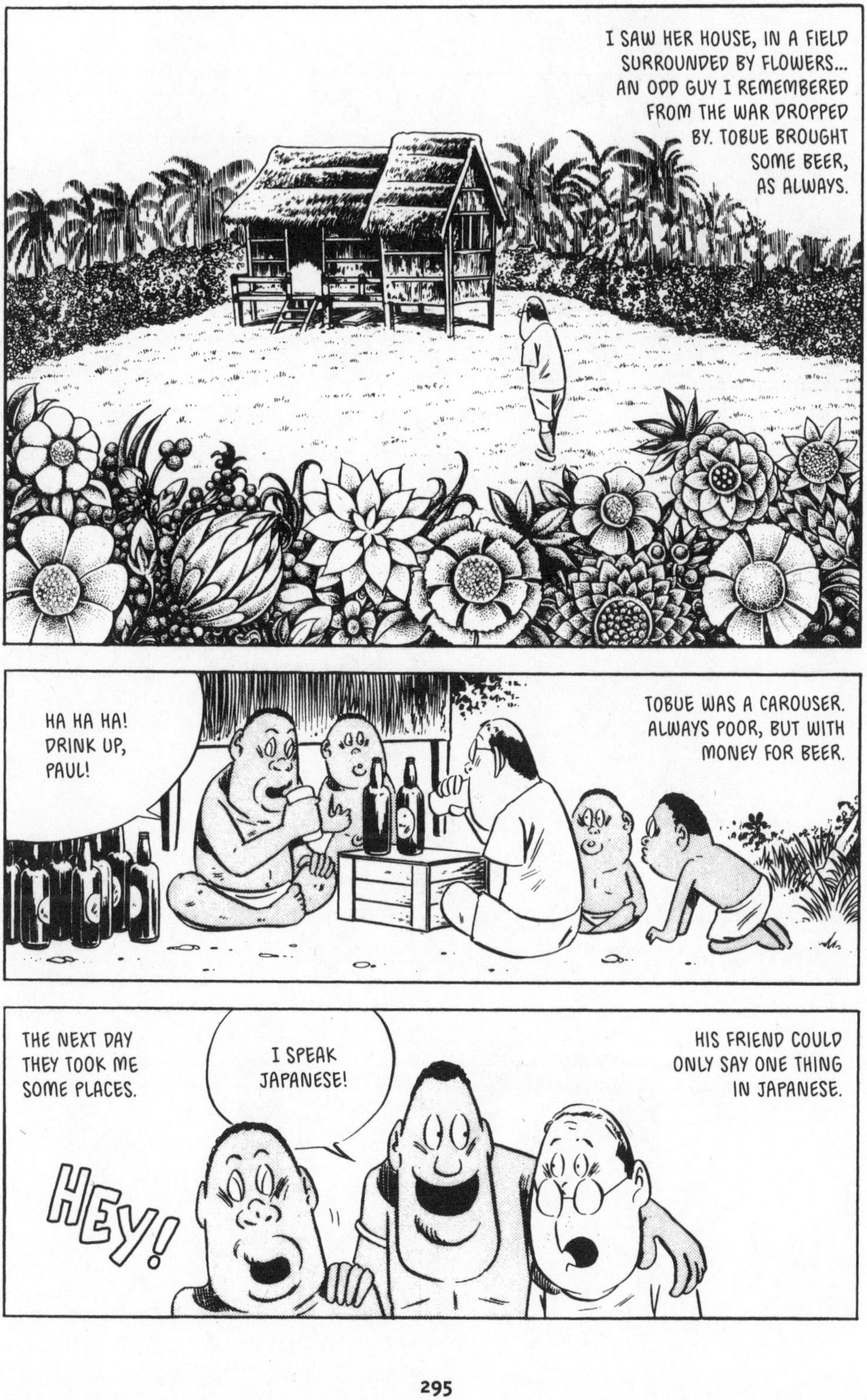
I SAW HER HOUSE, IN A FIELD SURROUNDED BY FLOWERS... AN ODD GUY I REMEMBERED FROM THE WAR DROPPED BY. TOBUE BROUGHT SOME BEER, AS ALWAYS.
TOBUE WAS A CAROUSER. ALWAYS POOR, BUT WITH MONEY FOR BEER.
HA HA HA! DRINK UP, PAUL!
HIS FRIEND COULD ONLY SAY ONE THING IN JAPANESE.
I SPEAK JAPANESE!
THE NEXT DAY THEY TOOK ME SOME PLACES.
HEY!

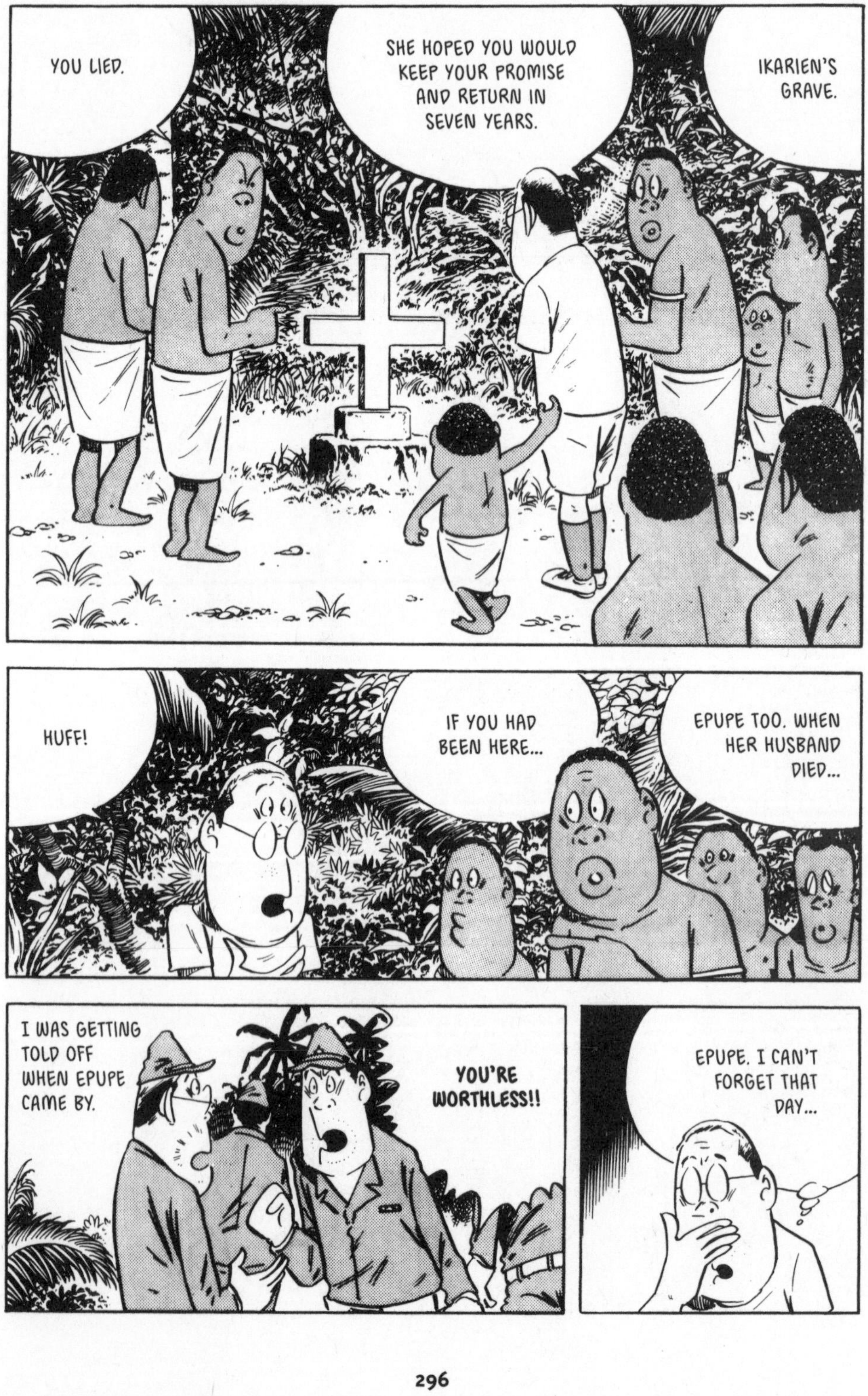
IKARIEN'S GRAVE.
SHE HOPED YOU WOULD KEEP YOUR PROMISE AND RETURN IN SEVEN YEARS.
YOU LIED.
EPUPE TOO. WHEN HER HUSBAND DIED...
IF YOU HAD BEEN HERE...
HUFF!
EPUPE. I CAN'T FORGET THAT DAY...
I WAS GETTING TOLD OFF WHEN EPUPE CAME BY.
YOU'RE WORTHLESS!!

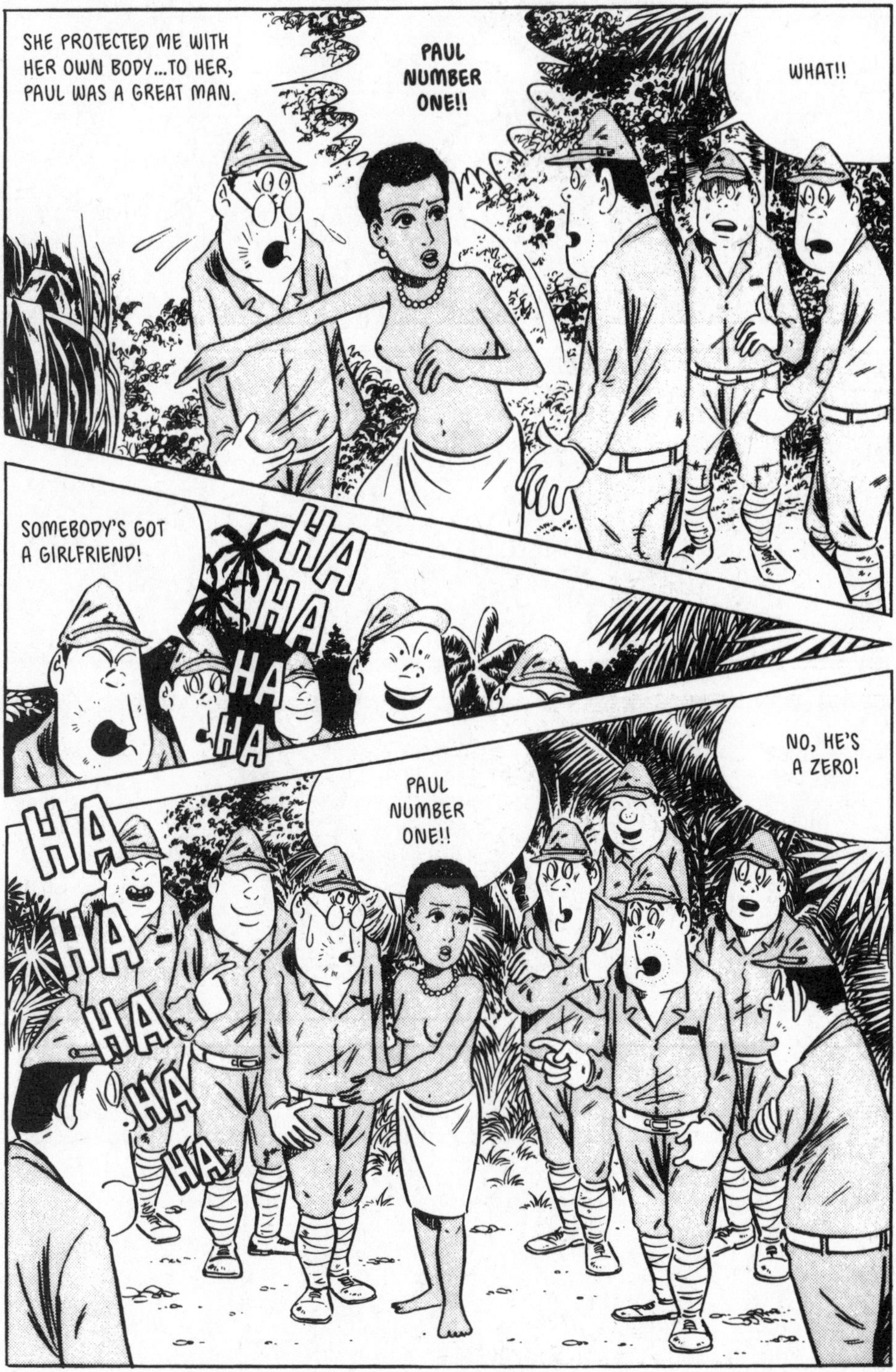
WHAT!!
PAUL NUMBER ONE!!
SHE PROTECTED ME WITH HER OWN BODY...TO HER, PAUL WAS A GREAT MAN.
HA HA HA HA
SOMEBODY'S GOT A GIRLFRIEND!
NO, HE'S A ZERO!
PAUL NUMBER ONE!!
HA HA HA HA HA HA

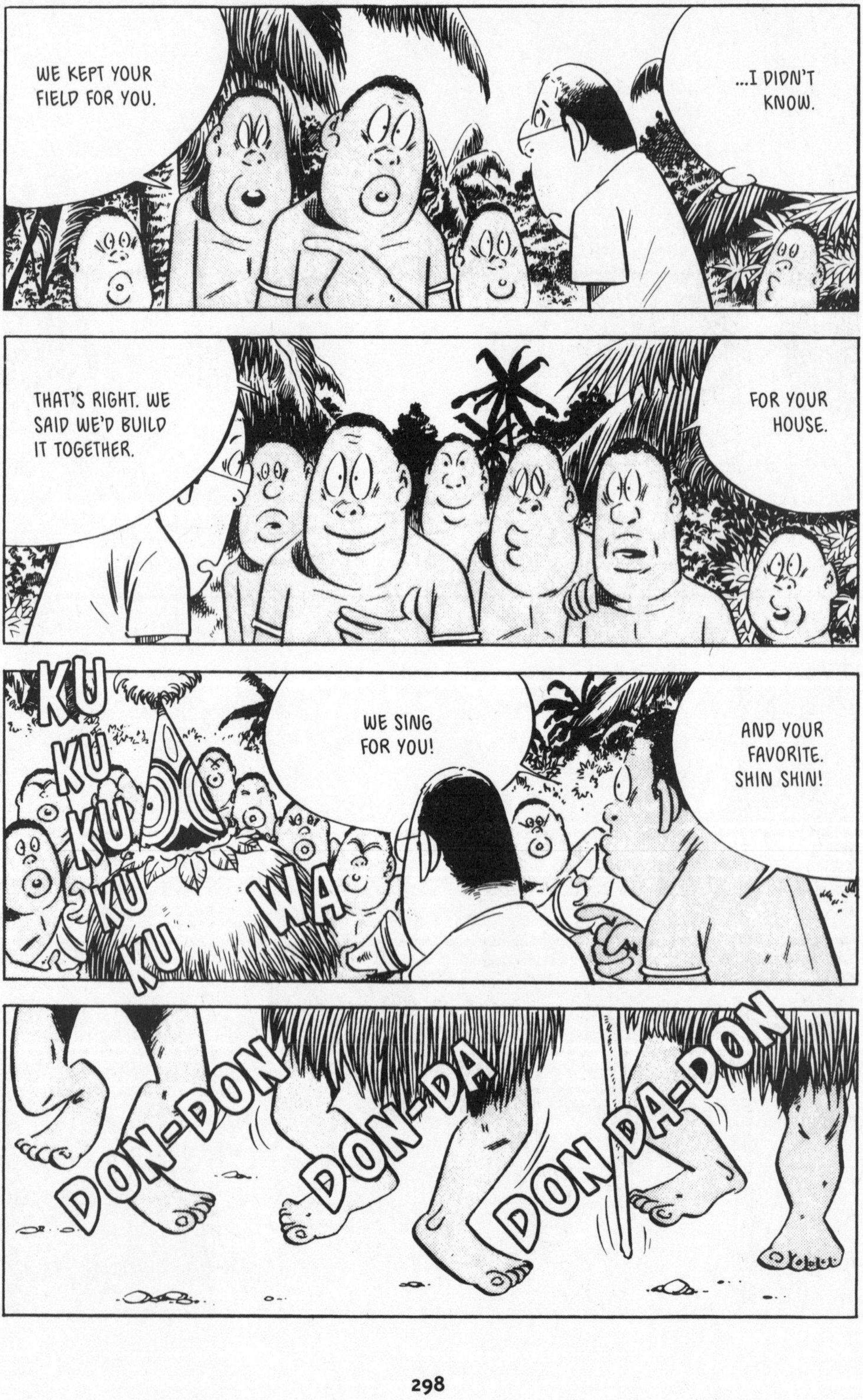
...I DIDN'T KNOW.
WE KEPT YOUR FIELD FOR YOU.
FOR YOUR HOUSE.
THAT'S RIGHT. WE SAID WE'D BUILD IT TOGETHER.
AND YOUR FAVORITE. SHIN SHIN!
WE SING FOR YOU!
WA
KU KU KU KU KU
DON DA-DON
DON-DA
DON-DON

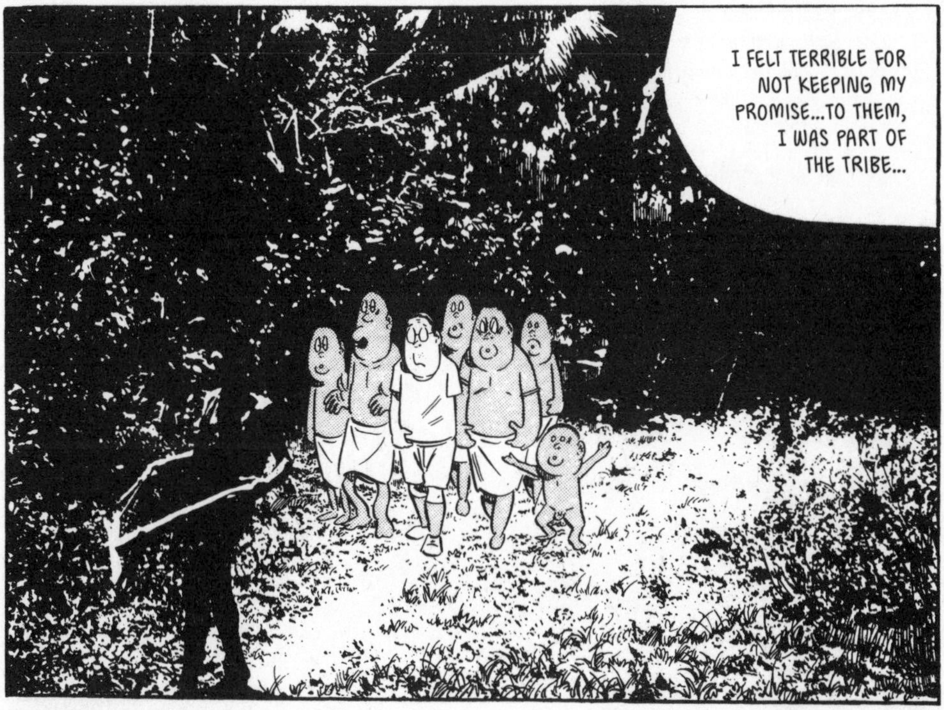
I FELT TERRIBLE FOR NOT KEEPING MY PROMISE...TO THEM, I WAS PART OF THE TRIBE...

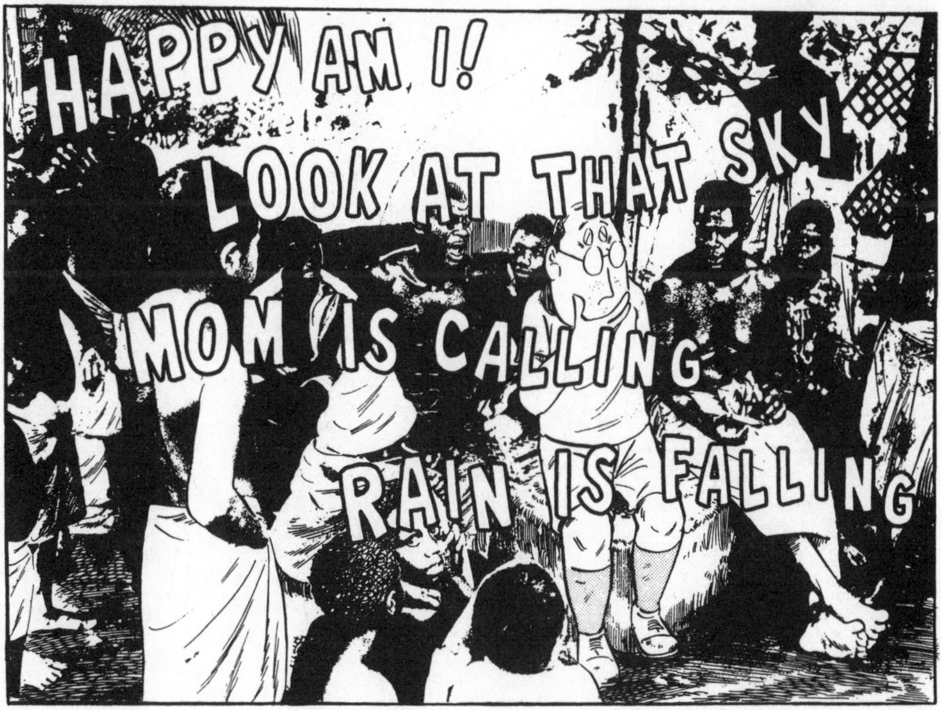
HAPPY AM I!
LOOK AT THAT SKY
MOM IS CALLING
RAIN IS FALLING

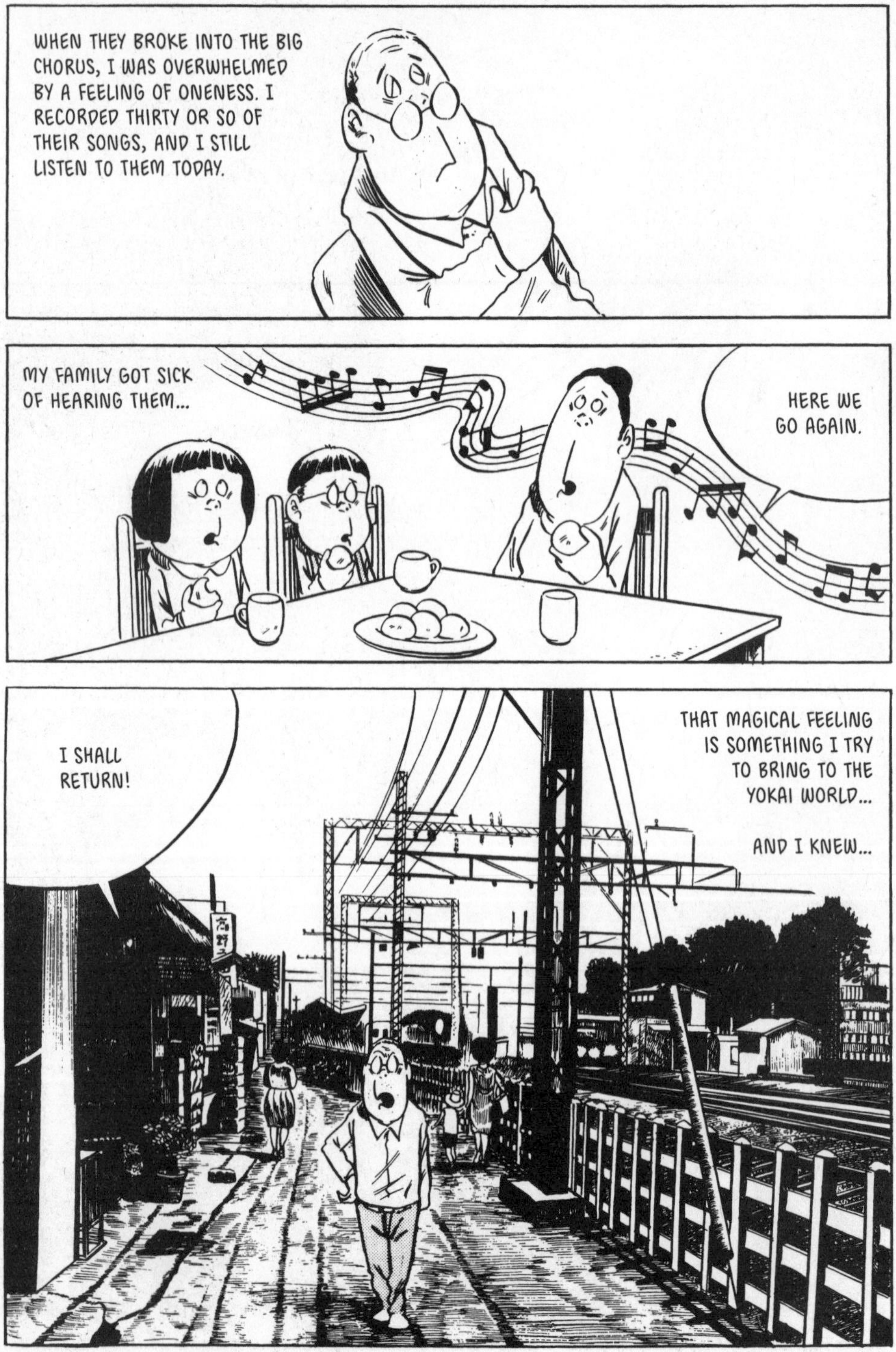
WHEN THEY BROKE INTO THE BIG CHORUS, I WAS OVERWHELMED BY A FEELING OF ONENESS. I RECORDED THIRTY OR SO OF THEIR SONGS, AND I STILL LISTEN TO THEM TODAY.
HERE WE GO AGAIN.
MY FAMILY GOT SICK OF HEARING THEM...
THAT MAGICAL FEELING IS SOMETHING I TRY TO BRING TO THE YOKAI WORLD...
AND I KNEW...
I SHALL RETURN!

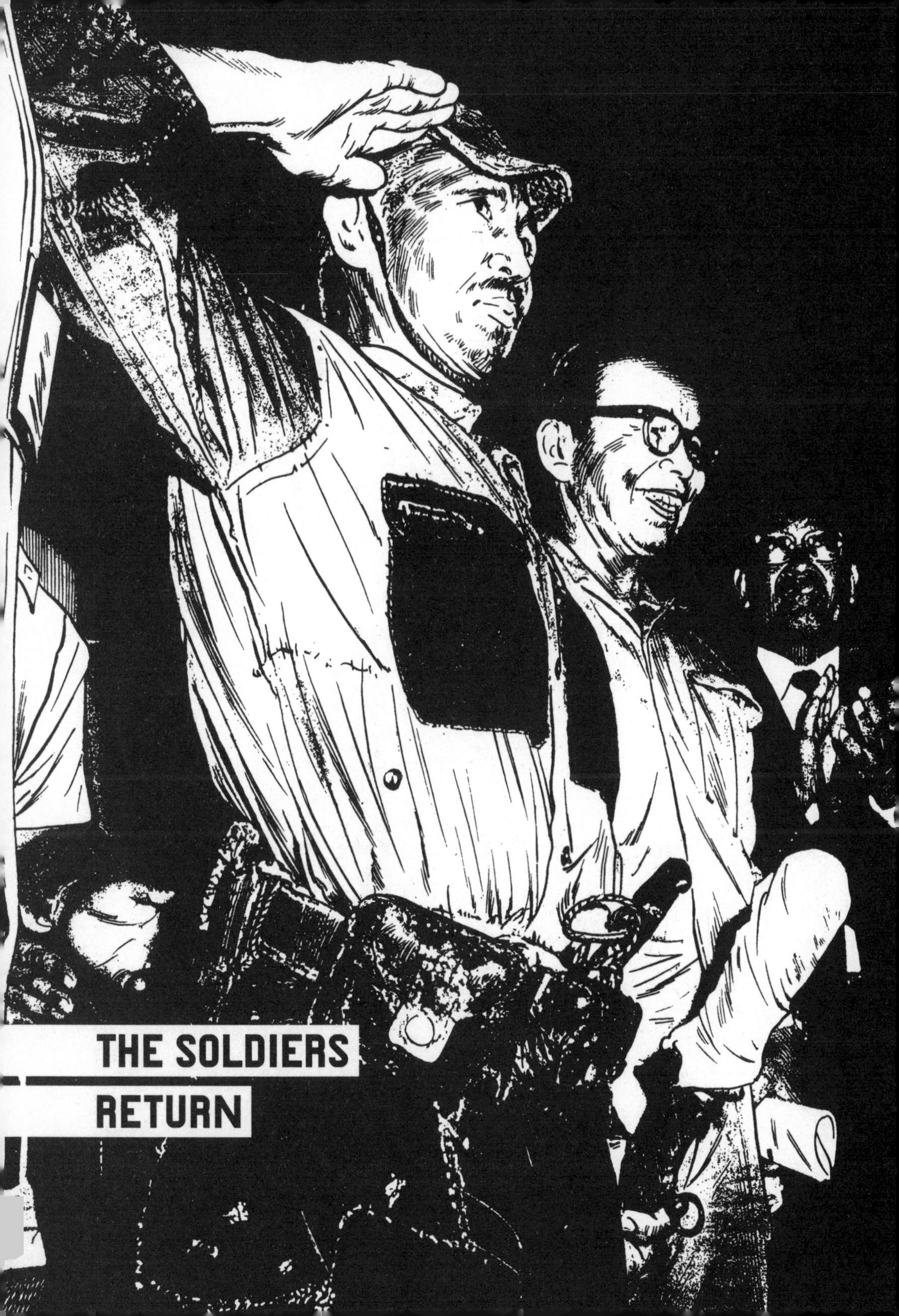
THE SOLDIERS
RETURN

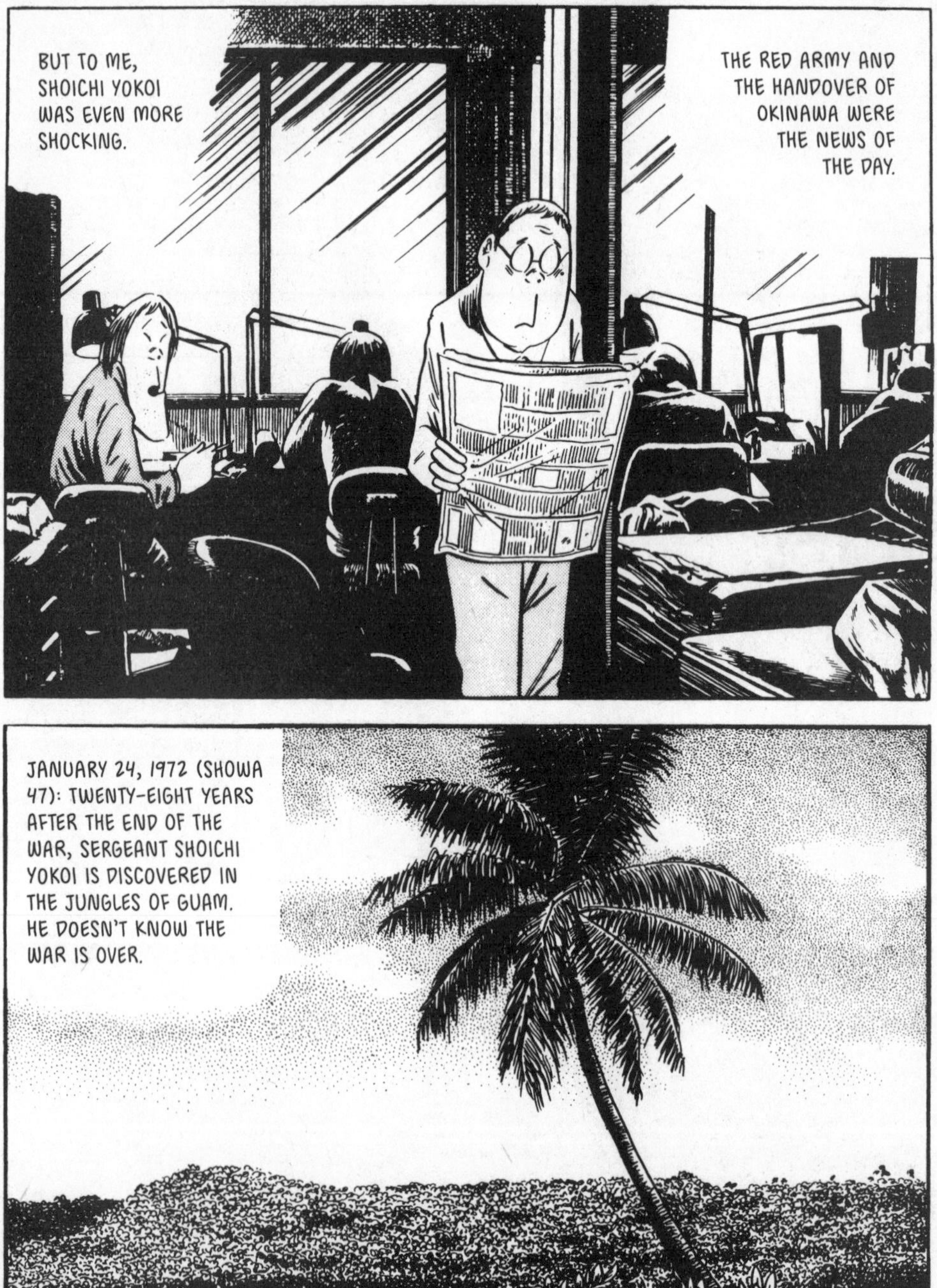
THE RED ARMY AND THE HANDOVER OF OKINAWA WERE THE NEWS OF THE DAY.
BUT TO ME, SHOICHI YOKOI WAS EVEN MORE SHOCKING.
JANUARY 24, 1972 (SHOWA 47): TWENTY-EIGHT YEARS AFTER THE END OF THE WAR, SERGEANT SHOICHI YOKOI IS DISCOVERED IN THE JUNGLES OF GUAM. HE DOESN'T KNOW THE WAR IS OVER.

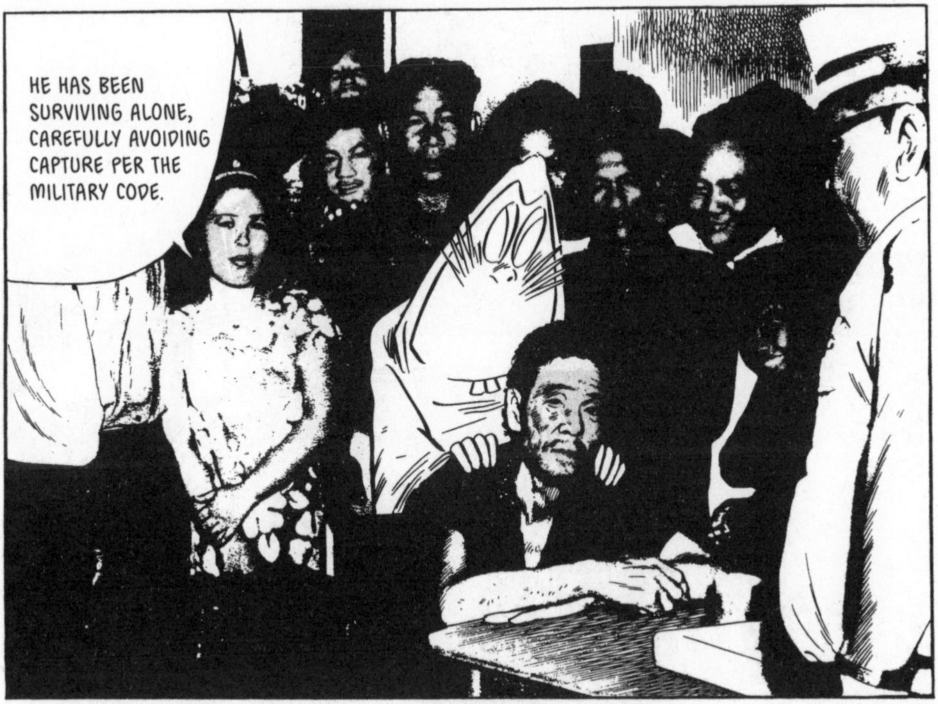
HE HAS BEEN SURVIVING ALONE, CAREFULLY AVOIDING CAPTURE PER THE MILITARY CODE.

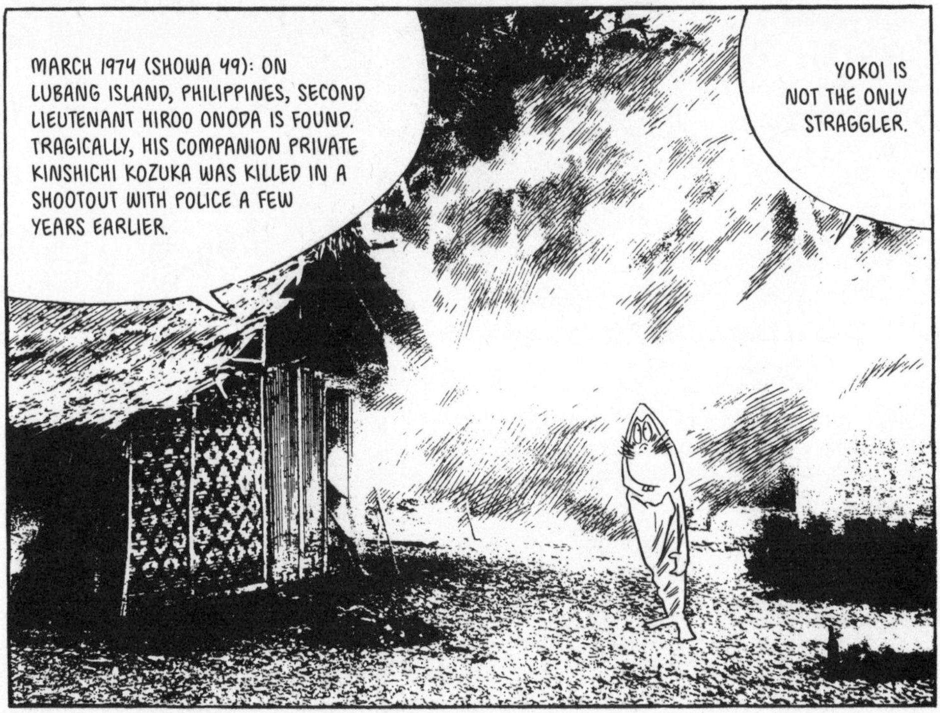
YOKOI IS NOT THE ONLY STRAGGLER.
MARCH 1974 (SHOWA 49): ON LUBANG ISLAND, PHILIPPINES, SECOND LIEUTENANT HIROO ONODA IS FOUND. TRAGICALLY, HIS COMPANION PRIVATE KINSHICHI KOZUKA WAS KILLED IN A SHOOTOUT WITH POLICE A FEW YEARS EARLIER.

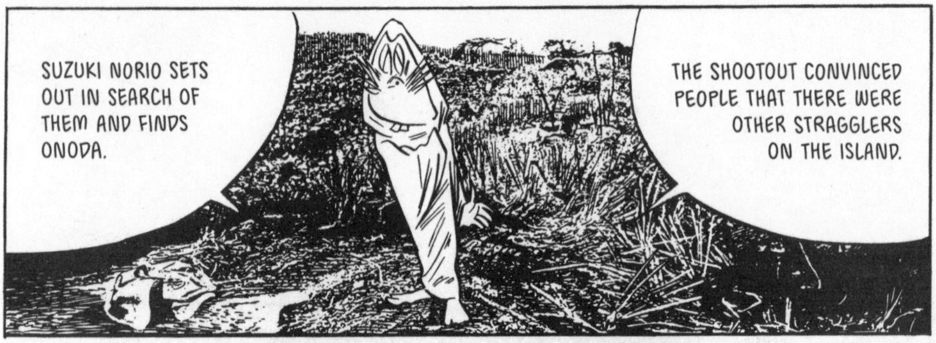
THE SHOOTOUT CONVINCED PEOPLE THAT THERE WERE OTHER STRAGGLERS ON THE ISLAND.
SUZUKI NORIO SETS OUT IN SEARCH OF THEM AND FINDS ONODA.

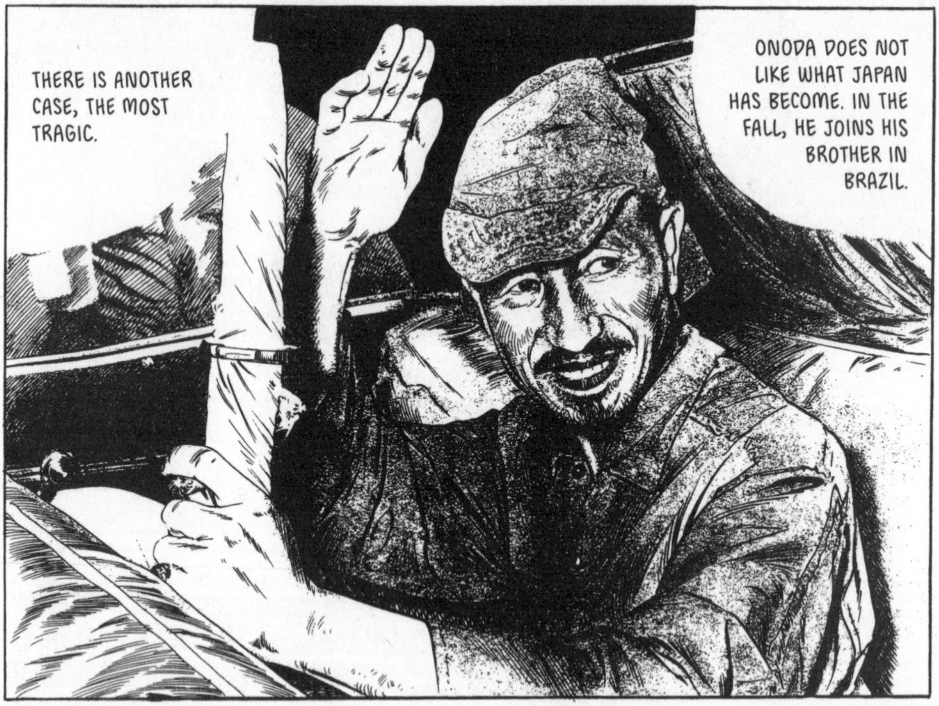
ONODA DOES NOT LIKE WHAT JAPAN HAS BECOME. IN THE FALL, HE JOINS HIS BROTHER IN BRAZIL.
THERE IS ANOTHER CASE, THE MOST TRAGIC.

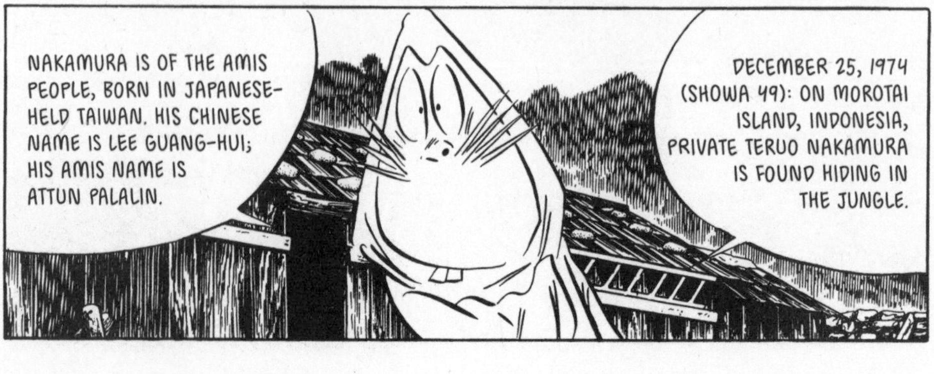
DECEMBER 25, 1974 (SHOWA 49): ON MOROTAI ISLAND, INDONESIA, PRIVATE TERUO NAKAMURA IS FOUND HIDING IN THE JUNGLE.
NAKAMURA IS OF THE AMIS PEOPLE, BORN IN JAPANESE-HELD TAIWAN. HIS CHINESE NAME IS LEE GUANG-HUI; HIS AMIS NAME IS ATTUN PALALIN.

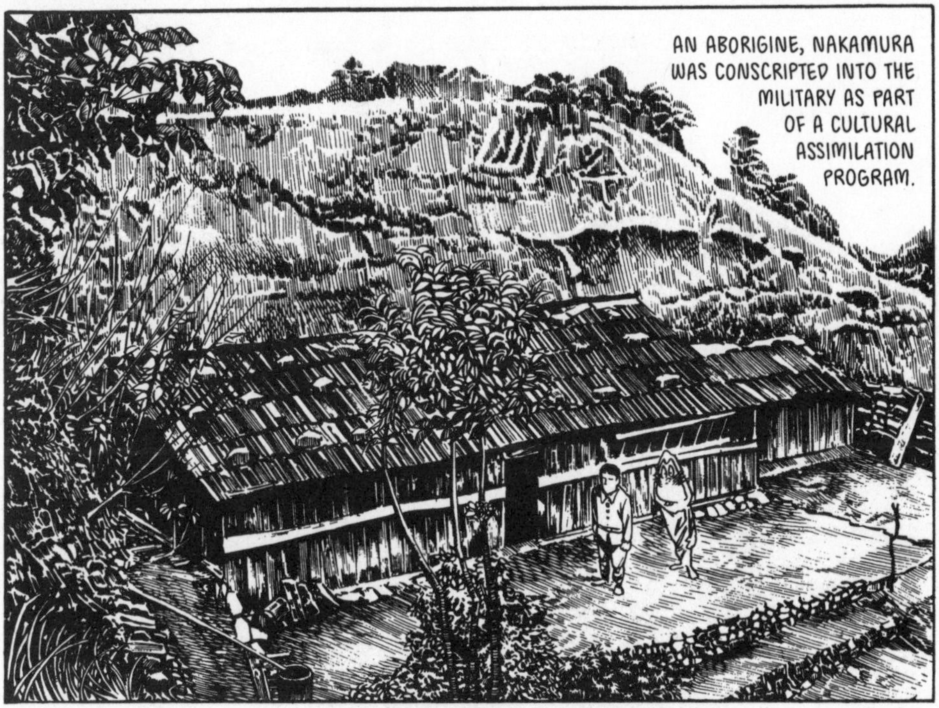
AN ABORIGINE, NAKAMURA WAS CONSCRIPTED INTO THE MILITARY AS PART OF A CULTURAL ASSIMILATION PROGRAM.

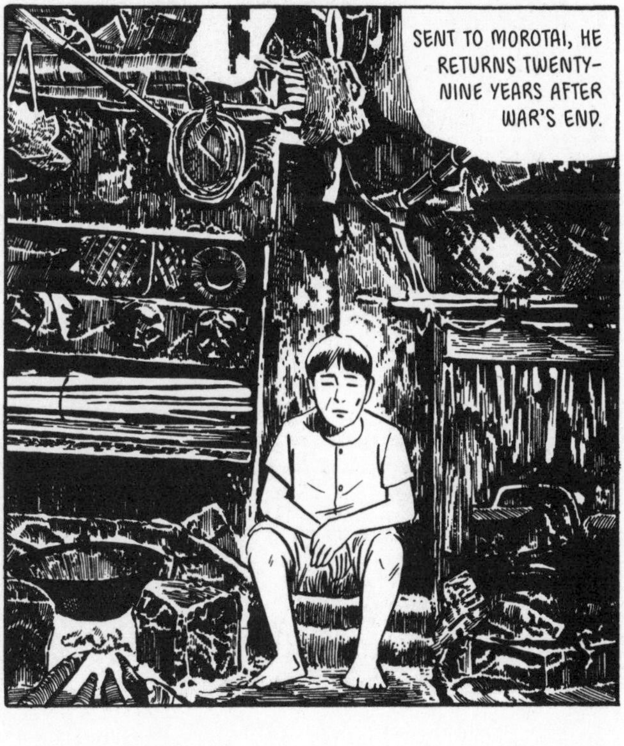
SENT TO MOROTAI, HE RETURNS TWENTY-NINE YEARS AFTER WAR'S END.

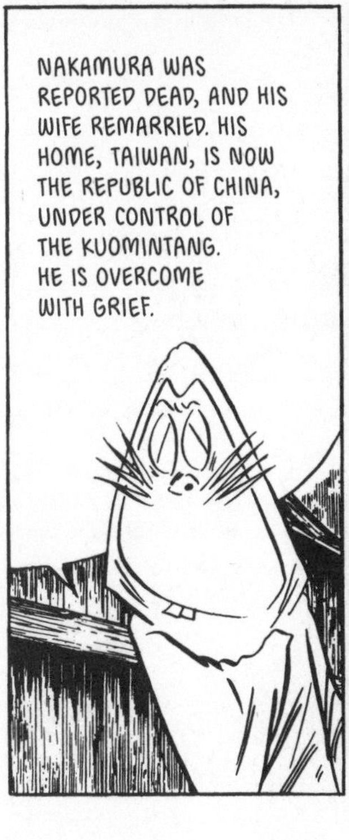
NAKAMURA WAS REPORTED DEAD, AND HIS WIFE REMARRIED. HIS HOME, TAIWAN, IS NOW THE REPUBLIC OF CHINA, UNDER CONTROL OF THE KUOMINTANG. HE IS OVERCOME WITH GRIEF.

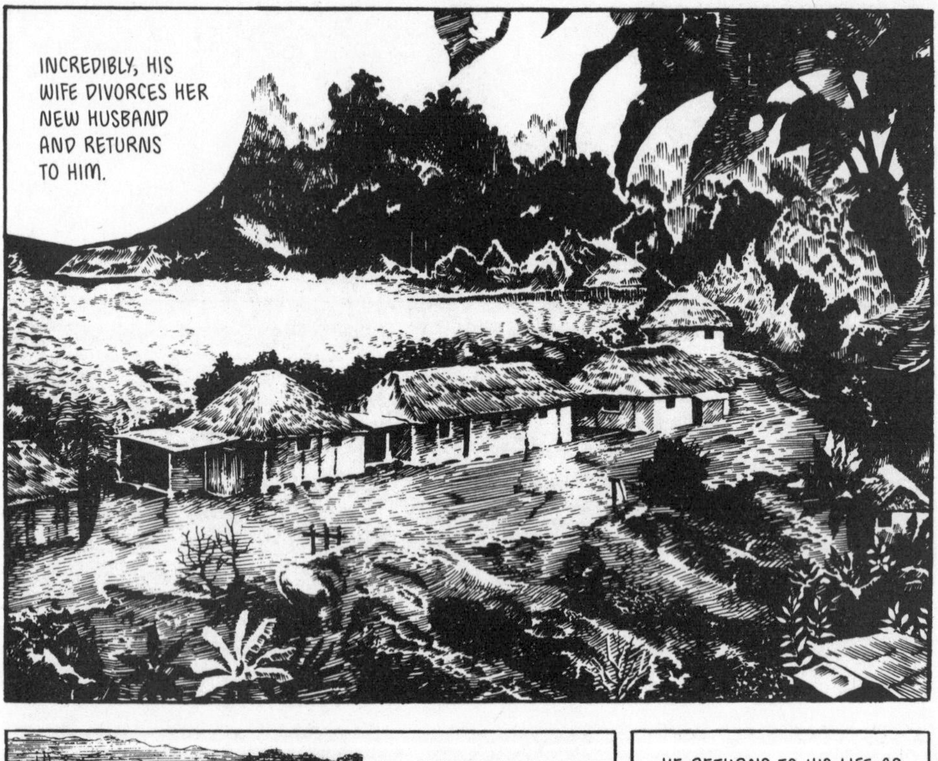
INCREDIBLY, HIS WIFE DIVORCES HER NEW HUSBAND AND RETURNS TO HIM.

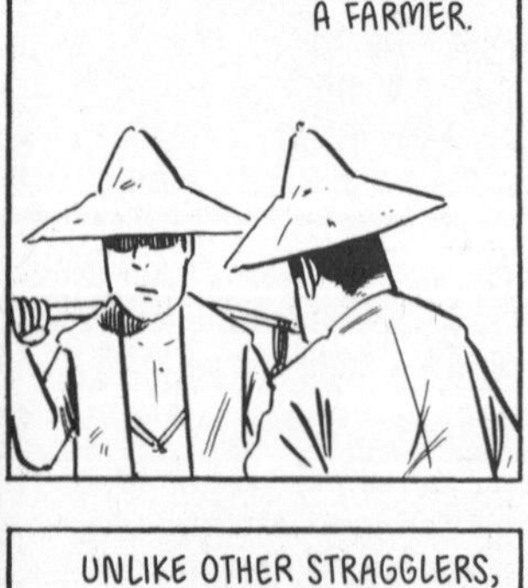
HE RETURNS TO HIS LIFE AS A FARMER.

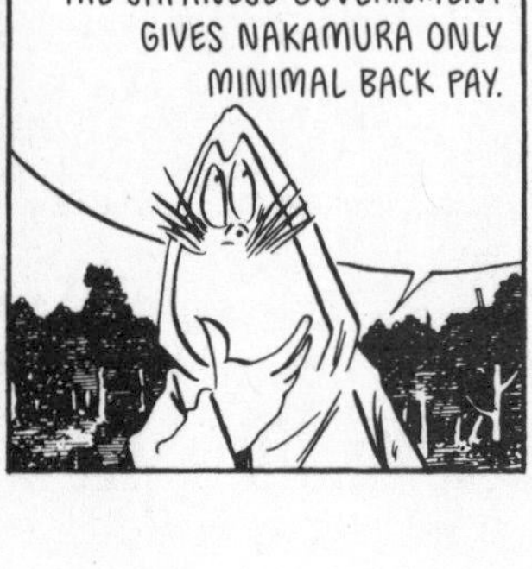
UNLIKE OTHER STRAGGLERS, THE JAPANESE GOVERNMENT GIVES NAKAMURA ONLY MINIMAL BACK PAY.

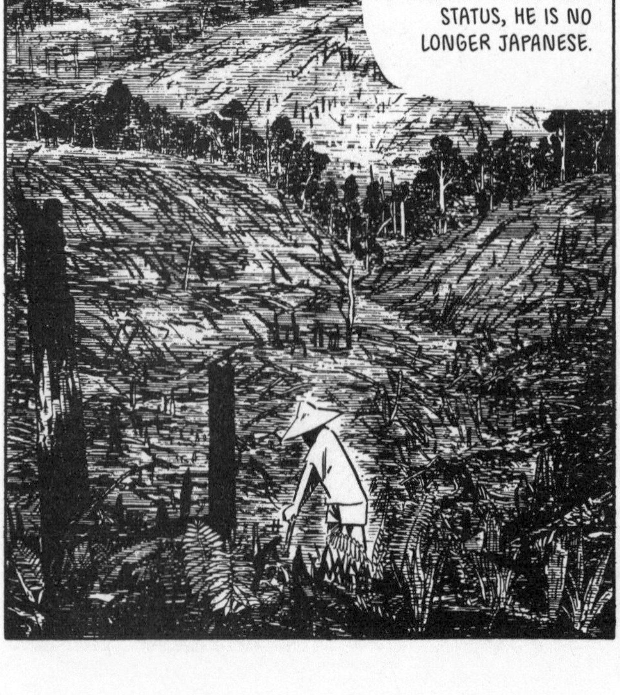
WITH TAIWAN'S NEW STATUS, HE IS NO LONGER JAPANESE.

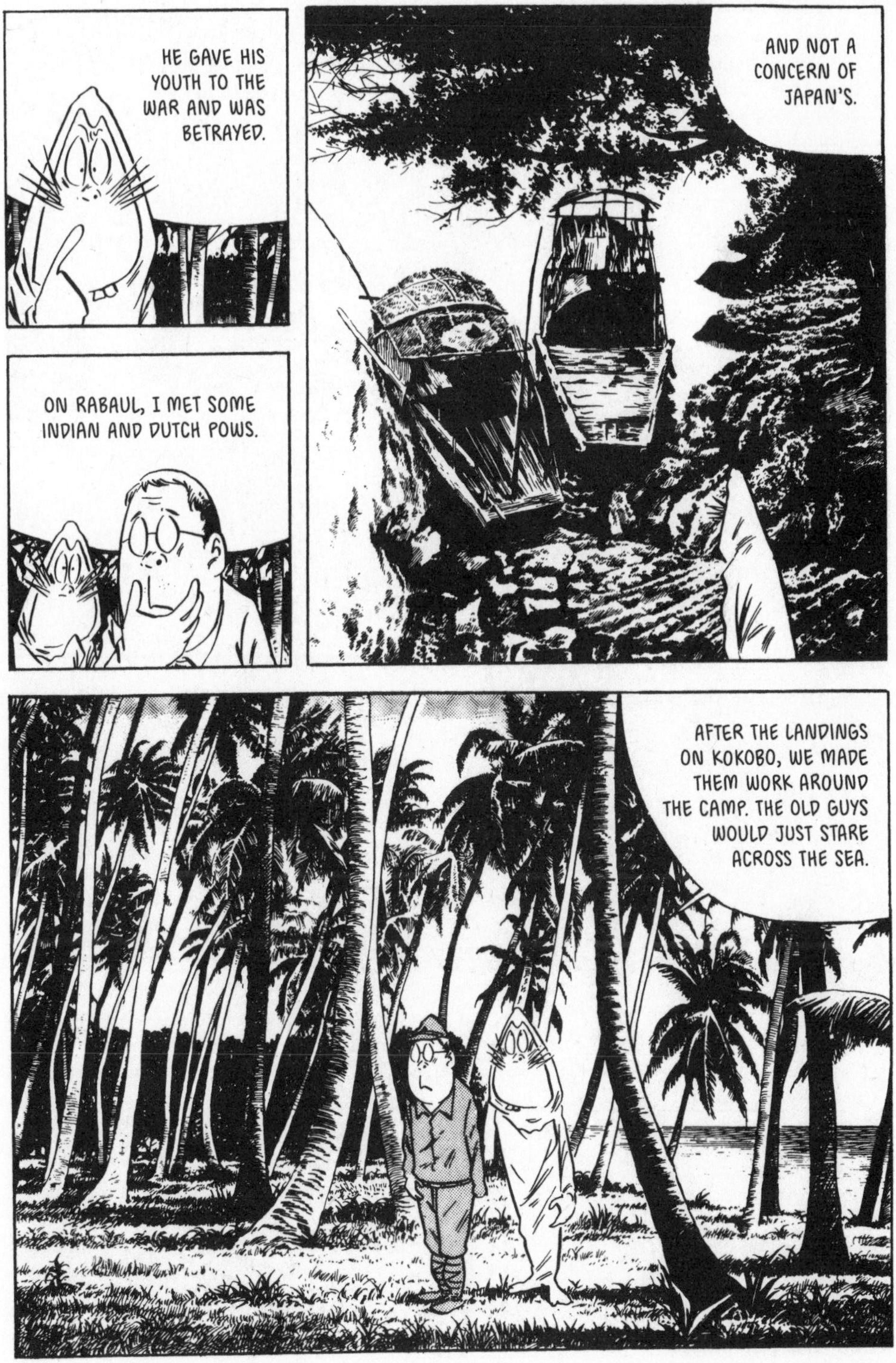
AND NOT A CONCERN OF JAPAN'S.
HE GAVE HIS YOUTH TO THE WAR AND WAS BETRAYED.
ON RABAUL, I MET SOME INDIAN AND DUTCH POWS.
AFTER THE LANDINGS ON KOKOBO, WE MADE THEM WORK AROUND THE CAMP. THE OLD GUYS WOULD JUST STARE ACROSS THE SEA.

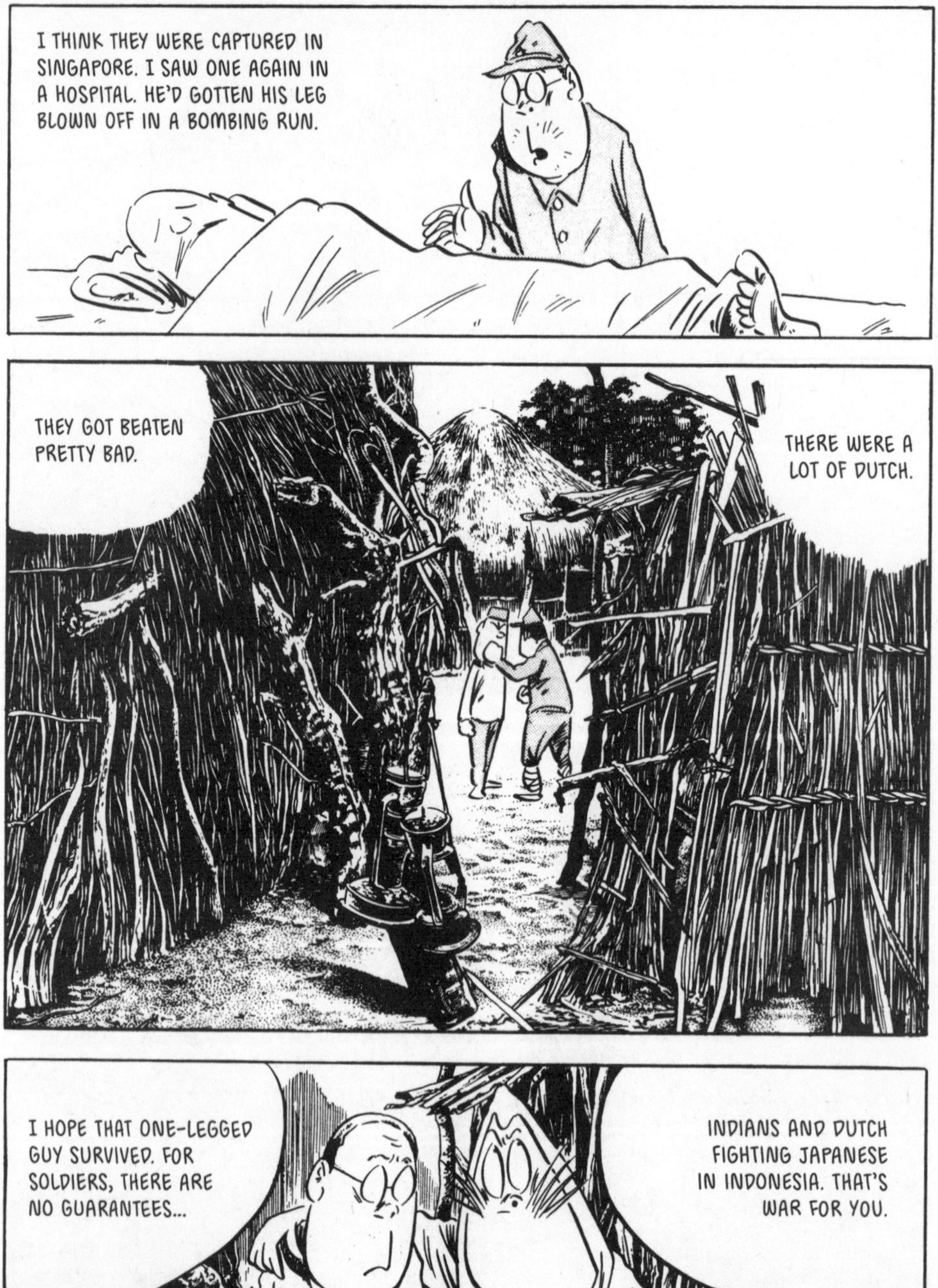
I THINK THEY WERE CAPTURED IN SINGAPORE. I SAW ONE AGAIN IN A HOSPITAL. HE'D GOTTEN HIS LEG BLOWN OFF IN A BOMBING RUN.
THERE WERE A LOT OF DUTCH.
THEY GOT BEATEN PRETTY BAD.
INDIANS AND DUTCH FIGHTING JAPANESE IN INDONESIA. THAT'S WAR FOR YOU.
I HOPE THAT ONE-LEGGED GUY SURVIVED. FOR SOLDIERS, THERE ARE NO GUARANTEES...

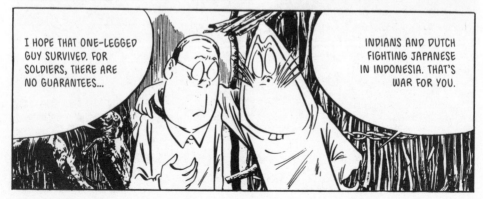

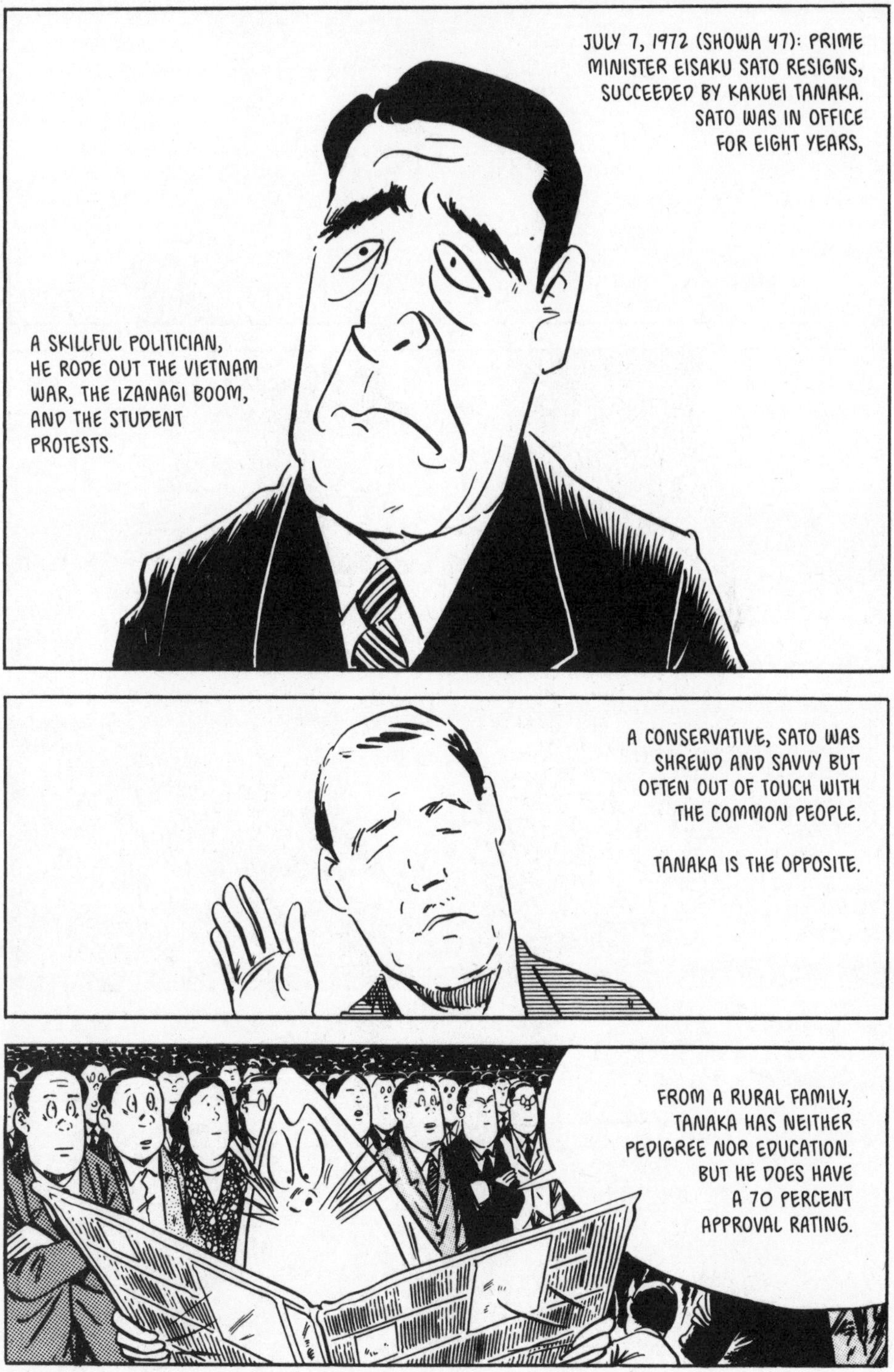
JULY 7, 1972 (SHOWA 47): PRIME MINISTER EISAKU SATO RESIGNS, SUCCEEDED BY KAKUEI TANAKA. SATO WAS IN OFFICE FOR EIGHT YEARS,
A SKILLFUL POLITICIAN, HE RODE OUT THE VIETNAM WAR, THE IZANAGI BOOM, AND THE STUDENT PROTESTS.
A CONSERVATIVE, SATO WAS SHREWD AND SAVVY BUT OFTEN OUT OF TOUCH WITH THE COMMON PEOPLE.
TANAKA IS THE OPPOSITE.
FROM A RURAL FAMILY, TANAKA HAS NEITHER PEDIGREE NOR EDUCATION. BUT HE DOES HAVE A 70 PERCENT APPROVAL RATING.

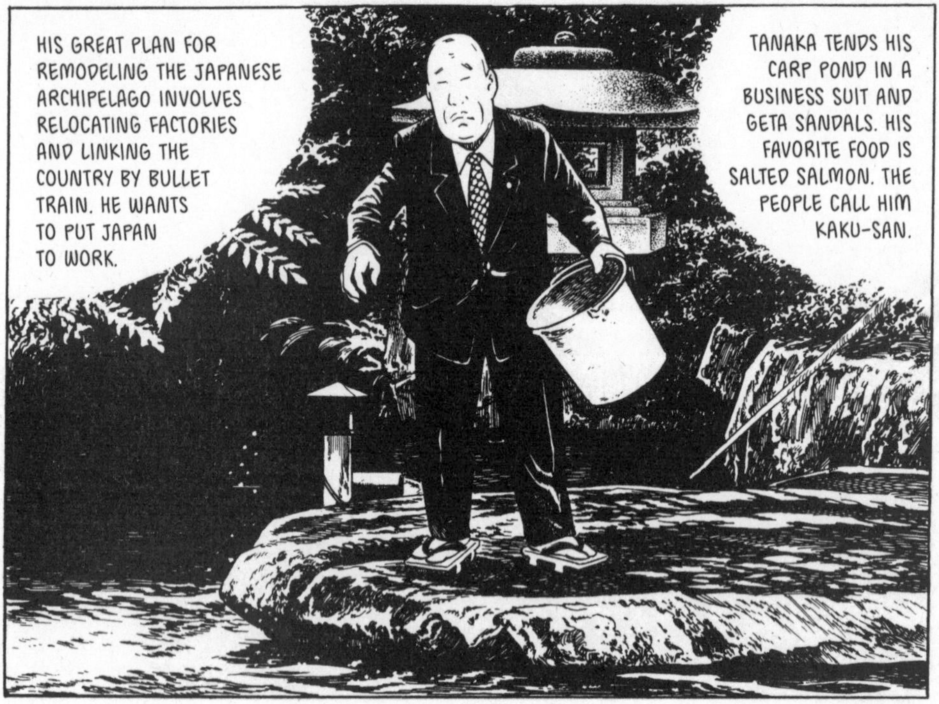
TANAKA TENDS HIS CARP POND IN A BUSINESS SUIT AND GETA SANDALS. HIS FAVORITE FOOD IS SALTED SALMON. THE PEOPLE CALL HIM KAKU-SAN.
HIS GREAT PLAN FOR REMODELING THE JAPANESE ARCHIPELAGO INVOLVES RELOCATING FACTORIES AND LINKING THE COUNTRY BY BULLET TRAIN. HE WANTS TO PUT JAPAN TO WORK.

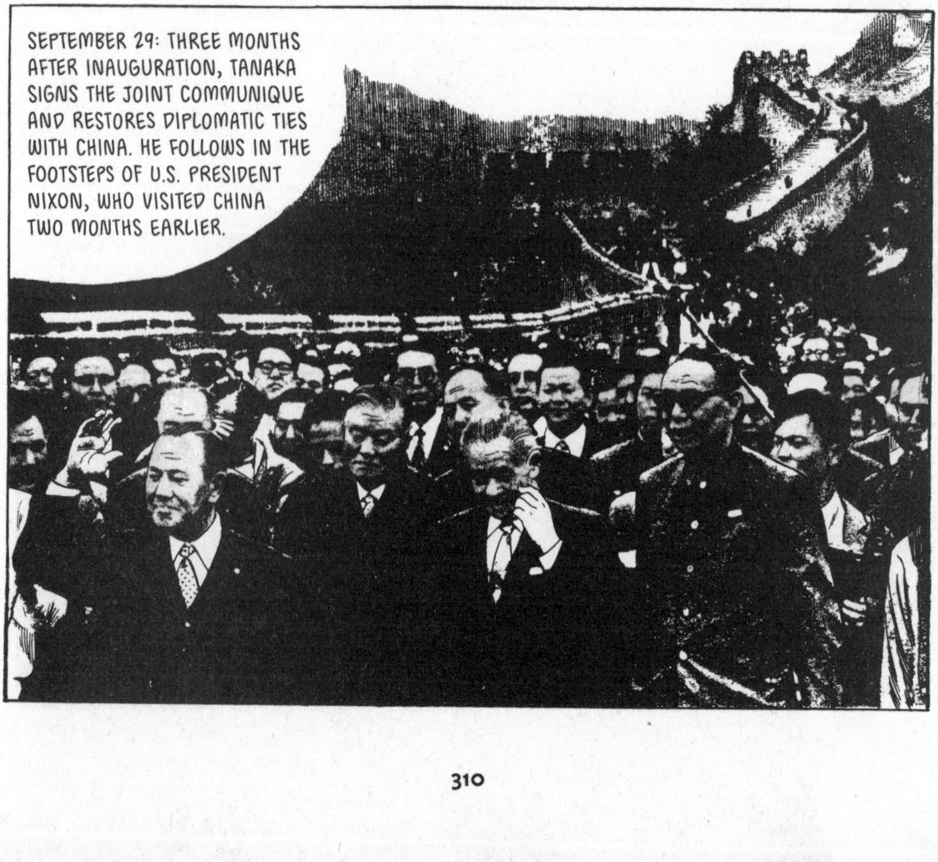
SEPTEMBER 29: THREE MONTHS AFTER INAUGURATION, TANAKA SIGNS THE JOINT COMMUNIQUE AND RESTORES DIPLOMATIC TIES WITH CHINA. HE FOLLOWS IN THE FOOTSTEPS OF U.S. PRESIDENT NIXON, WHO VISITED CHINA TWO MONTHS EARLIER.

BUILDING A NEW JAPAN

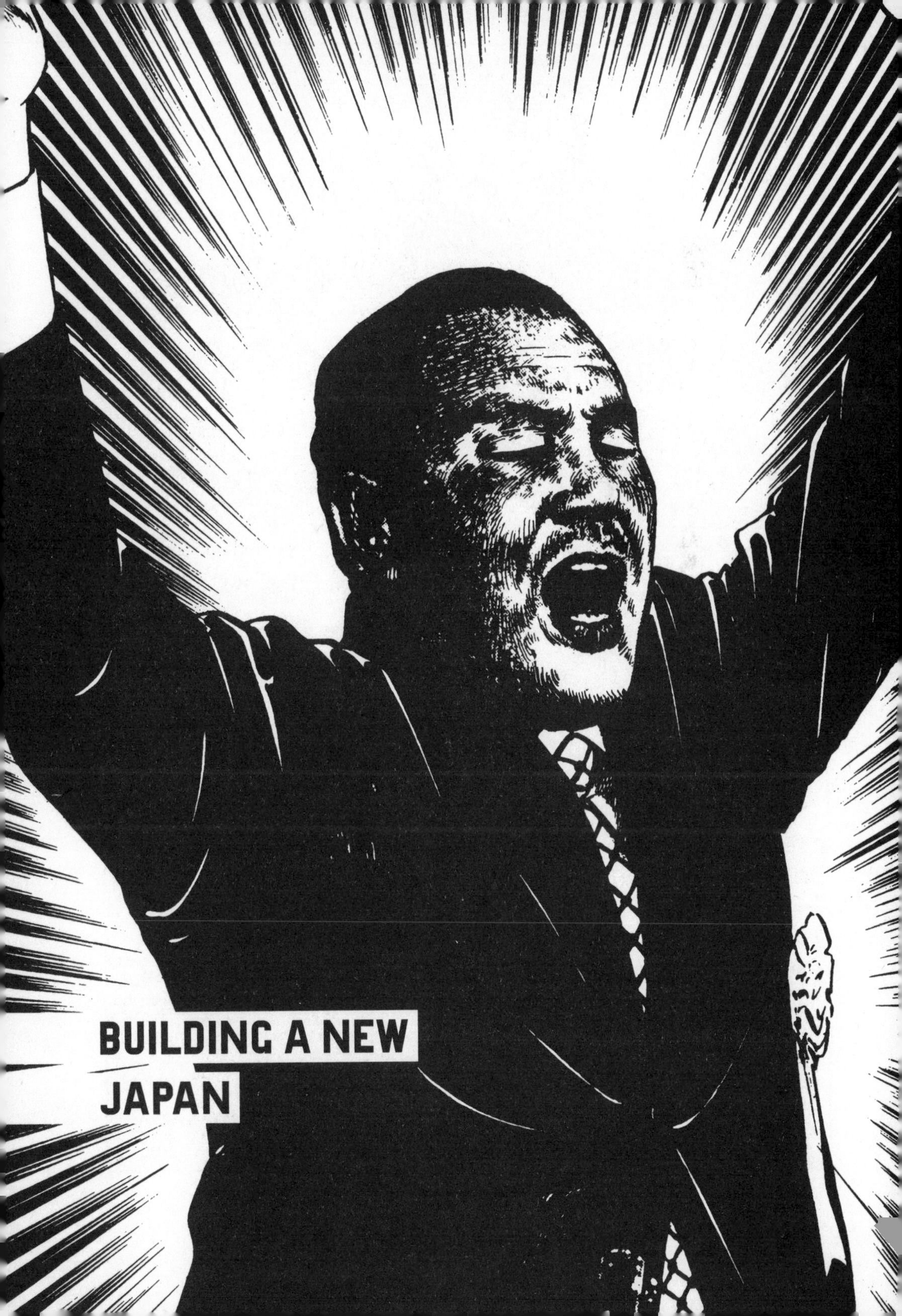

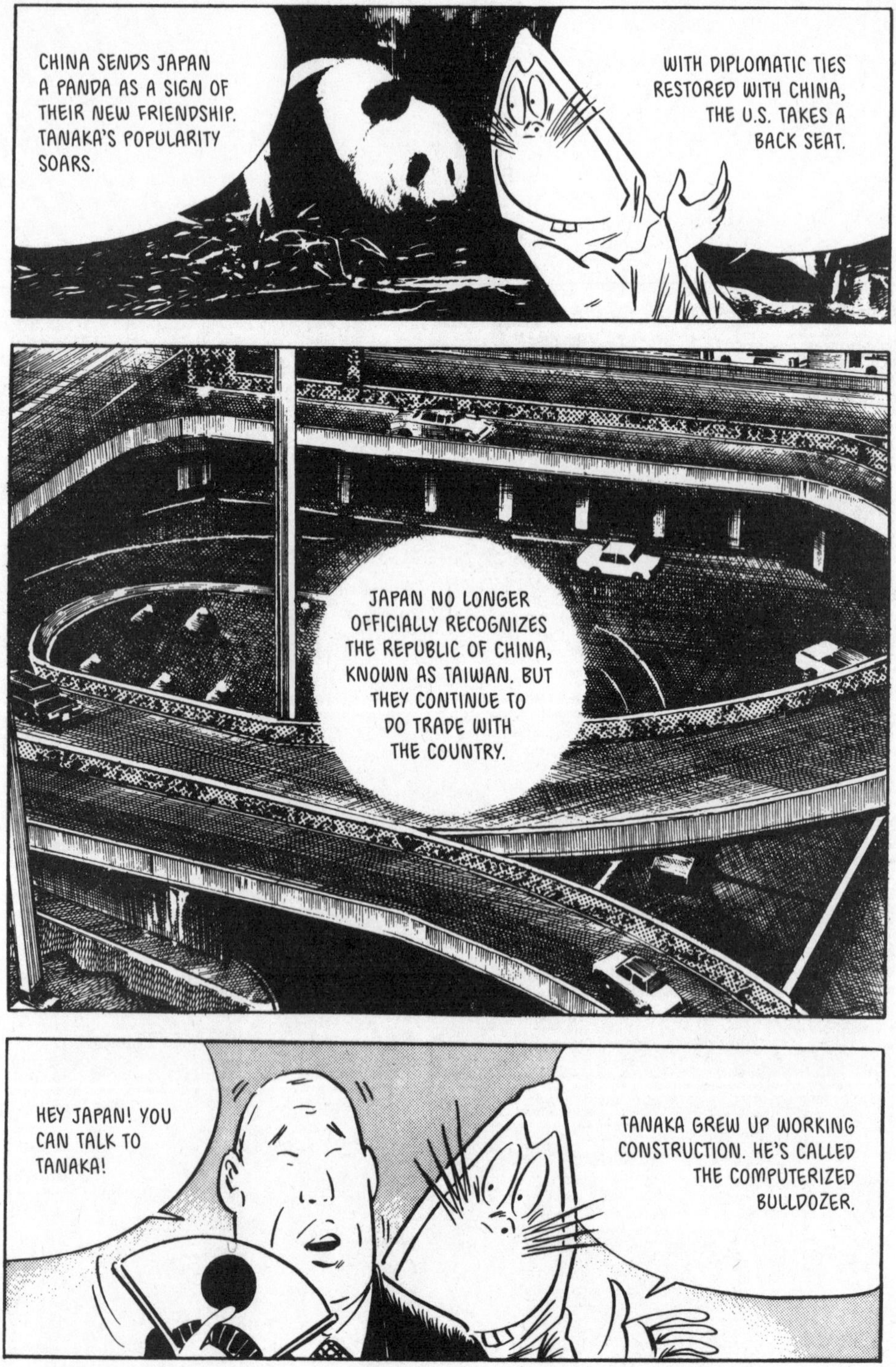
WITH DIPLOMATIC TIES RESTORED WITH CHINA, THE U.S. TAKES A BACK SEAT.
CHINA SENDS JAPAN A PANDA AS A SIGN OF THEIR NEW FRIENDSHIP. TANAKA'S POPULARITY SOARS.
JAPAN NO LONGER OFFICIALLY RECOGNIZES THE REPUBLIC OF CHINA, KNOWN AS TAIWAN. BUT THEY CONTINUE TO DO TRADE WITH THE COUNTRY.
TANAKA GREW UP WORKING CONSTRUCTION. HE'S CALLED THE COMPUTERIZED BULLDOZER.
HEY JAPAN! YOU CAN TALK TO TANAKA!

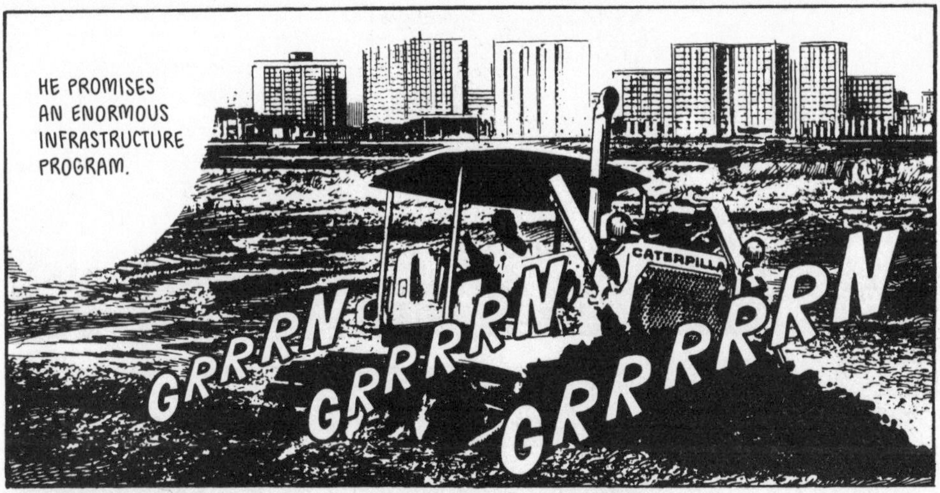
HE PROMISES AN ENORMOUS INFRASTRUCTURE PROGRAM.
CATERPILLA
GRRRN
GRRRRN
GRRRRRN

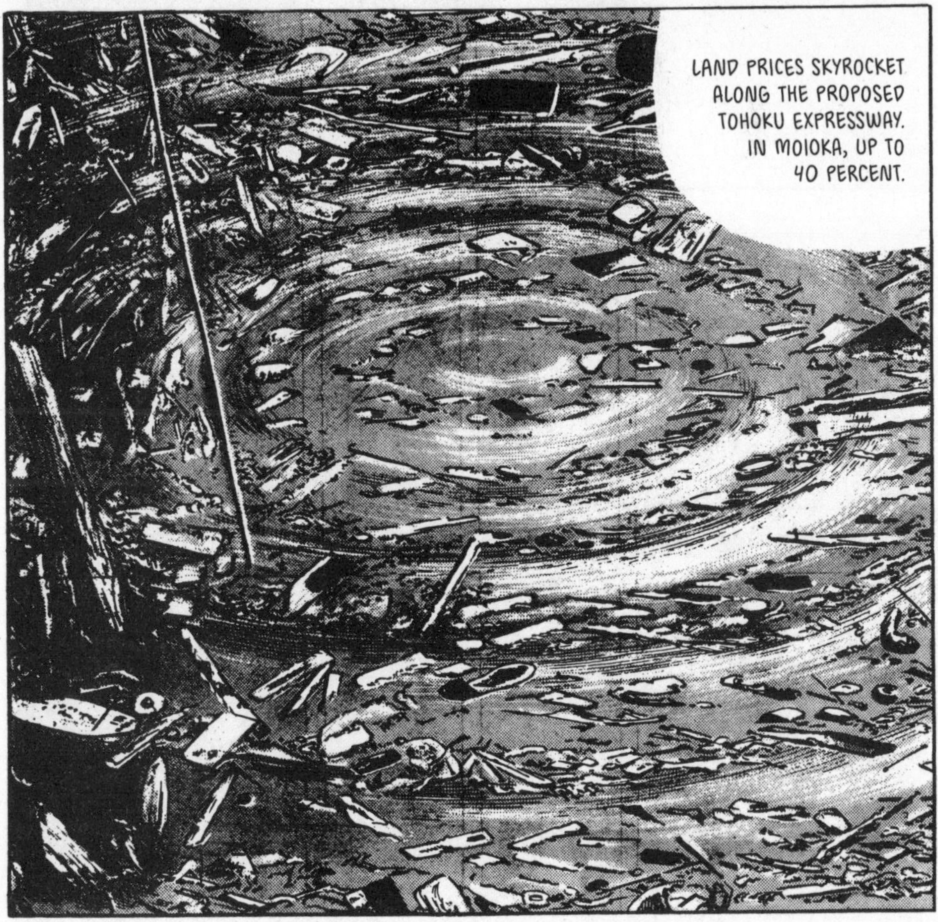
LAND PRICES SKYROCKET ALONG THE PROPOSED TOHOKU EXPRESSWAY. IN MOIOKA, UP TO 40 PERCENT.

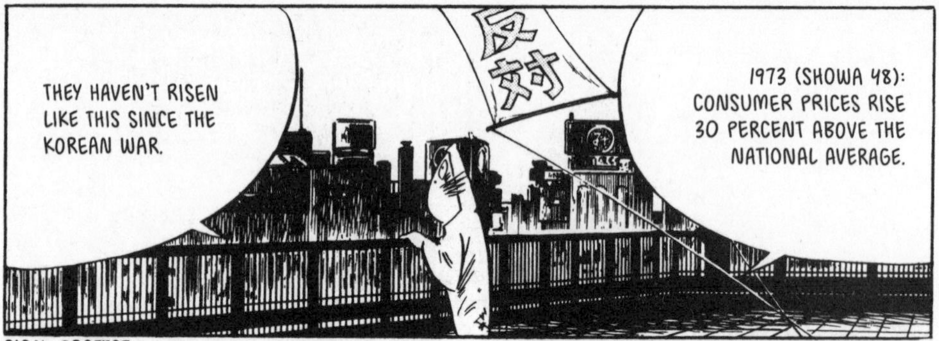
反対
1973 (SHOWA 48): CONSUMER PRICES RISE 30 PERCENT ABOVE THE NATIONAL AVERAGE.
THEY HAVEN'T RISEN LIKE THIS SINCE THE KOREAN WAR.
SIGN: PROTEST.

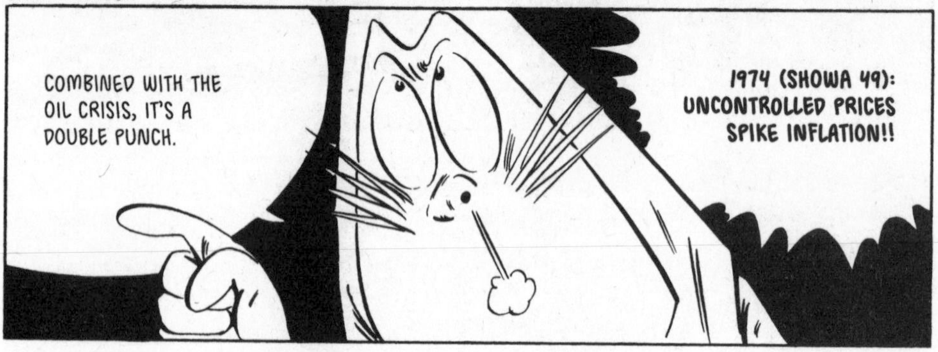
1974 (SHOWA 49): UNCONTROLLED PRICES SPIKE INFLATION!!
COMBINED WITH THE OIL CRISIS, IT'S A DOUBLE PUNCH.

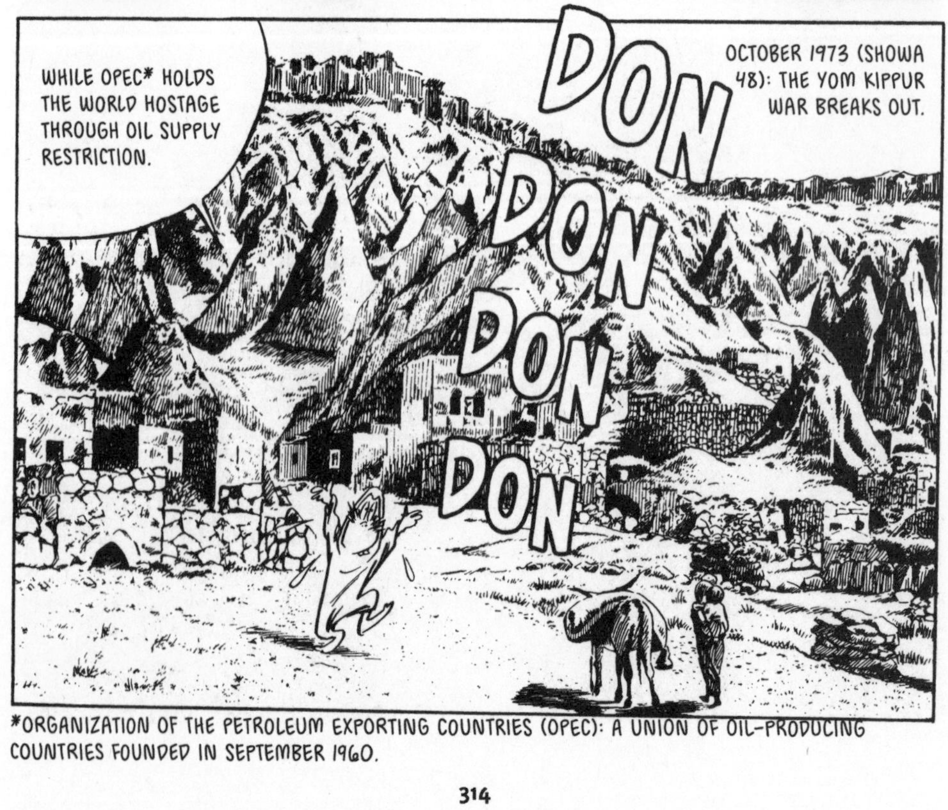
OCTOBER 1973 (SHOWA 48): THE YOM KIPPUR WAR BREAKS OUT.
DON DON DON DON DON
WHILE OPEC* HOLDS THE WORLD HOSTAGE THROUGH OIL SUPPLY RESTRICTION.
*ORGANIZATION OF THE PETROLEUM EXPORTING COUNTRIES (OPEC): A UNION OF OIL-PRODUCING COUNTRIES FOUNDED IN SEPTEMBER 1960.

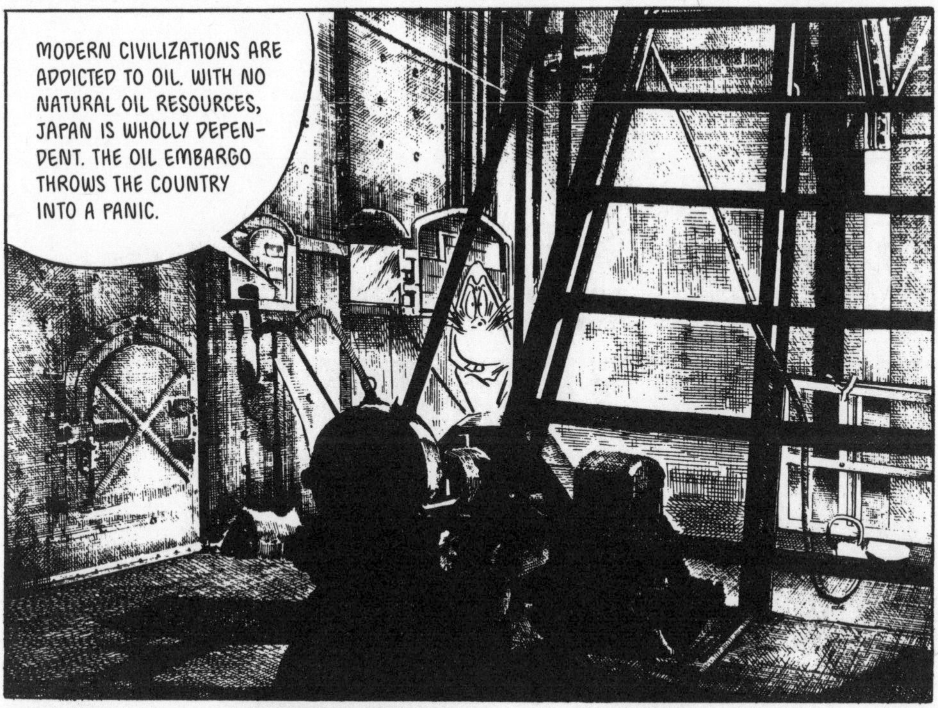
MODERN CIVILIZATIONS ARE ADDICTED TO OIL. WITH NO NATURAL OIL RESOURCES, JAPAN IS WHOLLY DEPENDENT. THE OIL EMBARGO THROWS THE COUNTRY INTO A PANIC.

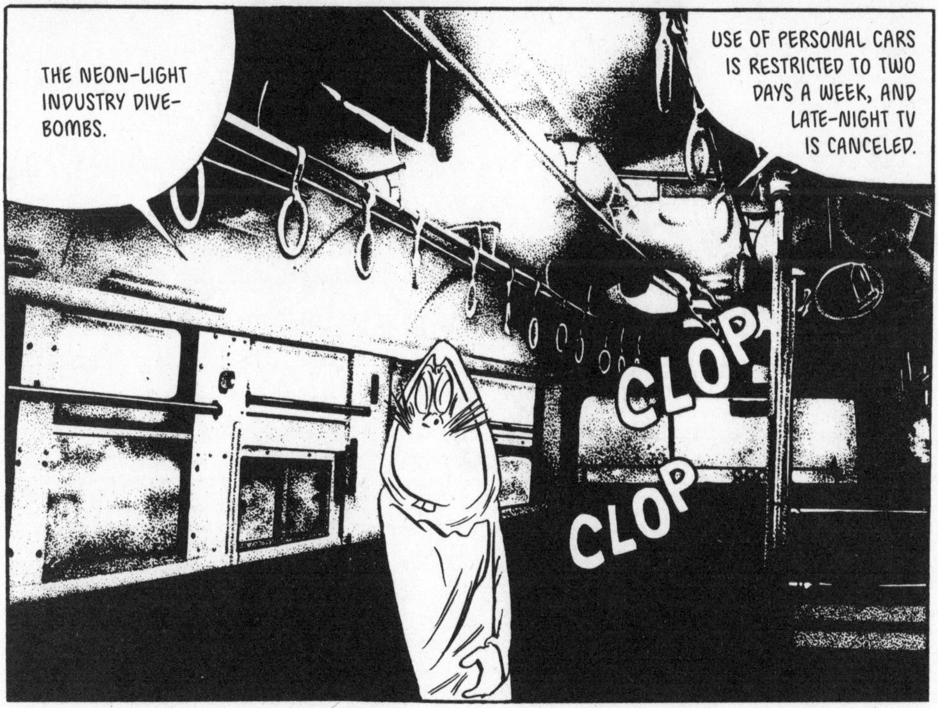
USE OF PERSONAL CARS IS RESTRICTED TO TWO DAYS A WEEK, AND LATE-NIGHT TV IS CANCELED.
THE NEON-LIGHT INDUSTRY DIVE-BOMBS.
CLOP
CLOP

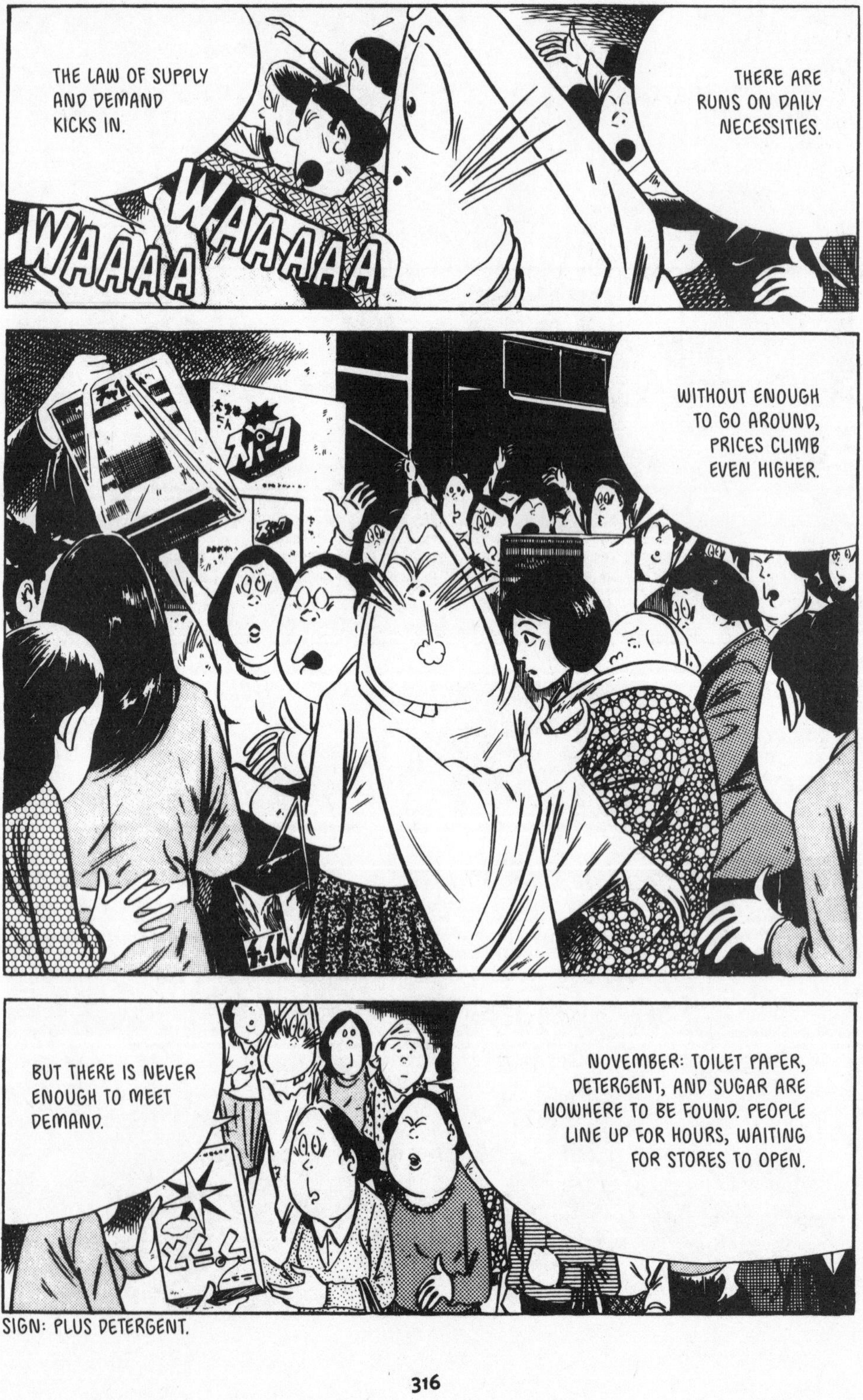
THERE ARE RUNS ON DAILY NECESSITIES.
THE LAW OF SUPPLY AND DEMAND KICKS IN.
WAAAAAA
WAAAAA
WITHOUT ENOUGH TO GO AROUND, PRICES CLIMB EVEN HIGHER.
NOVEMBER: TOILET PAPER, DETERGENT, AND SUGAR ARE NOWHERE TO BE FOUND. PEOPLE LINE UP FOR HOURS, WAITING FOR STORES TO OPEN.
BUT THERE IS NEVER ENOUGH TO MEET DEMAND.

SIGN: PLUS DETERGENT.

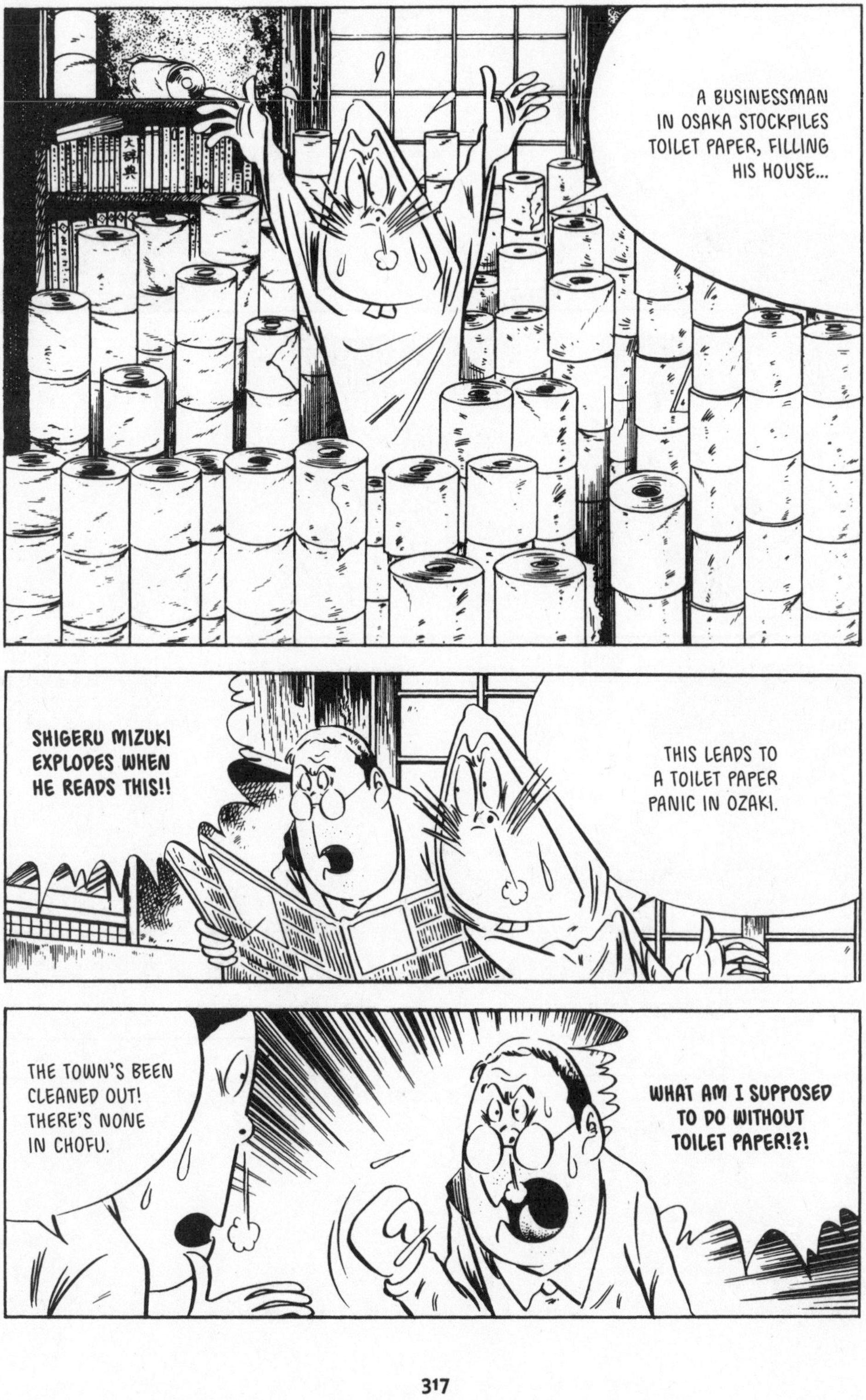
A BUSINESSMAN IN OSAKA STOCKPILES TOILET PAPER, FILLING HIS HOUSE...
THIS LEADS TO A TOILET PAPER PANIC IN OZAKI.
SHIGERU MIZUKI EXPLODES WHEN HE READS THIS!!
WHAT AM I SUPPOSED TO DO WITHOUT TOILET PAPER!?!
THE TOWN'S BEEN CLEANED OUT! THERE'S NONE IN CHOFU.

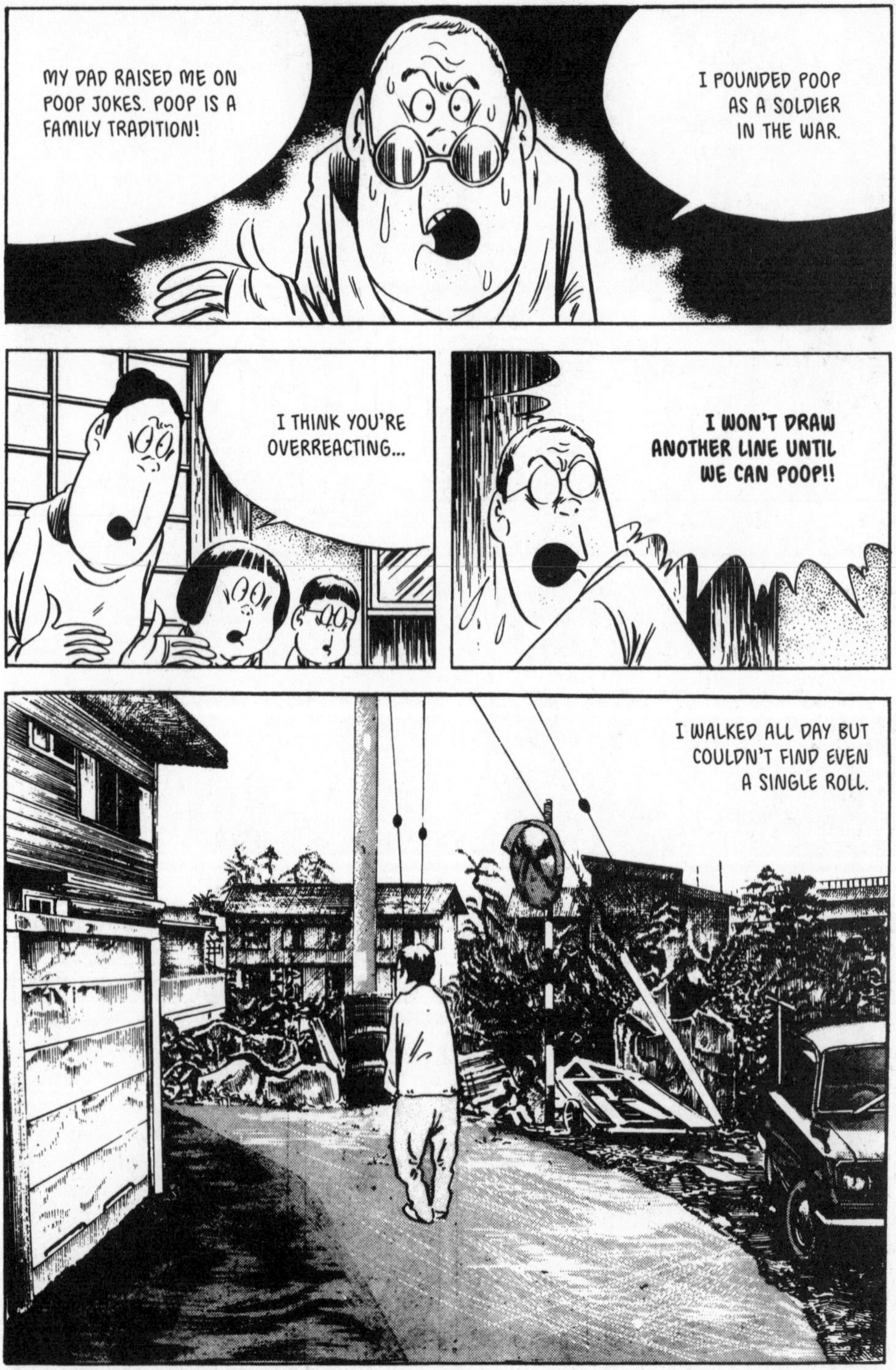
I POUNDED POOP AS A SOLDIER IN THE WAR.
MY DAD RAISED ME ON POOP JOKES. POOP IS A FAMILY TRADITION!
I WON'T DRAW ANOTHER LINE UNTIL WE CAN POOP!!
I THINK YOU'RE OVERREACTING...
I WALKED ALL DAY BUT COULDN'T FIND EVEN A SINGLE ROLL.

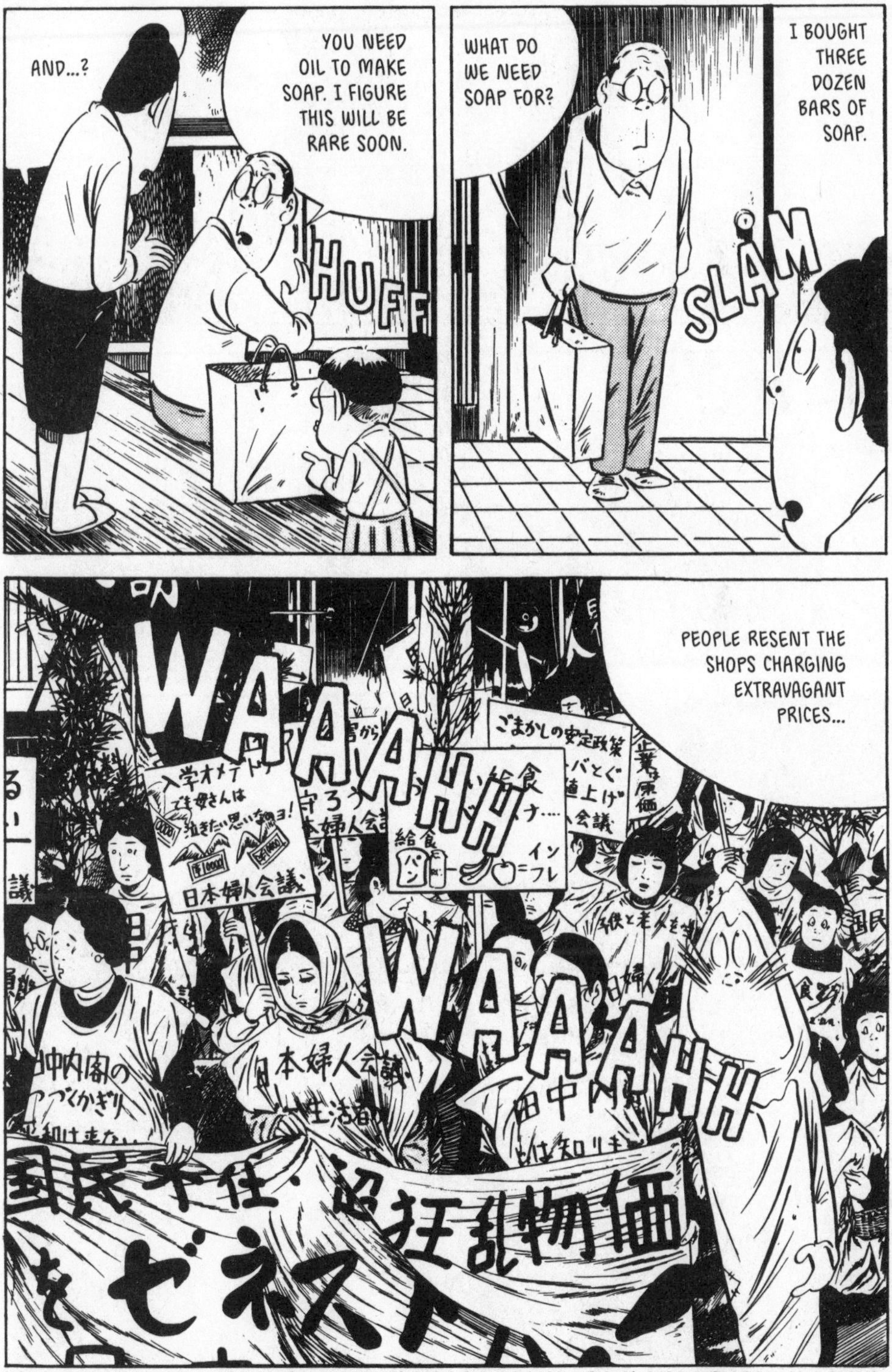
I BOUGHT THREE DOZEN BARS OF SOAP.
WHAT DO WE NEED SOAP FOR?
SLAM
YOU NEED OIL TO MAKE SOAP. I FIGURE THIS WILL BE RARE SOON.
AND...?
HUFF
PEOPLE RESENT THE SHOPS CHARGING EXTRAVAGANT PRICES...
WAAAHH
ごまかしの安定政策
入学オメデトウ でも母さんは 泣きたい思いなのヨ！
日本婦人会議
給食
パン
インフレ
WAAAAHH
日本婦人会議
田中内閣の
国民不在・超狂乱物価
をゼネスト

SIGNS: I WANT TO EAT GOOD SCHOOL LUNCHES! STOP FAKING HIGH PRICES! STOP INFLATION AND POLLUTION! CONGRATULATIONS ON GETTING INTO SCHOOL, BUT DON'T FORGET YOUR MOTHER! LET'S KEEP LIVING! JAPAN WOMEN'S COUNCIL. BLAME TANAKA'S CABINET. ZENEKON IS PRICE-FIXING!!

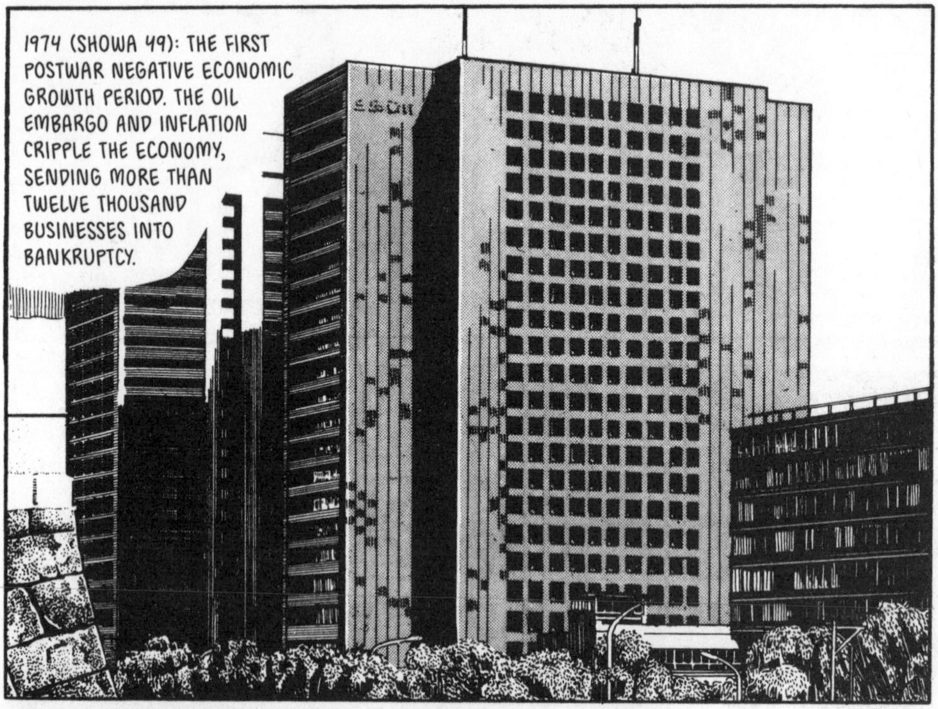
1974 (SHOWA 49): THE FIRST POSTWAR NEGATIVE ECONOMIC GROWTH PERIOD. THE OIL EMBARGO AND INFLATION CRIPPLE THE ECONOMY, SENDING MORE THAN TWELVE THOUSAND BUSINESSES INTO BANKRUPTCY.

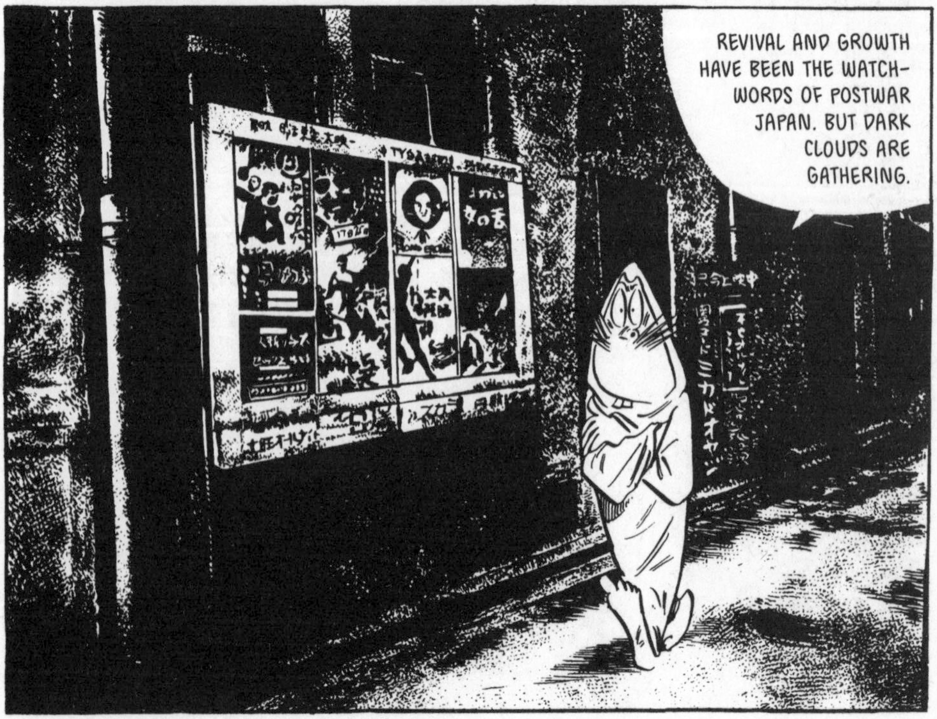
REVIVAL AND GROWTH HAVE BEEN THE WATCH-WORDS OF POSTWAR JAPAN. BUT DARK CLOUDS ARE GATHERING.

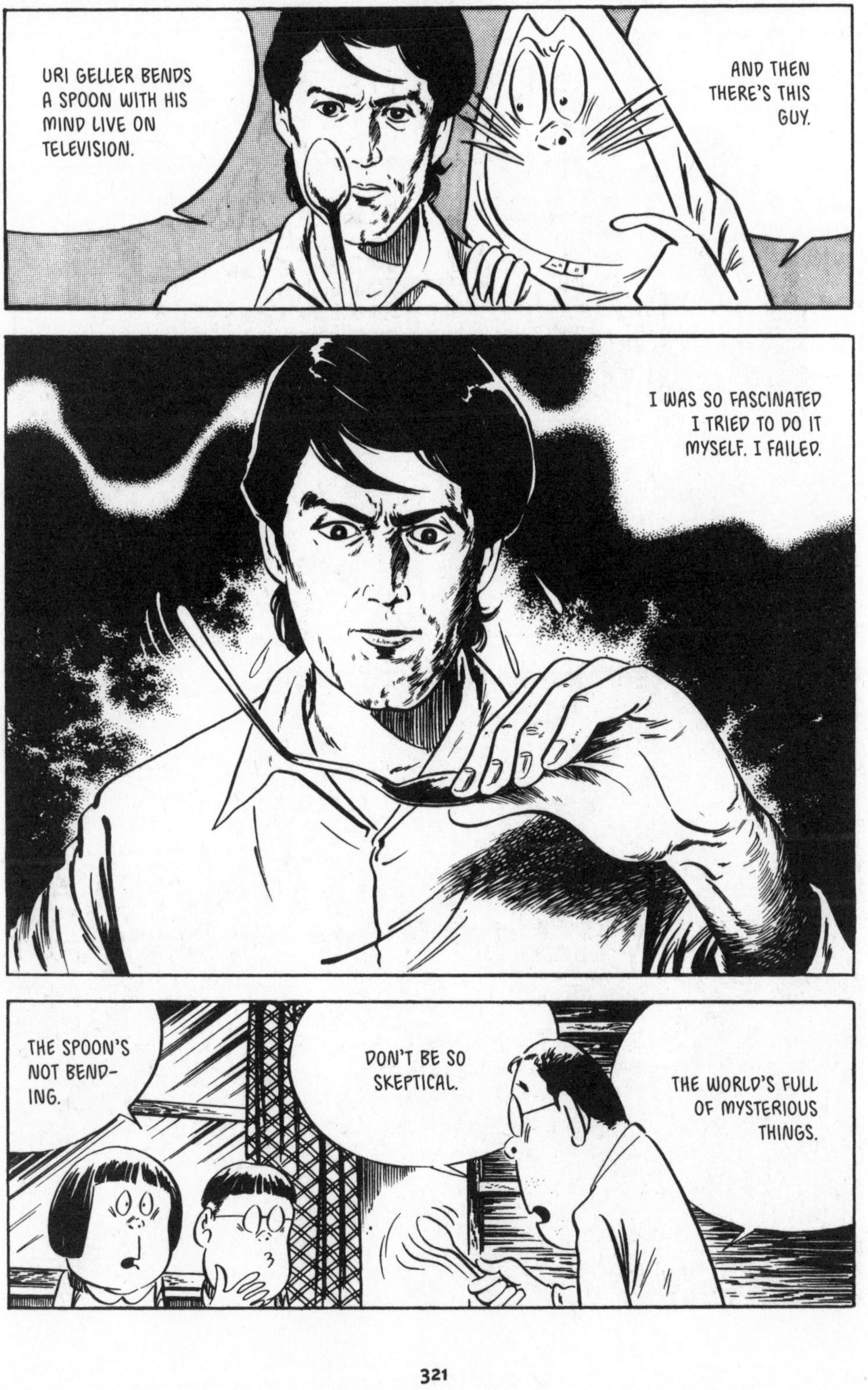
URI GELLER BENDS A SPOON WITH HIS MIND LIVE ON TELEVISION.
AND THEN THERE'S THIS GUY.
I WAS SO FASCINATED I TRIED TO DO IT MYSELF. I FAILED.
THE SPOON'S NOT BEND-ING.
DON'T BE SO SKEPTICAL.
THE WORLD'S FULL OF MYSTERIOUS THINGS.

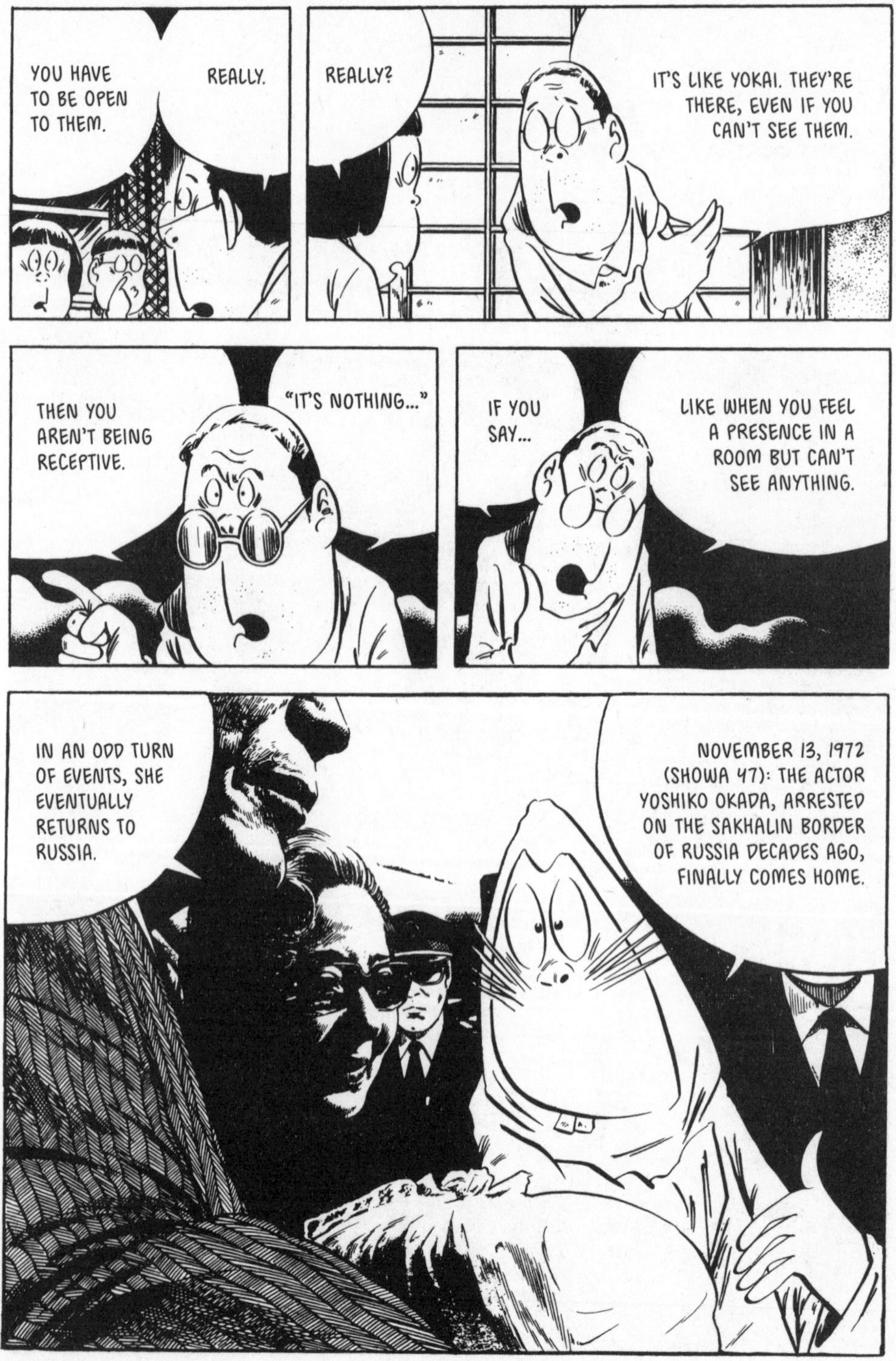
IT'S LIKE YOKAI. THEY'RE THERE, EVEN IF YOU CAN'T SEE THEM.
REALLY?
REALLY.
YOU HAVE TO BE OPEN TO THEM.
LIKE WHEN YOU FEEL A PRESENCE IN A ROOM BUT CAN'T SEE ANYTHING.
IF YOU SAY...
"IT'S NOTHING..."
THEN YOU AREN'T BEING RECEPTIVE.
NOVEMBER 13, 1972 (SHOWA 47): THE ACTOR YOSHIKO OKADA, ARRESTED ON THE SAKHALIN BORDER OF RUSSIA DECADES AGO, FINALLY COMES HOME.
IN AN ODD TURN OF EVENTS, SHE EVENTUALLY RETURNS TO RUSSIA.

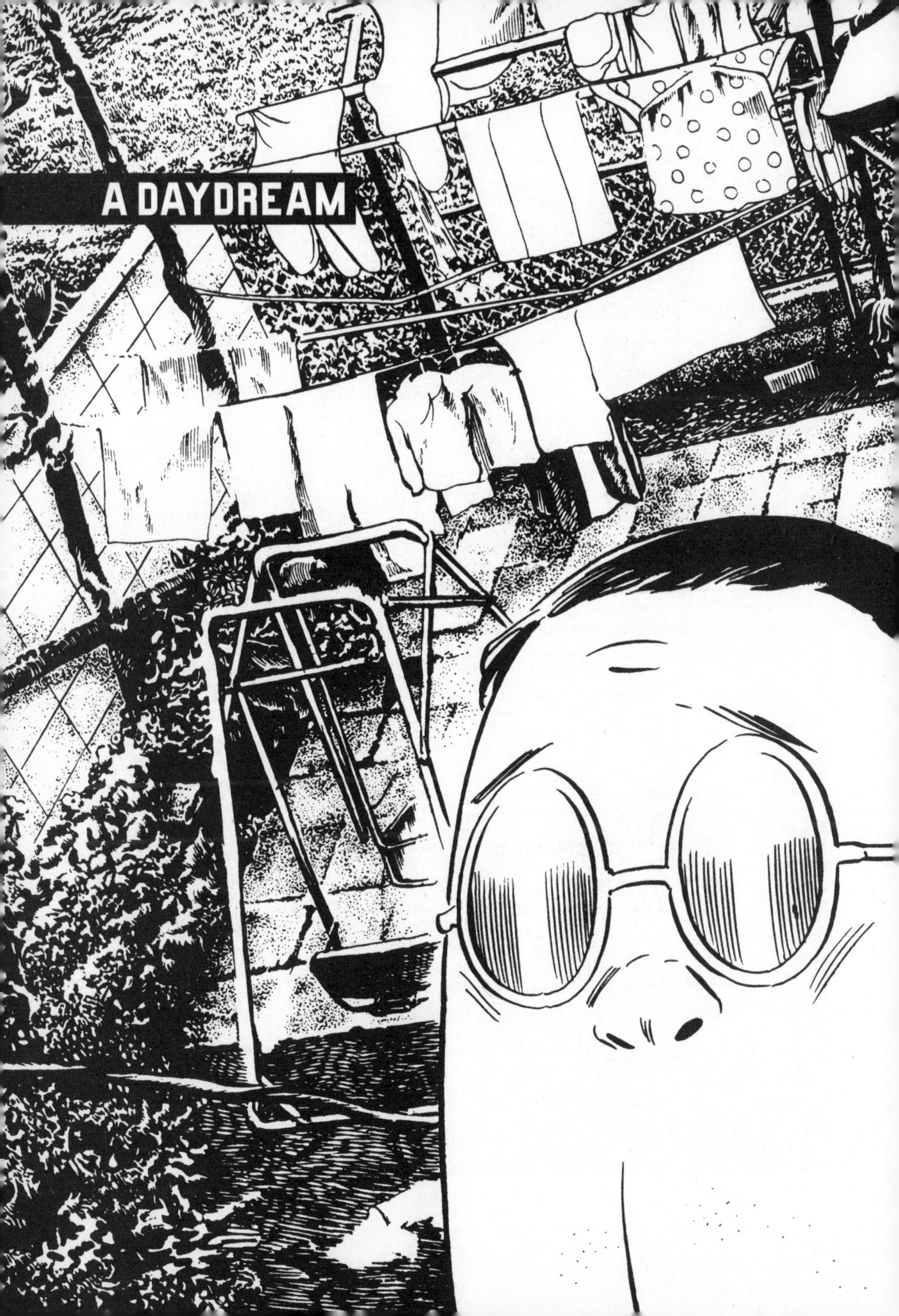
A DAYDREAM

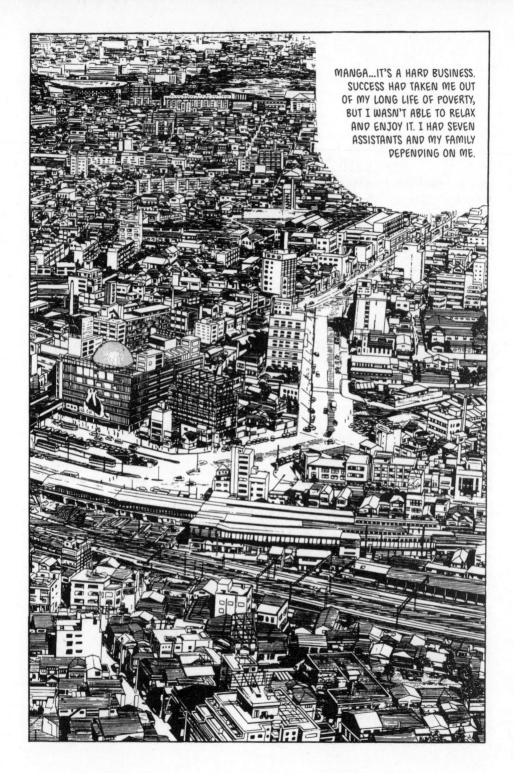

MANGA...IT'S A HARD BUSINESS. SUCCESS HAD TAKEN ME OUT OF MY LONG LIFE OF POVERTY, BUT I WASN'T ABLE TO RELAX AND ENJOY IT. I HAD SEVEN ASSISTANTS AND MY FAMILY DEPENDING ON ME.

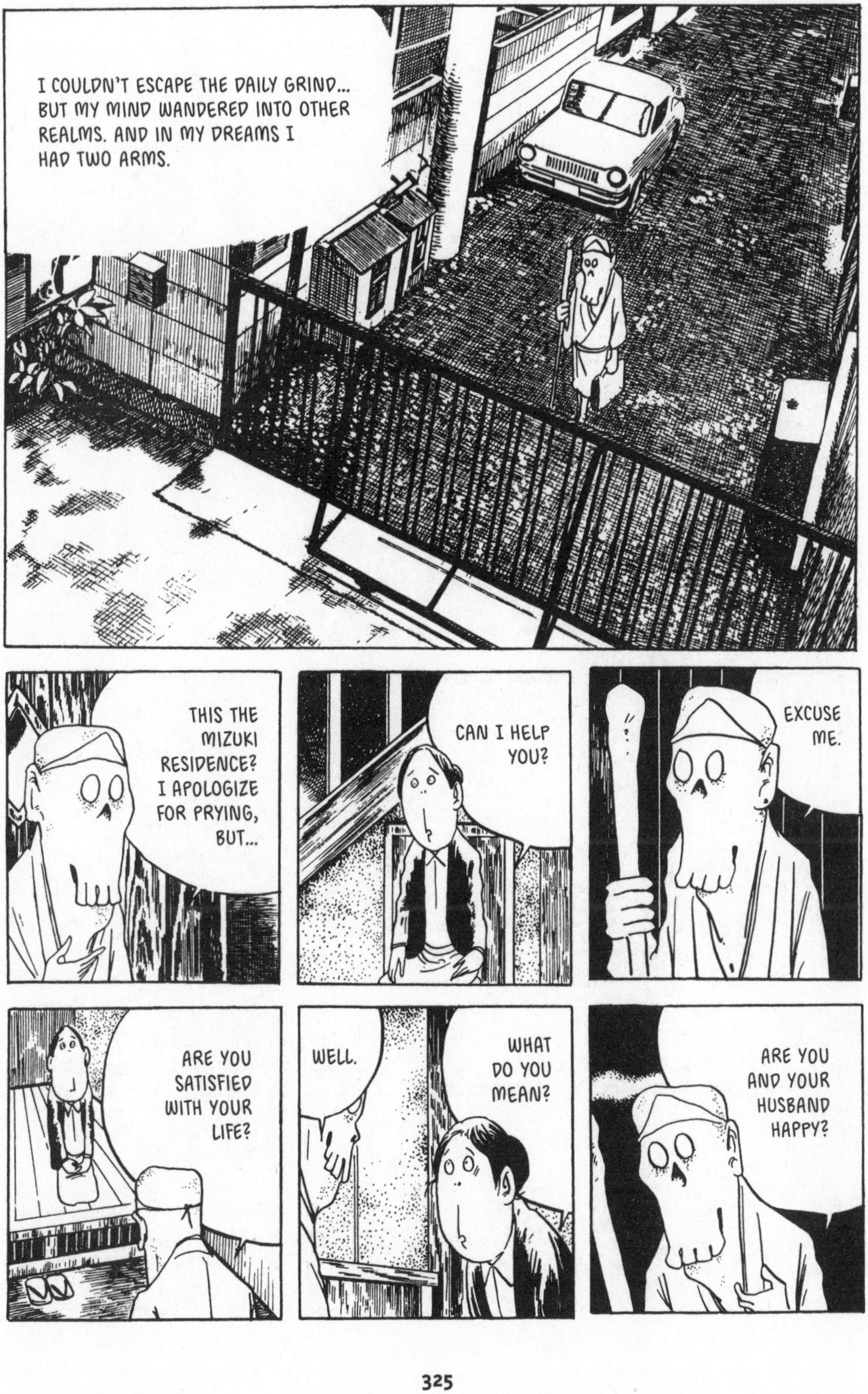
I COULDN'T ESCAPE THE DAILY GRIND... BUT MY MIND WANDERED INTO OTHER REALMS. AND IN MY DREAMS I HAD TWO ARMS.
EXCUSE ME.
CAN I HELP YOU?
THIS THE MIZUKI RESIDENCE? I APOLOGIZE FOR PRYING, BUT...
ARE YOU AND YOUR HUSBAND HAPPY?
WHAT DO YOU MEAN?
WELL.
ARE YOU SATISFIED WITH YOUR LIFE?

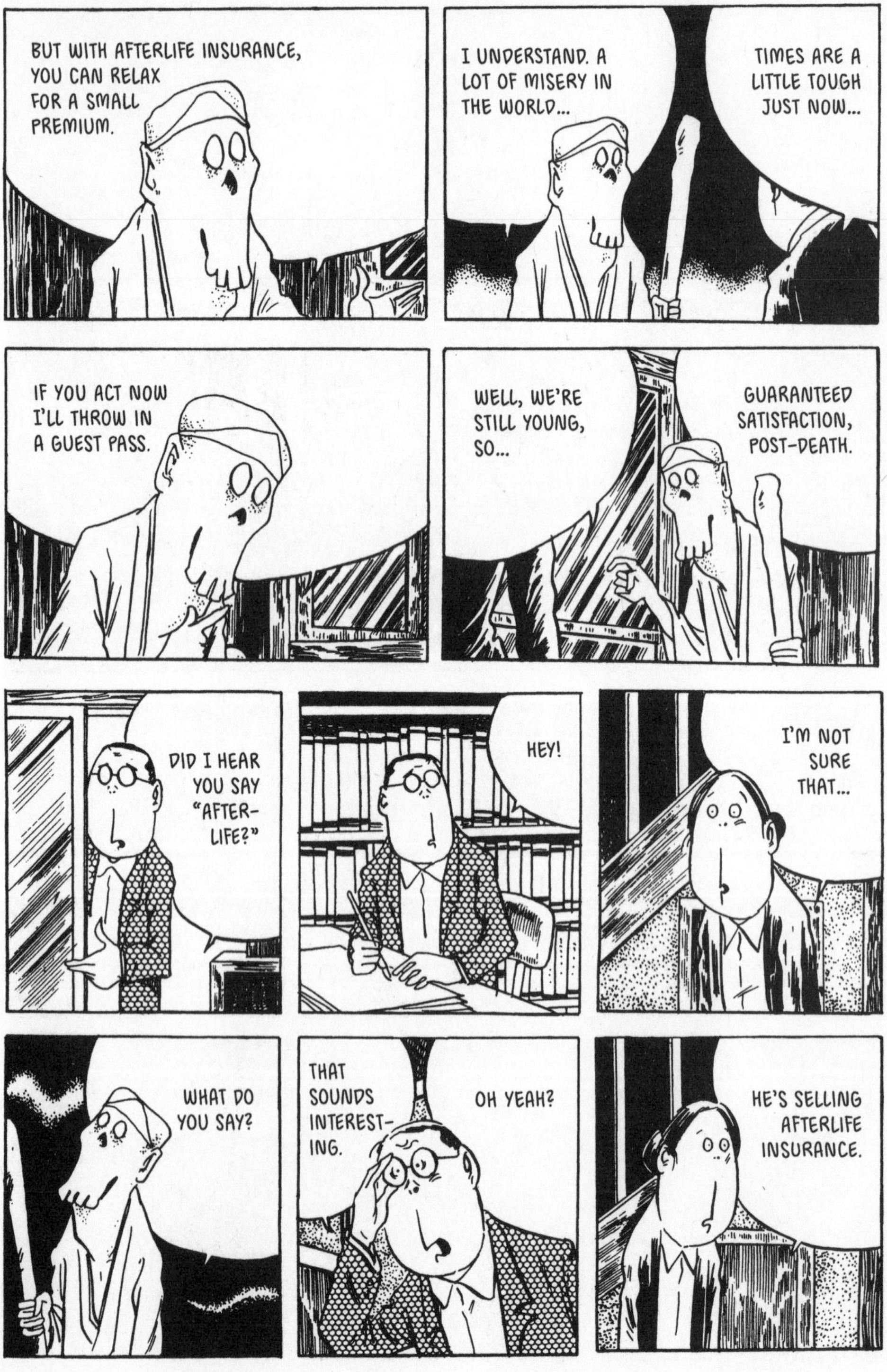
TIMES ARE A LITTLE TOUGH JUST NOW...
I UNDERSTAND. A LOT OF MISERY IN THE WORLD...
BUT WITH AFTERLIFE INSURANCE, YOU CAN RELAX FOR A SMALL PREMIUM.
GUARANTEED SATISFACTION, POST-DEATH.
WELL, WE'RE STILL YOUNG, SO...
IF YOU ACT NOW I'LL THROW IN A GUEST PASS.
I'M NOT SURE THAT...
HEY!
DID I HEAR YOU SAY "AFTER-LIFE?"
HE'S SELLING AFTERLIFE INSURANCE.
OH YEAH?
THAT SOUNDS INTEREST-ING.
WHAT DO YOU SAY?

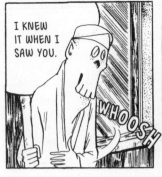

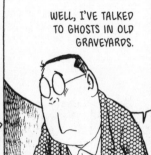

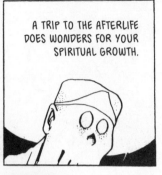

A TRIP TO THE AFTERLIFE DOES WONDERS FOR YOUR SPIRITUAL GROWTH.
WELL, I'VE TALKED TO GHOSTS IN OLD GRAVEYARDS.
I KNEW IT WHEN I SAW YOU.
WHOOSH
COME ON IN.
HEY! MAKE SOME COFFEE.
PEOPLE CRACK ME UP WHEN THEY TALK TO GRAVES.
MOST AREN'T PSYCHICALLY SENSITIVE ENOUGH TO HEAR THE ANSWERS.
I KNOW WHAT YOU MEAN.
SOMETIMES I FEEL LIKE THEY HAVEN'T QUITE EVOLVED.
LIVING ONLY IN THE PHYSICAL WORLD IS LIMITING.
EXACTLY...NOW THIS INSURANCE...
BUY NOW AND GET A SPECIAL GUEST PASS TO THE AFTERLIFE.
HOW MUCH MONEY ARE WE TALKING?
WE HAVE DIFFERENT PACKAGES.

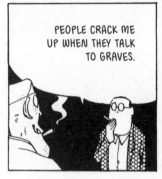

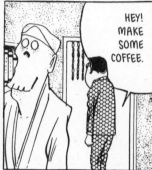

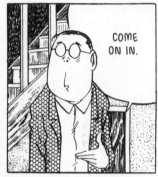

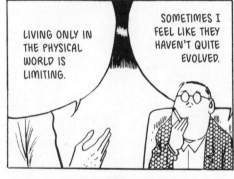

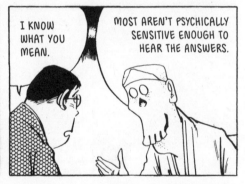

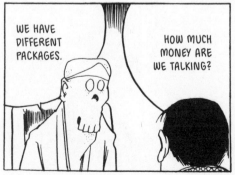

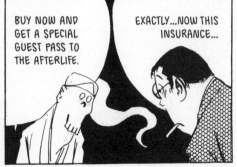

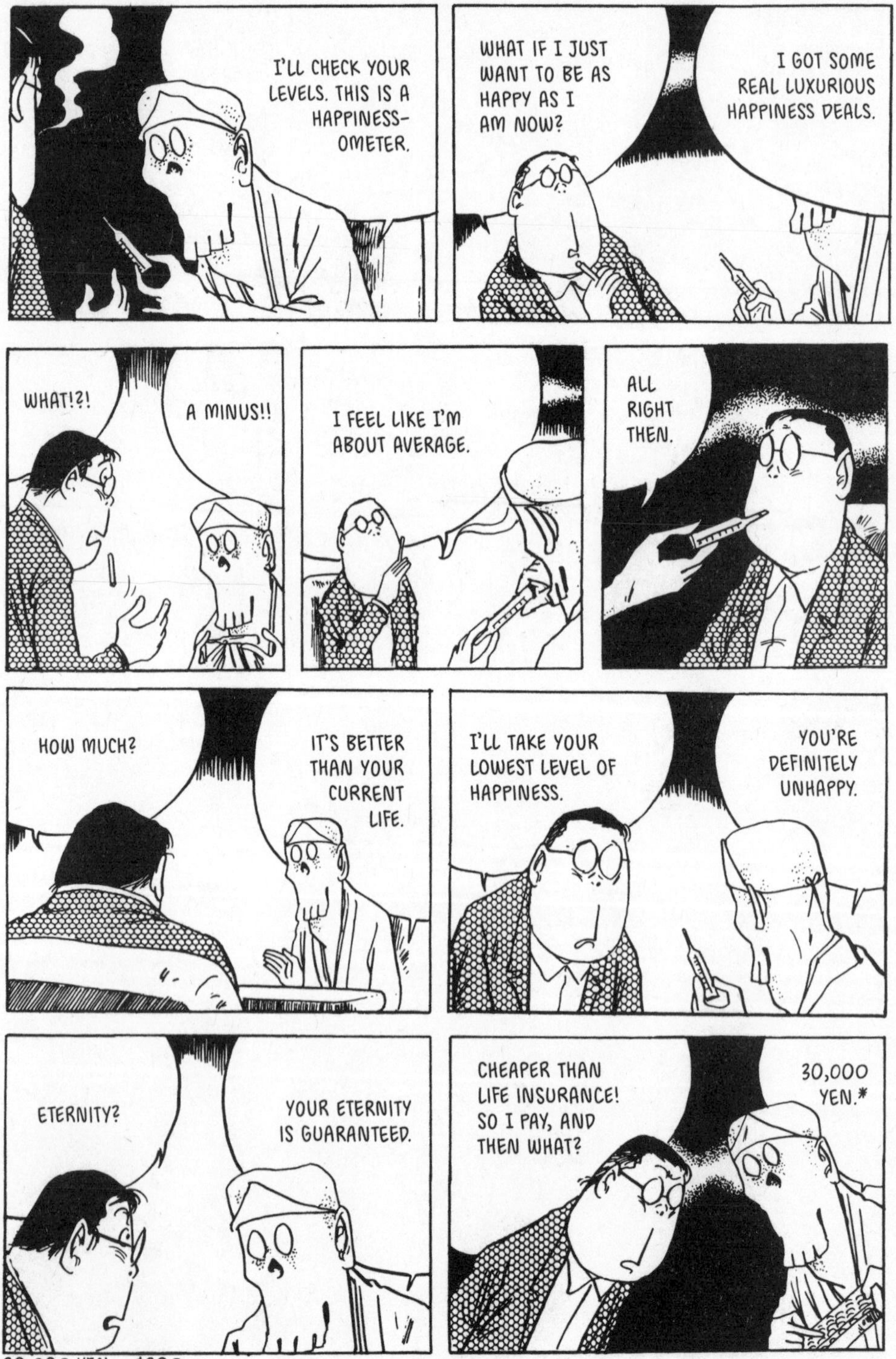
I GOT SOME REAL LUXURIOUS HAPPINESS DEALS.
WHAT IF I JUST WANT TO BE AS HAPPY AS I AM NOW?
I'LL CHECK YOUR LEVELS. THIS IS A HAPPINESS-OMETER.
ALL RIGHT THEN.
I FEEL LIKE I'M ABOUT AVERAGE.
A MINUS!!
WHAT!?!
YOU'RE DEFINITELY UNHAPPY.
I'LL TAKE YOUR LOWEST LEVEL OF HAPPINESS.
IT'S BETTER THAN YOUR CURRENT LIFE.
HOW MUCH?
30,000 YEN.*
CHEAPER THAN LIFE INSURANCE! SO I PAY, AND THEN WHAT?
YOUR ETERNITY IS GUARANTEED.
ETERNITY?

30,000 YEN = $300

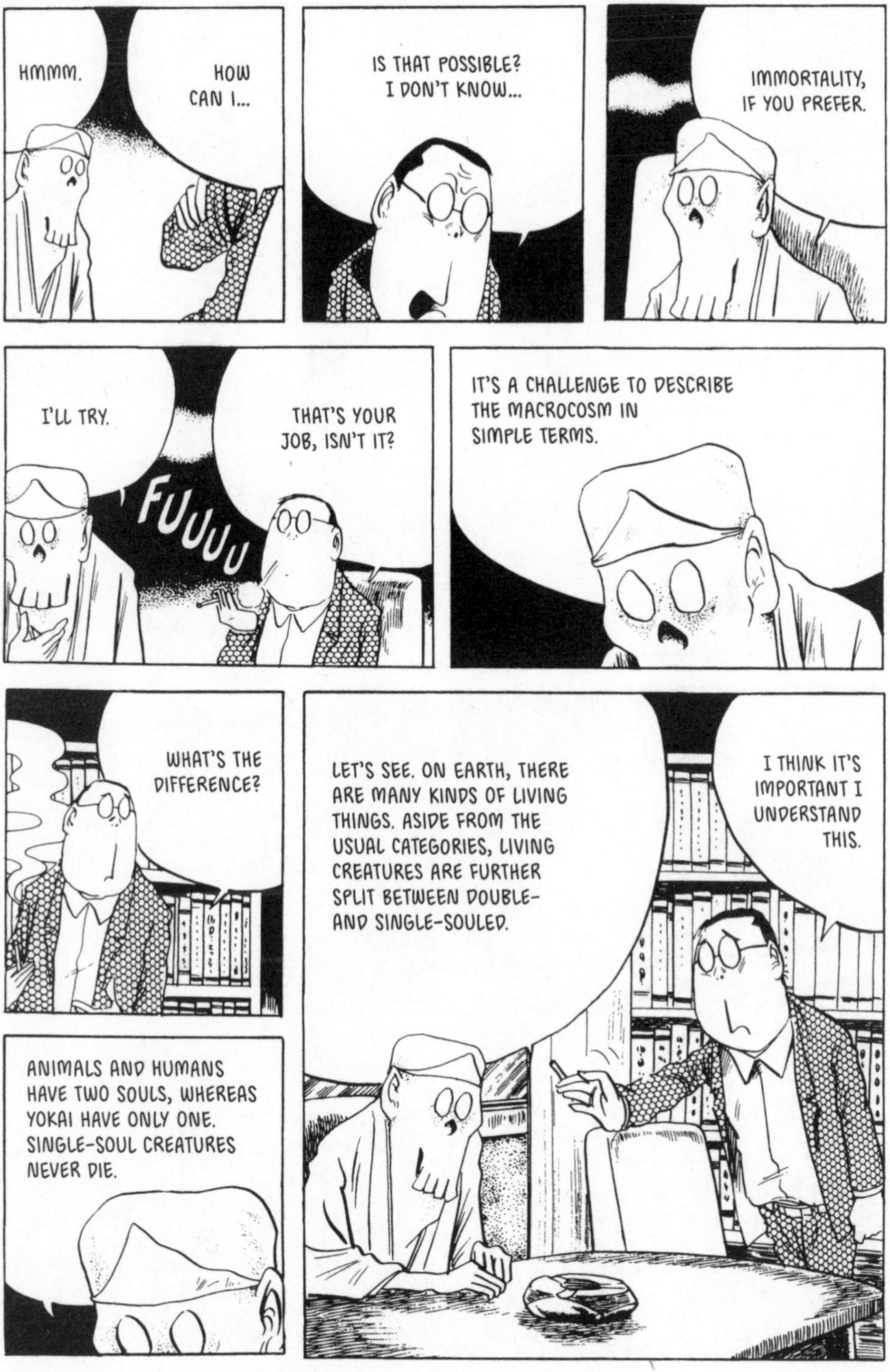
IMMORTALITY, IF YOU PREFER.
IS THAT POSSIBLE? I DON'T KNOW...
HOW CAN I...
HMMM.
IT'S A CHALLENGE TO DESCRIBE THE MACROCOSM IN SIMPLE TERMS.
THAT'S YOUR JOB, ISN'T IT?
I'LL TRY.
FUUUU
I THINK IT'S IMPORTANT I UNDERSTAND THIS.
LET'S SEE. ON EARTH, THERE ARE MANY KINDS OF LIVING THINGS. ASIDE FROM THE USUAL CATEGORIES, LIVING CREATURES ARE FURTHER SPLIT BETWEEN DOUBLE- AND SINGLE-SOULED.
WHAT'S THE DIFFERENCE?
ANIMALS AND HUMANS HAVE TWO SOULS, WHEREAS YOKAI HAVE ONLY ONE. SINGLE-SOUL CREATURES NEVER DIE.

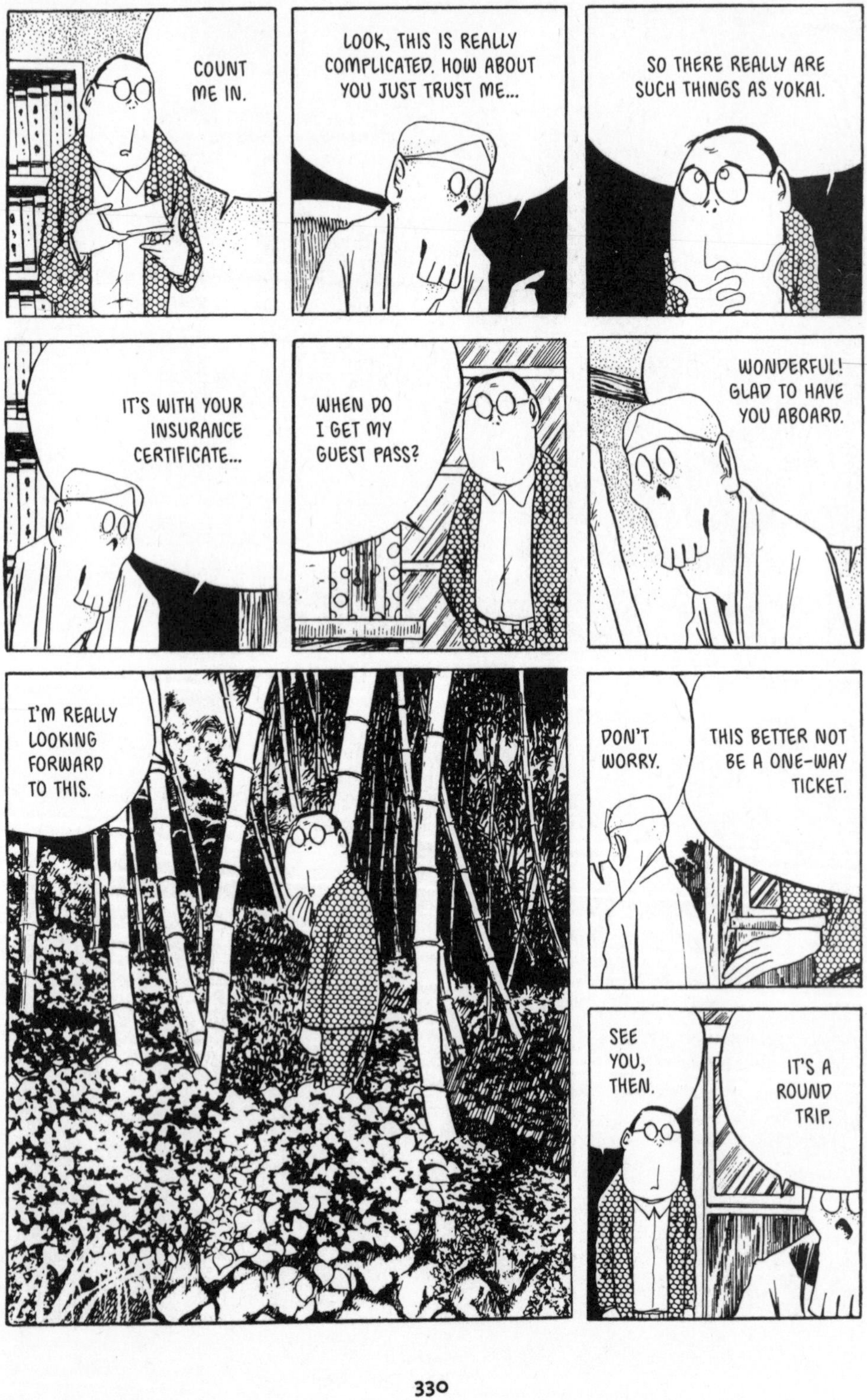
SO THERE REALLY ARE SUCH THINGS AS YOKAI.
LOOK, THIS IS REALLY COMPLICATED. HOW ABOUT YOU JUST TRUST ME...
COUNT ME IN.
WONDERFUL! GLAD TO HAVE YOU ABOARD.
WHEN DO I GET MY GUEST PASS?
IT'S WITH YOUR INSURANCE CERTIFICATE...
THIS BETTER NOT BE A ONE-WAY TICKET.
DON'T WORRY.
IT'S A ROUND TRIP.
SEE YOU, THEN.
I'M REALLY LOOKING FORWARD TO THIS.

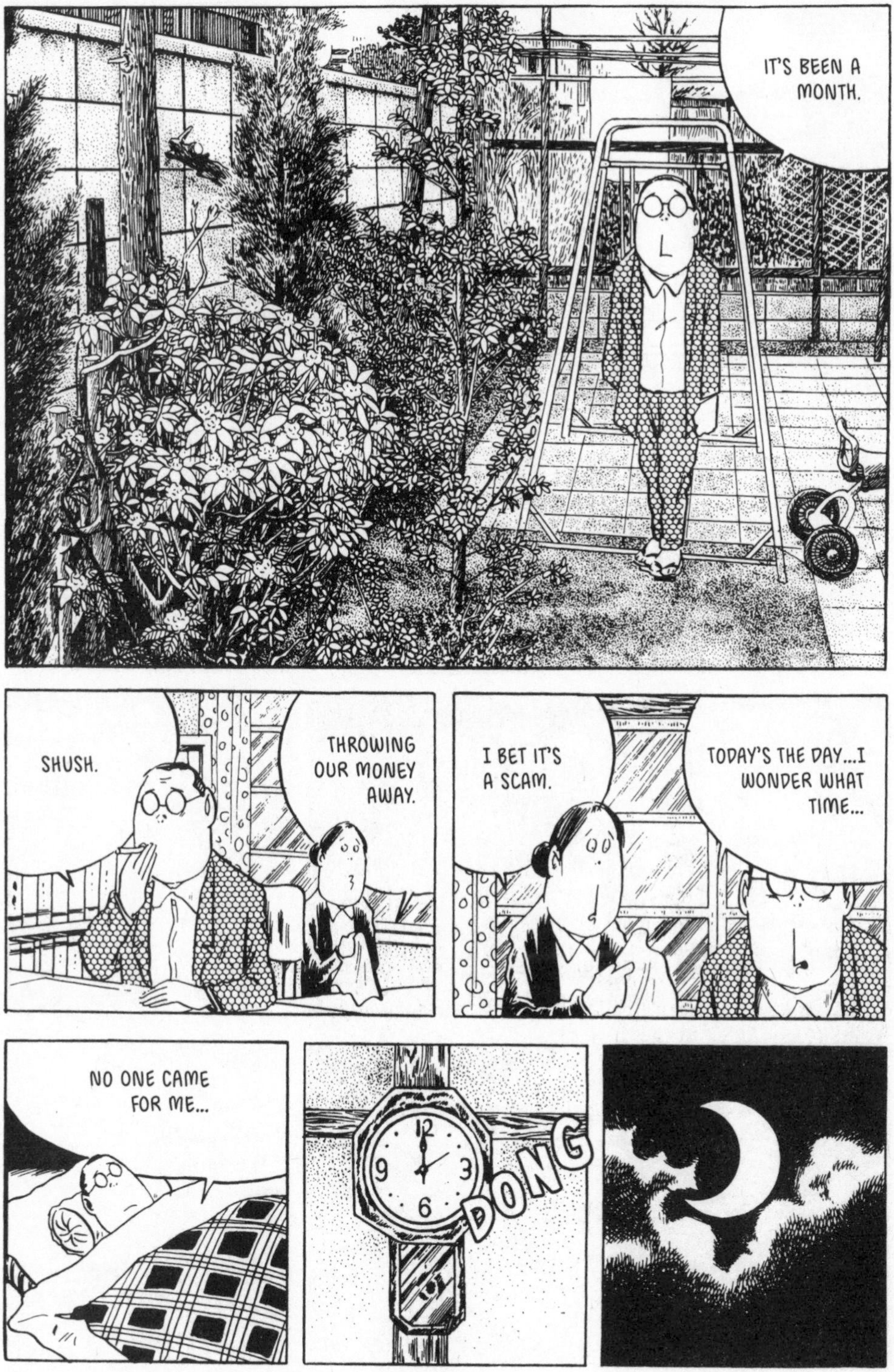
IT'S BEEN A MONTH.
TODAY'S THE DAY...I WONDER WHAT TIME...
I BET IT'S A SCAM.
THROWING OUR MONEY AWAY.
SHUSH.
DONG
NO ONE CAME FOR ME...

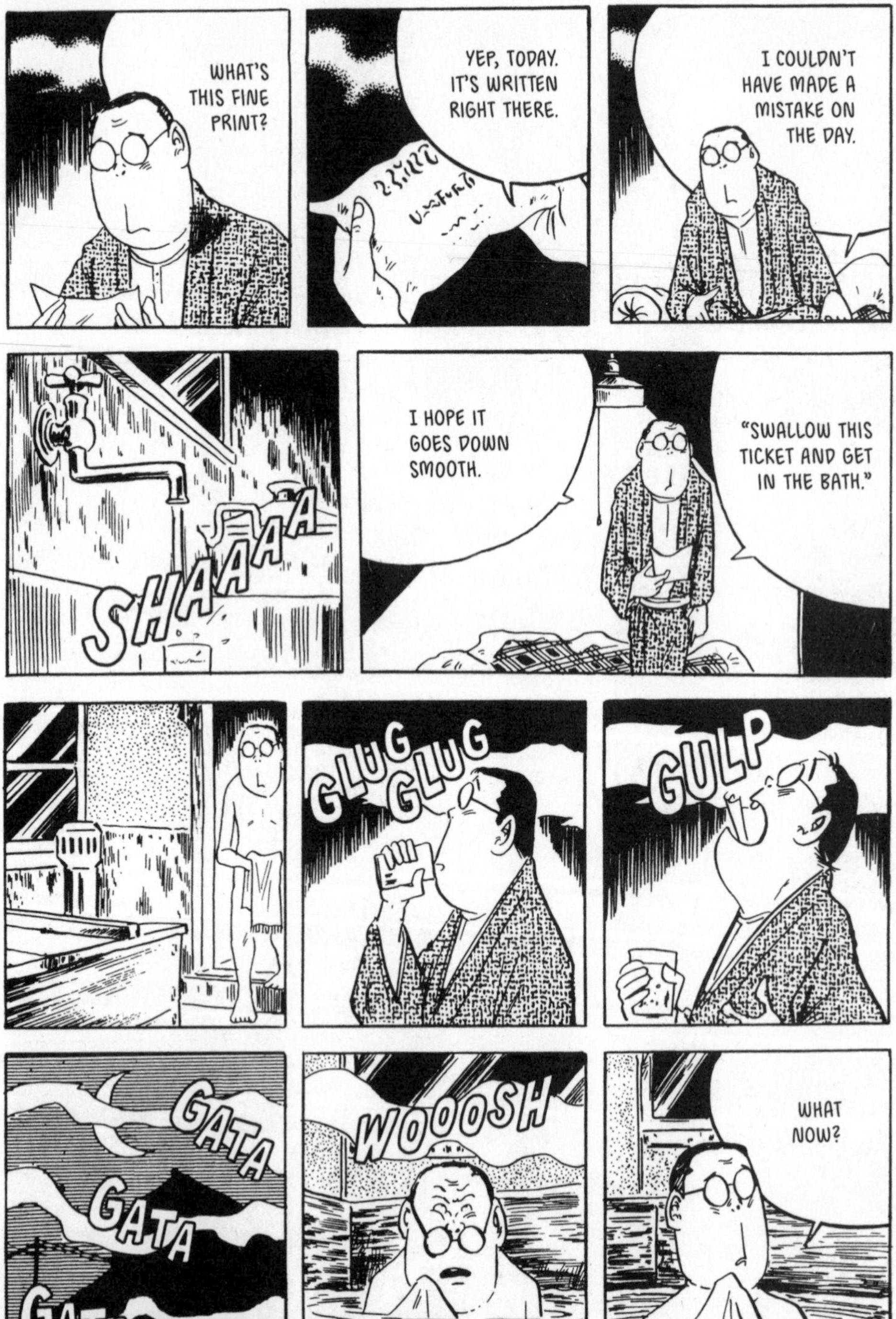
I COULDN'T HAVE MADE A MISTAKE ON THE DAY.
YEP, TODAY. IT'S WRITTEN RIGHT THERE.
WHAT'S THIS FINE PRINT?
"SWALLOW THIS TICKET AND GET IN THE BATH."
I HOPE IT GOES DOWN SMOOTH.
SHAAAAA
GULP
GLUG GLUG
WHAT NOW?
WOOOSH
GATA
GATA
GATA

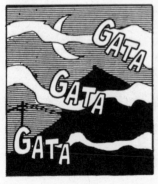

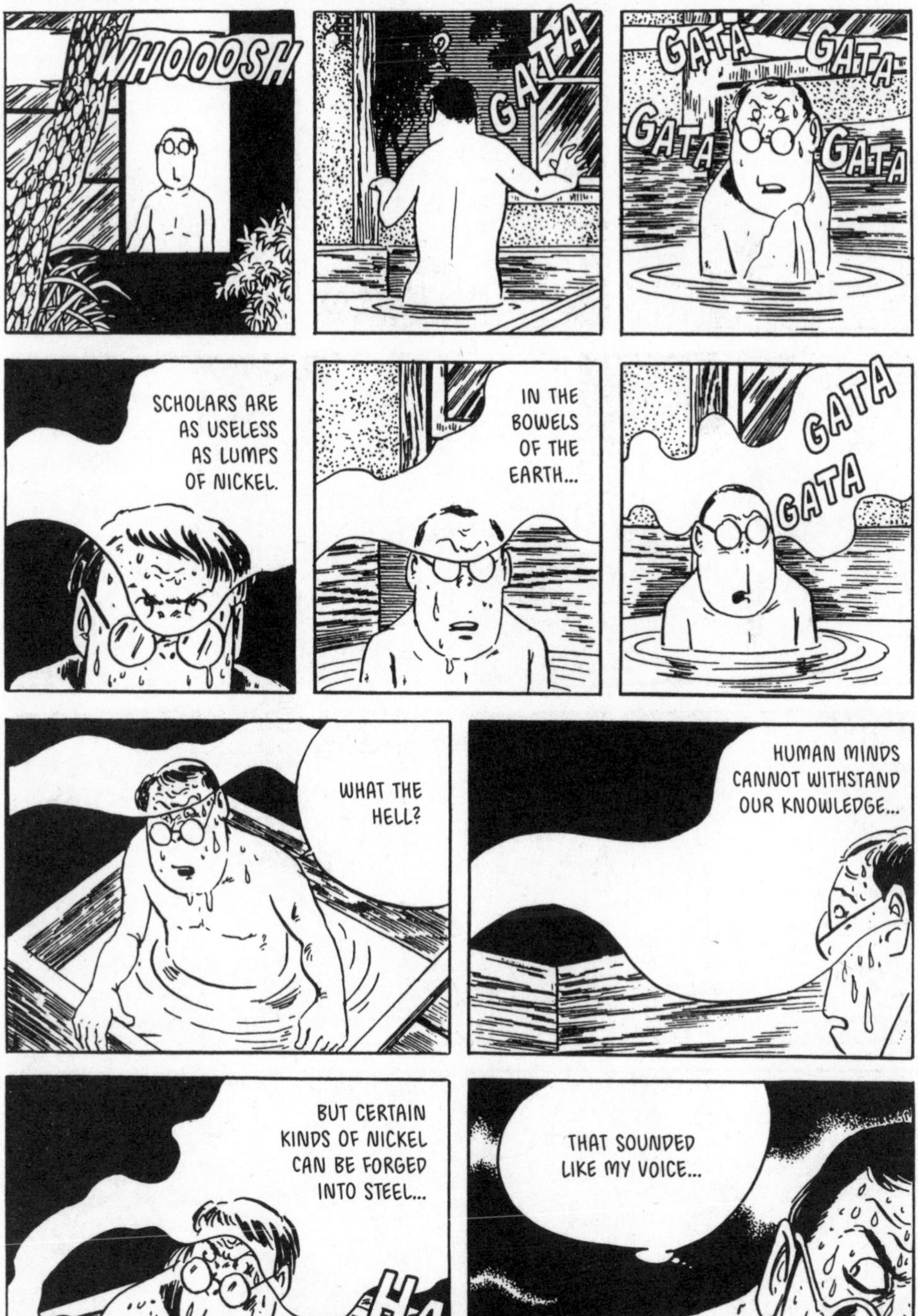
GATA
GATA
GATA
GATA
?
GATA
WHOOOSH
GATA
GATA
IN THE BOWELS OF THE EARTH...
SCHOLARS ARE AS USELESS AS LUMPS OF NICKEL.
HUMAN MINDS CANNOT WITHSTAND OUR KNOWLEDGE...
WHAT THE HELL?
THAT SOUNDED LIKE MY VOICE...
BUT CERTAIN KINDS OF NICKEL CAN BE FORGED INTO STEEL...
HA
HA

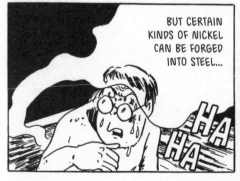

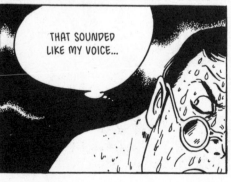

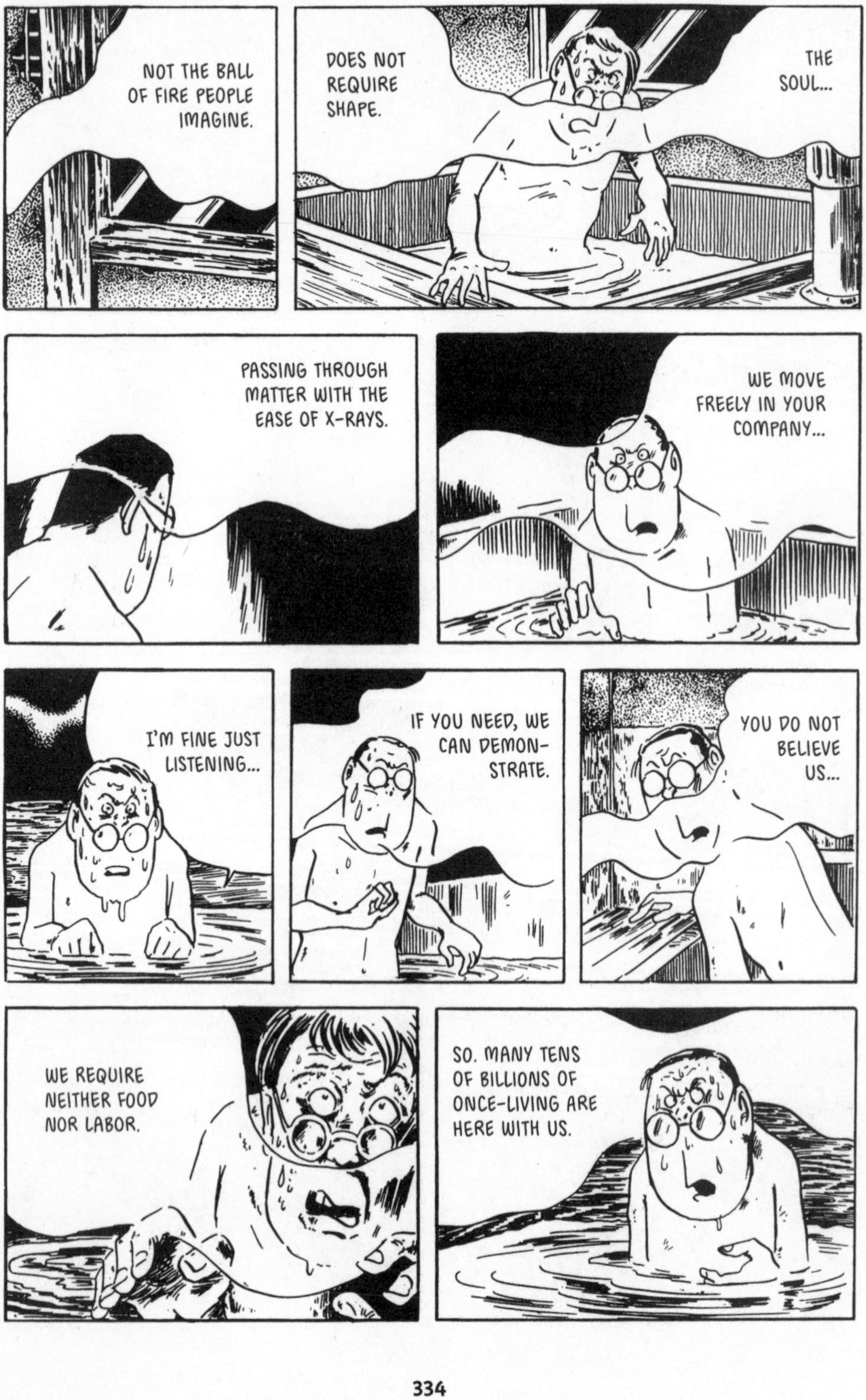
THE SOUL...
DOES NOT REQUIRE SHAPE.
NOT THE BALL OF FIRE PEOPLE IMAGINE.
WE MOVE FREELY IN YOUR COMPANY...
PASSING THROUGH MATTER WITH THE EASE OF X-RAYS.
YOU DO NOT BELIEVE US...
IF YOU NEED, WE CAN DEMON-STRATE.
I'M FINE JUST LISTENING...
SO. MANY TENS OF BILLIONS OF ONCE-LIVING ARE HERE WITH US.
WE REQUIRE NEITHER FOOD NOR LABOR.

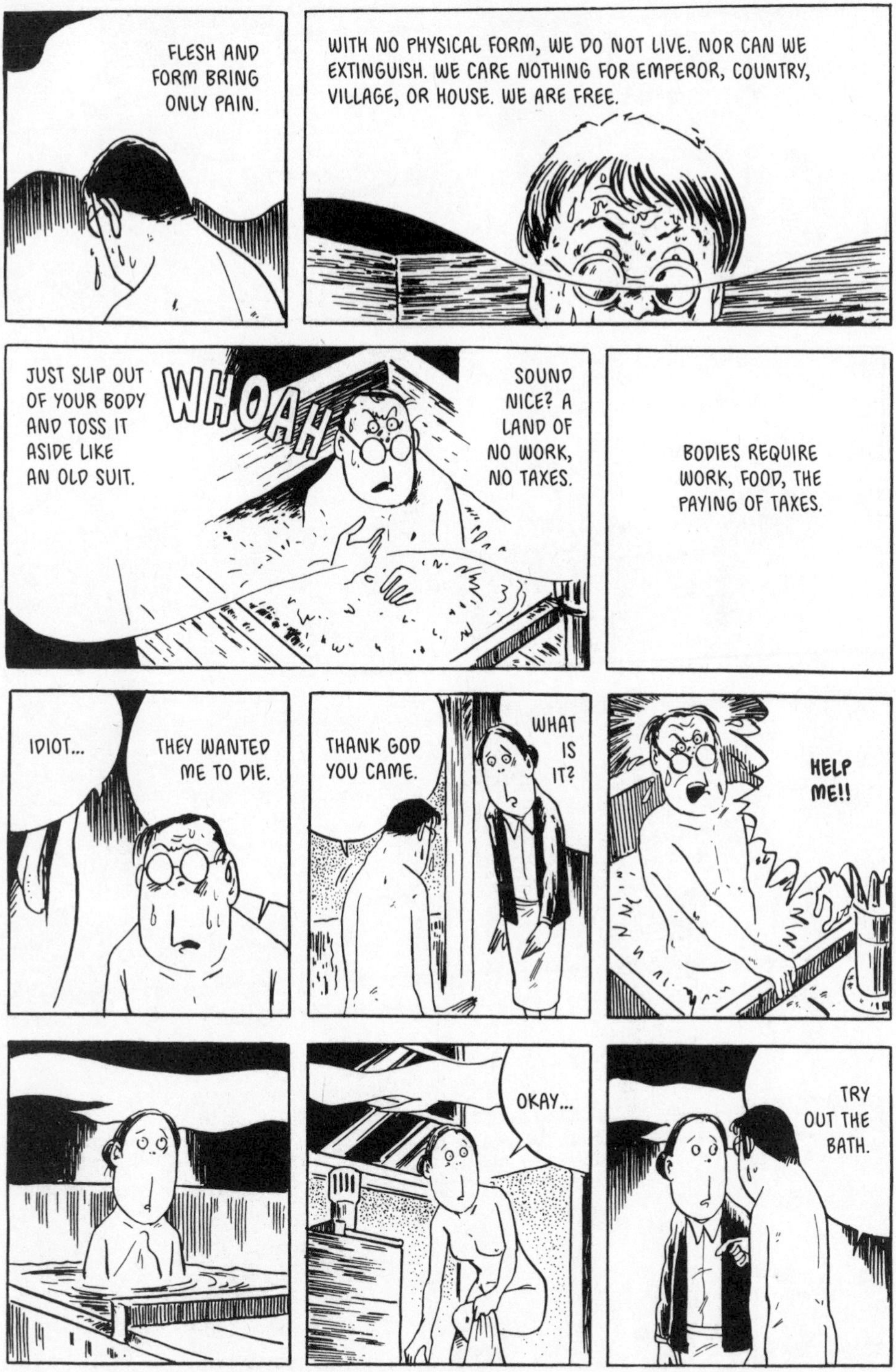
WITH NO PHYSICAL FORM, WE DO NOT LIVE. NOR CAN WE EXTINGUISH. WE CARE NOTHING FOR EMPEROR, COUNTRY, VILLAGE, OR HOUSE. WE ARE FREE.
FLESH AND FORM BRING ONLY PAIN.
BODIES REQUIRE WORK, FOOD, THE PAYING OF TAXES.
SOUND NICE? A LAND OF NO WORK, NO TAXES.
WHOAH
JUST SLIP OUT OF YOUR BODY AND TOSS IT ASIDE LIKE AN OLD SUIT.
HELP ME!!
WHAT IS IT?
THANK GOD YOU CAME.
THEY WANTED ME TO DIE.
IDIOT...
TRY OUT THE BATH.
OKAY...

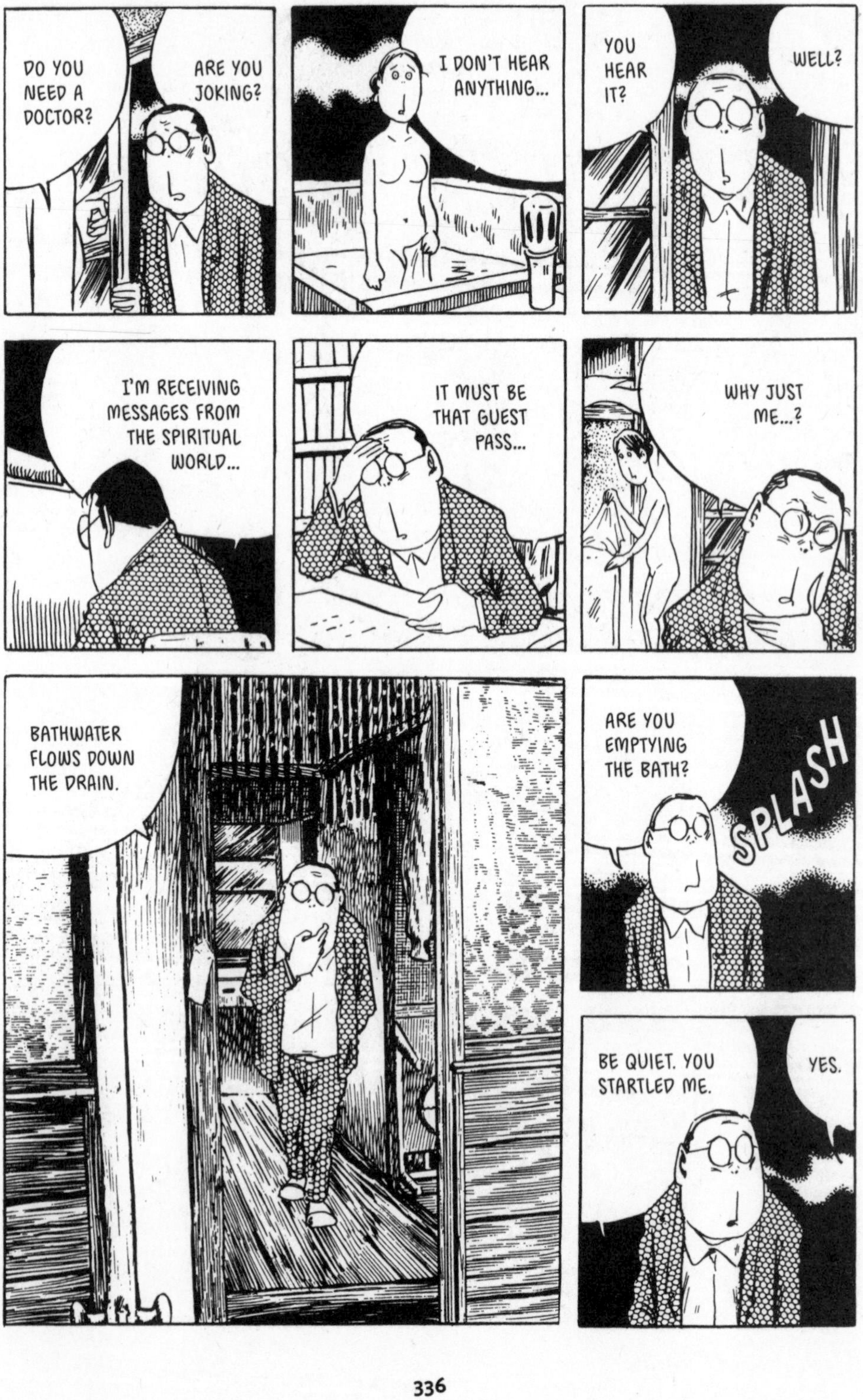
WELL?
YOU HEAR IT?
I DON'T HEAR ANYTHING...
ARE YOU JOKING?
DO YOU NEED A DOCTOR?
WHY JUST ME...?
IT MUST BE THAT GUEST PASS...
I'M RECEIVING MESSAGES FROM THE SPIRITUAL WORLD...
ARE YOU EMPTYING THE BATH?
SPLASH
YES.
BE QUIET. YOU STARTLED ME.
BATHWATER FLOWS DOWN THE DRAIN.

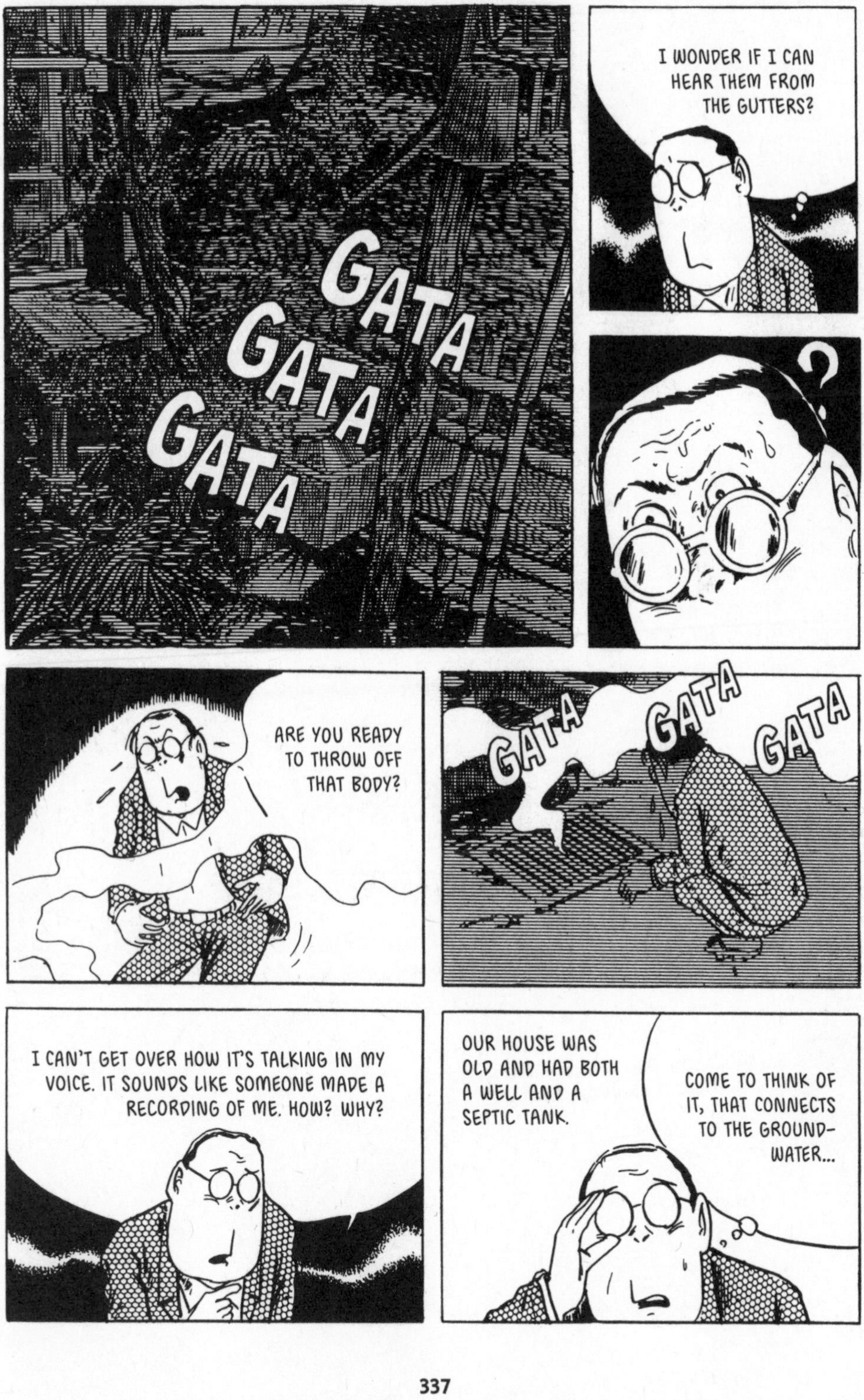
I WONDER IF I CAN HEAR THEM FROM THE GUTTERS?
?
GATA GATA GATA
GATA GATA GATA
ARE YOU READY TO THROW OFF THAT BODY?
OUR HOUSE WAS OLD AND HAD BOTH A WELL AND A SEPTIC TANK.
COME TO THINK OF IT, THAT CONNECTS TO THE GROUND-WATER...
I CAN'T GET OVER HOW IT'S TALKING IN MY VOICE. IT SOUNDS LIKE SOMEONE MADE A RECORDING OF ME. HOW? WHY?

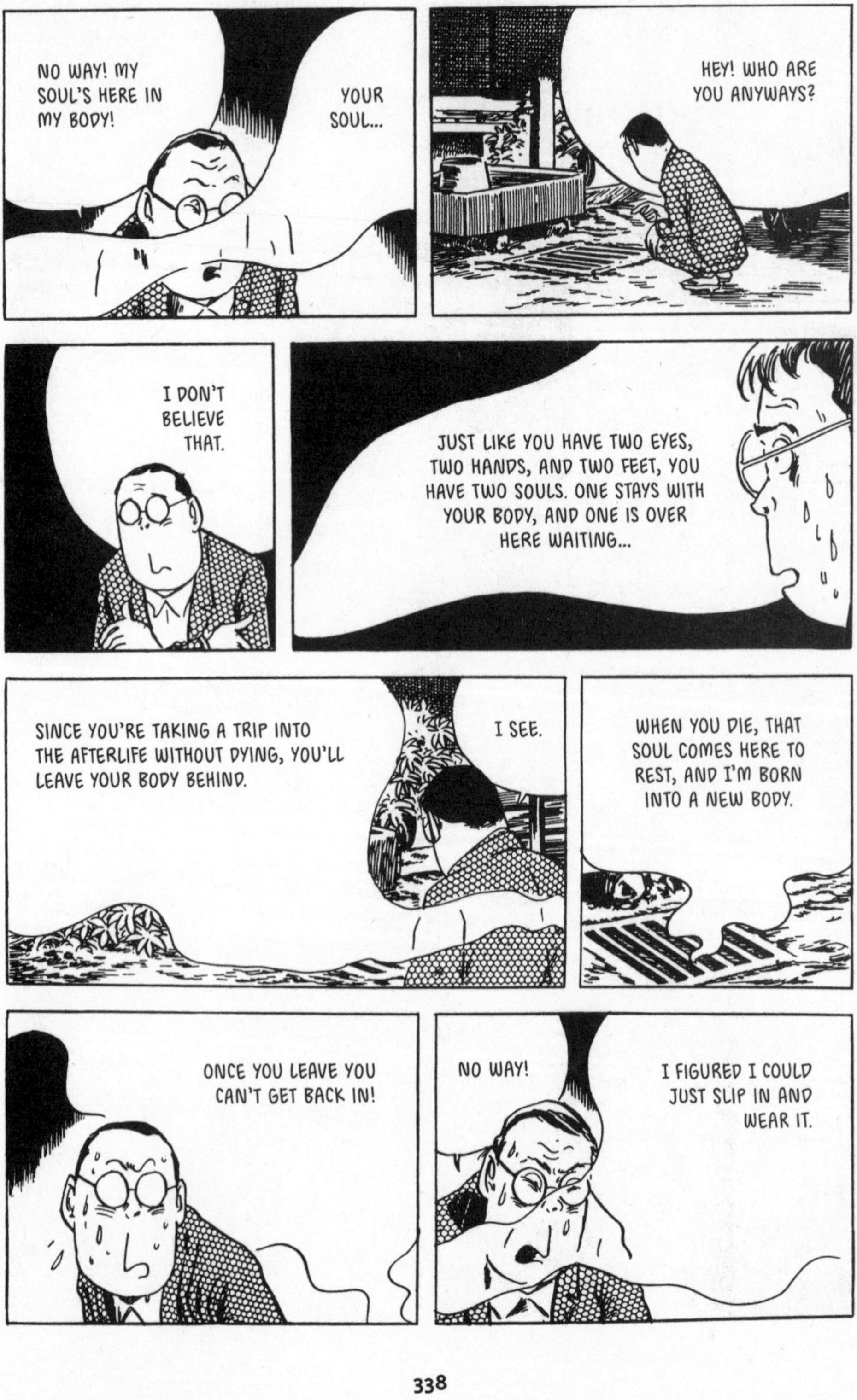
HEY! WHO ARE YOU ANYWAYS?
YOUR SOUL...
NO WAY! MY SOUL'S HERE IN MY BODY!
JUST LIKE YOU HAVE TWO EYES, TWO HANDS, AND TWO FEET, YOU HAVE TWO SOULS. ONE STAYS WITH YOUR BODY, AND ONE IS OVER HERE WAITING...
I DON'T BELIEVE THAT.
WHEN YOU DIE, THAT SOUL COMES HERE TO REST, AND I'M BORN INTO A NEW BODY.
I SEE.
SINCE YOU'RE TAKING A TRIP INTO THE AFTERLIFE WITHOUT DYING, YOU'LL LEAVE YOUR BODY BEHIND.
I FIGURED I COULD JUST SLIP IN AND WEAR IT.
NO WAY!
ONCE YOU LEAVE YOU CAN'T GET BACK IN!

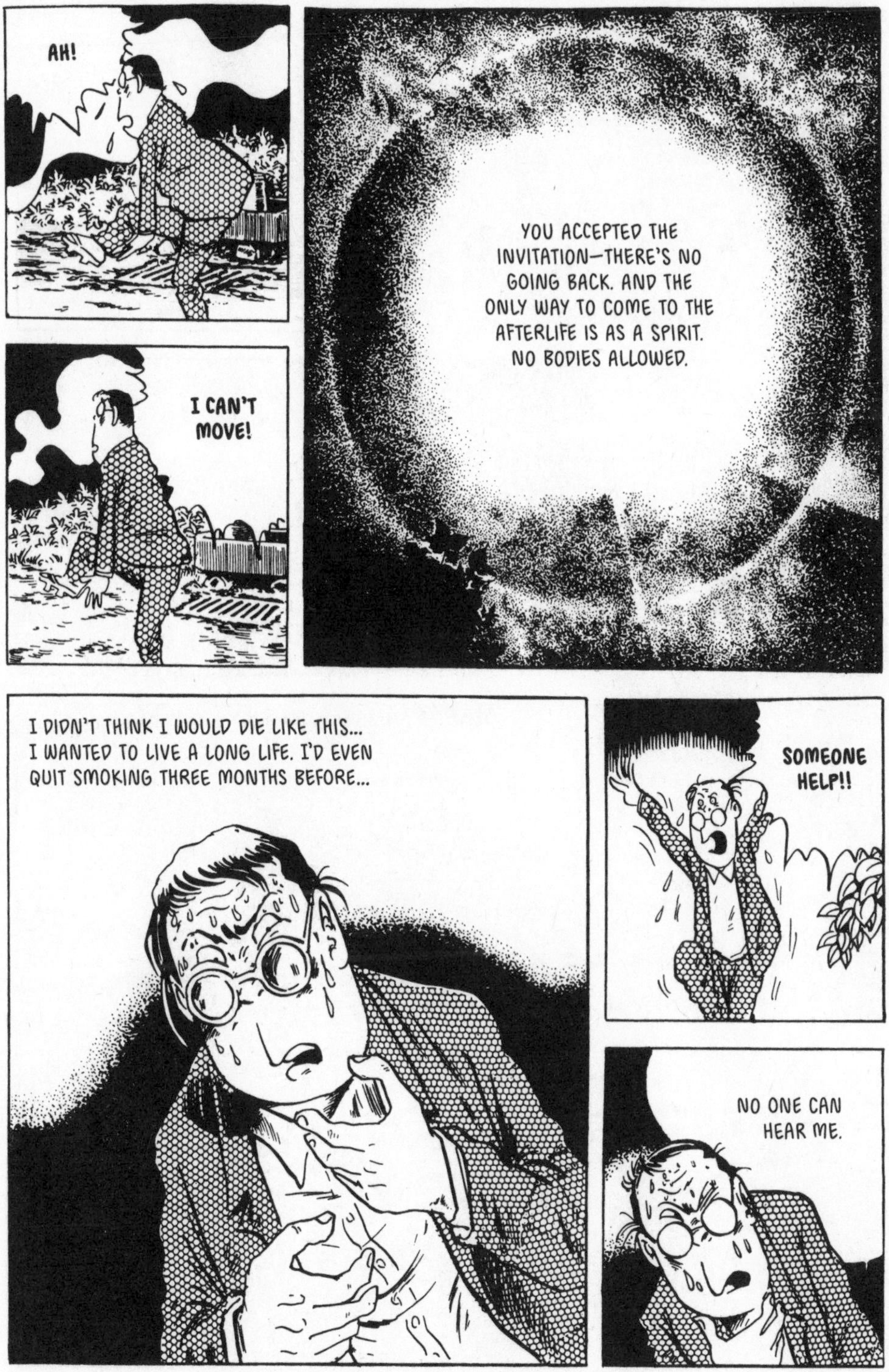
YOU ACCEPTED THE INVITATION—THERE'S NO GOING BACK. AND THE ONLY WAY TO COME TO THE AFTERLIFE IS AS A SPIRIT. NO BODIES ALLOWED.
AH!
I CAN'T MOVE!
SOMEONE HELP!!
NO ONE CAN HEAR ME.
I DIDN'T THINK I WOULD DIE LIKE THIS... I WANTED TO LIVE A LONG LIFE. I'D EVEN QUIT SMOKING THREE MONTHS BEFORE...

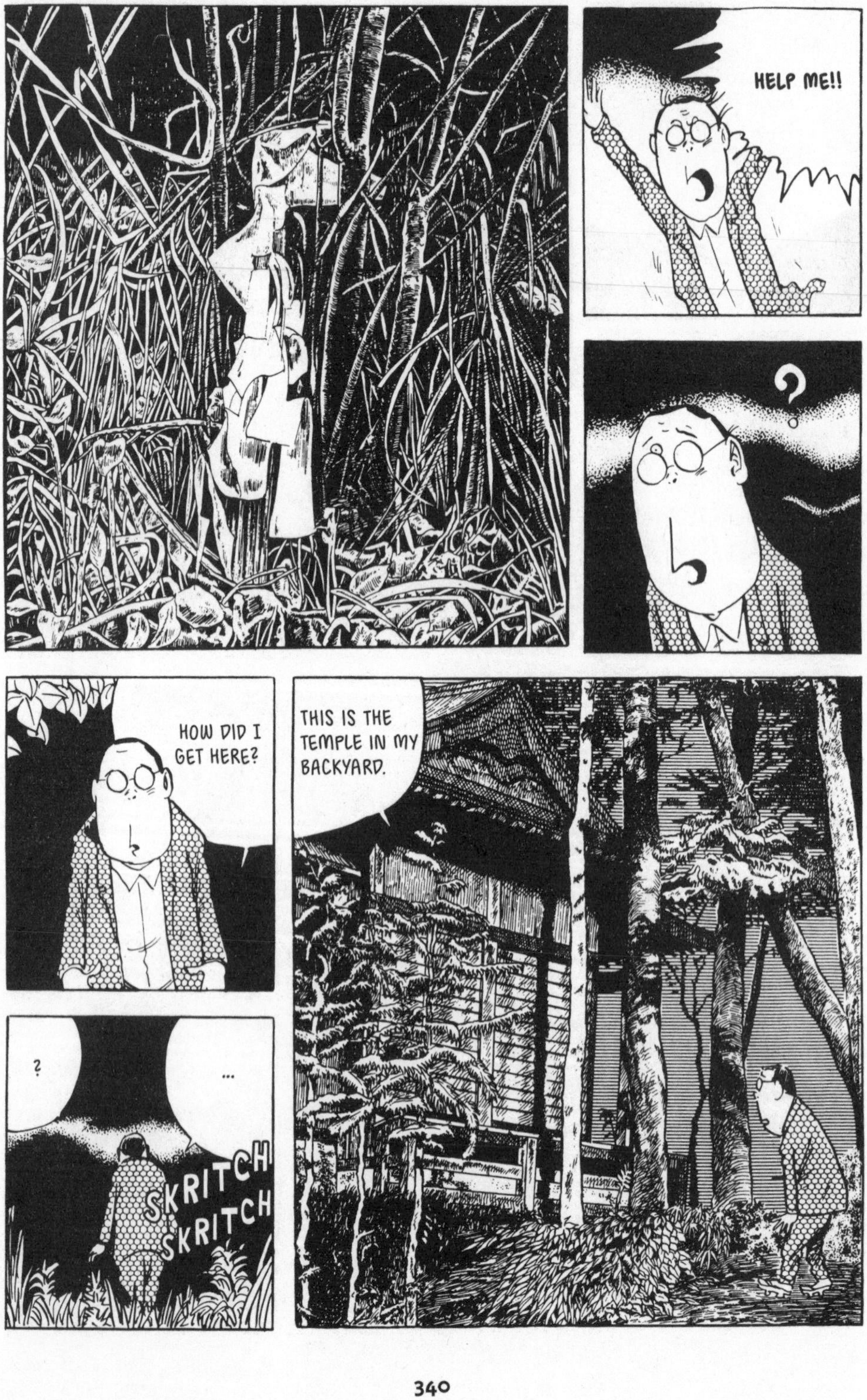
HELP ME!!
?
THIS IS THE TEMPLE IN MY BACKYARD.
HOW DID I GET HERE?
...
?
SKRITCH
SKRITCH

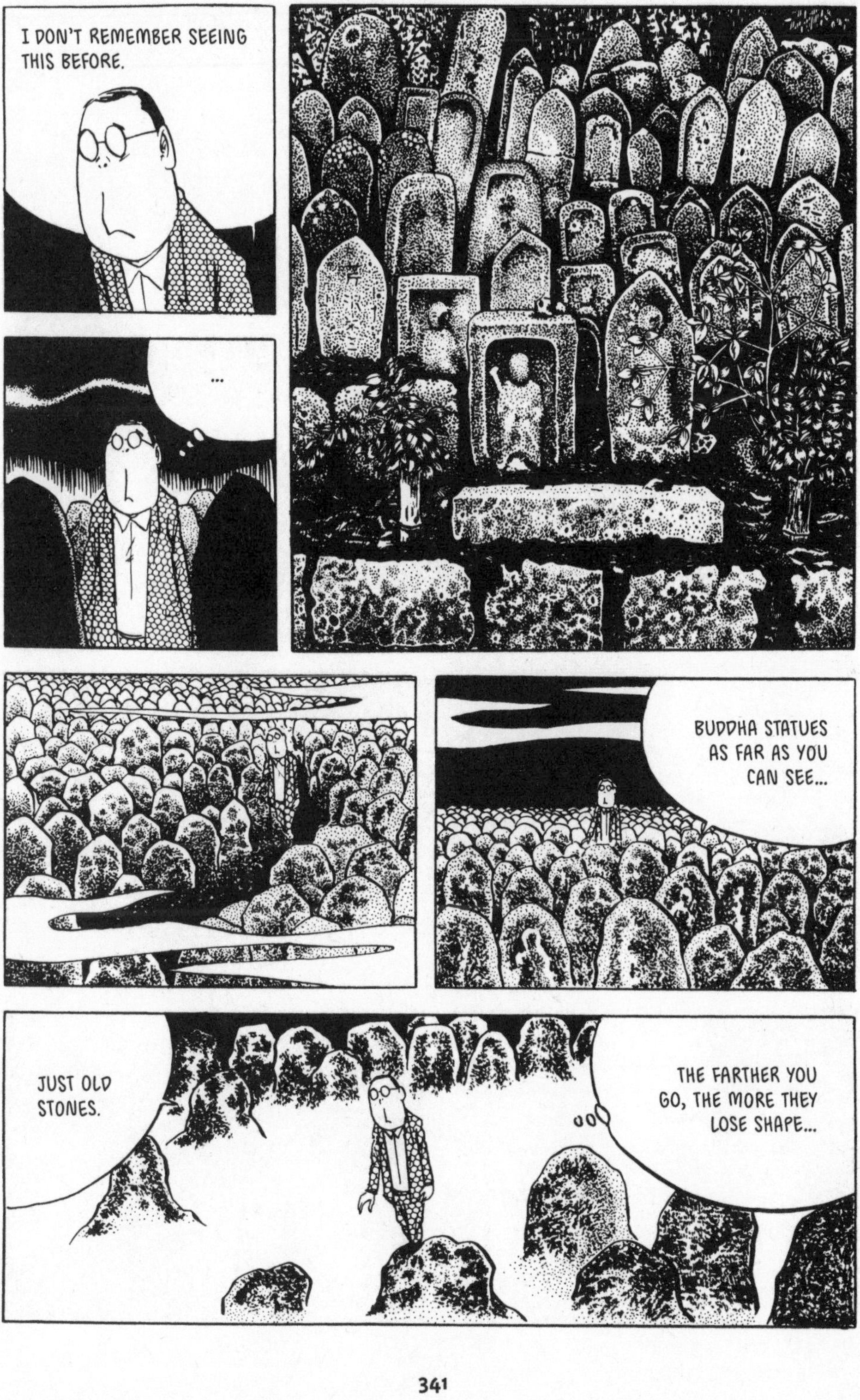
I DON'T REMEMBER SEEING THIS BEFORE.
...
BUDDHA STATUES AS FAR AS YOU CAN SEE...
THE FARTHER YOU GO, THE MORE THEY LOSE SHAPE...
JUST OLD STONES.

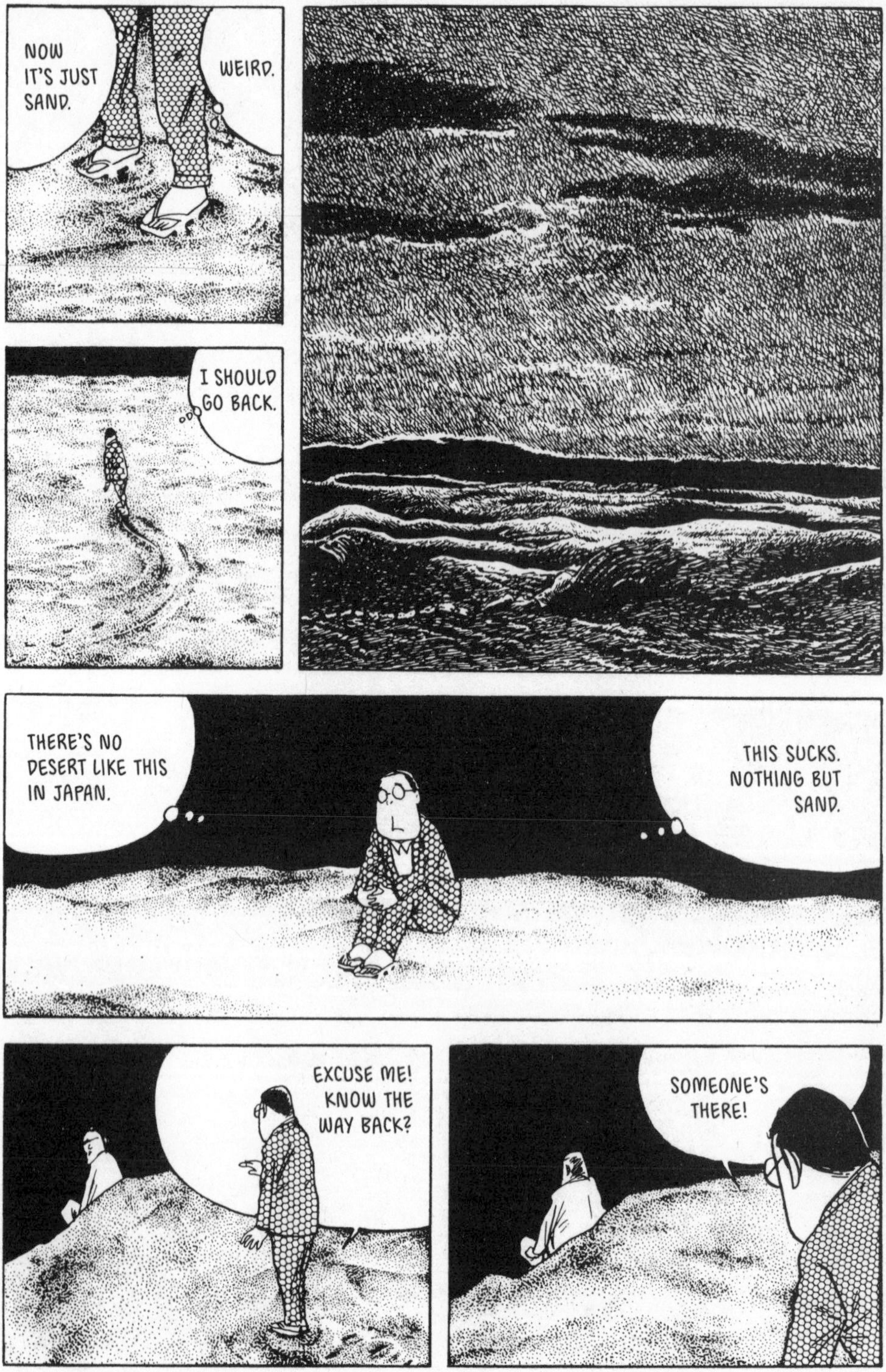
WEIRD.
NOW IT'S JUST SAND.
I SHOULD GO BACK.
THIS SUCKS. NOTHING BUT SAND.
THERE'S NO DESERT LIKE THIS IN JAPAN.
SOMEONE'S THERE!
EXCUSE ME! KNOW THE WAY BACK?

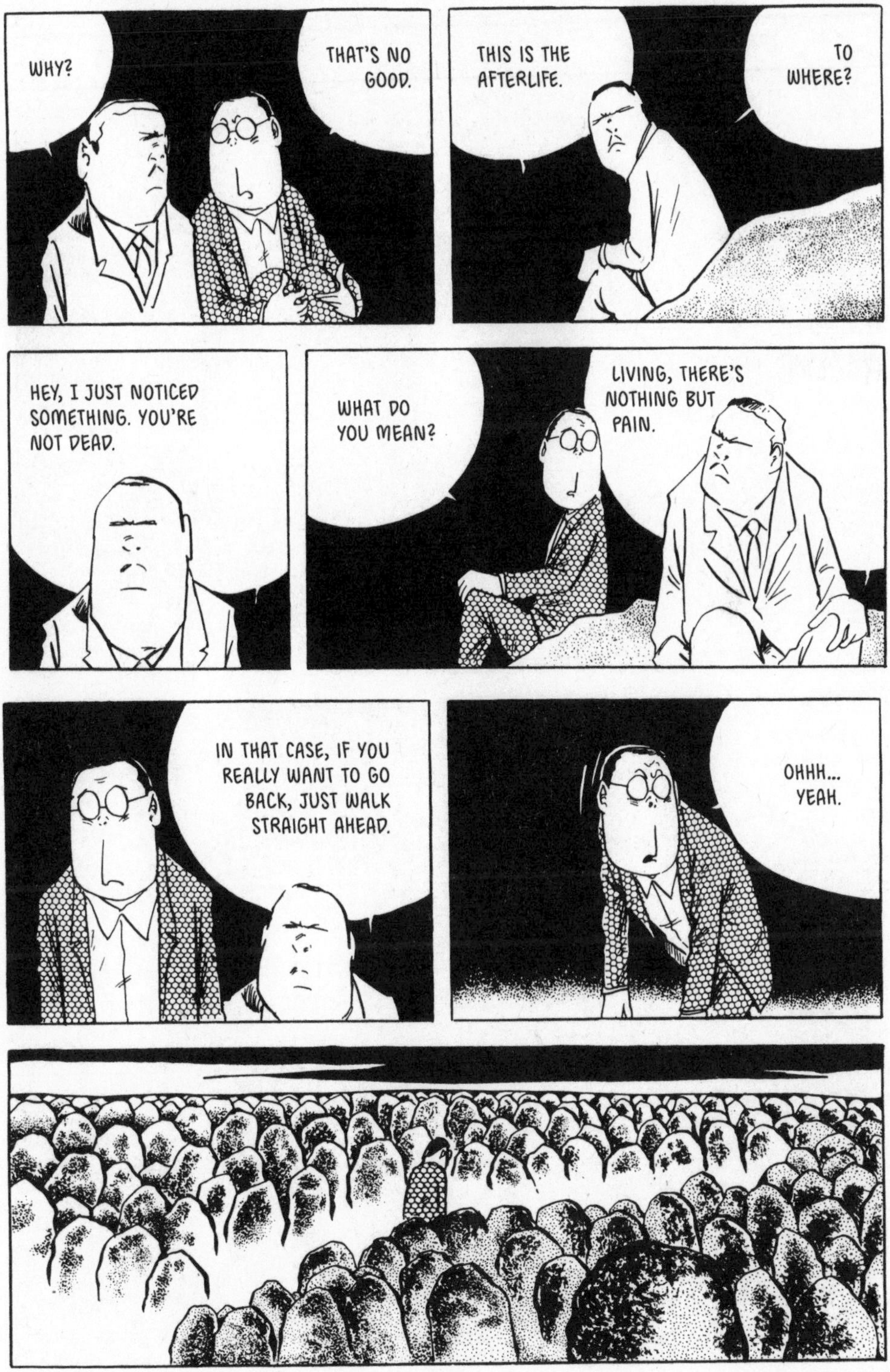
TO WHERE?
THIS IS THE AFTERLIFE.
THAT'S NO GOOD.
WHY?
LIVING, THERE'S NOTHING BUT PAIN.
WHAT DO YOU MEAN?
HEY, I JUST NOTICED SOMETHING. YOU'RE NOT DEAD.
OHHH... YEAH.
IN THAT CASE, IF YOU REALLY WANT TO GO BACK, JUST WALK STRAIGHT AHEAD.

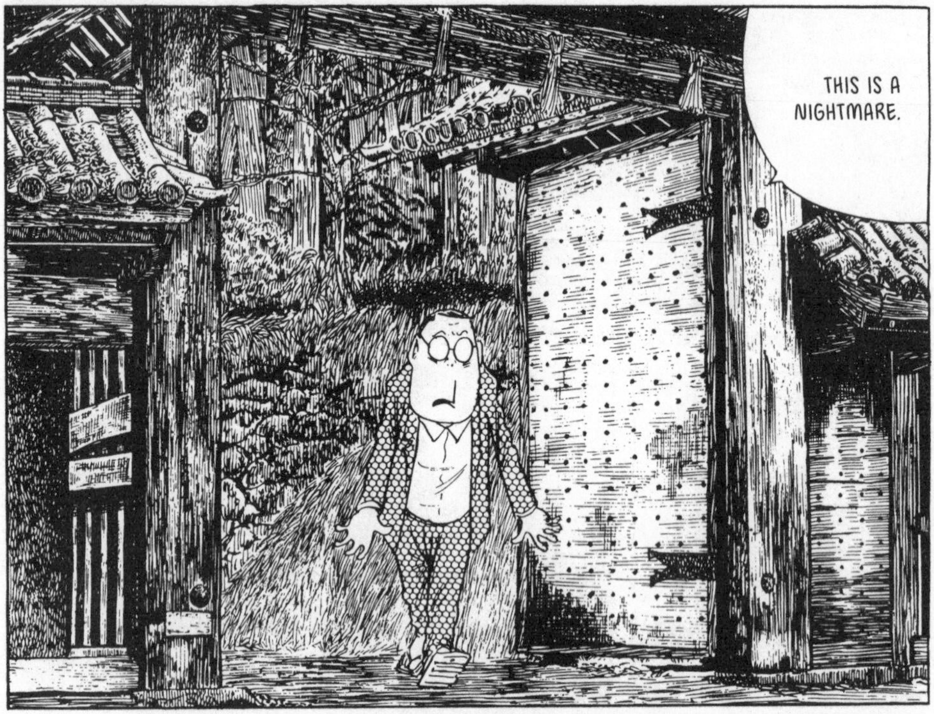
THIS IS A NIGHTMARE.

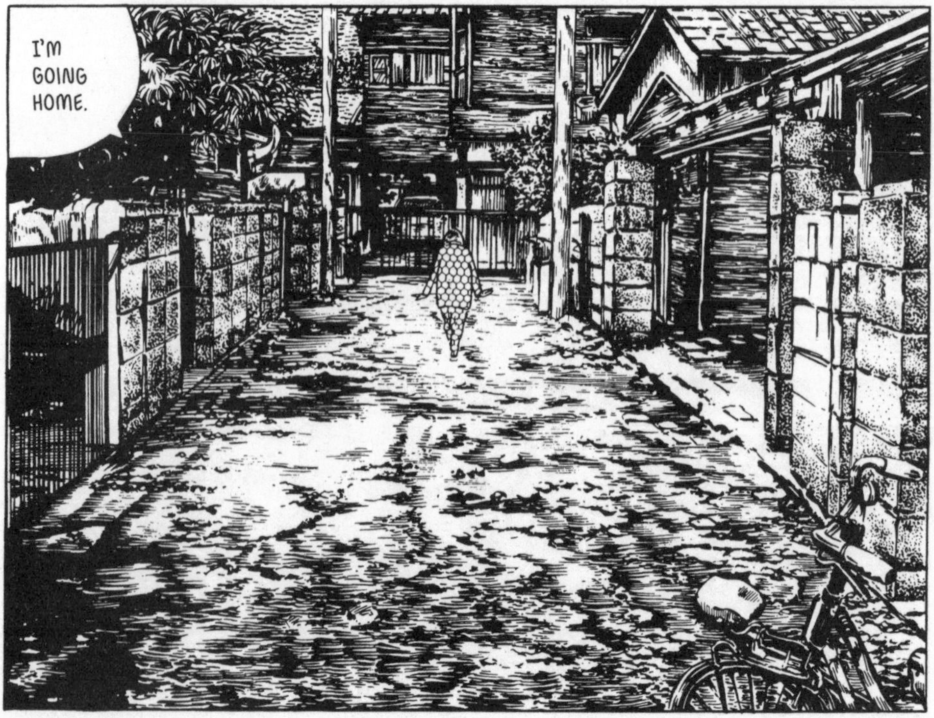
I'M GOING HOME.

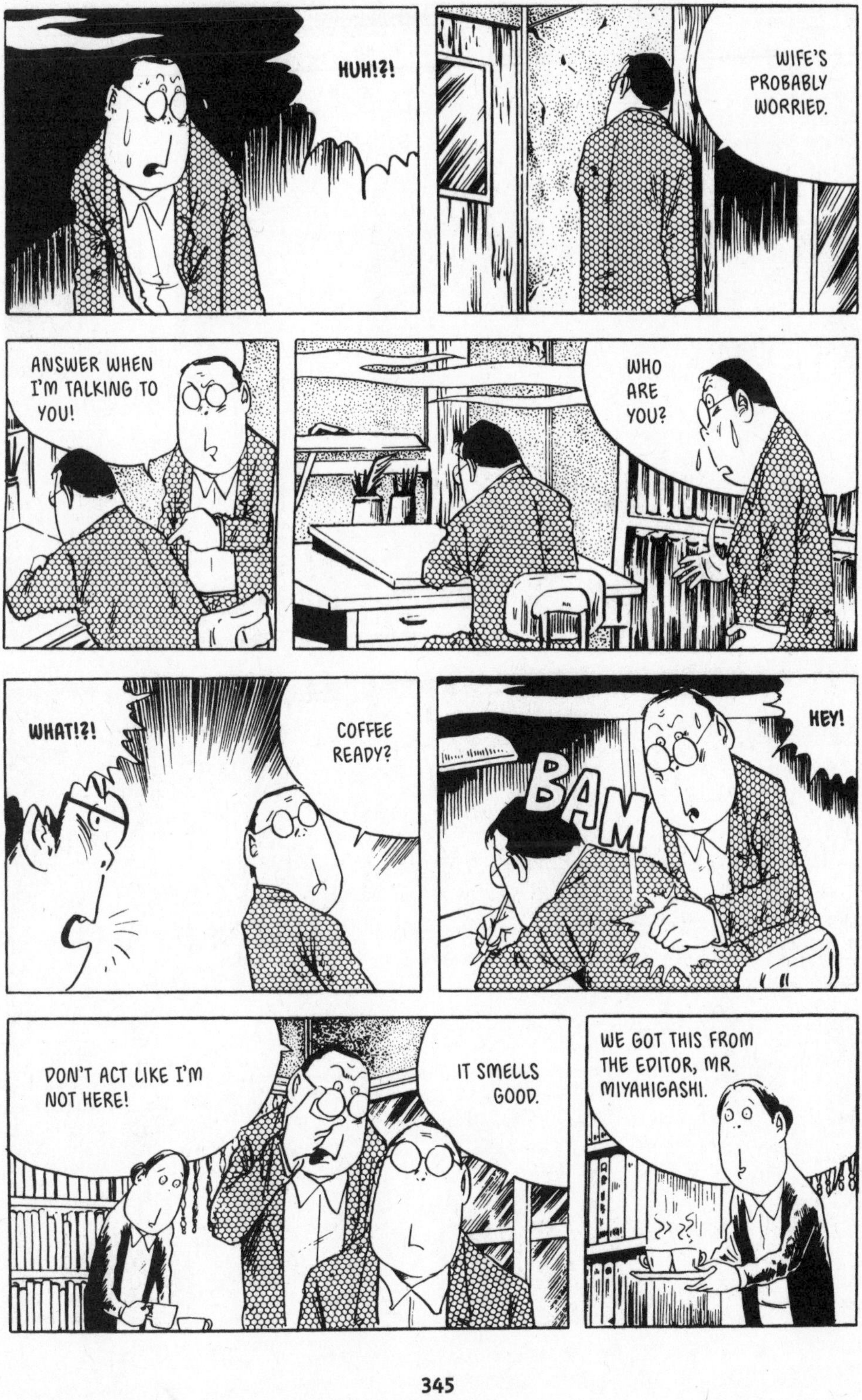
WIFE'S PROBABLY WORRIED.
HUH!?!
WHO ARE YOU?
ANSWER WHEN I'M TALKING TO YOU!
HEY!
BAM
COFFEE READY?
WHAT!?!
WE GOT THIS FROM THE EDITOR, MR. MIYAHIGASHI.
IT SMELLS GOOD.
DON'T ACT LIKE I'M NOT HERE!

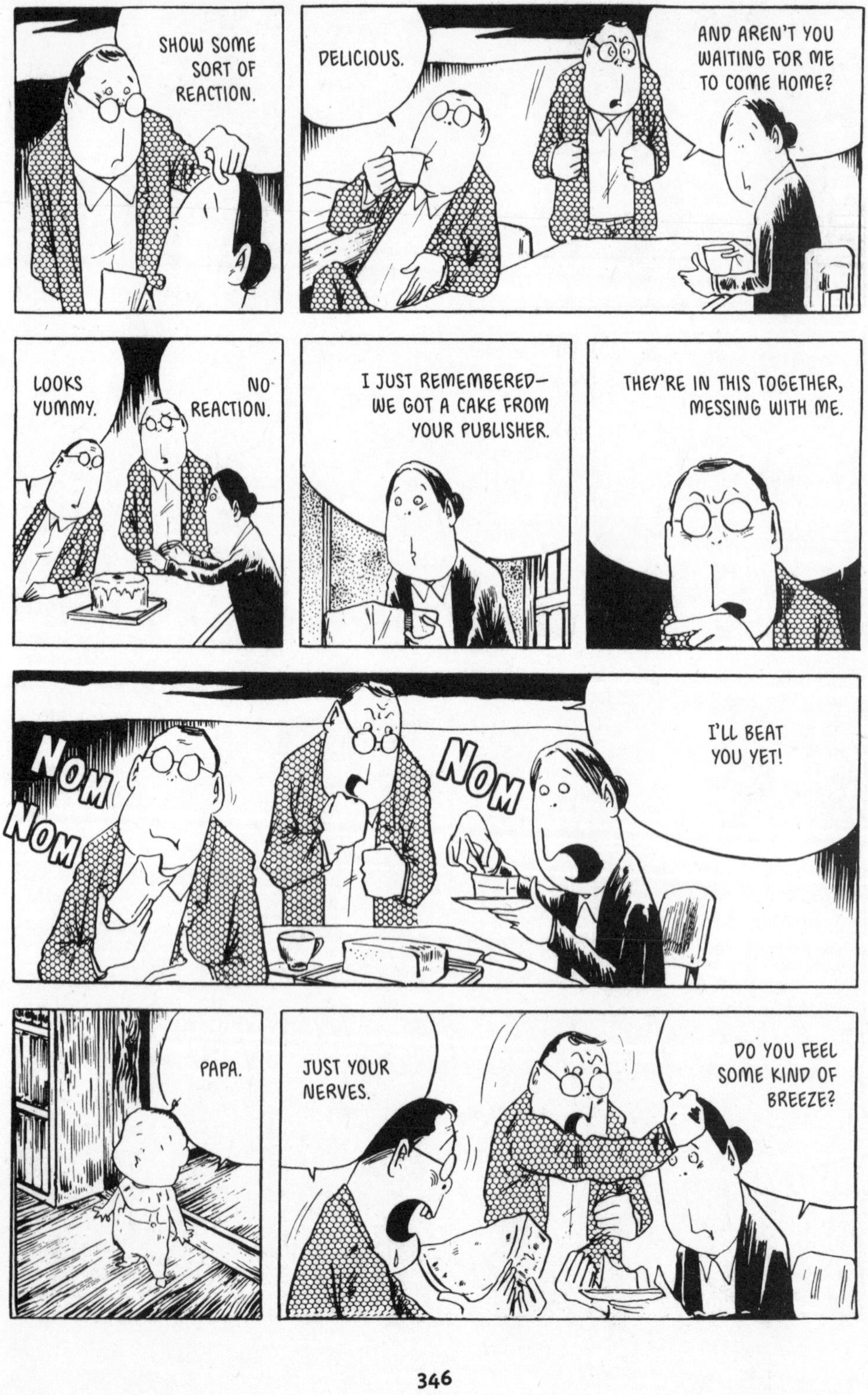
AND AREN'T YOU WAITING FOR ME TO COME HOME?
DELICIOUS.
SHOW SOME SORT OF REACTION.
THEY'RE IN THIS TOGETHER, MESSING WITH ME.
I JUST REMEMBERED— WE GOT A CAKE FROM YOUR PUBLISHER.
NO REACTION.
LOOKS YUMMY.
I'LL BEAT YOU YET!
NOM
NOM
NOM
DO YOU FEEL SOME KIND OF BREEZE?
JUST YOUR NERVES.
PAPA.

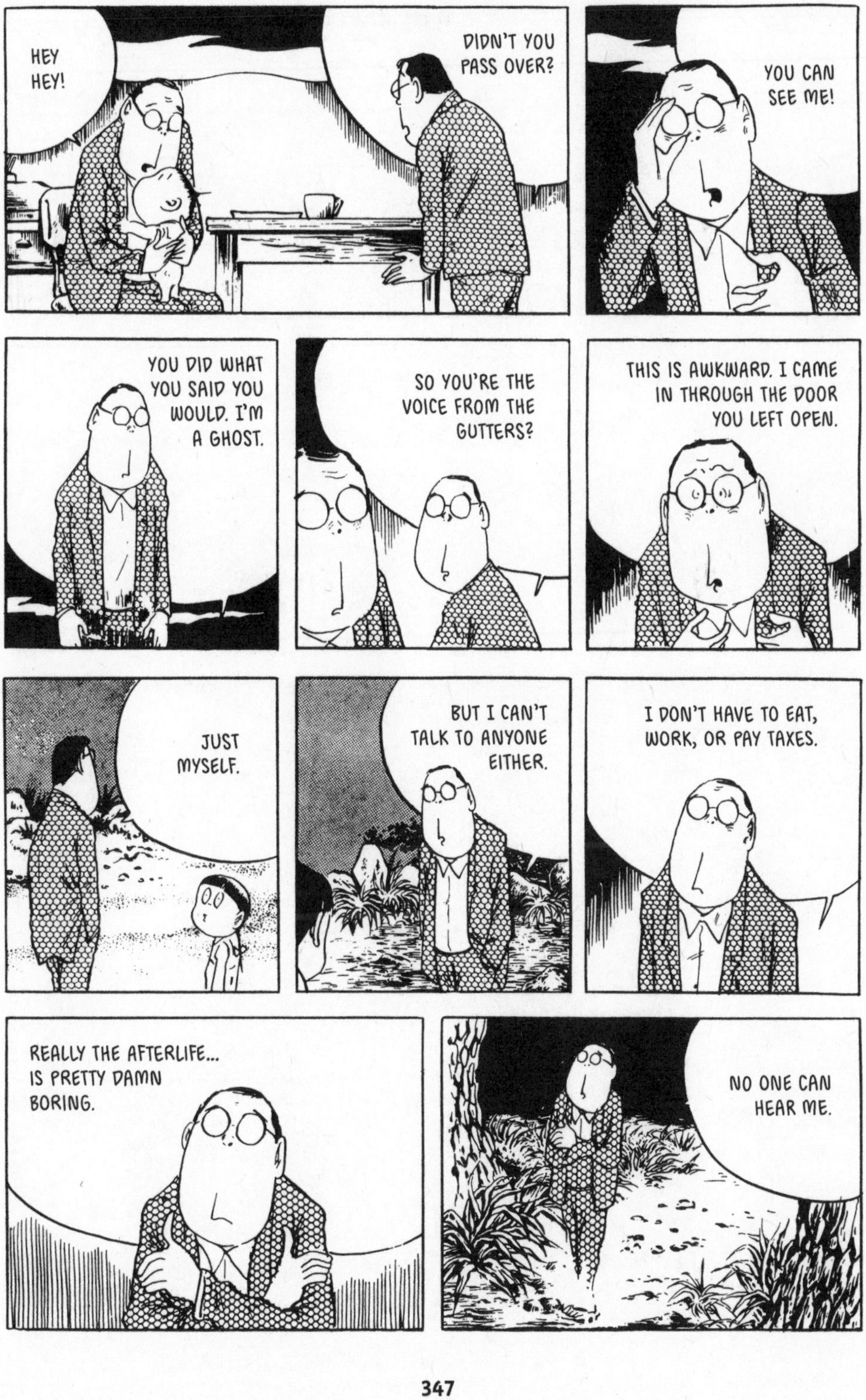
YOU CAN SEE ME!
DIDN'T YOU PASS OVER?
HEY HEY!
THIS IS AWKWARD. I CAME IN THROUGH THE DOOR YOU LEFT OPEN.
SO YOU'RE THE VOICE FROM THE GUTTERS?
YOU DID WHAT YOU SAID YOU WOULD. I'M A GHOST.
I DON'T HAVE TO EAT, WORK, OR PAY TAXES.
BUT I CAN'T TALK TO ANYONE EITHER.
JUST MYSELF.
NO ONE CAN HEAR ME.
REALLY THE AFTERLIFE... IS PRETTY DAMN BORING.

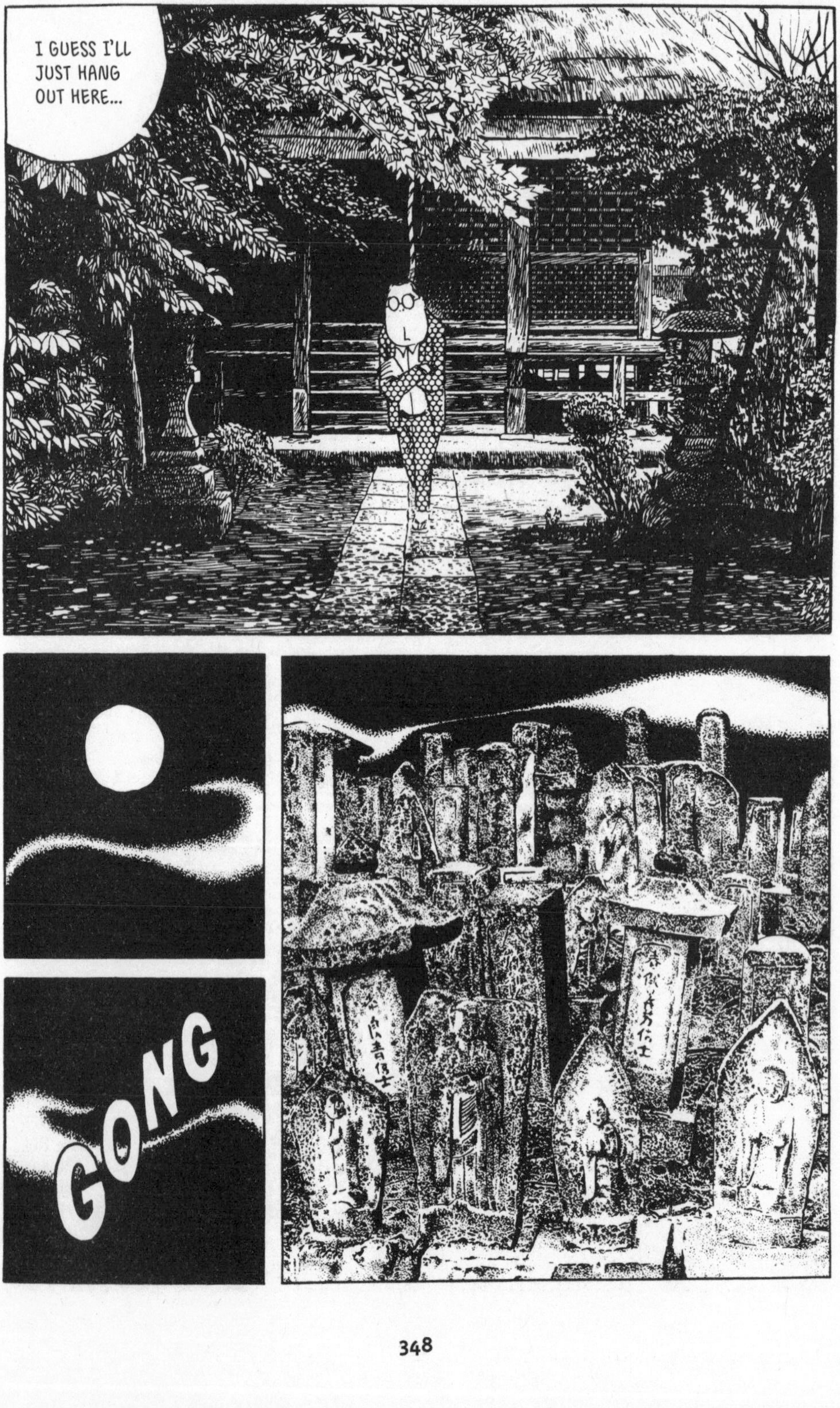
I GUESS I'LL JUST HANG OUT HERE...
GONG

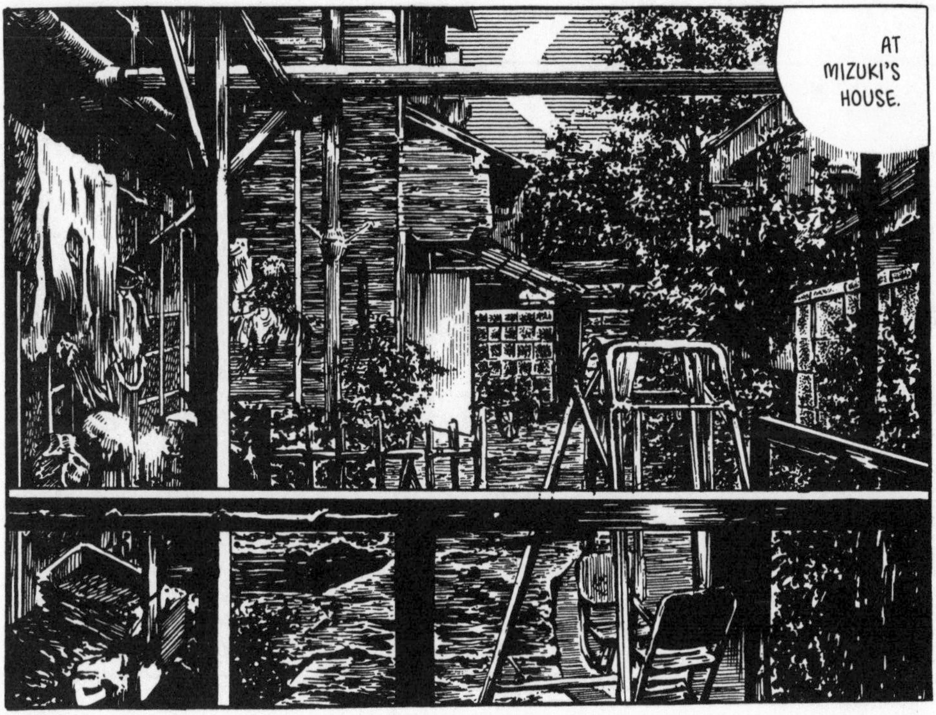
AT MIZUKI'S HOUSE.

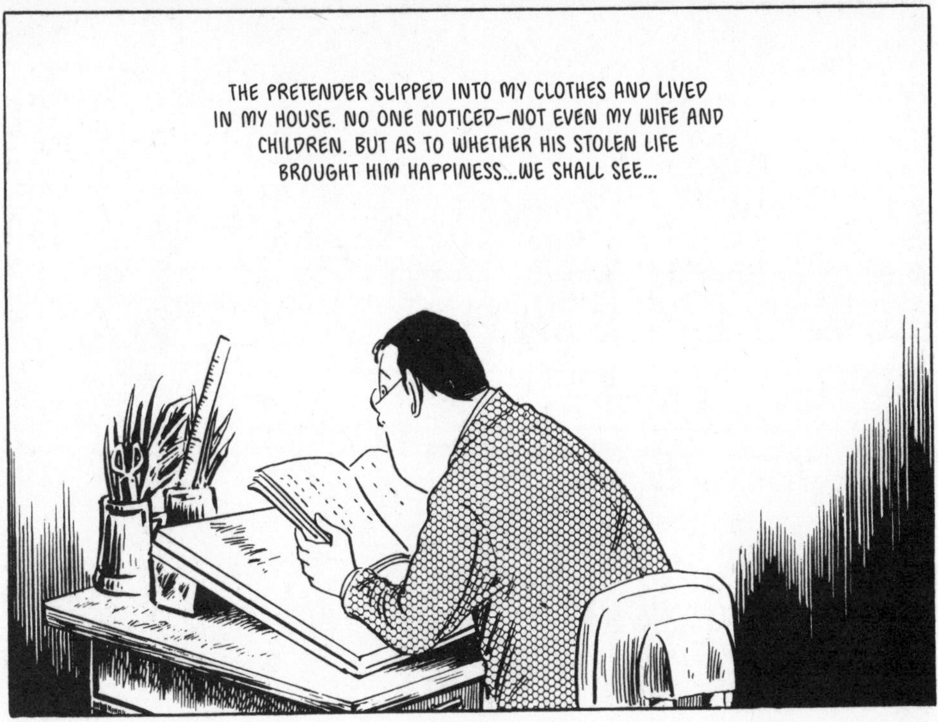
THE PRETENDER SLIPPED INTO MY CLOTHES AND LIVED IN MY HOUSE. NO ONE NOTICED—NOT EVEN MY WIFE AND CHILDREN. BUT AS TO WHETHER HIS STOLEN LIFE BROUGHT HIM HAPPINESS...WE SHALL SEE...

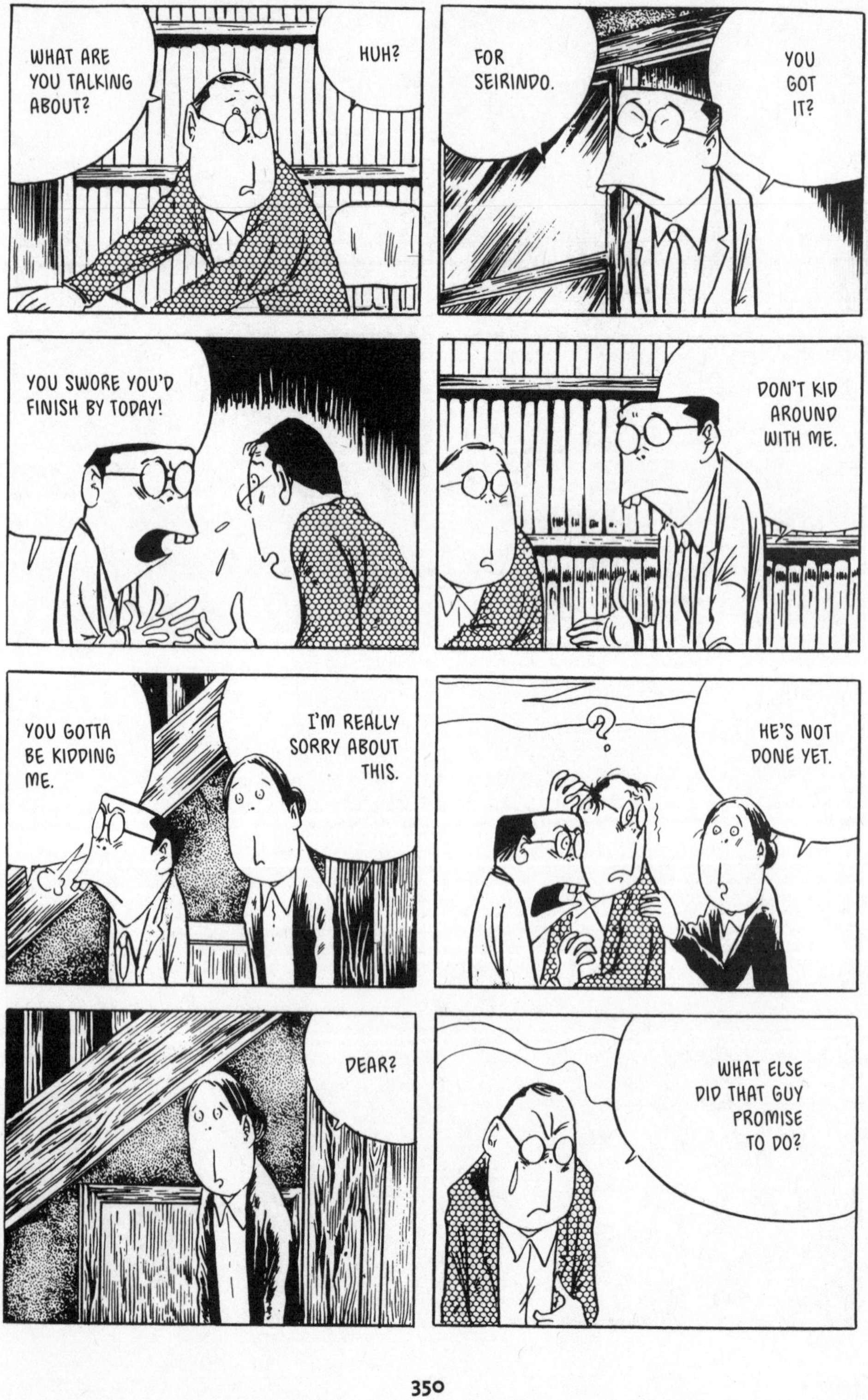
YOU GOT IT?
FOR SEIRINDO.
HUH?
WHAT ARE YOU TALKING ABOUT?
DON'T KID AROUND WITH ME.
YOU SWORE YOU'D FINISH BY TODAY!
HE'S NOT DONE YET.
?
I'M REALLY SORRY ABOUT THIS.
YOU GOTTA BE KIDDING ME.
WHAT ELSE DID THAT GUY PROMISE TO DO?
DEAR?

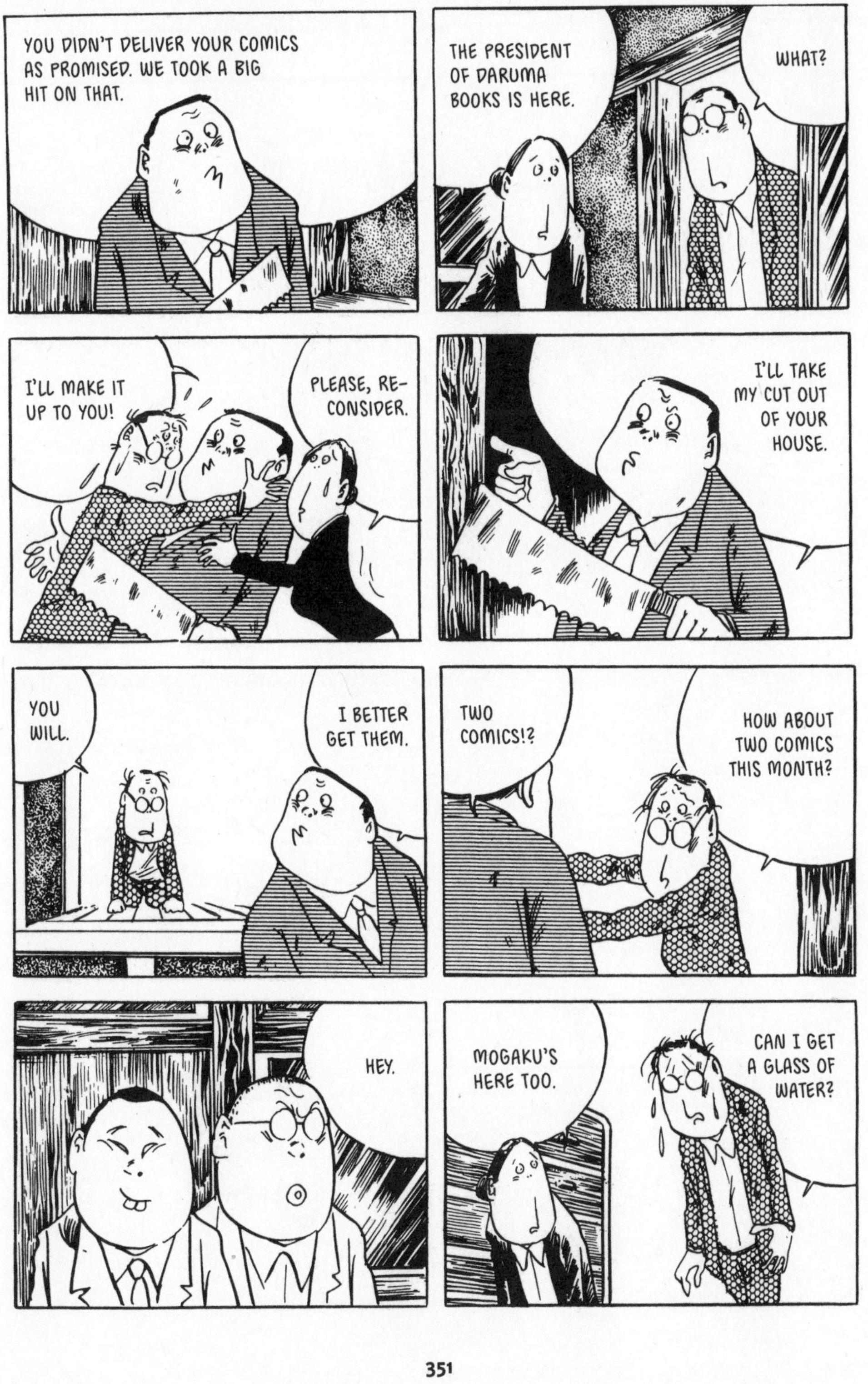
WHAT?
THE PRESIDENT OF DARUMA BOOKS IS HERE.
YOU DIDN'T DELIVER YOUR COMICS AS PROMISED. WE TOOK A BIG HIT ON THAT.
I'LL TAKE MY CUT OUT OF YOUR HOUSE.
PLEASE, RE-CONSIDER.
I'LL MAKE IT UP TO YOU!
HOW ABOUT TWO COMICS THIS MONTH?
TWO COMICS!?
I BETTER GET THEM.
YOU WILL.
CAN I GET A GLASS OF WATER?
MOGAKU'S HERE TOO.
HEY.

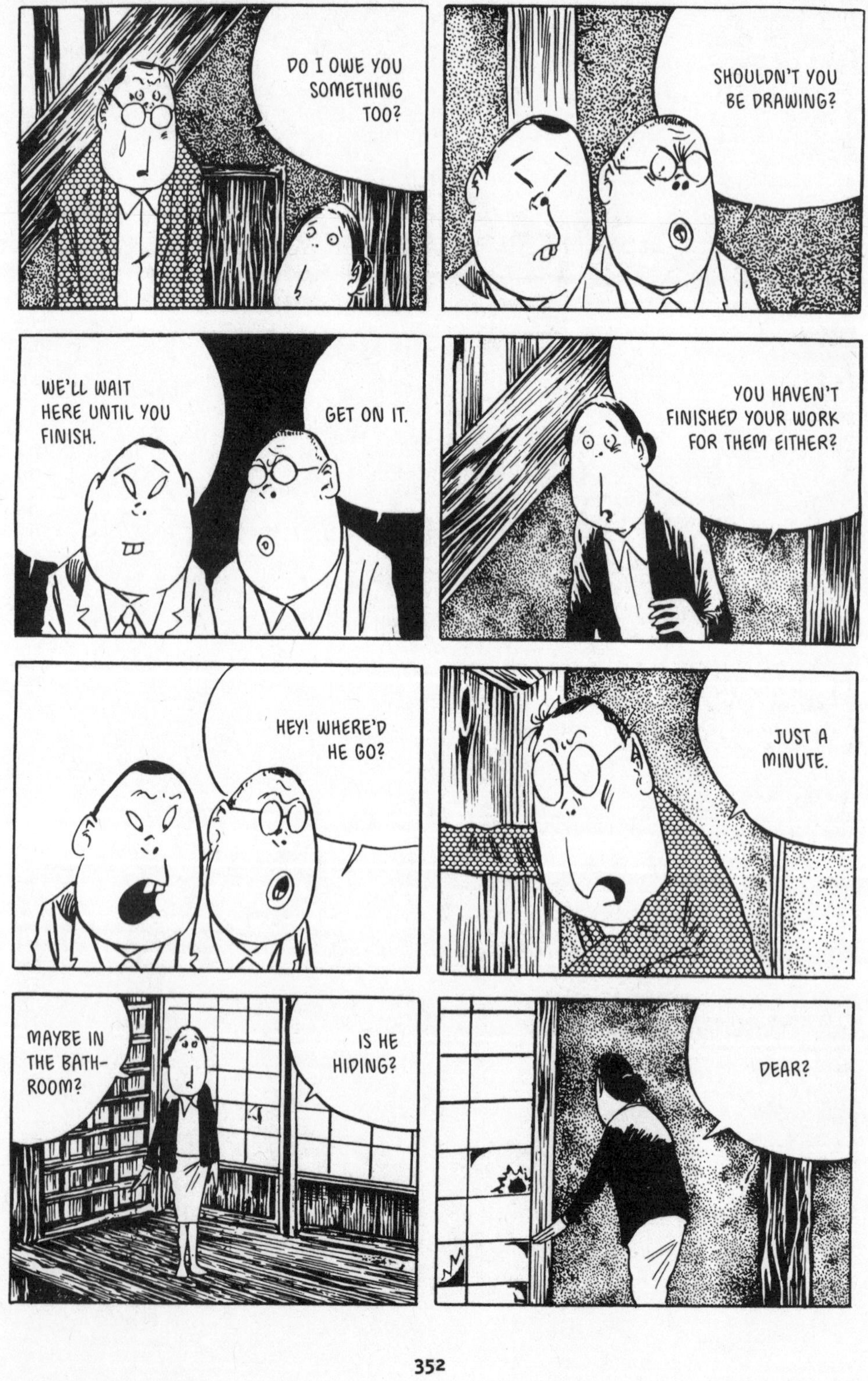
SHOULDN'T YOU BE DRAWING?
DO I OWE YOU SOMETHING TOO?
YOU HAVEN'T FINISHED YOUR WORK FOR THEM EITHER?
GET ON IT.
WE'LL WAIT HERE UNTIL YOU FINISH.
JUST A MINUTE.
HEY! WHERE'D HE GO?
DEAR?
IS HE HIDING?
MAYBE IN THE BATH-ROOM?

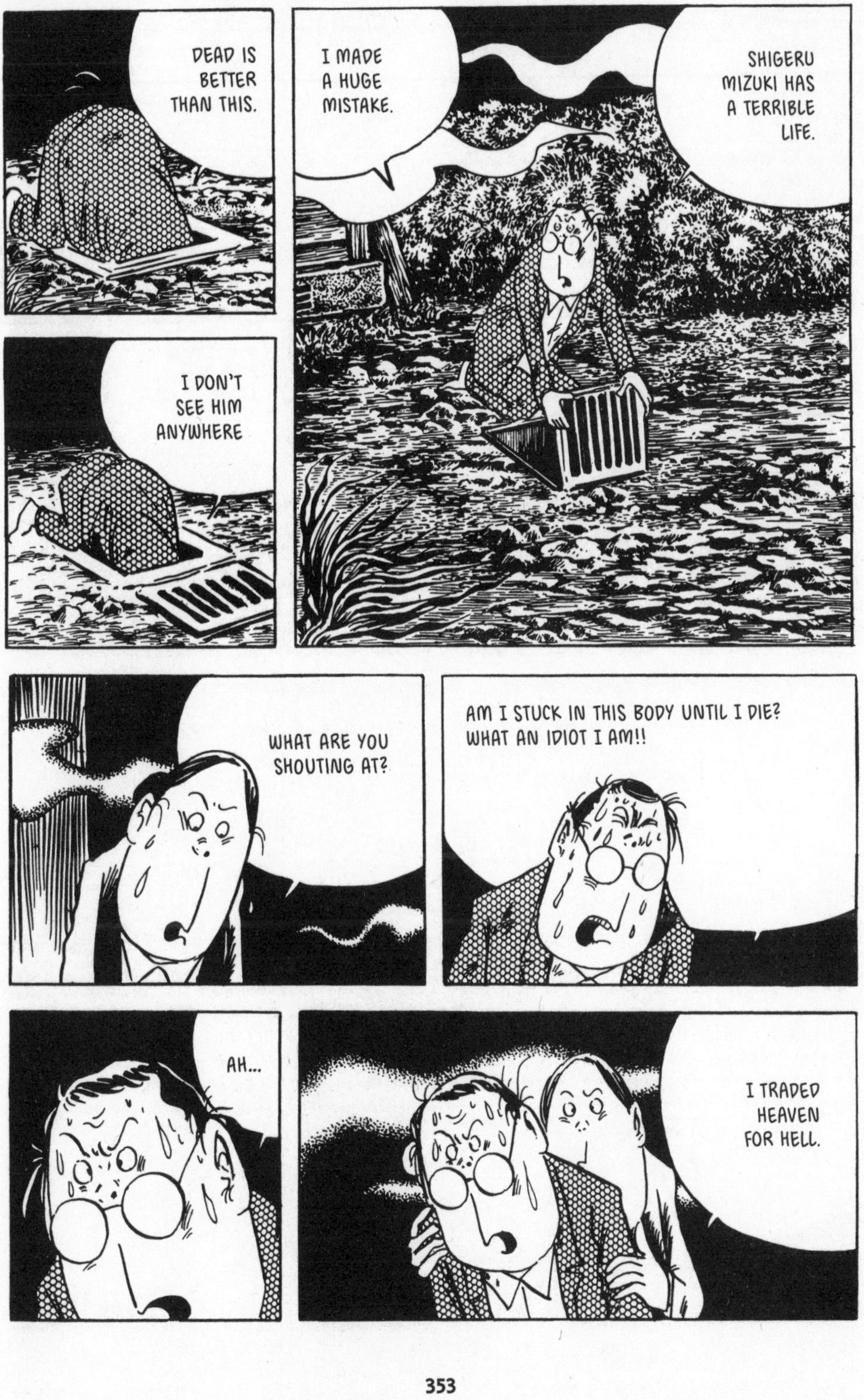
SHIGERU MIZUKI HAS A TERRIBLE LIFE.
I MADE A HUGE MISTAKE.
DEAD IS BETTER THAN THIS.
I DON'T SEE HIM ANYWHERE
AM I STUCK IN THIS BODY UNTIL I DIE? WHAT AN IDIOT I AM!!
WHAT ARE YOU SHOUTING AT?
I TRADED HEAVEN FOR HELL.
AH...

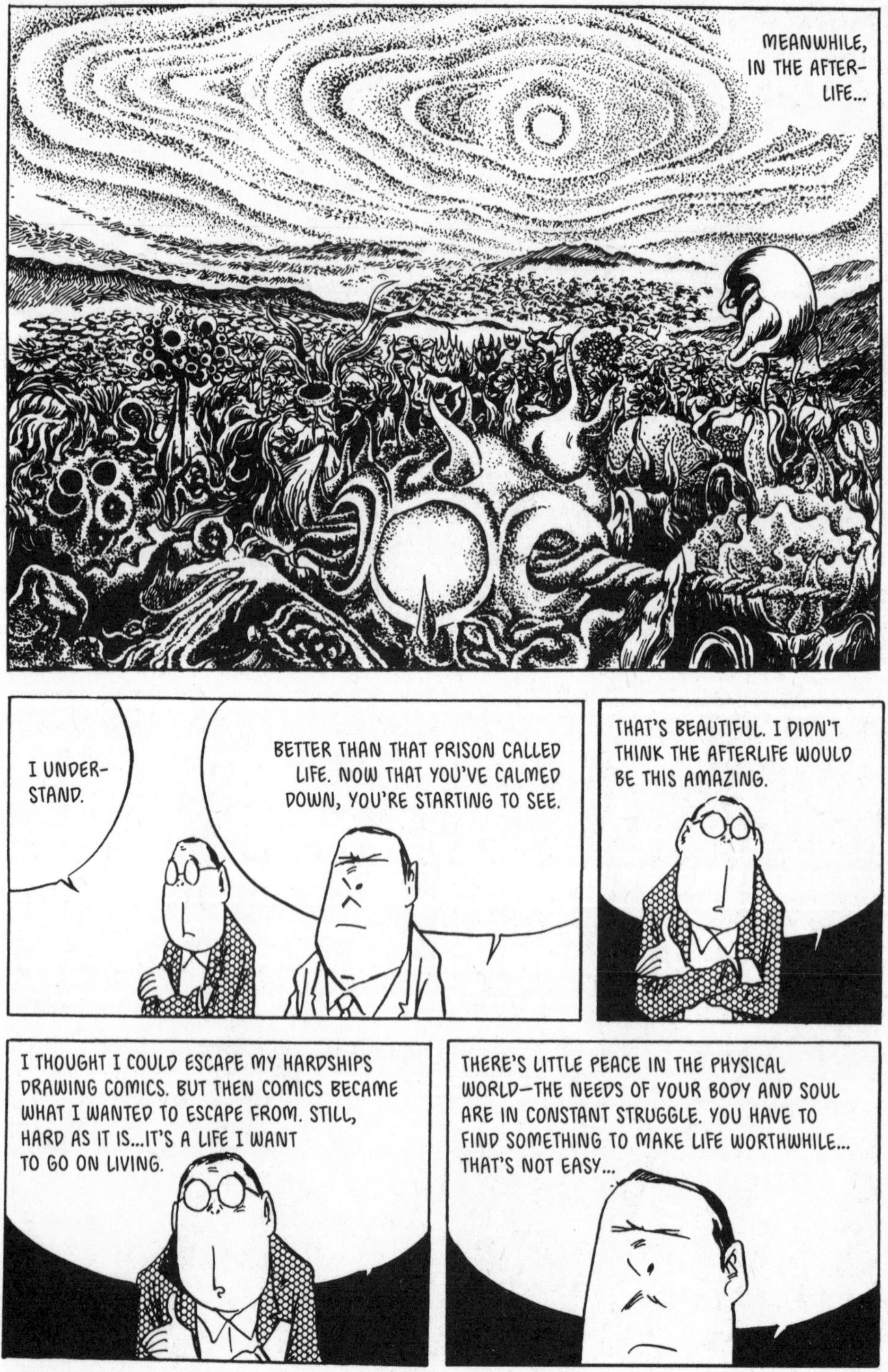
MEANWHILE, IN THE AFTER-LIFE...
THAT'S BEAUTIFUL. I DIDN'T THINK THE AFTERLIFE WOULD BE THIS AMAZING.
BETTER THAN THAT PRISON CALLED LIFE. NOW THAT YOU'VE CALMED DOWN, YOU'RE STARTING TO SEE.
I UNDER-STAND.
THERE'S LITTLE PEACE IN THE PHYSICAL WORLD—THE NEEDS OF YOUR BODY AND SOUL ARE IN CONSTANT STRUGGLE. YOU HAVE TO FIND SOMETHING TO MAKE LIFE WORTHWHILE... THAT'S NOT EASY...
I THOUGHT I COULD ESCAPE MY HARDSHIPS DRAWING COMICS. BUT THEN COMICS BECAME WHAT I WANTED TO ESCAPE FROM. STILL, HARD AS IT IS...IT'S A LIFE I WANT TO GO ON LIVING.

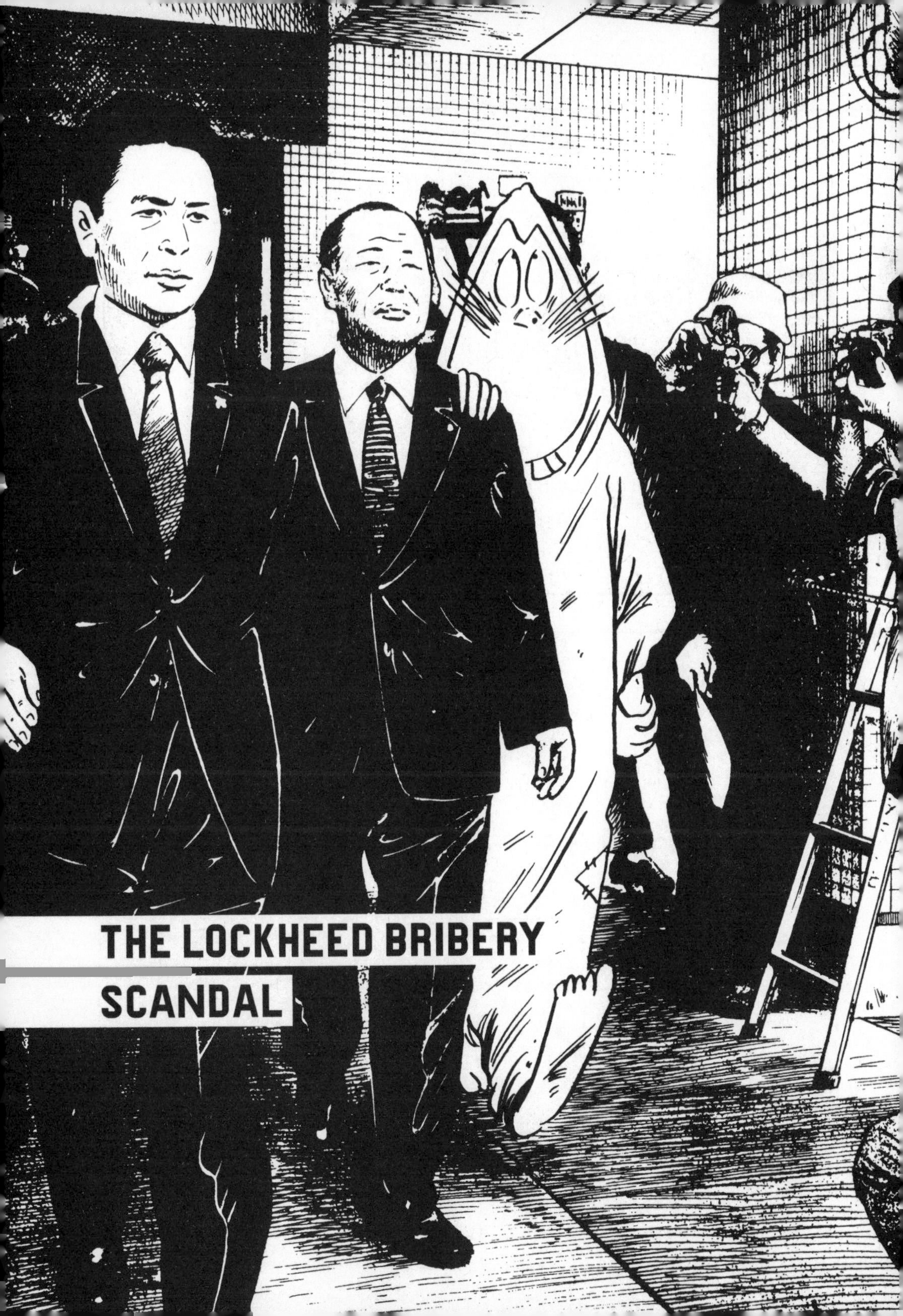
THE LOCKHEED BRIBERY
SCANDAL

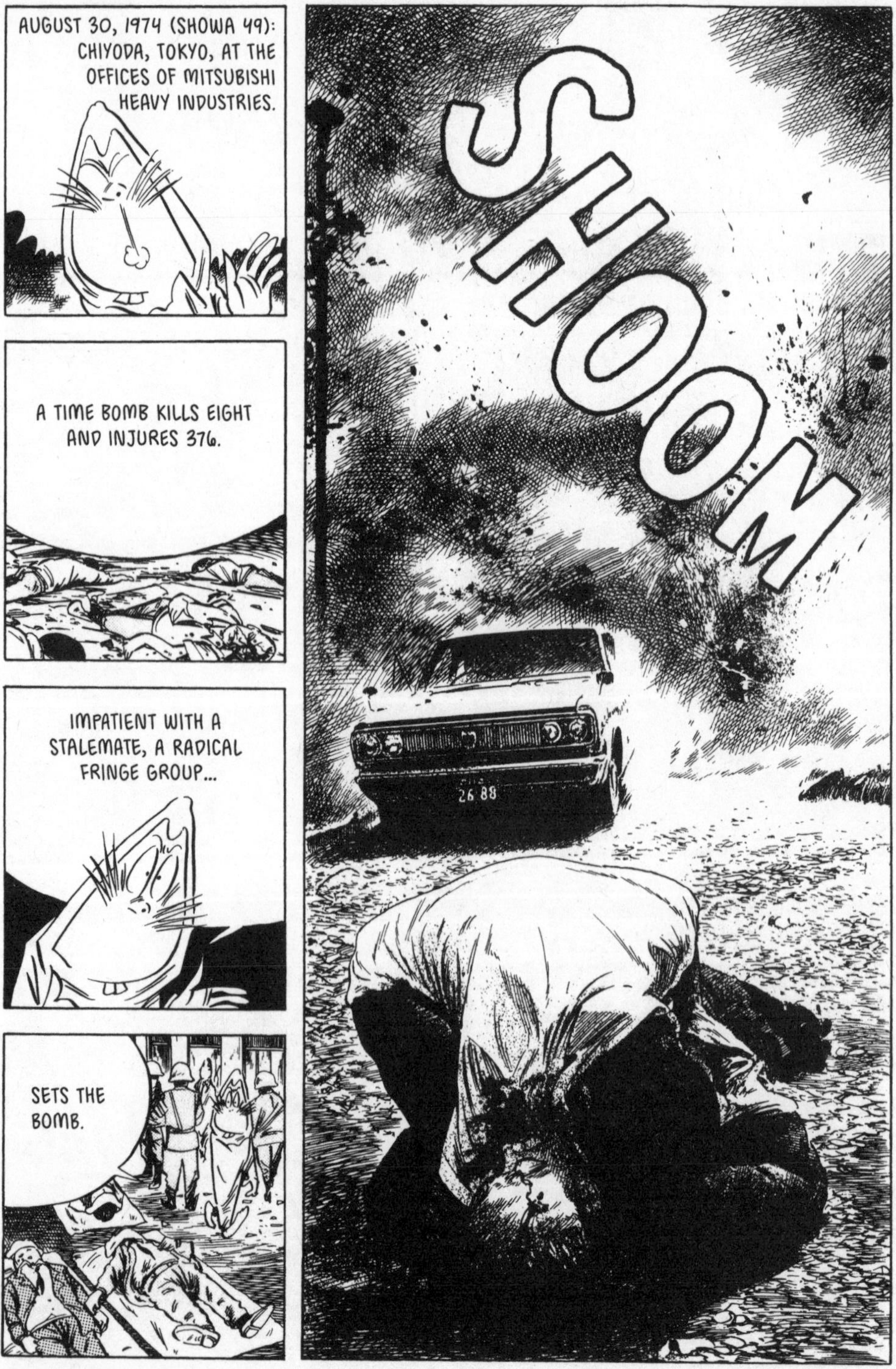
SHOOM
26 88
AUGUST 30, 1974 (SHOWA 49): CHIYODA, TOKYO, AT THE OFFICES OF MITSUBISHI HEAVY INDUSTRIES.
A TIME BOMB KILLS EIGHT AND INJURES 376.
IMPATIENT WITH A STALEMATE, A RADICAL FRINGE GROUP...
SETS THE BOMB.

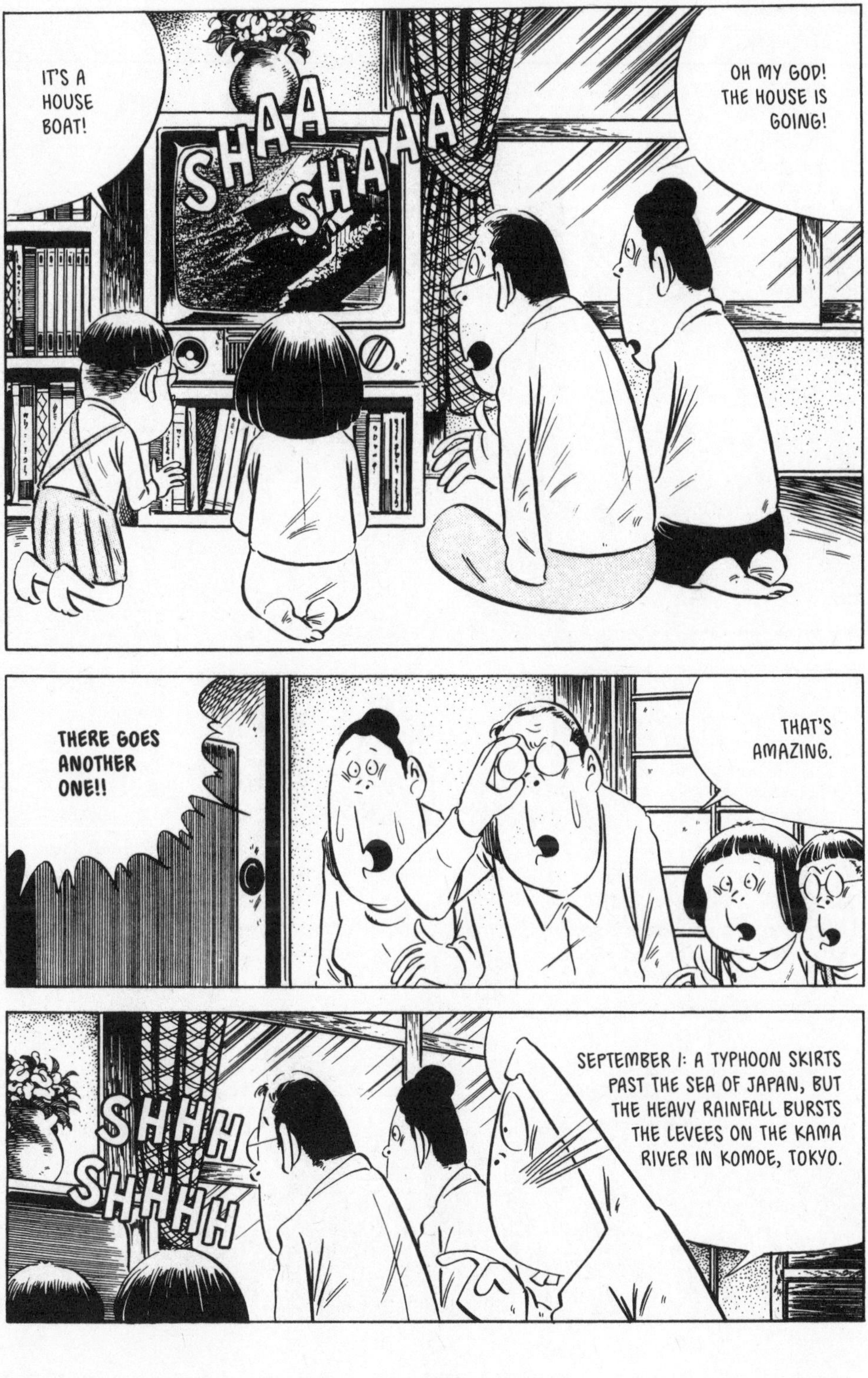
OH MY GOD! THE HOUSE IS GOING!
SHAA
SHAAA
IT'S A HOUSE BOAT!
THAT'S AMAZING.
THERE GOES ANOTHER ONE!!
SEPTEMBER 1: A TYPHOON SKIRTS PAST THE SEA OF JAPAN, BUT THE HEAVY RAINFALL BURSTS THE LEVEES ON THE KAMA RIVER IN KOMOE, TOKYO.
SHHH
SHHHH

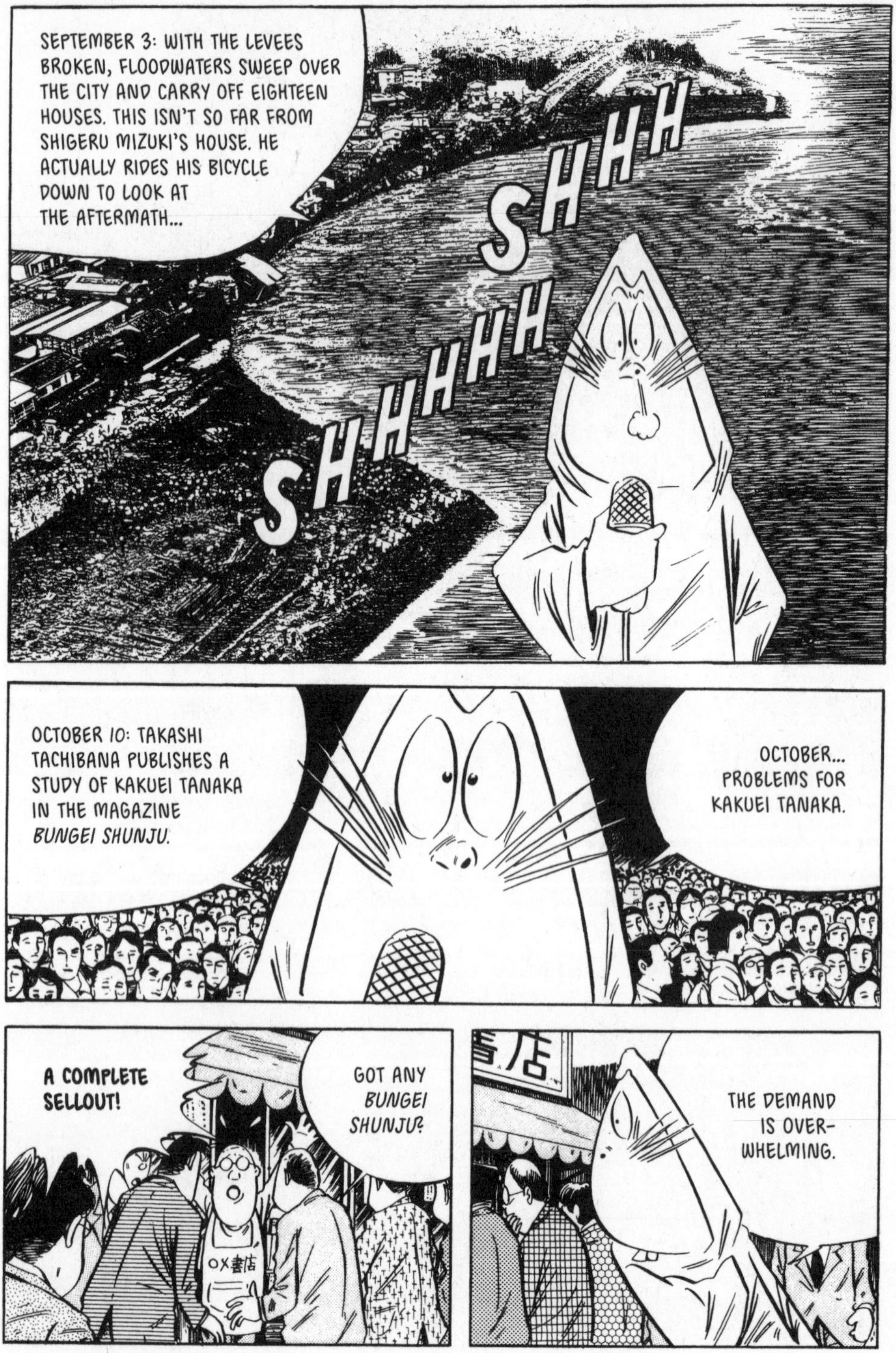
SEPTEMBER 3: WITH THE LEVEES BROKEN, FLOODWATERS SWEEP OVER THE CITY AND CARRY OFF EIGHTEEN HOUSES. THIS ISN'T SO FAR FROM SHIGERU MIZUKI'S HOUSE. HE ACTUALLY RIDES HIS BICYCLE DOWN TO LOOK AT THE AFTERMATH...
SHHHH SHHHHH
OCTOBER... PROBLEMS FOR KAKUEI TANAKA.
OCTOBER 10: TAKASHI TACHIBANA PUBLISHES A STUDY OF KAKUEI TANAKA IN THE MAGAZINE *BUNGEI SHUNJU*.
書店
THE DEMAND IS OVER-WHELMING.
GOT ANY *BUNGEI SHUNJU*?
A COMPLETE SELLOUT!
○×書店

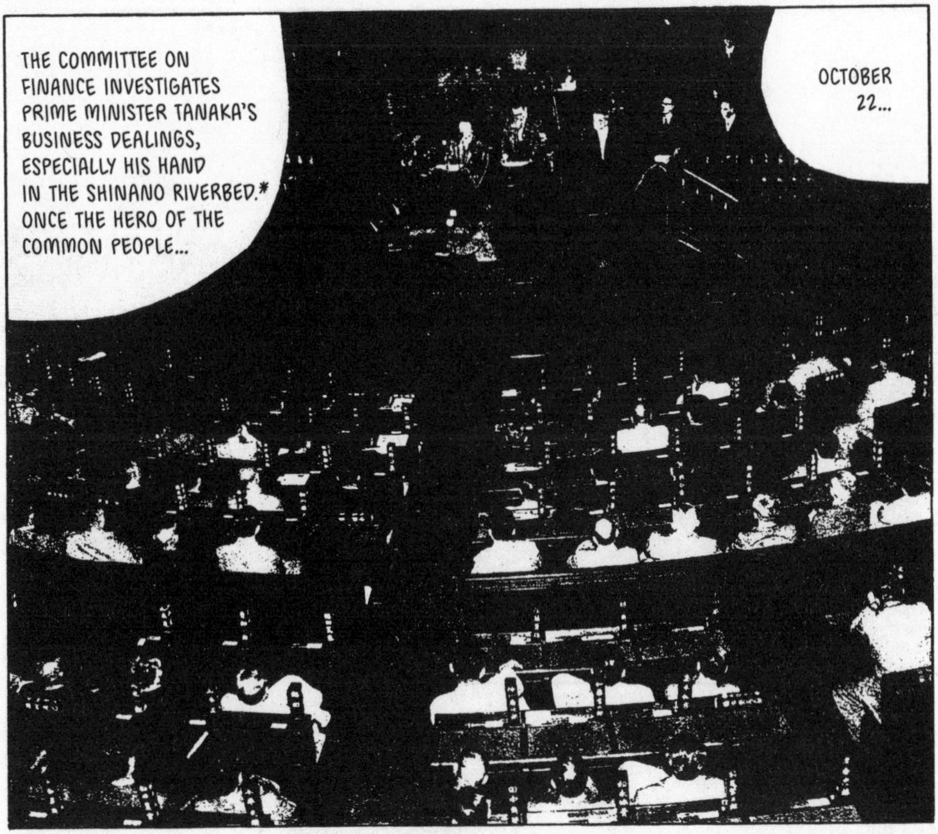
OCTOBER 22...
THE COMMITTEE ON FINANCE INVESTIGATES PRIME MINISTER TANAKA'S BUSINESS DEALINGS, ESPECIALLY HIS HAND IN THE SHINANO RIVERBED.* ONCE THE HERO OF THE COMMON PEOPLE...

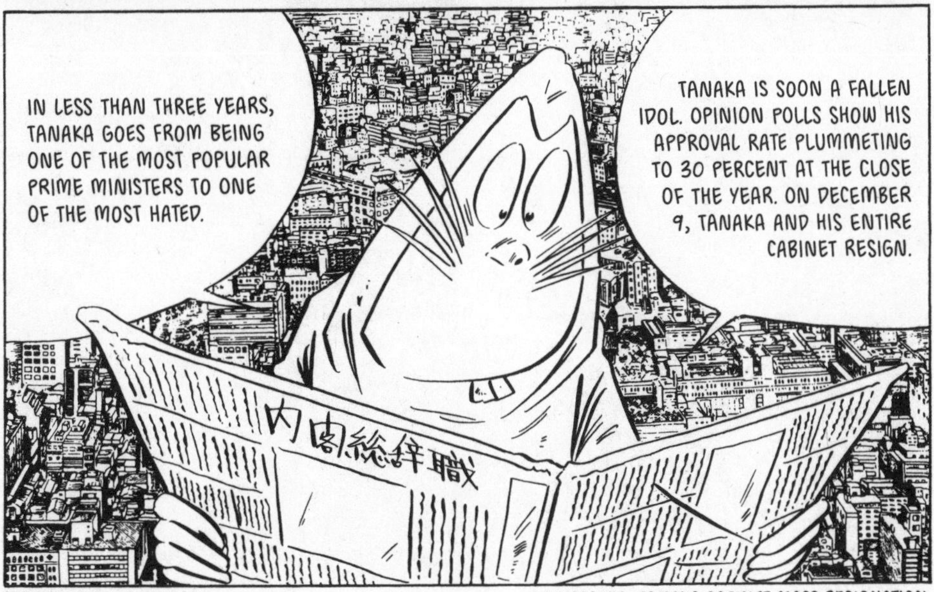
TANAKA IS SOON A FALLEN IDOL. OPINION POLLS SHOW HIS APPROVAL RATE PLUMMETING TO 30 PERCENT AT THE CLOSE OF THE YEAR. ON DECEMBER 9, TANAKA AND HIS ENTIRE CABINET RESIGN.
IN LESS THAN THREE YEARS, TANAKA GOES FROM BEING ONE OF THE MOST POPULAR PRIME MINISTERS TO ONE OF THE MOST HATED.
内閣総辞職

*SEE NOTE ON PAGE 535.

NEWSPAPER: TANAKA CABINET MASS RESIGNATION.

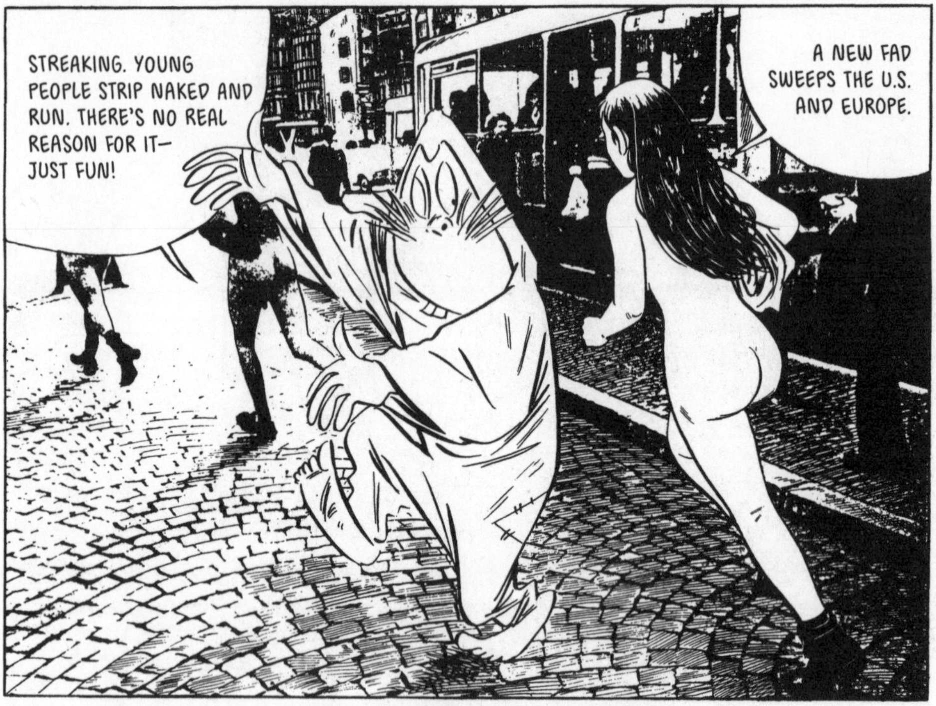
A NEW FAD SWEEPS THE U.S. AND EUROPE.
STREAKING. YOUNG PEOPLE STRIP NAKED AND RUN. THERE'S NO REAL REASON FOR IT— JUST FUN!

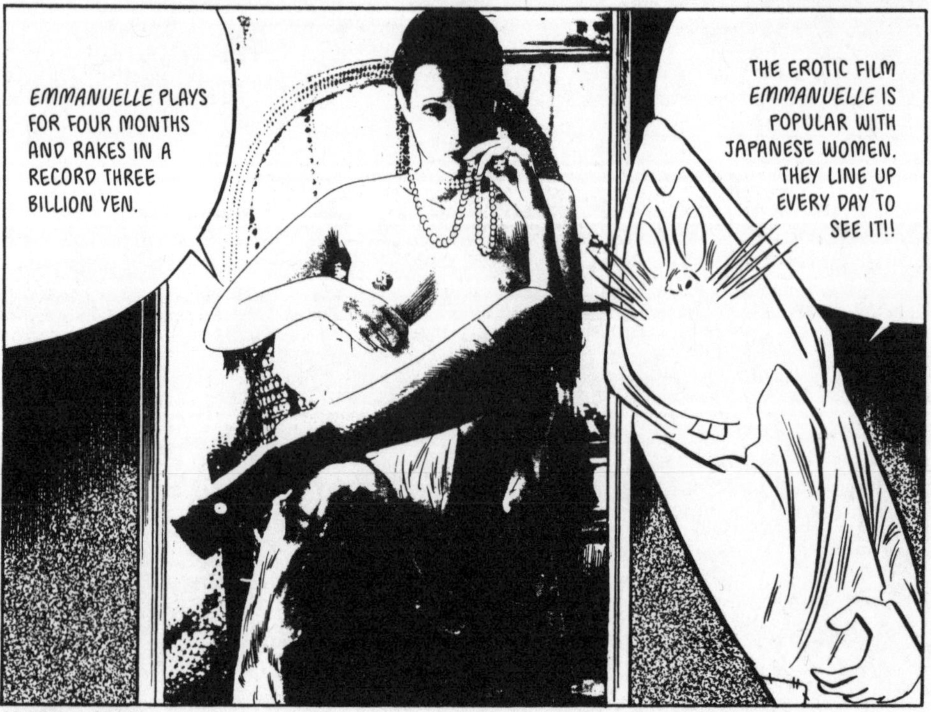
THE EROTIC FILM *EMMANUELLE* IS POPULAR WITH JAPANESE WOMEN. THEY LINE UP EVERY DAY TO SEE IT!!
EMMANUELLE PLAYS FOR FOUR MONTHS AND RAKES IN A RECORD THREE BILLION YEN.

3B YEN = $30M

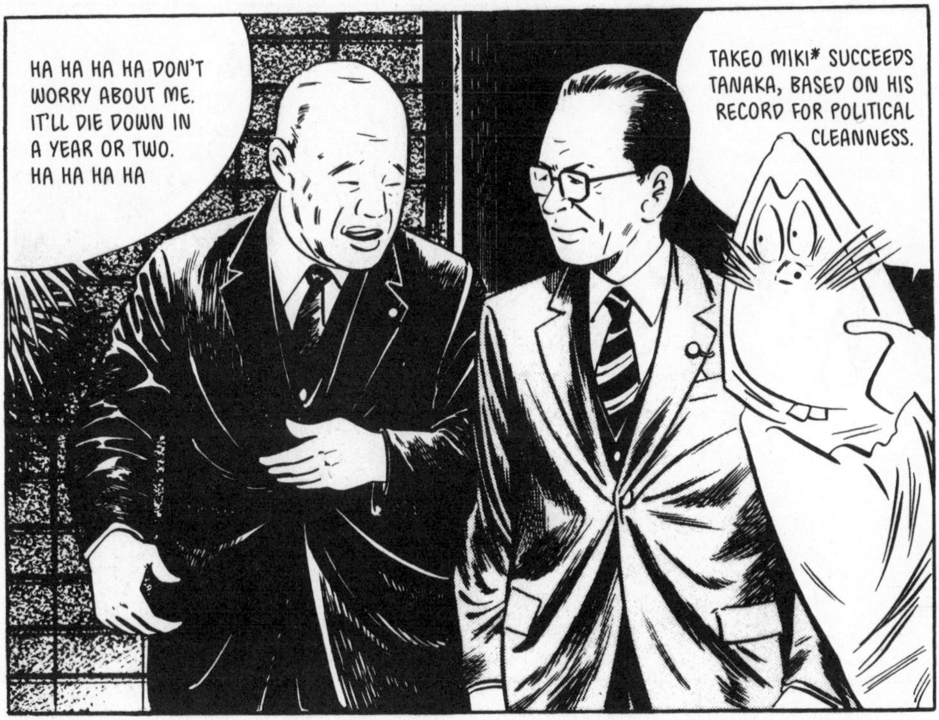
TAKEO MIKI* SUCCEEDS TANAKA, BASED ON HIS RECORD FOR POLITICAL CLEANNESS.
HA HA HA HA DON'T WORRY ABOUT ME. IT'LL DIE DOWN IN A YEAR OR TWO. HA HA HA HA

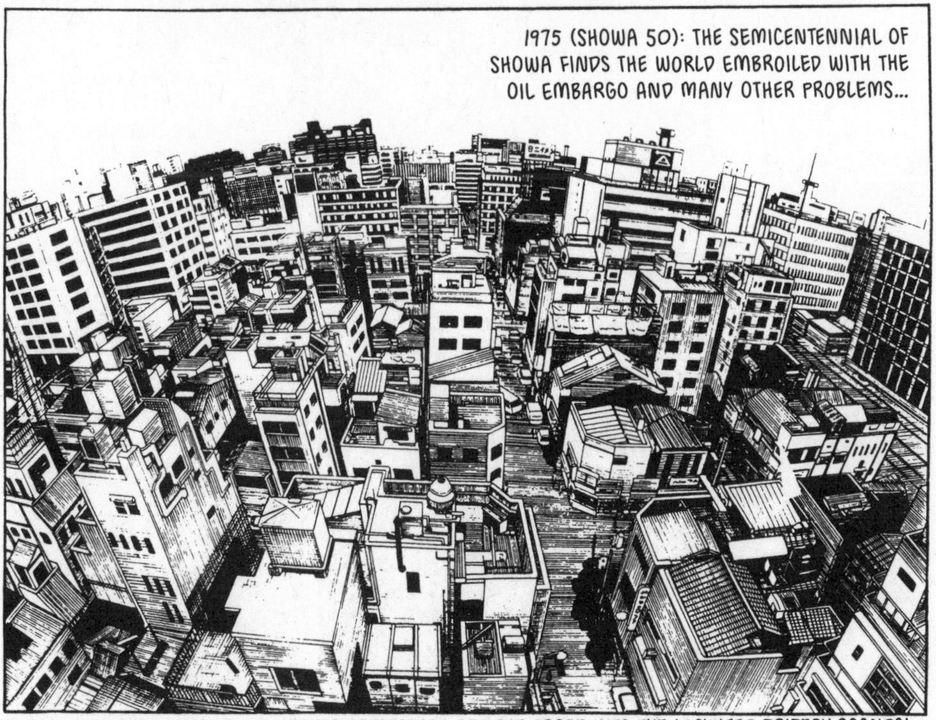
1975 (SHOWA 50): THE SEMICENTENNIAL OF SHOWA FINDS THE WORLD EMBROILED WITH THE OIL EMBARGO AND MANY OTHER PROBLEMS...

*TAKEO MIKI (1907–1988) B. TOKUSHIMA PREFECTURE. LED THE PROBE INTO THE LOCKHEED BRIBERY SCANDAL.

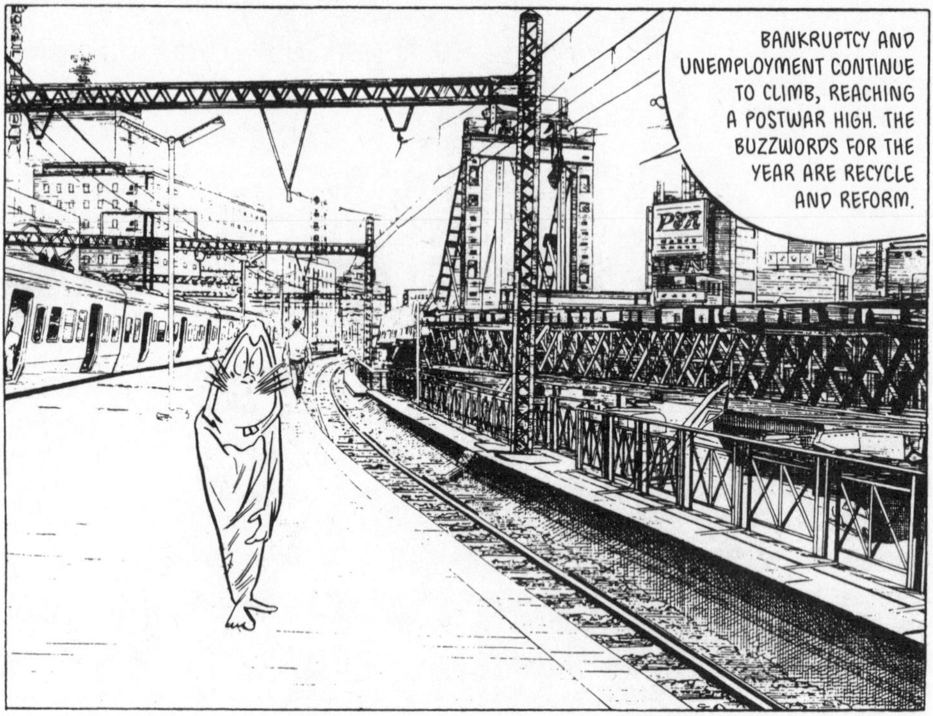
BANKRUPTCY AND UNEMPLOYMENT CONTINUE TO CLIMB, REACHING A POSTWAR HIGH. THE BUZZWORDS FOR THE YEAR ARE RECYCLE AND REFORM.

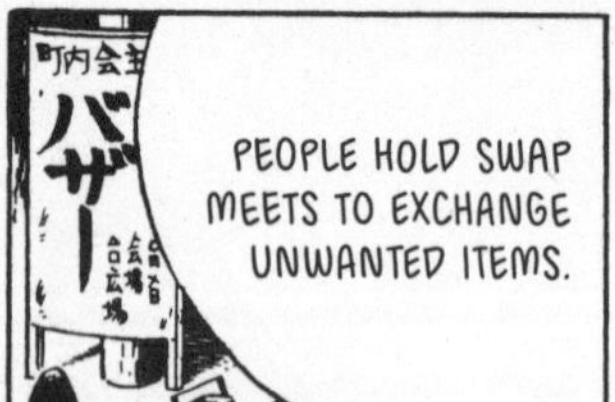
町内会主
バザー
PEOPLE HOLD SWAP MEETS TO EXCHANGE UNWANTED ITEMS.

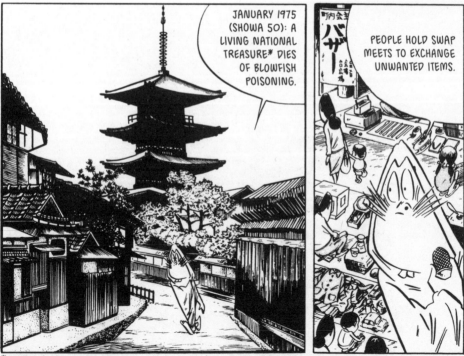

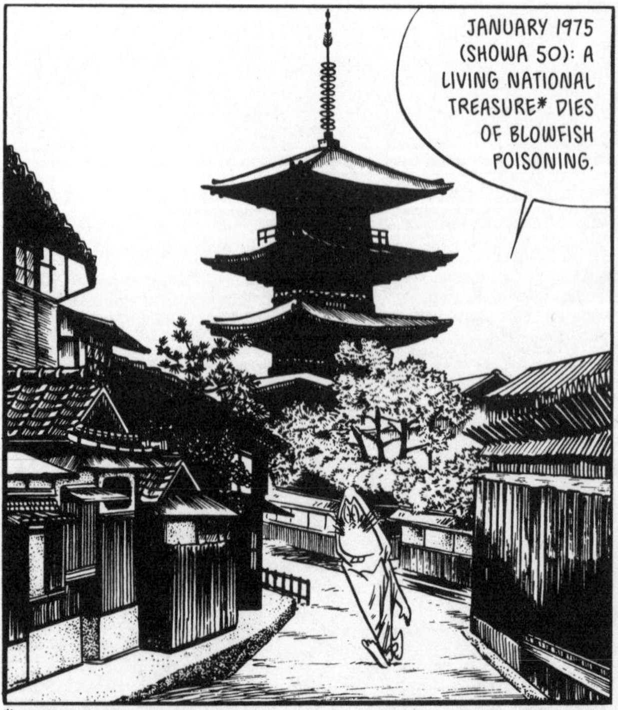
JANUARY 1975 (SHOWA 50): A LIVING NATIONAL TREASURE* DIES OF BLOWFISH POISONING.

*A TITLE AWARDED BY JAPAN TO EXCEPTIONAL ARTISANS WORKING IN PROTECTED TRADITIONAL CRAFTS AND ARTS THAT COMES WITH AN ANNUAL GRANT FROM THE GOVERNMENT.

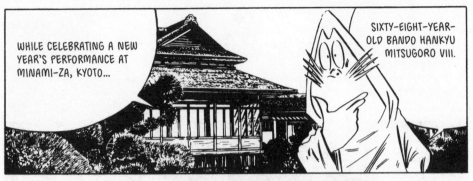

SIXTY-EIGHT-YEAR-OLD BANDO HANKYU MITSUGORO VIII.
WHILE CELEBRATING A NEW YEAR'S PERFORMANCE AT MINAMI-ZA, KYOTO...
I FEEL NUMB.
HE SUDDENLY SHOUTS AND COLLAPSES. HE IS DEAD TWO HOURS LATER FROM BLOWFISH POISONING.
ACCORDING TO THE POLICE REPORT, BANDO AND THREE FRIENDS HAD ORDERED THE BLOWFISH COURSE, BUT NO ONE WAS EATING THE POISONOUS LIVERS.
IF NO ONE'S BRAVE ENOUGH TO EAT THE LIVERS, I WILL...
THIS LIVING NATIONAL TREASURE ATE FOUR ENTIRE SERVINGS.
SOON, THE TREASURE WAS NO LONGER LIVING.
BBHH
BBHHU
BBBHUU

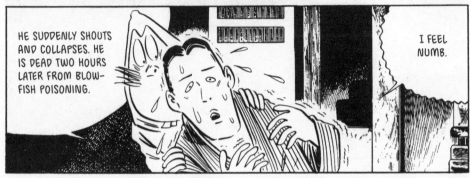

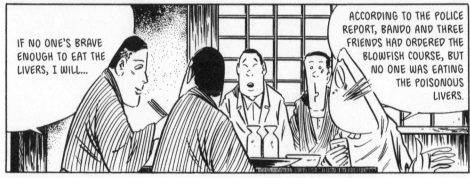

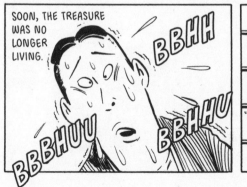

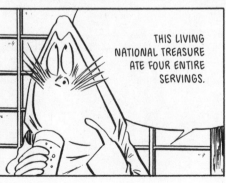

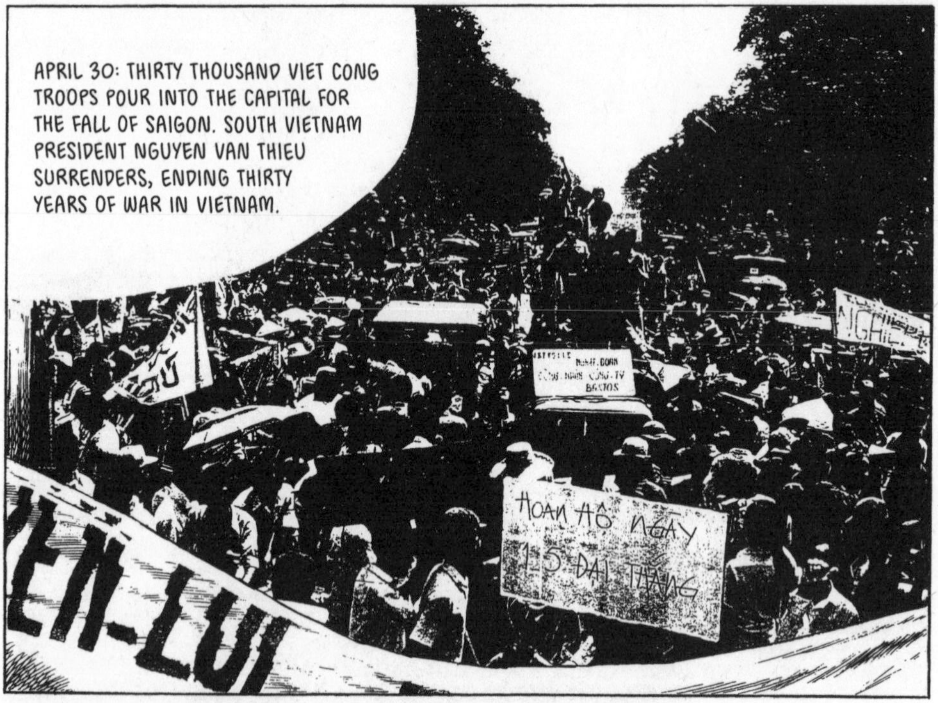
APRIL 30: THIRTY THOUSAND VIET CONG TROOPS POUR INTO THE CAPITAL FOR THE FALL OF SAIGON. SOUTH VIETNAM PRESIDENT NGUYEN VAN THIEU SURRENDERS, ENDING THIRTY YEARS OF WAR IN VIETNAM.

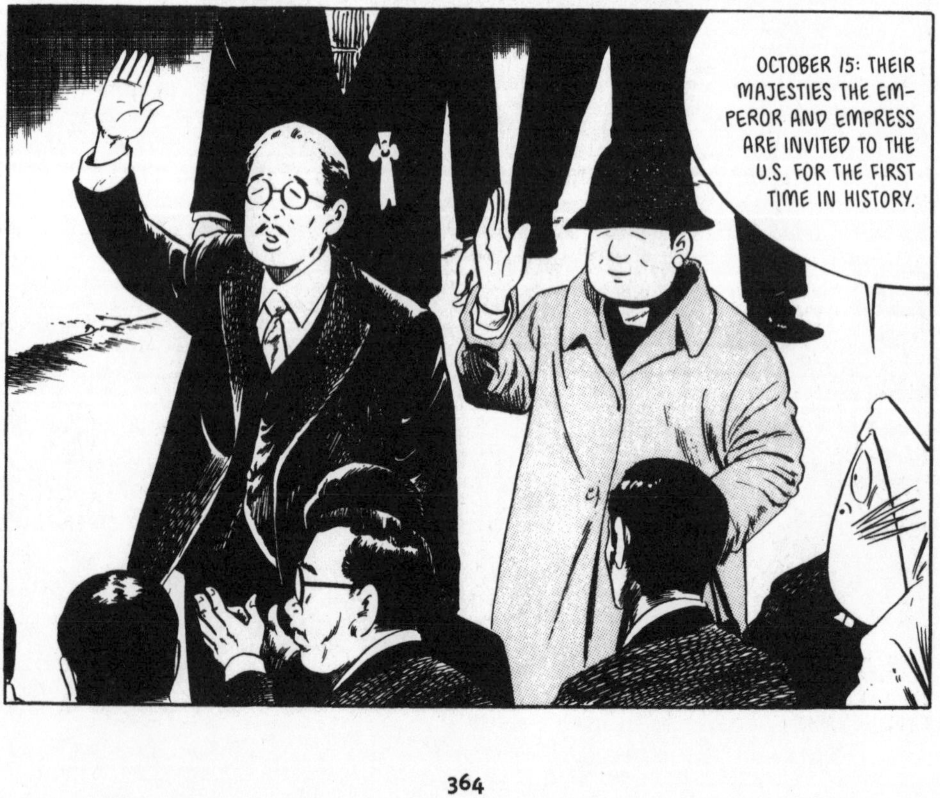
OCTOBER 15: THEIR MAJESTIES THE EMPEROR AND EMPRESS ARE INVITED TO THE U.S. FOR THE FIRST TIME IN HISTORY.

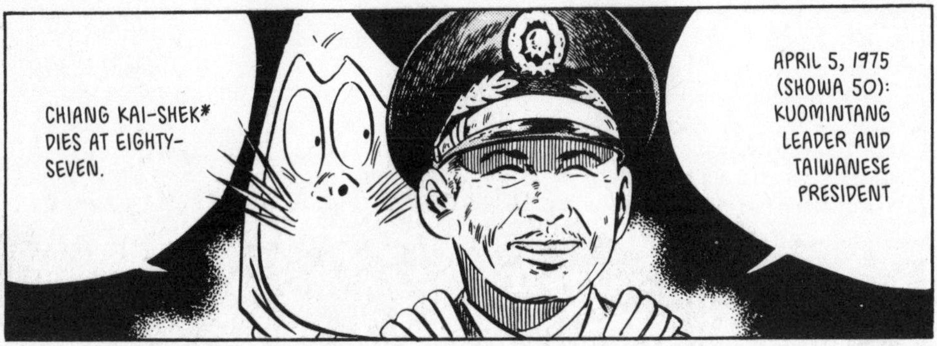
APRIL 5, 1975 (SHOWA 50): KUOMINTANG LEADER AND TAIWANESE PRESIDENT
CHIANG KAI-SHEK* DIES AT EIGHTY-SEVEN.

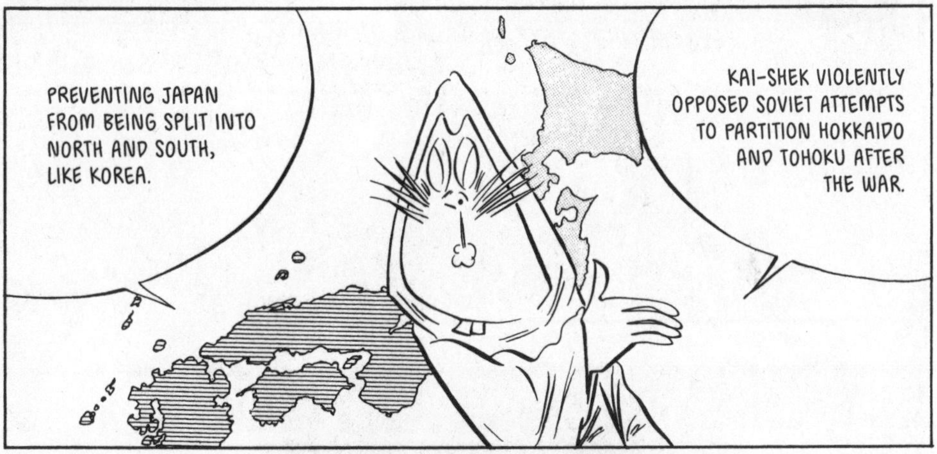
KAI-SHEK VIOLENTLY OPPOSED SOVIET ATTEMPTS TO PARTITION HOKKAIDO AND TOHOKU AFTER THE WAR.
PREVENTING JAPAN FROM BEING SPLIT INTO NORTH AND SOUTH, LIKE KOREA.

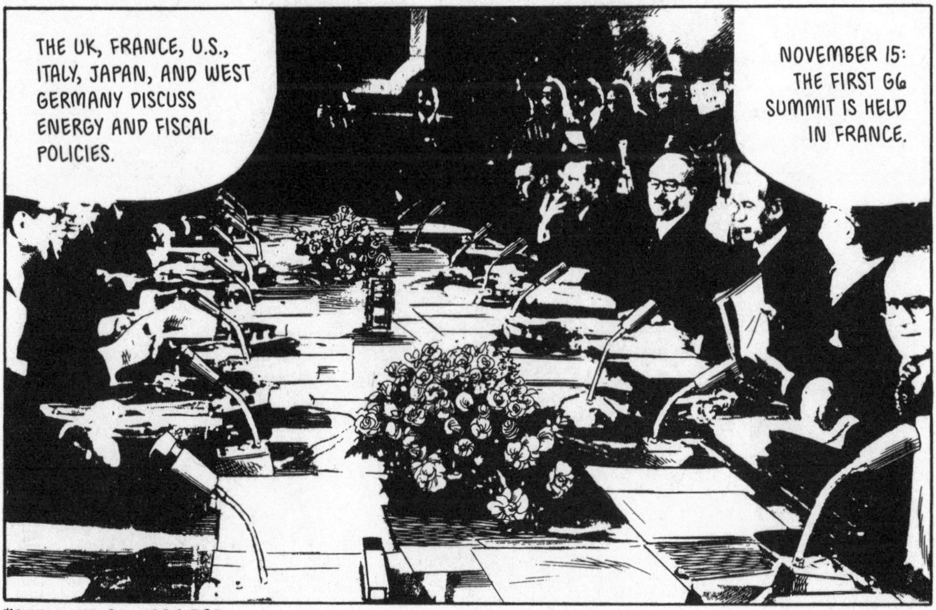
NOVEMBER 15: THE FIRST G6 SUMMIT IS HELD IN FRANCE.
THE UK, FRANCE, U.S., ITALY, JAPAN, AND WEST GERMANY DISCUSS ENERGY AND FISCAL POLICIES.

*SEE NOTE ON PAGE 535.

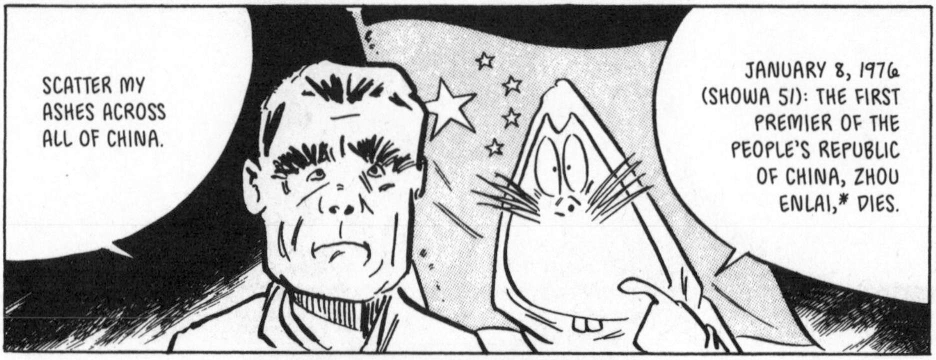

JANUARY 8, 1976 (SHOWA 51): THE FIRST PREMIER OF THE PEOPLE'S REPUBLIC OF CHINA, ZHOU ENLAI,* DIES.
SCATTER MY ASHES ACROSS ALL OF CHINA.

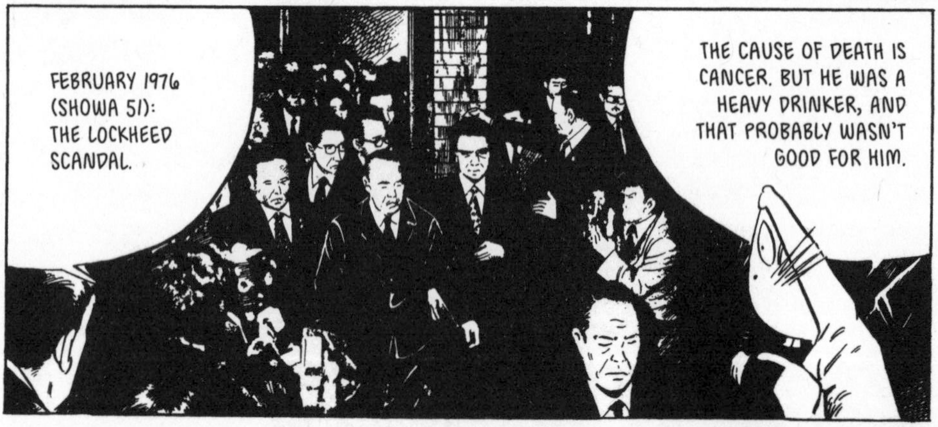

THE CAUSE OF DEATH IS CANCER. BUT HE WAS A HEAVY DRINKER, AND THAT PROBABLY WASN'T GOOD FOR HIM.
FEBRUARY 1976 (SHOWA 51): THE LOCKHEED SCANDAL.

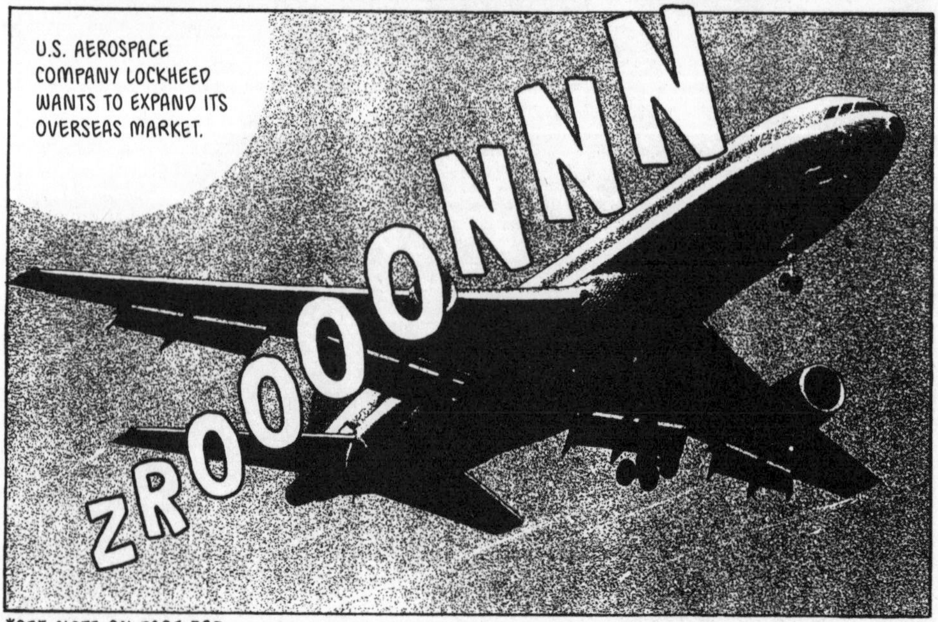

U.S. AEROSPACE COMPANY LOCKHEED WANTS TO EXPAND ITS OVERSEAS MARKET.
ZROOOOONNN

*SEE NOTE ON PAGE 535.

FEBRUARY 4: A U.S. SENATE FOREIGN RELATIONS SUBCOMMITTEE REVEALS...

THAT LOCKHEED HAS BEEN BRIBING KEY OFFICIALS IN SEVERAL COUNTRIES.

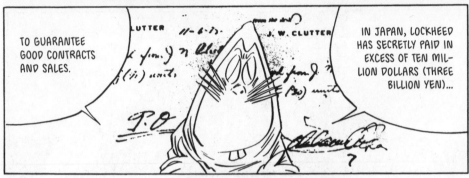

IN JAPAN, LOCKHEED HAS SECRETLY PAID IN EXCESS OF TEN MILLION DOLLARS (THREE BILLION YEN)...

TO GUARANTEE GOOD CONTRACTS AND SALES.

ACCOUNTANT WILLIAM FINDLEY BLOWS THE WHISTLE WHEN HE SEES...

RECEIPTS MADE OUT TO ULTRANATIONALIST GANGSTER YOSHIO KODAMA.

THE SUBCOMMITTEE GATHERS AND TRANSLATES KODAMA'S RECEIPTS.

ON THE SIXTH, HEARINGS ARE HELD.

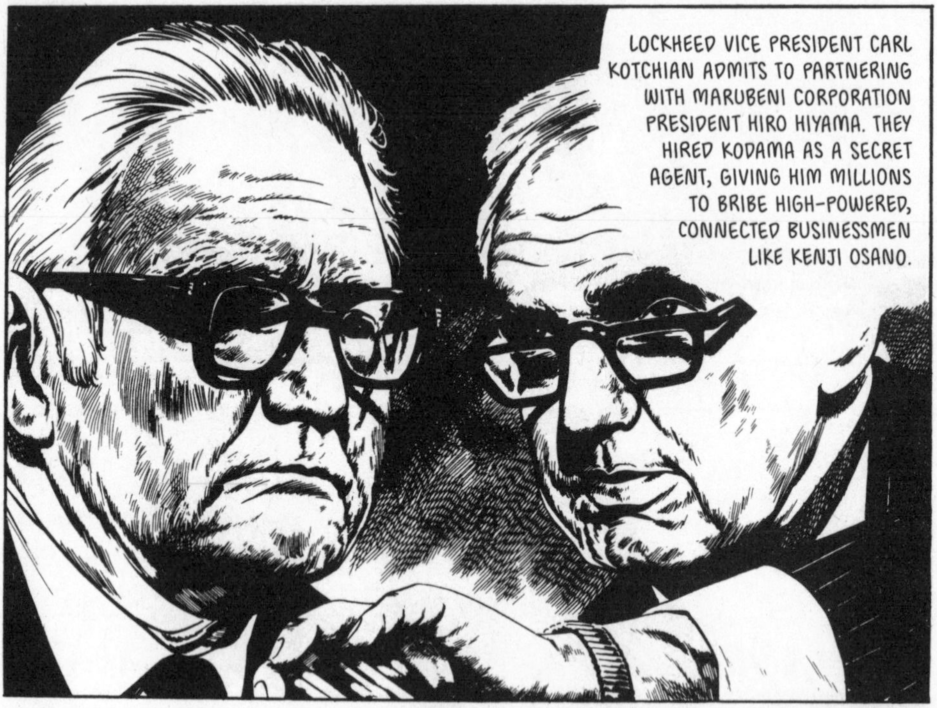
LOCKHEED VICE PRESIDENT CARL KOTCHIAN ADMITS TO PARTNERING WITH MARUBENI CORPORATION PRESIDENT HIRO HIYAMA. THEY HIRED KODAMA AS A SECRET AGENT, GIVING HIM MILLIONS TO BRIBE HIGH-POWERED, CONNECTED BUSINESSMEN LIKE KENJI OSANO.

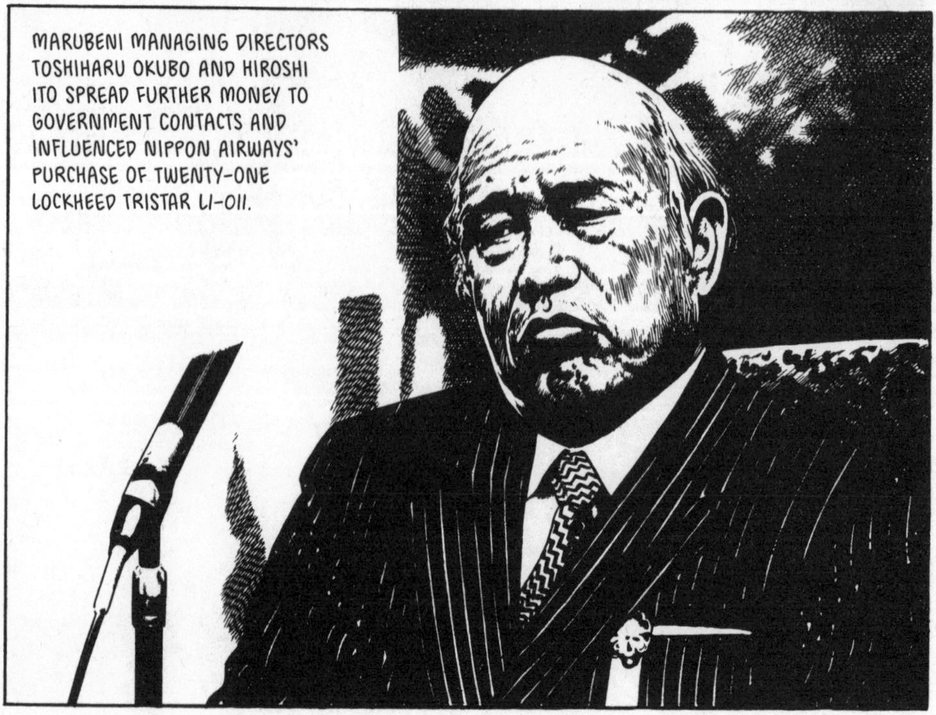
MARUBENI MANAGING DIRECTORS TOSHIHARU OKUBO AND HIROSHI ITO SPREAD FURTHER MONEY TO GOVERNMENT CONTACTS AND INFLUENCED NIPPON AIRWAYS' PURCHASE OF TWENTY-ONE LOCKHEED TRISTAR L1-011.

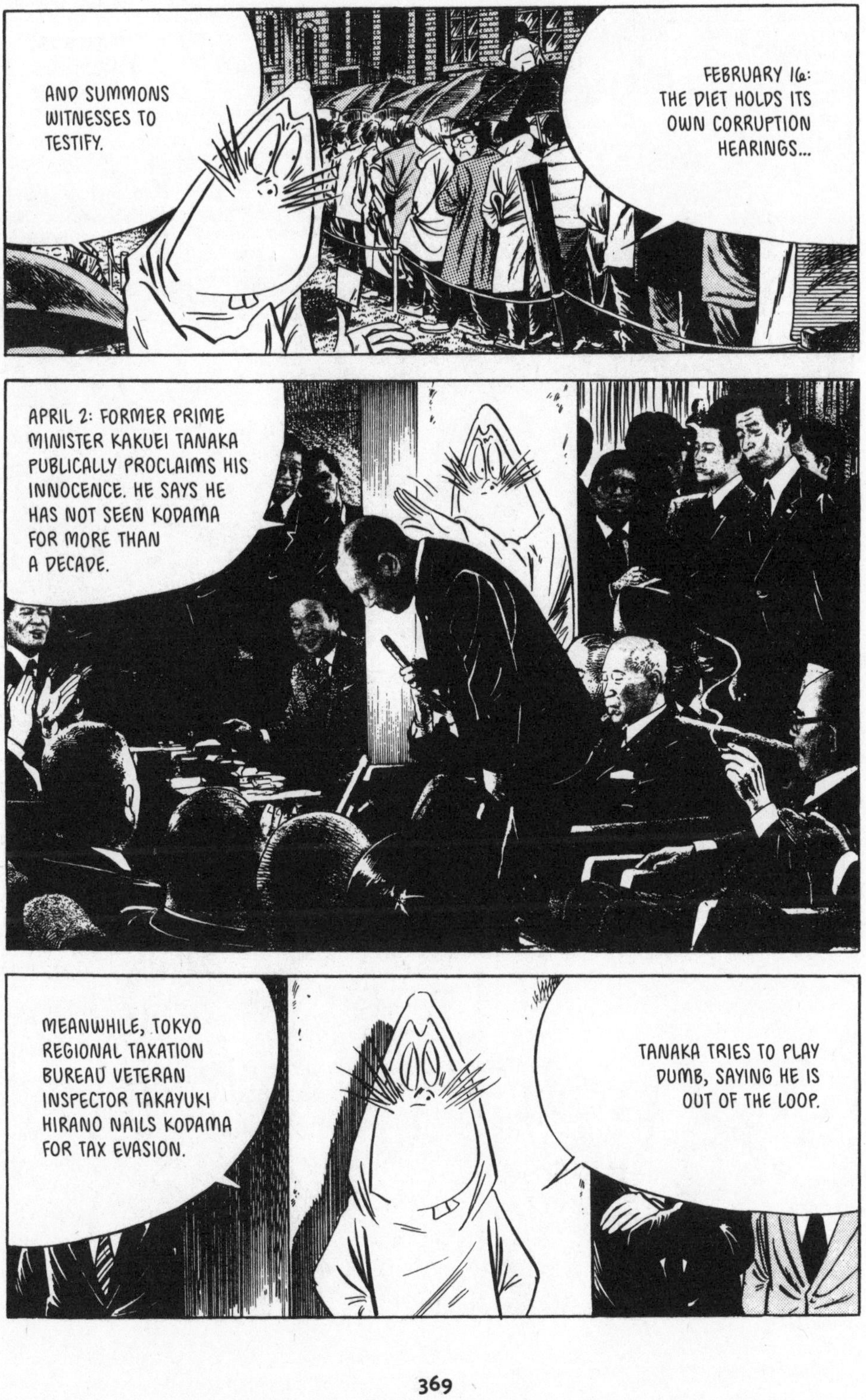
FEBRUARY 16: THE DIET HOLDS ITS OWN CORRUPTION HEARINGS...
AND SUMMONS WITNESSES TO TESTIFY.
APRIL 2: FORMER PRIME MINISTER KAKUEI TANAKA PUBLICALLY PROCLAIMS HIS INNOCENCE. HE SAYS HE HAS NOT SEEN KODAMA FOR MORE THAN A DECADE.
TANAKA TRIES TO PLAY DUMB, SAYING HE IS OUT OF THE LOOP.
MEANWHILE, TOKYO REGIONAL TAXATION BUREAU VETERAN INSPECTOR TAKAYUKI HIRANO NAILS KODAMA FOR TAX EVASION.

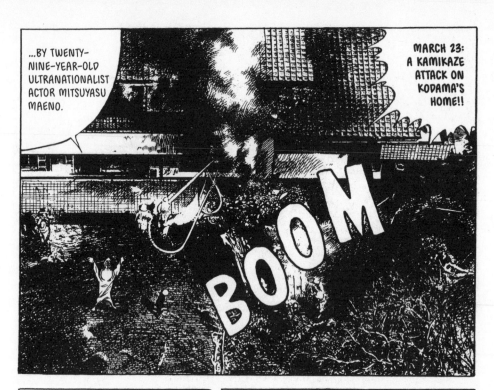

MARCH 23: A KAMIKAZE ATTACK ON KODAMA'S HOME!!
...BY TWENTY-NINE-YEAR-OLD ULTRANATIONALIST ACTOR MITSUYASU MAENO.
BOOM
HE ALWAYS ADMIRED THE KAMIKAZE AND EVEN DRESSED LIKE THEM.
ACROSS JAPAN, PEOPLE ARE STRUGGLING FINANCIALLY. THEY'RE ANGRY BEYOND BELIEF TO SEE POLITICIANS AND CORPORATIONS POCKETING MILLIONS IN BACKROOM DEALS WHILE THE COMMON PEOPLE SUFFER. MANY APPLAUD MAENO'S ATTACK—IT'S JUST TOO BAD HE FAILED.

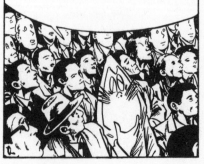

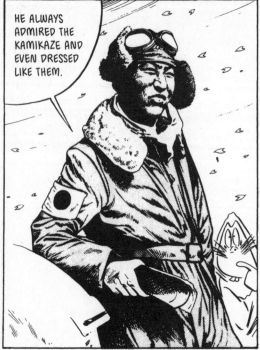

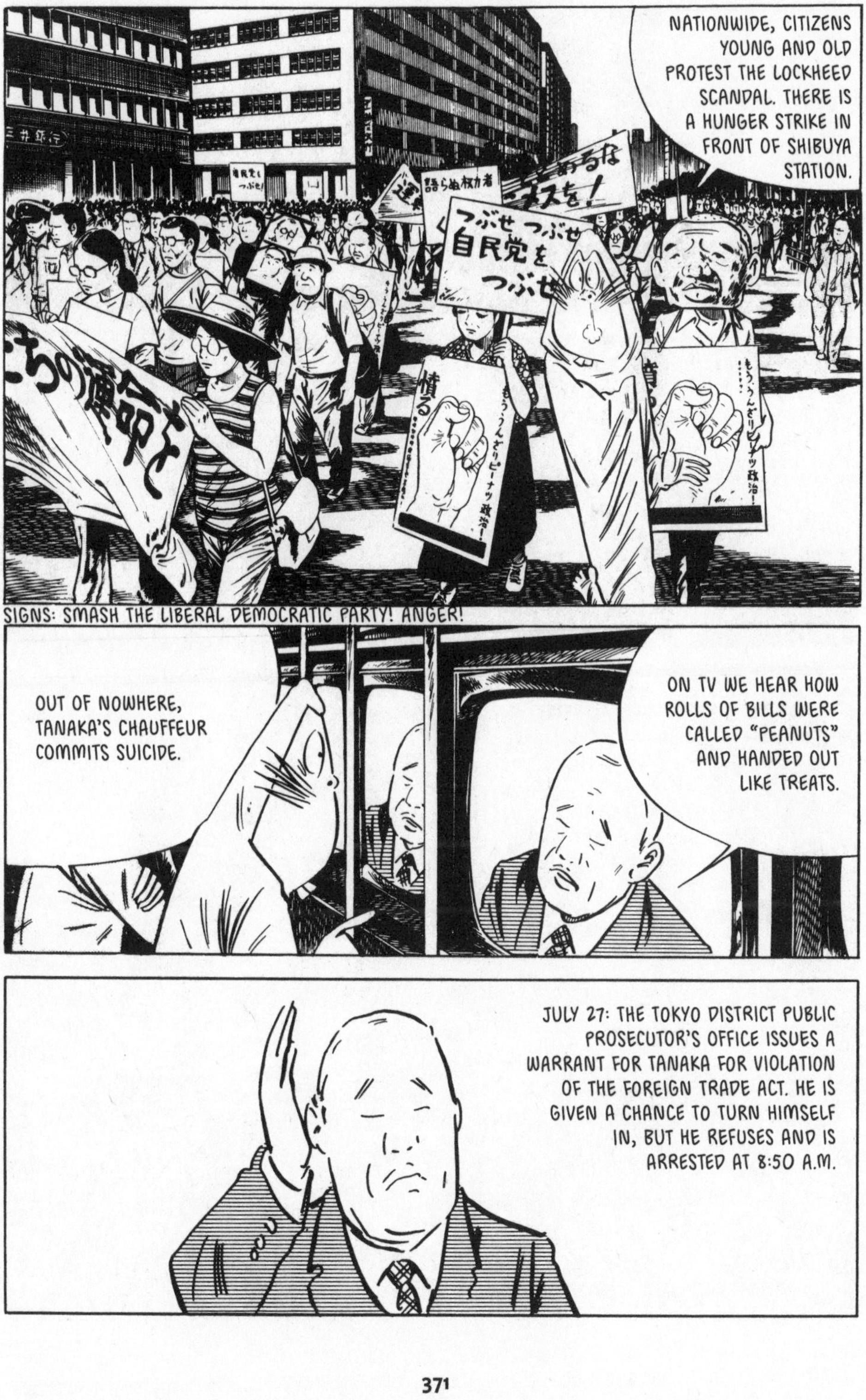
NATIONWIDE, CITIZENS YOUNG AND OLD PROTEST THE LOCKHEED SCANDAL. THERE IS A HUNGER STRIKE IN FRONT OF SHIBUYA STATION.
つぶせ つぶせ 自民党を つぶせ
SIGNS: SMASH THE LIBERAL DEMOCRATIC PARTY! ANGER!
ON TV WE HEAR HOW ROLLS OF BILLS WERE CALLED "PEANUTS" AND HANDED OUT LIKE TREATS.
OUT OF NOWHERE, TANAKA'S CHAUFFEUR COMMITS SUICIDE.
JULY 27: THE TOKYO DISTRICT PUBLIC PROSECUTOR'S OFFICE ISSUES A WARRANT FOR TANAKA FOR VIOLATION OF THE FOREIGN TRADE ACT. HE IS GIVEN A CHANCE TO TURN HIMSELF IN, BUT HE REFUSES AND IS ARRESTED AT 8:50 A.M.

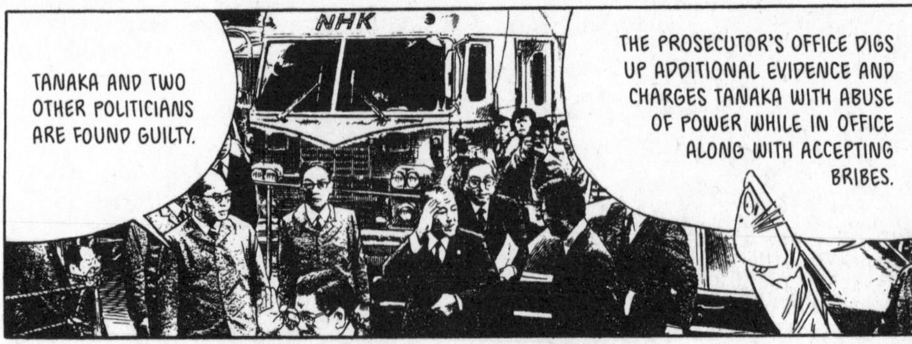
NHK
THE PROSECUTOR'S OFFICE DIGS UP ADDITIONAL EVIDENCE AND CHARGES TANAKA WITH ABUSE OF POWER WHILE IN OFFICE ALONG WITH ACCEPTING BRIBES.
TANAKA AND TWO OTHER POLITICIANS ARE FOUND GUILTY.

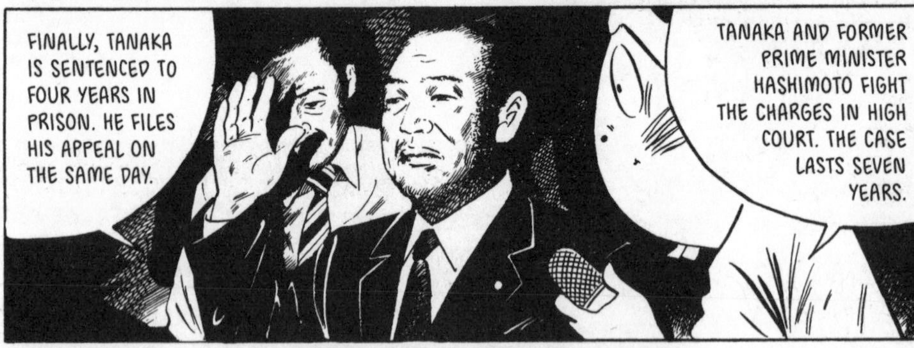
TANAKA AND FORMER PRIME MINISTER HASHIMOTO FIGHT THE CHARGES IN HIGH COURT. THE CASE LASTS SEVEN YEARS.
FINALLY, TANAKA IS SENTENCED TO FOUR YEARS IN PRISON. HE FILES HIS APPEAL ON THE SAME DAY.

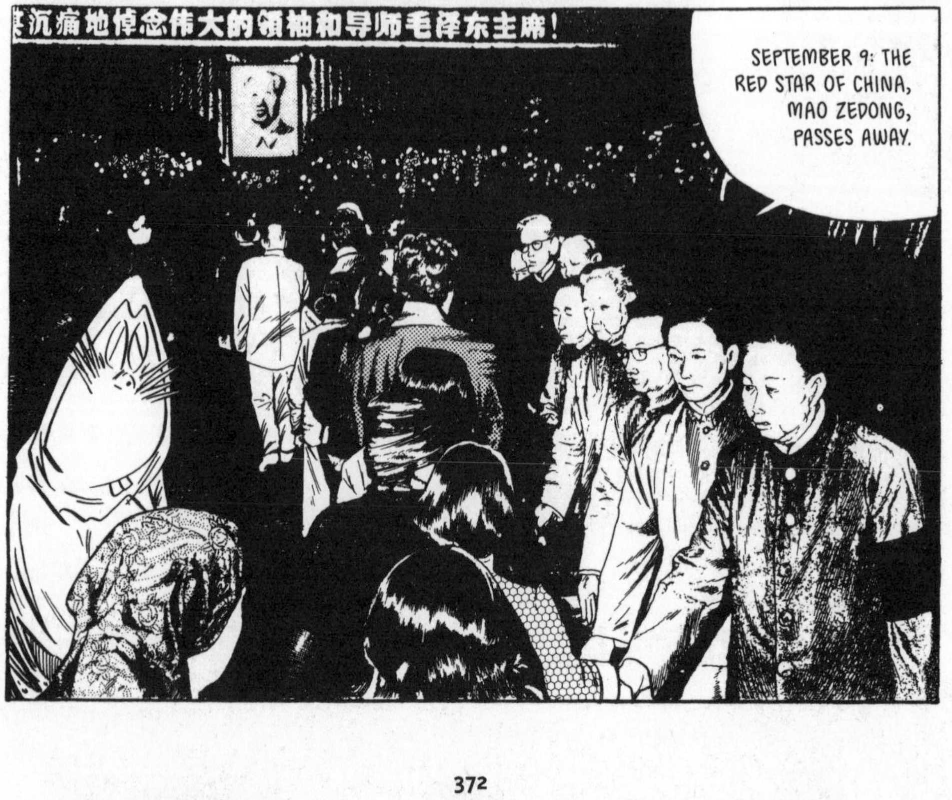
SEPTEMBER 9: THE RED STAR OF CHINA, MAO ZEDONG, PASSES AWAY.
沉痛地悼念伟大的领袖和导师毛泽东主席！

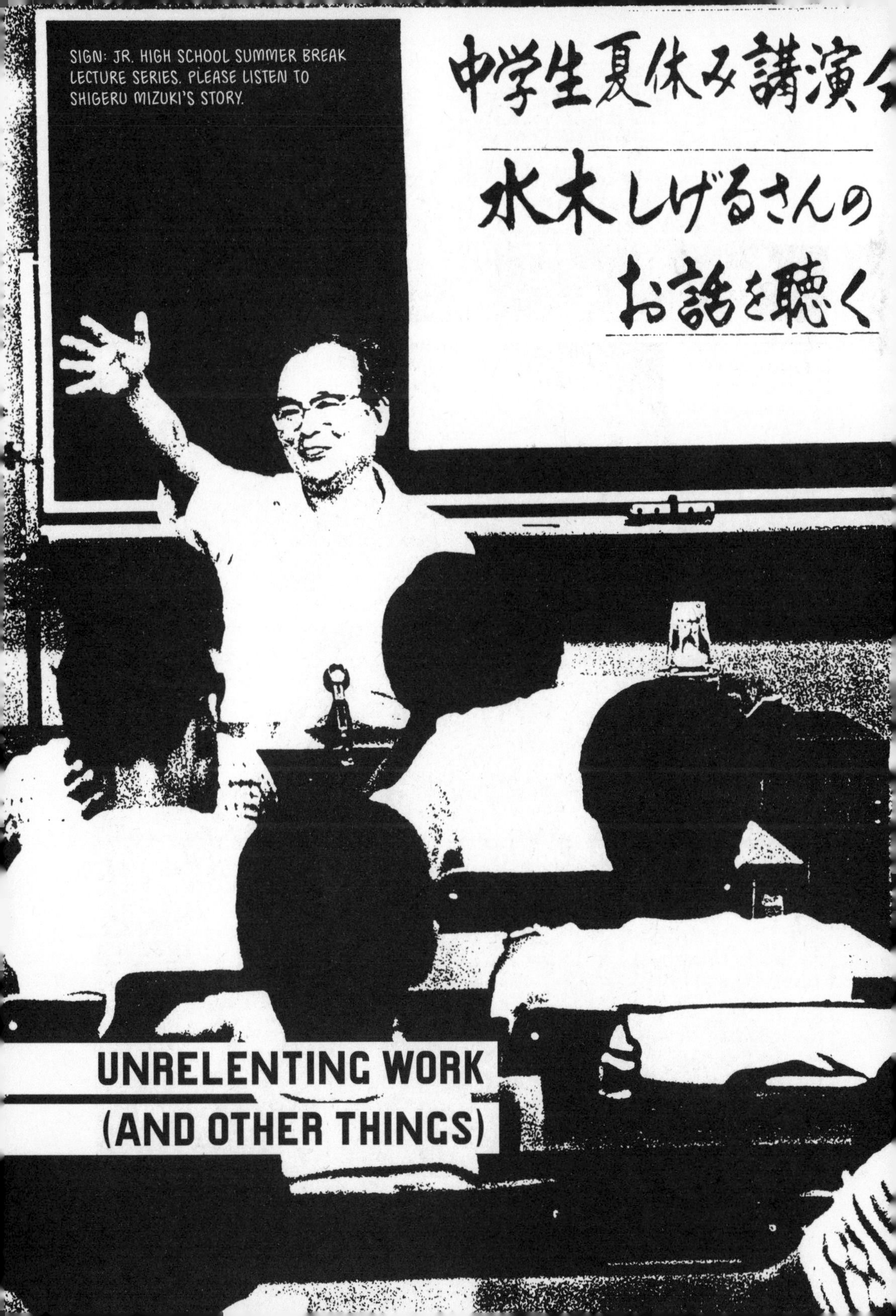
SIGN: JR. HIGH SCHOOL SUMMER BREAK LECTURE SERIES. PLEASE LISTEN TO SHIGERU MIZUKI'S STORY.
中学生夏休み講演会
水木しげるさんの
お話を聴く

UNRELENTING WORK (AND OTHER THINGS)

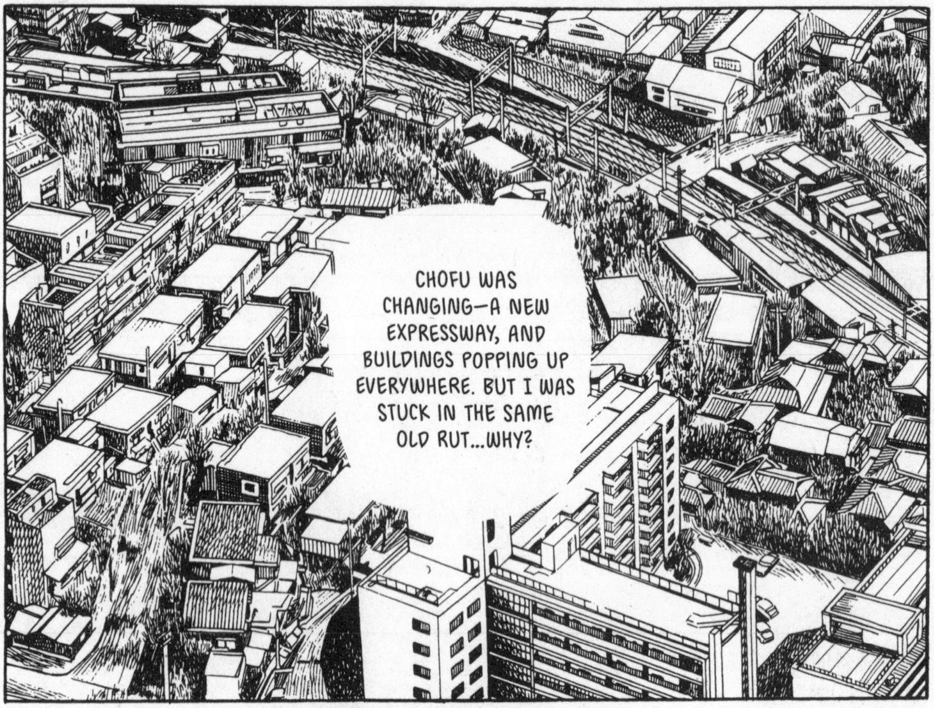
CHOFU WAS CHANGING—A NEW EXPRESSWAY, AND BUILDINGS POPPING UP EVERYWHERE. BUT I WAS STUCK IN THE SAME OLD RUT...WHY?

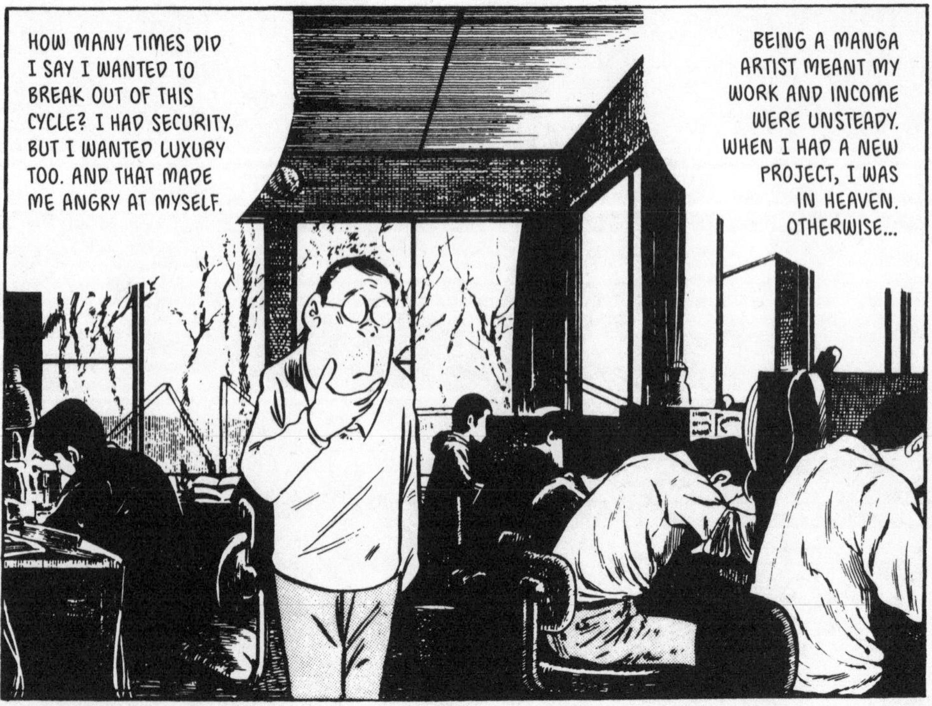
BEING A MANGA ARTIST MEANT MY WORK AND INCOME WERE UNSTEADY. WHEN I HAD A NEW PROJECT, I WAS IN HEAVEN. OTHERWISE...
HOW MANY TIMES DID I SAY I WANTED TO BREAK OUT OF THIS CYCLE? I HAD SECURITY, BUT I WANTED LUXURY TOO. AND THAT MADE ME ANGRY AT MYSELF.

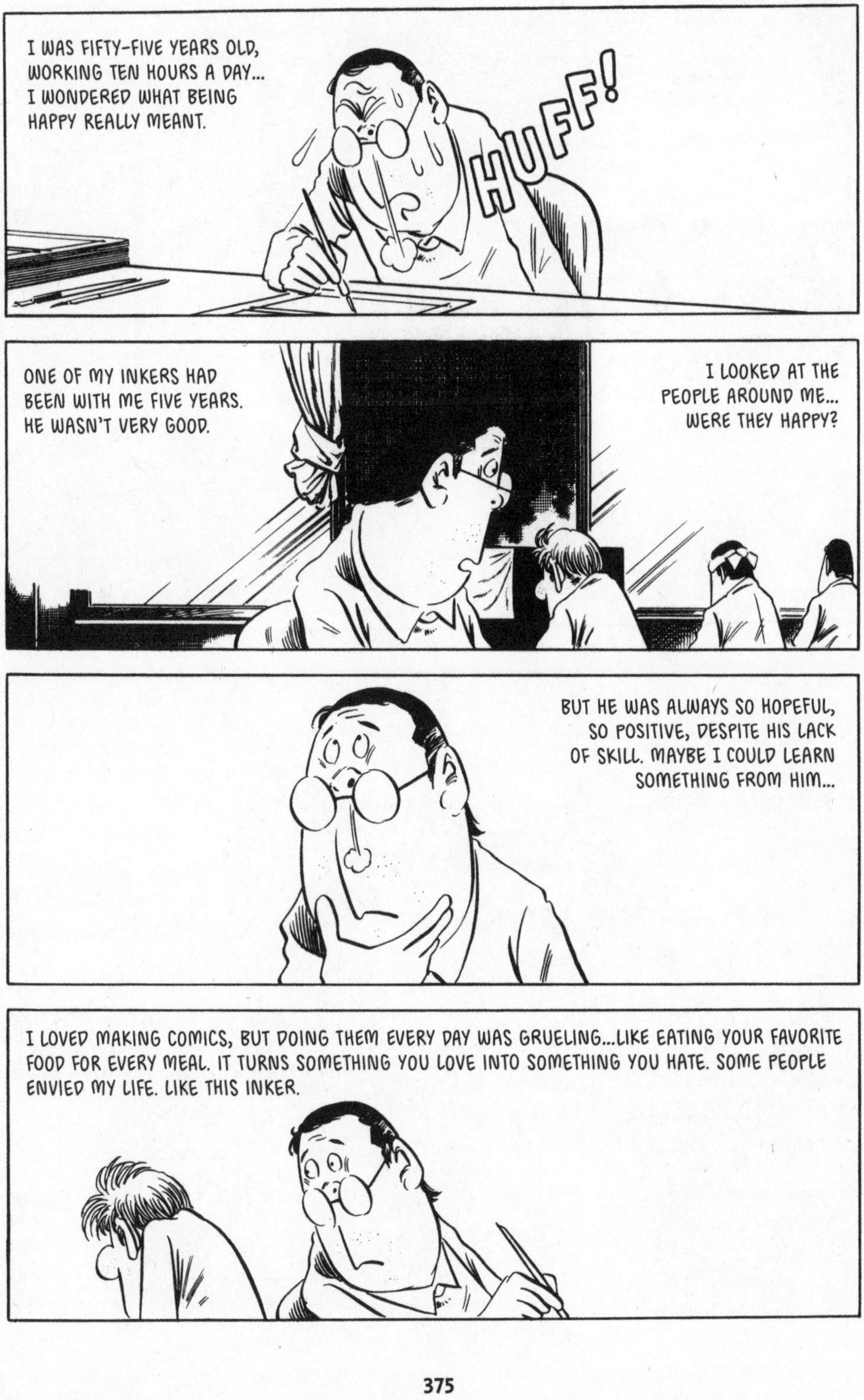
I WAS FIFTY-FIVE YEARS OLD, WORKING TEN HOURS A DAY... I WONDERED WHAT BEING HAPPY REALLY MEANT.
HUFF!
I LOOKED AT THE PEOPLE AROUND ME... WERE THEY HAPPY?
ONE OF MY INKERS HAD BEEN WITH ME FIVE YEARS. HE WASN'T VERY GOOD.
BUT HE WAS ALWAYS SO HOPEFUL, SO POSITIVE, DESPITE HIS LACK OF SKILL. MAYBE I COULD LEARN SOMETHING FROM HIM...
I LOVED MAKING COMICS, BUT DOING THEM EVERY DAY WAS GRUELING...LIKE EATING YOUR FAVORITE FOOD FOR EVERY MEAL. IT TURNS SOMETHING YOU LOVE INTO SOMETHING YOU HATE. SOME PEOPLE ENVIED MY LIFE. LIKE THIS INKER.

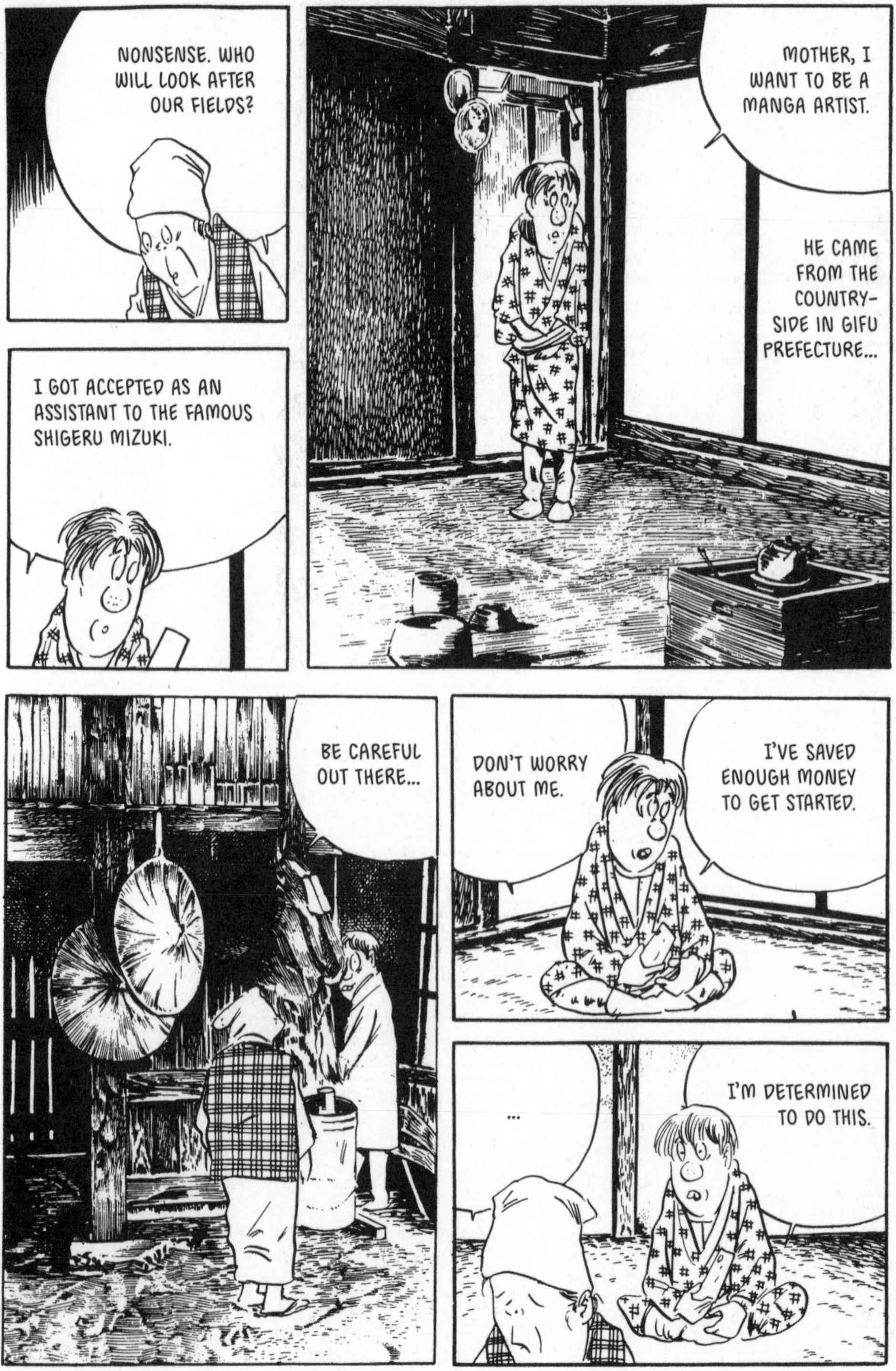
MOTHER, I WANT TO BE A MANGA ARTIST.
HE CAME FROM THE COUNTRY-SIDE IN GIFU PREFECTURE...
NONSENSE. WHO WILL LOOK AFTER OUR FIELDS?
I GOT ACCEPTED AS AN ASSISTANT TO THE FAMOUS SHIGERU MIZUKI.
I'VE SAVED ENOUGH MONEY TO GET STARTED.
DON'T WORRY ABOUT ME.
I'M DETERMINED TO DO THIS.
...
BE CAREFUL OUT THERE...

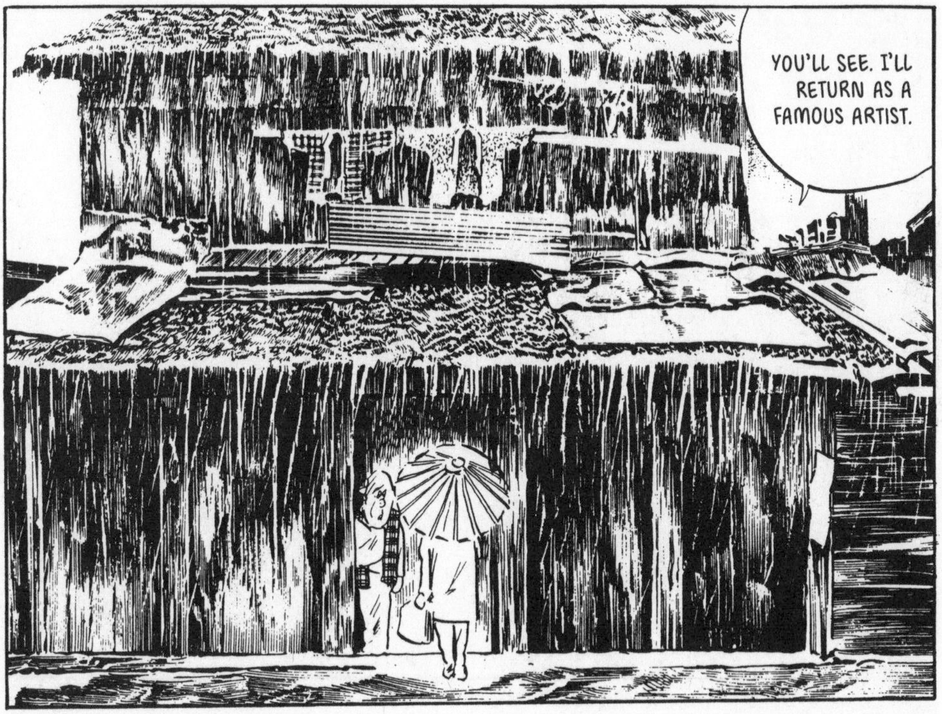
YOU'LL SEE. I'LL RETURN AS A FAMOUS ARTIST.

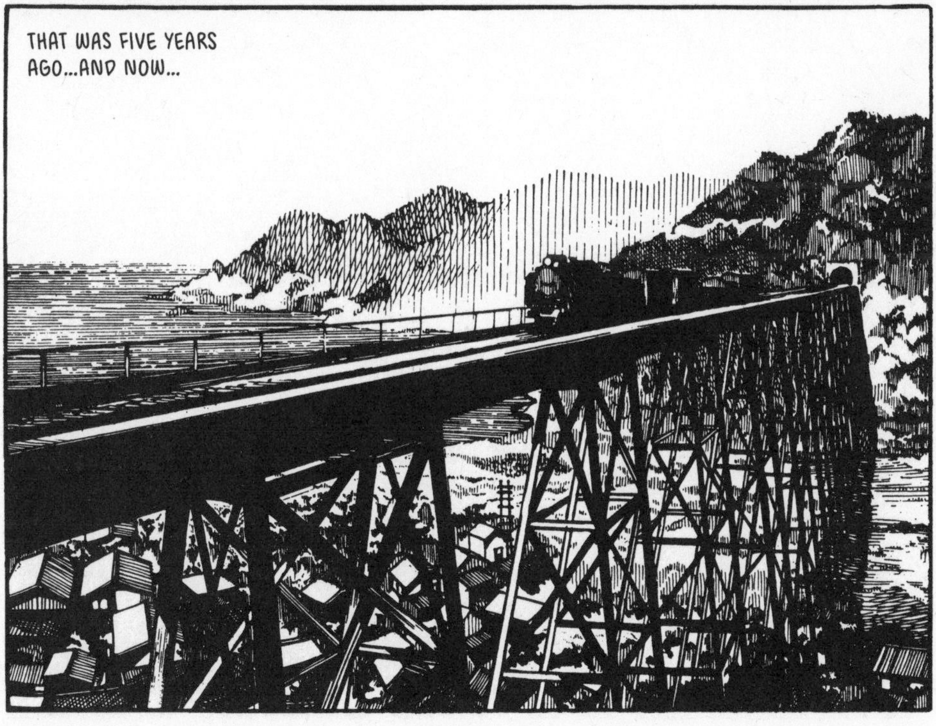
THAT WAS FIVE YEARS AGO...AND NOW...

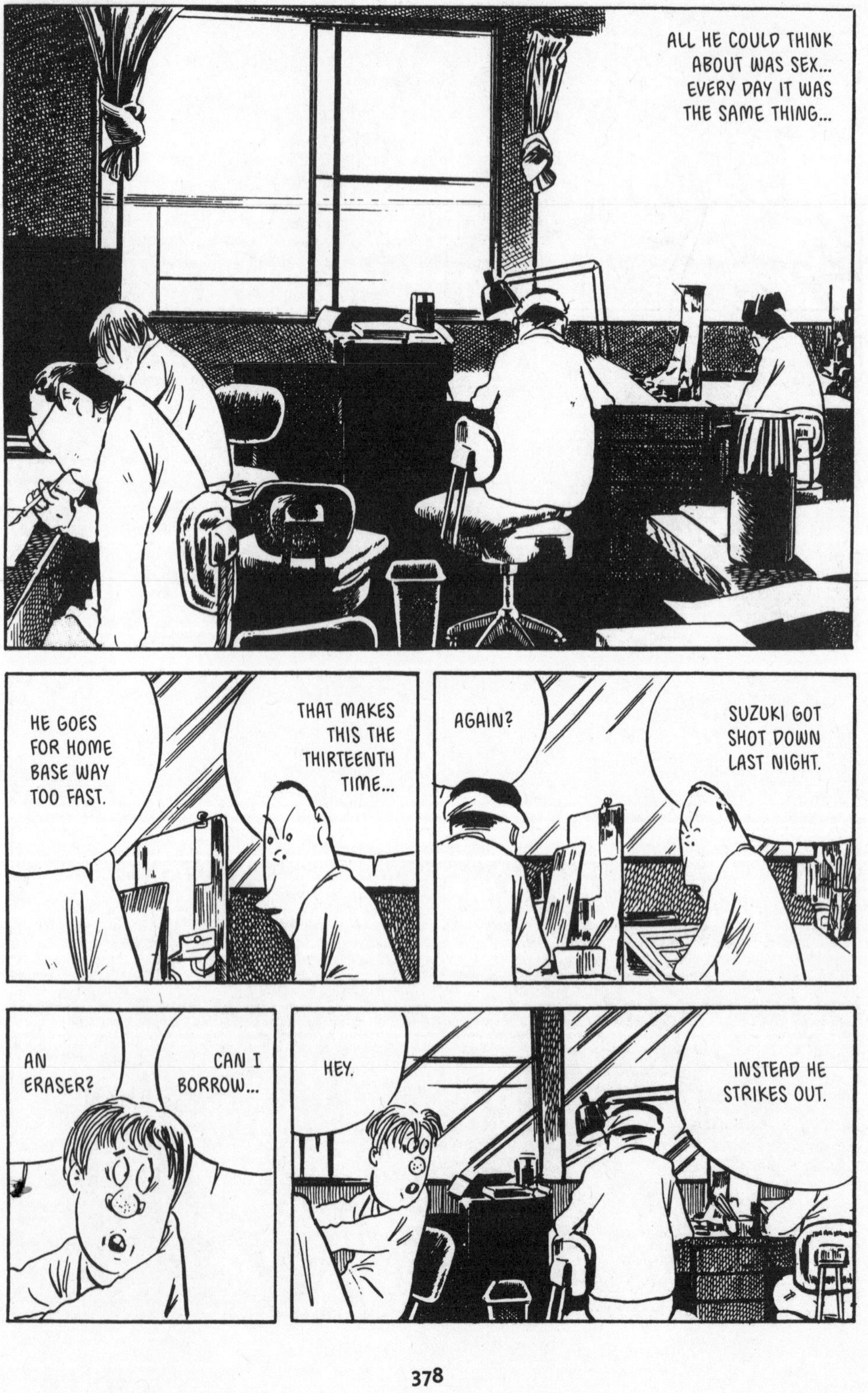
ALL HE COULD THINK ABOUT WAS SEX... EVERY DAY IT WAS THE SAME THING...
SUZUKI GOT SHOT DOWN LAST NIGHT.
AGAIN?
THAT MAKES THIS THE THIRTEENTH TIME...
HE GOES FOR HOME BASE WAY TOO FAST.
INSTEAD HE STRIKES OUT.
HEY.
CAN I BORROW...
AN ERASER?

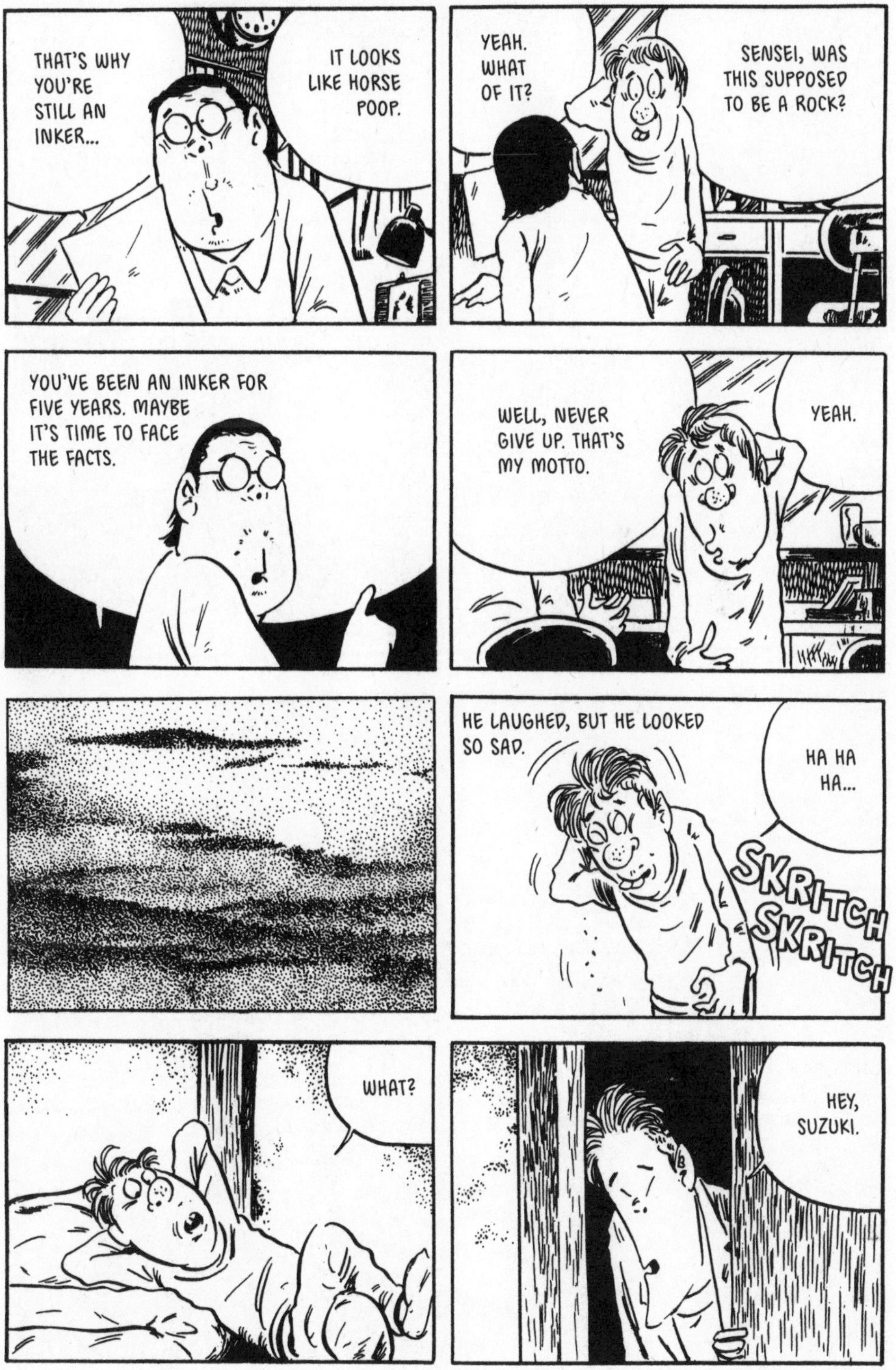
SENSEI, WAS THIS SUPPOSED TO BE A ROCK?
YEAH. WHAT OF IT?
IT LOOKS LIKE HORSE POOP.
THAT'S WHY YOU'RE STILL AN INKER...
YEAH.
WELL, NEVER GIVE UP. THAT'S MY MOTTO.
YOU'VE BEEN AN INKER FOR FIVE YEARS. MAYBE IT'S TIME TO FACE THE FACTS.
HA HA HA...
HE LAUGHED, BUT HE LOOKED SO SAD.
SKRITCH SKRITCH
HEY, SUZUKI.
WHAT?

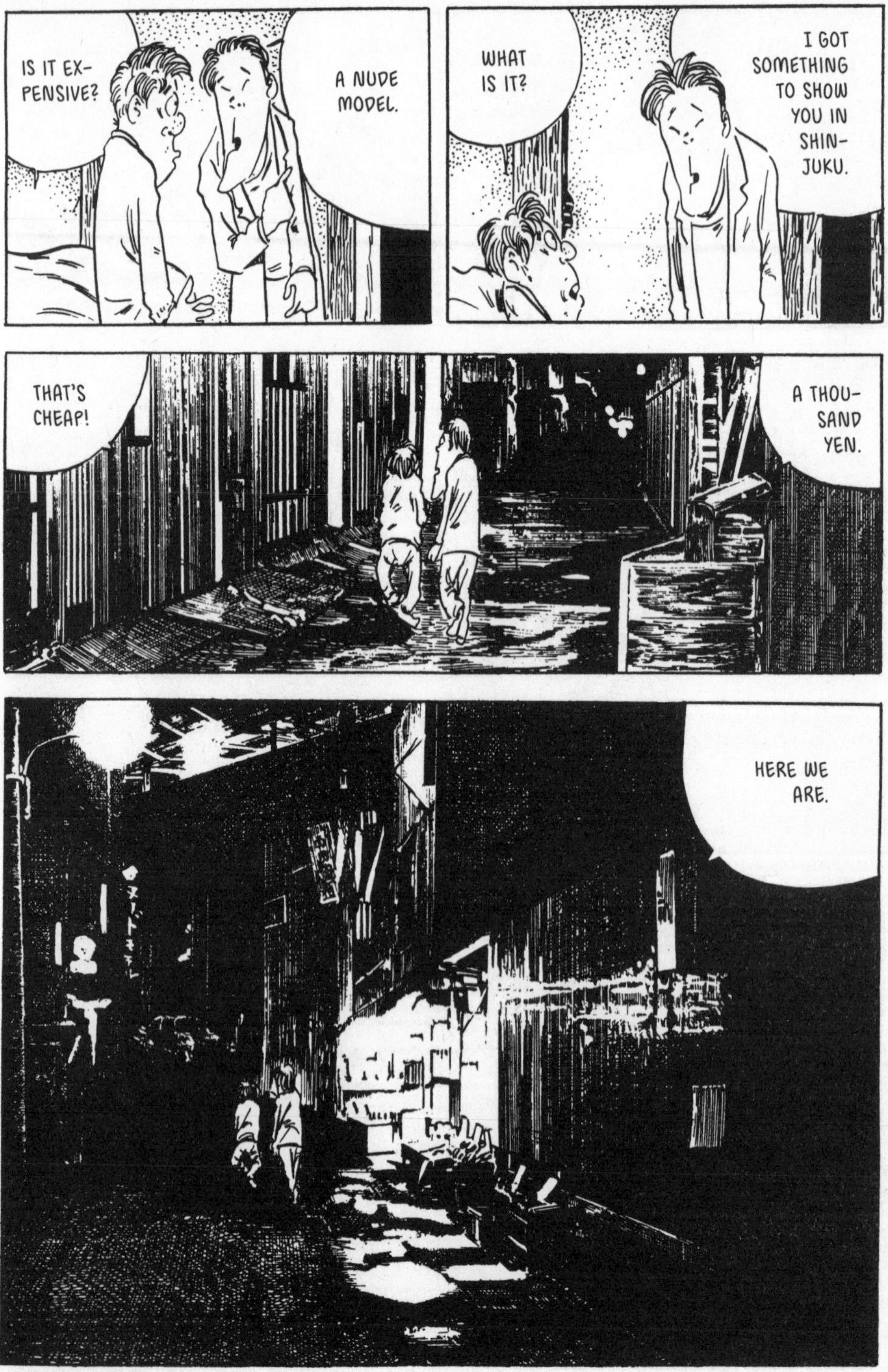
I GOT SOMETHING TO SHOW YOU IN SHIN-JUKU.
WHAT IS IT?
A NUDE MODEL.
IS IT EX-PENSIVE?
A THOU-SAND YEN.
THAT'S CHEAP!
HERE WE ARE.

1,000 YEN = $10

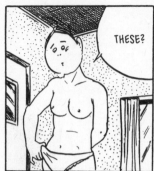

ARE YOU GUYS REALLY GONNA PRETEND TO DRAW?
WHEN DO YOU TAKE YOUR PANTIES OFF?
THESE?
THAT'S ANOTHER THOUSAND.
I'LL PAY FOR THAT.
CAN I TOUCH IT?
IF YOU PAY.

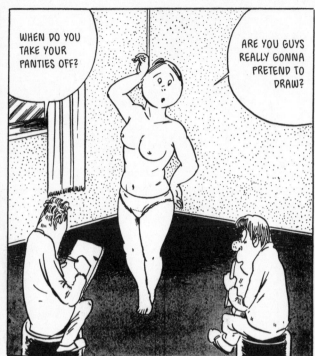

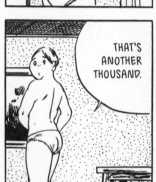

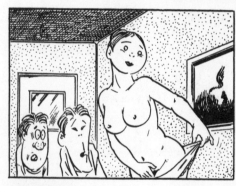

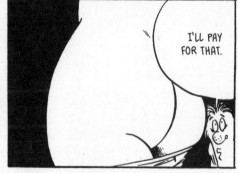

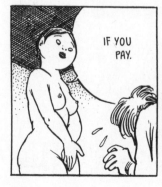

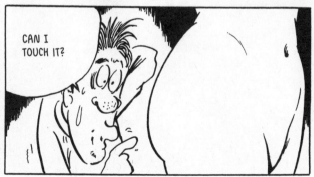

HELL YEAH.
SHIT! OUT OF CASH!
I'LL SPOT YOU.
THANKS! I OWE YOU MORE THAN MONEY.
I CAN'T WAIT!
THAT'S FIVE THOUSAND YEN TOTAL.
WHAT ELSE CAN WE BUY?
LET'S TALK ABOUT IT.
COME THIS WAY.

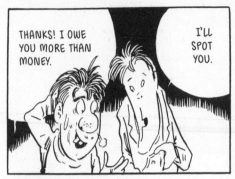

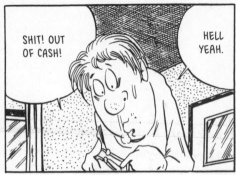

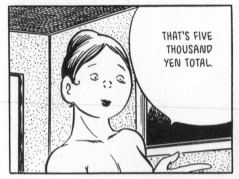

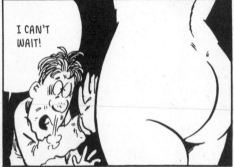

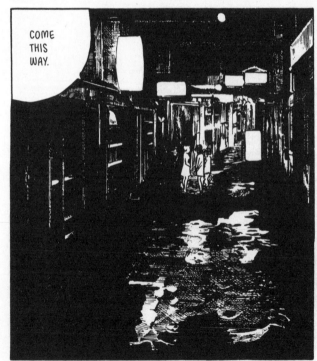

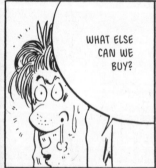

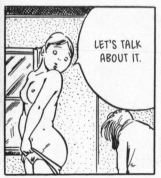

5,000 YEN = $50

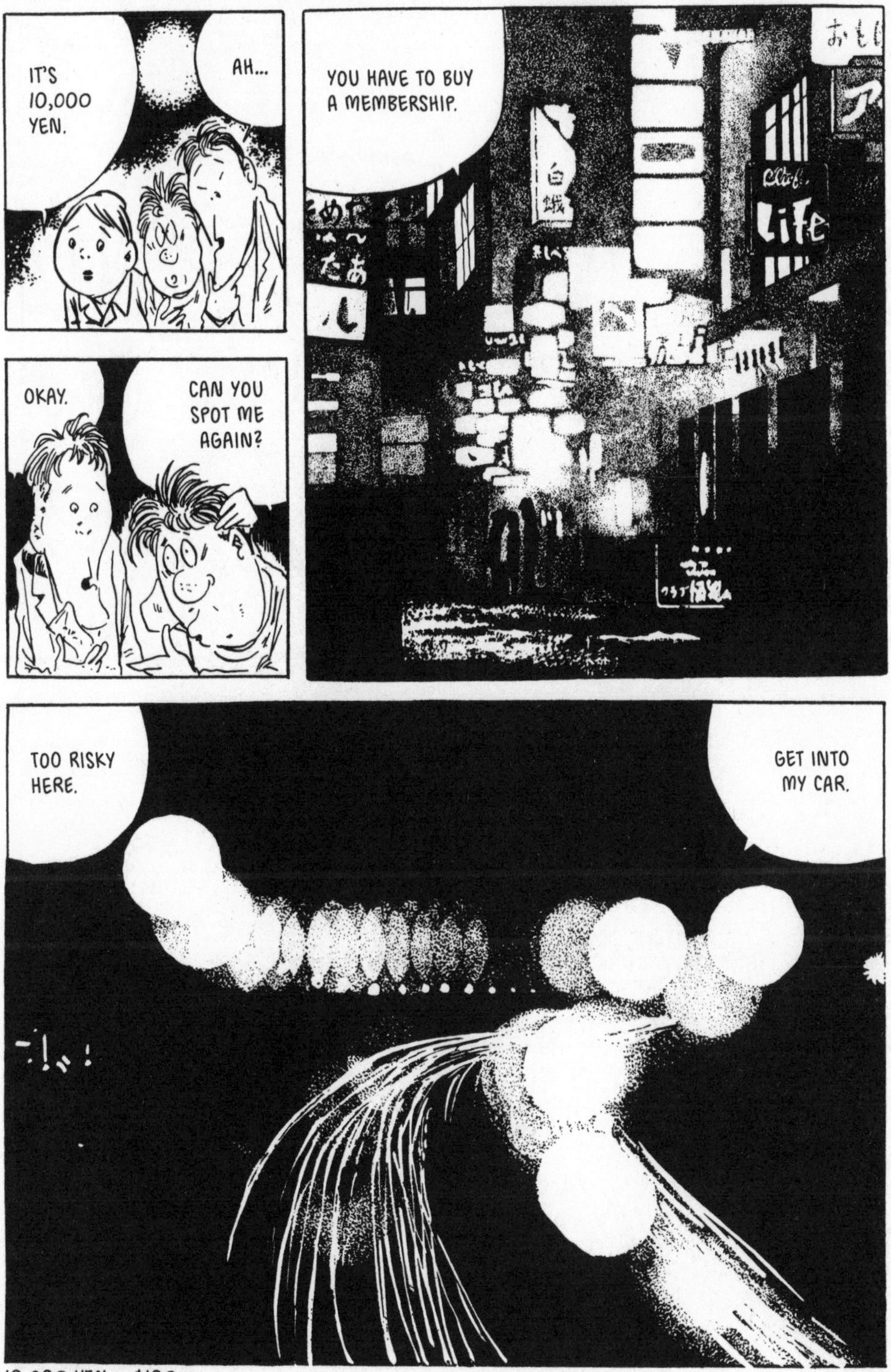
YOU HAVE TO BUY A MEMBERSHIP.
Life
AH...
IT'S 10,000 YEN.
CAN YOU SPOT ME AGAIN?
OKAY.
GET INTO MY CAR.
TOO RISKY HERE.

10,000 YEN = $100

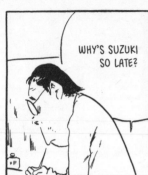

THE NEXT DAY.
WHY'S SUZUKI SO LATE?
AH...I TOOK HIM TO SHINJUKU LAST NIGHT.
WHAT? TO A HOOKER?
YEAH. AND HE BORROWED THIRTY THOU-SAND YEN.
THAT MUCH...
BANG
BONK
BASH
OUCH, OUCH.
HUH?
FELL DOWN THE STAIRS. CAN I TALK TO YOU IN PRIVATE?

30,000 YEN = $300

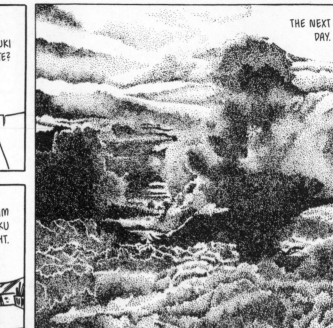

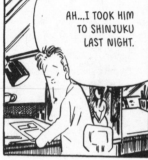

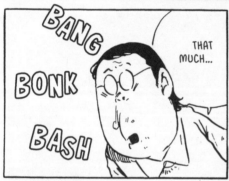

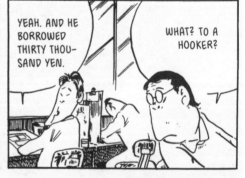

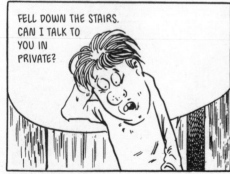

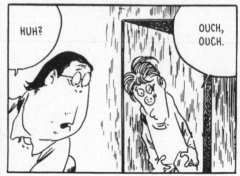

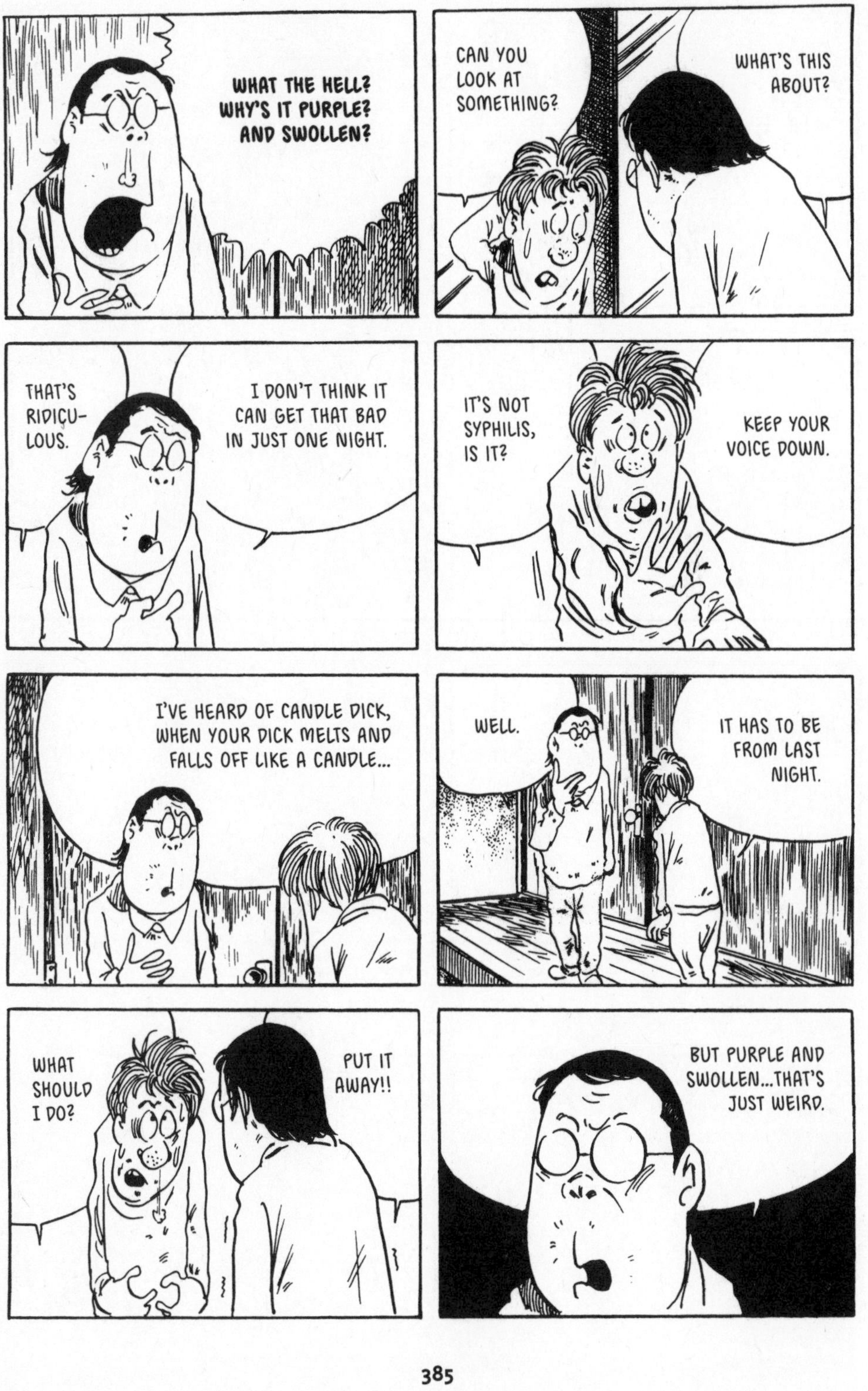
WHAT'S THIS ABOUT?
CAN YOU LOOK AT SOMETHING?
WHAT THE HELL? WHY'S IT PURPLE? AND SWOLLEN?
KEEP YOUR VOICE DOWN.
IT'S NOT SYPHILIS, IS IT?
I DON'T THINK IT CAN GET THAT BAD IN JUST ONE NIGHT.
THAT'S RIDICU-LOUS.
IT HAS TO BE FROM LAST NIGHT.
WELL.
I'VE HEARD OF CANDLE DICK, WHEN YOUR DICK MELTS AND FALLS OFF LIKE A CANDLE...
BUT PURPLE AND SWOLLEN...THAT'S JUST WEIRD.
PUT IT AWAY!!
WHAT SHOULD I DO?

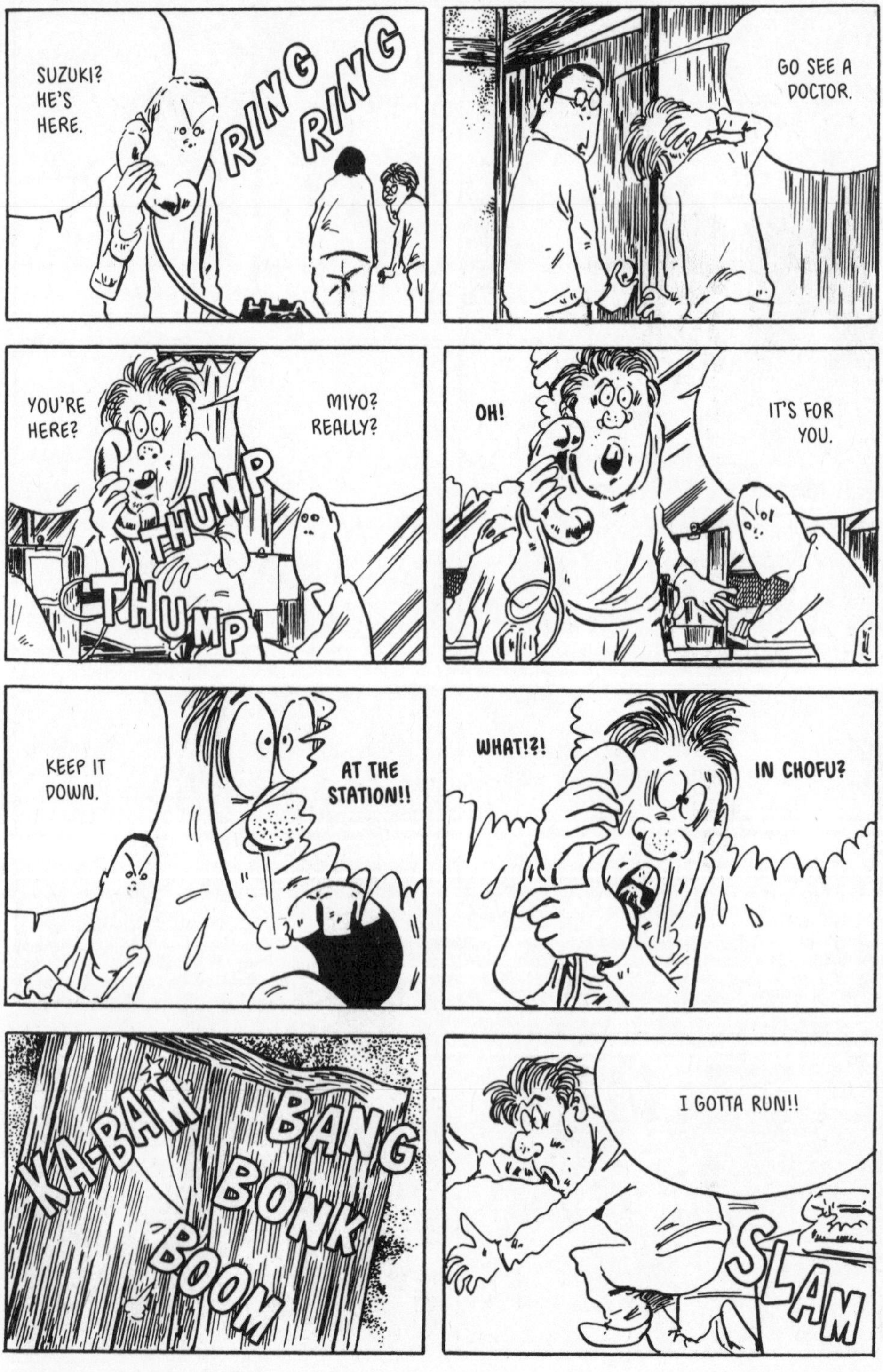
GO SEE A DOCTOR.
SUZUKI? HE'S HERE.
RING RING
IT'S FOR YOU.
OH!
MIYO? REALLY?
YOU'RE HERE?
THUMP THUMP
IN CHOFU?
WHAT!?!
AT THE STATION!!
KEEP IT DOWN.
I GOTTA RUN!!
SLAM
BANG
BONK
KA-BAM
BOOM

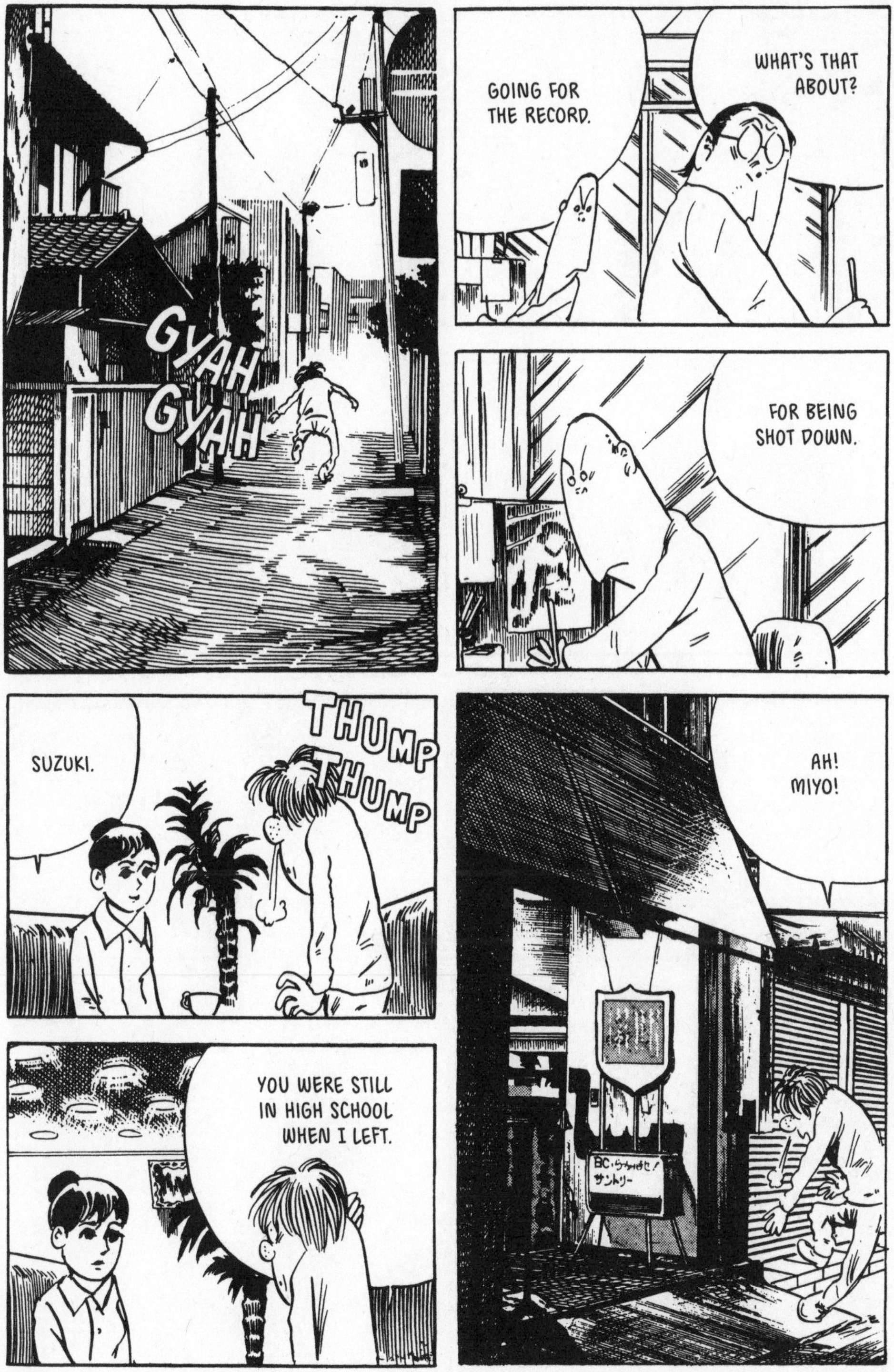
WHAT'S THAT ABOUT?
GOING FOR THE RECORD.
FOR BEING SHOT DOWN.
GYAH GYAH
AH! MIYO!
サントリー
THUMP THUMP
SUZUKI.
YOU WERE STILL IN HIGH SCHOOL WHEN I LEFT.

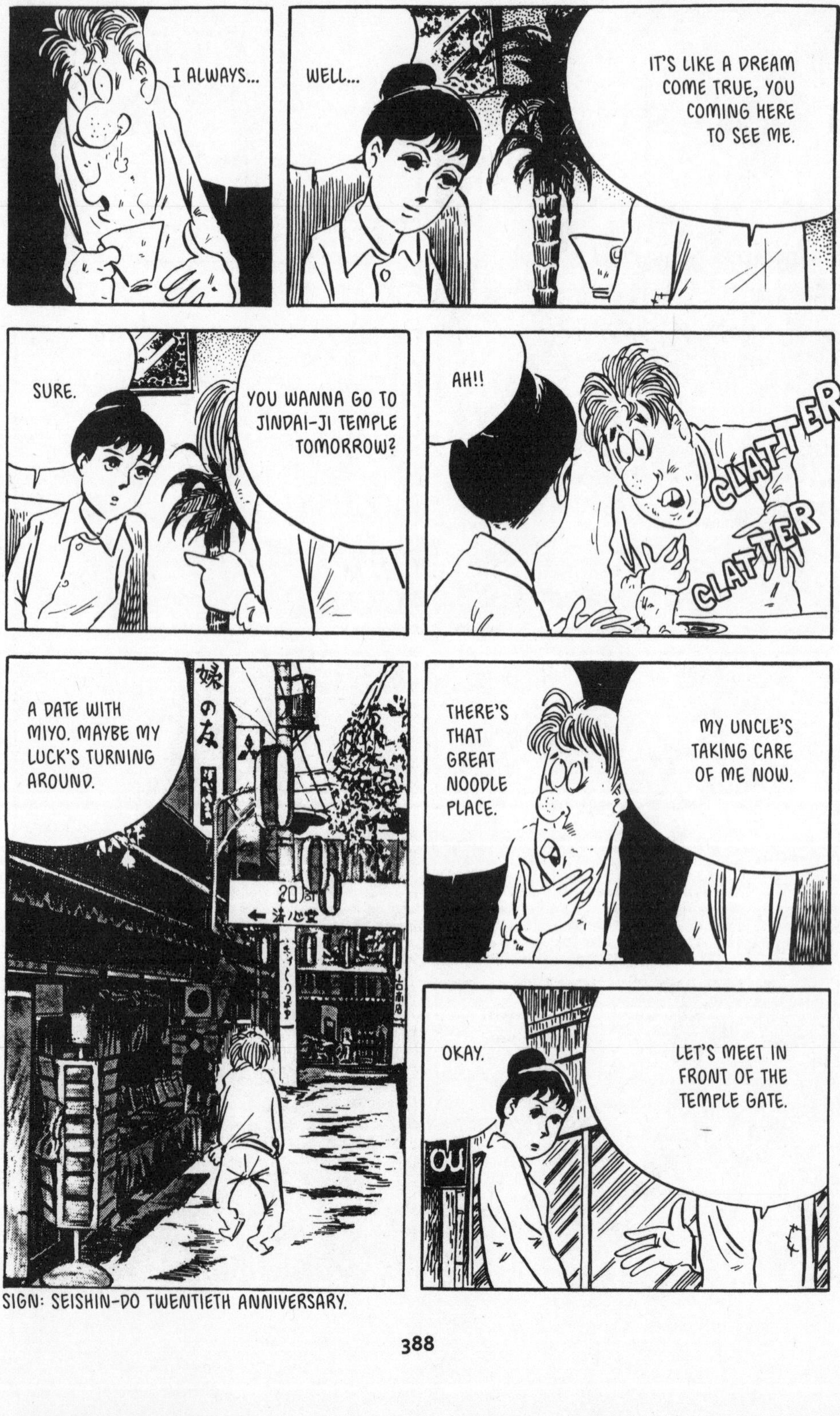
IT'S LIKE A DREAM COME TRUE, YOU COMING HERE TO SEE ME.
WELL...
I ALWAYS...
AH!!
CLATTER
CLATTER
YOU WANNA GO TO JINDAI-JI TEMPLE TOMORROW?
SURE.
MY UNCLE'S TAKING CARE OF ME NOW.
THERE'S THAT GREAT NOODLE PLACE.
LET'S MEET IN FRONT OF THE TEMPLE GATE.
OKAY.
A DATE WITH MIYO. MAYBE MY LUCK'S TURNING AROUND.
SIGN: SEISHIN-DO TWENTIETH ANNIVERSARY.

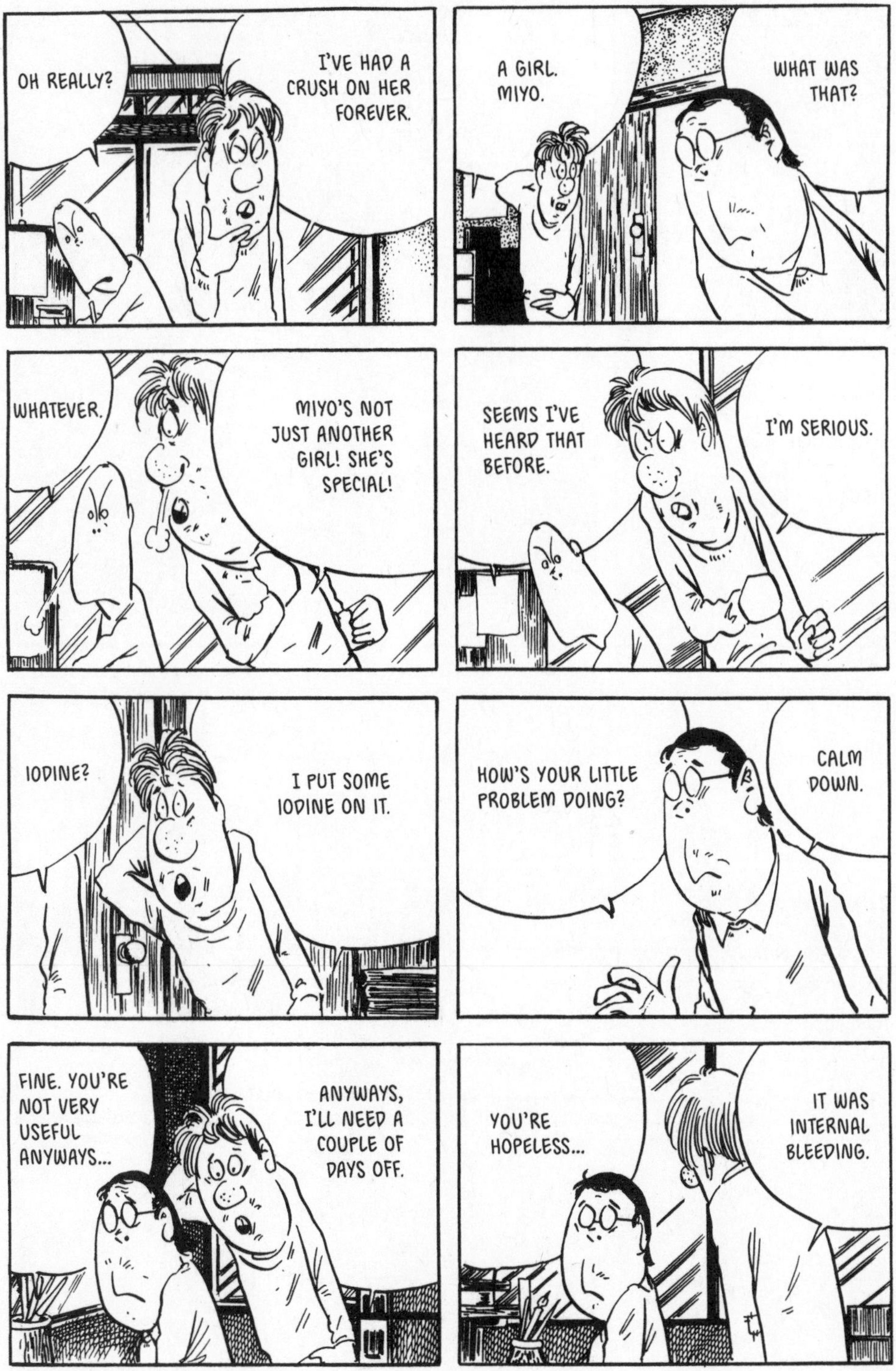
WHAT WAS THAT?
A GIRL. MIYO.
I'VE HAD A CRUSH ON HER FOREVER.
OH REALLY?
I'M SERIOUS.
SEEMS I'VE HEARD THAT BEFORE.
MIYO'S NOT JUST ANOTHER GIRL! SHE'S SPECIAL!
WHATEVER.
CALM DOWN.
HOW'S YOUR LITTLE PROBLEM DOING?
I PUT SOME IODINE ON IT.
IODINE?
IT WAS INTERNAL BLEEDING.
YOU'RE HOPELESS...
ANYWAYS, I'LL NEED A COUPLE OF DAYS OFF.
FINE. YOU'RE NOT VERY USEFUL ANYWAYS...

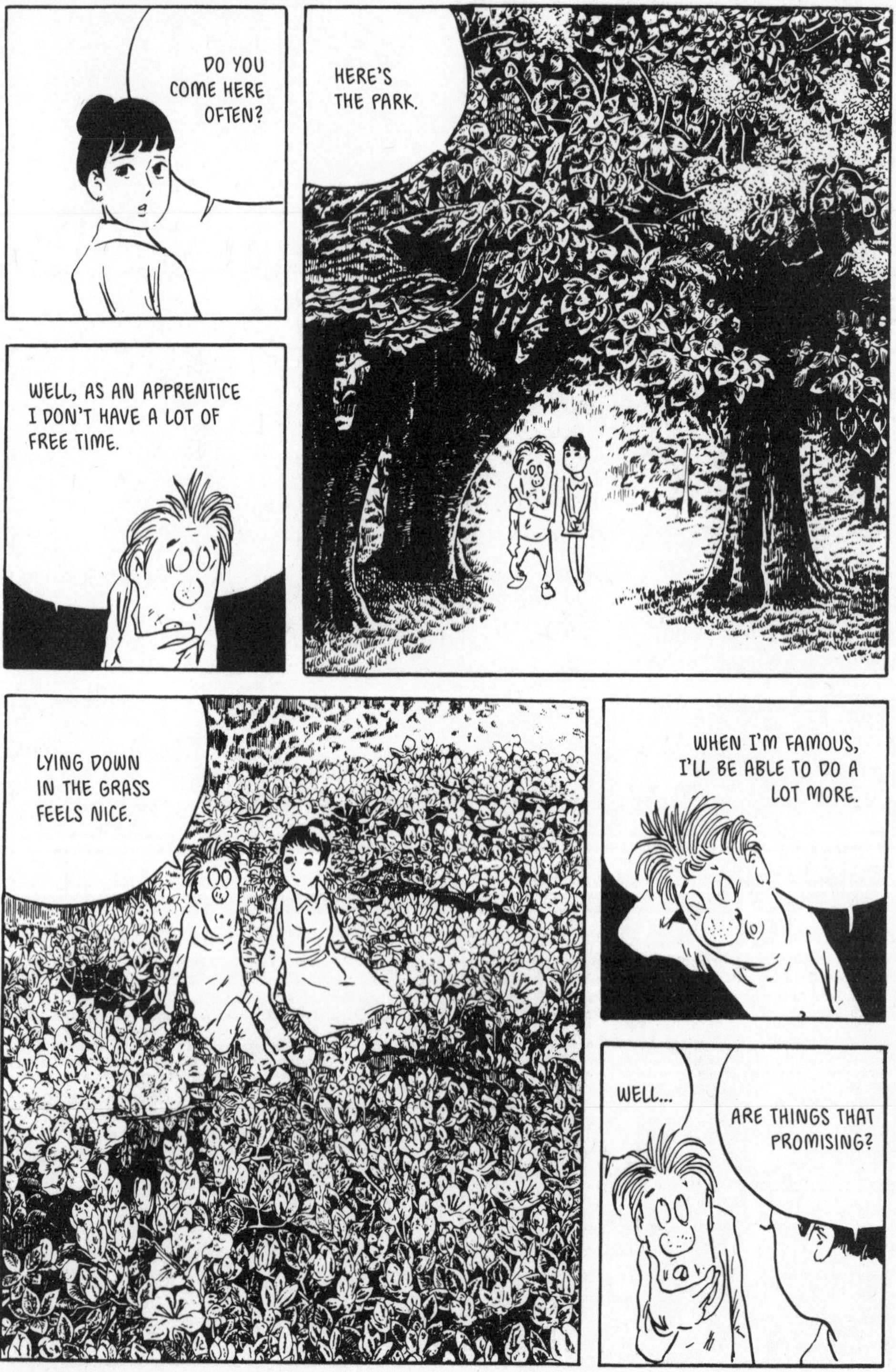
HERE'S THE PARK.
DO YOU COME HERE OFTEN?
WELL, AS AN APPRENTICE I DON'T HAVE A LOT OF FREE TIME.
WHEN I'M FAMOUS, I'LL BE ABLE TO DO A LOT MORE.
ARE THINGS THAT PROMISING?
WELL...
LYING DOWN IN THE GRASS FEELS NICE.

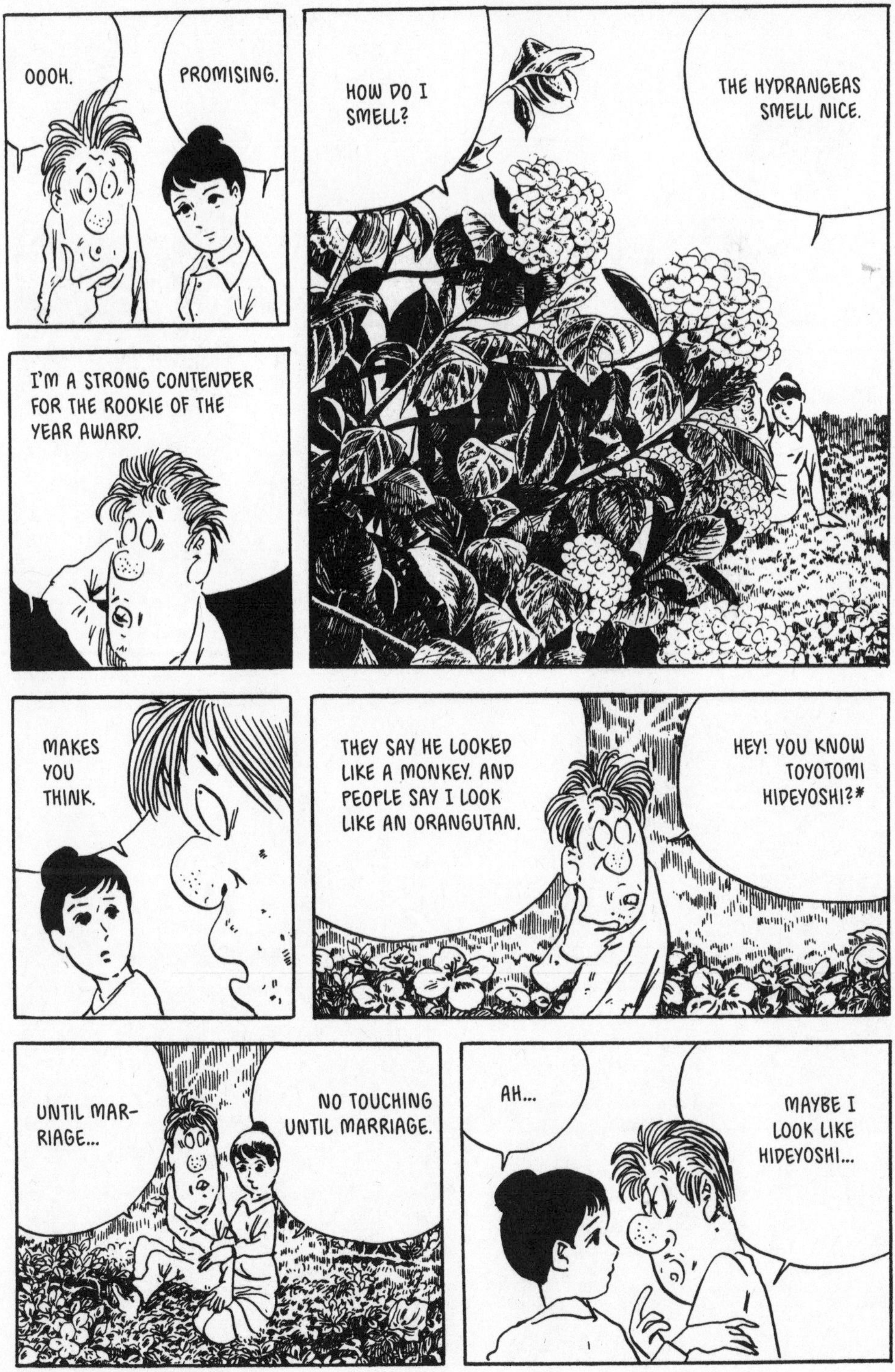
THE HYDRANGEAS SMELL NICE.
HOW DO I SMELL?
PROMISING.
OOOH.
I'M A STRONG CONTENDER FOR THE ROOKIE OF THE YEAR AWARD.
HEY! YOU KNOW TOYOTOMI HIDEYOSHI?*
THEY SAY HE LOOKED LIKE A MONKEY. AND PEOPLE SAY I LOOK LIKE AN ORANGUTAN.
MAKES YOU THINK.
MAYBE I LOOK LIKE HIDEYOSHI...
AH...
NO TOUCHING UNTIL MARRIAGE.
UNTIL MAR-RIAGE...

*SEE NOTE ON PAGE 535.

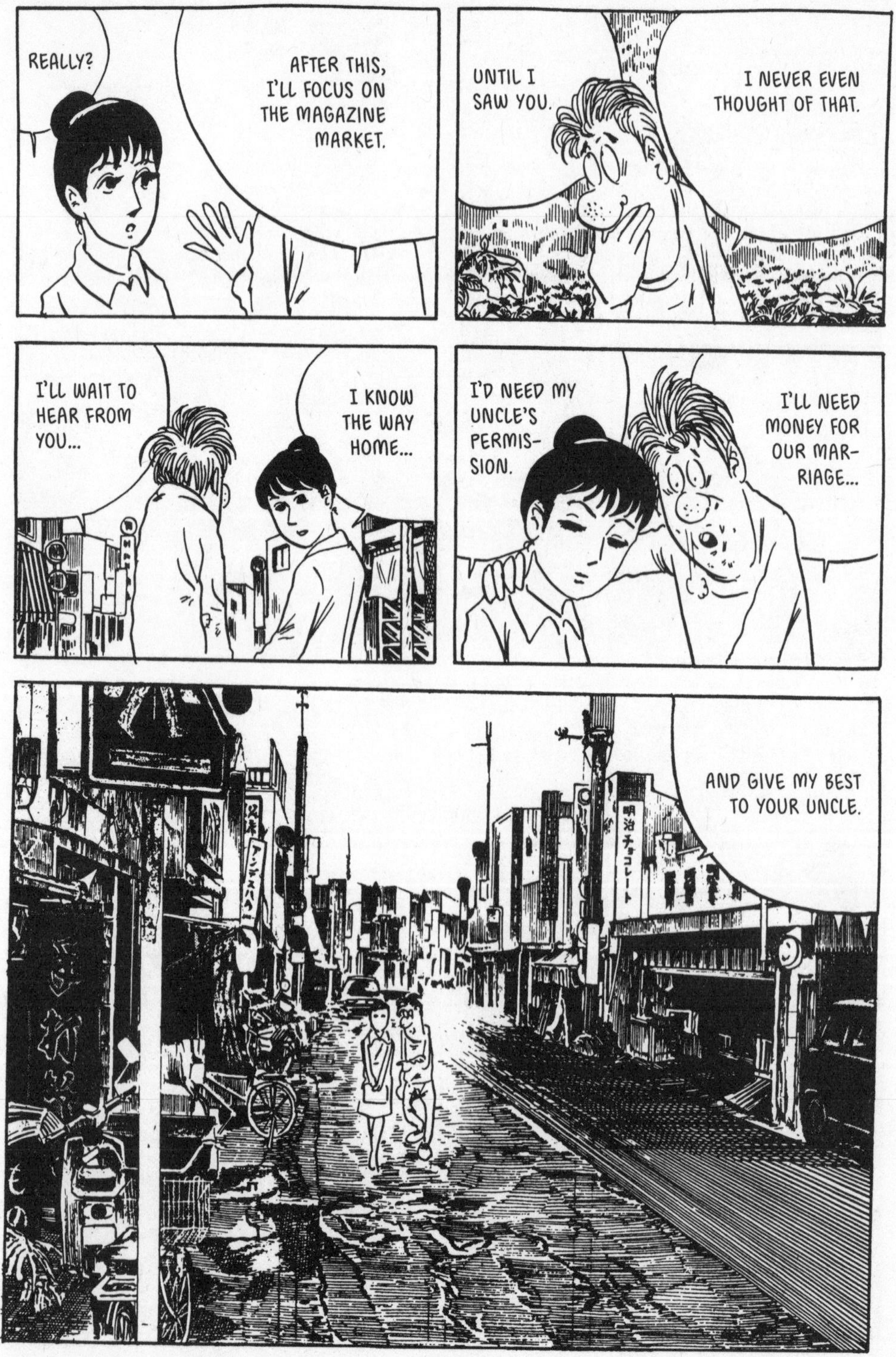
I NEVER EVEN THOUGHT OF THAT.
UNTIL I SAW YOU.
AFTER THIS, I'LL FOCUS ON THE MAGAZINE MARKET.
REALLY?
I'LL NEED MONEY FOR OUR MAR-RIAGE...
I'D NEED MY UNCLE'S PERMIS-SION.
I KNOW THE WAY HOME...
I'LL WAIT TO HEAR FROM YOU...
AND GIVE MY BEST TO YOUR UNCLE.
明治 チョコレート

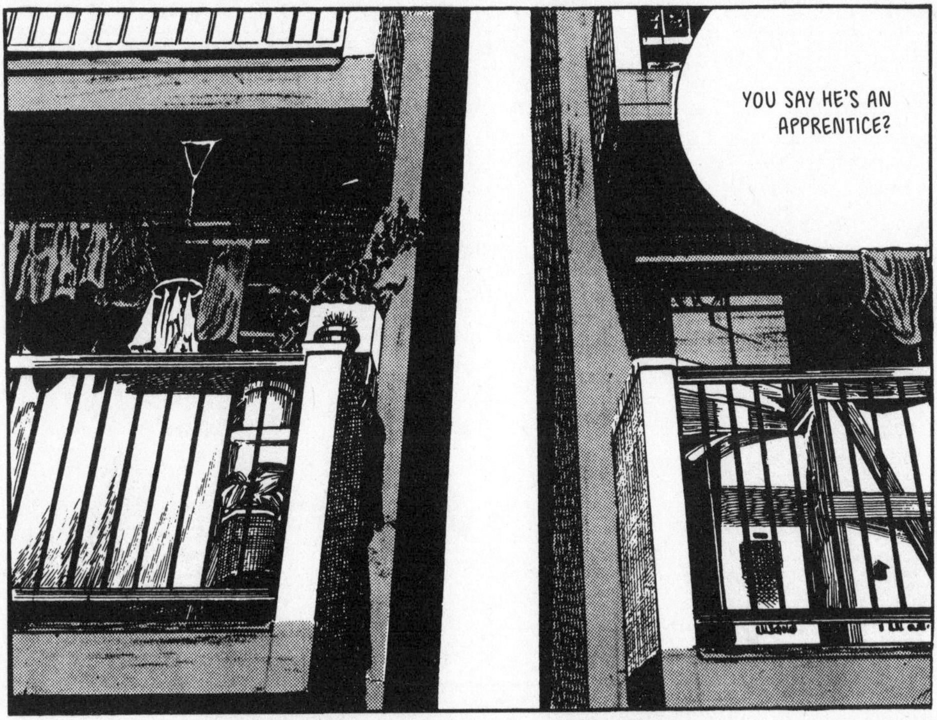
YOU SAY HE'S AN APPRENTICE?

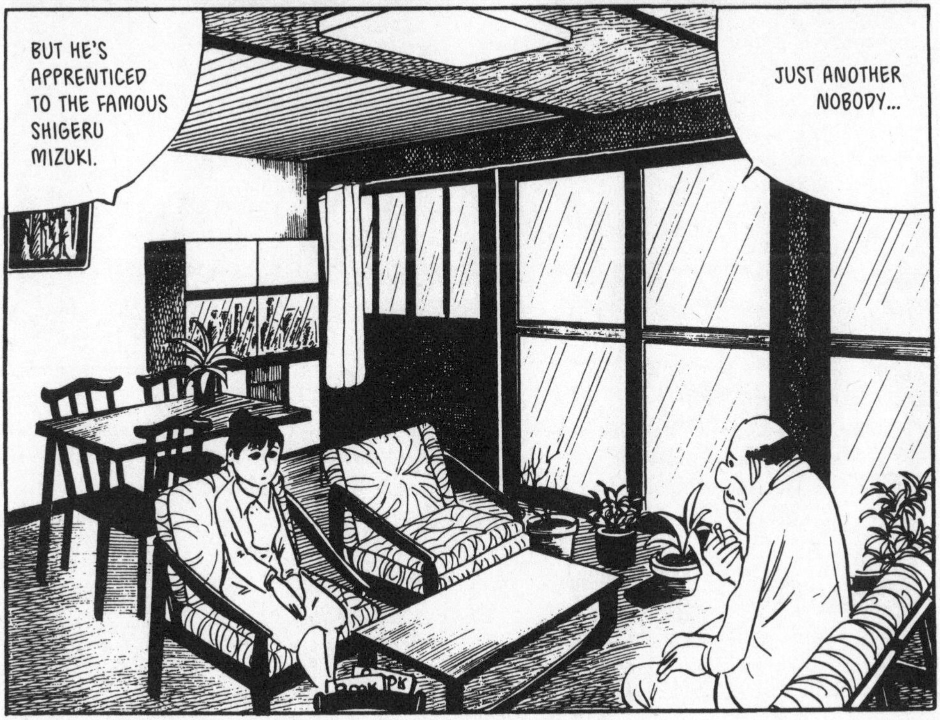
JUST ANOTHER NOBODY...
BUT HE'S APPRENTICED TO THE FAMOUS SHIGERU MIZUKI.

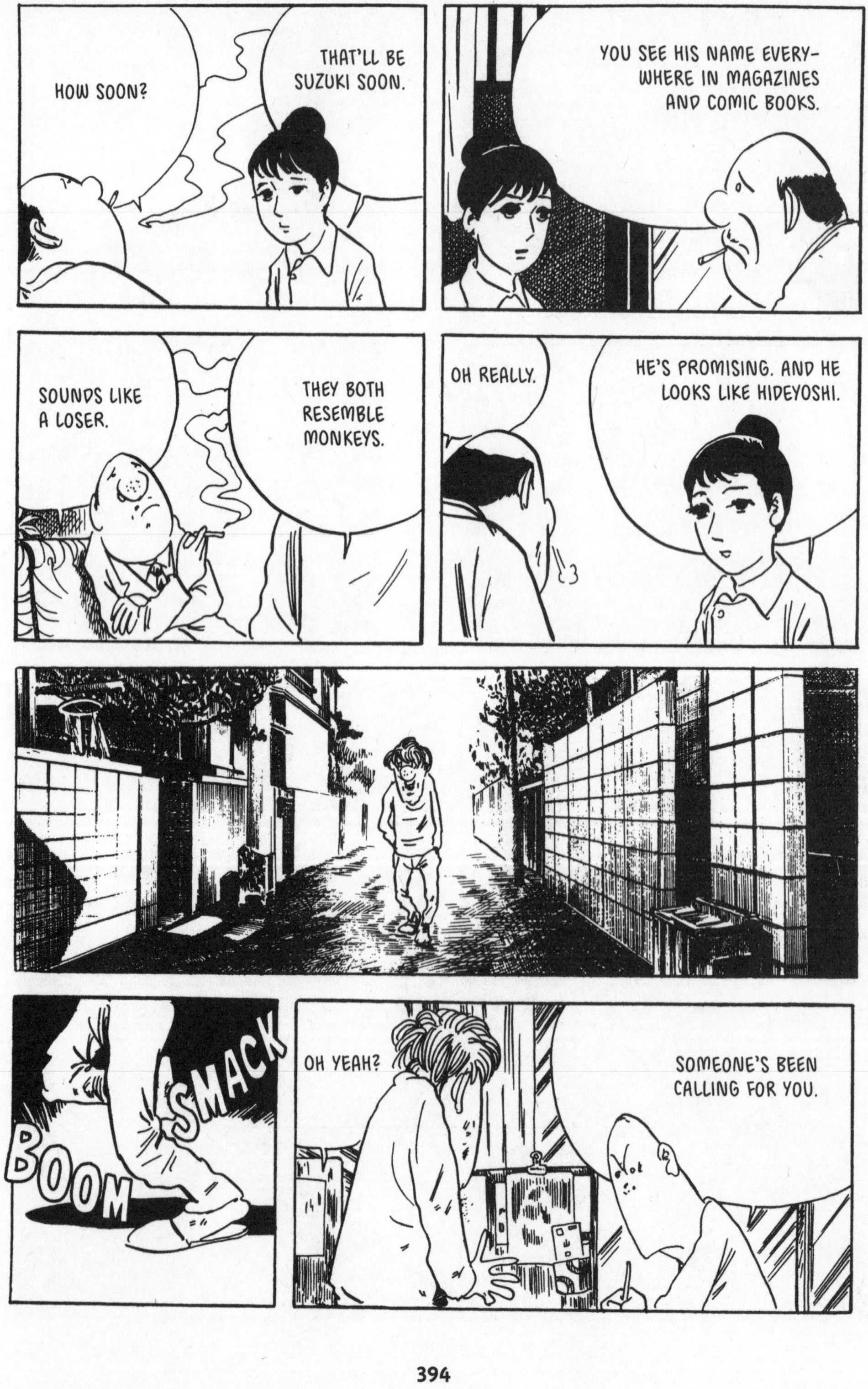
YOU SEE HIS NAME EVERY-WHERE IN MAGAZINES AND COMIC BOOKS.
THAT'LL BE SUZUKI SOON.
HOW SOON?
HE'S PROMISING. AND HE LOOKS LIKE HIDEYOSHI.
OH REALLY.
THEY BOTH RESEMBLE MONKEYS.
SOUNDS LIKE A LOSER.
SOMEONE'S BEEN CALLING FOR YOU.
OH YEAH?
SMACK
BOOM

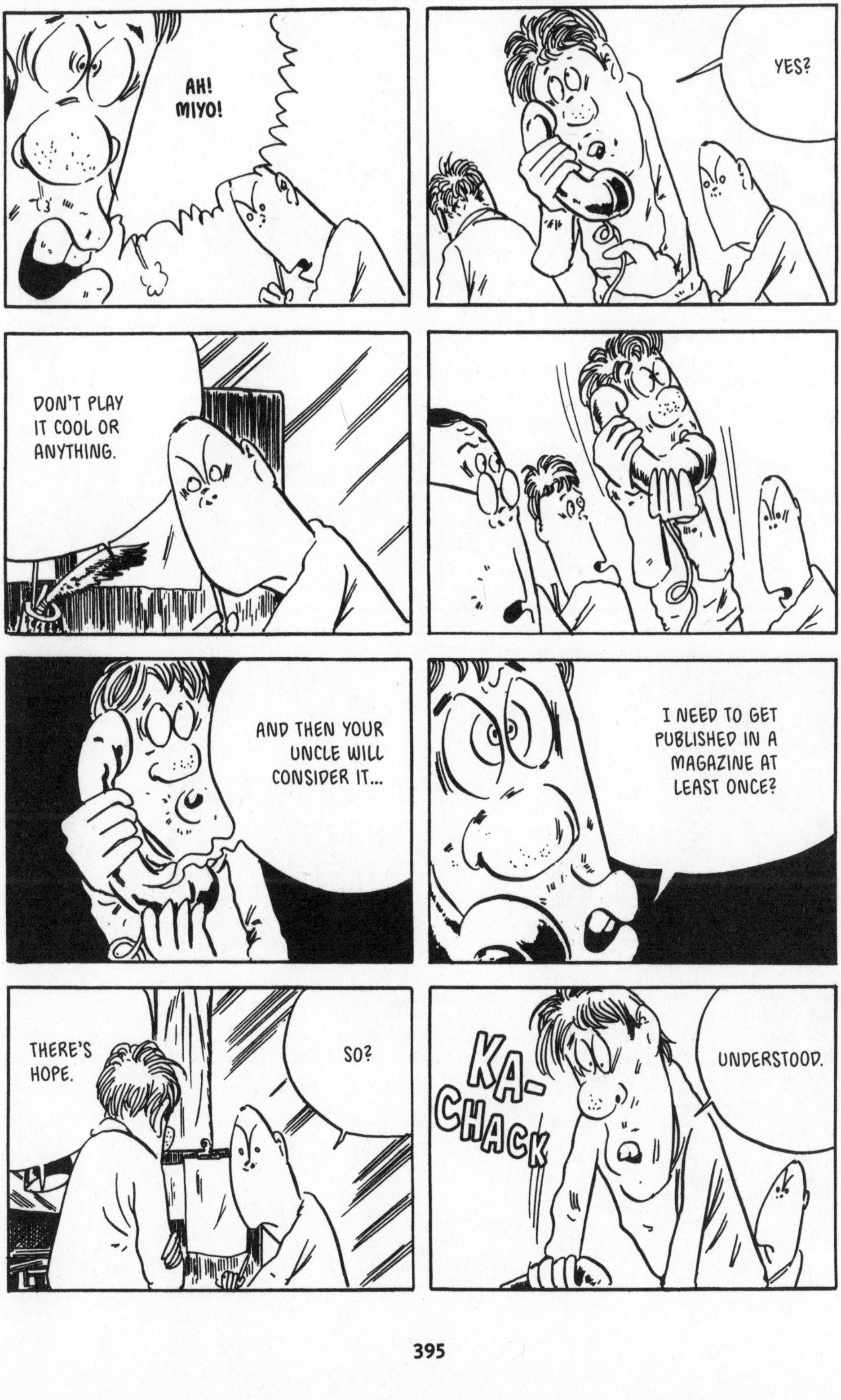

YES?
AH! MIYO!
DON'T PLAY IT COOL OR ANYTHING.
I NEED TO GET PUBLISHED IN A MAGAZINE AT LEAST ONCE?
AND THEN YOUR UNCLE WILL CONSIDER IT...
KA-CHACK
UNDERSTOOD.
SO?
THERE'S HOPE.

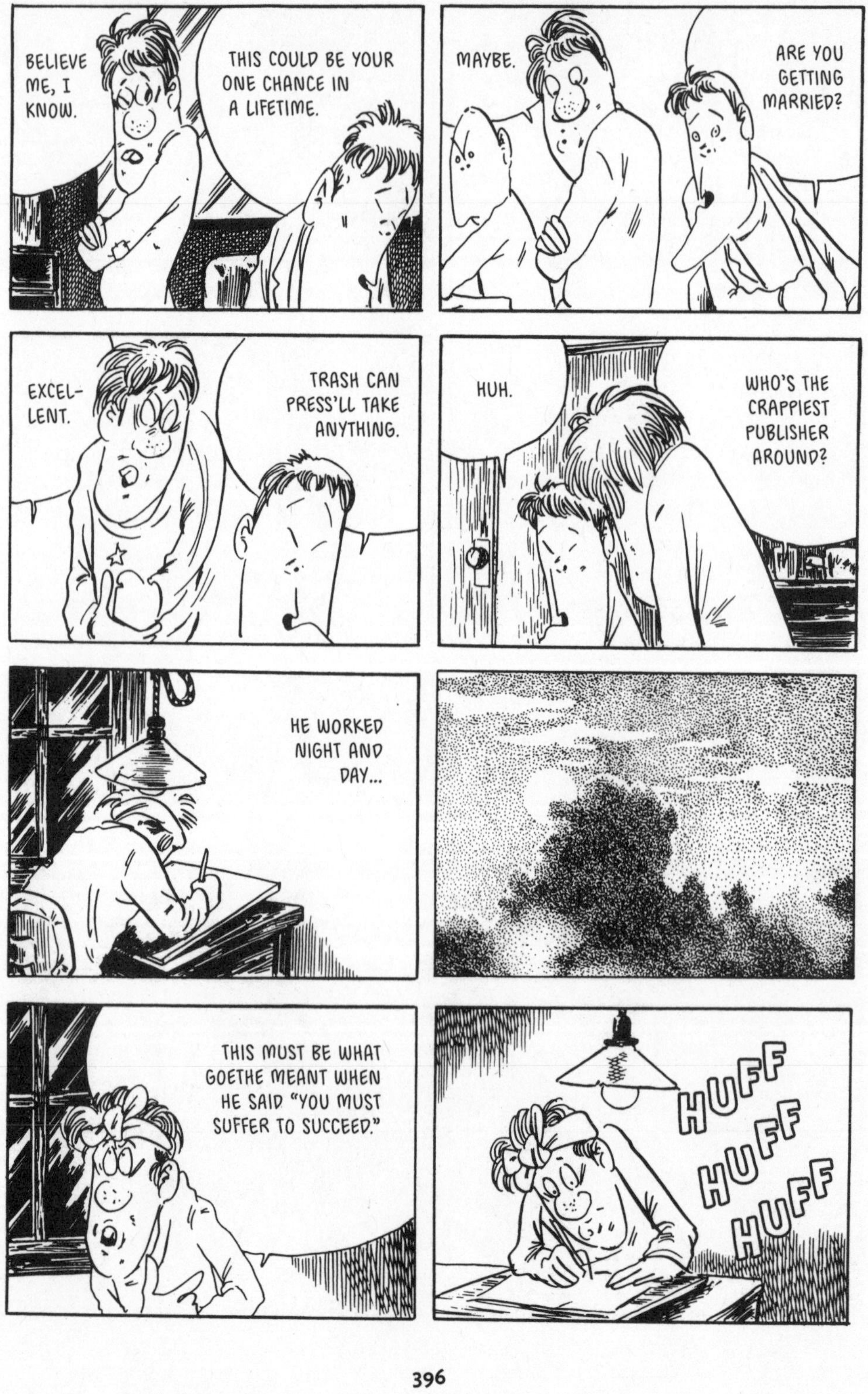
ARE YOU GETTING MARRIED?
MAYBE.
THIS COULD BE YOUR ONE CHANCE IN A LIFETIME.
BELIEVE ME, I KNOW.
WHO'S THE CRAPPIEST PUBLISHER AROUND?
HUH.
TRASH CAN PRESS'LL TAKE ANYTHING.
EXCEL-LENT.
HE WORKED NIGHT AND DAY...
HUFF HUFF HUFF
THIS MUST BE WHAT GOETHE MEANT WHEN HE SAID "YOU MUST SUFFER TO SUCCEED."

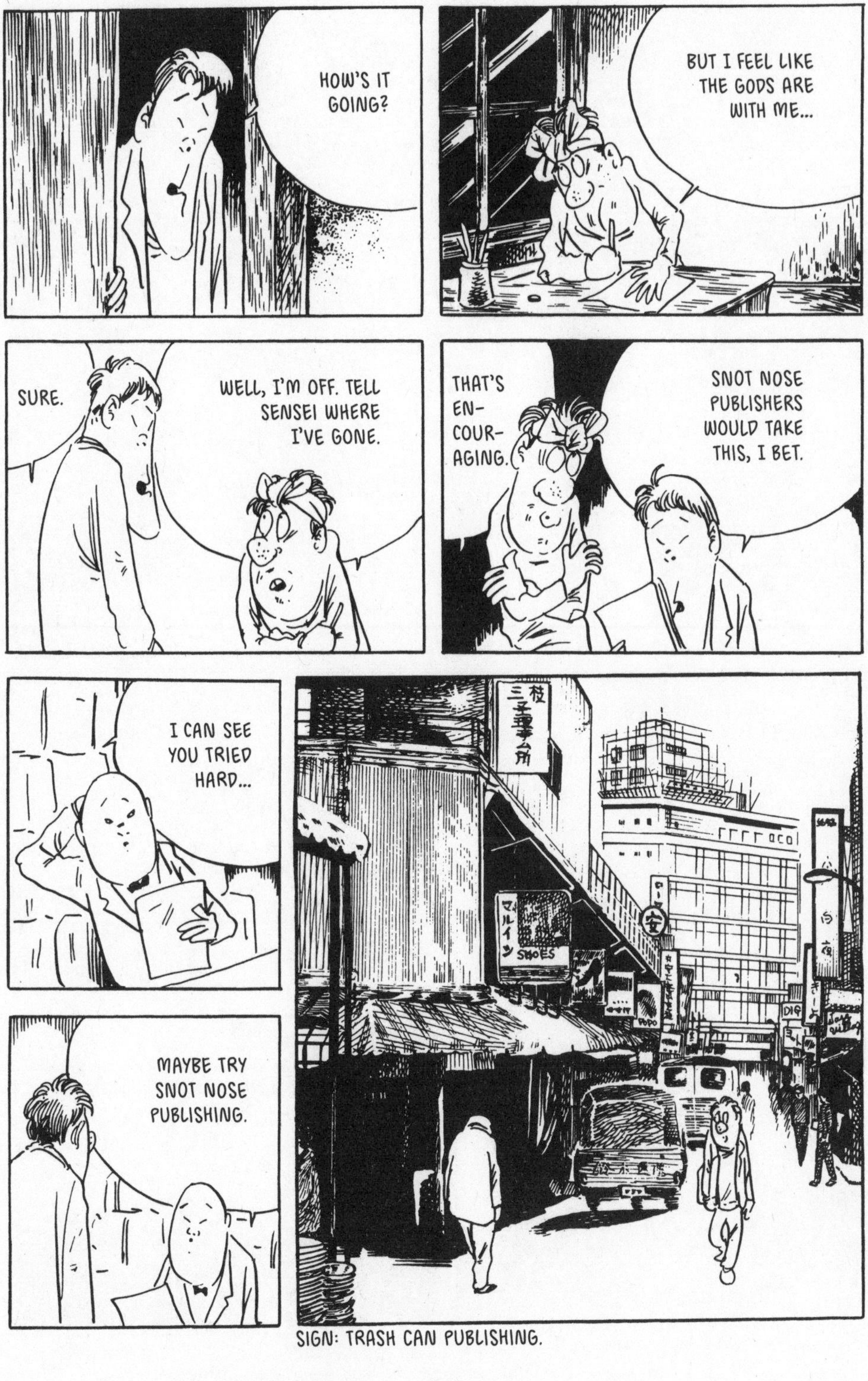
BUT I FEEL LIKE THE GODS ARE WITH ME...
HOW'S IT GOING?
SNOT NOSE PUBLISHERS WOULD TAKE THIS, I BET.
THAT'S EN- COUR- AGING.
WELL, I'M OFF. TELL SENSEI WHERE I'VE GONE.
SURE.
SHOES
I CAN SEE YOU TRIED HARD...
MAYBE TRY SNOT NOSE PUBLISHING.

SIGN: TRASH CAN PUBLISHING.

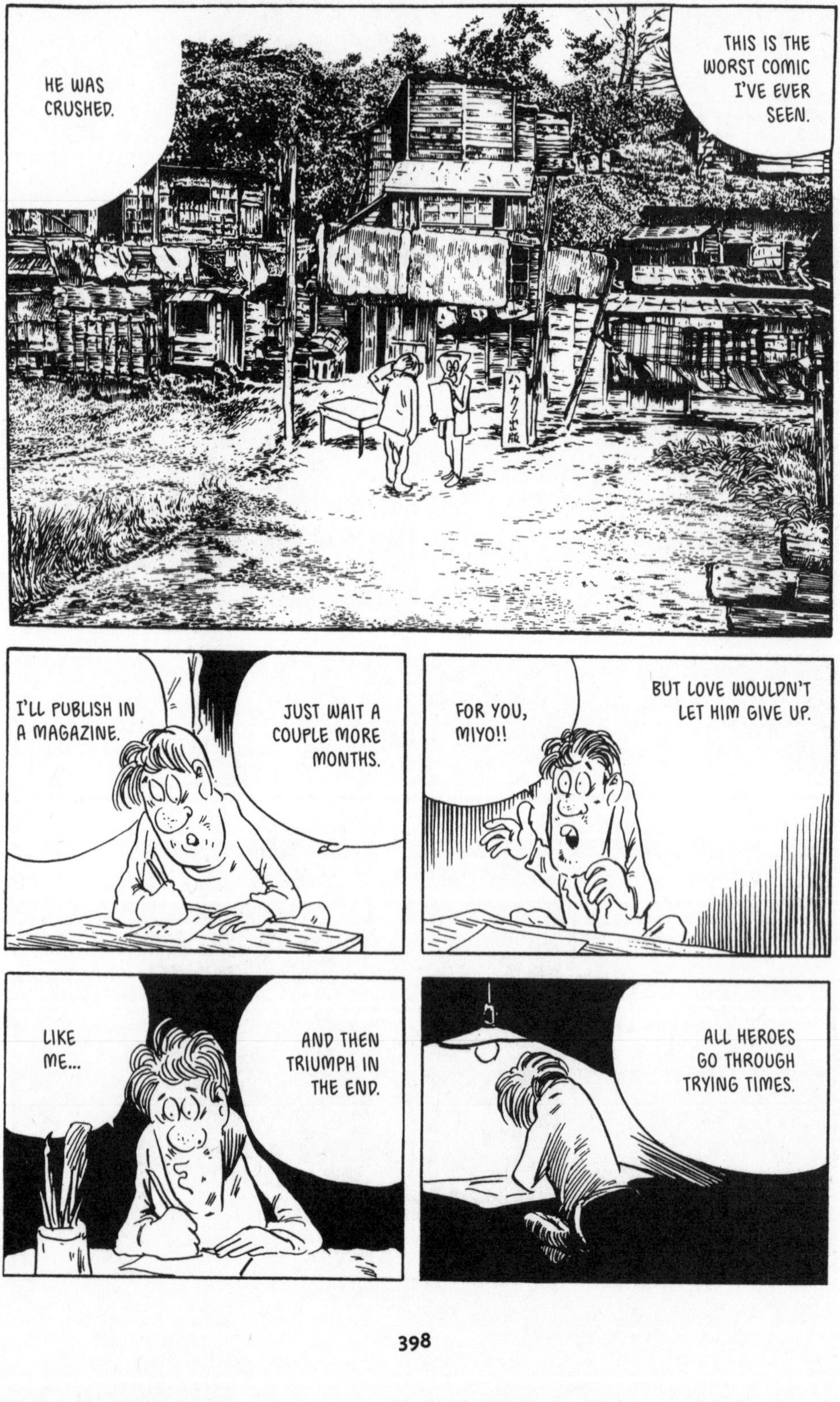
THIS IS THE WORST COMIC I'VE EVER SEEN.
HE WAS CRUSHED.
BUT LOVE WOULDN'T LET HIM GIVE UP.
FOR YOU, MIYO!!
JUST WAIT A COUPLE MORE MONTHS.
I'LL PUBLISH IN A MAGAZINE.
ALL HEROES GO THROUGH TRYING TIMES.
AND THEN TRIUMPH IN THE END.
LIKE ME...

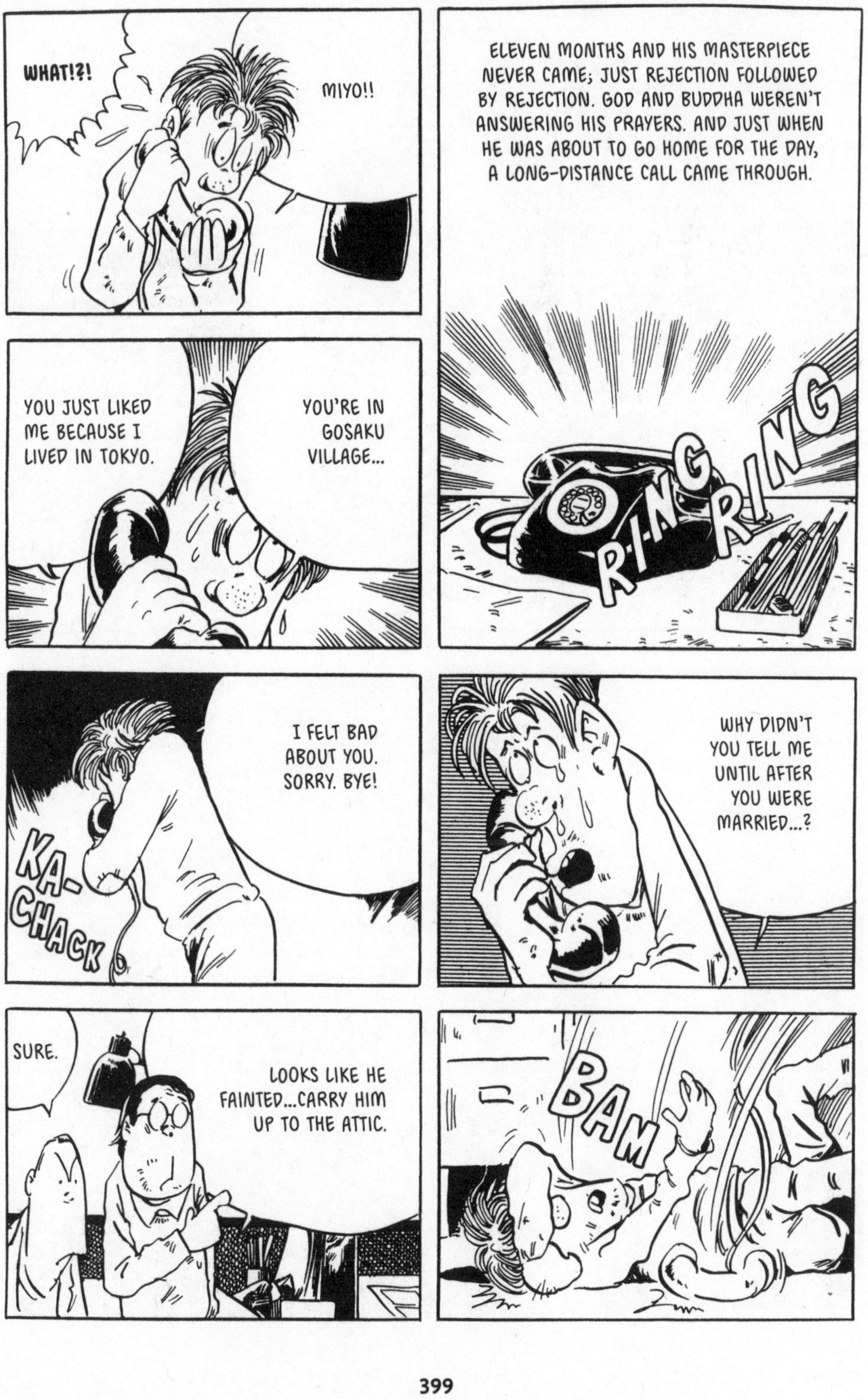
ELEVEN MONTHS AND HIS MASTERPIECE NEVER CAME; JUST REJECTION FOLLOWED BY REJECTION. GOD AND BUDDHA WEREN'T ANSWERING HIS PRAYERS. AND JUST WHEN HE WAS ABOUT TO GO HOME FOR THE DAY, A LONG-DISTANCE CALL CAME THROUGH.
RING RING
MIYO!!
WHAT!?!
YOU'RE IN GOSAKU VILLAGE...
YOU JUST LIKED ME BECAUSE I LIVED IN TOKYO.
WHY DIDN'T YOU TELL ME UNTIL AFTER YOU WERE MARRIED...?
I FELT BAD ABOUT YOU. SORRY. BYE!
KA-CHACK
BAM
LOOKS LIKE HE FAINTED...CARRY HIM UP TO THE ATTIC.
SURE.

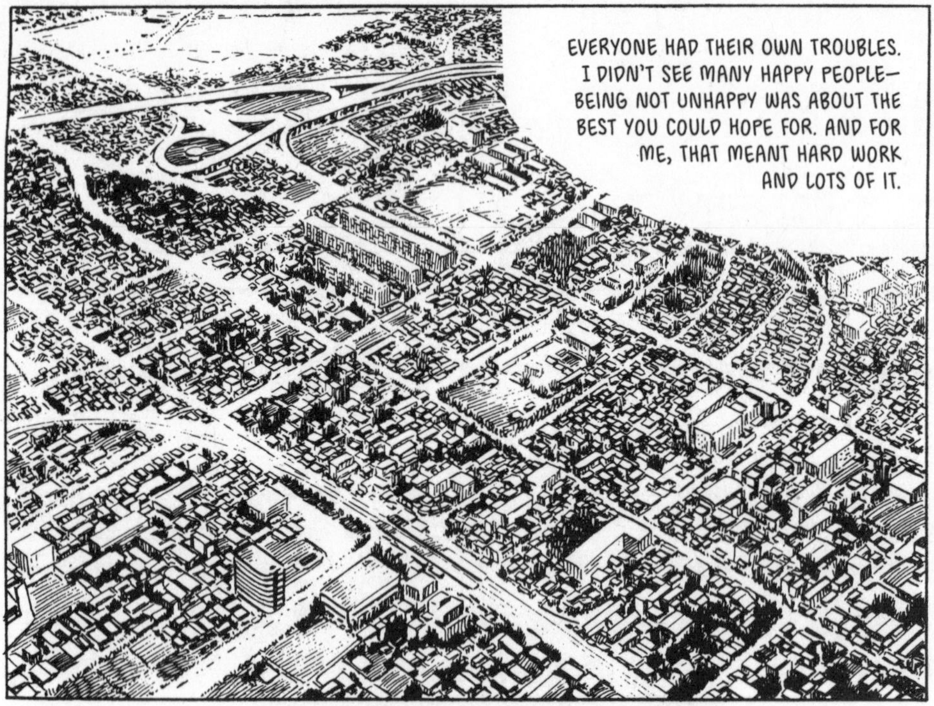
EVERYONE HAD THEIR OWN TROUBLES. I DIDN'T SEE MANY HAPPY PEOPLE—BEING NOT UNHAPPY WAS ABOUT THE BEST YOU COULD HOPE FOR. AND FOR ME, THAT MEANT HARD WORK AND LOTS OF IT.

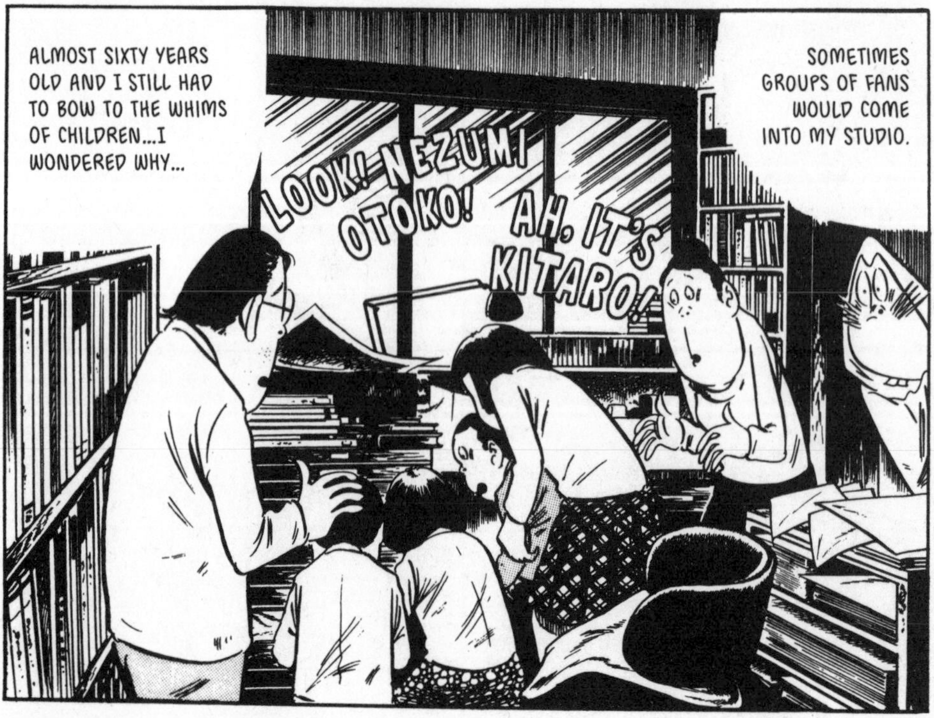
SOMETIMES GROUPS OF FANS WOULD COME INTO MY STUDIO.
AH, IT'S KITARO!
LOOK! NEZUMI OTOKO!
ALMOST SIXTY YEARS OLD AND I STILL HAD TO BOW TO THE WHIMS OF CHILDREN...I WONDERED WHY...

CORRUPTION AMIDST ECONOMIC GROWTH

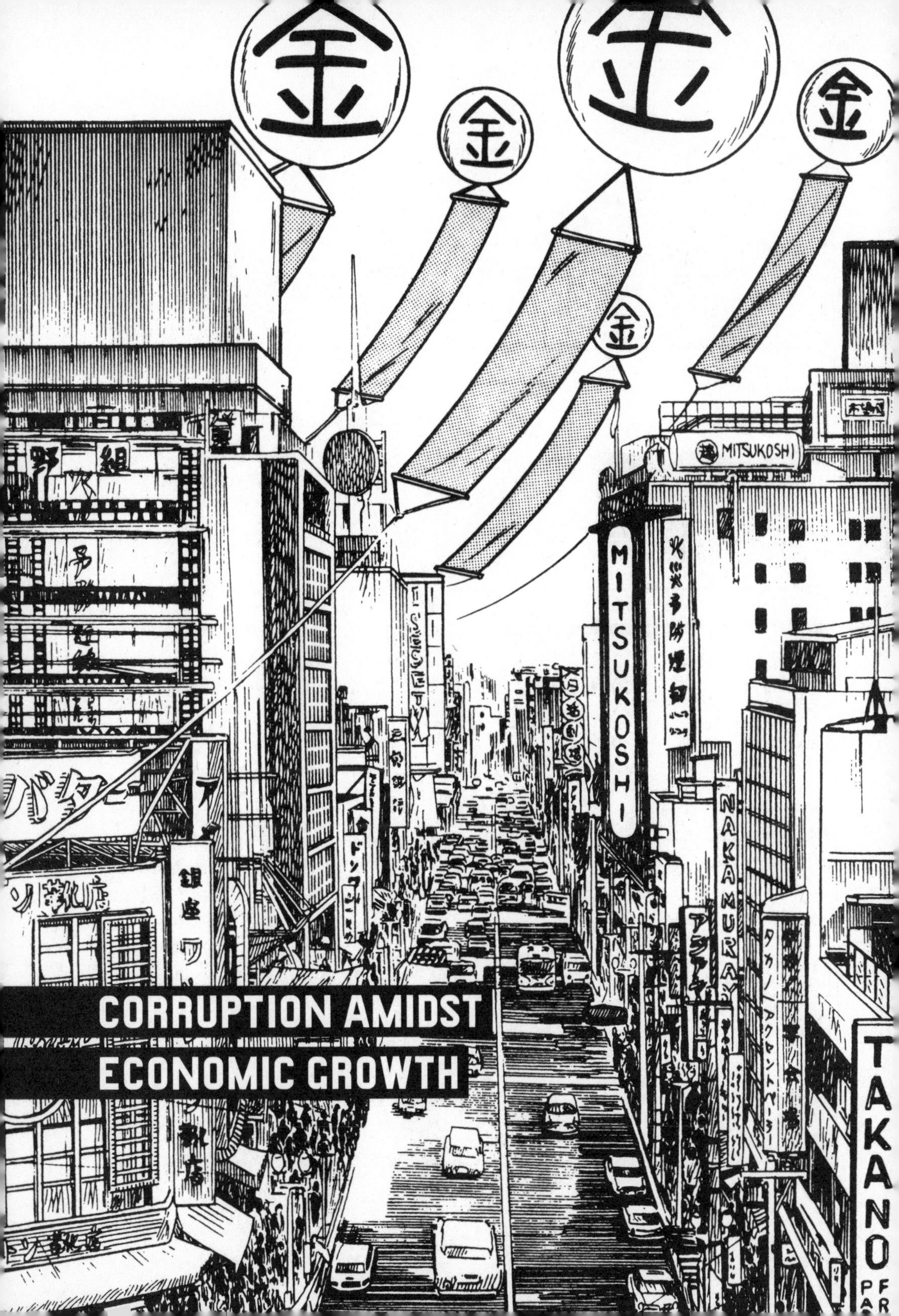
金
金
金
金
金
MITSUKOSHI
MITSUKOSHI
NAKAMURA
TAKANO

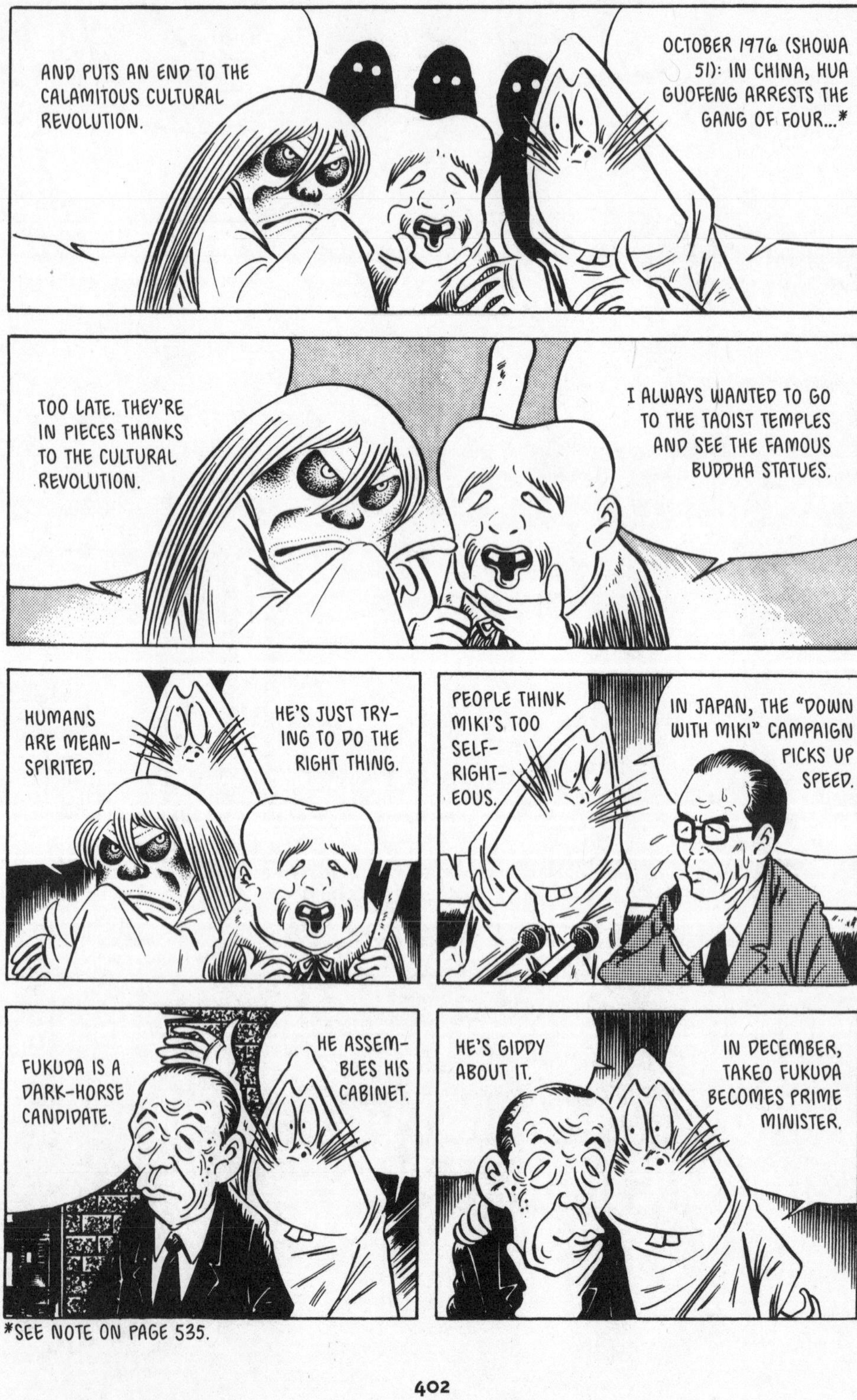
OCTOBER 1976 (SHOWA 51): IN CHINA, HUA GUOFENG ARRESTS THE GANG OF FOUR...*
AND PUTS AN END TO THE CALAMITOUS CULTURAL REVOLUTION.
I ALWAYS WANTED TO GO TO THE TAOIST TEMPLES AND SEE THE FAMOUS BUDDHA STATUES.
TOO LATE. THEY'RE IN PIECES THANKS TO THE CULTURAL REVOLUTION.
IN JAPAN, THE "DOWN WITH MIKI" CAMPAIGN PICKS UP SPEED.
PEOPLE THINK MIKI'S TOO SELF-RIGHTEOUS.
HE'S JUST TRYING TO DO THE RIGHT THING.
HUMANS ARE MEAN-SPIRITED.
IN DECEMBER, TAKEO FUKUDA BECOMES PRIME MINISTER.
HE'S GIDDY ABOUT IT.
HE ASSEMBLES HIS CABINET.
FUKUDA IS A DARK-HORSE CANDIDATE.

*SEE NOTE ON PAGE 535.

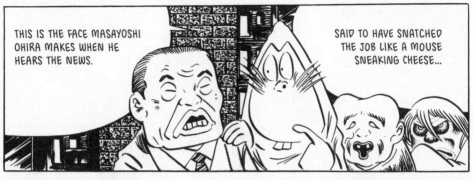

SAID TO HAVE SNATCHED THE JOB LIKE A MOUSE SNEAKING CHEESE...
THIS IS THE FACE MASAYOSHI OHIRA MAKES WHEN HE HEARS THE NEWS.
IT SHOULD HAVE BEEN ME.
YOU'LL GET YOUR CHANCE.
EASY COME, EASY GO.
MIKI WAS A DARK HORSE TOO.
JULY 1977 (SHOWA 52)...
TELEPHONE. A REPORTER FROM KYODO NEWS.
IT'S PAST MIDNIGHT.
THE RE-PORTER, NEKO-HACHI, CALLED TO TELL ME...
WHAT!?!
A DINOSAUR HAD BEEN DISCOVERED IN NEW ZEALAND.

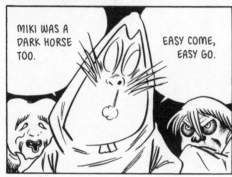

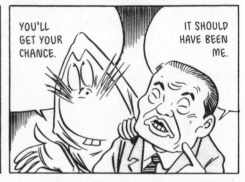

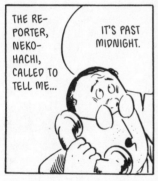

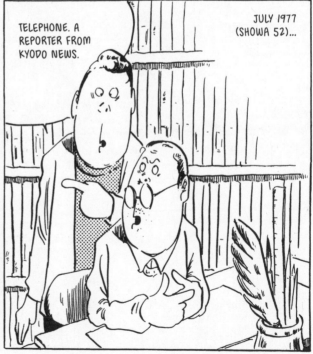

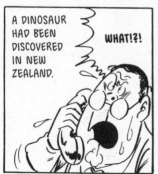

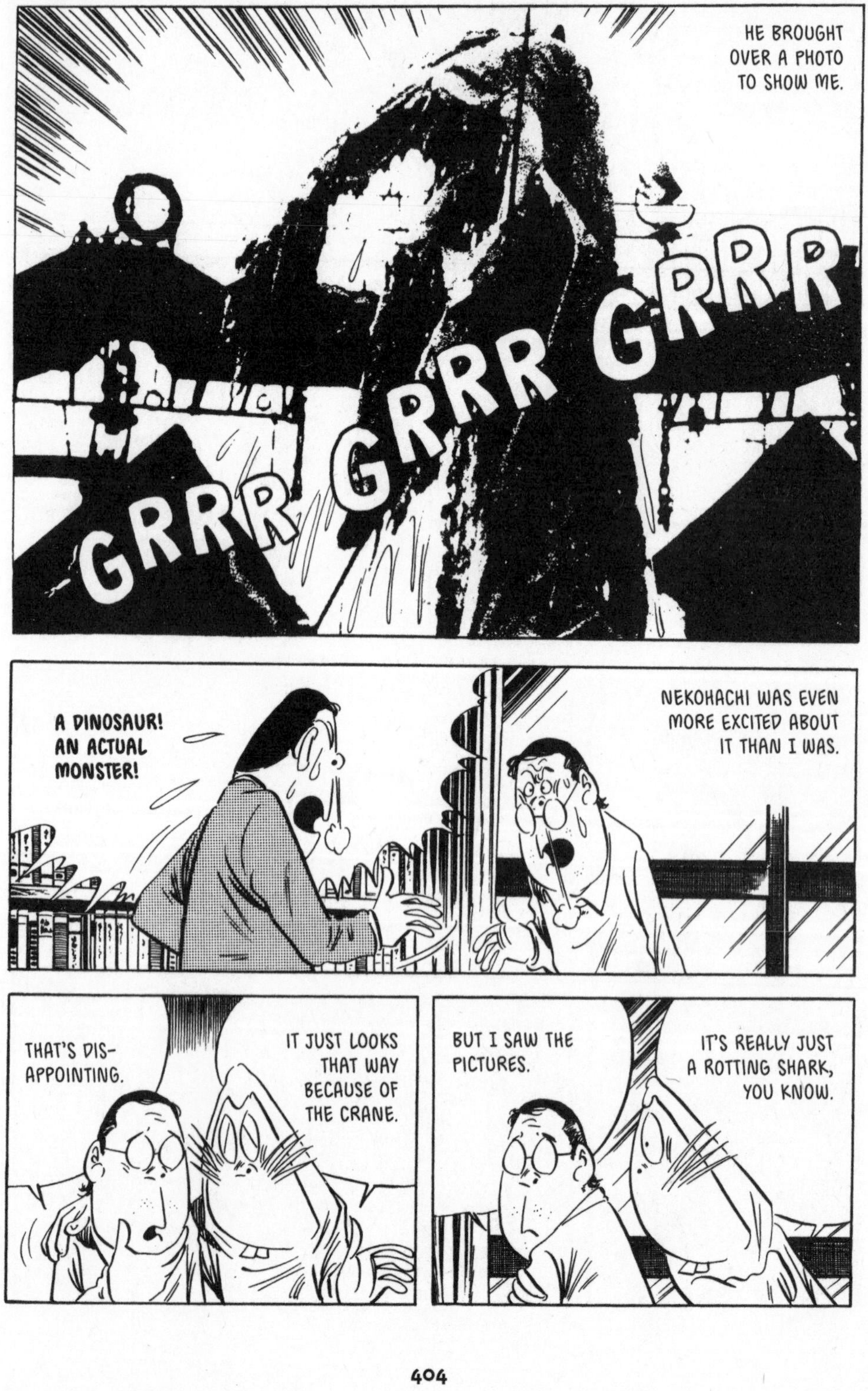
HE BROUGHT OVER A PHOTO TO SHOW ME.
GRRR GRRR GRRR GRRR
NEKOHACHI WAS EVEN MORE EXCITED ABOUT IT THAN I WAS.
A DINOSAUR! AN ACTUAL MONSTER!
IT'S REALLY JUST A ROTTING SHARK, YOU KNOW.
BUT I SAW THE PICTURES.
IT JUST LOOKS THAT WAY BECAUSE OF THE CRANE.
THAT'S DIS-APPOINTING.

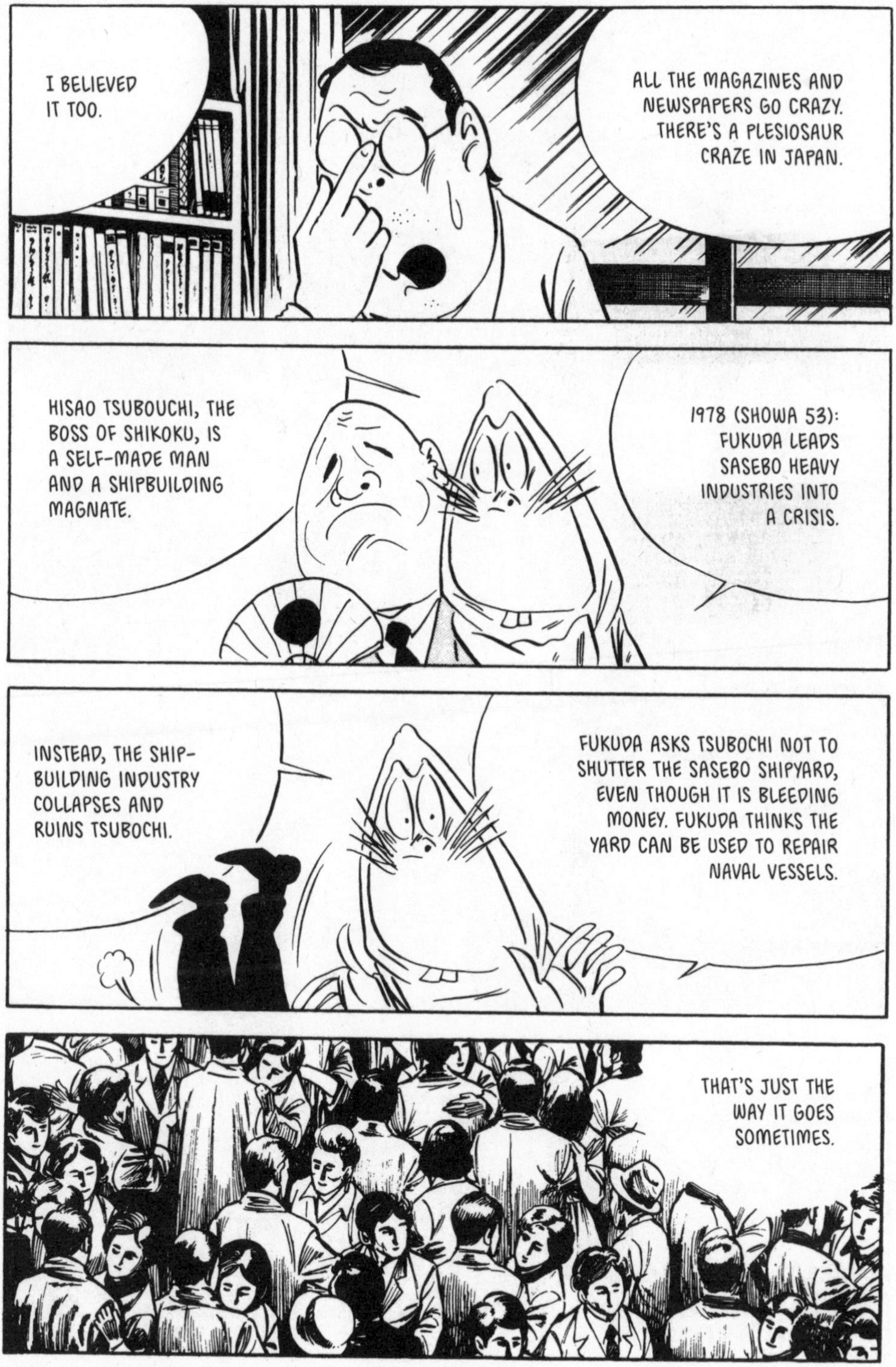
ALL THE MAGAZINES AND NEWSPAPERS GO CRAZY. THERE'S A PLESIOSAUR CRAZE IN JAPAN.
I BELIEVED IT TOO.
1978 (SHOWA 53): FUKUDA LEADS SASEBO HEAVY INDUSTRIES INTO A CRISIS.
HISAO TSUBOUCHI, THE BOSS OF SHIKOKU, IS A SELF-MADE MAN AND A SHIPBUILDING MAGNATE.
FUKUDA ASKS TSUBOCHI NOT TO SHUTTER THE SASEBO SHIPYARD, EVEN THOUGH IT IS BLEEDING MONEY. FUKUDA THINKS THE YARD CAN BE USED TO REPAIR NAVAL VESSELS.
INSTEAD, THE SHIP-BUILDING INDUSTRY COLLAPSES AND RUINS TSUBOCHI.
THAT'S JUST THE WAY IT GOES SOMETIMES.

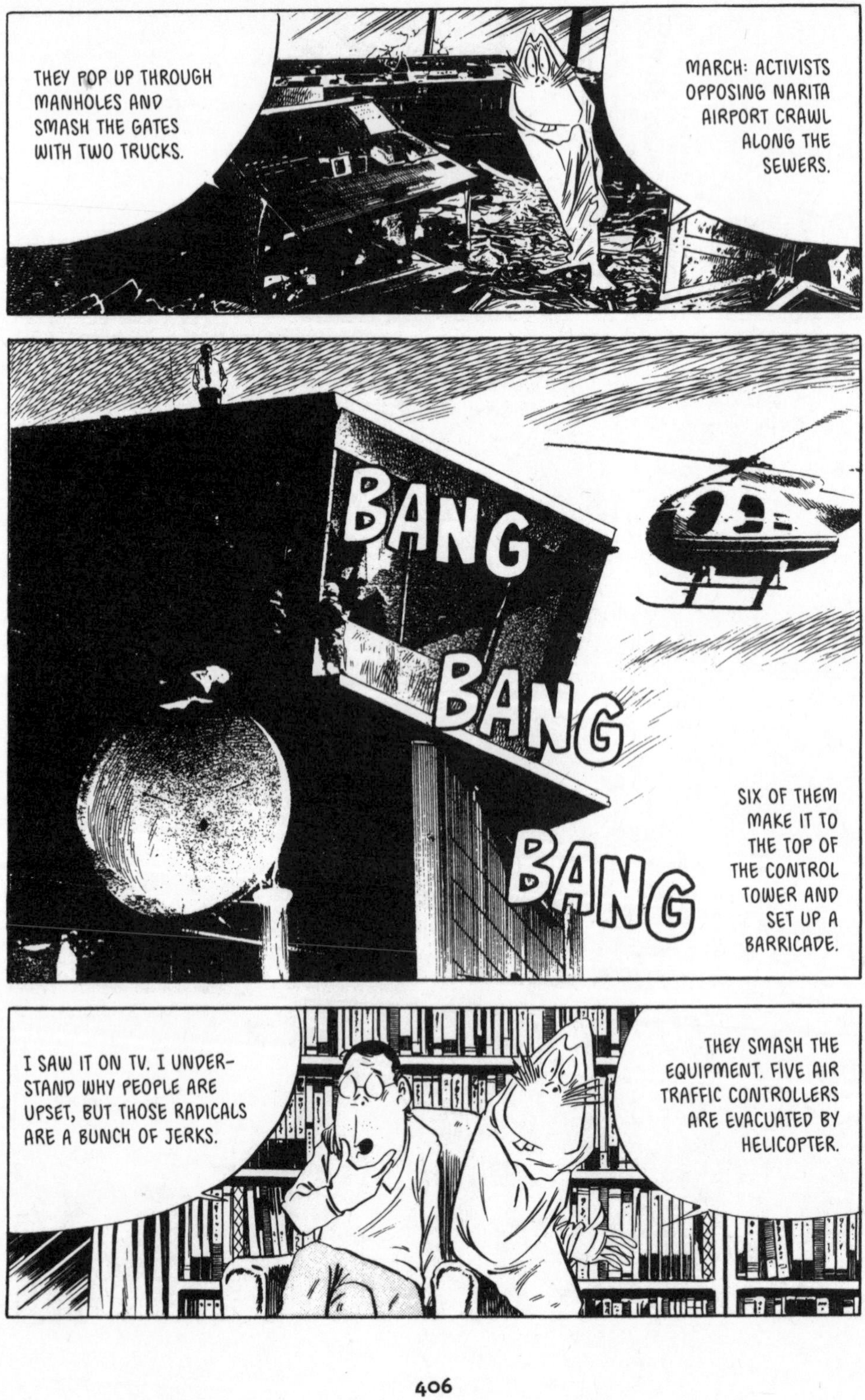
MARCH: ACTIVISTS OPPOSING NARITA AIRPORT CRAWL ALONG THE SEWERS.
THEY POP UP THROUGH MANHOLES AND SMASH THE GATES WITH TWO TRUCKS.
BANG
BANG
BANG
SIX OF THEM MAKE IT TO THE TOP OF THE CONTROL TOWER AND SET UP A BARRICADE.
THEY SMASH THE EQUIPMENT. FIVE AIR TRAFFIC CONTROLLERS ARE EVACUATED BY HELICOPTER.
I SAW IT ON TV. I UNDER-STAND WHY PEOPLE ARE UPSET, BUT THOSE RADICALS ARE A BUNCH OF JERKS.

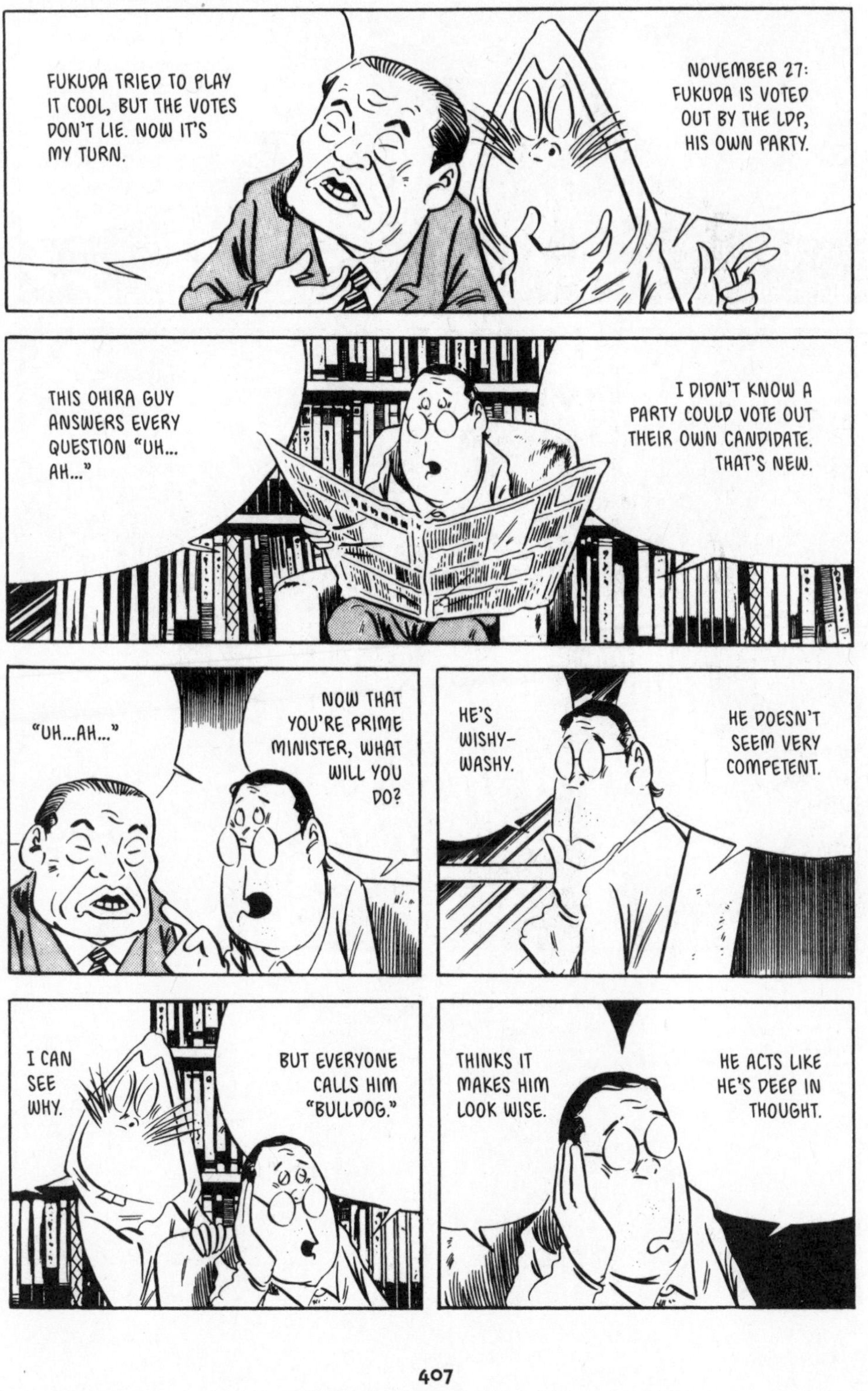
NOVEMBER 27: FUKUDA IS VOTED OUT BY THE LDP, HIS OWN PARTY.
FUKUDA TRIED TO PLAY IT COOL, BUT THE VOTES DON'T LIE. NOW IT'S MY TURN.
I DIDN'T KNOW A PARTY COULD VOTE OUT THEIR OWN CANDIDATE. THAT'S NEW.
THIS OHIRA GUY ANSWERS EVERY QUESTION "UH... AH..."
HE DOESN'T SEEM VERY COMPETENT.
HE'S WISHY-WASHY.
NOW THAT YOU'RE PRIME MINISTER, WHAT WILL YOU DO?
"UH...AH..."
HE ACTS LIKE HE'S DEEP IN THOUGHT.
THINKS IT MAKES HIM LOOK WISE.
BUT EVERYONE CALLS HIM "BULLDOG."
I CAN SEE WHY.

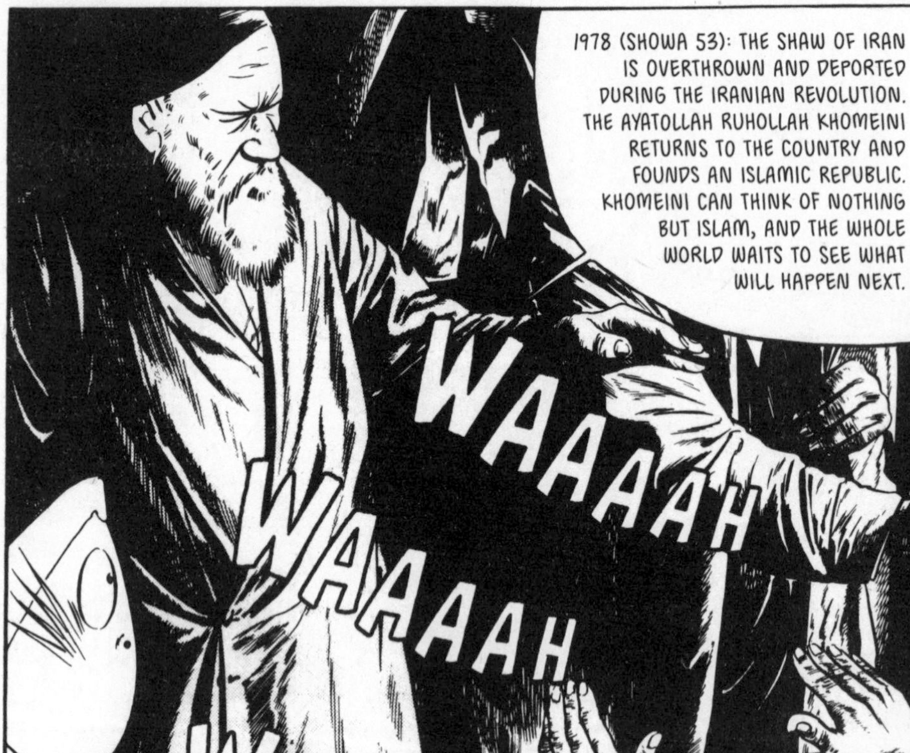
1978 (SHOWA 53): THE SHAW OF IRAN IS OVERTHROWN AND DEPORTED DURING THE IRANIAN REVOLUTION. THE AYATOLLAH RUHOLLAH KHOMEINI RETURNS TO THE COUNTRY AND FOUNDS AN ISLAMIC REPUBLIC. KHOMEINI CAN THINK OF NOTHING BUT ISLAM, AND THE WHOLE WORLD WAITS TO SEE WHAT WILL HAPPEN NEXT.
WAAAAAH
WAAAAAH
WAAAAAH

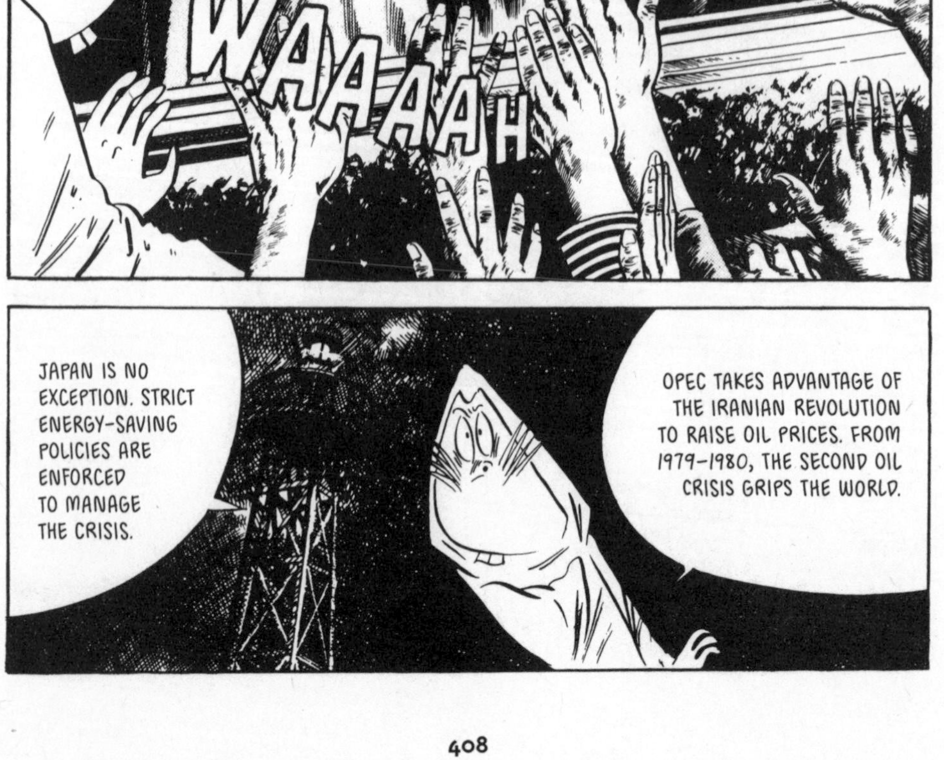
OPEC TAKES ADVANTAGE OF THE IRANIAN REVOLUTION TO RAISE OIL PRICES. FROM 1979–1980, THE SECOND OIL CRISIS GRIPS THE WORLD.
JAPAN IS NO EXCEPTION. STRICT ENERGY-SAVING POLICIES ARE ENFORCED TO MANAGE THE CRISIS.

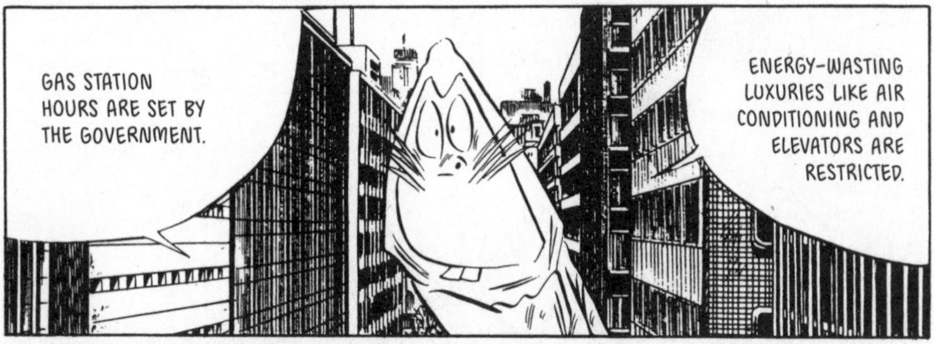
ENERGY-WASTING LUXURIES LIKE AIR CONDITIONING AND ELEVATORS ARE RESTRICTED.
GAS STATION HOURS ARE SET BY THE GOVERNMENT.

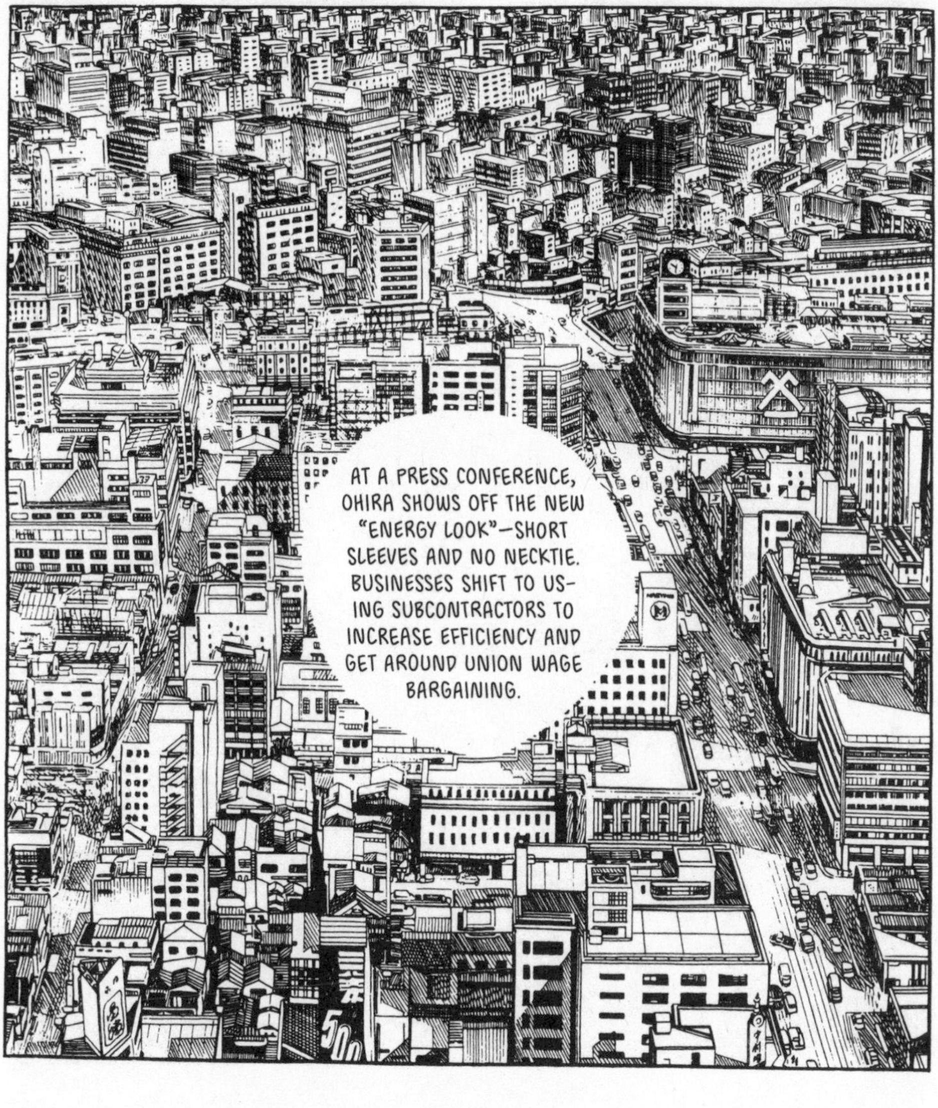
AT A PRESS CONFERENCE, OHIRA SHOWS OFF THE NEW "ENERGY LOOK"—SHORT SLEEVES AND NO NECKTIE. BUSINESSES SHIFT TO US-ING SUBCONTRACTORS TO INCREASE EFFICIENCY AND GET AROUND UNION WAGE BARGAINING.

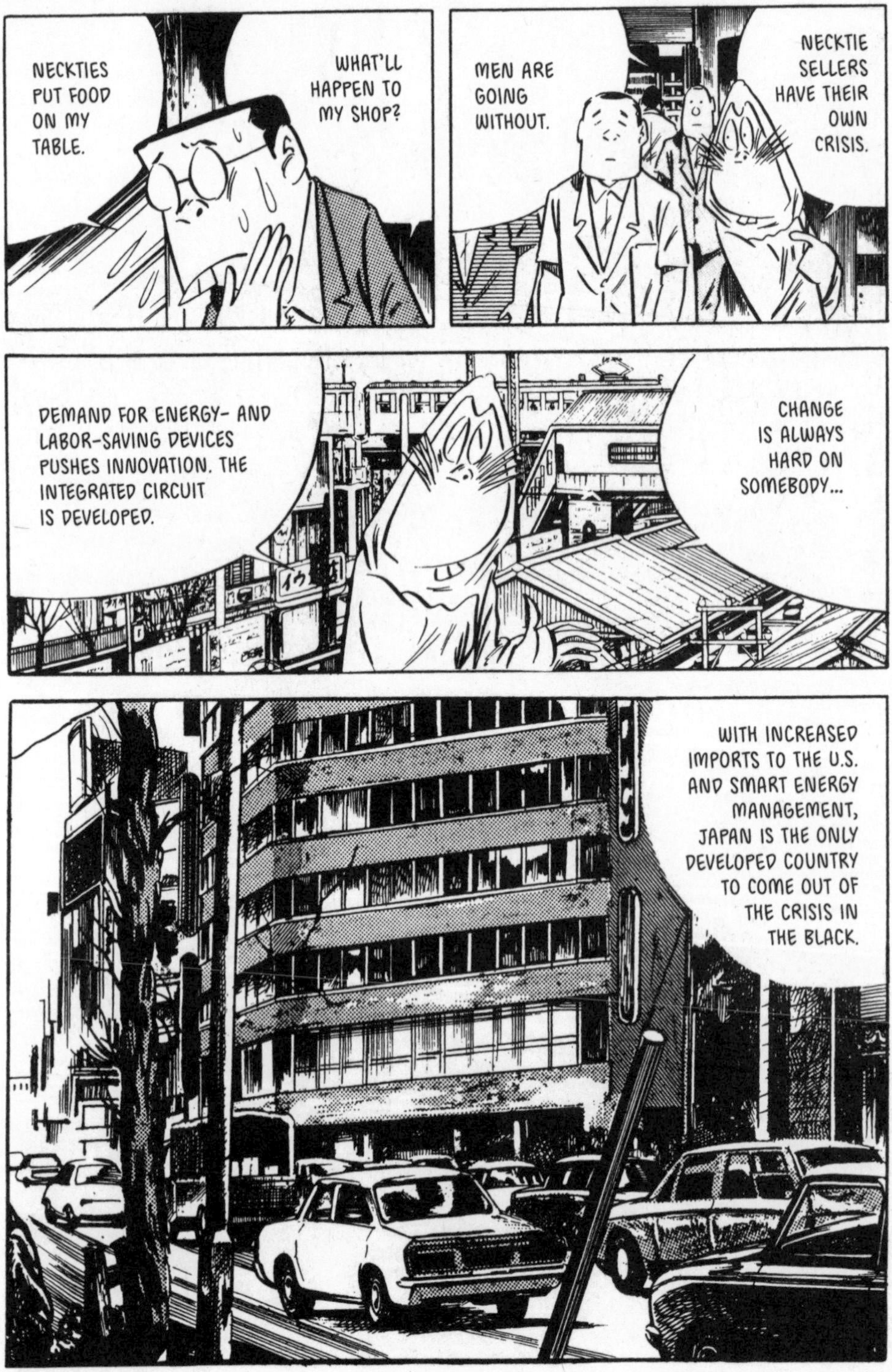
NECKTIE SELLERS HAVE THEIR OWN CRISIS.
MEN ARE GOING WITHOUT.
WHAT'LL HAPPEN TO MY SHOP?
NECKTIES PUT FOOD ON MY TABLE.
CHANGE IS ALWAYS HARD ON SOMEBODY...
DEMAND FOR ENERGY- AND LABOR-SAVING DEVICES PUSHES INNOVATION. THE INTEGRATED CIRCUIT IS DEVELOPED.
WITH INCREASED IMPORTS TO THE U.S. AND SMART ENERGY MANAGEMENT, JAPAN IS THE ONLY DEVELOPED COUNTRY TO COME OUT OF THE CRISIS IN THE BLACK.

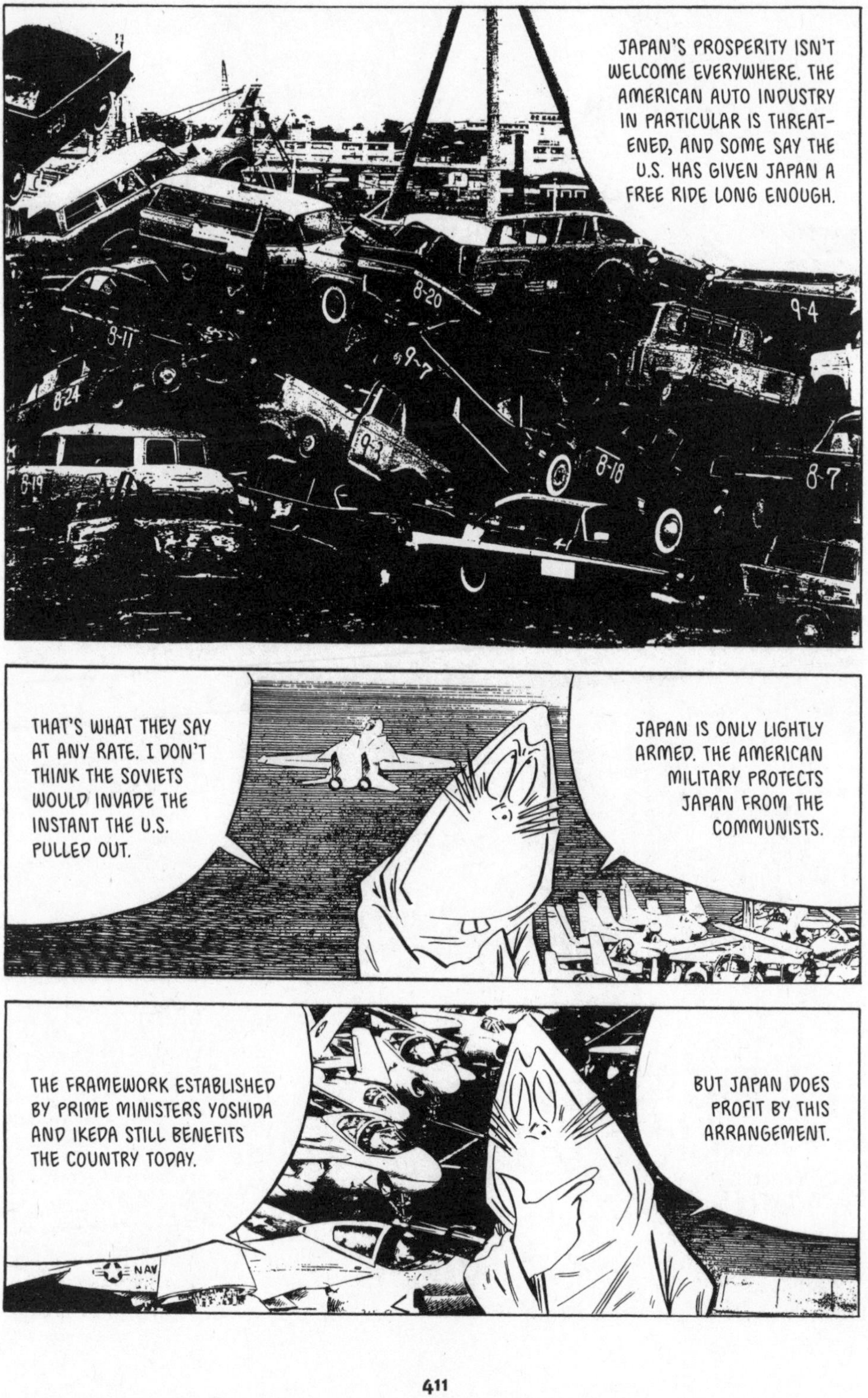
JAPAN'S PROSPERITY ISN'T WELCOME EVERYWHERE. THE AMERICAN AUTO INDUSTRY IN PARTICULAR IS THREATENED, AND SOME SAY THE U.S. HAS GIVEN JAPAN A FREE RIDE LONG ENOUGH.
JAPAN IS ONLY LIGHTLY ARMED. THE AMERICAN MILITARY PROTECTS JAPAN FROM THE COMMUNISTS.
THAT'S WHAT THEY SAY AT ANY RATE. I DON'T THINK THE SOVIETS WOULD INVADE THE INSTANT THE U.S. PULLED OUT.
BUT JAPAN DOES PROFIT BY THIS ARRANGEMENT.
THE FRAMEWORK ESTABLISHED BY PRIME MINISTERS YOSHIDA AND IKEDA STILL BENEFITS THE COUNTRY TODAY.

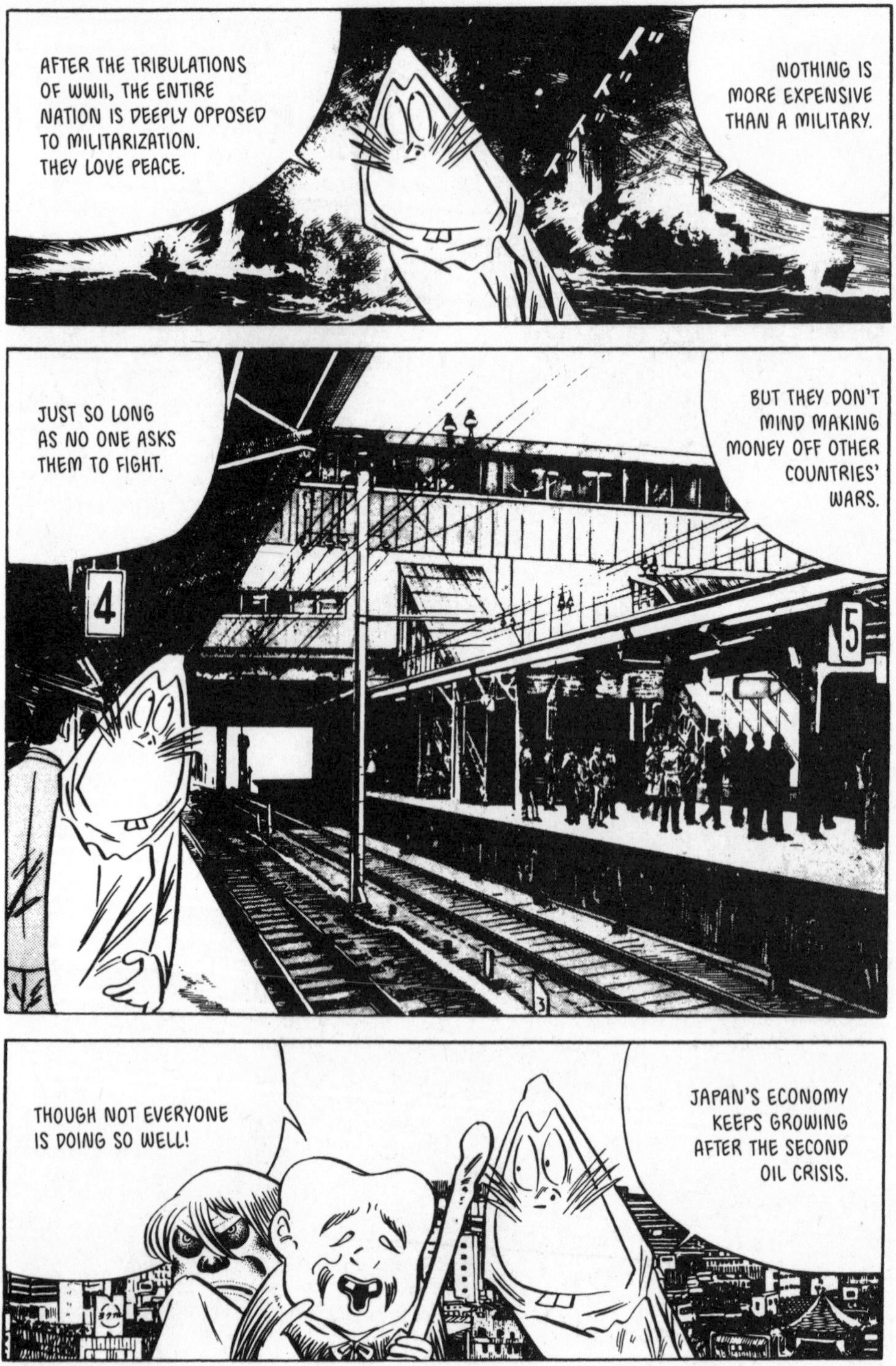

NOTHING IS MORE EXPENSIVE THAN A MILITARY.
ドドド
AFTER THE TRIBULATIONS OF WWII, THE ENTIRE NATION IS DEEPLY OPPOSED TO MILITARIZATION. THEY LOVE PEACE.
BUT THEY DON'T MIND MAKING MONEY OFF OTHER COUNTRIES' WARS.
5
4
JUST SO LONG AS NO ONE ASKS THEM TO FIGHT.
JAPAN'S ECONOMY KEEPS GROWING AFTER THE SECOND OIL CRISIS.
THOUGH NOT EVERYONE IS DOING SO WELL!

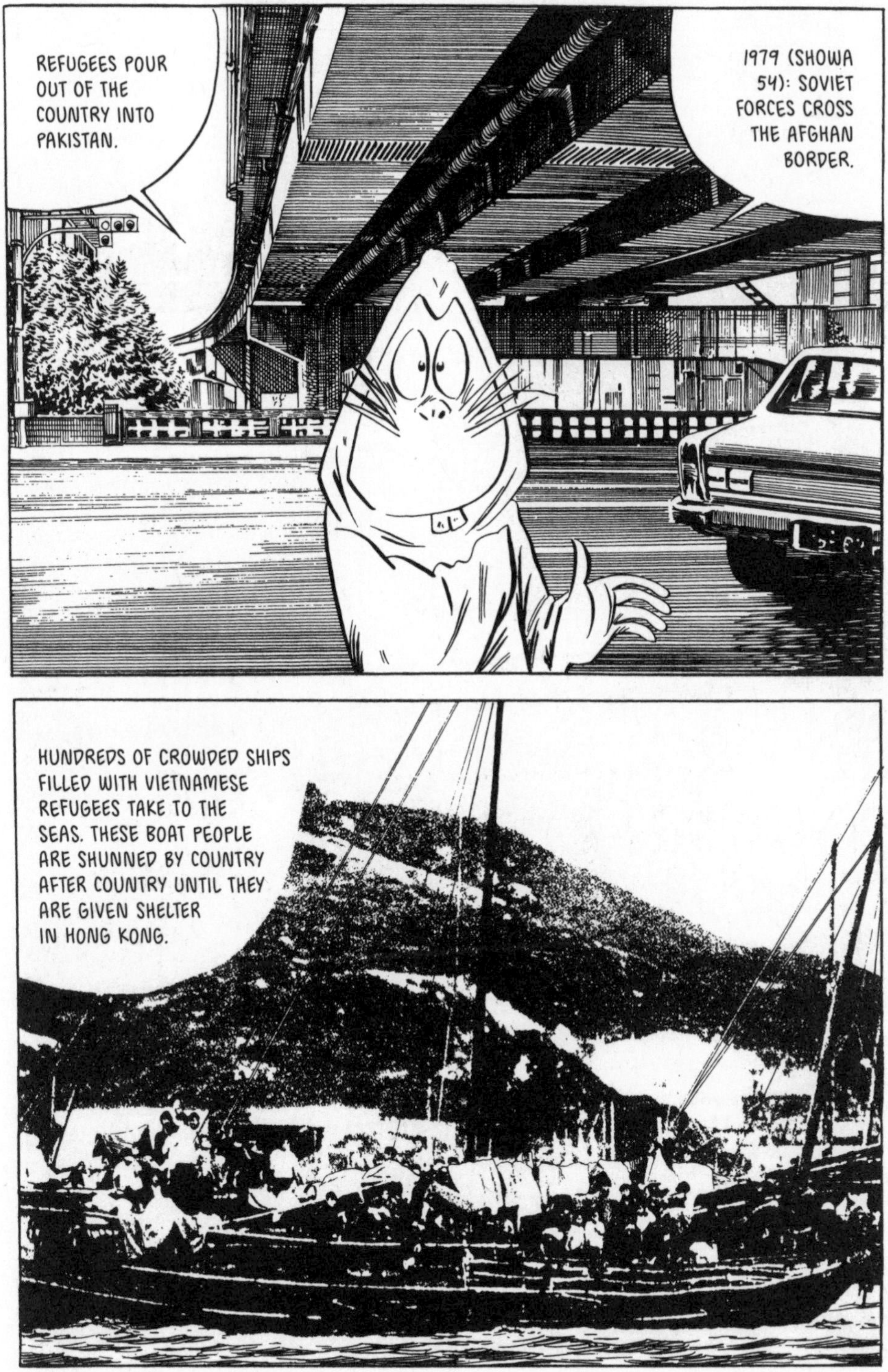
1979 (SHOWA 54): SOVIET FORCES CROSS THE AFGHAN BORDER.
REFUGEES POUR OUT OF THE COUNTRY INTO PAKISTAN.
HUNDREDS OF CROWDED SHIPS FILLED WITH VIETNAMESE REFUGEES TAKE TO THE SEAS. THESE BOAT PEOPLE ARE SHUNNED BY COUNTRY AFTER COUNTRY UNTIL THEY ARE GIVEN SHELTER IN HONG KONG.

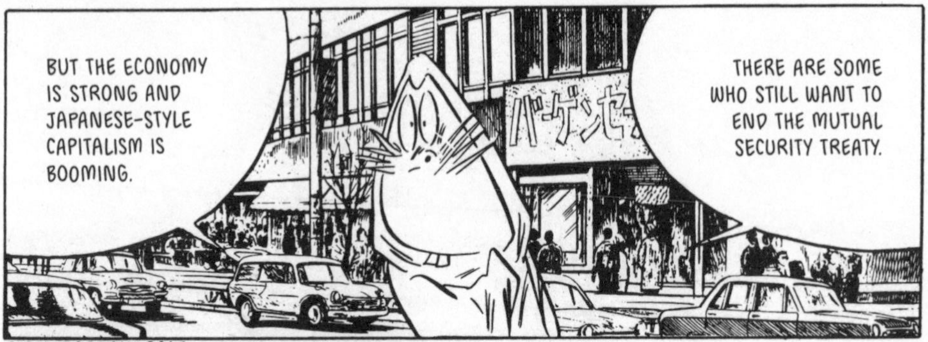
THERE ARE SOME WHO STILL WANT TO END THE MUTUAL SECURITY TREATY.
バーゲンセー
BUT THE ECONOMY IS STRONG AND JAPANESE-STYLE CAPITALISM IS BOOMING.
SIGN: BARGAIN SALE

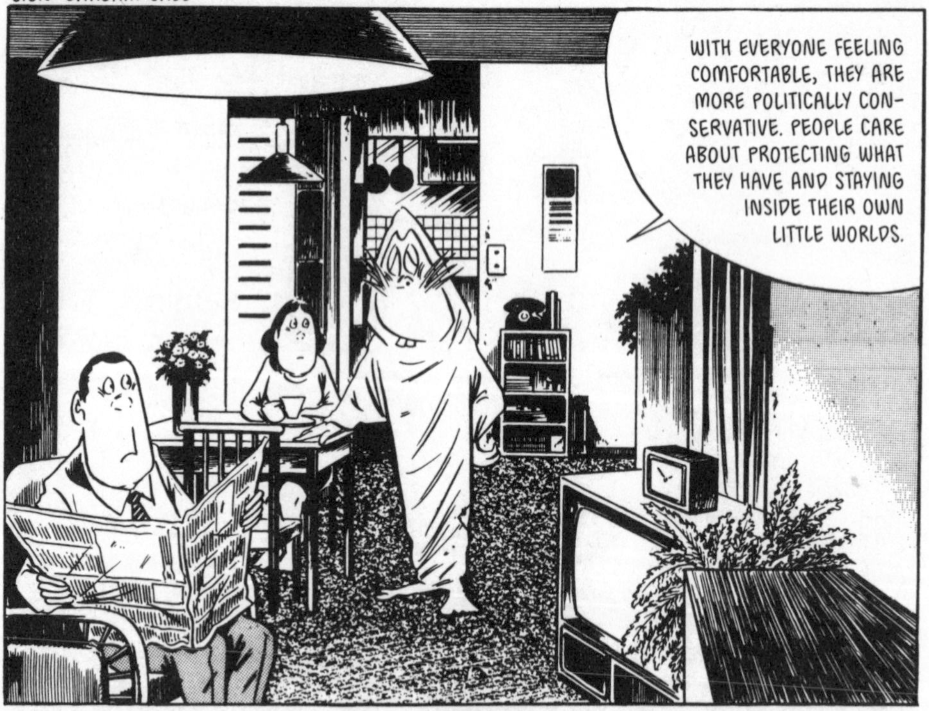
WITH EVERYONE FEELING COMFORTABLE, THEY ARE MORE POLITICALLY CON-SERVATIVE. PEOPLE CARE ABOUT PROTECTING WHAT THEY HAVE AND STAYING INSIDE THEIR OWN LITTLE WORLDS.

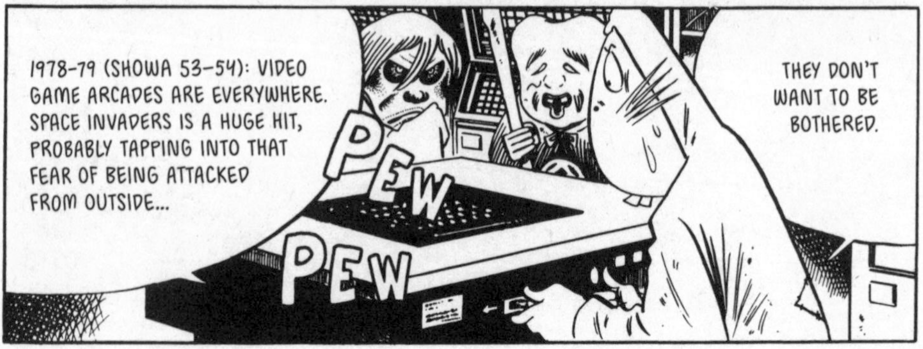
THEY DON'T WANT TO BE BOTHERED.
1978–79 (SHOWA 53–54): VIDEO GAME ARCADES ARE EVERYWHERE. SPACE INVADERS IS A HUGE HIT, PROBABLY TAPPING INTO THAT FEAR OF BEING ATTACKED FROM OUTSIDE...
PEW
PEW

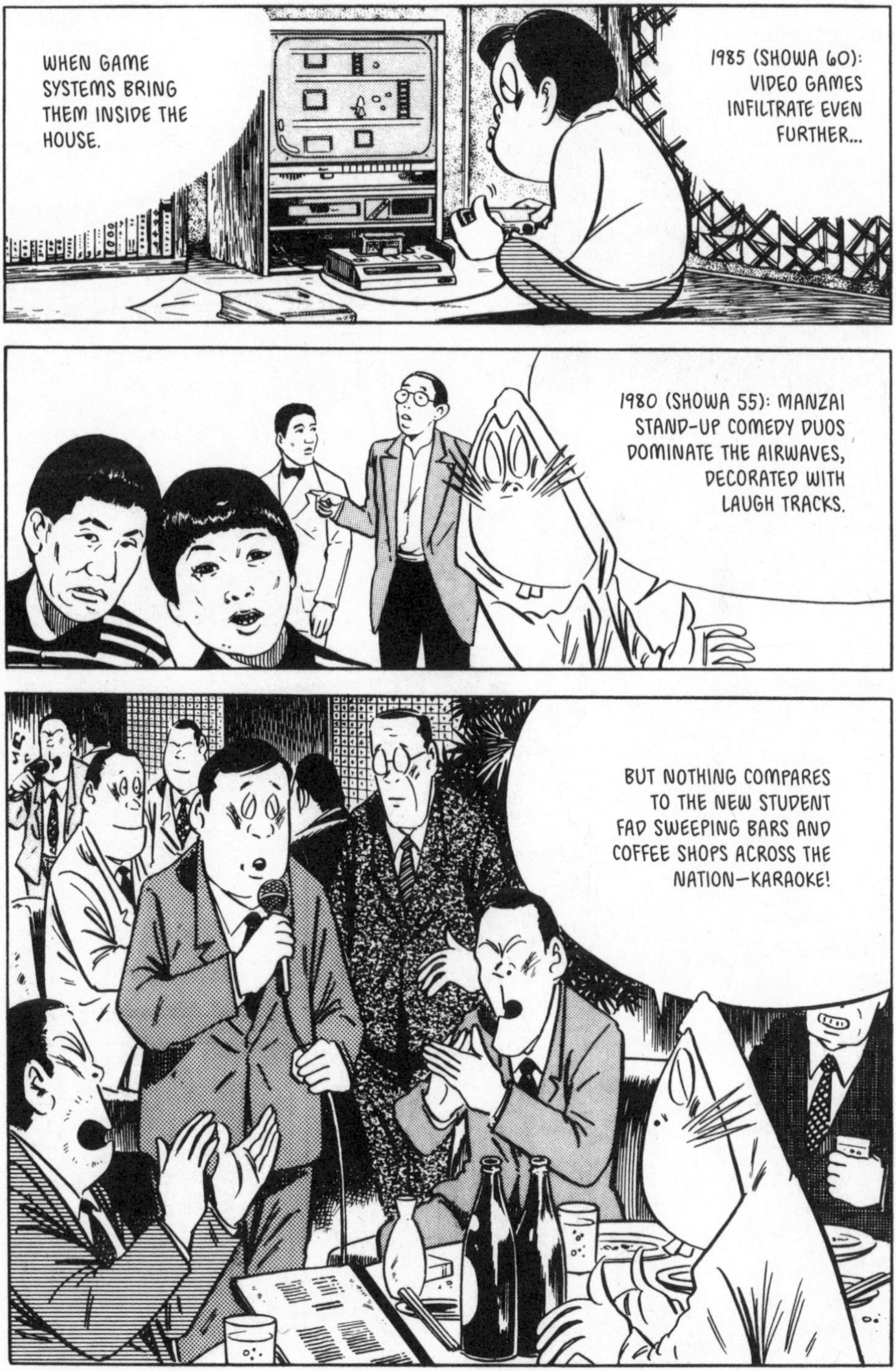
1985 (SHOWA 60): VIDEO GAMES INFILTRATE EVEN FURTHER...
WHEN GAME SYSTEMS BRING THEM INSIDE THE HOUSE.
1980 (SHOWA 55): MANZAI STAND-UP COMEDY DUOS DOMINATE THE AIRWAVES, DECORATED WITH LAUGH TRACKS.
BUT NOTHING COMPARES TO THE NEW STUDENT FAD SWEEPING BARS AND COFFEE SHOPS ACROSS THE NATION—KARAOKE!

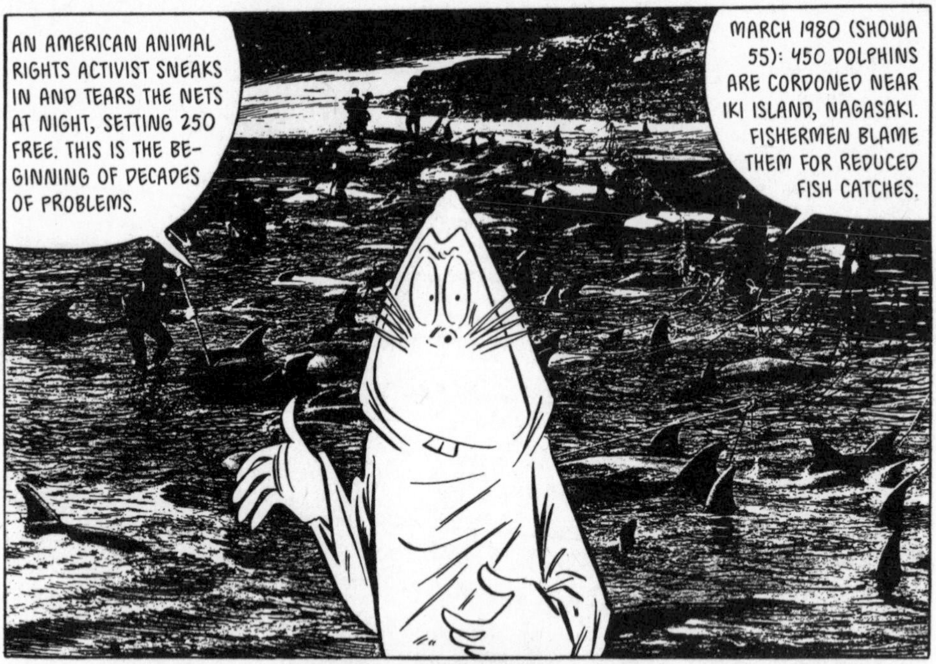
MARCH 1980 (SHOWA 55): 450 DOLPHINS ARE CORDONED NEAR IKI ISLAND, NAGASAKI. FISHERMEN BLAME THEM FOR REDUCED FISH CATCHES.
AN AMERICAN ANIMAL RIGHTS ACTIVIST SNEAKS IN AND TEARS THE NETS AT NIGHT, SETTING 250 FREE. THIS IS THE BE-GINNING OF DECADES OF PROBLEMS.

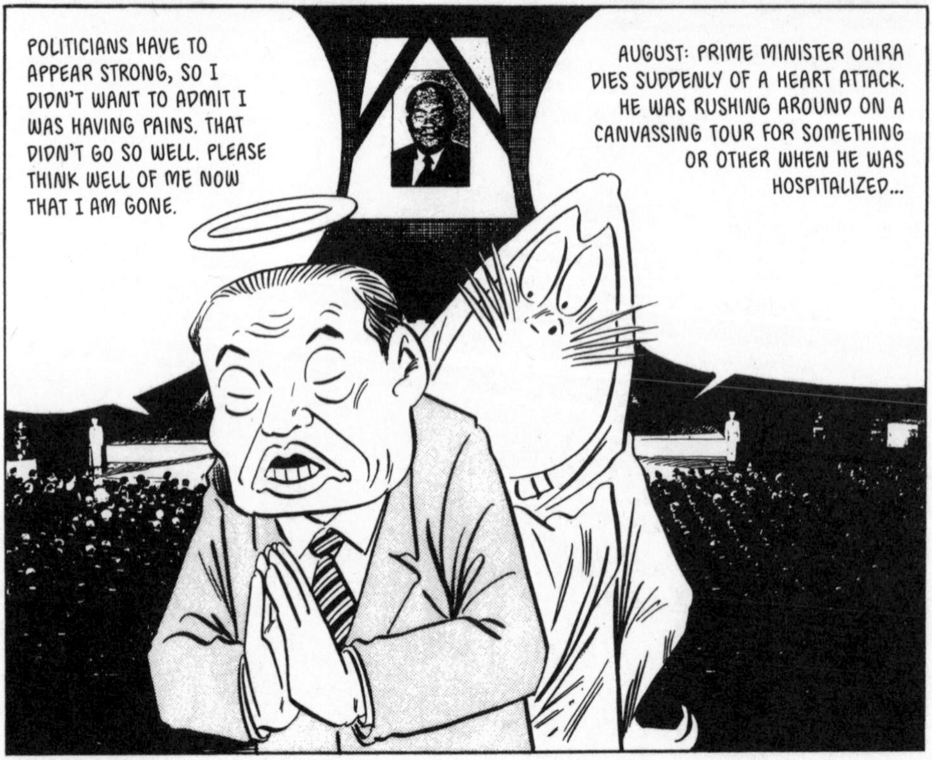
AUGUST: PRIME MINISTER OHIRA DIES SUDDENLY OF A HEART ATTACK. HE WAS RUSHING AROUND ON A CANVASSING TOUR FOR SOMETHING OR OTHER WHEN HE WAS HOSPITALIZED...
POLITICIANS HAVE TO APPEAR STRONG, SO I DIDN'T WANT TO ADMIT I WAS HAVING PAINS. THAT DIDN'T GO SO WELL. PLEASE THINK WELL OF ME NOW THAT I AM GONE.

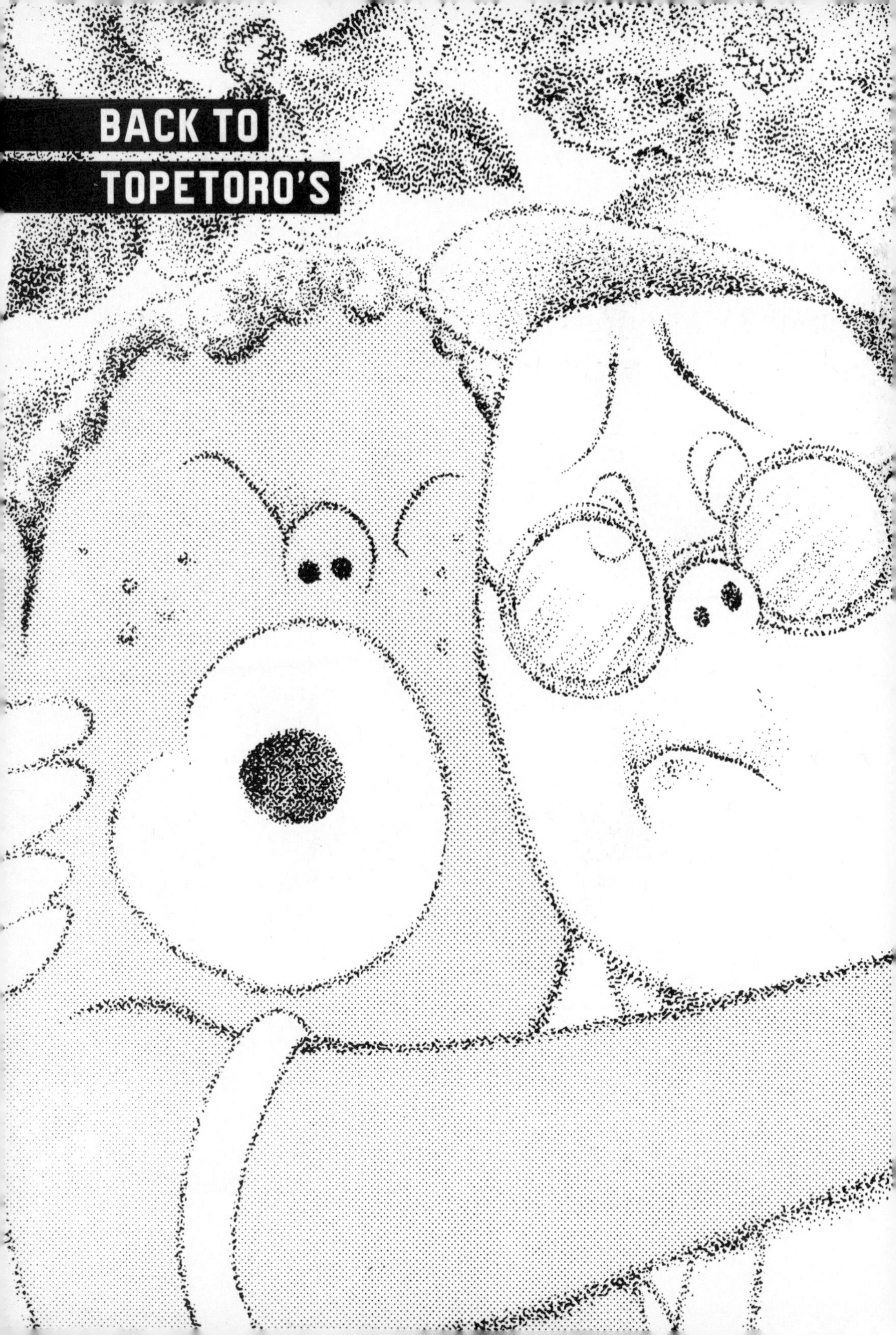
BACK TO
TOPETORO'S

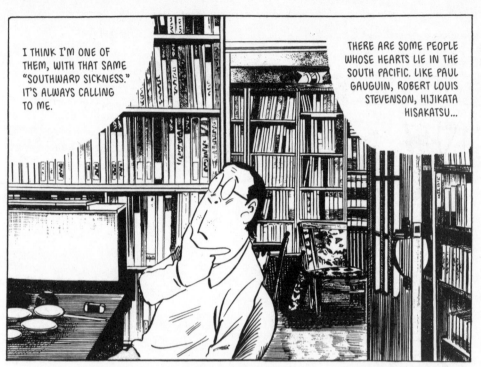

THERE ARE SOME PEOPLE WHOSE HEARTS LIE IN THE SOUTH PACIFIC. LIKE PAUL GAUGUIN, ROBERT LOUIS STEVENSON, HIJIKATA HISAKATSU...
I THINK I'M ONE OF THEM, WITH THAT SAME "SOUTHWARD SICKNESS." IT'S ALWAYS CALLING TO ME.
NATIVES ALWAYS SEEM SO AT PEACE WITH BEING ALIVE. THEY LOVE THE COLORS OF TREES, THE CALM SEAS, AND THE BEAUTY OF SUNSETS. WHEN MY SOUTHWARD SICKNESS GOT TOO BAD, I WENT TO SEE MY OLD SERGEANT IN TAKARAZUKA.

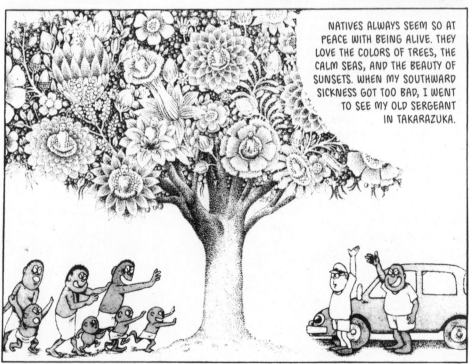

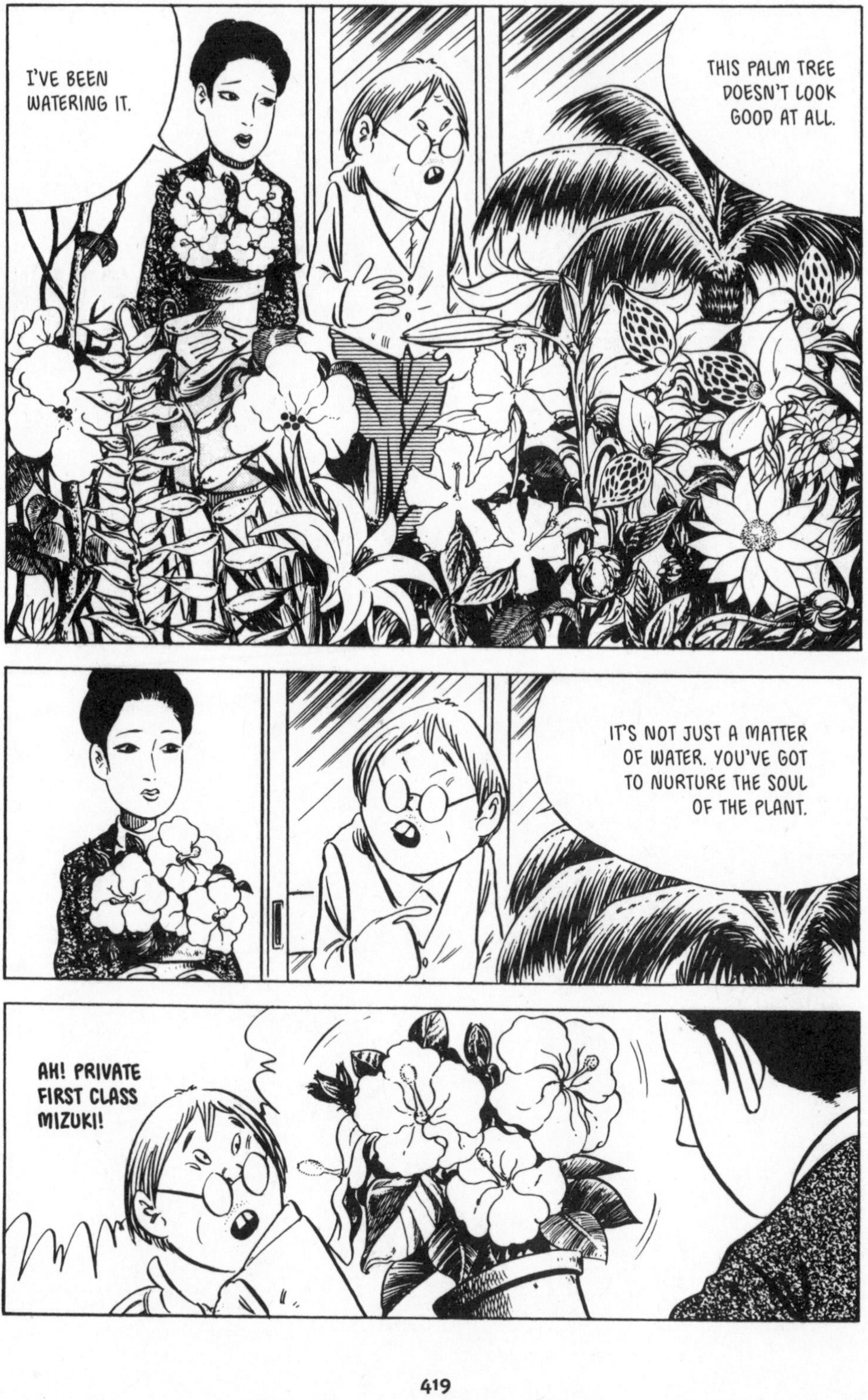
THIS PALM TREE DOESN'T LOOK GOOD AT ALL.
I'VE BEEN WATERING IT.
IT'S NOT JUST A MATTER OF WATER. YOU'VE GOT TO NURTURE THE SOUL OF THE PLANT.
AH! PRIVATE FIRST CLASS MIZUKI!

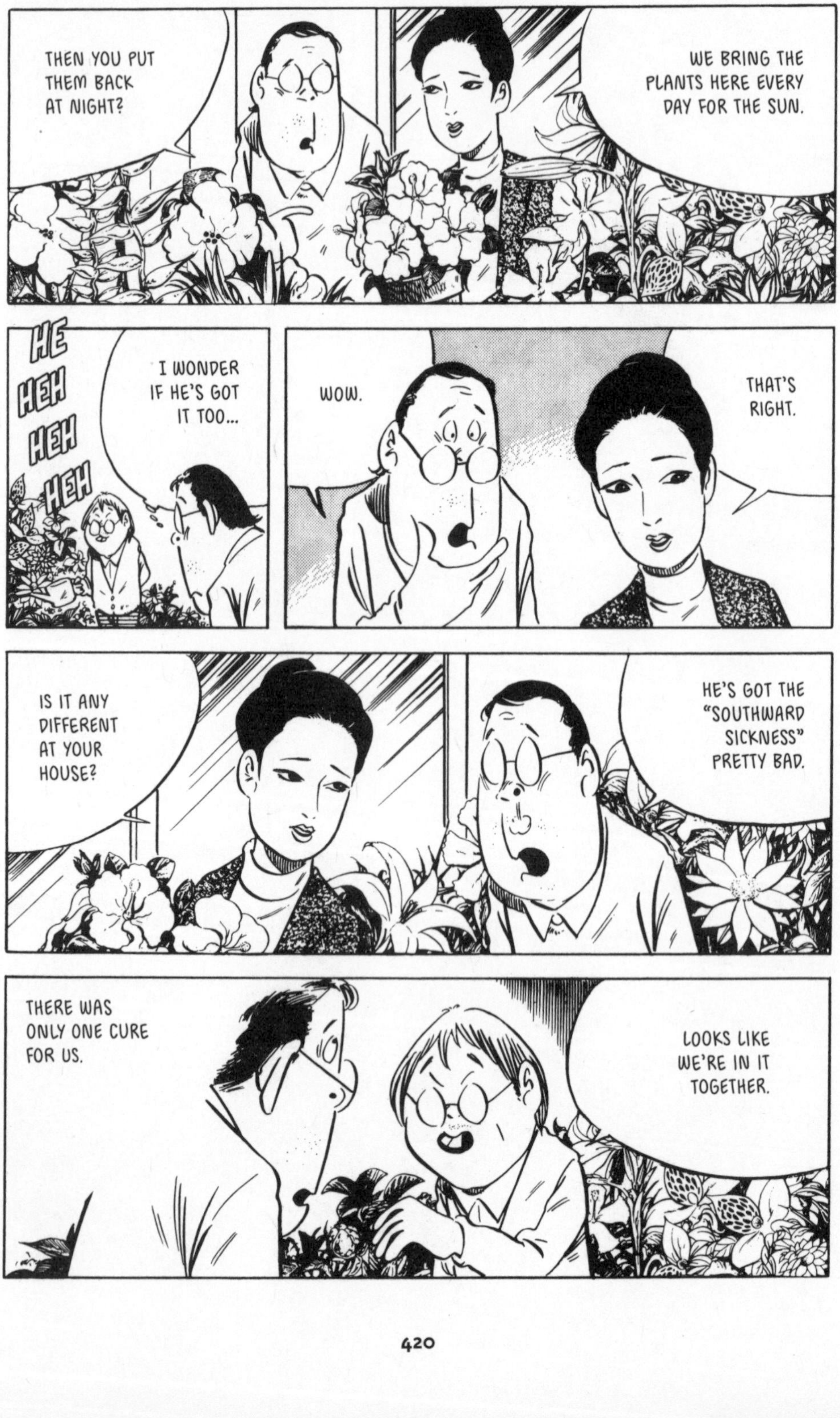
WE BRING THE PLANTS HERE EVERY DAY FOR THE SUN.
THEN YOU PUT THEM BACK AT NIGHT?
THAT'S RIGHT.
WOW.
I WONDER IF HE'S GOT IT TOO...
HE HEH HEH HEH
HE'S GOT THE "SOUTHWARD SICKNESS" PRETTY BAD.
IS IT ANY DIFFERENT AT YOUR HOUSE?
LOOKS LIKE WE'RE IN IT TOGETHER.
THERE WAS ONLY ONE CURE FOR US.

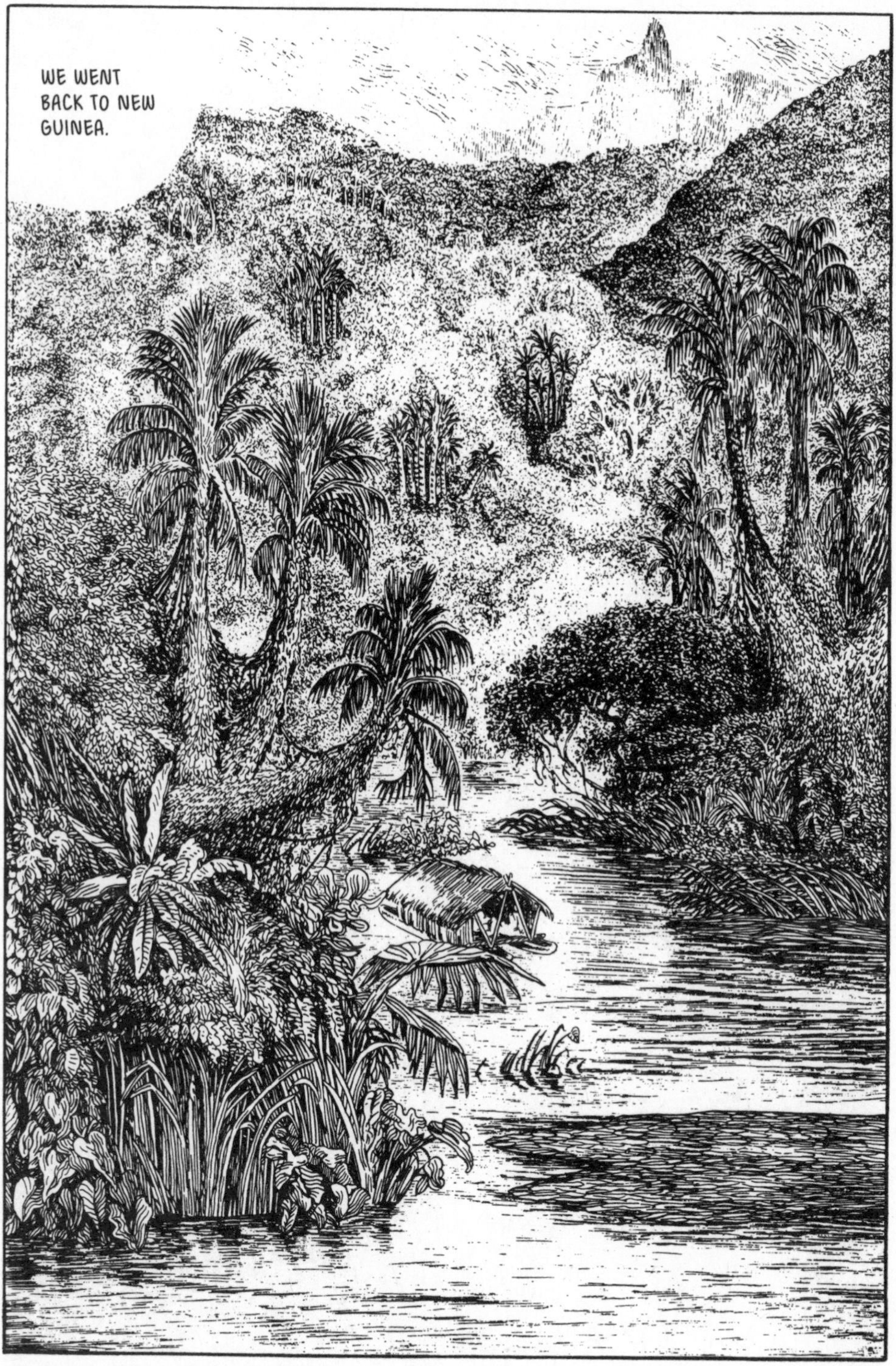
WE WENT
BACK TO NEW
GUINEA.

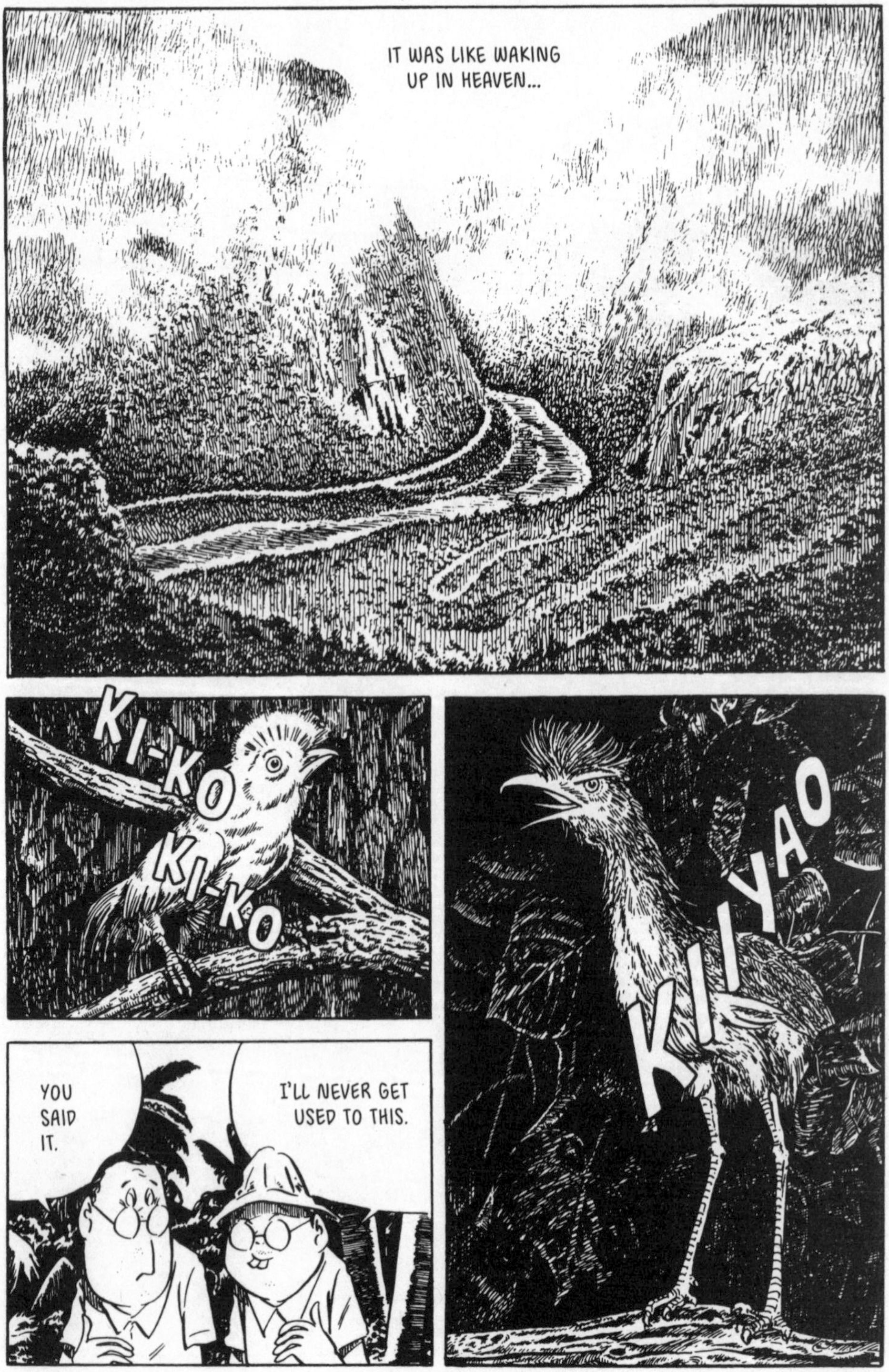
IT WAS LIKE WAKING UP IN HEAVEN...
KII YAO
KI-KO KI-KO
I'LL NEVER GET USED TO THIS.
YOU SAID IT.

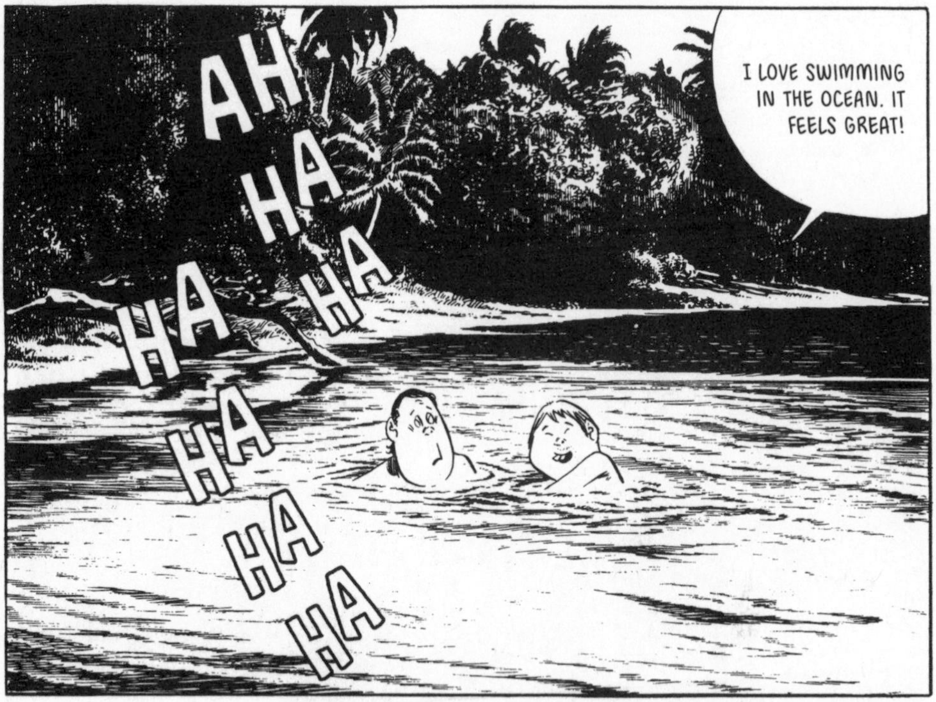
I LOVE SWIMMING IN THE OCEAN. IT FEELS GREAT!
AH HA HA HA HA HA HA HA HA

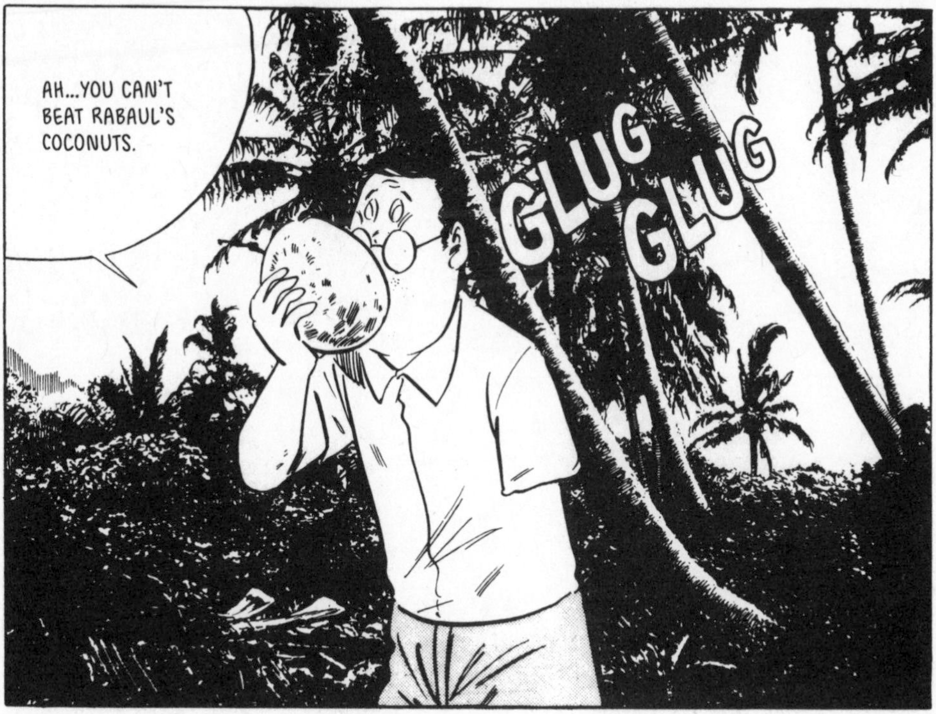
AH...YOU CAN'T BEAT RABAUL'S COCONUTS.
GLUG GLUG

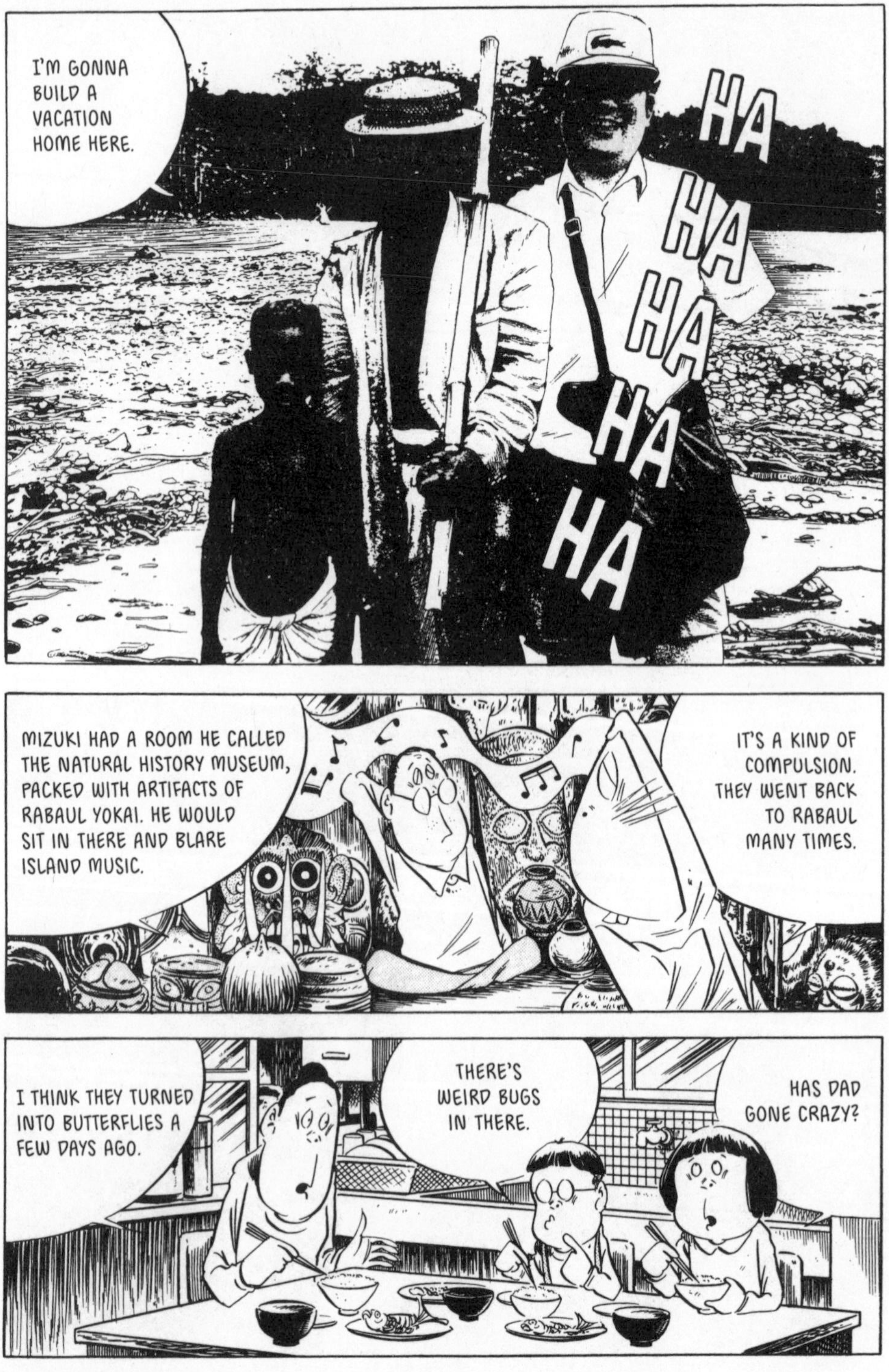
HA HA HA HA HA HA HA
I'M GONNA BUILD A VACATION HOME HERE.
IT'S A KIND OF COMPULSION. THEY WENT BACK TO RABAUL MANY TIMES.
MIZUKI HAD A ROOM HE CALLED THE NATURAL HISTORY MUSEUM, PACKED WITH ARTIFACTS OF RABAUL YOKAI. HE WOULD SIT IN THERE AND BLARE ISLAND MUSIC.
HAS DAD GONE CRAZY?
THERE'S WEIRD BUGS IN THERE.
I THINK THEY TURNED INTO BUTTERFLIES A FEW DAYS AGO.

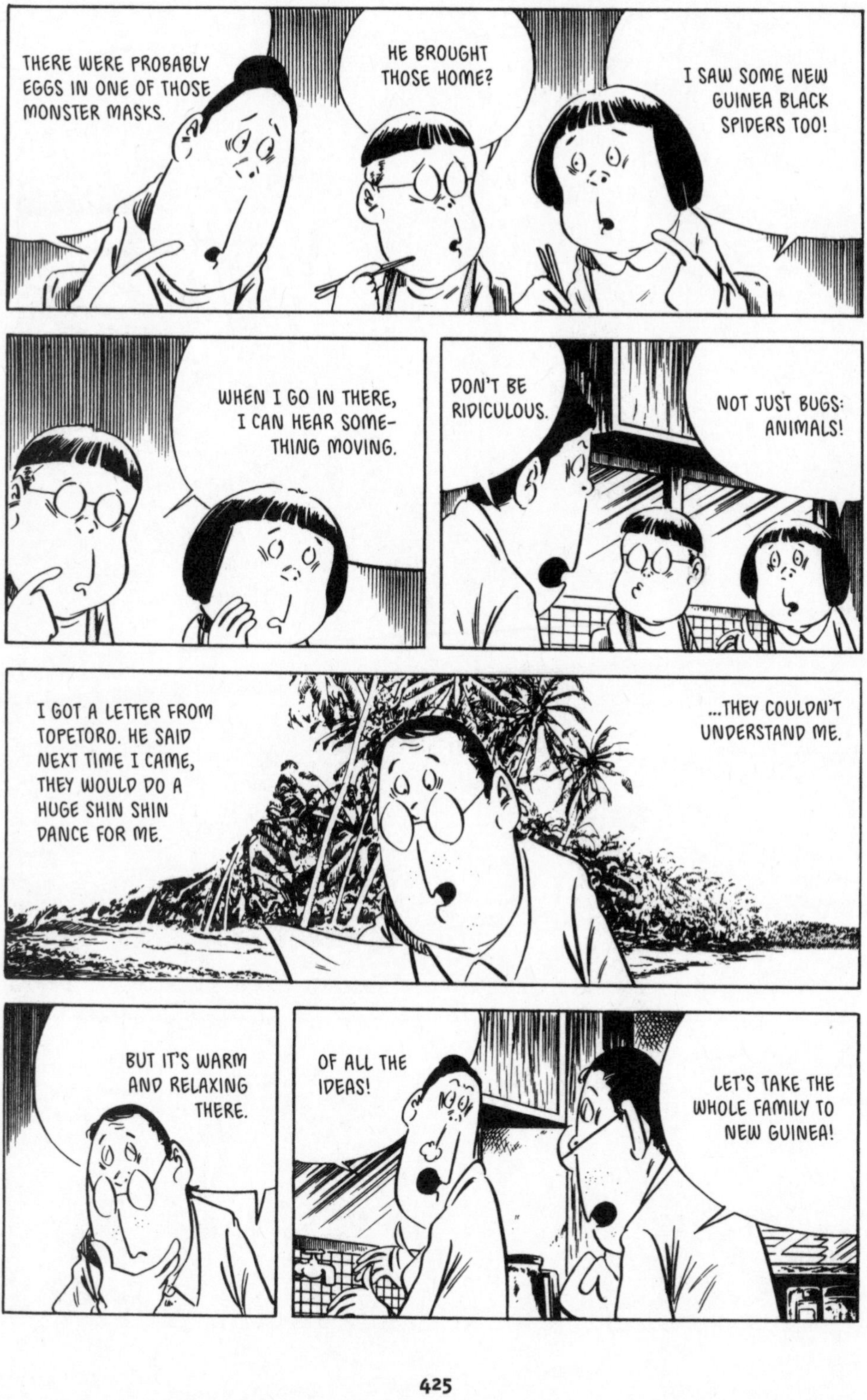
I SAW SOME NEW GUINEA BLACK SPIDERS TOO!
HE BROUGHT THOSE HOME?
THERE WERE PROBABLY EGGS IN ONE OF THOSE MONSTER MASKS.
NOT JUST BUGS: ANIMALS!
DON'T BE RIDICULOUS.
WHEN I GO IN THERE, I CAN HEAR SOME-THING MOVING.
...THEY COULDN'T UNDERSTAND ME.
I GOT A LETTER FROM TOPETORO. HE SAID NEXT TIME I CAME, THEY WOULD DO A HUGE SHIN SHIN DANCE FOR ME.
LET'S TAKE THE WHOLE FAMILY TO NEW GUINEA!
OF ALL THE IDEAS!
BUT IT'S WARM AND RELAXING THERE.

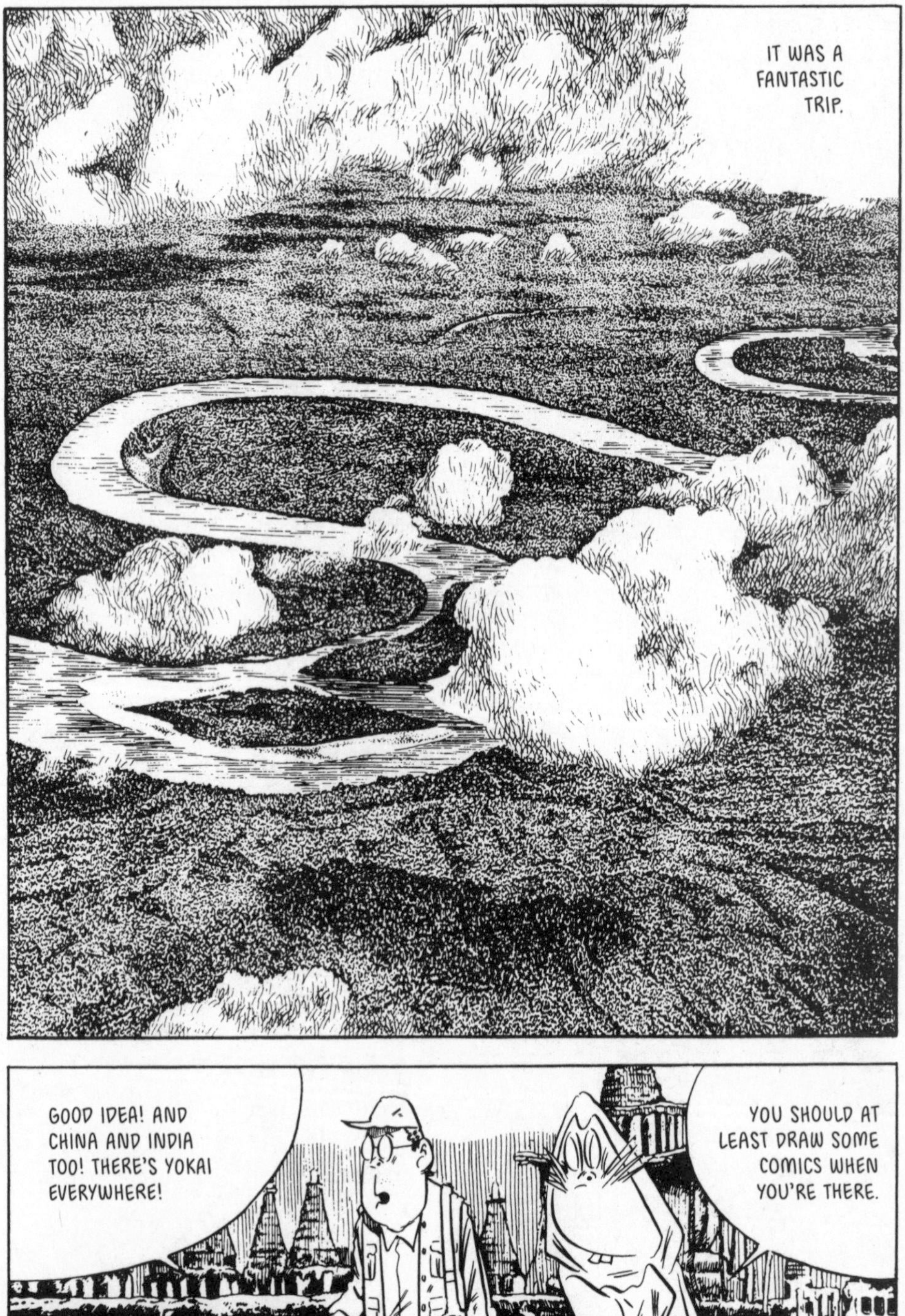
IT WAS A FANTASTIC TRIP.
YOU SHOULD AT LEAST DRAW SOME COMICS WHEN YOU'RE THERE.
GOOD IDEA! AND CHINA AND INDIA TOO! THERE'S YOKAI EVERYWHERE!

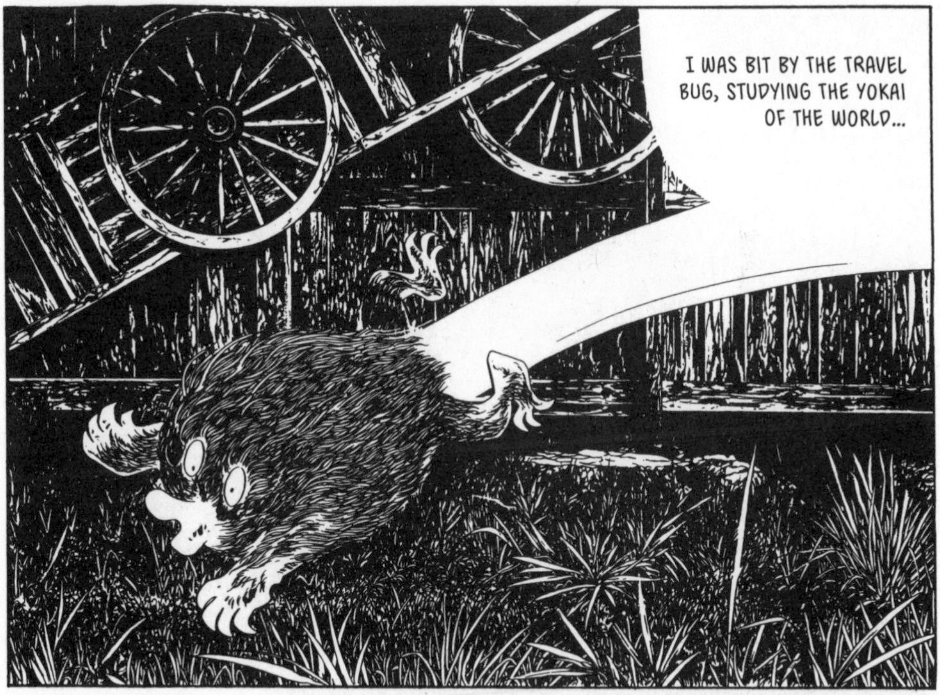
I WAS BIT BY THE TRAVEL BUG, STUDYING THE YOKAI OF THE WORLD...

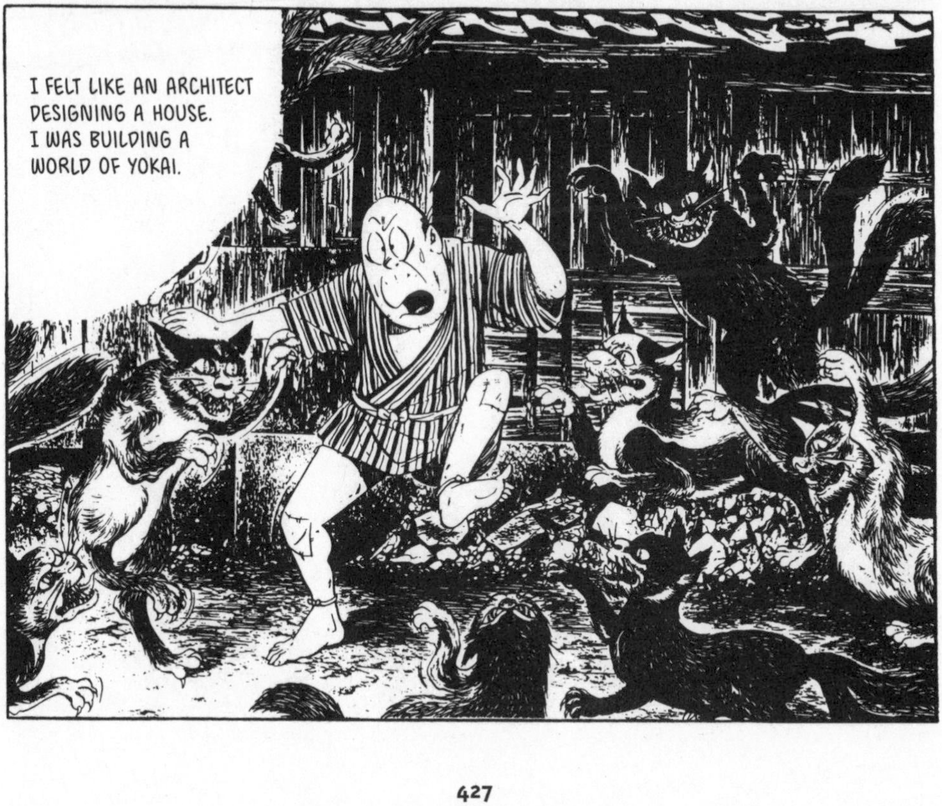
I FELT LIKE AN ARCHITECT DESIGNING A HOUSE. I WAS BUILDING A WORLD OF YOKAI.

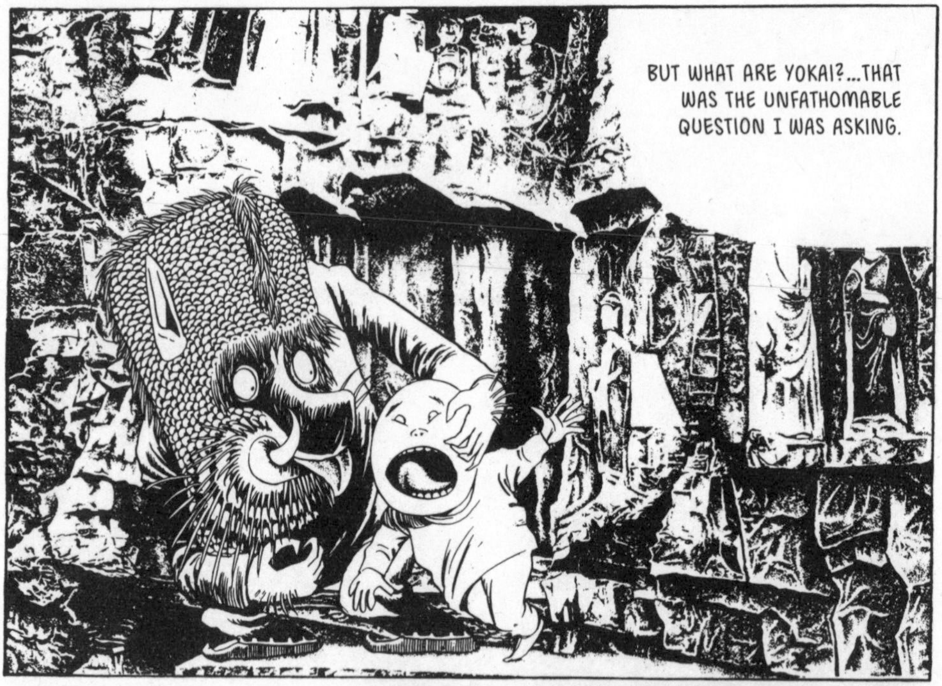
BUT WHAT ARE YOKAI?...THAT WAS THE UNFATHOMABLE QUESTION I WAS ASKING.

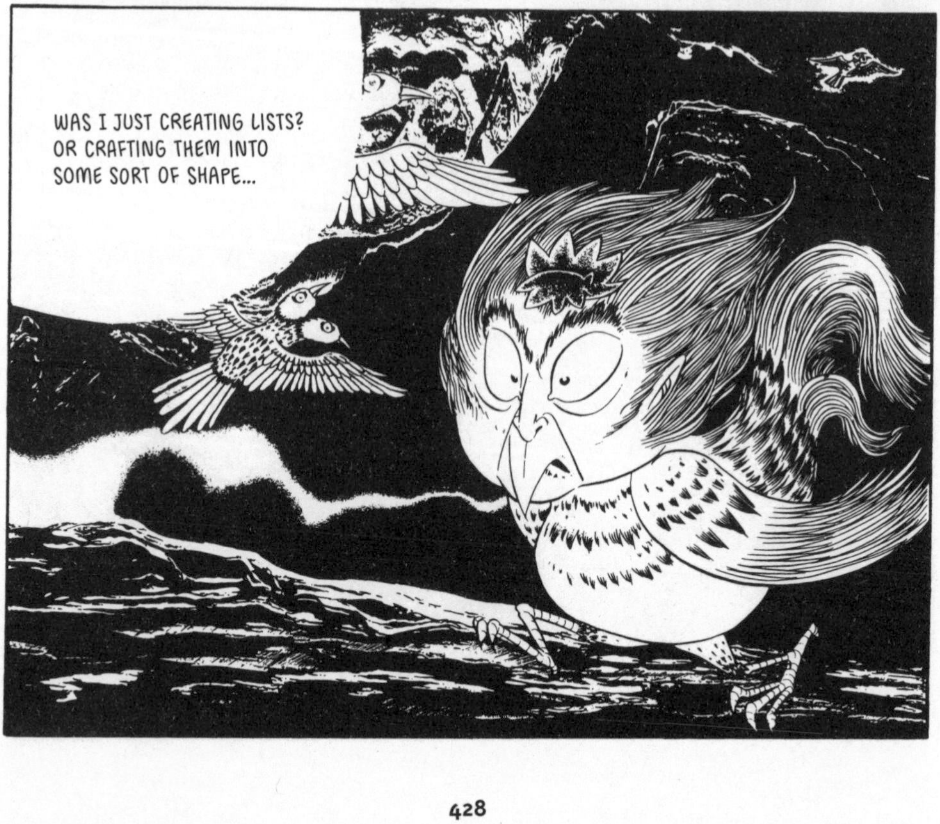
WAS I JUST CREATING LISTS? OR CRAFTING THEM INTO SOME SORT OF SHAPE...

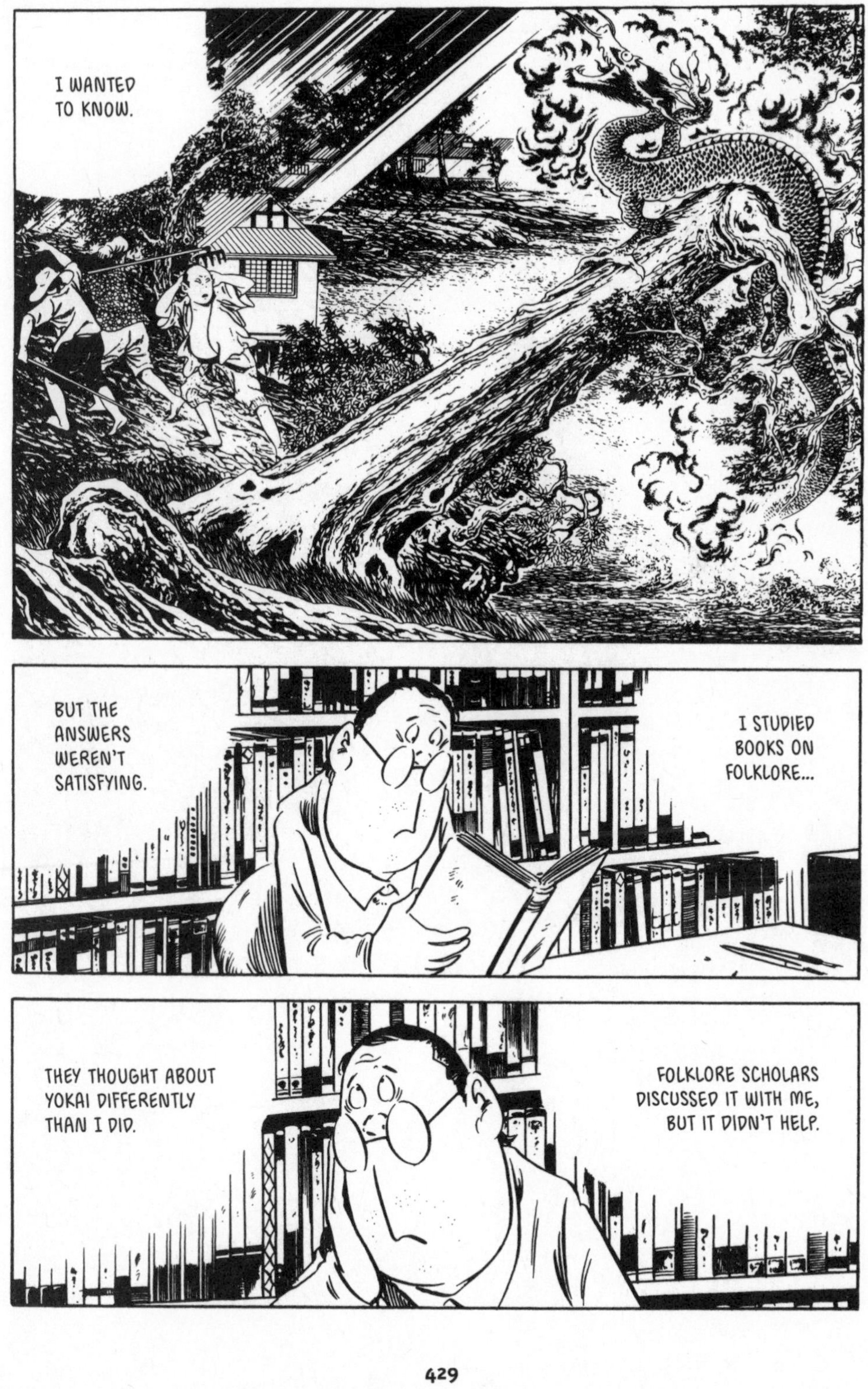
I WANTED TO KNOW.
I STUDIED BOOKS ON FOLKLORE...
BUT THE ANSWERS WEREN'T SATISFYING.
FOLKLORE SCHOLARS DISCUSSED IT WITH ME, BUT IT DIDN'T HELP.
THEY THOUGHT ABOUT YOKAI DIFFERENTLY THAN I DID.

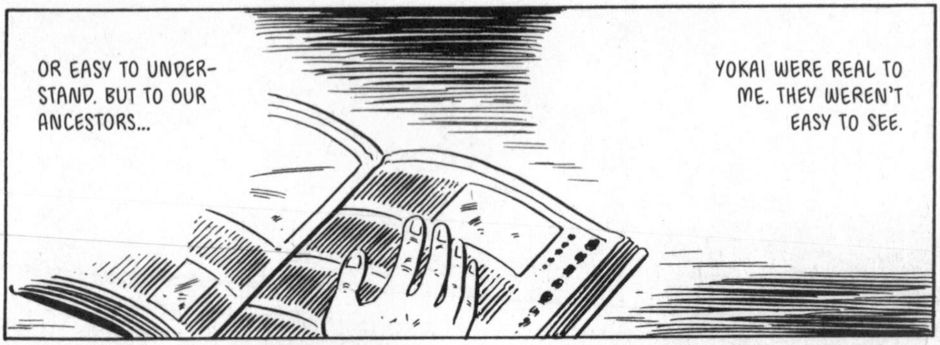
YOKAI WERE REAL TO ME. THEY WEREN'T EASY TO SEE.
OR EASY TO UNDER-STAND. BUT TO OUR ANCESTORS...

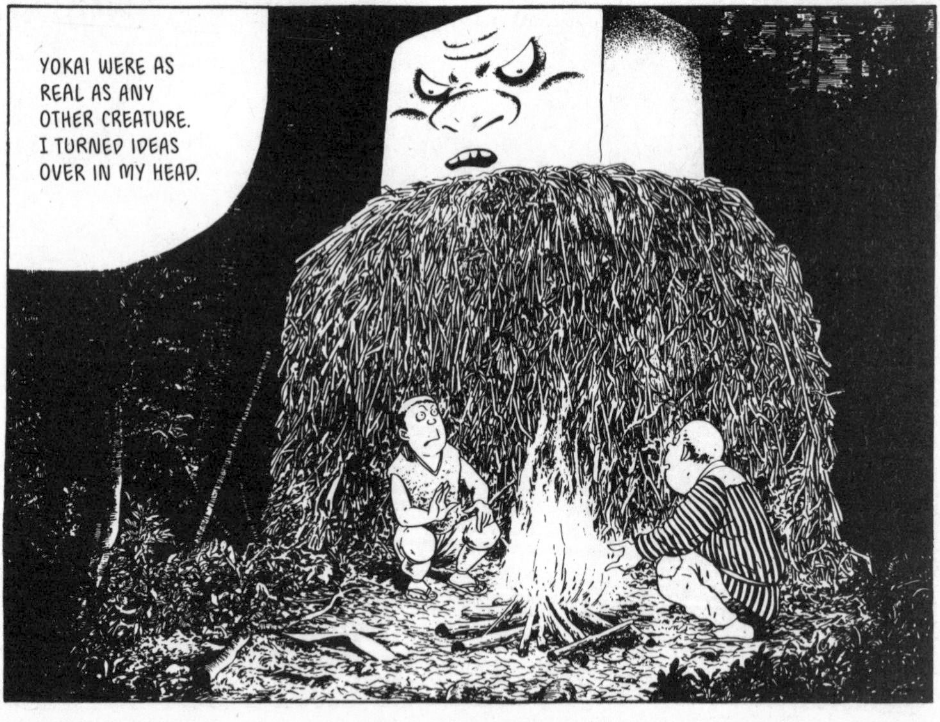
YOKAI WERE AS REAL AS ANY OTHER CREATURE. I TURNED IDEAS OVER IN MY HEAD.

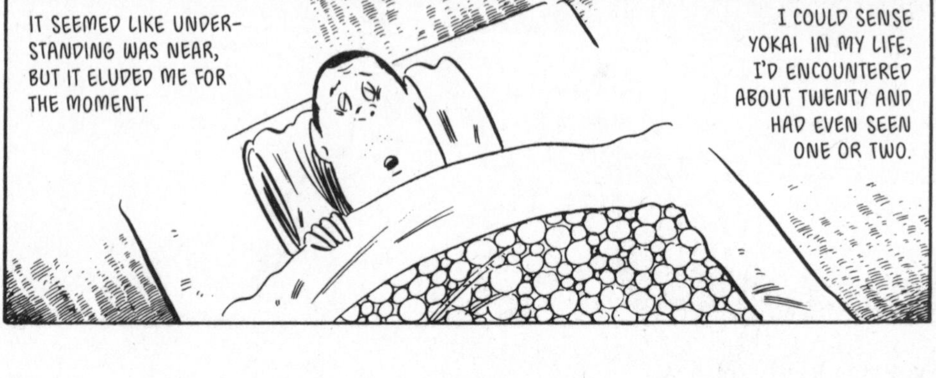
I COULD SENSE YOKAI. IN MY LIFE, I'D ENCOUNTERED ABOUT TWENTY AND HAD EVEN SEEN ONE OR TWO.
IT SEEMED LIKE UNDER-STANDING WAS NEAR, BUT IT ELUDED ME FOR THE MOMENT.

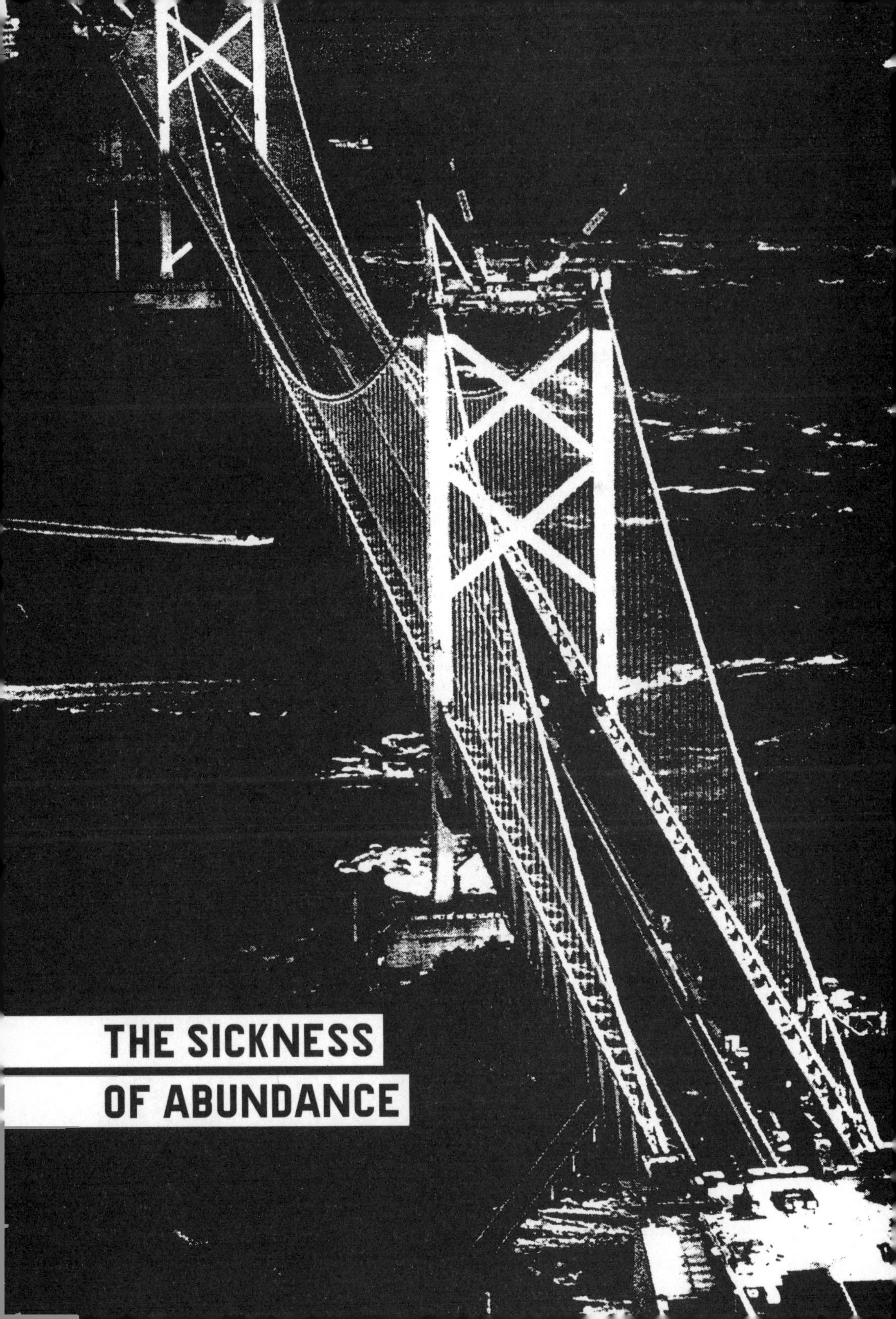

THE SICKNESS OF ABUNDANCE

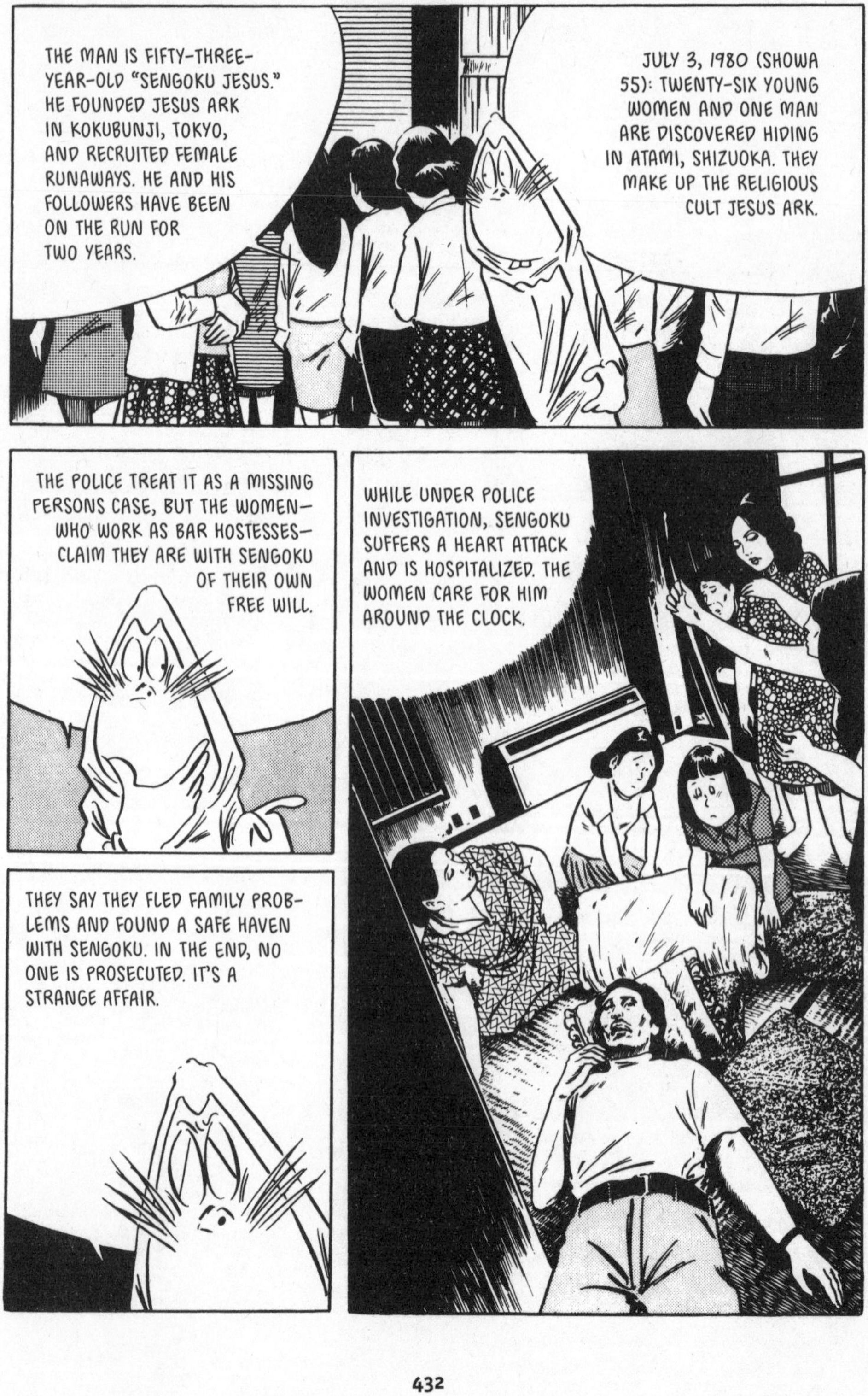
JULY 3, 1980 (SHOWA 55): TWENTY-SIX YOUNG WOMEN AND ONE MAN ARE DISCOVERED HIDING IN ATAMI, SHIZUOKA. THEY MAKE UP THE RELIGIOUS CULT JESUS ARK.
THE MAN IS FIFTY-THREE-YEAR-OLD "SENGOKU JESUS." HE FOUNDED JESUS ARK IN KOKUBUNJI, TOKYO, AND RECRUITED FEMALE RUNAWAYS. HE AND HIS FOLLOWERS HAVE BEEN ON THE RUN FOR TWO YEARS.
WHILE UNDER POLICE INVESTIGATION, SENGOKU SUFFERS A HEART ATTACK AND IS HOSPITALIZED. THE WOMEN CARE FOR HIM AROUND THE CLOCK.
THE POLICE TREAT IT AS A MISSING PERSONS CASE, BUT THE WOMEN—WHO WORK AS BAR HOSTESSES—CLAIM THEY ARE WITH SENGOKU OF THEIR OWN FREE WILL.
THEY SAY THEY FLED FAMILY PROBLEMS AND FOUND A SAFE HAVEN WITH SENGOKU. IN THE END, NO ONE IS PROSECUTED. IT'S A STRANGE AFFAIR.

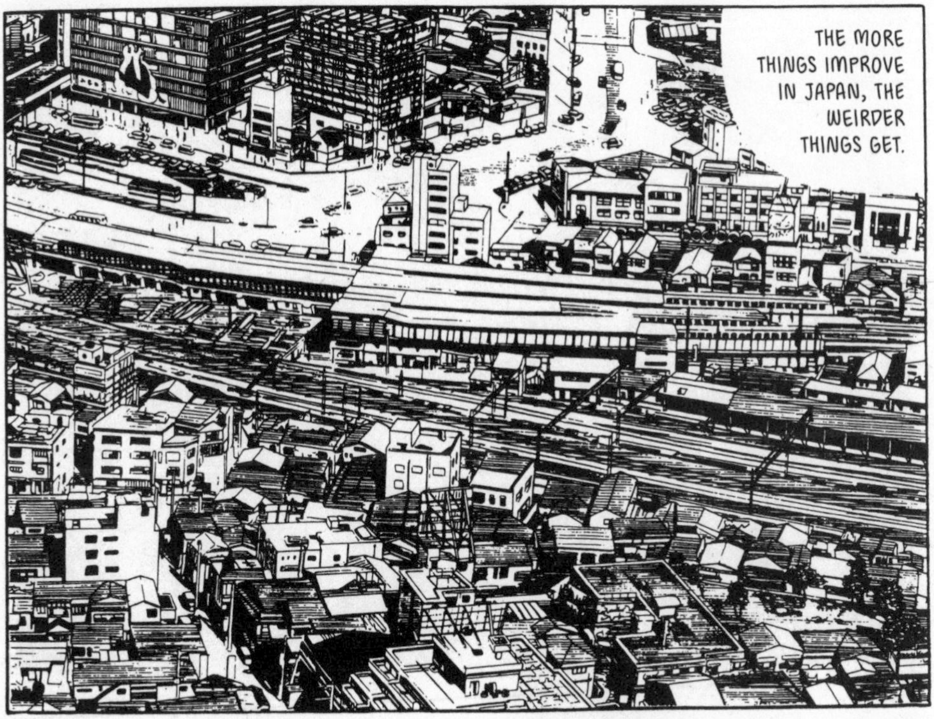
THE MORE THINGS IMPROVE IN JAPAN, THE WEIRDER THINGS GET.

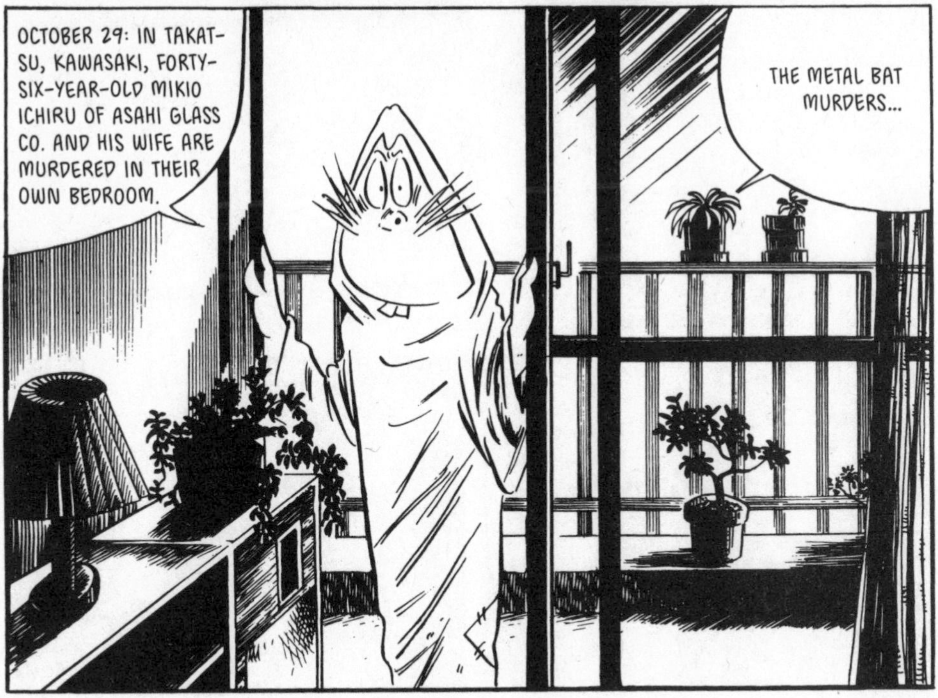
THE METAL BAT MURDERS...
OCTOBER 29: IN TAKATSU, KAWASAKI, FORTY-SIX-YEAR-OLD MIKIO ICHIRU OF ASAHI GLASS CO. AND HIS WIFE ARE MURDERED IN THEIR OWN BEDROOM.

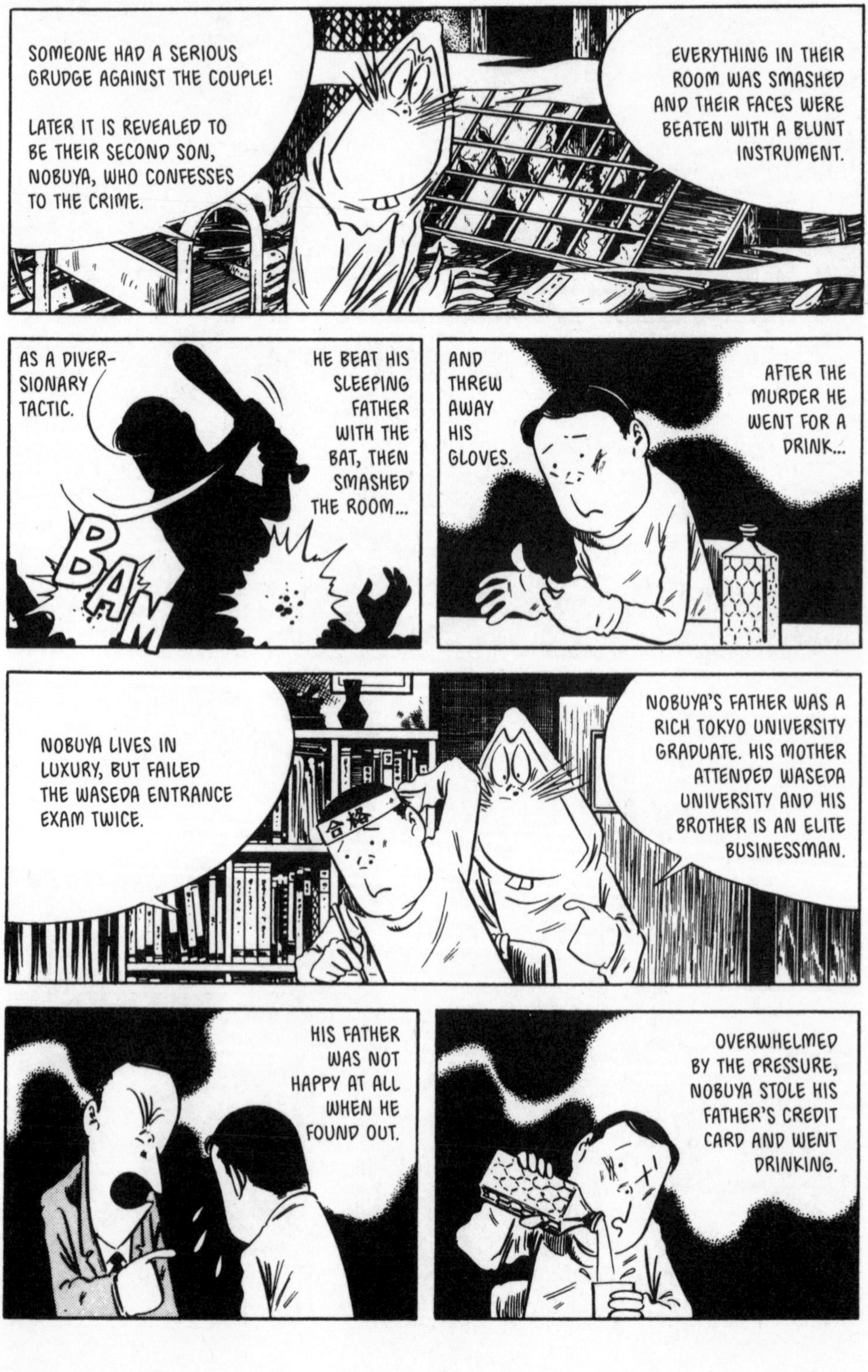
EVERYTHING IN THEIR ROOM WAS SMASHED AND THEIR FACES WERE BEATEN WITH A BLUNT INSTRUMENT.
SOMEONE HAD A SERIOUS GRUDGE AGAINST THE COUPLE!
LATER IT IS REVEALED TO BE THEIR SECOND SON, NOBUYA, WHO CONFESSES TO THE CRIME.
AFTER THE MURDER HE WENT FOR A DRINK...
AND THREW AWAY HIS GLOVES.
HE BEAT HIS SLEEPING FATHER WITH THE BAT, THEN SMASHED THE ROOM...
AS A DIVERSIONARY TACTIC.
BAM
NOBUYA'S FATHER WAS A RICH TOKYO UNIVERSITY GRADUATE. HIS MOTHER ATTENDED WASEDA UNIVERSITY AND HIS BROTHER IS AN ELITE BUSINESSMAN.
合格
NOBUYA LIVES IN LUXURY, BUT FAILED THE WASEDA ENTRANCE EXAM TWICE.
OVERWHELMED BY THE PRESSURE, NOBUYA STOLE HIS FATHER'S CREDIT CARD AND WENT DRINKING.
HIS FATHER WAS NOT HAPPY AT ALL WHEN HE FOUND OUT.

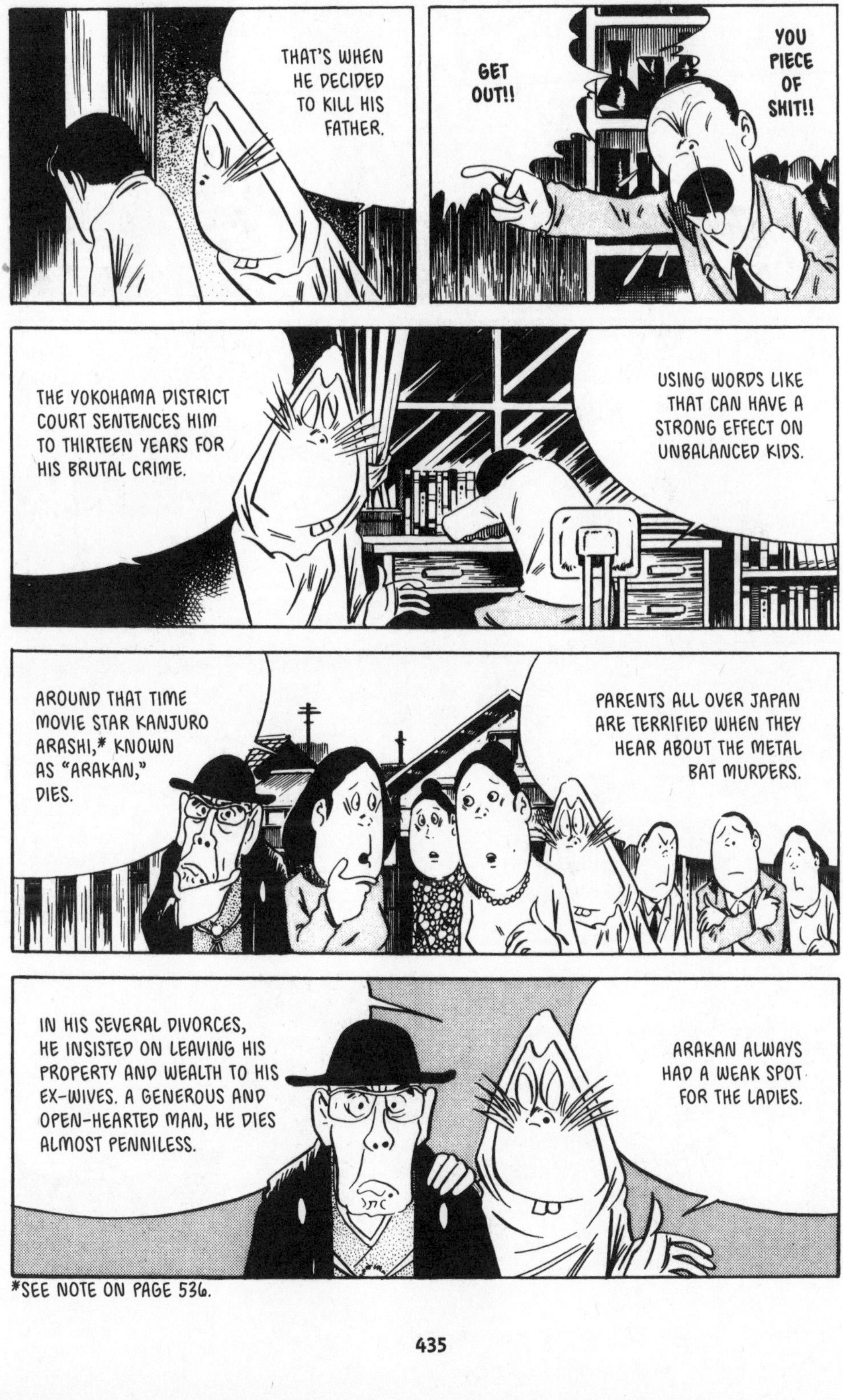
YOU PIECE OF SHIT!!
GET OUT!!
THAT'S WHEN HE DECIDED TO KILL HIS FATHER.
USING WORDS LIKE THAT CAN HAVE A STRONG EFFECT ON UNBALANCED KIDS.
THE YOKOHAMA DISTRICT COURT SENTENCES HIM TO THIRTEEN YEARS FOR HIS BRUTAL CRIME.
PARENTS ALL OVER JAPAN ARE TERRIFIED WHEN THEY HEAR ABOUT THE METAL BAT MURDERS.
AROUND THAT TIME MOVIE STAR KANJURO ARASHI,* KNOWN AS "ARAKAN," DIES.
ARAKAN ALWAYS HAD A WEAK SPOT FOR THE LADIES.
IN HIS SEVERAL DIVORCES, HE INSISTED ON LEAVING HIS PROPERTY AND WEALTH TO HIS EX-WIVES. A GENEROUS AND OPEN-HEARTED MAN, HE DIES ALMOST PENNILESS.

*SEE NOTE ON PAGE 536.

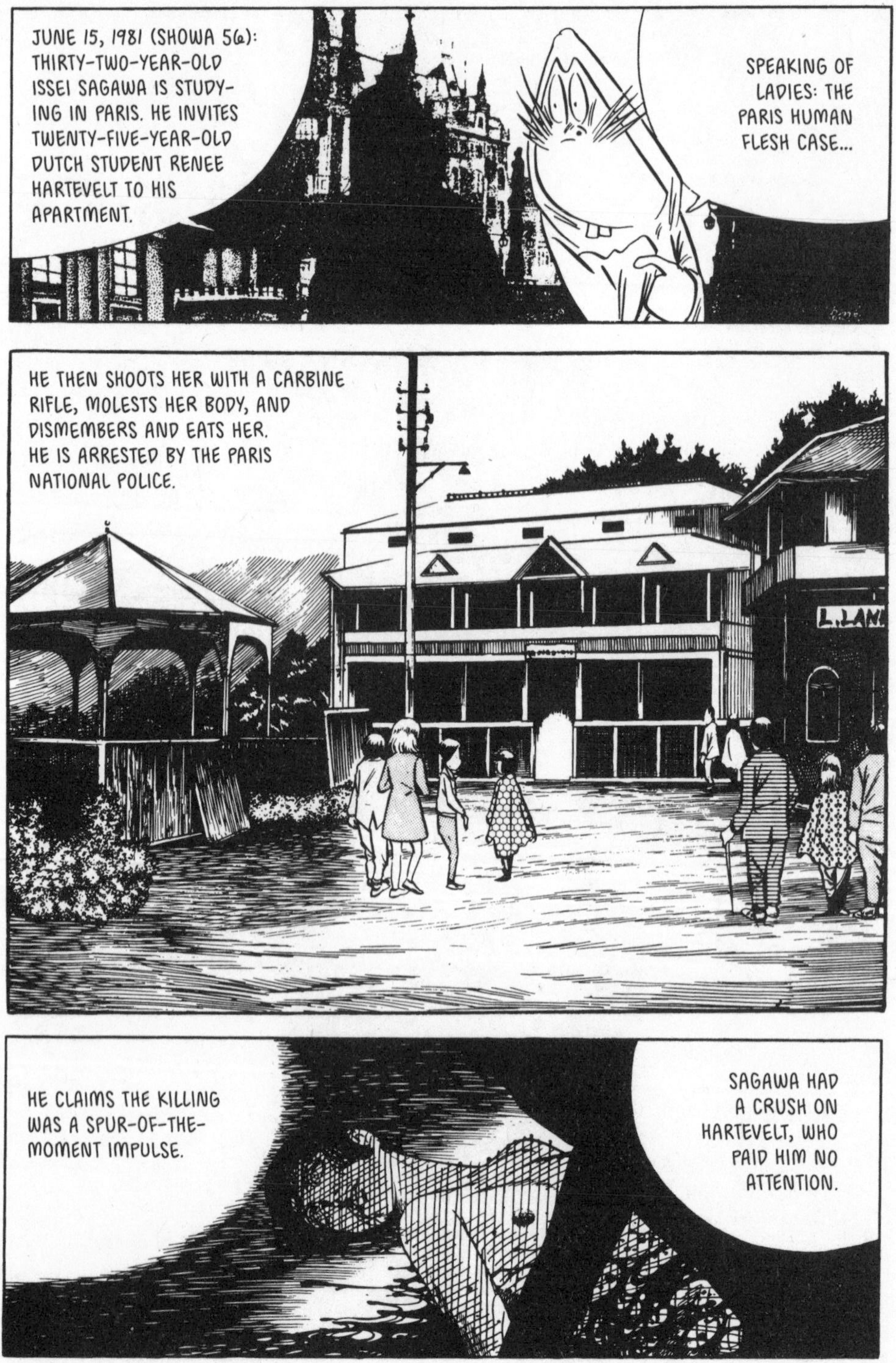
SPEAKING OF LADIES: THE PARIS HUMAN FLESH CASE...
JUNE 15, 1981 (SHOWA 56): THIRTY-TWO-YEAR-OLD ISSEI SAGAWA IS STUDYING IN PARIS. HE INVITES TWENTY-FIVE-YEAR-OLD DUTCH STUDENT RENEE HARTEVELT TO HIS APARTMENT.
HE THEN SHOOTS HER WITH A CARBINE RIFLE, MOLESTS HER BODY, AND DISMEMBERS AND EATS HER. HE IS ARRESTED BY THE PARIS NATIONAL POLICE.
L.LAN
SAGAWA HAD A CRUSH ON HARTEVELT, WHO PAID HIM NO ATTENTION.
HE CLAIMS THE KILLING WAS A SPUR-OF-THE-MOMENT IMPULSE.

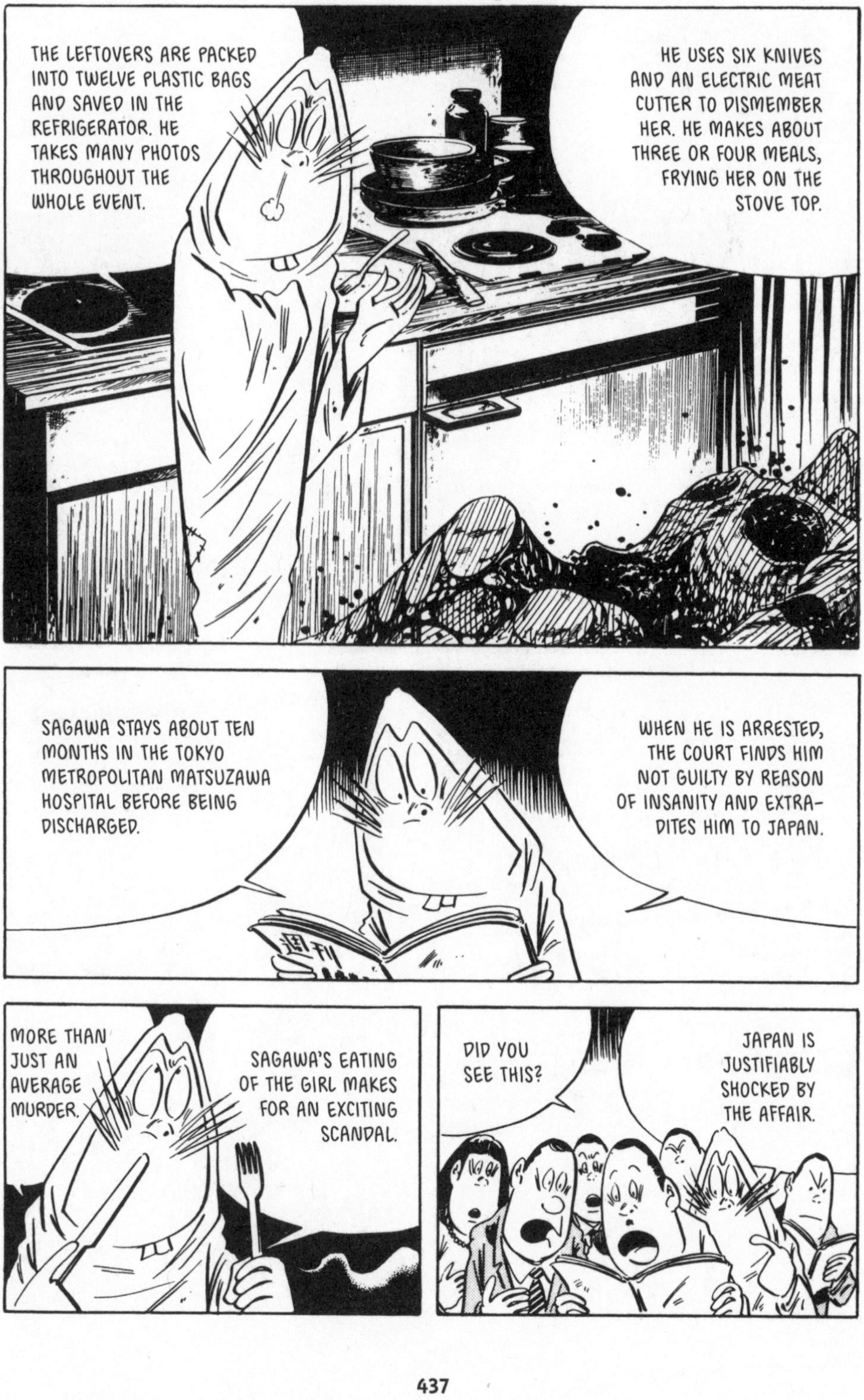

HE USES SIX KNIVES AND AN ELECTRIC MEAT CUTTER TO DISMEMBER HER. HE MAKES ABOUT THREE OR FOUR MEALS, FRYING HER ON THE STOVE TOP.
THE LEFTOVERS ARE PACKED INTO TWELVE PLASTIC BAGS AND SAVED IN THE REFRIGERATOR. HE TAKES MANY PHOTOS THROUGHOUT THE WHOLE EVENT.
WHEN HE IS ARRESTED, THE COURT FINDS HIM NOT GUILTY BY REASON OF INSANITY AND EXTRA-DITES HIM TO JAPAN.
SAGAWA STAYS ABOUT TEN MONTHS IN THE TOKYO METROPOLITAN MATSUZAWA HOSPITAL BEFORE BEING DISCHARGED.
週刊
JAPAN IS JUSTIFIABLY SHOCKED BY THE AFFAIR.
DID YOU SEE THIS?
SAGAWA'S EATING OF THE GIRL MAKES FOR AN EXCITING SCANDAL.
MORE THAN JUST AN AVERAGE MURDER.

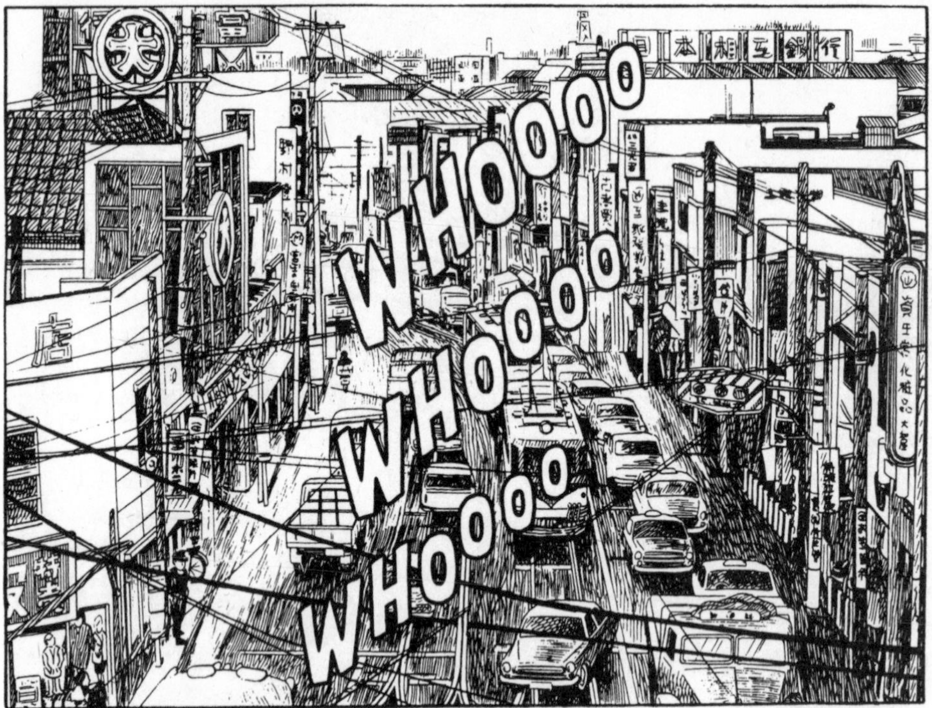
日本相互銀行
WHOOOO
WHOOOOO
WHOOOO
WHOOOO

SIGN: JAPAN MUTUAL BANK

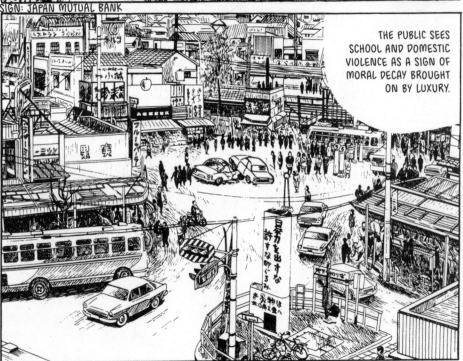

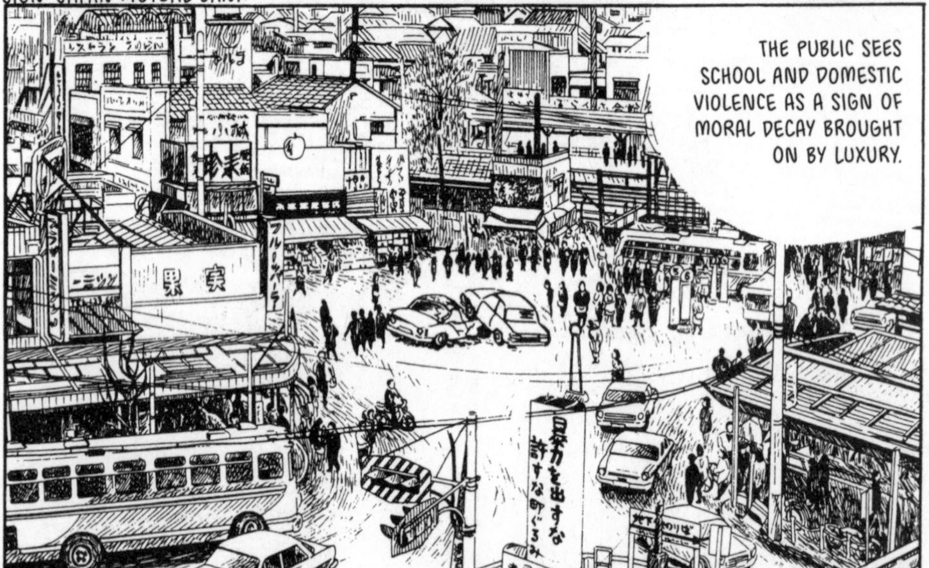
THE PUBLIC SEES SCHOOL AND DOMESTIC VIOLENCE AS A SIGN OF MORAL DECAY BROUGHT ON BY LUXURY.
暴力を出すな
許すな町ぐるみ

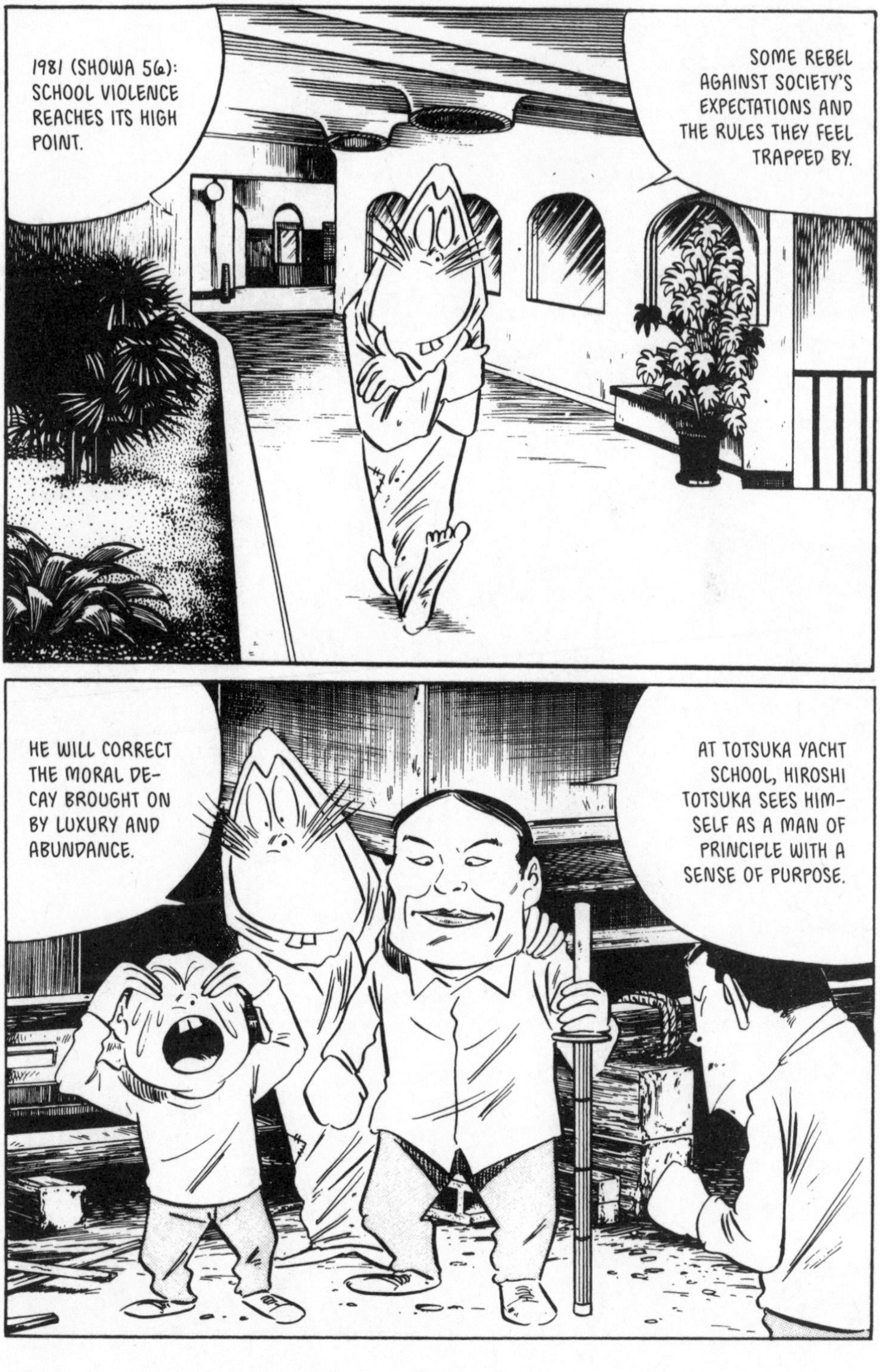
SOME REBEL AGAINST SOCIETY'S EXPECTATIONS AND THE RULES THEY FEEL TRAPPED BY.
1981 (SHOWA 56): SCHOOL VIOLENCE REACHES ITS HIGH POINT.
AT TOTSUKA YACHT SCHOOL, HIROSHI TOTSUKA SEES HIMSELF AS A MAN OF PRINCIPLE WITH A SENSE OF PURPOSE.
HE WILL CORRECT THE MORAL DECAY BROUGHT ON BY LUXURY AND ABUNDANCE.

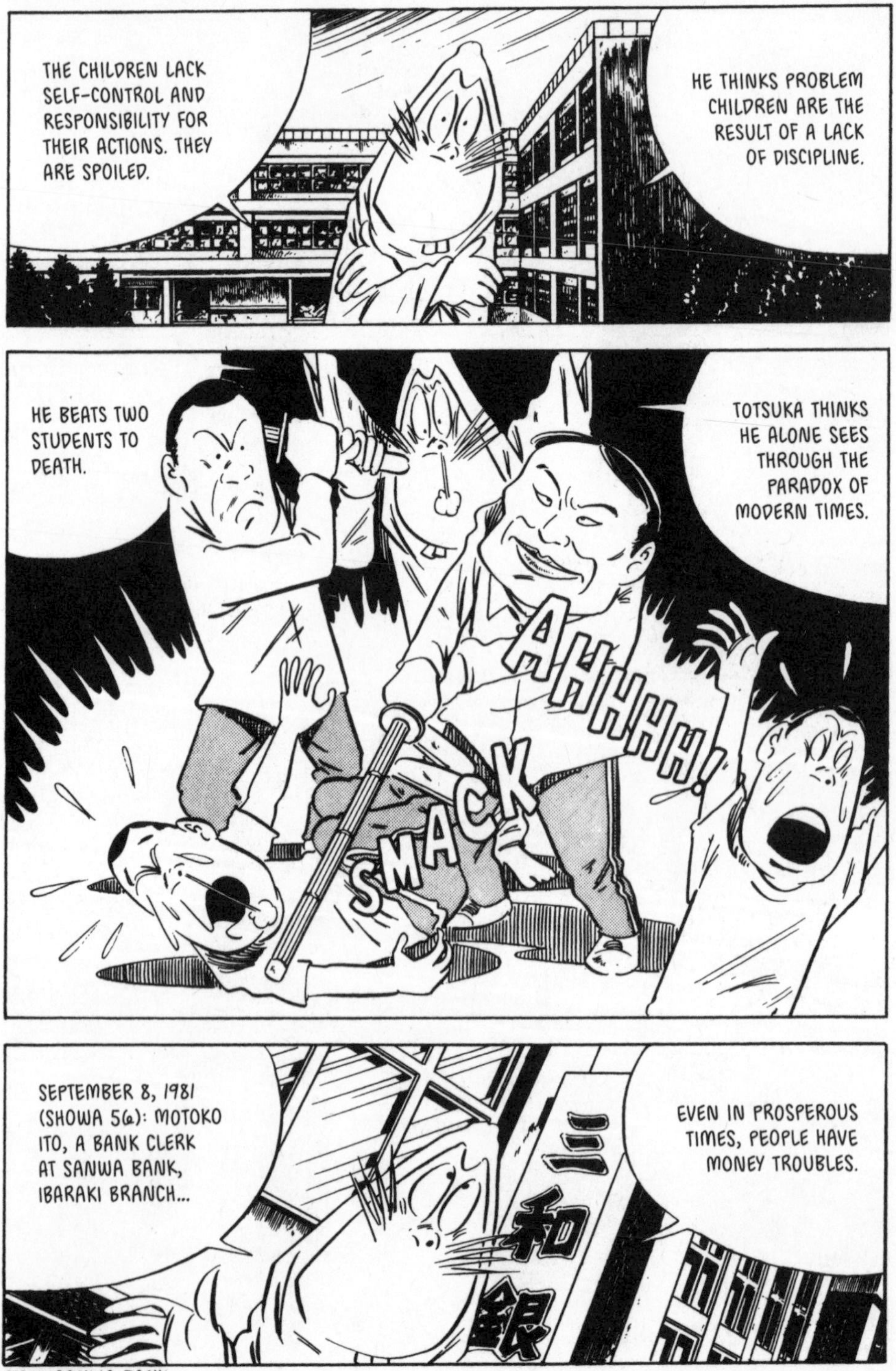
HE THINKS PROBLEM CHILDREN ARE THE RESULT OF A LACK OF DISCIPLINE.
THE CHILDREN LACK SELF-CONTROL AND RESPONSIBILITY FOR THEIR ACTIONS. THEY ARE SPOILED.
TOTSUKA THINKS HE ALONE SEES THROUGH THE PARADOX OF MODERN TIMES.
HE BEATS TWO STUDENTS TO DEATH.
AHHHHH!
SMACK
EVEN IN PROSPEROUS TIMES, PEOPLE HAVE MONEY TROUBLES.
三和銀
SEPTEMBER 8, 1981 (SHOWA 56): MOTOKO ITO, A BANK CLERK AT SANWA BANK, IBARAKI BRANCH...
SIGN: SANWA BANK.

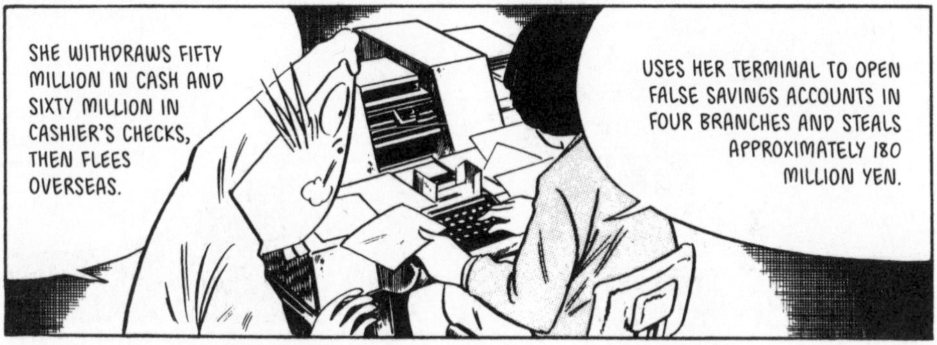
USES HER TERMINAL TO OPEN FALSE SAVINGS ACCOUNTS IN FOUR BRANCHES AND STEALS APPROXIMATELY 180 MILLION YEN.
SHE WITHDRAWS FIFTY MILLION IN CASH AND SIXTY MILLION IN CASHIER'S CHECKS, THEN FLEES OVERSEAS.

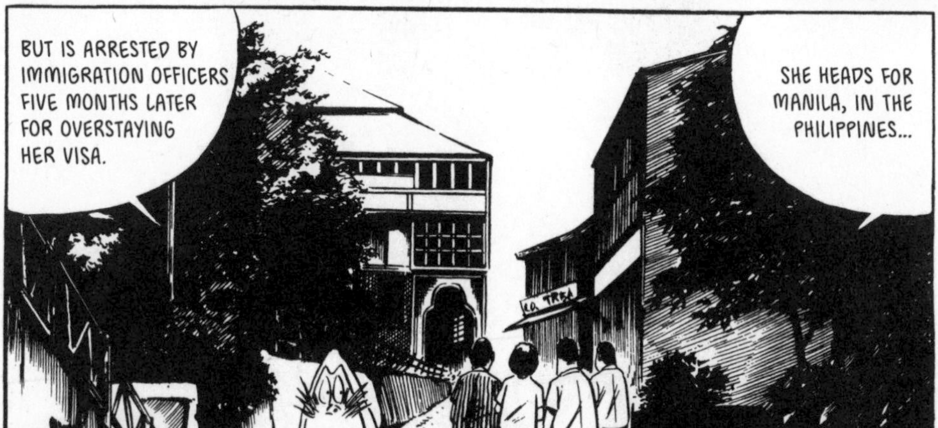
SHE HEADS FOR MANILA, IN THE PHILIPPINES...
BUT IS ARRESTED BY IMMIGRATION OFFICERS FIVE MONTHS LATER FOR OVERSTAYING HER VISA.

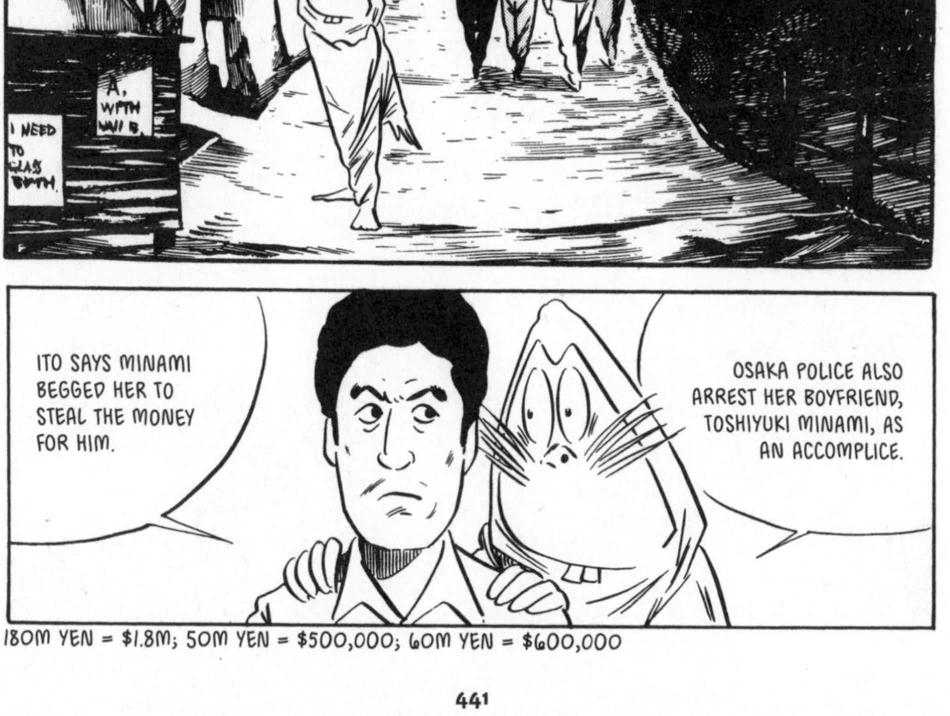
OSAKA POLICE ALSO ARREST HER BOYFRIEND, TOSHIYUKI MINAMI, AS AN ACCOMPLICE.
ITO SAYS MINAMI BEGGED HER TO STEAL THE MONEY FOR HIM.

180M YEN = $1.8M; 50M YEN = $500,000; 60M YEN = $600,000

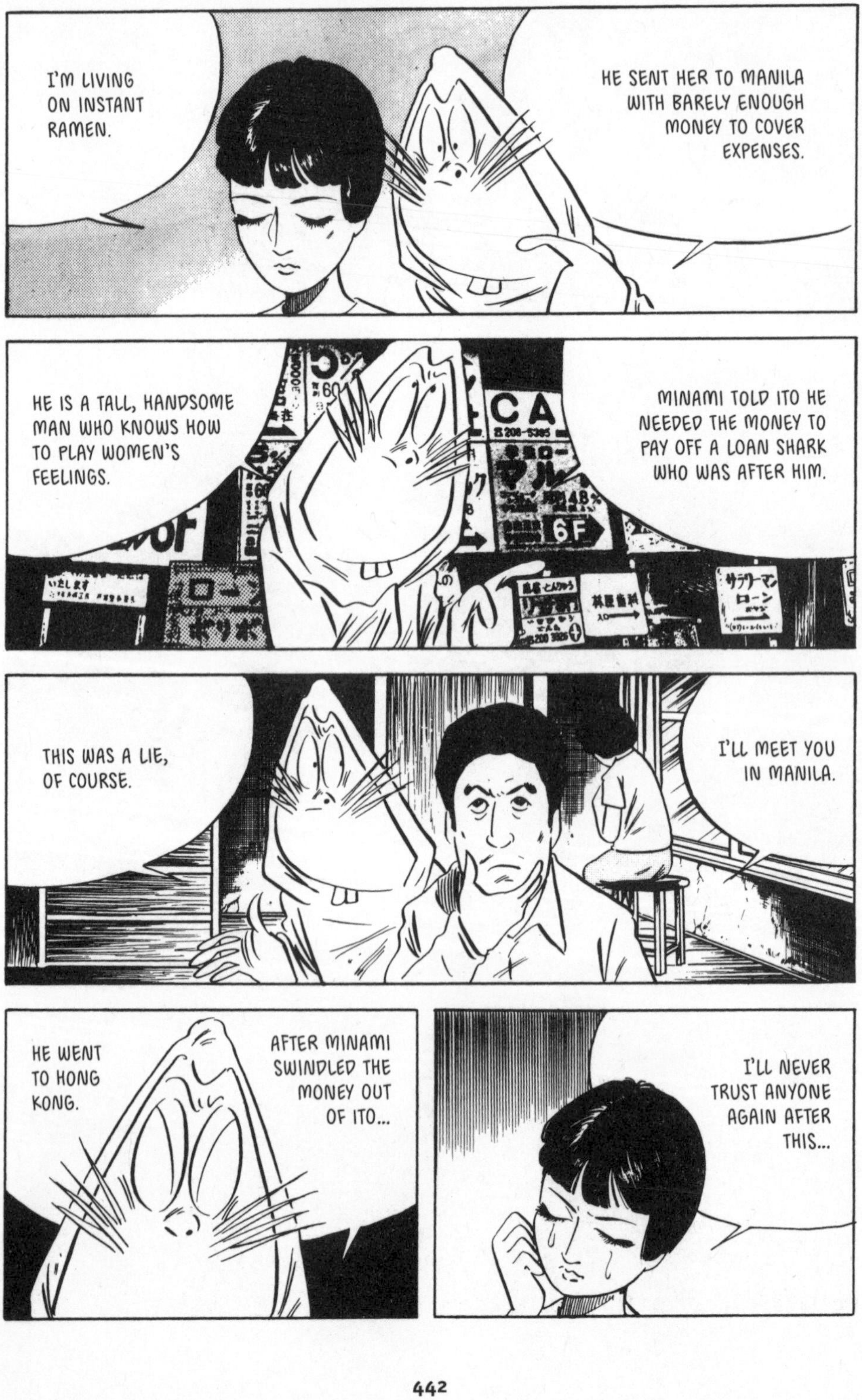
HE SENT HER TO MANILA WITH BARELY ENOUGH MONEY TO COVER EXPENSES.
I'M LIVING ON INSTANT RAMEN.
MINAMI TOLD ITO HE NEEDED THE MONEY TO PAY OFF A LOAN SHARK WHO WAS AFTER HIM.
HE IS A TALL, HANDSOME MAN WHO KNOWS HOW TO PLAY WOMEN'S FEELINGS.
I'LL MEET YOU IN MANILA.
THIS WAS A LIE, OF COURSE.
I'LL NEVER TRUST ANYONE AGAIN AFTER THIS...
AFTER MINAMI SWINDLED THE MONEY OUT OF ITO...
HE WENT TO HONG KONG.

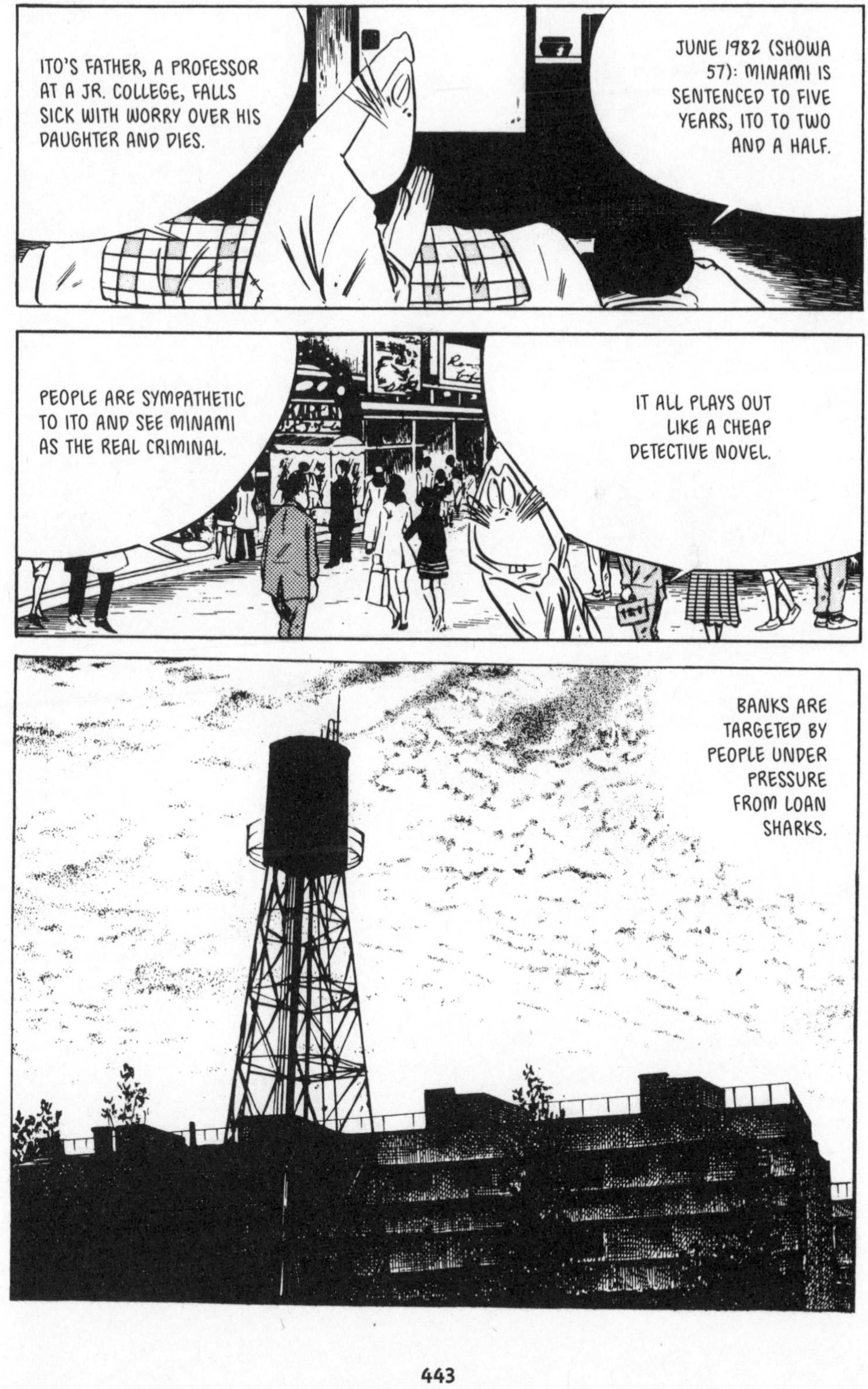
JUNE 1982 (SHOWA 57): MINAMI IS SENTENCED TO FIVE YEARS, ITO TO TWO AND A HALF.
ITO'S FATHER, A PROFESSOR AT A JR. COLLEGE, FALLS SICK WITH WORRY OVER HIS DAUGHTER AND DIES.
IT ALL PLAYS OUT LIKE A CHEAP DETECTIVE NOVEL.
PEOPLE ARE SYMPATHETIC TO ITO AND SEE MINAMI AS THE REAL CRIMINAL.
BANKS ARE TARGETED BY PEOPLE UNDER PRESSURE FROM LOAN SHARKS.

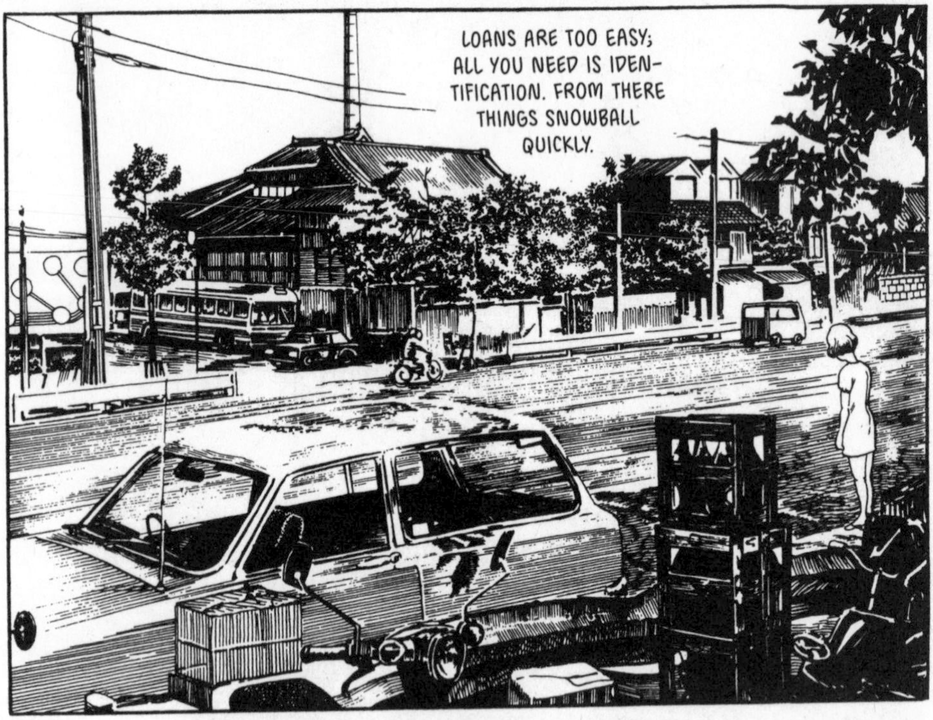
LOANS ARE TOO EASY; ALL YOU NEED IS IDEN- TIFICATION. FROM THERE THINGS SNOWBALL QUICKLY.

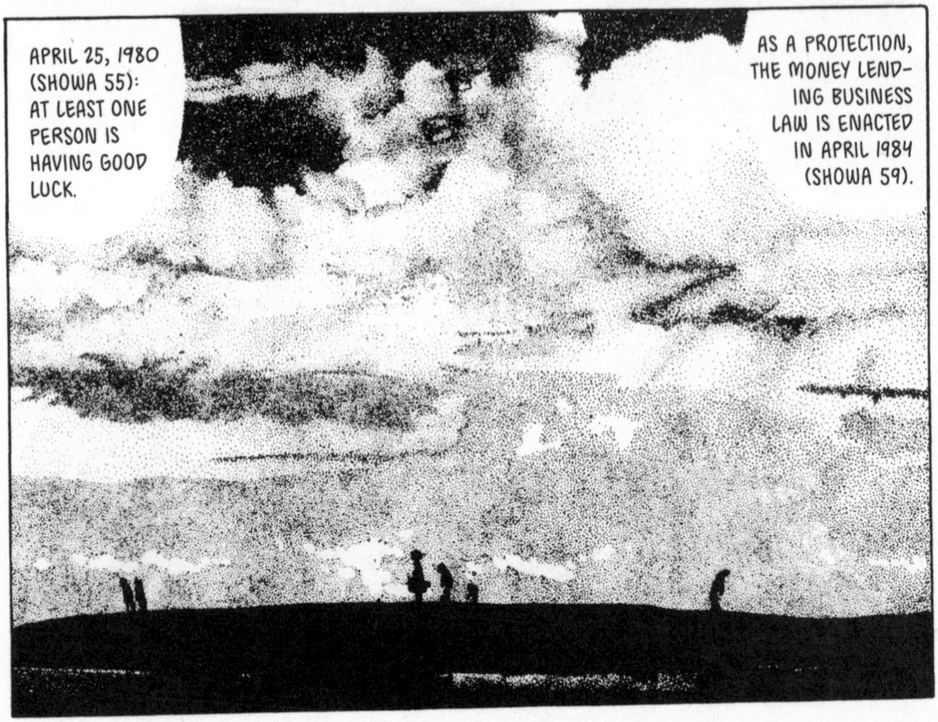
AS A PROTECTION, THE MONEY LEND- ING BUSINESS LAW IS ENACTED IN APRIL 1984 (SHOWA 59).
APRIL 25, 1980 (SHOWA 55): AT LEAST ONE PERSON IS HAVING GOOD LUCK.

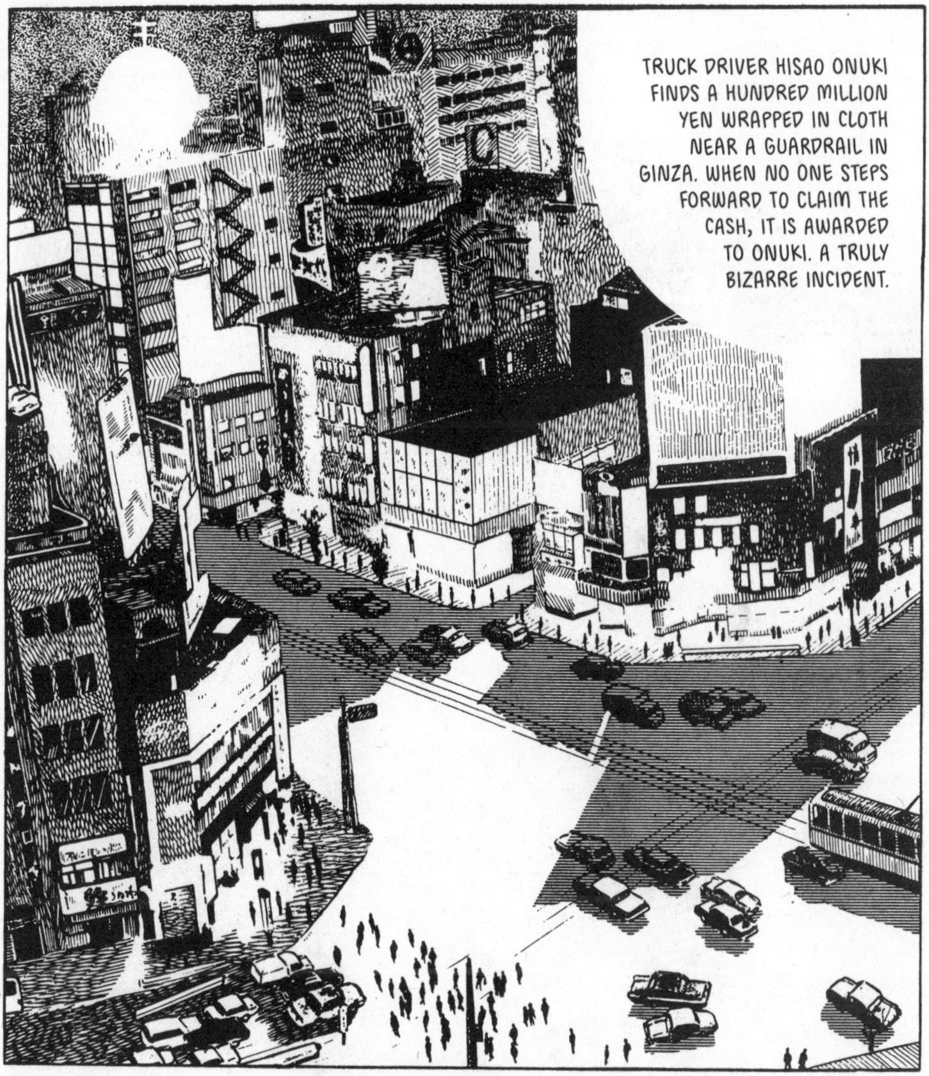
TRUCK DRIVER HISAO ONUKI FINDS A HUNDRED MILLION YEN WRAPPED IN CLOTH NEAR A GUARDRAIL IN GINZA. WHEN NO ONE STEPS FORWARD TO CLAIM THE CASH, IT IS AWARDED TO ONUKI. A TRULY BIZARRE INCIDENT.

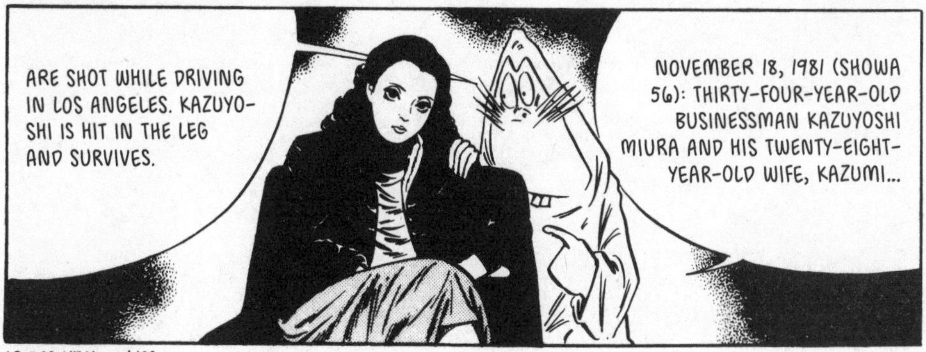
NOVEMBER 18, 1981 (SHOWA 56): THIRTY-FOUR-YEAR-OLD BUSINESSMAN KAZUYOSHI MIURA AND HIS TWENTY-EIGHT-YEAR-OLD WIFE, KAZUMI...
ARE SHOT WHILE DRIVING IN LOS ANGELES. KAZUYO-SHI IS HIT IN THE LEG AND SURVIVES.

100M YEN = $1M

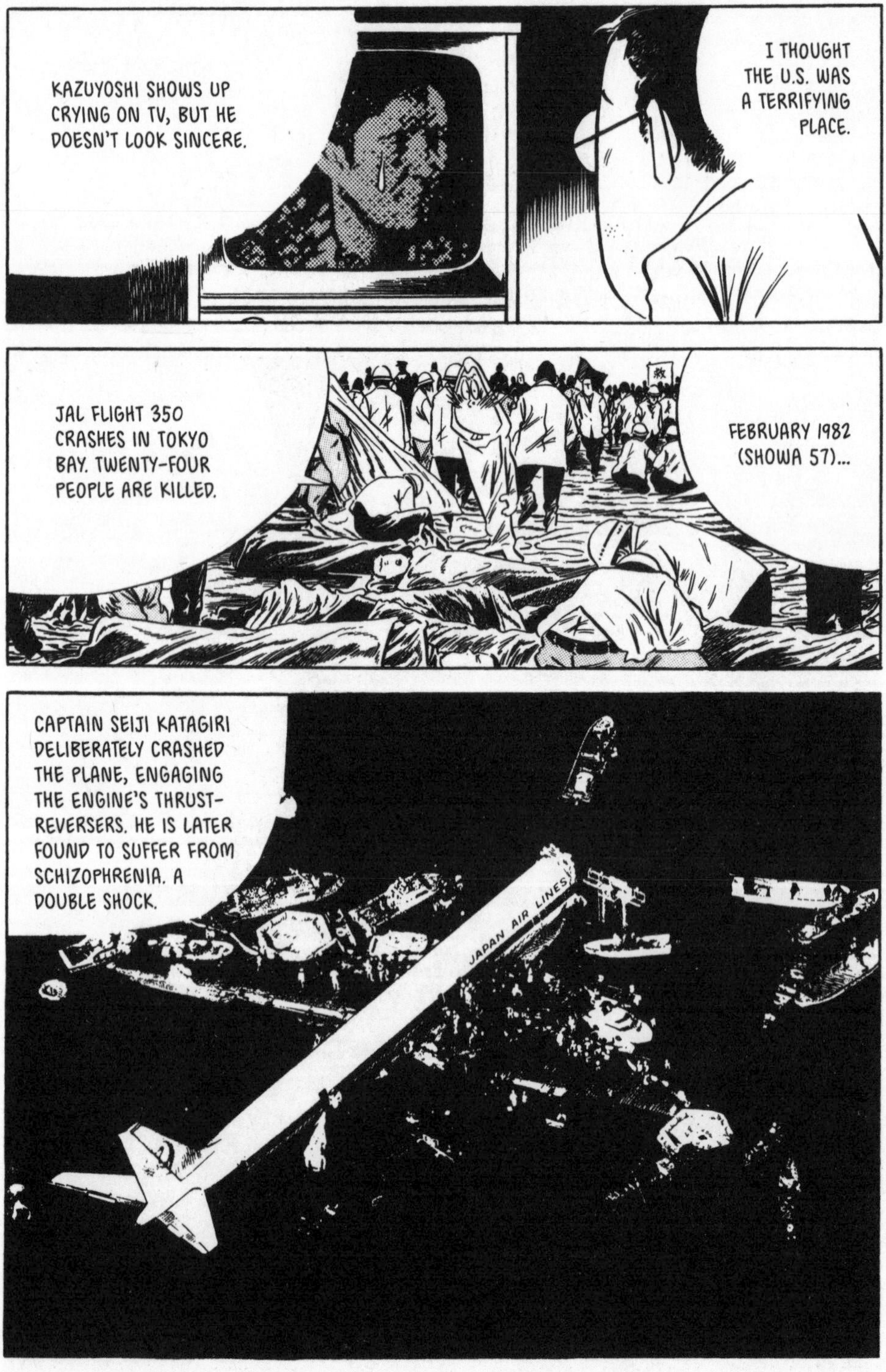
I THOUGHT THE U.S. WAS A TERRIFYING PLACE.
KAZUYOSHI SHOWS UP CRYING ON TV, BUT HE DOESN'T LOOK SINCERE.
FEBRUARY 1982 (SHOWA 57)...
JAL FLIGHT 350 CRASHES IN TOKYO BAY. TWENTY-FOUR PEOPLE ARE KILLED.
CAPTAIN SEIJI KATAGIRI DELIBERATELY CRASHED THE PLANE, ENGAGING THE ENGINE'S THRUST-REVERSERS. HE IS LATER FOUND TO SUFFER FROM SCHIZOPHRENIA. A DOUBLE SHOCK.
JAPAN AIR LINES

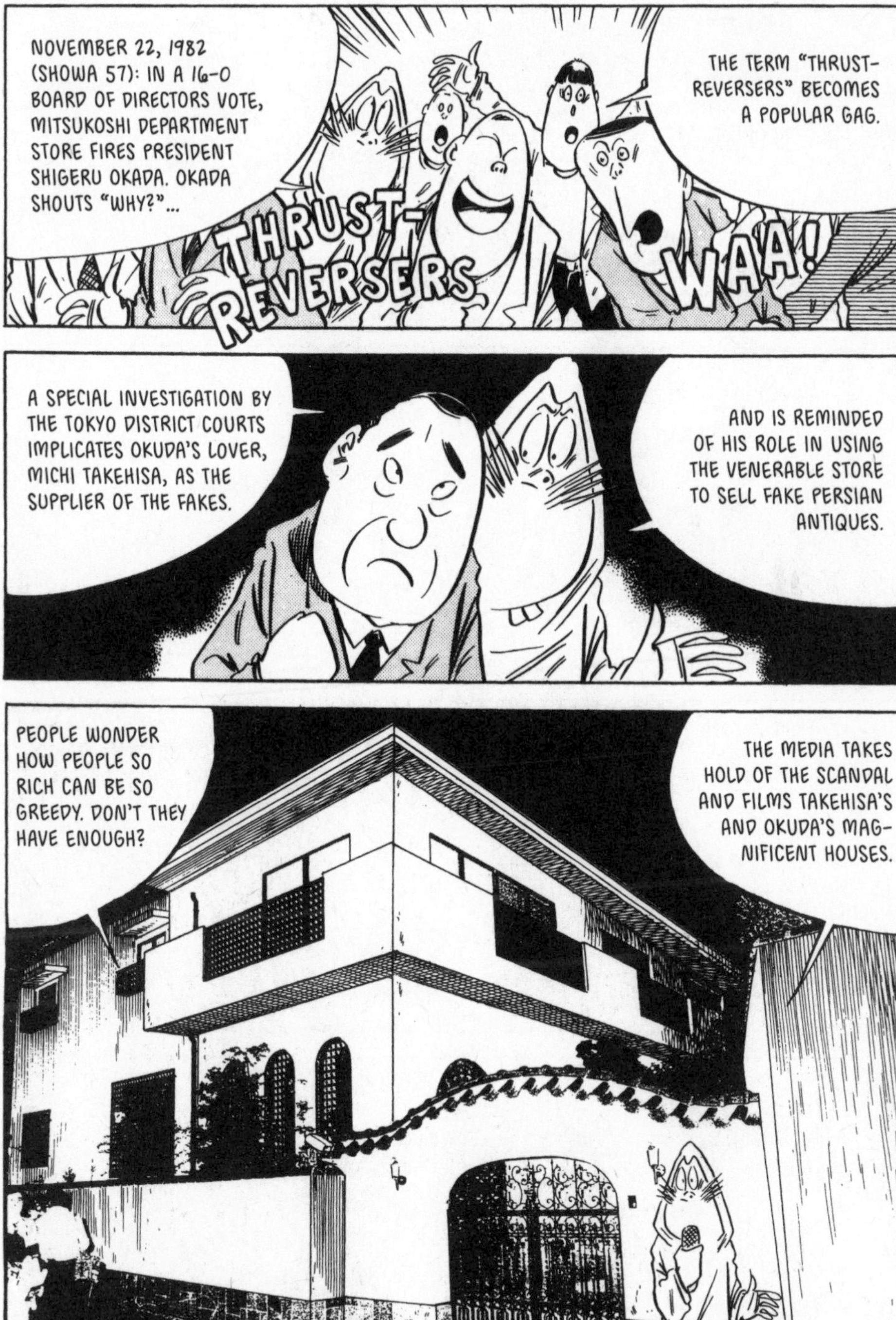
THE TERM "THRUST-REVERSERS" BECOMES A POPULAR GAG.
WAA!
THRUST-REVERSERS
NOVEMBER 22, 1982 (SHOWA 57): IN A 16-0 BOARD OF DIRECTORS VOTE, MITSUKOSHI DEPARTMENT STORE FIRES PRESIDENT SHIGERU OKADA. OKADA SHOUTS "WHY?"...
AND IS REMINDED OF HIS ROLE IN USING THE VENERABLE STORE TO SELL FAKE PERSIAN ANTIQUES.
A SPECIAL INVESTIGATION BY THE TOKYO DISTRICT COURTS IMPLICATES OKUDA'S LOVER, MICHI TAKEHISA, AS THE SUPPLIER OF THE FAKES.
THE MEDIA TAKES HOLD OF THE SCANDAL AND FILMS TAKEHISA'S AND OKUDA'S MAG-NIFICENT HOUSES.
PEOPLE WONDER HOW PEOPLE SO RICH CAN BE SO GREEDY. DON'T THEY HAVE ENOUGH?

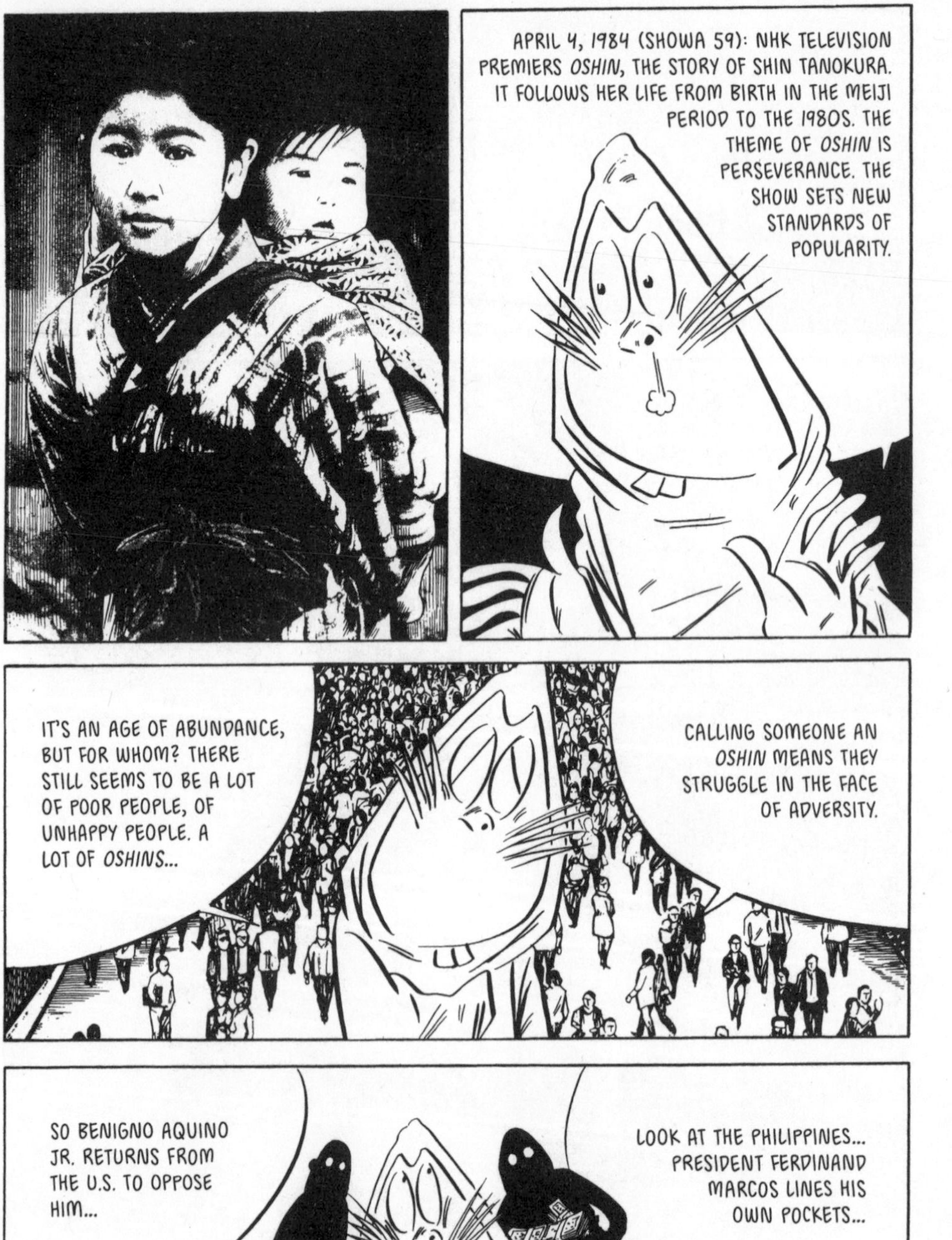
APRIL 4, 1984 (SHOWA 59): NHK TELEVISION PREMIERS *OSHIN*, THE STORY OF SHIN TANOKURA. IT FOLLOWS HER LIFE FROM BIRTH IN THE MEIJI PERIOD TO THE 1980S. THE THEME OF *OSHIN* IS PERSEVERANCE. THE SHOW SETS NEW STANDARDS OF POPULARITY.
CALLING SOMEONE AN *OSHIN* MEANS THEY STRUGGLE IN THE FACE OF ADVERSITY.
IT'S AN AGE OF ABUNDANCE, BUT FOR WHOM? THERE STILL SEEMS TO BE A LOT OF POOR PEOPLE, OF UNHAPPY PEOPLE. A LOT OF *OSHINS*...
LOOK AT THE PHILIPPINES... PRESIDENT FERDINAND MARCOS LINES HIS OWN POCKETS...
SO BENIGNO AQUINO JR. RETURNS FROM THE U.S. TO OPPOSE HIM...

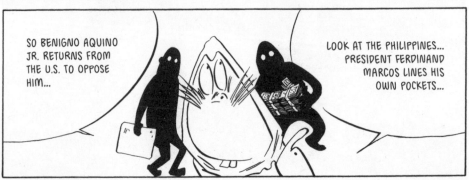

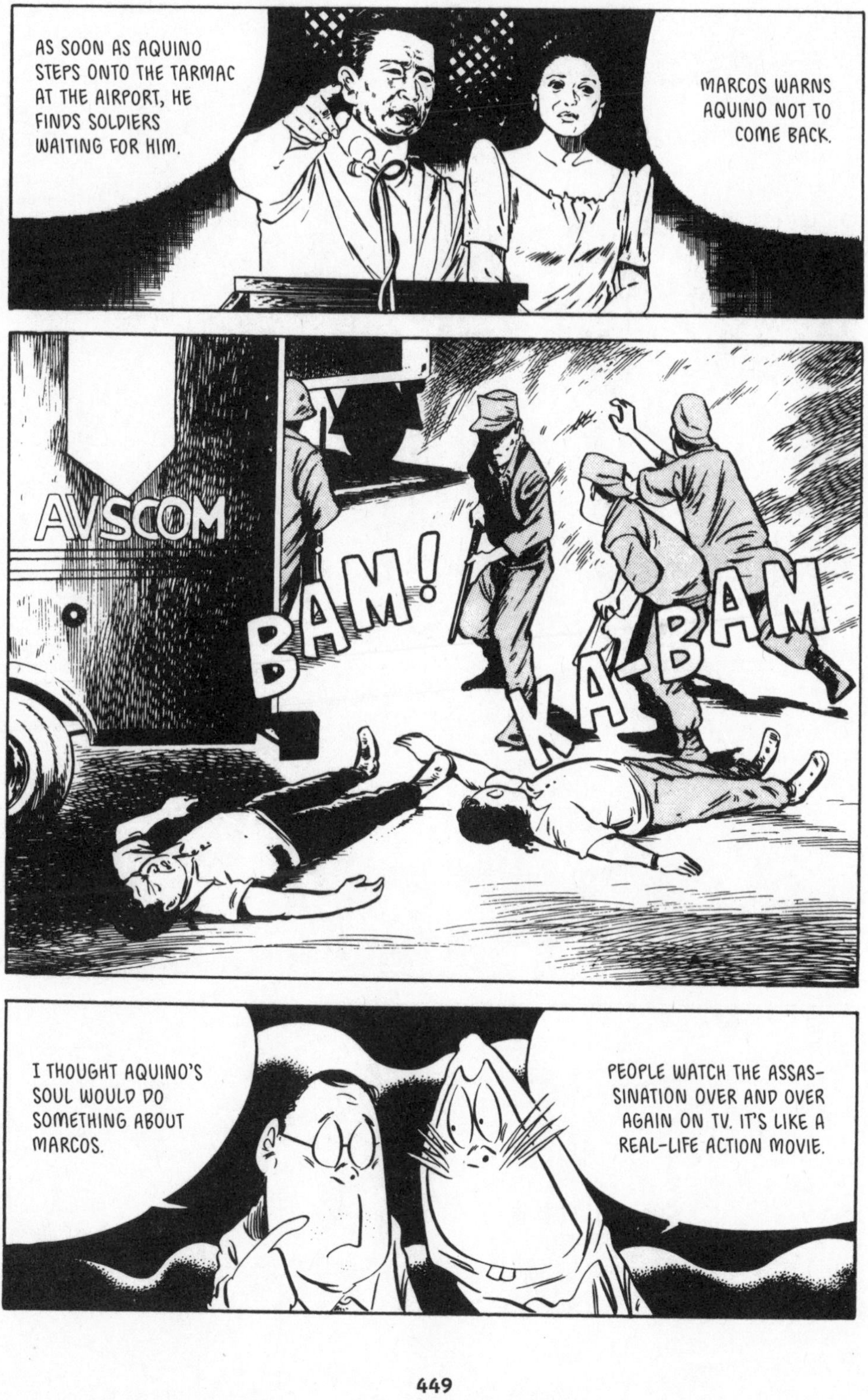
MARCOS WARNS AQUINO NOT TO COME BACK.
AS SOON AS AQUINO STEPS ONTO THE TARMAC AT THE AIRPORT, HE FINDS SOLDIERS WAITING FOR HIM.
AVSCOM
BAM!
KA-BAM
PEOPLE WATCH THE ASSAS-SINATION OVER AND OVER AGAIN ON TV. IT'S LIKE A REAL-LIFE ACTION MOVIE.
I THOUGHT AQUINO'S SOUL WOULD DO SOMETHING ABOUT MARCOS.

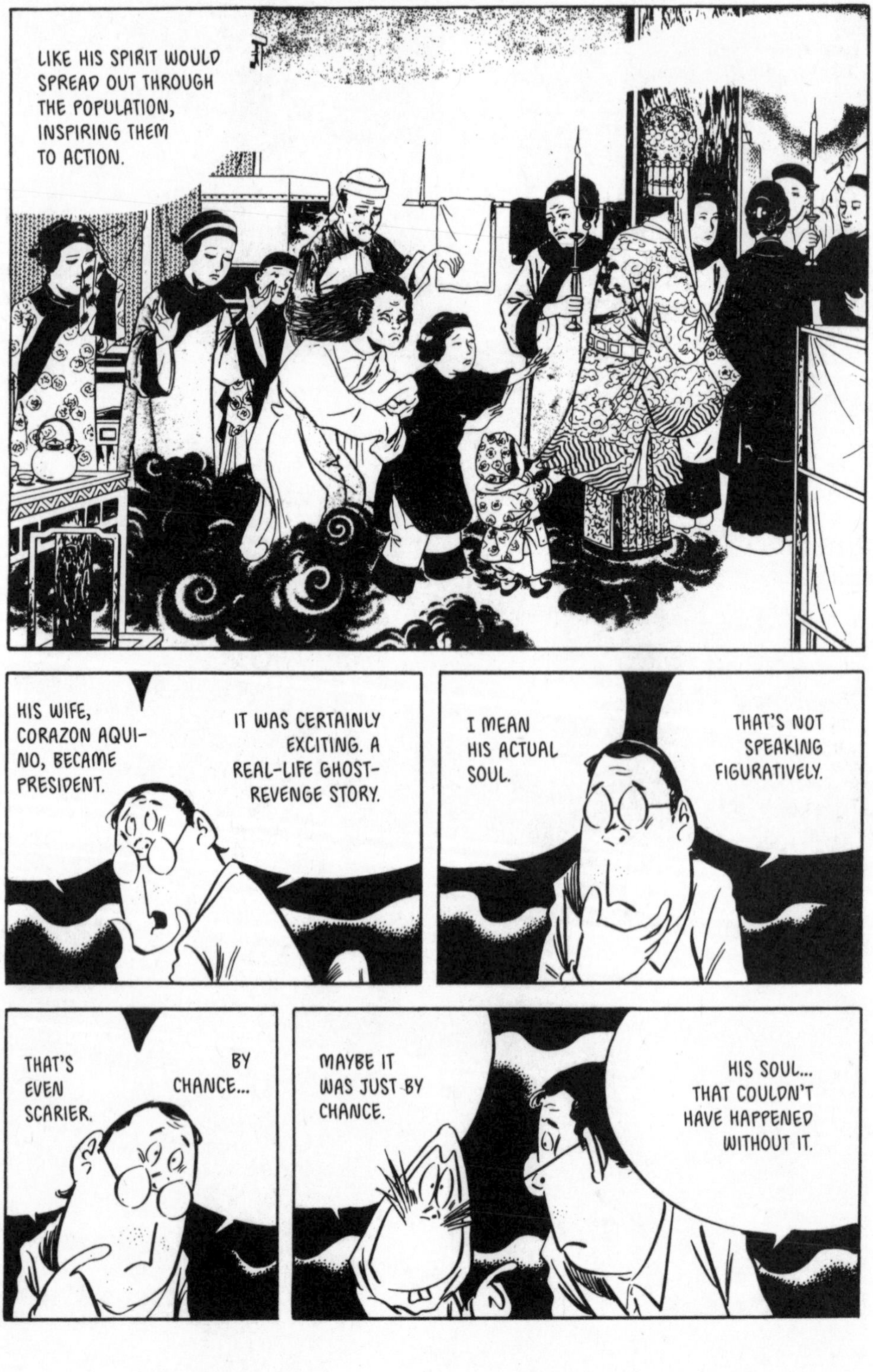
LIKE HIS SPIRIT WOULD SPREAD OUT THROUGH THE POPULATION, INSPIRING THEM TO ACTION.
THAT'S NOT SPEAKING FIGURATIVELY.
I MEAN HIS ACTUAL SOUL.
IT WAS CERTAINLY EXCITING. A REAL-LIFE GHOST-REVENGE STORY.
HIS WIFE, CORAZON AQUI-NO, BECAME PRESIDENT.
HIS SOUL... THAT COULDN'T HAVE HAPPENED WITHOUT IT.
MAYBE IT WAS JUST BY CHANCE.
BY CHANCE...
THAT'S EVEN SCARIER.

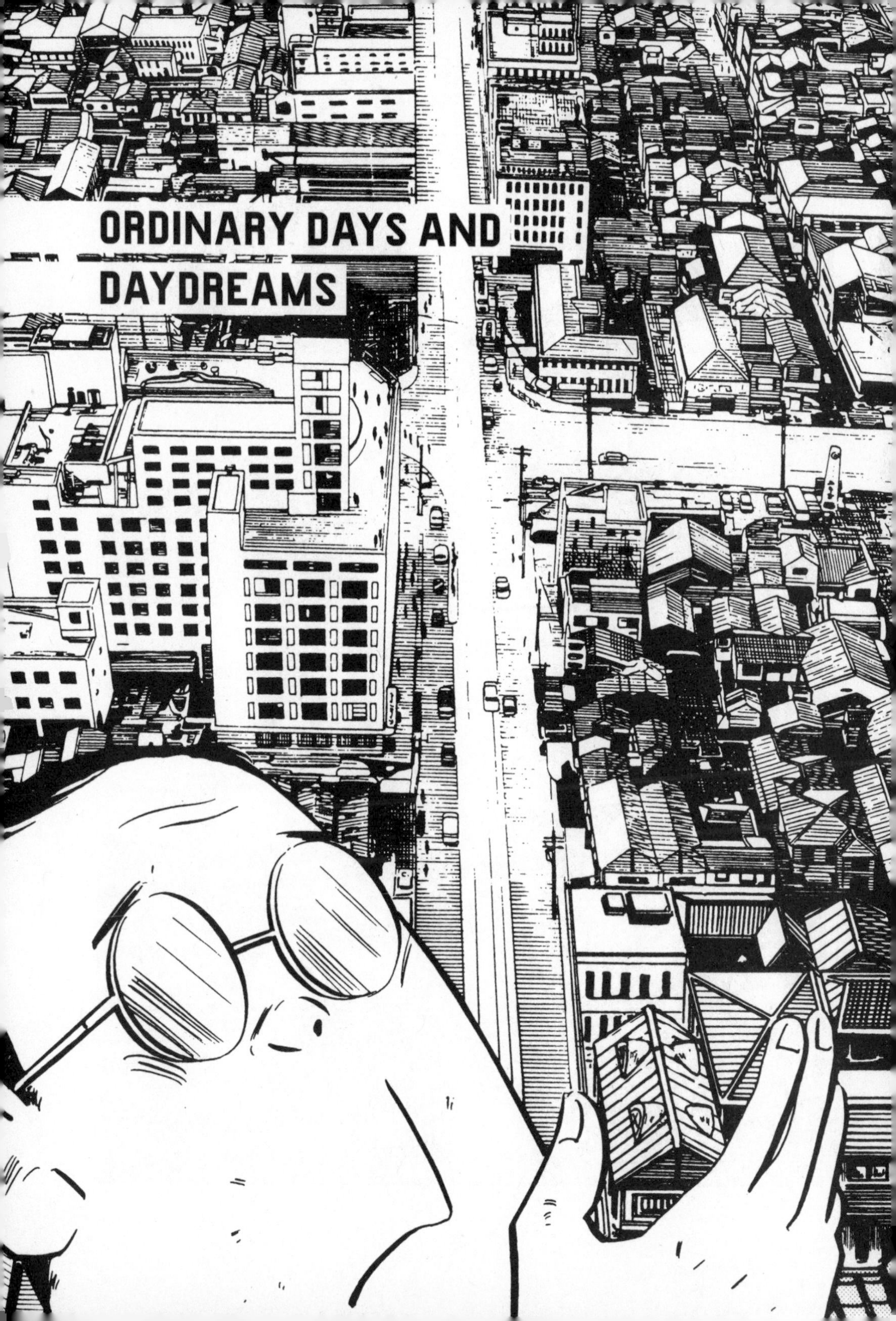
ORDINARY DAYS AND
DAYDREAMS

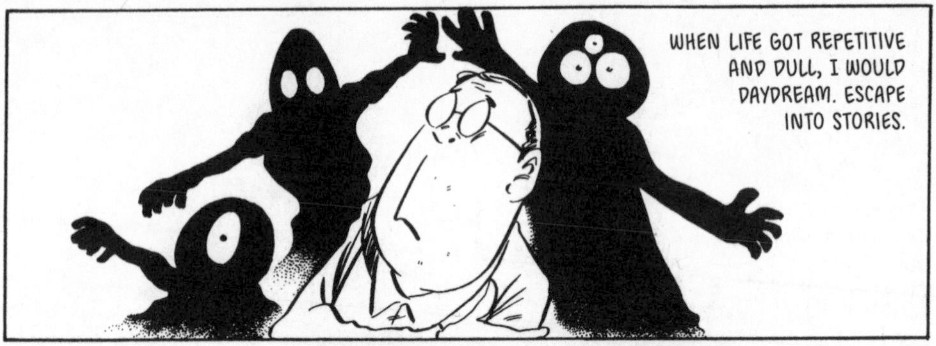
WHEN LIFE GOT REPETITIVE AND DULL, I WOULD DAYDREAM. ESCAPE INTO STORIES.

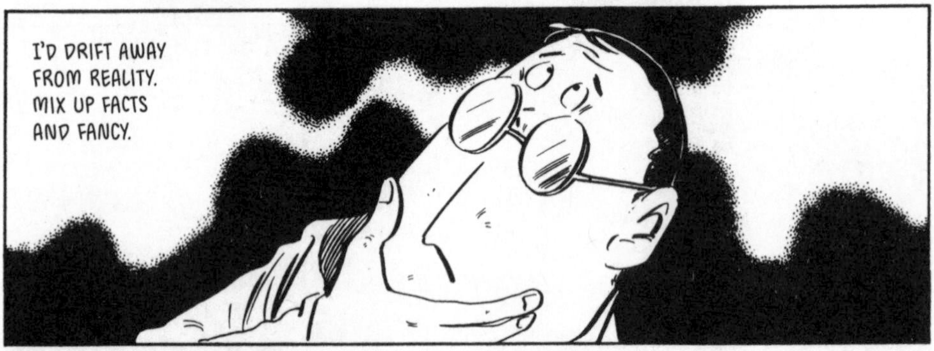
I'D DRIFT AWAY FROM REALITY. MIX UP FACTS AND FANCY.

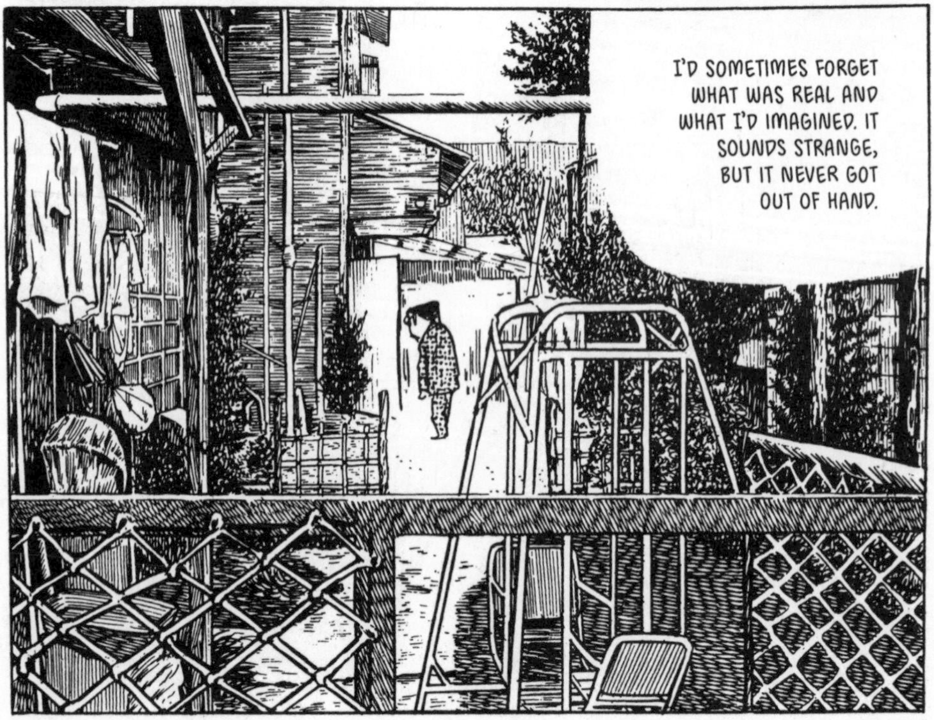
I'D SOMETIMES FORGET WHAT WAS REAL AND WHAT I'D IMAGINED. IT SOUNDS STRANGE, BUT IT NEVER GOT OUT OF HAND.

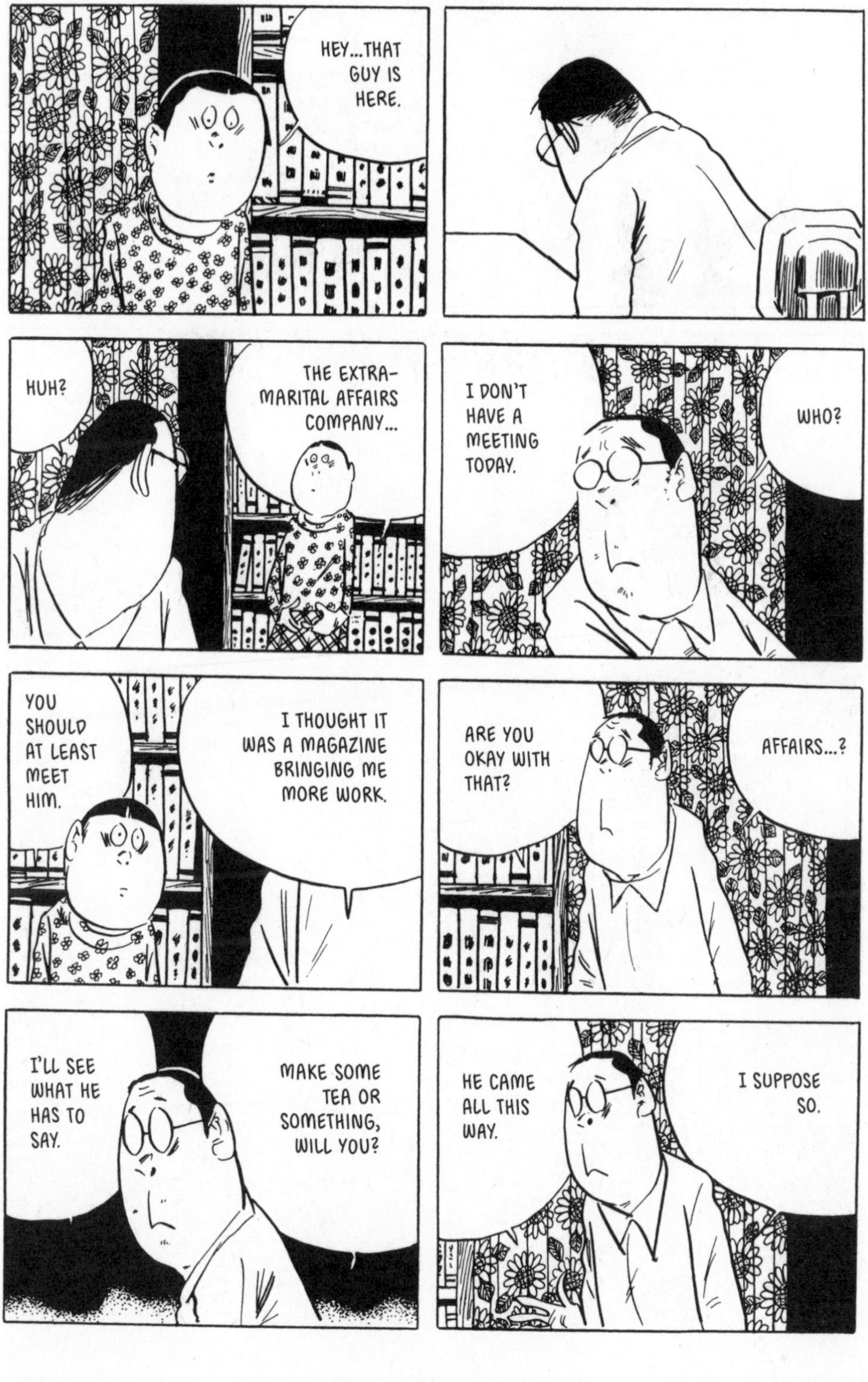
HEY...THAT GUY IS HERE.
WHO?
I DON'T HAVE A MEETING TODAY.
THE EXTRA-MARITAL AFFAIRS COMPANY...
HUH?
AFFAIRS...?
ARE YOU OKAY WITH THAT?
I THOUGHT IT WAS A MAGAZINE BRINGING ME MORE WORK.
YOU SHOULD AT LEAST MEET HIM.
I SUPPOSE SO.
HE CAME ALL THIS WAY.
MAKE SOME TEA OR SOMETHING, WILL YOU?
I'LL SEE WHAT HE HAS TO SAY.

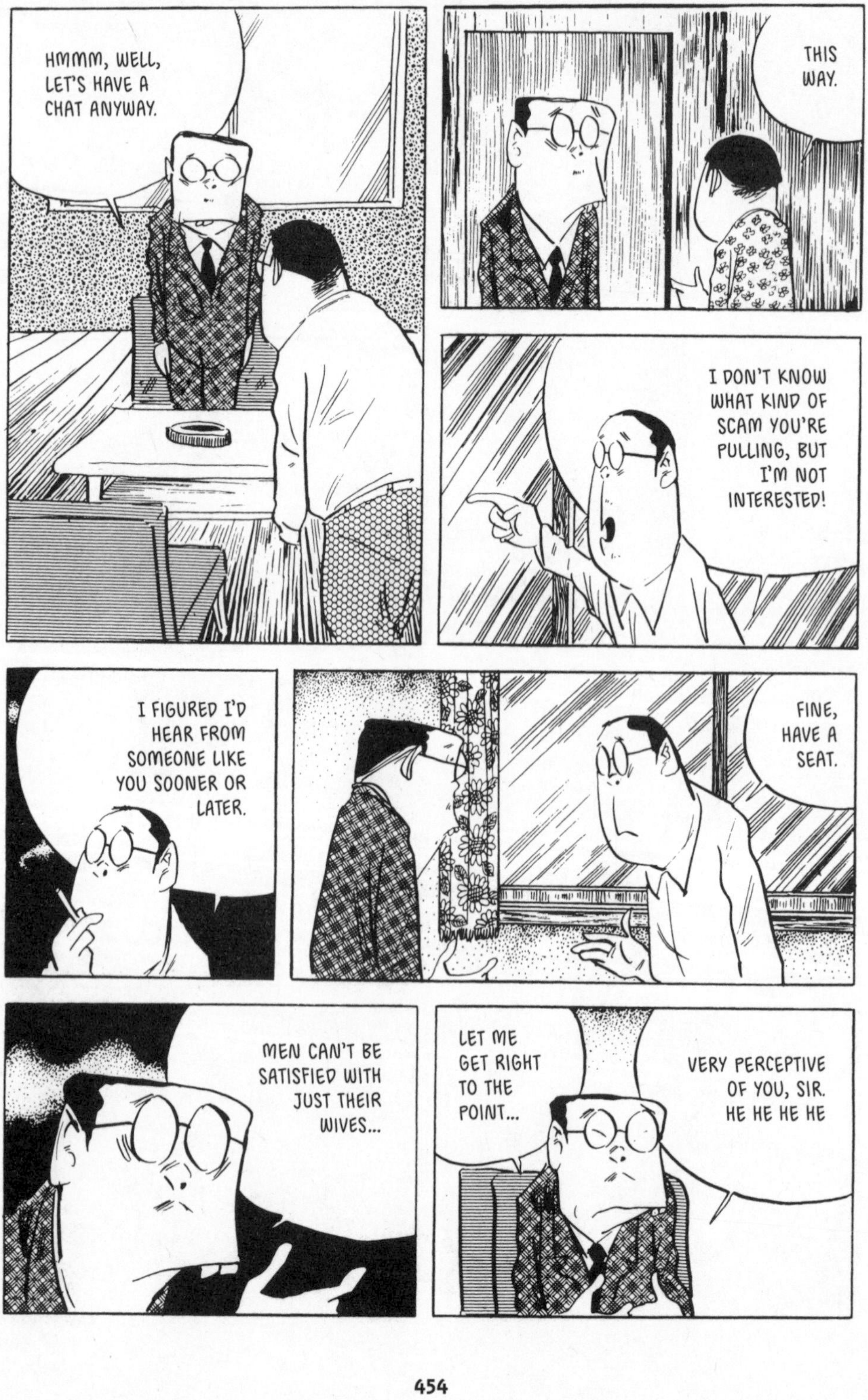
THIS WAY.
I DON'T KNOW WHAT KIND OF SCAM YOU'RE PULLING, BUT I'M NOT INTERESTED!
HMMM, WELL, LET'S HAVE A CHAT ANYWAY.
FINE, HAVE A SEAT.
I FIGURED I'D HEAR FROM SOMEONE LIKE YOU SOONER OR LATER.
VERY PERCEPTIVE OF YOU, SIR. HE HE HE HE
LET ME GET RIGHT TO THE POINT...
MEN CAN'T BE SATISFIED WITH JUST THEIR WIVES...

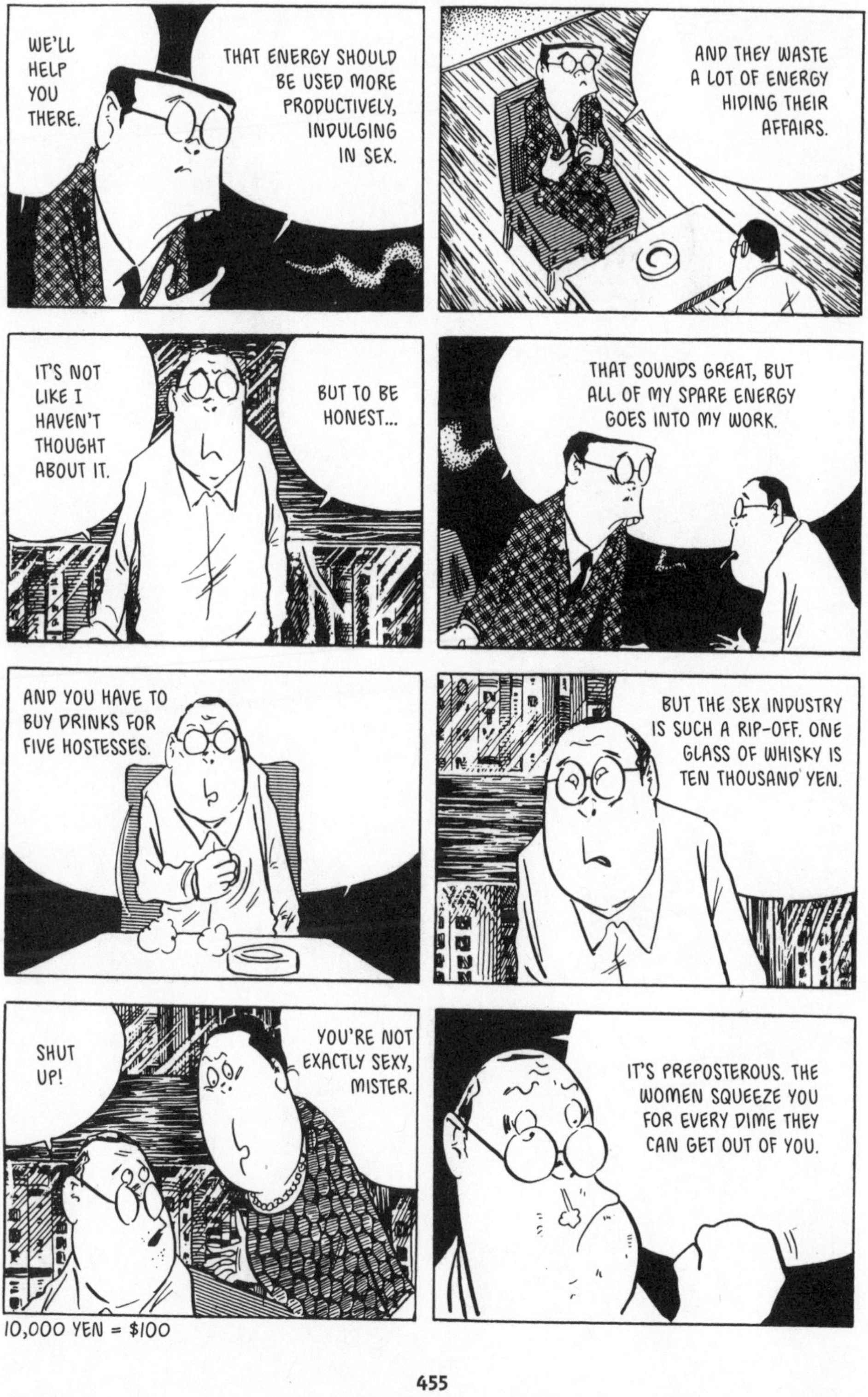
AND THEY WASTE A LOT OF ENERGY HIDING THEIR AFFAIRS.
THAT ENERGY SHOULD BE USED MORE PRODUCTIVELY, INDULGING IN SEX.
WE'LL HELP YOU THERE.
THAT SOUNDS GREAT, BUT ALL OF MY SPARE ENERGY GOES INTO MY WORK.
BUT TO BE HONEST...
IT'S NOT LIKE I HAVEN'T THOUGHT ABOUT IT.
BUT THE SEX INDUSTRY IS SUCH A RIP-OFF. ONE GLASS OF WHISKY IS TEN THOUSAND YEN.
AND YOU HAVE TO BUY DRINKS FOR FIVE HOSTESSES.
IT'S PREPOSTEROUS. THE WOMEN SQUEEZE YOU FOR EVERY DIME THEY CAN GET OUT OF YOU.
YOU'RE NOT EXACTLY SEXY, MISTER.
SHUT UP!

10,000 YEN = $100

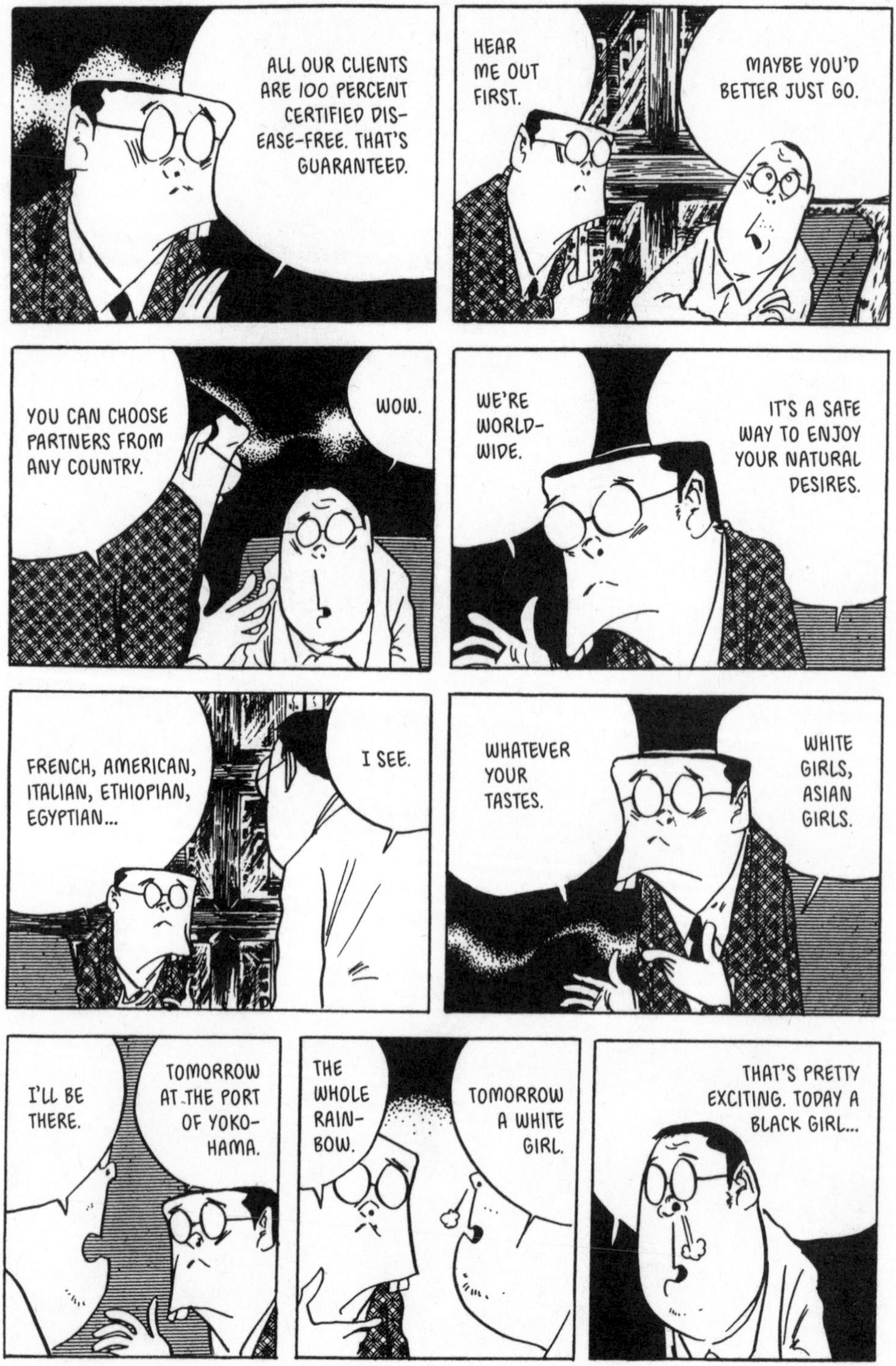
MAYBE YOU'D BETTER JUST GO.
HEAR ME OUT FIRST.
ALL OUR CLIENTS ARE 100 PERCENT CERTIFIED DISEASE-FREE. THAT'S GUARANTEED.
IT'S A SAFE WAY TO ENJOY YOUR NATURAL DESIRES.
WE'RE WORLDWIDE.
WOW.
YOU CAN CHOOSE PARTNERS FROM ANY COUNTRY.
WHITE GIRLS, ASIAN GIRLS.
WHATEVER YOUR TASTES.
I SEE.
FRENCH, AMERICAN, ITALIAN, ETHIOPIAN, EGYPTIAN...
THAT'S PRETTY EXCITING. TODAY A BLACK GIRL...
TOMORROW A WHITE GIRL.
THE WHOLE RAINBOW.
TOMORROW AT THE PORT OF YOKOHAMA.
I'LL BE THERE.

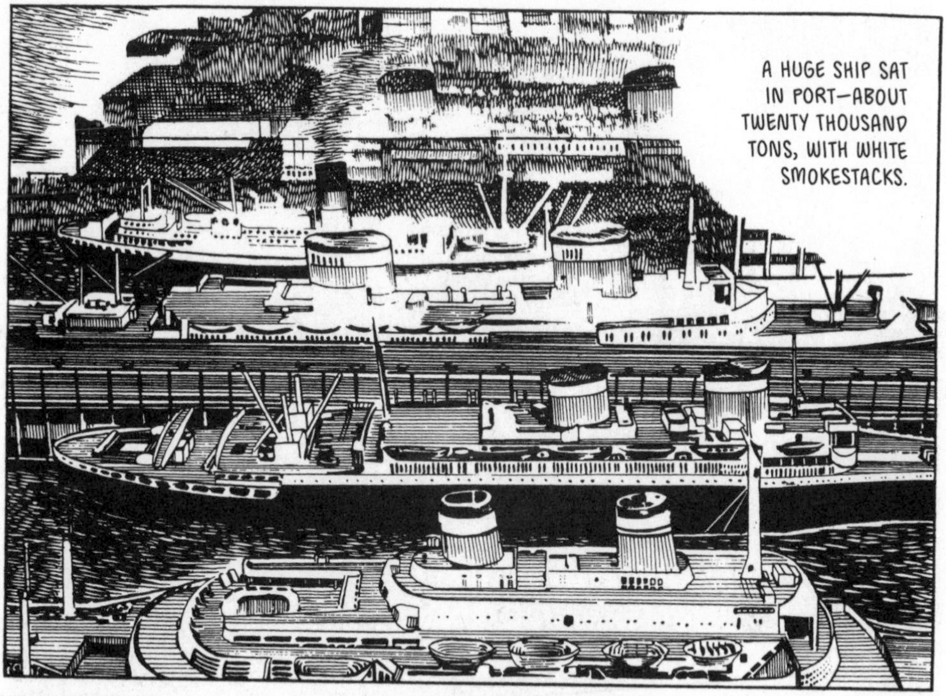
A HUGE SHIP SAT IN PORT—ABOUT TWENTY THOUSAND TONS, WITH WHITE SMOKESTACKS.

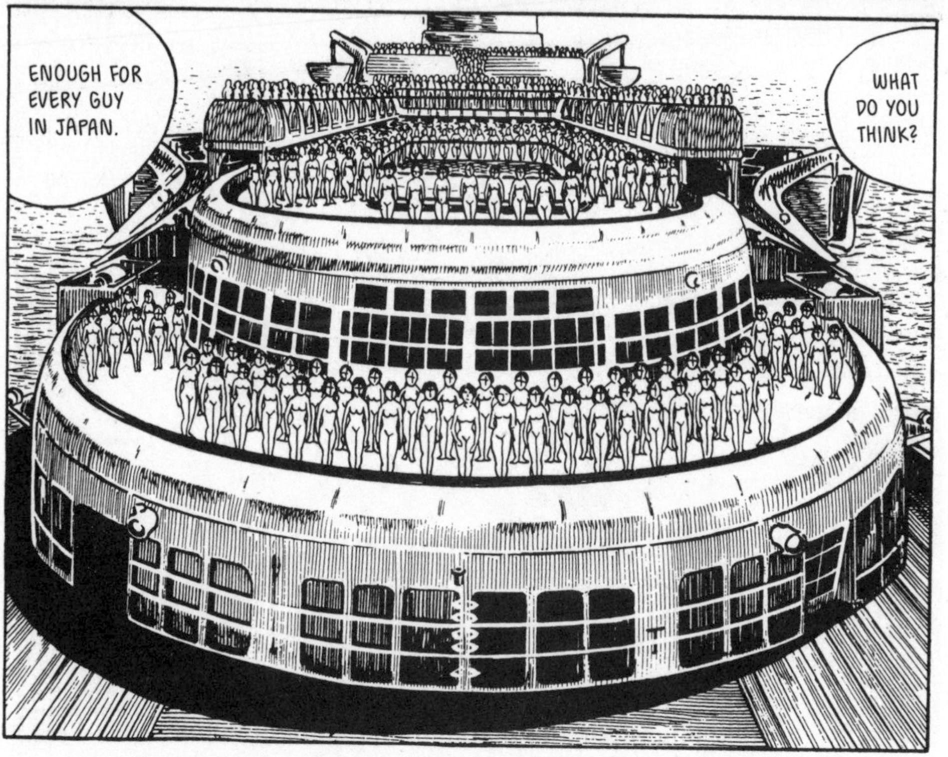
WHAT DO YOU THINK?
ENOUGH FOR EVERY GUY IN JAPAN.

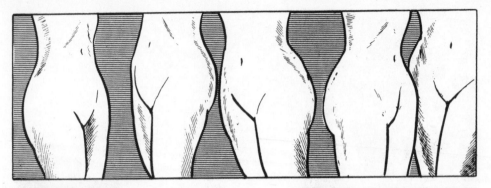

I HAD NO IDEA THE SEX INDUSTRY HAD ADVANCED THIS FAR.

OH YEAH.

NOW YOU SEE OUR SERVICE.

IT'S A HUNDRED-THOUSAND-YEN MEMBERSHIP FEE.

GOT THE FORM RIGHT HERE.

NOW HURRY UP WITH MY MEMBERSHIP.

OKAY.

100,000 YEN = $1,000

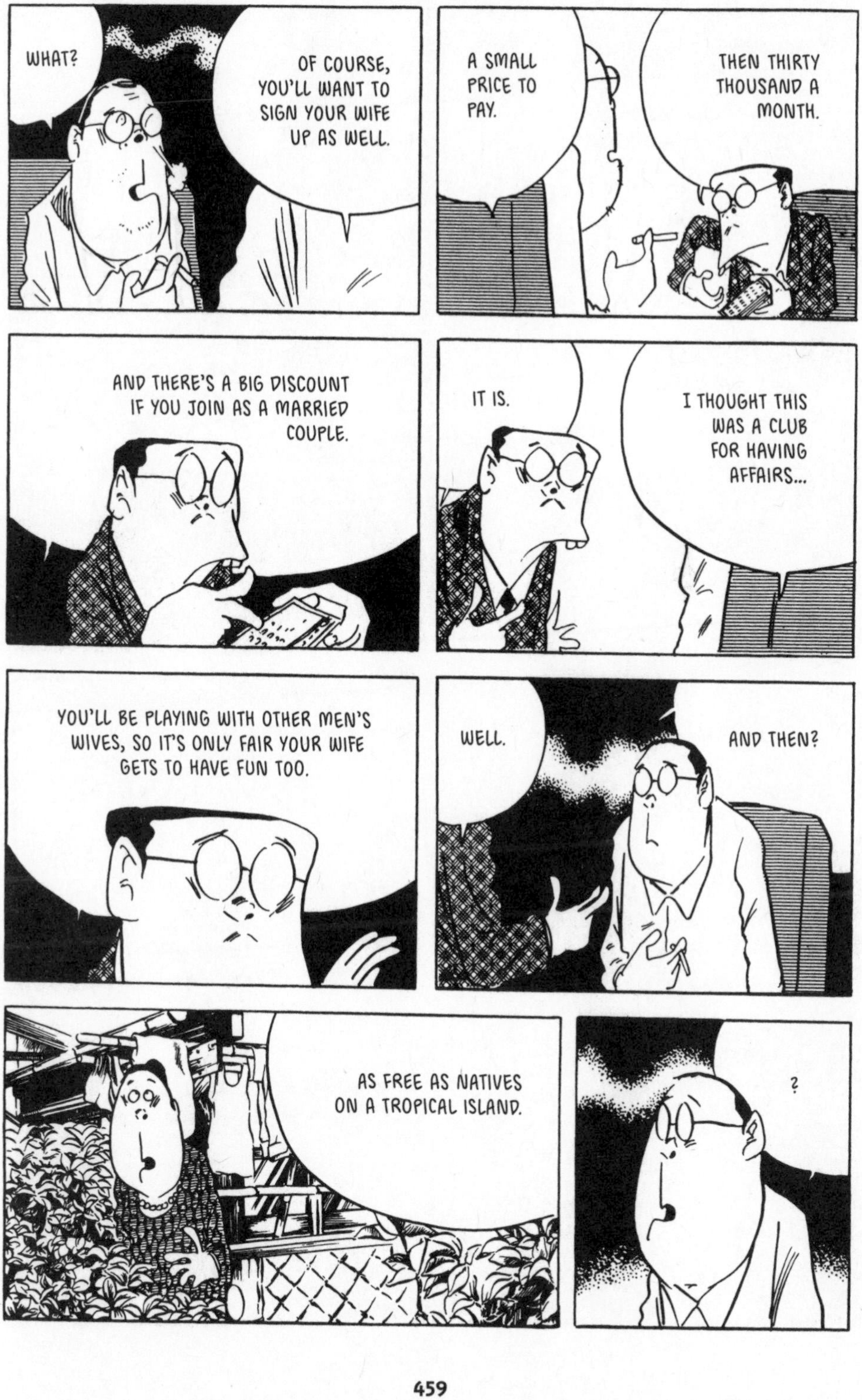
THEN THIRTY THOUSAND A MONTH.
A SMALL PRICE TO PAY.
OF COURSE, YOU'LL WANT TO SIGN YOUR WIFE UP AS WELL.
WHAT?
I THOUGHT THIS WAS A CLUB FOR HAVING AFFAIRS...
IT IS.
AND THERE'S A BIG DISCOUNT IF YOU JOIN AS A MARRIED COUPLE.
AND THEN?
WELL.
YOU'LL BE PLAYING WITH OTHER MEN'S WIVES, SO IT'S ONLY FAIR YOUR WIFE GETS TO HAVE FUN TOO.
?
AS FREE AS NATIVES ON A TROPICAL ISLAND.

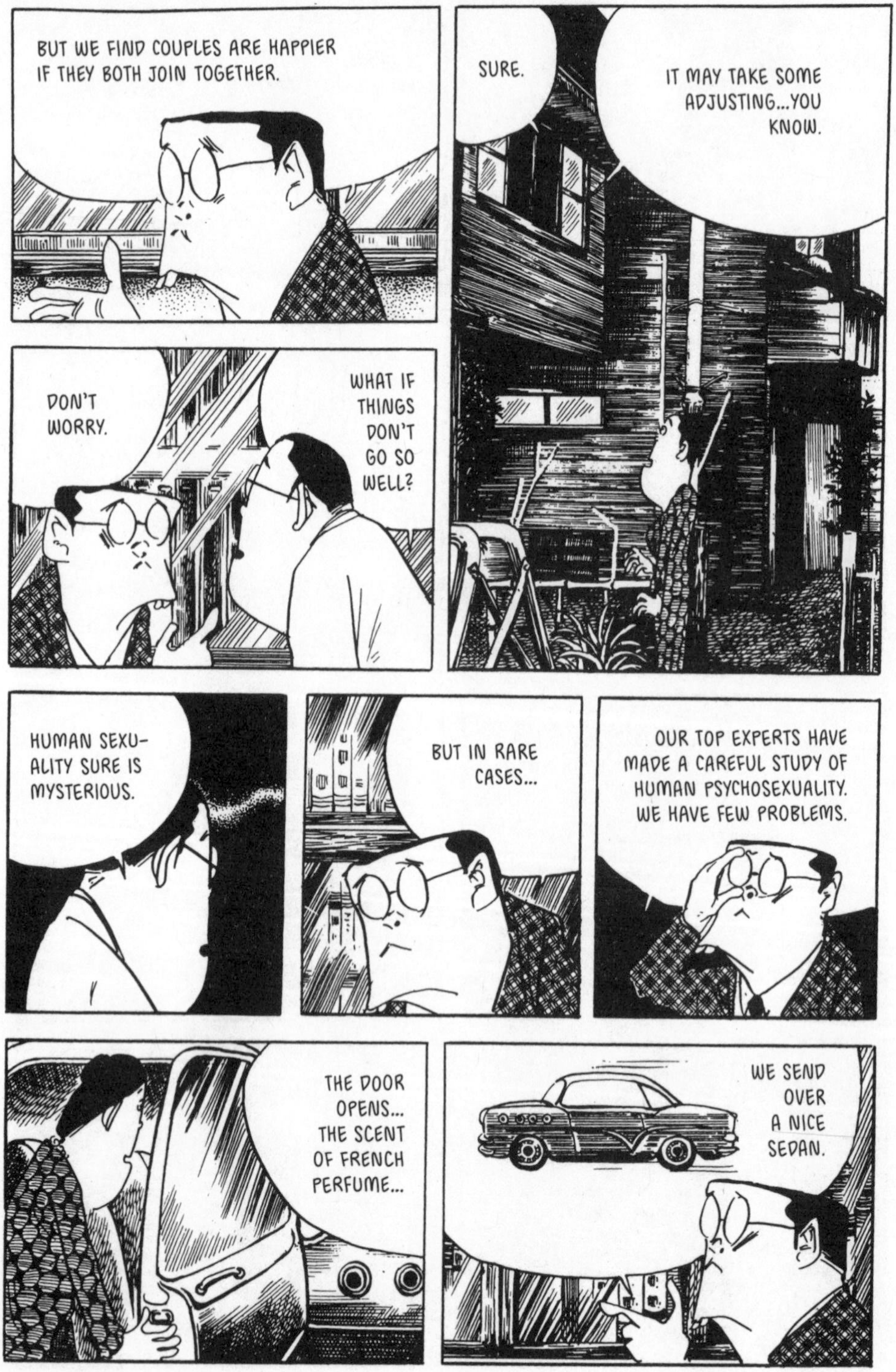
IT MAY TAKE SOME ADJUSTING...YOU KNOW.
SURE.
BUT WE FIND COUPLES ARE HAPPIER IF THEY BOTH JOIN TOGETHER.
WHAT IF THINGS DON'T GO SO WELL?
DON'T WORRY.
OUR TOP EXPERTS HAVE MADE A CAREFUL STUDY OF HUMAN PSYCHOSEXUALITY. WE HAVE FEW PROBLEMS.
BUT IN RARE CASES...
HUMAN SEXU-ALITY SURE IS MYSTERIOUS.
WE SEND OVER A NICE SEDAN.
THE DOOR OPENS... THE SCENT OF FRENCH PERFUME...

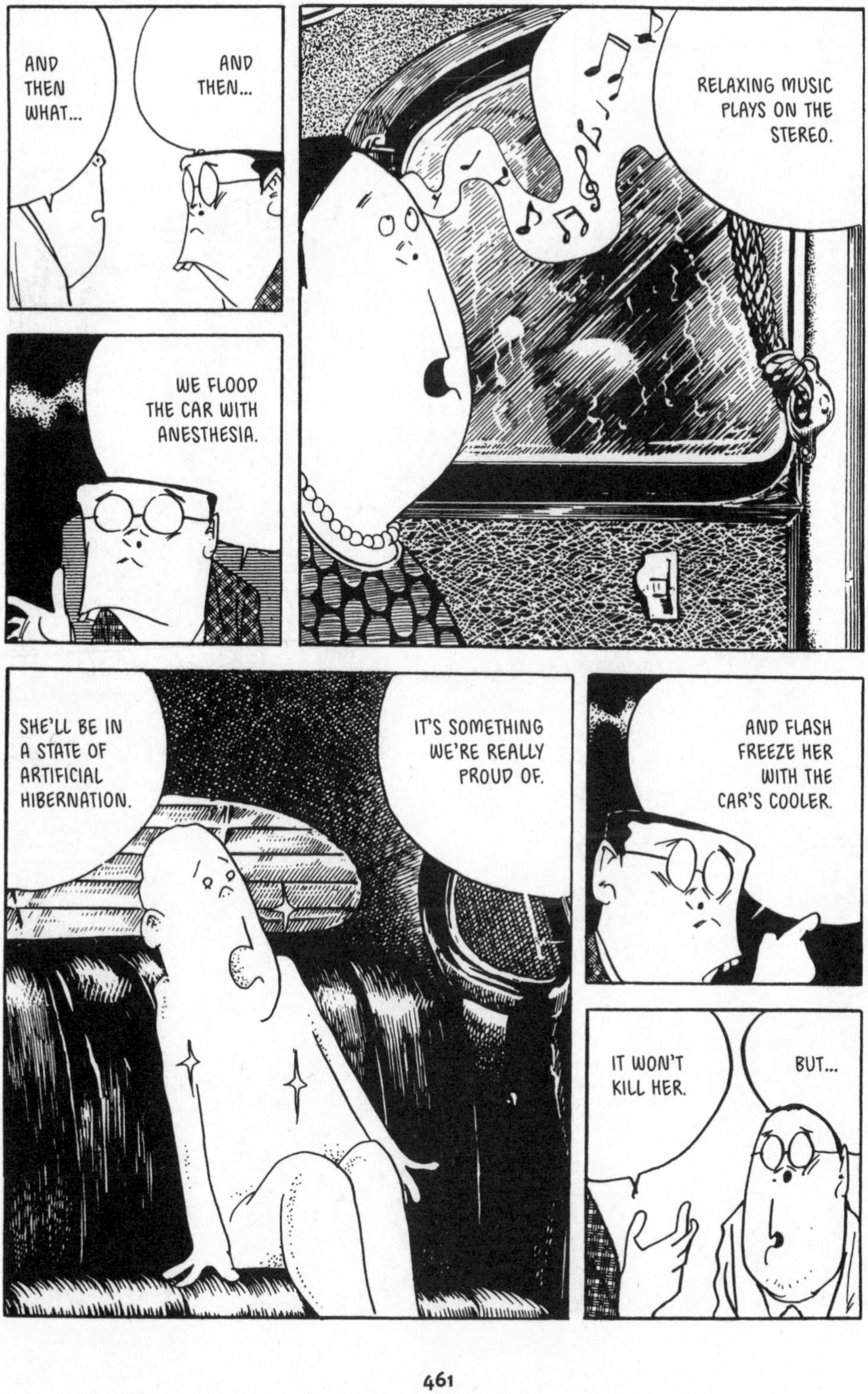
RELAXING MUSIC PLAYS ON THE STEREO.
AND THEN...
AND THEN WHAT...
WE FLOOD THE CAR WITH ANESTHESIA.
AND FLASH FREEZE HER WITH THE CAR'S COOLER.
BUT...
IT WON'T KILL HER.
IT'S SOMETHING WE'RE REALLY PROUD OF.
SHE'LL BE IN A STATE OF ARTIFICIAL HIBERNATION.

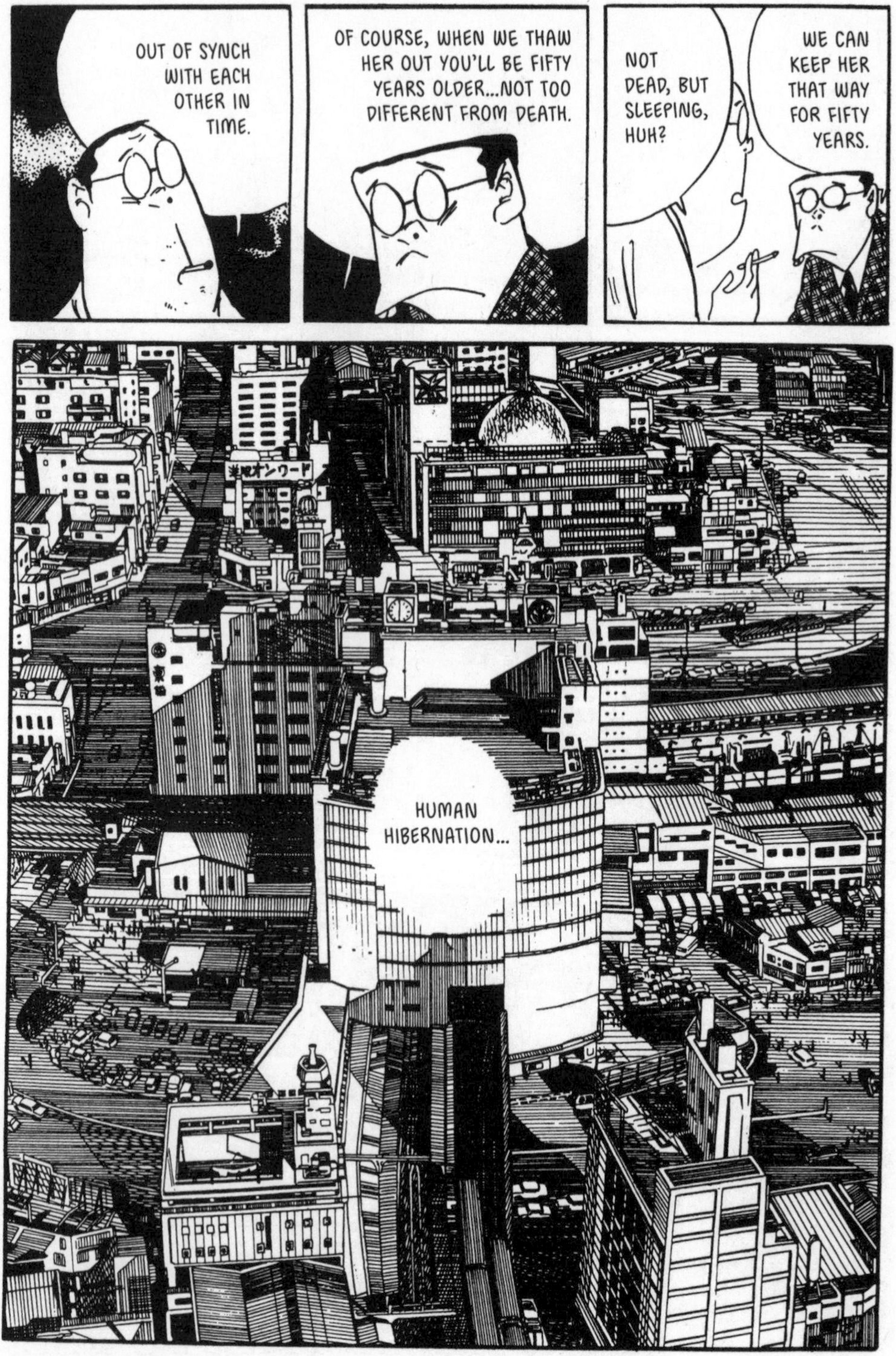
WE CAN KEEP HER THAT WAY FOR FIFTY YEARS.
NOT DEAD, BUT SLEEPING, HUH?
OF COURSE, WHEN WE THAW HER OUT YOU'LL BE FIFTY YEARS OLDER...NOT TOO DIFFERENT FROM DEATH.
OUT OF SYNCH WITH EACH OTHER IN TIME.
HUMAN HIBERNATION...

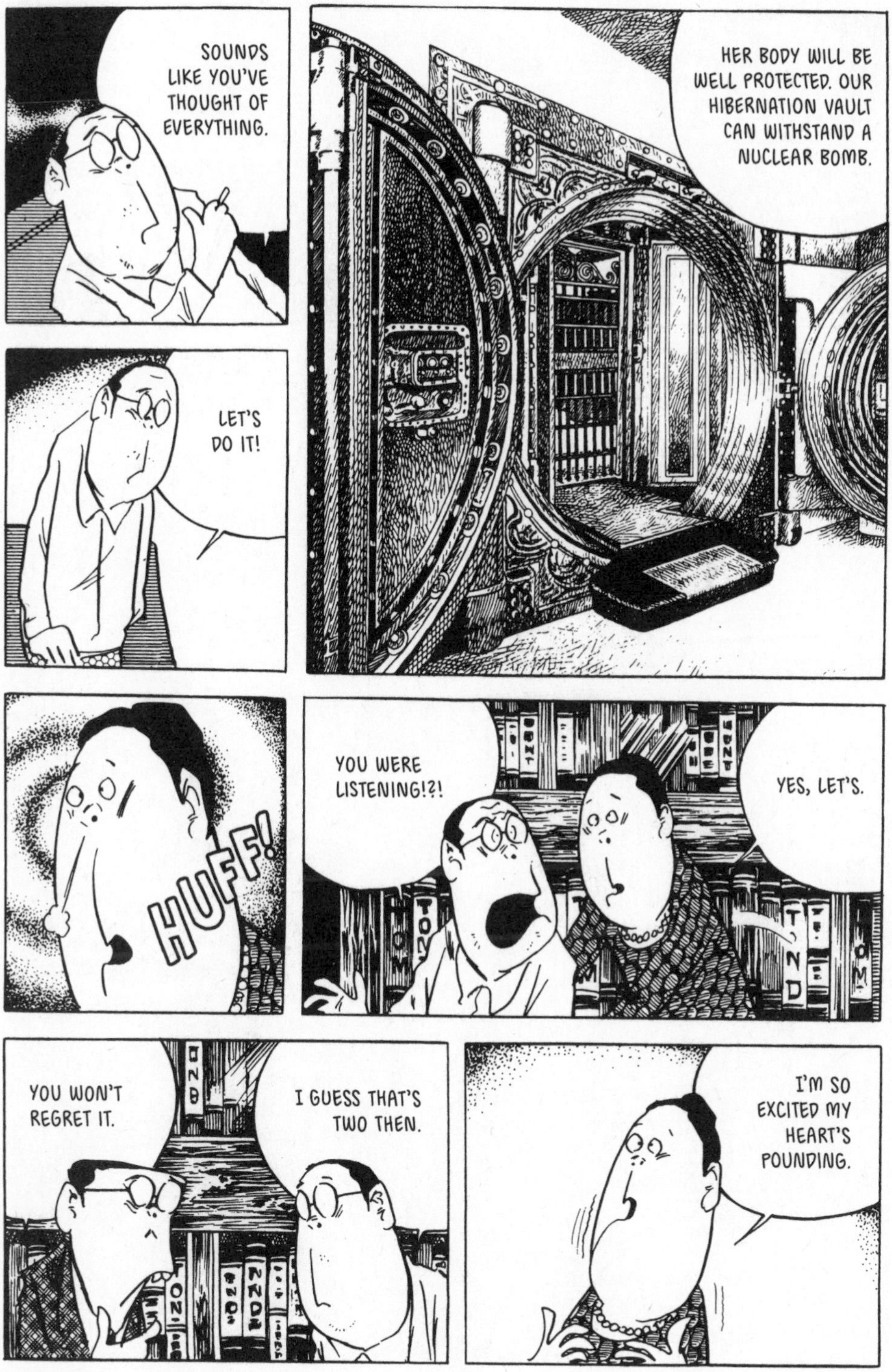
HER BODY WILL BE WELL PROTECTED. OUR HIBERNATION VAULT CAN WITHSTAND A NUCLEAR BOMB.
SOUNDS LIKE YOU'VE THOUGHT OF EVERYTHING.
LET'S DO IT!
YES, LET'S.
YOU WERE LISTENING!?!
HUFF!
I'M SO EXCITED MY HEART'S POUNDING.
I GUESS THAT'S TWO THEN.
YOU WON'T REGRET IT.

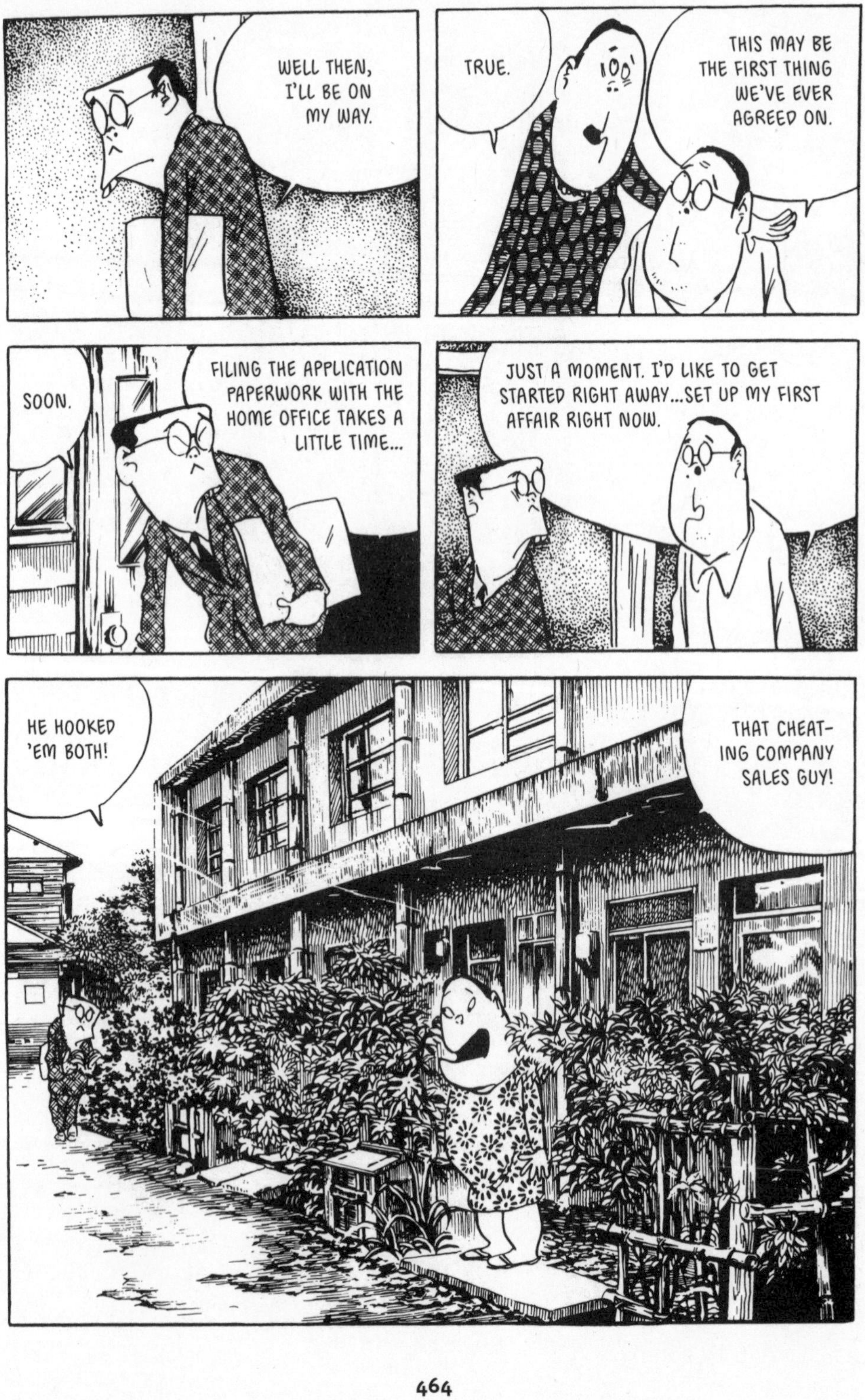
THIS MAY BE THE FIRST THING WE'VE EVER AGREED ON.
TRUE.
WELL THEN, I'LL BE ON MY WAY.
JUST A MOMENT. I'D LIKE TO GET STARTED RIGHT AWAY...SET UP MY FIRST AFFAIR RIGHT NOW.
FILING THE APPLICATION PAPERWORK WITH THE HOME OFFICE TAKES A LITTLE TIME...
SOON.
THAT CHEAT-ING COMPANY SALES GUY!
HE HOOKED 'EM BOTH!

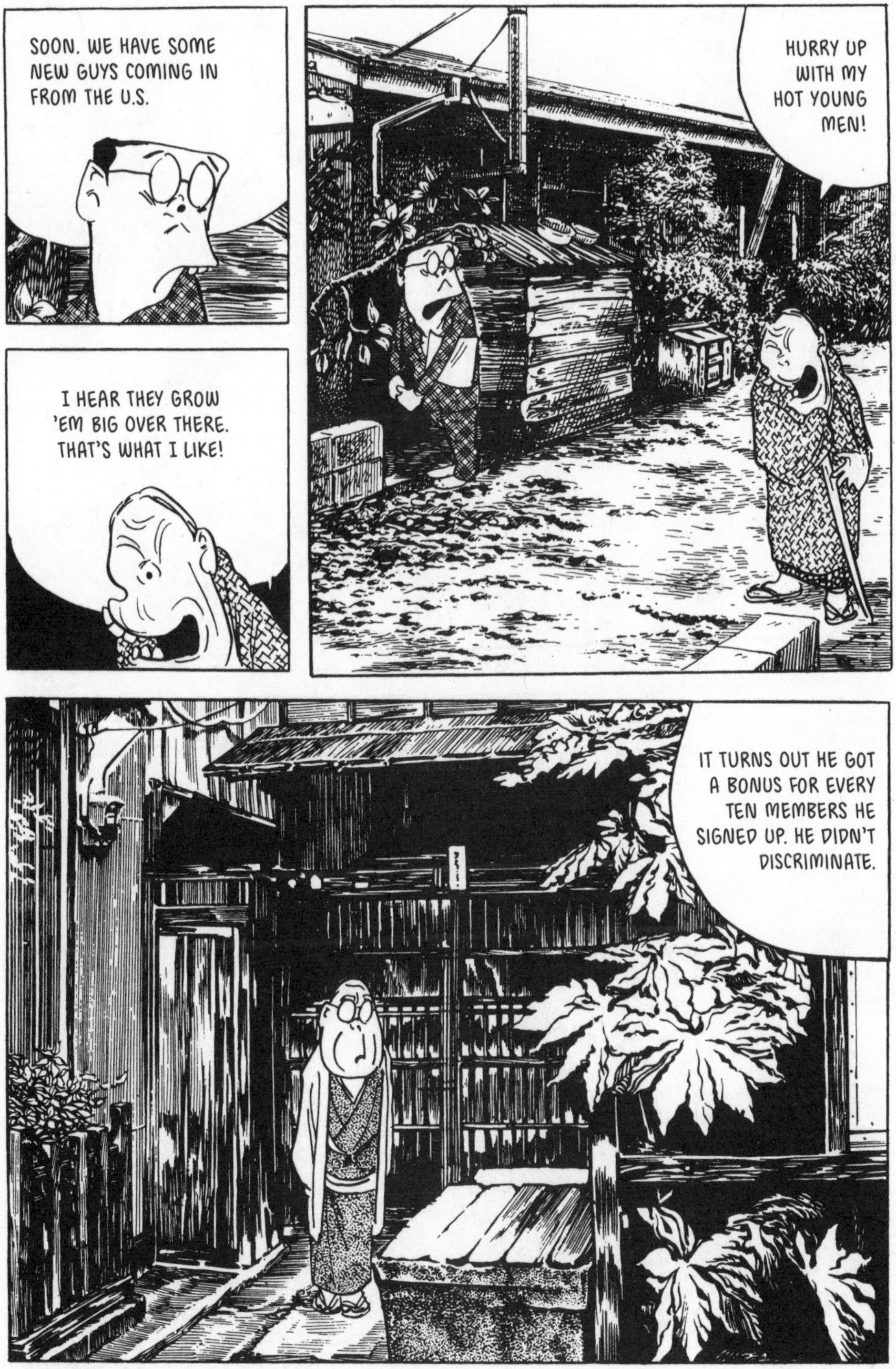
HURRY UP WITH MY HOT YOUNG MEN!
SOON. WE HAVE SOME NEW GUYS COMING IN FROM THE U.S.
I HEAR THEY GROW 'EM BIG OVER THERE. THAT'S WHAT I LIKE!
IT TURNS OUT HE GOT A BONUS FOR EVERY TEN MEMBERS HE SIGNED UP. HE DIDN'T DISCRIMINATE.

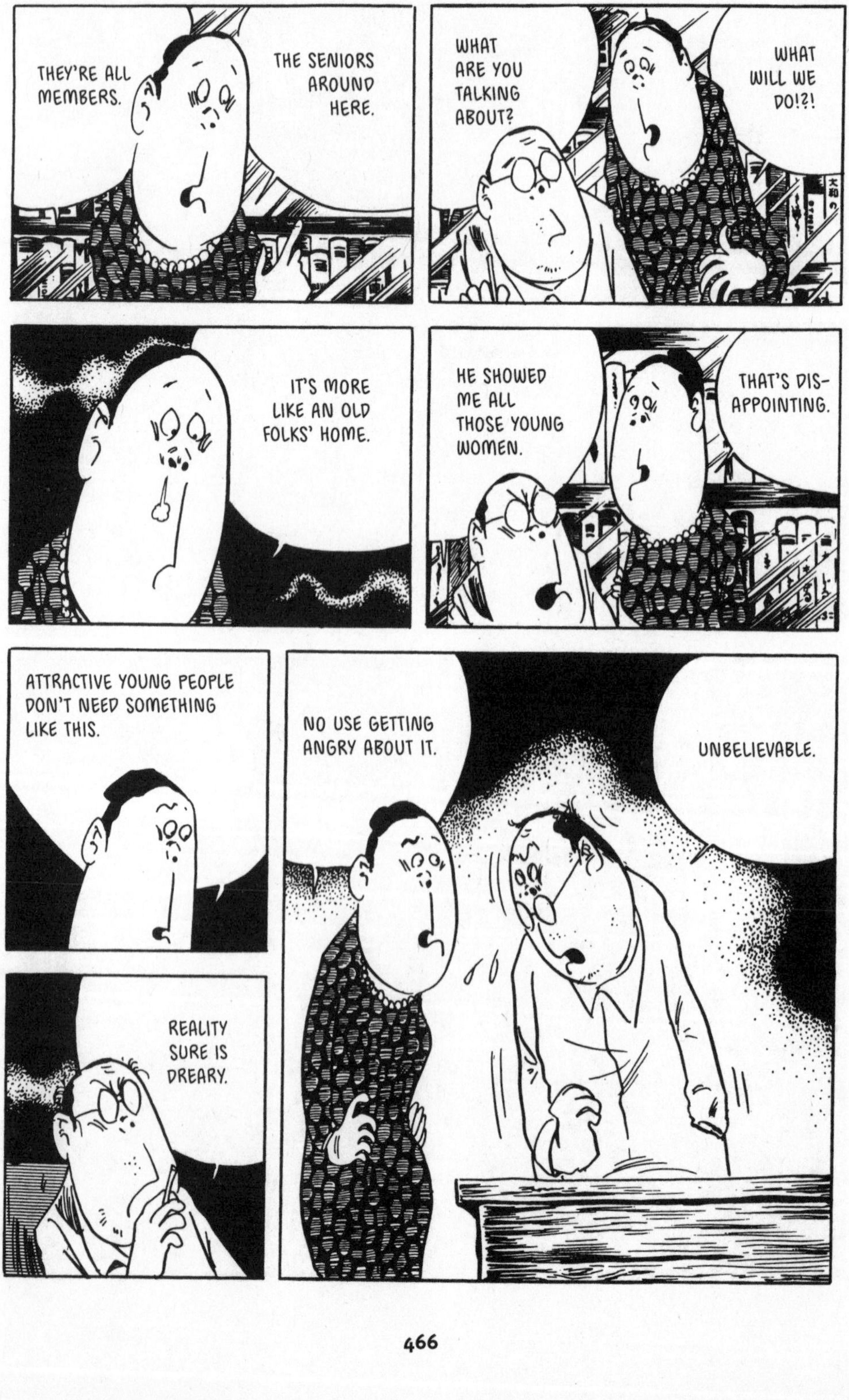
WHAT WILL WE DO!?!
WHAT ARE YOU TALKING ABOUT?
THE SENIORS AROUND HERE.
THEY'RE ALL MEMBERS.
THAT'S DIS-APPOINTING.
HE SHOWED ME ALL THOSE YOUNG WOMEN.
IT'S MORE LIKE AN OLD FOLKS' HOME.
UNBELIEVABLE.
NO USE GETTING ANGRY ABOUT IT.
ATTRACTIVE YOUNG PEOPLE DON'T NEED SOMETHING LIKE THIS.
REALITY SURE IS DREARY.

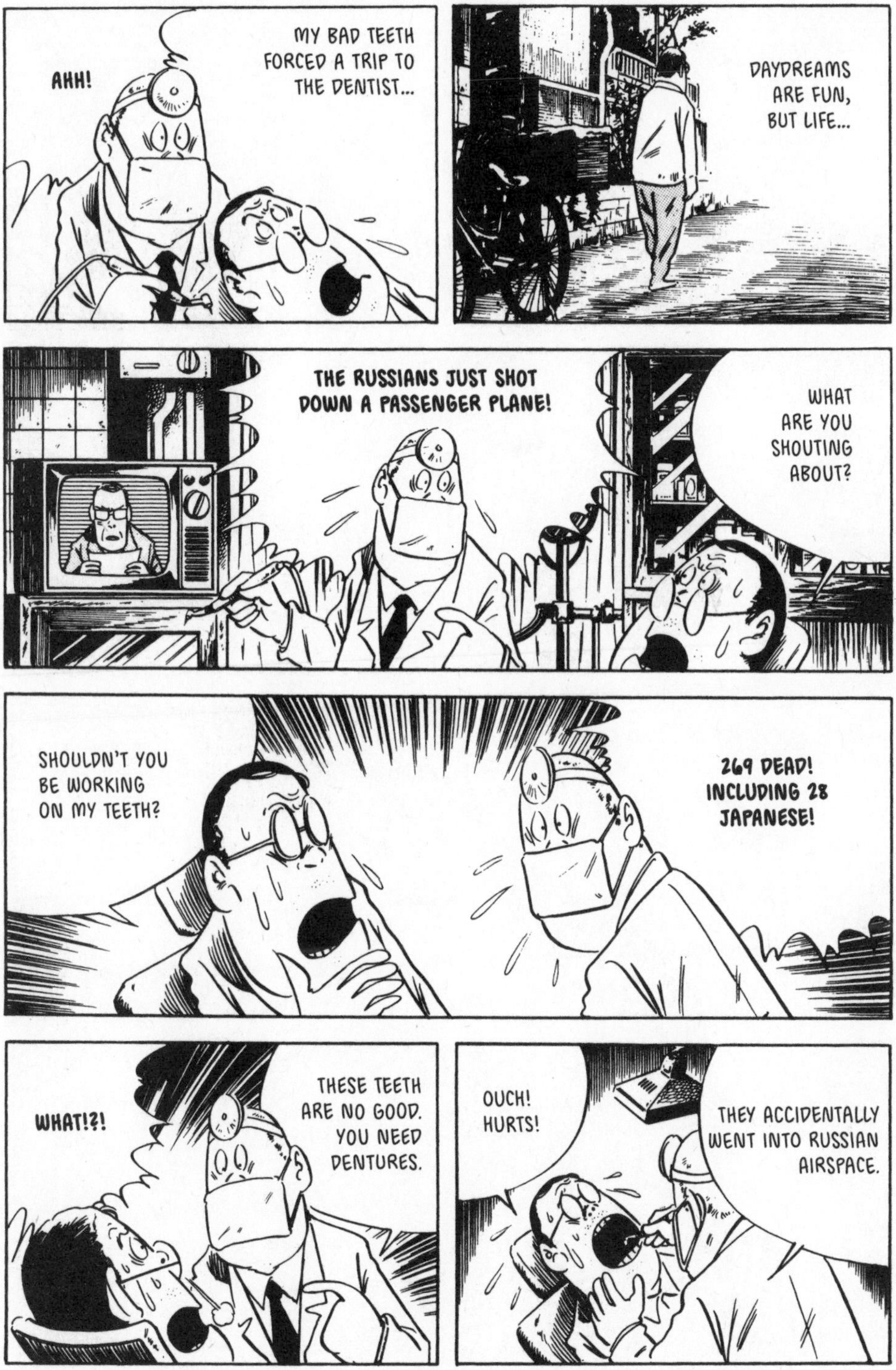
DAYDREAMS ARE FUN, BUT LIFE...
MY BAD TEETH FORCED A TRIP TO THE DENTIST...
AHH!
WHAT ARE YOU SHOUTING ABOUT?
THE RUSSIANS JUST SHOT DOWN A PASSENGER PLANE!
269 DEAD! INCLUDING 28 JAPANESE!
SHOULDN'T YOU BE WORKING ON MY TEETH?
THEY ACCIDENTALLY WENT INTO RUSSIAN AIRSPACE.
OUCH! HURTS!
THESE TEETH ARE NO GOOD. YOU NEED DENTURES.
WHAT!?!

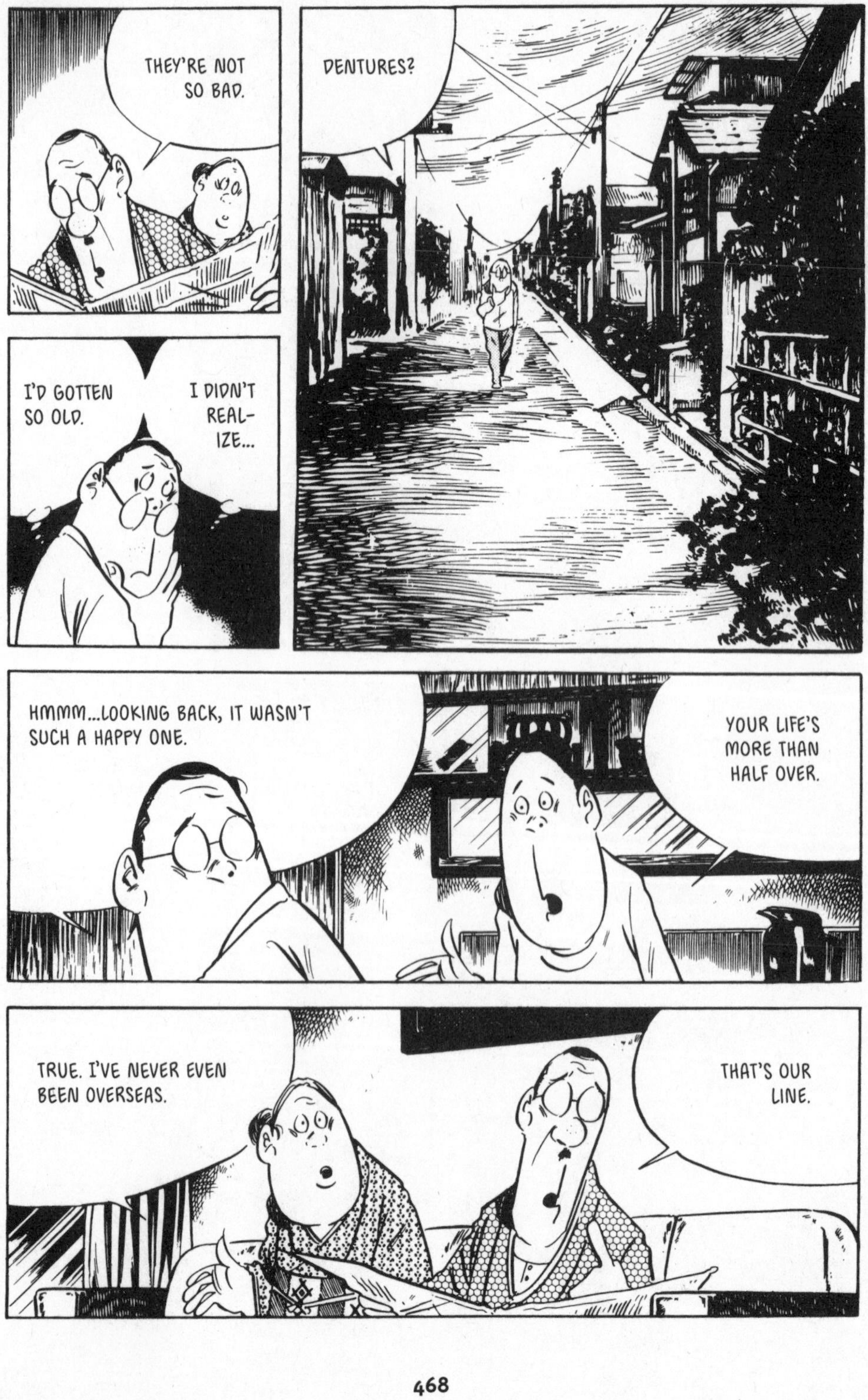
DENTURES?
THEY'RE NOT SO BAD.
I DIDN'T REALIZE...
I'D GOTTEN SO OLD.
YOUR LIFE'S MORE THAN HALF OVER.
HMMM...LOOKING BACK, IT WASN'T SUCH A HAPPY ONE.
THAT'S OUR LINE.
TRUE. I'VE NEVER EVEN BEEN OVERSEAS.

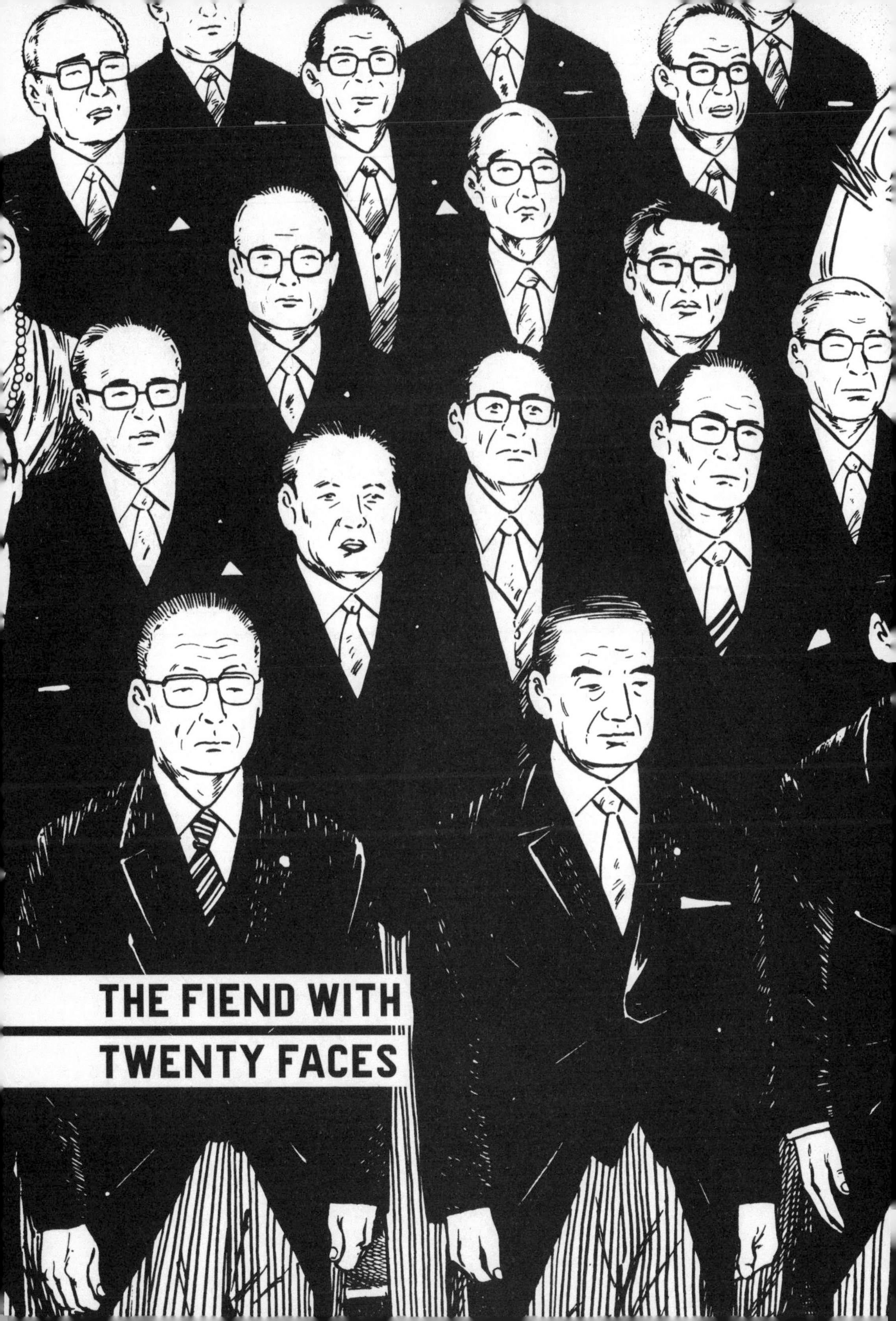

THE FIEND WITH TWENTY FACES

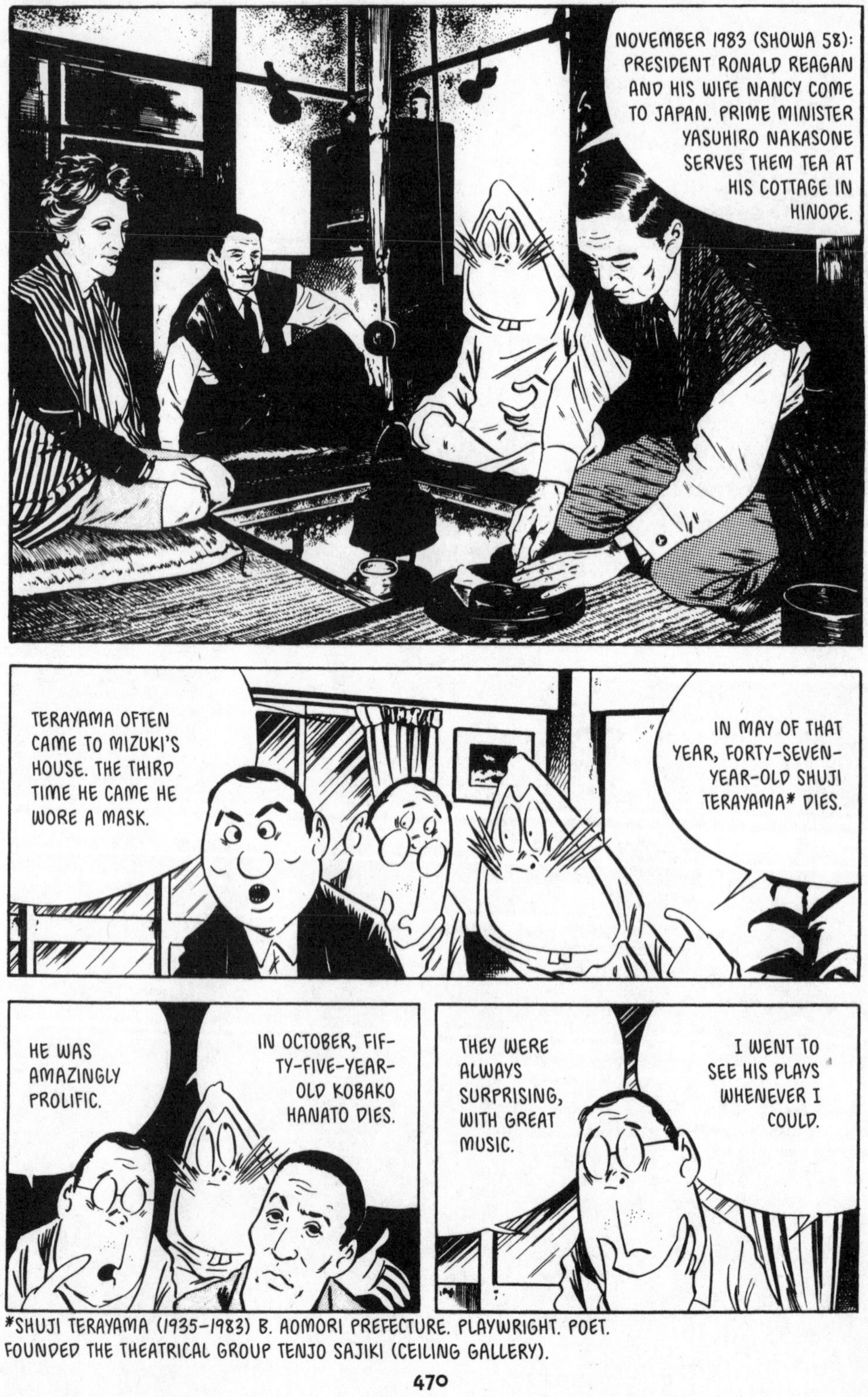
NOVEMBER 1983 (SHOWA 58): PRESIDENT RONALD REAGAN AND HIS WIFE NANCY COME TO JAPAN. PRIME MINISTER YASUHIRO NAKASONE SERVES THEM TEA AT HIS COTTAGE IN HINODE.
IN MAY OF THAT YEAR, FORTY-SEVEN-YEAR-OLD SHUJI TERAYAMA* DIES.
TERAYAMA OFTEN CAME TO MIZUKI'S HOUSE. THE THIRD TIME HE CAME HE WORE A MASK.
I WENT TO SEE HIS PLAYS WHENEVER I COULD.
THEY WERE ALWAYS SURPRISING, WITH GREAT MUSIC.
IN OCTOBER, FIFTY-FIVE-YEAR-OLD KOBAKO HANATO DIES.
HE WAS AMAZINGLY PROLIFIC.

*SHUJI TERAYAMA (1935–1983) B. AOMORI PREFECTURE. PLAYWRIGHT. POET. FOUNDED THE THEATRICAL GROUP TENJO SAJIKI (CEILING GALLERY).

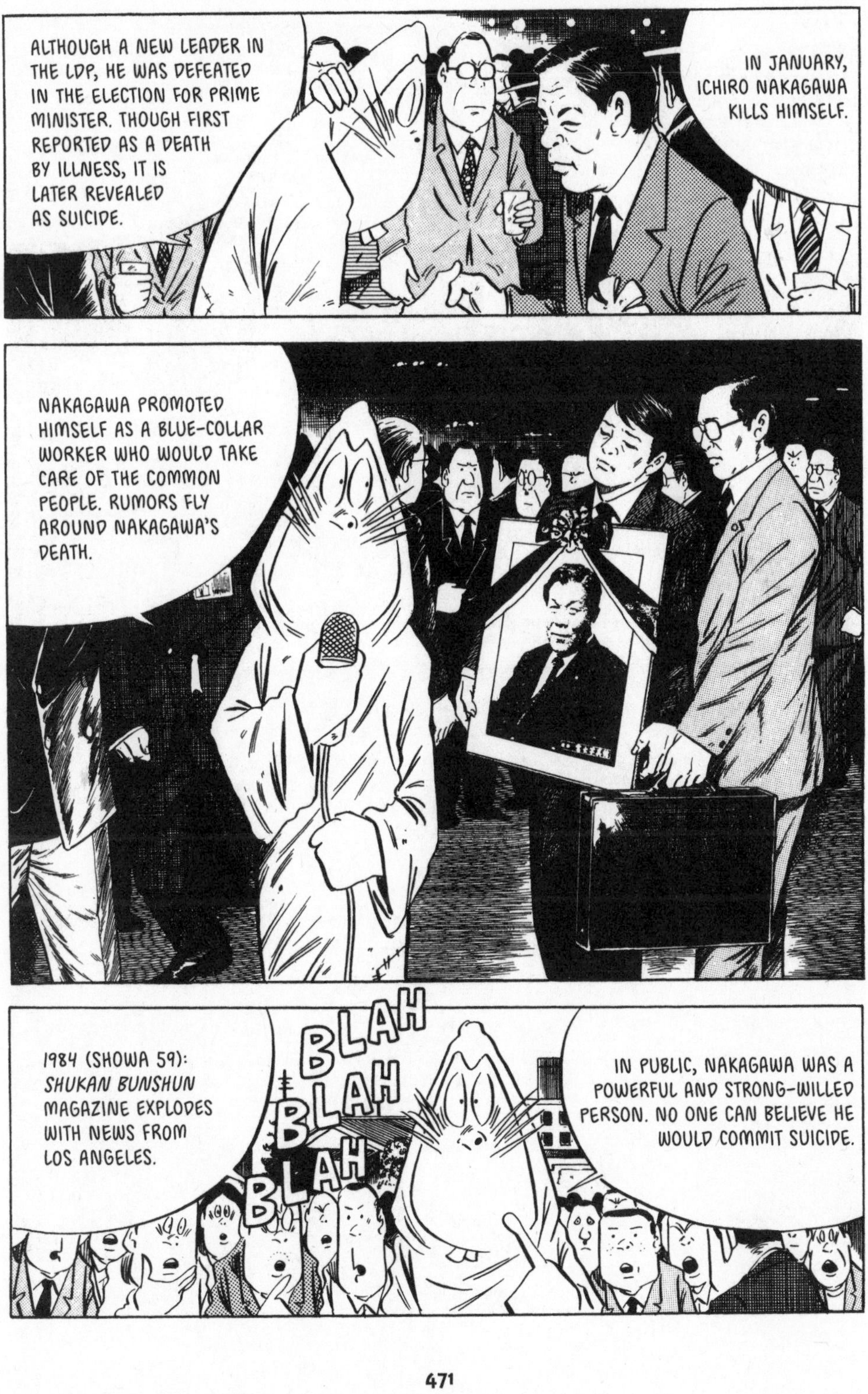
IN JANUARY, ICHIRO NAKAGAWA KILLS HIMSELF.
ALTHOUGH A NEW LEADER IN THE LDP, HE WAS DEFEATED IN THE ELECTION FOR PRIME MINISTER. THOUGH FIRST REPORTED AS A DEATH BY ILLNESS, IT IS LATER REVEALED AS SUICIDE.
NAKAGAWA PROMOTED HIMSELF AS A BLUE-COLLAR WORKER WHO WOULD TAKE CARE OF THE COMMON PEOPLE. RUMORS FLY AROUND NAKAGAWA'S DEATH.
IN PUBLIC, NAKAGAWA WAS A POWERFUL AND STRONG-WILLED PERSON. NO ONE CAN BELIEVE HE WOULD COMMIT SUICIDE.
BLAH BLAH BLAH BLAH
1984 (SHOWA 59): *SHUKAN BUNSHUN* MAGAZINE EXPLODES WITH NEWS FROM LOS ANGELES.

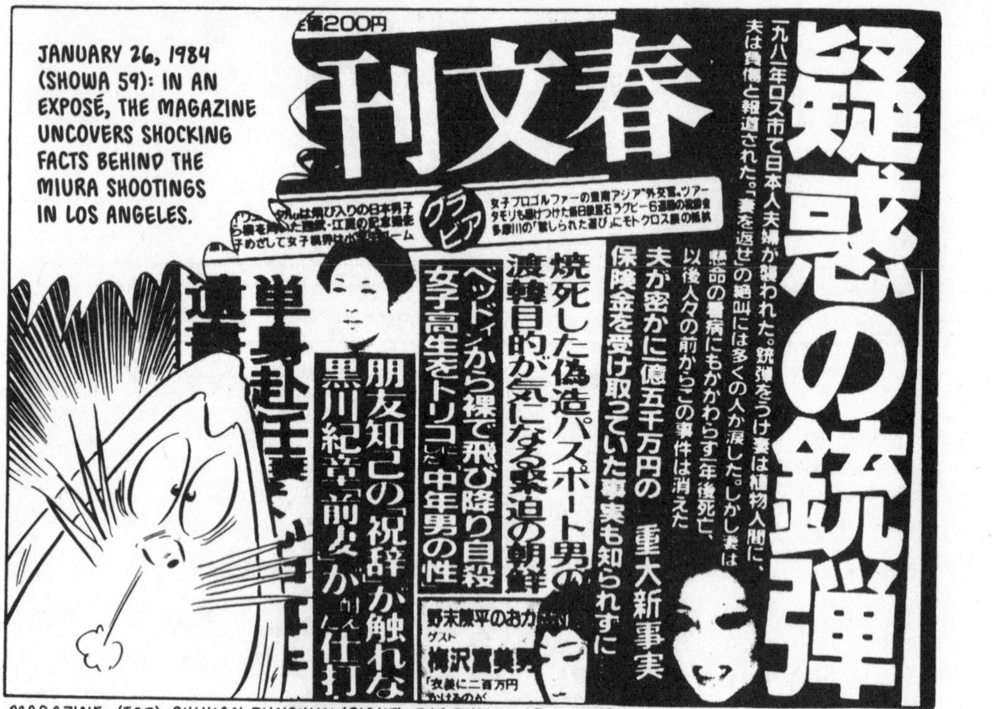
刊文春
疑惑の銃弾
一九八二年ロス市で日本人夫婦が襲われた。銃弾をうけ妻は植物人間に、夫は負傷と報道された。「妻を返せ」の絶叫には多くの人が涙した。しかし妻は懸命の看病にもかかわらず一年後死亡、以後人々の前からこの事件は消えた
夫が密かに一億五千万円の保険金を受け取っていた事実も知られずに
重大新事実
焼死した偽造パスポート男の渡韓目的が気になる緊迫の朝鮮
ベッドから裸で飛び降り自殺
JANUARY 26, 1984 (SHOWA 59): IN AN EXPOSÉ, THE MAGAZINE UNCOVERS SHOCKING FACTS BEHIND THE MIURA SHOOTINGS IN LOS ANGELES.

MAGAZINE: (TOP) *SHUKAN BUNSHUN* (RIGHT) *THE BULLET OF DOUBT!*

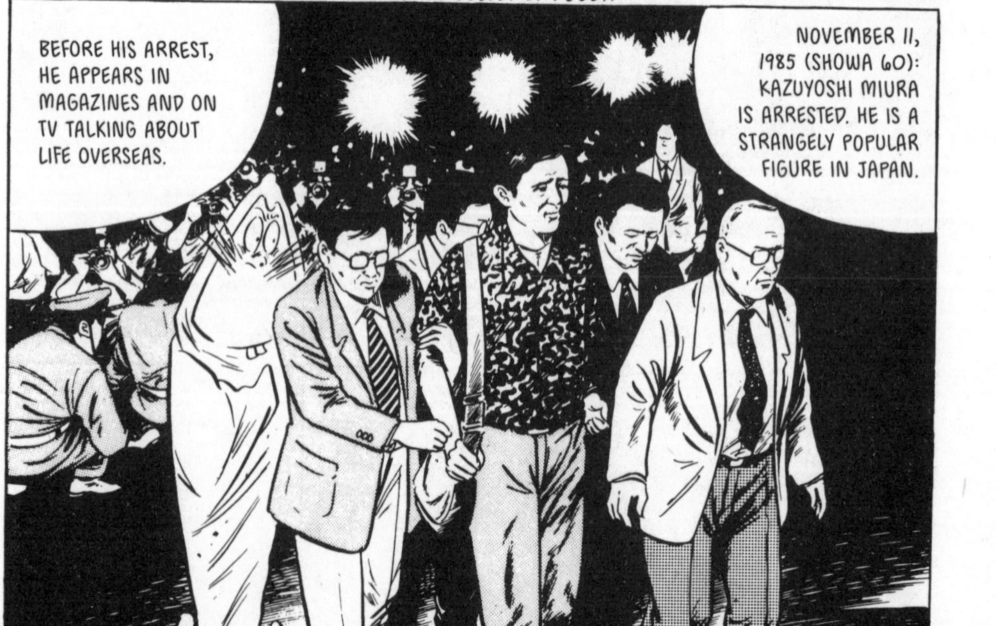
NOVEMBER 11, 1985 (SHOWA 60): KAZUYOSHI MIURA IS ARRESTED. HE IS A STRANGELY POPULAR FIGURE IN JAPAN.
BEFORE HIS ARREST, HE APPEARS IN MAGAZINES AND ON TV TALKING ABOUT LIFE OVERSEAS.

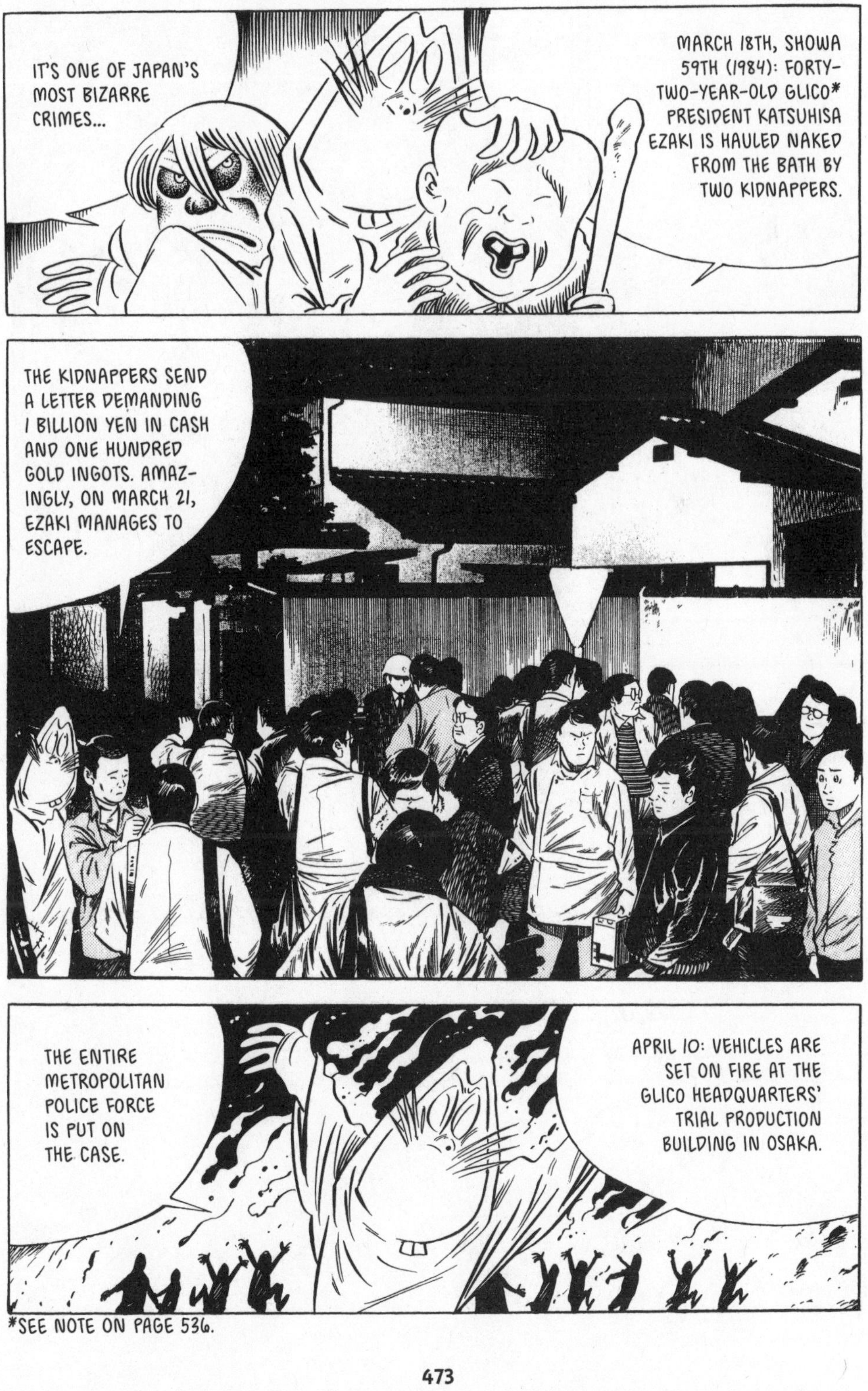
MARCH 18TH, SHOWA 59TH (1984): FORTY-TWO-YEAR-OLD GLICO* PRESIDENT KATSUHISA EZAKI IS HAULED NAKED FROM THE BATH BY TWO KIDNAPPERS.
IT'S ONE OF JAPAN'S MOST BIZARRE CRIMES...
THE KIDNAPPERS SEND A LETTER DEMANDING 1 BILLION YEN IN CASH AND ONE HUNDRED GOLD INGOTS. AMAZINGLY, ON MARCH 21, EZAKI MANAGES TO ESCAPE.
APRIL 10: VEHICLES ARE SET ON FIRE AT THE GLICO HEADQUARTERS' TRIAL PRODUCTION BUILDING IN OSAKA.
THE ENTIRE METROPOLITAN POLICE FORCE IS PUT ON THE CASE.

*SEE NOTE ON PAGE 536.

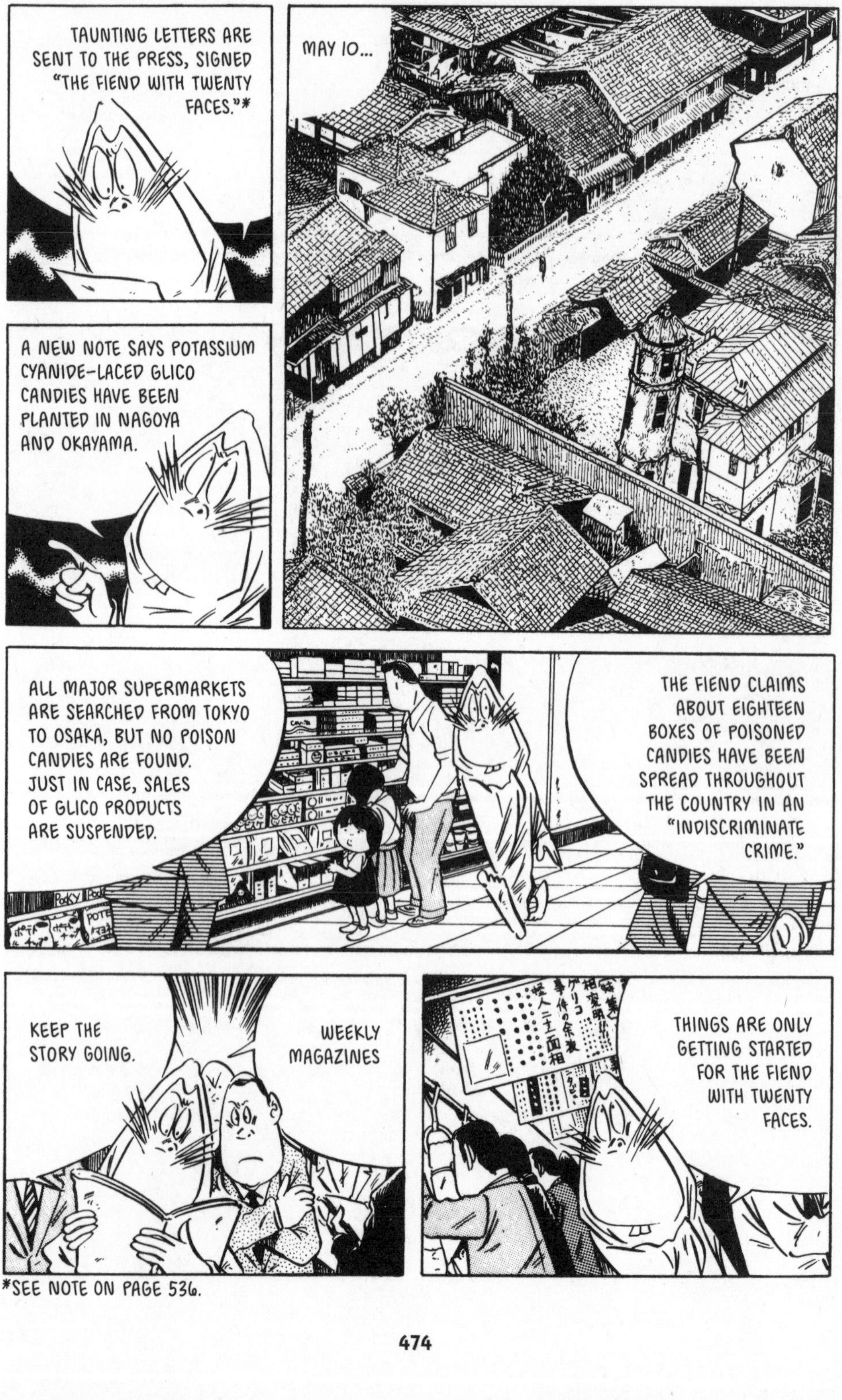
MAY 10...
TAUNTING LETTERS ARE SENT TO THE PRESS, SIGNED "THE FIEND WITH TWENTY FACES."*
A NEW NOTE SAYS POTASSIUM CYANIDE-LACED GLICO CANDIES HAVE BEEN PLANTED IN NAGOYA AND OKAYAMA.
THE FIEND CLAIMS ABOUT EIGHTEEN BOXES OF POISONED CANDIES HAVE BEEN SPREAD THROUGHOUT THE COUNTRY IN AN "INDISCRIMINATE CRIME."
ALL MAJOR SUPERMARKETS ARE SEARCHED FROM TOKYO TO OSAKA, BUT NO POISON CANDIES ARE FOUND. JUST IN CASE, SALES OF GLICO PRODUCTS ARE SUSPENDED.
THINGS ARE ONLY GETTING STARTED FOR THE FIEND WITH TWENTY FACES.
WEEKLY MAGAZINES
KEEP THE STORY GOING.

*SEE NOTE ON PAGE 536.

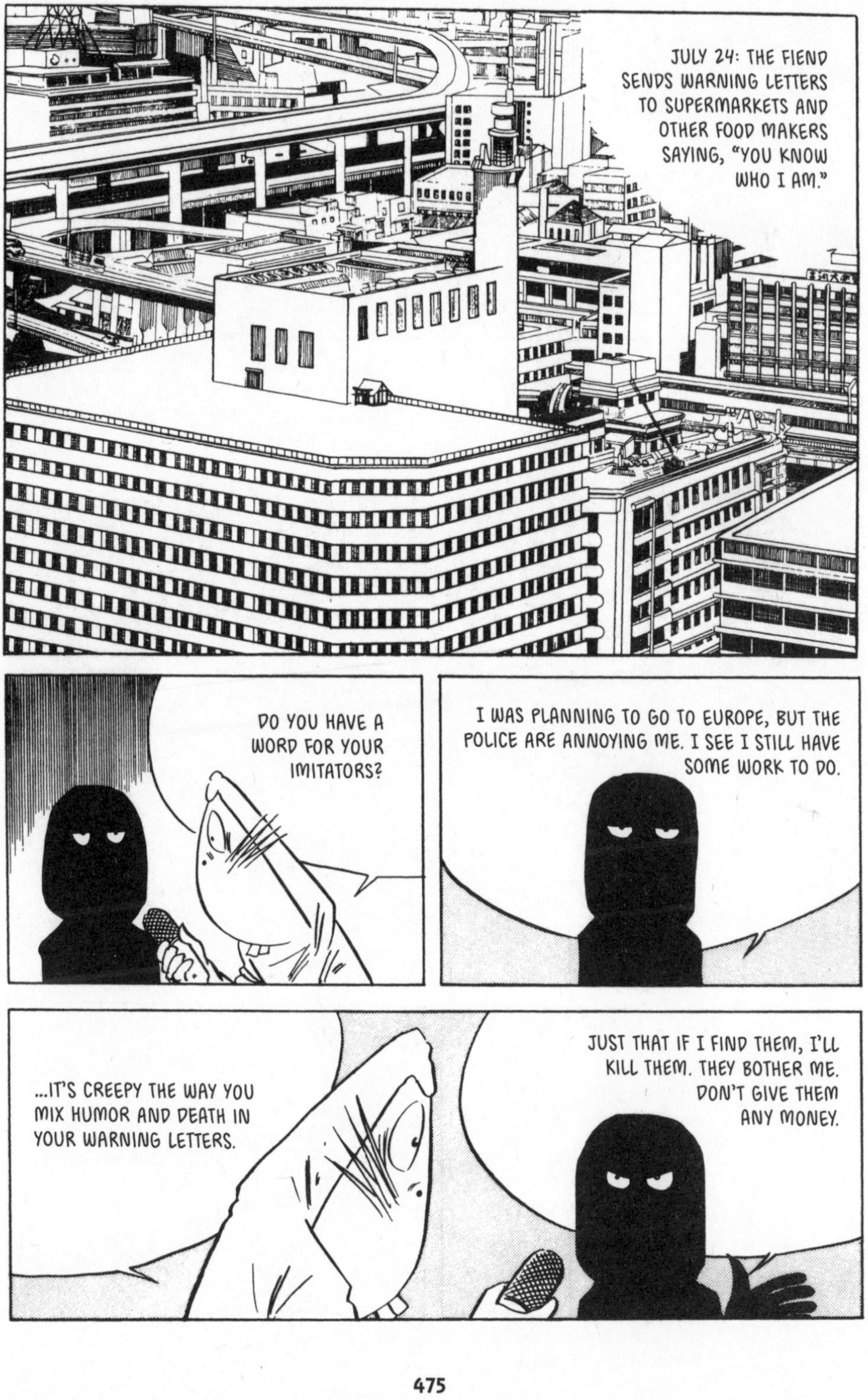
JULY 24: THE FIEND SENDS WARNING LETTERS TO SUPERMARKETS AND OTHER FOOD MAKERS SAYING, "YOU KNOW WHO I AM."
I WAS PLANNING TO GO TO EUROPE, BUT THE POLICE ARE ANNOYING ME. I SEE I STILL HAVE SOME WORK TO DO.
DO YOU HAVE A WORD FOR YOUR IMITATORS?
JUST THAT IF I FIND THEM, I'LL KILL THEM. THEY BOTHER ME. DON'T GIVE THEM ANY MONEY.
...IT'S CREEPY THE WAY YOU MIX HUMOR AND DEATH IN YOUR WARNING LETTERS.

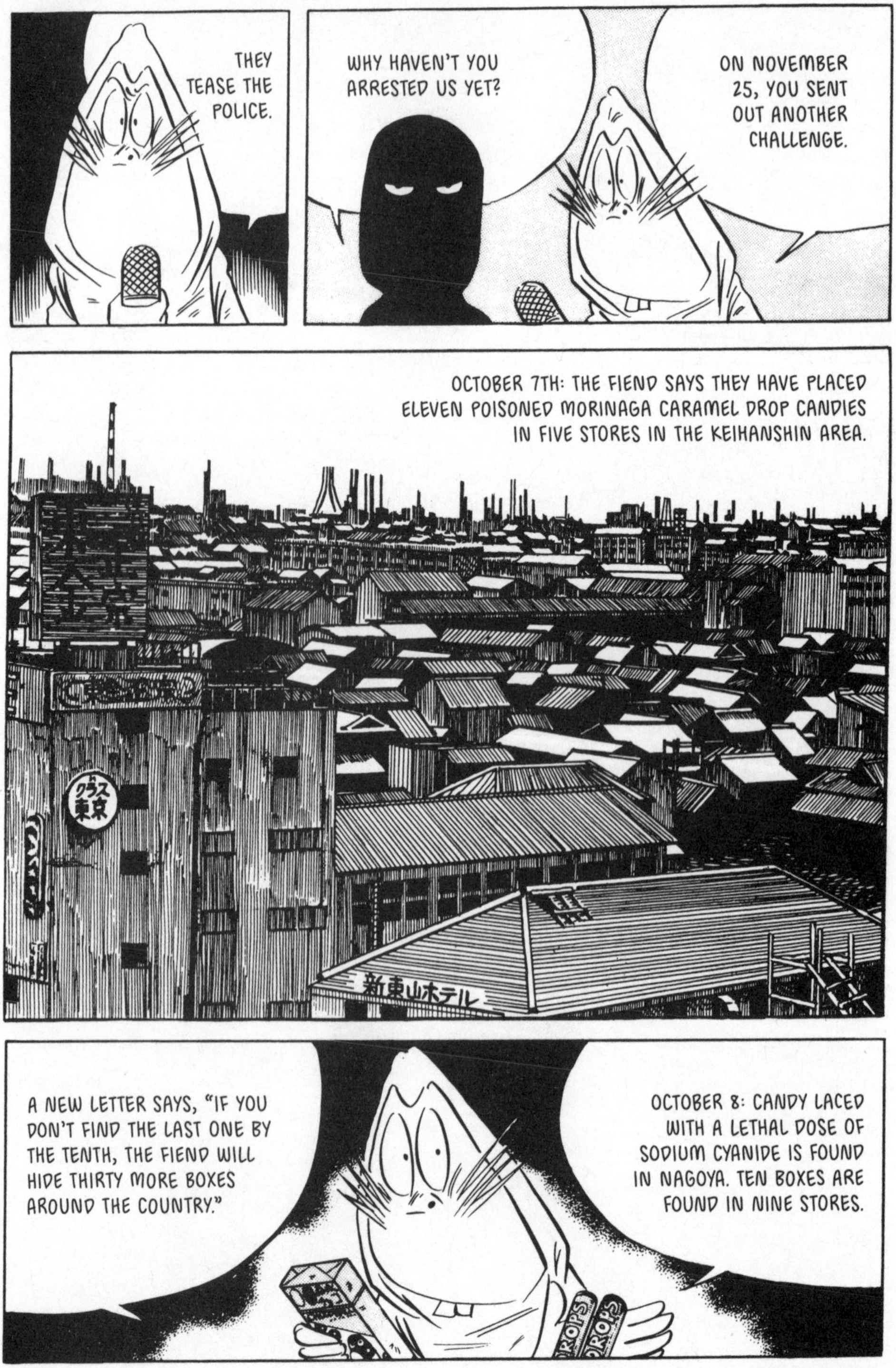
ON NOVEMBER 25, YOU SENT OUT ANOTHER CHALLENGE.
WHY HAVEN'T YOU ARRESTED US YET?
THEY TEASE THE POLICE.
OCTOBER 7TH: THE FIEND SAYS THEY HAVE PLACED ELEVEN POISONED MORINAGA CARAMEL DROP CANDIES IN FIVE STORES IN THE KEIHANSHIN AREA.
OCTOBER 8: CANDY LACED WITH A LETHAL DOSE OF SODIUM CYANIDE IS FOUND IN NAGOYA. TEN BOXES ARE FOUND IN NINE STORES.
A NEW LETTER SAYS, "IF YOU DON'T FIND THE LAST ONE BY THE TENTH, THE FIEND WILL HIDE THIRTY MORE BOXES AROUND THE COUNTRY."

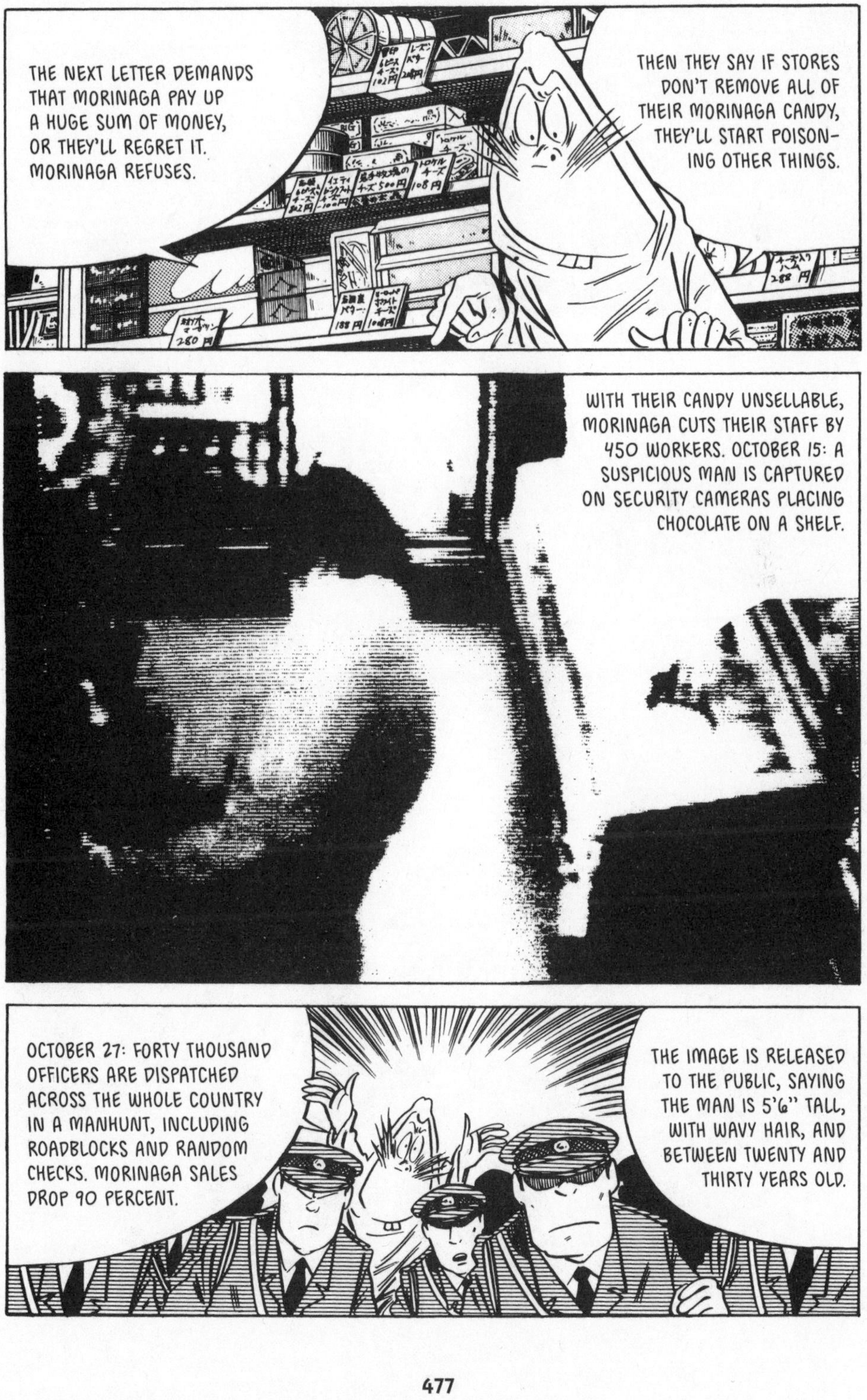
THEN THEY SAY IF STORES DON'T REMOVE ALL OF THEIR MORINAGA CANDY, THEY'LL START POISON-ING OTHER THINGS.
THE NEXT LETTER DEMANDS THAT MORINAGA PAY UP A HUGE SUM OF MONEY, OR THEY'LL REGRET IT. MORINAGA REFUSES.
WITH THEIR CANDY UNSELLABLE, MORINAGA CUTS THEIR STAFF BY 450 WORKERS. OCTOBER 15: A SUSPICIOUS MAN IS CAPTURED ON SECURITY CAMERAS PLACING CHOCOLATE ON A SHELF.
THE IMAGE IS RELEASED TO THE PUBLIC, SAYING THE MAN IS 5'6" TALL, WITH WAVY HAIR, AND BETWEEN TWENTY AND THIRTY YEARS OLD.
OCTOBER 27: FORTY THOUSAND OFFICERS ARE DISPATCHED ACROSS THE WHOLE COUNTRY IN A MANHUNT, INCLUDING ROADBLOCKS AND RANDOM CHECKS. MORINAGA SALES DROP 90 PERCENT.

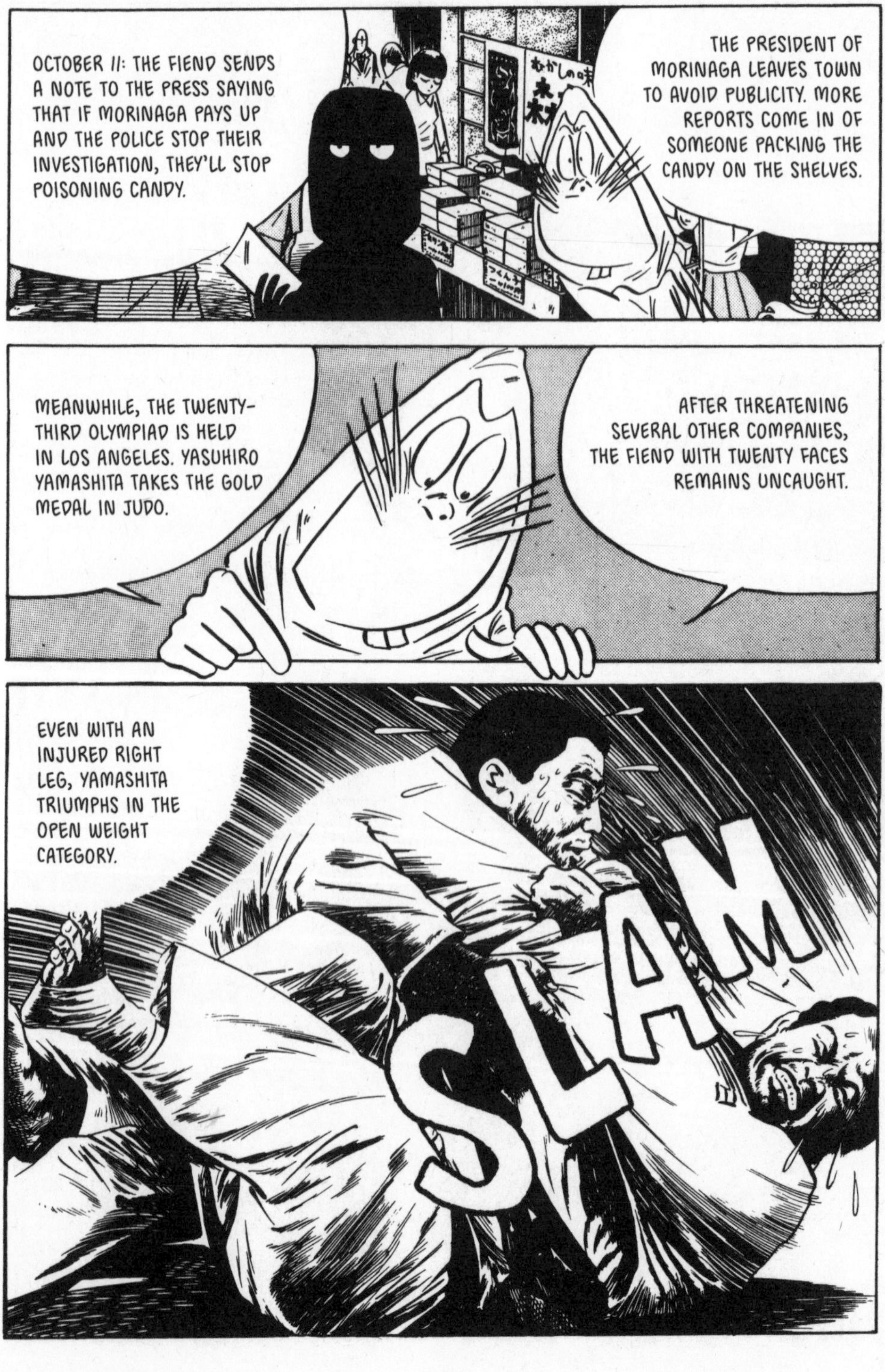
THE PRESIDENT OF MORINAGA LEAVES TOWN TO AVOID PUBLICITY. MORE REPORTS COME IN OF SOMEONE PACKING THE CANDY ON THE SHELVES.
OCTOBER 11: THE FIEND SENDS A NOTE TO THE PRESS SAYING THAT IF MORINAGA PAYS UP AND THE POLICE STOP THEIR INVESTIGATION, THEY'LL STOP POISONING CANDY.
AFTER THREATENING SEVERAL OTHER COMPANIES, THE FIEND WITH TWENTY FACES REMAINS UNCAUGHT.
MEANWHILE, THE TWENTY-THIRD OLYMPIAD IS HELD IN LOS ANGELES. YASUHIRO YAMASHITA TAKES THE GOLD MEDAL IN JUDO.
EVEN WITH AN INJURED RIGHT LEG, YAMASHITA TRIUMPHS IN THE OPEN WEIGHT CATEGORY.
SLAM

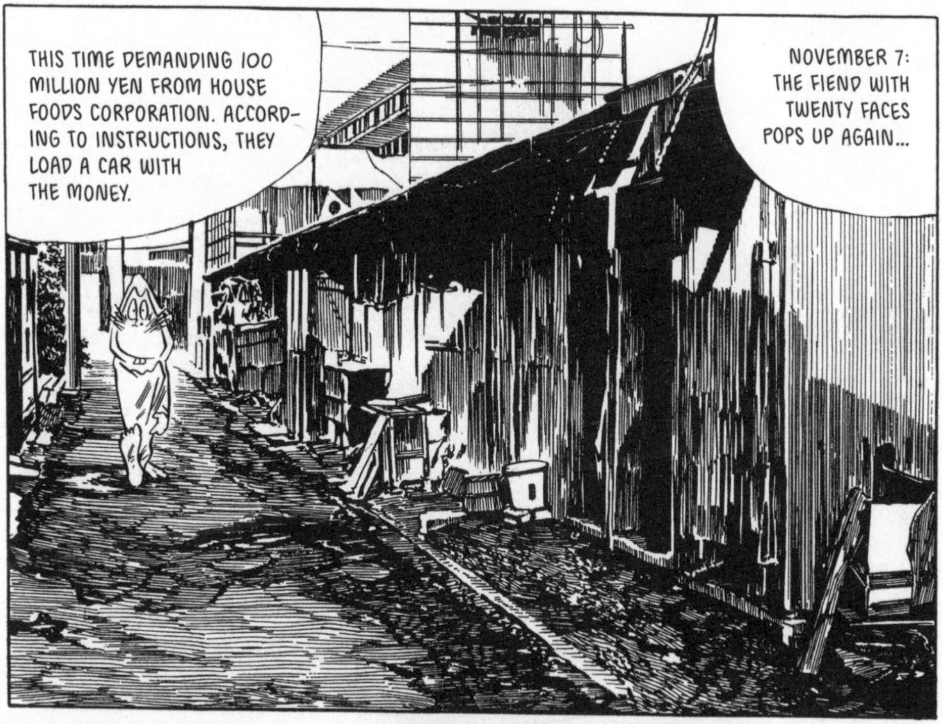
NOVEMBER 7: THE FIEND WITH TWENTY FACES POPS UP AGAIN...
THIS TIME DEMANDING 100 MILLION YEN FROM HOUSE FOODS CORPORATION. ACCORDING TO INSTRUCTIONS, THEY LOAD A CAR WITH THE MONEY.

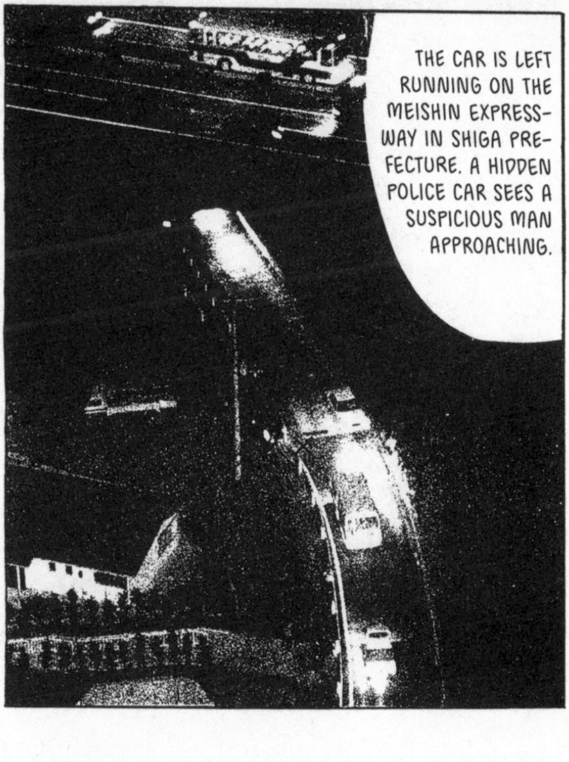
THE CAR IS LEFT RUNNING ON THE MEISHIN EXPRESSWAY IN SHIGA PREFECTURE. A HIDDEN POLICE CAR SEES A SUSPICIOUS MAN APPROACHING.

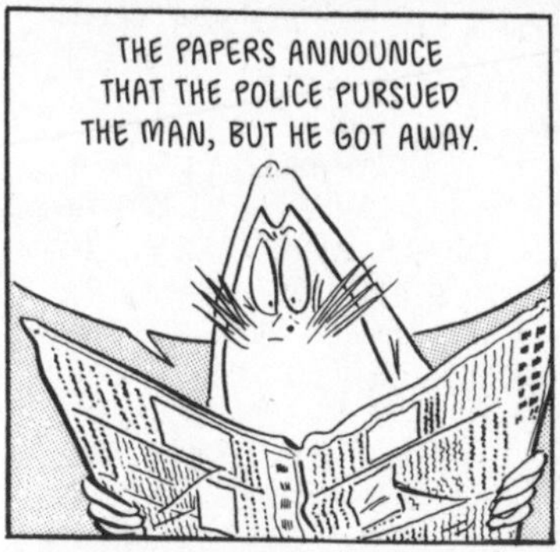
THE PAPERS ANNOUNCE THAT THE POLICE PURSUED THE MAN, BUT HE GOT AWAY.

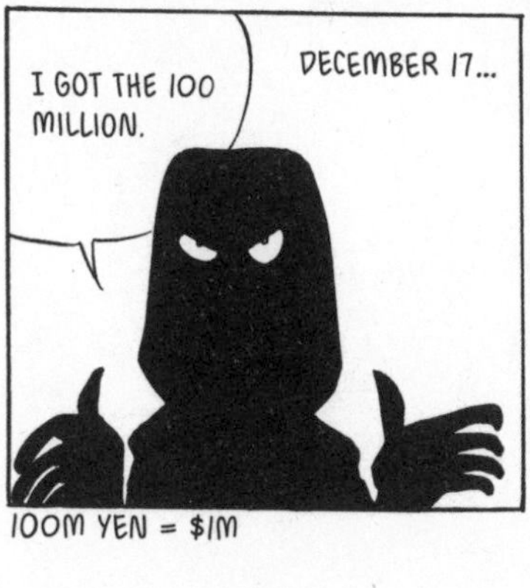
DECEMBER 17...
I GOT THE 100 MILLION.

100M YEN = $1M

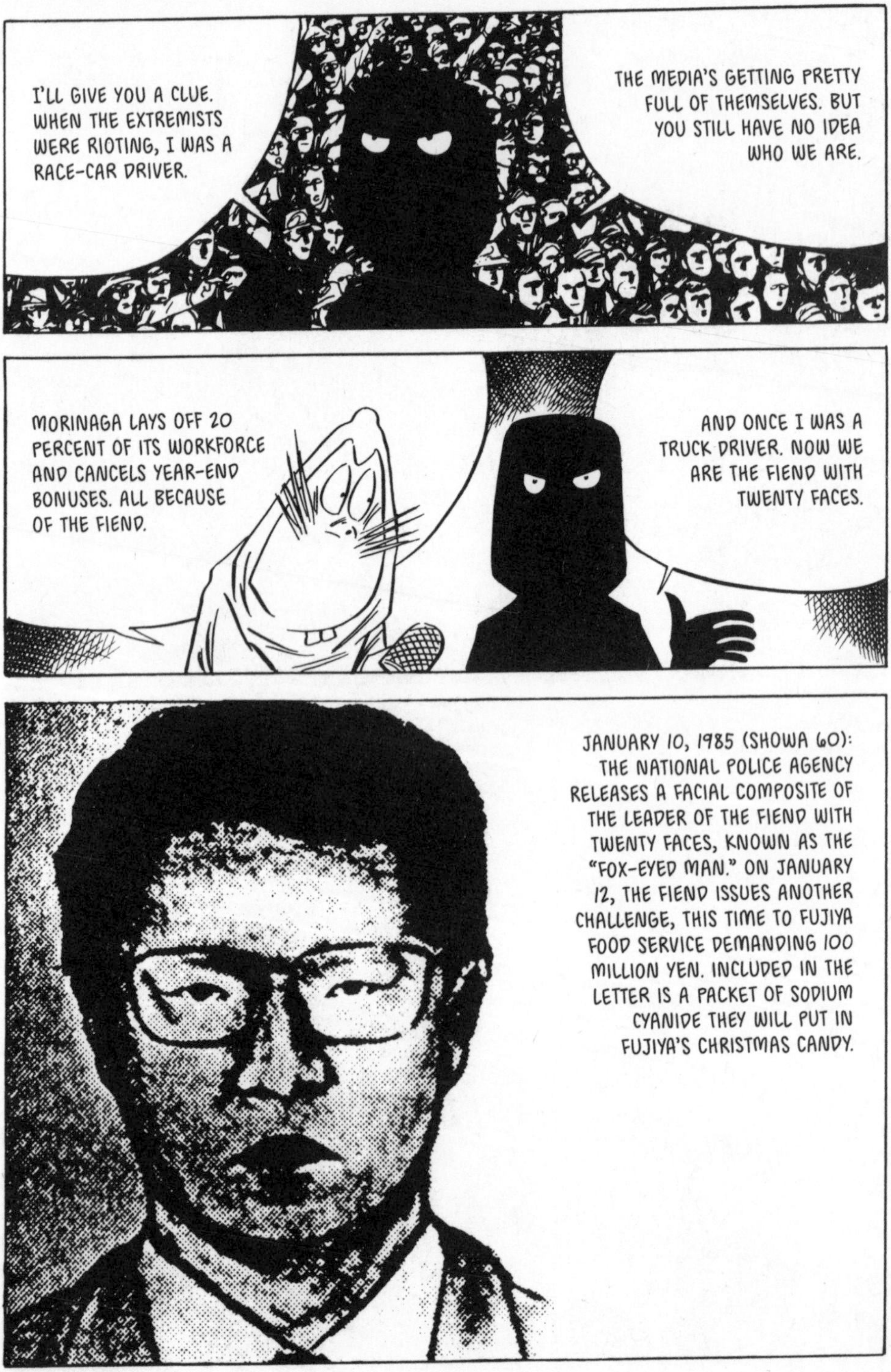
THE MEDIA'S GETTING PRETTY FULL OF THEMSELVES. BUT YOU STILL HAVE NO IDEA WHO WE ARE.
I'LL GIVE YOU A CLUE. WHEN THE EXTREMISTS WERE RIOTING, I WAS A RACE-CAR DRIVER.
AND ONCE I WAS A TRUCK DRIVER. NOW WE ARE THE FIEND WITH TWENTY FACES.
MORINAGA LAYS OFF 20 PERCENT OF ITS WORKFORCE AND CANCELS YEAR-END BONUSES. ALL BECAUSE OF THE FIEND.
JANUARY 10, 1985 (SHOWA 60): THE NATIONAL POLICE AGENCY RELEASES A FACIAL COMPOSITE OF THE LEADER OF THE FIEND WITH TWENTY FACES, KNOWN AS THE "FOX-EYED MAN." ON JANUARY 12, THE FIEND ISSUES ANOTHER CHALLENGE, THIS TIME TO FUJIYA FOOD SERVICE DEMANDING 100 MILLION YEN. INCLUDED IN THE LETTER IS A PACKET OF SODIUM CYANIDE THEY WILL PUT IN FUJIYA'S CHRISTMAS CANDY.

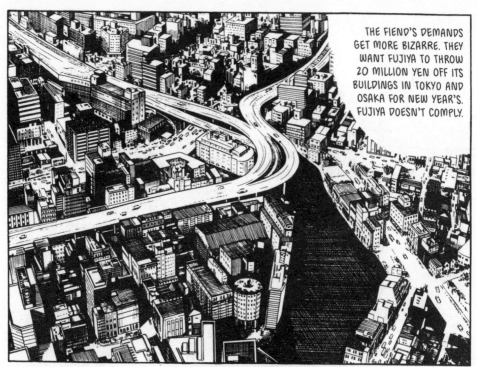

THE FIEND'S DEMANDS GET MORE BIZARRE. THEY WANT FUJIYA TO THROW 20 MILLION YEN OFF ITS BUILDINGS IN TOKYO AND OSAKA FOR NEW YEAR'S. FUJIYA DOESN'T COMPLY.
NOW THEY WANT 200 MILLION FROM MORINAGA, THIS TIME DELIVERED IN SECRET.
MORINAGA AND FUJIYA AGREE TO STOP COMPETING AND WORK TOGETHER TO PAY OFF THE FIEND.
JANUARY 16: THE FIEND DEMANDS 1.3 BILLION YEN IN TOTAL, FROM THIRTY-ONE DIFFERENT COMPANIES.
AND WE'RE GOING TO GET IT.

1.3B YEN = $13M

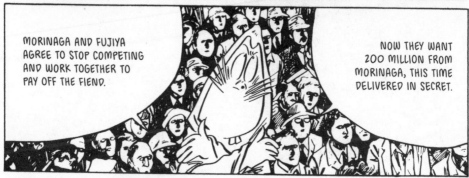

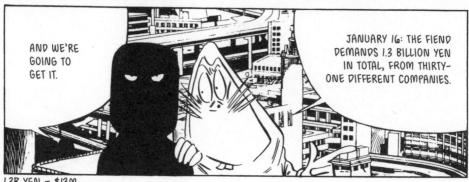

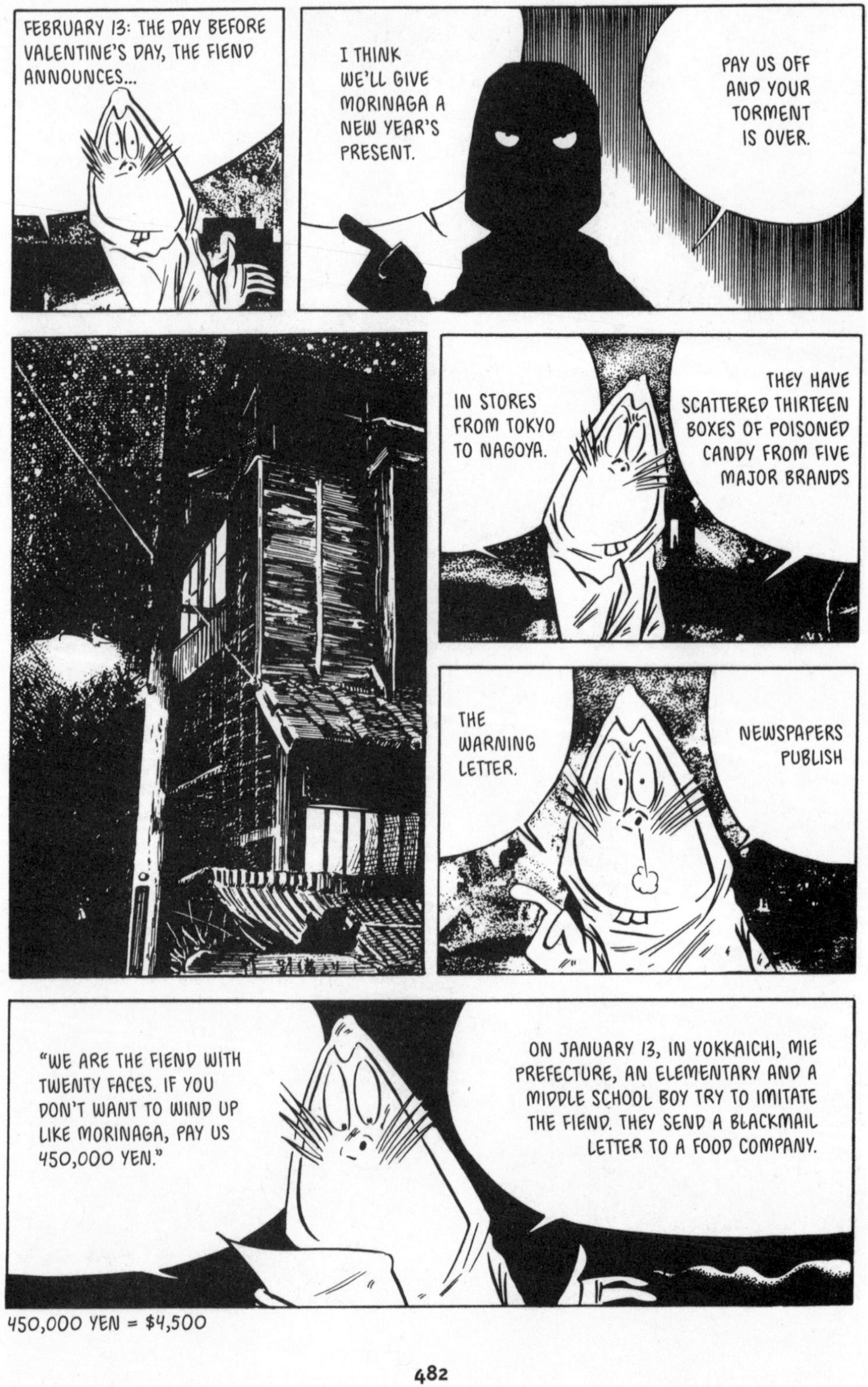
PAY US OFF AND YOUR TORMENT IS OVER.
I THINK WE'LL GIVE MORINAGA A NEW YEAR'S PRESENT.
FEBRUARY 13: THE DAY BEFORE VALENTINE'S DAY, THE FIEND ANNOUNCES...
THEY HAVE SCATTERED THIRTEEN BOXES OF POISONED CANDY FROM FIVE MAJOR BRANDS
IN STORES FROM TOKYO TO NAGOYA.
NEWSPAPERS PUBLISH
THE WARNING LETTER.
ON JANUARY 13, IN YOKKAICHI, MIE PREFECTURE, AN ELEMENTARY AND A MIDDLE SCHOOL BOY TRY TO IMITATE THE FIEND. THEY SEND A BLACKMAIL LETTER TO A FOOD COMPANY.
"WE ARE THE FIEND WITH TWENTY FACES. IF YOU DON'T WANT TO WIND UP LIKE MORINAGA, PAY US 450,000 YEN."

450,000 YEN = $4,500

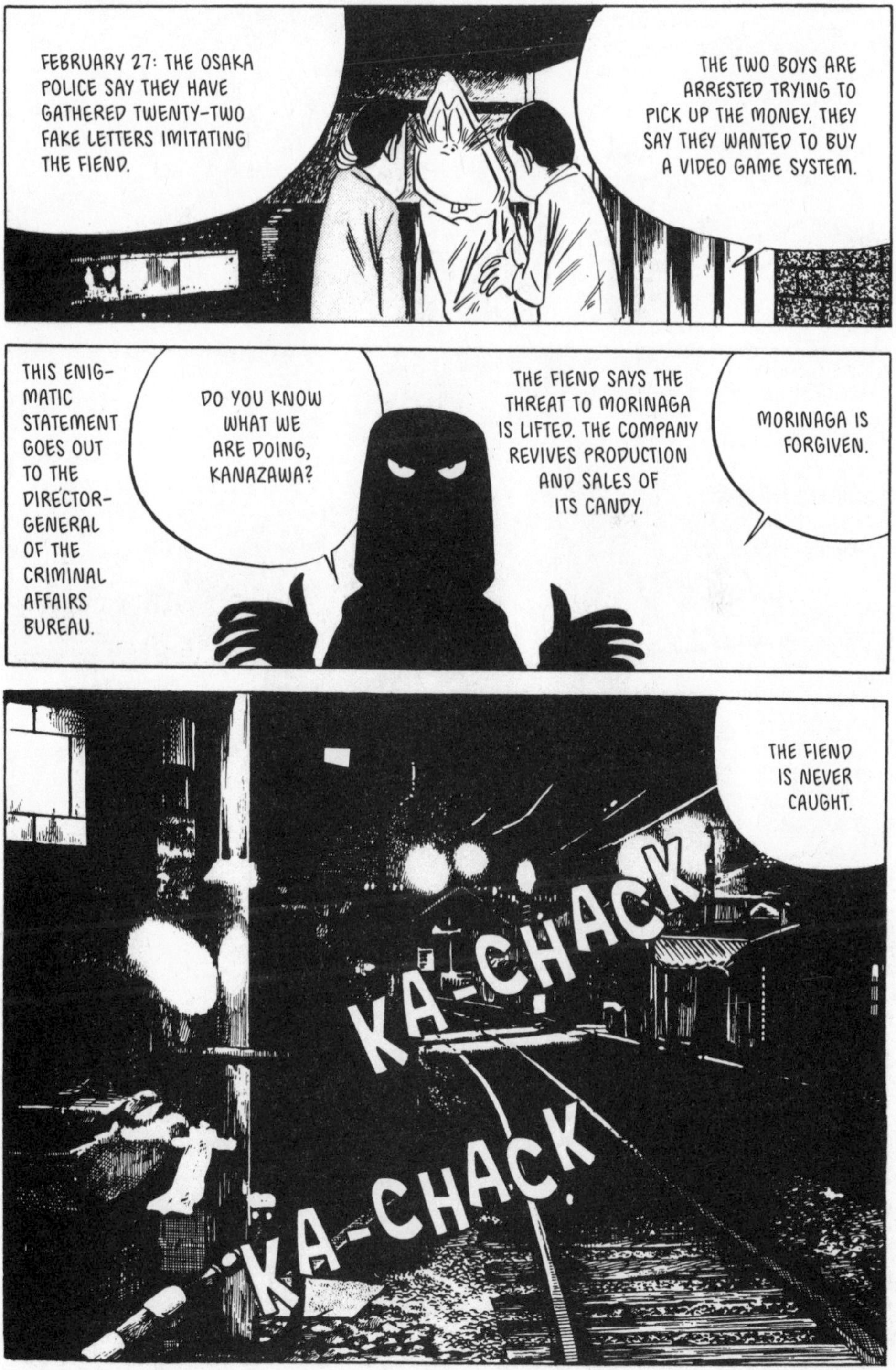
THE TWO BOYS ARE ARRESTED TRYING TO PICK UP THE MONEY. THEY SAY THEY WANTED TO BUY A VIDEO GAME SYSTEM.
FEBRUARY 27: THE OSAKA POLICE SAY THEY HAVE GATHERED TWENTY-TWO FAKE LETTERS IMITATING THE FIEND.
MORINAGA IS FORGIVEN.
THE FIEND SAYS THE THREAT TO MORINAGA IS LIFTED. THE COMPANY REVIVES PRODUCTION AND SALES OF ITS CANDY.
DO YOU KNOW WHAT WE ARE DOING, KANAZAWA?
THIS ENIGMATIC STATEMENT GOES OUT TO THE DIRECTOR-GENERAL OF THE CRIMINAL AFFAIRS BUREAU.
THE FIEND IS NEVER CAUGHT.
KA-CHACK
KA-CHACK

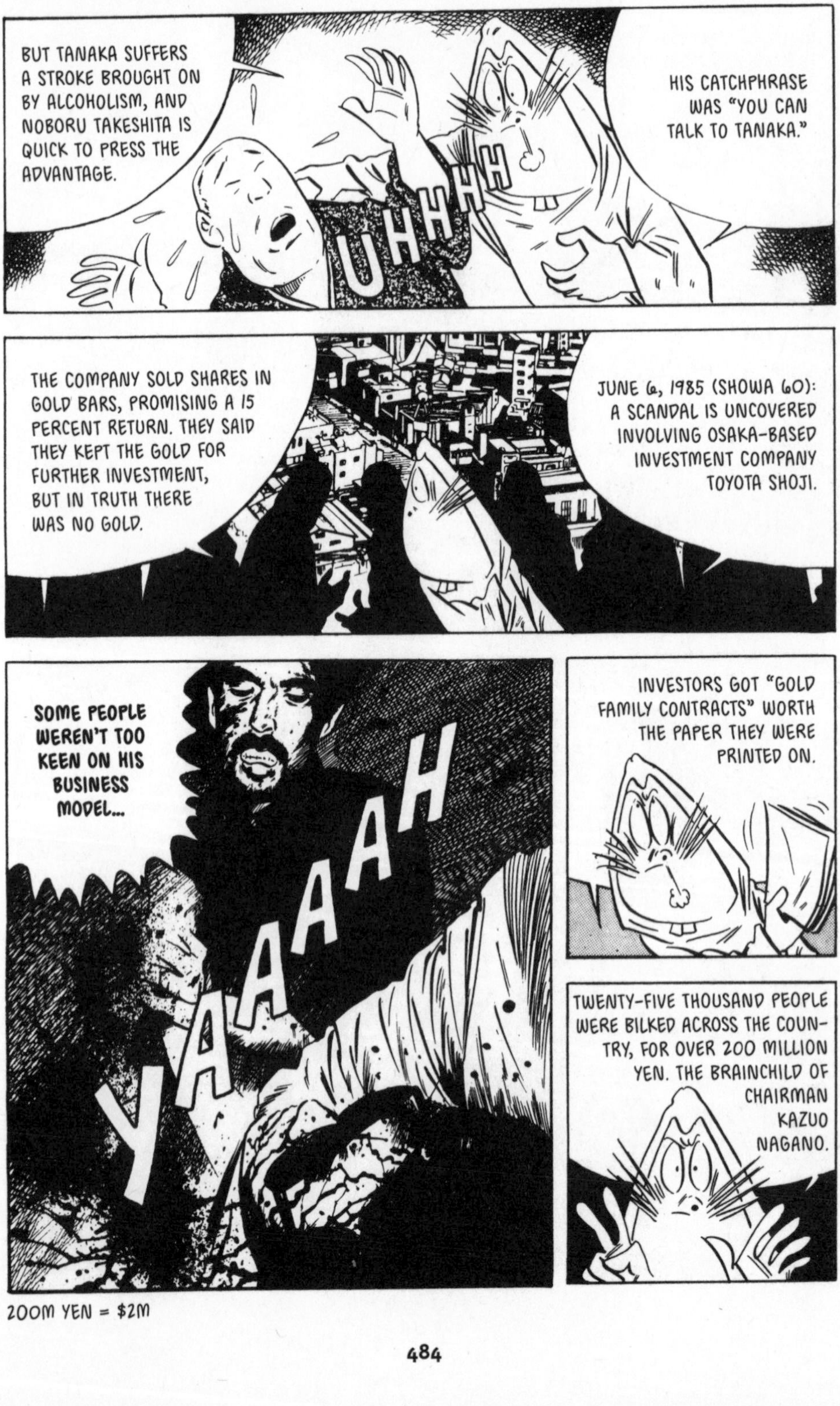
HIS CATCHPHRASE WAS "YOU CAN TALK TO TANAKA."
UHHHHH
BUT TANAKA SUFFERS A STROKE BROUGHT ON BY ALCOHOLISM, AND NOBORU TAKESHITA IS QUICK TO PRESS THE ADVANTAGE.
JUNE 6, 1985 (SHOWA 60): A SCANDAL IS UNCOVERED INVOLVING OSAKA-BASED INVESTMENT COMPANY TOYOTA SHOJI.
THE COMPANY SOLD SHARES IN GOLD BARS, PROMISING A 15 PERCENT RETURN. THEY SAID THEY KEPT THE GOLD FOR FURTHER INVESTMENT, BUT IN TRUTH THERE WAS NO GOLD.
INVESTORS GOT "GOLD FAMILY CONTRACTS" WORTH THE PAPER THEY WERE PRINTED ON.
TWENTY-FIVE THOUSAND PEOPLE WERE BILKED ACROSS THE COUNTRY, FOR OVER 200 MILLION YEN. THE BRAINCHILD OF CHAIRMAN KAZUO NAGANO.
SOME PEOPLE WEREN'T TOO KEEN ON HIS BUSINESS MODEL...
YAAAAAH

200M YEN = $2M

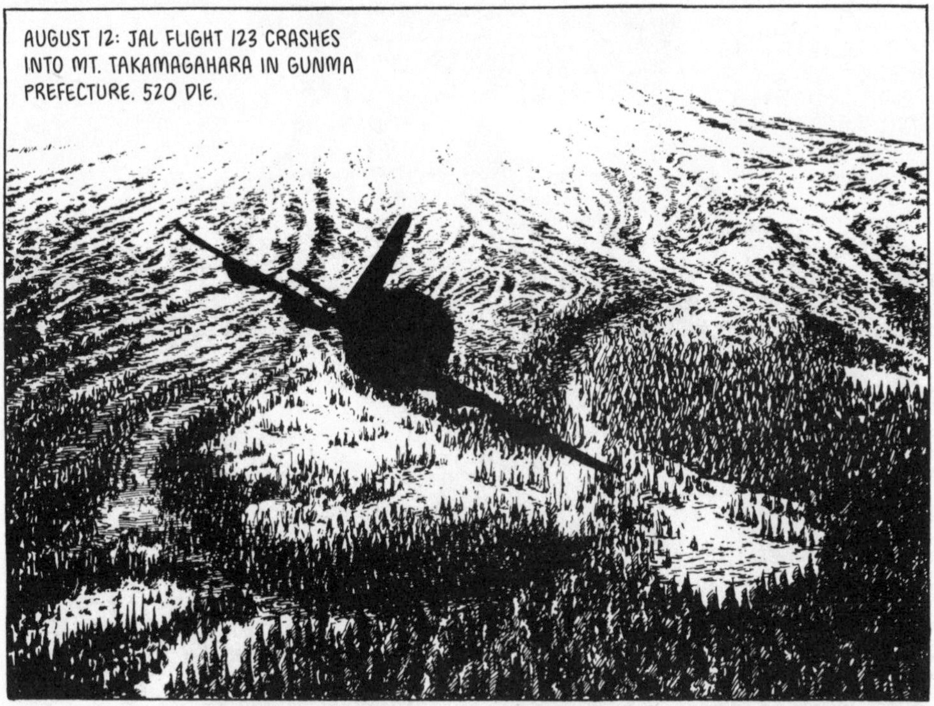
AUGUST 12: JAL FLIGHT 123 CRASHES INTO MT. TAKAMAGAHARA IN GUNMA PREFECTURE. 520 DIE.

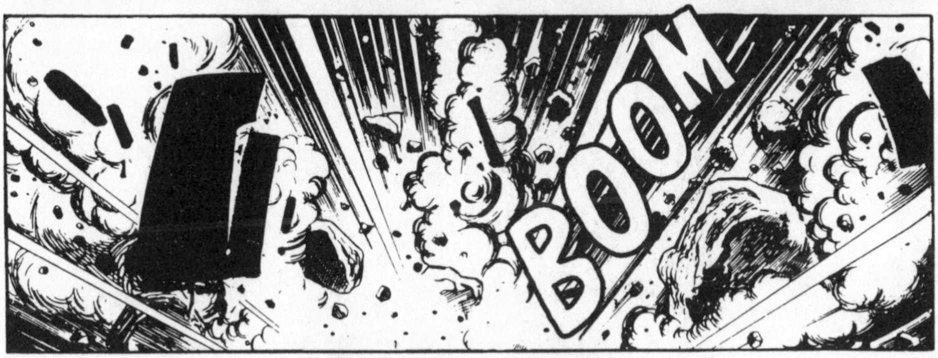
BOOM

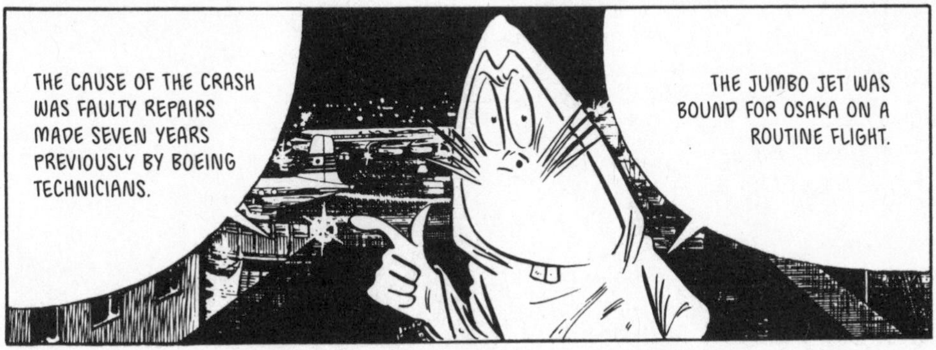
THE JUMBO JET WAS BOUND FOR OSAKA ON A ROUTINE FLIGHT.
THE CAUSE OF THE CRASH WAS FAULTY REPAIRS MADE SEVEN YEARS PREVIOUSLY BY BOEING TECHNICIANS.

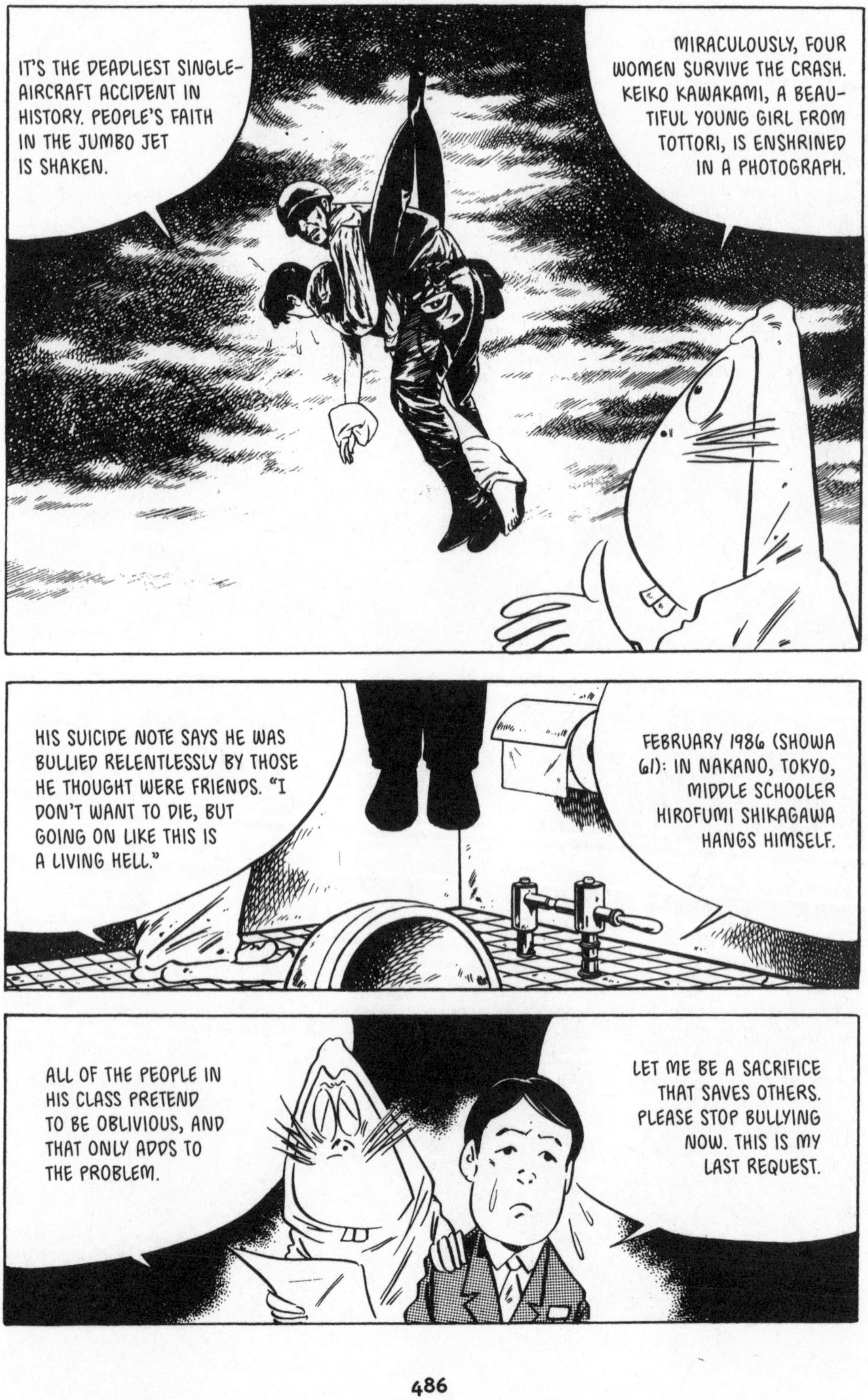
MIRACULOUSLY, FOUR WOMEN SURVIVE THE CRASH. KEIKO KAWAKAMI, A BEAU-TIFUL YOUNG GIRL FROM TOTTORI, IS ENSHRINED IN A PHOTOGRAPH.
IT'S THE DEADLIEST SINGLE-AIRCRAFT ACCIDENT IN HISTORY. PEOPLE'S FAITH IN THE JUMBO JET IS SHAKEN.
FEBRUARY 1986 (SHOWA 61): IN NAKANO, TOKYO, MIDDLE SCHOOLER HIROFUMI SHIKAGAWA HANGS HIMSELF.
HIS SUICIDE NOTE SAYS HE WAS BULLIED RELENTLESSLY BY THOSE HE THOUGHT WERE FRIENDS. "I DON'T WANT TO DIE, BUT GOING ON LIKE THIS IS A LIVING HELL."
LET ME BE A SACRIFICE THAT SAVES OTHERS. PLEASE STOP BULLYING NOW. THIS IS MY LAST REQUEST.
ALL OF THE PEOPLE IN HIS CLASS PRETEND TO BE OBLIVIOUS, AND THAT ONLY ADDS TO THE PROBLEM.

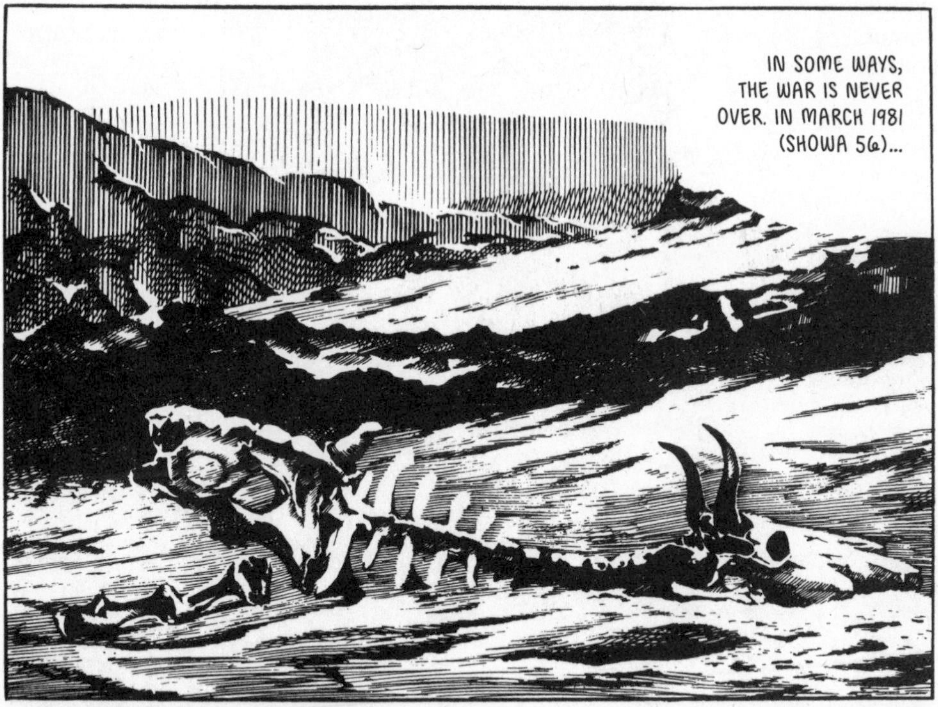
IN SOME WAYS, THE WAR IS NEVER OVER. IN MARCH 1981 (SHOWA 56)...

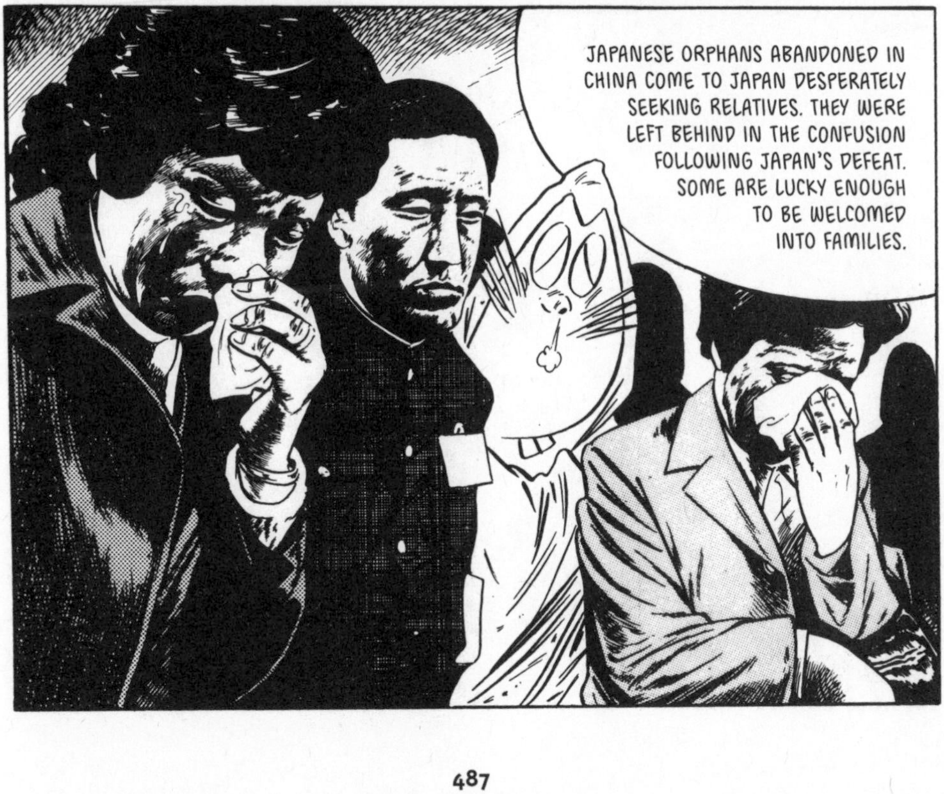
JAPANESE ORPHANS ABANDONED IN CHINA COME TO JAPAN DESPERATELY SEEKING RELATIVES. THEY WERE LEFT BEHIND IN THE CONFUSION FOLLOWING JAPAN'S DEFEAT. SOME ARE LUCKY ENOUGH TO BE WELCOMED INTO FAMILIES.

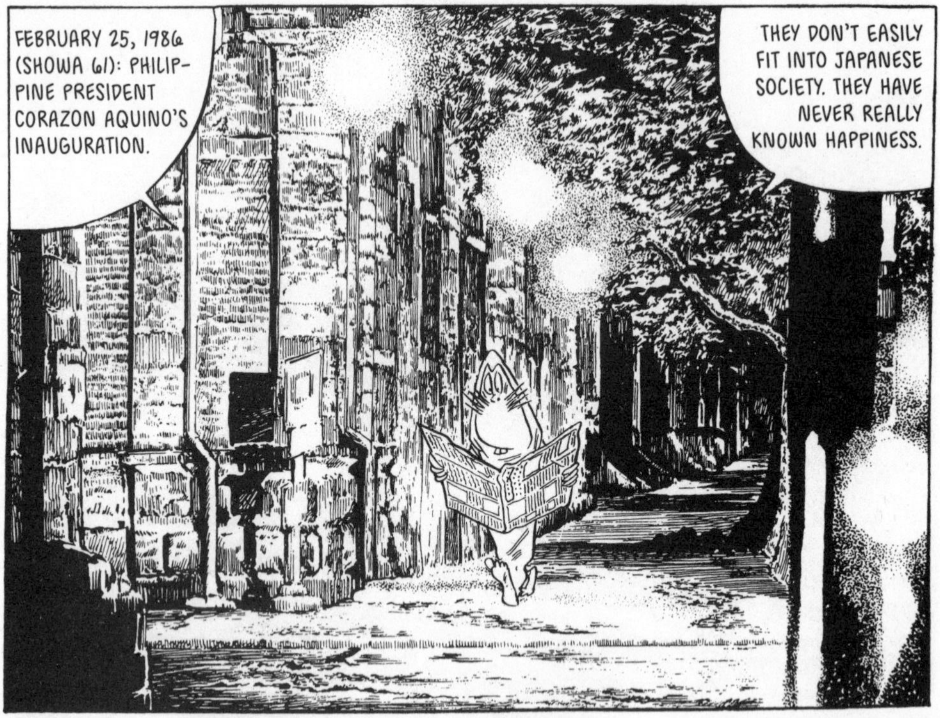
THEY DON'T EASILY FIT INTO JAPANESE SOCIETY. THEY HAVE NEVER REALLY KNOWN HAPPINESS.
FEBRUARY 25, 1986 (SHOWA 61): PHILIP-PINE PRESIDENT CORAZON AQUINO'S INAUGURATION.

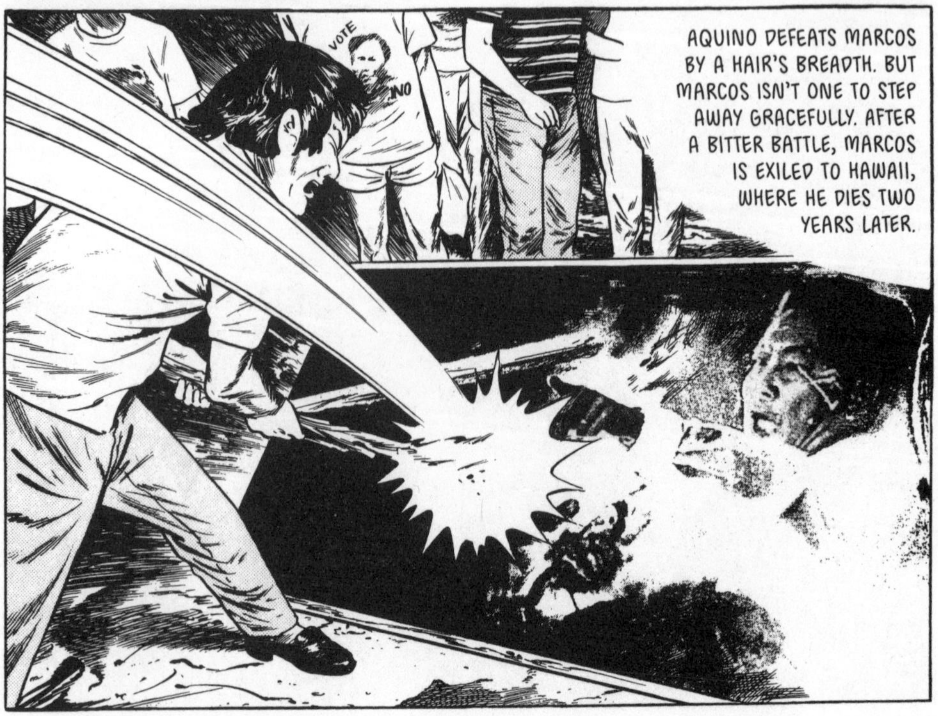
AQUINO DEFEATS MARCOS BY A HAIR'S BREADTH. BUT MARCOS ISN'T ONE TO STEP AWAY GRACEFULLY. AFTER A BITTER BATTLE, MARCOS IS EXILED TO HAWAII, WHERE HE DIES TWO YEARS LATER.
VOTE

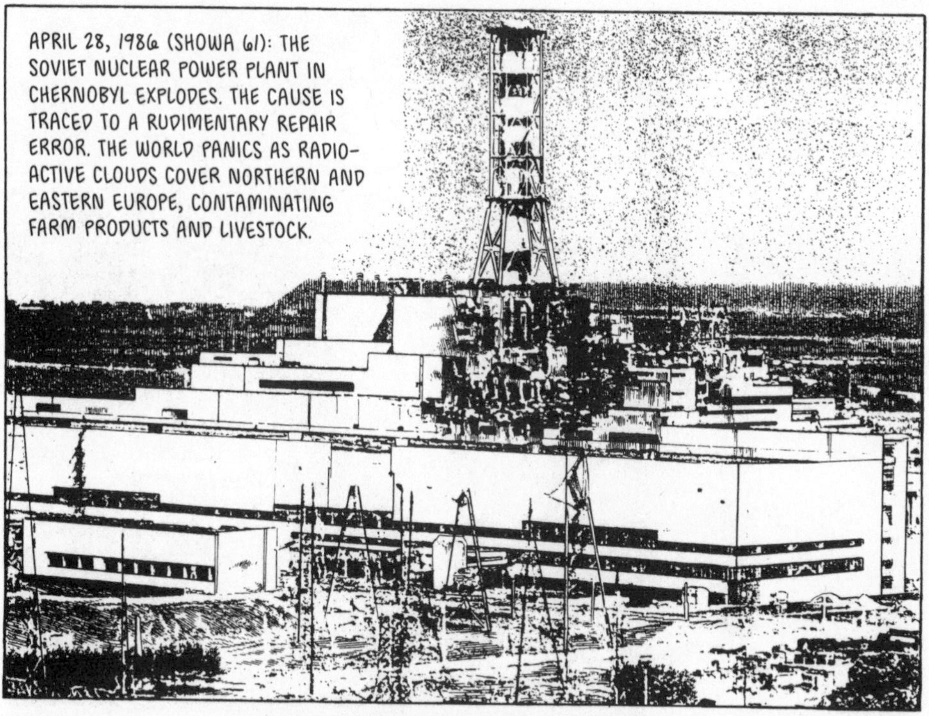
APRIL 28, 1986 (SHOWA 61): THE SOVIET NUCLEAR POWER PLANT IN CHERNOBYL EXPLODES. THE CAUSE IS TRACED TO A RUDIMENTARY REPAIR ERROR. THE WORLD PANICS AS RADIO-ACTIVE CLOUDS COVER NORTHERN AND EASTERN EUROPE, CONTAMINATING FARM PRODUCTS AND LIVESTOCK.

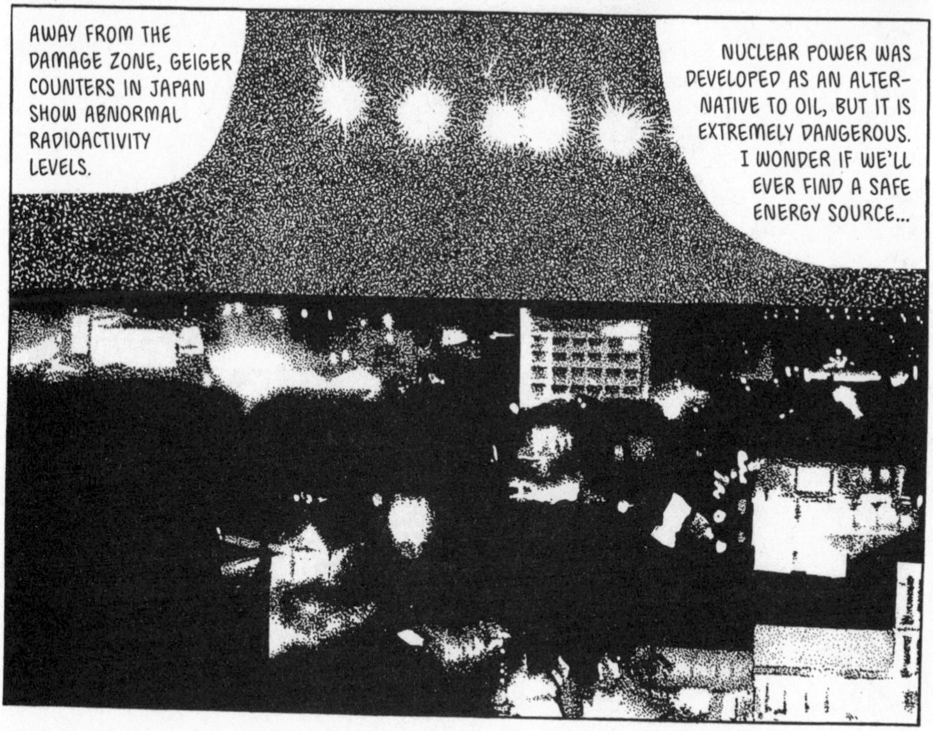
NUCLEAR POWER WAS DEVELOPED AS AN ALTER-NATIVE TO OIL, BUT IT IS EXTREMELY DANGEROUS. I WONDER IF WE'LL EVER FIND A SAFE ENERGY SOURCE...
AWAY FROM THE DAMAGE ZONE, GEIGER COUNTERS IN JAPAN SHOW ABNORMAL RADIOACTIVITY LEVELS.

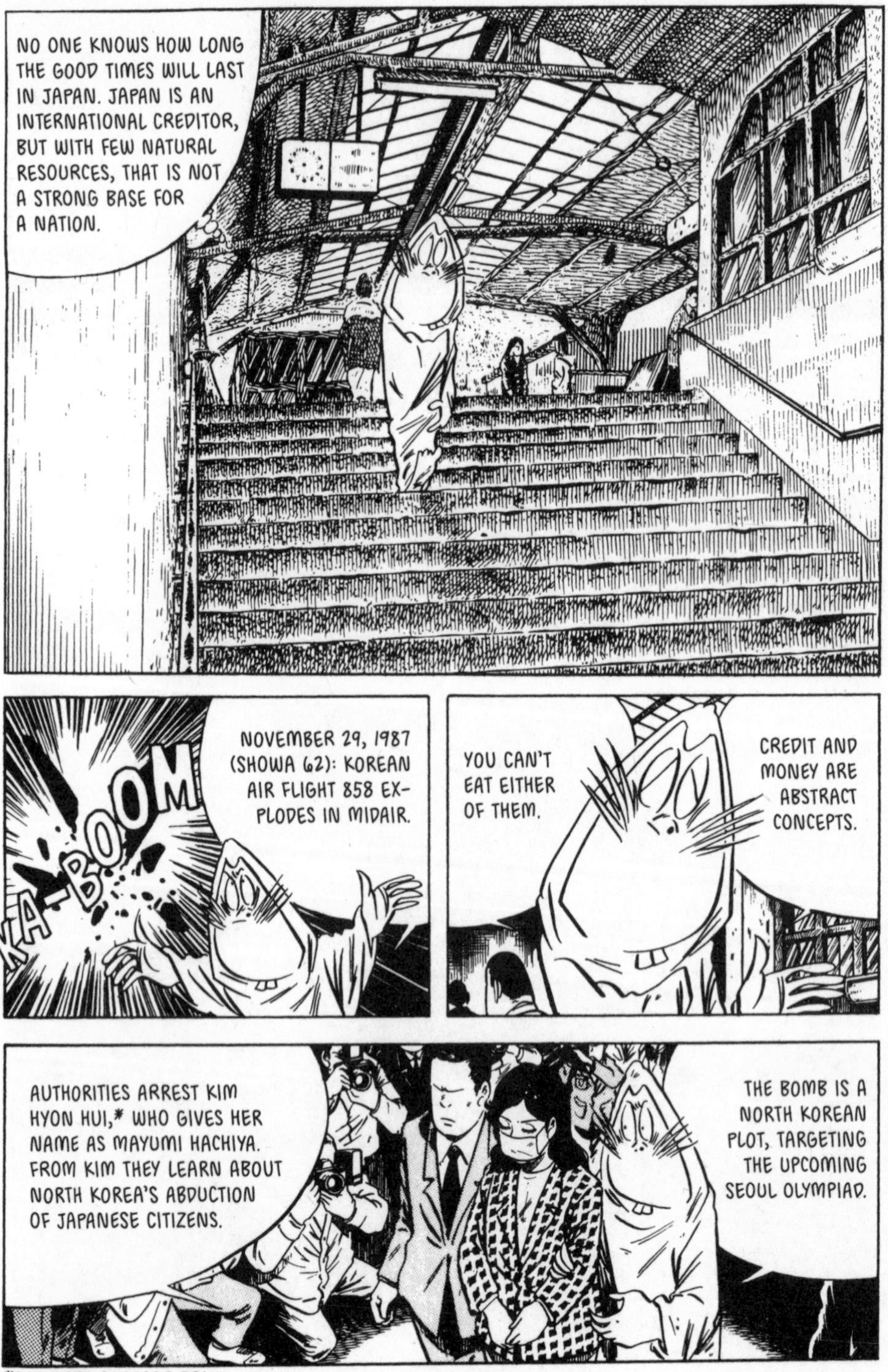
NO ONE KNOWS HOW LONG THE GOOD TIMES WILL LAST IN JAPAN. JAPAN IS AN INTERNATIONAL CREDITOR, BUT WITH FEW NATURAL RESOURCES, THAT IS NOT A STRONG BASE FOR A NATION.
CREDIT AND MONEY ARE ABSTRACT CONCEPTS.
YOU CAN'T EAT EITHER OF THEM.
NOVEMBER 29, 1987 (SHOWA 62): KOREAN AIR FLIGHT 858 EXPLODES IN MIDAIR.
KA-BOOM
THE BOMB IS A NORTH KOREAN PLOT, TARGETING THE UPCOMING SEOUL OLYMPIAD.
AUTHORITIES ARREST KIM HYON HUI,* WHO GIVES HER NAME AS MAYUMI HACHIYA. FROM KIM THEY LEARN ABOUT NORTH KOREA'S ABDUCTION OF JAPANESE CITIZENS.

*SEE NOTE ON PAGE 536.

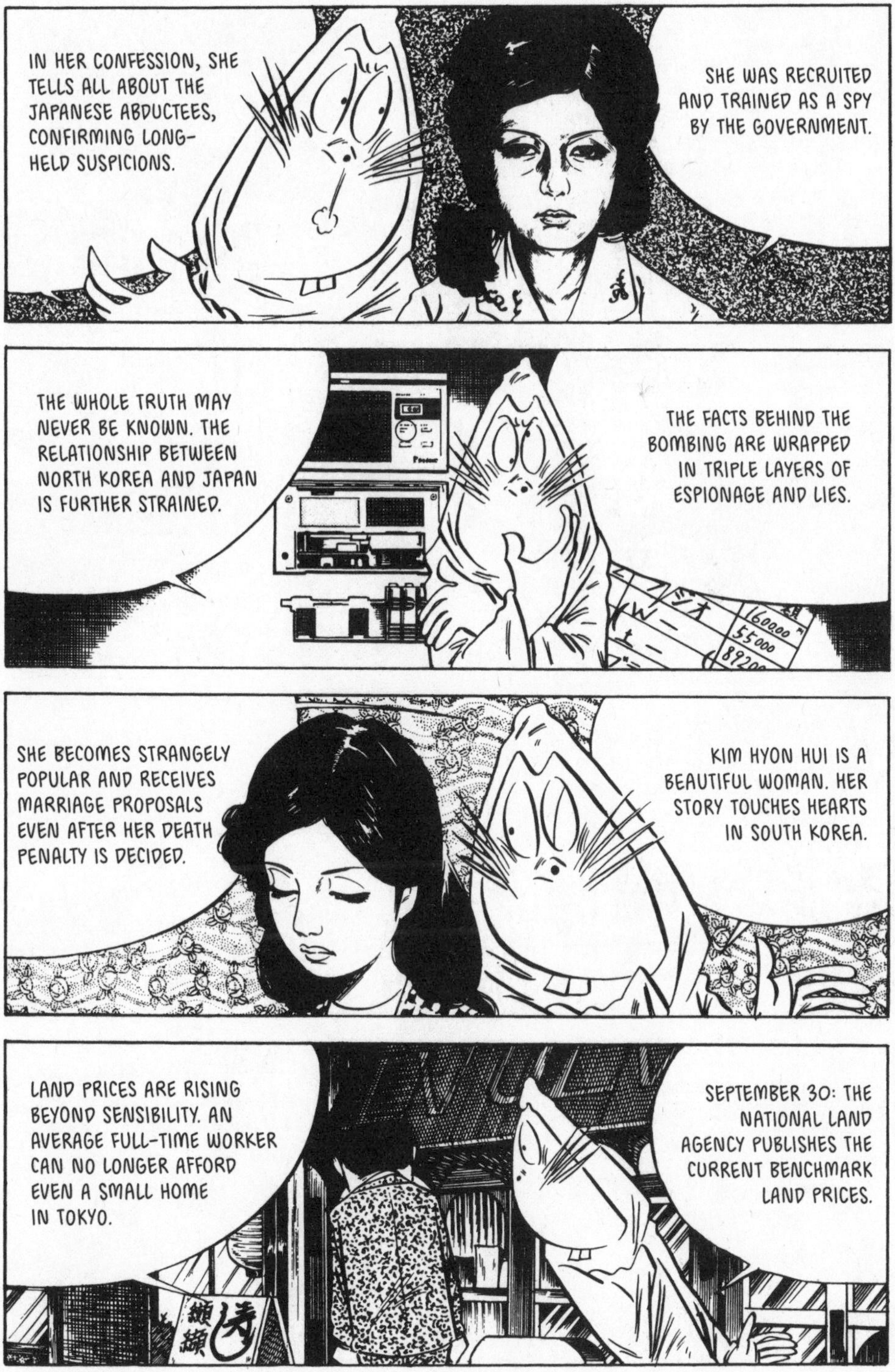
SHE WAS RECRUITED AND TRAINED AS A SPY BY THE GOVERNMENT.
IN HER CONFESSION, SHE TELLS ALL ABOUT THE JAPANESE ABDUCTEES, CONFIRMING LONG-HELD SUSPICIONS.
THE FACTS BEHIND THE BOMBING ARE WRAPPED IN TRIPLE LAYERS OF ESPIONAGE AND LIES.
THE WHOLE TRUTH MAY NEVER BE KNOWN. THE RELATIONSHIP BETWEEN NORTH KOREA AND JAPAN IS FURTHER STRAINED.
KIM HYON HUI IS A BEAUTIFUL WOMAN. HER STORY TOUCHES HEARTS IN SOUTH KOREA.
SHE BECOMES STRANGELY POPULAR AND RECEIVES MARRIAGE PROPOSALS EVEN AFTER HER DEATH PENALTY IS DECIDED.
SEPTEMBER 30: THE NATIONAL LAND AGENCY PUBLISHES THE CURRENT BENCHMARK LAND PRICES.
LAND PRICES ARE RISING BEYOND SENSIBILITY. AN AVERAGE FULL-TIME WORKER CAN NO LONGER AFFORD EVEN A SMALL HOME IN TOKYO.

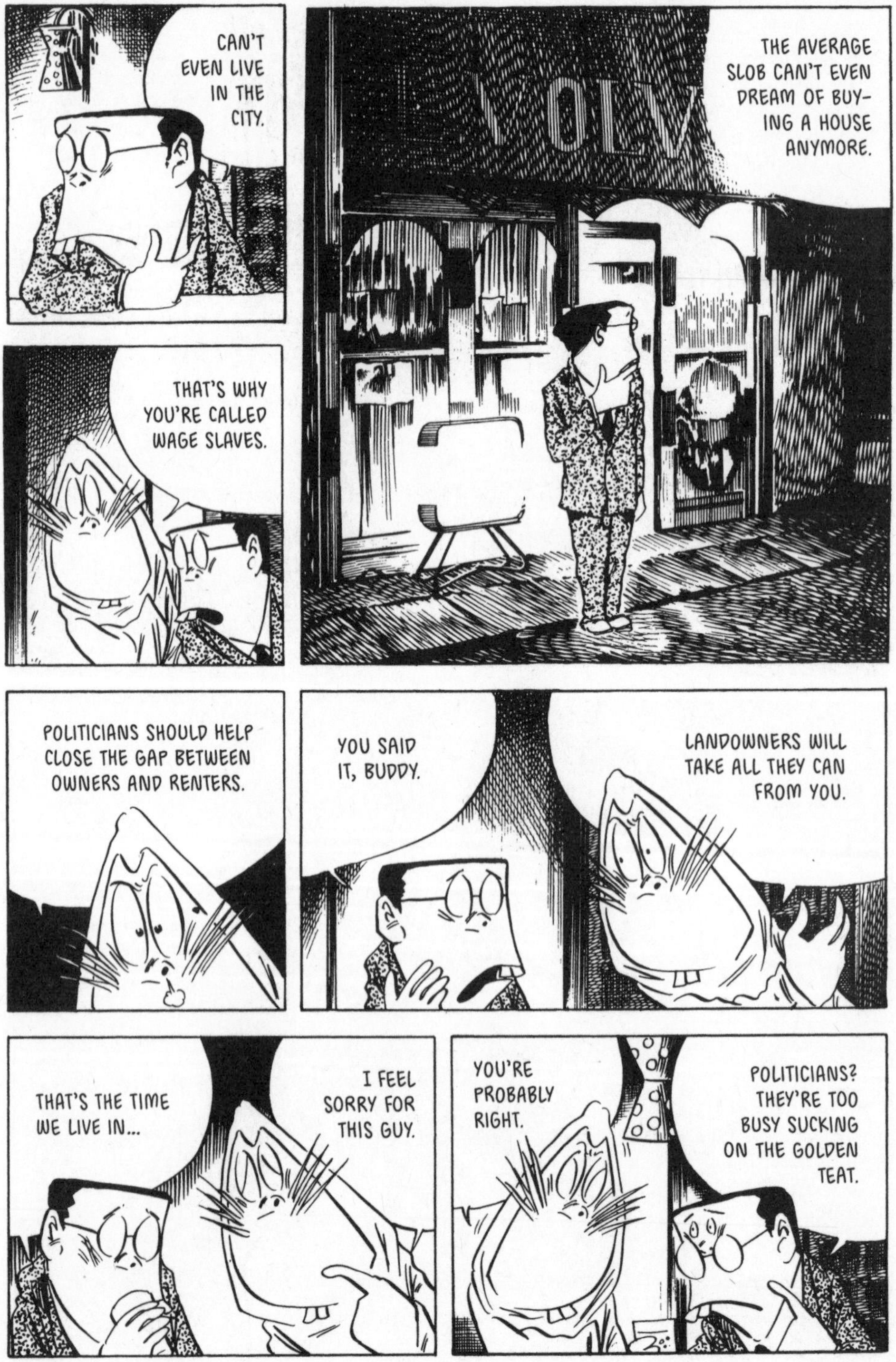
VOLV
THE AVERAGE SLOB CAN'T EVEN DREAM OF BUYING A HOUSE ANYMORE.
CAN'T EVEN LIVE IN THE CITY.
THAT'S WHY YOU'RE CALLED WAGE SLAVES.
LANDOWNERS WILL TAKE ALL THEY CAN FROM YOU.
YOU SAID IT, BUDDY.
POLITICIANS SHOULD HELP CLOSE THE GAP BETWEEN OWNERS AND RENTERS.
POLITICIANS? THEY'RE TOO BUSY SUCKING ON THE GOLDEN TEAT.
YOU'RE PROBABLY RIGHT.
I FEEL SORRY FOR THIS GUY.
THAT'S THE TIME WE LIVE IN...

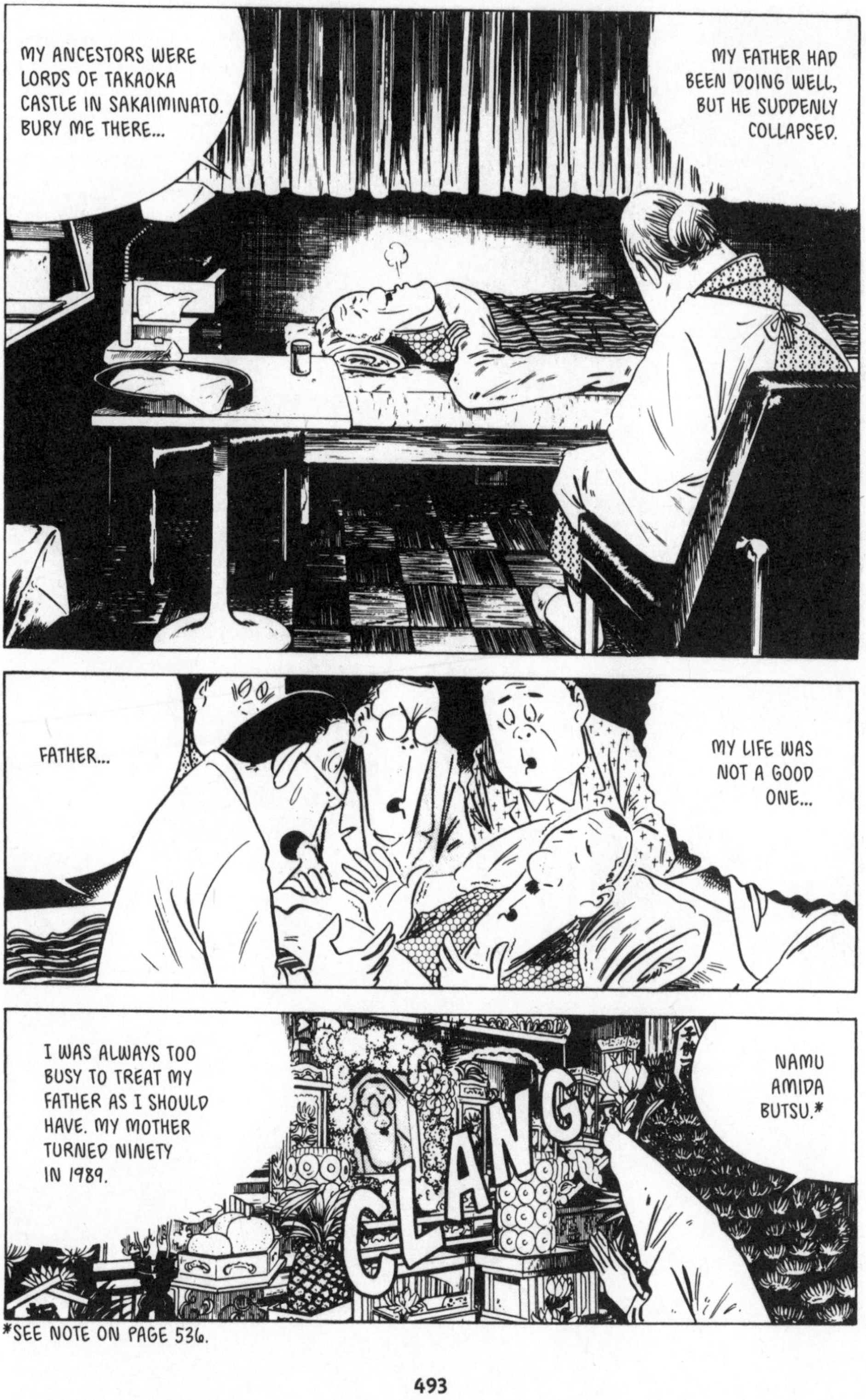
MY FATHER HAD BEEN DOING WELL, BUT HE SUDDENLY COLLAPSED.
MY ANCESTORS WERE LORDS OF TAKAOKA CASTLE IN SAKAIMINATO. BURY ME THERE...
MY LIFE WAS NOT A GOOD ONE...
FATHER...
NAMU AMIDA BUTSU.*
CLANG
I WAS ALWAYS TOO BUSY TO TREAT MY FATHER AS I SHOULD HAVE. MY MOTHER TURNED NINETY IN 1989.

*SEE NOTE ON PAGE 536.

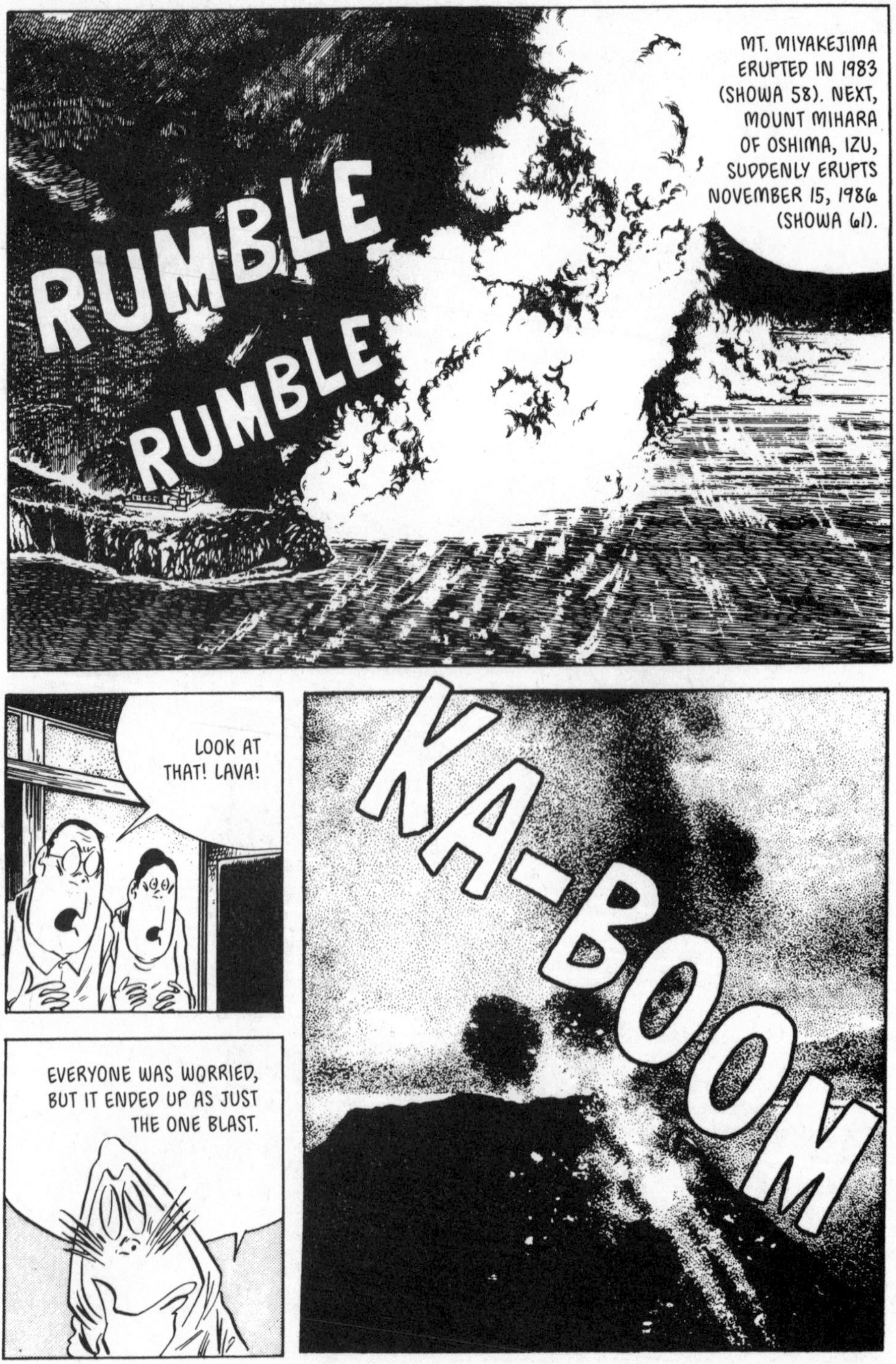
MT. MIYAKEJIMA ERUPTED IN 1983 (SHOWA 58). NEXT, MOUNT MIHARA OF OSHIMA, IZU, SUDDENLY ERUPTS NOVEMBER 15, 1986 (SHOWA 61).
RUMBLE
RUMBLE
KA-BOOM
LOOK AT THAT! LAVA!
EVERYONE WAS WORRIED, BUT IT ENDED UP AS JUST THE ONE BLAST.

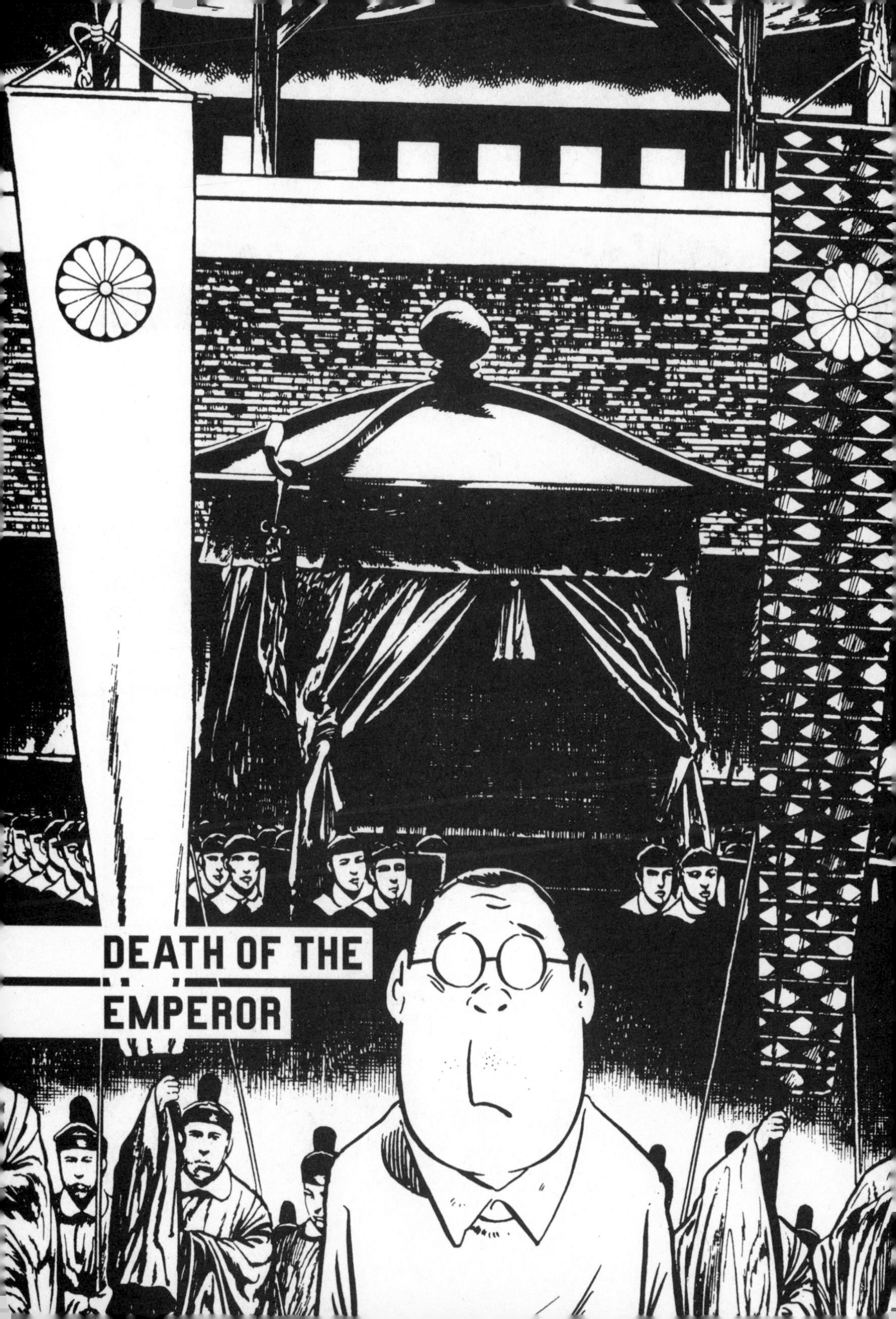
DEATH OF THE EMPEROR

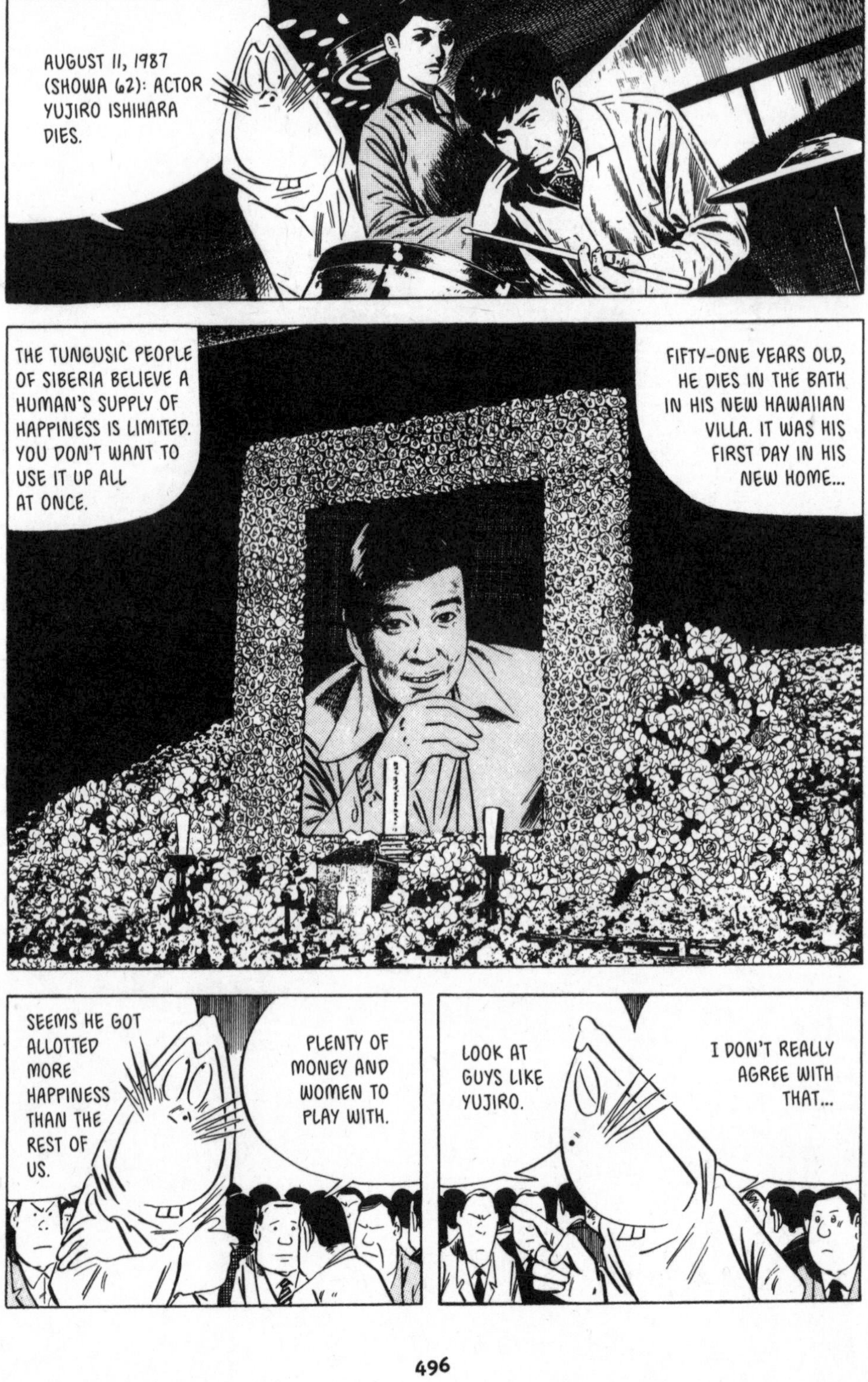
AUGUST 11, 1987 (SHOWA 62): ACTOR YUJIRO ISHIHARA DIES.
FIFTY-ONE YEARS OLD, HE DIES IN THE BATH IN HIS NEW HAWAIIAN VILLA. IT WAS HIS FIRST DAY IN HIS NEW HOME...
THE TUNGUSIC PEOPLE OF SIBERIA BELIEVE A HUMAN'S SUPPLY OF HAPPINESS IS LIMITED. YOU DON'T WANT TO USE IT UP ALL AT ONCE.
I DON'T REALLY AGREE WITH THAT...
LOOK AT GUYS LIKE YUJIRO.
PLENTY OF MONEY AND WOMEN TO PLAY WITH.
SEEMS HE GOT ALLOTTED MORE HAPPINESS THAN THE REST OF US.

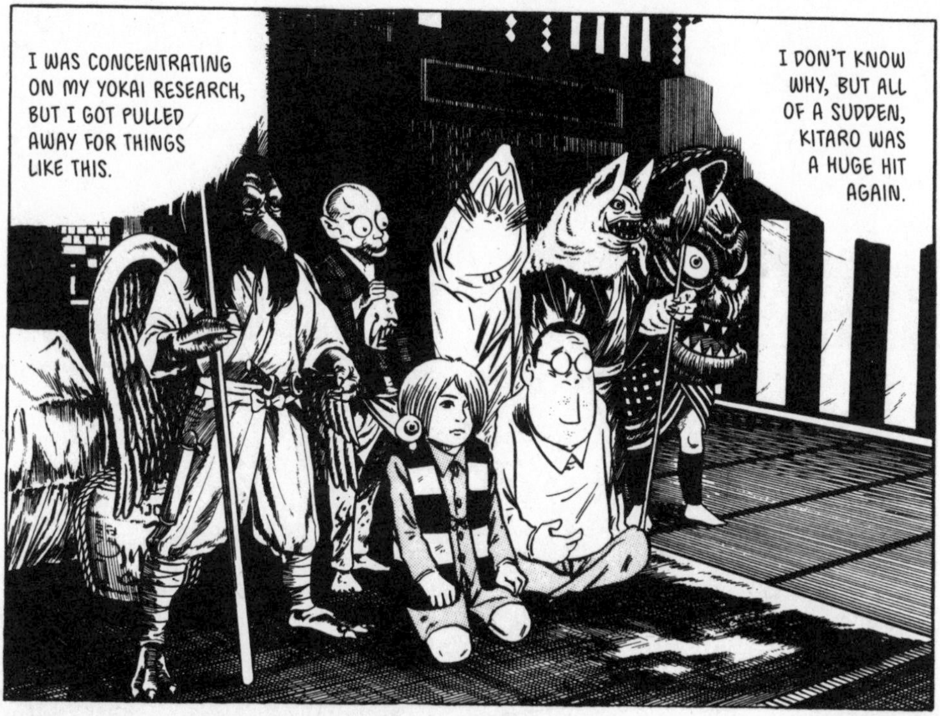
I DON'T KNOW WHY, BUT ALL OF A SUDDEN, KITARO WAS A HUGE HIT AGAIN.
I WAS CONCENTRATING ON MY YOKAI RESEARCH, BUT I GOT PULLED AWAY FOR THINGS LIKE THIS.

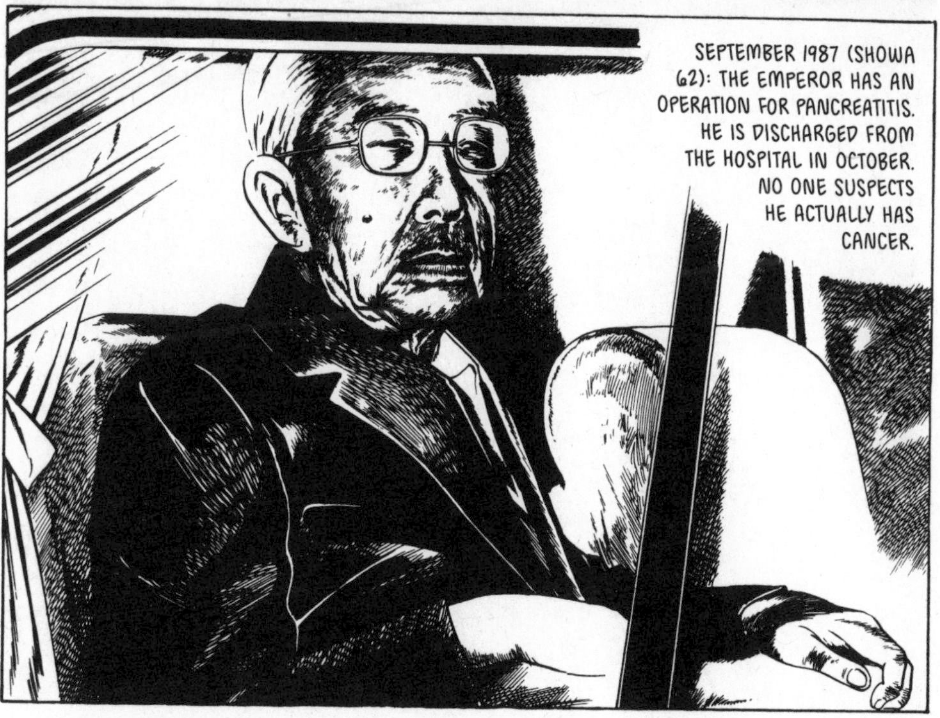
SEPTEMBER 1987 (SHOWA 62): THE EMPEROR HAS AN OPERATION FOR PANCREATITIS. HE IS DISCHARGED FROM THE HOSPITAL IN OCTOBER. NO ONE SUSPECTS HE ACTUALLY HAS CANCER.

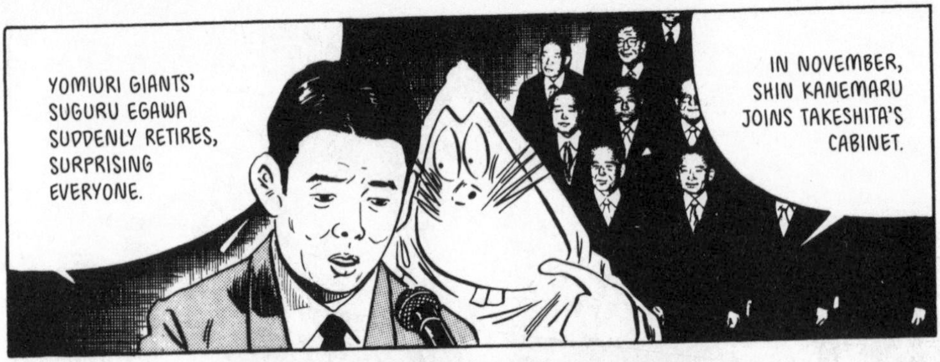
IN NOVEMBER, SHIN KANEMARU JOINS TAKESHITA'S CABINET.
YOMIURI GIANTS' SUGURU EGAWA SUDDENLY RETIRES, SURPRISING EVERYONE.

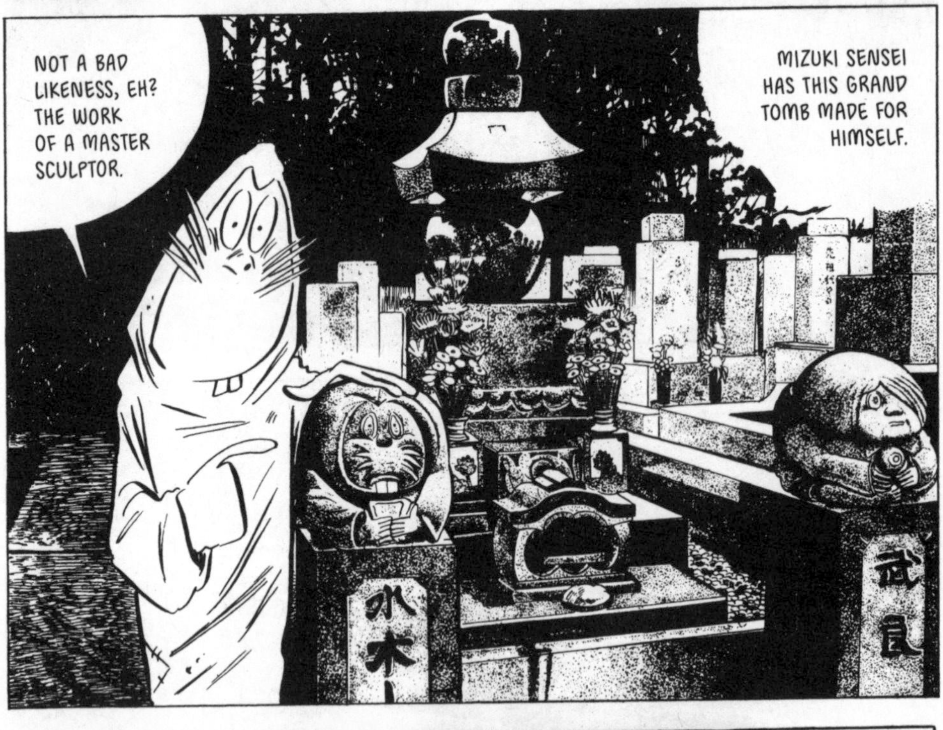
MIZUKI SENSEI HAS THIS GRAND TOMB MADE FOR HIMSELF.
NOT A BAD LIKENESS, EH? THE WORK OF A MASTER SCULPTOR.

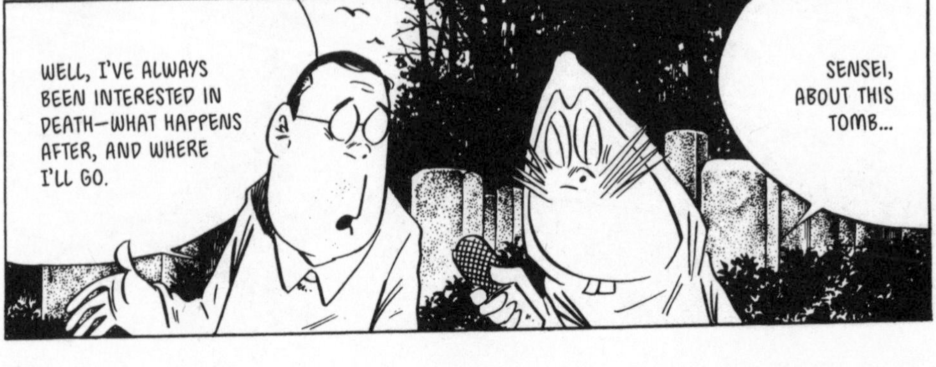
SENSEI, ABOUT THIS TOMB...
WELL, I'VE ALWAYS BEEN INTERESTED IN DEATH—WHAT HAPPENS AFTER, AND WHERE I'LL GO.

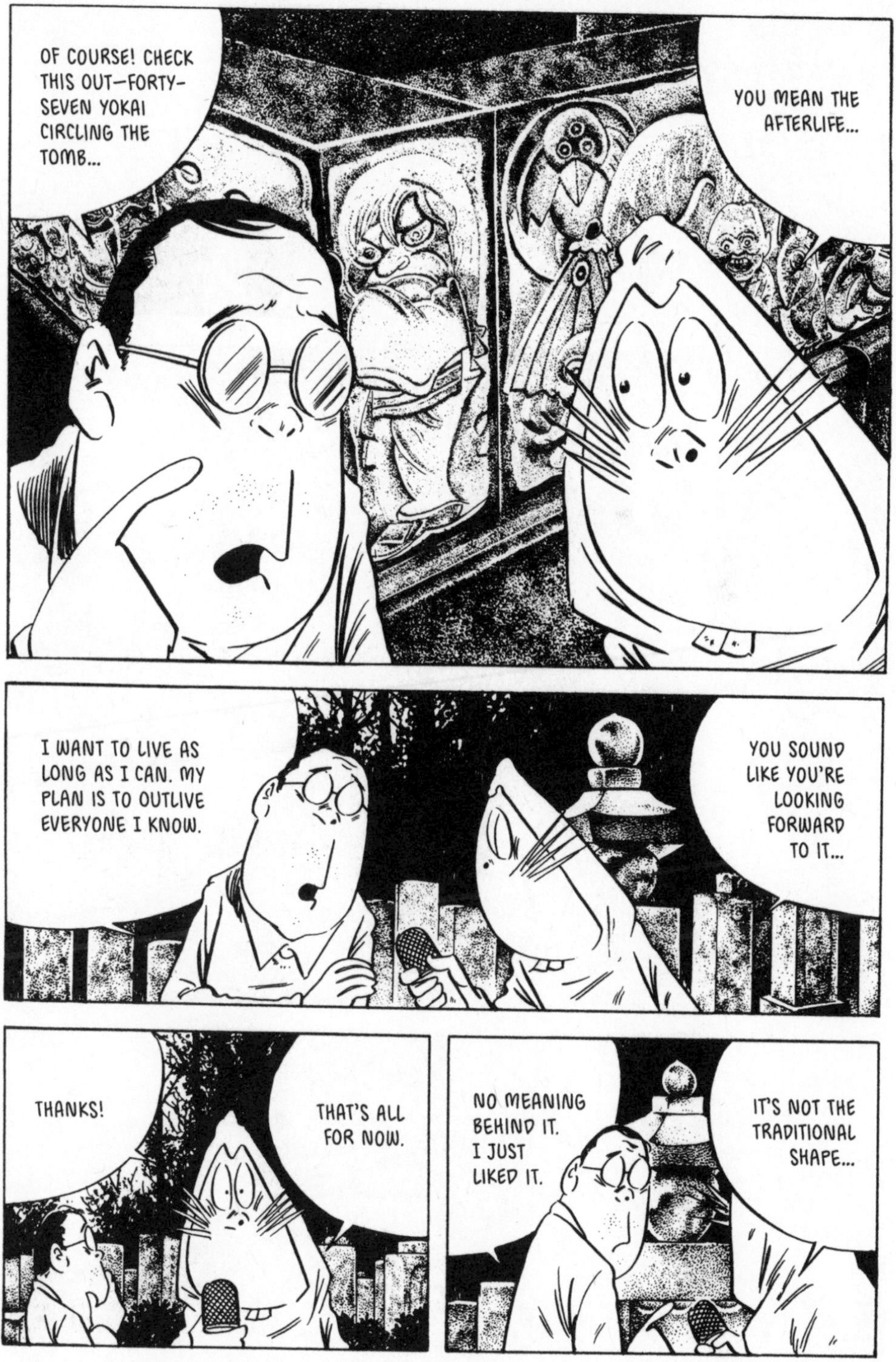
YOU MEAN THE AFTERLIFE...
OF COURSE! CHECK THIS OUT—FORTY-SEVEN YOKAI CIRCLING THE TOMB...
YOU SOUND LIKE YOU'RE LOOKING FORWARD TO IT...
I WANT TO LIVE AS LONG AS I CAN. MY PLAN IS TO OUTLIVE EVERYONE I KNOW.
IT'S NOT THE TRADITIONAL SHAPE...
NO MEANING BEHIND IT. I JUST LIKED IT.
THAT'S ALL FOR NOW.
THANKS!

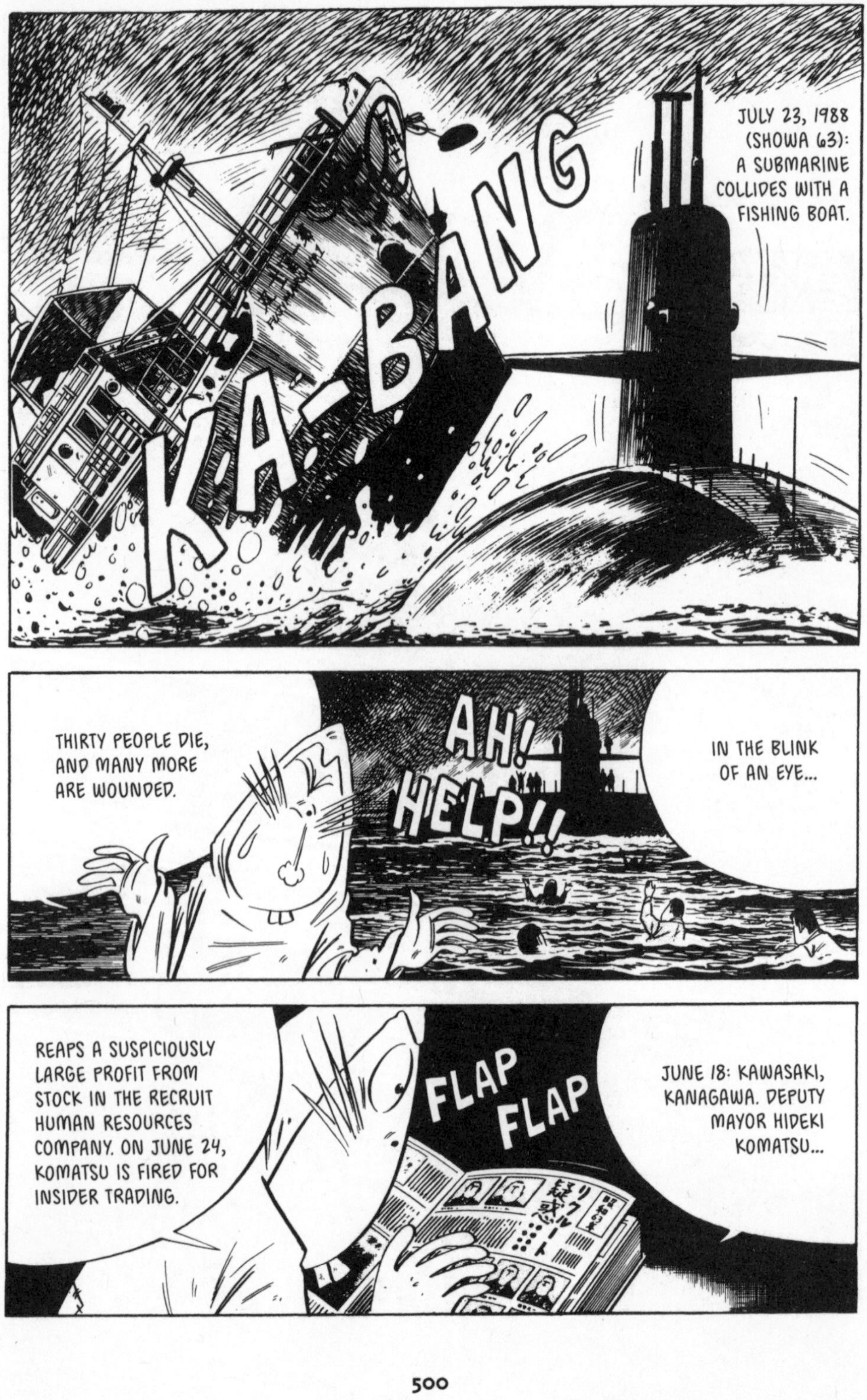
JULY 23, 1988 (SHOWA 63): A SUBMARINE COLLIDES WITH A FISHING BOAT.
KA-BANG
IN THE BLINK OF AN EYE...
AH! HELP!!
THIRTY PEOPLE DIE, AND MANY MORE ARE WOUNDED.
JUNE 18: KAWASAKI, KANAGAWA. DEPUTY MAYOR HIDEKI KOMATSU...
FLAP FLAP
REAPS A SUSPICIOUSLY LARGE PROFIT FROM STOCK IN THE RECRUIT HUMAN RESOURCES COMPANY. ON JUNE 24, KOMATSU IS FIRED FOR INSIDER TRADING.

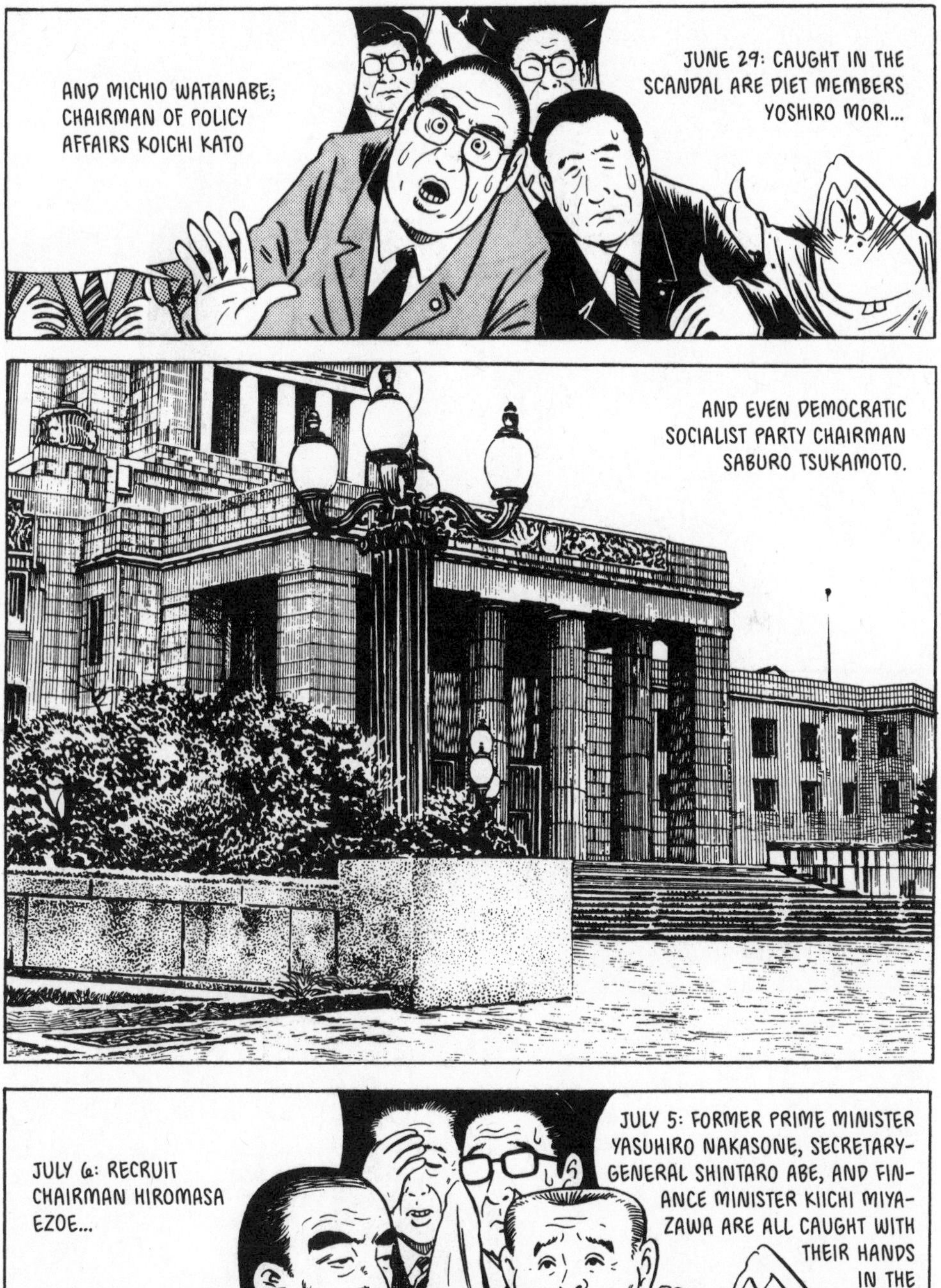
JUNE 29: CAUGHT IN THE SCANDAL ARE DIET MEMBERS YOSHIRO MORI...
AND MICHIO WATANABE; CHAIRMAN OF POLICY AFFAIRS KOICHI KATO
AND EVEN DEMOCRATIC SOCIALIST PARTY CHAIRMAN SABURO TSUKAMOTO.
JULY 5: FORMER PRIME MINISTER YASUHIRO NAKASONE, SECRETARY-GENERAL SHINTARO ABE, AND FIN-ANCE MINISTER KIICHI MIYA-ZAWA ARE ALL CAUGHT WITH THEIR HANDS IN THE COOKIE JAR.
JULY 6: RECRUIT CHAIRMAN HIROMASA EZOE...

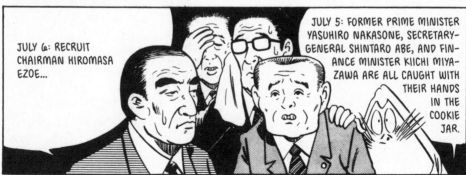

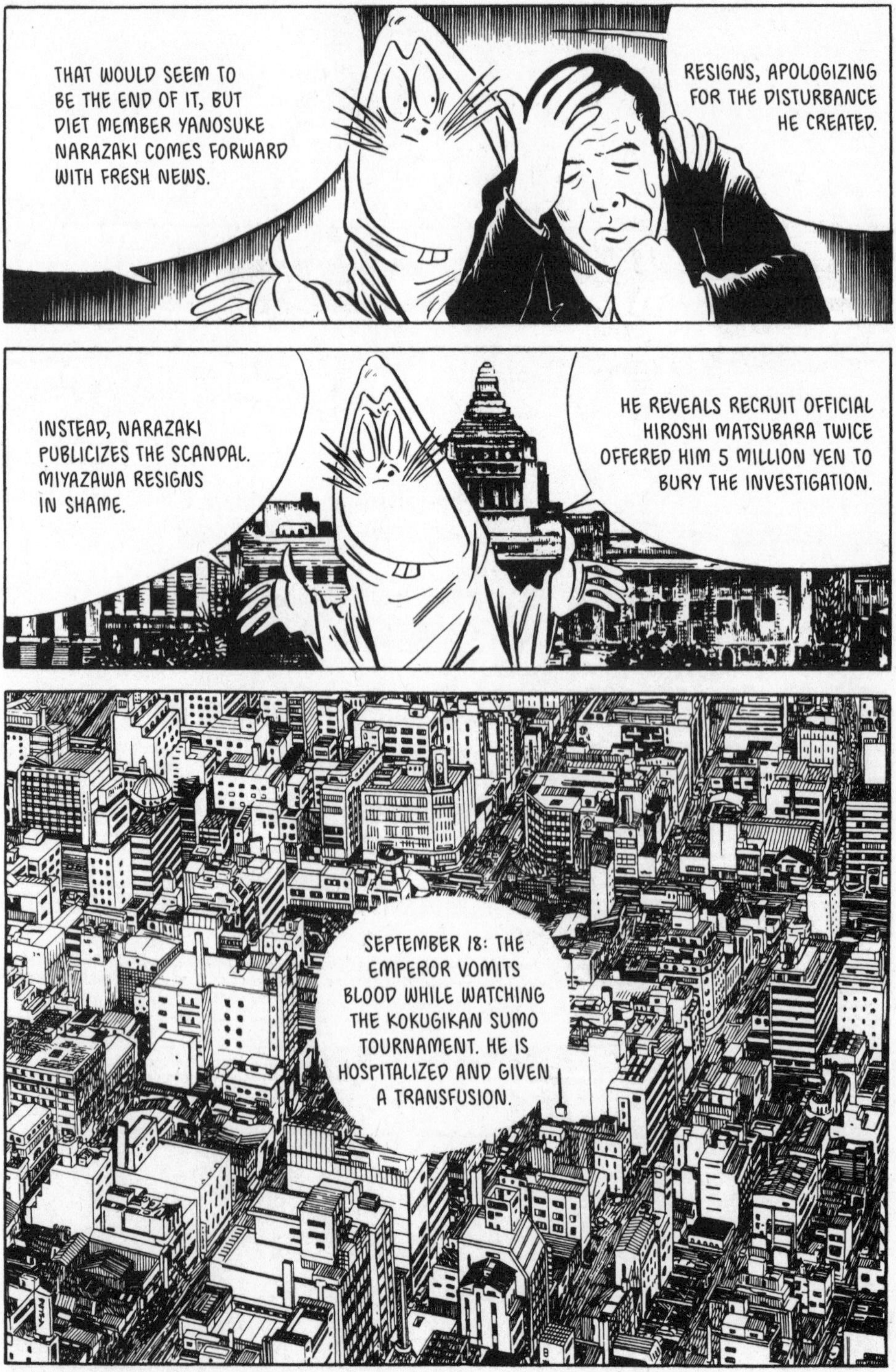
RESIGNS, APOLOGIZING FOR THE DISTURBANCE HE CREATED.
THAT WOULD SEEM TO BE THE END OF IT, BUT DIET MEMBER YANOSUKE NARAZAKI COMES FORWARD WITH FRESH NEWS.
HE REVEALS RECRUIT OFFICIAL HIROSHI MATSUBARA TWICE OFFERED HIM 5 MILLION YEN TO BURY THE INVESTIGATION.
INSTEAD, NARAZAKI PUBLICIZES THE SCANDAL. MIYAZAWA RESIGNS IN SHAME.
SEPTEMBER 18: THE EMPEROR VOMITS BLOOD WHILE WATCHING THE KOKUGIKAN SUMO TOURNAMENT. HE IS HOSPITALIZED AND GIVEN A TRANSFUSION.

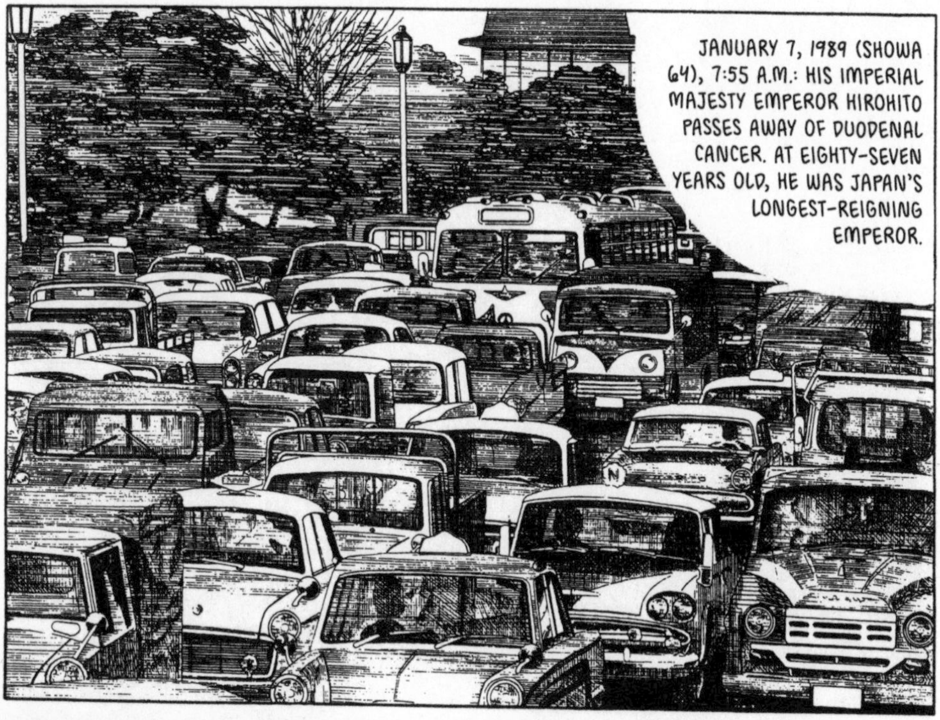
JANUARY 7, 1989 (SHOWA 64), 7:55 A.M.: HIS IMPERIAL MAJESTY EMPEROR HIROHITO PASSES AWAY OF DUODENAL CANCER. AT EIGHTY-SEVEN YEARS OLD, HE WAS JAPAN'S LONGEST-REIGNING EMPEROR.

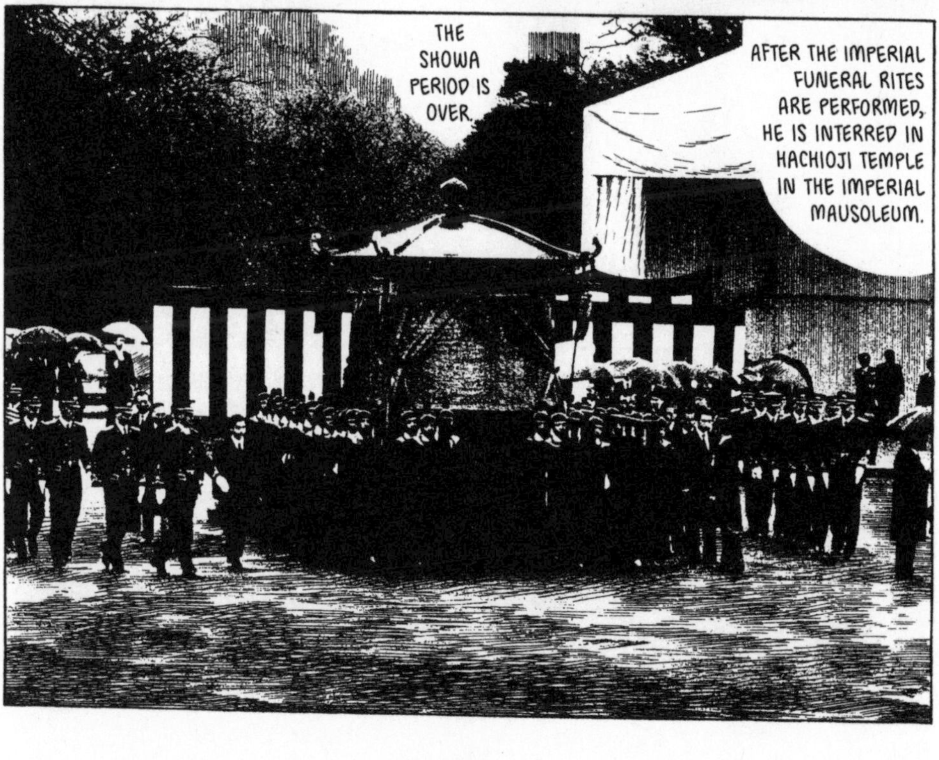
AFTER THE IMPERIAL FUNERAL RITES ARE PERFORMED, HE IS INTERRED IN HACHIOJI TEMPLE IN THE IMPERIAL MAUSOLEUM.
THE SHOWA PERIOD IS OVER.

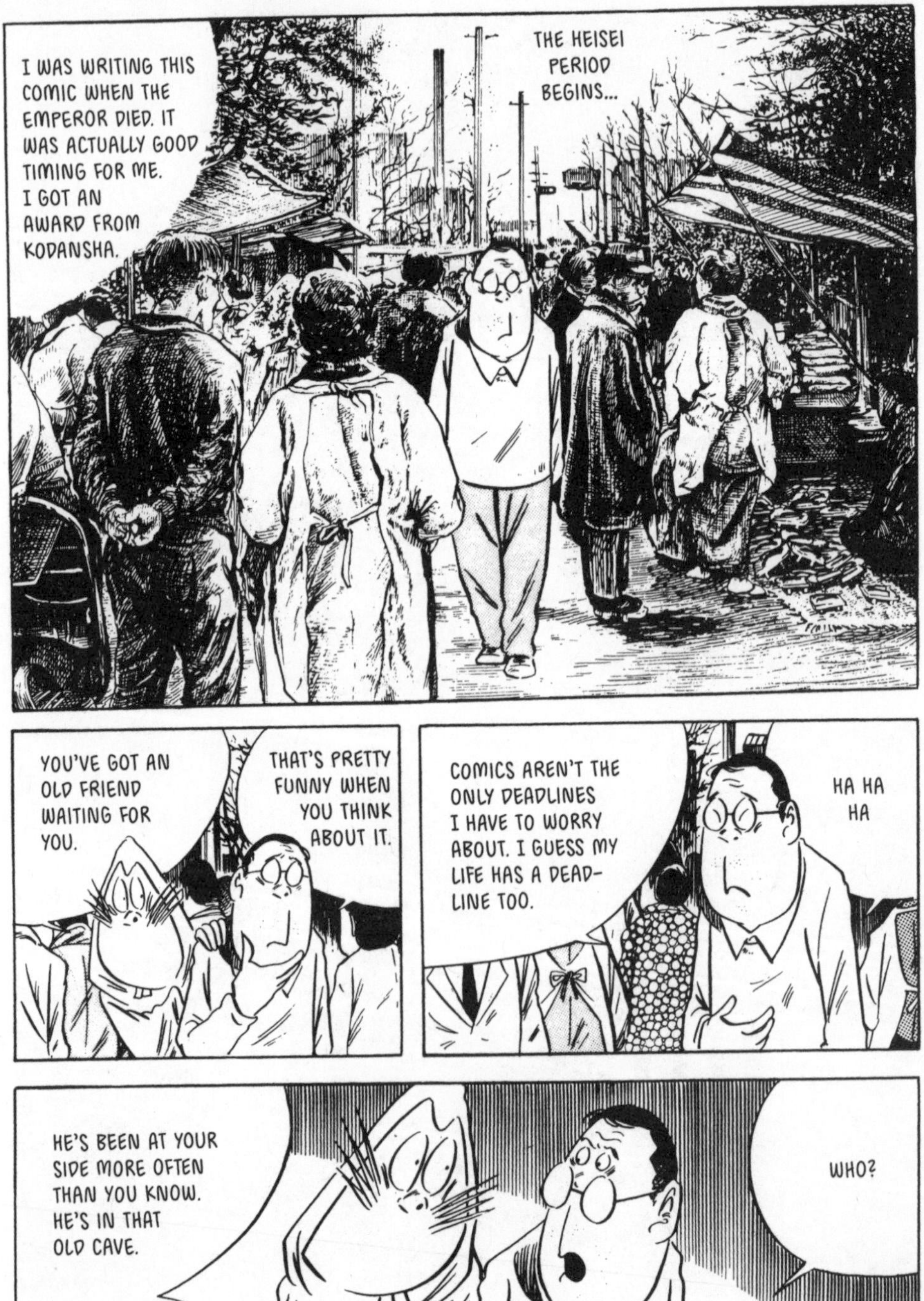
I WAS WRITING THIS COMIC WHEN THE EMPEROR DIED. IT WAS ACTUALLY GOOD TIMING FOR ME. I GOT AN AWARD FROM KODANSHA.
THE HEISEI PERIOD BEGINS...
YOU'VE GOT AN OLD FRIEND WAITING FOR YOU.
THAT'S PRETTY FUNNY WHEN YOU THINK ABOUT IT.
COMICS AREN'T THE ONLY DEADLINES I HAVE TO WORRY ABOUT. I GUESS MY LIFE HAS A DEAD-LINE TOO.
HA HA HA
HE'S BEEN AT YOUR SIDE MORE OFTEN THAN YOU KNOW. HE'S IN THAT OLD CAVE.
WHO?

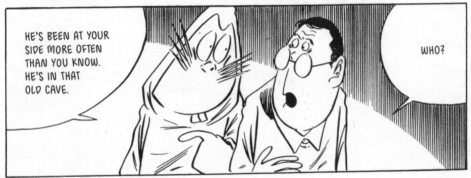

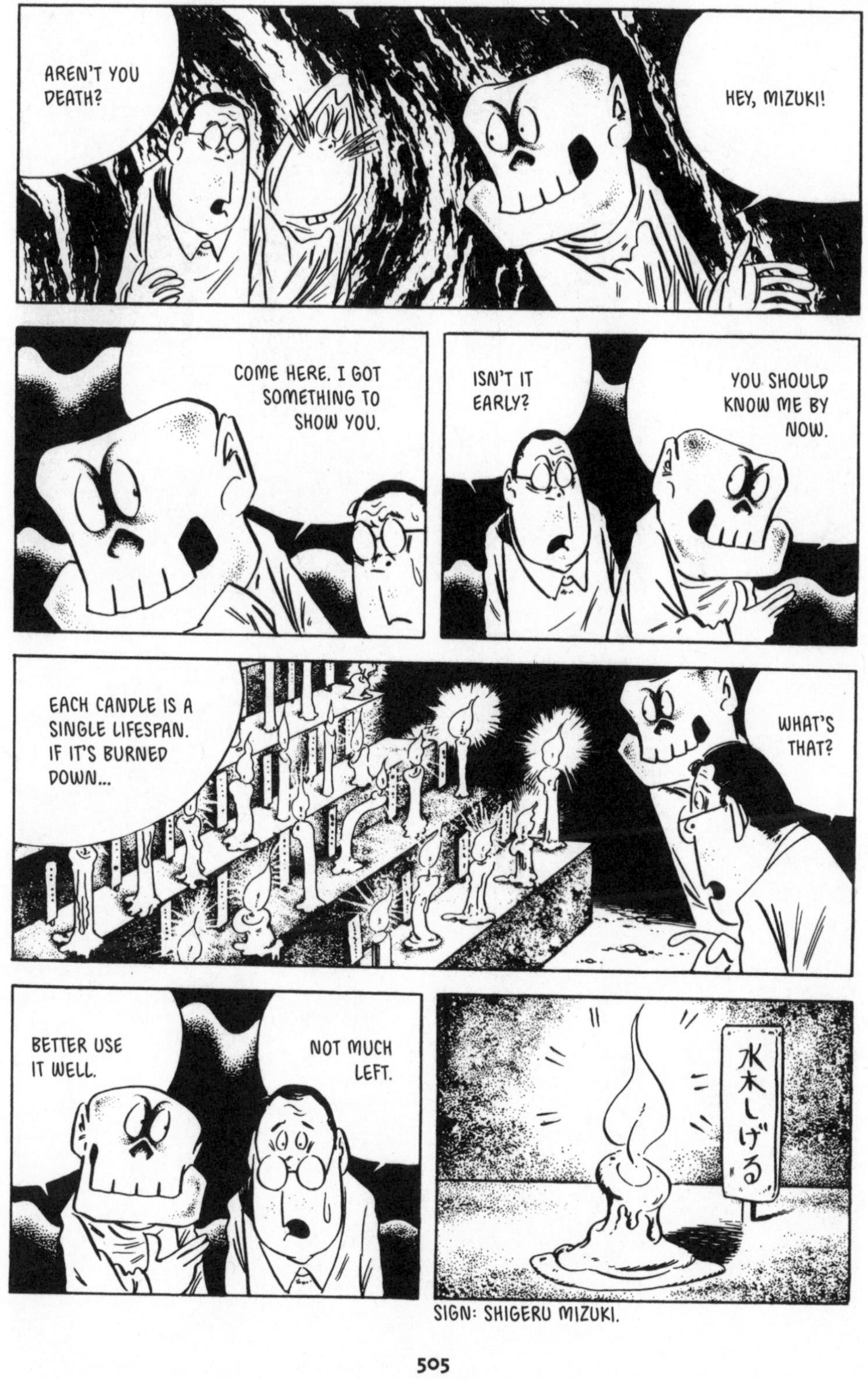
HEY, MIZUKI!
AREN'T YOU DEATH?
YOU SHOULD KNOW ME BY NOW.
ISN'T IT EARLY?
COME HERE. I GOT SOMETHING TO SHOW YOU.
WHAT'S THAT?
EACH CANDLE IS A SINGLE LIFESPAN. IF IT'S BURNED DOWN...
水木しげる
NOT MUCH LEFT.
BETTER USE IT WELL.
SIGN: SHIGERU MIZUKI.

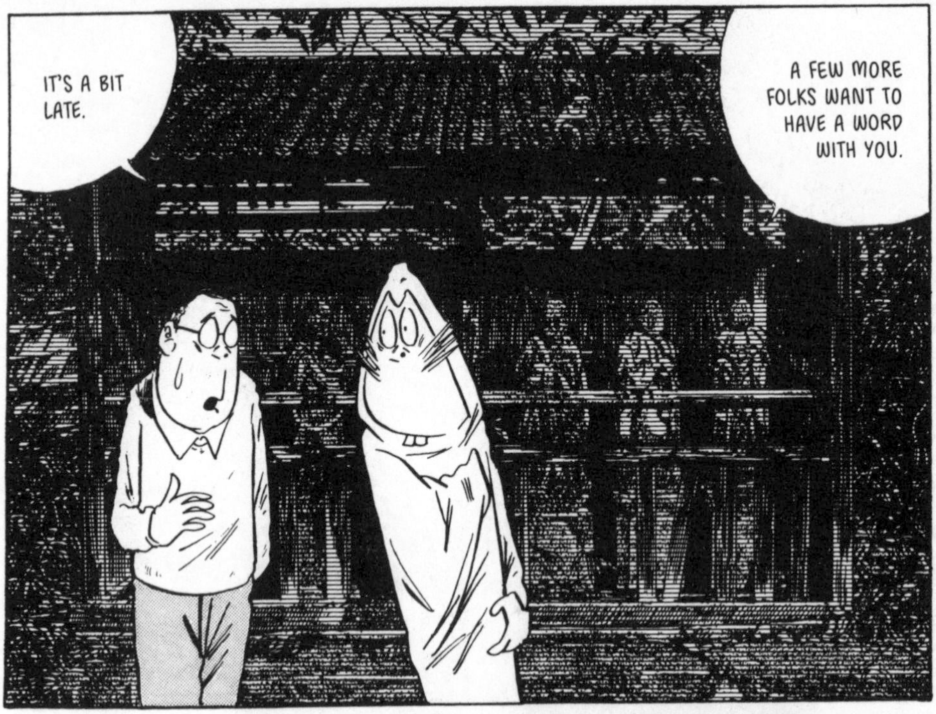
A FEW MORE FOLKS WANT TO HAVE A WORD WITH YOU.
IT'S A BIT LATE.

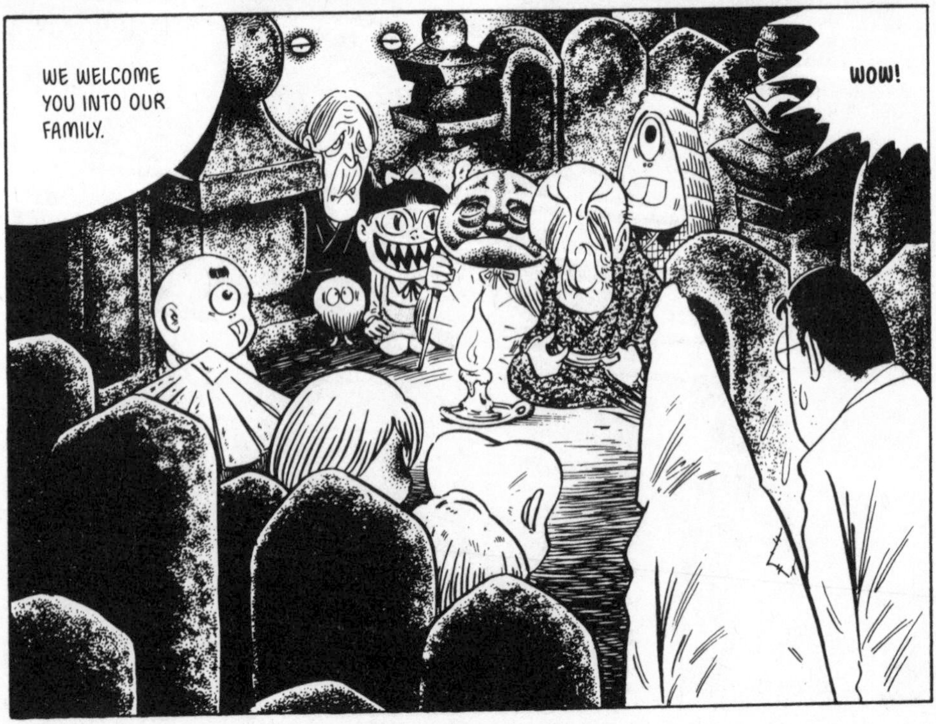
WOW!
WE WELCOME YOU INTO OUR FAMILY.

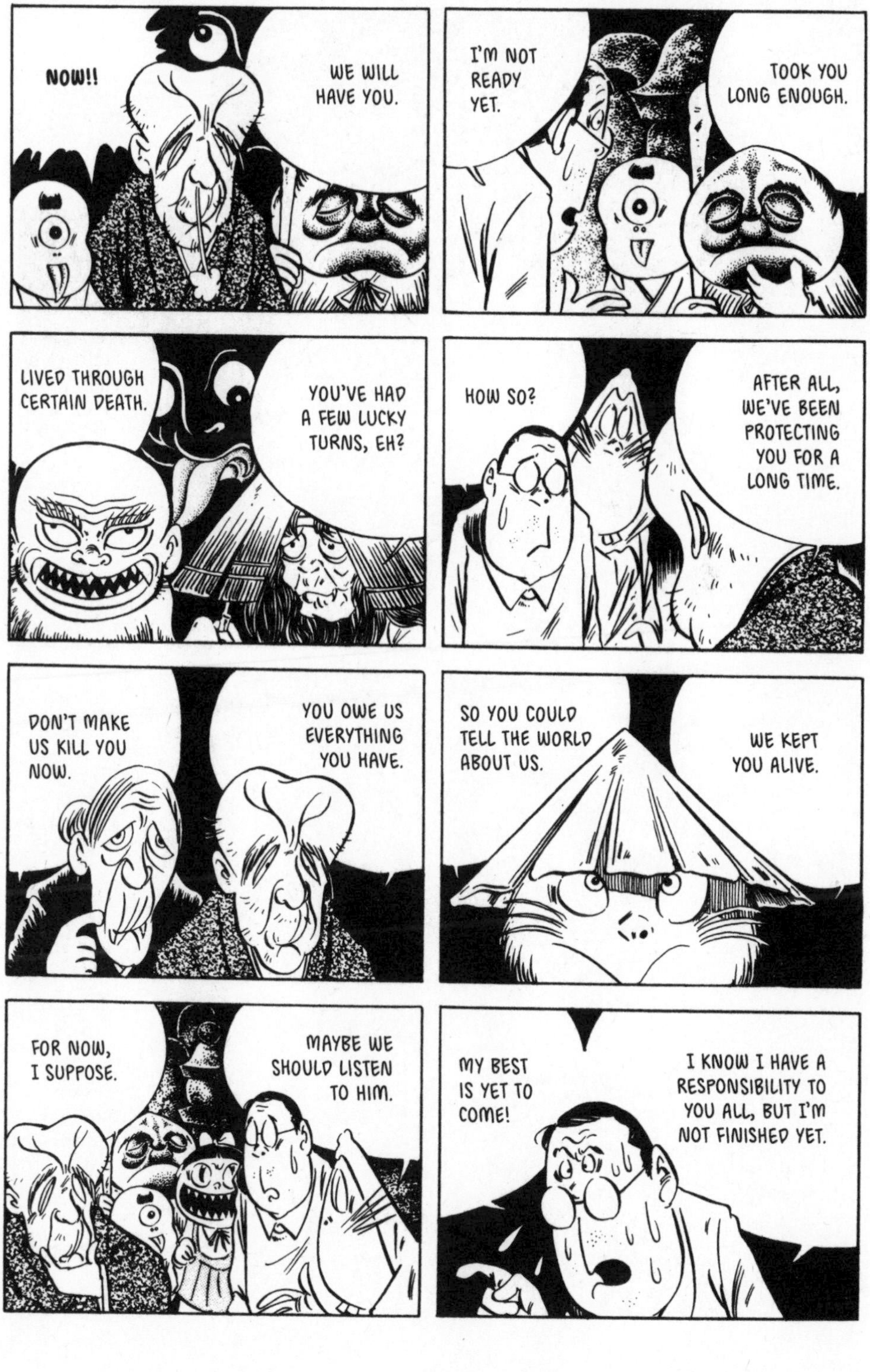
TOOK YOU LONG ENOUGH.
I'M NOT READY YET.
WE WILL HAVE YOU.
NOW!!
AFTER ALL, WE'VE BEEN PROTECTING YOU FOR A LONG TIME.
HOW SO?
YOU'VE HAD A FEW LUCKY TURNS, EH?
LIVED THROUGH CERTAIN DEATH.
WE KEPT YOU ALIVE.
SO YOU COULD TELL THE WORLD ABOUT US.
YOU OWE US EVERYTHING YOU HAVE.
DON'T MAKE US KILL YOU NOW.
I KNOW I HAVE A RESPONSIBILITY TO YOU ALL, BUT I'M NOT FINISHED YET.
MY BEST IS YET TO COME!
MAYBE WE SHOULD LISTEN TO HIM.
FOR NOW, I SUPPOSE.

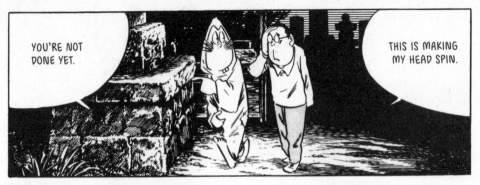

THIS IS MAKING MY HEAD SPIN.
YOU'RE NOT DONE YET.
THE HOUSE WE MADE FOR YOU IS EMPTY.
PAUL, DID YOU EVER REALLY INTEND TO LIVE WITH US?
I'LL RETURN! I PROMISE!!
WHAT GOES ON IN YOUR FATHER'S HEAD?
THEY'RE BUILDING YOU A MUSEUM.
I NEED TO DO SOMETHING...A ROUND-THE-WORLD TRIP, MAYBE...
SCRISH SCRISH
聖飢魔II
NOT BEFORE YOU DELIVER YOUR NEW SERIES! YOU GOT DEADLINES, YOU KNOW!!
...I KNOW ALL ABOUT DEADLINES. I THINK IT'S TIME I PUT SOME THINGS IN ORDER. I DON'T HAVE ALL THE TIME IN THE WORLD.

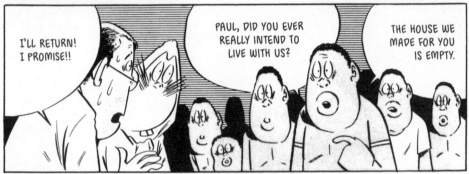

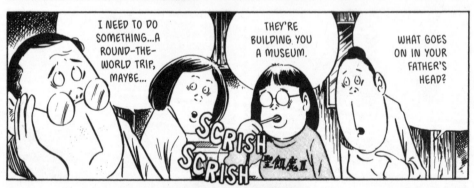

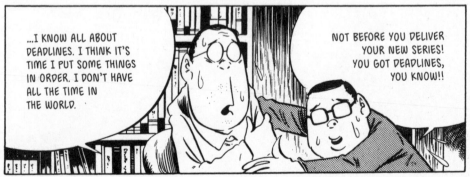

PAYING BACK MY WAR DEBT

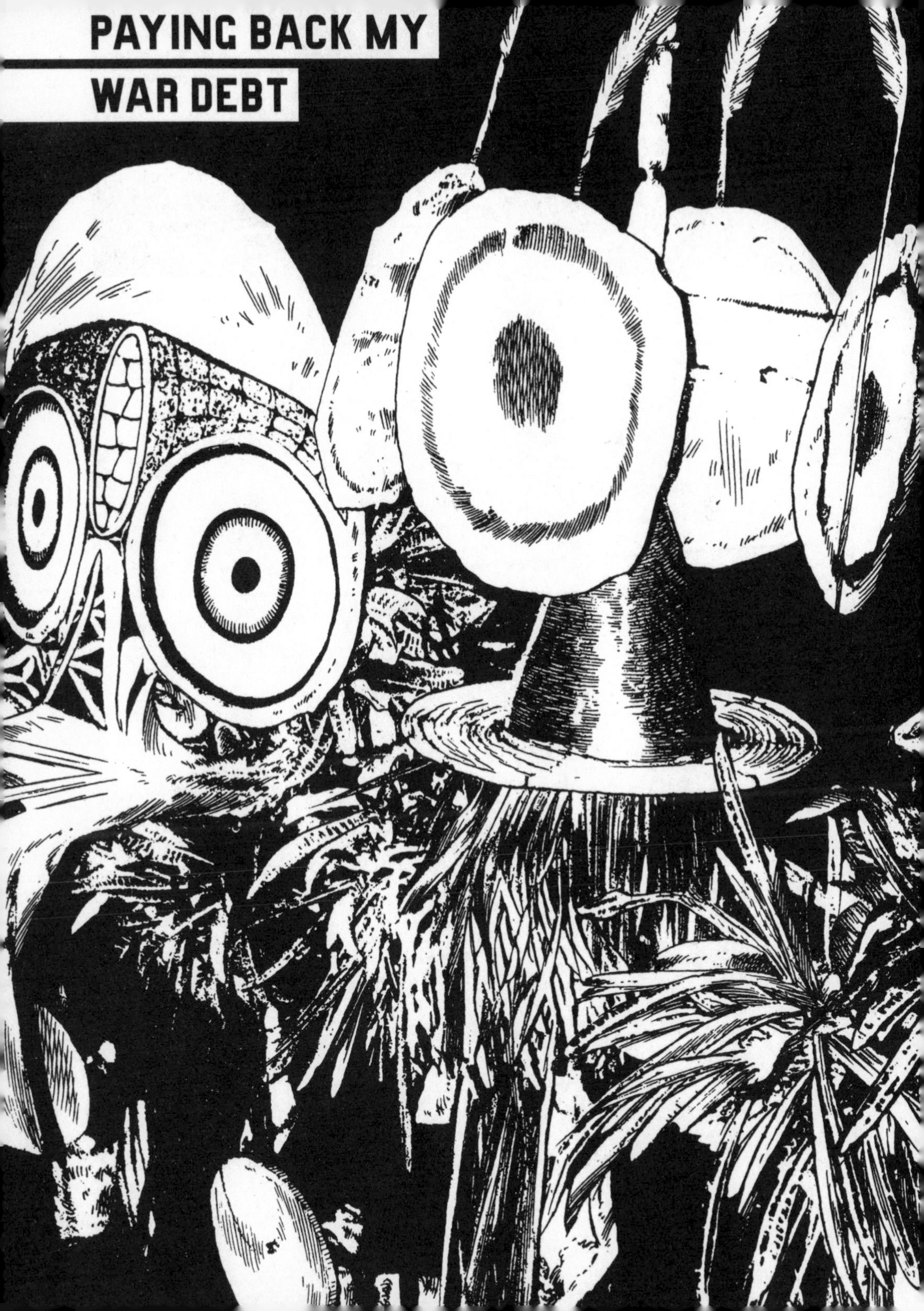

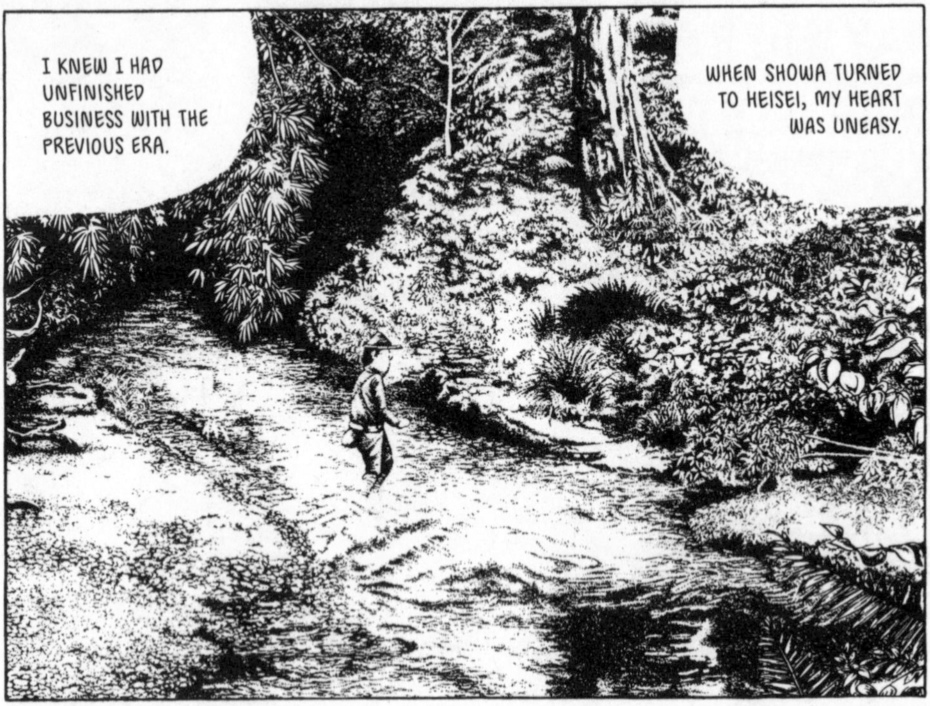
WHEN SHOWA TURNED TO HEISEI, MY HEART WAS UNEASY.
I KNEW I HAD UNFINISHED BUSINESS WITH THE PREVIOUS ERA.

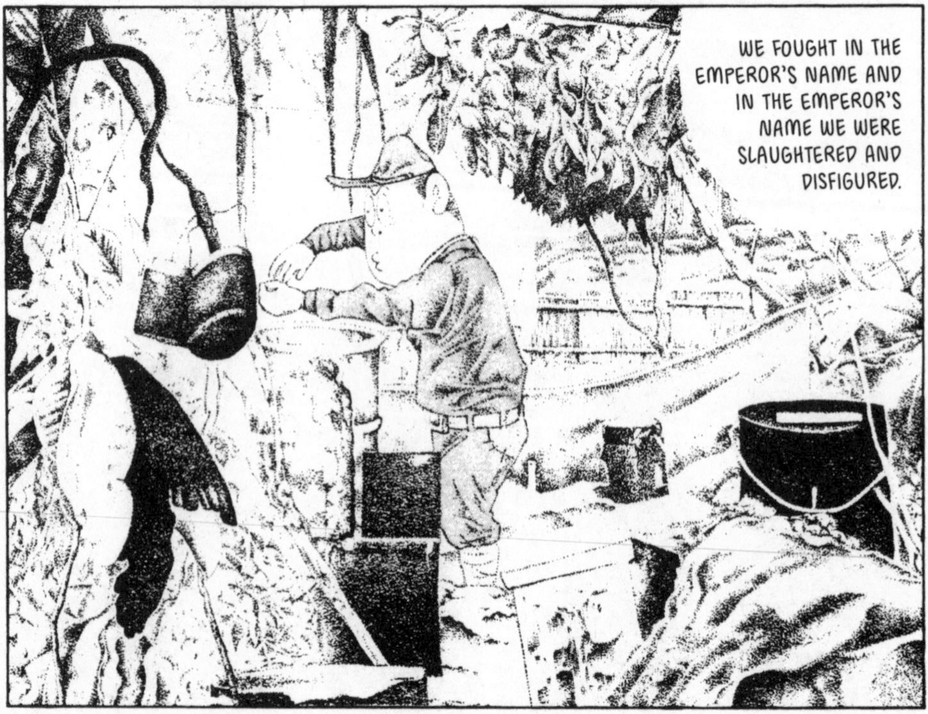
WE FOUGHT IN THE EMPEROR'S NAME AND IN THE EMPEROR'S NAME WE WERE SLAUGHTERED AND DISFIGURED.

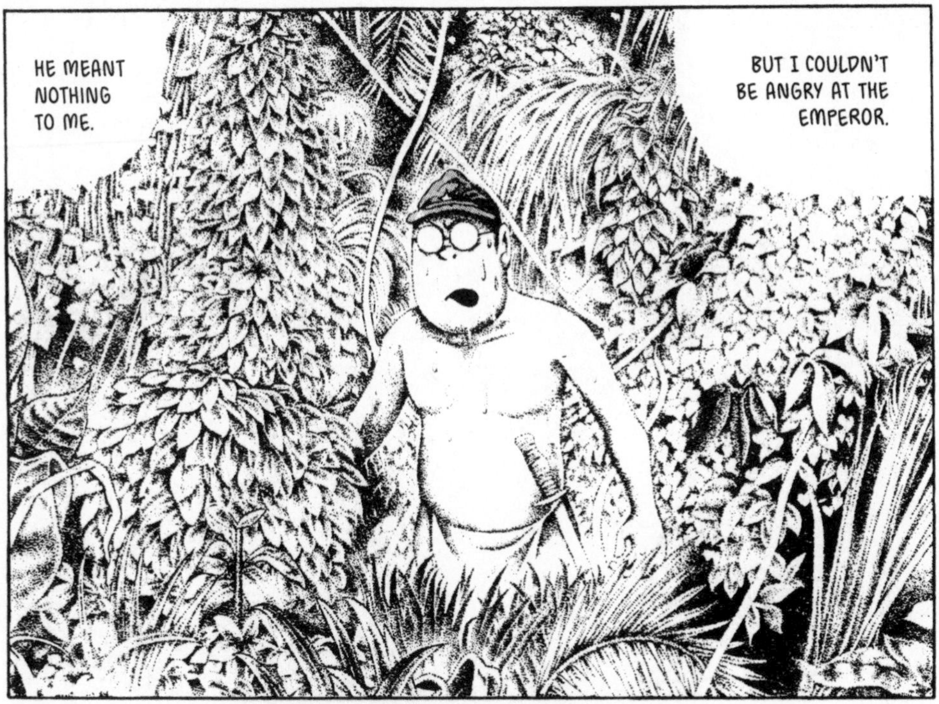
BUT I COULDN'T BE ANGRY AT THE EMPEROR.
HE MEANT NOTHING TO ME.

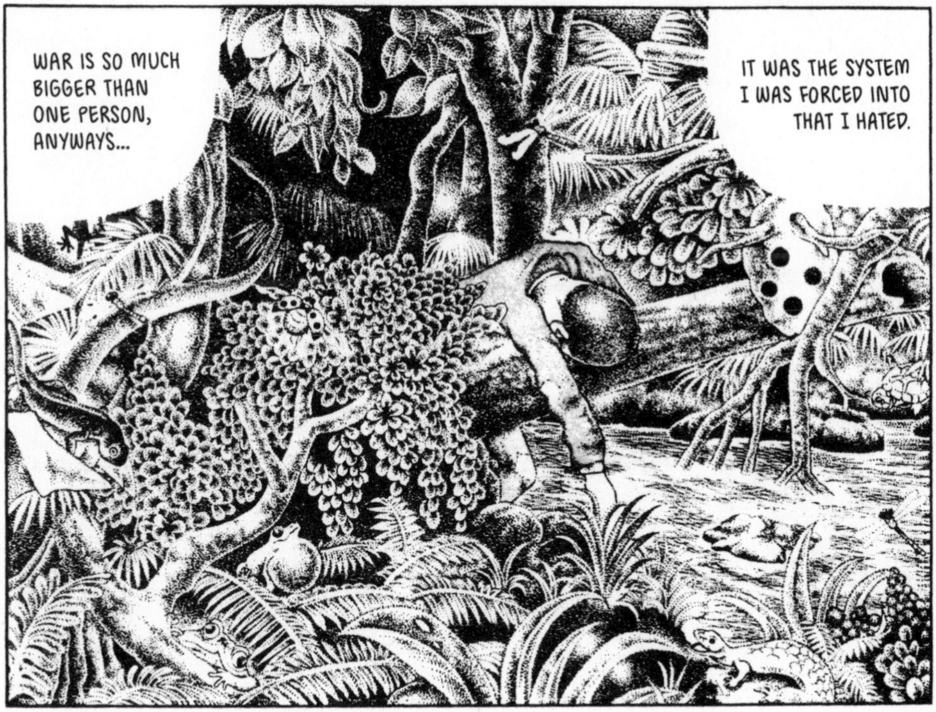
IT WAS THE SYSTEM I WAS FORCED INTO THAT I HATED.
WAR IS SO MUCH BIGGER THAN ONE PERSON, ANYWAYS...

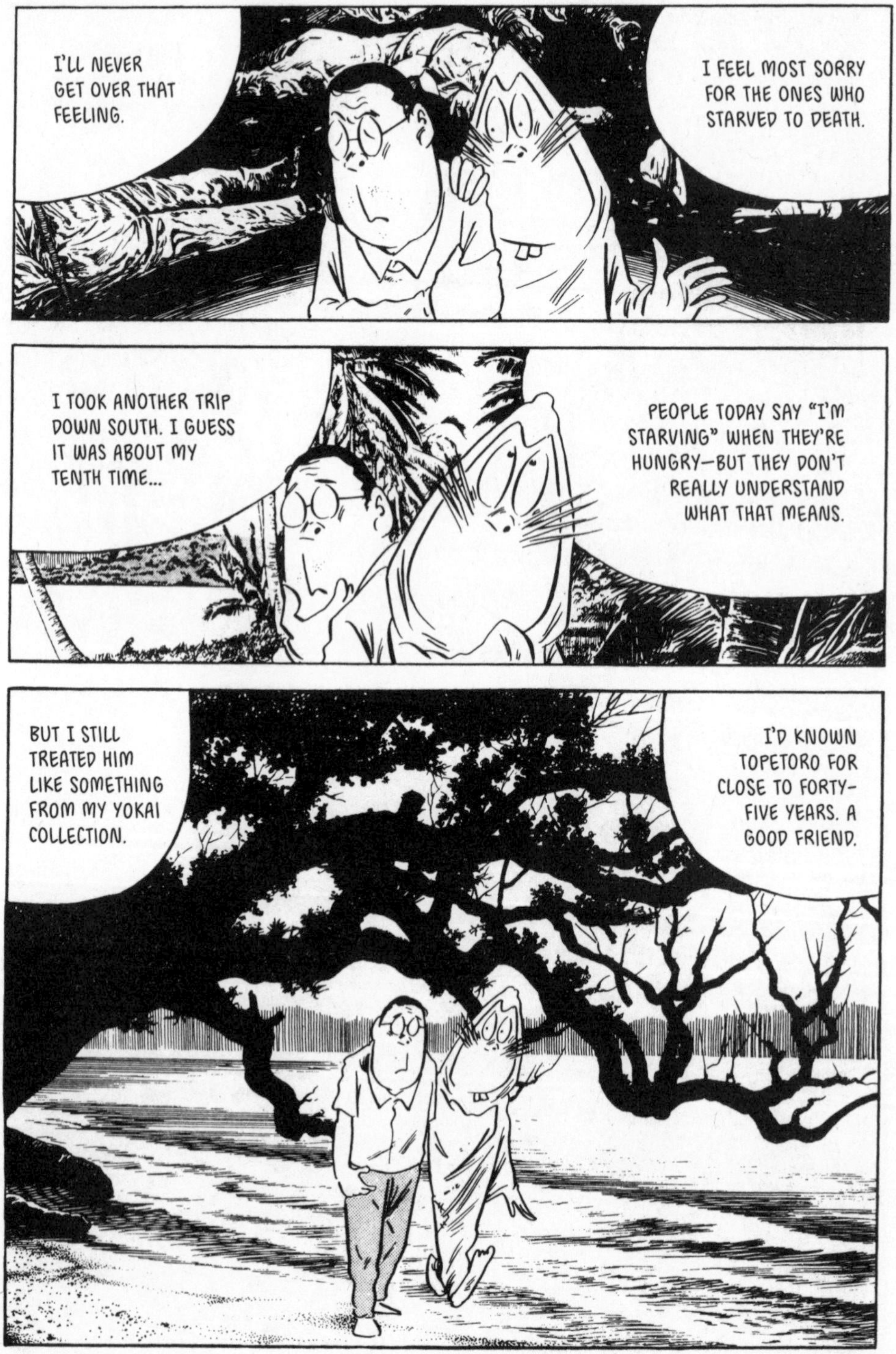
I FEEL MOST SORRY FOR THE ONES WHO STARVED TO DEATH.
I'LL NEVER GET OVER THAT FEELING.
PEOPLE TODAY SAY "I'M STARVING" WHEN THEY'RE HUNGRY—BUT THEY DON'T REALLY UNDERSTAND WHAT THAT MEANS.
I TOOK ANOTHER TRIP DOWN SOUTH. I GUESS IT WAS ABOUT MY TENTH TIME...
I'D KNOWN TOPETORO FOR CLOSE TO FORTY-FIVE YEARS. A GOOD FRIEND.
BUT I STILL TREATED HIM LIKE SOMETHING FROM MY YOKAI COLLECTION.

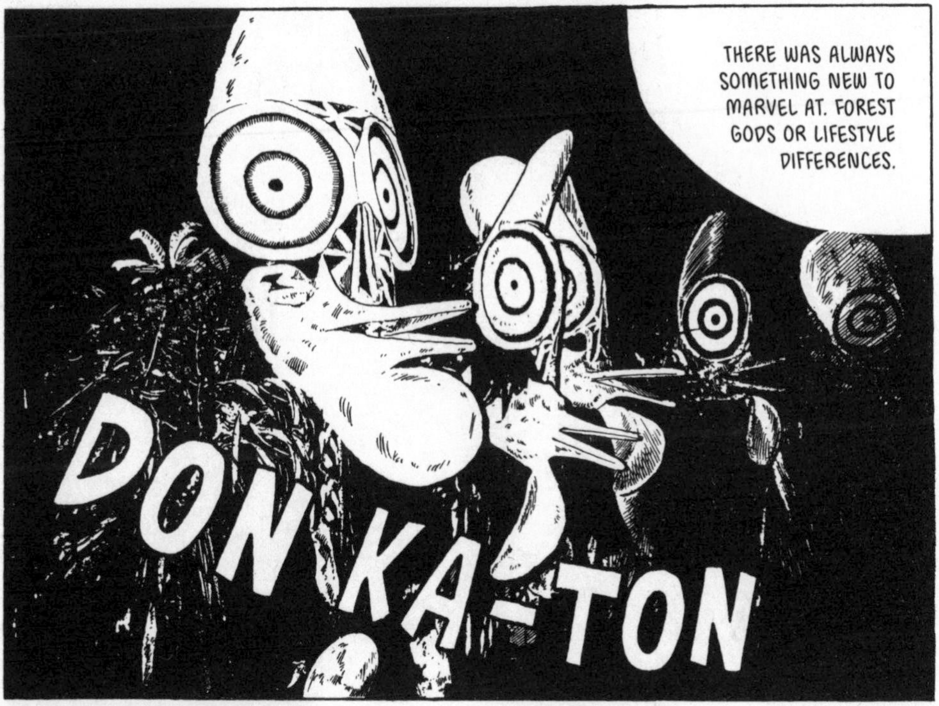
THERE WAS ALWAYS SOMETHING NEW TO MARVEL AT. FOREST GODS OR LIFESTYLE DIFFERENCES.
DON KA-TON

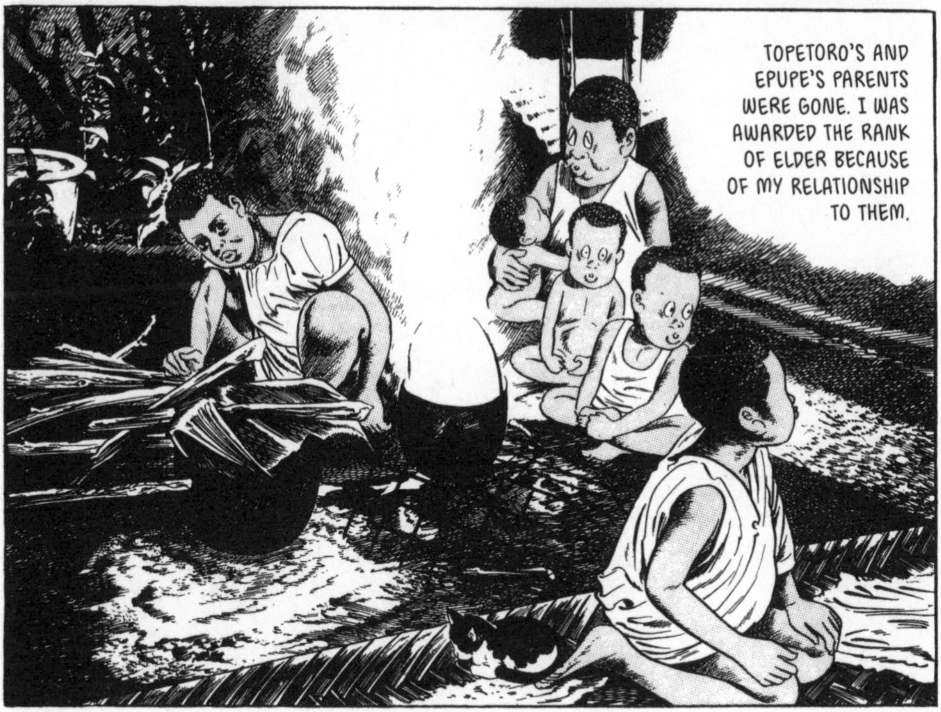
TOPETORO'S AND EPUPE'S PARENTS WERE GONE. I WAS AWARDED THE RANK OF ELDER BECAUSE OF MY RELATIONSHIP TO THEM.

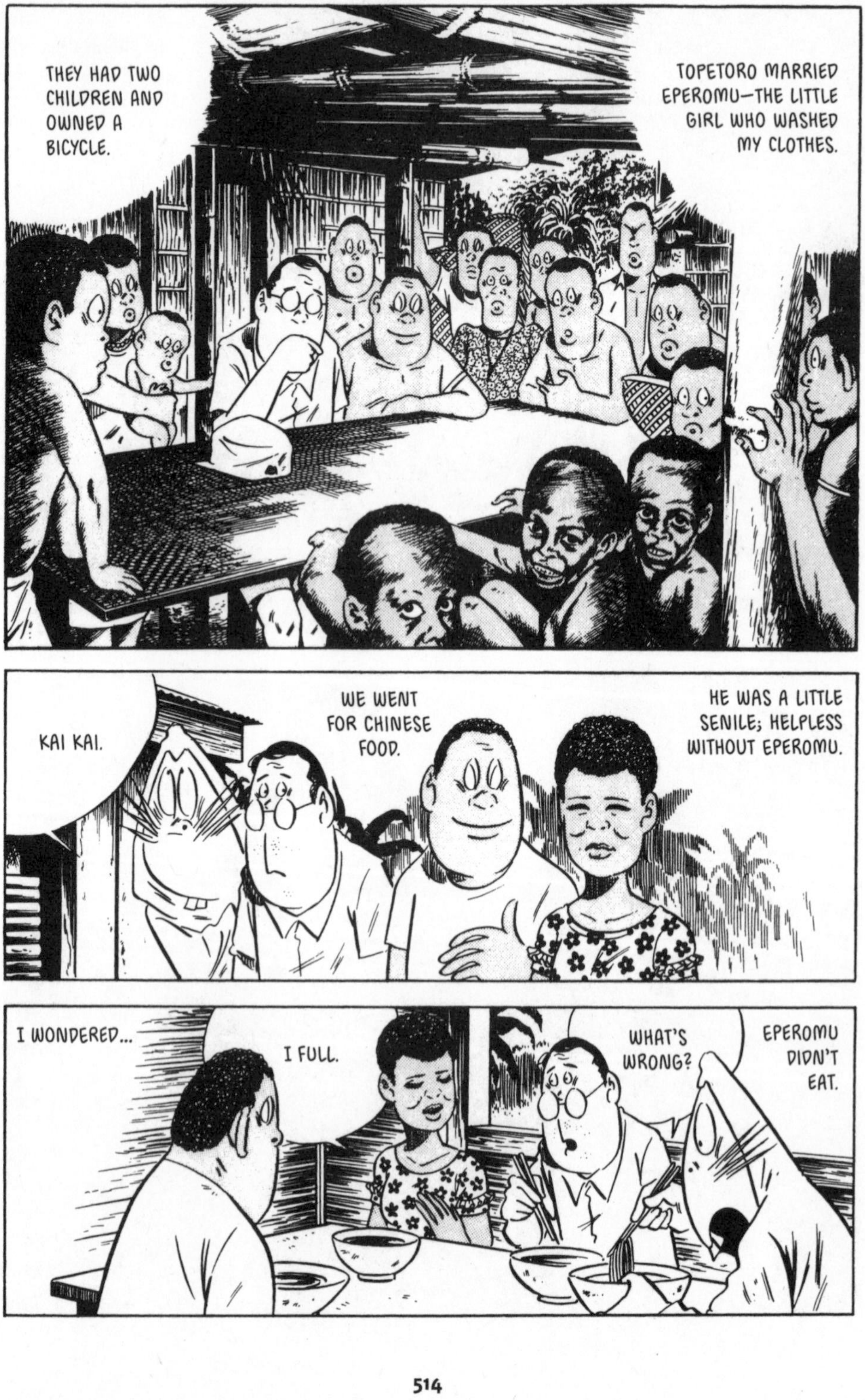
TOPETORO MARRIED EPEROMU—THE LITTLE GIRL WHO WASHED MY CLOTHES.
THEY HAD TWO CHILDREN AND OWNED A BICYCLE.
HE WAS A LITTLE SENILE; HELPLESS WITHOUT EPEROMU.
WE WENT FOR CHINESE FOOD.
KAI KAI.
EPEROMU DIDN'T EAT.
WHAT'S WRONG?
I FULL.
I WONDERED...

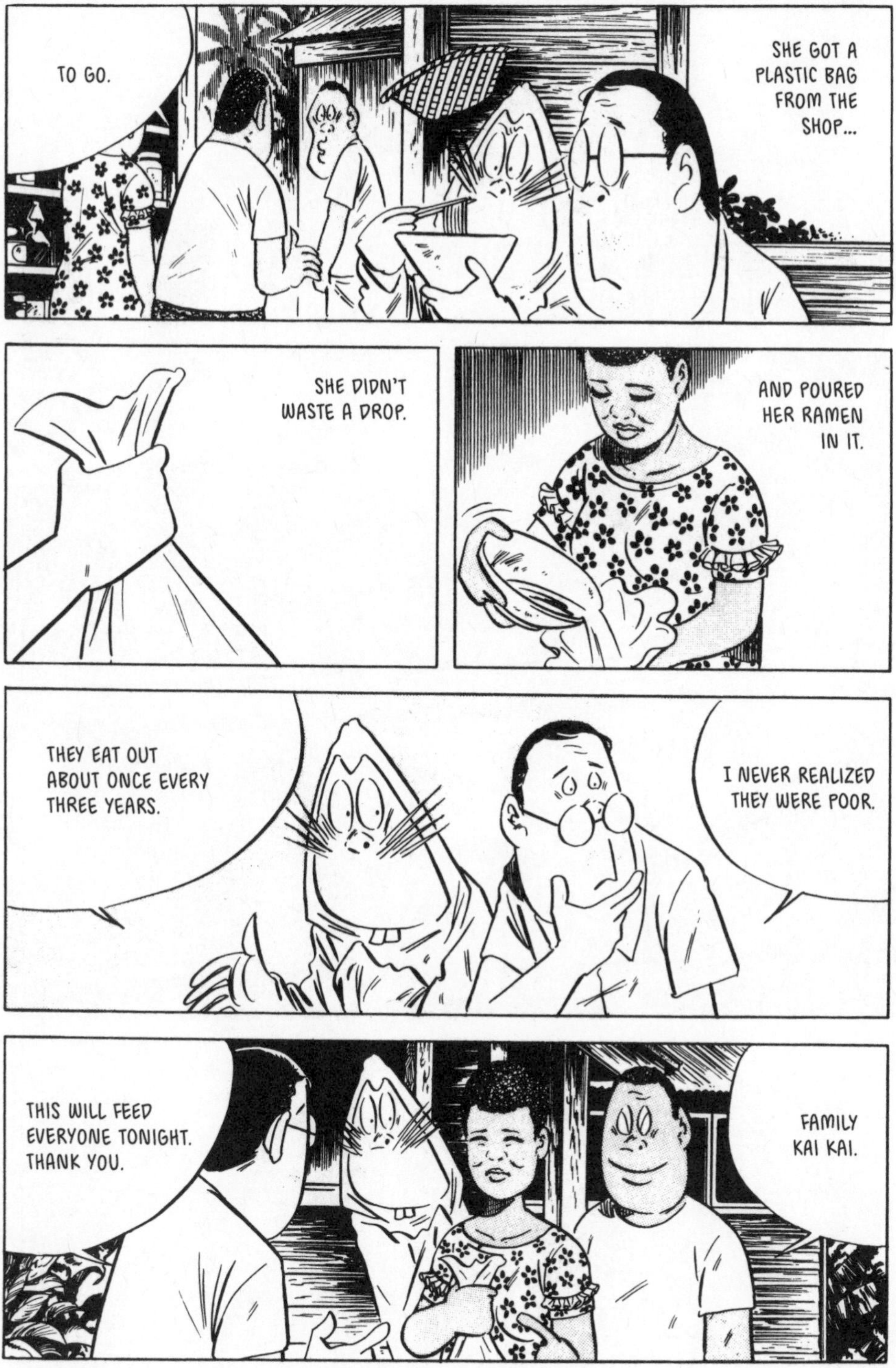
SHE GOT A PLASTIC BAG FROM THE SHOP...
TO GO.
AND POURED HER RAMEN IN IT.
SHE DIDN'T WASTE A DROP.
I NEVER REALIZED THEY WERE POOR.
THEY EAT OUT ABOUT ONCE EVERY THREE YEARS.
FAMILY KAI KAI.
THIS WILL FEED EVERYONE TONIGHT. THANK YOU.

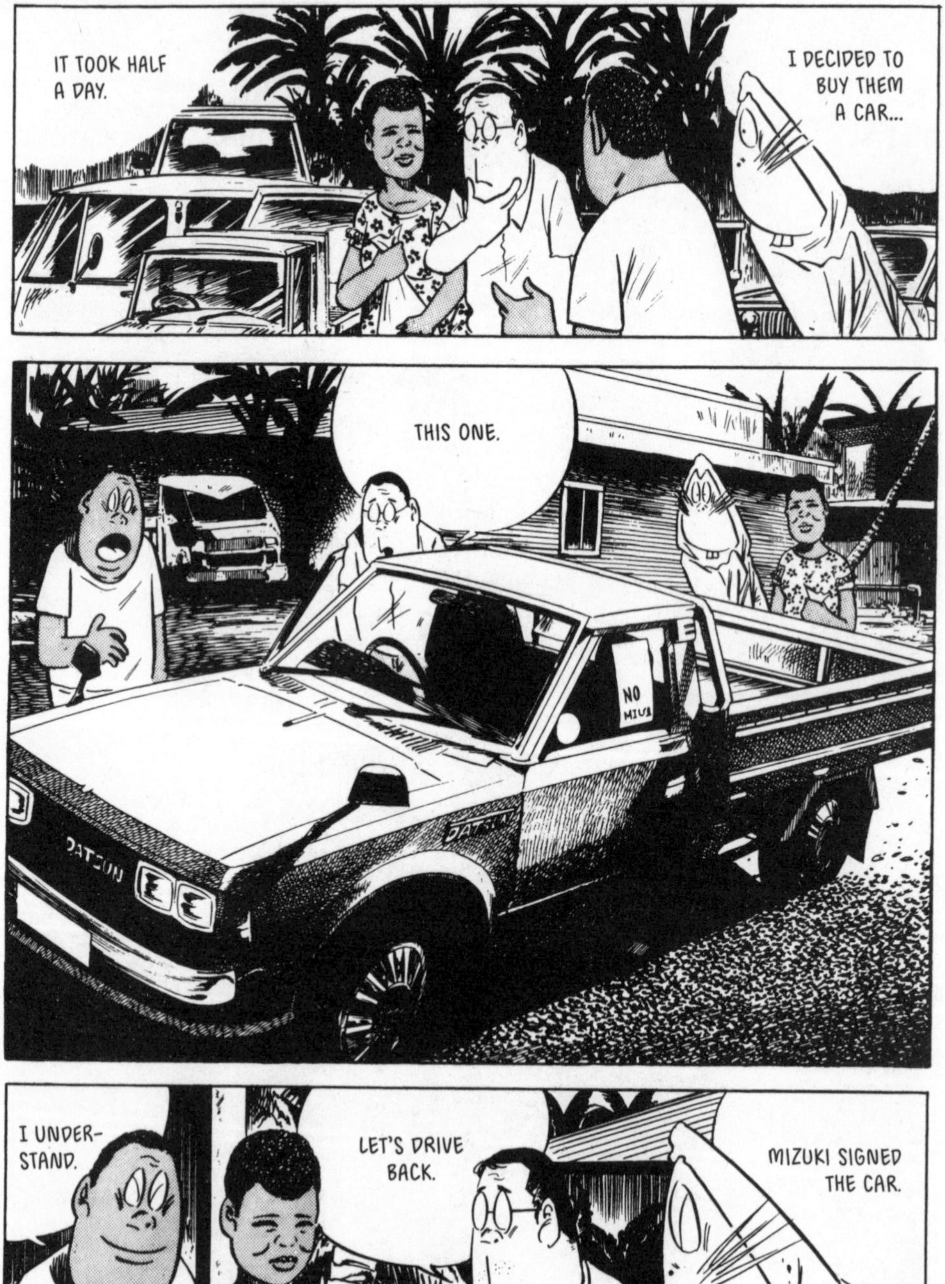
I DECIDED TO BUY THEM A CAR...
IT TOOK HALF A DAY.
THIS ONE.
DATSUN
MIZUKI SIGNED THE CAR.
LET'S DRIVE BACK.
I UNDER-STAND.

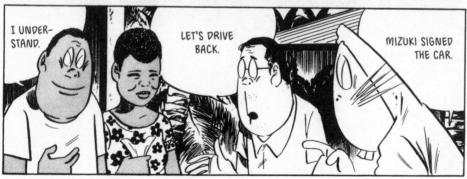

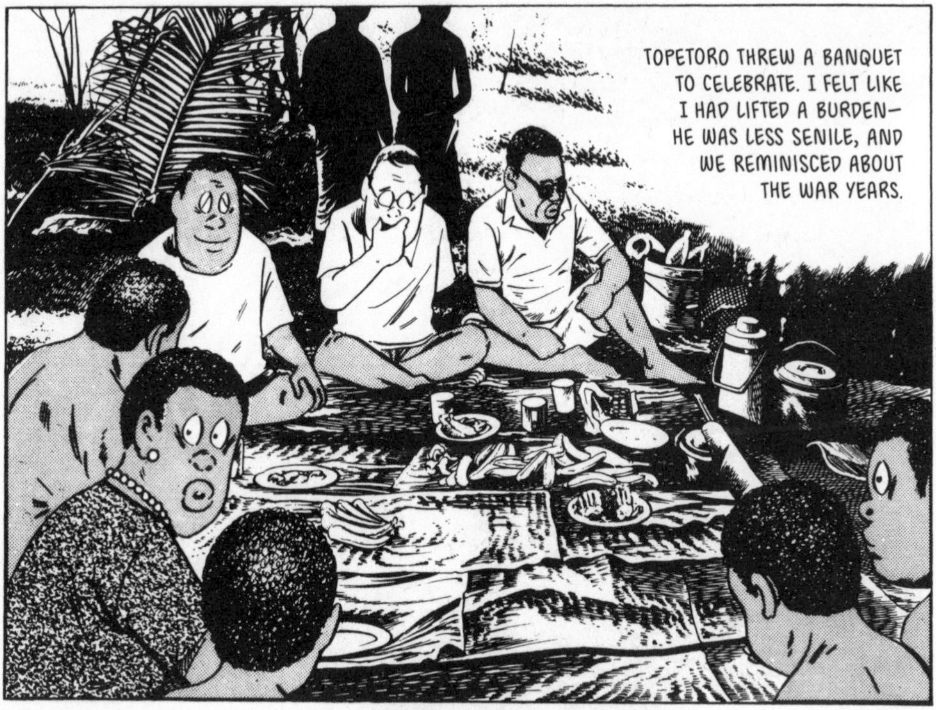
TOPETORO THREW A BANQUET TO CELEBRATE. I FELT LIKE I HAD LIFTED A BURDEN— HE WAS LESS SENILE, AND WE REMINISCED ABOUT THE WAR YEARS.

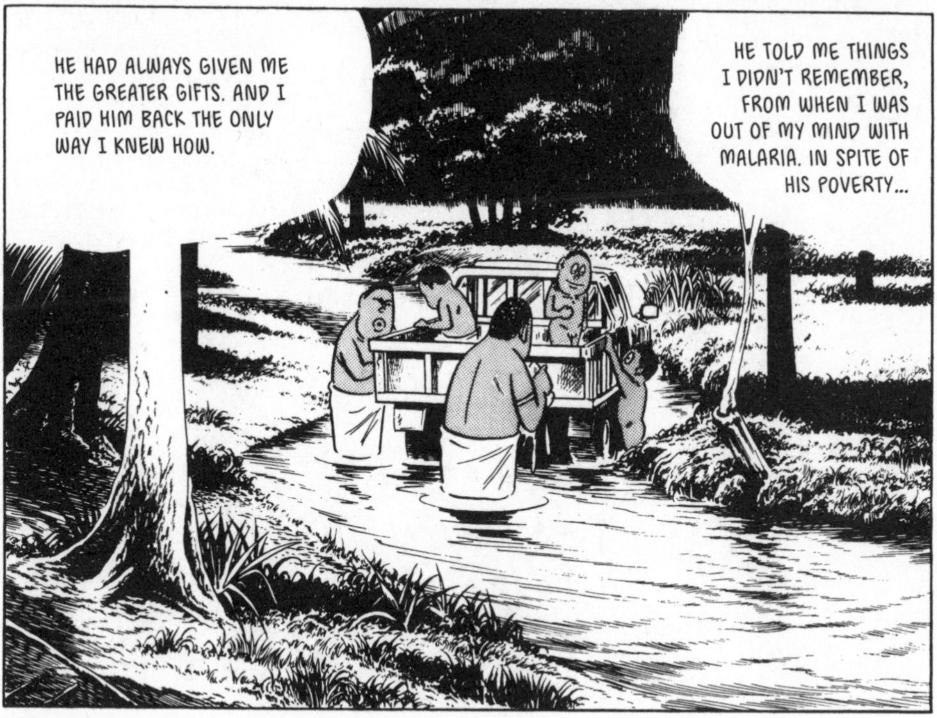
HE TOLD ME THINGS I DIDN'T REMEMBER, FROM WHEN I WAS OUT OF MY MIND WITH MALARIA. IN SPITE OF HIS POVERTY...
HE HAD ALWAYS GIVEN ME THE GREATER GIFTS. AND I PAID HIM BACK THE ONLY WAY I KNEW HOW.

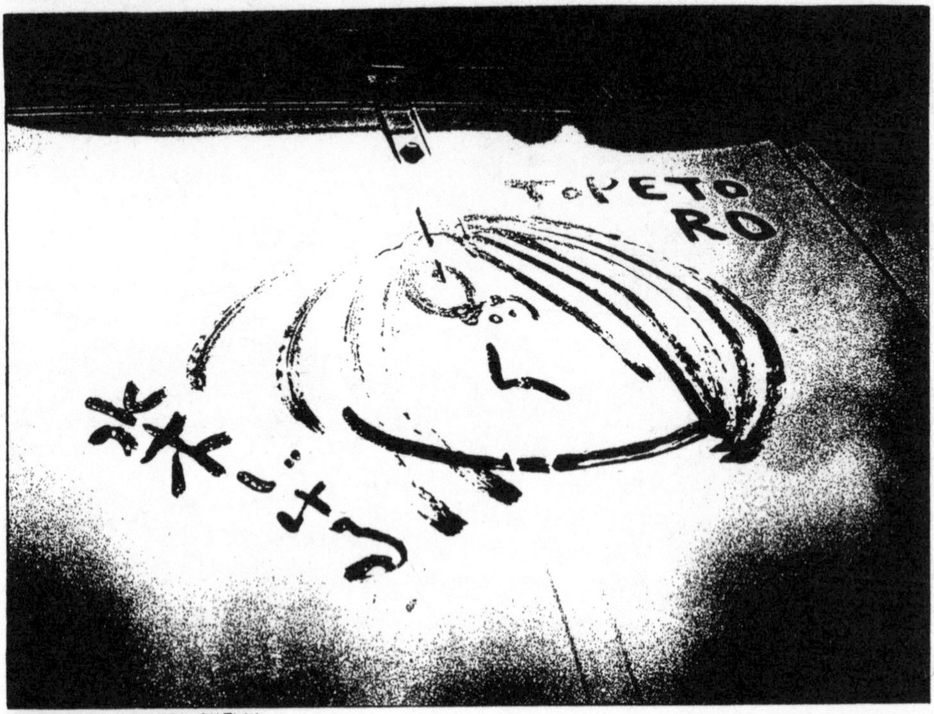

SIGNATURE: SHIGERU MIZUKI.

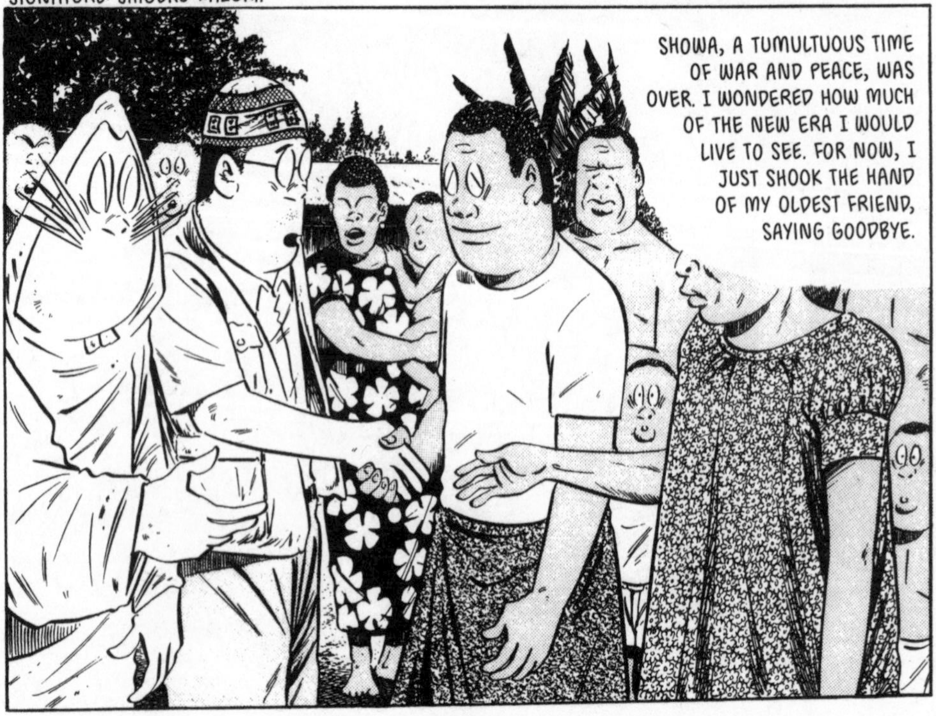
SHOWA, A TUMULTUOUS TIME OF WAR AND PEACE, WAS OVER. I WONDERED HOW MUCH OF THE NEW ERA I WOULD LIVE TO SEE. FOR NOW, I JUST SHOOK THE HAND OF MY OLDEST FRIEND, SAYING GOODBYE.

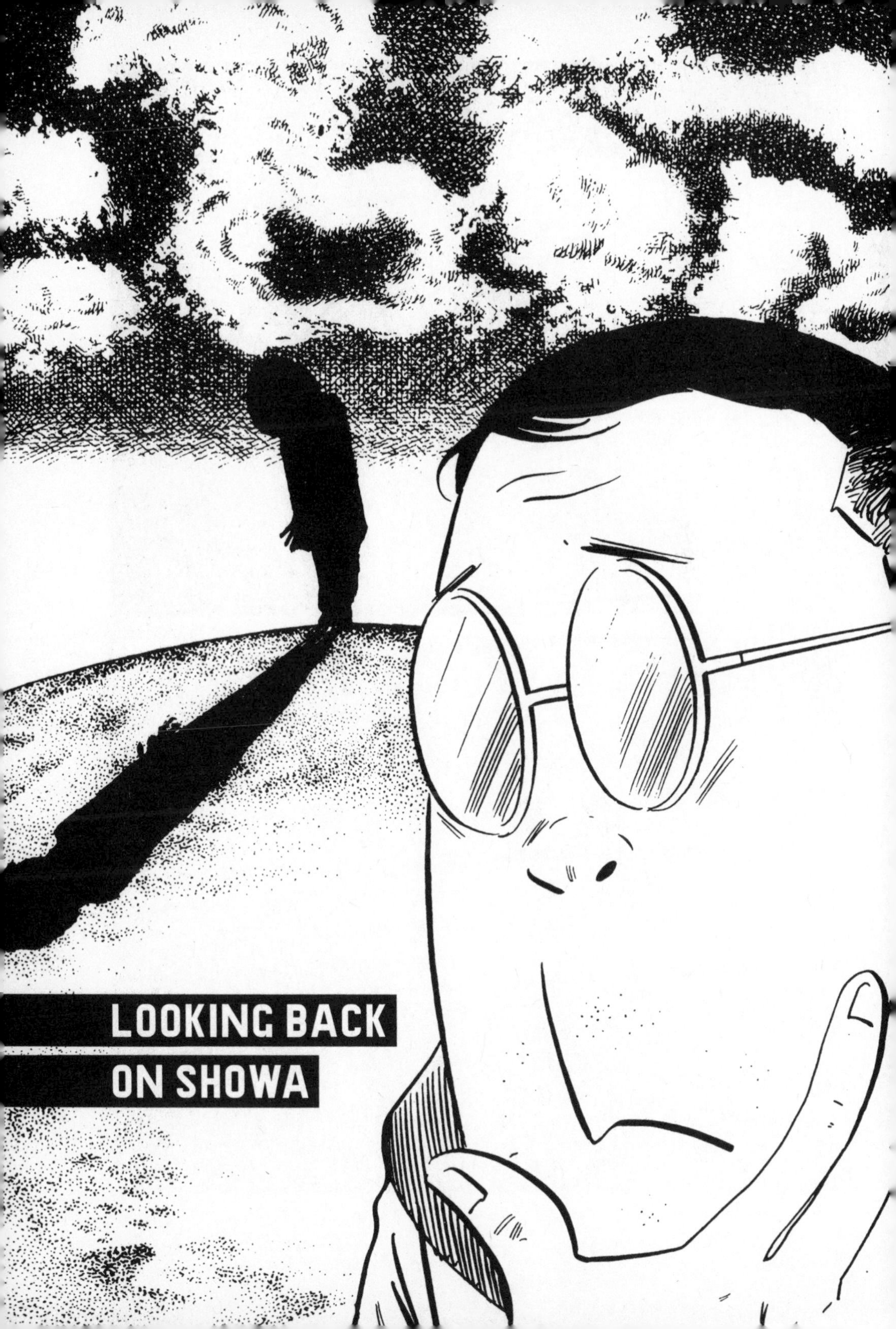
LOOKING BACK
ON SHOWA

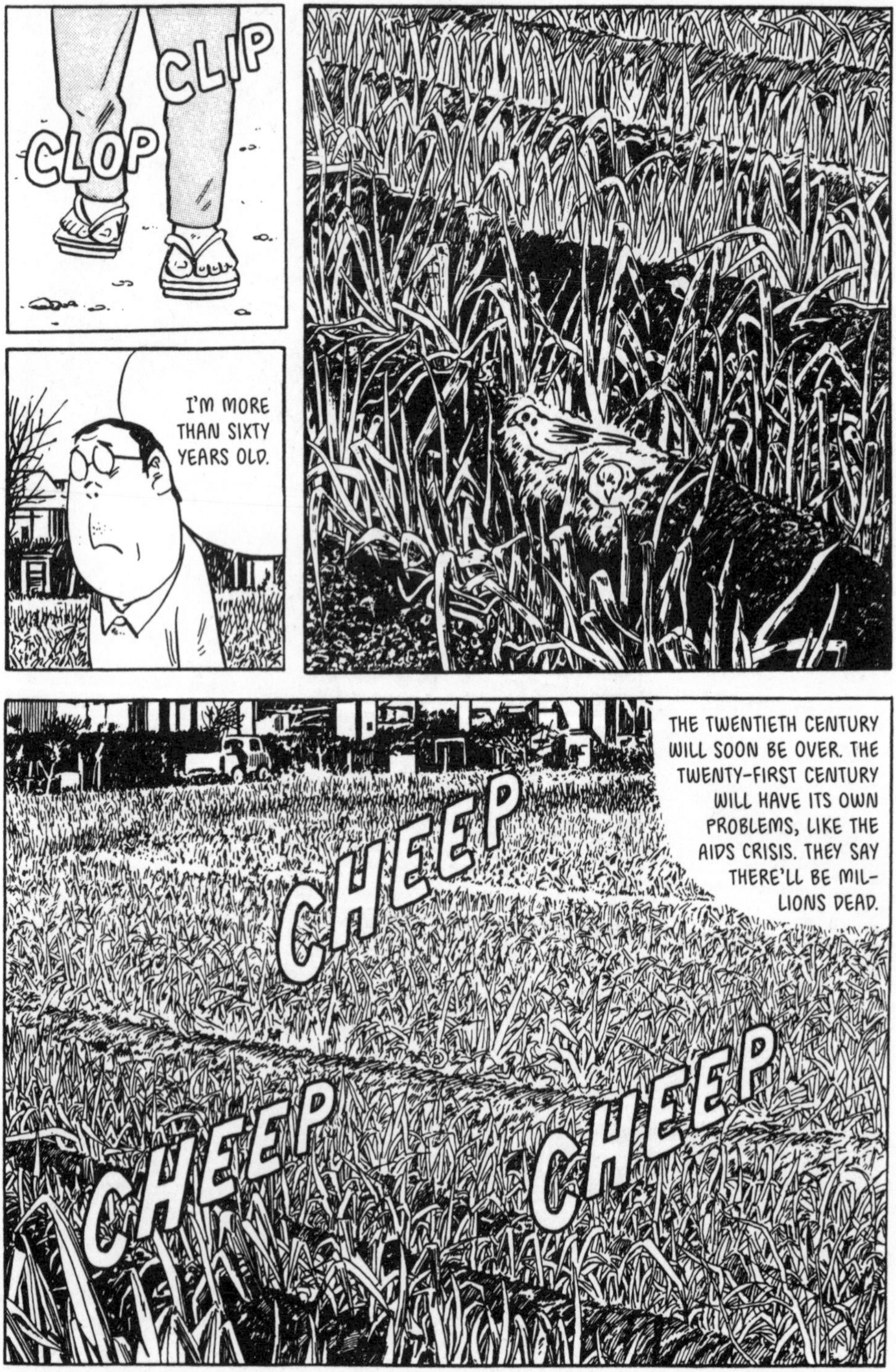
CLIP
CLOP
I'M MORE THAN SIXTY YEARS OLD.
THE TWENTIETH CENTURY WILL SOON BE OVER. THE TWENTY-FIRST CENTURY WILL HAVE ITS OWN PROBLEMS, LIKE THE AIDS CRISIS. THEY SAY THERE'LL BE MIL-LIONS DEAD.
CHEEP
CHEEP
CHEEP

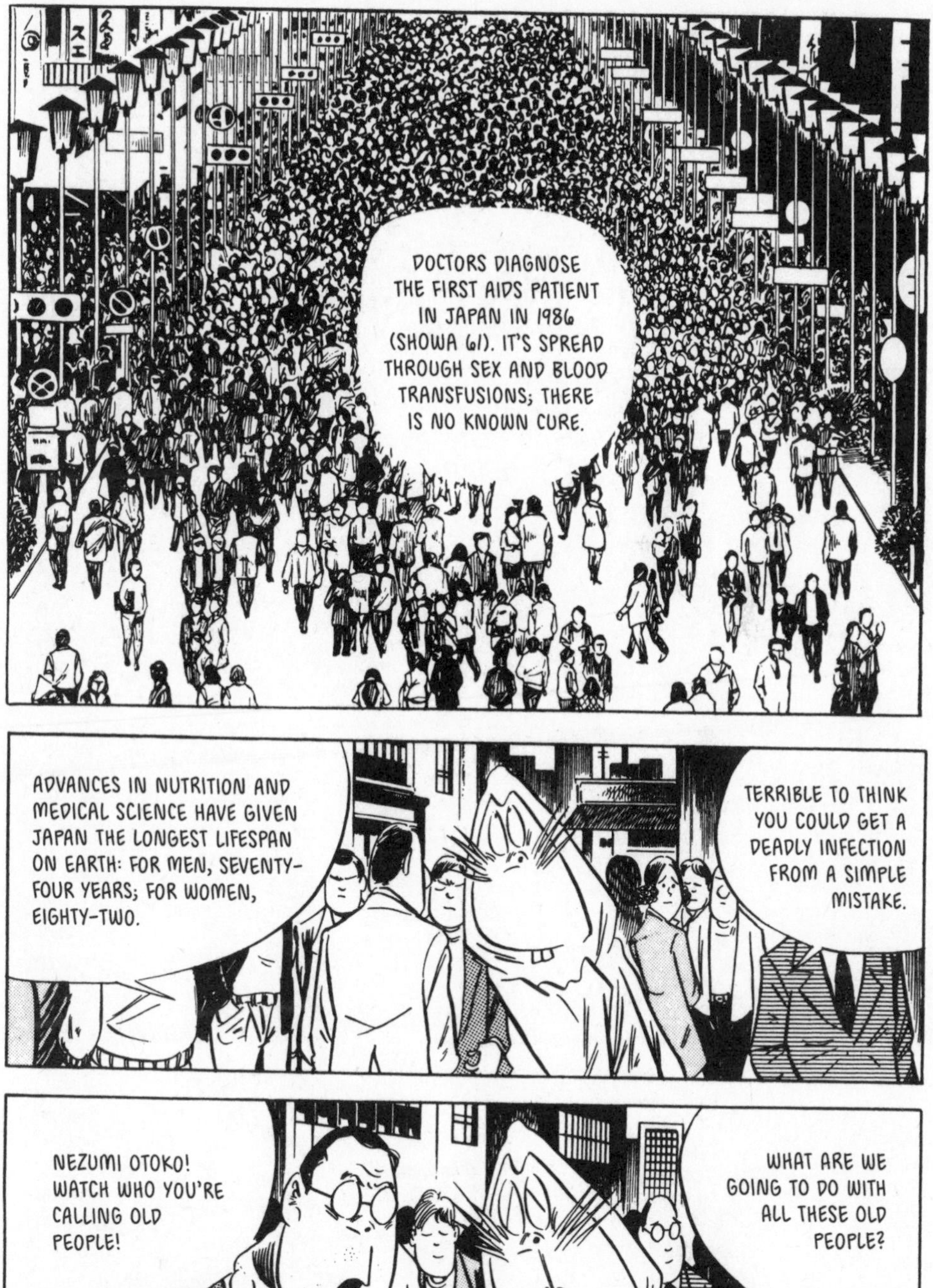
DOCTORS DIAGNOSE THE FIRST AIDS PATIENT IN JAPAN IN 1986 (SHOWA 61). IT'S SPREAD THROUGH SEX AND BLOOD TRANSFUSIONS; THERE IS NO KNOWN CURE.
TERRIBLE TO THINK YOU COULD GET A DEADLY INFECTION FROM A SIMPLE MISTAKE.
ADVANCES IN NUTRITION AND MEDICAL SCIENCE HAVE GIVEN JAPAN THE LONGEST LIFESPAN ON EARTH: FOR MEN, SEVENTY-FOUR YEARS; FOR WOMEN, EIGHTY-TWO.
WHAT ARE WE GOING TO DO WITH ALL THESE OLD PEOPLE?
NEZUMI OTOKO! WATCH WHO YOU'RE CALLING OLD PEOPLE!

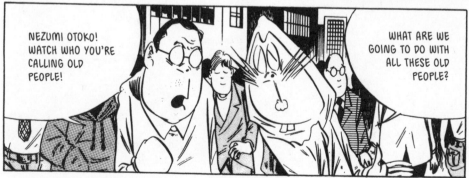

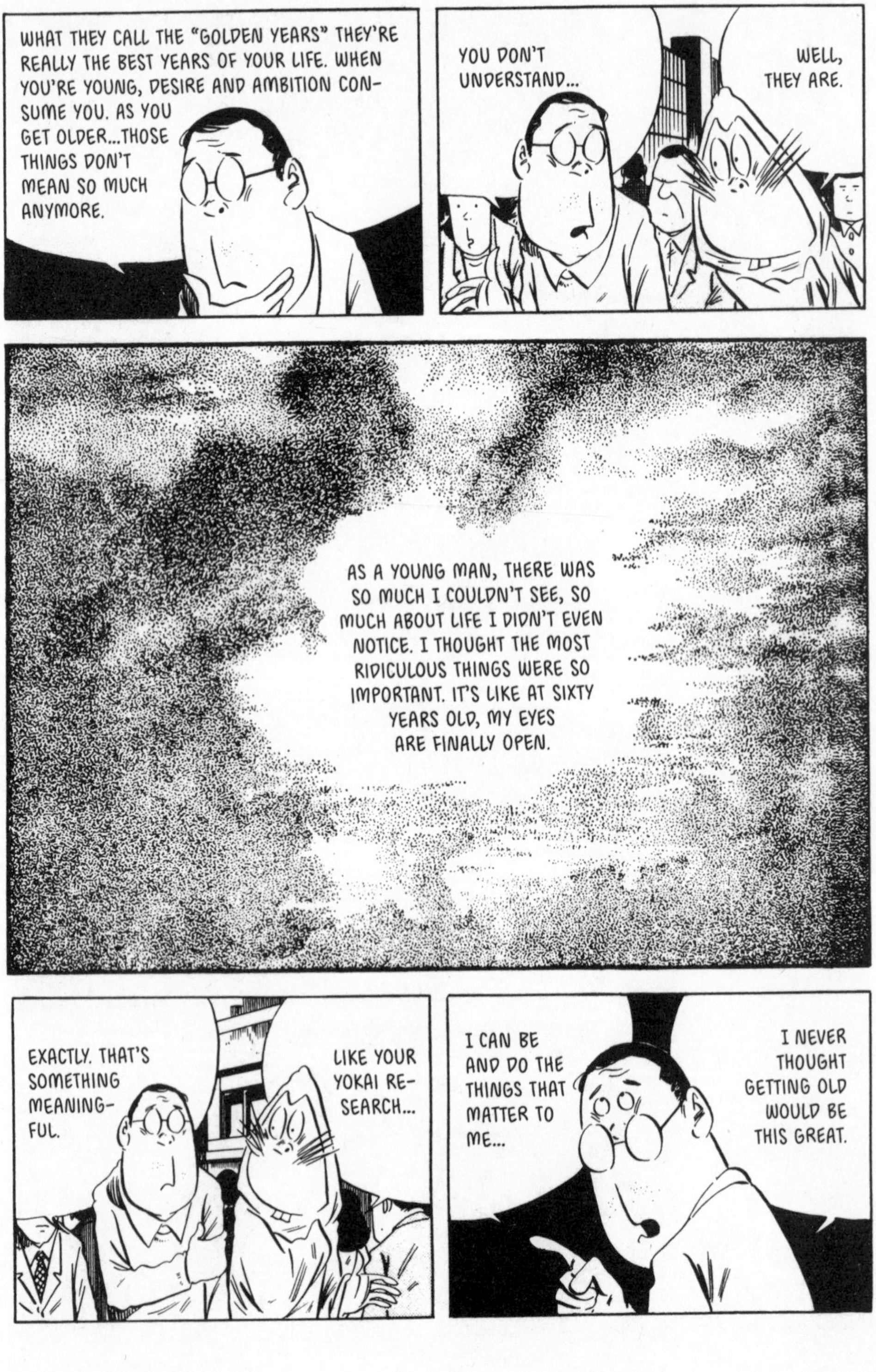
WELL, THEY ARE.
YOU DON'T UNDERSTAND...
WHAT THEY CALL THE "GOLDEN YEARS" THEY'RE REALLY THE BEST YEARS OF YOUR LIFE. WHEN YOU'RE YOUNG, DESIRE AND AMBITION CONSUME YOU. AS YOU GET OLDER...THOSE THINGS DON'T MEAN SO MUCH ANYMORE.
AS A YOUNG MAN, THERE WAS SO MUCH I COULDN'T SEE, SO MUCH ABOUT LIFE I DIDN'T EVEN NOTICE. I THOUGHT THE MOST RIDICULOUS THINGS WERE SO IMPORTANT. IT'S LIKE AT SIXTY YEARS OLD, MY EYES ARE FINALLY OPEN.
I NEVER THOUGHT GETTING OLD WOULD BE THIS GREAT.
I CAN BE AND DO THE THINGS THAT MATTER TO ME...
LIKE YOUR YOKAI RESEARCH...
EXACTLY. THAT'S SOMETHING MEANINGFUL.

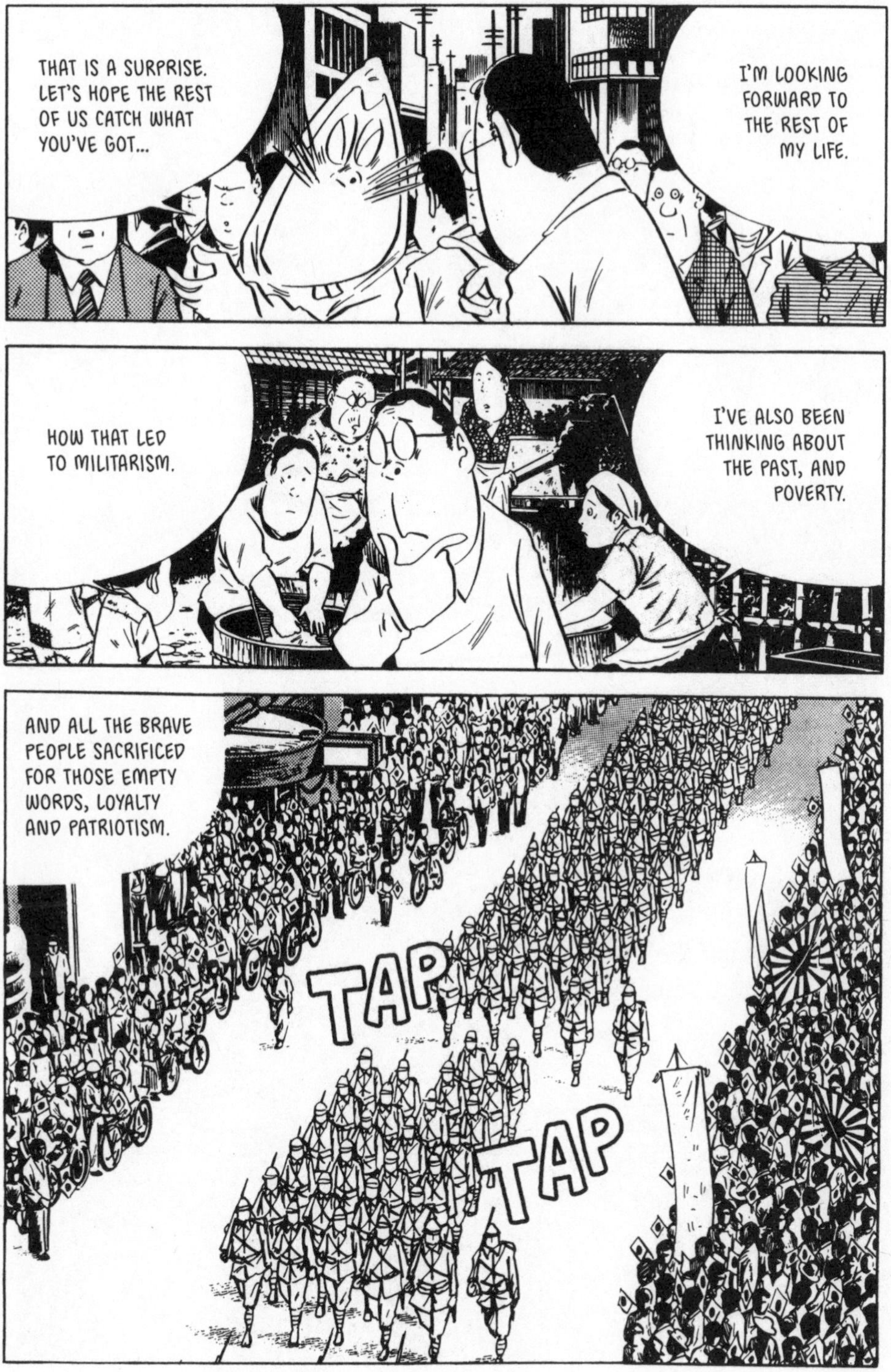
I'M LOOKING FORWARD TO THE REST OF MY LIFE.
THAT IS A SURPRISE. LET'S HOPE THE REST OF US CATCH WHAT YOU'VE GOT...
I'VE ALSO BEEN THINKING ABOUT THE PAST, AND POVERTY.
HOW THAT LED TO MILITARISM.
AND ALL THE BRAVE PEOPLE SACRIFICED FOR THOSE EMPTY WORDS, LOYALTY AND PATRIOTISM.
TAP
TAP

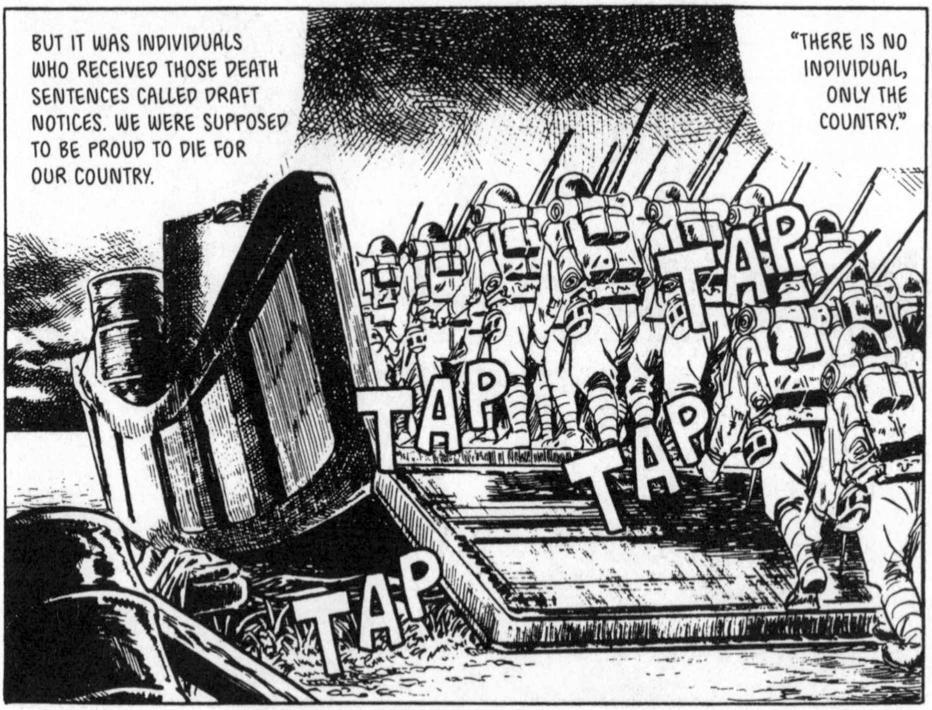
"THERE IS NO INDIVIDUAL, ONLY THE COUNTRY."
BUT IT WAS INDIVIDUALS WHO RECEIVED THOSE DEATH SENTENCES CALLED DRAFT NOTICES. WE WERE SUPPOSED TO BE PROUD TO DIE FOR OUR COUNTRY.
TAP
TAP
TAP
TAP

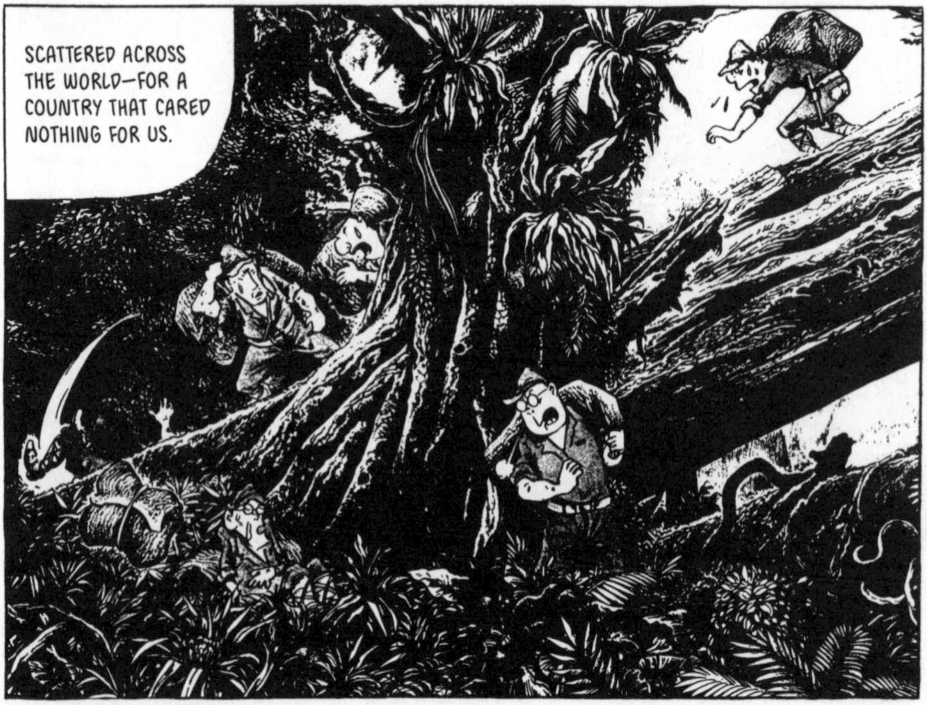
SCATTERED ACROSS THE WORLD—FOR A COUNTRY THAT CARED NOTHING FOR US.

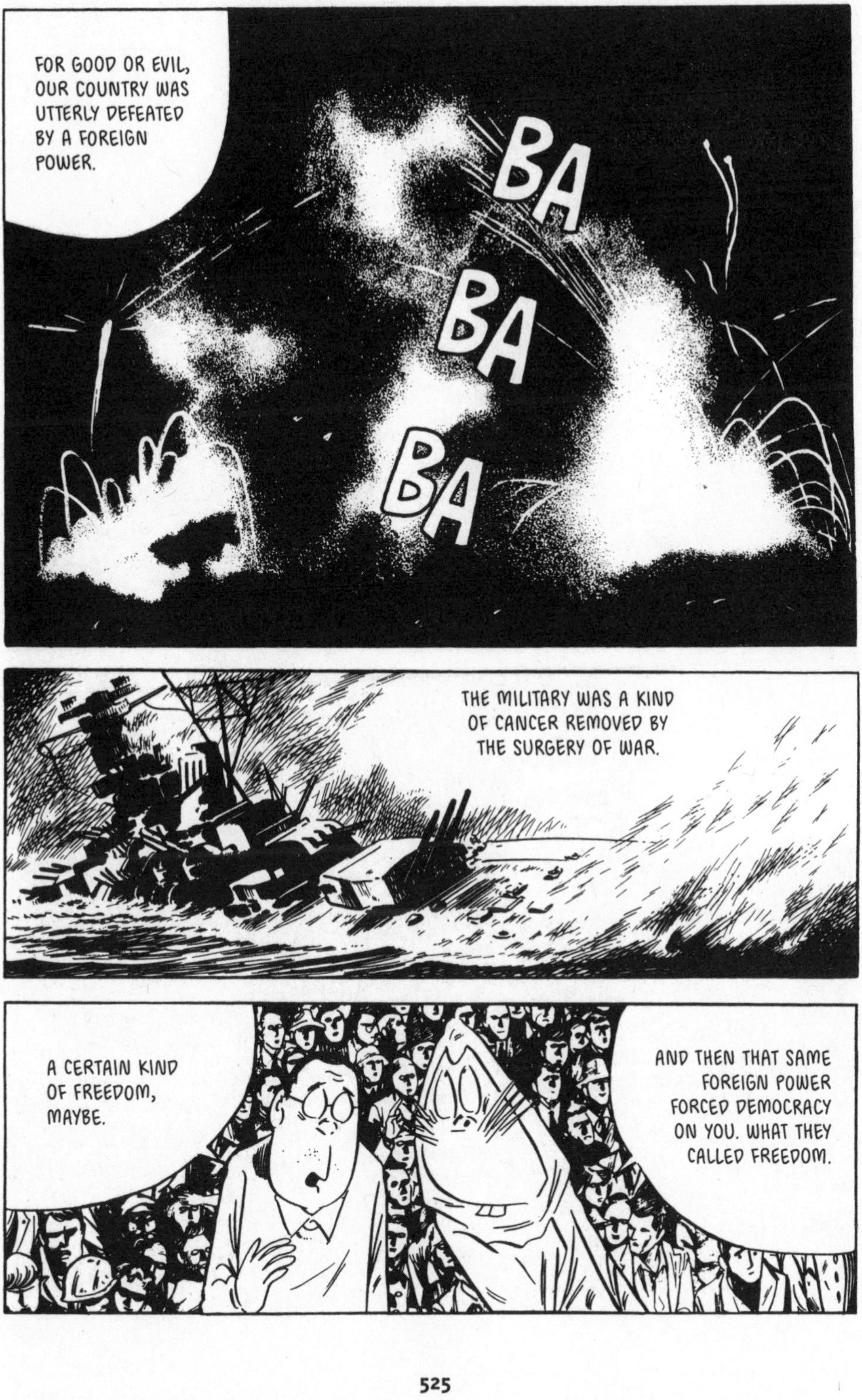
FOR GOOD OR EVIL, OUR COUNTRY WAS UTTERLY DEFEATED BY A FOREIGN POWER.
BA
BA
BA
THE MILITARY WAS A KIND OF CANCER REMOVED BY THE SURGERY OF WAR.
AND THEN THAT SAME FOREIGN POWER FORCED DEMOCRACY ON YOU. WHAT THEY CALLED FREEDOM.
A CERTAIN KIND OF FREEDOM, MAYBE.

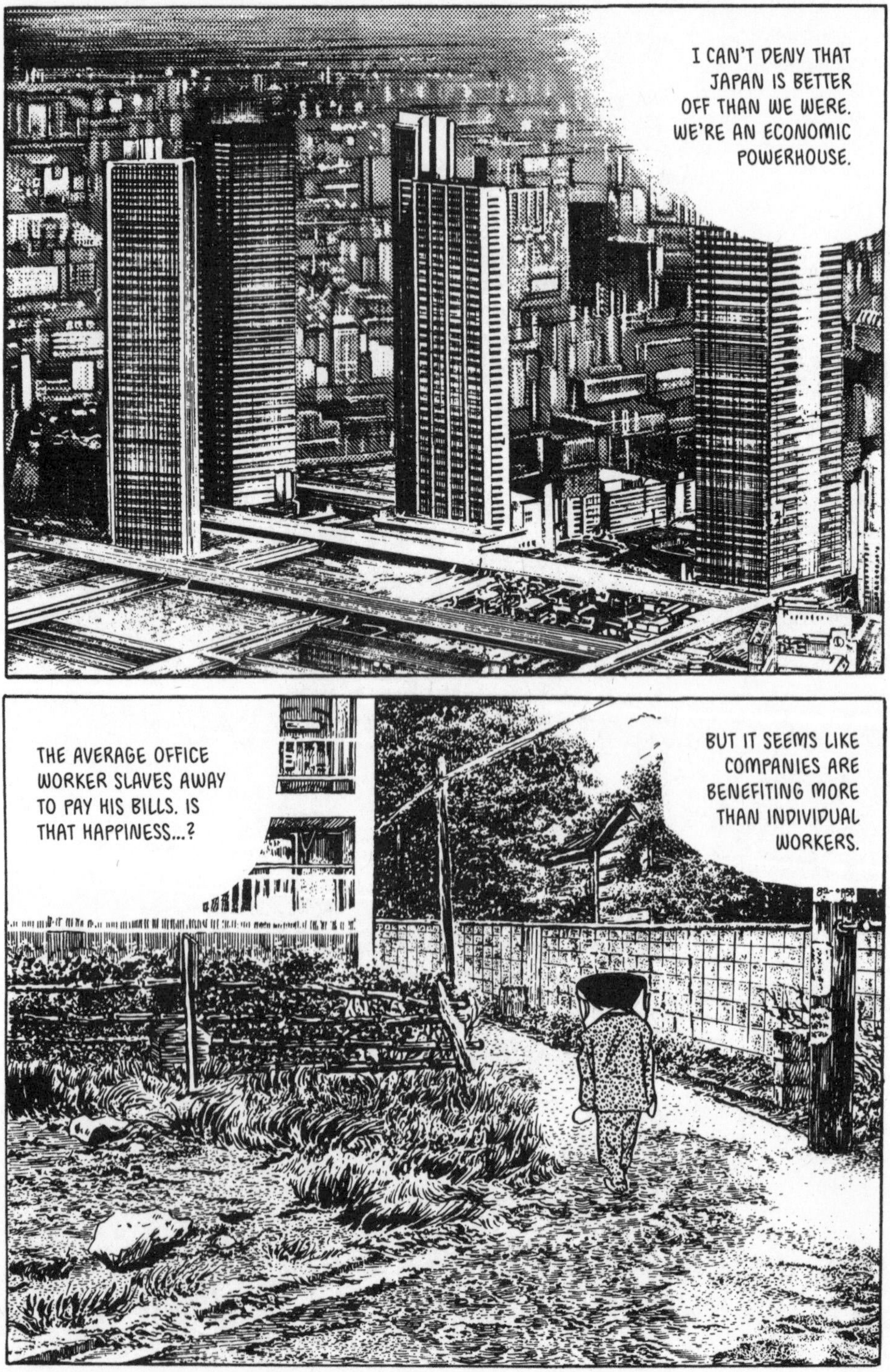
I CAN'T DENY THAT JAPAN IS BETTER OFF THAN WE WERE. WE'RE AN ECONOMIC POWERHOUSE.
BUT IT SEEMS LIKE COMPANIES ARE BENEFITING MORE THAN INDIVIDUAL WORKERS.
THE AVERAGE OFFICE WORKER SLAVES AWAY TO PAY HIS BILLS. IS THAT HAPPINESS...?

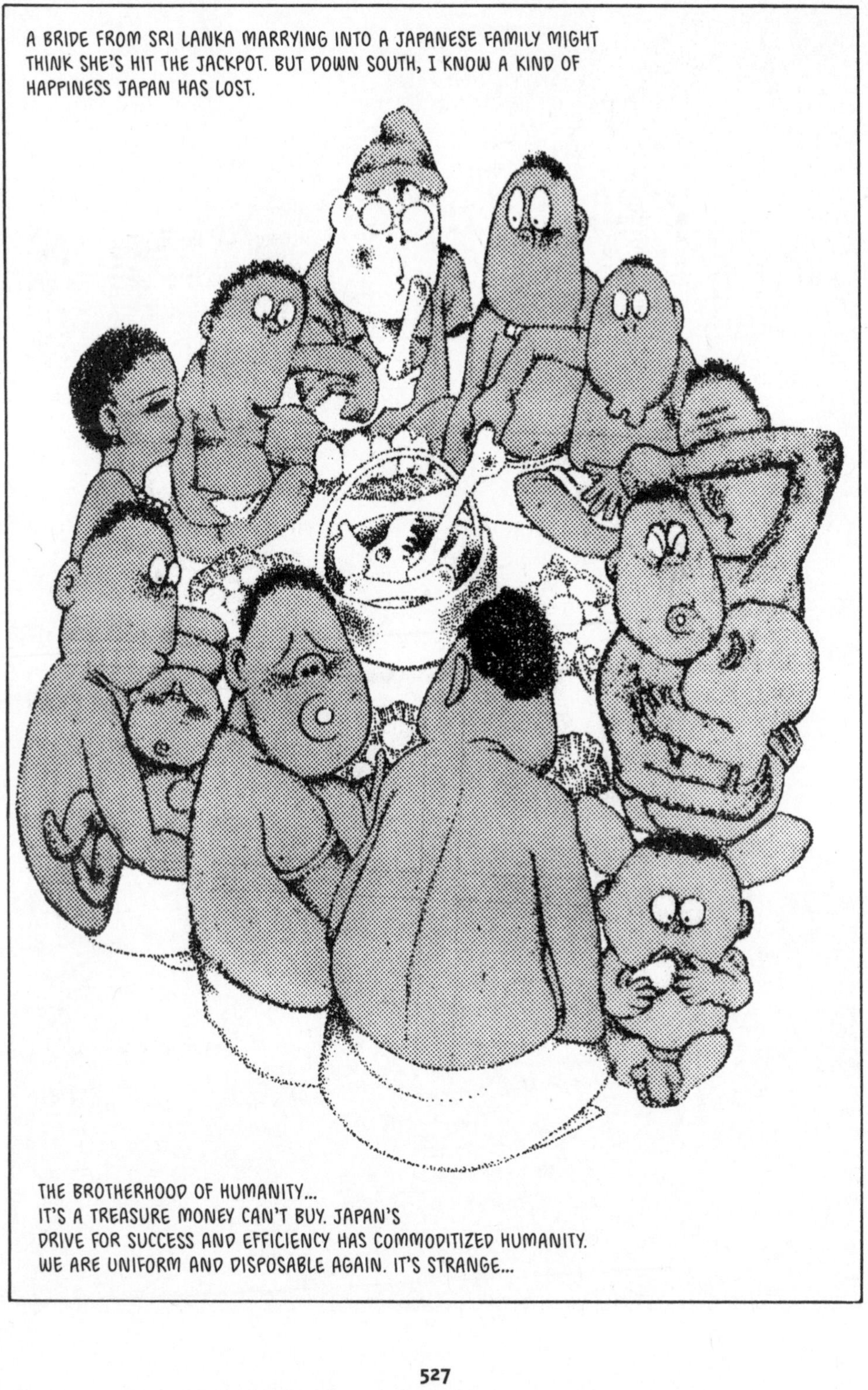
A BRIDE FROM SRI LANKA MARRYING INTO A JAPANESE FAMILY MIGHT THINK SHE'S HIT THE JACKPOT. BUT DOWN SOUTH, I KNOW A KIND OF HAPPINESS JAPAN HAS LOST.
THE BROTHERHOOD OF HUMANITY... IT'S A TREASURE MONEY CAN'T BUY. JAPAN'S DRIVE FOR SUCCESS AND EFFICIENCY HAS COMMODITIZED HUMANITY. WE ARE UNIFORM AND DISPOSABLE AGAIN. IT'S STRANGE...

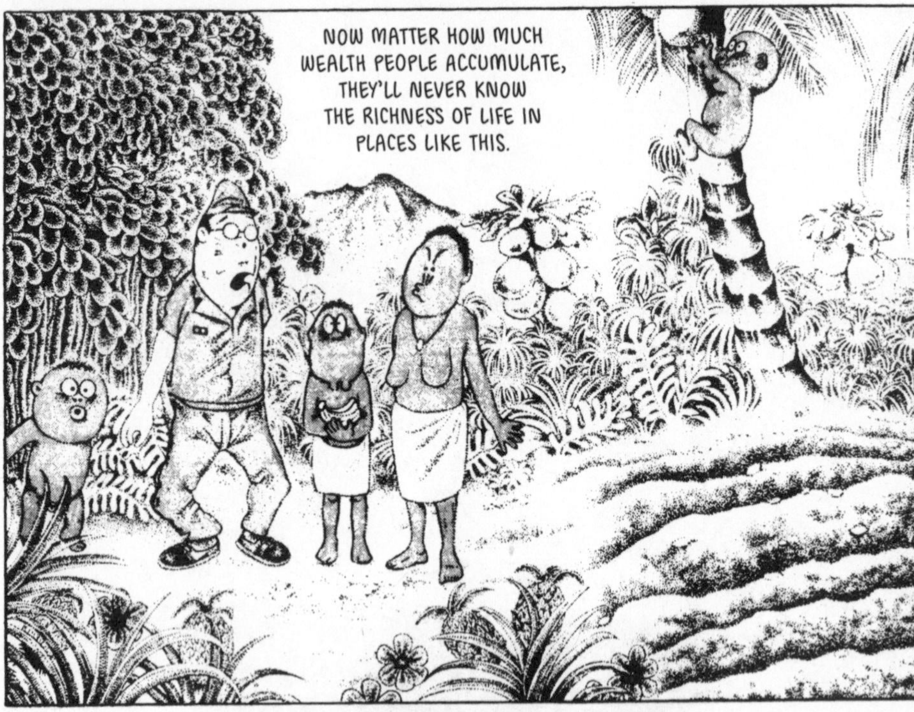
NOW MATTER HOW MUCH WEALTH PEOPLE ACCUMULATE, THEY'LL NEVER KNOW THE RICHNESS OF LIFE IN PLACES LIKE THIS.

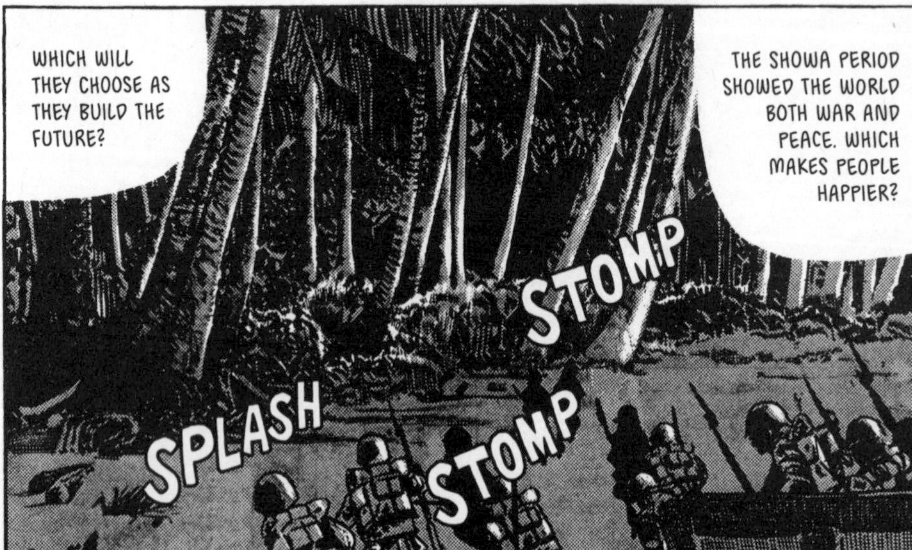
THE SHOWA PERIOD SHOWED THE WORLD BOTH WAR AND PEACE. WHICH MAKES PEOPLE HAPPIER?
WHICH WILL THEY CHOOSE AS THEY BUILD THE FUTURE?
STOMP
STOMP
SPLASH
SPLASH

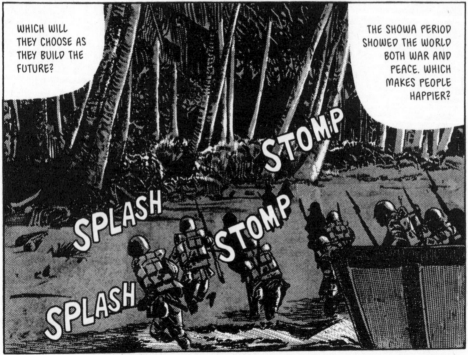

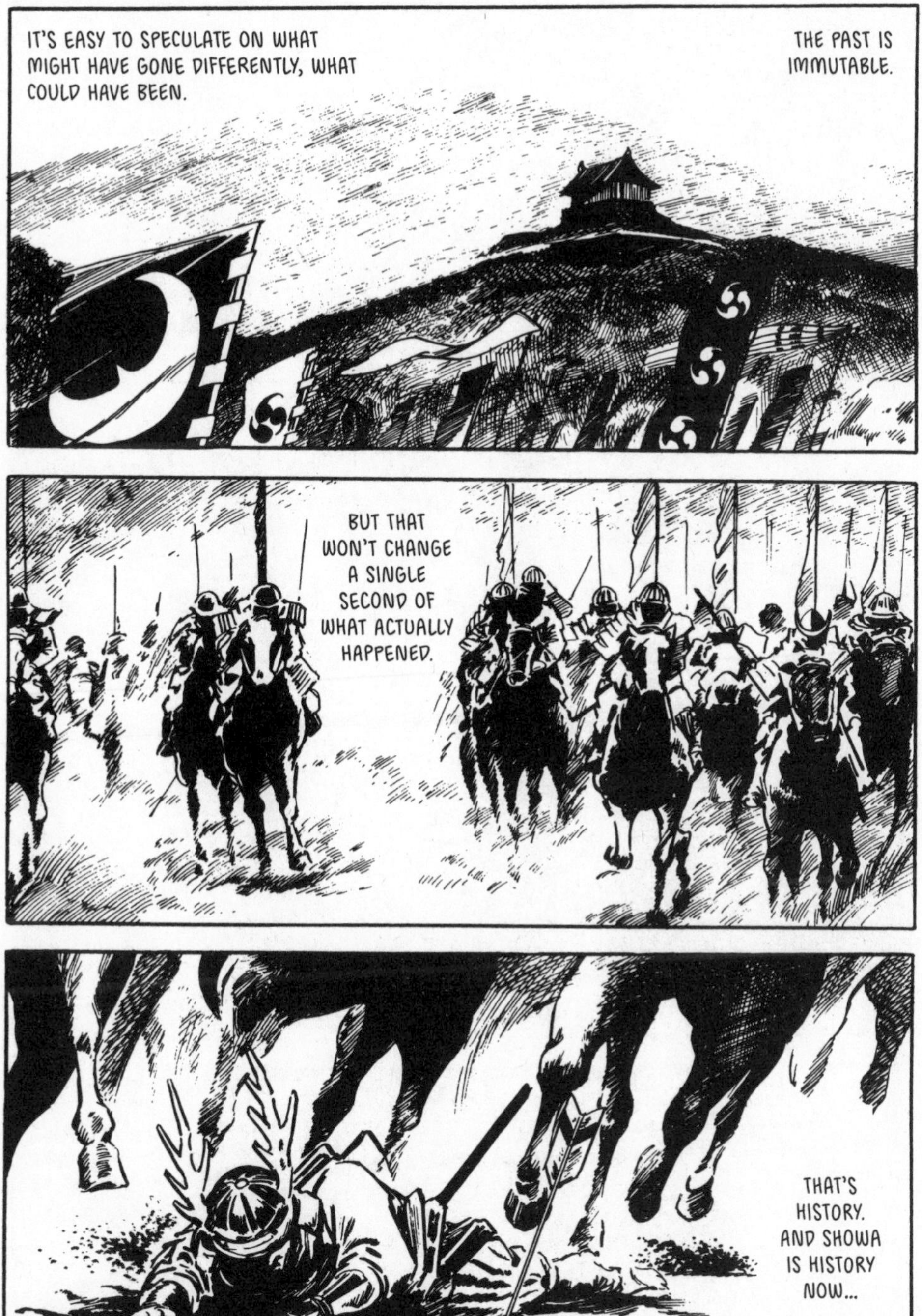
THE PAST IS IMMUTABLE.
IT'S EASY TO SPECULATE ON WHAT MIGHT HAVE GONE DIFFERENTLY, WHAT COULD HAVE BEEN.
BUT THAT WON'T CHANGE A SINGLE SECOND OF WHAT ACTUALLY HAPPENED.
THAT'S HISTORY. AND SHOWA IS HISTORY NOW...

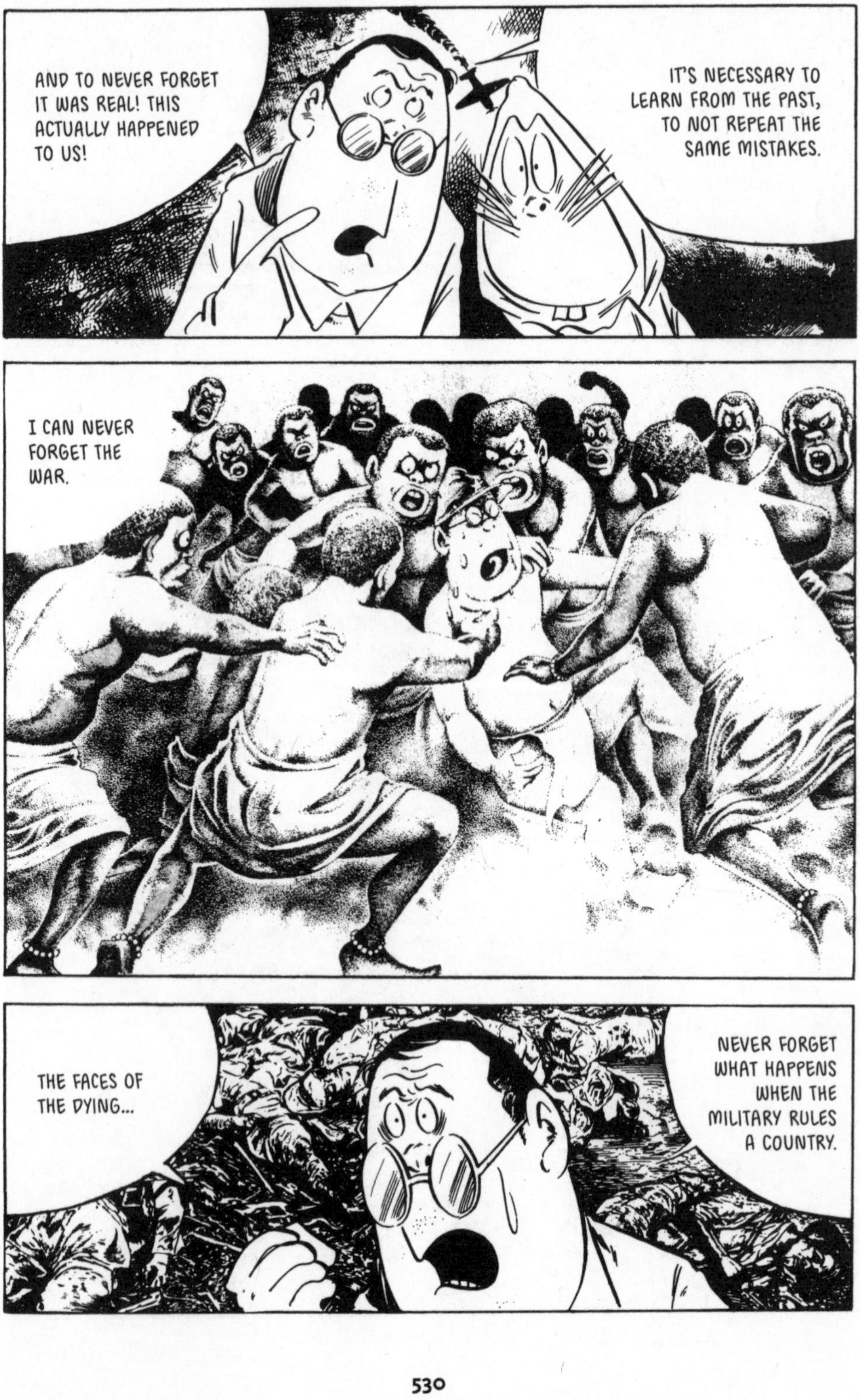
IT'S NECESSARY TO LEARN FROM THE PAST, TO NOT REPEAT THE SAME MISTAKES.
AND TO NEVER FORGET IT WAS REAL! THIS ACTUALLY HAPPENED TO US!
I CAN NEVER FORGET THE WAR.
NEVER FORGET WHAT HAPPENS WHEN THE MILITARY RULES A COUNTRY.
THE FACES OF THE DYING...

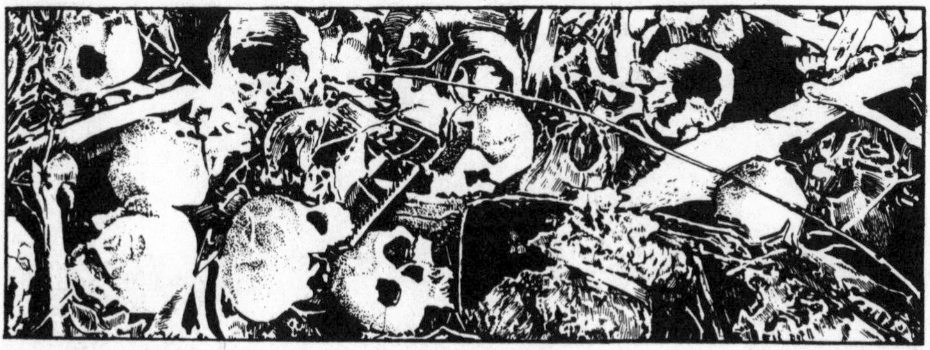
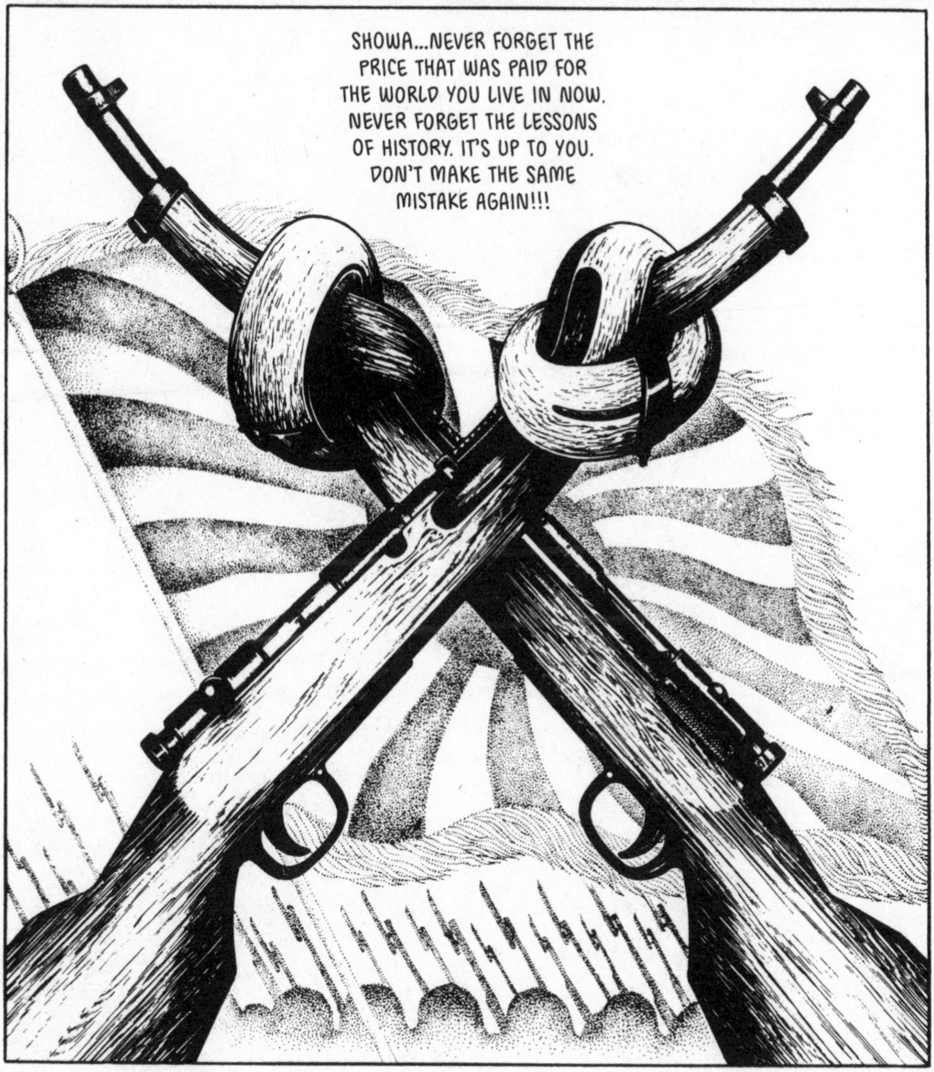
SHOWA...NEVER FORGET THE PRICE THAT WAS PAID FOR THE WORLD YOU LIVE IN NOW. NEVER FORGET THE LESSONS OF HISTORY. IT'S UP TO YOU. DON'T MAKE THE SAME MISTAKE AGAIN!!!

NOTES

16 India Abstention: India abstained from the treaty as it felt it infringed on Japan's sovereignty and national independence. The country signed a separate treaty—the Treaty of Peace Between Japan and India—that respected Japan's rights as a free country.

16 Shigeru Yoshida: (1878–1967) b. Tokyo City. Diplomat. Politician. Ambassador to Italy and the UK. Minister of foreign affairs. Elected prime minister five separate times.

19 Kyuichi Tokuda: (1894–1953) b. Okinawa Prefecture. Politician. Founder and first chairman of the Japanese Communist Party. 1950 (Showa 25): kicked out of the party for extremist views. 1953 (Showa 28): died as an exile in China.

44 Jinmu Boom: Economic booms at the time were named after auspicious figures from Japanese mythology. The Jinmu Boom was named after the mythical first emperor of Japan; the Iwato Boom after Amano-Iwato, the heavenly rock cave of the sun goddess Amaterasu; and the Izanagi Boom after a major deity in Japan's creation myth.

47 Zengakuren: The All-Japan Federation of Students' Self-Governing Associations. Founded 1948 (Showa 23), Zengakuren (short for Zen Nihon Gakusei Jichikai So Rengo) is a nation-wide communist/anarchist league of students that gained prominence in 1960 with large-scale protests against the Japan–US Security Treaty.

95 Treaty of Mutual Cooperation and Security between the United States and Japan: In 1951 (Showa 26), the security treaty between the United States and Japan was signed. Japan granted the US territorial rights for military bases, and the US guaranteed Japan's protection. The treaty was revised in 1960, becoming the Treaty of Mutual Cooperation and Security between the United States and Japan. Many Japanese were upset with Japan being militarily tied to the US and protested the treaties. These protests are also known as the Ampo Struggle.

99 Nobusuke Kishi: (1896–1987) b. Yamaguchi prefecture. Politician. Minister of commerce and industry. He was Prime Minister during the signing of the Treaty of Mutual Cooperation and Security.

100 Syngman Rhee: (1875–1965) Korean politician. Active in establishing an independent South Korea after Japan's defeat. Elected first president of the First Republic of South Korea. Left office in 1960.

104 Miike Dispute: (1960) Violent labor dispute over attempts to reduce size of workforce. Gang members were brought in as strike breakers. Union members disagreed over the strike, leading to the factionalizing and weakening of the labor unions.

105 Central Labor Relations Commission: An outside agency authorized to mediate and arbitrate labor disputes. Each prefecture has its own labor relations commission, which reports to the Central Labor Relations Commission.

146 Akuma-kun: Shigeru Mizuki's first real success as a manga artist. The name translates to Devil Boy. After the initial three volumes, Mizuki revised the character and not only published several series, but also adapted the character for a live-action TV show and several animated series.

150 Sympathy Payments: In the Japanese court system, people and corporations can offer "sympathy payments" in lieu of an official judgment for any number of crimes. If the victims accept the money, they are considered to have forgiven the perpetrator.

158 Special Procurement: Military lingo. Under the Treaty of Mutual Cooperation and Security, the US can establish military bases and resupply in Japan. This has traditionally been good for Japan's economy, creating markets and jobs. During both the Korean and Vietnam wars, Japan experienced an economic boom.

162 Kondo Isami: (1834–1868) Vassal of the Shogun. Director-general of the Shinsengumi (New Model Army) in Kyoto. Active in the revolution against the Shogunate and the Meiji Restoration. Captured by government forces and beheaded.

212 Ryokichi Minobe: (1904–1984) b. Tokyo City. Governor of Tokyo. Legislator of the House of Councillors. Worked for twenty years to reform the Tokyo government. Son of constitutional scholar Tatsukichi Minobe (see *Showa 1939–1944: A History of Japan*).

214 Eisaku Sato: (1901–1975) b. Yamaguchi prefecture. Politician. Became prime minister in 1964 (Showa 39) following Hayato Ikeda's resignation. Received the Nobel Peace Prize in 1974 (Showa 49) with Nobusuke Kishi.

218 The Shinjuku Turmoil Incident: On October 21, 1968 (Showa 43), International Anti-War Day, 290,000 protesters occupy Shinjuku Station. A thousand members of Zengakuren force their way into the station house and stop all train traffic.

268 Taro Okamoto: (1911–1996) b. Tokyo City. Artist. Eldest son of manga artist Ippei Okamoto and tanka poet and writer Kanoko Okamoto.

276 Yukio Mishima: (1915–1970) b. Tokyo City. The most important postwar novelist. Famous works include *Confessions of a Mask*, *Temple of the Golden Pavilion*, *The Sea of Fertility*, and *The Sailor Who Fell from Grace with the Sea*.

359 Shinano Riverbed Scandal: In 1963, Kakuei Tanaka, then the minister of finance, bought swampland for bargain prices from farmers along the Shinano Riverbed. Tanaka then used his government influence to rush through construction projects such as a dam on the Shinano River and a bridge connecting the region to Nagaoka City. This caused property values to skyrocket.

365 Chiang Kai-shek: (1887–1975) Chinese militant. Politician. Succeeded Sun Yat-sen as leader of the Kuomintang (KMT) Nationalist Party. After WWII, he lost the Chinese Civil War and retreated to Taiwan, where he ruled as the self-declared president of the Republic of China.

366 Zhou Enlai: (1898–1976) Chinese politician. Revolutionary. With Mao Zedong, a leader of the Chinese Communist party. First premier of the People's Republic of China, and achieved great strides for China as foreign minister.

391 Toyotomi Hideyoshi: (1585–1591) b. Nagoya Prefecture. Along with Oda Nobunaga and Tokugawa Ieyasu, one of the three leaders who unified Japan. His nickname was "Little Monkey."

402 Gang of Four: The driving forces behind the Cultural Revolution, the Gang of Four consisted of Mao Zedong's wife, Jiang Qing, and her close associates Zhang Chunqiao, Yao Wenyuan, and Wang Hongwen.

435 Kanjuro Arashi: (1902–1980) b. Kyoto Prefecture. Appeared in more than three hundred films. One of the biggest movie stars of his generation.

473 Glico: A hugely popular candy company in Japan, Glico is best known for Pocky and Pretz. Glico is famous for its corporate logo, the Glico running man.

474 The Fiend with Twenty Faces: A character from a series of detective novels by Edogawa Ranpo. The Fiend is the antagonist for detective Akechi Kogoro in much the same way as Professor Moriarty is for Sherlock Holmes.

490 Kim Hyon Hui: (b. 1962) North Korean spy. One of two agents who planted time bombs on Korean Air Flight 858, deplaning in Bahraini. Sentenced to death for her actions, she was later pardoned in 1998.

493 Namu Amida Butsu: In the Pure Land sect of Mahayana Buddhism, repetition of Namu Amida Butsu helps a soul achieve rebirth in the pure lands. The words have no meaning, but come from the Sanskrit *buddhanusmrti* meaning "mindfulness of the Buddha."

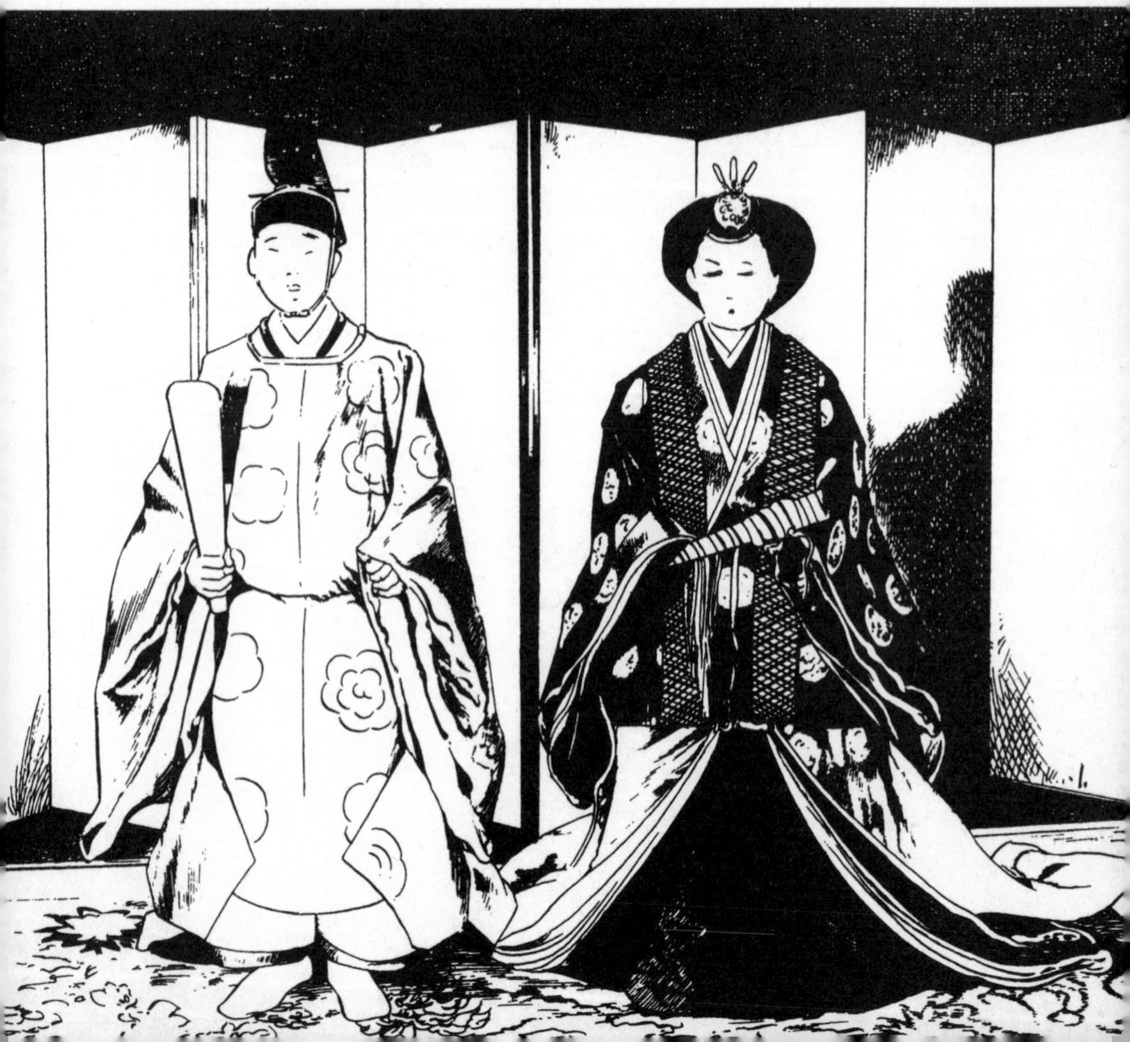

Showa: A History of Japan was originally published as an eight-volume series between November 1988 and December 1989 under the title of *Showa-shi: Komiku* (*A History of Showa: The Comic*). Unusual for a comic in Japan, *Showa* was published directly in the deluxe *tankobon* format, instead of being first serialized in magazines. Each volume was prefaced by several full-color pages.

The series was republished in *bunkobon* mass-market pocketbook format from August 1 to November 4, 1994. The color pages were removed, and the series was retitled *Komiku Showa-Shi* (*A Comic History of Showa*). This version was packaged as a box set on December 14, 1994, and has been the most commonly available version ever since.

In 2015, as part of the Shigeru Mizuki Complete Collection, *Showa* was republished as a four-volume series and the tankobon color pages were restored. The complete set of color pages are included here, in their original order. Enjoy!

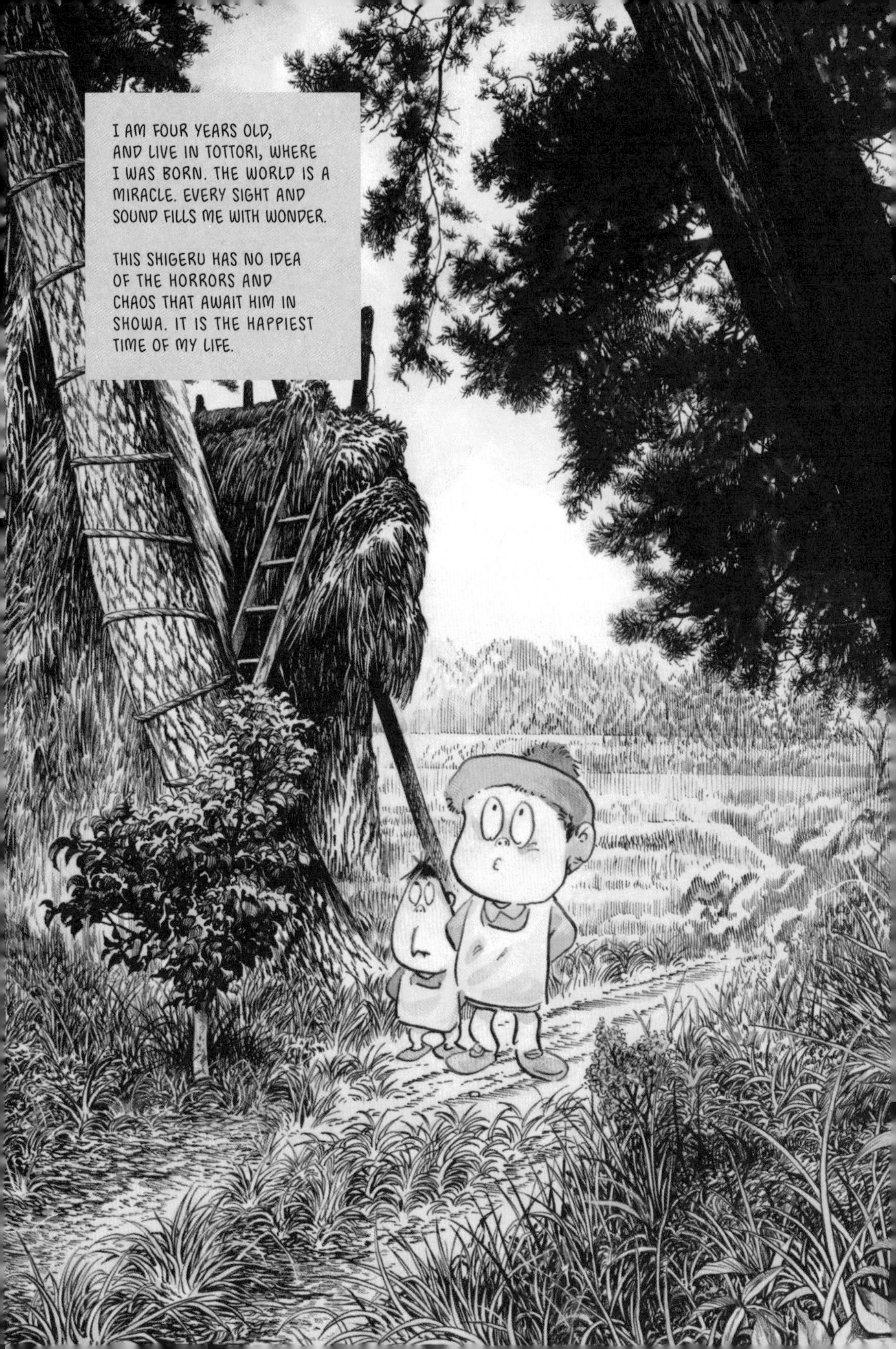
I AM FOUR YEARS OLD, AND LIVE IN TOTTORI, WHERE I WAS BORN. THE WORLD IS A MIRACLE. EVERY SIGHT AND SOUND FILLS ME WITH WONDER.
THIS SHIGERU HAS NO IDEA OF THE HORRORS AND CHAOS THAT AWAIT HIM IN SHOWA. IT IS THE HAPPIEST TIME OF MY LIFE.

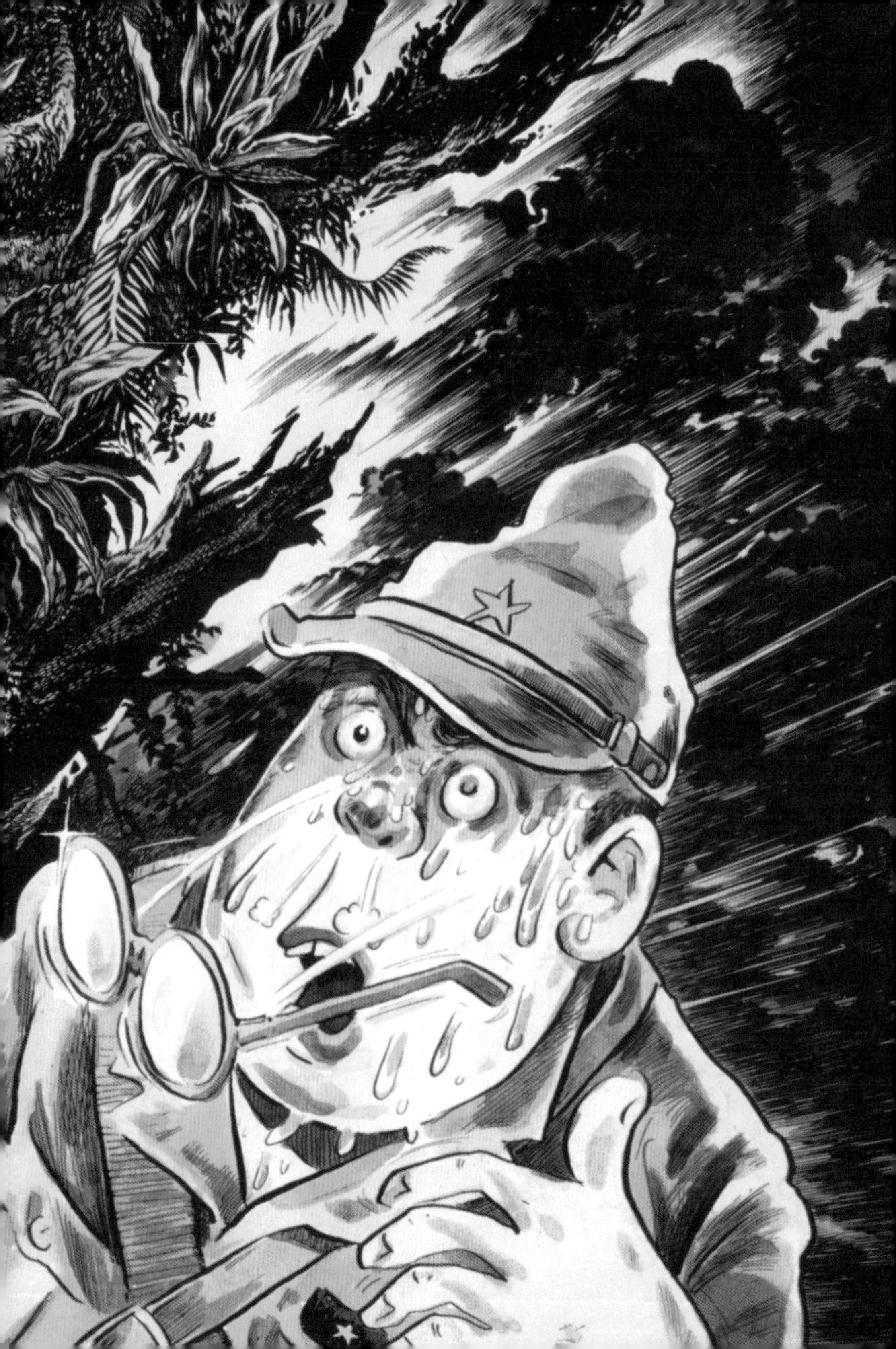

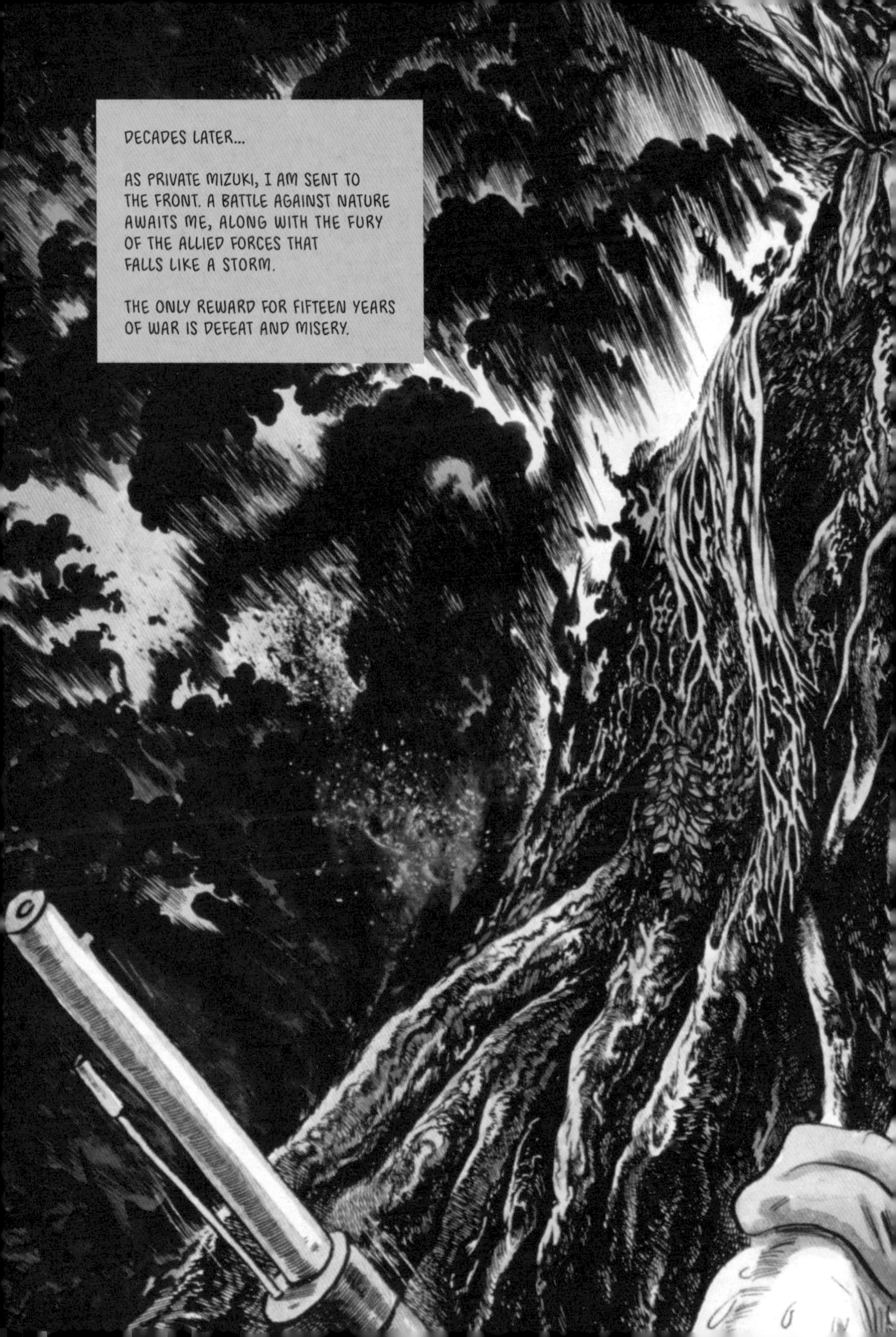
DECADES LATER...
AS PRIVATE MIZUKI, I AM SENT TO THE FRONT. A BATTLE AGAINST NATURE AWAITS ME, ALONG WITH THE FURY OF THE ALLIED FORCES THAT FALLS LIKE A STORM.
THE ONLY REWARD FOR FIFTEEN YEARS OF WAR IS DEFEAT AND MISERY.

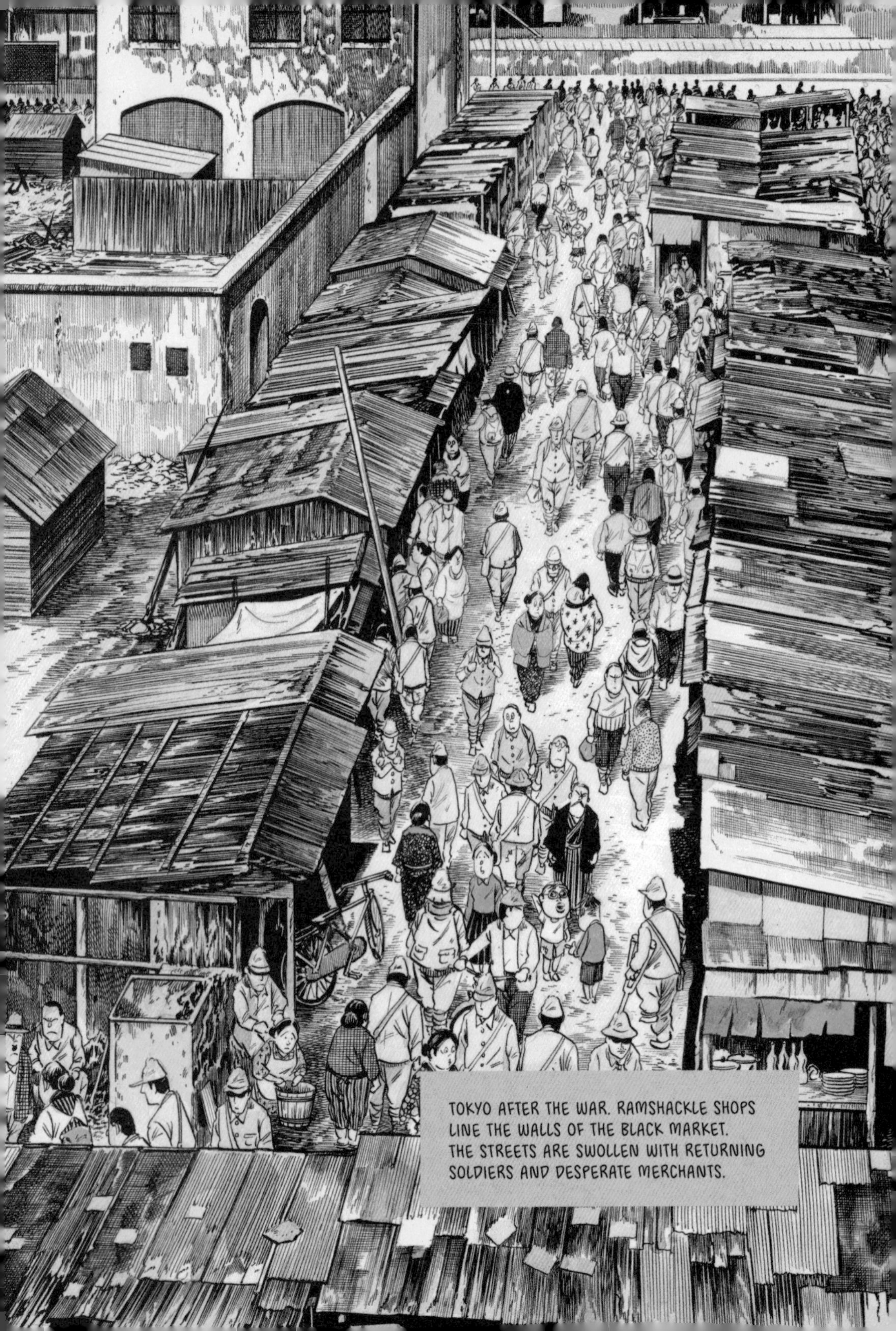
TOKYO AFTER THE WAR. RAMSHACKLE SHOPS LINE THE WALLS OF THE BLACK MARKET. THE STREETS ARE SWOLLEN WITH RETURNING SOLDIERS AND DESPERATE MERCHANTS.

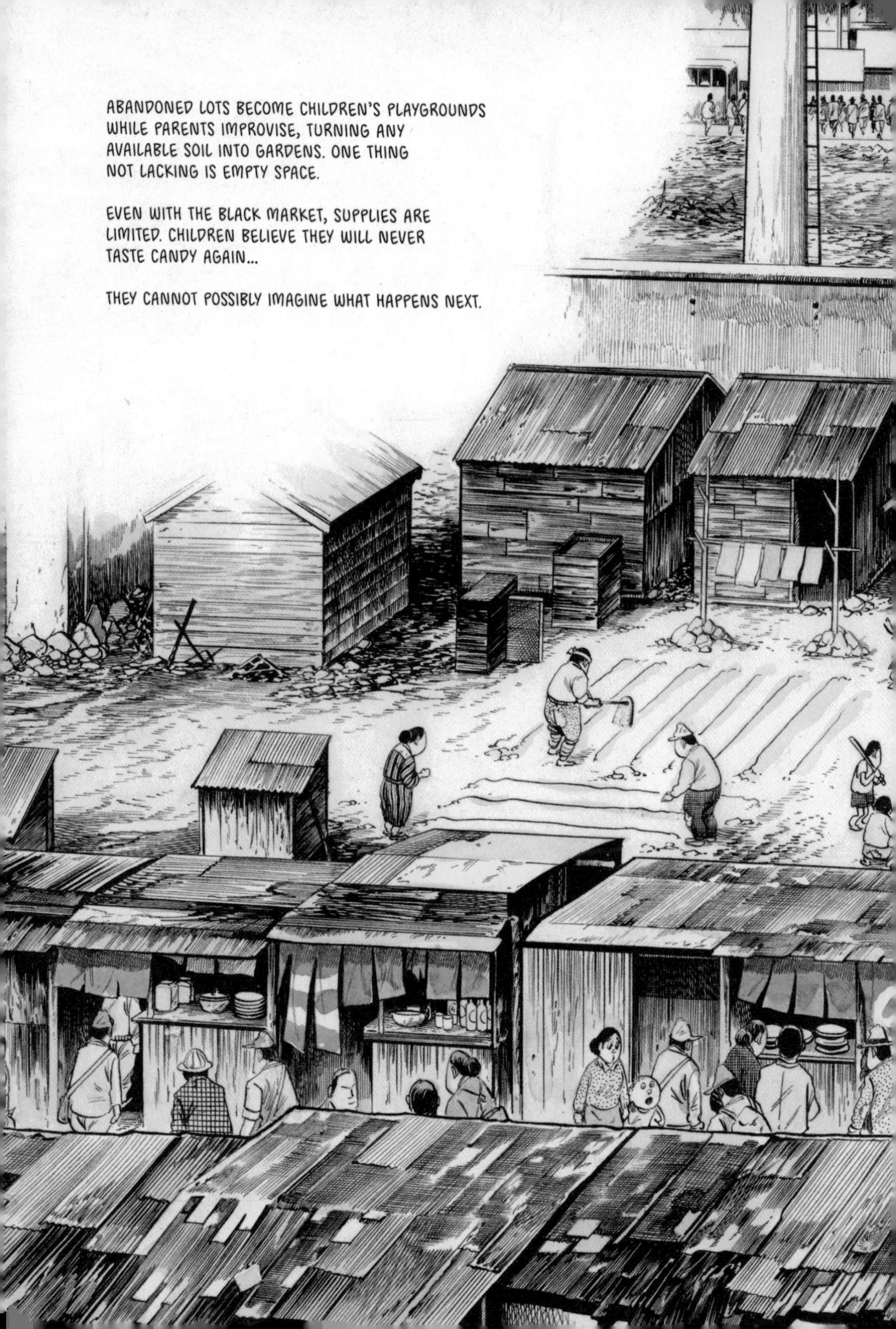
ABANDONED LOTS BECOME CHILDREN'S PLAYGROUNDS WHILE PARENTS IMPROVISE, TURNING ANY AVAILABLE SOIL INTO GARDENS. ONE THING NOT LACKING IS EMPTY SPACE.
EVEN WITH THE BLACK MARKET, SUPPLIES ARE LIMITED. CHILDREN BELIEVE THEY WILL NEVER TASTE CANDY AGAIN...
THEY CANNOT POSSIBLY IMAGINE WHAT HAPPENS NEXT.

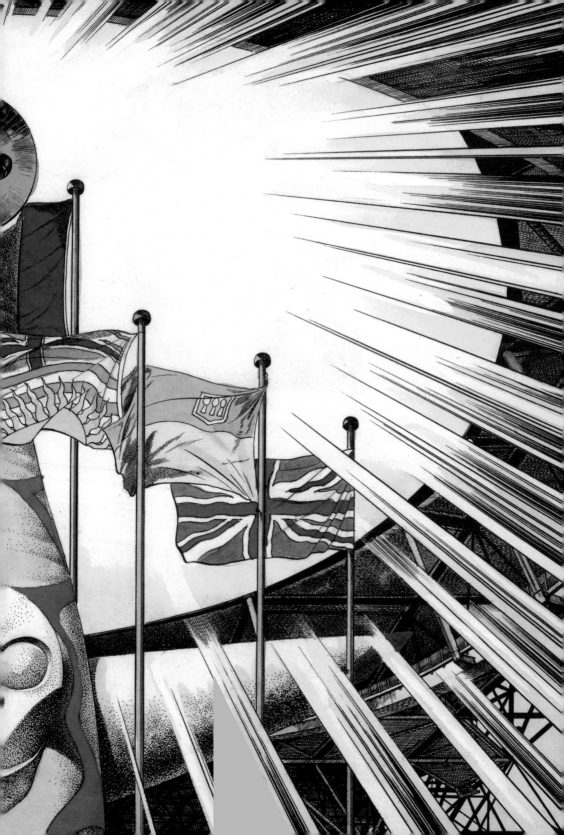

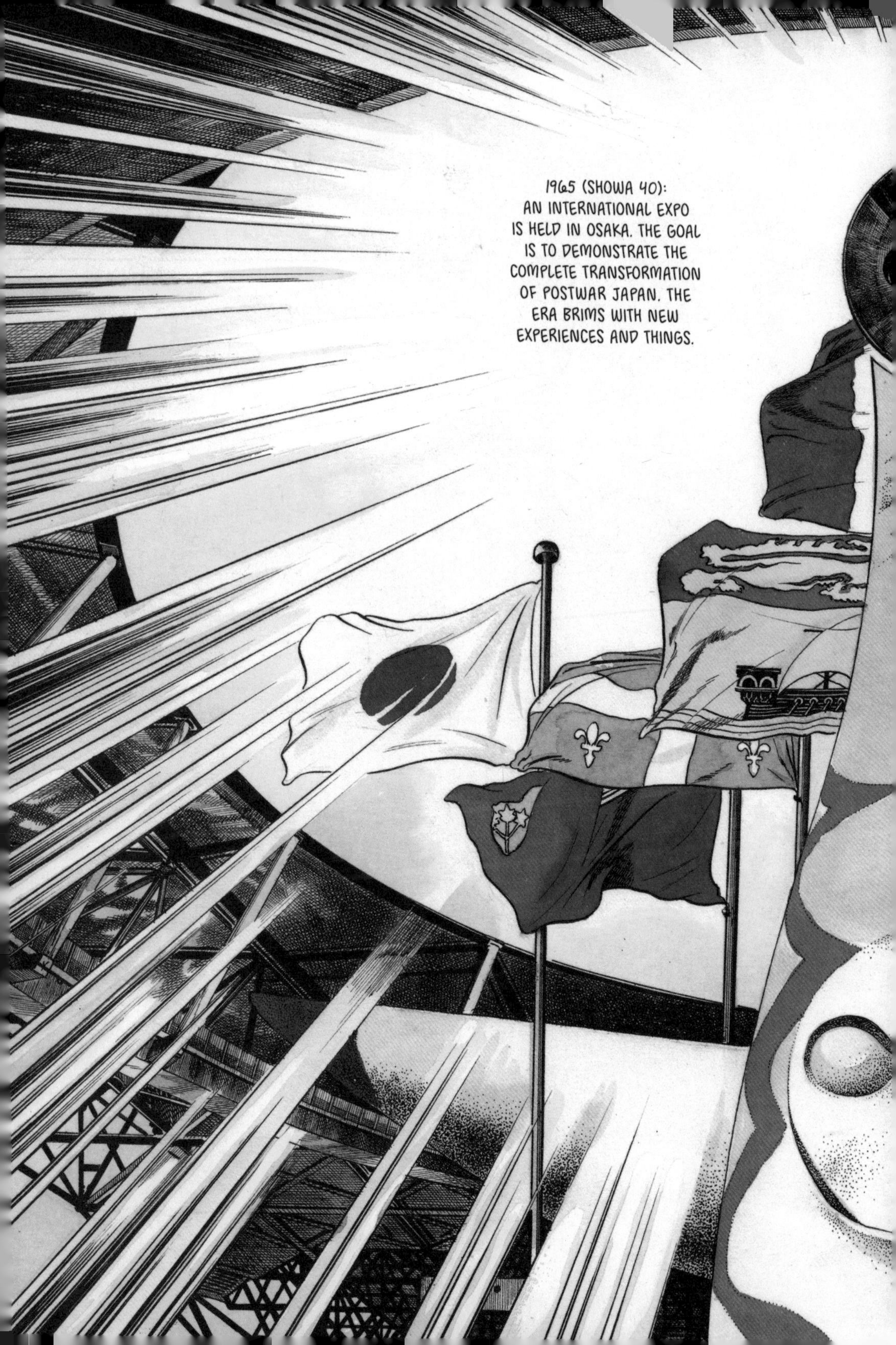
1965 (SHOWA 40):
AN INTERNATIONAL EXPO IS HELD IN OSAKA. THE GOAL IS TO DEMONSTRATE THE COMPLETE TRANSFORMATION OF POSTWAR JAPAN. THE ERA BRIMS WITH NEW EXPERIENCES AND THINGS.

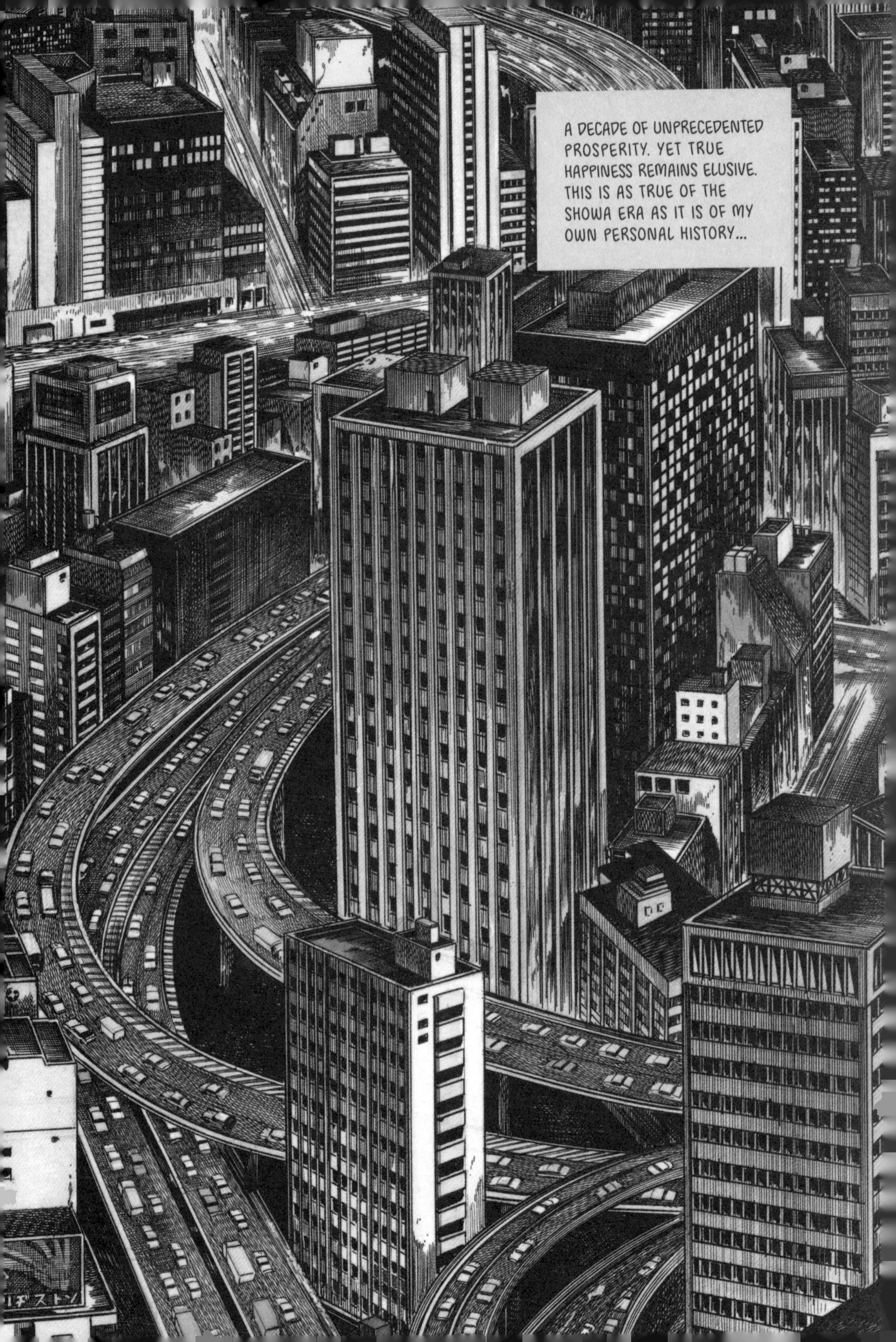
A DECADE OF UNPRECEDENTED PROSPERITY. YET TRUE HAPPINESS REMAINS ELUSIVE. THIS IS AS TRUE OF THE SHOWA ERA AS IT IS OF MY OWN PERSONAL HISTORY...

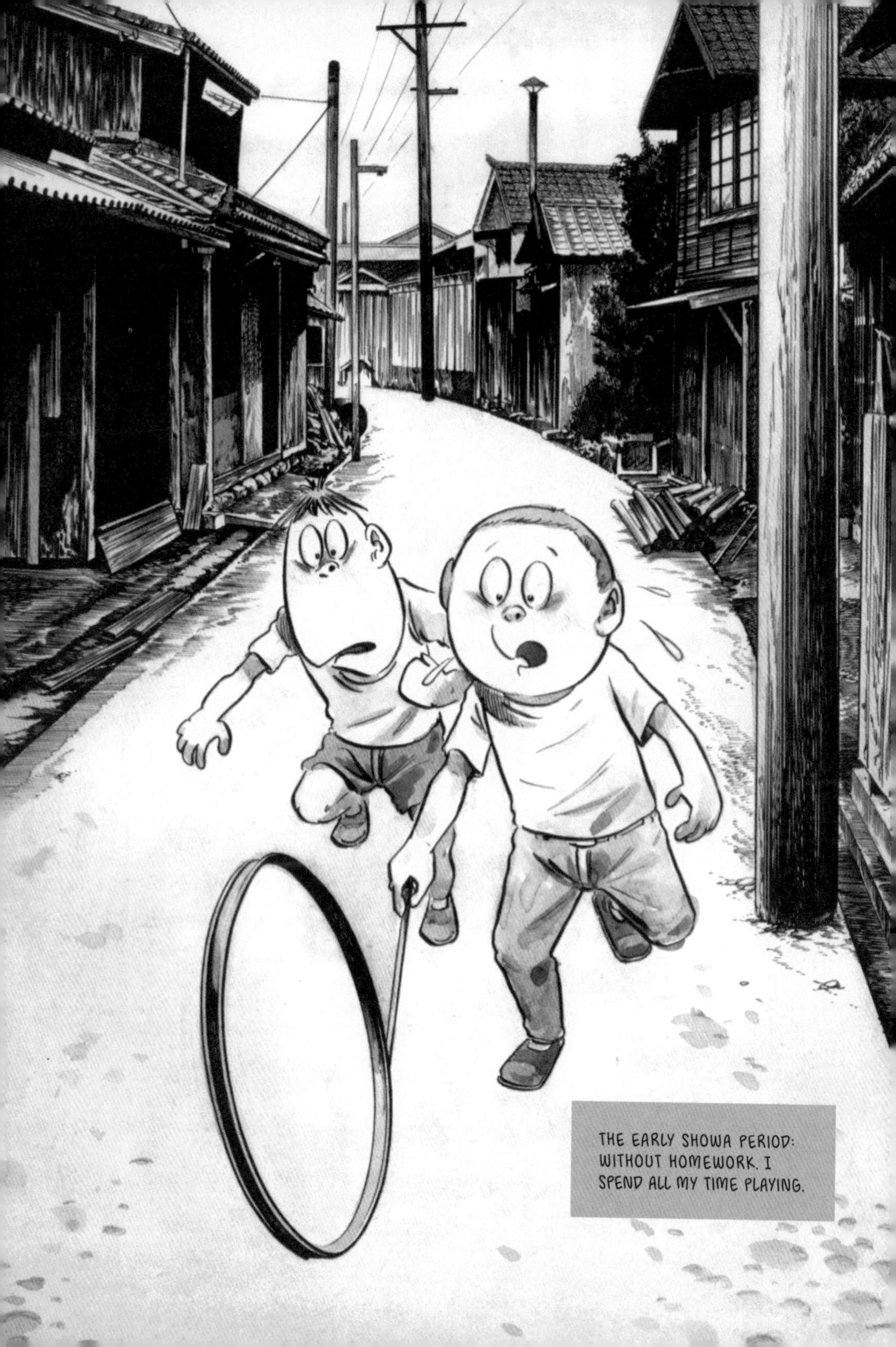
THE EARLY SHOWA PERIOD: WITHOUT HOMEWORK. I SPEND ALL MY TIME PLAYING.

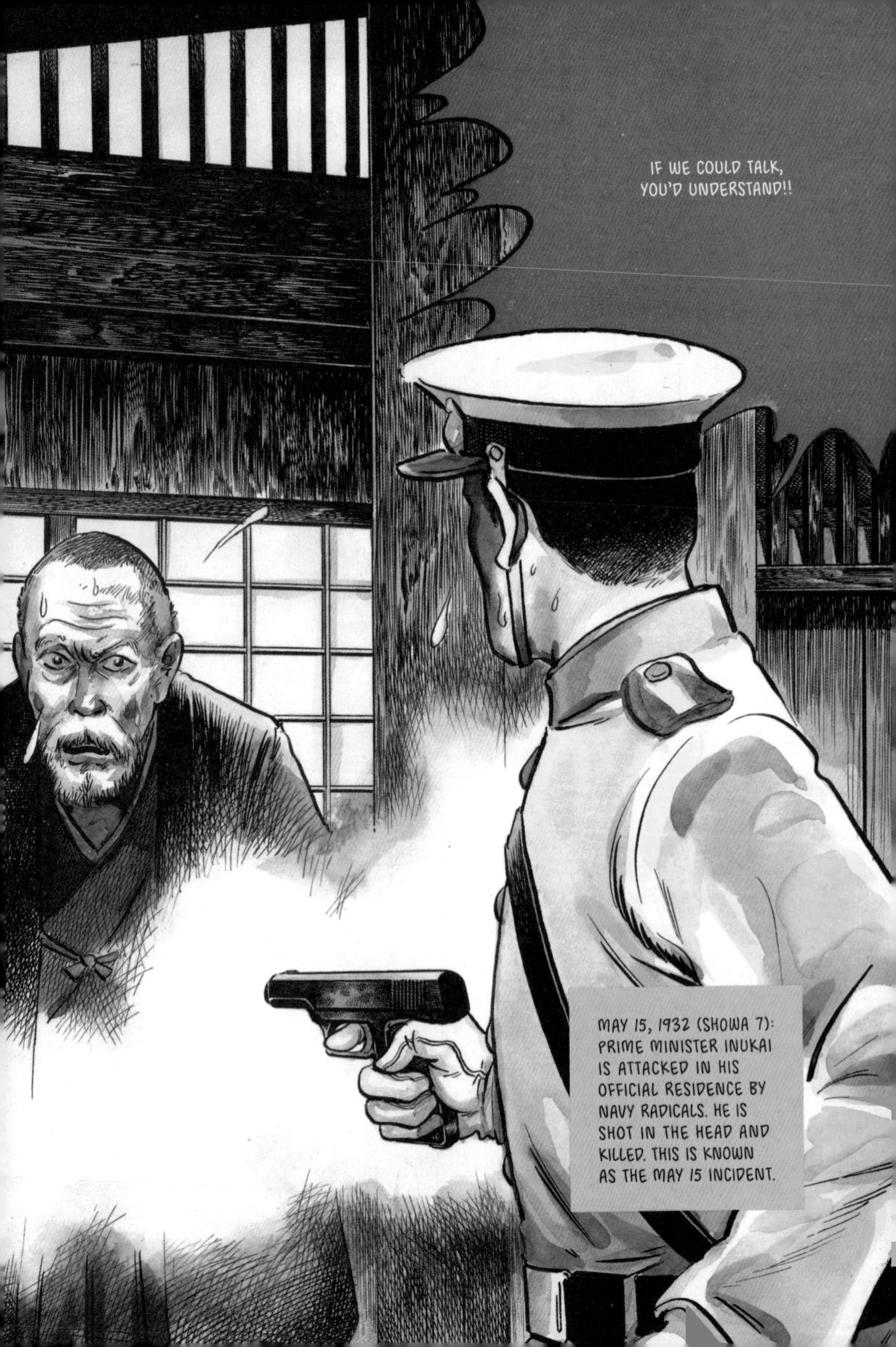
IF WE COULD TALK,
YOU'D UNDERSTAND!!
MAY 15, 1932 (SHOWA 7): PRIME MINISTER INUKAI IS ATTACKED IN HIS OFFICIAL RESIDENCE BY NAVY RADICALS. HE IS SHOT IN THE HEAD AND KILLED. THIS IS KNOWN AS THE MAY 15 INCIDENT.

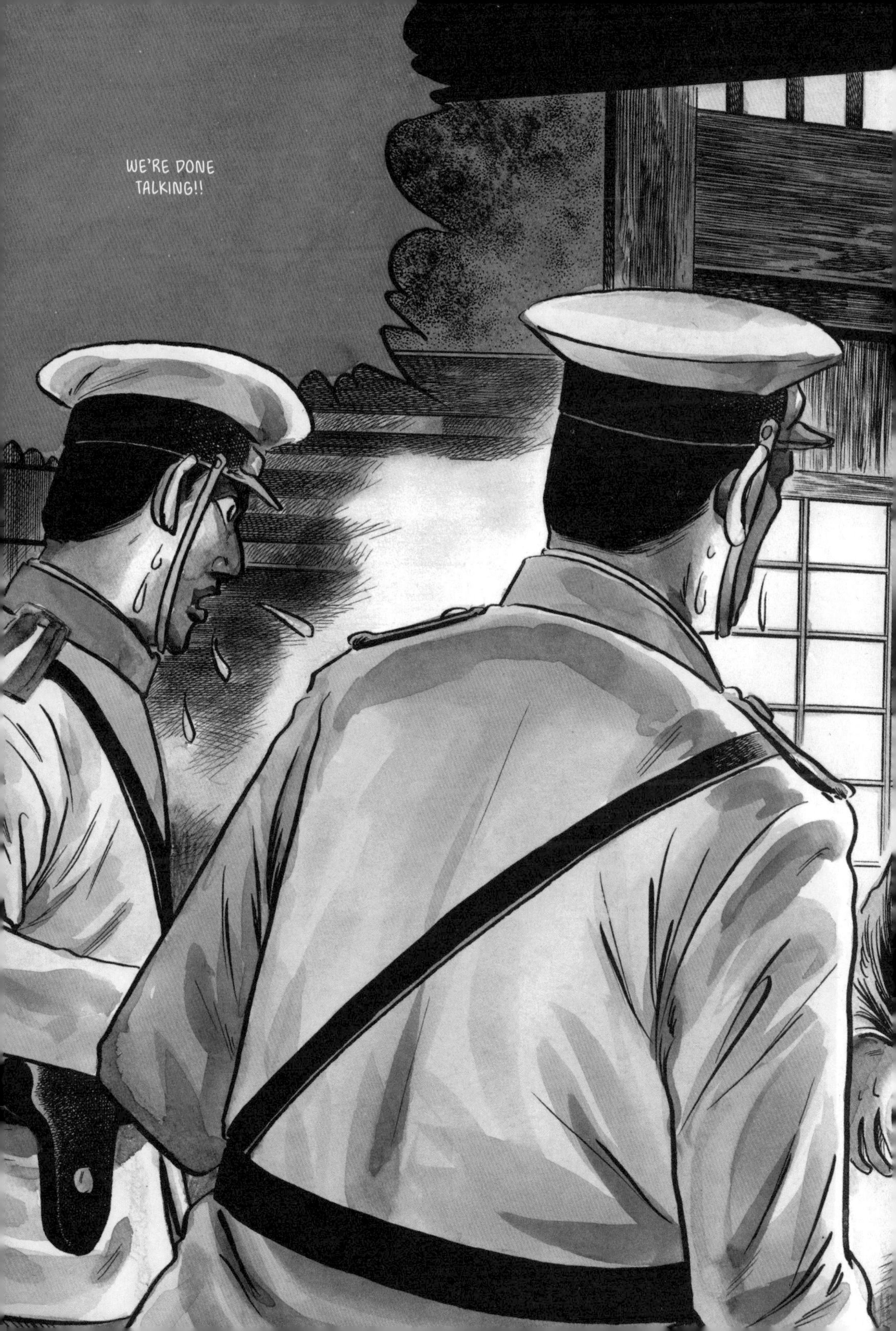
WE'RE DONE TALKING!!

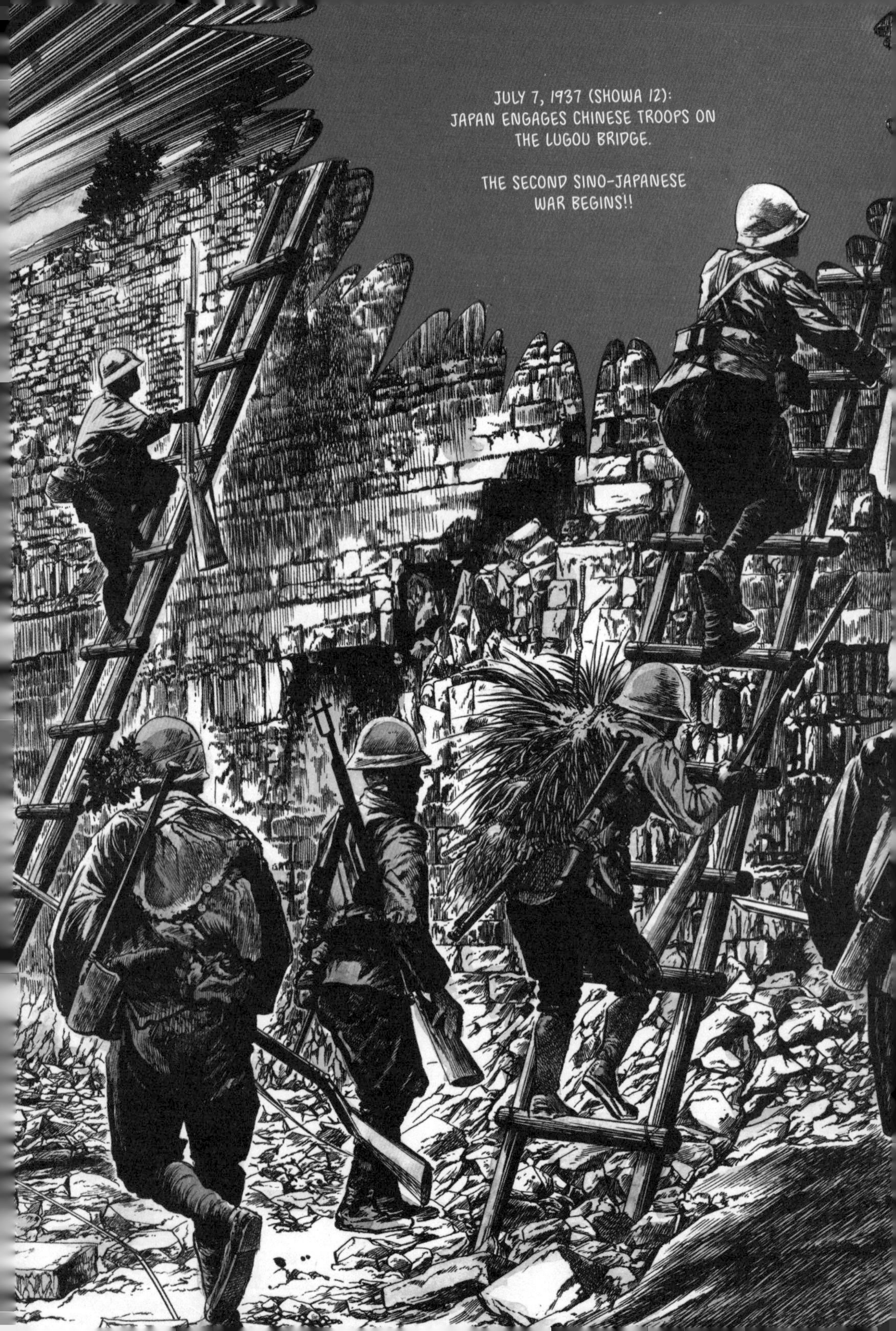
JULY 7, 1937 (SHOWA 12): JAPAN ENGAGES CHINESE TROOPS ON THE LUGOU BRIDGE.
THE SECOND SINO-JAPANESE WAR BEGINS!!

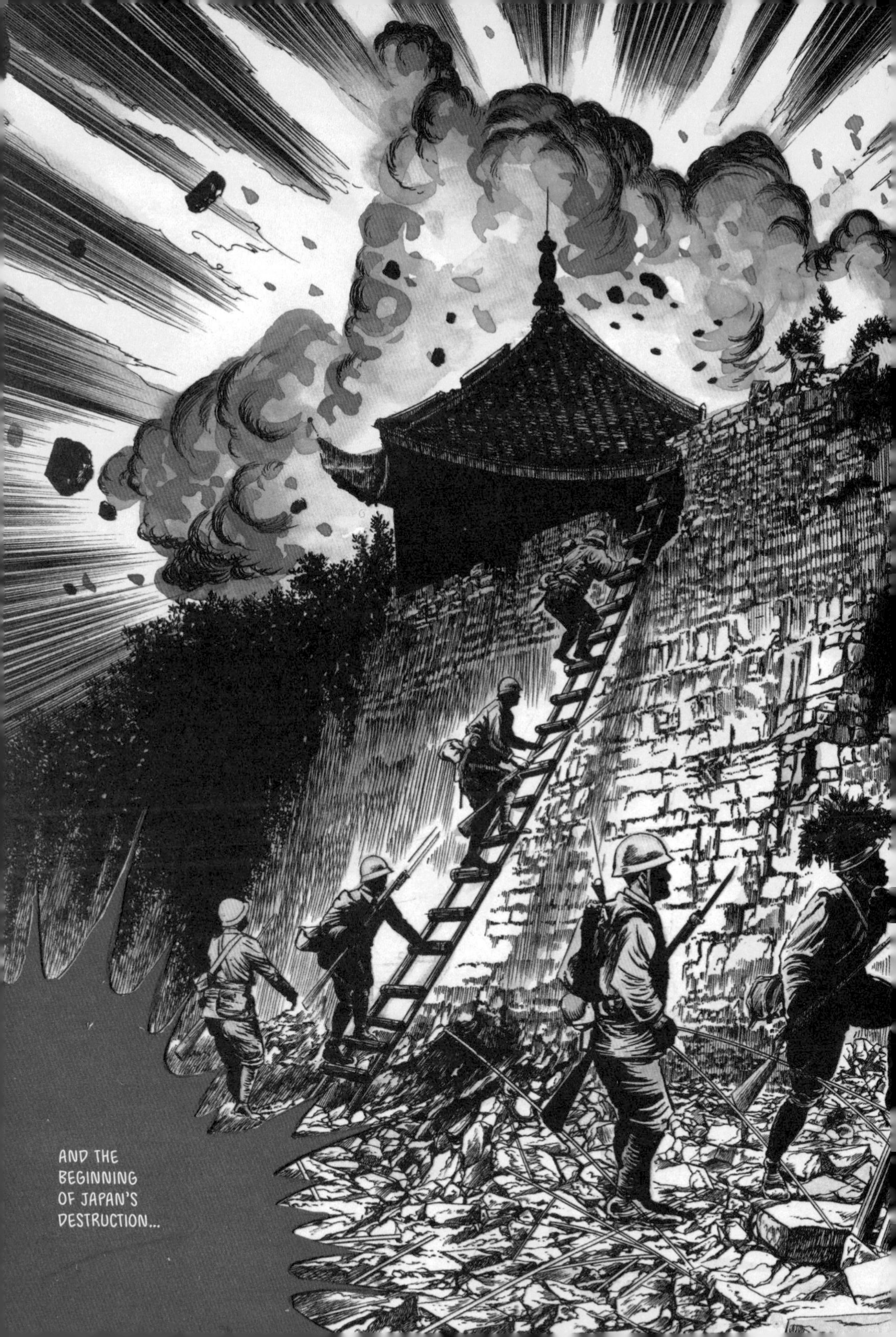
AND THE BEGINNING OF JAPAN'S DESTRUCTION...

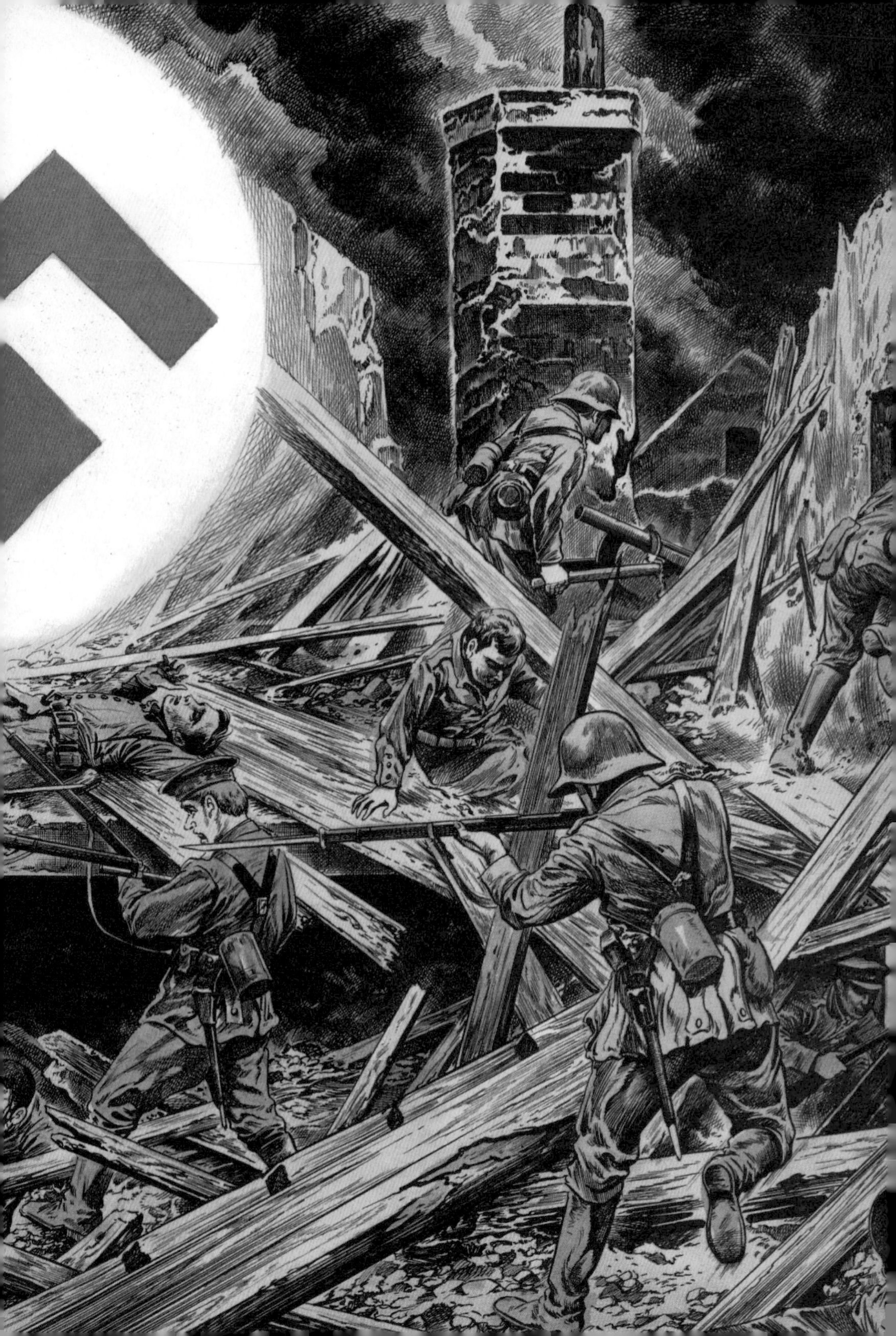

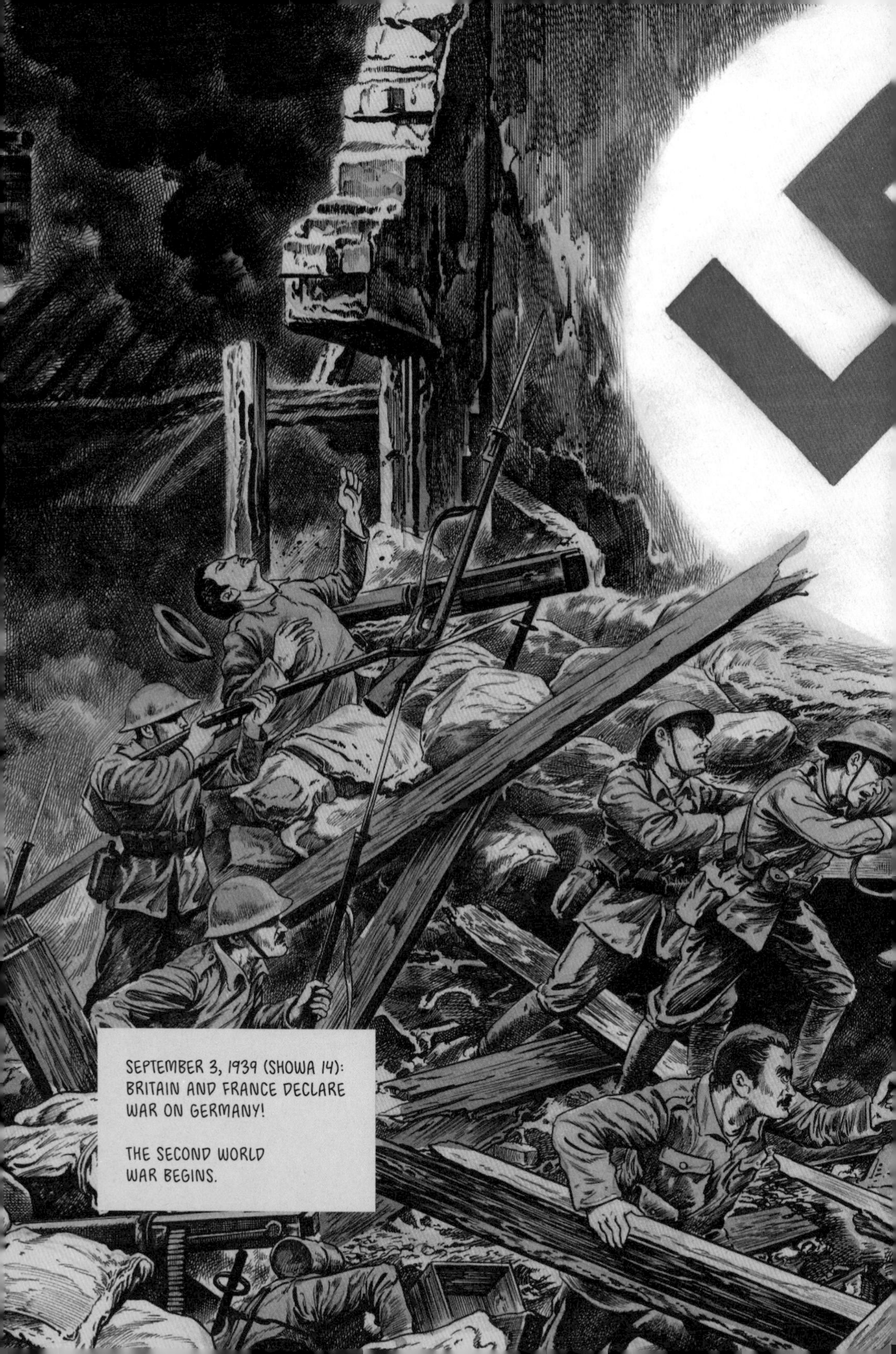
SEPTEMBER 3, 1939 (SHOWA 14): BRITAIN AND FRANCE DECLARE WAR ON GERMANY!
THE SECOND WORLD WAR BEGINS.

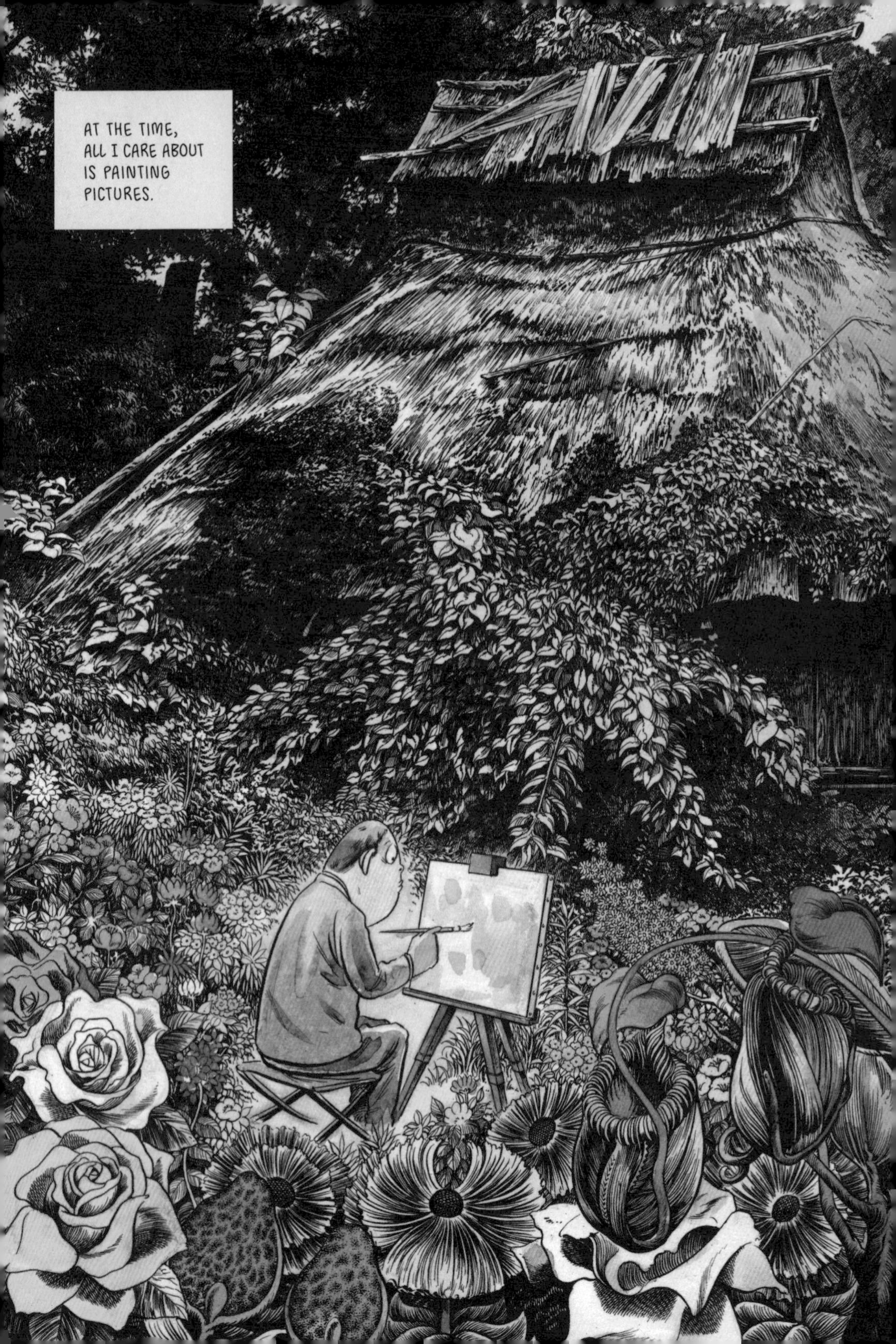
AT THE TIME, ALL I CARE ABOUT IS PAINTING PICTURES.

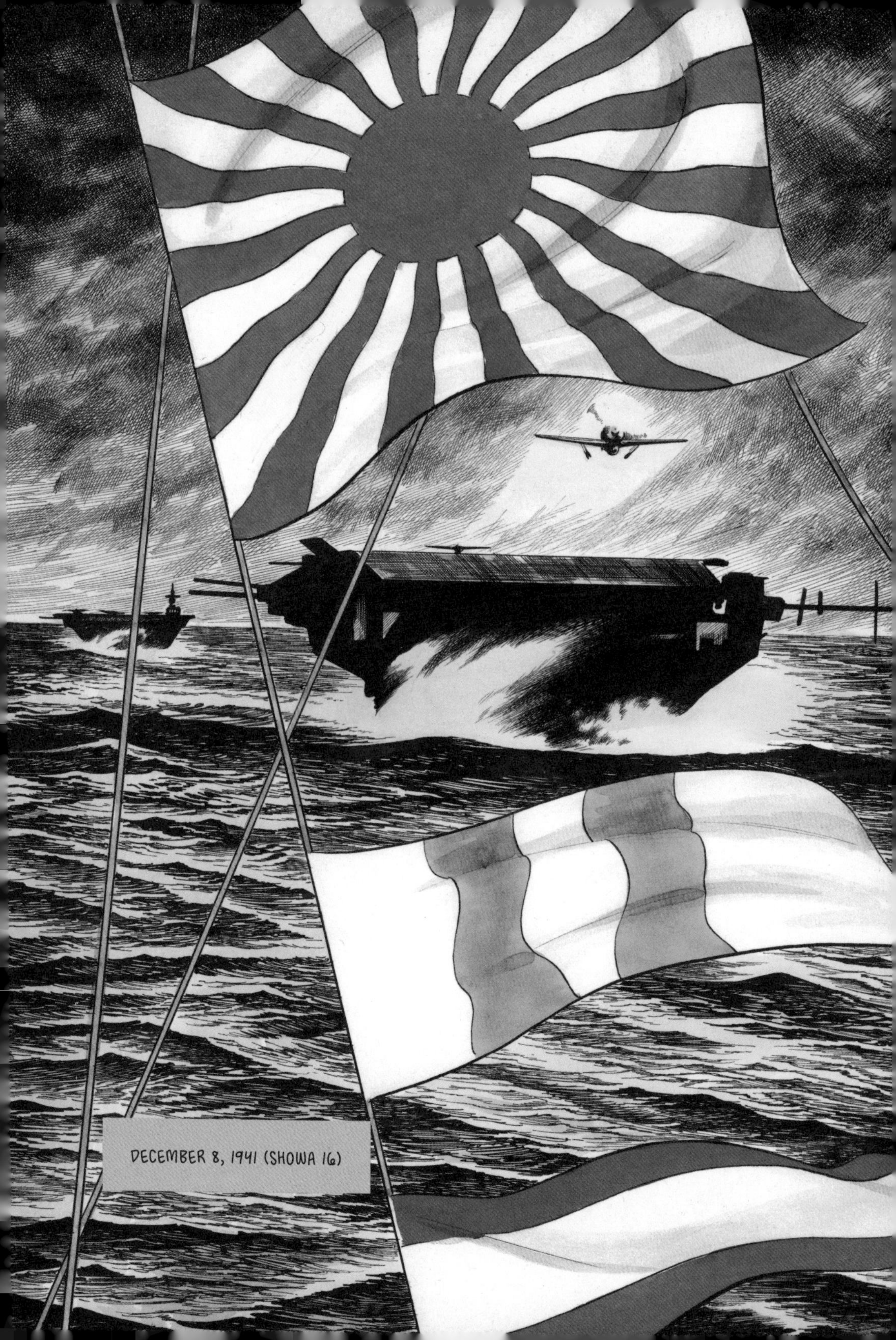
DECEMBER 8, 1941 (SHOWA 16)

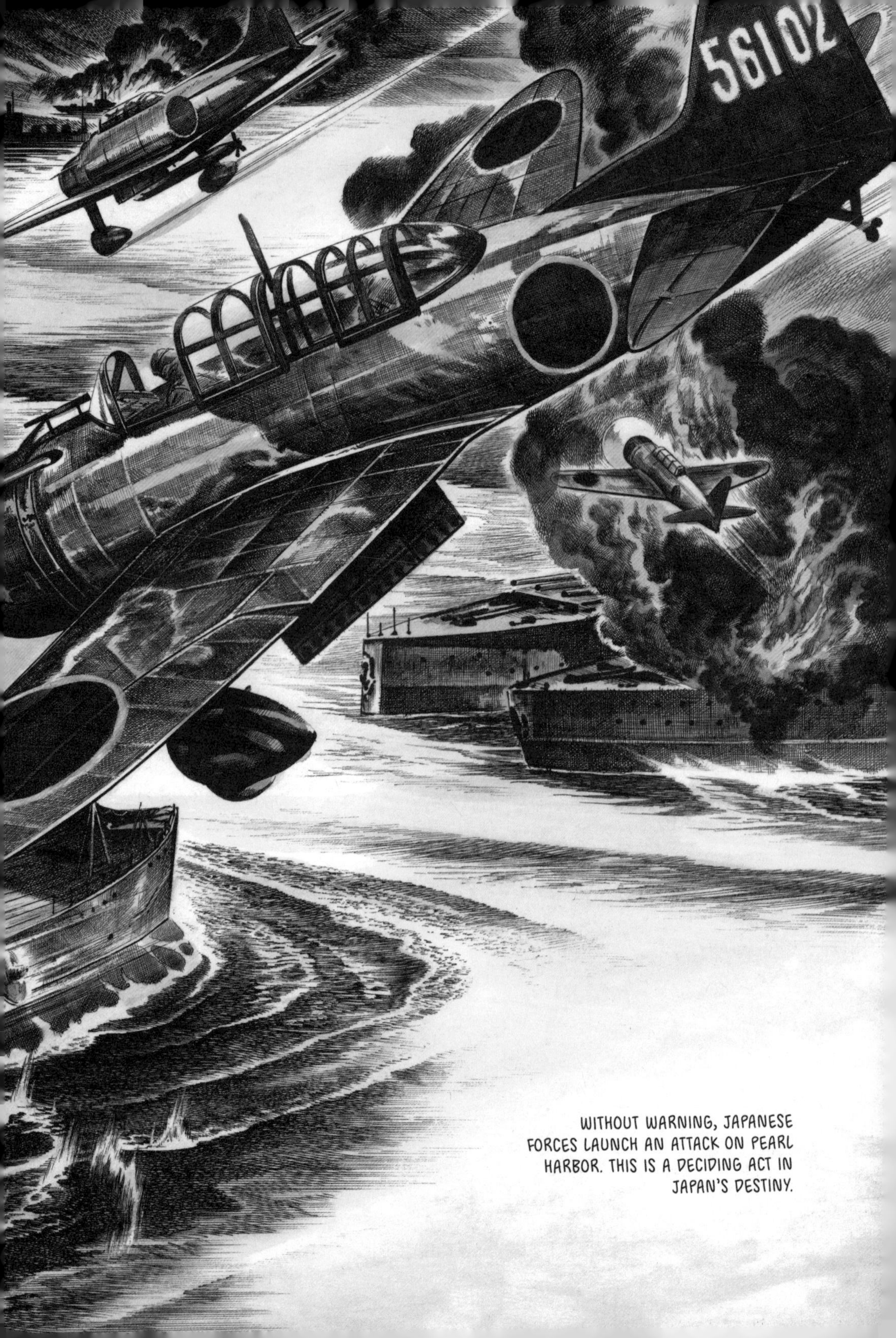
56102
WITHOUT WARNING, JAPANESE FORCES LAUNCH AN ATTACK ON PEARL HARBOR. THIS IS A DECIDING ACT IN JAPAN'S DESTINY.

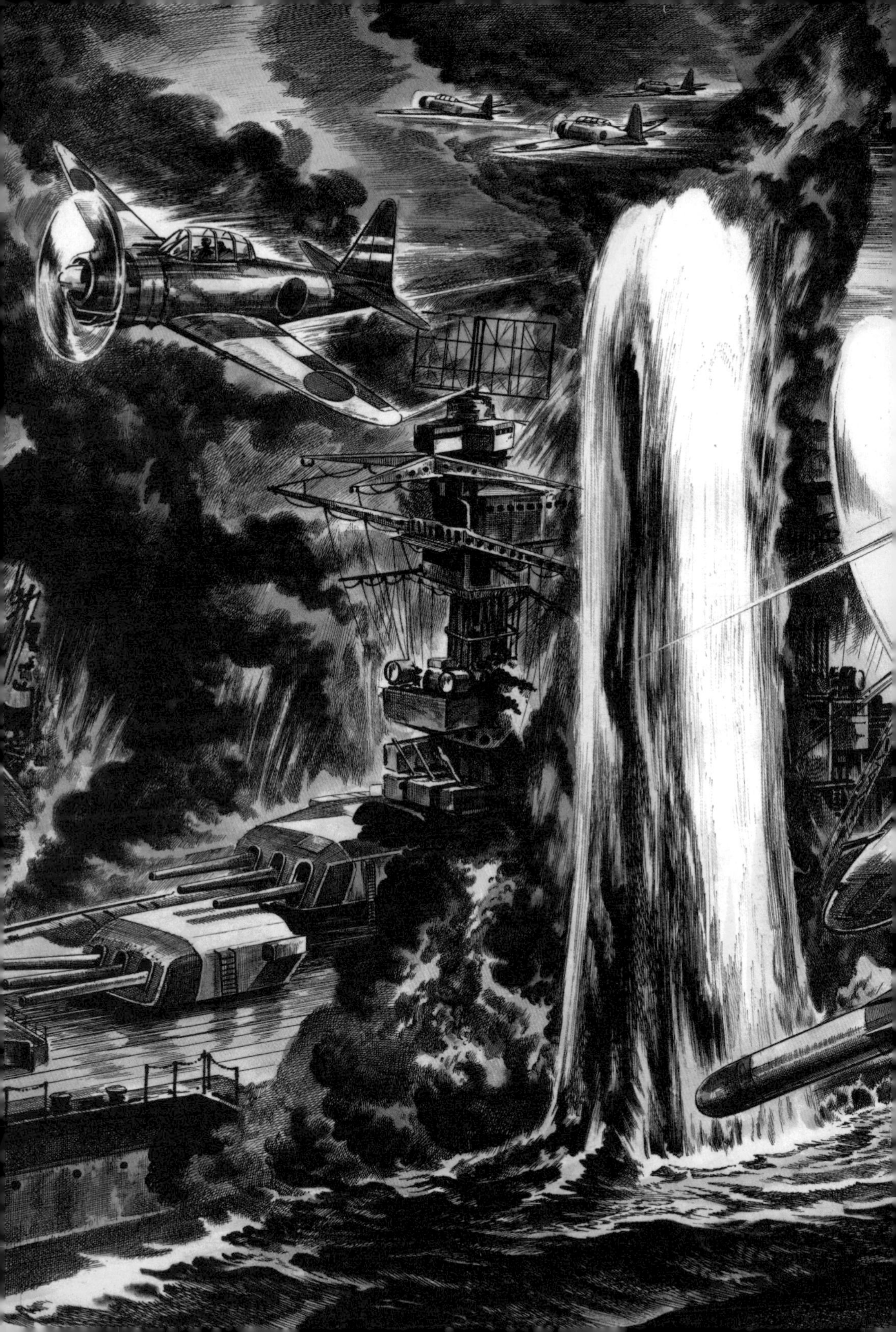

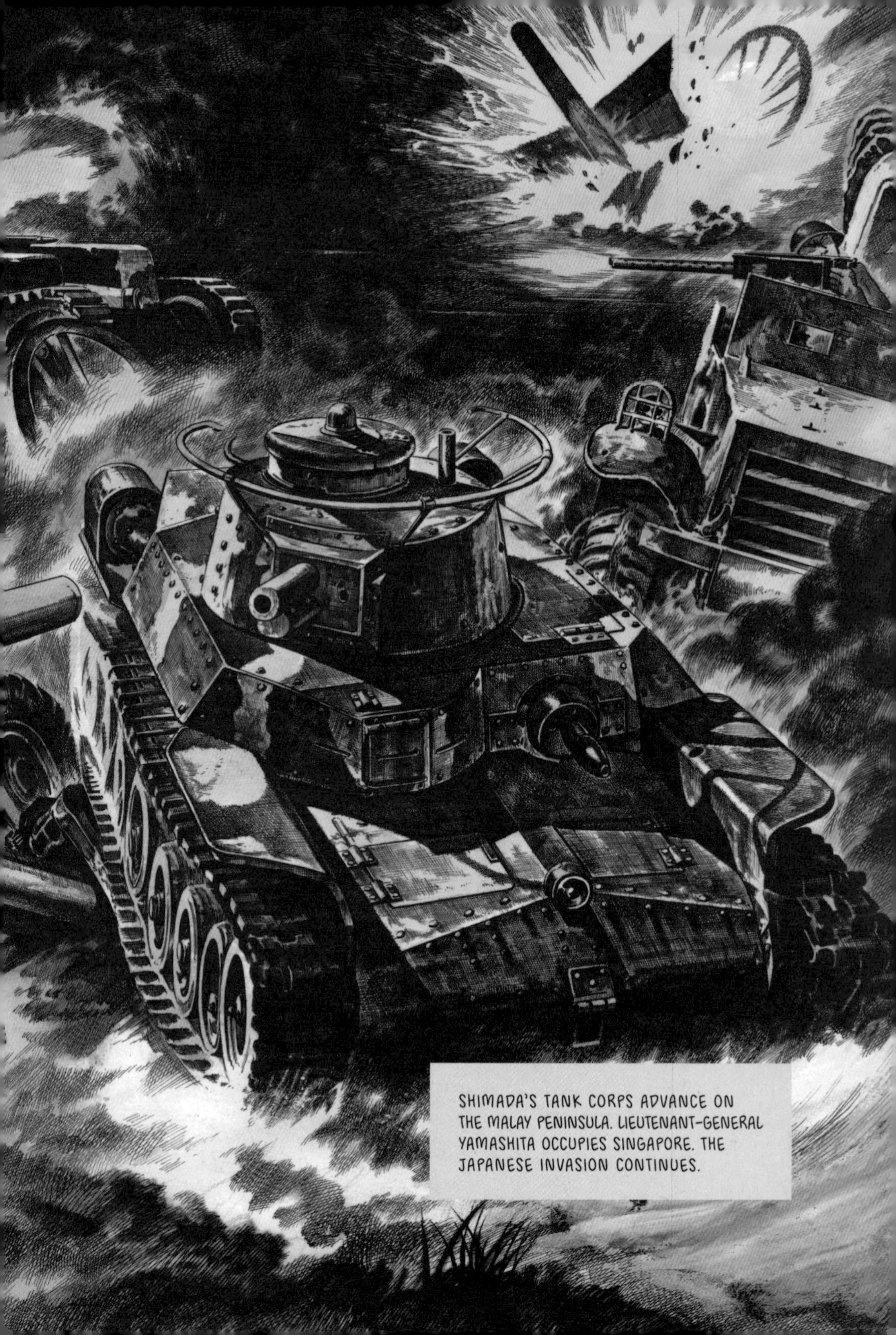
SHIMADA'S TANK CORPS ADVANCE ON THE MALAY PENINSULA. LIEUTENANT-GENERAL YAMASHITA OCCUPIES SINGAPORE. THE JAPANESE INVASION CONTINUES.

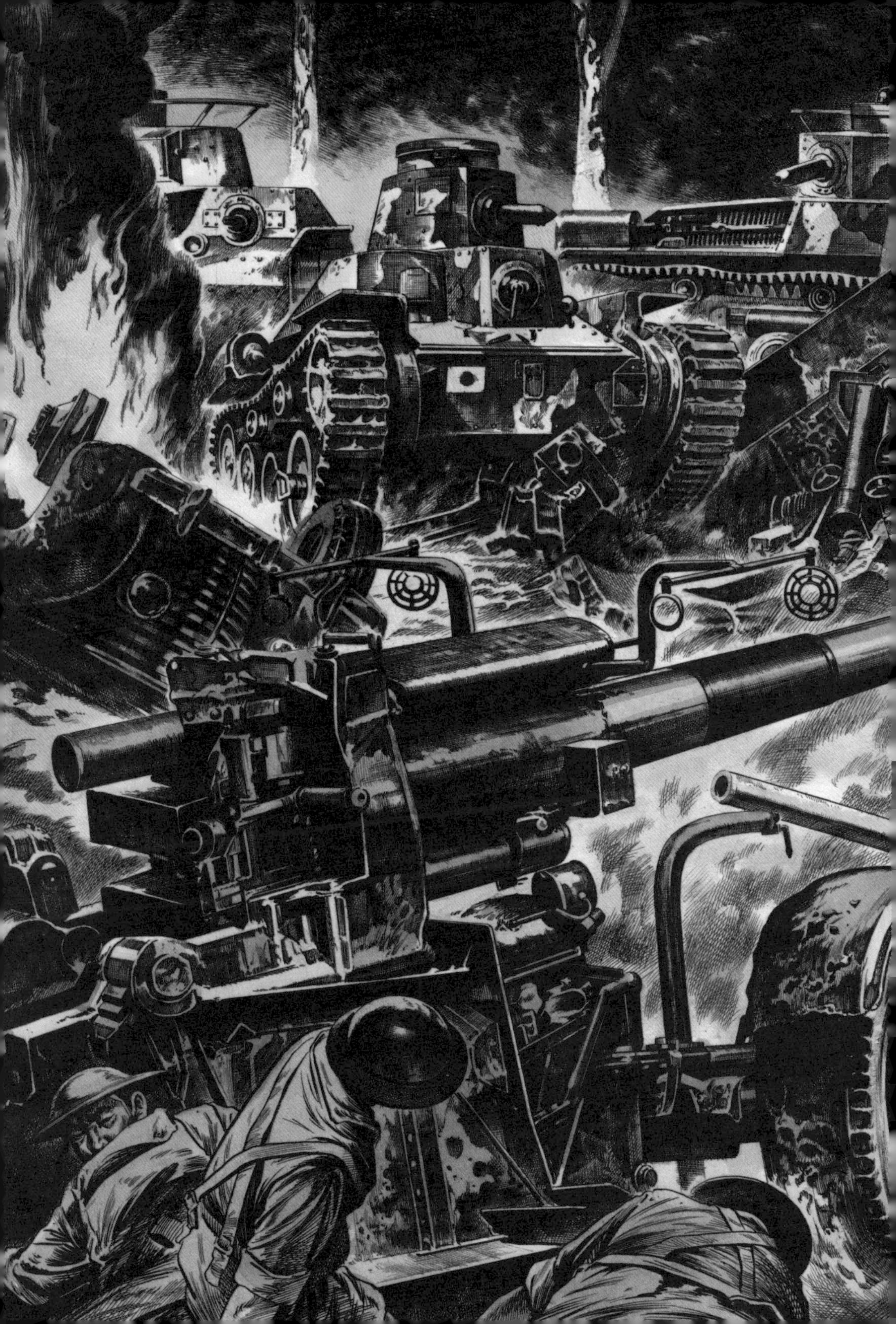

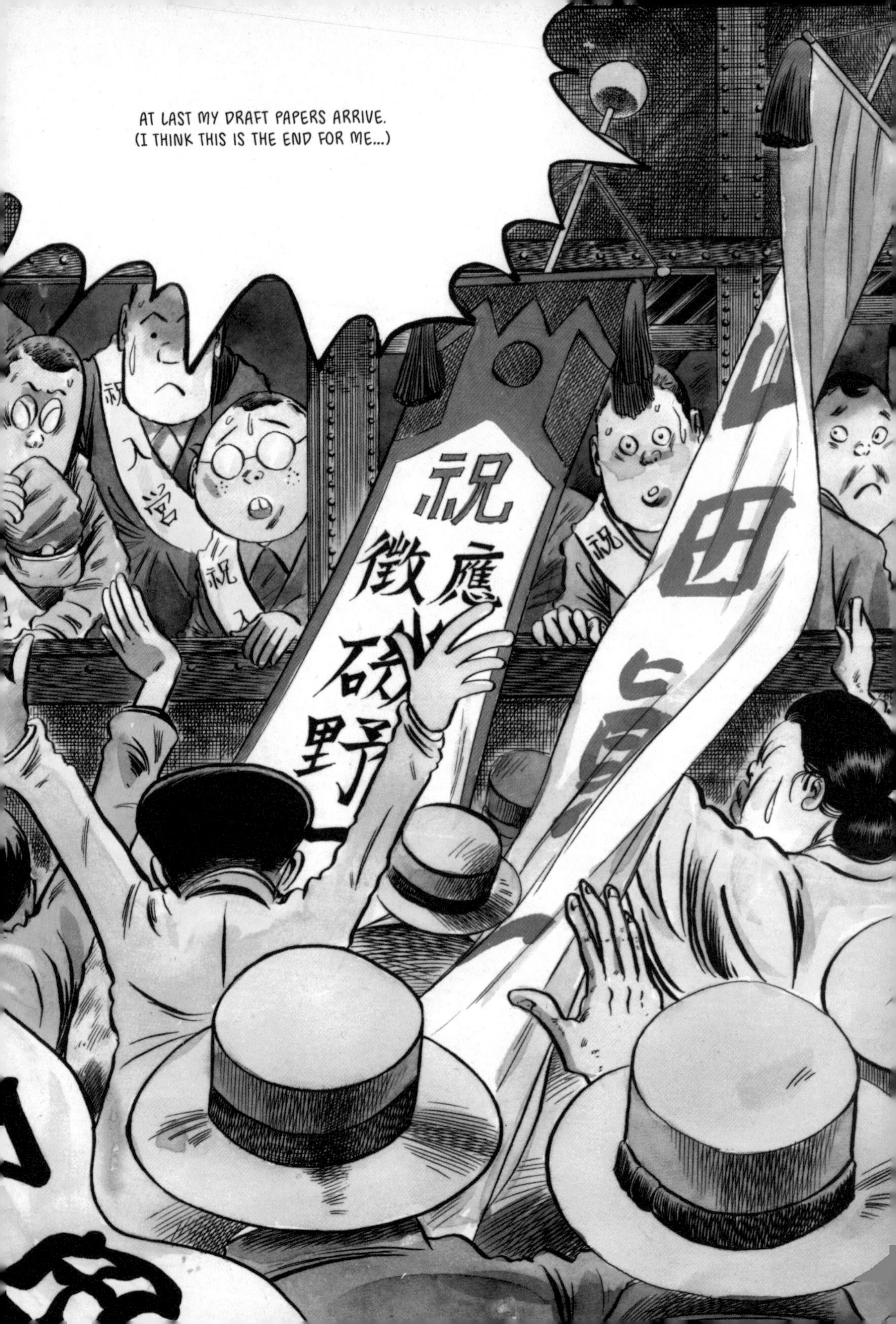
AT LAST MY DRAFT PAPERS ARRIVE.
(I THINK THIS IS THE END FOR ME...)

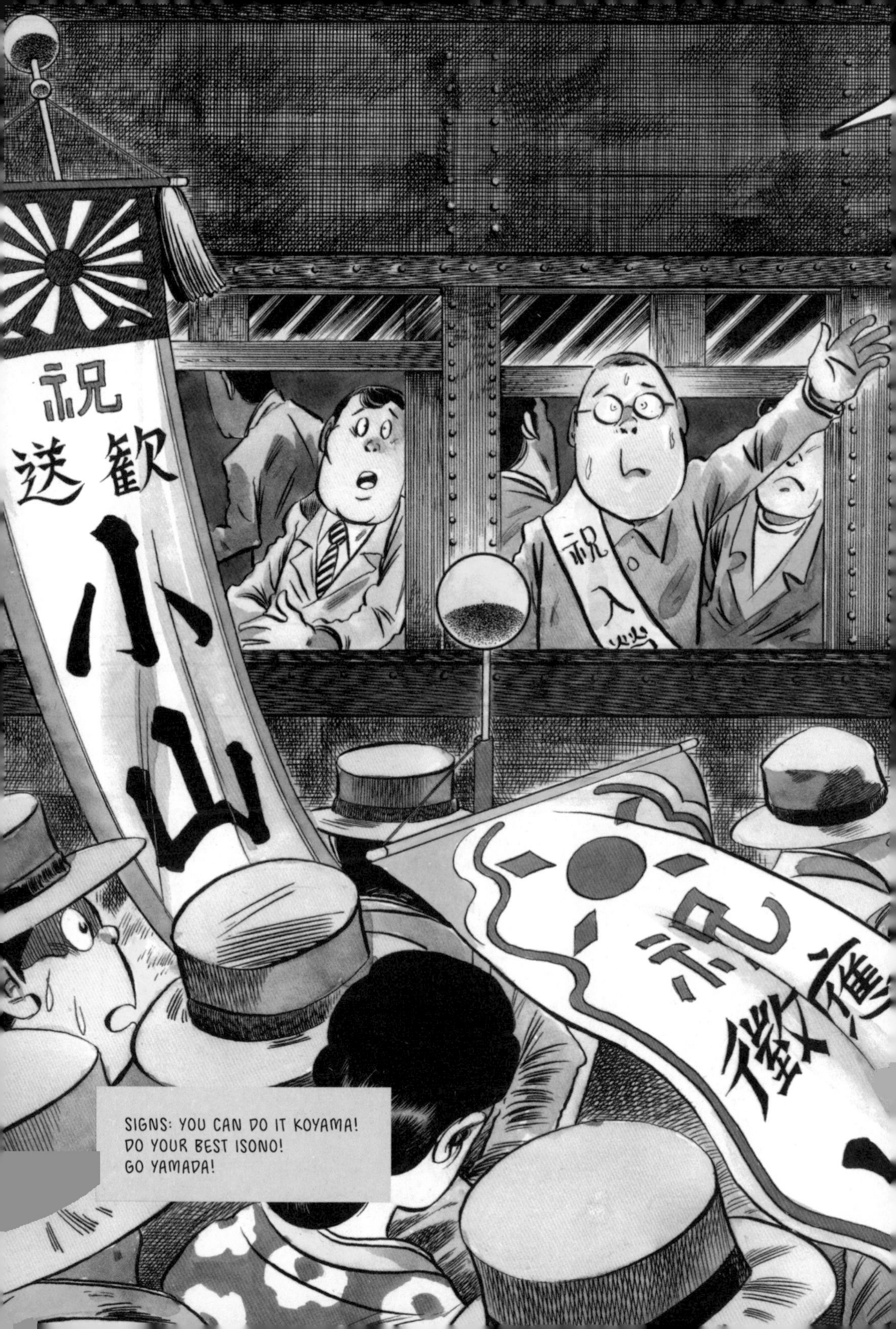
SIGNS: YOU CAN DO IT KOYAMA!
DO YOUR BEST ISONO!
GO YAMADA!

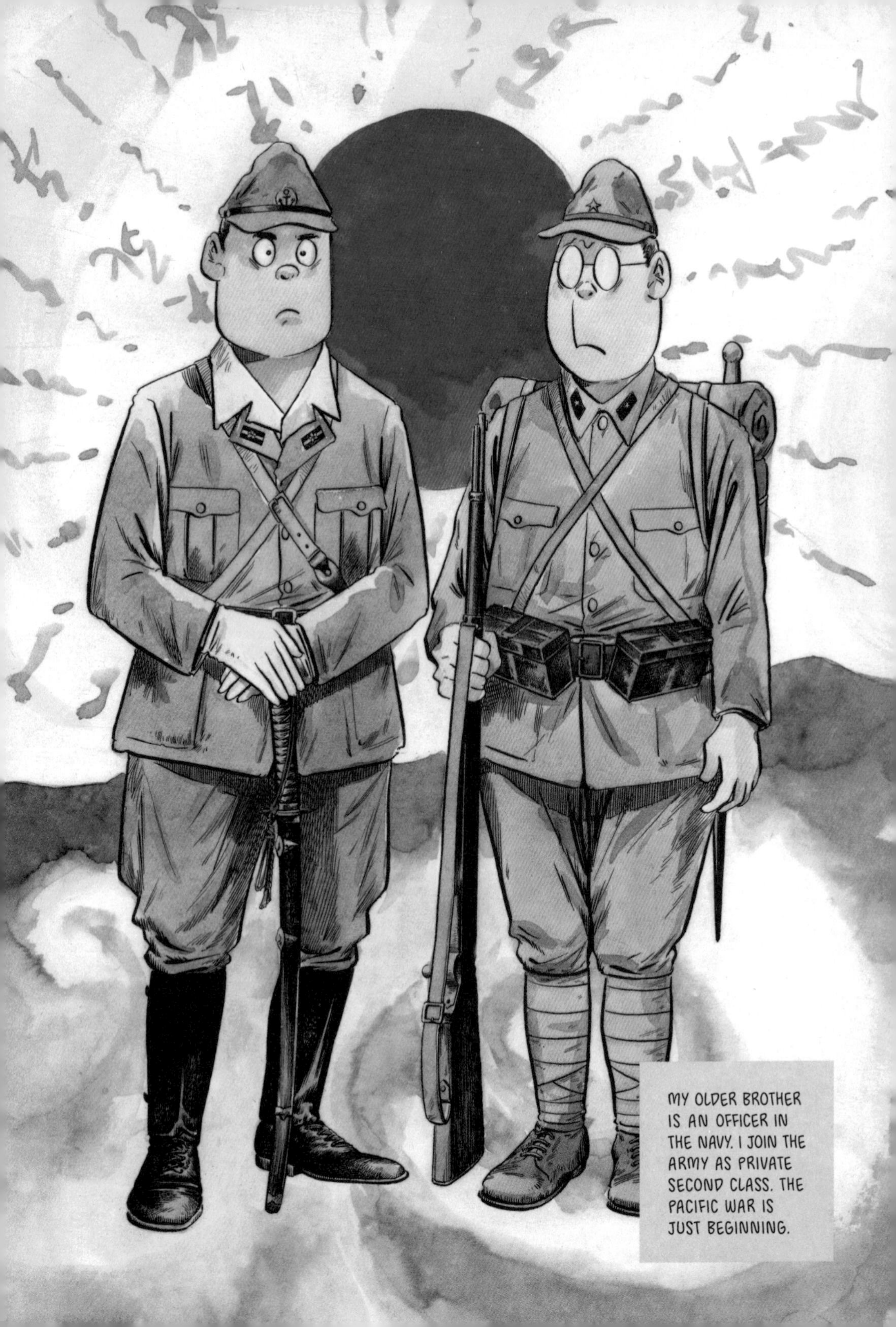
MY OLDER BROTHER IS AN OFFICER IN THE NAVY. I JOIN THE ARMY AS PRIVATE SECOND CLASS. THE PACIFIC WAR IS JUST BEGINNING.

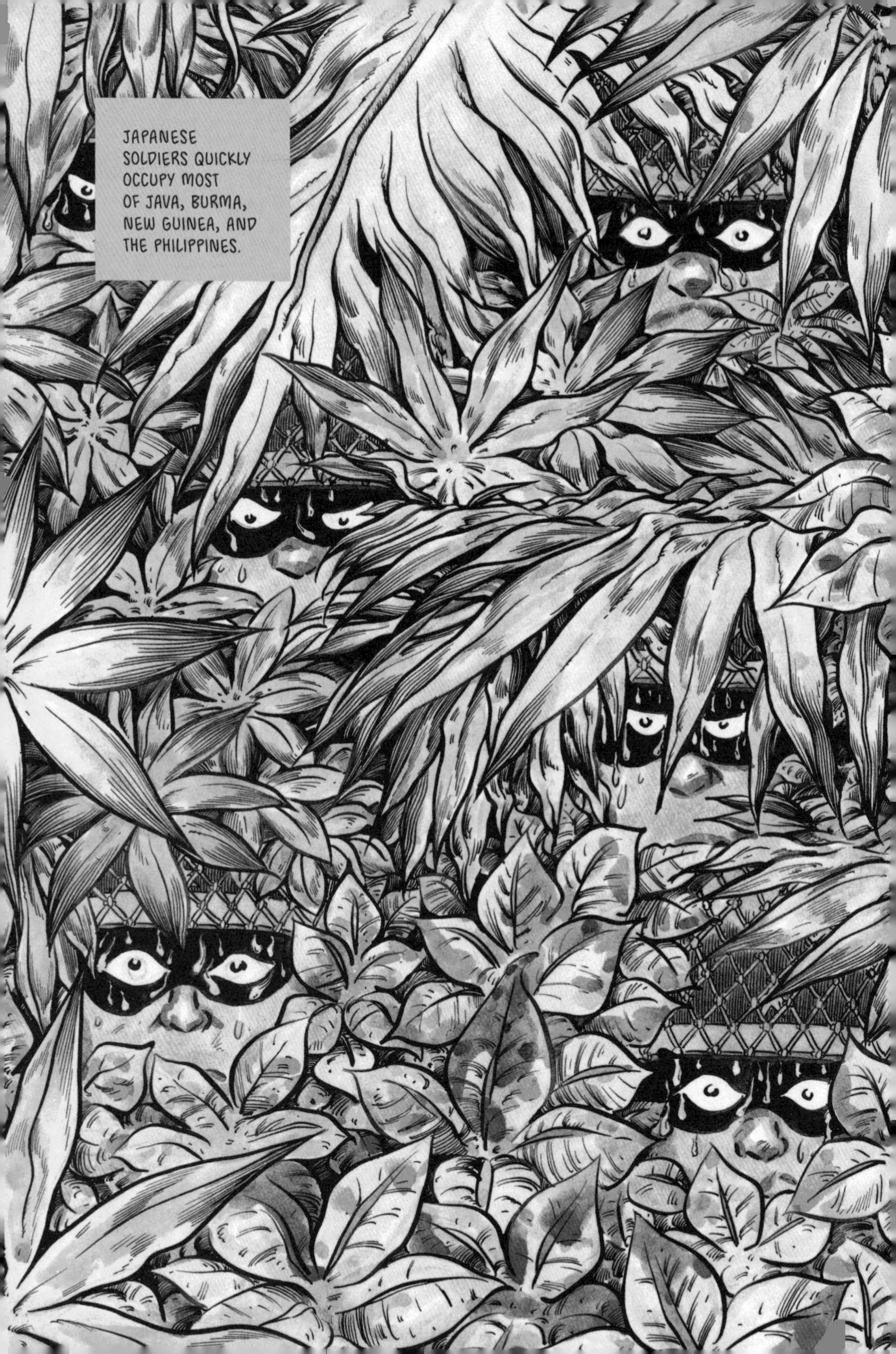
JAPANESE SOLDIERS QUICKLY OCCUPY MOST OF JAVA, BURMA, NEW GUINEA, AND THE PHILIPPINES.

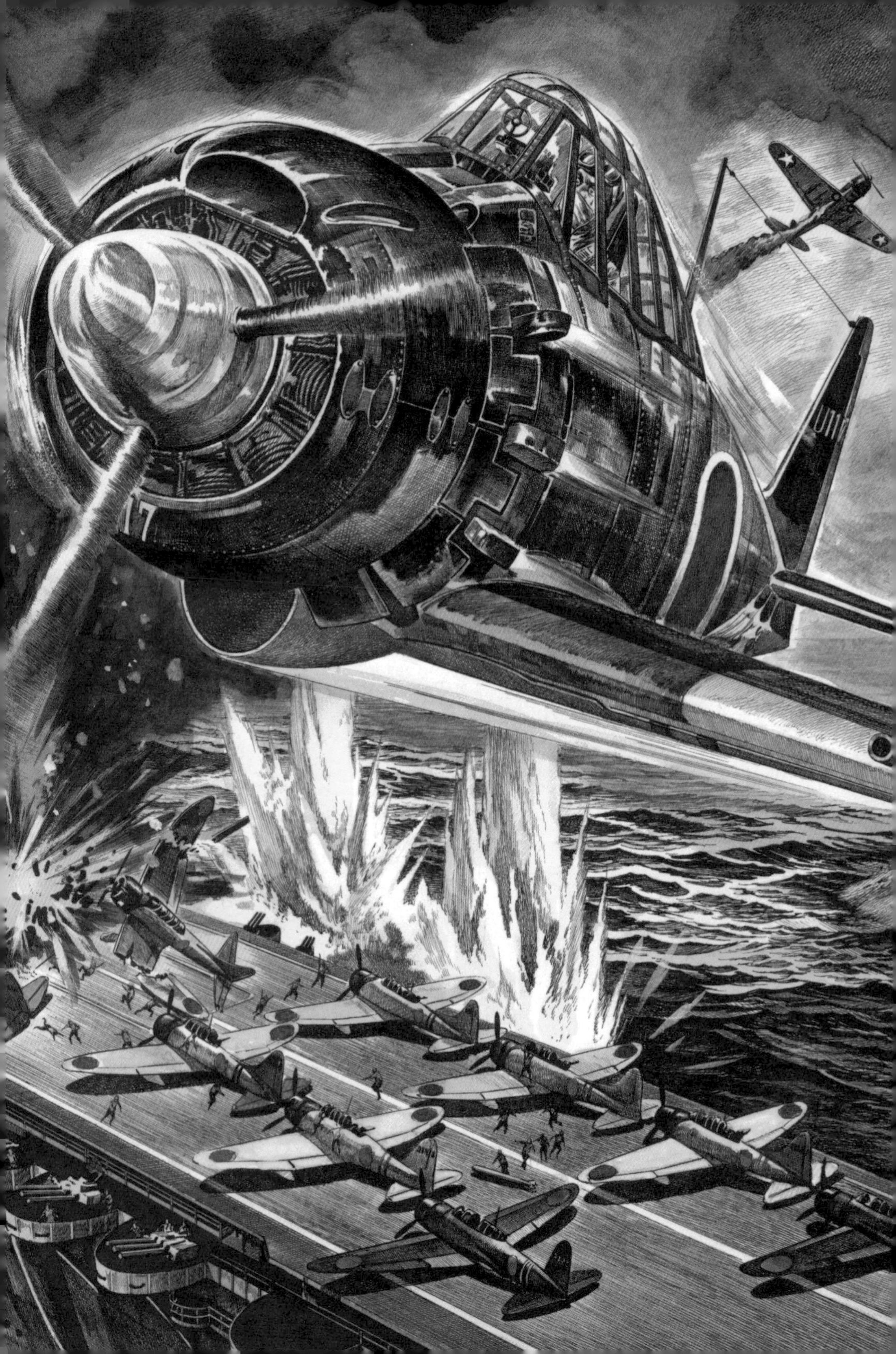

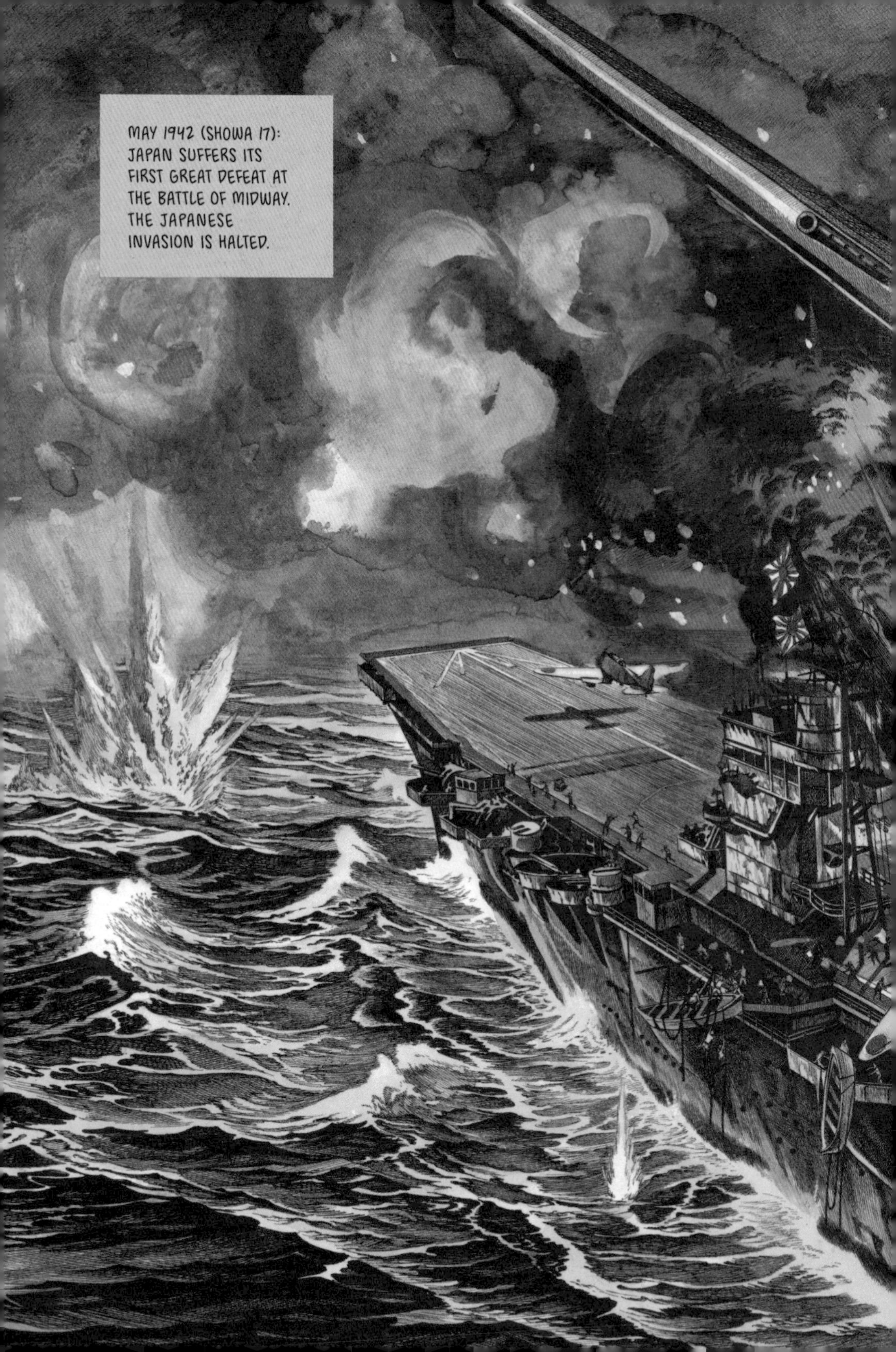
MAY 1942 (SHOWA 17): JAPAN SUFFERS ITS FIRST GREAT DEFEAT AT THE BATTLE OF MIDWAY. THE JAPANESE INVASION IS HALTED.

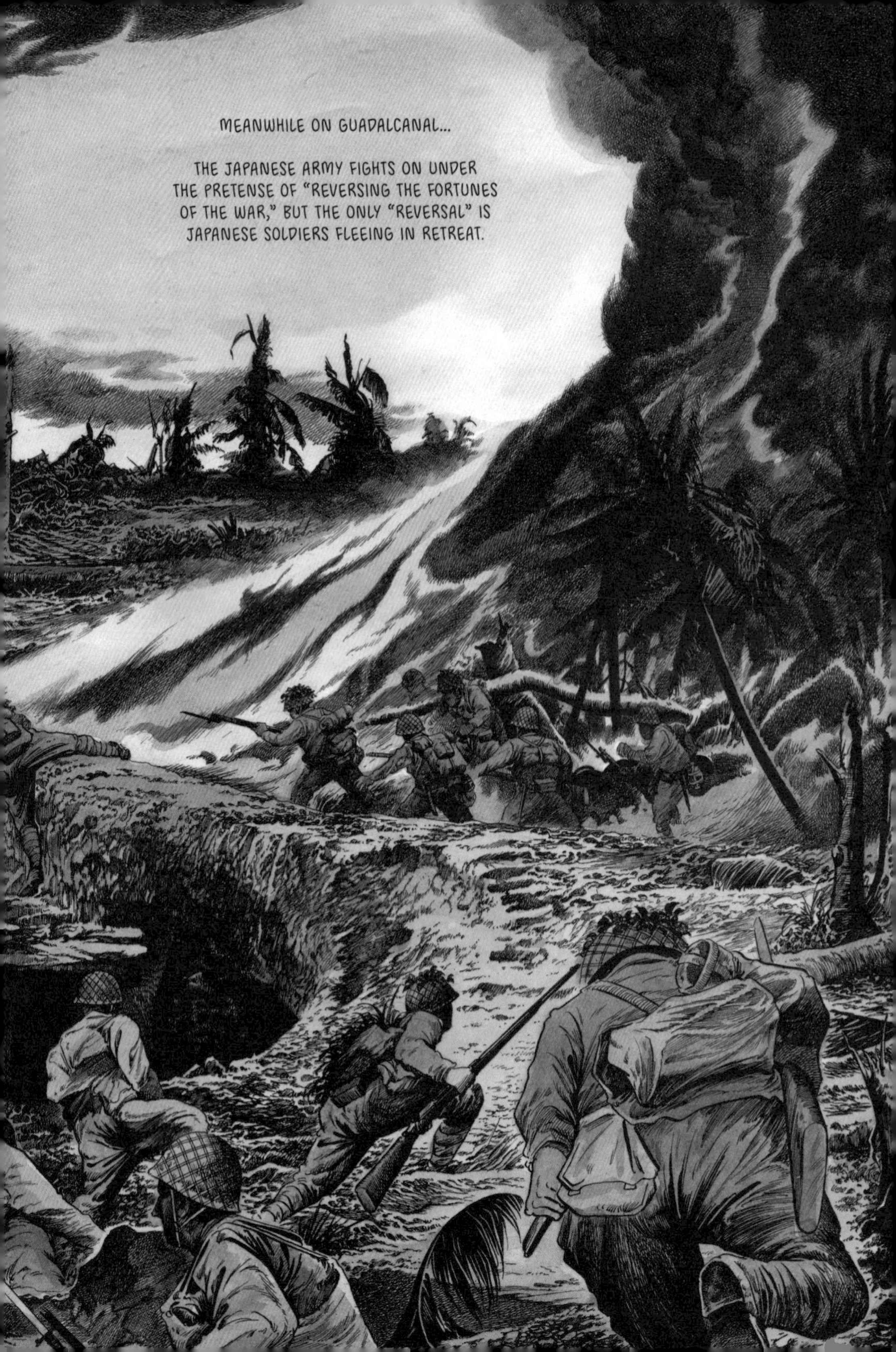
MEANWHILE ON GUADALCANAL...
THE JAPANESE ARMY FIGHTS ON UNDER THE PRETENSE OF "REVERSING THE FORTUNES OF THE WAR," BUT THE ONLY "REVERSAL" IS JAPANESE SOLDIERS FLEEING IN RETREAT.

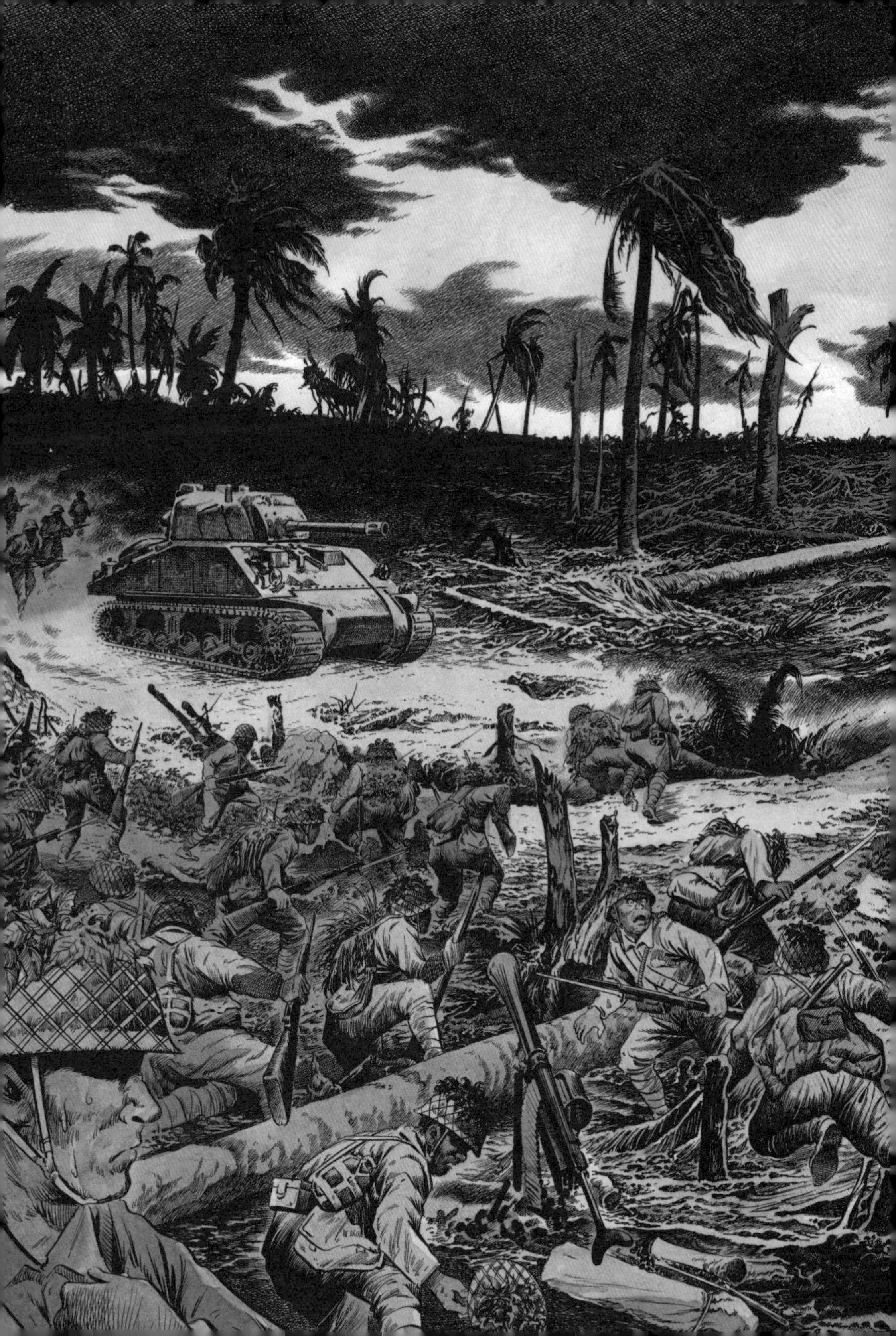

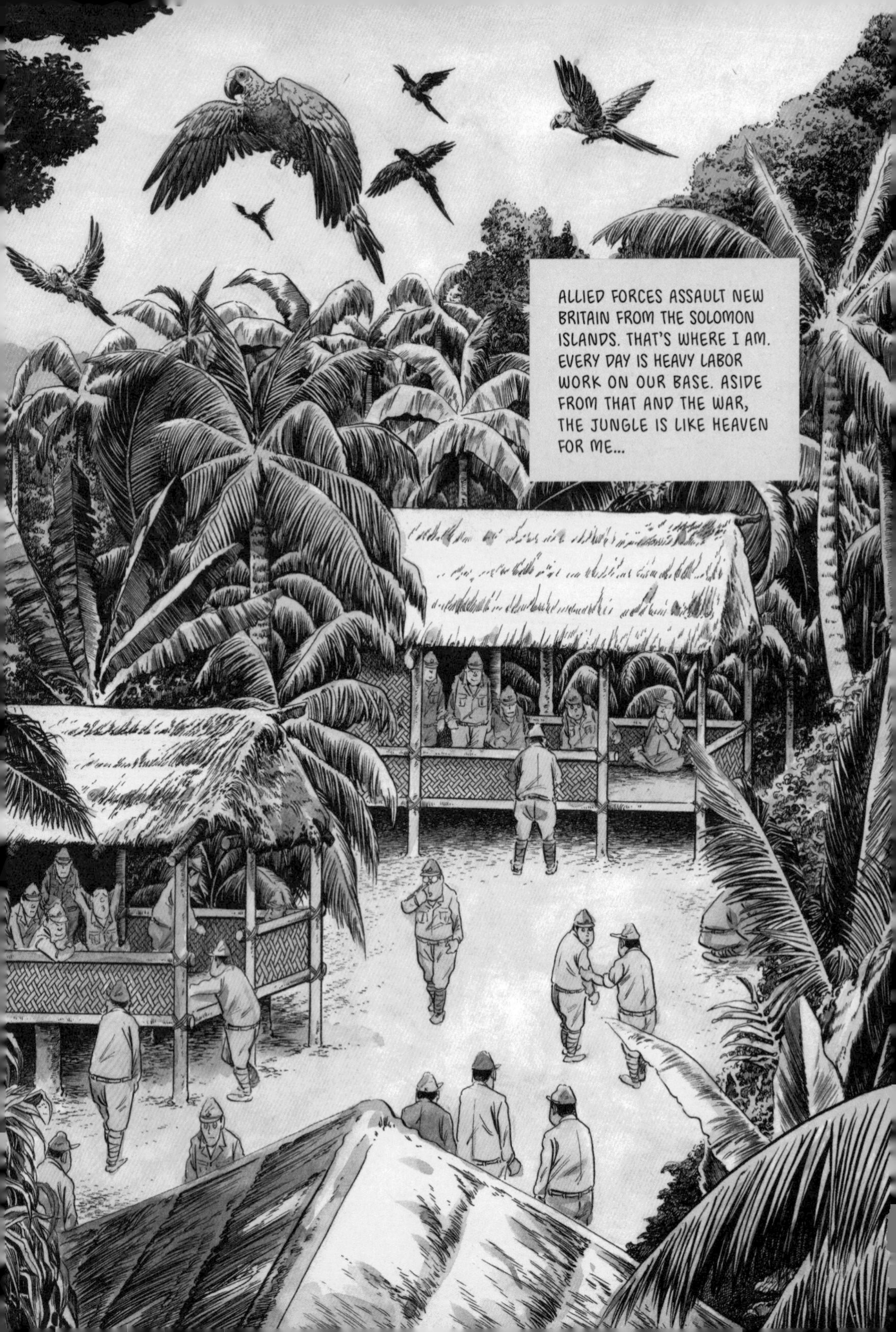
ALLIED FORCES ASSAULT NEW BRITAIN FROM THE SOLOMON ISLANDS. THAT'S WHERE I AM. EVERY DAY IS HEAVY LABOR WORK ON OUR BASE. ASIDE FROM THAT AND THE WAR, THE JUNGLE IS LIKE HEAVEN FOR ME...

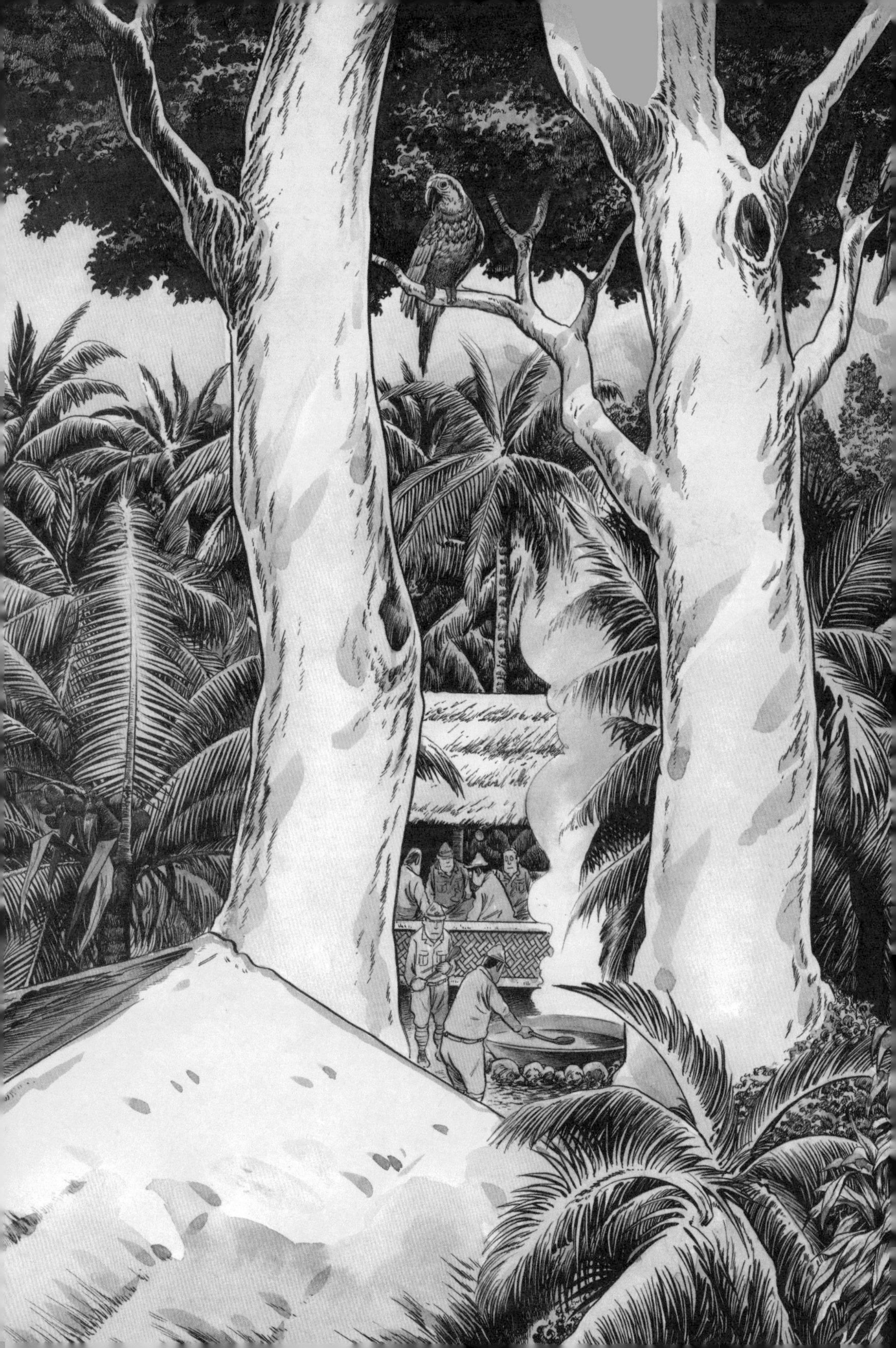

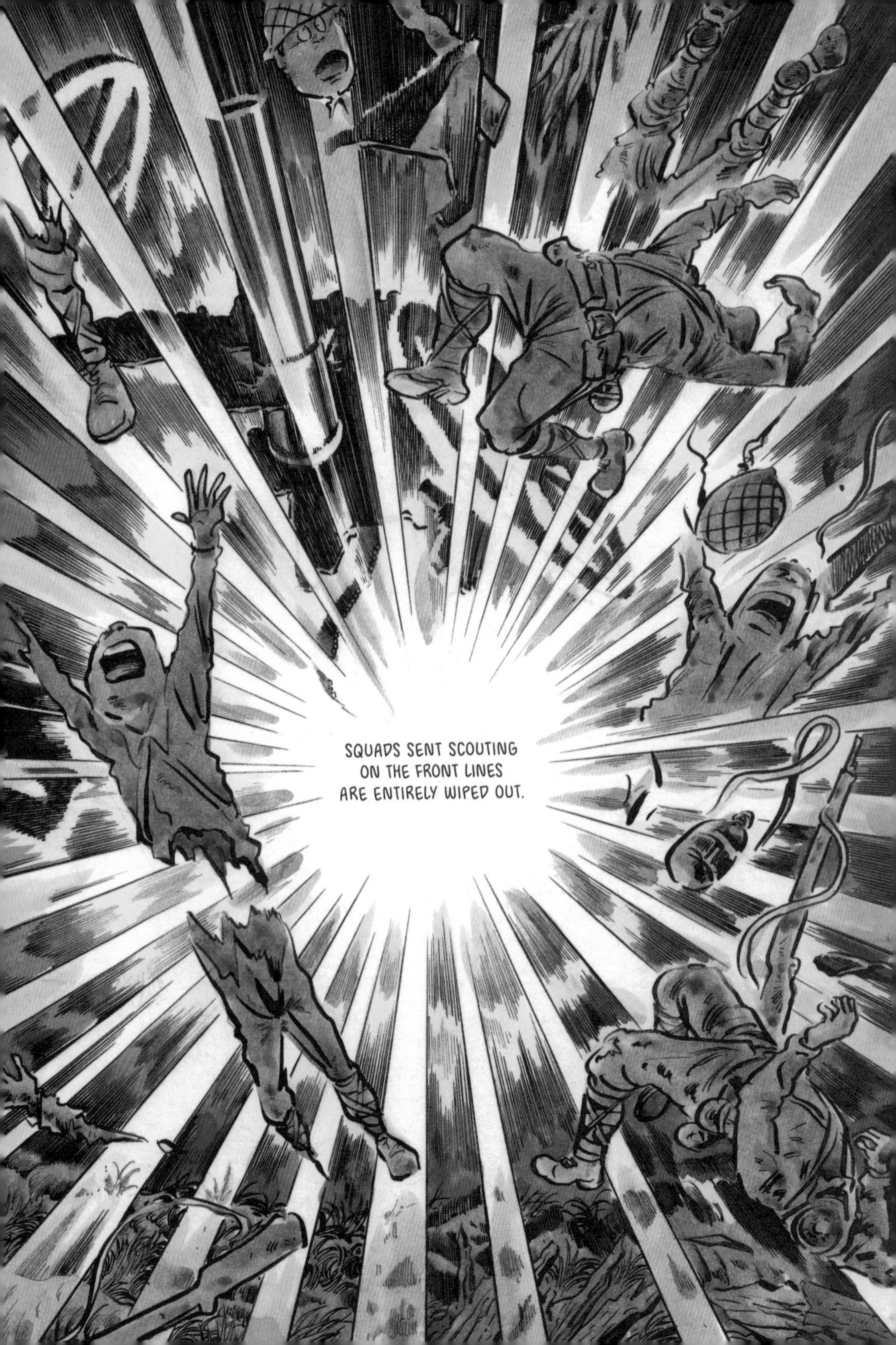
SQUADS SENT SCOUTING
ON THE FRONT LINES
ARE ENTIRELY WIPED OUT.

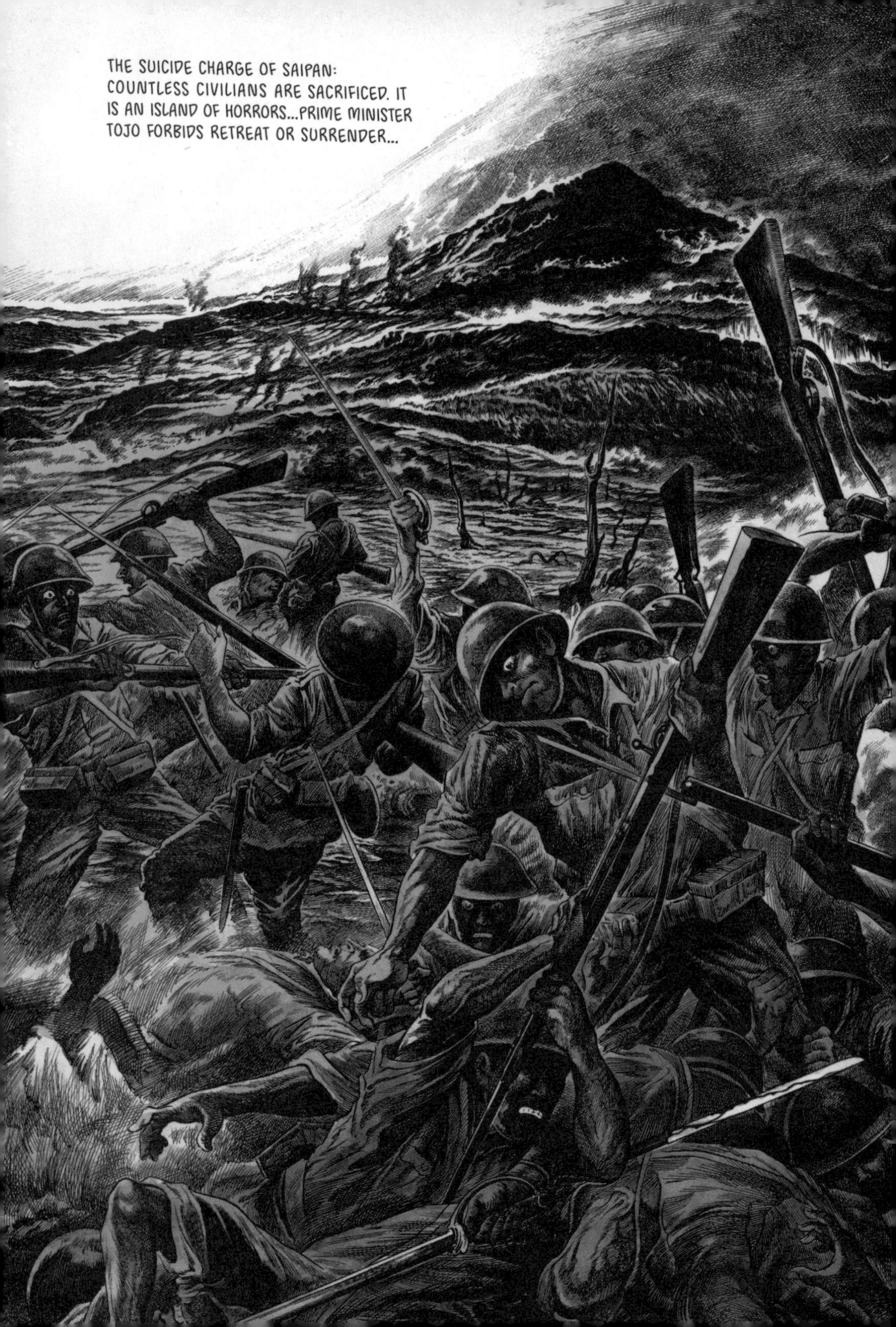
THE SUICIDE CHARGE OF SAIPAN: COUNTLESS CIVILIANS ARE SACRIFICED. IT IS AN ISLAND OF HORRORS...PRIME MINISTER TOJO FORBIDS RETREAT OR SURRENDER...

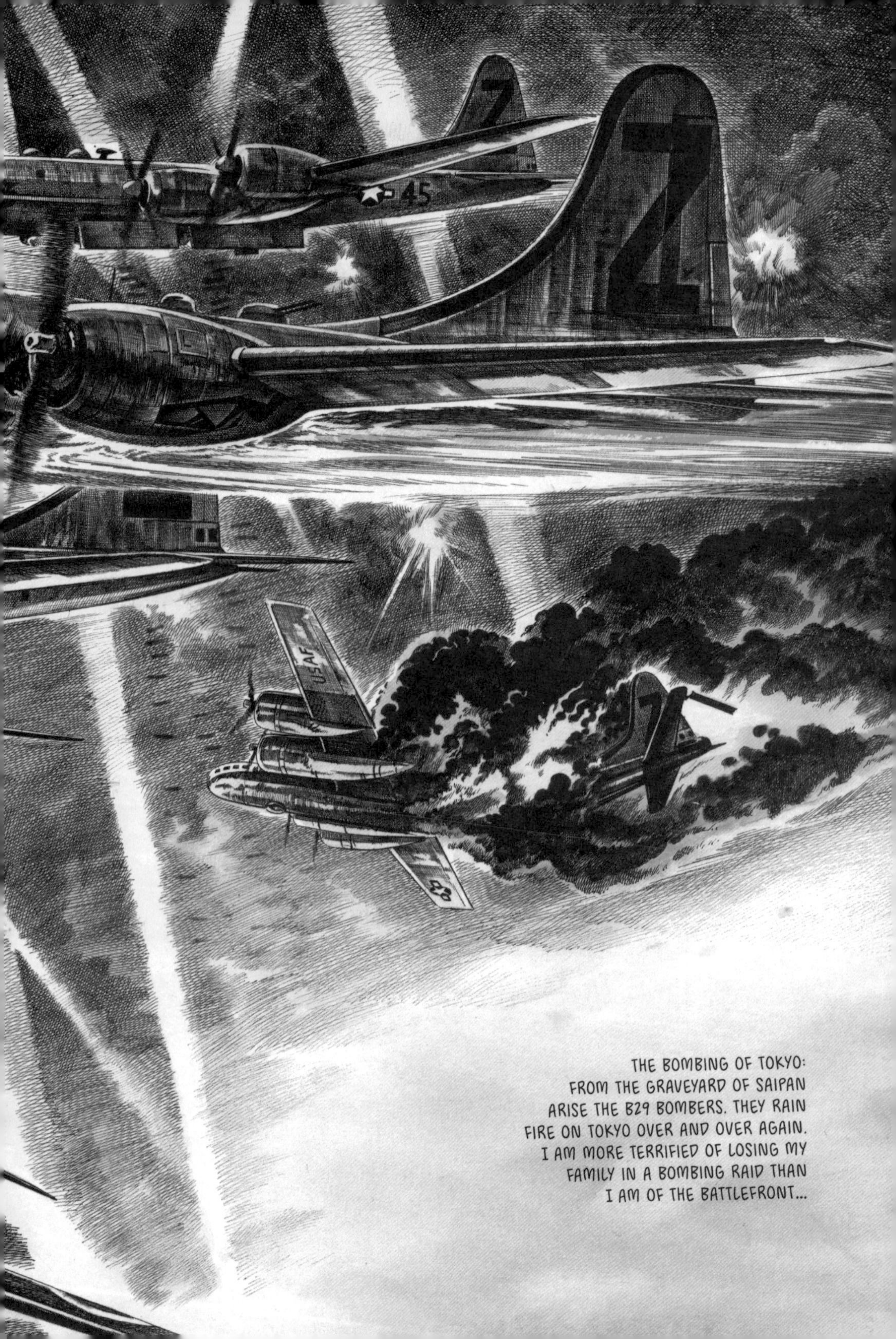
USAF
THE BOMBING OF TOKYO:
FROM THE GRAVEYARD OF SAIPAN
ARISE THE B29 BOMBERS. THEY RAIN
FIRE ON TOKYO OVER AND OVER AGAIN.
I AM MORE TERRIFIED OF LOSING MY
FAMILY IN A BOMBING RAID THAN
I AM OF THE BATTLEFRONT...

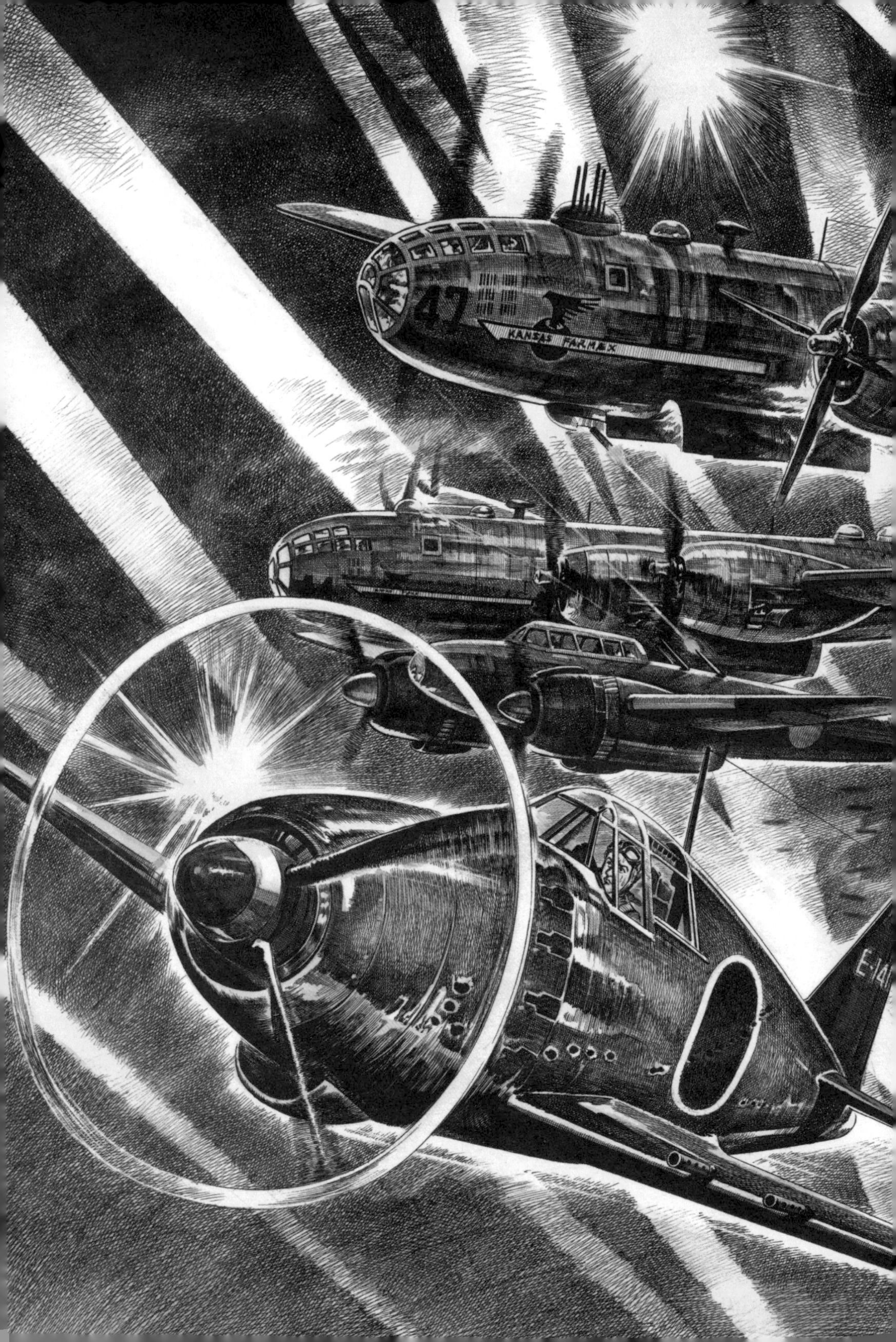
47
KANSAS FARMER

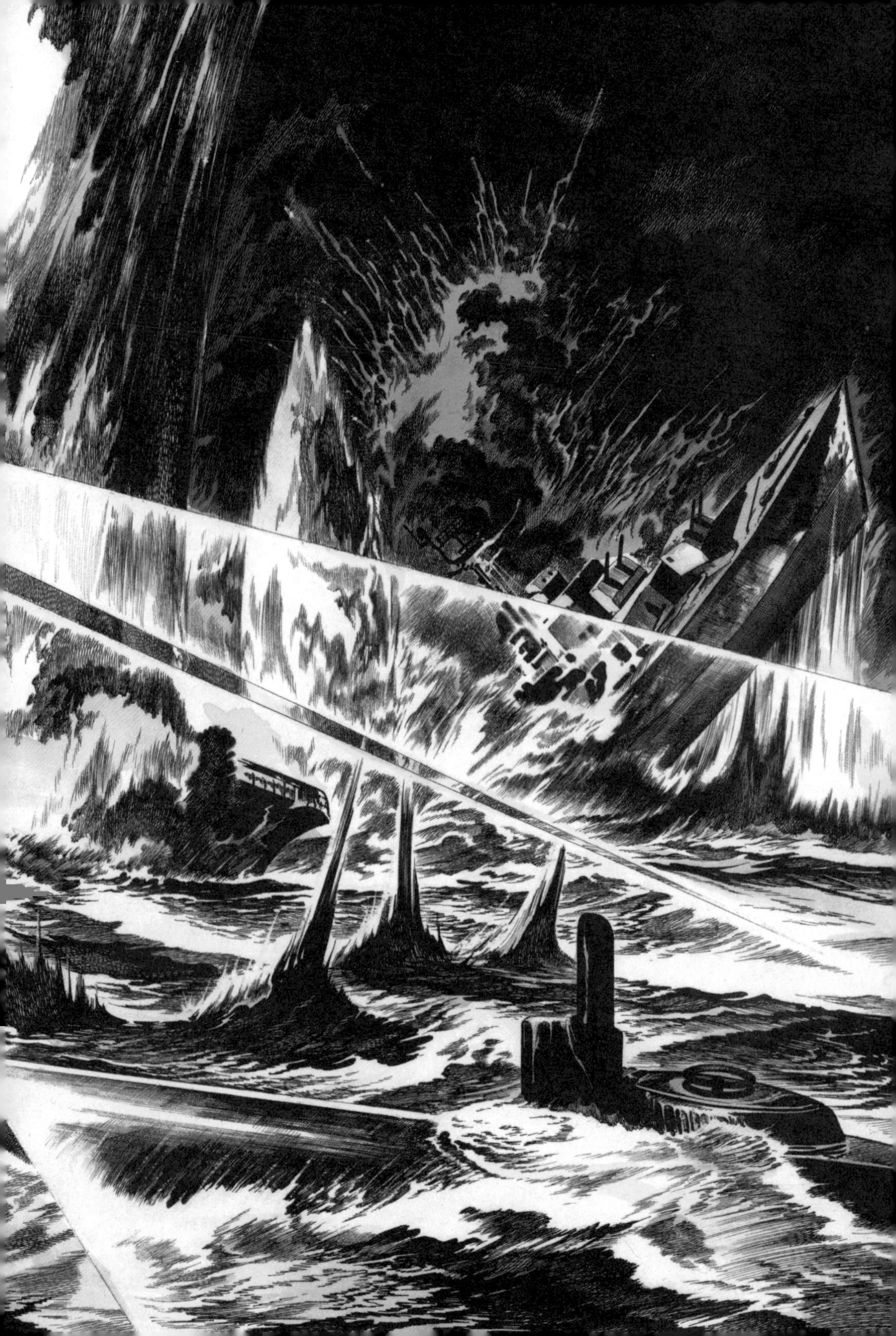

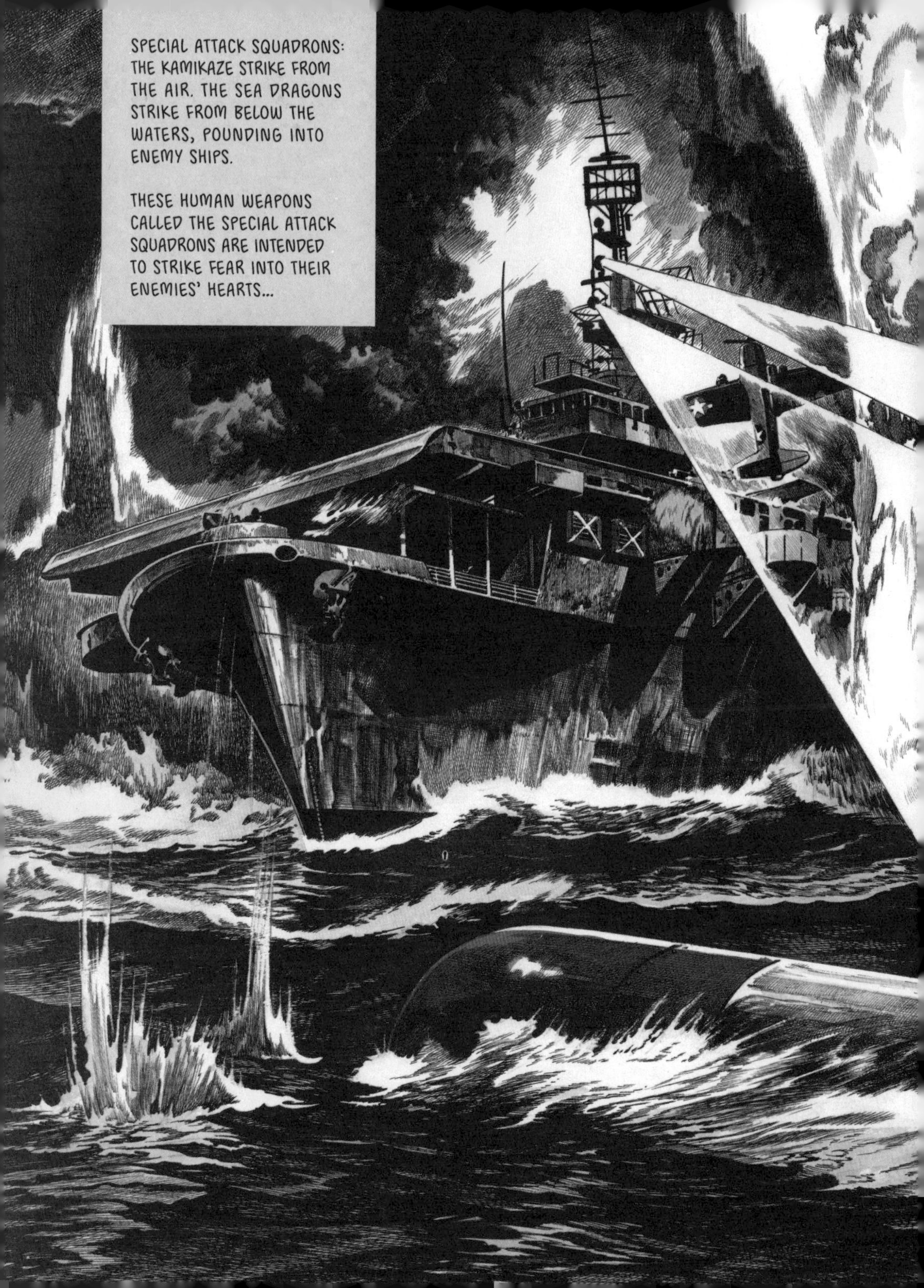
SPECIAL ATTACK SQUADRONS: THE KAMIKAZE STRIKE FROM THE AIR. THE SEA DRAGONS STRIKE FROM BELOW THE WATERS, POUNDING INTO ENEMY SHIPS.
THESE HUMAN WEAPONS CALLED THE SPECIAL ATTACK SQUADRONS ARE INTENDED TO STRIKE FEAR INTO THEIR ENEMIES' HEARTS...

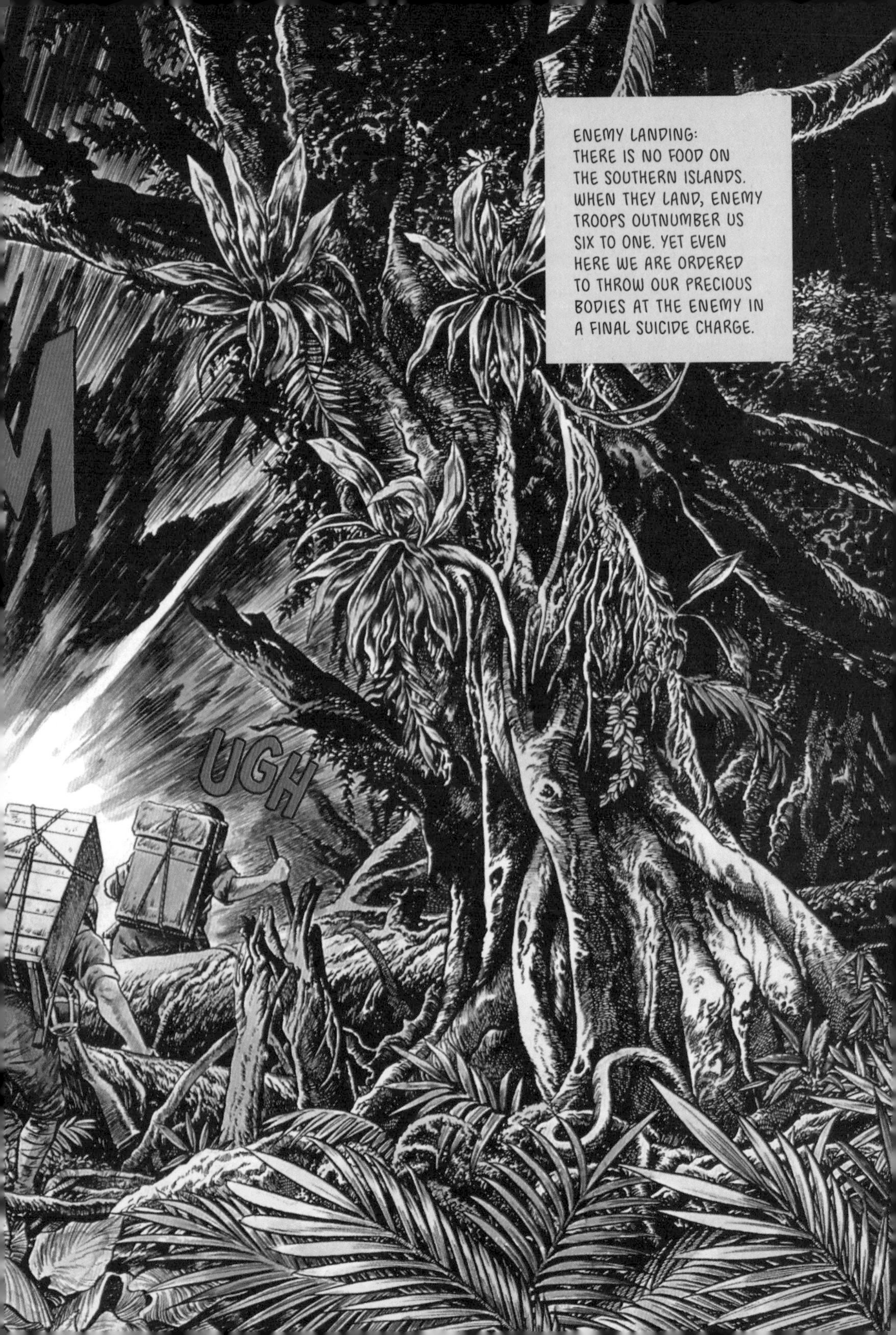
ENEMY LANDING:
THERE IS NO FOOD ON THE SOUTHERN ISLANDS. WHEN THEY LAND, ENEMY TROOPS OUTNUMBER US SIX TO ONE. YET EVEN HERE WE ARE ORDERED TO THROW OUR PRECIOUS BODIES AT THE ENEMY IN A FINAL SUICIDE CHARGE.
UGH

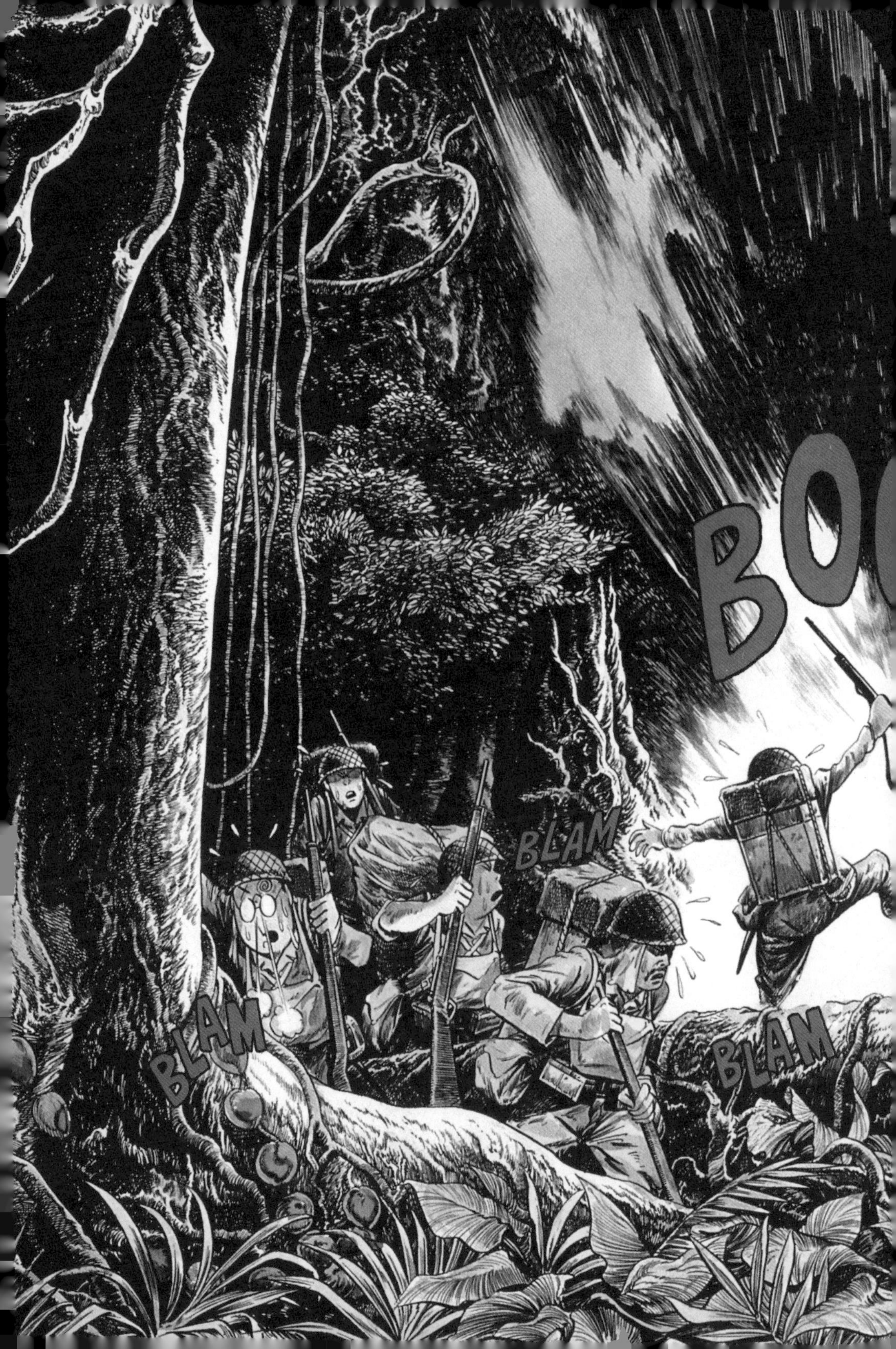
BLAM
BLAM
BLAM

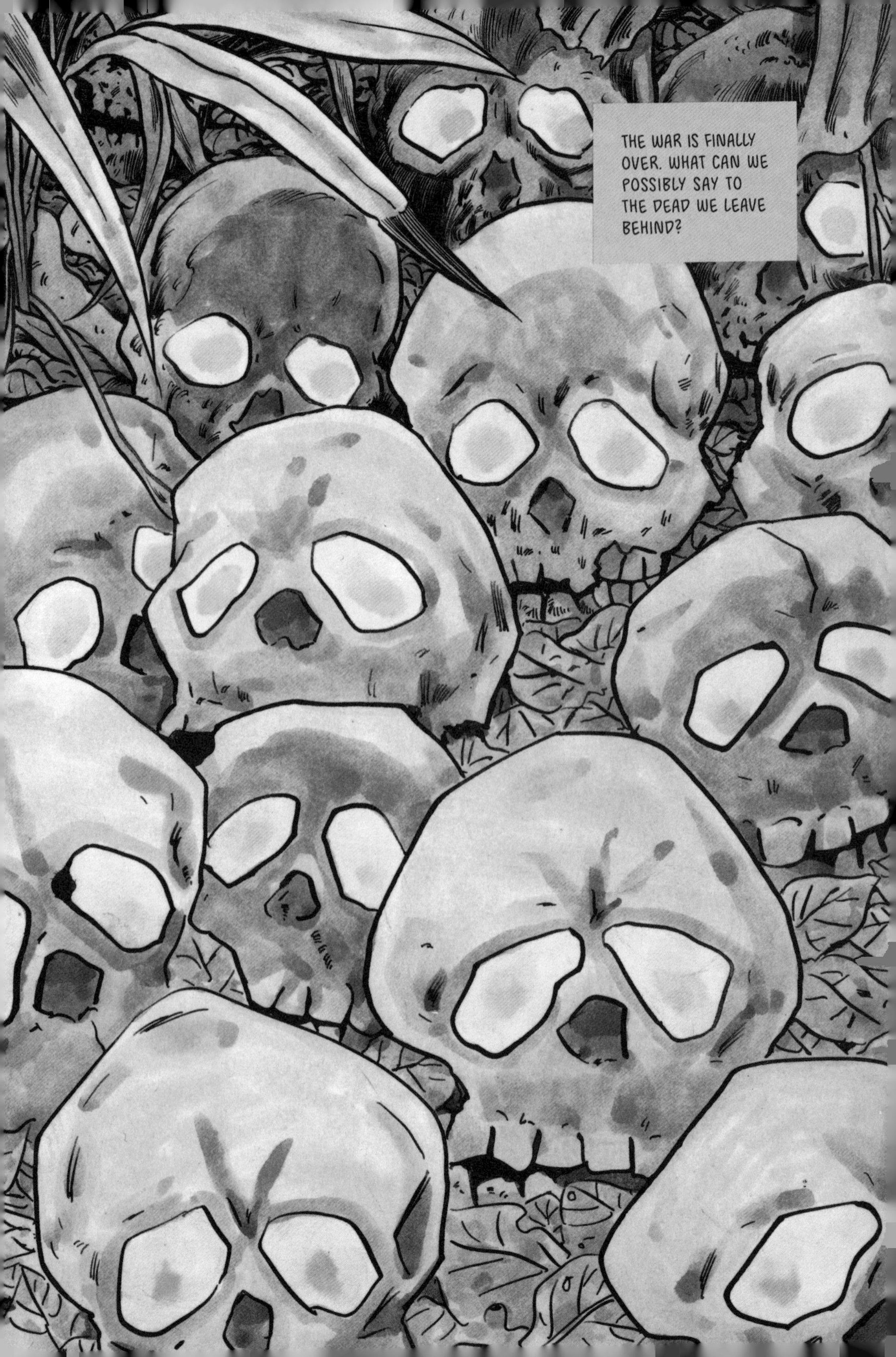
THE WAR IS FINALLY OVER. WHAT CAN WE POSSIBLY SAY TO THE DEAD WE LEAVE BEHIND?

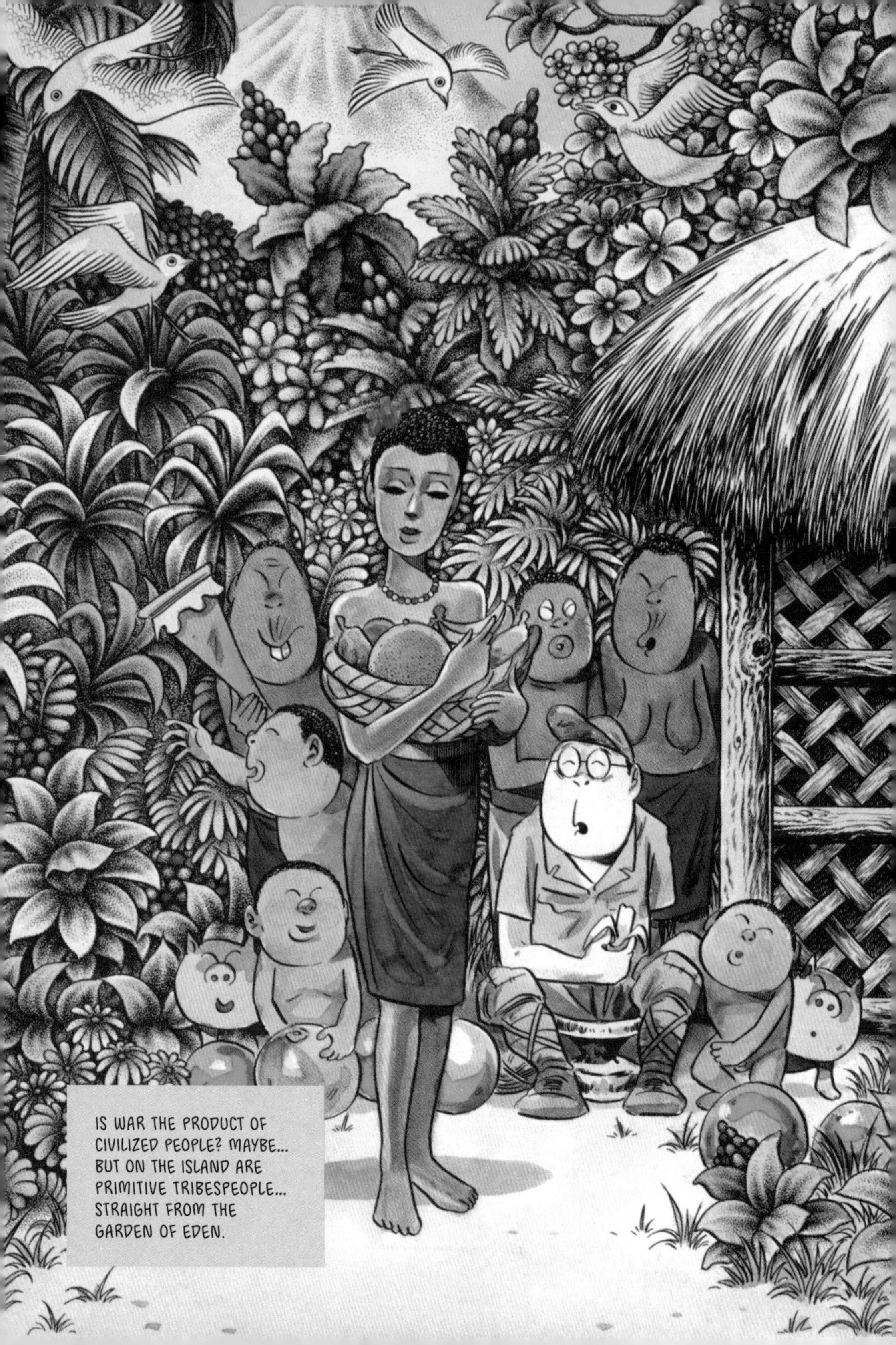
IS WAR THE PRODUCT OF CIVILIZED PEOPLE? MAYBE... BUT ON THE ISLAND ARE PRIMITIVE TRIBESPEOPLE... STRAIGHT FROM THE GARDEN OF EDEN.

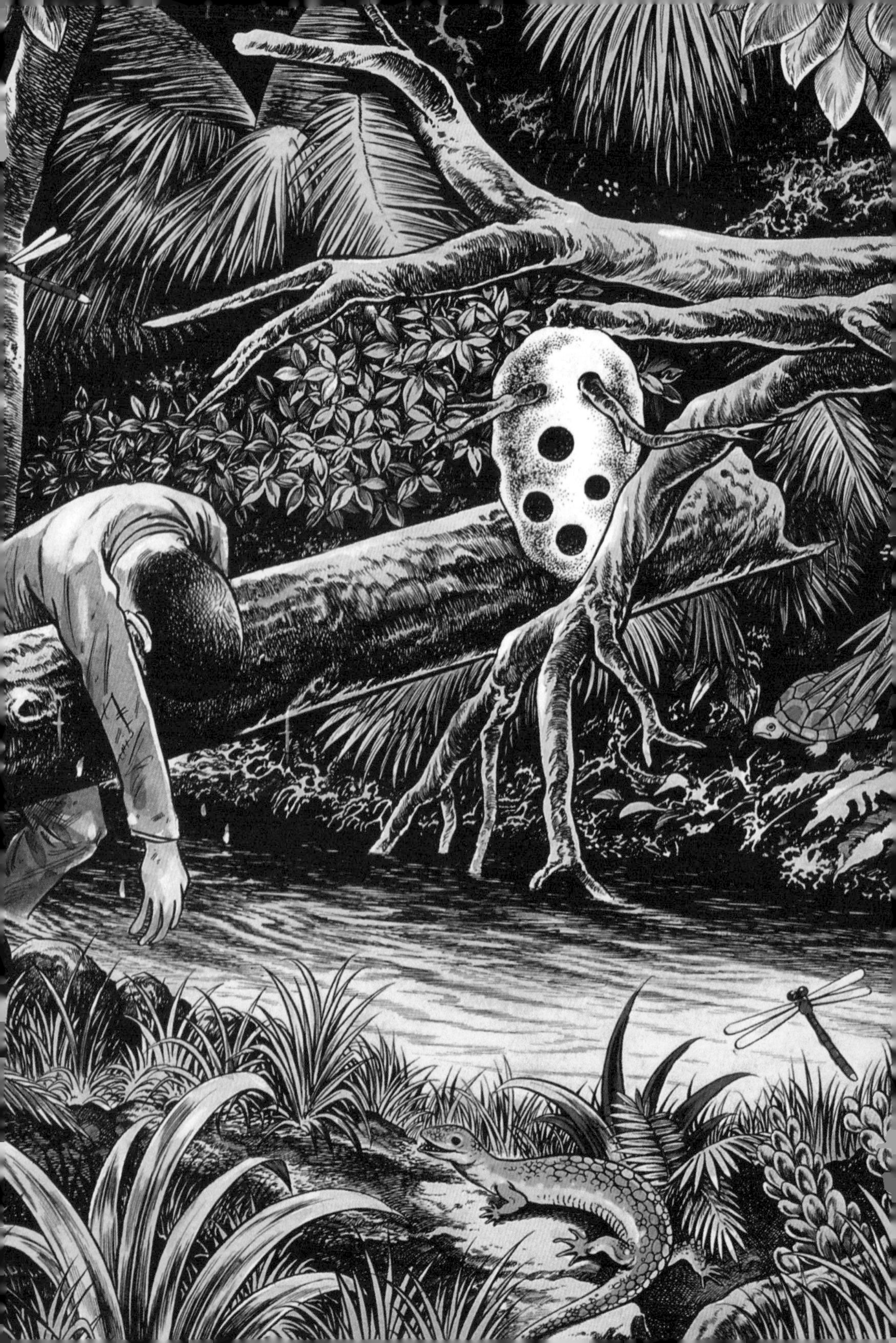

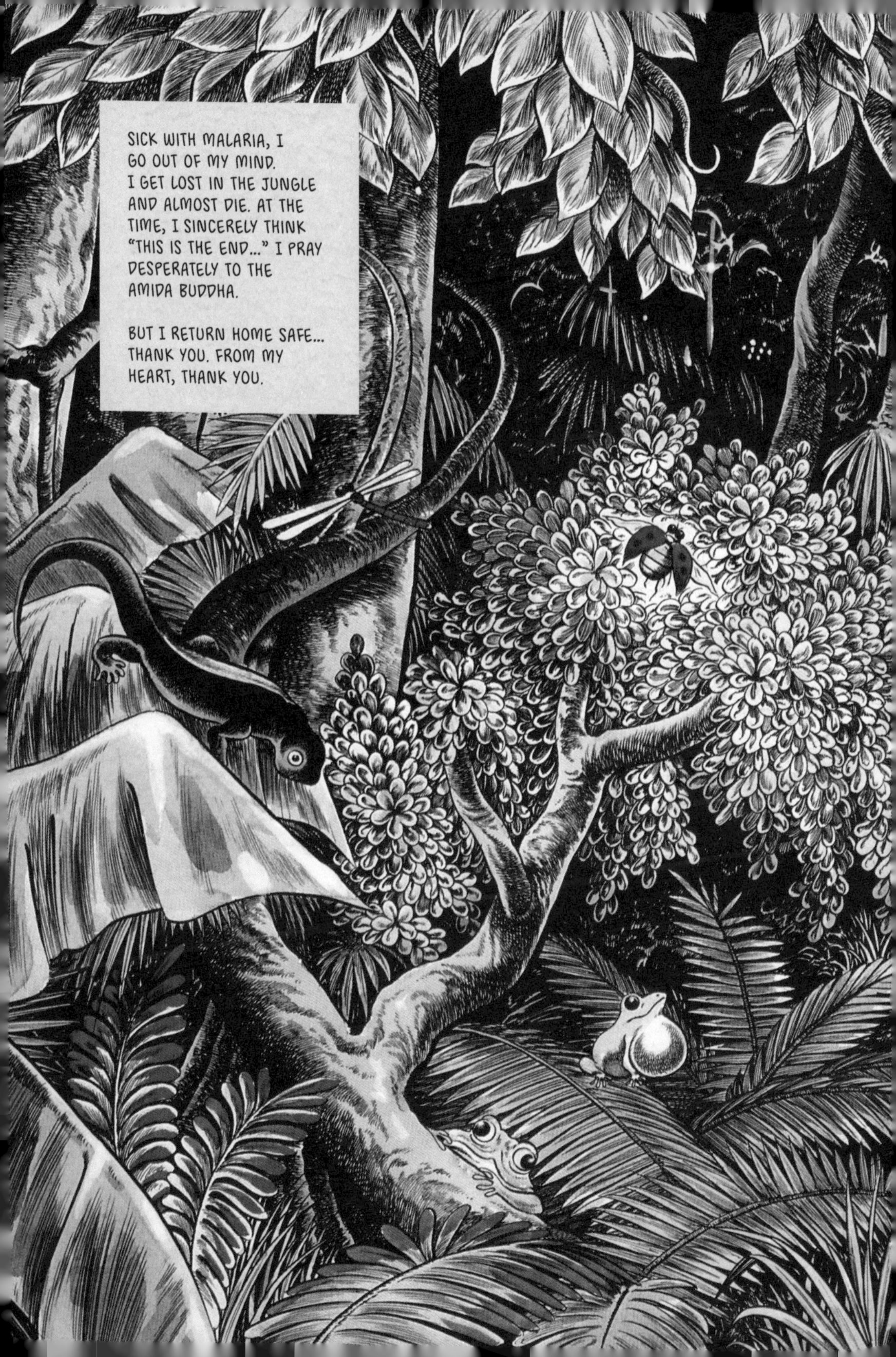
SICK WITH MALARIA, I GO OUT OF MY MIND. I GET LOST IN THE JUNGLE AND ALMOST DIE. AT THE TIME, I SINCERELY THINK "THIS IS THE END..." I PRAY DESPERATELY TO THE AMIDA BUDDHA.
BUT I RETURN HOME SAFE... THANK YOU. FROM MY HEART, THANK YOU.

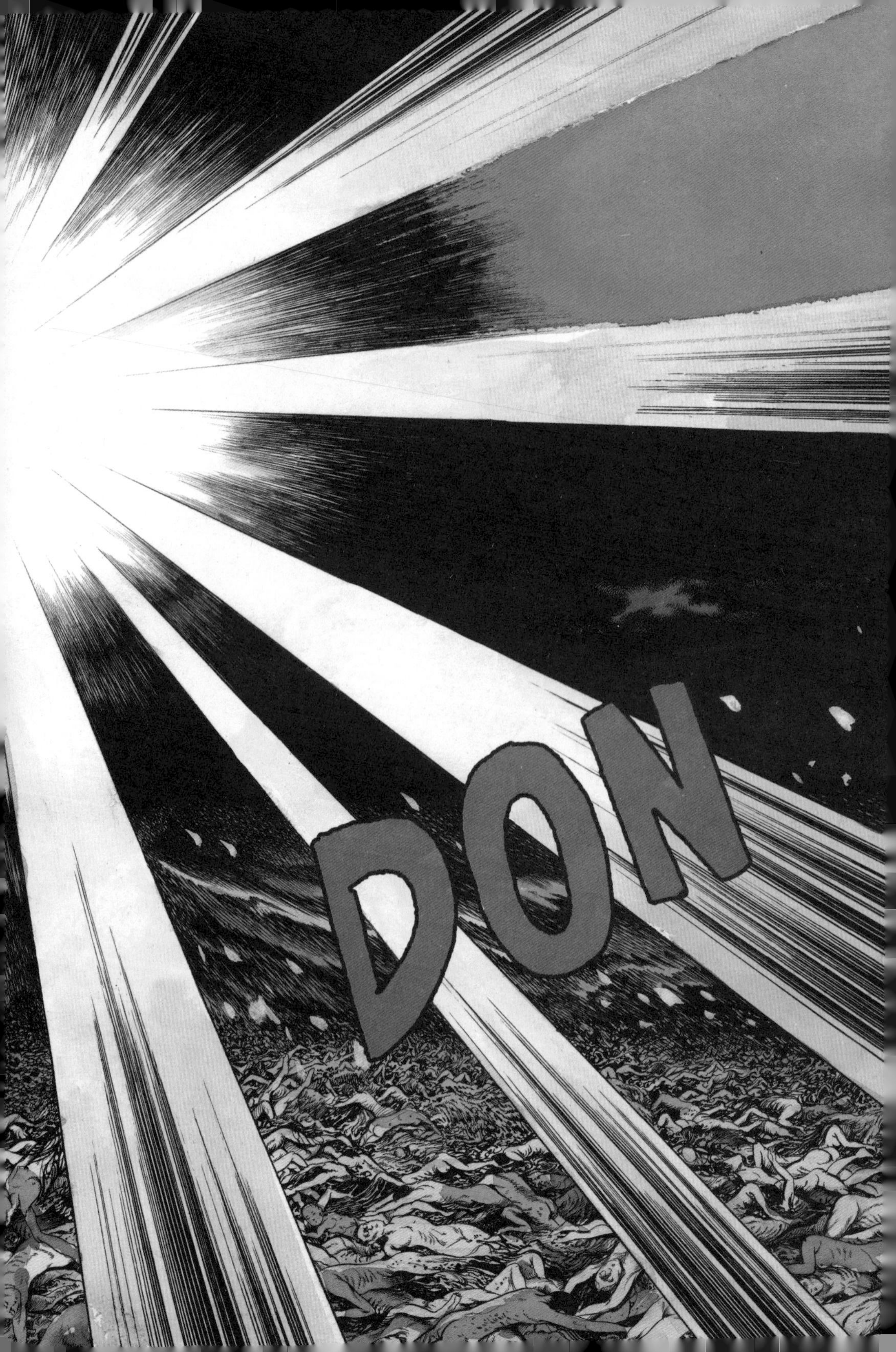
DON

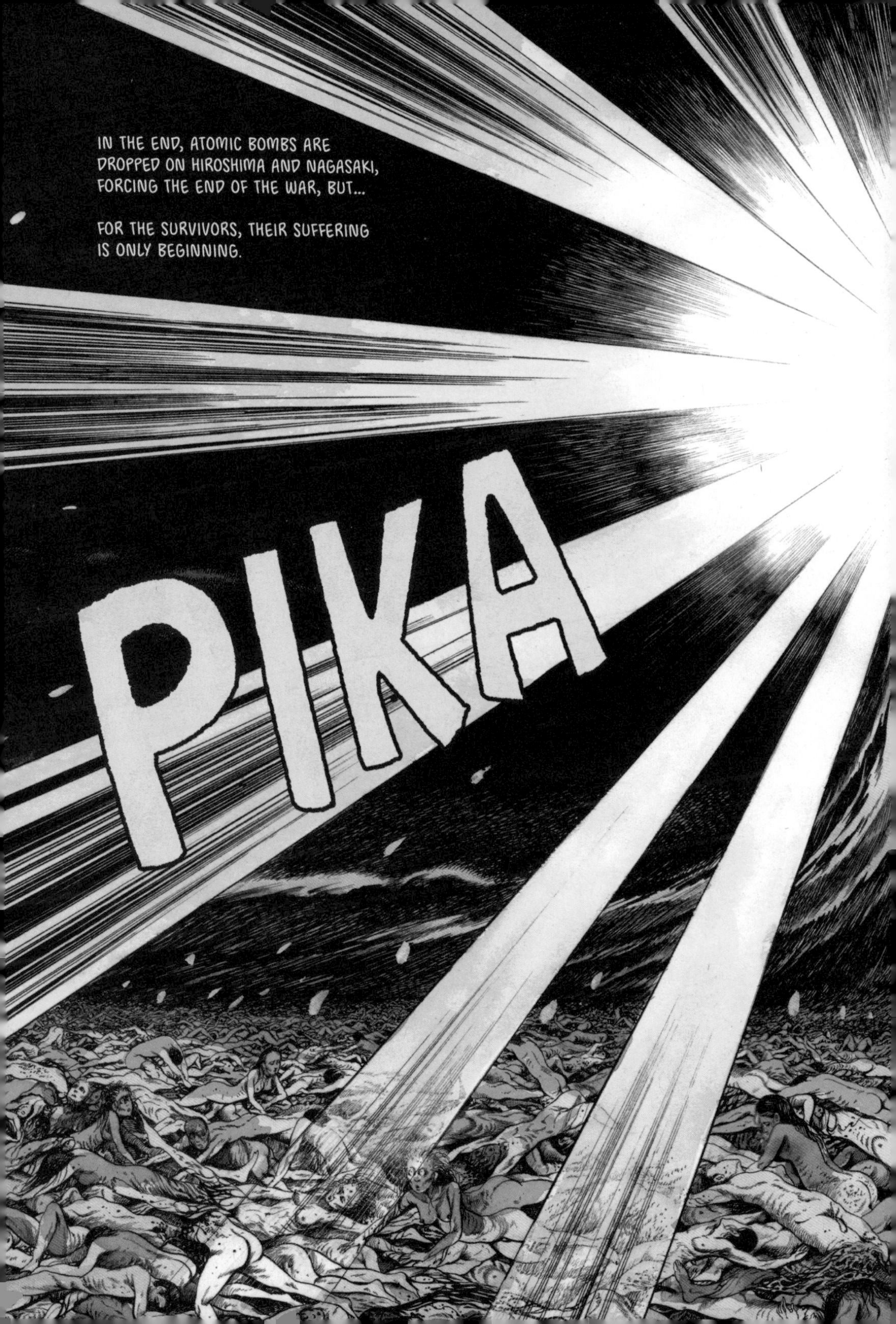
IN THE END, ATOMIC BOMBS ARE DROPPED ON HIROSHIMA AND NAGASAKI, FORCING THE END OF THE WAR, BUT...
FOR THE SURVIVORS, THEIR SUFFERING IS ONLY BEGINNING.
PIKA

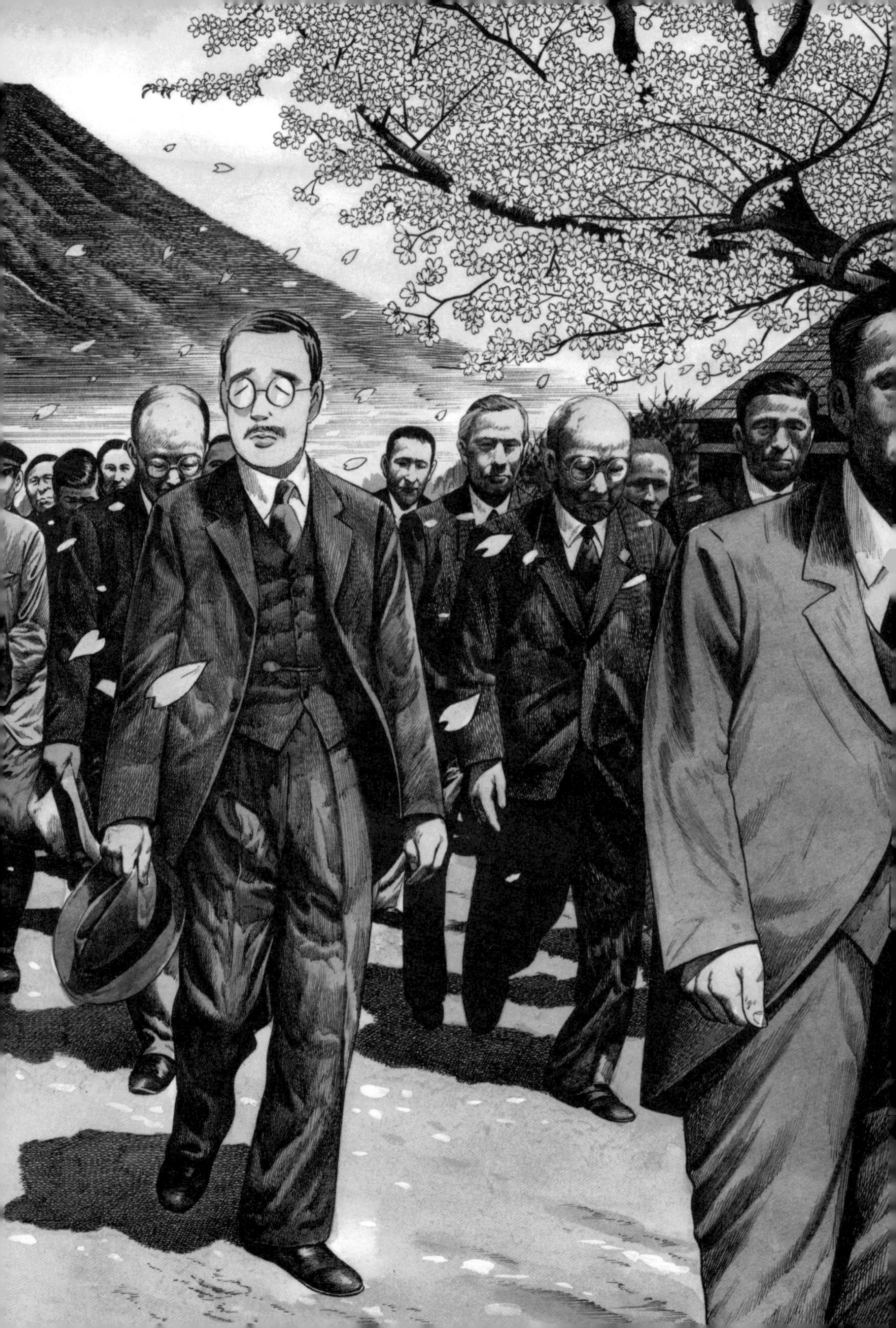

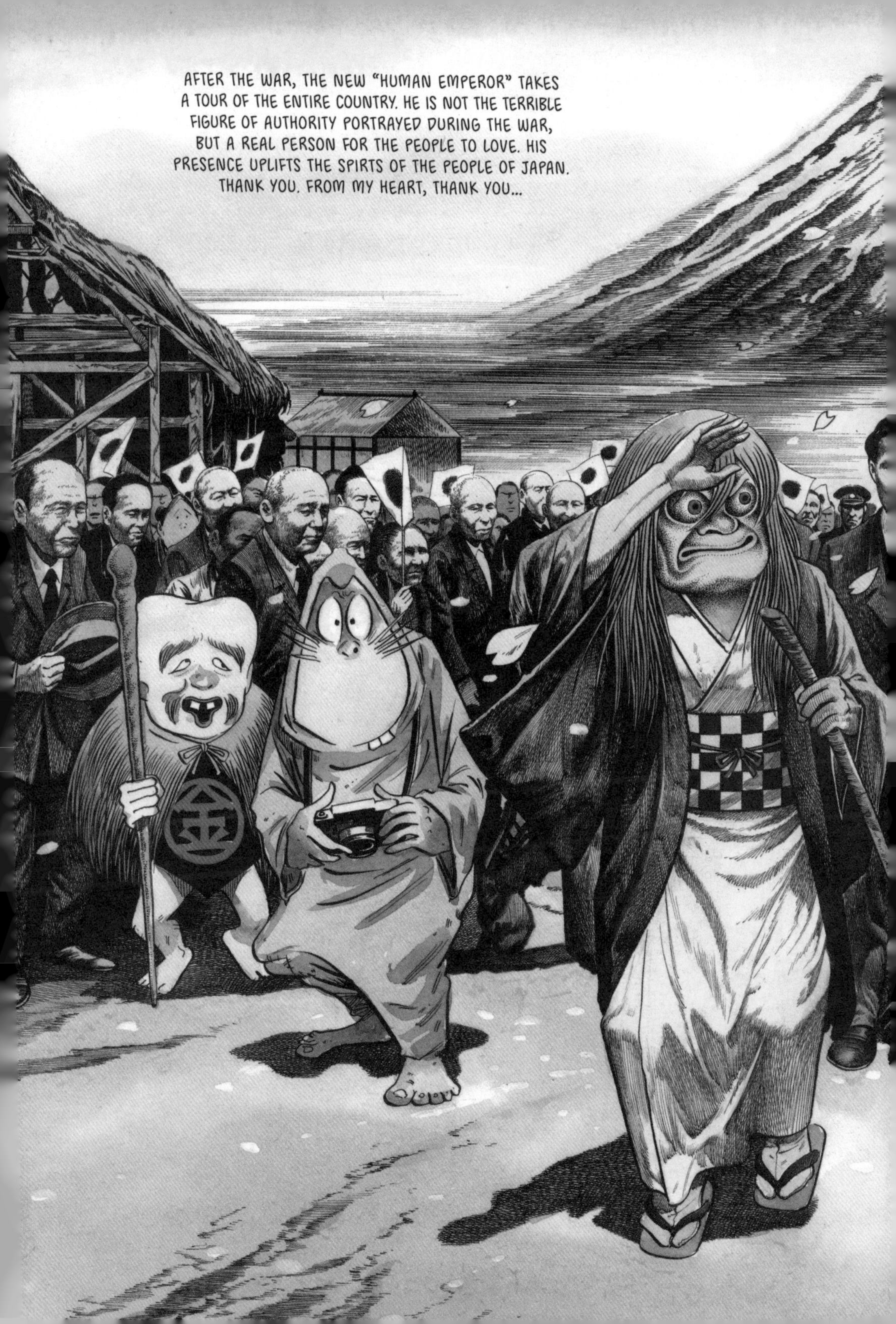
AFTER THE WAR, THE NEW "HUMAN EMPEROR" TAKES A TOUR OF THE ENTIRE COUNTRY. HE IS NOT THE TERRIBLE FIGURE OF AUTHORITY PORTRAYED DURING THE WAR, BUT A REAL PERSON FOR THE PEOPLE TO LOVE. HIS PRESENCE UPLIFTS THE SPIRTS OF THE PEOPLE OF JAPAN. THANK YOU. FROM MY HEART, THANK YOU...

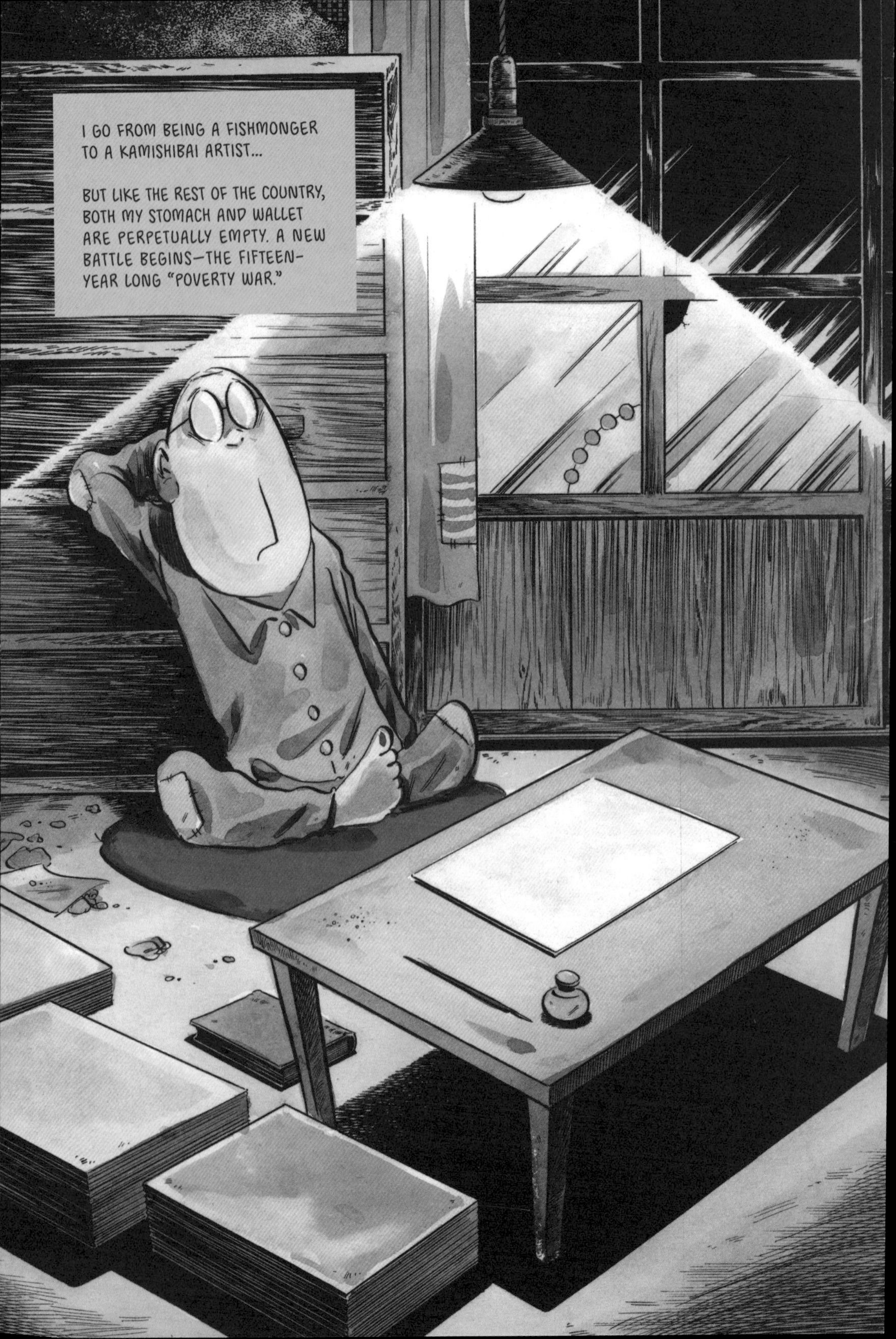
I GO FROM BEING A FISHMONGER TO A KAMISHIBAI ARTIST...
BUT LIKE THE REST OF THE COUNTRY, BOTH MY STOMACH AND WALLET ARE PERPETUALLY EMPTY. A NEW BATTLE BEGINS—THE FIFTEEN-YEAR LONG "POVERTY WAR."

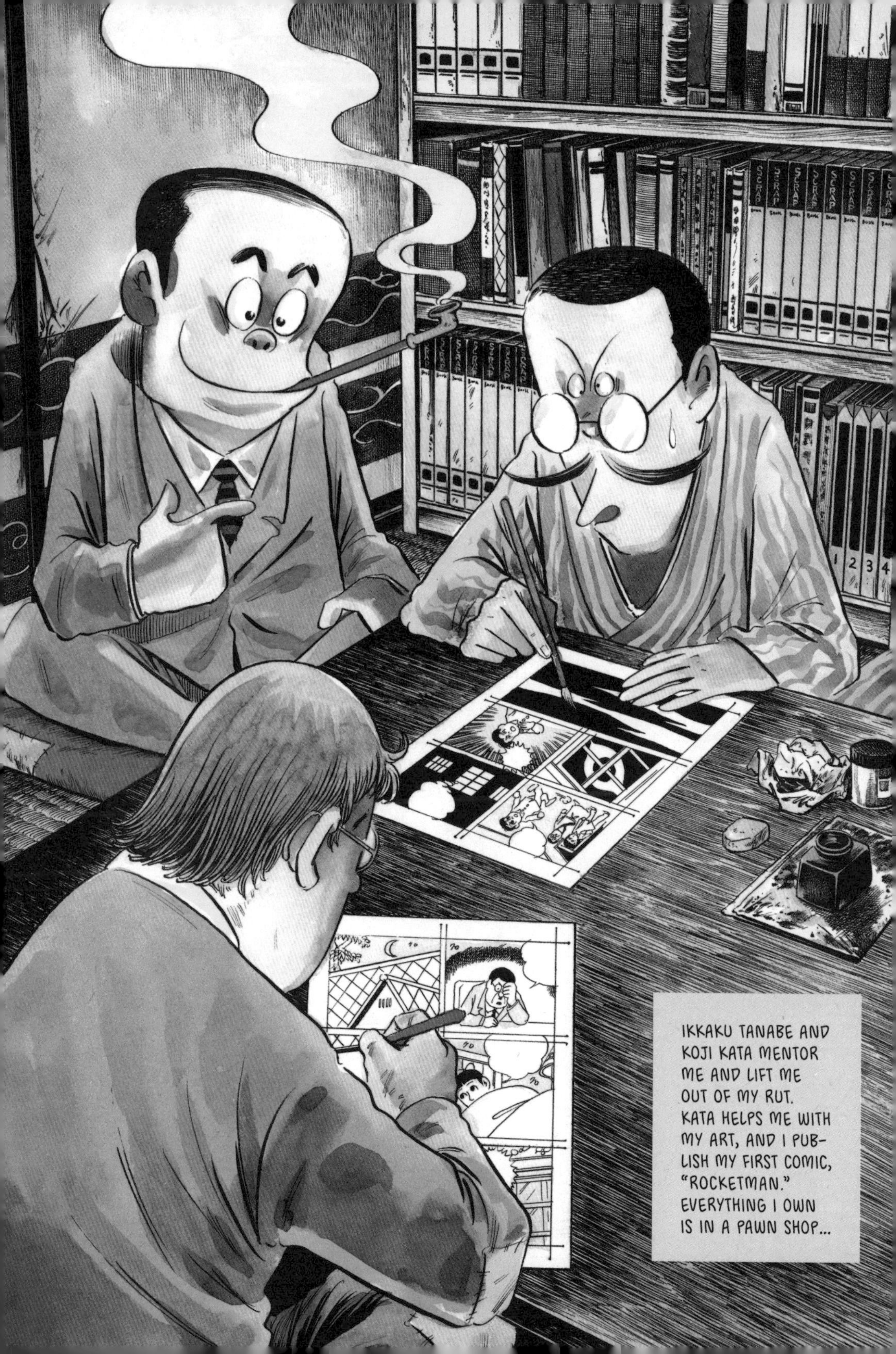
IKKAKU TANABE AND KOJI KATA MENTOR ME AND LIFT ME OUT OF MY RUT. KATA HELPS ME WITH MY ART, AND I PUBLISH MY FIRST COMIC, "ROCKETMAN." EVERYTHING I OWN IS IN A PAWN SHOP...

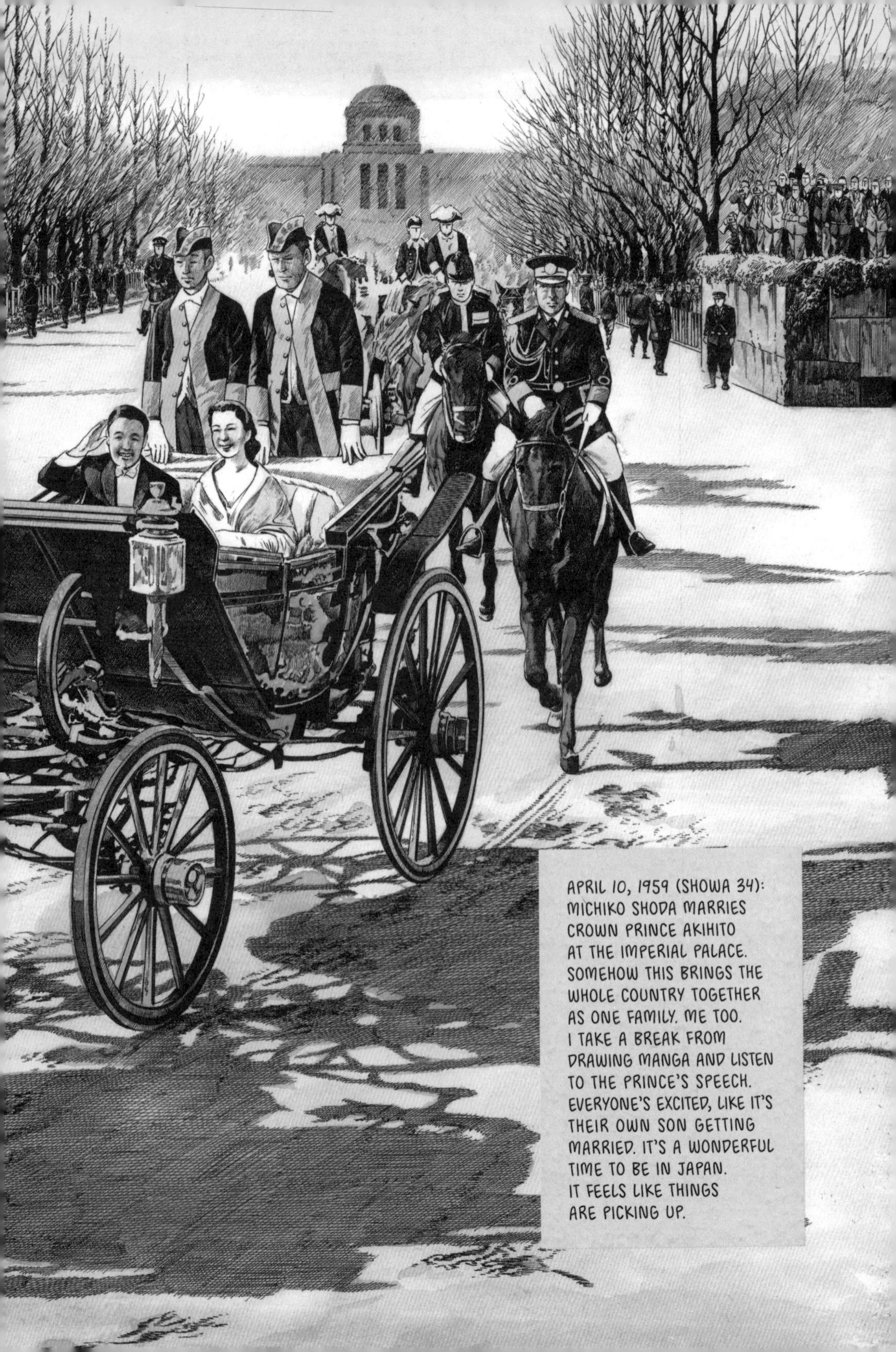
APRIL 10, 1959 (SHOWA 34): MICHIKO SHODA MARRIES CROWN PRINCE AKIHITO AT THE IMPERIAL PALACE. SOMEHOW THIS BRINGS THE WHOLE COUNTRY TOGETHER AS ONE FAMILY. ME TOO. I TAKE A BREAK FROM DRAWING MANGA AND LISTEN TO THE PRINCE'S SPEECH. EVERYONE'S EXCITED, LIKE IT'S THEIR OWN SON GETTING MARRIED. IT'S A WONDERFUL TIME TO BE IN JAPAN. IT FEELS LIKE THINGS ARE PICKING UP.

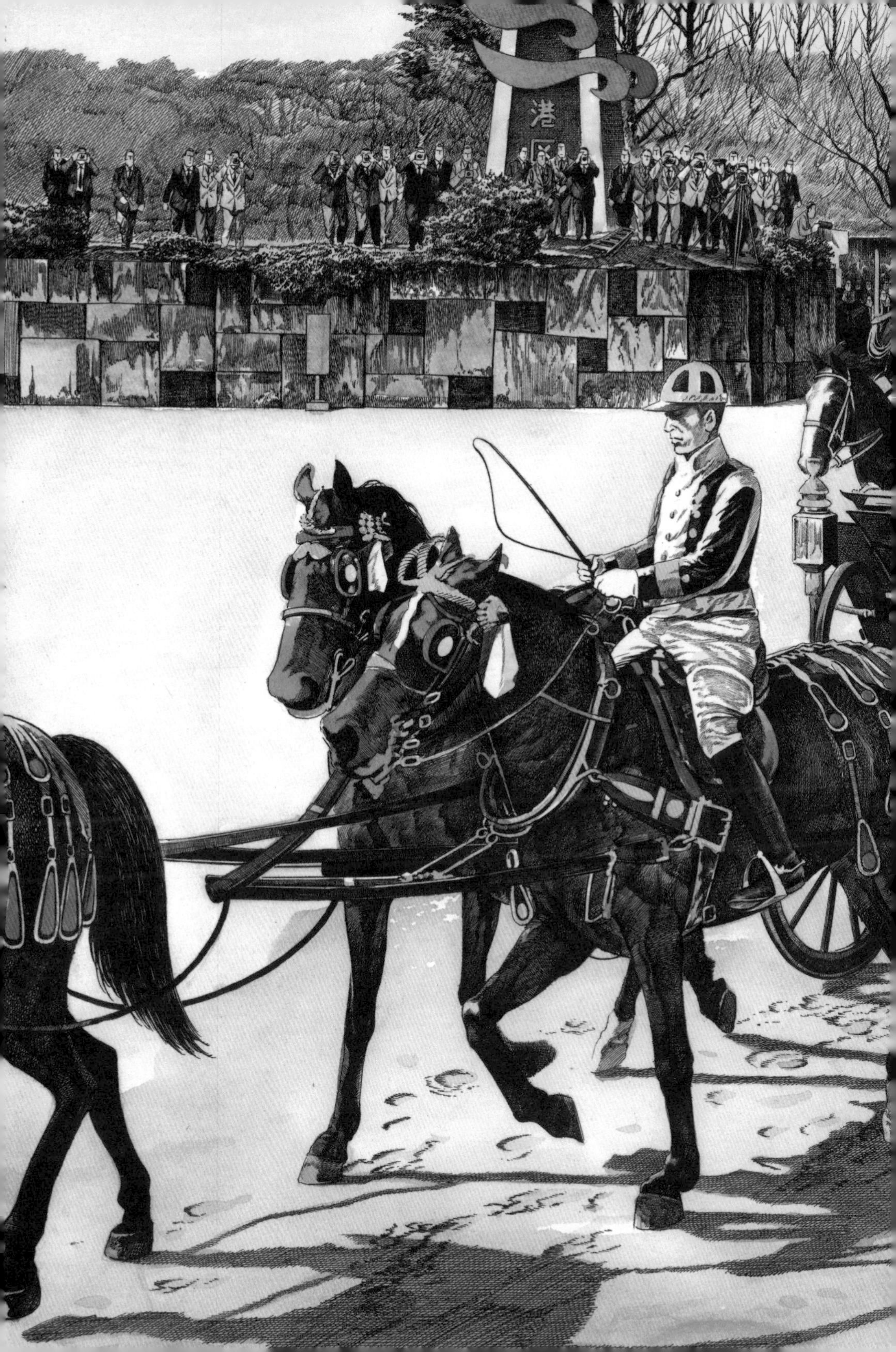
港

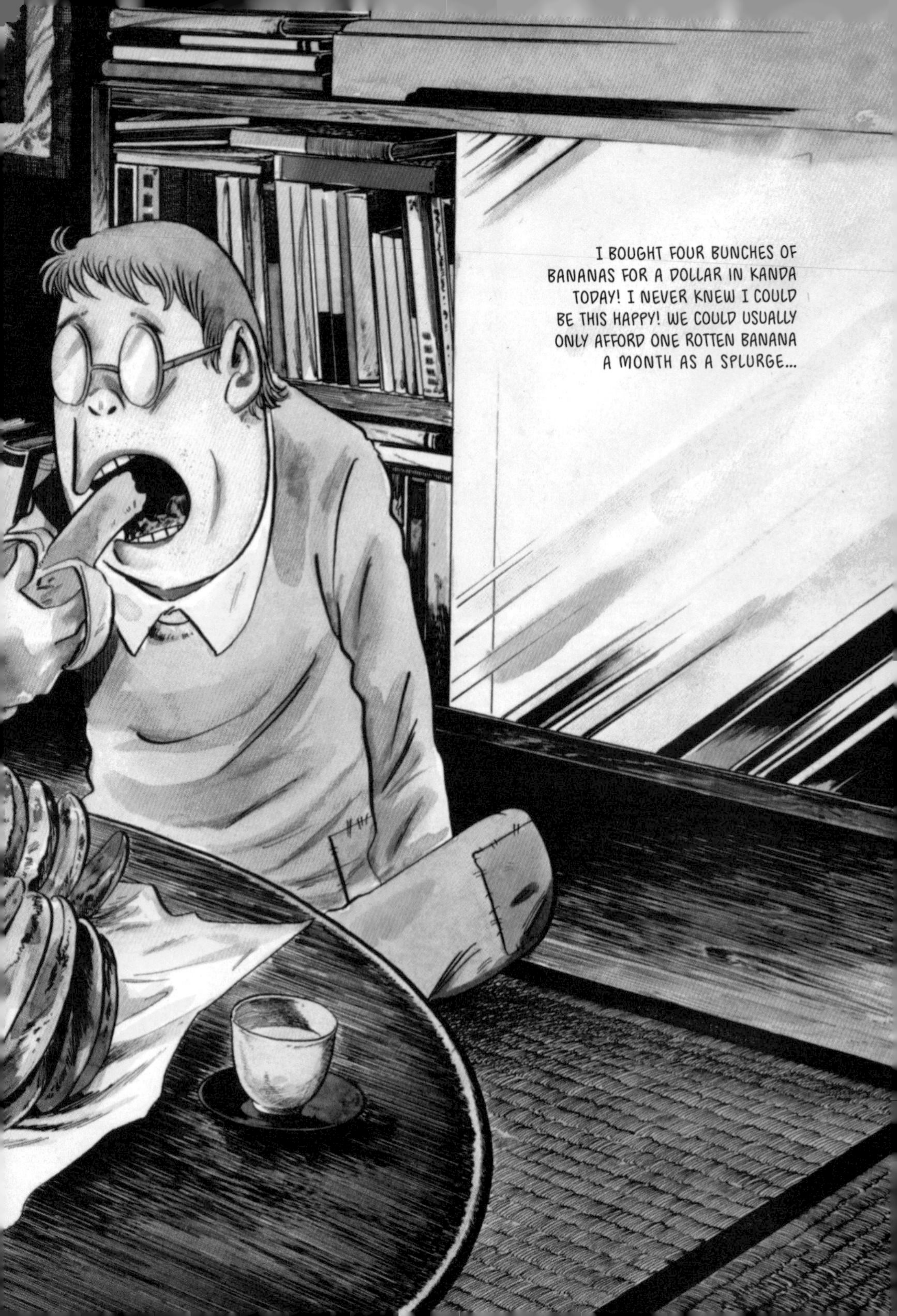
I BOUGHT FOUR BUNCHES OF BANANAS FOR A DOLLAR IN KANDA TODAY! I NEVER KNEW I COULD BE THIS HAPPY! WE COULD USUALLY ONLY AFFORD ONE ROTTEN BANANA A MONTH AS A SPLURGE...

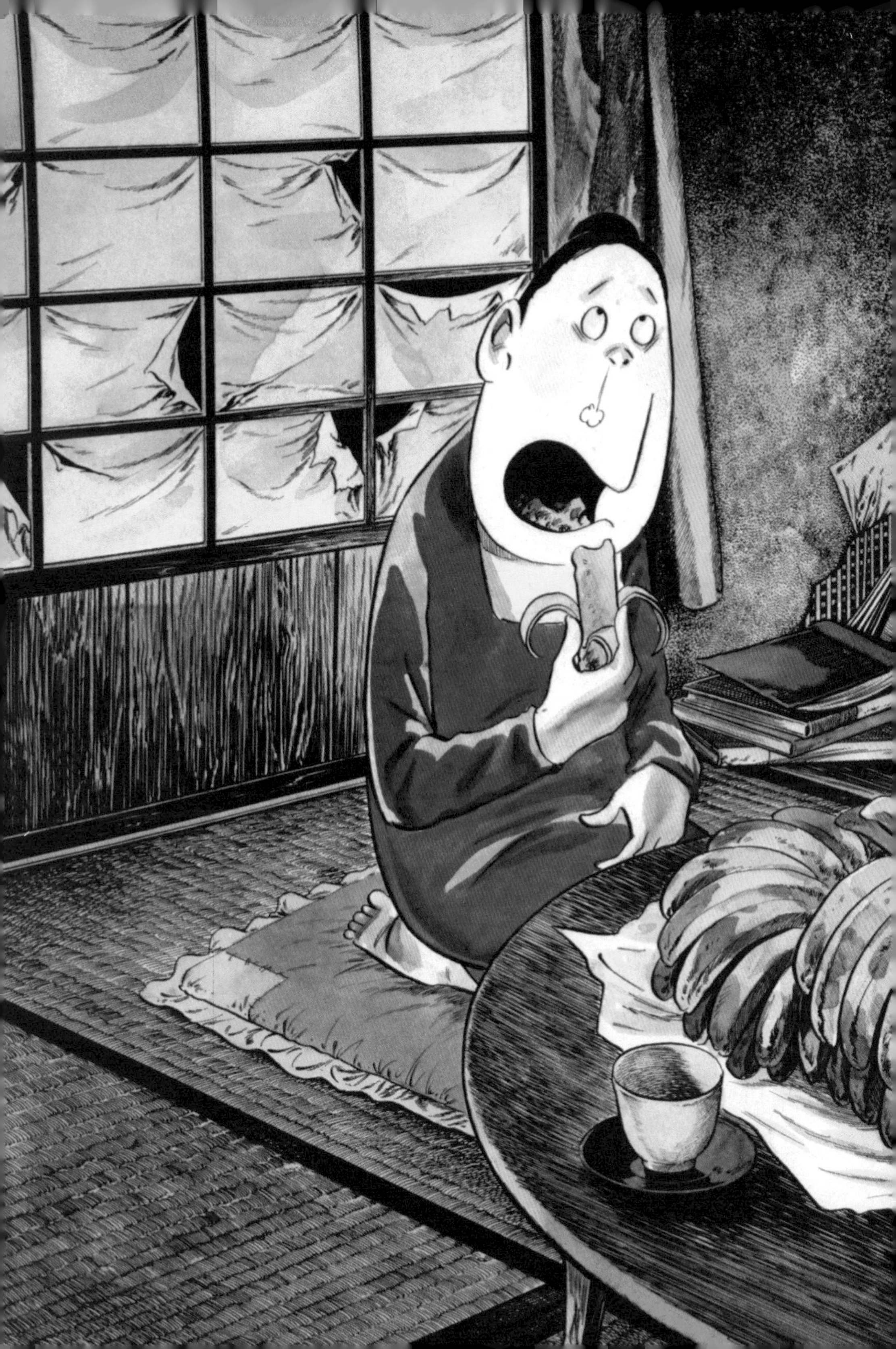

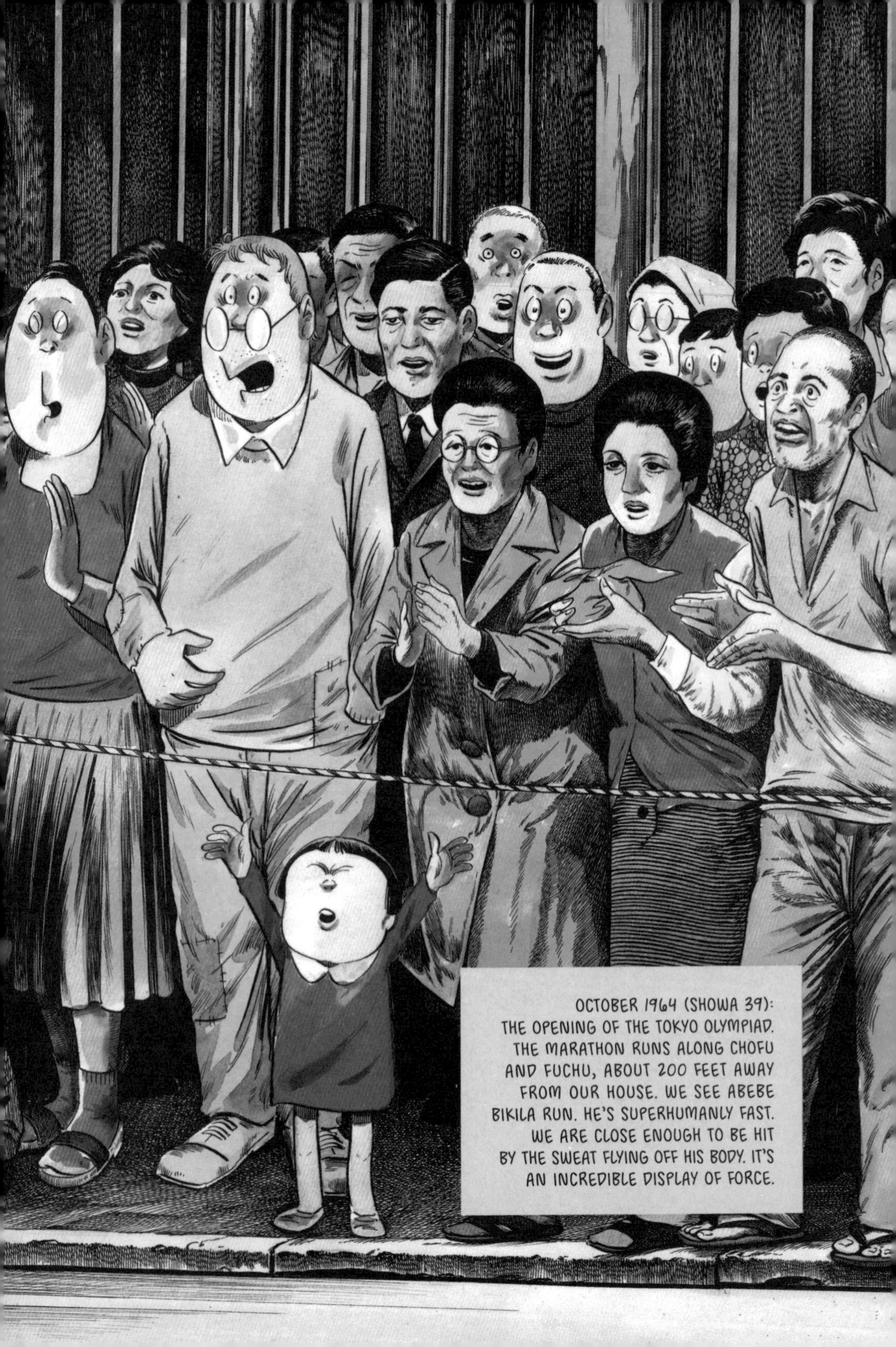
OCTOBER 1964 (SHOWA 39): THE OPENING OF THE TOKYO OLYMPIAD. THE MARATHON RUNS ALONG CHOFU AND FUCHU, ABOUT 200 FEET AWAY FROM OUR HOUSE. WE SEE ABEBE BIKILA RUN. HE'S SUPERHUMANLY FAST. WE ARE CLOSE ENOUGH TO BE HIT BY THE SWEAT FLYING OFF HIS BODY. IT'S AN INCREDIBLE DISPLAY OF FORCE.

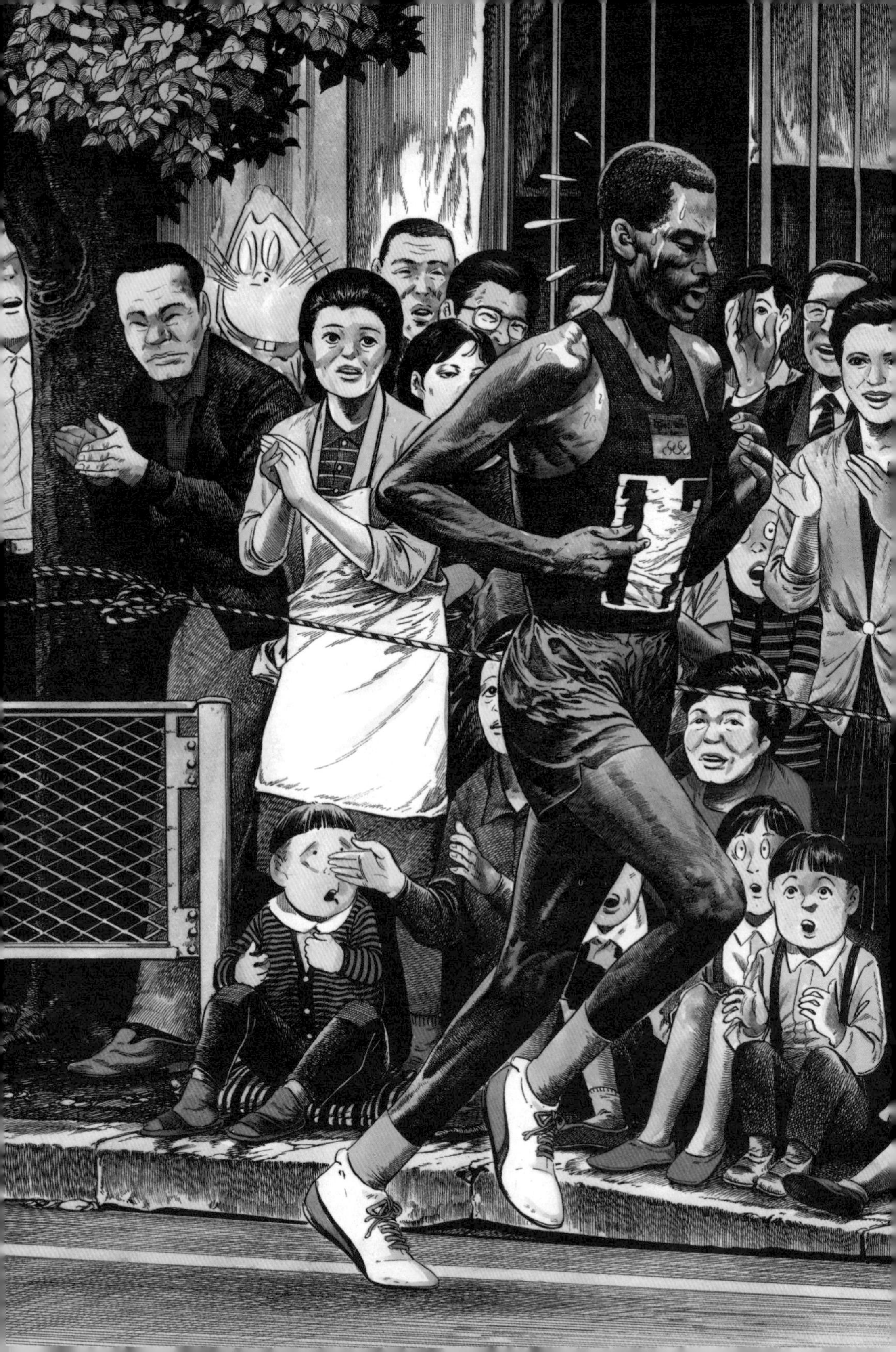

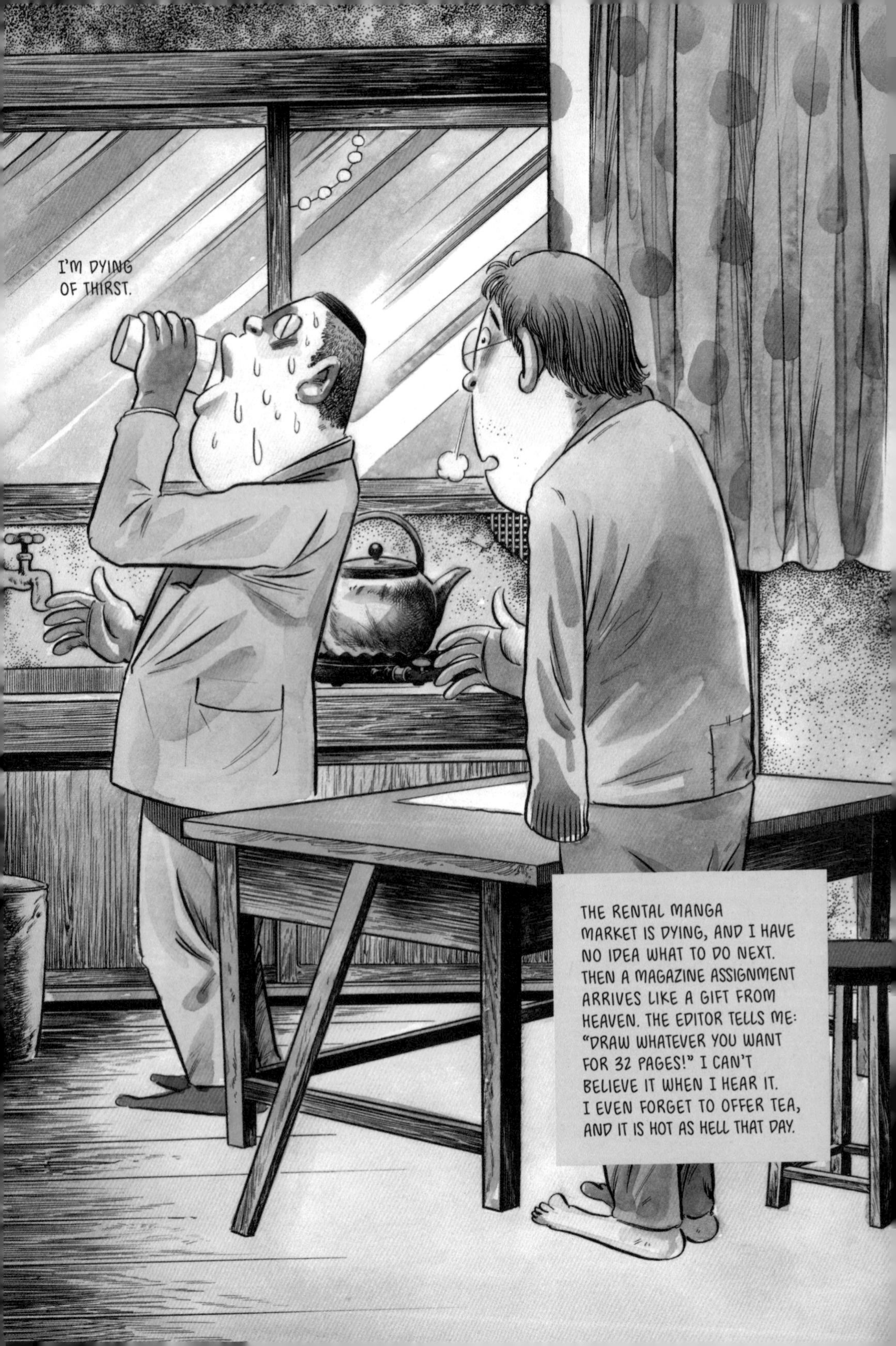
I'M DYING OF THIRST.
THE RENTAL MANGA MARKET IS DYING, AND I HAVE NO IDEA WHAT TO DO NEXT. THEN A MAGAZINE ASSIGNMENT ARRIVES LIKE A GIFT FROM HEAVEN. THE EDITOR TELLS ME: "DRAW WHATEVER YOU WANT FOR 32 PAGES!" I CAN'T BELIEVE IT WHEN I HEAR IT. I EVEN FORGET TO OFFER TEA, AND IT IS HOT AS HELL THAT DAY.

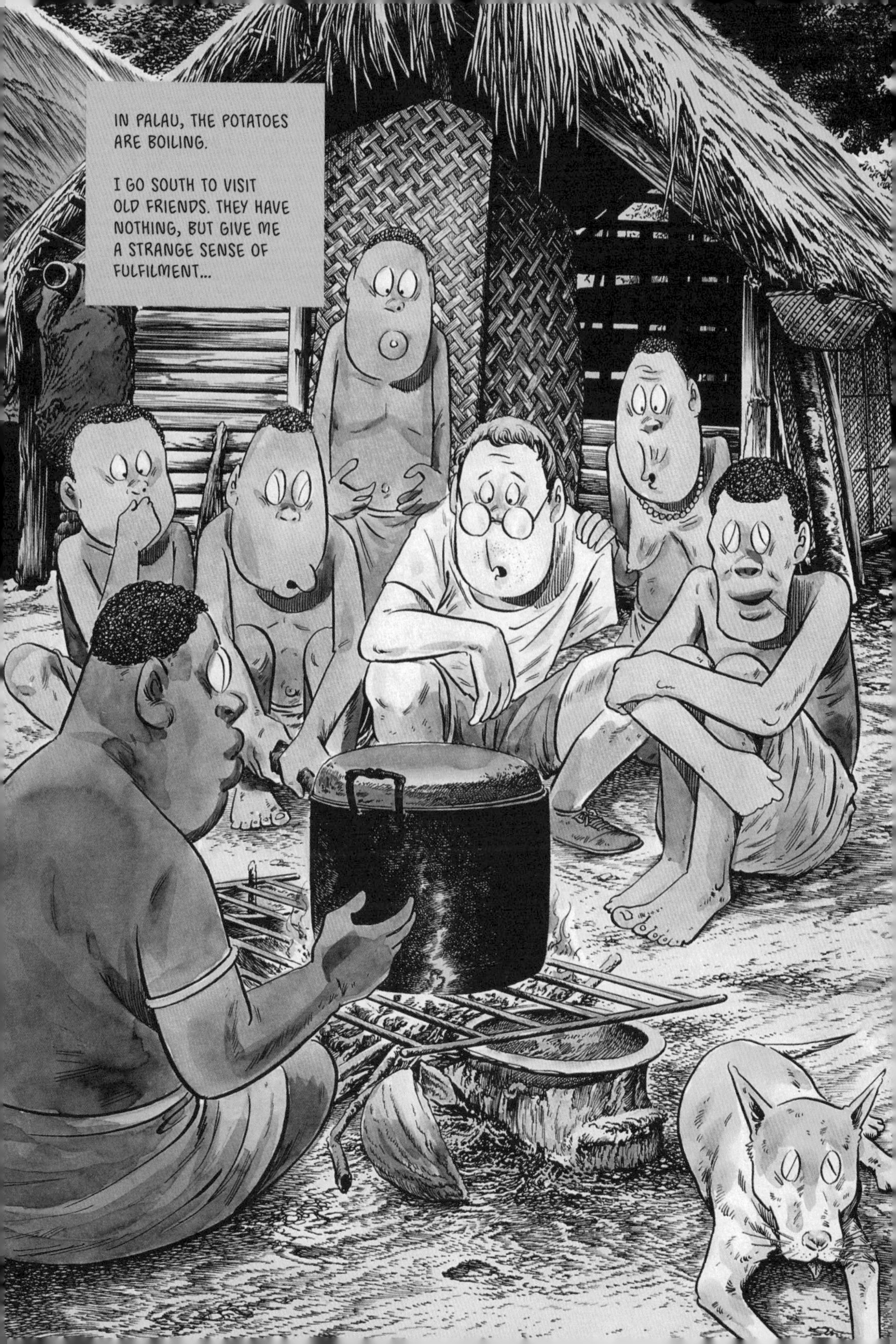
IN PALAU, THE POTATOES ARE BOILING.

I GO SOUTH TO VISIT OLD FRIENDS. THEY HAVE NOTHING, BUT GIVE ME A STRANGE SENSE OF FULFILMENT...

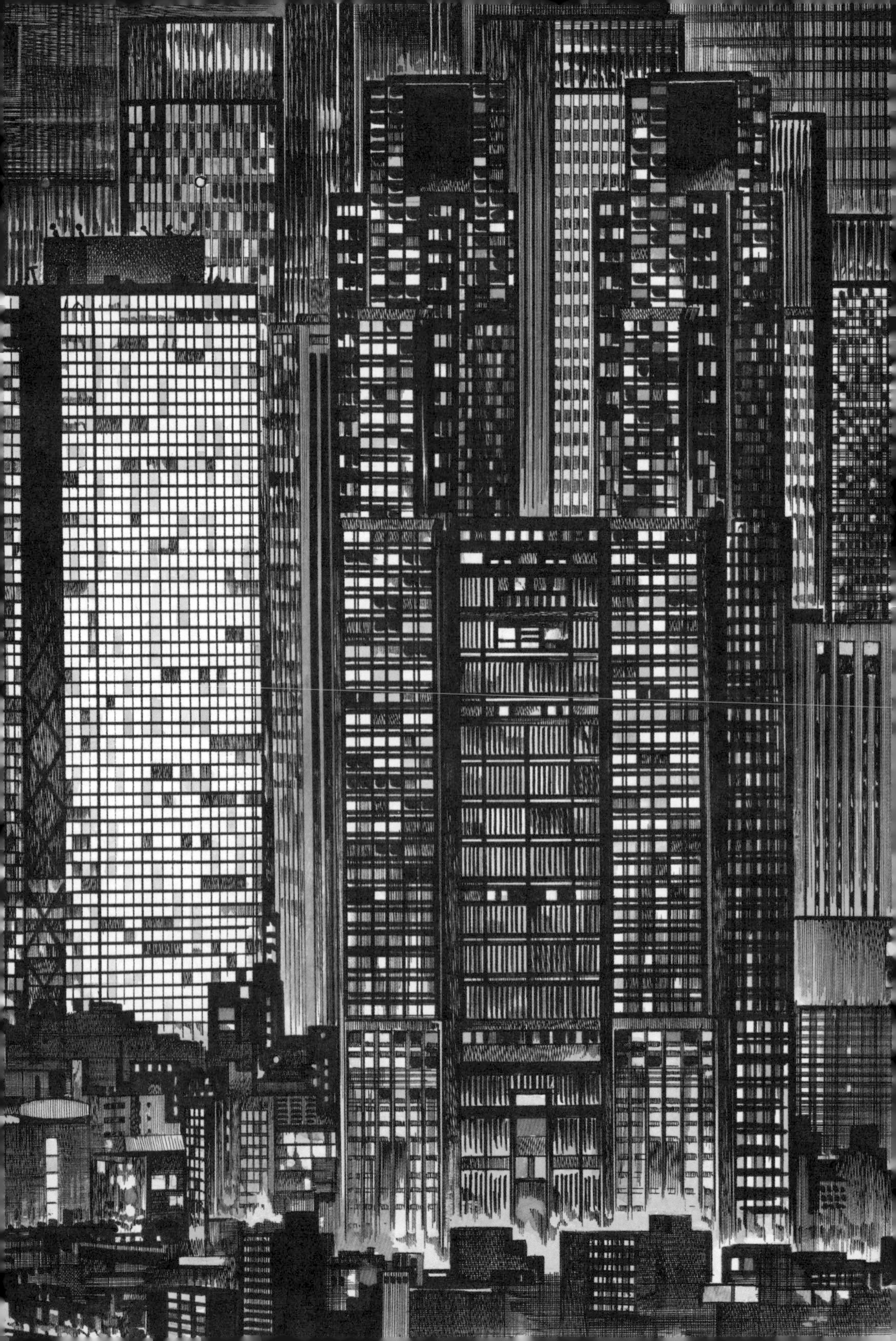

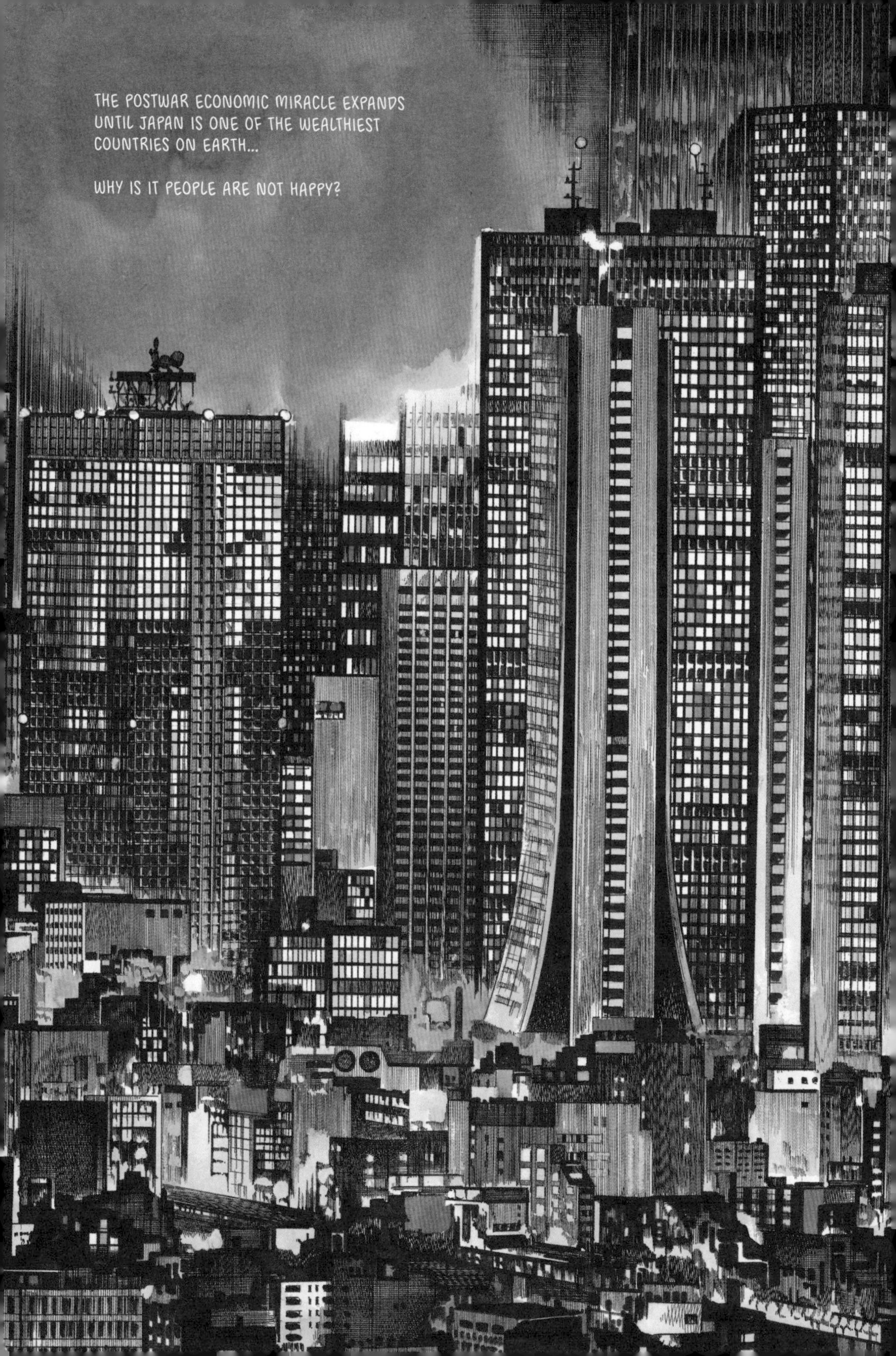
THE POSTWAR ECONOMIC MIRACLE EXPANDS UNTIL JAPAN IS ONE OF THE WEALTHIEST COUNTRIES ON EARTH...
WHY IS IT PEOPLE ARE NOT HAPPY?

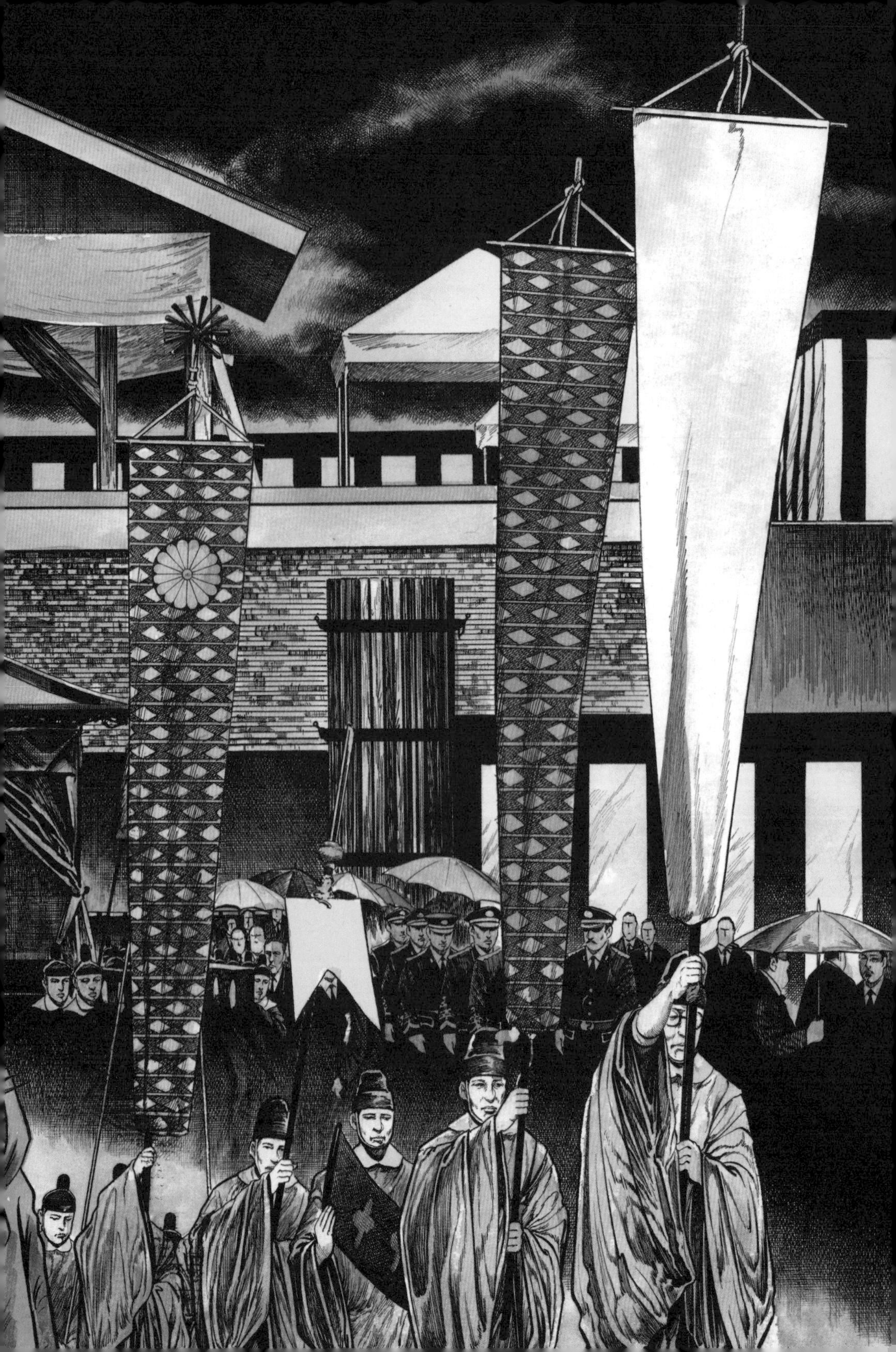

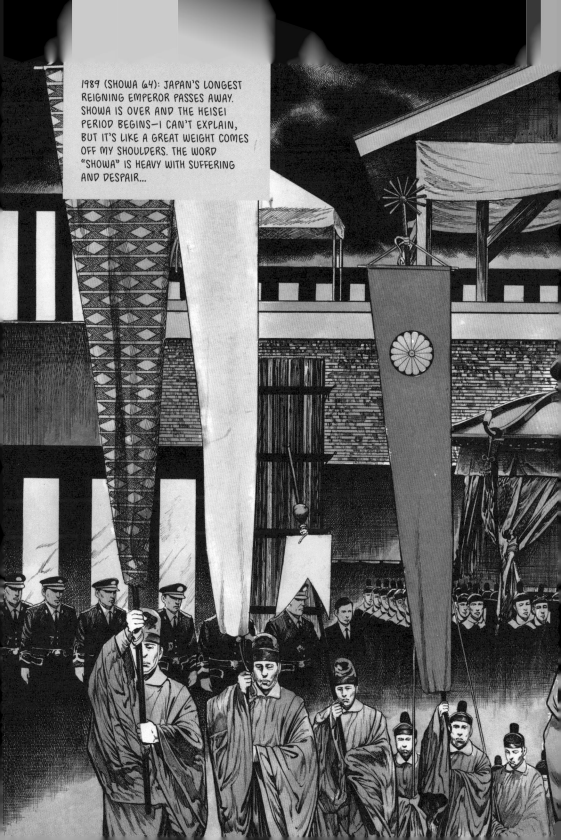

1989 (SHOWA 64): JAPAN'S LONGEST REIGNING EMPEROR PASSES AWAY. SHOWA IS OVER AND THE HEISEI PERIOD BEGINS—I CAN'T EXPLAIN, BUT IT'S LIKE A GREAT WEIGHT COMES OFF MY SHOULDERS. THE WORD "SHOWA" IS HEAVY WITH SUFFERING AND DESPAIR...

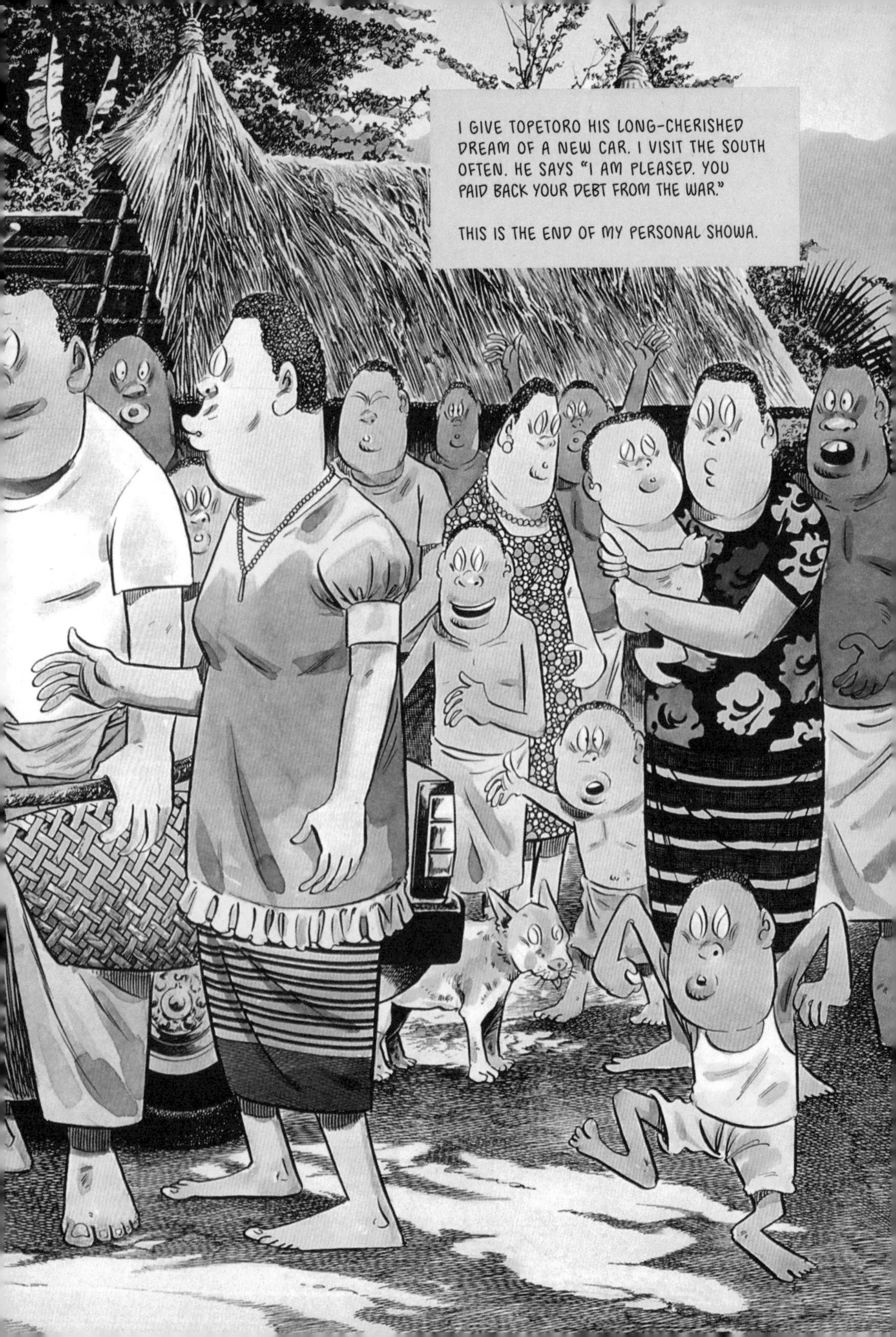
I GIVE TOPETORO HIS LONG-CHERISHED DREAM OF A NEW CAR. I VISIT THE SOUTH OFTEN. HE SAYS "I AM PLEASED. YOU PAID BACK YOUR DEBT FROM THE WAR."
THIS IS THE END OF MY PERSONAL SHOWA.

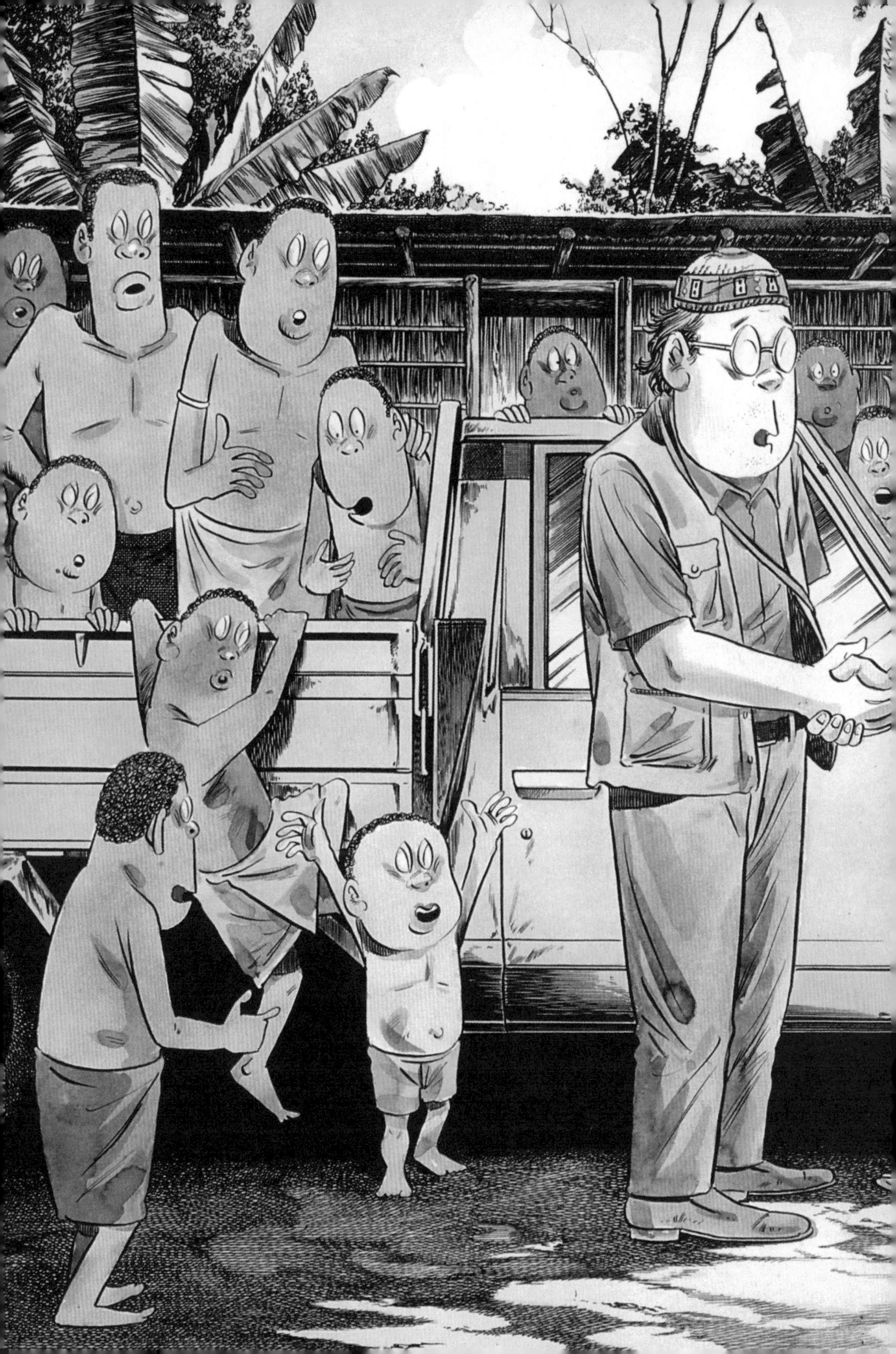

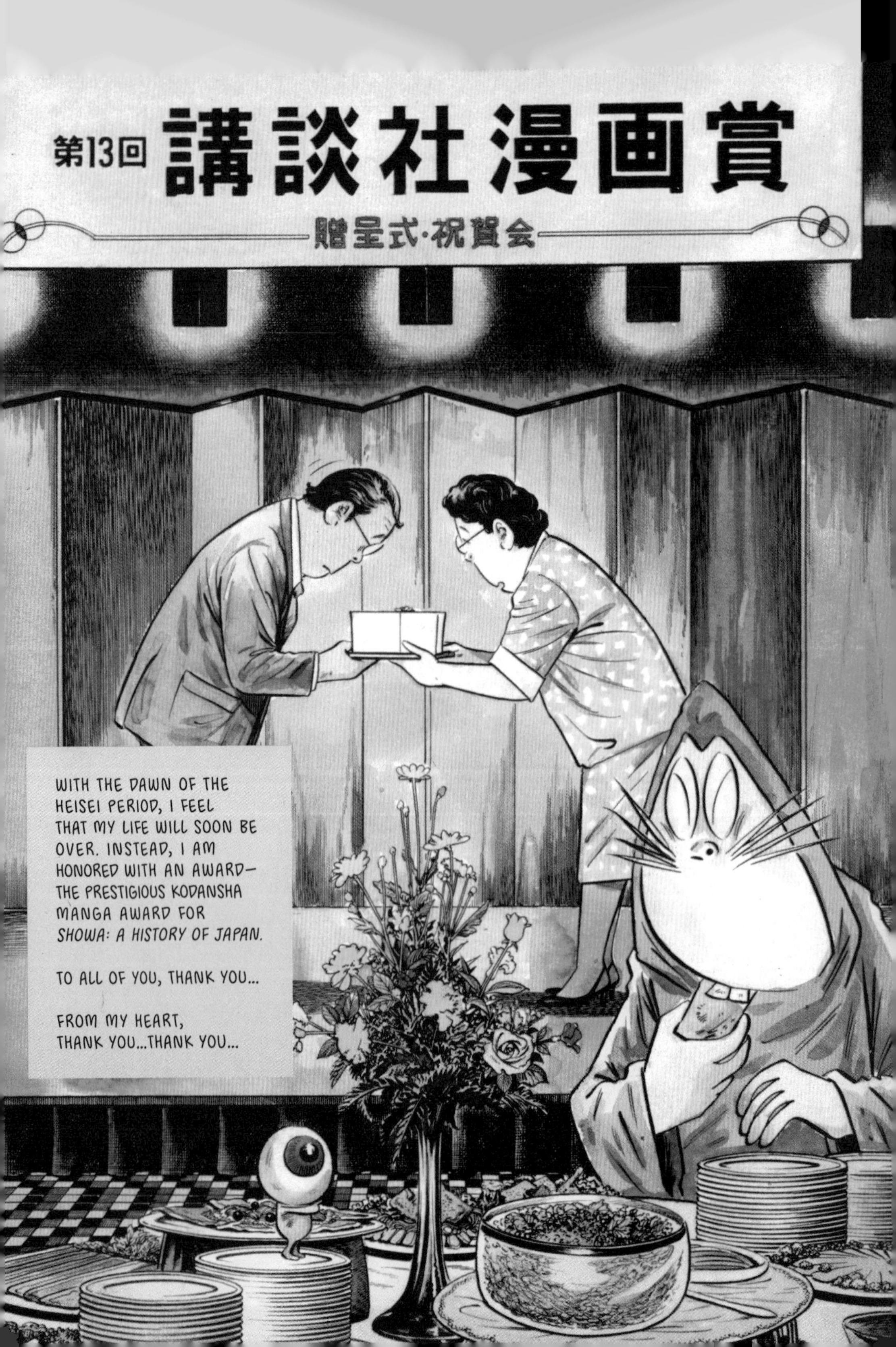
第13回 講談社漫画賞
贈呈式・祝賀会
WITH THE DAWN OF THE HEISEI PERIOD, I FEEL THAT MY LIFE WILL SOON BE OVER. INSTEAD, I AM HONORED WITH AN AWARD— THE PRESTIGIOUS KODANSHA MANGA AWARD FOR *SHOWA: A HISTORY OF JAPAN.*
TO ALL OF YOU, THANK YOU...
FROM MY HEART, THANK YOU...THANK YOU...

This book is presented in the traditional Japanese manner and is meant to be read from right to left. The cover at the opposite end is considered the front of the book.

To begin reading, please flip over and start at the other end, making your way "backward" through the book, starting at the top right corner and reading the panels (and the word balloons) from right to left. Continue on to the next row and repeat.

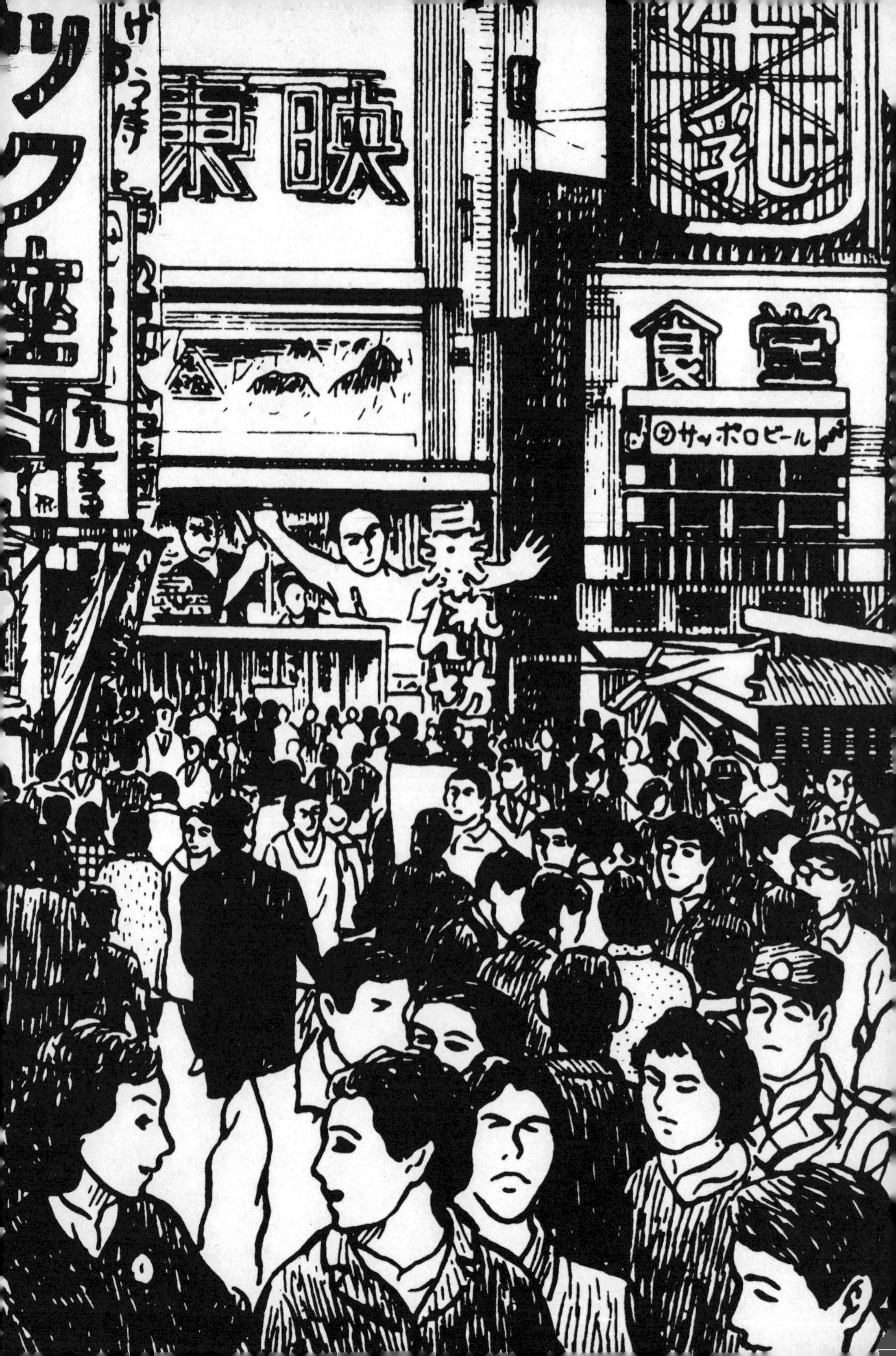
東映
食堂
サッポロビール

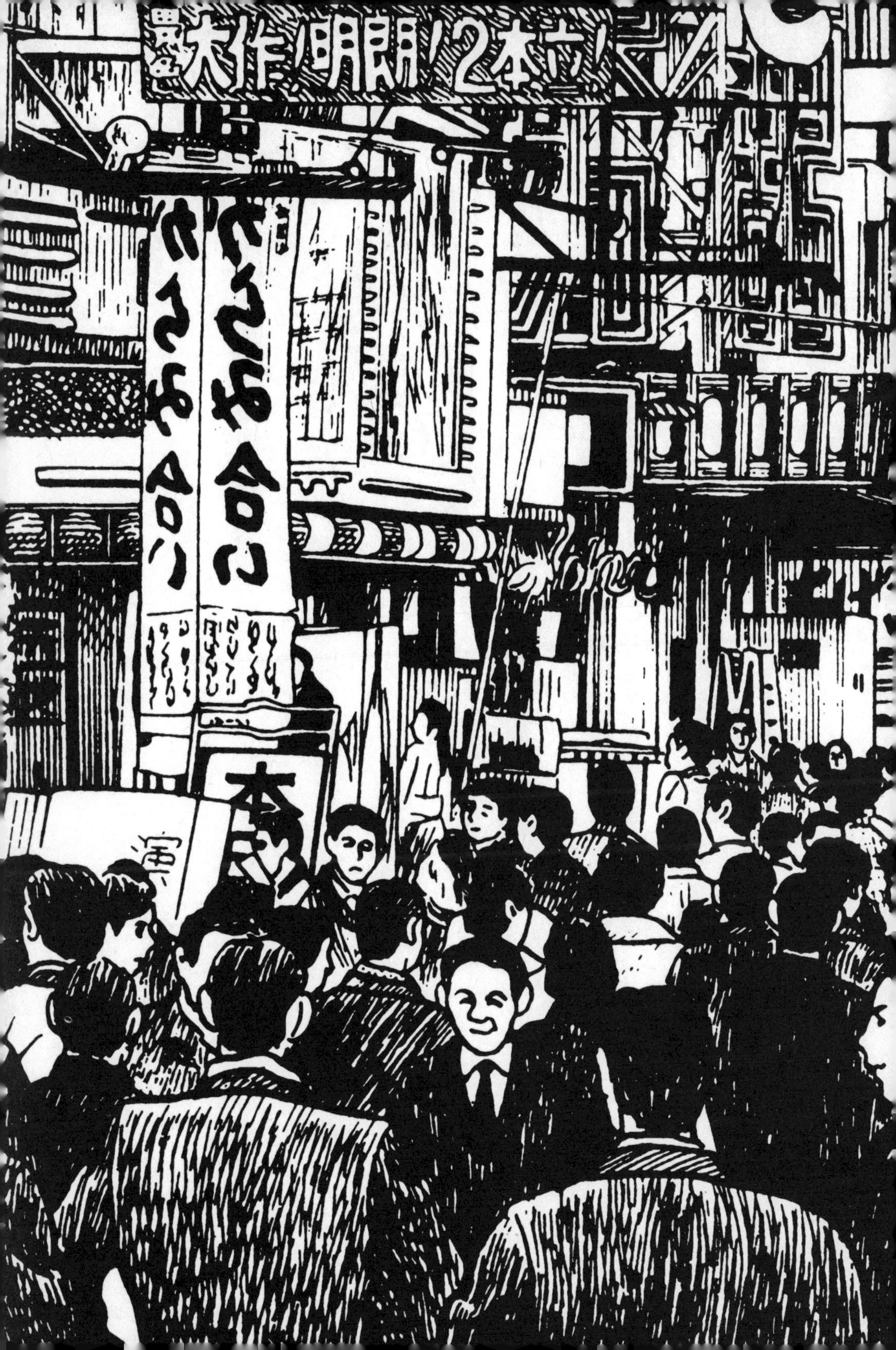
大作！明朗！2本立！
本